EU BUSINESS LAW

ANDRE FIEBIG

Business Law Section
AMERICAN BAR ASSOCIATION

Cover design by Jill Tedhams.

Page layout by Quadrum Solutions.

The materials contained herein represent the opinions of the author and should not be construed to be the views or opinions of the law firm or any other entity with whom the author is in partnership with, associated with, or employed by, nor of the American Bar Association or the Business Law Section unless adopted pursuant to the bylaws of the Association.

Nothing contained in this book is to be considered as the rendering of legal advice for specific cases, and readers are responsible for obtaining such advice from their own legal counsel. This book and any forms and agreements herein are intended for educational and informational purposes only.

© 2015 American Bar Association. All rights reserved. No part of this publication may be reproduced, stored in a retrieval system, or transmitted in any form or by any means, electronic, mechanical, photocopying, recording, or otherwise, without the prior written permission of the publisher. For permission contact the ABA Copyrights & Contracts Department, copyright@americanbar.org or via fax at 312 988-6030, or complete the online form at www.americanbar.org/utility/reprint.

Printed in the United States of America.
19 18 17 16 15   5 4 3 2 1

Library of Congress Cataloging-in-Publication Data

Fiebig, André, 1964– author.
    EU business law / by Andre Fiebig; Business Law Section, American Bar Association.
        pages cm
    Includes index.
    ISBN 978-1-62722-976-0 (alk. paper)
 1. Commercial law—European Union countries. I. American Bar Association. Section of Business Law, sponsoring body. II. Title. III. Title: European Union business law.
  KJE2045.F54 2015
  346.24'065—dc23
                                2015017215

Discounts are available for books ordered in bulk. Special consideration is given to state bars, CLE programs, and other bar related organizations. Inquire at Book Publishing, ABA Publishing, American Bar Association, 321 N. Clark Street, Chicago, Illinois 60654-7598.

www.ShopABA.org

Contents

Foreword v

Abbreviations and Acronyms vii

Chapter I
Institutional and Legal Context of EU Business Law 01

Chapter II
Internal Trade 57

Chapter III
Regulation of Competition 127

Chapter IV
Regulation of External Trade 293

Chapter V
Corporate Law 369

Chapter VI
Securities Law 429

Chapter VII
Insolvency Law 467

Chapter VIII
Sales Agency Law 479

Chapter IX
Labor Law 489

Chapter X
Intellectual Property 529

Chapter XI
The Regulation of Electronic Commerce 651

Chapter XII
Consumer Protection 701

Index of Legislation and Common Names 739

Index 755

About the Author 795

Foreword

To the outsider, the law of the European Union (EU) can appear confusing and opaque. However, the legal system of the EU is, to a certain extent, similar to that of the United States. Like the United States, the EU is an amalgamation of 28 individual countries each with its own legal system and traditions. Just as federal laws in the United States do not replace state laws, the laws of the EU potentially apply parallel and in addition to the laws of the member states. Despite these general similarities, there are significant differences. For starters, unlike the United States, the EU legal system covers both civil and common law countries, 24 official languages and even more cultures. It is inevitable that the content and the application of law in this context reflect the real imperative of maintaining the cohesion of this rather young experiment. A recognition of this reality helps to avoid frustration when trying to come to terms with the legal system of the European Union.

After returning to the United States from Brussels over two decades ago, it immediately became apparent to me that there is a need for a greater understanding of EU business law among practitioners, academics and students in the United States. *EU Business Law* is an attempt to enhance the understanding of the EU in the United States or at least create a reference source where answers could be found. The book is based on of many years practicing and teaching EU law in the United States and in Europe. The two basic objectives of the book are to make EU business law accessible to readers with only a cursory understanding of the EU legal system as well as serve as a practical handbook for practicing lawyers and students. The work is based almost exclusively on primary materials, i.e., EU primary and secondary legislation as well as the case law of the European Court of Justice and General Court. To the extent that a particular area of EU is administratively applied, I have relied on the decisions reached by the respective administrative bodies. This would include, for example, EU competition law which is primarily applied by the European Commission, intellectual property law which is primarily applied by the Office for Harmonization in the Internal Market and external trade law which is primarily applied by the European Commission and Council. To a lesser extent I have relied on case law from the courts of the EU member states. However, the application of EU law in the member states is not the primary focus of this work. Although I have included references to national laws and judicial decisions, I recognized early on that too much of a reliance on national cases would distort the objective nature of the book to the benefit of those jurisdictions to which I had linguistic access.

A book of this scope and length is not an individual undertaking. There are many people to whom I owe a significant debt of gratitude in particular Professor David Gerber (IIT/Chicago-Kent College of Law) who originally piqued my curiosity in EU law many years ago and who has supported and encouraged me ever since. I still consider him my teacher and academic role model. I would also like to thank David Braun (Quarles & Brady LLP) and Professor Spencer Weber Waller (Loyola University Chicago School of Law) and who have served not only as mentors over the years but also sources of ideas, inspirations and guidance. It has been a personal and professional privilege knowing them over the years. David Flint of MacRoberts LLP lent the manuscript a critical read at an important moment in the book's creation. The publishing staff and editors at the American Bar Association have done a considerable amount of excellent work under tight time deadlines and I would like to commend and thank them for their professionalism and hard work. Valuable research assistance was provided by Sam Stevenson, Isabelle Stevenson, Esther Fiebig and Abigail Stevenson. Lastly, but most importantly, I would like to thank Tricia Van Eck for many years of patience and support in writing this book. Without her encouragement, spontaneity and curiosity, I would have never been able to complete the task which I started many years ago. It is to her that I dedicate this book.

Abbreviations and Acronyms

BTI	binding tariff information
CCT	Common Customs Tariff
CN	Combined Nomenclature
CSPs	certification service providers
DSB	WTO Dispute Settlement Body
DSM	WTO Dispute Settlement Mechanism
ECJ	European Court of Justice
EEA	European Economic Area
EEIG	European Economic Interest Grouping
ESMA	European Securities and Markets Authority
EU	European Union
GATT	General Agreement on Tariffs and Trade
HCDCS	Harmonized Commodity Description and Coding System
MET	Market economy treatment
OHIM	Office for Harmonization in the Internal Market
SE	Societas Europaea
TFEU	Treaty on the Formation of the European Union
WCO	World Customs Organization
WTO	World Trade Organization

CHAPTER **1**

Institutional and Legal Context of EU Business Law

An understanding of the field of European Union (EU or Union) business law necessitates a brief discussion of the historical, institutional, and macro-legal context in which the specific business laws and regulations are applied. The discussion in this Chapter is not intended to be exhaustive. Indeed, there are other, more comprehensive works on the history and institutions of the EU. Instead, the discussion is designed to enhance the accessibility of later Chapters for those readers not already familiar with the structure of the EU.

1. From the EEC to the EU

1.1 The Three European Communities

The formal beginnings of the European Union may be traced to the Treaty of Paris signed on April 18, 1951.[1] This international treaty—often referred to as the ECSC Treaty—between six countries (Belgium, the Netherlands, Luxembourg, France, Germany, and Italy) established the European Coal and Steel Community. As the duration of the ECSC Treaty was limited to 50 years, it is primarily of historical interest today. The member states allowed it to expire in 2002.

In 1957, the same six countries that established the European Coal and Steel Community entered into the Treaty of Rome establishing the European Economic Community[2] and the Euratom Treaty establishing the European Atomic Energy Community.[3] Upon creation of the Euratom Community and the European Economic Community in 1957, three separate European Communities existed, each based on its own treaty and having its own institutions: European Coal and Steel Community, Euratom Community, and the European Economic Community.

---

1. Treaty establishing the European Coal and Steel Community, Apr. 18, 1951, 261 U.N.T.S. 140 [hereinafter ECSC Treaty].
2. 298 U.N.T.S. 11.
3. 298 U.N.T.S. 167. Similar to the ECSC Treaty, the Euratom Treaty was limited to a specific sector of the economy. The six members intended to coordinate nuclear energy policies.

```
                    ┌─────────────┐
                    │    The      │
                    │  European   │
                    │ Communities │
                    └──────┬──────┘
          ┌────────────────┼────────────────┐
┌─────────┴────────┐ ┌─────┴──────┐ ┌───────┴────────┐
│ European Coal and│ │  Euratom   │ │European Economic│
│  Steel Community │ │ Community  │ │   Community    │
└─────────┬────────┘ └─────┬──────┘ └───────┬────────┘
        △               △                 △
      ECSC            Euratom             EEC
      Treaty          Treaty             Treaty
      (1951)          (1957)             (1957)
```

By the early 1960s, it was widely recognized that certain economies of scale could be achieved by merging the executive institutions of the three European Communities. This was accomplished in 1965 by the signing of the Merger Treaty.[4] The effect of the Merger Treaty was to establish one commission and one council for the three legally independent communities that existed at the time. It is important to remember, however, that the treaties themselves were not merged. The three European Communities continued to exist for several decades even after 1965, based essentially on three different legal regimes.

1.2 The European Union

For EU business law, the most important treaty is the Treaty Establishing the European Community, i.e., the EEC Treaty. The EEC Treaty has been amended a number of times since it was signed in 1957. As the EEC Treaty is an international convention, it can only be amended by a subsequent international treaty and ratified by all of the member states.[5] One of the most significant amendments to the EEC Treaty came in 1992 when the members of the European Economic Community signed the EU Treaty (sometimes referred to as the Maastricht Treaty in reference to the Dutch town where it was signed).[6] The EU Treaty amended the EEC Treaty by adding new substantive provisions and modifying some of the existing provisions.

---

4. Treaty Establishing a Single Council and Single Commission of the European Communities, April 8, 1965, 4 I.L.M. 776 (1965).
5. EU Treaty at art. 48(4).
6. Treaty on European Union, Feb. 7, 1992, O.J. 1992 (C 191) 1 [hereinafter EU Treaty].

The EU is currently based on the EU Treaty and the Treaty on the Functioning of the European Union (TFEU).[7] Both of these treaties, which have equal value,[8] have been amended several times. The main amending treaties are:

- Treaty of Lisbon[9]
- Treaty of Nice[10]
- Treaty of Amsterdam[11]
- Single European Act[12]
- Merger Treaty[13]

The most recent amendment to the EEC Treaty was the Lisbon Treaty. With the ratification of the Lisbon Treaty in 2009, the term "Union" officially replaced "Community."[14] Reference is now made to the European Union rather than the European Community. The Lisbon Treaty also renamed the Treaty Establishing the European Community to the Treaty on the Functioning of the European Union. The constitutional structure of the EU may be depicted as follows:

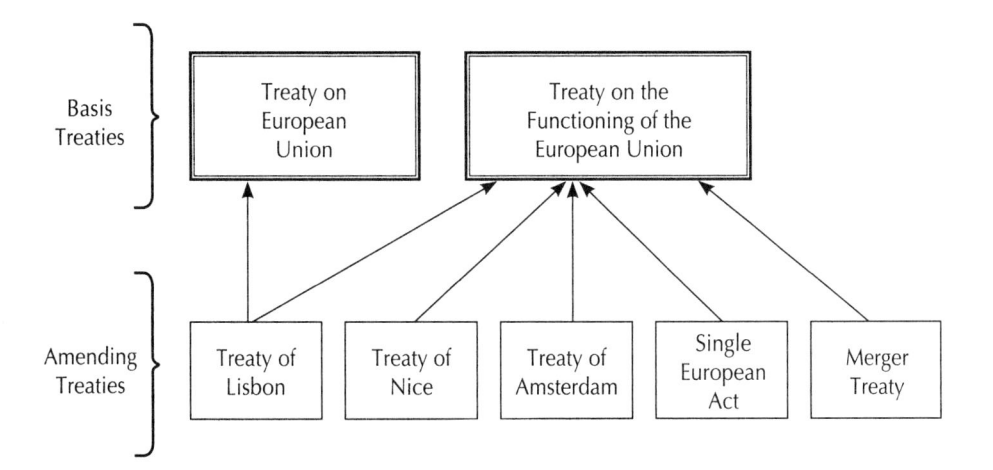

```
Basis        ⎱  Treaty on           Treaty on the
Treaties     ⎰  European            Functioning of the
                Union               European Union
                  ↑                   ↑  ↑  ↑  ↑
Amending     ⎱  Treaty of  Treaty of  Treaty of   Single      Merger
Treaties     ⎰  Lisbon     Nice       Amsterdam   European    Treaty
                                                  Act
```

---

7. Consolidated versions of the EU Treaty and the TFEU can be found at 2010 O.J. (C 83) 13 and 2010 O.J. (C 83) 47 respectively.
8. EU Treaty at art. 1.
9. Treaty of Lisbon amending the Treaty on European Union and the Treaty establishing the European Community, signed at Lisbon, 13 December 2007, 2007 O.J. (C 306) 1.
10. Treaty of Nice amending the Treaty on European Union, the Treaties establishing the European Communities, and certain related acts, 2001 O.J. (C 80) 1.
11. Treaty of Amsterdam amending the Treaty on European Union, the Treaties establishing the European Communities and certain related acts, 1997 O.J. (C 340) 3.
12. 1986 O.J. (L 163) 1.
13. Treaty Establishing a Single Council and Single Commission of the European Communities, April 8, 1965, 4 I.L.M. 776 (1965).
14. EU Treaty at art. 1.

2. Membership

2.1 Accession

The success of the economies of the initial six member states made membership in the European Economic Community attractive to European countries who were not members. From the original six member states, the EU has grown to 28 countries. As the EU was created by international treaty, the act of "joining" the EU refers to the accession by that state to the treaties. Currently, the EU is comprised of the following 28 member states: Austria, Belgium, Bulgaria, Croatia. Cyprus, Czech Republic, Denmark, Estonia, Finland, France, Germany, Greece, Hungary, Ireland, Italy, Latvia, Lithuania, Luxembourg, Malta, the Netherlands, Poland, Portugal, Romania, the Slovak Republic, Slovenia, Spain, Sweden, and United Kingdom.

Nations Online Project

The requirements for membership in the EU, which are codified in the EU Treaty and the "Copenhagen Criteria,"[15] are geographic, political, economic, and legal. Article 49 of the EU Treaty provides that membership in the EU is open to "any European State." It is unclear geographically which states qualify as "European." Although the EU has been unable or unwilling to provide a definition of "Europe," Morocco's application for membership in the 1970s was rejected because it was generally perceived that this country was outside Europe.[16] The basic political criterion is that the state accepts and respects the principles set out in Article 2 of the EU Treaty (i.e., democratic principles, respect for human rights and the rule of law, etc.). The economic criterion requires that the state must have a functioning market economy. Finally, the legal criterion requires the state to assume and observe the EU laws and legal system.

Meeting these requirements gives the country the right to apply to the EU Council. Once the Council has received the application, it must consult with the European Commission and secure the consent of the European Parliament to admit the applicant. The Council must then unanimously decide to accept the applicant. The precise terms of admission are then codified in a treaty between the EU and the applicant state. As a last step, all of the member states must ratify the accession treaty with that applicant. It is a cumbersome process, but achievable when the necessary political consensus is reached.

2.2 Withdrawal

Article 50(1) of the EU Treaty gives each member state the right to withdraw from the EU at any time. That member state must first notify the European Council of its intention to withdraw and negotiate an agreement with the EU regulating the terms of the withdrawal.[17] The European Parliament must consent to the agreement of withdrawal which is then concluded on behalf of the EU by the Council (acting by a qualified majority excluding the withdrawing member state). In the event that no agreement on the terms of withdrawal is reached,

---

15. At their summit in Copenhagen in June 1993, the member states agreed upon certain political, economic, and legal criteria they would use to approve future applications for membership into the European Community: "Membership requires that the candidate country has achieved stability of institutions guaranteeing democracy, the rule of law, human rights and respect for and protection of minorities, the existence of a functioning market economy as well as the capacity to cope with competitive pressure and market forces within the Union. Membership presupposes the candidate's ability to take on the obligations of membership including adherence to the aims of political, economic, and monetary union." These rather loose requirements are commonly known as the "Copenhagen Criteria."
16. The Commission, in its Report on Europe and the Challenge of Enlargement, Bull. Eur. Communities Supp., 3-1992, at 11, indicated that the "European" requirement cannot be condensed into a single definition, but rather refers to the "shared experience of proximity, ideas, values, and historical interaction" comprised of geographical, historical, and cultural elements."
17. EU Treaty at art. 50(2).

the withdrawal is automatically effective two years after the initial notification to the Council.[18]

2.3 Suspension of Membership

Although the Treaties do not provide for the expulsion of a member state from the EU, Article 7 of the EU Treaty creates the possibility for the EU to suspend the rights of a member state under the treaties. The process, which has yet to be exercised, starts with a reasoned proposal for suspension from the European Commission, the European Parliament, or one third of the member states. The Council, acting by a majority of four-fifths of its members, must then determine that there is a clear risk of a serious breach by a member state of the fundamental values of the EU.[19] Assuming that the Council determines that such a risk exists, and the European Parliament has consented, it is up to the Council to decide whether there is a clear risk of a serious breach by a member state of the EU's fundamental values. Before making this determination, the Council must invite the member state in question to submit its observations. The decision of the Council is taken by unanimity, excluding the member state concerned. Only then may the Council, acting by a qualified majority, decide to suspend the rights of that member state.

3. Other Pan-European Legal Systems

It is important to recognize that the EU is different from the European Free Trade Association (EFTA) and the European Economic Area (EEA). In 1959, Denmark, Norway, Portugal, Sweden, Switzerland, and the United Kingdom (Finland joined later) established the EFTA as a free trade area in which tariffs on the cross-border flow of goods were reduced or eliminated.[20] The EFTA establishes a much less integrated relationship among its members compared to the relationship among the EU member states. The EFTA is not part or an institution of the EU; nor does its membership overlap with that of the EU. As some of the EFTA countries joined the EU, they necessarily relinquished their membership in the EFTA. Only Iceland, Liechtenstein, Norway, and Switzerland remain members of the EFTA.

---

18. *Id.* at art. 50(3). The Council and the withdrawing member state may agree to extend this two-year period.
19. The fundamental values are set forth in Article 2 of the EU Treaty.
20. North American Free Trade Agreement, done Dec. 17, 1992, 32 I.L.M. 630 (1993).

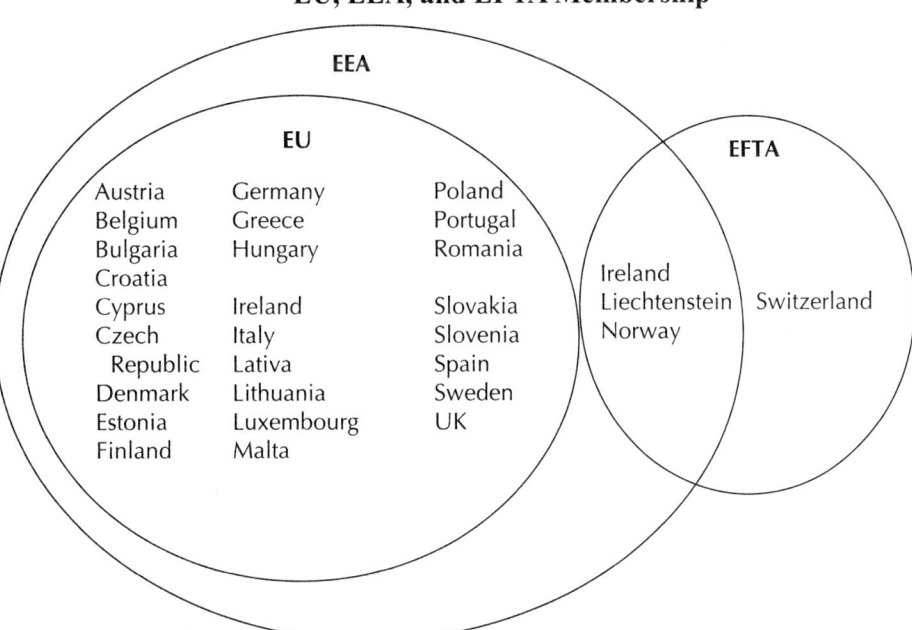

EU, EEA, and EFTA Membership

```
                    EEA
         ┌──────────────────────┐
         │   EU                 │    EFTA
         │  Austria  Germany  Poland │
         │  Belgium  Greece   Portugal │
         │  Bulgaria Hungary  Romania │
         │  Croatia                  │  Ireland
         │  Cyprus   Ireland  Slovakia │ Liechtenstein  Switzerland
         │  Czech    Italy    Slovenia │ Norway
         │   Republic Lativa  Spain   │
         │  Denmark  Lithuania Sweden │
         │  Estonia  Luxembourg UK    │
         │  Finland  Malta           │
         └──────────────────────┘
```

The EEA was created in 1994 by treaty of the 12 EC member states and the then six EFTA member states (Austria, Finland, Iceland, Norway, Switzerland, and Sweden).[21] The fundamental aim of the EEA Treaty was to expand the four freedoms (free movement of goods, persons, services, and capital) to the EFTA states. The EEA Treaty also covers several "flanking" policy areas such as competition, education, consumer protection, and environment. The provisions of the EEA Treaty regulating these areas are almost identical to the parallel provisions in the TFEU. For example, the prohibition of bilateral restraints of competition contained in Article 53 of the EEA Agreement is identical to the wording of Article 101 of the TFEU. The EEA does not cover a number of politically sensitive areas, such as agriculture and fisheries and taxation.

Another political organization which must be distinguished from the EU is the Council of Europe based on the European Convention on Human Rights.[22] This organization, which was created in 1949 and is based in Strasbourg, France, is focused on the protection of human rights, parliamentary democracy, and the rule of law. Although all of the member states of the EU are also members of this organization, its membership is much broader, encompassing 46 countries in western, central, and eastern Europe. Similar to the EU, it has a Court (European Court of Human Rights), a Council (Council of Europe) and a Parliament (Parliamentary Assembly).

Although it is outside the framework of the EU and deals with human rights, the Council of Europe can be of relevance for EU business law. According to

---

21. 1994 O.J. (L 1) 1. Although Switzerland signed the EEA Treaty, it never ratified it and is consequently not a member.
22. European Convention for the Protection of Human Rights and Fundamental Freedoms, Nov. 4, 1950, 213 U.N.T.S. 221.

Article 6(1) of the EU Treaty, for example, the European Convention on Human Rights is part of the EU legal system and the decisions of the European Court of Human Rights are frequently relied upon by the EU courts as evidence that a principle is a generally accepted fundamental right.[23] As discussed in greater detail in Chapter III, fundamental rights frequently arise in competition law cases.

4. The Nature of the European Union

The EEC was created by agreement between sovereign nations. It has sovereignty and legal personality under international law. In this respect, it is quite similar to the United States. Indeed, Winston Churchill, in a famous speech on September 19, 1948, at the University of Zürich, envisaged that the EEC would become the "United States of Europe." Although the EU is heading in that direction, it has failed to reach the same level of political, economic, and social integration as the United States. In order to understand the level of integration achieved by the EU, the following discussion will address its three dimensions: economic, political, and legal.

4.1 Economic Dimension

The EU represents an economic union between its members.[24] It is similar to the United States in this respect and may be distinguished from other forms of economic integration such as free trade areas, customs unions, and common markets.

A free trade area is a geographic area comprised of at least two sovereign states in which the duties on the sale of goods across borders has been broadly reduced or eliminated. Mercosur (derived from the words Mercado (market) and Sur (South)), NAFTA (North American Free Trade Agreement), and EFTA (European Free Trade Agreement) are examples of free trade areas. As discussed further in Chapter II, the member states of the EU have abolished customs duties and similar charges on the trade in goods across borders within the EU. However, the level of economic integration achieved by the EU is greater than that of a typical free trade area. It is also a customs union.

A customs union is similar to a free trade area in that it involves the reduction or elimination of duties on the flow of goods originating in the territory of the other members. In addition to the removal of customs duties on products originating from other member states, however, a customs union involves the introduction of a common external customs tariff on goods imported from

---

23. *See, e.g.*, Case C-36/02, Omega Spielhallen- und Automatenaufstellungs-GmbH v. Oberbürgermeisterin der Bundesstadt Bonn, 2004 E.C.R. I-9609, 9652 ¶33; Case C-327/02, Lili Georgieva Panayotova v. Minister voor Vreemdelingenzaken en Integratie, 2004 E.C.R. I-11055, 11099 ¶27; Joined cases T-67/00, T-68/00, T-71/00 and T-78/00, JFE Engineering Corp. v. Comm'n, 2004 E.C.R. II-2501, 2582 ¶178.
24. The economic system adopted by the EU is that of a "social market economy." EU Treaty at art. 3(3). At other points, however, the EU Treaty and the TFEU refer to an "open market economy with free competition." TFEU at arts. 119 and 120.

outside the customs union. The EU exhibits both of these characteristics: The TFEU (Article 30) prevents the member states from imposing duties on goods imported from other member states. At the same time, the TFEU (Article 31) introduces a common external customs tariff.

The EU is also a common market. A common market shares all of the characteristics of a customs union, but it also provides for the freedom of movement of services and capital based on the notion of equal treatment for nationals of the participating states. As discussed in Chapter II, the TFEU secures free movement of these factors of production among the member states. Nonetheless, the concept of common market does not capture all of the attributes of the economic integration achieved by the EU.

The EU is not only a common market, but also an economic community as it establishes the framework for a common economic policy separate from and superior to the policies of the individual member states. In addition, the TFEU establishes several EU institutions to which responsibility for economic policy is assigned. For example, the European Commission is entrusted with the task of maintaining competition within the EU through the application of the competition laws. The member states are generally bound to observe the decision of the Commission in this field.

4.2 Political Dimension

In the treaties, the member states have agreed to relinquish certain sovereign rights to the EU. For example, the member states have ceded their authority over trade with third countries to the EU. Consequently, in matters of external trade, the EU speaks as a single and independent actor.[25] This applies to all fields that the member states have ceded exclusively to the EU.

Although the EU is a self-declared "representative democracy,"[26] there is no commonly elected body. The European Parliament is a collection of representatives elected by constituencies in the respective member states and not by the EU as a whole. Moreover, the Parliament is imbued with relatively few independent legislative powers. The Commission, which is charged with protecting the interests of the EU, is made up of officials indirectly nominated by the individual member states. The absence of a commonly elected body and the limited legislative role given to the European Parliament is sometimes referred to as the democratic deficit of the EU.

4.3 Legal Dimension

(a) Legal Personality

Article 47 of the EU Treaty grants the EU legal personality. This grant of legal personality has two important ramifications. The first is that the EU, as an entity separate from its constituent parts, has the power to sign treaties binding on itself and its members (assuming, of course, that the subject matter of the treaty is

---

25. TFEU at art. 2(2).
26. EU Treaty at art. 10(1).

within the authority of the EU).[27] Once the treaty is entered into by the EU, it is binding on the EU institutions and the member states.[28] The member states are precluded from entering into treaties with other states on matters that fall within the competence of the EU. However, treaties entered into by the member states prior to their accession to the EU remain in force.[29] In such cases, the member states are required by EU law to interpret the respective pre-EU treaties in such a way that they are compatible with EU law.[30]

The second important ramification of having legal personality is that the EU becomes subject to international law. This aspect of legal personality is important for EU business law. As the European Court of Justice held in *Portugal v. Council*, for example, the EU institutions, when implementing a particular obligation assumed by the EU in the context of the World Trade Organization (WTO),[31] or where an EU law expressly refers to a WTO agreement, the application of the EU legislation must conform to the WTO rules.[32] Similarly, the jurisdiction of the EU institutions is limited by international law. For example, the European Commission's ability to review mergers under the Merger Control Regulation outside the EU must conform to public international law standards of jurisdiction.[33]

(b) Separate Legal System

The TFEU establishes a legal system sui generis. According to the European Court of Justice (ECJ):

> It is apparent from the Court's settled case-law that the founding treaties of the European Union, unlike ordinary international treaties, established a new legal order, possessing its own institutions, for the benefit of which the States have limited their sovereign rights, in ever wider fields, and the

---

27. TFEU at art. 218. The EU is exclusively responsible for concluding international agreements in three instances: (1) if the competence is provided for in a legislative act of the EU, (2) if the competence is necessary to enable the EU to exercise an internal comptence or (3) if the conclusion of the international agreement may affect common rules or their scope. TFEU at art. 3(2). The treaty or international agreement will be declared void if its subject matter does not fall within the competencies of the EU. Case C-327/91, French Republic v. Comm'n, 1994 E.C.R. I-3641, 3674 ¶24.
28. International treaties entered into by a member state prior to its accession to the EU remain valid and binding as against that member state. TFEU at art. 307.
29. TFEU at art. 351.
30. Case C-245/02, Anheuser-Busch Inc. v. Budejovický Budvar, národní podnik, 2004 E.C.R. I-10989, 11040 ¶55.
31. Agreement Establishing the World Trade Organization in Final Act Embodying the Results of the Uruguay Round of Multilateral Trade Negotiations, Apr. 15, 1994, 33 I.L.M. 1125, 1144-1154 (1994) [hereinafter WTO Agreement].
32. Case C-149/96, Portugal v. Council, 1999 E.C.R. I-8395, 8439 ¶49. One should note, however, that because of the political sensitivity of such issues, the European Court of Justice has never held that the community courts have blanket authority to review the conformity of community law with international law.
33. Case T-102/96, Gencor Ltd. v. Comm'n, 1999 E.C.R. II-753, 788 ¶101.

subjects of which comprise not only Member States but also their nationals.[34]

Although the EU legal system is dependent upon the legal systems of the member states, it did not replace the national legal systems. According to Article 4(1) of the EU Treaty, "competencies not conferred upon the Union in the Treaties remain with the Member States." The recognition that businesses in Europe may be exposed to both EU and national law depending on whether the EU has exclusive competence or shared competence, and whether the EU legislation is in the form of a directive or regulation, is practically and theoretically important for EU business law. For example, EU company law, as discussed in Chapter V, is a combination of EU secondary legislation and national law. In order to determine the capitalization requirements for establishing a public company in a particular member state, for example, reference needs to be made to both Council Directive 77/91/EEC[35] and the national company law implementing that directive.

According to Article 3(1) of the TFEU, the EU has *exclusive* competence in the following areas:

- customs union;
- the establishing of the competition rules necessary for the functioning of the internal market;
- monetary policy for the member states whose currency is the euro;
- the conservation of marine biological resources under the common fisheries policy; and
- common commercial policy.

The EU and the member states *share* competencies in the following areas:

- internal market;
- social policy;
- economic, social, and territorial cohesion;
- agriculture and fisheries, excluding the conservation of marine biological resources;
- environment;
- consumer protection;
- transport;
- trans-European networks;

---

34. Opinion 1/09 of the Court 8 March 2011, 2011 E.C.R. I-1137, 1168 ¶65.
35. Second Council Directive 77/91/EEC of 13 December 1976 on coordination of safeguards which, for the protection of the interests of members and others, are required by member states of companies within the meaning of the second paragraph of Article 58 of the Treaty, with regard to the formation of public limited liability companies and the maintenance and alteration of their capital, with a view to making such safeguards equivalent, 1977 O.J. (L 26) 1.

- energy;
- area of freedom, security, and justice; and
- common safety concerns in public health matters.

In these areas of shared competence, both the EU and the member states may legislate and adopt legally binding acts. However, the member states may only exercise their competence to the extent that the EU has not exercised its competence.[36] In some areas, EU law will expressly preempt the application of national law, much the same way as federal law in the United States can preempt state law. The EU Merger Control Regulation, for example, expressly preempts the application of national merger control laws to business transactions which fall within the scope of the EU Merger Control Regulation.[37] In other areas, EU legislation may implicitly preempt the application of national law. The EU Directive on Comparative Advertising, for example, preempts the application of national law to prevent comparative advertising if that same comparative advertising is permitted by the Directive. This preemption is not expressly stated in the Directive but implied as, according to the European Court of Justice, preemption is necessary to achieve the objective of the Directive.[38]

In yet other legal fields, the EU and the member states may have mutually exclusive competencies. In these areas, both the EU and member states may legislate as they deem appropriate, and the EU cannot preempt the member states. For example, the EU and member states share mutually exclusive jurisdiction over trademarks. The adoption of the Trademark Regulation[39] by the EU did not preclude the parallel application of the trademark regimes of the member states.[40]

In the event that EU law does not regulate a particular field, the member states have the authority to legislate and administer laws as they deem appropriate, subject to the principles of equivalence and effectiveness.[41] According to the principle of equivalence, the member states must apply their rules without distinction to the elements of the case that involve other member states. The principle of effectiveness, on the other hand, requires the member states to refrain from making it difficult for individuals and businesses to exercise their rights.

---

36. TFEU at art. 2(2).
37. Council Regulation (EC) No. 139/2004 of 20 January 2004 on the Control of Concentrations between undertakings, 2004 O.J. (L 24) 1.
38. Case C-44/01, Pippig Augenoptik v. Hartlauer Handelsgesellschaft mbH, 2003 E.C.R. I-3095, 3146 ¶44.
39. Council Regulation (EC) No. 207/2009 of 26 February 2009 on the Community trade mark, 2009 O.J. (L 78) 1.
40. According to Article 345 of the TFEU, the Treaty "shall in no way prejudice the rules in the member states governing the system of property ownership."
41. Case C-246/09, Bulicke v. Deutsche Büro Service GmbH, 2010 E.C.R. I-7003, 7017 ¶25.

5. European Monetary Union

5.1 From Common Market to Monetary Union

On January 1, 2002, the euro was introduced into circulation in Europe. As of July 1, 2002, the national currencies of the member states making up the "Euro Group" ceased to be legal tender. These events represent a significant milestone on the road to complete European integration. The EEC was initially envisaged and constituted as an economic union in which goods and services flow freely across borders. Although the idea of a monetary union can be traced back to the October 24, 1962, proposal of the European Commission referred to as the Marjolin Memorandum,[42] the more contemporary impetus behind the current monetary union was the Werner Report of October 8, 1970, (named after the chair of the Working Group, Pierre Werner) in which the creation of a monetary union was envisaged in stages.[43] This staged approach to monetary union was subsequently formalized by resolution of the member states.[44]

Although this resolution was never implemented, it influenced the creation of a committee in 1988, chaired by Jacques Delors, then president of the Commission, to prepare a report on the stages to monetary union. The resulting "Delors Report" followed the Werner Report and proposed to achieve monetary union in three stages. The third stage of economic and monetary union (EMU) started on January 1, 1999. This marked the irrevocable fixing of the exchange rates of the currencies of the 11 member states which the Council had determined in 1998 had fulfilled the necessary conditions for adopting the single currency.[45]

5.2 Euro Group Membership

Although Article 3(4) of the EU Treaty declares the EU a monetary union, not all of the member states have achieved the same level of monetary integration. The term Euro Group refers to the member states that have qualified and adopted the euro as their national currency. Only 18 of the 28 member states are members of the Euro Group. The member states where the euro is not the currency are

---

42. In this document, the Commission envisaged that the customs union would eventually develop into a system with irrevocably fixed exchange rates between the member states' currencies by 1970. What the Commission did not envisage was the creation of a common currency and new institutions to serve as a basis for such system. No concrete steps were taken on the Marjolin Memorandum. The initial Treaty of Rome did not envisage a common currency.
43. Report of the Council and Commission on the Realization by Stages of Economic and Monetary Union in Community, 3 Bull. E.C. No. 11 (Supp. 1970).
44. Resolution of the Council and of the Representatives of the Governments of the Member States of 22 March 1971 on the attainment by stages of economic and monetary union in the Community, 1971 O.J. (C 28) 1.
45. Council Decision of 3 May 1998 in accordance with Article 109j(4) of the Treaty, 1998 O.J. (L 139) 30. The member states were Belgium, Germany, Spain, France, Ireland, Italy, Luxembourg, the Netherlands, Austria, Portugal, and Finland.

referred to as member states with a derogation. To qualify for membership in the Euro Group, the member state must meet the convergence criteria set forth in Article 140(1) of the TFEU and the Protocol on the Convergence Criteria.[46] The four convergence criteria are:

- A high degree of price stability measured by the attainment of an inflation rate close to that (i.e., within 1.5 percent) of the three best performing member states (inflation rate criterion);

- The long-term interest rate in the preceding year cannot exceed more than 2 percent of the level achieved by the three best performing member states (interest rate criterion).

- The national currency must have been within the European Monetary System band for the previous two years (exchange rate criterion).

- The government deficit cannot exceed 3 percent of that country's gross domestic product (GDP) and the accumulated total government debt should not exceed 60 percent of GDP (public deficit criterion).[47]

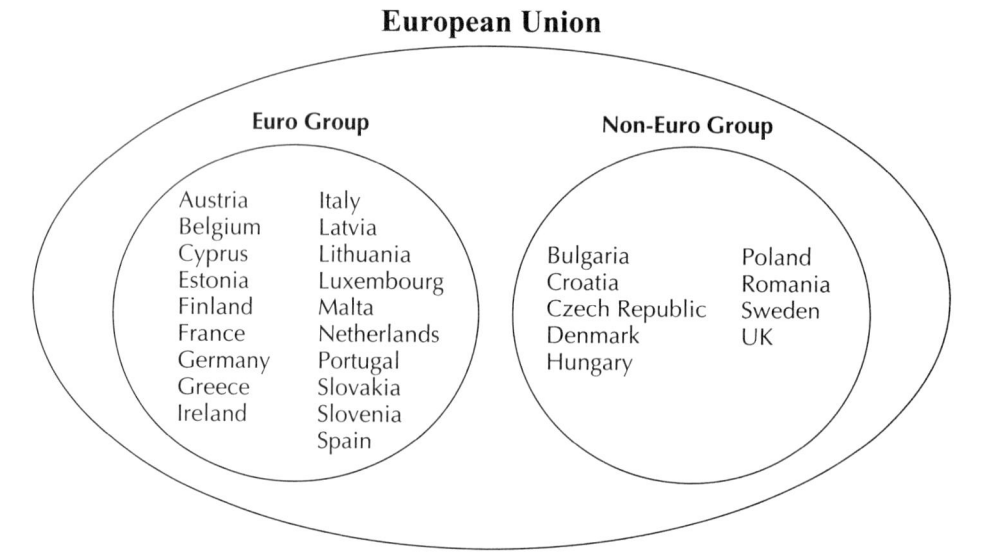

European Union

Euro Group

Austria, Belgium, Cyprus, Estonia, Finland, France, Germany, Greece, Ireland, Italy, Latvia, Lithuania, Luxembourg, Malta, Netherlands, Portugal, Slovakia, Slovenia, Spain

Non-Euro Group

Bulgaria, Croatia, Czech Republic, Denmark, Hungary, Poland, Romania, Sweden, UK

Of the 28 member states, 19 have met the convergence criteria and joined the Euro Group. Initially only Belgium, Germany, Spain, France, Ireland, Italy, Luxembourg, the Netherlands, Austria, Portugal, and Finland qualified

---

46. Protocol (No. 13) on the Convergence Criteria, 2010 O.J. (C 83) 281.
47. The "deficit" is the amount by which the government's expenditures exceed its revenue in a given year. It should be distinguished from "debt" which is the government's total indebtedness at a moment in time. In other words, the debt is the accumulation of previous deficits together with any unpaid interest accrued on these deficits. "GDP" is the gross domestic product, i.e., the total output of goods and services produced within a given country in a particular time period. It is equal to the sum of the value added by each industry, net of all inputs, including imported intermediate goods. It is different from the gross national product (GNP) which is the GDP plus net property income from abroad.

and decided to join the third stage of the monetary union.[48] Greece initially failed to meet the criteria but was later admitted on January 1, 2001.[49] Although it was later discovered that Greece was able to meet the qualifications for membership by manipulating the numbers it provided to Eurostat (the EU agency responsible for collecting the statistics used to apply the convergence criteria),[50] it was allowed to remain in the Euro Group. The following member states have subsequently joined the Euro Group: Slovenia (2007),[51] Cyprus (2008),[52] Malta (2008),[53] Slovakia (2009),[54] Estonia (2011),[55] Latvia (2014) and Lithuania (2015).

Although all EU member states are legally obligated to strive to meet the convergence criteria and join the Euro Group, the member states in the Non-Euro Group all have "derogations." Some of these member states have affirmatively decided not to join (i.e., Denmark, Sweden, and the UK) while others (Bulgaria, Romania, the Czech Republic, Hungary, and Poland) have not qualified to join.

5.3   Enforcement of Fiscal Discipline

The European monetary union establishes a central monetary policy but not a uniform economic or fiscal policy.[56] The member states retain individual authority to set their own fiscal policies. Nonetheless, the success of the monetary union depends on the fiscal discipline of the member states which each retain authority to tax and spend money. Consequently, member states are limited in their fiscal policies by Article 126(1) of the TFEU which requires the member states to "avoid excessive government deficits."

The excessive deficit procedure, codified in a combination of Article 126 of the TFEU, the Protocol on the Excessive Deficit Procedure,[57] Council

---

48. Council Decision of 3 May 1998 in accordance with Article 109j(4) of the Treaty, 1998 O.J. (L 139) 30.
49. Council Decision of 19 June 2000 in accordance with Article 122(2) of the Treaty on the adoption by Greece of the single currency on 1 January 2001, 2000 O.J. (L 167) 19.
50. See Commission reports on Greek statistics, starts infringement procedure, IP/04/1431 (Dec. 1, 2004).
51. Council Decision of 11 July 2006 in accordance with Article 122(2) of the Treaty on the adoption by Slovenia of the single currency on 1 January 2007, 2006 O.J. (L 195) 25.
52. Council Decision of 10 July 2007 in accordance with Article 122(2) of the Treaty on the adoption by Cyprus of the single currency on 1 January 2008, 2007 O.J. (L 186) 29.
53. Council Decision of 10 July 2007 in accordance with Article 122(2) of the Treaty on the adoption by Malta of the single currency on 1 January 2008, 2007 O.J. (L 186) 32.
54. Council Decision of 8 July 2008 in accordance with Article 122(2) of the Treaty on the adoption by Slovakia of the single currency on 1 January 2009, 2008 O.J. (L 195) 24.
55. Council Decision of 13 July 2010 in accordance with Article 122(2) of the Treaty on the adoption by Estonia of the single currency on 1 January 2011, 2010 O.J. (L 196) 24.
56. Whereas the term "monetary policy" refers generally to the control over interest rates and money supply, the term "fiscal policy" refers to the taxation and expenditure policies of a government.
57. Protocol (No. 12) on the Excessive Deficit Procedure, 2010 O.J. (C 83) 279.

Regulation 479/2009,[58] and Council Regulation 1467/97,[59] is the mechanism by which the EU may impose discipline among the member states in exercising their fiscal policies. The member states are required to periodically submit data to the Commission[60]. The Commission uses the data to monitor the budgetary discipline of the member states on the basis of two reference values:

- The first reference value is the ratio of the planned or actual government deficit[61] to gross domestic product. This ratio must not exceed 3 percent (i.e., the deficit may not be more than 3 percent of GDP) unless (1) the ratio has declined substantially and continuously and reached a level that comes close to the reference value or (2) the excess is only temporary and exceptional.[62]

- The second reference value is the ratio of government debt[63] to gross domestic product. This ratio must not exceed 60 percent (i.e., the government debt may not be more than 60 percent of GDP) unless the ratio is sufficiently diminishing and approaching the reference value at a satisfactory pace.[64]

If a member state which has already fulfilled the convergence criteria no longer fulfills the requirements, the first step is for the Commission to prepare

---

58. Council Regulation (EC) No. 479/2009 of 25 May 2009 on the application of the Protocol on the excessive deficit procedure annexed to the Treaty establishing the European Community, 2009 O.J. (L 145) 1.
59. Council Regulation (EC) No. 1467/97 of 7 July 1997 on speeding up and clarifying the implementation of the excessive deficit procedure, 1997 O.J. (L 209) 6 as last amended by Council Regulation (EU) No 1177/2011.
60. The effectiveness of this oversight depends, of course, on the veracity of the data reporting. The member states are required to report their data to the Commission pursuant to the rules codified in Council Regulation (EC) No. 2223/96 of 25 June 1996 on the European system of national and regional accounts in the Community, 1996 O.J. (L 310) 1, and Council Regulation (EC) No. 479/2009 of 25 May 2009 on the application of the Protocol on the excessive deficit procedure annexed to the Treaty establishing the European Community, 2009 O.J. (L 145) 1. Nonetheless, these accounting rules are vulnerable to manipulation by the member states. *See, e.g.*, George Parker & Peter Larsen, "*EU States Accused of Using Budget Deficit 'Ruse,'*" FINANCIAL TIMES, Oct. 6, 2005, at 2 col. 3.
61. The term "deficit" in this context is defined as net borrowing consolidated for all levels of government in the particular member state (federal, state, and local).
62. TFEU at art. 126(2). The excess is considered "exceptional" if it results from an unusual event outside the control of the member state having a major impact on the financial position of the general government or when resulting from a severe economic downturn and the Commission Forecasts show that the deficit will fall below the reference value following the severe economic downturn or unusual event. Council Regulation (EC) No. 1467/97 of 7 July 1997 on speeding up and clarifying the implementation of the excessive deficit procedure, 1997 O.J. (L 209) 6, art. 2(1).
63. The term "debt" in this context is defined as total gross debt at nominal value outstanding at the end of the year consolidated for all levels of government (federal, state, and local).
64. TFEU at art. 126(2)(b).

a report which examines whether the government deficit exceeds government investment expenditure. In preparing the report, the Commission must take into account "all relevant factors," such as the medium-term economic and budgetary position of the member state and the efforts of the member state to maintain budgetary discipline.[65] In order to make the system more flexible to accommodate noncomplying member states, the Council adopted legislation which requires the Commission to consider other excuses given by the member state as to its excess.[66]

The Monetary Committee of the European Central Bank[67] then (within two weeks) prepares an opinion on the Commission's report. If the Commission considers that a situation of excessive deficit still exists, the Commission may address an opinion to the Council.[68] The Council then reviews the situation, allows the member state to submit observations, and decides after an "overall assessment" whether an excessive deficit exists.[69] If the Council decides that an excessive deficit exists, it issues a recommendation to the member state concerned with a view to bringing that situation to an end within a given period.[70] If the member state fails to implement the recommendation, the Council may (but is not required to)[71] give notice to the member state to take specific deficit reduction measures within a specific timeframe.[72]

---

65. TFEU at art. 126(3); Regulation (EC) No 1467/97 of 7 July 1997 on speeding up and clarifying the implementation of the excessive deficit procedure, 1997 O.J. (L 209) 6, art. 2(3).
66. According to Regulation (EC) No 1467/97 of 7 July 1997 on speeding up and clarifying the implementation of the excessive deficit procedure, 1997 O.J. (L 209) 6, art. 2(3) as amended by Council Regulation (EC) No. 1177/2011, the Commission is required to also consider any other factors which, in the opinion of the member state concerned, are relevant in order to comprehensively assess compliance with deficit and debt criteria. That would include such broad consideration as financial contributions to fostering international solidarity and achieving the policy goals of the EU, the debt incurred in the form of bilateral and multilateral support between member states in the context of safeguarding financial stability, and the debt related to financial stabilization operations during major financial disturbances.
67. The Monetary Committee is established by Article 134 of the TFEU. It is comprised of members elected by the member states (two per member state) and two members elected by the Commission.
68. TFEU at art. 126(3).
69. *See, e.g.*, Council Decision of 27 April 2009 on the existence of an excessive deficit in France, 2009 O.J. (L 135) 19.
70. TFEU at art. 126(7). Although the terms of the recommendation are not made public, if the member state does not take adequate steps to comply with the recommendation, the terms of the recommendation may be made public. TFEU at art. 126(8).
71. Case C-27/04, Comm'n v. Council, 2004 E.C.R. I-6649, 6699 ¶34. The inability to achieve a majority in the Council means that a contestable decision in the meaning of Article 230 of the TFEU has not been reached.
72. TFEU at art. 126(9). *See, e.g.*, Council Decision of 16 February 2010 giving notice to Greece to take measures for the deficit reduction judged necessary in order to remedy the situation of excessive deficit, 2010 O.J. (L 83) 13.

If the member state takes appropriate steps to correct its excessive deficit, the Council may abrogate its decision.[73] If, however, the Council decides to give notice, and the member state fails to comply with the Council's notice within four months after the Council's notice,[74] the Council has the authority (by qualified weighted majority vote excluding the votes of the member state concerned) to apply one or more of the following measures:[75]

- require the member state to publish additional information before issuing bonds and securities;
- invite the European Investment Bank to reconsider its lending policy towards the member state concerned;
- require the member state to make a non-interest-bearing deposit of an appropriate size with the EU until the excessive deficit has been corrected; or
- impose fines in an "appropriate" amount.[76]

Because of political considerations, the imposition of sanctions as a result of the excessive deficit procedure is highly unlikely. Moreover, the Council has the discretion to abrogate an excessive deficit decision if the member state reports that it has complied with the Council's decision,[77] or extend the time period in which the member state has to comply with the decisions.[78] Nonetheless, if sanctions are imposed and the member state refuses to take remedial action, the EU institutions do not have additional options to compel compliance. Expulsion from the Euro Group is not a legal or political option. The political realities of the EU dictate more pragmatic solutions. The sanction mechanisms available

---

73. TFEU at art. 126(12). *See, e.g.*, Council Decision of 5 June 2007 abrogating Decision 2003/89/EC on the existence of an excessive deficit in Germany, 2007 O.J. (L 183) 23.
74. Council Regulation (EC) No. 1467/97 of 7 July on speeding up and clarifying the implementation of the excessive deficit procedure, 1997 O.J. (L 209) 6, art. 6(2), as amended by Council Regulation (EC) No. 1177/2011. The Council can extend the time deadline by revising the notice to take account of "unexpected adverse economic events with major unfavorable consequences for government finances" occurring after the Council's notice. *Id.* art. 5(2).
75. TFEU at art. 126(11).
76. According to Article 11 of Council Regulation (EC) No. 1467/97 of 7 July 1997, 1997 O.J. (L 209) 6 as amended by Council Regulation (EU) No 1177/11, fines are to be imposed on the member state "as a rule." According to Article 12, the fine is to include a fixed component equal to 0.2 percent of GDP and a variable component up to a maximum of 0.5 percent of GDP. The variable component is 10 percent of the absolute value of the difference between the balance as a percentage of GDP in the preceding year and either the reference value for government balance or, if noncompliance with budgetary discipline includes the debt criterion, the government balance as a percentage of GDP that should have been achieved in the same year according to the notice issued under Article 126(9) of the TFEU.
77. *See, e.g.*, Council Decision of 21 June 2013 abrogating Decision 2010/286/EU on the existence of an excessive government deficit in Italy, 2013 O.J. (C 173) 41.
78. *See, e.g.*, Council Recommendation of 21 June 2013 with a view to bringing an end to the situation of an excessive government deficit in Spain, 2013 O.J. (C 180) 4.

to the Council have not been employed even in situations in which they would have been legally appropriate.

The experience with France, which ultimately necessitated the involvement of the ECJ in *Commission v. Council*,[79] provides a good illustration of how the excessive deficit procedure works and its limitations. France had repeatedly breached the deficit ratio limit of 3 percent of GDP discussed above.[80] In 2003, the Council issued a recommendation to France that it should take all appropriate measures to ensure that its government deficit does not exceed 3 percent. Despite numerous public and private admonitions, the French Finance Minister, Francis Mer, informed the Council its deficit would reach 4 percent of GDP in 2003 and 3.6 percent in 2004. As discussed above, if a member state persists in failing to put into practice the recommendations of the Council, the Council may decide to give notice to the member state to take measures for the deficit reduction which is judged necessary by the Council in order to remedy the situation.[81] The next step would have been for the Council to give France notice under Article 126(9) of the TFEU. Because of political considerations, however, the Council did not adopt a decision to give notice as the Commission had recommended (the required majority for a decision was not achieved). It decided to hold the excessive deficit procedure in abeyance, pending France's compliance with the Council's requirements. Although the Commission continued to pressure France to adopt appropriate measures to bring its deficit into line, the Commission recognized "off the record" that there was little it could do because of political constraints.[82]

The Commission took the rather bold step of bringing an action against the Council under Article 263 of the TFEU to annul the decision of the Council not to adopt a decision against France. The ECJ held that the lack of a decision, even though it may have had the effect of rejecting the Commission's recommendations, was not a contestable decision within the meaning of Article 263 of the TFEU. The decision to hold the excessive deficit procedure in abeyance was, however, illegal because it made the resumption of the procedure conditional on conduct of the member state, thereby illegitimately relinquishing

---

79. Case C-27/04, Comm'n v. Council, 2004 E.C.R. 6649.
80. *See, e.g.*, Council Decision of 3 June 2003 on the existence of an excessive deficit in France, 2003 O.J. (L 165) 29. Germany was also involved in this case but adopted a much more conciliatory approach.
81. TFEU at art. 126(9).
82. George Parker & Daniel Dombey, *Commission powerless as Paris defies euro rules*, THE FINANCIAL TIMES, Oct. 4/5, 2003, at 2 col 1.

the Council's authority to resume the procedure as it deemed appropriate.[83] In the end, no sanctions were imposed on France, and it remains a member of the Euro Group.

5.4 Non-Euro Group Member States

As indicated above, the following nine EU member states have not (yet) joined the Euro Group: Bulgaria, Czech Republic, Denmark, Hungary, Lithuania, Poland, Romania, Sweden, and the UK. These non-Euro Group member states are referred to as member states with a derogation.[84] The member states with a derogation are required to strive to meet the convergence criteria and join the Euro Group. In the meantime, however, they retain their own currencies.

To prevent wide fluctuations in the exchange rates between the Euro and the currencies of the respective non-Euro Group member states, the ECB has established an exchange rate mechanism referred to as ERM II. Two of the member states with a derogation are members of the ERM II: Denmark and Lithuania.[85] The ERM II establishes a target exchange rate for each of the national currencies participating in the EMR II. Those currencies are allowed to fluctuate within a band of 15 percent above or below that target exchange rate. The ECB and the national central banks are required to intervene if the exchange rate threatens to move outside that band. As discussed below, the General Counsel of the ECB is responsible for coordinating with the national central banks to implement the ERM II.

5.5 Institutions of the European Monetary Union

(a) *European System of Central Banks*

The European System of Central Banks (ESCB) was established on January 1, 1999, and is comprised of the European Central Bank (ECB) and the national central banks of all of the member states (and not just the 16 member states who are members of the Euro Group). However, the non-Euro Group member states do not take part in the decisions affecting the Euro Group. The operations

---

83. Case C-27/04, Comm'n v. Council, 2004 E.C.R. I-6649, 6711 ¶88. This case served to illustrate the legal constraints imposed on the politicians by the legal system that they had initially established. At that time, they did not envisage the political problems that the strict application of the legal standards would introduce. The constraints on the Council have since been loosened somewhat by the adoption of Council Regulation (EC) No. 1056/2005 of 27 June 2005 (2005 O.J. (L 174) 5) which amends Council Regulation (EC) No. 1467/97 of 7 July 1997 on speeding up and clarifying the implementation of the excessive deficit procedure 1997 O.J. (L 209) 6) and introduces longer time periods and more flexible standards for the Council and Commission.
84. TFEU at art. 122(1).
85. Joining the ERM II requires the member state to sign and ratify the Agreement of 16 March 2006 between the European Central Bank and the national central banks (NCBs) of the member states outside the euro area, laying down the operating procedures for an exchange rate mechanism in stage three of EMU, 2006 O.J. (C 73) 21. Bulgaria, Czech Republic, Hungary, Poland, Romania, Sweden, and the UK are the only member states that are neither in the Euro Group nor in the ERM II.

of the ESCB are governed by certain provisions of the TFEU and the Statute of the ESCB and ECB.[86]

The ESCB is not an institution per se, but rather a system of coordination between the ECB and the national central banks of the member states. The decision-making bodies of the ECB are the Executive Board and Governing Council.[87] The general objective of the ESCB is to maintain price stability (i.e., prevent excessive inflation).[88] In pursuing this objective, it relies on the monetary policy instruments which have been entrusted to it. The monetary policy instruments are open market operations (such as reverse transactions, outright transactions, foreign exchange swaps, and fixed-term deposits), standing facilities (such as marginal lending facilities and deposit facilities), and minimum reserves requirements. Each of these monetary policy instruments allows the ESCB to influence inflation within Europe.

(b) *European Central Bank*

The central institution in the ESCB is the European Central Bank. The ECB, which has legal personality, is charged with implementing the tasks conferred upon the ESCB.[89] The ECB (as well as the national central banks) are required to be independent from political or national influence. This equally applies to the governing organs of the ECB. They are prohibited by law from taking instructions from any EU institutions or bodies or from any member state.[90] Although the ESCB has three bodies (Executive Board, Governing Council, and General Counsel), only two of these (Executive Board and Governing Council) have decision-making authority.[91]

The Executive Board is made up of a president, vice-president, and four other members, all appointed by the European Council for a nonrenewable period of eight years.[92] The Executive Board is responsible for the implementation of the monetary policy set by the Governing Council and for the daily management of the ECB. The Executive Board meets once a week.

The most important body of the ECB in terms of setting monetary policy is the Governing Council, consisting of the six members of the Executive Board and

---

86. Protocol on the Statute of the European System of Central Banks and of the ECB, 1992 O.J. (C 191) 68 [hereinafter Statute of the ESCB and ECB].
87. TFEU at art. 129(1).
88. *Id.* at art. 127(1). The general target is to keep inflation under (but close to) 2 percent based on a year-on-year comparison of the harmonized index of consumer prices.
89. Statute of the ESCB and ECB at art. 9.2.
90. Statute of the ESCB and ECB at art. 7.
91. The ESCB has several committees, created by the Governing Council, which support the work of the Executive Board and the Governing Council. At present, the committees are as follows: the Accounting and Monetary Income Committee, the Banking Supervision Committee, the Banknote Committee, the Budget Committee, the Eurosystem/ESCB Communications Committee, the Information Technology Committee, the Internal Auditors Committee, the International Relations Committee, the Legal Committee, the Market Operations Committee, the Monetary Policy Committee, the Payment and Settlement Systems Committee, and the Statistics Committee.
92. TFEU at art. 283.

the governors of the national central banks of the member states. The Governing Council, which meets at least 10 times annually, is responsible for all decisions except for those expressly reserved to the Executive Board.[93] It defines monetary policy and establishes the necessary guidelines for its implementation.

The last of the three main ECB bodies is the General Council consisting of the president and vice-president of the ECB and the governors of the central banks of the member states.[94] The General Council has no decision-making authorities with regard to monetary policy. Its primary task is to monitor the progress of the non-Euro Group member states toward entry into the Euro Group. In particular it carries out the work necessary for the possible accession of those countries to the Euro Group and ERM II.

(c) Eurosystem

As discussed above, all EU member states participate in the ESCB through their respective central banks (Denmark and the UK have special status). However, the fact that certain member states have fulfilled the necessary requirements for adoption of the euro while others have not necessitated the establishment of a separate "sub-system" within the ESCB called the Eurosystem. The Eurosystem is comprised of representatives of the ECB and the national central banks of the 15 Euro Group member states. It shares the same governing bodies as the ESCB. However, the composition of the bodies differs depending on the issues being addressed.

(d) Single Supervisory Mechanism

For many politicians, the banking crisis of 2007-2008 was at least in part due to the absence of a pan-EU banking regulator. The ECB was never granted jurisdiction by the member states to fulfill the role of a central bank regulator. The responsibility and authority for regulating banks remained in the hands of the member states. Some EU and member state politicians then pressed for movement in the direction of an integrated banking union. The Single Supervisory Mechanism (SSM) is the first legislative step in this direction.[95] Membership in the SSM is mandatory for all member states in the Euro Group and voluntary for all other member states. It is important to remember that the SSM is (merely) a mechanism and not an institution. Ultimate decision-making authority lies with the ECB's Governing Council.

---

93. Statute of the ESCB and the ECB at art. 12.1.
94. The operations of the General Council are governed by the Decision of the European Central Bank adopting rules of procedure of the General Council of the European Central Bank, 2004 O.J. (L 230) 61.
95. The primary legislative instruments on which the Single Supervisory Mechanism are based are Regulation (EU) No 1022/2013 of the European Parliament and of the Council of 22 October 2013 amending Regulation (EU) No 1093/2010 establishing a European Supervisory Authority (European Banking Authority) as regards the conferral of specific tasks on the European Central Bank pursuant to Council Regulation (EU) No 1024/2013, 2013 O.J. (L 287) 5 and Council Regulation (EU) No 1024/2013 of 15 October 2013 conferring specific tasks on the European Central Bank concerning policies relating to the prudential supervision of credit institutions, 2013 O.J. (L 287) 63.

In general, the SSM shifts some responsibility to regulate banks of a certain size (referred to as "significant banks") to the SSM Supervisory Board. The responsibility for regulating the other banks remains with the member states. A bank is deemed significant if the value of its assets is over €30 billion, or the value of its assets is over €30 billion and 20 percent of the GDP of the member state where it is located, or the bank is one of the three most significant banks in the member state where it is located, or the bank has large cross-border activities or the bank has applied for Eurozone bailout funds.

The "significant banks" are regulated by the Supervisory Board consisting of representatives of the member states and the ECB. The SSM gives the ECB certain exclusive authorities, such as the authority to authorize credit institutions and to withdraw authorizations of credit institutions, to assess notifications of the acquisition and disposal of qualifying holdings in credit institutions, to ensure compliance with funds requirements, securitization, large exposure limits, liquidity, and leverage, to carry out stress tests, and to supervise troubled credit institutions.[96]

6. Institutional Structure of European Union

6.1 Main Institutions

The institutional structure of the EU is comprised of seven institutions and a number of agencies. The fundamental differences between an EU institution and agency are that the institutions are created by the EU Treaty and the TFEU, responsible for a broad range of subject matters and have their own legal personality, whereas the agencies are created by secondary legislation—typically to address specific issues—and do not have legal personality. The institutions of the EU are:

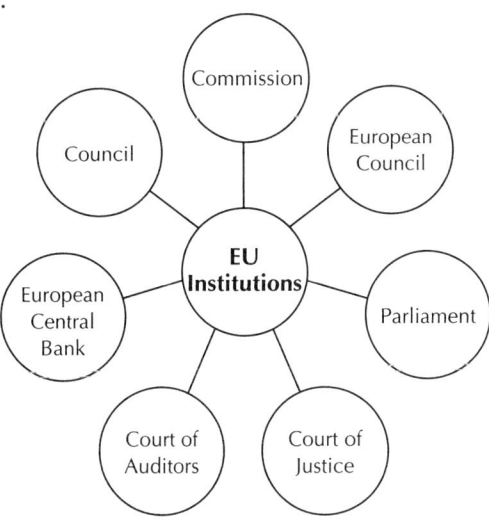

---

96. Council Regulation (EU) No 1024/2013 of 15 October 2013 conferring specific tasks on the European Central Bank concerning policies relating to the prudential supervision of credit institutions, 2013 O.J. (L 287) 63 at art. 4.

(a) Commission

A discussion of the EU institutions in a publication on EU business law appropriately begins with the European Commission. Until 2019, the Commission, which is located in Brussels, Belgium, consists of 28 members. After 2019, the number of commissioners is to be reduced to a number of members equal to two-thirds of the number of member states.[97] The commissioners are indirectly appointed by the member states for terms of five years and include the High Representative of the Union for Foreign Affairs.[98] The nomination and election of the Commission members start with the European Council, acting by a qualified majority, proposing to the European Parliament a candidate for president of the Commission. If the president-elect is approved by Parliament, he or she—together with the Council—then compiles a list of other Commission members. These individuals are selected on the basis of the suggestions made by member states. The complete Commission is then subject as a body to a vote of consent by the Parliament. On the basis of this consent, the Commission is then appointed by the Council, acting by a qualified majority.

Legally, the members of the Commission are required to act "completely independent" of the member states. According to Article 17(3) of the EU Treaty, "the members of the Commission shall neither seek nor take instructions from any Government or other institution, body, office or entity." The Commission members may be removed individually or as a body. A member of the Commission must resign if requested by the president of the Commission to do so.[99] In addition, the European Parliament may censure the Commission. If such a motion is carried, the members of the Commission must resign as a body.

The Commission acts by simple majority of the members present at a meeting with a quorum.[100] The College of Commissioners (i.e., a meeting of all 28 commissioners) meets once a week in Brussels. The work of the Commission (e.g., drafting the Commission's legislative proposals) is largely delegated to 41 Directorate Generals (each responsible for a particular subject matter, such as competition or economic affairs) and services (such as the Legal Service). Each of the Directorate Generals reports to a specific commissioner. The Commission president determines which commissioner is responsible for which portfolio.[101] As the responsibility for drafting legislation is assumed by the respective Directorate Generals, businesses desiring to influence legislation work closely with the staff of the Directorate Generals. By the time the legislation is presented to the College of Commissioners, it is typically too late to exert much influence. Each Directorate General is subdivided into directorates and further into units.

---

97. EU Treaty at art. 17(5).
98. *Id.* at art. 17(3).
99. *Id.* at art. 17(6).
100. TFEU at art. 250.
101. Commission Rules of Procedure, 2010 O.J. (L 55) 60 at art. 3.

```
         College of Commissioners
            /              \
Directorate Generals    Services
(e.g., competition)    (e.g., legal)
         |
     Directorates
         |
       Units
```

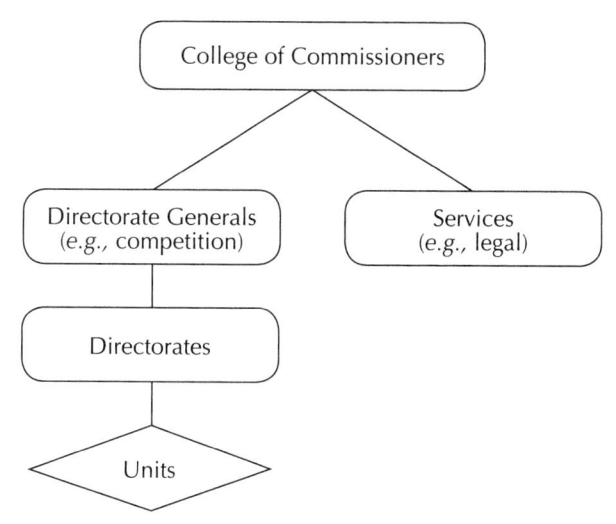

The legislative functions of the Commission are limited to initiating legislative acts and adopting nonlegislative acts. Although the Commission does not have the authority to adopt legislative acts on its own, an EU legislative act may only be adopted on the basis of a Commission proposal except where the treaties provide otherwise.[102] The power of initiation should not be underestimated. As the drafter of the legislation, the Commission has an influence on the start—and hence the outcome—of EU laws. The Council may only amend the proposal of the Commission by acting unanimously.[103] In addition, if the legislation is not introduced by the Commission, it cannot be adopted in most instances. Moreover, the Commission participates in the legislative process through its power to withdraw a legislative proposal before the Council makes a final decision.

Although the Commission does not have the authority to adopt legislative acts, it does have the authority to adopt nonlegislative acts. There are two types of nonlegislative acts: delegated acts and implementing acts.[104] When adopting a legislative act, the Council and Parliament may delegate to the Commission the authority to adopt nonlegislative acts of general application to supplement or amend certain nonessential elements of the legislative act.[105] For example, in the Prospectus Directive, the Council set out the fundamental requirements for the issuance of prospectuses in public offerings of securities, but delegated to the Commission the authority to adopt legislation governing the format of the prospectuses.[106] In reliance on this authority, the Commission adopted

---

102. EU Treaty at art. 17(2).
103. TFEU at art. 293(1).
104. *Id.* at art. 291.
105. *Id.* at art. 290.
106. Article 5(5) of the Directive 2003/71/EC of the European Parliament and of the Council of 4 November 2003 on the prospectus to be published when securities are offered to the public or admitted to trading and amending Directive 2001/34/EC, 2003 O.J. (L 345) 64.

Regulation 809/2004 setting forth the specific format of prospectuses.[107] The Council and Parliament retain negative control over delegated nonlegislative acts of the Commission as the delegated act may enter into force only if no objection has been expressed by the Council and Parliament and they can revoke the delegated authority at any time.[108]

In addition, the Commission may adopt implementing nonlegislative acts when authorized by the appropriate EU institution. For example, in Directive 2009/65, the Parliament and Council promulgated the rule that the prospectus of an undertaking for collective investment in transferrable securities does not necessarily have to be provided to investors on paper and authorized the Commission to adopt implementing measures which define the specific conditions that need to be met when providing the prospectus in a durable medium other than paper or by means of a website which does not constitute a durable medium.[109] The Commission subsequently relied on this authority to adopt Regulation 583/2010.[110] Whereas a delegated nonlegislative act is designed to give the Commission the authority to fill in the nonessential details of a particular legislative act, the purpose of implementing a nonlegislative legislative act is to establish uniform implementing conditions for the member states.[111]

The Commission also serves as the executive branch of the EU. As it is entrusted with supervision and enforcement of TFEU,[112] the Commission is sometimes referred to as the Guardian of the Treaty. According to the ECJ, "the Commission's function is to ensure, in its own motion and in the general interest, that the member states give effect to EU law."[113] For example, if a member state fails to fulfill its obligations under the TFEU or secondary legislation, the Commission has the authority to bring a claim against that member state before the European Court of Justice. As discussed below, if the ECJ then concludes

---

107. Commission Regulation (EC) No 809/2004 of 29 April 2004 implementing Directive 2003/71/EC of the European Parliament and of the Council as regards information contained in prospectuses as well as the format, incorporation by reference and publication of such prospectuses and dissemination of advertisements, 2004 O.J. (L 149) 1.
108. TFEU at art. 290(2).
109. Directive 2009/65/EC of the European Parliament and of the Council of 13 July 2009 on the coordination of laws, regulations and administrative provisions relating to undertakings for collective investment in transferable securities, 2009 O.J. (L 302) 32 art. 75.
110. Commission Regulation (EU) No 583/2010 of 1 July 2010 implementing Directive 2009/65/EC of the European Parliament and of the Council as regards key investor information and conditions to be met when providing key investor information or the prospectus in a durable medium other than paper or by means of a website, 2010 O.J. (L 176) 1.
111. Communication from the Commission to the European Parliament and the Council—Implementation of Article 290 of the Treaty on the Functioning of the European Union, COM/2009/0673 final.
112. TFEU at art. 258.
113. Case C-20/09, Comm'n v. Portugal, 2011 E.C.R. I-2637, 2675 ¶41.

that a member state has failed to fulfill an obligation under the treaties, it can ultimately impose a monetary fine on the member state.[114]

The Commission also acts on behalf of the EU in making sure that the other EU institutions act within their authorities. Article 263 of the TFEU allows the Commission to bring an action to the ECJ challenging EU acts which do not conform with EU law. In *Commission v. Council*, for example, the Commission successfully brought a claim against the Council when the Council exceeded its authority by restraining the ability of the Commission to negotiate an international agreement.[115]

The executive authority of the Commission is not limited to enforcing compliance by the member states and EU institutions with the treaties. The Commission is also charged with enforcing EU law vis-à-vis private actors. For example, Article 105 of the TFEU entrusts the Commission with ensuring the application of the competition laws codified in Articles 101 and 102 of the TFEU. As will become evident in Chapter III, the Commission is an important institution for businesses operating in Europe because of this authority.

(b) European Council

The European Council consists of the heads of state of the member states, together with the Council's president and the president of the Commission. The Council is primarily a political body as it has no legislative functions. It is charged with defining the general political direction and priorities of the EU.[116] It meets at least twice every six months in Brussels, Belgium.[117] Decisions of the Council are generally taken by consensus.[118]

The president of the European Council is elected by qualified majority of the members of the Council for a term of 30 months. The president is responsible for chairing the work of the Council. The president is also responsible for representing the EU externally, subject to the authorities of the High Representative of the Union for Foreign Affairs and Security Policy.

The High Representative of the Union for Foreign Affairs and Security Policy is elected (and removed) by the European Council, acting by a qualified majority, with the agreement of the President of the Commission.[119] The High Representative is responsible for conducting the EU common foreign, defense, and security policy as one of the vice-presidents of the Commission.

(c) Council

The European Council should be distinguished from the Council of the European Union. Whereas the European Council is comprised of the heads of state of the respective member states, the Council, which meets when convened by its president on his or her own initiative or at the request of one of its members or

---

114. TFEU at art. 260(2).
115. Case C-114/12, Comm'n v. Parliament, 2014 E.C.R. I-____.
116. EU Treaty at art. 15.
117. Rules of Procedure of the European Council, 2009 O.J. (L 315) 52 art. 1(1) [hereinafter European Council Rules of Procedure].
118. European Council Rules of Procedure at art. 6(1).
119. EU Treaty at art. 18(1).

of the Commission,[120] is comprised of the ministers of the respective member states responsible for a specific subject matter.[121] For example, if the topic to be addressed is in the field of transportation, the respective transportation ministers from the governments of each of the member states meet to form the Council. There are 10 different Council configurations:[122]

- General Affairs
- Foreign Affairs
- Economic and Financial Affairs
- Justice and Home Affairs
- Employment, Social Policy, Health, and Consumer Affairs
- Competitiveness (Internal Market, Industry, Research, and Space)
- Transport, Telecommunications, and Energy
- Agriculture and Fisheries
- Environment
- Education, Youth, Culture, and Sport

The main tasks of the Council are to adopt legislation introduced by the Commission and to ratify international agreements negotiated by the Commission. It also has the authority to adopt the budget for the EU. It is also the forum in which the member states coordinate their economic policies (in the context of the Economic and Financial Affairs configuration).

Unless otherwise specified in the TFEU, the Council acts by qualified majority voting, with each country having one vote.[123] For the period from November 1, 2014, to March 31, 2017, a qualified majority will be as at least 55 percent of the members of the Council, comprising at least 15 of them and representing member states comprising at least 65 percent of the population of the Union.[124]

The presidency of the Council, which should be distinguished from the President of the European Council, is made up of a group of three member states based on a rotation of 18 months.[125] This "group presidency" does not have competence for foreign affairs—that is left to the president of the European Council and the High Representative. Each six months, these three member states rotate as chairs of the respective Council configurations (except for Foreign Affairs which is chaired by the High Representative).

---

120. TFEU at art. 237
121. EU Treaty at art. 16.
122. Decision of the Council of 1 December 2009 establishing the list of Council configurations in addition to those referred to in the second and third subparagraphs of Article 16(6) of the Treaty on European Union, 2009 O.J. (L 315) 46.
123. EU Treaty at art. 16(3).
124. *Id.* at art. 16(4).
125. European Council Decision of 1 December 2009 on the exercise of the Presidency of the Council, 2009 O.J. (L 315) 50 at art. 1.

As the Council is comprised of representatives of the member states at the ministerial level, there is a need for a permanent administration in Brussels to address the issues on a daily basis and deal with the details required in the formation and drafting of legislation. This function is exercised by the General Secretariat, under the responsibility of a Secretary-General appointed by the Council, and the Committee of Permanent Representatives of the Governments of the Member States (often referred to as COREPER).[126] Each member state has a permanent ambassador to the EU. These ambassadors, who meet on a weekly basis in the context of the COREPER meetings, are charged with negotiating the details of the Council's work. By the time the Council formally meets, most, if not all, of the issues have been addressed in the context of COREPER. The COREPER is chaired by the member state chairing the General Affairs configuration of the Council.[127]

(d) Parliament

The European Parliament, formally located in Strasbourg, France, but with offices in Brussels and Luxembourg, is comprised of 785 members who are elected every five years.[128] The monthly meetings are held in Strasbourg, the committee meetings in Brussels, and the administrative offices are located in Luxembourg.[129]

The powers of the European Parliament are less than one would expect in a typical parliamentary democracy. Its primary powers are legislative, supervisory, fiscal, and political. Although the Parliament has the right to request the Commission to initiate legislation,[130] it does not have the authority to initiate legislation itself. Nor does it have the authority to adopt legislative acts independently. As discussed in greater detail below, there are two basic processes by which legislative acts are adopted: ordinary legislative procedure and the special legislative procedure. In neither of these procedures can the Parliament adopt legislation by itself. Under the ordinary legislative procedure, the legislative act is adopted jointly by the Parliament and Council on a proposal from the Commission.[131] Under the special legislative procedure, the Parliament only has a consultative role.[132]

In its supervisory role, the Parliament has the ability to bring an action before the ECJ against an EU institution for failure of that institution to observe the formalities in which Parliament has a role.[133] For example, if the Council fails to consult with the Parliament in adopting legislation on a matter in which consultation is required under the TFEU, the Parliament may initiate proceedings

---

126. EU Treaty at art. 16(7); TFEU at art. 240.
127. European Council Decision of 1 December 2009 on the exercise of the Presidency of the Council, 2009 O.J. (L 315) 50 at art. 2.
128. EU Treaty at art. 14(3).
129. Protocol (No 6) on the Location of the Seats of the Institutions and of Certain Bodies, Offices, Agencies, and Departments of the European Union.
130. TFEU at art. 225.
131. *Id.* at art. 289(1).
132. *Id.* at art. 289(2).
133. *Id.* at art. 263(3).

against the Council. The Parliament may also seek a prior opinion from the ECJ on the compatibility of an international agreement with the TFEU.[134]

The Parliament also has influence on the EU's budget. As a supranational form of government with thousands of employees, the EU requires substantial funds in order to operate. There are four basic sources of funds for the EU. First, each member state is required to contribute a certain amount annually based on that member state's gross national product up to a maximum of 1.27 percent. This source of funds comprises approximately 75 percent of the EU's revenue. Second, the agricultural levies and customs duties (which include any anti-dumping duties) collected on imports into the EU of products from third countries belong to the Union. This source of funds makes up approximately 10 percent of the Union's revenues. Third, the EU receives a portion of the value-added tax (VAT), i.e., sales tax, revenues which are collected by the member states. VAT constitutes approximately 14 percent of the Union's revenues. Finally, the fines imposed by the Commission in competition law cases are paid into the EU budget. For example, the €497.2 million fine imposed by the Commission on Microsoft in 2004 for abusing its dominant position in the market for operating systems was paid into the EU coffers.

The Parliament has influence over how these funds are then spent as it must adopt or reject the EU's budget. The Commission submits a draft budget to the Parliament and the Council.[135] The Council then forwards its position on the draft budget to the Parliament. The Parliament then has 42 days in which to amend or approve the draft budget (failure to amend or approve the draft budget in the 42 days means that it is adopted). If the Parliament decides to amend the draft budget, it must send the amendments to the Council and the Commission. A Conciliation Committee comprised of equal representatives of the Parliament and Council is then convened to work out a joint text. If the Conciliation Committee is unable to agree on a joint text, the Commission is required to submit a new budget proposal.[136]

Finally, the Parliament enjoys certain political powers which give it significant influence over the policies of the Union. As discussed above, for example, the Parliament has the power to elect the Commission president.[137] The Parliament has been willing to use this power as a means to block the nomination of particular Commission members. As the president of the Commission customarily presents to the Parliament his or her Commission as a whole, the Parliament can withhold its approval of the Commission president if there is an individual selected by the president for membership in the Commission which Parliament does not approve. In 2004, Commission President José Manuel Barroso was required to withdraw three of his nominations for Commission members because of fundamental political differences with the Parliament.

---

134. *Id.* at art. 300(6).
135. *Id.* at art. 314(2).
136. *Id.* at art. 314(8).
137. EU Treaty at art. 14(1).

(e) Court of Auditors

The Court of Auditors, located in Luxembourg, is made up of one national from each of the member states appointed for terms of six years. Its primary responsibility is overseeing the EU budget by auditing the accounts of the institutions and agencies.[138]

6.2 European Courts

The EU courts have played a critical role in the legal and political development of the European Union. The often precarious stability of the EU has required a pragmatic approach to the adjudication of disputes. The judicial branch of the EU is frequently called upon to determine the extent of the authority ceded to the EU and the limits placed on the EU institutions. In *Costa v. Enel*, for example, the ECJ was called upon to determine the relationship between EU law and national law.[139] The ECJ concluded that EU law had supremacy over conflicting national law. It is important to remember that EU business law operates in the context of an evolving legal system which rests on a delicate political balance between the interests of the EU and those of the individual member states. The doctrines developed by the EU courts and the results attained are often explicable by this reality.

(a) Structure, Composition, and Function

The judicial branch of the EU consists of the ECJ and the General Court, both of which are located in Luxembourg. In addition, the Parliament and Council have the authority to appoint specialized courts but have yet to exercise this authority.[140] The basic function of the courts is to ensure that the law is observed when the EU Treaty is interpreted and applied. The ECJ and General Court are each composed of 28 judges (one from each member state).[141] Eight advocates general are assigned to the ECJ. The General Court does not have any advocates general. The judges are selected by common accord of the governments of the member states for six-year terms which can be renewed.[142] The political reality is that each member state appoints a judge. The two necessary qualifications are (1) their independence must be beyond doubt and (2) they must possess the qualifications required for appointment to the highest judicial office in the member state appointing the judge.[143] Prior to their appointment by the member states, a panel of seven jurists chosen from among former members of the Court of Justice and the General Court, members of national supreme courts, and lawyers of recognized competence gives its opinion on the ability

---

138. TFEU at art. 248.
139. Case 6/64, Costa v. ENEL, 1964 E.C.R. 585.
140. TFEU at art. 257.
141. EU Treaty at art. 19(2).
142. *Id.* at art. 19(2); TFEU at art. 254.
143. TFEU at art. 253.

of the respective candidates to perform their anticipated duties as a member of the Court.[144]

The president of the ECJ and the president of the General Court are elected for three-year terms by the respective courts.[145] The judges are assisted in their work by advocates general. The advocates general are responsible for examining the case and presenting their opinion on its resolution to the court.[146] The ECJ may sit in full (all judges), in grand chamber (13 judges), or in chamber (three or five judges).[147] Most cases are heard in chambers of three or five judges. In certain cases, however, an EU institution or member state that is a party to the proceedings may request that the court sit in grand chamber.[148] The court only sits as a full court where cases are brought before it pursuant to Article 228(2), Article 245(2), Article 247, or Article 286(7) of the TFEU.[149]

The procedure of the EU courts—even when hearing a case in the first instance—resembles that of a U.S. appellate court rather than a U.S. trial court.[150] The first step in the procedure in a direct action is the initiation of proceedings by filing the application with the appropriate court. Notice is then served on the defendant who has 30 days (in cases before the ECJ) or 60 days (in cases before the General Court) to file a response. The president of the court then assigns the case to an advocate general. A date is then set for oral arguments. During the oral arguments, the judges and assigned advocate general may ask questions of the parties. Art. 67 Although the applicant may choose the language of the case, the judges may use any of the official languages when they conduct the oral hearing.[151]

No independent discovery, as it is known in the United States., is made by the courts or the parties.[152] The gathering of evidence is primarily within the purview of the national courts. The ECJ and General Court may ex officio or upon the request of the parties request information and documents, hear oral testimony,

---

144. *Id.* at art. 255. Council Decision of 25 February 2010 relating to the operating rules of the panel provided for in Article 255 of the Treaty on the Functioning of the European Union, 2010 O.J. (L 50) 18.
145. Article 8(1) Rules of Procedure of the Court of Justice, 2012 O.J. (L 265) 1 [hereinafter ECJ Rules of Procedure] and Article 7 of the Rules of Procedure of the General Court, 2010 O.J. (C 177) 37 [hereinafter General Court Rules of Procedure].
146. TFEU at art. 252.
147. *Id.* at art. 251; Statute of the Court of Justice of the European Union, 2010 O.J. (C 83) 210 at art. 16 [hereinafter ECJ Statute]; ECJ Rules of Procedure at arts. 27 and 28 and General Court Rules of Procedure at art. 11.
148. ECJ Statute at art 16.
149. *Id.* at art. 16(4).
150. The procedure before the European courts is regulated primarily by the ECJ Statute, the ECJ Rules of Procedure, and the General Court Rules of Procedure.
151. ECJ Rules of Procedure at art. 38(8) and General Court Rules of Procedure at art. 35.
152. The ECJ and General Court have the authority to require the parties to produce all documents and to supply all information that the court considers desirable. ECJ Statute at art. 64(2). The courts cannot compel discovery from third parties, except that member states and institutions can be required to supply information which the court considers "necessary" even if they are not party to the case. ECJ Statute at art. 24.

commission expert reports, or conduct a physical inspection outside the court.[153] The scope of the information or documentary request is within the discretion of the court. The EU courts cannot compel discovery from third parties, except that member states and institutions can be required to supply information which the court considers "necessary" even if they are not party to the case.[154]

Shortly after the oral hearing, the advocate general prepares his or her opinion on how the case should be decided and delivers that written opinion to the court. Although the advocate general's opinion does not have the force of law, it is often closely followed by the court in formulating its opinion because the advocate general is the person who typically devotes the most attention to the issues.

The next step is for one of the judges designated to be the rapporteur to circulate a draft of a judgment. The chamber or plenary of judges then deliberate and agree to a final text of the judgment. Contrary to the U.S. judicial system, there are no dissenting opinions, and the author of the judgment remains anonymous. The judgments are taken by simple majority vote of the judges assigned to the case.[155] The judgment is then given in open court.

(b) Jurisdiction

Similar to the authorities of the other EU institutions, the authorities granted to the EU courts are limited. The limited jurisdiction of the EU courts is conceptually analogous to that of the U.S. federal courts: the ECJ and General Court only have jurisdiction in those instances specifically granted to them by the TFEU.

(1) Preliminary Rulings

The most common basis of jurisdiction for cases before the EU courts is the preliminary ruling. The ECJ has the authority to issue preliminary rulings on the interpretation of the treaties or the validity of acts of an EU institution or the ECB.[156] If, for example, an unsettled issue requiring the application of EU law arises in domestic litigation, the domestic court may stay the proceedings and refer the issue to the ECJ. The basic requirement is that the ruling is necessary for the resolution of a dispute involving EU law.[157] Hypothetical legal issues will not be resolved by the ECJ.

Preliminary rulings are of critical importance because each of the member states has retained its own judicial system. The ability to grant preliminary rulings promotes the uniform application of EU law throughout the EU by the national judiciaries. In fact, the EU courts have the obligation to hear and opine on references for preliminary rulings. A reference from a national court may be refused by the ECJ only if it is quite obvious that the interpretation of EU law

---

153. ECJ Rules of Procedure at arts. 63-67 and General Court Rules of Procedure at arts. 65-73.
154. ECJ Statute at art. 24.
155. If the case is assigned to a chamber of only three judges, however, the decision of the chamber requires the consensus of all three judges. Article 17 of the ECJ Statute.
156. EU Treaty at art. 19(3)(b); TFEU at art. 267.
157. Case C-313/12, Romeo v. Regione Siciliana, 2013 E.C.R. I-____, at ¶40.

sought bears no relation to the actual facts of the main action or to its purpose, the issue is hypothetical, or the ECJ court is not provided with the factual or legal material necessary to give a useful ruling.[158]

The success of the system is dependent on the willingness of national courts to refer cases to the ECJ. The decision on whether to refer a particular issue in a national court to the EU courts is within the discretion of the national court which is confronted with the issue.[159] The mere fact that the issue involves the application of EU law does not necessarily result in a reference to the EU courts. If the resolution of the issue is already clear, the national court is not required to refer that issue to the EU courts.[160] In a case before the German Supreme Court, for example, a German national claimed that he had the right to be admitted to practice law in Germany based on the fact that he was a member of the New York bar.[161] One of the issues was whether the refusal of Germany to allow him to practice law in Germany infringed his right to provide services as guaranteed by the TFEU. After all, he was working in London and was prohibited from offering services in Germany. The German Supreme Court held that this refusal did not violate EU law and it refused to refer the issue to the ECJ as, in its view, the issue was clear under EU law.

The effective operation of the referral procedure also depends on the ability or willingness of the national judges to comply with the subsequent decision of the EU courts. In preliminary ruling cases, the ECJ does not decide the case, but only the narrow issue on the meaning of EU law. Judicial independence or ambiguity of the judgment may challenge the proper application by the national court. In *Arsenal Football Club v. Reed*, an English court referred to the ECJ a question on the applicability of the EU Trademark Directive. The specific issue was whether Mr. Reed was infringing the trademark of the Arsenal soccer team by selling paraphernalia with the Arsenal team logo. The ECJ held that Arsenal could rely on the trademark to prevent the sale.[162] The English court refused to apply the decision of the ECJ on the basis that the ECJ had disagreed with the finding of facts in the case and consequently exceeded its authority.[163]

(2) *Other Bases of Jurisdiction*

In addition to preliminary rulings, the ECJ has the competence to hear the following types of cases:

- Proceedings brought by a member state against another member state for infringement of the TFEU (Article 259 TFEU).

---

158. Case C-238/05, Asnef-Equifax, Servicios de Información sobre Solvencia y Crédito, SL v. Asociación de Usuarios de Servicios Bancarios, 2006 E.C.R. I-11125, 11153 ¶17; Case C-344/04, IATA and ELFAA, 2006 E.C.R. I-403, 419 ¶24.
159. Case C-103/08, Gottwald v. Bezirkshauptmannschaft Bregenz, 2009 E.C.R. I-9117, 9121 ¶16.
160. Case T-47/02, Danzer v. Council, 2006 E.C.R. II-1779, 1798 ¶44.
161. Decision of the German Bundesgerichtshof of Sept. 19, 2003, *reported in* 50 Recht der Internationalen Wirtschaft 75 (2004).
162. Case C-206/01, Arsenal Football Club v. Reed, 2002 E.C.R. I-10273.
163. Arsenal Football Club v. Reed [2002] EWHC 2695 (CH); 34 IIC 542 (2003). The holding of the English court was overturned on appeal. Decision of the Court of Appeal (Civil Division) of May 21, 2003, 34 IIC 983 (2003).

- Proceedings brought by an EU institution against a member state for infringement of the TFEU (Article 258 TFEU).
- Proceedings brought by a member state against an EU institution for infringement of the TFEU (Article 263 TFEU).
- Proceedings for annulment brought by individuals against a decision addressed to that person or a regulation or decision addressed to another person which is of direct and individual concern to that individual (Article 263(4) TFEU).[164]
- Proceedings for failure to act brought by a member state or other EU institution against the Council, Commission, or Parliament (Article 265 TFEU).
- Proceedings for the noncontractual liability of the EU (Article 268 and 340 TFEU).
- Proceedings by the Commission for noncompliance with a previous ruling (Article 260 TFEU).
- Proceedings involving special agreements between member states (Article 273 TFEU).[165]
- Appeals of General Court rulings.[166]
- Advisory opinions on the conclusion of international agreements between the EU and third countries or organizations (Article 318(11) TFEU).

The ECJ has the authority to impose a lump sum or penalty payment on a member state which fails to comply with the findings reached by the ECJ.[167] However, the ECJ is not authorized to impose these sanctions on its own initiative. As a first step, the Commission must bring the case to the ECJ if the Commission has concluded that the member state has failed to comply with the ECJ's opinion. Although the Commission proposes the amount of the lump

---

164. In order to be the subject of an annulment proceeding, the contested measures must be binding on the applicant and capable of affecting the interests of, the applicant. Case T-377/00, Philip Morris International v. Comm'n, 2003 E.C.R. II-1, 27 ¶77. In the *Philip Morris* case, the General Court held that the decision taken by the Commission to institute legal proceedings in the United States against the U.S. tobacco maker did not produce legal effects itself because only the outcome of the case would produce legal effects. Case T-377/00, Philip Morris International v. Comm'n, 2003 E.C.R. II-1, 27 ¶77. The individual concern requirement makes it difficult for individuals to challenge the illegality of regulations and directives as these types of secondary community law are typically of general application. *See, e.g.*, Case C-263/02 P, Comm'n v. Jégo-Quéré & Cie SA, 2004 E.C.R. I-3425, 3458 ¶33.
165. For example, the ECJ has jurisdiction over disputes regarding the Brussels Convention on jurisdiction and the enforcement of judgments in civil and commercial matters, 1262 UNTS 153; 8 ILM 229 (1969).
166. ECJ Statute at art. 56. An appeal to the Court of Justice is limited to points of law, on the grounds of lack of competence of the General Court, a breach of procedure before it which adversely affects the interests of the appellant, or the infringement of EU law by the General Court. *Id.* at art. 58.
167. TFEU at art. 260.

sum or penalty payment, the ECJ ultimately has the discretion to determine the form of payment (i.e., lump sum or penalty payment), the amount, and the conditions of payment.[168] The sanction may only be imposed if the member state continues to fail to observe the decision of the ECJ up to the date of the ECJ's examination of the facts.[169] Consequently, a member state could delay compliance up to that point in time without any risk of sanctions.

(3) *Jurisdiction of the General Court*

The jurisdiction of the General Court is more limited than that of the European Court of Justice. For example, the General Court does not have the general authority to grant preliminary rulings.[170] The General Court has jurisdiction only over those types of actions referred to in the TFEU (Art. 225 TFEU). In general terms, these are cases involving natural or legal persons challenging acts of the EU institutions. The General Court has jurisdiction to hear cases involving an EU measure which produces effects vis-à-vis third parties (Art. 230 and Art. 225 TFEU). The most prominent example is competition decisions.

The General Court also has jurisdiction over damages actions against the EU for noncontractual liability (Art. 268 TFEU and Art. 340 TFEU). Article 340(2) of the TFEU requires the EU to compensate an injured party for any damage caused by its institutions or servants. Article 268, together with Article 256 of the TFEU, grants the General Court jurisdiction to hear such cases in the first instance. Another type of case over which the General Court has jurisdiction, and is increasingly common, is appeals from decisions of the Office for Harmonization in the Internal Market (OHIM). Although the bulk of its work involves claims brought by natural or legal persons, the General Court also has the jurisdiction to adjudicate claims brought by a member state or EU institution actions against the Council, Commission, or Parliament for failure to act (Art. 265 TFEU). Although of little relevance for EU businesses, the General Court has jurisdiction over employment matters of communities' own staff (Art. 270 TFEU) and arbitration clauses in contracts concluded by the Union (Art. 272 TFEU).

(c) *Methods of Interpretation*

As discussed below, the EU legal system is based on codified legal norms composed of primary and secondary law. The EU courts are responsible for interpreting and applying these laws. Rules of interpretation are important in the EU legal system for several reasons. First, the wording of EU legislation is often vague. There is a political incentive (by no means limited to the EU) to draft vague legislation. Moreover, as the diversity of the constituencies in the EU is much greater than in most other polities, it is much more difficult to achieve political consensus. To achieve a consensus in a legal system comprised of 28 member states, EU legislation may be intentionally drafted in vague terms. This allows each politician to declare victory or explain the legislation to his

---

168. Case C-496/09, Comm'n v. Italy, 2011 E.C.R. I-11483, 11508 ¶46.
169. *Id.* at ¶42.
170. The General Court only has jurisdiction to hear preliminary rulings which are brought under Article 267 of the TFEU. TFEU at art. 256(3).

or her advantage. Hence, much of the burden associated with its interpretation falls on the ECJ and General Court.

Second, codified legal norms are by necessity formulated in abstract terms as they are designed to apply to events the details of which cannot be foreseen with certainty by the legislator. It would be impossible for the legislature to adopt laws that apply specifically to every fact pattern which may arise.

Third, codified legal norms rely on language which is inherently imprecise. Words themselves have no inherent meaning. Their meaning is subjective and acquired by humans through experience. The same language used in a particular statute can mean different things to different courts as understanding is a subjective process.

Finally, the EU legal system is faced with the additional challenge that all legislation needs to be translated into 23 different languages. Moreover, the judges charged with the interpretation and application of the law come from quite different social and legal cultures. These aspects of the EU legal system exacerbate the challenges which are inherent in all other legal systems due to the law's dependence on language. Although there is no one language that takes precedence over the others,[171] the statutory texts are sometimes inconsistent. For example, in *In re X*, the issue was whether EU legislation[172] allowed a member state to charge a fee to a person who requested access to personal data which that member state collected on this person. The fee in this case was designed to cover the costs of providing the information to the person. The problem was, however, that the English, Swedish, and Dutch versions of the EU legislation stated that such information had to be provided "without excessive delay or expense." The French and German versions stated that the information had to be provided "without unreasonable delay or excessive expense." In other words, the case turned on which language version was used. Some versions suggested that no expense could be charged, whereas other versions suggested that expenses could be charged provided they were not excessive.[173]

The TFEU does not identify a specific method of interpretation to be used by the EU courts in applying primary and secondary EU law. Although the primacy of international law in the EU legal system also requires legislation to be interpreted in a way that conforms to international law,[174] it does not mandate a particular method of interpretation. Contemporary international law only provides that treaties are to be interpreted "in good faith in accordance with the ordinary meaning to be given to the terms of the treaty in their context

---

171. Case C-488/11, Brusse v. Jahani BV, 2013 E.C.R. I-____, at ¶26.
172. Directive 95/46/EC of the European Parliament and of the Council of 24 October 1995 on the protection of individuals with regard to the processing of personal data and on the free movement of such data, 1995 O.J. (L 281) 31.
173. The ECJ ultimately held that the member states could impose a fee provided that it was not excessive. Case C- 486/12, *In re* X, 2013 E.C.R. I-____, at ¶22.
174. Case C-76/00 P, Petrotub and Republica v. Council, 2003 E.C.R. I-79, 142 ¶57; Case T-199/04, Gul Ahmed Textile Mills Ltd. v. Council, 2011 E.C.R. II-321, 343 ¶54.

and in light of its object and purpose."[175] In the absence of precise rules of interpretation, the EU courts have developed a very pragmatic approach to statutory interpretation.

As a review of the case law demonstrates, the EU courts will rely on the method of interpretation which in its view is appropriate. The ECJ and General Court have relied on various methods of statutory interpretation including literal, original intent, contextual, and teleological. In some cases, the EU courts will rely on the *ratio legis* to interpret and apply the law.[176] In other cases, the courts may refer to the original intent of the drafters.[177] Although the ECJ has not expressly recognized the principle of stare decisis, the basic principles of EU law require that "comparable situations must not be treated differently, and different situations must not be treated in the same way, unless such treatment is objectively justified."[178]

As discussed above, the interpretation of statutory text in a multilingual legal system presents a number of challenges. As language is an imprecise method of communication, it is impossible for translations to capture the exact meaning in each language. When a comparison of two or more authentic texts of a treaty reveals a difference in meaning, the Vienna Convention on the Law of Treaties provides that the institution charged with the interpretation and application of that treaty must choose the best interpretation that reconciles the texts "having regard to the object and purpose of the treaty."[179] This reconciliation approach is apparent in the case law of the EU courts. The starting point is the recognition that one language version of a multilingual text of EU law does not take precedence over all other versions, since the uniform application of EU rules requires that they be interpreted in the light of all the versions.[180] In determining

---

175. Article 31(1) of the Vienna Convention on the Law of Treaties, done at Vienna, May 23, 1969, 1155 UNTS 331, 8 I.L.M. 679. The customary international law rules codified in the Vienna Convention on the Law of Treaties are binding on the EU institutions. Case C-386/08, Brita GmbH v. Hauptzollamt Hamburg-Hafen, 2010 E.C.R. I-1289, 1336 ¶42.
176. Case C-53/05, Comm'n v. Portugal, 2006 E.C.R. I-6215, 6222 ¶20; Joined cases T-22/02 & T-23/02, Sumitomo Chemical Co. Ltd. v. Comm'n, 2005 E.C.R. II-4065, 4088 ¶47.
177. Case C-72/03, Carbonati Apuani Srl v. Comune di Carrara, 2004 E.C.R. I-8027, 8060 ¶22; Case C-11/00, Comm'n v. European Central Bank, 2003 E.C.R. I-7147, 7256 ¶100.
178. Case T-24/05, Alliance One International, Inc. v. Comm'n, 2010 E.C.R. II-5329, 5380 ¶157 *aff'd on appeal* Joined Cases C-628/10 P and C-14/11 P, Alliance One International, Inc. v. Comm'n (reported only in the electronic reports of cases ECLI:EU:C:2012:479); *see also* Case C-38/06, Comm'n v. Portugal, 2010 E.C.R. I-1569, 1592 ¶58 ("It must be stated at the outset that the Court has ruled in several recent judgments on questions identical to those raised in the present case. The principles developed in those judgments must therefore be applied.").
179. Article 31(1) of the Vienna Convention on the Law of Treaties, done at Vienna, May 23, 1969, 1155 UNTS 331, 8 I.L.M. 679.
180. C-268/99, Aldona Malgorzata Jany and Others v. Staatssecretaris van Justitie, 2001 E.C.R. I-8615, 8678 ¶47; Case C-219/95 P, Ferriere Nord v. Comm'n, 1997 E.C.R. I-4411, 4435 ¶15.

the meaning of a provision of the TFEU or secondary law which is apparently inconsistent, the EU courts may look to the meaning in the other languages and adopt the interpretation which is consistent with the meaning in the other languages.[181] In other cases where there is a difference in the translations of the statutory texts, the EU courts have adopted an interpretation by reference to the purpose and general scheme of the rules of which it forms a part.[182]

(d) Enforcement

As discussed above, the Commission and the member states each have the authority to bring a claim before the ECJ that a member state has failed to fulfill its obligations under the treaties. Before doing so, however, there is a specific procedure they must follow. If the Commission is bringing the claim,[183] it is required to notify the member state and give the member state an opportunity to explain its position. The Commission then delivers a "reasoned opinion" on the matter to the member state.[184] If the member state is bringing the claim, it is required to first raise the matter with the Commission. The Commission then gives each of the member states involved the opportunity to explain their positions. It then issues a "reasoned opinion."[185]

If the Commission finds that the member state has not complied with its obligations under the treaties, it may instruct the member state to take measures to comply within a specific time frame. If the member state concerned does not comply with the Commission's opinion within the required time frame, the Commission may bring the matter before the ECJ. If the ECJ finds that a member state has failed to fulfill an obligation under the treaties, it sets forth the necessary measures the member state needs to take.[186] If the Commission considers that the member state concerned has not taken the necessary measures to comply with the judgment of the ECJ,[187] it may bring the case before the court after giving that member state the opportunity to submit its observations. If the court finds that the member state concerned has not complied with its judgment, it may impose a lump sum or penalty payment on it.

---

181. Case T-174/01, Goulbourn v. OHIM, 2003 E.C.R. II-789, 805 ¶37; Case C-327/91, French Republic v. Comm'n, 1994 E.C.R. I-3641, 3676 ¶35.
182. Case C-463/09, CLECE SA v. Valor, 2011 E.C.R. I-95, at ¶29; C-215/10, Pacific World Limited v. The Commissioners for Her Majesty's Revenue & Customs, 2011 E.C.R. I-7255, 7273 ¶48; Case C-151/09, Federación de Servicios Públicos de la UGT v. Ayuntamiento de La Línea de la Concepción, 2010 E.C.R. I-7591, 7633 ¶39; Case C-511/08, Handelsgesellschaft Heinrich Heine GmbH v. Verbraucherzentrale Nordrhein-Westfalen eV, 2010 E.C.R. I-3047, 3088 ¶51.
183. Case C-280/08 P, Deutsche Telekom AG v. Comm'n, 2010 E.C.R. I-9555, 9628 ¶47.
184. TFEU at art. 258.
185. *Id.* at art. 259.
186. *Id.* at art. 260(1).
187. Although the TFEU does not set forth a specific time frame in which the member state is required to comply, the standard adopted by the ECJ is that the compliance efforts of the member state must begin "immediately and be completed as soon as possible." Case C-407/09, Comm'n v. Greece, 2011 E.C.R. I-2467, 2492 ¶34 (A period of 29 months was determined to be too long.).

7. Sources of EU Law

7.1 International Law

International law is the highest source of law in the European Union.[188] This derives from the recognition that the EU is a creation of and based on international law. The EU (then the European Economic Community) was created by an international agreement between sovereign states. Adherence to that agreement is an issue of international law.[189] International law therefore prevails when in conflict with EU law. This applies both to customary international law[190] as well as international conventions.[191]

7.2 Primary Law

In the hierarchy of legal norms within the EU legal system, primary law follows international law. The term "primary law" refers to the treaties which serve as the foundation for the EU and its legal system. This includes the EU Treaty and the TFEU as well as the Charter of Fundamental Rights of the European Union (Article 6(1) EU Treaty).

7.3 Secondary Law

Secondary law refers to the collection of legislative acts taken by the EU institutions based on the authority granted by a provision of primary law. Secondary law follows primary law in the EU legal system. There are three forms of binding secondary law: regulations, directives, and decisions (Art. 288 TFEU).

(a) Regulations

Regulations are binding in their entirety, self-executing, and directly applicable throughout the EU. Regulations have immediate effect and operate to confer rights on individuals which the national courts have a duty to protect.[192] They are not dependent upon transposition by the member states. The European Merger Control Regulation,[193] for example, is a form of law which does not require transposition into national law. Companies involved in mergers and acquisitions

---

188. Case C-366/10, Air Transport Association of America v. Secretary of State for Energy and Climate Change, 2011 E.C.R. I-13833, 13871 ¶50. This includes customary international law. *Id.* at 13886 ¶101.
189. Case 6/64, Costa v. ENEL, 1964 E.C.R. 585, 594. Whether the EU can enter into a treaty, however, is an issue subject to EU judicial review. Opinion 1/09 of the Court 8 March 2011, 2011 E.C.R. I-1137 ¶60.
190. Case C-366/10, Air Transport Association of America v. Secretary of State for Energy and Climate Change, 2011 E.C.R. I-13755, 13886 ¶101.
191. Case C-76/00 P, Petrotub and Republica v. Council, 2003 E.C.R. I-79, 141 ¶53.
192. Joined Cases C-4/10 and C-27/10, Bureau national interprofessionel du Cognac v. Gust. Ranin Oy, 2011 E.C.R. I-6131.
193. Council Regulation No. 139/2004 of 20 January 2004 on the control of concentrations between undertakings, 2004 O.J. (L 24) 1.

exceeding certain monetary thresholds set forth in the Merger Control Regulation are required to notify the transaction to the European Commission regardless of the application of national law. The obvious benefit of regulations is that they establish a uniform set of laws throughout the EU. As is discussed below, other forms of secondary legislation create the possibility for differences among the member states and consequently cause some legal uncertainty.

(b) Directives

Another type of secondary law is directives. Directives are only binding in terms of their results to be achieved, and addressed to the member states, which are free to choose the best forms and methods of implementation.[194] Directives are commonly used to harmonize the law of the member states as they apply to certain conduct. For example, Directive 98/44 on the legal protection of biotechnological inventions requires the member states to adjust their laws to make sure that biotechnological inventions are protected under national patent law.[195] Although there are still 28 different sets of laws applicable to the biotechnological inventions, there is a degree of uniformity among these laws because of the Directive. A regulation, on the other hand, would establish a separate law which applies by itself—without the need for transposition by the member states. As discussed in greater detail below, the TFEU determines when the EU institutions can adopt a regulation and when they can adopt a directive.

The effectiveness of directives is dependent on the willingness of the member states to transpose them into national law, and to do so correctly. The Commission is entrusted with the responsibility of making sure the member states comply with their responsibility to transpose the directives into national law. The TFEU (Article 258) grants the Commission the authority to bring an action against a member state before the ECJ for failure to transpose a directive. Before doing so, however, the Commission must notify the member state of its alleged infringement, allow the member state to respond, and then deliver a reasoned opinion to that member state. If the member state fails to conform to the reasoned opinion of the Commission, the case may be brought to the Court of Justice.

For practical purposes, it is important to recognize that directives do not necessarily completely harmonize the laws of the member states. First, the member states are not required to transpose a directive literally.[196] The only requirement is that the national legislation achieves the results envisaged by the directive. Consequently, the laws of the member states transposing a particular directive differ in their wording. These differences often lead to different judicial and administrative interpretations. Of course, if the affected parties contend

---

194. The fact that directives are directed at the member states means that they cannot be relied on by individuals in private litigation against other individuals. Case C-12/08, Mono Car Styling SA v. Dervis Odemis, 2009 E.C.R. I-6653, 6674 ¶59.
195. Directive 98/44/EC of the European Parliament and of the Council of 6 July 1998 on the legal protection of biotechnological inventions, 1998 O.J. (L 213) 13.
196. Case C-321/05, Kofoed v. Skatteministeriet, 2007 E.C.R. I-5795, 5809 ¶44.

that the interpretation of the national law does not conform to the directive, they can challenge the validity of the national law.

Second, noncomprehensive directives allow the member states to adopt legislation offering greater protection than that required by the applicable directive. Generally, there are two types of directives: those that do not leave the member states any latitude in their transposition into national law (comprehensive directives)[197] and those that allow the member states to adopt stricter measures than those set forth in the directive (noncomprehensive directives).[198] For example, the ECJ has held that the biotechnology directive[199] is comprehensive and, consequently, member states are not able to grant greater protection to biotechnology patent holders than is set forth in the directive.[200] The Directive on Transparency Requirements for Issuers of Public Securities expressly provides that the member state where the issuer is located may impose more stringent requirements on the issuer than those set forth in the Directive.[201] Similarly, the Data Privacy Directive and consumer protection legislation set only the minimum standards for protecting personal data and consumers; the member states are not precluded from granting greater protection.[202] The consequences of noncomprehensive directives for businesses are obvious.

Directives that do not fully harmonize an area of law increase legal uncertainty because they lead to divergent outcomes among the member states. Consequently, doing business in Europe may require compliance with a panoply of different laws even where the EU has adopted a directive. Determining when a transaction triggers employee rights provides a good example. The Transfer Directive insures that the rights of an employee transfer along with a transfer of an undertaking, business, or part of a business.[203] According to the ECJ, however, the member states can grant the employees greater protections and in

---

197. *See, e.g.*, Case C-421/12, Comm'n v. Belgium, 2014 E.C.R. I-____, at ¶63; Joined cases C-261/07 & 299/07, VTB-VAB NV v. Total Belgium NV, 2009 E.C.R. I-2949, 2968 ¶52.
198. *See, e.g.*, Case C-328/13, Österreichischer Gewerkschaftsbund v. Wirtschaftskammer Österreich, 2014 E.C.R. I-____, at ¶22; Case C-205/07, Gysbrechts v. Santurel Inter BVBA, 2008 E.C.R. I-9947, 9961 ¶34.
199. Directive 98/44/EC of the European Parliament and of the Council of 6 July 1998 on the legal protection of biotechnological inventions, 1998 O.J. (L 213) 13.
200. Case C-428/08, Monsanto Technology LLC v. Cefetra BV, 2010 E.C.R. I-6765, 6810 ¶62.
201. Directive 2004/109/EC of the European Parliament and of the Council of 15 December 2004 on the harmonization of transparency requirements in relation to information about issuers whose securities are admitted to trading on a regulated market, 2004 O.J. (L 390) 38 at art. 3(1).
202. According to Article 169(4) of the TFEU, the member states, as a general rule, may adopt legislation that imposes greater protection for consumers than the requirements set forth in EU consumer protection legislation.
203. Council Directive 2001/23 of 12 March 2001 on the approximation of the laws of the member states relating to the safeguarding of employees' rights in the event of transfers of undertakings, businesses or parts of undertakings, or businesses, 2001 O.J. (L82) 16. The Transfer Directive is discussed in detail in Chapter IX.

a broader range of circumstances than are set forth in the Transfer Directive.[204] Consequently, the legal situation regarding employees in the context of business transactions differs among the member states. For local transactions involving a small number of employees all in one member state, this panoply of rules does not present a significant challenge. In multi-jurisdictional transactions, however, the parties to the transaction need to address all potentially applicable laws (and their judicial interpretation), most of which differ and some of which contradict each other.

(c) Decisions

The third form of binding secondary law is decisions. This type of legislation is binding in its entirety upon those to whom it is addressed. Article 105(2) of the TFEU, for example, allows the Commission to adopt decisions regarding infringements of the competition rules. As discussed in Chapter III, when the Commission finds that a firm has infringed the competition rules, the Commission will adopt a formal decision addressed specifically to the firms involved. The TFEU (Article 296) requires the EU institution to provide its reasoning for adopting a decision. The standard is whether the statement of reasons "disclose[s] in a clear and unequivocal fashion the reasoning followed by the institution which adopted the measure in question in order to enable the persons concerned to ascertain the reasons for the measure."[205] Failure to adequately state its reasoning can lead to the annulment of the decision by the EU courts.[206]

(d) Recommendations

Recommendations are of less importance than regulations, directives, and decisions because they are not binding.[207] The Council and the Commission may unilaterally adopt recommendations as authorized in the treaties.[208] As the Commission can unilaterally adopt recommendations, this form of quasi-legislation is often employed when the necessary political consensus cannot be achieved to adopt a regulation or directive. Even though recommendations lack binding character, they are important in two respects. First, a recommendation may be a necessary precondition to the EU institutions taking a binding action. For example, for the Council to sanction a member state for excessive deficits under the EMU, the Council must first receive a recommendation from the Commission.[209] Second, recommendations (even though not binding) can be influential in prompting the member states to observe them. For example, in response to perceived excesses in the remuneration of directors of large EU companies, the Commission adopted a recommendation suggesting that the member states should create greater transparency in this respect so that

---

204. Case C-458/12, Amatori v. Telecom Italia SrL, 2014 E.C.R. I-___, at ¶40.
205. Case T-144/99, Institute of Professional Representatives before the EPO v. Comm'n, 2001 E.C.R. II-1087, 1102 ¶41.
206. *See, e.g.*, Case T-206/99, Mètropole Tèlèvision SA v. Comm'n, 2001 E.C.R. II-1061.
207. TFEU at art. 288.
208. *Id.* at art. 292.
209. *Id.* at art. 104(5). Case C-27/04, Comm'n v. Council, 2004 E.C.R. I-6649.

the shareholders of these companies could more effectively monitor the remuneration of the directors.[210] Within a very short period of time, most of the member states had adopted legislation along the lines recommended by the Commission in its recommendation.

(e) Notices and Guidelines

Mention should also be made of several additional quasi-legislative measures which may be adopted by the EU institutions.[211] Of particular importance for lawyers and businesses are the notices and guidelines which the Commission has adopted to clarify its position in enforcing primary and secondary EU law. Although these notices and guidelines do not qualify as rules which the EU administration or member states are bound to observe,[212] they are nonetheless considered indirectly binding. The indirectly binding nature of notices and guidelines arises from the application of the general principles of legal certainty and equal treatment. Once an EU institution adopts such notices, that institution is required by the recognized principles of legal certainty and equal application to consistently apply them.[213] For example, failure by the Commission to adhere to its Guidelines on the Method of Setting Fines for Violations of the Competition Laws[214] caused the General Court to partially annul the Commission decision imposing fines on a company for serious competition law violations.[215] If the Commission intends to depart from the notice or guidelines, it must provide reasons why this departure conforms to the principle of equal treatment.[216]

The binding effect of notices and guidelines on the courts of the member states is a different issue, and one whose resolution is uncertain. As discussed above, the member states may have the authority (and in some cases the obligation) to apply EU law. For example, the courts of the member states

---

210. Comm'n Recommendation of 30 April 2009 as regards the regime for the remuneration of directors of listed companies, 2009 O.J. (L 120) 28.
211. In addition to the measures discussed here, it is possible for the Council to adopt resolutions. Similar to recommendations of the Commission, resolutions of the Council are not binding on the member states. They are often adopted to address political issues which call for a quick response. For example, in order to prompt the member states into adopting a uniform solution to the problem of football hooliganism, the Council adopted a resolution that "invited" the member states "to examine the possibility of introducing provisions establishing a means of banning individuals guilty of violent conduct at football matches from stadiums at which football matches are to be held." Council Resolution of 17 November 2003 on the use by member states of bans on access to venues of football matches with an international dimension, 2003 O.J. (C 281) 1.
212. Case C-226/11, Expedia Inc. v. Autorité de la concurrence, 2012 E.C.R. I-___, at ¶29; Case C-360/09, Pfleiderer AG v. Bundeskartellamt, 2011 E.C.R. I-5161, 5198 ¶21.
213. Case T-461/07, Visa Europe Ltd v. Comm'n, 2011 E.C.R. II-1729, 1807 ¶246; Case C-3/06 P, Groupe Danone v. Comm'n, 2007 E.C.R. I-1331, 1343 ¶23.
214. 1998 O.J. (C 9) 1.
215. Joined cases T-67/00, T-68/00, T-71/00 and T-78/00, JFE Engineering Corp v. Comm'n, 2004 E.C.R. II-2501, 2694 ¶537.
216. Case C-167/04 P, JCB Service v. Comm'n, 2006 E.C.R. I-8935, 9029 ¶207; Joined cases C-189/02 P, C-202/02 P, C-205/02 P to C-208/02 P and C-213/02 P, Dansk Rørindustri A/S v. Comm'n, 2005 E.C.R. I-5425, 5483 ¶209.

have the authority to apply Article 101 of the TFEU to agreements which restrain competition and there is an effect on trade between member states. The Commission has adopted several guidelines and notices designed to assist in the application of the prohibition codified in Article 101. In particular, the Commission has adopted Guidelines on the Effect on Trade Concept contained in Articles 101 and 102 of the TFEU.[217] In *Filigranbetondecken*, one of the issues before the German court was whether the cooperation between two cement products manufacturers in northern Germany had an effect on trade between member states.[218] The German Cartel Office had previously held that the cooperation violated Article 101 of the TFEU. The defendants claimed that Article 101 of the TFEU was not applicable because there was no effect on trade between member states as required by Article 101 of the TFEU. The Düsseldorf Appeals Court held that although the Interstate Trade Guidelines adopted by the Commission suggested that there was an effect on trade between member states, guidelines adopted by the Commission are not necessarily binding on the national courts. The court concluded that in view of the type of product involved in the case—cement products—and the limited geographic scope of the cooperation, there was no effect on trade between member states as required by Article 101 of the TFEU. This issue of the binding effect of Commission guidelines and notices on national courts has not been decided by the ECJ or General Court.

(f) *Legislative Procedures*

There are two basic processes by which legislative acts are adopted (both of which necessarily involve other EU institutions).[219] The ordinary legislative procedure refers to the joint adoption by the Parliament and Council on a proposal from the Commission.[220] The ordinary legislative procedure codified in Article 294 of the TFEU starts with the Commission submitting a proposal to the Parliament and Council. The Parliament communicates its position on the proposal to the Council. The Council may then adopt the wording of the legislative act as communicated by the Parliament. If the Council does not approve the Parliament's position, it communicates this lack of approval to the Parliament. It is then up to the Parliament to either approve, reject, or propose amendments to the Council's position. In the instances where the Parliament

---

217. Commission Guidelines on the effect on trade concept contained in Articles 81 and 82 of the Treaty, 2004 O.J. (C 101) 81, 83 ¶21.
218. Decision of the OLG Düsseldorf of June 10, 2005, VI – 2 Kart 12/04, *reported in* Wirtschaft und Wettbewerb 62 (2006).
219. The term "legislative act" only refers to laws adopted by one of these two procedures. TFEU at art. 289(3). A legislative act may authorize the Commission to adopt delegated nonlegislative acts or implementing nonlegislative acts. TFEU at art. 290. The procedures for adopting these nonlegislative acts are discussed in Communication from the Commission to the European Parliament and the Council—Implementation of Article 290 of the Treaty on the Functioning of the European Union, COM/2009/0673 final; and Council Decision of 28 June 1999 laying down the procedures for the exercise of implementing powers conferred on the Commission, 1999 O.J. (L 184) 23.
220. TFEU at art. 289.

proposes amendments, it must communicate the amendments not only to the Council but also to the Commission. It is then up to the Council to approve or reject the amendments (but unanimity is required for amendments for which the Commission has given a negative opinion). If the Council does not approve the amendments proposed by the Parliament, the proposed legislation enters the conciliation process.

The Council and Parliament are required to establish a Conciliation Committee comprised of an equal number of representatives of the Council and the Parliament.[221] If the Conciliation Committee does not approve the proposed legislation within six weeks of being convened, the proposed act is deemed not adopted. If the Conciliation Committee does approve a joint text, the Council and the Parliament have six weeks to approve the joint text. Otherwise, it is deemed not to have been adopted.

The other basic process by which legislation is adopted is the special legislative procedure. This refers to the adoption of legislative acts by the Parliament with the participation of the Council or by the Council with the participation of the Parliament.[222] The instances in which the Parliament can adopt legislative acts with the (mere) participation of the Council are limited to:

- The adoption of a statute for the members of the Parliament (Articles 223(2) TFEU);
- The establishment of a committee to inquire into alleged contraventions in the implementation of EU law (Article 226 TFEU); and
- The adoption of the statute of the EU ombudsman (Article 228(4) TFEU).

The more common type of special legislative procedure is where the Council has the right to adopt the legislative act after seeking the participation of the Parliament. Notable examples include Article 115 TFEU authorizing the Council to adopt directives directly affecting the internal market; Article 262 TFEU authorizing the Council to define the jurisdiction of the EU courts; and Article 64 TFEU giving the Council the exclusive right to adopt legislative acts which constitute a step backwards in the liberalization of the movement of capital to or from third countries.

The growth of the EU from the initial six member states to 28 member states meant that consensus on legislation was increasingly difficult to reach. This challenge often led to the inability of the EU to adopt legislation which at least some member states opposed. For example, the introduction of a financial transaction tax on transactions between financial institutions was blocked by the opposition of the UK and Sweden to the tax. The recognition that the difficulty of achieving consensus would hamper the growth of the EU led to the introduction of the enhanced cooperation procedure. This procedure, codified in Article 20 of the EU Treaty and Articles 326 to 334 of the TFEU, allows a minimum of nine member states to adopt legislation applicable only to them through a special

---

221. *Id.* at art. 294(10).
222. *Id.* at art. 289(2).

procedure. This avoids the situation where a minority of member states can prevent others from moving ahead with EU legislation. The basic requirement for employing the enhanced cooperation procedure is that it be used "as a last resort, when it has been established that the objectives of such cooperation cannot be attained within a reasonable period by the Union as a whole."[223] This typically means that the EU has been unable to adopt legislation after attempting to reach a consensus using the traditional legislative procedures.

The creation of the unitary patent and the EU patent court is a good example of the use of the enhanced procedure to overcome political deadlock. For many years, the EU struggled with the creation of a unitary patent and a corresponding EU patent court due to the lack of consensus over the official languages. Although, as discussed in Chapter 10, inventors could take advantage of the European Patent Convention, this procedure was outside the parameters of the European Union. Moreover, the European Patent Convention offers only a bundle of rights and not a unitary patent. Most of the EU member states recognized the need for a unitary patent. However, in order to make the EU unitary patent successful, the EU legislators knew that they would have to limit the official languages in which the applications must be filed and the working language of the EU patent court. Spain and Italy blocked the adoption of the necessary legislation because the official languages were to be English, French, and German. The enhanced cooperation procedure allowed the EU to avoid this deadlock and adopt the necessary legislation without the inclusion of Spain and Italy.[224]

7.4 General Principles of Law

Not all sources of EU law are codified in primary or secondary legislation. General principles of law form an integral part of the EU legal system. These are noncodified legal principles common to most or all of the member states, which have been recognized as a general principle by the EU courts. They would include, for example, proportionality, equal treatment, legal certainty, legitimate expectations, and fundamental rights. As discussed throughout the following Chapters, these principles play an important role in EU business law. For example, the European Commission is required to respect the fundamental rights of individuals when conducting competition law investigations.[225]

7.5 Importance of the Hierarchy of Norms

A proper understanding of the hierarchy of legal norms in the EU is essential for a proper understanding of EU business law. In *Institute of Professional Representatives before the EPO v. Commission*, for example, one of the issues

---

223. EU Treaty at art. 20(2).
224. Council Decision 2011/167/EU of 10 March 2011 authorizing enhanced cooperation in the area of the creation of unitary patent protection, 2011 O.J. (L 76) 53. The use of the enhanced cooperation procedure in this instance was challenged but approved by the ECJ. Joined cases C-274/11 and 295/11, Spain v. Council, 2013 E.C.R. I-____.
225. Case C-411/04, Salzgitter Mannesmann GmbH v. Comm'n, 2007 E.C.R. I-959, 972 ¶41.

was whether the conduct of an association of undertakings which conformed to a Council Directive could nonetheless violate Article 101 of the TFEU. The General Court held that a norm of secondary EU law (the Directive in this case) could not preclude the application of primary law.[226]

In *Schmidberger v. Austria*, the issue concerned the relationship between fundamental rights (freedom of speech) and the principle of free movement of goods.[227] Austria had granted a permit to environmental groups to demonstrate on a major highway through Austria. The plaintiff, a transportation company, incurred significant damage resulting from its inability to transport products from Italy to Germany because of the demonstration, which lasted 30 hours. The plaintiff claimed that the approval of Austria infringed Article 34 of the TFEU (which prohibits state measures restricting the free movement of goods between member states). The ECJ concluded, however, that the fundamental right of free speech took precedence over the free movement of goods rules.

The plethora of laws adopted by the EU institutions creates the possibility that two legal norms apply to the same conduct. In such cases, the EU courts will apply the principle of *lex specialis,* i.e., the more specific law applies to the conduct. In *Gottfried Linhart v. Hans Biffl*, for example, the issue concerned labeling and selling of cosmetic products.[228] Both the Council Directive 76/768/EEC of 27 July 1976 on the approximation of the laws of the member states relating to cosmetic products[229] and Council Directive 84/450/EEC of 10 September 1984 relating to the approximation of the laws, regulations, and administrative provisions of the member states concerning misleading advertising[230] could have applied to the particular facts. Because the former directive specifically applied to the conduct, the ECJ held that it was applicable to the facts (even though technically both directives were applicable).[231]

8. Fundamental Legislative Principles

8.1 Principle of Conferral

The principle of conferral, codified in Article 5 of the EU Treaty, is comprised of two components. The first component is the limitation placed on the authority of the EU to act only when the treaties confer that right on the Union. The TFEU, similar to the U.S. Constitution, expressly enumerates the powers granted by the member states to the EU. Powers not conferred upon the Union in the treaties remain with the member states.[232] The second component of the principle of conferral is the limitation that the content and form of action by the EU may not

---

226. Case T-144/99, Institute of Professional Representatives before the EPO v. Comm'n, 2001 E.C.R. II-1087, 1105 ¶50.
227. Case C-112/00, Schmidberger v. Austria, 2003 E.C.R. I-5659.
228. Case C-99/01, Gottfried Linhart v. Hans Biffl, 2002 E.C.R. I-9372.
229. 1976 O.J. (L 262) 169.
230. 1984 O.J. (L 250) 17.
231. Case C-99/01, Gottfried Linhart v. Hans Biffl, 2002 E.C.R. I-9375, 9402 ¶20.
232. EU Treaty at art. 4(1).

exceed what is necessary to achieve the objective. Whether a body may act and what measures it may adopt if it does act and the procedures they must follow are all matters deriving from the EU Treaty and the TFEU. When an institution acts, it must identify which legal provision it is relying on as authority for its act.[233] Failure to do so will lead to the invalidity of the legislation.[234]

The provision of the EU Treaty or TFEU that serves as the source of authority to act also determines the form of legislation—regulation, directive, or decision. In certain instances, e.g., Article 48 (legislation in the field of social security for workers) and Article 103 (legislation to give effect to the competition rules), the institutions have the choice between adopting legislation in the form of a regulation or a directive. In other instances, the EU Treaty or TFEU stipulates the precise form of legislation to be employed. For example, if the Council wants to rely on the authority to act granted by Article 50 (legislation to secure the freedom of establishment), Article 114 (legislation approximating the laws affecting the functioning of the internal market), or Article 59 (legislation to liberalize a specific service), it can only adopt legislation in the form of a directive. If the EU institution relies on Article 105(2) (infringements of competition law) or Article 108(2) (infringement of the state aid rules), it is required to act in the form of a decision.

The application of the principle of conferral is illustrated in *French Republic v. Commission*.[235] In that case, the Commission had entered into an agreement with the United States concerning cooperation in competition law matters. The basic issue was whether the Commission exceeded its authority in doing so. France challenged the act of the Commission. The ECJ concluded that even though the Commission had the authority to apply the competition rules as codified in the TFEU, the Commission lacked the authority to conclude this cooperation treaty with the United States as the TFEU reserves such authority to the Council. A similar conclusion was reached by the ECJ in *Parliament v. European Data Protection Supervisor*.[236] In this case, the Commission entered into an administrative agreement with the United States that allowed airlines to share personal information on airline passengers with the United States.[237] The ECJ held that the Commission failed to properly identify the legal basis for its conduct, and consequently annulled the agreement with the United States.

---

233. TFEU at art. 253.
234. *See, e.g.*, Case C-94/03, Comm'n v. Council, 2006 E.C.R. I-1
235. Case C-327/91, French Republic v. Comm'n, 1994 E.C.R. I-3641. *See also* similar cases in the area of international environmental treaties, Case C-36/98, Spain v. Council, 2001 E.C.R. I-779; Case C-281/01, Comm'n v. Council, 2002 E.C.R. I-12049, or in the area of the regulation of food supplements, Joined cases C-154/04 and C-155/04, Alliance for Natural Health v. Secretary of State for Health, 2005 E.C.R. I-6451.
236. Joined cases C-317/04 and C-318/04, Parliament v. European Data Protection Supervisor, 2006 E.C.R. I-4721.
237. Decision 2004/535/EC of 14 May 2004 on the conclusion of an Agreement between the European Community and the United States of America on the processing and transfer of passenger name record (PNR) data by air carriers to the United States Department of Homeland Security, Bureau of Customs and Border Protection, 2004 O.J. (L 183) 83.

8.2 Principle of Subsidiarity for Shared Authorities

In exercising the authorities conferred upon it, the EU must observe the principle of subsidiarity. The principle of subsidiarity only applies to the authorities which are not exclusively conferred upon the Union. According to Article 5(3) of the EU Treaty, the EU may only act if and insofar as the objectives of the proposed action cannot be sufficiently achieved by the member states and can be better achieved at EU level. The principle of subsidiarity requires the EU institutions to justify the necessity of legislating at an EU level as opposed to the national level. This justification must be embodied in a statement included in the legislation itself. The member states may challenge the legislation by bringing a case before the ECJ that the legislation violates the principle of subsidiarity.[238]

8.3 Principle of Proportionality

Similar to the principle of subsidiarity, the principle of proportionality limits the authority of the EU in adopting legislative acts. According to Article 5(4) of the EU Treaty, the content and form of EU action may not exceed what is necessary to achieve the objectives of the treaties.[239] There are two prongs to this test. First, the measure employed by the EU institution must be appropriate to achieve the objective which legitimatizes the measure. In those areas where the EU institution enjoys broad discretion—such as external trade—the standard is whether the measures are manifestly inappropriate.[240] Second, the measures employed must be narrowly tailored to achieve that objective. If there are less onerous measures, the EU institution is required to employ the less onerous measure. The member states have the authority to challenge the legislation based on the failure to conform to the principle of proportionality.[241]

9. Application of EU Law at the National Level

9.1 Direct Applicability

The principle of direct applicability means that certain EU laws may be directly applicable in the legal system of the member state without an additional transposing act of the national legislature. Treaty provisions and EU regulations

---

238. Article 8 of the Protocol (No 2) on the Application of the Principles of Subsidiarity and Proportionality.
239. EU Treaty at art. 5(4).
240. Case T-119/06, Usha Martin Ltd. v. Council, 2010 E.C.R. II-4335, 4355 ¶45 *aff'd on appeal* Case C-552/10 P, Usha Martin Ltd v Council (reported in the electronic reports of cases ECLI:EU:C:2012:736).
241. Article 8 of the Protocol (No 2) on the Application of the Principles of Subsidiarity and Proportionality.

are directly applicable in all member states.[242] Direct applicability means that legal effect of the EU law is not dependent upon the acceptance of that law by the legal system of the member states.[243] Moreover, the principle of direct applicability imposes an obligation on the member states to cooperate to give effect to the directly applicable measures.[244] National laws which conflict with EU law are automatically inapplicable.[245]

The principle of direct applicability is enforced in two ways. First, the Commission may act against a member state to secure compliance with directly applicable EU law.[246] For example, in *Commission v. Italian Republic*,[247] the Commission successfully brought an action against Italy on the basis that Italy failed to appropriately transpose the Biotechnology Directive[248] into domestic Italian law.

Second, the principle of direct applicability creates rights and obligations of individuals on which they may rely against other individuals in national courts. In *Consorzio del Prosciutto di Parma v. Asda Stores Ltd*,[249] for example, an Italian association of Parma ham producers brought an action in the UK against a UK grocery store chain called Asda for violation of Council Regulation (EEC) No 2081/92 of 14 July 1992 on the protection of geographical indications and designations of origin for agricultural products and foodstuffs[250] and of Commission Regulation (EC) No 1107/96 of 12 June 1996 on the registration of geographical indications and designations of origin under the procedure laid down in Article 17 of Regulation No 2081/92.[251] The Italian association claimed that the ham being sold at the Asda stores in the UK as "Prosciutto di Parma" was not sliced and packaged in Parma in accordance with the regulations. Although the association ultimately lost the case, the ECJ recognized that the

---

242. Case C-455/01, Comm'n v. Italian Republic, 2003 E.C.R. I-12,023, 12,034 ¶25. International treaties between the EU and nonmember states also are directly applicable in the member states. Case C-240/09, Lesoochranárske zoskupenie VLK v. Ministerstvo životného prostredia Slovenskej republiky, 2011 E.C.R. I-1255, 1305 ¶44.
243. Case C-92/02, Nina Kristiansen v. Rijksdienst voor Arbeidsvoorziening, 2003 E.C.R. I-14597, 14631 ¶32; Case C-108/01, Consorzio del Prosciutto di Parma v. Asda Stores Ltd, 2003 E.C.R. I-5121, 5191 ¶87; Case C-469/00, Ravil SARL v. Bellon import SARL, 2003 E.C.R. I-5053, 5114 ¶91.
244. Case C-92/02, Nina Kristiansen v. Rijksdienst voor Arbeidsvoorziening, 2003 E.C.R. I-14597, 14610 ¶32.
245. Case C-409/06, Winner Wetten GmbH v. Bürgermeisterin des Stadt Bergheim, 2010 E.C.R. I-8015, 8061 ¶53.
246. TFEU at art. 258.
247. Case C-456/03, Comm'n v. Italian Republic, 2005 E.C.R. I-5335.
248. Directive 98/44/EC of the European Parliament and of the Council of 6 July 1998 on the legal protection of biotechnological inventions, 1998 O.J. (L 213) 13.
249. Case C-108/01, Consorzio del Prosciutto di Parma v. Asda Stores Ltd, 2003 E.C.R. I-5121.
250. 1992 O.J. (L 208) 1.
251. 1996 O.J. (L 148) 1.

association had the right to bring the claim in the UK courts even though the claim rested on a violation of EU law and not UK law.[252]

9.2 Direct Effect

The principles of direct applicability and direct effect are similar. They both address the issue when an EU law can be relied upon by individuals at the national level. Hence, they are both essential to the effective implementation of EU law. The difference between the two principles is that the principle of direct applicability relates to the applicability of an entire legislative act (or provision of the TFEU), whereas the principle of direct effect relates to specific rights contained in a particular provision of a legislative act or the TFEU. For example, regulations are directly applicable, but directives are not. Directives are (merely) orders given to the member states to make sure that their national laws conform to the principles codified in the directive. However, the existence of political constraints in the respective member states means that directives are not always transposed into national law in a timely fashion. In other cases, the member state may incorrectly transpose the directive into national law or interpret national law in a manner inconsistent with the directive. As discussed above, the Commission has the authority to bring an action as "Guardian of the Treaty" against a member state based on Article 258 of the TFEU for failure to correctly transpose a directive.

In contrast to the principle of direct applicability, the principle of direct effect provides that an individual (legal or natural person) may rely on EU law vis-à-vis their member state (referred to as vertical direct effect) or vis-à-vis other natural and legal persons (referred to as horizontal direct effect). Primary EU law as well as regulations may have both horizontal and vertical direct effect.[253] Directives, however, only have vertical direct effect.[254] Primary EU

---

252. The principle of direct applicability is not readily commensurate with dualist legal systems such as the United Kingdom. In a dualist legal system, international law such as treaties needs to be adopted into national law by the legislature before it becomes part of the national legal system. In a monist legal system, no additional step is needed to bring international law into the domestic system. In the UK, it is not readily apparent that the domestic legal system would even allow the Italian association in *Consorzio del Prosciutto di Parma v. Asda Stores Ltd.*, even if, from an EU legal perspective, the regulations were directly applicable. However, when joining the EU in 1972, the UK adopted the European Communities Act which essentially recognized the direct applicability of EU law. Other dualist member states have adopted similar legislation.
253. Case C-453/99, Courage Ltd v. Bernard Crehan, 2001 E.C.R. I-6297, 6323 ¶24.
254. Case C-555/07, Kücükdeveci v. Swedex GmbH & Co. KG, 2010 E.C.R. I-365, 392 ¶46. Although directives do not have horizontal direct effect (i.e., they cannot be relied on by a legal or natural person in a national court against another legal or natural person), the national courts are required to apply (or not apply) national law commensurate with the directives. Therefore, a legal or natural person may indirectly rely on a directive in a case against another legal or natural person by claiming that the applicable national law at issue needs to be interpreted in conformity with the particular directive. *Id.* at 393 ¶51.

law and regulations and directives have horizontal and vertical direct effect (except directives which only have vertical direct effect) if (1) the law is clear and unconditional, in the sense that its implementation must not be subject to any substantive condition, and (2) its implementation must not depend on the adoption of subsequent measures which either the EU institutions or the member states may take in the exercise of a discretionary power of assessment.[255]

Although the application of these requirements will depend on the particular case, and may be influenced by political considerations, the requirements embody a basic respect for the retained sovereignty of the member states. These requirements ensure that a provision of EU law only has direct effect at the national level if it is clear that this was the intent of the drafters of the particular EU law. If, for example, the EU law gives the member state discretion in its application, then the resolution of the legal issue is more appropriately left to the member states.[256]

The principle of direct effect is more than an abstract principle of EU business law as it facilitates claims by and against businesses based on EU law. Article 45(2) of the TFEU, for example, prohibits discrimination based on nationality between workers. The principle of direct effect could be used by an employee against an employer in the EU which contemplates the adoption of an employee policy that discriminates based on nationality in breach of Article 45(2) of the TFEU.[257] Moreover, the doctrine of direct effect may allow a company to initiate legal proceedings against another company based on primary EU law. In *Courage Ltd v. Bernard Crehan*, for example, the ECJ held that an individual could rely on Article 101 of the TFEU (i.e., prohibiting restraints of competition) in an action against another individual in proceedings before the national courts.[258]

9.3 Noncontractual Liability of Member States

The member states are required to conform their national laws to EU primary and secondary law. As mentioned above, the Commission can bring an action before the ECJ against a member state for failure to implement a directive.[259] Individuals assist the Commission in this respect by bringing private actions against their member state for infringements of EU law.[260] A member state

---

255. Case C-486/08, Zentralbetriebsrat der Landeskrankenhäuser Tirols v. Land Tirol, 2010 E.C.R. I-3530, 3542 ¶22; Joined cases C-471/07 and C-472/07, Association générale de lindustrie du médicament v. État belge, 2010 E.C.R. I-113, 145 ¶26.
256. Joined cases C-471/07 and C-472/07, Association générale de l'industrie du médicament v. État belge, 2010 E.C.R. I-113, 146 ¶28.
257. Case C-281/98, Angonese v. Cassa di Risparmino, 2000 E.C.R. I-4139 (Employee exercises rights codified in TFEU directly against his employer).
258. Case C-453/99, Courage Ltd v. Bernard Crehan, 2001 E.C.R. I-6297, 6323 ¶24.
259. TFEU at art. 260(2).
260. *See, e.g.*, C-224/01, Köbler v. Republik Österreich, 2003 E.C.R. I-10239, 10305 ¶30.

(or a public authority within that member state)[261] incurs liability to an individual for breaches of EU rules (e.g., failure to implement a directive) if:

- the EU legislation is intended to confer individual rights on the particular parties (as opposed to rights extended to the general public);
- the content of the individual right is capable of being identified;
- the breach by the member state is sufficiently serious; and
- there is a causal link between the noncompliance of the member state and the injury incurred by the plaintiff.[262]

Liability of member states has been recognized when the member state infringes "directly applicable" rules of the TFEU,[263] when the member state incorrectly transposed an EU directive into national law,[264] when a public administration violates directly applicable Treaty provisions,[265] and when a member state implemented the directive in national law but only after the time period provided for in the directive.[266]

9.4 Primacy of EU Law

The principle of primacy of EU law serves as the basis for the principles of direct applicability, direct effect, and noncontractual liability. For example, to recognize that EU law is directly applicable only solves half of the problem. The second half of the problem is whether the EU or the national law takes precedence in a particular case. This issue arises because the EU is a supranational organization which exists parallel to (and not in place of) the laws of the member states. It is the creation of an agreement between sovereign states according to which the member states agreed to imbue the EU institutions with certain limited authorities. Nonetheless, the member states continue to retain authority over those areas which have not been ceded to the Union.

The retention of two separate legal systems potentially applicable to the same factual constellation presents the possibility of conflict between those laws. The principle of primacy of EU law resolves this issue by recognizing

---

261. Case C-118/00, Larsy v. Institut national d'assurances sociales pour travailleurs indépendants, 2001 E.C.R. I-5063, 5098 ¶35; Case C-302/97, Konle v. Austria, 1999 E.C.R. I-3099, 3140 ¶62.
262. C-398/11, Hogan v. Minister for Family Affairs, 2013 E.C.R. I-___, at ¶49; Joined cases C-6/90 and C-9/90, Francovich v. Italy, 1991 E.C.R. I-5357, 5414 ¶35.
263. Joined cases C-46/93 and 48/93, Brasserie du Pêcheur and Factortame, 1996 E.C.R. I-1029, 1144 ¶31.
264. C-398/11, Hogan v. Minister for Family Affairs, 2013 E.C.R. I-___, at ¶49; Case C-392/93 British Telecommunications, 1996 E.C.R. I-1631, 1667 ¶38.
265. Case C-5/94, Hedley Lomas, 1996 E.C.R. I-2553, 2612 ¶24.
266. Joined cases C-178/94, C-179/94, C-188/94, C-189/94 and C-190/94, Dillenkofer v. Federal Republic of Germany, 1996 E.C.R. I-4845, 4878 ¶20.

that in cases of conflict, a provision of EU law prevails over national law.[267] The national provision is not automatically void, but rather inapplicable in that instance. In *Debra Allonby v. Accrington & Rossendale College*, for example, a female college lecturer claimed that the application of the UK pension laws resulted in her being compensated at a lower level than comparable male colleagues.[268] As Article 157(1) of the TFEU prohibits gender discrimination in the compensation of workers, and has direct effect, the ECJ recognized that where there is conflict between an EU law and national law, the national law "must be disapplied."[269]

---

267. Case C-409/06, Winner Wetten GmbH v. Bürgermeisterin des Stadt Bergheim, 2010 E.C.R. I-8015, 8064 ¶61 (The primacy of EU law applies even as against national constitutional law.); Case C-555/07, Kücükdeveci v. Swedex GmbH & Co. KG, 2010 E.C.R. I-365, 392 ¶54.
268. Case C-256/01, Debra Allonby v. Accrington & Rossendale College, 2004 E.C.R. I-873.
269. *Id.* at 931 ¶77.

CHAPTER **II**

Internal Trade

1. Introduction to the Internal Market

The efforts to create an internal market (or a "common market" as it was called prior to the Single European Act) are directed to achieve economic integration among the member states. The various forms of integration range from agreements to grant preferential tariff treatment to full economic and monetary union.

Between the two poles, there are different levels of economic integration. There may be circumstances when a country agrees to reduce the tariffs on goods imported from another country without integrating its economy with that other country or relinquishing any sovereignty. For example, the European Union (EU) unilaterally grants certain developing countries preferential tariff treatment as part of the EU's development policy. Import duties imposed on imports of products from these countries are generally lower than the duties imposed on products imported from other countries.

Granting preferential trade treatment is a less intense level of economic integration than establishing a free trade area. In a free trade area, the countries involved agree to a removal (or substantial reduction) of tariff barriers to trade, but each member retains the right to set tariffs vis-à-vis third countries. For example, the United States, Mexico, and Canada have entered into the North American Free Trade Agreement. Although tariffs were largely reduced and eliminated in many cases, these three countries did not agree on a common external customs tariff and system.

In a customs union, the participating countries go one step further than a free trade area: they agree to remove or reduce tariffs on trade between them *and* establish a common external tariff.[1] As discussed below, the EU is a customs union. Regardless of whether goods are imported to Sweden or Greece or any other member state, the duties imposed on those goods are the same. The EU

---

1. According to Article 24 (a) of the General Agreement on Tariffs and Trade, a "customs territory" refers to "any territory with respect to which separate tariffs or other regulations of commerce are maintained for a substantial part of the trade of such territory with other territories." Agreement Establishing the World Trade Organization in Final Act Embodying the Results of the Uruguay Round of Multilateral Trade Negotiations, Apr. 15, 1994, 33 I.L.M. 1125, 1144-1154 (1994) [hereinafter GATT].

has one tariff schedule used by all of the member states.[2] In a customs union, however, the participating countries retain their autonomy to adopt their own economic policies. For example, in a customs union the members may still adopt and implement their own industrial policy to promote certain industries. A customs union that goes one step further, and in which the members agree to relinquish sovereignty over economic policies (e.g., competition policy, industrial policy, agricultural policy, etc.), is referred to as an economic union. The EU is an example of an economic union. The member states have agreed to cede sovereignty over a wide range of economic and monetary policies to the EU institutions.

The internal market refers to just one component of EU integration. The EU is based on a customs union and an internal market. The legal parameters of the customs union are discussed in Chapter IV on external trade. The term "internal market" refers to the free trade in goods, services, labor, and capital within the EU. The internal market is based on the four fundamental freedoms: free movement of goods, free movement of labor, freedom to establish a business or provide services, and free movement of capital.

The legality of the creation of the internal market, which involved the removal of tariffs on goods traded between member states, was not altogether clear. The establishment of the internal market meant a reduction of tariffs vis-à-vis the other member states of the EU. Article 1 of the General Agreement on Tariffs and Trade (GATT) requires that "any advantage, favor, privilege or immunity granted by any contracting party to any product originating in or destined for any other country shall be accorded immediately and unconditionally to the like product originating in or destined for the territories of all other contracting parties." However, there is a codified derogation in GATT for customs unions and free trade areas.[3] The general rule is that signatory states may create a free trade area (i.e., reduce customs duties on the importation of goods from some countries) as long as there is no increase of customs duties on the importation of goods from third countries that are not part of that customs union or free trade area.

---

2. As discussed in Chapter IV, the member states are responsible for implementing the customs law and collecting the tariffs when goods are imported into their territory.
3. Article XXIV of GATT provides that GATT shall not prevent, the formation of a customs union or of a free trade area if three conditions are fulfilled: (1) notification of the agreement must be given to the GATT signatories (Article XXIV: 7a); (2) the agreement applies to substantially all trade between the countries (Article XXIV: 8b); and (3) the duties and other regulations of commerce imposed at the institution of any such union or maintained in each of the constituent territories in respect of trade with contracting parties not parties to such union shall not on the whole be higher or more restrictive than the general incidence of the duties and regulations of commerce applicable in the constituent territories prior to the formation of such union or territory.

2. Free Movement of Goods

The free movement of goods principle is based on two basic prohibitions imposed on the member states by the Treaty on the Functioning of the European Union (TFEU). Articles 28 and 30 of the TFEU (which contain the same prohibition) prohibit customs duties and charges having an effect equivalent to a customs duty, and Articles 34 and 35 of the TFEU prohibit quantitative restrictions on imports (Article 34) and on exports (Article 35) and measures having an effect equivalent to a quantitative restriction. These provisions only apply to goods. The term "goods" is not defined in the TFEU. It generally refers to products that are capable of forming the subject of commercial transactions.[4] It would, for example, even include waste.[5] According to the European Court of Justice (ECJ), however, not everything "which can be valued in money and which is capable, as such, of forming the subject of commercial transactions ... necessarily falls within the scope of application of those Treaty provisions."[6] Fishing rights, for example, would not fall under the concept of goods even if they are embodied in a fishing permit that can be bought and sold.[7] The same applies to intellectual property rights even though they can be integrally tied to physical products.[8]

2.1 Abolition of Customs Duties and Charges Having Equivalent Effect

(a) Prohibition of Customs Duties

The first component of Article 30 of the TFEU (Article 28 contains the same prohibition) is the prohibition of customs duties on the trade of goods. The terms "tariff" and "customs duties" are used synonymously in trade law. They both refer to a fee levied on goods as they cross certain identified boundaries (usually national). Although they share certain characteristics, customs duties should be distinguished from taxes. The predominant purpose of customs duties is not financial but protectionist. Whereas taxes are generally imposed to increase a country's revenue, duties are imposed to protect domestic industries from foreign competition.

The prohibition applies not only to the trade of goods between member states, but also between a member state and a non-member state.[9] For example, Ireland could not impose customs duties on goods imported from the United States. This is because the authority for external trade has been relinquished

---

4. Case C-65/05, Comm'n v. Greece, 2006 E.C.R. I-10341, 10354 ¶23; Case 7/68, Italian Art Treasures, 1968 E.C.R. 617, 626.
5. Case C-221/06, Stadtgemeinde Frohnleiten v. Bundesminister für Land- und Forstwirtschaft, Umwelt und Wasserwirtschaft, 2007 E.C.R. I-9643, 9656 ¶37.
6. Case C-97/98, Jägerskiöld v. Gustafsson, 1999 E.C.R. I-7319, 7319 ¶33.
7. *Id.* at 7319 ¶36.
8. *Id.* at 7319 ¶38.
9. Case C-173/05, Comm'n v. Italy, 2007 E.C.R. I-4917, 4927 ¶40.

by the member states to the EU. As discussed above, the EU has adopted a common external tariff. The system would not work if each member state retained the authority to impose its own customs duties.[10] This also applies to goods in transit. For example, Italy could not impose a charge on gas transported in pipelines from Algeria to certain member states.[11] Allowing such charges would seriously undermine the customs union that characterizes the EU.

(b) Prohibition of Charges Having an Effect Equivalent to a Customs Duty

As discussed above, Article 30 of the TFEU prohibits customs duties and charges having an effect equivalent to a customs duty. In most cases involving Article 30, the issue is not whether a particular charge constitutes a customs duty, but rather whether the charge has an effect equivalent to a customs duty. The concept of "charge" in the context of Article 30 implies the payment of some sort of fee. For example, a quota on the import of goods from another member state is not technically a charge for purposes of Article 30, although both are prohibited by Article 30.

The standard definition of a "charge equivalent to a customs duty" employed by the ECJ is: Any pecuniary charge, however small and whatever its designation and mode of application, which is imposed unilaterally on domestic or foreign goods by reason of the fact that they cross a frontier, and which is not a customs duty, even if it is not imposed for the benefit of the State.[12] The requirement of crossing a territorial frontier distinguishes prohibited charges from internal tax measures which are within the authorities of the member states.[13] If, for example, Poland imposed a charge on the initial registration of automobiles in Poland regardless of their origin or place of purchase, the Polish law would not be a charge having an equivalent effect because it does not apply by reason of the fact that the products cross a frontier.[14]

The prohibition on customs duties and charges having equivalent effect applies to exports as well as imports. In *Kapniki Mikhailidis v. Idrima Kinonikon Asphaliseon*, for example, a fee imposed on the export of tobacco from a member state (for the purpose of financially supporting a tobacco

---

10. *Id.* at 4926 ¶30.
11. *Id.* at 4926 ¶32.
12. Case C-254/13, Orgacom BVBA v. Vlaamse Landmaatschappij, 2014 E.C.R. I-____, at ¶22; Case C-313/05, Brzeziński v. Dyrektor Izby Celnej w Warszawie, 2007 E.C.R. I-513, 549 ¶22; Joined Cases C-290/05 and C-333/05, Ákos Nádasdi v. Vám- és Pénzügyőrség Észak-Alföldi Regionális Parancsnoksága, 2006 E.C.R. I-10115, 10173 ¶39.
13. Case C-254/13, Orgacom BVBA v. Vlaamse Landmaatschappij, 2014 E.C.R. I-____, at ¶28.
14. Case C-313/05, Brzeziński v. Dyrektor Izby Celnej w Warszawie, 2007 E.C.R. I-513, 549 ¶23.

workers' welfare fund) was considered a charge having an effect equivalent to a customs duty.[15]

(c) *Limitation of Prohibition*

(1) *General System of Internal Taxation*

In contrast to the prohibitions codified in Article 34 and Article 35 of the TFEU which are discussed below, there are no exceptions in the TFEU to the prohibition contained in Article 25.[16] However, not all "fees" imposed by the member states are prohibited by Article 30 of the TFEU. In the EU legal system, the member states retain the power to impose pecuniary charges under a general system of internal taxation.[17] Hence, internal tax measures adopted by the member states do not fall under Article 30 even though their effect may be equivalent to that of a customs duty.[18] Instead, such charges are scrutinized under Article 110 of the TFEU. The fundamental requirement of Article 110 is that the tax must be applied equally to domestic and foreign products. If the internal tax measure is "in excess of that imposed directly or indirectly on similar domestic products" (Article 110(1)), it is prohibited by Article 110 (and not by Article 30 because the latter does not apply to internal tax measures.)

The challenge is to identify whether a particular charge is a charge having equivalent effect as a customs duty (and therefore falls under Article 30 of the TFEU) or an internal tax measure (and therefore falls under Article 110 of the TFEU). The essential feature of a charge having an effect equivalent to a customs duty which distinguishes it from an internal tax is that it applies only to imported products or is triggered by the fact that the product is imported.[19] Conversely, a charge whose application does not depend on whether a good crosses a border is likely to be considered an internal tax measure.[20] In *De Danske Bilimportører v. Skatteministeriet, Told- og Skattestyrelsen*, for example, the ECJ characterized a Danish tax on new vehicle registrations as part of the Danish system of internal taxation because it was not triggered by the vehicle crossing "the frontier of

---

15. Case C-441/98, Kapniki Mikhailidis v. Idrima Kinonikon Asphaliseon, 2000 E.C.R. I-7145, 7172 ¶15. *See also* Case C-347/95, Fazenda Pública v. Ucal, 1997 E.C.R. I-4911, 4929 ¶18; Case C-426/92, Germany v. Deutsches Milch-Kontor, 1994 E.C.R. I-2757, 2784 ¶50.
16. Case C-173/05, Comm'n v. Italy, 2007 E.C.R. I-4917, 4927 ¶42.
17. Case C-334/02, Comm'n v. France, 2004 E.C.R. I-2229, 2251 ¶21; Case C-347/95, Fazenda Pública v. Unico, 1997 E.C.R. I-4911. The term "internal taxation" is derived from Article III(2) of the GATT.
18. Joined Cases C-290/05 and C-333/05, Ákos Nádasdi v. Vám- és Pénzügyőrség Észak-Alföldi Regionális Parancsnoksága, 2006 E.C.R. I-10115, 10173 ¶¶40-41.
19. Case C-313/05, Brzeziński v. Dyrektor Izby Celnej w Warszawie, 2007 E.C.R. I-513, 549 ¶23; C-109/98, CRT France Int'l. SA v. Directeur Regional des Impôts de Bourgogne, 1999 E.C.R. I-2237, 2271 ¶11.
20. Joined Cases C-290/05 and C-333/05, Ákos Nádasdi v. Vám- és Pénzügyőrség Észak-Alföldi Regionális Parancsnoksága, 2006 E.C.R. I-10115, 10173 ¶40.

the member state which imposed the charge."[21] Consequently, the applicable legal norm was Article 110 of the TFEU. As the internal tax measure was not discriminatory, the ECJ held it was consistent with the TFEU even though there may have been a negative effect on trade between member states.

(2) Compensatory Fee

In addition to internal tax measures, the other limitation on the scope of the prohibition contained in Article 30 of the TFEU is that it does not cover fees or charges which are directly related to services rendered.[22] For example, a fee imposed by a member state on an importer of ice cream to reimburse the member state for costs incurred by that member state as a result of providing refrigerated storage for the goods during customs clearance would not necessarily be prohibited by Article 30. This limitation is to be interpreted narrowly. There must be some sort of service actually rendered to the specific trader in proportion to the services which that trader receives. If the returns to the state through the imposition of the fees exceed the costs incurred by the state in providing such services, the fee assumes the character of a prohibited charge.[23]

2.2 Elimination of Quantitative Restrictions and Measures Having Equivalent Effect

The second prohibition that forms the basis of the free movement of goods principle is the elimination of quantitative restrictions on the import or export of goods within the EU and measures having an equivalent effect (Articles 34 and 35 TFEU). The prohibition contained in Article 30 of the TFEU on customs duties and charges having equivalent effect would not on its face prevent Germany, for example, from introducing a quota on foreign-brewed beer sold in Germany. This is because a quota is not a customs duty or a charge. As indicated above, the concept of charge in the context of Article 30 implies payment by the importer or exporter or receipt of payment by the state. Yet the proper functioning of the internal market necessitates the elimination of all barriers to trade. This is the purpose of the prohibitions codified in Articles 34 and 35 of the TFEU.

In securing the internal market, the prohibitions contained in Articles 34 and 35 complement the prohibition on customs duties and equivalent

---

21. Case C-383/01, De Danske Bilimportører v. Skatteministeriet, Told- og Skattestyrelsen, 2003 E.C.R. I-6065, 6097 ¶34. *See also* Joined Cases C-34/01 to C-38/01, Enirisorse SpA v. Ministero delle Finanze, 2003 E.C.R. I-14243, 14308 ¶60.
22. C-109/98, CRT France Int'l. v. Directeur Regional des Impots de Bourgogne, 1999 E.C.R. I-2237, 2271 ¶11.
23. Case C-209/89, Comm'n v. Italy, 1991 E.C.R. I-1575.

charges.[24] Articles 34 and 35 prohibit two acts: quantitative restrictions on imports (Article 34) and exports (Article 35) of goods between member states and measures having an effect equivalent to a quantitative restriction. As discussed above, the threshold requirement for the application of both Article 34 and Article 35 is that the restriction or measure must relate to goods. For example, Articles 34 and 35 would not apply to a Spanish law prohibiting the transport to another member state of more than €1 million in cash without the prior approval of the Spanish authorities because banknotes and other forms of payment are not considered goods.[25]

(a) Quantitative Restrictions

Quantitative restrictions limit or reduce the volume of goods directly imported into or exported from a country. Perhaps the most obvious example of a quantitative restriction is a quota or the outright suspension of imports from another member state.[26]

(b) Measures Having Equivalent Effect

Articles 34 and 35 of the TFEU also prohibit measures having an effect equivalent to a quantitative restriction on imports or exports. For example, a Finnish law that requires Finnish residents to apply for and secure a transfer license if they want to buy an automobile from another member state is a measure having an equivalent effect because it reduces the quantity of automobiles exported from other member states into Finland.[27] The prohibition on measures having an effect equivalent to a quantitative restriction has been the subject of significantly more litigation than the definition of quantitative restrictions. As the case law demonstrates, this stems not only from the ambiguity of the phrase but also the use by the European Commission and the EU courts of the prohibition as an instrument to achieve greater economic integration.

(1) State Measure

Articles 34 and 35 of the TFEU apply only to state measures. As is discussed in Chapter III, Articles 101 and 102 of the TFEU apply to restraints of trade stemming from activities of private firms and individuals. Articles 34 and 35 complement Articles 101 and 102 as the latter do not directly apply to the

---

24. Although a charge in the context of Article 30 of the TFEU may be considered a measure, and therefore both Article 30 and Article 34 are potentially applicable, the legal principle *lex specialis derogat legi generali* would apply. *See, e.g.*, Case C-96/00, *In re* Rudolf Gabriel, 2002 E.C.R. I-6367, 6399 ¶36. This principle of statutory interpretation, which applies when two legal norms apply to the same factual situation, requires that the special norm, or the norm specifically addressed to that circumstance, applies over the more general legal norm.
25. *See, e.g.*, Joined cases C-358/93 and C-416/93, *In re* Bordessa, 1995 E.C.R. I-361, 383 ¶12.
26. Case 7/61, Comm'n v. Italy, 1961 E.C.R. 317.
27. Case C-54/05, Comm'n v. Finland, 2007 E.C.R. I-2473, 2507 ¶32.

various measures adopted by the member states. When taken together, they essentially prohibit public and private restrictions on the trade of good between member states.

The requirement of a state measure has two components. The first component is the existence of a measure. The obvious example is a law of a member state that prohibits the sale of goods from other member states: the adoption of a law by France which prohibits the sale of non-French wine in France would violate Article 34 of the TFEU. But there are more subtle, indirect ways by which trade between member states may be restricted. In *Commission v. Ireland*, the Irish government adopted a "Buy Irish" campaign designed to promote the sale of Irish products. To that end, the Irish government provided exhibition facilities and a publicity campaign for Irish products. Although the activities of the Irish government did not directly prevent the sale of goods from other member states, the ECJ held that the campaign violated Article 34 of the TFEU because it reduced the quantity of goods from other member states sold in Ireland.[28] This case illustrates that indirect means of restraining trade between member states may constitute state measures in the context of Article 34 of the TFEU.

The facts in *Commission v. France* illustrate how difficult it is to identify a state measure.[29] In that case, the French government had regularly received complaints concerning the passivity of the French authorities in the face of violent acts committed by private individuals and by protest movements of French farmers directed against agricultural products from other member states. Groups of French farmers launched a systematic campaign to restrict the supply of agricultural products from other member states. For example, the farmers intercepted produce (strawberries and tomatoes) trucks from Spain and Belgium into France and destroyed their loads. Although these acts were prohibited by French law, the French authorities failed to take remedial measures. Hence, the issue was not whether the activity of the state (in this case France) constituted a state measure, but rather whether inactivity by the state could constitute a measure in the context of Article 34 of the TFEU. Although the conduct restricting the flow of goods in this case was undertaken by private individuals, the ECJ imposed an affirmative duty on the member state to intervene: "As an indispensable instrument for the realization of a market without internal frontiers, Article [34] therefore does not prohibit solely measures emanating from the State which, in themselves, create restrictions on trade between Member States. It also applies where a Member State abstains from adopting the measures required in order to deal with obstacles to the free movement of goods which are not caused by the State."[30]

Second, the measure must be that of the state. The term "state" refers to public authorities and agencies at whatever level (national, regional or local).

---

28. Case 249/81, Comm'n v. Ireland, 1982 E.C.R. 4005.
29. Case C-265/95, Comm'n v. France, 1997 E.C.R. I-6959.
30. *Id.* at ¶30.

The prohibition also applies to measures adopted by the EU institutions.[31] Even restrictions imposed by private groups may constitute "state measures" if the state has granted regulatory powers to the group, the function of the group is to carry out a public interest which the state would otherwise fulfill, the state mandates the public interest criteria and essential rules with which the group must comply, and the state retains the power to adopt decisions of last resort.[32]

Commission v. Germany involved a German law which established a central fund to promote the German food industry.[33] Private German firms were required by law to contribute to the fund. The administration of the fund was assigned to a German limited liability company (GmbH). The supervisory board of this company was composed of representatives of the various professional associations active in the German food industry. The ECJ held that the promotional activities of this entity constituted state measures. In coming to that conclusion, the ECJ focused on the following facts: The entity was a creation of the state; the state retained some control over the activity of the entity; and although the entity was financed by contributions of private firms, the contributions were compulsory.[34]

In *Fra.bo SpA v. DVGW*, the involvement of the state was even more indirect.[35] In this case, a private standardization body in Germany adopted a certification standard for copper fittings. The private association was not mandated by law, nor were companies selling copper fittings required by law to conform to the private standards. However, German law recognized certifications by the private association to be compliant by German law.[36] According to the ECJ, the prohibition on state measures codified in Art. 29 applied to the standards adopted by the private association.[37]

(2) Effect Equivalent to a Quantitative Restriction

A measure having an effect equivalent to a quantitative restriction is defined as "all trading rules enacted by Member States which are capable of hindering, directly or indirectly, actually or potentially intra-Community trade."[38] This is often referred to as the Dassonville Formula. It is the *effect* of the state measure

---

31. Joined Cases C-154/04 and C-155/04, Alliance for Natural Health v. Secretary of State for Health, 2005 E.C.R. I-6451, 6503 ¶47; Case C-469/00, Ravil SARL v. Bellon Import SARL, 2003 E.C.R. I-5085, 5113 ¶86; Case C-169/99, Schwarzkopf, 2001 E.C.R. I-5901, 5938 ¶37. This rule has little practical effect as the EU will generally assume that the EU institutions are acting commensurate with one of the public policy exceptions enumerated in the TFEU or case law. *See, e.g.*, Case C-210/03, Swedish Match AB v. Secretary of State for Health, 2004 E.C.R. I-11900, 11922 ¶61.
32. Case C-1/12, Ordem dos Técnicos Oficiais de Contas v. Autoridade da Concorrência, 2013 E.C.R. I-____, at ¶54.
33. Case C-325/00, Comm'n v. Germany, 2002 E.C.R. I-9977.
34. *Id.* at 10000 ¶17.
35. Case C-171/11, Fra.bo SpA v. DVGW, 2012 E.C.R. I-____.
36. *Id.* at ____, at ¶27.
37. *Id.* at ____, at ¶32.
38. Case 8/74, Procurer du Roi v. Dassonville, 1974 E.C.R. 837, 840 ¶5.

rather than its *purpose* which is determinative. A member state cannot therefore justify a state measure by arguing that it was not the purpose of the measure to restrict the trade of goods between member states. This applies to restrictions on imports as well as exports. In *Jersey Produce Marketing Organization Ltd. v. State of Jersey*, for example, a state measure hindering the export of potatoes was deemed to violate Article 31 of the TFEU as it had an effect equivalent to a quantitative restriction on the export of goods.[39]

The term "restriction" has traditionally been interpreted broadly in this context. The promotion of domestic products may have the effect of reducing the amount of foreign products sold in a member state and hence be deemed a measure having an effect equivalent to a quantitative restriction even though there is no absolute barrier to the importation of the foreign goods.[40] Thus, state measures which merely make the marketing of foreign products more difficult are considered a measure having an effect equivalent to a quantitative restriction.[41]

Based on the jurisprudence of the ECJ, there are two types of state measures that may have an effect equivalent to a quantitative restriction. A state measure which distinctly applies to goods from other member states is referred to as distinctly applicable. A Maltese law which required olives from outside Malta to be in green bottles would be an example of a distinctly applicable state measure. There are state measures which, although they apply equally to foreign and domestic goods, restrict the flow of goods that are lawfully sold in other member states. These are referred to as indistinctly applicable state measures. For example, a German law requiring liqueur to have at least 25 percent alcohol content in order to be sold as a liqueur is indistinctly applicable as it applies equally to alcohol produced in Germany as well as in other member states.[42] It can, however, have a restrictive effect on trade if, for example, that same alcohol is lawfully produced and sold as liqueur in France even with an alcohol content of 20 percent. The German law would then be a restriction on the flow of products from one member state to the other. As the ECJ held in the seminal case *Rewe-Zentral v. Bundesmonopolverwaltung für Branntwein*, such indistinctly applicable measures violate Article 34 of the TFEU because they prevent a product lawfully manufactured and sold in one member state from being lawfully sold in another member state without justification (rule of equivalence).[43]

There are three practical implications of the distinction between distinctly and indistinctly applicable measures. Whereas indistinctly applicable measures

---

39. Case C-293/02, Jersey Produce Marketing Organization Ltd. v. State of Jersey, 2005 E.C.R. I-9543, 9807 ¶85.
40. Case C-443/10, Bonnarde v. Agence de Services et de Paiement, 2011 E.C.R. I-9327, 9340 ¶26.
41. Case C-448/98, Tribunal de Police v. Jean-Pierre Guimon, 2000 E.C.R. I-10663.
42. See Case 120/78, Rewe-Zentral v. Bundesmonopolverwaltung für Branntwein, 1979 E.C.R. 649.
43. *Id.* at 664 ¶14. As discussed below, such indistinctly applicable measures may be justified by imperative requirements in the public interest.

may be justified by imperative requirements of public interest (discussed below), distinctly applicable measures are prohibited per se under Articles 34 and 35 of the TFEU. Although distinctly applicable measures may technically benefit from an exception under Article 36 of the TFEU, it is unlikely that they will meet the nondiscrimination requirement as discussed below.

Second, the selling arrangements doctrine only applies to state measures that are indistinctly applicable. As discussed below, a state measure that merely regulates how the product is sold (selling arrangements) does not fall under Article 34 of the TFEU provided it is indistinctly applicable to domestic products and products from other member states.[44]

The third implication of the distinction between distinctly and indistinctly applicable measures is that ECJ has not extended the rule of equivalence to Article 35 of the TFEU (i.e., restrictions on exports). Indistinctly applicable state measures restricting exports are generally commensurate with Article 35 even if they are capable of hindering, directly or indirectly, actually or potentially intra-EU trade. The standard under Article 29 is, rather, whether there is a difference in treatment between domestic trade of a member state and its export trade, in such a way as to provide a particular advantage for national production or for the domestic market of the state in question, at the expense of the trade or production of other member states.[45]

(c) Effect on Trade Between Member States

Articles 34 and 35 of the TFEU only apply if there is an effect on trade between member states. This requirement is construed broadly. In most cases, the existence of a quantitative restriction or a measure having equivalent effect will mean ipso facto that the inter-state trade requirement is fulfilled. In *Jersey Produce Marketing Organization Ltd. v. State of Jersey*, the Isle of Jersey, a part of the UK, passed a local law requiring all sellers of potatoes to some other place in the UK to be registered with the Jersey Potato Export Marketing Board. The ECJ held that this restriction, even though it only applied to trade within one member state, had an effect on trade between member states as those same potatoes could be subsequently sold to other member states.[46] In *Carbonati Apuani SrL v. Comune di Carrara*, the ECJ held that a charge imposed by a region within a member state to exports of marble even to other parts of that same member state was a prohibited charge having an effect equivalent to a quantitative restriction.[47]

There is no de minimis threshold for the interstate trade requirement. In *Commission v. France*, the issue was whether a French law that required gold not meeting a particular fineness criterion to be sold as "gold alloy" violated Article 34 of the TFEU because that same gold could lawfully be sold as gold in

---

44. Case C-267/91, Keck and Mithouard, 1993 E.C.R. I-6097, 6131 ¶16.
45. Case C-205/07, Gysbrechts v. Santurel Inter BVBA, 2008 E.C.R. I-9947, 9992 ¶40; Case C-293/02, Jersey Produce Marketing Organization Ltd. v. State of Jersey, 2005 E.C.R. I-9543, 9603 ¶73.
46. *Id.* at 9601 ¶65.
47. Case C-72/03, Carbonati Apuani SrL v. Comune di Carrara, 2004 E.C.R. I-8027.

other member states.[48] France argued that the impact on trade between member states, if any, was not appreciable. The ECJ held that the French law was a measure having an effect equivalent to a quantitative restriction "without it being necessary to prove that it has had an appreciable effect on intra-Community trade."[49]

Moreover, it is not necessary that trade between member states be directly affected. In *Administration des douanes et droit indirects v. Rioglass SA*, the French customs authorities (on the basis of French intellectual property law) had stopped a shipment of automobile windows lawfully produced in Spain and destined for Poland (which at the time was not a member of the EU).[50] The French authorities believed the goods violated the trademark rights of a third party under French intellectual property law. The ECJ held that even if the goods are intended for a non-EU country, they come within the scope of Article 34 of the TFEU.[51]

2.3 Attempts by the Court to Limit the Scope of the Prohibition

The expansive interpretation of Article 34 of the TFEU—which may have been considered appropriate at the time as a means of promoting the integration of the member states—has necessitated the introduction of certain limitations by the ECJ. The dogmatic application of the Dassonville Formula (that all state measures which are capable of hindering, directly or indirectly, actually or potentially intra-EU trade are prohibited)[52] leads to politically difficult results as it results in the EU courts annulling member state laws. The integration of Europe has not achieved a level that would allow the EU institutions—and even the EU courts—to ignore the political implications of their decisions. The ECJ has consequently promulgated two important limitations on the traditional application of the prohibitions codified in Articles 34 and 35 of the TFEU. These limitations have been introduced by the EU courts to either supplement or expand the exceptions codified in Article 36 of the TFEU. As they are examples of state measures that are not prohibited by Articles 34 or 35, however, they technically cannot be considered exceptions.

(1) Selling Arrangements

In *Keck and Mithouard*, the ECJ limited the scope of the prohibition contained in Articles 34 and 35 of the TFEU by introducing into the free movement of goods jurisprudence the concept of selling arrangements.[53] In that case, Messrs. Keck and Mithouard were prosecuted by the French authorities for selling coffee

---

48. Case C-166/03, Comm'n v. France, 2004 E.C.R. I-6535.
49. *Id.* at 6550 ¶15.
50. Case C-115/02, Administration des douanes et droits indirects v. Rioglass SA, 2003 E.C.R. I-12705.
51. *Id.* at 12714 ¶20.
52. Case 8/74, Procurer du Roi v. Dassonville, 1974 E.C.R. 837.
53. Case C-267/91, Keck and Mithouard, 1993 E.C.R. I-6097.

and beer at a price lower than the price at which they purchased the coffee and beer. They argued that the French law violated Article 34 of the TFEU.

In holding the French law was consistent with Article 34, the ECJ introduced the selling arrangements doctrine.[54] The regulation of selling arrangements which have an effect equivalent to a quantitative restriction on trade between member states can be regulated by the member states (i.e., fall outside the prohibitions of Articles 34 and 35)[55] provided that (1) those regulations apply to all relevant traders operating within that member state (i.e., are indistinctly applicable) and (2) they affect the marketing of domestic products and those from other member states equally. The rationale subsequently offered by the ECJ for the introduction of this selling arrangements concept is that such measures do not impede access of imported goods any more than they impede domestic products from being offered on the market.[56]

Reconciling the selling arrangements doctrine with prior case law is not always easy. Many of the prior cases decided by the ECJ seem to have involved state measures regulating selling arrangements. However, subsequent case law of the EU courts has assisted in clarifying which activities qualify as selling arrangements. State measures applicable to selling arrangements essentially regulate how, when, or where products are sold. For example, the state measure at issue in *Hünermund v. Landesapothekerkammer* was a German pharmacy association rule prohibiting the advertising of certain pharmaceutical products outside of the pharmacy. Several pharmacists in Germany were sanctioned for advertising these products outside their stores. The ECJ concluded that this state measure qualified as the regulation of selling arrangements and therefore fell outside of Article 34 of the TFEU.[57] In another case, an Austrian law which prohibited door-to-door selling of jewelry was deemed a regulation of selling arrangements.[58] In general, any regulation of a marketing method (and not the characteristics of the products)[59] will fall outside the scope of Article 34 if it applies to all relevant traders operating within that member state and equally

---

54. *Id.* at 6131 ¶16.
55. The selling arrangement doctrine should be considered as narrowing the scope of Articles 34 and 35 and not an exception to these TFEU provisions. This classification arises from the recognition that the doctrine does not apply to state measures that "prevent access to the market by products from another Member State or impede access any more than they impede the access of domestic products." Case C-405/98, Konsumentombudsmannen (KO) v. Gourmet Int'l. Products AB, 2001 E.C.R. I-1795, 1823 ¶18. This requirement for the application of the selling arrangements doctrine would be superfluous if the doctrine were characterized as an exception because the same thing is prohibited by Article 34 of the TFEU.
56. Case C-416/00, Tommaso Morellato v. Comune di Padove, 2003 E.C.R. I-9343, 9369 ¶31.
57. Case C-292/92, Hünermund v. Landesapothekerkammer, 1993 E.C.R. I-6787, 6823 ¶24.
58. Case C-441/04, A-Punkt Schmuckhandels GmbH v. Schmidt, 2006 E.C.R. I-2093, 20,101 ¶17.
59. Case C-141/07, Comm'n v. Germany, 2008 E.C.R. I-6935, 6979 ¶31.

affects the marketing of domestic products and those from other member states.[60]

A state measure which in effect requires goods from other member states to be altered or repackaged in order to comply with that state measure do not qualify as selling arrangements.[61] In *Dynamic Medien Vertriebs GmbH v. Avides Media*, for example, the ECJ held that a German law effectively requiring certain DVDs purchased over the Internet to be relabeled "Not suitable for young persons" when those same DVDs were already labeled "suitable only for 15 years and over" in the UK in accordance with UK law was not the regulation of a selling arrangement.[62]

At issue in *Tommaso Morellato v. Comune di Padove* was an Italian law which required that bread made from partially baked bread (for example, deep-frozen bread that is then baked and sold by the baker) be sold in pre-prepared packaging. An Italian baker sold bread that he had imported pre-cooked, deep-frozen from France. However, he did not sell it in packages, but rather put it in a bag and stapled it shut when the customer came into the bakery and indicated a desire to purchase the bread. After he was fined for infringing the Italian law, he argued that the law violated Article 34 of the TFEU. The ECJ held that "legislation of a Member State which prohibits a product that is lawfully manufactured and marketed in another Member State from being put on sale in the first Member State without being subjected to new packaging of a specific type that complies with the requirements of that legislation cannot be held to concern selling arrangements within the meaning of *Keck and Mithouard*."[63]

As indicated above, the application of the selling arrangements doctrine requires that the state measure regulating the selling arrangement (1) applies equally to all relevant traders operating within that member state (i.e., is indistinctly applicable), and (2) affects the marketing of domestic products and those from other member states equally (i.e., does not have a differential effect).[64] The indistinctly applicable requirement means that the state measure must apply equally to both domestic and foreign products. The differential effect standard goes one step further and examines the actual effect of the indistinctly

---

60. Case C-20/03, *In re* Burmanjer, 2005 E.C.R. I-4133, 4161 ¶25.
61. Case C-244/06 Dynamic Medien Vertriebs GmbH v. Avides GmbH, 2008 E.C.R. 505, 545 ¶32; Case C-217/99, Comm'n v. Belgium, 2000 E.C.R. I-10251, 10272 ¶16 (Labeling of nutrients in foodstuffs was not considered a selling arrangement.); Case C-12/00, Comm'n v. Spain, 2003 E.C.R. I-459, 505 ¶76 (Spanish law requiring chocolate products containing vegetable fats other than cocoa butter to contain the term "chocolate substitute" was not a selling arrangement).
62. Case C-244/06, Dynamic Medien Vertriebs GmbH v. Avides GmbH, 2008 E.C.R. I-505, 545 ¶31.
63. Case C-416/00, Tommaso Morellato v. Comune di Padove, 2003 E.C.R. I-9343, 9368 ¶30. The ECJ left it up to the national court to determine whether the law actually restricted the sale of goods in Italy.
64. Case C-108/09, Ker-Optika bt v. ÀNTSZ Dél-dunántúli Regionális Intézete, 2010 E.C.R. I-12213, 12260 ¶51; Case C-441/04, A-Punkt Schmuckhandels GesmbH v. Schmidt, 2006 E.C.R. I-2093, 2101 ¶15; Case C-292/92, Hünermund v. Landesapothekerkammer, 1993 E.C.R. I-6787, 6823 ¶21.

applicable state measure. The state measure must not prevent access to the market by products from another member state any more than they impede the access of domestic products.[65]

Many state measures qualifying as selling arrangements fail to meet the differential effect requirement. In *Ker-Optika bt v. ÀNTSZ Dél-dunántúli Regionális Intézete*, a Hungarian law prohibiting the sale of contact lenses was considered by the ECJ as a regulation of a selling arrangement.[66] However, the ECJ concluded that the law did not qualify for the selling arrangements exception because it had a different effect on sellers from outside Hungary compared to sellers within Hungary who were not as dependent upon the Internet to reach customers in Hungary.[67]

In *Fachverband der Buch- und Medienwirtschaft v. LIBRO Handelsgesellschaft mbH*, an Austrian law prohibited Austrian book retailers from selling imported books at prices below the price recommended by the publisher located in another member state. The purpose of the law was to provide an incentive for publishers of low-volume books by allowing these publishers to ensure a higher profit margin. The effectiveness of the law was possible because the primary member state from which books were imported into Austria was Germany, which shares the same language and had a similar law on book prices. According to the ECJ, the Austrian law treated imported books less favorably than books published in Austria "since it prevents Austrian importers and foreign publishers from fixing minimum retail prices according to the conditions of the import market, whereas the Austrian publishers are free to fix themselves, for their goods, such minimum retail prices for the national market."[68]

(2) Imperative Requirements

In *Rewe-Zentral v. Bundesmonopolverwaltung für Branntwein*, the ECJ held that indistinctly applicable state measures which otherwise violate Article 34 or 35 of the TFEU may be justified by imperative requirements of public interest, provided such measures apply without discrimination to both domestic and imported products.[69] There is no exhaustive catalog of what constitutes imperative requirements. It is probably best considered as an open-ended public policy exception. Based on the case law of the ECJ, the imperative requirements doctrine may preclude the application of Article 34 or Article 35[70] of the TFEU

---

65. Case C-405/98, Konsumentombudsmannen v. Gourmet Int'l. Products *AB*, 2001 E.C.R. I-1795, 1823 ¶18.
66. Case C-108/09, Ker-Optika bt v. ÀNTSZ Dél-dunántúli Regionális Intézete, 2010 E.C.R. I-12213, 12260 ¶51.
67. *Id.*
68. Case C-531/07, Fachverband der Buch- und Medienwirtschaft v. LIBRO Handelsgesellschaft mbH, 2009 E.C.R. I-3717, 3778 ¶21.
69. Case 120/78, Rewe-Zentral v. Bundesmonopolverwaltung für Branntwein, 1979 E.C.R. 649, 662 ¶8. The ECJ sometimes uses the terms "mandatory requirements" or "overriding requirements" to refer to the same concept. *See, e.g.*, Case C-265/06, Comm'n v. Portugal, 2008 E.C.R. 2245, 2279 ¶37.
70. Case C-205/07, Gysbrechts v. Sandoval Inter BVBA, 2008 E.C.R. I-9947, 9994 ¶45.

to state measures relating to road safety,[71] consumer protection,[72] cultural diversity,[73] law enforcement,[74] protection against misleading advertising,[75] public safety,[76] the prevention of unfair commercial practices (sometimes expressed as the promotion of fair trading or the prevention of unfair competition), environmental protection,[77] improvement of working conditions, and the plurality of the media. By contrast, state measures based on purely economic grounds cannot benefit from this exception.[78]

As discussed below, Article 36 of the TFEU codifies certain public policy exceptions to the prohibitions set forth in Articles 34 and 35. It was unclear from *Rewe-Zentral v. Bundesmonopolverwaltung für Branntwein* whether this imperative requirements doctrine should be considered merely a characterization of the objective which Article 36 pursues rather than a source of additional exceptions independent of the statutory exception enumerated in Article 30 of the TFEU. In subsequent cases, however, the ECJ has been clear that the imperative requirements exception is in addition to the exceptions enumerated in Article 36.[79] In *Fachverband der Buch- und Medienwirtschaft v. LIBRO Handelsgesellschaft mbH*, for example, the ECJ held that an Austrian law which ostensibly protected cultural diversity by prohibiting book retailers in Austria from selling books published in other member states from being sold below the publisher's fixed price could not be justified under Article 36 of the TFEU but could be justified as required by imperative requirements in the public interest.[80]

(3) Certain and Direct Requirement

Another judicially created limitation to the prohibitions set forth in Articles 34 and 35 of the TFEU on quantitative restrictions and measures having an equivalent effect is the requirement that the restrictive effect be certain and

---

71. Case C-110/05, Comm'n v. Italy, 2009 E.C.R. I-519, 598 ¶60.
72. Case C-423/13, UAB Vilniaus energija v. Lietuvos metrologijos inspekcijos Vilniaus apskrities skyrius, 2014 E.C.R. I-___, at ¶50; Case C-205/07, Gysbrechts v. Sandolval BVBA, 2008 E.C.R. I-9947, 9994 ¶47.
73. Case C-531/07, Fachverband der Buch- und Medienwirtschaft v. LIBRO Handelsgesellschaft mbH, 2009 E.C.R. I-3717, 3782 ¶34.
74. Case C-265/06, Comm'n v. Portugal, 2008 E.C.R. I- 2245, 2279 ¶38.
75. Case C-470/93, Verein gegen Unwesen in Handel und Gewerbe Köln e.V. v. Mars, 1995 E.C.R. I-1936, 1941 ¶15.
76. Case C-265/06, Comm'n v. Portugal, 2008 E.C.R. I- 2245, 2279 ¶38.
77. Case C-443/10, Bonnarde v. Agence de Services et de Paiement, 2011 E.C.R. I-9327, 9342 ¶34.
78. Case C-456/10, Asociación Nacional de Expendedores de Tabaco y Timbre v. Administración del Estado, 2012 E.C.R. I-___, at ¶53.
79. Case C-161/09, Kakavetsos-Fragkopoulos AE Epexergasias kai Emporias Stafidas v. Nomarchiaki Aftodioikisi Korinthias, 2011 E.C.R. I-946, 968 ¶51; Case C-88/07, Comm'n v. Spain, 2009 E.C.R. I-1359, at ¶85; Case C-524/07, Comm'n v. Austria, 2008 E.C.R. I-187, at ¶54; Case C-297/05, Comm'n v. Netherlands, 2007 E.C.R. I-7467, 7491 ¶75.
80. Case C-531/07, Fachverband der Buch- und Medienwirtschaft v. LIBRO Handelsgesellschaft mbH, 2009 E.C.R. I-3717, 3782 ¶34.

direct.[81] If one were to literally apply the standard set forth in *Dassonville*, all measures with a potential, indirect effect on trade between member states would violate Article 34 or 35 of the TFEU. One need not be familiar with the case law to recognize that this standard would capture a broad range of measures. The certain and direct standard sets a minimum threshold to filter those restrictions which, although they may theoretically fulfill the Dassonville formula, are just too speculative to attract concern.

The issue in *BASF v. Präsident des Deutschen Patentamts* was whether a German law which required patent specifications to be translated into German if they were filed with the German Patent Office restricted the free movement of goods.[82] BASF had filed a patent application with the German Patent Office in English but failed to provide a German translation within the prescribed three months. BASF argued that the high costs of translating patent specifications caused the patent holders to be selective as to the member states where they file an application. This effectively would result in a division of the EU into "protected zones" (i.e., where the patent holder decided to incur the costs of a transaction and submit a patent application) and "free zones" (i.e., where the patent holder did not file for patent protection because of the high costs of the translation). According to BASF, this would inevitably result in less trade in goods between the protected zone and the free zone as the prices for the goods in the free zone would likely be lower than in the protected zone (because of the competition the patent holder would face in the free zone). The ECJ held, however, that the potential effect argued by BASF was "too indirect to be considered to be an obstacle within the meaning of Article [34] of the Treaty."[83]

2.4 Exceptions Enumerated in the TFEU

In addition to the exceptions or limitations to Articles 34 and 35 of TFEU created by the EU courts, the TFEU contains express exceptions from the prohibition on quantitative restrictions and measures having equivalent effect. These exemptions, which are codified in Article 36 of the TFEU,[84] only relate to import restrictions and export restrictions falling under Article 34 or 35. There are no equivalent exceptions to the prohibition on customs duties and charges having equivalent effect in Article 30 of the TFEU.

---

81. Case C-291/09, Francesco Guarnieri & Cie v. Vandevelde Eddy VOF, 2011 E.C.R. I-2700, 2707 ¶17; Case C-412/97, ED Srl v. Fenocchio, 1999 E.C.R. I-3874, 3879 ¶11. This does not mean, however, that there is a quantative de minimis threshold. A restriction on any free movement is prohibited "even if it is limited in scope or minor importance." Case C-498/10, X NV v. Staatssecretaris, 2012 E.C.R. I-___, at ¶30.
82. Case C-44/98, BASF v. Präsident des Deutschen Patentamts, 1999 E.C.R. I-6269.
83. *Id.* at 6295 ¶21.
84. The TFEU (Article 114(4)) provides a procedure by which a member state can request a determination from the Commission as to whether a particular state measure falls under Article 36 of the TFEU.

(a) Public Morality, Public Policy, and Public Security

State measures which are based on grounds of public morality, public policy, or public security are exempted from the prohibitions contained in Articles 34 and 35 of the TFEU. In *Regina v. Henn and Darby*, the ECJ held that a member state could prohibit the sale and importation of pornographic material on the basis of the protection of public morality.[85] The very nature of the terms "public morality, public policy or public security" indicate that this exception is vulnerable to abuse by the member states and difficult to apply. For example, the difference between a legitimate public policy concern and a protectionist measure will differ among the member states. The ECJ has recognized this relative characteristic of the exception and granted the member states a margin of discretion.[86]

In *Dynamic Medien Vertriebs GmbH v. Avides Media AG*, for example, the ECJ held that Germany may rely on the protection of children to justify a law that required certain warnings to be placed on DVDs coming from the UK.[87] In *Commission v. Denmark*, the issue was whether a Danish law which required containers for soft drinks to be reusable and returnable violated Article 34 of the TFEU.[88] Sellers of soft drinks from member states where such laws were not in place argued that this law restricted the sale of their soft drinks in Denmark. The ECJ held that the restraint was justified by legitimate environmental protection concerns.[89]

(b) Protection of Health

A state measure having an effect equivalent to a quantitative restriction may be justified on grounds that it is necessary to protect public health. For example, the ECJ recognized in *Konsumentombudsmannen v. Gourmet International Products* that the prevention of alcohol abuse may be a legitimate public health concern. In that case, Sweden had adopted a law which prohibited the advertising of alcoholic beverages in magazines and on television. As this law made it more difficult for sellers of alcohol from other member states to break into the Swedish market, it was considered a violation of Article 34 of the TFEU. However, the ECJ held that the objective of the law—to reduce the incidents of alcohol abuse in Sweden—was a legitimate public health concern. Consequently, the law benefited from the exception provided under Article 36 of the TFEU.[90] In *Commission v. Italian Republic*, however, the ECJ held that an Italian law which prohibited the marketing in Italy of energy drinks containing caffeine

---

85. Case 34/79, Regina v. Henn and Darby, 1979 E.C.R. 3795.
86. Case C-244/06, Dynamic Medien Vertriebs GmbH v. Avides Media AG, 2008 E.C.R. I-505, 549 ¶44.
87. *Id.* at ¶52.
88. Case 302/86, Comm'n v. Denmark, 1988 E.C.R. 4607.
89. 1988 E.C.R. 4607, 4632 ¶21 (The law did not benefit from Article 36 because it failed the proportionality test).
90. Case C-405/98, Konsumentombudsmannen v. Gourmet Int'l. Products, 2001 E.C.R. I-1795, 1825 ¶27. *See also* Case C-434/04, Jan-Erik Anders Ahokainen v. Virallinen syyttäjä, 2006 E.C.R. I-9171.

in excess of a certain limit was not justified as necessary for the protection of public health.[91] In *Morellato v. Comune di Padova*, the ECJ similarly held that the public health exemption cannot justify an Italian law which required that bread which was made from partially baked bread (e.g., deep-frozen) to be sold in pre-prepared packaging as the purpose of the law was to protect bakers who used the traditional methods of baking breads.[92]

The existence of a public health exception presents the possibility of abuse by the member states because of the lack of an objective standard as to what constitutes a public health threat. It is clear that a state measure cannot be justified under the exceptions on pure speculation.[93] In *Commission v. Germany*, for example, the ECJ held that a German law which prohibited beer from being sold as "Bier" in Germany if it contained anything except malted barley, hops, yeast, and water—and consequently prohibited the sale of beer in Germany which had been lawfully produced and sold in other member states—could not be justified on the basis of Article 36 of the TFEU because there was no scientific evidence that the additives commonly used in beer in other member states was a health threat.[94]

On the other hand, it is not always necessary for a member state to adduce scientific evidence justifying the state measure. If there exists uncertainty in the scientific community as to the potential threat, a member state may rely on the precautionary principle to prevent the importation of the particular product into its country.[95] The precautionary principle is a rule of international law that allows member states to restrict the flow of goods even in the absence of scientific evidence of a threat to the public (environment or human, plant or animal health) if the risk of the realization of the threat is so great as to outweigh the disruption incurred by the imposition of the restriction until sufficient scientific evidence is available to adequately assess the risk.[96]

Although it is not expressly provided for by the TFEU, the ECJ has held that it may justify restrictions on the free movement of goods based on public health grounds where there is uncertainty in the scientific evidence relating to

---

91. Case C-420/01, Comm'n v. Italian Republic, 2003 E.C.R. I-6445.
92. Case C-416/00, Morellato v. Comune di Padova, 2003 E.C.R. I-9343, 9371 ¶40.
93. Case C-333/08, Comm'n v. France, 2010 E.C.R. I-757, at ¶91; Case C-270/02, *Comm'n v. Italian Republic*, 2004 E.C.R. I-1559, 1569 ¶24.
94. Case 178/84, Comm'n v. Germany, 1987 E.C.R. I-1227, 1274 ¶44.
95. Case C-333/08, Comm'n v. France, 2010 E.C.R. I-757, at ¶91; Case C-41/02, Comm'n v. The Netherlands, 2004 E.C.R. I-11375, 11412 ¶44; Case C-387/99, Comm'n v. Germany, 2004 E.C.R. I-3751, 3794 ¶68; Case C-95/01, *In re* Greenham & Abel, 2004 E.C.R. I-1333, 1365 ¶39; Case C-192/01, Comm'n v. Denmark, 2003 E.C.R. I-9693, 9740 ¶52.
96. *See* Communication from the Commission on the Precautionary Principle, COM (2000) 1 (Feb. 2, 2000).

a particular threat.[97] For example, a member state may impose restrictions (a system of prior authorization) on the sale of foodstuffs enhanced with particular nutrients if the scientific evidence is inconclusive about the health effects of those nutrients even if the same foodstuffs are lawfully sold in another member state.[98] To justify its measure, however, the member state must proffer some scientific evidence indicating a minimum level of uncertainty in the scientific community.[99]

(c) *Protection of Intellectual Property Rights*

Intellectual property rights perform important functions in market economies. A trademark allows a company to benefit from goodwill and allows a customer to identify the maker of a product. A patent rewards an inventor for his or her inventive efforts. Because of the beneficial uses of intellectual property, states grant certain exclusive rights to the creators of intellectual property as a reward or incentive. Hence, intellectual property rights by their very nature are restrictive on trade. This creates an apparent contradiction with Articles 34 and 35 of the TFEU which seek to promote trade. For example, the holder of a Greek patent could prohibit companies from other member states from selling products in Greece which violate that patent even though the goods were lawfully manufactured and sold in other member states. The state measure in such a case, the Greek patent law, would violate Article 34.

According to Article 36 of the TFEU, Articles 34 and 35 shall not be applied to preclude restrictions on exports or imports if such restrictions are justified on grounds of the protection of industrial and commercial property.[100] As stated by the ECJ in *Commission v. French Republic*, the purpose of this limitation on the application of Articles 34 and 35 is to reconcile the apparent conflict between the retention by the member states of sovereignty in the field of intellectual property rights and the free movement of goods principle.[101] However, instead

---

97. Case C-95/01, *In re* Greenham & Abel, 2004 E.C.R. I-1333, 1366 ¶43; Case C-192/01, Comm'n v. Denmark, 2003 E.C.R. I-9693, 9739 ¶48. Reliance on this justification requires that it be proportional to the chosen level of protection, nondiscriminatory, consistent with measures already taken, based on an examination of the potential costs and benefits, subject to review in light of new scientific data, and capable of assigning responsibility for producing the scientific evidence necessary for a more comprehensive risk assessment. For example, a system of prior authorization may be permitted whereas an absolute prohibition may not.
98. Case C-333/08, Comm'n v. France, 2010 E.C.R. I-757, at ¶95; Case C-95/01, *In re* Greenham & Abel, 2004 E.C.R. I-1333, 1366 ¶43.
99. Case C-41/02, Comm'n v. The Netherlands, 2004 E.C.R. I-11375, 11416 ¶59.
100. The term "industrial and commercial property" includes patents, trademarks, copyrights, design rights, and other customary forms of intellectual property protected by statute. The protection of geographical indications and designations of origin under Council Regulation 2081/92 for agricultural products and foodstuffs, 1992 O.J. (L 208) 1 is also considered a form of intellectual property for purposes of Article 30 TFEU. Case C-161/09, Kakavetsos-Fragkopoulos AE Epexergasias kai Emporias Stafidas v. Nomarchiaki Aftodioikisi Korinthias, 2011 E.C.R. I-946, 964 ¶37.
101. Case C-23/99, Comm'n v. France, 2000 E.C.R. I-7653, 7686 ¶37.

of recognizing that Article 36 exempts *all* state measures involving intellectual property, the ECJ relied on a distinction which it introduced in earlier cases.

According to the EJC, the exception provided for in Article 36 relating to intellectual property rights only applies to state measures, the purpose of which are to protect the subject matter of the particular intellectual property right.[102] The subject matter of an intellectual property right is the specific purpose that it serves and that justifies the grant of exclusivity by the state. For example, the essential function of the trademark is to guarantee to the consumer or end user the identity of the trademarked product's origin by enabling him or her to distinguish it without any risk of confusion from products of different origin.[103] Therefore, "[t]he right attributed to a trademark proprietor of preventing any use of the trademark which is likely to impair the guarantee of origin so understood is therefore part of the specific subject-matter of the trademark rights."[104] In *Commission v. French Republic*, the transit of products (as opposed to merely their sale) was held not to be within the specific "subject matter" of a design right. Therefore, France could not detain the goods which had been lawfully entered into circulation in another member state.

2.5 Prerequisites for the Application of the Exceptions

(a) *Proportionality*

In order for a state measure to benefit from the exemptions identified in Article 36 of the TFEU or any of the judicially created exceptions, it must meet the proportionality requirement. This requires that a state measure which violates either Article 34 or 35 of the TFEU but falls under Article 36 or any of the judicially created exceptions must be suitable for attaining the legitimate objective and must not go beyond what is necessary to attain that objective.[105] As indicated by the ECJ in *Commission v. Germany*, the fact that a restriction may serve a legitimate function is not enough if there are other less restrictive means of achieving the same objectives.[106]

In that case, the German *Reinheitsgebot* (beer purity law) requiring beer to be manufactured only from malted barley, hops, yeast, and water (and no additives) was at issue. The European Commission considered this law to be a violation of Article 34 of the TFEU as it precluded beer lawfully manufactured

---

102. Case C-5/11, *In re* Donner, 2012 E.C.R. I-___, at ¶33.
103. Case C-143/00, Boehringer Ingelheim KG v. Swingward Ltd., 2002 E.C.R. I-3759, 3772 ¶12.
104. Case T-6/01, Matratzen Concord GmbH v. OHIM, 2002 E.C.R. II-4335, 4356 ¶58.
105. Case C-531/07, Fachverband der Buch- und Medienwirtschaft v. LIBRO Handelsgesellschaft mbH, 2009 E.C.R. I-3717, 3782 ¶34 (imperative requirements); Case C-387/99, Comm'n v. Germany, 2004 E.C.R. I-3751, 3794 ¶71 (Article 30).
106. Case 178/84, Comm'n v. Germany, 1987 E.C.R. I-1227. The mere fact that another member state imposes less restrictive rules to the goods does not necessarily mean that the state measure at issue is not proportionate. It is, however, a relevant consideration. Case C-421/09, Humanplasma GmbH v. Austria, 2010 E.C.R. 12869, at ¶40.

and sold in other member states from being sold in Germany. According to the German government, the law was justified on the basis that it served to protect the German consumer. In the absence of the law, German consumers would not know whether their beer was "pure" or with additives. The ECJ concluded, however, that while this consumer protection argument may be legitimate, the same objective could be achieved by less restrictive means such as requiring the contents of the beer to be on the label.[107]

A similar issue arose in *Rosengren v. Riksåklagaren*.[108] In this case, a group of Swedish residents argued that the Swedish law which prevented Swedish residents from ordering alcohol from sellers outside of Sweden violated Article 34 of the TFEU. Although Swedish law did not prohibit importing alcohol, if Swedish residents wanted to do so, they were required to submit their order to the Systembolaget (state-owned alcohol stores which had a monopoly on the sale of alcohol in Sweden). The law clearly restricted trade between member states. However, Sweden argued that the law was justified because it protected public health by limiting alcohol consumption by young people in Sweden. The ECJ held that although this may be a legitimate reason, the law went beyond what was necessary to achieve this objective. The ECJ held that the law "applies to everyone, irrespective of age. Accordingly, it goes manifestly beyond what is necessary for the objective sought."[109]

(b) *Preemption*

A member state may not rely on Article 36 of the TFEU to justify infringements of Articles 34 or 35 if the particular concern justifying the state measure is preempted by EU harmonizing legislation.[110] Article 115 of the TFEU authorizes the EU to adopt directives designed to harmonize the laws of the member states regarding issues that directly affect the establishment or functioning of the internal market. The EU institutions have relied on this authority to adopt a large number of directives applicable to various sectors of the economy. In adopting these directives, the EU often addresses the concerns expressed in the exceptions codified in Article 36. In such cases, the EU legislation may effectively preempt a member state from justifying its national legislation on public policy concerns as codified in Article 36 because the EU has already comprehensively addressed these concerns in the directive.[111] Consequently, stricter measures imposed by the member state are not necessary.[112] For example, a directive on labeling foodstuffs may address the public health issues related

---

107. Case 178/84, Comm'n v. Germany, 1987 E.C.R. 1262, 1271 ¶36.
108. Case C-170/04, Rosengren v. Riksåklagaren, 2007 E.C.R. I-4107.
109. *Id.* at 4125 ¶51.
110. Case C-132/08, Lidl Magyarország Kereskedelmi bt v. Nemzeti Hírközlési Hatóság Tanácsa, 2009 E.C.R. I-3841, 3863 ¶42; Case 72/83, Campus Oil v. Minister for Industry and Energy, 1984 E.C.R. 2727, 2749 ¶27.
111. Case C-421/12, Comm'n v. Belgium, 2014 E.C.R. I-____, at ¶63; Case C-132/08, Lidl Magyarország Kereskedelmi bt v. Nemzeti Hírközlési Hatóság Tanácsa, 2009 E.C.R. I-3841, 3864 ¶43; Case C-205/07, Gysbrechts v. Santurel Inter BVBA, 2008 E.C.R. I-9947, 9991 ¶33.
112. Case C-421/09, Humanplasma GmbH v. Austria, 2010 E.C.R. 12871, 12886 ¶43.

to the consumption of the particular foods that fall under the directive. Hence, a national law which imposes stricter requirements based on public health concerns would not benefit from the exception codified in Article 36.[113] The rationale in many ways resembles that which serves as the basis of the federal law preemption doctrine in the United States.

There are two basic requirements for the application of the preemption doctrine. First, the EU legislation must apply to the specific conduct at issue. Member states may rely on the exceptions if the conduct regulated by the state measure are external to the field covered by the EU legislation.[114] In *Commission v. Portugal*, for example, Portuguese law prohibited the affixing of tinted film to automobile windows. Although the EU already had adopted legislation governing tinted windows in automobiles, that legislation (Directive 92/22) only applied to windows originally fitted to those vehicles and not to the subsequent affixing of film to the windows. Hence, the EU legislation did not preempt the Portuguese law which regulated the tinted film to be affixed to the windows.[115] Similarly in *Schwarz v. Bürgermeister der Landeshauptstadt Salzburg*, the issue was whether the EC Directive on the Hygiene of Foodstuffs preempted Austria's reliance on Article 36 to justify an Austrian law which prohibited candy from being distributed via vending machines unless the candy was wrapped.[116] Because the Directive did not specifically require that candy dispensed via vending machines be wrapped, the ECJ concluded that the EU legislation did not preempt the application of Article 36 in the case.[117]

Second, the EU legislation must comprehensively regulate the particular conduct.[118] There are basically two types of directives: Those directives that allow the member states to adopt stricter measures than those set forth in the directive (noncomprehensive directives)[119] and those that do not leave the member states any latitude in its transposition into national law (comprehensive directives).[120] If the directive comprehensively regulates the issue, the member states may not rely on Article 36 of the TFEU to justify the measure; they must

---

113. *See* Case C-239/02, Douwe Egberts NV v. Westrom Pharma NV, 2004 E.C.R. I-7007, 7060 ¶56.
114. Case C-132/08, Lidl Magyarország Kereskedelmi bt v. Nemzeti Hírközlési Hatóság Tanácsa, 2009 E.C.R. I-3841, 3864 ¶45.
115. Case C-265/06, Comm'n v. Portugal, 2008 E.C.R. I-2245, 2277 ¶28.
116. Case C-366/04, Schwarz v. Bürgermeister der Landeshauptstadt Salzburg, 2005 E.C.R. I-10139.
117. *Id.* at 10163 ¶26.
118. Case C-132/08, Lidl Magyarország Kereskedelmi bt v. Nemzeti Hírközlési Hatóság Tanácsa, 2009 E.C.R. I-3841, 3864 ¶43; Case C-205/07, Gysbrechts v. Santurel Inter BVBA, 2008 E.C.R. I-9947, 9991 ¶33; Case C-12/00, Comm'n v. Spain, 2003 E.C.R. I-459, 502 ¶65.
119. *See, e.g.*, Case C-205/07, Gysbrechts v. Santurel Inter BVBA, 2008 E.C.R. I-9947, 9991 ¶34.
120. Case C-319/05, Comm'n v. Germany, 2007 E.C.R. I-9841, 9866 ¶83.

rely on the directive.[121] If, however, the directive is not comprehensive, the member states may still claim that the measure is justified under Article 36 of the TFEU. In *A-Punkt Schmuckhandels GesmbH v. Schmidt*, for example, an Austrian law which prohibited door-to-door sales was applied to prohibit a German jewelry shop owner from having a jewelry party in Austria at a private home and selling her jewelry.[122] The Distance Selling Directive specifically allowed the member states to adopt more stringent consumer protection measures than codified in the Distance Selling Directive.[123] Consequently, the application of Article 36 was not preempted by the EU legislation.[124]

(c) Arbitrary Discrimination

Another requirement for the application of Article 36 of the TFEU is that the state measure not "constitute a means of arbitrary discrimination."[125] In other words, a member state cannot use the exceptions provided for in Article 36 to discriminate between foreign and domestic products in an arbitrary manner. For example, a German law which prohibited foreign cars from being sold in Germany would not fall under Article 36 even if it were motivated by concerns that the Black Forest is being decimated by acid rain.

The arbitrary discrimination standard is different from the differential effect standard applied as a requirement to the application of the selling arrangements doctrine. As the ECJ held in *Konsumentombudsmannen v. Gourmet International Products AB*,[126] a mere differential effect (which would be sufficient to preclude the application of the "selling arrangement exception") is insufficient to preclude the application of Article 36 of the TFEU. In this case, a Swedish law prohibiting advertisements for the sale of alcohol except for point of sale advertisements, which was indistinctly applicable to domestic and foreign goods, did not meet the requirements of the selling arrangement doctrine because it had an unequal effect on products from outside of Sweden (i.e., the prohibition on advertising made it more difficult for foreign alcohol to compete because local people were already more familiar with local brands). Despite this differential effect, the ECJ recognized that it did not "constitute a means of arbitrary discrimination" and hence could qualify for an exception under Article 36 of the TFEU.[127]

---

121. A state measure which is adopted in response to a directive does not fall under Article 34 of the TFEU even if it has the effect of restricting the free movement of goods. Case C-88/07, Comm'n v. Spain, 2009 E.C.R. I-1353, 1392 ¶68.
122. Case C-441/04, A-Punkt Schmuckhandels GmbH v. Schmidt, 2006 E.C.R. I-2093.
123. Council Directive 85/577/EEC of 20 December 1985 to protect the consumer in respect of contracts negotiated away from business premises, 1985 O.J. (L 372) 31, art. 8.
124. Case C-441/04, A-Punkt Schmuckhandels GmbH v. Schmidt, 2006 E.C.R. I-2093, 2100 ¶11.
125. Case C-170/04, Rosengren v. Riksåklagaren, 2007 E.C.R. I-4071, 4123 ¶41.
126. Case C-405/98, Konsumentombudsmannen v. Gourmet Int'l. Products AB, 2001 E.C.R. I-1795.
127. The ECJ instructed the national court to determine whether the proportionality requirement was met in this particular case.

A similar situation arose in *Deutscher Apotheker Verbund v. 0800 DocMorris*.[128] At issue was a German law that prohibited Internet sales of prescription and nonprescription drugs. Although the ECJ recognized that "the prohibition does not affect the sale of domestic medicines in the same way as it affects the sale of those coming from other Member States,"[129] it held that the part of the law prohibiting Internet sales of prescription drugs could be justified on public health grounds under Article 36 of the TFEU.[130]

2.6 Categories of Goods Benefiting from Free Movement

Foreign goods do not automatically benefit from the protection that these provisions of primary EU law offer. If, for example, a Hungarian law prohibits U.S. beer from being sold in Hungary, a U.S. beer exporter to Hungary cannot refer to Article 34 of the TFEU to challenge the law. The free movement rights only apply to (1) goods originating in the member states and (2) goods coming from third countries placed into free circulation in the EU (Article 28 TFEU). A good is "in free circulation" in the EU if its importation complied with applicable import formalities, and any customs duties have been paid (Article 29 TFEU). The basic idea is that once the goods have been imported, the foreign goods should be able to move freely throughout the EU. The nationality of the owner of the goods is not determinative of whether the goods benefit from the free movement rules.

For example, a can of Budweiser beer produced in the United States benefits from the free movement of goods principle only after it has been admitted into free circulation in the EU.[131] A state measure restricting its sale in other parts of the EU may violate Article 34 of the TFEU. Using the earlier example of the Hungarian prohibition on U.S. beer, the U.S. beer manufacture may rely on Article 34 to challenge the Hungarian law once the beer is in free circulation in, for example, Austria.

The determination of whether goods are to be deemed as originating in a member state should be made by reference to the secondary law which forms part of the EU's external trade policy. The issue typically arises concerning goods partially produced in the EU or produced in the EU from parts manufactured outside the EU. If a good is produced entirely within a member state from inputs from a member state, it is considered to be originating in a member state.[132] If the production of a good involves more than one country, the good is considered to originate in the country where it underwent its last, "substantial,

---

128. Case C-322/01, Deutscher Apothekerverband v. 0800 Doc Morris, 2003 E.C.R. I-14887.
129. *Id.* at 14987 ¶75.
130. *Id.* at 15001 ¶124.
131. Case C-216/01, Budejovický Budvar, národní podnik v. Rudolf Ammersin GmbH, 2003 E.C.R. I-13617, 13690 ¶95.
132. Regulation (EC) No. 450/2008 of the European Parliament and of the Council of 23 April 2008 laying down the Community Customs Code, 2008 O.J. (L 145) 1 at art. 36(1) [hereinafter Union Customs Code].

economically justified processing or working in an undertaking equipped for that purpose and resulting in the manufacture of a new product or representing an important stage of manufacture."[133]

3. Free Movement of Labor/Workers

One of the other four principles upon which the internal market is based is the free movement of labor and workers. According to Article 45 of the TFEU, the member states must secure the freedom of movement for workers within the EU. The European Council has the authority to adopt regulations and directives to secure this right (Article 46 TFEU). The Council has relied on this right on numerous occasions to adopt secondary legislation which now forms an integral part of the free movement of labor and workers.[134] The application of this freedom is discussed in detail in Chapter VIII.

4. Freedom to Conduct Business

4.1 Legal Bases

Although the phrase "free movement of business" is not generally used in EU parlance, it is used in this Chapter to refer to both the freedom of establishment and the free movement of services. These freedoms often overlap with each other and are designed to achieve the same objective: the right of EU nationals to do business in another member state.[135] If the business is in the form of a fixed business in the other member state, the rules relating to the freedom of

---

133. Id. at art. 36(2).
134. *See, e.g.*, Council Directive 64/221/EC of 25 February 1964 on the coordination of special measures concerning the movement and residence of foreign nationals that are justified on grounds of public policy, public security, or public health, 1964 O.J. (L 56) 850; Council Regulation (EC) No. 1612/68 of 15 October 1968 on freedom of movement for workers within the Community, 1968 O.J. (L 257), 2, as amended by Council Regulation (EC) No. 312/76 of 9 February 1976, 1976 O.J. (L 39) 2; Council Directive 68/360/EC of 15 October 1968 on the abolition of restrictions on movement and residence within the Community for workers of member states and their families, 1968 O.J. (L 257) 13; Commission Regulation (EC) No. 1251/70 of 29 June 1970 on the right of workers to remain in the territory of a member state after having been employed in that state, 1970 O.J. (L 142) 24; Council Directive 72/194/EC of 18 May 1972 extending to workers exercising the right to remain in the territory of a member state after having been employed in that state the scope of Directive 64/221/EC, 1972 O.J. (L 121) 32; Council Directive 77/486/EC of 25 July 1977 on the education of the children of migrant workers, 1977 O.J. (L 199) 32.
135. Although Charter of Fundamental Rights of the European Union, O.J. 2000 (C 364) 1, also protects "the freedom to conduct a business," the European courts interpret this right as being equivalent to the freedom of establishment and the freedom to provide services as codified in the TFEU. Case C-367/12, *In re* Sokoll-Seebacher, 2014 E.C.R. I-____, at ¶22.

establishment are relevant (Article 49 TFEU). According to the ECJ, "the concept of establishment within the meaning of the Treaty provisions on freedom of establishment involves the actual pursuit of an economic activity through a fixed establishment in that State for an indefinite period. Consequently, it presupposes actual establishment of the company concerned in the host Member State and the pursuit of genuine economic activity there."[136]

If, on the other hand, an individual or company merely wants to provide services in another member state without establishing a business there, then the TFEU provisions relating to the freedom to provide services are relevant (Article 56 TFEU). The term "services" is defined as "ordinarily provided for remuneration and that remuneration constitutes consideration for the service in question and is agreed upon between the provider and the recipient of the service."[137] According to the Council and Parliament:

> Where an operator travels to another Member State to exercise a service activity there, a distinction should be made between situations covered by the freedom of establishment and those covered, due to the temporary nature of the activities concerned, by the free movement of services. As regards the distinction between the freedom of establishment and the free movement of services, according to the case law of the Court of Justice the key element is whether or not the operator is established in the Member State where it provides the service concerned. If the operator is established in the Member State where it provides its services, it should come under the scope of application of the freedom of establishment. If, by contrast, the operator is not established in the Member State where the service is provided, its activities should be covered by the free movement of services. The Court of Justice has consistently held that the temporary nature of the activities in question should be determined in the light not only of the duration of the provision of the service, but also of its regularity, periodical nature or continuity. The fact that the activity is temporary should not mean that the provider may not equip itself with some forms of infrastructure in the Member State where the service is provided, such as an office, chambers or consulting rooms, in so far as such infrastructure is necessary for the purposes of providing the service in question.[138]

The distinction between the freedom of establishment and the free movement of services is not always easy to apply. Indeed, the ECJ has expressly

---

136. Case C-196/04, Cadbury Schweppes plc v. Commissioners of Inland Revenue, 2006 E.C.R. I-7995, 8048 ¶54.
137. Case C-169/08, Presidente del Consiglio del Ministri v. Regione Sardegna, 2009 E.C.R. ECLI:EU:C:2009:709 at ¶23.
138. Directive 2006/123/EC of the European Parliament and of the Council of 12 December 2006 on services in the internal market, 2006 O.J. (L 376) 36, 46 recital ¶77.

recognized that both legal norms can apply to the same facts.[139] The ECJ has repeatedly recognized that particular conduct may be classified as services and establishment. In *Commission v. Spain*, for example, the ECJ recognized that a Spanish law requiring that all companies providing private security services in Spain have a minimum share of capital implicates *both* the free movement of services as well as freedom of establishment.[140]

The standard used by the ECJ to distinguish between services and establishment is as follows:[141]

> As regards the delimitation of the scope, respectively, of the principles of freedom to provide services and freedom of establishment, it is necessary to establish whether or not the economic operator is established in the Member State in which it offers the service in question (citations omitted). Where that operator is established in the Member State in which it offers the service, it falls within the scope of the principle of freedom of establishment, as defined in Article [49 TFEU]. On the other hand, where the economic operator is not established in the Member State of destination, it is a cross-border service provider covered by the principle of freedom to provide services laid down in Article [56 TFEU] (citations omitted).

Distinguishing restrictions on the free movement of services and restrictions on the free movement of labor (discussed in Chapter IX) can be equally challenging (particularly when the person is trying to provide services as a self-employed person).[142] For example, a French resident who goes to Finland to seek employment will benefit from the free movement of labor codified in Article 45 of the TFEU and not the free movement of services. However, a French self-employed painter who drives to Finland to paint houses will benefit from the free movement of services codified in Article 56 of the TFEU.

The basic distinction is that services are commonly provided for a foreseeable duration not in a relationship of direct subordination whereas employment is for an indefinite duration and characterized by a relationship of subordination.[143] In *Ritter-Coulais v. Finanzamt Germersheim*, for example, a German law preventing two German teachers who were teaching in France

---

139. Joined Cases C-357/10 to 359/10, Duomo Gpa Srl v. Comune di Baranzate, ECLI:EU:C:2012:283 at ¶38.
140. Case C-470/11, Comm'n v. Spain, 2012 E.C.R. I-___, at ¶29; Case C-514/03, Comm'n v. Spain, 2006 E.C.R. I-963, 1007 ¶22; Case C-314/08, Filipiak v. Dyrektor Izby Skarbowej w Poznaniu, 2009 E.C.R. I-11049, 11070 ¶57.
141. Case C-470/11, Garkalns SIA v. Rigas dome, ECLI:EU:C:2012:505 at ¶26.
142. It is possible that a particular state measure constitutes a restriction on the free movement of services, the freedom of establishment, and the free movement of labor. Case C-150/04, Comm'n v. Denmark, 2007 E.C.R. I-1163, 1210 ¶45.
143. Joined Cases C-151/04 and C-152/04, *In re* Nadin and Durré, 2005 E.C.R. I-11203, 11229 ¶31; Case C-456/02, Michel Trojani v. Centre public d'aide sociale de Bruxelles, 2004 E.C.R. I-7573, 7607 ¶27.

from deducting costs associated with their apartment in Germany was analyzed under Article 45 of the TFEU and not the freedom of establishment rules as the teachers were employees and not self-employed persons.[144]

The TFEU grants the EU the authority to adopt directives regarding the freedom of establishment (Article 50) and free movement of services (Article 59) in a number of different situations. The Council has relied on this authority to give greater clarity to the freedom of establishment and services by secondary legislation.[145]

4.2 Substantive Standard

The abstract definition of "restriction" provided by the ECJ in the context of the free movement of services and the freedom of establishment is "all measures which prohibit, impede or render less attractive the freedom of establishment or the freedom to provide services."[146] As applied by the ECJ, this definition captures two types of restrictions: (1) restrictions that discriminate based on nationality and (2) restrictions that are not discriminatory but have the effect of impeding the establishment of a business or the provision of services.[147] Each of these scenarios is discussed below.

(a) Equal Treatment

The basic principle codified in Articles 49 and 56 of the TFEU is that of nondiscrimination: nationals of other member states must be treated equally as a member state treats its own nationals.[148] In *Commission v. Belgium*, for example, a Belgian law required Belgian employers to secure social insurance

---

144. Case C-152/03, Ritter-Coulais v. Finanzamt Germersheim, 2006 E.C.R. I-1711, 1745 ¶20.
145. The main instruments of secondary EU law related to the free movement of business are: Directive 2006/48/EC of the European Parliament and of the Council of 14 June 2006 relating to the taking up and pursuit of the business of credit institutions (recast), 2006 O.J. (L 177) 1; Directive 2005/36/EC of the European Parliament and of the Council of 7 September 2005 on the recognition of professional qualifications, 2005 O.J. (L 255) 22; Directive 2004/38/EC of the European Parliament and of the Council of 29 April 2004 on the right of citizens of the Union and their family members to move and reside freely within the territory of the member states, 2004 O.J. (L 158) 77; Council Directive 98/5 of the European Parliament and of the Council of 16 February 1998 to facilitate practice of the profession of lawyer on a permanent basis in a member state other than that in which the qualification was obtained, 1998 O.J. (L 77) 36; Directive 77/249 to facilitate the effective exercise by lawyers of freedom to provide services, 1977 O.J. (L 78) 17.
146. Case C-518/06, Comm'n v. Italy, 2009 E.C.R. I-3491, 3555 ¶62.
147. Case C-244/04, Comm'n v. Germany, 2006 E.C.R. I-885, 911 ¶30. There is no de minimis exception, Case C-170/05, Denkavit Int'l. BV v. Ministre de l'Économie, des Finances et de l'Industrie, 2006 E.C.R. I-11949, 11984 ¶50.
148. Case C-371/10, National Grid Indus BV v. Inspecteur van de Belastingdienst Rijnmond, 2011 E.C.R. I-12307, 12318 ¶25; Case C-310/09, Ministre du Budget, des Comptes publics et de la Fonction publique v. Accor SA, 2011 E.C.R. I-8150, 8164 ¶40; Case C-231/05, *In re* Oy AA, 2007 E.C.R. I-6373, 6902 ¶29; Case C-157/05, Holböck v. Finanzamt Salzburg-Land, 2007 E.C.R. I-4051, 4063 ¶27.

for their employees. Employers could deduct these contributions from their income taxes, but only if the insurance company providing the social insurance was located in Belgium. As this law did not treat Belgian insurance companies and non-Belgian insurance companies equally, it was considered by the ECJ as a restriction on the freedom to provide services.[149] In another case, the ECJ overturned a German law imposing a requirement on foreign companies providing services in Germany to establish an office or branch in Germany.[150]

The prohibition extends beyond forms of direct discrimination. It captures state measures which apply equally to domestic and nationals from other member states but which disproportionately affect the nationals from other member states.[151] This is sometimes referred to as indirect discrimination.

(b) Deterring Exercise of Right

The prohibitions codified in these two provisions of the TFEU are not limited to instances of discrimination. The ECJ has repeatedly held that national measures liable to hinder or make less attractive the exercise of fundamental freedoms guaranteed by the EU Treaty are prohibited unless otherwise justified even if those measures apply equally to nationals of that member state and nationals of other member states.[152] In *Commission v. Hellenic Republic*, a Greek law which required that all optician shops be personally managed by a licensed optician, and a licensed optician could only manage one shop, was deemed an infringement of Article 49 of the TFEU even though it did not distinguish between Greek opticians and opticians from other member states.[153] In *Commission v. France*, a French law prohibiting nonbiologists from holding more than 25 percent of a company operating biomedical analysis laboratories was held to be a restriction on the freedom of establishment even though it applied equally to French and non-French investors.[154] According to the ECJ, "by prohibiting a non-biologist from holding more than 25% of the shares, hence of the voting rights, in a SELARL operating biomedical analysis laboratories, the provisions ... restrict the possibility for natural or legal persons who are not biologists and are established in other Member States to hold capital in such a company."[155]

Almost every law, of course, makes doing business in that jurisdiction less attractive for companies. Consequently, pragmatism requires there to be some limitation to this standard. If the domestic law is based on EU legislation or is established to legitimately cover administrative costs, it will not be deemed a restriction on the freedom to do business unless it does not apply

---

149. Case C-522/04, Comm'n v. Belgium, 2007 E.C.R. I-5701.
150. Case C-546/07, Comm'n v. Germany, 2010 E.C.R. I-439 (summary), at ¶39 (full version of case reported in the electronic reports of cases ECLI:EU:C:2010:25).
151. Joined Cases C-570/07 and C-571/07, Pérez v. Consejería de Salud y Servicios Sanitarios, 2010 E.C.R. I-4653, 4690 ¶119.
152. Case C-400/08, Comm'n v. Spain, 2011 E.C.R. I-1952, 1980 ¶70; Case C-287/10, Tankreederei I SA V. Directeur de l'administration des contributions directes, 2011 E.C.R. I-14235, 14241 ¶15.
153. Case C-140/03, Comm'n v. Hellenic Republic, 2005 E.C.R. I-3177, 3202 ¶27.
154. Case C-89/09, Comm'n v. France, 2011 E.C.R. I-12984, 13001 ¶49.
155. *Id.* at 13001 ¶46.

equally to domestic companies and companies from other member states. In *In re innoventif Limited*, the issue was whether a German law which required companies registering a branch office in Germany to pay a fee to cover the administrative costs of publishing the appropriate notices violated Article 49 of the TFEU.[156] In this particular case, an English company wanted to register a branch in Germany and claimed that the German fee violated the TFEU. The ECJ held, however, that EU company law required the member states to publish certain information on companies doing business in their respective jurisdictions, and the law requiring a payment for registration merely reflected the administrative costs of publication. Hence, according to the ECJ, "it cannot constitute a restriction on the freedom of establishment in so far as it neither prohibits, impedes nor renders less attractive the exercise of that freedom."[157]

In other cases, the ECJ simply interprets the notion of "restriction" narrowly. This creates a challenge in deciphering a consistent application of the jurisprudence and suggests that the ECJ is sensitive to political realities of the EU. The issue in *Commission v. Italy*, for example, was whether an Italian law which imposed a cap on the fees of lawyers practicing in Italy violated the free movement of services and the freedom of establishment principles. As discussed above, the ECJ has repeatedly held that national laws which could even potentially make the exercise of the free movement of services or the freedom of establishment less attractive are prohibited.[158]

In this case, one could plausibly make the argument that the existence of a cap on the fees which lawyers can charge makes the provision of legal services by firms from other member states less attractive. The ECJ somewhat confusingly held, however, that the Italian law was not a restriction within the meaning of the free movement rules: "The existence of a restriction within the meaning of the Treaty cannot therefore be inferred from the mere fact that lawyers established in Member States other than the Italian Republic must become accustomed to the rules applicable in that latter Member State for the calculation of their fees for services provided in Italy."[159]

(c) Prohibited Restrictions

There is no exhaustive catalog of prohibited restrictions on the freedom of establishment or the free movement of services. Moreover, there is no de minimis threshold.[160] A nonexhaustive list of examples of state measures which the European Commission considers to violate the freedom of establishment or freedom to provide services can be found in the Services Directive.[161]

---

156. Case C-453/04, *In re* innoventif Limited, 2006 E.C.R. I-4931.
157. *Id.* at 4942 ¶38.
158. Case C-400/08, Comm'n v. Spain, 2011 E.C.R. I-1952, 1980 ¶70; Case C-287/10, Tankreederei I SA V. Directeur de l'administration des contributions directes, 2011 E.C.R. I-14235, 14241 ¶15.
159. Case C-565/08, Comm'n v. Italy, 2011 E.C.R. I-2115, 2129 ¶50.
160. Case C-233/09, Dijkman v. Belgische Staat, 2010 E.C.R. I-6652, 6665 ¶42.
161. Directive 2006/123/EC of the European Parliament and of the Council of 12 December 2006 on services in the internal market, 2006 O.J. (L 276) 36, art. 14 (establishment) and art. 16(2) (services).

4.3 Sphere of Application

(a) Right of Establishment

(1) EU Nationality

Article 49 of the TFEU prohibits restrictions on the freedom of establishment of nationals of a member state in the territory of another member state. Hence, the scope of the protection only applies to nationals of a member state. For example, a U.S. company would not be able to rely on this provision of the TFEU to establish a business in the EU;[162] its EU affiliates would, however, be able to rely on the right of establishment to challenge national legislation.[163] The requirements for a legal person to have EU nationality are set forth in Article 48 of the TFEU.

The legal entity (1) must be formed in accordance with the laws of a member state, and (2) have its registered office, central administration, or principal place of business within the EU. The right of a foreign company to set up an office in a member state is a matter of national law. In other words, if a U.S. company, for example, wants to take advantage of the freedom of establishment, it would first need to form a subsidiary in a member state pursuant to the law of that member state. The other member states would then have to recognize that subsidiary as having EU nationality even if ultimately controlled by a U.S. company.[164]

The exercise of these freedoms might incidentally benefit non-EU nationals. For example, the right to transfer a business from one member state to another and to bring along the employees of the business may also extend to employees who are not nationals of a member state. If a company decides to transfer its business from Germany to Poland, it has the right under Article 56 of the TFEU to relocate its employees from Germany to Poland.[165] This even applies to employees who are not nationals of a member state provided that they were employees prior to the transfer of the business to the other member state.[166]

(2) Establishment

The right protected under Article 49 of the TFEU is the actual pursuit of an economic activity through a fixed establishment in another member state for an indefinite period.[167] The reference to "fixed establishment" in the context of

---

162. *See* Case C-157/05, Holböck v. Finanzamt Salzburg-Land, 2007 E.C.R. I-4051, 4064 ¶28; Case C-524/04, Test Claimants in the Thin Cap Group Litigation v. Commissioners of Inland Revenue, 2007 E.C.R. I-2107, 2198 ¶98.
163. C-80/12, Felixstowe Dock and Railway Co. Ltd. v. The Commissioners for Her Majesty's Revenue & Customs, 2014 E.C.R. I-____, at ¶40.
164. Case C-524/04, 2007 E.C.R. I-2107, 2197 ¶95.
165. Case C-113/89, Rush Portuguesa v. Office National d'Immigration, 1990 E.C.R. I-1417, 1443 ¶12.
166. Case C-43/94, Vander Elst v. Office de Migrations Internationales, 1994 E.C.R. I-3803, 3827 ¶26.
167. Case C-196/04, Cadbury Schweppes plc v. Commissioners of Inland Revenue, 2006 E.C.R. I-7995, 8048 ¶54; Case C-221/89, The Queen v. Secretary of State for Transport, 1991 E.C.R. I-3905, 3965 ¶20.

defining the right should not be interpreted to require the creation of a separate legal entity. It is clear that the prohibition applies not only to restrictions on the formation of subsidiaries by nationals of any member state established in the territory of any member state, but also to agencies, branches, and offices.[168] According to the ECJ, "the maintenance of a permanent presence in a Member State by an undertaking established in another Member State may fall within the provisions of the Treaty on the freedom of establishment even if that presence does not take the form of a branch or agency, but consists merely of an office managed by a person who is independent but authorised to act on a permanent basis for that undertaking."[169] Moreover, the concept of fixed establishment does not require a factory or a minimum level of assets. According to Article 49(2) of the TFEU, the freedom of establishment even includes "the right to take up and pursue activities as self-employed persons and to set up and manage undertakings." For example, the ECJ has indicated that the freedom of establishment applies to self-employed persons such as prostitutes.[170] It does, however, require a physical presence. The ECJ has held, for example, that doing business via the Internet in another member state does not constitute the exercise of the freedom of establishment.[171]

The prohibition of restrictions on the freedom of establishment applies not only to restrictions placed by a member state on foreign nationals doing business in their country. It also prohibits member states from restricting their own nationals from exercising the freedom of establishment in other member states.[172]

(b) *Right to Provide Services*

(1) *EU Nationality*

As a corollary to the prohibition of restrictions on the freedom of establishment, Article 56(1) of the TFEU prohibits restrictions on the freedom of EU nationals established in a member state to provide services to other legal or natural persons in other member states. Similar to the right of establishment, the right to provide services protected by this provision of the TFEU extends only to nationals of member states. For example, a company established in Switzerland cannot rely on the right to provide services to customers in Germany.[173]

---

168. Case C-284/06, Finanzamt Hamburg-Am Tierpark v. Burda GmbH, 2008 E.C.R. I-4571, 4629 ¶76; Case C-414/06, Lidl Belgium GmbH & Co. KG v. Finanzamt Heilbronn, 2008 E.C.R. I-3601, 3625 ¶18.
169. Case C-409/06, Winner Wetten GmbH v. Bürgermeisterin des Stadt Berghcim, 2010 E.C.R. I-8041, 8059 ¶46.
170. Case C-268/99, Aldona Malgorzata Jany v. Staatssecretaris, 2001 E.C.R. I-8615.
171. Case C-42/07, Liga Portuguesa de Futebol Professional v. Departamento de Jogos da Santa Casa da Misericórdia de Lisboa, 2009 E.C.R. I-7633, 7713 ¶46.
172. Case C-247/08, Gaz de France v. Bundeszentralamt für Steuern, 2009 E.C.R. I-9225, 9260 ¶55; Case C-414/06, Lidl Belgium GmbH & Co. KG v. Finanzamt Heilbronn, 2008 E.C.R. I-3617, 3625 ¶18.
173. Case C-452/04, Fidium Finanz AG v. Bundesanstalt für Finanzdienstleistungsaufsicht, 2006 E.C.R. I-9521, 9574 ¶25.

The right to provide services, however, adds an additional requirement not required by Article 49 of the TFEU: the provider of the service must be established in a different member state than the recipient.[174] As discussed above, the term establishment generally refers to the actual pursuit of an economic activity through a fixed establishment in another member state for an indefinite period. Therefore, a law which restricts only a domestic service provider in providing services within that member state would fall outside the prohibition.

(2) Services

The free movement of services extends only to the provision of services that "are normally provided for remuneration" (Article 50). The remuneration requirement means that volunteer activities or work done for free do not fall under the free movement of services protection codified in Article 56 of the TFEU.[175] Moreover, the notion of providing services implies a temporary character.[176] This distinguishes the freedom to provide services from the freedom of establishment which implies a permanent or at least indefinite character.

Article 56 of the TFEU includes the right to provide services in another member state (sometimes called active freedom to provide services) and the right of recipients of services to go to another member state in order to receive a service there (sometimes called passive freedom to provide services).[177] The right of a patent lawyer to provide legal counseling in another member state is an example of the exercise of the active freedom to provide services.[178] The right of a Swedish national to receive Internet gambling services from a service provider outside of Sweden is an example of the passive freedom to receive services arising from Article 56.[179]

4.4 State Measures

Articles 49 and 56 of the TFEU do not specify whether they apply to all restrictions on the freedom of establishment and the freedom to provide services or just state measures that produce such effects. As the free movement rules are directed at the member states, the implication arising from the structure of the TFEU is that application Articles 49 and 56 require a state measure. In *GlaxoSmithKline Services Unlimited v. Commission*, the General Court specifically refused to apply Article 49 of the TFEU to private conduct because

---

174. Joined Cases C-357/10 to 359/10, Duomo Gpa Srl v. Comune di Baranzate, 2012 E.C.R. I-___, at ¶30.
175. Case C-281/06, Jundt v. Finanzamt Offenburg, 2007 E.C.R. I-12,231, 12,256 ¶32.
176. Case C-55/94, Gebhard v. Consiglio dell'Ordine degli Avvocati e Procuratori di Milano, 1995 E.C.R. I-4165, 4198 ¶39.
177. Case C-444/05, Aikaterini Stamatelaki v. NPDD Organismos Asfaliseos Eleftheron Epangelmation, 2007 E.C.R. I-3185, 3218 ¶20; Case C-262/02, Comm'n v. France, 2004 E.C.R. I-6569, 6605 ¶22.
178. Case C-478/01, Comm'n v. Luxembourg, 2003 E.C.R. I-2351.
179. Joined Cases C-447/08 and 448/08, *In re* Sjöberg and Gerdin, 2010 E.C.R. I-6942, 6955 ¶34.

the conduct did not constitute a state measure.[180] Hence, although the ECJ has not specifically articulated the requirement of a state measure, the prohibition on restrictions of the freedom of establishment or the right to provide services will generally require a state measure.[181]

The EU courts have nonetheless been willing to apply a pragmatic approach to this requirement. Although they are not state measures, the ECJ has repeatedly applied Articles 49 and 56 to the internal rules of private associations and trade unions which had the effect of restricting the freedom of establishment or the free movement of services.[182] The rationale applied by the ECJ is that a strict limitation of the application of Articles 49 and 56 to state measures would create a loophole; private associations could effectively achieve the same result which Articles 49 and 56 are trying to prevent.[183] Consequently, Articles 49 and 56 apply not only to state measures but also to associations which regulate certain professions or commercial activities.

4.5 Cross-Border Element

The right of establishment and the right to provide services both require a cross-border effect.[184] Article 49 of the TFEU (right of establishment) only applies to restrictions imposed on nationals of a member state "in the territory of *another* Member State" [emphasis added]. Article 56 of the TFEU (freedom to provide services) only applies to services provided by nationals established in one member state to persons in another member state "other than that of the person for whom the services are intended." Hence, the service provider and the service recipient must be established in different member states. For example, the prohibition on restrictions of the freedom of establishment does not apply

---

180. Case T-168/01, GlaxoSmithKline Services Unlimited v. Comm'n, 2006 E.C.R. II-2969, 3039 ¶206.
181. *See* Case C-318/10, Société d'investissement pour l'agriculture tropicale SA v. Belgium, 2012 E.C.R. I-___, at ¶18 ("Restrictions on the freedom to provide services are national measures which prohibit, impede or render less attractive the exercise of that freedom."); Case C-498/10, X NV v. Staatssecretaris van Financiën, 2012 E.C.R. I-___, at ¶22 ("Restrictions on the freedom to provide services are national measures which prohibit, impede or render less attractive the exercise of that freedom.").
182. C-356/08, Comm'n v. Austria, 2009 E.C.R. I-108 (summary), at ¶37 (rules of a physicians' association) (full version of case reported in the electronic reports of cases ECLI:EU:C:2009:401); Case C-438/05, Int'l. Transport Workers' Federation v. Viking Line ABP, 2007 E.C.R. I-10,779, 10,830 ¶58 (rules of a labor union); Case 36/74, Walrave and Koch v. Association Union Cycliste Internationale, 1974 E.C.R. 1405, 1418 ¶17 (internal rules of bicycling association); Case C-51/96 and 191/87, Christelle Deliége v. Ligue Francophone de dudo et Disciplines Associées, 2000 E.C.R. I-2549, 2614 ¶47 (internal rules of private judo association).
183. C-356/08, Comm'n v. Austria, 2009 E.C.R. I-108 (summary), at ¶37 (full version of case reported in the electronic reports of cases ECLI:EU:C:2009:401).
184. Joined Cases C-357/10 to 359/10, Duomo Gpa Srl v. Comune di Baranzate, 2012 E.C.R. I-___, at ¶26; Case 17/94, *In re* Gervais, 1995 E.C.R. I-4353, 4377 ¶24.

to a Finnish law prohibiting a Finnish pharmacy from relocating its operations from one town in Finland to another town in Finland.[185]

Although the prohibitions are not applicable to activities which are confined in all respects within a member state,[186] this rule should be interpreted narrowly. If the activity has an effect on trade between member states, it is likely to fall under Article 49 even though the activity itself is confined to one member state. In *In re Donatella Calfa*, for example, the activity—the provision of tourist services—occurred in one member state, and yet the measure adopted by that member state was deemed to violate Article 49 of the TFEU.[187]

In *Alpine Investments v. Minister Van Financien*, the application of a national rule to nationals of that same member state was deemed to have a sufficient cross-border element.[188] The restriction in that case (a prohibition under Dutch law on contacting individuals by telephone without their prior consent) was not on foreign service providers but on service providers within the Netherlands and the law hindered them in providing services outside the Netherlands. The provision of those services in the other states was not prohibited by the member states where the recipient of the services was located. Nonetheless, the ECJ held that Article 56 applies to restrictions imposed by the state of origin as well as the state of destination.[189]

The increased reliance on the Internet as a means of doing business has expanded the scope of the freedoms even further. For example, a service provider established in one member state exercises its freedom to do business in another member state merely by offering its services to customers in other member states without ever even going to those states. In fact, the service provider does not even have to offer services in the member state where it is established as long as it is established in one member state and offers services to customers in other member states.[190]

The prohibitions are not limited to restrictions imposed on nationals of other member states. Even a national measure which restricts nationals of that state from setting up an establishment or securing services in another member state is prohibited.[191] In *Hughes de Lasteyrie du Saillant v. Ministère de l'Économie*, for example, a French national claimed that a French law violated his right to establish a business in another member state and was therefore

---

185. Case C-84/11, *In re* Susisalo, ECLI:EU:C:2012:374 at ¶19.
186. Joined cases C-162/12 and 163/12, Airport Shuttle Express scarl v. Comune di Grottaferrata, 2014 E.C.R. I-____, at ¶42; Case C-245/09, Omalet NV V. Rijksdienst voor Sociale Zekerheid, 2011 E.C.R. I-13773, 13780 ¶15.
187. Case C-348/96, *In re* Calfa, 1999 E.C.R. I-11.
188. Case C-384/93, Alpine Investments v. Minister Van Financien, 1995 E.C.R. I-1141.
189. In that same case, the ECJ concluded that although it restricts the freedom to provide services, the restriction may be justified on grounds of public policy. *Id.* at ¶44.
190. C-46/08, Carmen Media Group Ldt. v. Land Schleswig-Holstein, 2010 E.C.R. I-8175, 8197 ¶43.
191. Case C-418/07, Société Papillon v. Ministère du Budget, des Comptes publics et de la Fonction publique, 2008 E.C.R. I-8947, 8972 ¶16.

contrary to Article 49 of the TFEU.[192] According to the French law at issue, if a French resident wanted to move his or her residence to another member state, that resident would have to pay capital gains taxes on investments which he or she had regardless of whether the person sold those investments and realized the gain at the time of the change of residence. The ECJ held: "Even if, like the other provisions concerning freedom of establishment, Article [49] of the Treaty is, according to its terms, aimed particularly at ensuring that foreign nationals are treated in the host Member State in the same way as nationals of that State, it also prohibits the Member State of origin from hindering the establishment in another Member State of one of its own nationals."[193] The ECJ went on to conclude that the French law violates Article 49 of the TFEU as it discourages French persons from exercising their right of establishment.[194]

4.6 Exceptions

As discussed above, the free movement of business rules codified in the TFEU not only prohibit overt restrictions, but also measures of a member state that hinder or make the establishment of a business or the provision of a service across member state borders less attractive. According to the ECJ, the exceptions codified in the TFEU theoretically apply to both categories of restrictions (discriminatory and equally applicable restrictions).[195] In most cases, however, the discriminatory restriction will not meet the requirements of the relevant exception.[196]

(a) *Public Policy, Security, and Health*

According to Article 52 of the TFEU, a state measure which restricts the freedom of establishment may be justified on grounds of public policy, public security, and public health. This same exception is extended to the freedom to provide services by Article 62 of the TFEU. For example, although the French law prohibiting nonbiologists from holding more than 25 percent of a company operating biomedical analysis laboratories discussed above in *Commission v. France* was held to be a restriction within the meaning of Article 56 of the TFEU, the ECJ concluded that it was justified on grounds of public health.[197] In *Colegio de Ingenieros de Caminos v. Administracion del Estado*, a Spanish law requiring certain minimum qualifications for licensed civil engineers which had the effect of precluding a licensed Italian civil engineer from providing civil engineering services in Spain was justified because it protected the recipients of those services.[198] In *Hartlauer Handelsgesellschaft mbH v. Wiener*

---

192. Case C-9/02, Hughes de Lasteyrie du Saillant v. Ministère de l'Économie, 2004 E.C.R. I-2409.
193. *Id.* at 2452 ¶42.
194. *Id.* at 2452 ¶46.
195. Case C-153/08, Comm'n v. Spain, 2009 E.C.R. I-9735, 9776 ¶37.
196. *See, e.g.*, Case C-153/08, Comm'n v. Spain, 2009 E.C.R. I-9735, 9778 ¶47.
197. Case C-89/09, Comm'n v. France, 2011 E.C.R. I-12984, 13014 ¶89.
198. Case C-330/03, Colegio de Ingenieros de Caminos v. Administracion del Estado, 2006 E.C.R. I-826, 843 ¶39.

Landesregierung, an Austrian law requiring persons from other member states who wanted to establish a medical clinic in Austria to secure prior authorization from the Austrian government was considered to protect public health even though it otherwise violated the prohibition of restrictions on the freedom of establishment.[199]

(b) Exercise of Official Authority

As discussed in greater detail in Chapter IX, Article 45(4) of the TFEU allows member states to restrict workers from other member states from holding certain positions in the public service. The basic idea is that certain portions require a greater level of trust and loyalty to the state, and citizens are more likely to observe that loyalty than non-citizens. The same rationale is embodied in Article 45 of the TFEU which provides an exception to the prohibition on restrictions on the free movement of business if the restriction concerns activities connected with the exercise of official authority.

Neither the ECJ nor the European Commission has provided a definition of "official authority" or a list of activities that may be considered "official authority."[200] The fact that a profession is regulated by the state does not necessarily mean that it is the exercise of official authority.[201] The classification implies the ability to compel certain behavior on behalf of the state or acceptance of fiduciary responsibilities vis-à-vis the state. A judge, police officer, or military officer would be exercising official authority because they can compel behavior on behalf of the state. Civil law notaries, however, are not exercising official authority.[202]

In *Reyners v. Belgium*, the ECJ similarly held that the profession of an attorney is not the exercise of official authority.[203] At issue in that case was a Belgian law that required persons entering the Belgian bar to be Belgian nationals. Although the plaintiff, a Dutch national, had fulfilled all the educational requirements, he was denied membership in the Belgian bar. The ECJ held that Belgium could not justify this restriction on the basis that attorneys exercise official authority of the state. In *Commission v. Kingdom of Spain*, Spain unsuccessfully argued that a law requiring all employees who perform private security services to be Spanish was justified because it involved the exercise of official authority and

---

199. Case C-169/07, Hartlauer Handelsgesellschaft mbH v. Wiener Landesregierung, 2009 E.C.R. I-1721, 1767 ¶48.
200. Case C-54/08, Comm'n v. Germany, 2011 E.C.R. I-4360, 4383 ¶85 (The exercise of official authority exception "must be restricted to activities which in themselves are directly and specifically connected with the exercise of official authority."
201. Case C-53/08, Comm'n v. Austria, 2011 E.C.R. I-4314, 4339 ¶95.
202. Case C-51/08, Comm'n v. Luxembourg, 2011 E.C.R. I-4235, 4268 ¶126.
203. Case 2/74, Reyners v. Belgium, 1974 E.C.R. 631. *See also* Case C-309/99, *J. C. J. Wouters, J. W. Savelbergh and Price Waterhouse Belastingadviseurs BV v. Algemene Raad van de Nederlandse Orde van Advocaten*, 2002 E.C.R. I-1577, 1677 ¶50, in which the ECJ held that Dutch attorneys are "undertakings" when they exercise their profession for compensation and therefore subject to the competition laws applicable to private undertakings.

the nationality requirement is necessary to allow the government to oversee the activities of the security companies.[204]

The source of remuneration is not the decisive criterion. Not all services directly or indirectly paid by the state would constitute the exercise of official authority. In *Jundt v. Finanzamt Offenburg*, for example, a lawyer who taught a course at a state university (University of Strasbourg) was held not to be exercising official authority even though his remuneration for the teaching services came from the state.[205]

(c) Judicially Created Exceptions

As discussed above, the ECJ introduced an "overriding requirements" exception to the prohibition on the free movement of goods, which appears redundant to the exceptions codified in Article 30 of the TFEU. Similarly, the ECJ has repeatedly held that restrictions on the free movement of services and the freedom of establishment may be justified on the basis of overriding requirements of public interest[206] in addition to the exceptions codified in the TFEU.[207] The concept of overriding requirements is not defined in the TFEU.[208] Its malleable character essentially allows the EU courts discretion in accepting certain restrictions imposed by the member states on the freedom to do business. As in the context of the free movement of goods, the introduction of the concept of overriding requirements was probably unnecessary in light of the public policy exception codified in Article 52 of the TFEU.

Similar to the application of the overriding requirements exception in the context of the free movement of goods, the ECJ has indicated that the exception only applies if the restriction at issue applies without distinction to all persons and undertakings operating in the member state concerned.[209] A law that is discriminatory cannot be justified on the basis of overriding requirements.[210]

---

204. Case C-114/97, Comm'n v. Spain, 1998 E.C.R. I-6717. Spain subsequently amended the law by removing the nationality requirement but requiring that the company be constituted as a legal entity, to have a minimum share capital, pay a security to a Spanish agency, and employ a minimum number of workers. The ECJ subsequently held that these requirements also restricted the free movement of services in contravention of Article 56 of the TFEU. Case C-514/03, Comm'n v. Spain, 2006 E.C.R. I-963.
205. Case C-281/06, Jundt v. Finanzamt Offenburg, 2007 E.C.R. I-12246, 12256 ¶38.
206. Case C-400/08, Comm'n v. Spain, 2011 E.C.R. I-1952, 1980 ¶73 (freedom of establishment); Case C-42/07, Liga Portuguesa de Futebol Profissional v. Departamento de Jogos da Santa Casa da Misericórdia de Lisboa, 2009 E.C.R. I-7633, 7716 ¶56 (free movement of services).
207. It is clear from the case law of the ECJ that the overriding requirements are in addition to the exception codified in the TFEU. Case C-384/08, Attanasio Srl v. Comune di Carbognano, 2010 E.C.R. I-2059, 2074 ¶50; Case C-567/07, Minister voor Wonen v. Woningstichting Sint Servatius, 2009 E.C.R. I-9021, 9036 ¶25.
208. Case C-42/07, Liga Portuguesa de Futebol Profissional v. Departamento de Jogos da Santa Casa da Misericórdia de Lisboa, 2009 E.C.R. I-7633 ¶46.
209. Case C-470/11, SIA Garkalns v Rīgas dome, 2012 E.C.R. I-___, at ¶37; Case C-400/08, Comm'n v. Spain, 2011 E.C.R. I-1952, 1980 ¶73; Case C-219/08, Comm'n v. Belgium, 2009 E.C.R. I-9213, 9221 ¶14.
210. Case C-153/08, Comm'n v. Spain, 2009 E.C.R. I-9735, 9775 ¶36.

This distinguishes the overriding requirements justification from the exceptions codified in the TFEU. According to the ECJ, even a discriminatory restriction can be justified if it falls under one of the exceptions in the TFEU.[211]

The overriding requirements exception could be viewed as a judicial creation to catch those situations that do not fall squarely under the public policy, health, and security exception codified in Article 52 of the TFEU. For example, the regulation of the legal profession to prohibit conflicts of interest may not neatly be characterized as public policy, security, or health within the meaning of Article 52. However, the ECJ has held that it may justify certain restrictions on the freedom to do business as, for example, a prohibition on lawyers sharing fees with accountants.[212] The overriding requirements exception, as well as the codified exceptions to the free movement of services and establishment, are relative. According to the ECJ, "the specific circumstances which may justify recourse to the concept of public policy may vary from one country to another and from one era to another."[213] This attribute of the rule makes an exhaustive assessment of its application difficult, if not impossible.

There is no exhaustive catalog of overriding requirements sufficient to legitimatize a restriction on the freedom to do business. In *Commission v. Germany*, the protection of workers was recognized as an overriding reason of public interest capable of justifying a restriction on the freedom to provide services.[214] At issue in that case was a German law requiring foreign construction companies operating in Germany to translate into German the employment contract, pay slips, time sheets, and proof of payment of wages for the employees working in Germany. The German government argued that the requirement was necessary to ensure effective protection for employees. However, the law had the effect of making it more difficult to employ foreign workers at constructions sites in Germany. Up to that point, German construction workers were finding it difficult to compete with migrant workers from other member states and even outside the EU. According to the ECJ:

> "By requiring the relevant documents in the language of the host Member State to be kept on the building site, [the German law] is designed to enable the competent authorities of that Member State to carry out the monitoring, at the building site, necessary to ensure compliance with the national provisions regarding worker protection, in particular those relating to pay and working hours. This type of on-site supervision would become extremely difficult, even impossible, in practice, if those documents could be presented in the language of the

---

211. *Id.* at 9776 ¶37.
212. Case C-309/99, J. C. J. Wouters, J. W. Savelbergh and Price Waterhouse Belastingadviseurs BV v. Algemene Raad van de Nederlandse Orde van Advocaten, 2002 E.C.R. I-1577, 1695 ¶122.
213. Case C-36/02, Omega Spielhallen- und Automatenaufstellungs-GmbH v. Oberbürgermeister der Bundesstadt Bonn, 2004 E.C.R. I-9609, 9652 ¶31.
214. Case C-490/04, Comm'n v. Germany, 2007 E.C.R. I-6095, 6146 ¶70.

Member State in which the undertaking is established, as that language would not necessarily be understood by the civil servants of the host Member State. It follows that the obligation laid down in [German law] is justified."[215]

Additional examples of legitimate overriding requirements are consumer protection, preserving the financial equilibrium of the social security system, protection of workers, prevention of fraud, environmental protection, intellectual property, prevention of gambling addiction, the conservation of the national historic and artistic heritage, social policy and cultural policy objectives, and ensuring the proper administration of justice.[216]

Administrative efficiency or the protection of purely economic interests will not qualify as overriding requirements sufficient to justify a restriction on the freedom to do business.[217] In *Commission v. Austria*, Austria tried to justify a rule that required doctors practicing in Austria to have a bank account with a specific bank in Austria on the basis that it was easier to administer the state-funded insurance if all the accounts were at one bank. The ECJ refused to recognize this as an overriding requirement with the reasoning that considerations of administrative nature cannot justify a restriction on the free movement of services.[218]

In *Commission v. Germany*, the ECJ held that a German law requiring foreign companies to have an office or branch in Germany in order to provide services in German areas with high unemployment was an impermissible restriction on the freedom to provide services.[219] According to the ECJ, the economic justifications advanced by Germany were irrelevant for justifying the restriction. *Hughes de Lasteyrie du Saillant v. Ministère de l'Économie* involved a French law which required French residents to pay capital gains taxes on certain investments if they wanted to change their residence to another country, regardless of whether the person sold those investments and realized the gain at the time of the change of residence.[220] One of the arguments raised in defense of the French law was that it was necessary on public interest grounds because it prevented an erosion of the French tax base by deterring French residents from moving to other member states with lower taxes. The ECJ held, however, that the diminution of tax receipts "cannot be regarded as a matter of overriding

---

215. *Id.* at 6146 ¶¶71-72.
216. *See* art. 4(8) Directive 2006/123/EC of the European Parliament and of the Council of 12 December 2006 on services in the internal market, 2006 O.J. (L 376) 36.
217. Joined cases C-72/10 and C-77/10, *In re* Costa and Cifone, 2012 E.C.R. I-___, at ¶59; Case C-400/08, Comm'n v. Spain, 2011 E.C.R. I-1952, 1981 ¶74; Case C-384/08, Attanasio Srl v. Comune di Carbognano, 2010 E.C.R. I-2059, 2076 ¶55.
218. C-356/08, Comm'n v. Austria, 2009 E.C.R. I-108 (summary), at ¶46 (full version of case reported in the electronic reports of cases ECLI:EU:C:2009:401).
219. Case C-546/07, Comm'n v. Germany, 2010 E.C.R. I-439 (summary), at ¶48 (full version of case reported in the electronic reports of cases ECLI:EU:C:2010:25).
220. Case C-9/02, Huges de Lasteyrie du Saillant v. Ministere de l'Economie, 2004 E.C.R. I-2409.

general interest which may be relied upon in order to justify a measure which is in principle contrary to a fundamental freedom."[221]

Further complicating matters is the apparent overlap with the exceptions codified in Article 52 of the TFEU. As discussed above, Article 52 expressly permits the member states to impose restrictions on the freedom of establishment in order to protect the public interest. The ECJ continues to consider the overriding requirements exception to be (at least conceptually) in addition to the exceptions codified in the TFEU.[222] However, the ECJ has recognized a certain degree of overlap between the two. In *Hartlauer Handelsgesellschaft mbH v. Wiener Landesregierung*, for example, the issue was whether an Austrian law requiring persons from other member states to secure prior approval in order to set up a medical clinic in Austria was justified by Article 52 (public health) or by overriding reasons in the general interest. In recognizing the legitimate objective of the law, the ECJ stated "the protection of public health is one of the overriding reasons in the general interest which can, under Article 52(1) [of the TFEU], justify restrictions of freedom of establishment."[223]

(d) Preconditions for the Exceptions

The application of the codified and judicially created exemptions must also conform to the proportionality requirement.[224] As discussed above, this principle requires that the restriction be suitable for securing the attainment of the objective which it pursues and must not go beyond what is necessary in order to attain that objective.[225] In *In re Sevic Systems*, the ECJ held that a German corporate law prohibiting all mergers of non-German companies into German companies was not proportionate because, even though it may have had some legitimate objectives, it was not narrowly tailored to achieve these objectives and prohibited mergers that did not threaten the interests of Germany.[226] In *Presidente del Consiglio dei Ministri v. Regione Sardegna*, the region of Sardinia attempted to justify a regional law imposing a tax on aircraft stopovers where the aircraft was registered outside the region by arguing that the tax was to compensate for the pollution caused by such aircraft. According to the ECJ, the law did

---

221. *Id.* at 2456 ¶60.
222. Case C-567/07, Minister voor Wonen v. Woningstichting Sint Servatius, 2009 E.C.R. I-9021, 9036 ¶25.
223. Case C-169/07, Hartlauer Handelsgesellschaft mbH v. Wiener Landesregierung, 2009 E.C.R. I-1721, 1767 ¶46.
224. Case C-42/07, Liga Portuguesa de Futebol Profissional v. Departamento de Jogos da Santa Casa da Misericórdia de Lisboa, 2009 E.C.R. I-7698, 7716 ¶58; Case C-169/07, Hartlauer Handelsgesellschaft mbH v. Wiener Landesregierung, 2009 E.C.R. I-1721, at ¶50.
225. Case C-294/00, Deutsche Paracelsusschulen für Naturheilverfahren GmbH v. Kurt Gräbner, 2002 E.C.R. I-6515, 6553 ¶39; Case C-100/01, Ministre de l'Interieur v. Aitor Oteiza Olazabal, 2002 E.C.R. I-10981, 11015 ¶43.
226. Case C-411/03, *In re* Sevic Systems AG, 2005 E.C.R. I-10805.

not meet the proportionality test because the pollution was caused equally by aircraft registered in the region (which did not have to pay the tax).[227]

If there are other means to achieve the same objective, and those means impose less of a burden on the free movement of services or the freedom of establishment, the measure will not qualify for an exception. In *Commission v. Hellenic Republic*, the ECJ concluded that a Greek law which required that all optician shops be personally managed by a licensed optician, and a licensed optician may only manage one shop, was not justified on overriding requirements of public interest. The ECJ noted that "the objective of protecting public health upon which the Hellenic Republic relies may be achieved by measures which are less restrictive of the freedom of establishment both for natural and legal persons, for example by requiring the presence of qualified, salaried opticians or associates in each optician's shop, rules concerning civil liability for the actions of others, and rules requiring professional indemnity insurance."[228]

Prior administrative authorization schemes (e.g., a law requiring construction companies from other member states to secure a license prior to providing construction services) can only be justified if they are based on objective, nondiscriminatory criteria known in advance in such a way that they adequately circumscribe the discretion of the authorities when applying such criteria.[229] As a general rule, state measures which require prior authorization will not be deemed proportionate because the authorities have too much discretion in granting the authorization[230] or there are typically other less restrictive means of securing the same objective.[231] If, for example, a member state requires businesses from other member states to secure prior approval of the local authorities before opening a business in that member state, the law is unlikely to be proportionate because a system of notification (which does not leave it to the discretion of the local authorities whether to grant the approval) would be less restrictive.

The ECJ has also stated that the application of the public interest exception for restrictions on the right of establishment or the freedom to provide services requires "that the public interest is not already protected by the rules of the state of establishment."[232] For example, a member state may not maintain a law that requires patent attorneys to have a residence or place of business in that member state if the legitimate public interest objective of such legislation is already protected by requirements imposed on the patent attorney in that attorney's home member state.[233] Whether this is a requirement to be applied in every case is uncertain.

---

227. Case C-169/08, Presidente del Consiglio dei Ministri v. Regione Sardegna, ECLI:EU:C:2009:709 at ¶44.
228. C-140/03, Comm'n v. Hellenic Republic, 2005 E.C.R. I-3193, 3205 ¶35.
229. C-458/08, Comm'n v. Portugal, 2010 E.C.R. I-11601, 11642 ¶107.
230. *Id.*
231. Case C-219/08, Comm'n v. Belgium, 2009 E.C.R. I-9213, 9223 ¶21. *But see* Case C-400/08, Comm'n v. Spain, 2011 E.C.R. I-1952, 1985 ¶92.
232. Case C-131/01, Comm'n v. Italy, 2003 E.C.R. I-1659, 1689 ¶43 (establishment); Case C-355/98, Comm'n v. Belgium, 2000 E.C.R. I-1221, 1248 ¶37.
233. Case C-131/01, Comm'n v. Italy, 2003 E.C.R. I-1659.

In *Deutsche Paracelsus Schulen für Naturheilverfahren GmbH v. Gräbner*, the ECJ held that Austria's prohibition on the practice of natural medicine was justified on the basis of public health, even though that profession was allowed in Germany.[234] The ECJ did not accept the argument of the plaintiffs that the prohibition was not proportional because Austria could have achieved the protection of public health through less restrictive means (i.e., the introduction of a formal examination for such practitioners).

Finally, a member state may not rely on any of the public interest exceptions addressed above if EU legislation already exists that takes into account the same concerns that are expressed in the national measure.[235] If, for example, the Council adopted legislation regulating the advertising of alcoholic beverages on television during sporting events, a member state may not justify on public health grounds a national law which prohibits all television advertising of alcohol. This is essentially the same requirement discussed above in the context of the free movement of goods.

If the EU legislation is in the form of a directive, the directive must exhaustively harmonize the member state laws. An EU directive exhaustively harmonizes if it does not leave the member states discretion as to the level of protections they must achieve in their national legislation. The Unfair Commercial Practices Directive,[236] for example, is considered to exhaustively harmonize the law relating to business-to-consumer commercial practices because it prohibits the member states from adopting more restrictive rules than those established in the Directive.[237] If, however, the Directive only prescribes a minimum level of protection, it is considered partial harmonization and the public policy exceptions discussed above can potentially be used to justify the state measure.[238] The Money Laundering Directive, for example, allows the member states to adopt stricter laws regulating money laundering and is therefore considered partial harmonization.[239]

4.7 Relationship to Free Movement of Goods

In many businesses, the sale of a product is closely intertwined with the provision of services. For example, the selling of mobile telephones is just as

---

234. Case C-294/00, Deutsche Paracelsus Schulen für Naturheilverfahren GmbH v. Gräbner, 2002 E.C.R. I-6515.
235. Case C-244/04, Comm'n v. Germany, 2006 E.C.R. I-885, 912 ¶31; Case C-445/03, Comm'n v. Luxembourg, 2004 E.C.R. I-10191, 10216 ¶21; Case C-262/02, Comm'n v. France, 2004 E.C.R. I-6569, 6606 ¶25.
236. Directive 2005/29/EC of the European Parliament and of the Council of 11 May 2005 concerning unfair business-to-consumer commercial practices in the internal market, 2005 O.J. (L 149) 22.
237. Case C-265/12, Citroën Belux NV v. Federatie voor Verzekerings- en Financiële Tussenpersonen, ECLI:EU:C:2013:489 at ¶20.
238. Case C-212/11, Jyske Bank Gibraltar Ltd. v. Administración del Estado, ECLI:EU:C: 2013:270 at ¶60; Case C-265/12, Citroën Belux NV v. Federatie voor Verzekerings- en Financiële Tussenpersonen, ECLI:EU:C:2013:489 at ¶31.
239. Case C-212/11, Jyske Bank Gibraltar Ltd. v. Administración del Estado, ECLI:EU:C: 2013:270 at ¶61.

much about the sale of the accompanying services as it is about the phone itself. Hence, a restriction on the ability of that business to provide its services will also be a restriction on its ability to sell its goods. Consequently, Articles 34 (free movement of goods) and 56 (free movement of services) may apply to the same facts. In *In re Burmanjer*, for example, a Belgian law prohibiting itinerant salesmen from selling magazines in Belgium had the effect of preventing the free movement of goods as well as the free movement of services.[240] The general rule is that both legal norms can be applied to the same facts.

In *Konsumentombudsmannen v. Gourmet International Products AB*,[241] for example, Swedish law prohibited the marketing of alcoholic beverages in certain media (such as magazines) but allowed advertising at point of sale (such as a sign at the liquor store). The Swedish consumer ombudsman sought to enjoin Gourmet International from publishing its magazine which contained advertisements for alcoholic beverages. The ECJ held that because the law had a differential impact on products from other member states (it gave local sellers an advantage because it allowed for point-of-sale advertising), the law violated *both* Article 34 and Article 56 of the TFEU (it reduced the cross-border purchase and sale of advertising space). However, the ECJ recognized the health benefits and exempted the law under Article 30 and Article 52.

The ECJ has introduced an exception to the general rule in cases where the application of one of these legal norms is clearly more appropriate than the other. According to the ECJ, "where a national measure relates to both the free movement of goods and freedom to provide services, the Court will in principle examine it in relation to only one of those two fundamental freedoms if it appears that one of them is entirely secondary in relation to the other and may be considered together with it."[242]

In *Ker-Optika bt v. ÀNTSZ Dél-dunántúli Regionális Intézete*, for example, one of the issues was whether both the rules governing the free movement of goods and the rules governing the freedom to provide services applied to a Hungarian law prohibiting the sale of contact lenses over the Internet. The ECJ held that the rules governing the freedom to provide services did not apply because they were wholly secondary to the application of Article 34 of the TFEU in this case.[243] In *Omega Spielhallen- und Automatenaufstellungs-GmbH v. Oberbürgermeister der Bundesstadt Bonn*, a German law prohibited the operation of a "laserdrome" using electronic laser guns and sensory tags placed on the players. The operators of the laserdrome argued that the prohibition of their business violated the free movement of goods and services. The ECJ, in applying the rule stated above, held that the free movement of goods did not

---

240. Case C-20/03, *In re* Burmanjer, 2005 E.C.R. I-4133.
241. Case C-405/98, Konsumentombudsmannen v. Gourmet Int'l. Products *AB*, 2001 E.C.R. I-1795.
242. Case C-403/08, Football Association Premier League v. QC Leisure, 2011 E.C.R. I-9159, 9209 ¶78.
243. Case C-108/09, Ker-Optika bt v. ÀNTSZ Dél-dunántúli Regionális *Intézete*, 2010 E.C.R. I-12213, 12258 ¶44.

apply because the goods in this case (i.e., the laser equipment purchased from other member states) were only incidental to the provision of the services.[244]

5. Free Movement of Capital

The final of the free movement principles is the free movement of capital. Similar to the other free movement principles, this rule is anchored in the TFEU and consists of a basic prohibition on restrictions on the free movement (Article 63) combined with codified exceptions (Article 65) and judicially created exceptions. As discussed in greater detail below, the free movement of capital differs from the other free movement principles in that it applies not only to the movement of capital between member states, but also between a member state and a third country.

5.1 Basic Prohibition

(a) Capital

Article 63 of the TFEU prohibits restrictions on the movement of capital between member states and between member states and third countries.[245] Although the TFEU does not define the term "capital," it is generally understood in a narrow sense to refer to financial capital (i.e., money and investments which can readily be converted into money). Other types of capital, such as physical capital (the physical assets used by a business to produce goods or provide services), natural capital (e.g., the natural environment), and human capital (e.g., the value of employees) are generally not considered capital in the sense of Article 63 of the TFEU.

(b) Restriction

As indicated above, Article 63 of the TFEU prohibits (1) restrictions on the movement of capital between member states and (2) restrictions on the movement of capital between a member state and third countries. Perhaps the most obvious example of a restriction on the free movement of capital between member states would be a national law prohibiting nationals of other member states from investing in domestic companies.[246] The basic principle of nondiscrimination—that comparable situations must not be treated differently and that different situations must not be treated in the same way—which applies to the other free movement rights also applies to the free movement

---

244. Case C-36/02, Omega Spielhallen- und Automatenaufstellungs-GmbH v. Oberbürgermeister der Bundesstadt Bonn, 2004 E.C.R. I-9609, 9651 ¶27.
245. Although Article 63, in a separate subparagraph, also prohibits "all restrictions on payments," according to the ECJ this prohibition on restrictions on payments is subsumed under the general prohibition on restrictions on the free movement of capital. See Case C-503/99, Comm'n v. Belgium, 2002 E.C.R. I-4809, 4830 ¶37.
246. Case C-367/98, Comm'n v. Portugal, 2002 E.C.R. I-4731.

of capital.[247] For example, a member state law that taxes corporate dividends at a different rate depending on whether or not the shareholder is a national of that member state constitutes a restriction on the free movement of capital.[248] Even a law which makes it more difficult to invest in another member state (as opposed to an outright prohibition) would constitute a restriction on the free movement of capital.[249] For example, a national law requiring a citizen from another member state to secure the prior approval of a particular agency in order to invest in real estate[250] or to live on the property[251] would constitute restrictions on the movement of capital. *In re Trummer and Mayer* illustrates a slightly more disguised restriction.[252] In that case, an Austrian law required mortgages registered in Austria to be denominated in Austrian schillings (prior to the introduction of the euro in Austria). A German who was acquiring land in Austria wanted to register a mortgage in German marks. The German argued, and the ECJ agreed, that the Austrian law amounted to a restriction on the free movement of capital. Although it did not establish an absolute prohibition, by imposing such a requirement the law made it more difficult for Austrians to get mortgages from lenders from other member states such as Germany.

In determining what constitutes a capital movement for purposes of Article 63 of the TFEU, the ECJ commonly relies on Council Directive 88/361/EC.[253] Although it is not an exhaustive list of what qualifies as a capital movement,[254] some of the examples of capital movements provided in Directive 88/361 are direct investments such as acquiring or investing in a legal entity or in real estate, capital market transactions such as purchasing equity or bonds in a public company and admission of securities to the capital market, depositing funds in a bank account, and extending loans and credits.

---

247. Joined cases C-578/10 to C-580/10, Staatssecretaris van Financiën v. L.A.C. van Putten, 2012 E.C.R. I-___, at ¶43.
248. Case C-190/72, Emerging Markets Series of DFA Investment Trust Co. v. Dyrektor Izby Skarbowej w Bydgoszczy, 2014 E.C.R. I-___, at ¶42.
249. Case C-493/09, Comm'n v. Portugal, 2011 E.C.R. I-9264, 9273 ¶28; Case C-377/07, Finanzamt Speyer-Germersheim v. Steko Industriemontage GmbH, 2009 E.C.R. I-299, 309 ¶23.
250. Case C-300/01, *In re* Salzman, 2003 E.C.R. I-4899.
251. Case C-370/05, *In re* Festersen, 2007 E.C.R. I-1129.
252. Case C-222/97, *Tr*ummer and Mayer, 1999 E.C.R. I-1661.
253. Council Directive 88/361/EC of 24 June 1988 for the implementation of Article 67 of the Treaty, 1988 O.J. (L 178) 5. *See, e.g.*, Joined Cases C-578/10 to C-580/10, Staatssecretaris van Financiën v. L.A.C. van Putten, 2012 E.C.R. I-___, at ¶28; Case C-132/10, Halley v. Belgium, 2011 E.C.R. I-8355, 8361 ¶19; Case C-543/08, Comm'n v. Portugal, 2010 E.C.R. I-11245, at ¶46; Case C-510/08, Mattner v. Finanzamt Velbert, 2010 E.C.R. I-3553, at ¶19; Case C-43/07, D.M.M.A. Arens-Sikken v. Staatssecretaris van Financiën, 2008 E.C.R. I-6887, 6923 ¶29.
254. In Case C-35/98, Staatssecretaris van Financiën v. B.G.M. Verkooijen, 2000 E.C.R. I-4071, for example, the ECJ held that the receipt of dividends from foreign investments, which was not listed in the Annex to Directive 88/361, was nonetheless a form of capital movement.

The free movement of capital rules are not limited to member state measures restricting foreigners from investing in that country (inbound restrictions), but extends also to measures that prohibit or discourage its own nationals from investing in other member states (outbound restrictions).[255] For example, a Latvian law discouraging Latvians from investing in property in Estonia would violate the prohibition on restrictions of the free movement of capital.

(c) Indistinctly Applicable Restrictions

In order to fall under the prohibition on restrictions on the free movement of capital, the measure does not have to overtly discriminate between nationals of other member states.[256] Even indistinctly applicable measures may be caught by the prohibition if they restrict the flow of capital from or into other member states. In the "Golden Share" cases, the issue was whether domestic laws in the Netherlands, France, and Germany which secured special rights (i.e., golden shares) for the government as a shareholder in certain companies violated Article 63 of the TFEU. The state measures securing these special rights did not discriminate between domestic and foreign investors. They were indistinctly applicable. Nonetheless, the ECJ held that they restricted the free movement of capital between member states because the existence of special rights held by the state had the effect of dissuading investors from other member states from investing in these companies.[257] In *Commission v. United Kingdom*, the ECJ similarly concluded that the special shareholder rights retained by the UK government in the British Airports Authority (BAA) when it was privatized constituted a restriction on the free movement of capital because it deterred private investment from other member states (even though private investors were not prevented from investing in the BAA).[258] The state measures securing these special rights were indistinctly applicable to domestic and foreign investors.

(d) Geographic Scope

Article 63 of the TFEU prohibits restrictions on the flow of capital not only between member states but also between member states and third countries. For example, an Austrian law imposing a higher rate of tax on dividends from investments in Swiss companies as opposed to dividends from companies in other member states is prohibited by Article 63 (subject, of course, to the exceptions discussed below).[259]

---

255. Case C-101/05, Skatteverket v. A, 2007 E.C.R. I-11531, 11583 ¶40; Case C-370/05, *In re* Festersen, 2007 E.C.R. I-1129, 1154 ¶24.
256. Case C-543/08, Comm'n v. Portugal, 2010 E.C.R. I-11245, 11272 ¶68; Case C-98/01, Comm'n v. United Kingdom, 2003 E.C.R. I-4641, 4662 ¶43.
257. Case C-112/05, Comm'n v. Germany, 2007 E.C.R. I-8995, 9040 ¶66; Joined cases C-282/04 and C-283/04, Comm'n v. Netherlands, 2006 E.C.R. I-9141, 9165 ¶23; Case C-483/99, Comm'n v. French Republic, 2002 E.C.R. I-4781, 4831 ¶41.
258. Case C-98/01, Comm'n v. United Kingdom, 2003 E.C.R. I-4641.
259. Joined Cases C-436/08 and C-436/08, Haribo Lakritzen Hans Riegel BetriebsGmbH v. Finanzamt Linz, 2011 E.C.R. I-355, 387 ¶81; Case C-157/05, Holböck v. Finanzamt Salzburg-Land, 2007 E.C.R. I-4051, 4064 ¶30 (The state measure in this case qualified for an exception under Article 64(1) of the TFEU.).

(e) Relationship to Other Free Movement Principles

There is, of course, potential for overlap between the free movement of capital rules and the other free movement rights—particularly the freedom of establishment and services. For example, a Hungarian law restricting the ability of Irish citizens to establish a company in Hungary would violate the freedom of establishment rights of the Irish as well as their free movement of capital rights because it limits the ability of Irish citizens to invest in Hungary. A German law restricting foreign lenders from offering credit via the Internet may restrict the ability of those foreign lenders to provide services in Germany as well as restrict the flow of capital between member states. The resolution of the overlap issue could have significant impact in particular cases. Using the German law restricting foreign lenders from offering credit via the Internet as an example, a Swiss company would not be able to challenge the German law on the basis of the freedom to provide services, but would be able to challenge the law on the basis of the free movement of capital.[260] This is because the prohibition on restrictions on the free movement of capital applies also to capital movements with nonmember states such as Switzerland.

The significance of the distinction also applies to the overlap between the freedom of establishment and the free movement in capital. At issue in *Itelcar v. Fazenda Pública* was whether a Portuguese law applicable to the taxation of dividends to non-EU shareholders was prohibited by the free movement principles. If the case were analyzed as a restriction on the freedom of establishment, as argued by Portugal, the restriction would be permissible as the freedom of establishment rules do not apply to restrictions on commerce with non-member states. However, the ECJ concluded that the case involved the movement of capital and concluded that the Portuguese law was a restriction of the free movement of capital.[261]

In the context of apparent overlapping application of the freedom of establishment and the free movement of capital rules, the distinguishing characteristic used by the ECJ is whether the investment gives the investor a substantial influence over the entity in which the investment is made.[262] If the investment gives the investor a substantial influence over the company's decisions, then the TFEU provisions on the freedom of establishment apply.[263] If, however, it is merely a financial investment, the free movement of capital rules apply.

---

260. *See, e.g.,* Case C-452/04, Fidium Finanz AG v. Bundesanstalt für Finanzdienstleistungsaufsicht, 2006 E.C.R. I-9521.
261. C-282/12, Itelcar v. Fazenda Pública, 2013 E.C.R. I-___, at ¶27.
262. Case C-314/08, Filipiak v. Dyrektor Izby Skarbowej w Poznaniu, 2009 E.C.R. I-11049, 11070 ¶57; Case C-231/05, *In re* Oy AA, 2007 E.C.R. I-6373, 6400 ¶20; Case C-196/04, Cadbury Schweppes plc v. Commissioners of Inland Revenue, 2006 E.C.R. I-7995, 8042 ¶31. Sometimes reference is made to "definite influence" instead of "substantial influence." C-282/12, Itelcar v. Fazenda Pública, 2013 E.C.R. I-___, at ¶17. However, these concepts are synonymous.
263. Case C-168/11, Beker v. Finanzamt Heilbronn, 2013 E.C.R. I-___, at ¶25; Case C-543/08, Comm'n v. Portugal, 2010 E.C.R. I-11245, 11264 ¶41.

Nonetheless, the ECJ has repeatedly recognized that it is possible that the prohibition of restrictions on the free movement of capital and the prohibition of restrictions on the freedom of establishment may all be applied to the same facts.[264] However, if one of the freedoms is primarily applicable in the particular circumstances, then the ECJ will apply only that freedom.[265] Unfortunately, there are no clear guidelines as to when one freedom is "primarily applicable" in particular circumstances. In *Fidium Finanz AG v. Bundesanstalt für Finanzdienstleistungsaufsicht*, the issue was whether the freedom to provide services rules or the free movement of capital rules were applicable to a German law that essentially required financial service providers providing services to customers in Germany to have their central administration in Germany.[266] The ECJ reasoned that the freedom to provide services rules were primarily applicable—and thereby preempted the application of the free movement of capital rules—because the restriction on the movement of capital was merely an "unavoidable consequence of the restriction on the freedom to provide services."[267]

5.2 State Measure

Unlike the TFEU provisions prohibiting restrictions on the free movement of goods, the prohibition on restrictions on the free movement of capital codified in the TFEU is not expressly limited to restrictions imposed by the member states. Hence, the question arises whether the prohibition also applies to *private restrictions* on the free movement of capital. For example, a clause in a distribution agreement prohibiting the distributor from investing in competitors would reduce the movement of capital in the EU.[268] There is no clear indication that Article 63 of the TFEU would apply to prohibit a restriction on the free movement of capital imposed by a private party. The text and structure of the TFEU suggests that Article 63 should be limited to state measures. Private restrictions, if appreciable, are more appropriately the concern of the competition law provisions of the TFEU. Moreover, the exceptions provided for in Article 65 of the TFEU as discussed below expressly apply only to the conduct of the member states.[269] An extension of the prohibition on restrictions on the free

---

264. Case C-212/09, Comm'n v. Portugal, 2011 E.C.R. I-10892, 10906 ¶44; Case C-310/09, Ministre du Budget, des Comptes publics et de la Fonction publique v. Accor SA, 2011 E.C.R. I-8150, 8163 ¶34. The applicability of the legal norms can have significant practical implications as the exceptions to the respective prohibitions differ.
265. Case C-233/09, Dijkman v. Belgische Staat, 2010 E.C.R. I-6652, 6663 ¶33; Case C-524/04, Test Claimants for the Thin Cap Group Litigation v. Commissioners of Inland Revenue, 2007 E.C.R. I-2107, 2176 ¶33; Case C-452/04, Fidium Finanz AG v. Bundesanstalt für Finanzdienstleistungsaufsicht, 2006 E.C.R. I-9521, 9576 ¶34.
266. Case C-452/04, Fidium Finanz AG v. Bundesanstalt für Finanzdienstleistungsaufsicht, 2006 E.C.R. I-9521, 9576 ¶34.
267. *Id.* at 9580 ¶48.
268. Joined Cases C-163/94, C-165/94 and C-250/94, Criminal Proceedings against Lucas Emilio Sanz de Lera, 1995 E.C.R. I-4821, 4841 ¶41.
269. "The provisions of Article [63] shall be without prejudice to *the right of Member States* ..." [emphasis added].

movement of capital to private conduct would leave these parties without recourse to the exceptions offered in Article 65. Therefore, the application of the prohibition on restrictions on the free movement of capital probably requires a state measure.

The requirement of a state measure is implicit in *Commission v. Germany*.[270] In that case, the Commission challenged the interest held by one of the German states in Volkswagen as restricting the free movement of capital. The rights held by the German state were based on a contract between the German state and Volkswagen. The German government argued that the absence of a state measure precluded the application of Article 63 of the TFEU in this case. The ECJ held, however, that the subsequent legislative codification of the contractual rights made them a state measure.[271] The implication of the case is that the application of Article 63 requires a state measure. Otherwise, the legislative codification of the rights held by the German state would not even have been an issue.

5.3 Exceptions

(a) Public Policy and Security and Overriding Requirements

Similar to the other free movement principles, there are exceptions to the prohibition of restrictions on the free movement of capital. According to Article 65(1)(b) of the TFEU, restrictions based on public policy or security are not prohibited by Article 63 of the TFEU. The TFEU does not define what types of issues qualify as legitimate public policy or public security concerns. The safeguarding of supplies of petroleum, electricity, gas, post, and telecommunication have been recognized as constituting a legitimate public security concern.[272] Even the protection of workers and shareholders and regional planning have been recognized as legitimate public security concerns potentially justifying a restriction on the free movement of capital.[273] In *Hans Reisch v. Bürgermeister der Landeshauptstadt Salzburg*, the ECJ held that an Austrian law prohibiting the use of certain property as a secondary residence "may be regarded as contributing to an objective in the public interest."[274] The basic idea behind the Austrian law was to make sure that certain areas had a minimum level of permanent population (rather than being dominated by vacation homes).

---

270. Case C-112/05, Comm'n v. Germany, 2007 E.C.R. I-8995.
271. *Id.* at 9030 ¶29.
272. Case C-212/09, Comm'n v. Portugal, 2011 E.C.R. I-10892, 10817 ¶82; Case C-463/00, Comm'n v. Spain, 2003 E.C.R. I-4581, 4634 ¶71; Case C-503/99, Comm'n v. Belgium, 2002 E.C.R. I-4809, 4832 ¶46; Case C-483/99, Comm'n v. French Republic, 2002 E.C.R. I-4781, 4804 ¶47.
273. C-112/05, Comm'n v. Germany, 2007 E.C.R. I-8995, 9042 ¶74 & ¶77; Case C-515/99, Hans Reisch v. Bürgermeister der Landeshauptstadt Salzburg, 2002 E.C.R. I-2157, 2205 ¶34.
274. Case C-515/99, Hans Reisch v. Bürgermeister der Landeshauptstadt Salzburg, 2002 E.C.R. I-2157, 2205 ¶34.

Not all justifications asserted by the member states have been accepted by the ECJ. The ECJ has consistently held that state measures restricting the free movement of capital cannot be justified purely on economic grounds or to safeguard the financial interests of the particular member state.[275] The ECJ has also held that a restriction on the free movement of capital cannot be justified by the interest of the state in protecting its banks or tobacco companies.[276]

There is no catalog of state interests that would justify a restriction on the free movement of capital under Article 65(1)(b) of the TFEU. According to the ECJ, the justification only applies "if there is a genuine and sufficiently serious threat to a fundamental interest of society and, moreover, those grounds must not serve purely economic ends."[277] Clearly the promotion of purely revenue interests would not justify a restriction.[278] Beyond that, the ECJ has been reluctant to provide a useful catalog of legitimate and illegitimate public interests. In *Commission v. Italy*, the ECJ even went so far as to broadly state that "the minimum supply of energy resources and goods essential to the public as a whole, the continuity of public service, national defense, the protection of public policy and public security and health emergencies ... may warrant certain restrictions of the exercise of fundamental freedoms."[279]

Further complicating the analysis is the extension of the "public policy" exception to include "overriding requirements of the general interest." The ECJ has repeatedly held that overriding requirements can justify restrictions imposed by member states on the free movement of capital between member states[280] as well as between a member state and a third country.[281] Although the ECJ considers the overriding requirements exception to be in addition to the justifications codified in Article 65(1)(b) of the TFEU,[282] the ECJ has failed to clarify the relationship between this exception and that provided for in Article 65(1)(b) (public policy or security). The overriding requirements exception was pragmatically introduced and maintained to give the member states broader discretion in complying with the free movement rules. From a practical and theoretical perspective, therefore, it should be viewed as broader than the statutory exceptions. In *Minister voor Wonen v. Woningstichting Sint Servatius*, for example, the issue was whether a Dutch law requiring prior approval of a

---

275. Case C-367/98, Comm'n v. Portugal, 2002 E.C.R. I-4756, 4775 ¶52.
276. Case C-463/00, Comm'n v. Spain, 2003 E.C.R. I-4581.
277. Case C-39/11, VBV Vorsorgekasse AG v. Finanzmarktaufsichtsbehörde, 2012 E.C.R. I-___, at ¶29.
278. Case 10/10, Comm'n v. Austria, 2011 E.C.R. I-5416, 5431 ¶40.
279. Case C-326/07, Comm'n v. Italy, 2009 E.C.R. I-2291, 2332 ¶45.
280. Case C-543/08, Comm'n v. Portugal, 2010 E.C.R. I-11245, 11277 ¶83; Case C-377/07, Finanzamt Speyer-Germersheim v. Steko Industriemontage GmbH, 2009 E.C.R. I-299, 311 ¶30.
281. Case C-101/05, Skatteverket v. A, 2007 E.C.R. I-11,531, 11587 ¶53. The ECJ gives greater deference to the member states in cases involving restrictions on the movement of capital between a member state and a third country. *Id.* at ¶60.
282. Case C-39/11, VBV Vorsorgekasse AG v. Finanzmarktaufsichtsbehörde, 2012 E.C.R. I-___, at ¶28; Case C-493/09, Comm'n v. Portugal, 2011 E.C.R. I-9264, 9274 ¶33; Case C-112/05, Comm'n v. Germany, 2007 E.C.R. I-8995, 9041 ¶72.

cross-border investment in public housing fell within one of the exceptions to the free movement of capital codified in Article 65 of the TFEU. The ECJ held that although the Dutch law could not benefit from the Article 65 exceptions, it could benefit from the overriding requirements exception.[283]

(b) Supervision of Financial Institutions

Responsibility for the supervision of financial institutions (e.g., banks) operating in the EU remains primarily with the member states even though there has been wide harmonization of the laws applicable to financial institutions.[284] Obviously, the regulation of financial institutions by the member states will have an impact on the flow of capital among member states. Member states are permitted to restrict the free movement of capital if this effect is ancillary to the legitimate (i.e., in conformity with applicable EU directives) supervision of financial institutions (Article 65(1)(b) TFEU). These member state measures are scrutinized for conformity with the applicable EU secondary law rather than the free movement of capital.

(c) Permitted Restrictions on the Right of Establishment

According to Article 65(2) of the TFEU, the prohibition of restrictions on the movement of capital does not apply to prevent restrictions on the right of establishment which the TFEU permits. In other words, if a member state measure restricts the freedom of establishment but qualifies for an exception to the prohibition on restrictions on the freedom of establishment, the prohibition of restrictions on the free movement of capital may not be applied to that measure.

This exception for permitted restrictions on the right of establishment has been of little import because of the similarity of the exceptions. In other words, if it falls under the exceptions to the freedom of establishment, it will probably also fall under the exceptions on free movement of capital. As discussed above, the TFEU (Article 65(1)(b)) already provides for a general public policy exception. The ECJ generally assumes that the same public policy concerns, such as public order, public security, and public health, apply equally to both the right of establishment and the free movement of capital.[285] Moreover, the ECJ has recognized that overriding requirements of the public interest may justify

---

283. Case C-567/07, Minister voor Wonen v. Woningstichting Sint Servatius, 2009 E.C.R. I-9021, 9037 ¶29.
284. *See, e.g.*, Directive 2000/12/European Community of the European Parliament and of the Council of 20 March 2000, relating to the taking up and pursuit of the business of credit institutions, 2000 O.J. (L 126) 1; Council Directive 86/635/EC of 8 December 1986 on the annual accounts and consolidated accounts of banks and other financial institutions, 1986 O.J. (L 372) 1; Council Directive 91/308/EC of 10 June 1991 on prevention of the use of the financial system for the purpose of money laundering, 1991 O.J. (L 166) 77; Council Directive 93/6/EC of 15 March 1993 on the capital adequacy of investments firms and credit institutions, 1993 O.J. (L 141) 1.
285. Case C-463/00, Comm'n v. Spain, 2003 E.C.R. I-4581, 4623 ¶34; Case C-503/99, Comm'n v. Belgium, 2002 E.C.R. I-4809, 4836 ¶59.

restrictions on the free movement of capital as they justify restrictions on the freedom of establishment.[286] Hence, it would be difficult to identify a scenario which qualified for an exception under one prohibition but not the other.

(d) Exceptions Applicable to Third Countries

Although the free movement of capital applies to capital movements between member states as well as between member states and third countries, there are several exceptions exclusively applicable to capital movements involving third countries.[287] First, the prohibition on restrictions on the free movement of capital does not apply to certain types of restrictions if such restriction existed on December 31, 1993.[288] The types of restrictions to which this exception applies are restrictions on direct investment to or from third countries, the provision of financial services, or the admission of securities to capital markets. In *Holböck v. Finanzamt Salzburg-Land*, for example, an Austrian tax law adopted in 1988 which imposed a higher rate of taxes on income from investments in companies in non-member states as opposed to income from investments in companies in member states qualified for this exception.[289]

Second, Article 66 of the TFEU authorizes the Council to take short-term steps which may restrict the flow of capital between the EU and third countries if serious difficulties arise in the operation of the European Monetary Union. For example, if it became necessary to stabilize the euro against the currency of a third country, the Council could adopt legislation limiting the ability of EU nationals to exchange euros for the currency of that third country.

Third, as part of the Common Foreign and Security Policy, the Council is authorized under Article 215 of the TFEU to take urgent measures affecting economic relations with third countries. For example, the Council may decide to impose economic sanctions against a third country in order to achieve certain political objectives. Such measures are expressly permitted under Article 75 of the TFEU even if they restrict the flow of capital between the EC and third countries. In Regulation 329/2007, for example, the Council imposed a ban on exports of goods and technology to North Korea which could contribute to North Korea's nuclear weapons program.[290] Although this technically restricted the flow of goods between the EU and a third country, it was permissible under Article 75 which provides an exception to the free movement of capital requirement.

---

286. Case C-463/00, Comm'n v. Spain, 2003 E.C.R. I-4581, 4633 ¶68.
287. The exceptions codified in Article 65(1)(a) and (b) of the TFEU apply both to the free movement of capital between member states as well as between a member state and a third country. Case C-101/05, Skatteverket v. A, 2007 E.C.R. I-11531, 11581 ¶35.
288. Article 64(1) TFEU. *See, e.g.*, Case C-541/08, Fokus Invest AG v. Finanzierungsberatung-Immobilientreuhand und Anlageberatung GmbH, 2010 E.C.R. I-1025.
289. Case C-157/05, Holböck v. Finanzamt Salzburg-Land, 2007 E.C.R. I-4054, 4068 ¶45.
290. Council Regulation (EC) No. 329/2007 of 27 March 2007 concerning restrictive measures against the Democratic People's Republic of Korea, 2007 O.J. (L 88) 1.

(e) Requirements for the Application of the Exceptions

The exceptions to the prohibition of restrictions on the free movement of capital are to be interpreted strictly.[291] There are two basic requirements for the application of the exceptions. First, there must not be any EU harmonizing legislation addressing the same concerns. If EU harmonizing legislation exists which exhaustively addresses the same concerns, then the member state cannot rely on the exception.[292] In such cases, the legitimacy of the member state measure is examined for conformity with the EU secondary legislation and not for conformity with the free movement of capital primary law.

Second, the restriction on the free movement of capital must conform to the proportionality principle.[293] As discussed throughout this book, the proportionality principle is an important component of the EU legal system that appears in practically all areas of law. In general, proportionality requires that (1) the measure must be appropriate for attaining the legitimizing objective it pursues and (2) it must not go beyond what is necessary to attain that objective. In *Commission v. Germany*, for example, the ECJ held that a law giving the German state of Lower Saxony special rights in Volkswagen was not appropriate for protecting the employees of Volkswagen even though the interest of protecting employees may be adequate justification for a restriction on the free movement of capital.[294] Germany failed to show the connection between the state measure and the legitimate objective of protecting employees.

The availability of less restrictive means to achieve the same objective will likely mean that the measure is not proportional.[295] In *Idrima Tipou AE v. Ipourgos Tipou kai Meson Mayikis Enimerosis*, for example, Greece had adopted a law which allowed the Greek television regulatory body to impose fines for breaches of applicable regulations not only on the legal entity which committed the breach, but also directly on shareholders of that entity who held more than 2.5 percent interest in the entity. The public policy justification for the law was to make sure companies observed the law designed to protect individuals who might appear on television. The ECJ held that the law violated the free movement of capital (the potential for personal liability had the potential to deter investors from other member states) and, although the public policy concern may be legitimate, was not proportional because there were other less restrictive

---

291. Case C-242/03, Ministre des Finances v. Weidert, 2004 E.C.R. I-7379, 7400 ¶20; Case C-463/00, Comm'n v. Spain, 2003 E.C.R. I-4581, 4634 ¶72.
292. Case C-212/11, Jyske Bank Gibraltar Ltd. v. Administración del Estado, 2013 E.C.R. I-___, at ¶61; Case C-463/04, Federconsumatori v. Comune di Milano, 2007 E.C.R. I-10419, 10448 ¶39; Joined Cases C-282/04 and C-283/04, Comm'n v. Netherlands, 2006 E.C.R. I-9141, 9167 ¶32.
293. Case C-39/11, VBV Vorsorgekasse AG v. Finanzmarktaufsichtsbehörde, 2012 E.C.R. I-___, at ¶32; Case C-326/07, Comm'n v. Italy, 2009 E.C.R. I-2291, 2332 ¶43.
294. Case C-112/05, Comm'n v. Germany, 2007 E.C.R. I-8995, 9042 ¶74.
295. Case C-39/11, VBV Vorsorgekasse AG v. Finanzmarktaufsichtsbehörde, 2012 E.C.R. I-___, at ¶33.

means of achieving the same objective.[296] As pointed out by the ECJ, Greece could (merely) suspend or revoke a broadcast license as a sanction without having to impose a penalty on the shareholders.

The proportionality principal was a central issue in the Golden Share cases. This series of cases involved the special rights that certain member states retained or held in formerly state-owned companies once they were privatized. The types of rights retained by the member states over these companies varied from case to case, but in each case the member states held rights that went beyond those rights which a minority shareholder would normally have. In each case, the existence of special rights had the effect of deterring investment from other member states because investors would be less willing to invest in a company that granted certain minority shareholders rights exceeding their shareholdings.[297] The central issue, however, was whether the particular rights held by the respective member states were justified based on public policy grounds and, if so, whether they conformed to the proportionality principle. As discussed above, the ECJ has accepted the safeguarding of supplies of petroleum, electricity, gas, post, and telecommunication as legitimate public security concerns.[298]

Whether the particular state measures were proportionate depended on the particular facts of the case. The special rights held by the member state are less likely to be deemed proportionate if they allow the member state to veto decisions of the company in advance (ex ante authorization) as opposed to ex post regimes which merely require the company to notify the state once a particular event has occurred.[299] Even ex ante notification systems may be proportionate if they are structured as opposition regimes.

In *Commission v. Belgium*, for example, Belgian law attached special rights to the shares that the Belgian state held in the Belgian national gas company.[300] According to the Belgian law, certain events involving the respective companies (such as the sale of strategic assets) had to be reported to the Belgian state prior to implementing such transactions. The ECJ held that although the decrees restricted the free movement of capital (because they deterred investors from other member states), the objective of safeguarding energy supplies was legitimate. As the notification regime required by the decrees was an "opposition" regime (i.e., it was approved as long as the state did not oppose it), the ECJ concluded that it was proportionate to the legitimate objective. If prior approval is required, the decision to approve must be based on objective

---

296. Case C-81/09, Idrima Tipou AE v. Ipourgos Tipou kai Meson Mayikis Enimerosis, 2010 E.C.R. I-10206, 10227 ¶65.
297. Joined cases C-282/04 and C-283/04, Comm'n v. Netherlands, 2006 E.C.R. I-9141, 9166 ¶27; Case C-483/99, Comm'n v. French Republic, 2002 E.C.R. I-4781, 4831 ¶41.
298. Case C-463/00, Comm'n v. Spain, 2003 E.C.R. I-4581, 4634 ¶71; Case C-503/99, Comm'n v. Belgium, 2002 E.C.R. I-4809, 4832 ¶46; Case C-483/99, Comm'n v. France, 2002 E.C.R. I-4781, 4804 ¶47.
299. Case C-483/99, Comm'n v. France, 2002 E.C.R. I-4781; Case C-54/99, Association Église de Scientologie de Paris v. The Prime Minister, 2000 E.C.R. I-1335.
300. Case C-503/99, Comm'n v. Belgium, 2002 E.C.R. I-4809.

criteria, which are known by all companies in advance, and the decision of the state not to approve is subject to judicial review.[301]

6. Taxation and the Free Movement Principles

6.1 Allocation of Taxing Authority Between EU and Member States

As discussed in Chapter I, the EU is based on the principle of limited powers. The EU institutions only have those authorities that have been directly or indirectly granted to them by the treaties. Authorities that have not been ceded by the member states to the EU are retained by the member states. The member states have retained their authorities in the field of taxation. The EU does not have the authority to impose direct or social security taxes. As discussed in Chapter I, the EU's budget is financed through other resources (agricultural levies, customs duties, a portion of the VAT revenues collected by the member states, and contributions of the member states).[302]

Although the EU does not have the authority to impose and collect direct, indirect, or social security taxes, it does have some legislative authority in the field of taxation. The EU has the authority—expressly granted by the TFEU—to adopt harmonization measures for indirect taxes "to the extent that such harmonization if necessary to ensure the establishment and the functioning of the internal market and to avoid distortion of competition."[303] For example, the EC has adopted a directive harmonizing the types of transactions in the member states to which value-added taxes apply.[304] The term indirect taxes refers to those taxes that are imposed indirectly on the taxpayer by levy on production and consumption (for example, value-added taxes and excise taxes). Indirect taxes are collected by commercial establishments or industry and passed on to the taxpayer in connection with the payment of the price of the product or service. The term direct taxes, on the other hand, refers to the taxes that are imposed directly on the taxpayer such as income tax, wealth taxes, corporate taxes, and most local taxes. The EU does not have the authority to impose direct taxes or to harmonize the direct taxes of the member states. The member states retain

---

301. Joined Cases C-282/04 and C-283/04, Comm'n v. Netherlands, 2006 E.C.R. I-9141, 9168 ¶40; Case C-463/00, Comm'n v. Spain, 2003 E.C.R. I-4581, 4634 ¶78; Case C-483/99, Comm'n v. French Republic, 2002 E.C.R. I-4781, 4831 ¶50.
302. TFEU at art. 269.
303. TFEU at art. 113.
304. Sixth Council Directive 77/388/EEC of 17 May 1977 on the harmonization of the laws of the member states relating to turnover taxes—common system of value- added tax, 1977 O.J. (L 145) 1.

the right to impose direct taxes as well as the right to impose indirect taxes in the absence of any EU harmonizing legislation.[305]

6.2 Tension Between Free Movement and Taxation Authorities Retained by the Member States

The exercise by a member state of its retained taxation authority may restrict the flow of goods, services, labor, or capital between the member states. If, for example, Germany grants a tax exemption for dividend income received by individuals with investments in German corporations (but not other corporations), this may distort the flow of capital between member states even though it is a form of direct taxation reserved to the member states. If Sweden imposes a tax on wine (a product not produced in Sweden) but not on beer (a product which is produced in Sweden), this may have the effect of reducing the volume of wine imported from other member states into Sweden and constitute a restriction on the free movement of goods.[306]

To resolve the conflict between the legitimate exercise of taxing authorities and respect for the free movement principles, the ECJ has introduced the rule that although the authority to impose and collect taxes continues to reside with the member states, they are required to exercise this authority consistent with EU law.[307] For example, the free movement rules may void a tax law of a member state which allows the parent company of a corporate group to only deduct losses of its subsidiaries in that particular member state and not losses of subsidiaries located in other member states.[308] By creating a tax disadvantage of having subsidiaries in other member states, the law deters the exercise of the freedom of establishment and violates Article 49 of the TFEU even though the authority to impose and collect taxes remains with the member states.

The practical application of this rule that the member states exercise their taxing authorities consistent with EU law means that member state tax measures are tested against the free movement rules similar to other restrictions. However, the politically sensitive nature of voiding national tax measures has forced the ECJ to be much more lenient on tax-related restrictions on the free movement principles than it has with other restrictions imposed by the member states.

---

305. Joined cases C-578/10 to C-580/10, Staatssecretaris van Financiën v. L.A.C. van Putten, 2012 E.C.R. I-___, at ¶37; C-194/06, Staatssecretaris van Financiën v. Orange European Smallcap Fund NV, 2008 E.C.R. I-3747, 3800 ¶32.
306. *See* Case C-167/05, Comm'n v. Sweden, 2008 E.C.R. I-2127.
307. Case C-310/09, Ministre du Budget, des Comptes publics et de la Fonction publique v. Accor SA, 2011 E.C.R. I-8150, 8165 ¶43; Case C-337/08, X Holding BV v. Staatssecretaris van Financiën, 2010 E.C.R. I-1237, 1246 ¶16; Case C-182/08, Glaxo Wellcome GmbH & Co KG v. Finanzamt München II, 2009 E.C.R. I-8591, 8642 ¶34; Case C-153/08, Comm'n v. Spain, 2009 E.C.R. I-9735, 9773 ¶28; Case C-347/04, Rewe Zentralfinanz eG v.v Finanzamt Köln-Mitte, 2007 E.C.R. I-2668, 2678 ¶21.
308. Case C-446/03, Marks & Spencer v. David Halsey, 2005 E.C.R. I-10866, 10875 ¶29. As discussed below, there are certain justifications for such restrictions.

The ECJ tends to give more scrutiny to the issue of whether the tax constitutes a restriction of one of the free movement principles. Taxes that indistinctly apply to foreign and domestic products or activities do not always constitute restrictions even though they may have a disparate effect.

In *Viacom Outdoor SrL v. Giotto Immobilier SARL*,[309] for example, a local Italian government imposed a tax on billboard advertising in that region of Italy. Although the law had the effect of restricting service providers in other member states from providing billboard services in Italy, the ECJ held that the tax did not violate Article 56 of the TFEU because it applied equally regardless of the nationality of the billboard advertiser and it was not disproportionately high related to the public costs of such billboard advertising.[310]

In *Commission v. Sweden*, the ECJ also took a more lenient approach to the tax measure. In that case, Sweden imposed taxes on wine but not beer.[311] Coincidentally, Sweden did not have much of a wine industry, but did have a stronger beer industry. The Commission argued that the tax on wine had the effect of placing the Swedish beer industry in an advantageous position vis-à-vis wine sellers from other member states. However, the ECJ concluded that the increase in the price of wine resulting from the tax was so insignificant that it would not influence the decisions of customers.[312] Consequently, the tax was held to be permissible under the TFEU.

A different outcome may have resulted in these cases if the state measure at issue were not a tax measure. In *Konsumentombudsmannen v. Gourmet International Products AB*, for example, a Swedish law prohibiting advertisements for alcohol was held to be a restriction on the free movement of goods because it made it more difficult for non-Swedish sellers of alcohol to enter the Swedish market.[313] In contrast to *Commission v. Sweden*, the ECJ did not address whether the effect was significant or not.

Another case that illustrates the lenient approach taken by the ECJ in applying the free movement principles to tax measures of member states is *Heirs of M.E.A. van Hilten-van der Heijden v. Inspecteur van de Belastingdienst/ Particulieren/Ondernemingen buitenland te Heerlen*.[314] At issue in that case was a Dutch tax law which stated that for purposes of inheritance taxes, the Netherlands would be deemed to be the place of residence for Dutch nationals who die within 10 years after having moved from the Netherlands. In this particular case, Ms. Van Hilten-van der Heijden, a national of the Netherlands, moved away from the Netherlands in 1988 and died in 1997. The heirs of

---

309. Case C-134/03, Viacom Outdoor SrL v. Giotto Immobilier SARL, 2005 E.C.R. I-1167.
310. *Id.* at ¶38.
311. Case C-167/05, Comm'n v. Sweden, 2008 E.C.R. I-2127.
312. *Id.* at 2170 ¶58.
313. Case C-405/98, Konsumentombudsmannen v. Gourmet Int'l Products AB, 2001 E.C.R. I-1795, 1825 ¶25.
314. Case C-513/03, Heirs of M.E.A. van Hilten-van der Heijden v. Inspecteur van de Belastingdienst/Particulieren/Ondernemingen buitenland te Heerlen, 2006 E.C.R. I-1957.

Ms. Hilten-van der Heijden argued that the Dutch law violated the free movement of capital under the TFEU because it had the effect of affecting the flow of capital in the EU. However, the ECJ concluded that the tax law did not have an effect on the free movement of capital.[315] This conclusion would likely have been different if the case had not involved the exercise of a taxing authority by a member state.

6.3 Justifications

Tax laws that violate one of the free movement principles are not automatically prohibited. There are several important judicially created bases as well as some statutorily based justifications for national tax measures which would otherwise violate the TFEU provisions on the free movement of goods, services, labor, or establishment.

(a) Judicially Created Justifications

(1) Imperative Requirements in the Public Interest

As stated above, the general rule applicable to the relationship between the free movement principles and the right to tax retained by the member states is that the member states are required to observe the TFEU rules in exercising their taxation authorities. The introduction of this rule clarified that the taxation authorities retained by the member states are not absolute. This limitation of the sovereign right of the member states causes some consternation at the national level when it is applied in individual cases. Sensitive political circumstances often require pragmatic judicial solutions. As discussed above, the ECJ has developed the doctrine of imperative requirements to employ in those cases where the dogmatic application of EU law may result in a politically unacceptable or difficult situation. The inherent tension between the free movement principles and the retained taxation authorities of the member states has resulted in the extension of this imperative requirements doctrine—first introduced by the ECJ in *Rewe-Zentral AG v. Bundesmonopolverwaltung für Branntwein*[316] in the context of nontax restrictions on the free movement of goods—to the field of taxation.[317]

Based on imperative requirements in the public interest, the ECJ has justified tax-related restrictions on the free movement principles where the situations of the resident and nonresident are not objectively comparable, or where the tax measure was necessary to counter abuse or tax avoidance, to ensure the effectiveness of fiscal supervision, or to safeguard the coherence of the tax system. Similar to the imperative requirements doctrine applicable to nontax measures, the imperative requirements in the public interest justification is a

---

315. *Id.* at ¶47.
316. Case 120/78 Rewe-Zentral AG v. Bundesmonopolverwaltung für Branntwein, 1979 E.C.R. 649, 662 ¶8.
317. Case C-10/10, Comm'n v. Austria, 2011 E.C.R. I-5416, 5429 ¶37; Case C-287/10, Tankreederei I SA v. Directeur de l'administration des contributions directes, 2011 E.C.R. I-14235, 14242 ¶19.

malleable concept which is not susceptible to precise delineation. Only some of the reoccurring themes are discussed here.

(2) Counteract Abuse or Tax Avoidance

A member state tax measure that restricts one of the free movement principles may be justified if the purpose of the tax measure is to counteract tax avoidance or abuse. The EU courts have consistently held that the mere avoidance of a loss of tax revenue does not in itself justify a restriction on one of the fundamental freedoms.[318] At issue in *X v. Staatssecretaris van Financiën* was a Dutch law that applied a 12-year statute of limitations for tax evasion using accounts or assets outside of the Netherlands. The standard duration of the statute of limitations was five years. A Dutch national opened an account in Luxembourg in 1993. He used the account to avoid taxes in the Netherlands. In 2002, the Dutch tax authorities discovered the account and imposed back taxes and penalties on the Dutch national. In his defense, the Dutch national argued that the Dutch law imposing a different statute of limitations for tax evasion using foreign accounts violated the free movement of services because it dissuaded Dutch nationals from seeking financial services outside of the Netherlands. The ECJ held that, although the Dutch law restricted the free movement of services, it was justified by imperative requirements in the public interest because it "contributes to the effectiveness of fiscal supervision and to the prevention of tax evasion."[319]

In order to benefit from this exception, the specific objective of the measure must be "to prevent conduct involving the creation of wholly artificial arrangements which do not reflect economic reality with a view to escaping the tax normally due on the profits generated by activities carried out on national territory.[320] In addition, the tax measure must be narrowly tailored to address tax avoidance. A measure generally addressed at compensating for lower tax rates in other member states will not benefit from this exception. The ECJ has repeatedly referred to "artificial arrangements" aimed at circumventing the application of the legislation of the member state concerned.[321]

In *Cadbury Schweppes plc v. Commissioners of Inland Revenue*, the UK passed a law that taxed UK companies on income of their subsidiaries in other member states where taxes were lower than in the UK.[322] The purpose of the law was to prevent UK companies from creating subsidiaries in low-tax member states (in this case Ireland) and shifting income to those subsidiaries from the

---

318. Case C-190/72, Emerging Markets Series of DFA Investment Trust Co. v. Dyrektor Izby Skarbowej w Bydgoszezy, 2014 E.C.R. I-___, ___ ¶102.
319. Joined cases C-155/08 and C-157/08, X v. Staatssecretaris van Financiën, 2009 E.C.R. I-5093, 5116 ¶52.
320. C-80/12, Felixstowe Dock and Railway Co. Ltd. v. The Commissioners for Her Majesty's Revenue & Customs, 2014 E.C.R. I-___, at ¶33.
321. Case C-318/10, Société d'investissement pour l'agriculture tropicale SA v. Belgium, 2012 E.C.R. I-___, at ¶40; Case C-311/08, Société de Gestion Industriielle SA v. État belge, 2010 E.C.R. I-511, 531 ¶65; Case C-196/04, Cadbury Schweppes plc v. Commissioners of Inland Revenue, 2006 E.C.R. I-7995, 8047 ¶51.
322. Case C-196/04, Cadbury Schweppes plc v. Commissioners of Inland Revenue, 2006 E.C.R. I-7995.

UK. A strict application of the freedom of establishment would have prevented the UK from implementing the tax law because it had the effect of dissuading UK companies from exercising the freedom of establishment in other member states.[323] However, the ECJ held that Ireland was justified in imposing such a restriction on the freedom of establishment to prevent abuse by companies of this freedom.[324] If, however, the establishment involves "genuine economic activities," the member state cannot rely on the abuse exception even if the purpose of the establishment was to reduce the tax burden of the company. The ECJ remanded the case to the national court to make this determination.

(3) *Effectiveness of Fiscal Supervision Justification*

As early as the *Cassis de Dijon* case, the ECJ has recognized the effectiveness of fiscal supervision to be an imperative requirement in the public interest justifying a restriction on the free movement principles.[325] The ECJ has extended this same justification to tax measures adopted by the member states.[326] The rationale behind the justification is that certain tax measures are simply necessary in order to allow the member states to effectively enforce their tax laws. At issue in *Futura Participations SA v. Administration des contributions* was a Luxembourg law requiring nonresident taxpayers to keep accounts in Luxembourg in accordance with the bookkeeping rules of Luxembourg if they wanted to deduct losses from their income when calculating their income tax. In this case, the application of the Luxembourg law required Futura, a French company, to maintain separate records for its Luxembourg branch office if it wanted to be able to write off the losses sustained by that branch office in Luxembourg. Although the ECJ considered this to be a restriction on the freedom of establishment,[327] it agreed with Luxembourg in that the tax measure was necessary for effective fiscal supervision. The rule was considered necessary for Luxembourg to make sure that the losses which Futura wished to set off against its income in Luxembourg did in fact arise from its Luxembourg activities and that the amount of the losses corresponded, under Luxembourg rules relating to the calculation of income and losses, to the amount of losses actually incurred

---

323. *Id.* 8046 ¶46.
324. *Id.* at 8047 ¶51. *See also* Case C-231/05, *In re* Oy AA, 2007 E.C.R. I-6393, 6413 ¶67 in which the ECJ came to the same conclusion regarding a similar Finnish law.
325. Case 120/78 Rewe-Zentral AG v. Bundesmonopolverwaltung für Branntwein, 1979 E.C.R. 649, 662 ¶8.
326. Case C-318/07, Persche v. Finanzamt Lüdenscheid, 2009 E.C.R. I-359, 408 ¶52.
327. Case C-250/95, Futura Participations v. Administration des contributions, 1997 E.C.R. I-2471, 2500 ¶24 ("It means in practice that if such a company or firm wishes to carry forward any losses incurred by its branch, it must keep, in addition to its own accounts which must comply with the tax accounting rules applicable in the Member State in which it has its seat, separate accounts for its branch's activities complying with the tax accounting rules applicable in the State in which its branch is established. Furthermore, those separate accounts must be held, not at the company's seat, but at the place of establishment of its branch. Consequently, the imposition of such a condition, which specifically affects companies or firms having their seat in another Member State, is in principle prohibited by Article 52 of the Treaty.").

by the taxpayer. According to the ECJ, "the effectiveness of fiscal supervision constitutes an overriding requirement of general interest capable of justifying a restriction on the exercise of fundamental freedoms guaranteed by the Treaty. A Member State may therefore apply measures which enable the amount of both the income taxable in that State and of the losses which can be carried forward there to be ascertained clearly and precisely."[328]

The application of the *Futura* case to other factual constellations is limited. In most cases, the ECJ is unwilling to recognize the effectiveness of fiscal supervision as a justification for a restriction on the free movement principles.[329] This is because Council Directive 77/799[330] and its subsequent amendments address many of the tax supervision loopholes created by the member states retaining separate taxing authority.[331] For example, Directive 77/799 allows the national tax authorities to exchange information on a person's income in order to detect any tax avoidance schemes. Hence, it becomes difficult for a member state to justify a tax law based on the argument that it is a necessary component of its fiscal supervision activities.[332]

(4) Safeguarding the Coherence of the Tax System

The ECJ has also recognized an exception to the free movement principles for measures that are necessary to ensure the coherence of the national tax system.[333] In *Bachmann v. Belgium*, for example, Belgian income tax legislation recognized tax deductions for life insurance premiums paid by individuals to insurance companies but only if the life insurance company was established in Belgium. Bachmann, a German who happened to work in Belgium, tried to deduct from his Belgian income tax the insurance premiums that he paid to his German insurance company. After Bachmann's deduction was not recognized by the Belgian tax authorities, he challenged the law as an infringement of the freedom of movement for insurance services. The ECJ held that the Belgian law had the effect of dissuading an individual residing in Belgium from dealing with an

---

328. Case C-250/95, Futura Participations v. Singer, 1997 E.C.R. I-2471, 2501 ¶31.
329. Case C-254/97, Société Baxter v. Premier Ministre, 1999 E.C.R. I-4809; Case C-55/98, Skatteministeriet v. Vestergaard, 1999 E.C.R. I-7641.
330. Council Directive 77/799/EEC of 19 December 1977 concerning mutual assistance by the competent authorities of the member states in the field of direct taxation and taxation of insurance premiums, 1977 O.J. (L 336) 1.
331. *See, e.g.*, Case C-55/98, Skatteministeriet v. Vestergaard, 1999 E.C.R. I-7641, 7667 ¶26.
332. As Council Directive 77/799 does not apply to the non-EU countries that are part of the European Economic Area (EEA), national tax laws which may not be justified as applied to EU countries, may be justified if they apply to non-EU EEA countries such as Liechtenstein. Case C-72/09, Établissements Rimbaud SA v. Directeur général des impôts, 2010 E.C.R. I-10680, 10698 ¶51. This is because the EU member states do not have the same enforcement tools vis-à-vis the non-EU EEA countries as they do vis-à-vis the EU member states.
333. Case C-493/09, Comm'n v. Portugal, 2011 E.C.R. I-9264, 9274 ¶35; Case C-169/08, Presidente del Consiglio del Ministri v. Regione Sardegna, ECLI:EU:C:2009:709 at ¶47; Case C-182/08, Glaxo Wellcome GmbH & Co KG v. Finanzamt München II, 2009 E.C.R. I-8591, 8652 ¶77.

insurer established abroad rather than with an insurer established in Belgium and therefore constituted a restriction on the free movement of services. However, the ECJ followed the argument of the Belgian government and held that the Belgian law was justified because it was necessary to ensure the cohesion of the national tax system.[334]

The coherence exception is a recognition that a strict application of the free movement principles could challenge the cohesiveness of the tax system. The meaning of cohesion is best explained by reference to the underlying facts of the *Bachmann* case. Although Hanns-Martin Bachmann worked in Belgium, it was likely that he would return to Germany, where he maintained his residence and where he would likely receive the insurance benefits.[335] In other words, if the Belgian tax system allowed Bachmann to deduct his insurance payments while working in Belgium, it would have no way of taxing the payments later when paid out to Bachmann (or his heirs) later in Germany. This possibility was enough to convince the ECJ that the cohesion of the Belgian tax system would be threatened if the free movement principles were applied to prevent the application of the Belgian law. Consequently, the application of the coherence justification is subject to the requirement of a direct link between the tax advantage and the offsetting of that tax advantage by the particular tax.[336]

In *Bachmann*, for example, the deduction of the insurance contributions was linked to the taxation of insurance payouts.[337] In other words, the system granting a tax benefit (i.e., the tax deduction) would only make sense if Belgium were able to tax the proceeds which that taxpayer received from the insurance company related to the policy for which the taxpayer received the deduction. If the insurer were located outside Belgium, it would be very difficult for Belgium to track and tax these payouts. Consequently, there was a direct link between the tax advantage and the offsetting of that advantage by the particular tax.

In *Presidente del Consiglio del Ministri v. Regione Sardegna*, the region of Sardinia argued that a tax imposed on aircraft stopovers where the aircraft was registered outside the region was justified by the need to secure the cohesion of its tax system. The tax was not imposed on resident aircraft because they paid other taxes. According to the ECJ, however, there was no direct link between the nonimposition of the aircraft tax on those resident aircraft and the pollution abatement efforts as the other taxes paid by the resident aircraft "serve to fund the State budget in a general way and thereby to finance all the activities of the Region of Sardinia.[338]

---

334. Case C-204/90, Bachmann v. Belgium, 1992 E.C.R. I-249, 283 ¶28.
335. *Id.* at 280 ¶11.
336. Case C-190/72, Emerging Markets Series of DFA Investment Trust Co. v. Dyrektor Izby Skarbowej w Bydgoszezy, 2014 E.C.R. I-___, at ¶92; Case C-493/09, Comm'n v. Portugal, 2011 E.C.R. I-9264, 9274 ¶36; Case C-104/06, Comm'n v. Sweden, 2007 E.C.R. I-671, 683 ¶26.
337. Case C-204/90, Bachmann v. Belgium, 1992 ECR I-249, 282 ¶23.
338. Case C-169/08, Presidente del Consiglio del Ministri v. Regione Sardegna, 2009 E.C.R. ECLI:EU:C:2009:709 at ¶48.

In contrast to tax abuse or avoidance cases, reliance on the cohesion justification does not require the inference of an illicit intent on behalf of the taxpayer.[339] There is no indication in the *Bachmann* case that the taxpayer selection of residence was motivated by the desire to avoid taxes. This explains why, although the member states continue to attempt to justify their tax laws by claiming that they are necessary to ensure the cohesion of their tax systems, the ECJ has consistently rejected such arguments.[340] In other words, the ECJ is more receptive to national tax laws which are designed to counter some malfeasance. Reliance on the cohesion exception has been successful in only one other case.[341] There is a general consensus that the cohesion exception introduced in the *Bachmann* case is of limited use and may be limited to those particular facts.[342]

(b) Justifications Codified in the TFEU

In addition to the judicially created justifications discussed above, the TFEU expressly permits certain tax laws which restrict the free movement of capital. According to Article 81(1)(a) of the TFEU, the free movement of capital rule cannot be applied to prevent a member state from adopting tax laws that distinguish between taxpayers who are not in the same situation with regard to their place of residence or with regard to the place where their capital is invested. The fundamental requirement is that the national tax measure must not constitute a form of arbitrary discrimination. If the unequal treatment can be explained by situations that are not objectively comparable, the national tax measure is justified.[343] According to the ECJ, for example, in relation to income taxes, the situations of residents and nonresidents within a member state are generally not comparable because the income received in that member state by a nonresident is typically only a small portion of that nonresident's overall income.[344] Consequently, a tax law which treats residents and nonresidents differently for income tax purposes is not arbitrarily discriminatory.

---

339. The application of the tax avoidance justification requires proof of an aim to circumvent the tax law. Case C-540/07, Comm'n v. Italy, 2009 E.C.R. I-11007, 11025 ¶58.
340. C-293/06, Deutsche Shell GmbH v. Finanzamt für Großunternehmen in Hamburg, 2008 E.C.R. I-1147, 1161 ¶40; Case C-281/06, Jundt v. Finanzamt Offenburg, 2007 E.C.R. I-12246, 12267 ¶73; Case C-379/05, Amurta SGPS v. Inspecteur van de Belastingdienst, 2007 E.C.R. I-9569.
341. Case C-300/90, Comm'n v. Belgium, 1992 E.C.R. I-305.
342. The ECJ has been unwilling to apply the cohesion justification in other cases. *See, e.g.*, Case C-168/01, Bosal Holding BV v. Staatssecretaris van Financiën, 2003 E.C.R. I-9430; Case C-136/00, Danner v. Finland, 2002 E.C.R. I-8147; Case C-251/98, Baars v. Inspecteur der Belastingen Particulieren, 2000 E.C.R. I-2787.
343. Case C-10/10, Comm'n v. Austria, 2011 E.C.R. I-5416, 5427 ¶29; Case C-337/08, X Holding BV v. Staatssecretaris van Financiën, 2010 E.C.R. I-1237, 1247 ¶20; Case C-440/08, Gielen v. Staatssecretaris van Financiën, 2010 E.C.R. I-2345, 2357 ¶43.
344. Case C-562/07, Comm'n v. Spain, 2009 E.C.R. I-9553, 9571 ¶46.

In *J.E.J. Blanckaert v. Inspecteur van de Belastingdients*,[345] the Netherlands disallowed tax credits for a Belgian whose only income in the Netherlands was from a vacation home in the Netherlands which he rented out. The rental income in the Netherlands was subject to Dutch taxes. To qualify for a tax credit for expenses related to this home under Dutch law, the Belgian would have had to be employed in the Netherlands and be paying into the social security system in the Netherlands. Blanckaert, a Belgian, claimed that this violated the principle of free movement of capital as it deterred foreign investors by treating them differently than Dutch residents. The ECJ held, however, that the unequal treatment was justified by the objective difference in residency between Blanckaert (residing in Belgium) and Dutch citizens who were employed and paying taxes in Holland into the social security system.[346]

In *Margaretha Bouanich v. Skatteverket*, Bouanich, a French citizen and resident, was a shareholder of Ratos, a Swedish publicly listed company.[347] Ratos then announced a reduction in its share capital and repurchased the shares held by Bouanich for €917,000. A legal issue arose, however, because Swedish tax law distinguished between resident shareholders and nonresident shareholders. Under Swedish law, the income derived from a repurchase of shares by a Swedish company from a resident shareholder was taxed as a capital gain to the shareholder. For nonresident shareholders, however, the income derived from the repurchase was treated as a dividend distribution by the company.

This different treatment created a significant difference in tax liability as taxes on capital gains are only imposed on the difference between the price at which the shares were purchased and the price at which they were sold. Taxes on dividends are imposed on the full amount of the dividend. After holding that this presented a case of unequal treatment, the ECJ addressed the issue of whether the exception codified in Article 81(1)(a) of the TFEU (justification based on recognition that the unequally treated taxpayers are in different situations) was applicable. The ECJ concluded that the situations of the resident Swedish shareholder and the nonresident Swedish shareholder were objectively comparable. Consequently, the unequal treatment was considered arbitrary discrimination and outside the scope of the exception codified in Article 81(1)(a) of the TFEU.[348]

The issue in *In re Petri Manninen* was whether a Finnish income tax law which granted a tax credit for dividend income received by Finnish taxpayers only from Finnish corporations should be considered permitted unequal treatment or arbitrary discrimination.[349] Manninen, a Finnish national and resident, held shares in a Swedish company. Under Swedish law, Manninen had to pay taxes in Sweden on the dividends issued to him by the Swedish company. Because

---

345. Case C-512/03, J.E.J. Blanckaert v. Inspecteur van de Belastingdients, 2005 E.C.R. I-7685.
346. *Id.* at 7721 ¶51.
347. Case C-265/04, Margaretha Bouanich v. Skatteverket, 2006 E.C.R. I-923, 956 ¶¶36-38.
348. *Id.* at 957 ¶43.
349. Case C-319/02, *In re* Petri Manninen, 2004 E.C.R. I-7477.

the Finnish tax credit only extended to dividends issued by Finnish companies, which meant that he had to pay taxes twice on the same dividend income, Manninen argued that the Finnish law violated Article 63 of the TFEU. The ECJ first recognized that the law had the effect of deterring Finnish taxpayers from investing in companies located in other member states and created an obstacle to companies from other member states raising capital in Finland. Hence, the law was characterized as a restriction on the free movement of capital. The ECJ concluded that because Finnish shareholders and shareholders from other member states were in objectively comparable situations in view of the purpose of the law (which was to prevent double taxation), the restriction created by the Finnish law was not justified.[350]

7. Harmonization

7.1 Harmonizing Directives

In recognition of the fact that legitimate differences in national laws and regulations may hinder trade between member states, the EU has attempted to harmonize the laws of the member states by issuing directives applicable to a wide array of commerce. Although these differences are prohibited in many instances based on the free movement principles discussed above, the various exceptions codified in the TFEU still permit the member states to maintain some of these differences. Many of these national laws and regulations are justified based on public concerns that are common throughout the EU. For example, whether the inclusion of particular artificial preservatives in foodstuffs presents a public health threat presents the same issue for all member states. Such foods present the same threat to a Swedish citizen as they do to a Greek citizen. Therefore, many of the national laws and regulations which are justified by the exemptions are amenable to harmonization by the EU.

Article 114 of the TFEU expressly gives the EU the authority to adopt directives designed to harmonize the laws of the member states. As discussed above, the harmonizing directives adopted by the EU may preempt the application of national law and the reliance by the member state on one of the exemptions to the free movement principles.[351] For example, a member state may not rely on public health grounds to justify a restriction on the free movement of goods if the public health concerns presented by the product at issue are already addressed in an EU directive. The basic idea is that the EU institutions, in adopting the legislation, took into account the legitimate concerns of the member states as relates to the public policy concerns that may otherwise justify the reliance on

---

350. *Id.* at 7509 ¶37.
351. Case C-100/13, Commission v. Germany, 2014 E.C.R. I-___, at ¶62; Case C-322/01, Deutscher Apothekerverband v. 0800 Doc Morris, 2003 E.C.R. I-14887, 15006 ¶139; Case C-99/01, Gottfried Linhart v. Hans Biffl, 2002 E.C.R. I-9375, 9401 ¶18.

an exemption. Preemption requires that the directive seeks to establish a fully harmonized system of rules to replace the existing national rules.[352]

7.2 Technical Standards

The harmonizing directives applicable to goods set forth essential requirements which the goods must fulfill before they are introduced on the market in the EU. This applies regardless of whether the products are manufactured in a member state or outside the EU.[353] A good is placed on the market when it is made available (free or for a price) for the first time in the EU. Products manufactured in the EU which are made for export are not considered to be placed on the market in the EU. Moreover, the mere manufacture and stocking of the product in inventory by the manufacturer does not constitute placing the goods on the market.

The essential requirements only provide the results to be attained relating to certain public concerns. They do not offer any specific guidance for manufacturers as to the technical characteristics which address these concerns. In order to facilitate compliance with these essential requirements and provide manufacturers with some legal certainty, the European standards bodies (European Committee for Standardization (CEN), European Committee for Electrotechnical Standardization (CENELEC) and European Telecommunications Standards Institute (ETSI)) have established a system of harmonized technical standards relating to specific products.[354] Compliance with a harmonized standard establishes a presumption of compliance with the applicable essential requirements. The member states must then recognize the compliance of that product with the essential requirements set forth in the applicable directive.

There are standards that exist for an extremely large number of products in the EU.[355] National standards are only relevant if European harmonized standards have not been adopted for the particular product. Although compliance with the essential requirements is mandatory, compliance with the technical standards relating to a particular product is voluntary. A manufacturer may still introduce products into the stream of commerce in the EU provided that the products comply with the essential requirements. In such cases, the manufacturer must conduct a demonstration of conformity with a third party certification body.

---

352. Case C-12/00, Comm'n v. Spain, 2003 E.C.R. I-459, 502 ¶65.
353. The directives generally apply to new products manufactured in the EU or outside the EU as well as second-hand goods imported into the EU.
354. The task of adopting technical specifications to meet the essential requirements established in the directives is entrusted by the EU Commission to the three European standards bodies: European Committee for Standardization (CEN); European Committee for Electrotechnical Standardization (CENELEC); and European Telecommunications Standards Institute (ETSI).
355. The absence of a European standard does not mean that the member states are free to adopt whatever standards they deem appropriate. National standards must still comply with the free movement rules. Case C-484/10, Asociación para la Calidad de los Forjados v. Administración del Estado, 2012 E.C.R. I-___, at ¶50.

These are independent bodies, designated by the respective member states, which have the technical capacity to determine whether the essential requirements are fulfilled even though the product at issue does not technically conform to the standards adopted by the European standardization bodies.

In both instances—conformity with the standards or demonstration of conformity—the manufacturer will then issue a declaration of conformity. The CE marking (Conformité Européenne) can then be affixed to the products. The legal significance of the CE mark is that it indicates that a product complies with the applicable essential requirements. The member states are not allowed to prohibit or hinder the sale of products with a CE marking regardless of their origin. As the United States relies on a similar system of technical standards, the EU and the United States have entered into a Mutual Recognition Agreement which alleviates the necessity to comply with many of the steps in the process.

CHAPTER **III**

Regulation of Competition

1. The Context of European Competition Law

1.1 Purpose of Competition Law

All societies must deal with the issue of the proper allocation of scarce resources. This arises from the realization that not everyone can have everything they want all of the time. Consequently, there must be some method by which scarce resources are allocated. The European Union (EU) and its member states generally rely on the market to allocate scarce resources. The proper functioning of the market, however, depends on competition between the market actors. Competition is considered to be the mechanism by which consumers ensure that they are receiving the best quality goods and services at the lowest possible prices. Consequently, competition is worthy of protection.

There is a general consensus in market economies that competition is not self-regulating. Because the potential rewards to companies of distorting or eliminating competition are high, there is an incentive for market actors to engage in anticompetitive conduct. For example, it may be beneficial for two paper producers to agree to set a minimum price for their paper rather than to compete with one another on price for customers. In such circumstances, they may be able to charge a higher price for their products than in the absence of an agreement. This results in a detriment to society (sometimes referred to as welfare loss) in the form of artificially high prices.

Competition law, as a form of state intervention in the market, is based on the recognition that competition is not self-regulating. By protecting competition, the law secures the benefits of the market and avoids the detriments of market distortions. It is important to remember that competition law is a form of market intervention by the state. The legitimacy of competition law rests on the consensus that state intervention in the market is necessary. This consensus is present in most market economies, including the EU member states. The central challenge of competition law is not *whether* the state should intervene in the market, but rather *when* the state should do so. This is ultimately a political decision. A recognition of the political context of competition law is necessary to understanding the EU competition law regime because it has an influence on how the law is applied.

It is difficult to discern one goal of EU competition law. Economic efficiency, market integration, justice and fairness, commercial freedom, and industrial policy have all been used to justify or at least influence the application of EU competition law by the European Commission and the EU courts. The presence of these considerations in the decisional practice of the Commission and EU courts, together with the lack of clear guidance as to when they apply, adds to the legal uncertainty surrounding the application of the EU competition laws to business practices.

1.2 Unique Character of Competition Law

EU competition law differs from other legal fields addressed in the Treaty on the Functioning of the European Union (TFEU) in two important respects. First, the Commission has the authority to enforce the competition rules directly (i.e., without having to seek the approval of the other EU institutions). This authority is granted in Article 105 of the TFEU. In other fields of law, the Commission does not enjoy this authority. For example, the Commission has the authority to initiate anti-dumping investigations, but the ultimate decision to impose definitive anti-dumping sanctions is with the Council. Second, the Commission has the authority to adopt secondary competition legislation without the involvement (and sometimes with the involvement) of the European Council. This authority is granted in Article 106(3) of the TFEU. One of the Commission's main tasks in this area, for example, is to adopt decisions directed toward undertakings. When a company violates the EU competition laws, the Commission issues a decision addressed specifically to the companies involved.

1.3 Relationship to Free Movement Rules

Assume that a French car manufacturer agrees with each of its EU distributors (who are each assigned exclusive territories based on national boundaries) that they may not sell to foreign buyers, including buyers from other member states. For example, the Spanish distributor may not sell cars to anyone in Portugal even if someone from Portugal orders one while on a holiday in Spain. This conduct has essentially the same effect as that which Article 34 of the TFEU is trying to prohibit: it is a barrier to commerce between member states. However, Articles 34 and 35 of the TFEU do not apply to this conduct because, as discussed in Chapter III, Article 34 applies only to *state measures* which restrict the flow of goods between member states.

The inapplicability of Article 34 to such facts does not mean the conduct is necessarily legal. The TFEU also contains competition rules which are addressed to the conduct of companies (as opposed to the conduct of states). As stated by the European Court of Justice (ECJ), Articles 101 and 102 of the TFEU "are concerned solely with the conduct of undertakings and not with laws or regulations emanating from Member States."[1] In the example above, the competition rules and not the free movement rules would apply. In this respect, the competition rules, which are codified in Articles 101 to 106 of the

---

1. Case C-393/08, Sbarigia v. Azienda USL RM/A, 2010 E.C.R. I-6360, 6372 ¶31.

TFEU, complement the four freedoms by serving the same general objective: to remove and deter barriers to trade between member states.

2. Taxonomy of Competition Law

The most basic distinction made by competition law practitioners and regulators is among bilateral, unilateral, and structural restraints of competition. The term bilateral restraint generally refers to agreements or concerted practices between two or more entities that restrict competition. An agreement between competing sugar producers to offer their products at certain target prices is an example of a bilateral restraint of competition.[2] A unilateral restraint, on the other hand, refers to conduct by one entity that has the effect of restraining competition. A unilateral restraint of competition exists, for example, when a dominant software manufacturer refuses to sell its dominant software unless customers also purchase another product from the dominant manufacturer.[3] As discussed below, the fundamental prerequisite for the ability to unilaterally restrain competition is market power.

The third and final type of restraint of competition is structural restraints. This category refers to those transactions that reduce competition through a change in the competitive relationships between firms. The change in competitive relationship typically results from a change in control over a business. For example, if McDonald's were to acquire Burger King, for purposes of competition law the competitive relationship between those two entities would change even if they were subsequently operated as separate entities. The assumption is that firms belonging to the same corporate group do not compete with each other. Although these types of restraints, similar to multilateral restraints, involve agreements between two or more firms, they are generally treated separately because of the perceived need to subject transactions having a potential anticompetitive structural effect to ex ante control.

The categorical distinctions between these three types of restraints of competition are important to understand because there is a difference between the legal norms that apply to each: Bilateral restraints are examined under Article 101 of the TFEU. Unilateral restraints are usually examined under Article 102. Structural restraints are examined under secondary legislation known as the Merger Control Regulation.

---

2. *See, e.g.*, British Sugar, 1999 O.J (L 76) 1.
3. Case T-201/04, Microsoft Corp. v. Comm'n, 2007 E.C.R. II-3601.

3. Subjects of the Law: Undertakings

The EU competition rules apply only to undertakings.[4] The term "undertaking" is broader than the notions of corporation or legal entity. According to the ECJ, the choice of the term undertaking by the drafters of the Treaty of Rome represents a conscious decision to expand the scope of the competition laws to more than just "companies" as that term is used in Article 54 of the TFEU.[5] The general definition applied by the EU courts is "any entity engaged in an economic activity, regardless of its legal status and the way in which it is financed."[6] An economic activity consists of offering goods or services on a given market.[7] The concept of undertaking may include more than one legal entity.[8]

In *Knauf Gips KG v. Commission*, for example, the ECJ held that the various companies owned by the Knauf family all belonged to the same economic unit and were therefore to be considered constituent elements of one undertaking for purposes of EU competition law.[9] Whether separate legal entities all belong to the same undertaking is a factual determination to be made in each case. The relevant factors mentioned by the ECJ in *Knauf Gips KG v. Commission* were overlap in shareholders, overlap in management, access to its own personal and financial resources to operate on its market, and the existence of coordination between the shareholders as to the operation of the legal entities.[10] As discussed below in greater detail, the expansive interpretation of undertaking to potentially include more than one legal entity has important implications on identifying an

---

4. The use of the English term "undertaking" is a result of the influence of the Germans in the early development of competition law. The first English-speaking countries (the United Kingdom and Ireland) did not join the EEC until 1973. Consequently, the early development of EU competition law, including its nomenclature, was heavily influenced by the Germans. The term undertaking is a literal translation of the German term *Unternehmen* which is an established German legal concept. § 14 German Civil Code [Bürgerliches Gesetzbuch].
5. Case C-231/11P to 233/11P, Comm'n v. Siemens AG Österreich, 2014 E.C.R. I-___, at ¶42; Case C-501/11P, Schindler Holding Ltd. v. Comm'n, 2013 E.C.R. I-___, at ¶102.
6. Case C-444/11/P, Team Relocations NV v. Comm'n, 2013 E.C.R.; Case C-520/09P, Arkema SA v. Comm'n, 2011 E.C.R. I-8918, 8930 ¶37; Case C-350/07, Kattner Stahlbau GmbH v. Maschinenbau- und Metall-Berufsgenossenschaft, 2009 E.C.R. I-1513, 1551 ¶34.
7. Case C-437/09, AG2R Prévoyance v. Beaudout Père et Fils SARL, 2011 E.C.R. I-1003, 1022 ¶42; Case C-113/07 P, Selex Sistemi Integrati SpA v. Comm'n, 2009 E.C.R. I-2207, 2273 ¶69. In Cases T-117/07 and 121/07, Areva SA v. Comm'n, 2011 E.C.R. II-649, 670 ¶63 *aff'd on appeal* Joined cases C-247/11P and 253/11P, Alstom SA v. Comm'n, 2014 E.C.R. I-___, the General Court stated that the "economic unit" must "consist of a unitary organisation of personal, tangible and intangible elements which pursues a specific economic aim on a long-term basis and can contribute to the commission of an infringement of the kind referred to in that provision."
8. Case T-325/01, DaimlerChrysler v. Comm'n, 2005 E.C.R. II-3319, 3357 ¶85.
9. Case C-407/08 P, Knauf Gips KG v. Comm'n, 2010 E.C.R. I-6415, 6445 ¶72.
10. *Id.* at 6443-4 ¶¶66-69.

agreement between undertakings, the imposition of liability on parent companies for competition law violations of their subsidiaries, and the determination of fines in competition law cases.

The fact that an entity is not for profit does not preclude it from qualifying as an undertaking. The competition rules apply to nonprofit undertakings as long as they are engaged in economic activities.[11] Moreover, the mere fact that a particular economic activity is regulated by the state does not mean that it falls outside the scope of the EU competition laws. Lawyers, for example, are considered undertakings even though their conduct is regulated by the member states.[12]

An undertaking may be a natural person or a legal entity. In *RAI/UNITEL*, the competition laws of the TFEU were applied to opera singers. In the *French Beef* decision, the Commission concluded that individual farmers are to be considered undertakings because they engage in an economic activity.[13] However, the extension of the concept of undertakings to natural persons has its limits. A strict application of the "engaged in economic activity" standard would mean that an employee would also be considered an undertaking for purposes of EU competition law. After all, an employee is merely selling his or her services on a long-term basis to one customer. Taken one step further, a labor union or a group of employees who have banded together to collectively negotiate their wages and terms of employment would then be considered a cartel because it is concerted conduct between undertakings to set a minimum price (i.e., salary, benefits, and the terms of trade).

The Commission and the EU courts are not prepared to extend the broad definition of undertaking to employees or workers in the sense of Article 45 of the TFEU.[14] According to the ECJ, a worker is a natural person, employed by another entity, and is under the direction of that entity regarding his or her commercial activities and the time, place and substance of his or her work.[15] Consequently, collective bargaining agreements between employers and employees do not fall under Article 101(1) even though they may set

---

11. Case C-49/07, Motosykletisitiki Omospondia Ellados v. Dimosio, 2008 E.C.R. I-4863, 4902 ¶27; UEFA Broadcasting Regulations, 2001 O.J. (L 171) 12, 22 ¶47; French Beef, 2003 O.J. (L 209) 12, 30 ¶111. Nonetheless, the fact the entity does not have a profit motive is a relevant factor in the analysis. Case C-350/07, Kattner Stahlbau GmbH v. Maschinenbau- und Metall-Berufsgenossenschaft, 2009 E.C.R. I-1538, 1552 ¶35.
12. Case T-193/02, Piau v. Comm'n, 2005 E.C.R. II-209, 238 ¶69; Case C-309/99, J.C.J. Wouters, J.W. Savelbergh, Price Waterhouse Belastingadviseurs BV. v. Algemene Raad van de Nederlandse Orde van Advocaten, 2002 E.C.R. I-1653. However, as discussed below, undertakings may not be held responsible for their anticompetitive conduct if such conduct was compelled by the state.
13. French Beef, 2003 O.J. (L 209) 12, 30 ¶105.
14. Case C-22/98, BECU v. Comm'n, 1999 E.C.R. I-5665, 5692 ¶26.
15. Case C-413/13, FNV Kunsten Informatie en Media v. The Netherlands, 2014 E.C.R. I-___, at ¶36; Case C-109/04, Kranemann v. Land Nordrhein-Westfalen, 2005 E.C.R. I-2421, 2438 ¶12.

the prices which the employees are charging for their services.[16] A different conclusion results, however, when the members of the collective are themselves undertakings. In the *French Beef* decision, the prices for beef were set by a trade union comprised of farmers. After concluding that the farmers were to be considered undertakings, the Commission went on to hold that the trade union was an association of undertakings for purposes of the EU competition rules.[17]

Members of the liberal professions such as lawyers, notaries, accountants, physicians, architects, engineers, and pharmacists are not considered employees.[18] In *Pavel Pavlov v. Stichting Pensioenfonds Medische Specialisten*, a group of self-employed medical specialists established a foundation to collect and administer their pension contributions.[19] They then convinced the Dutch government to make contributions to this pension fund compulsory for all medical specialists admitted to practice in the Netherlands. Several medical specialists objected to the mandatory character of the contributions and claimed that the agreement to establish the fund violated Article 101 of the TFEU. In distinguishing this case from earlier employee collective bargaining cases, the ECJ held:[20]

> Article [101](1) of the Treaty must be interpreted as meaning that a decision taken by the members of a liberal profession to set up a pension fund responsible for managing a supplementary pension scheme and to request the public authorities to make membership of that fund compulsory for all the members of that profession does not, by reason of its nature or purpose, fall outside the scope of that provision. ...
> In the present cases, the medical specialists ... provide, in their capacity as self-employed economic operators, services on a market, namely the market in specialist medical services. They are paid by their patients for the services they provide and assume the financial risks attached to the pursuit of their activity. The self-employed medical specialists ... therefore carry on an economic activity and are thus undertakings... The complexity and technical nature of the services they provide and the fact that the practice of their profession is regulated cannot alter that conclusion.

---

16. Case C-437/09, AG2R Prévoyance v. Beaudout Père et Fils SARL, 2011 E.C.R. I-1003, 1017 ¶29.
17. French Beef, 2003 O.J. (L 209) 12, 31 ¶117.
18. Case C-1/12, Ordem dos Técnicos Oficiais de Contas v. Autoridade da Concorrência, 2013 E.C.R. I-___, at ¶38; Case C-309/99, Wouters v. Nederlandse Orde van Advocaten, 2002 E.C.R. I-1653, 1680 ¶64.
19. Joined Cases C-180/98 to C-184/98, Pavel Pavlov v. Stichting Pensioenfonds Medische Specialisten, 2000 E.C.R. I-6451.
20. *Id.* at 6519 ¶70.

Independent contractors fall somewhere between employees and the liberal professions and present a challenge for competition law as it is difficult to distinguish between employees and independent contractors. In *FNV Kunsten Informatie en Media v. The Netherlands*, for example, the issue was whether substitute musicians which were engaged by orchestras on an ad hoc basis were employees (and hence outside the scope of the competition laws when negotiating collective bargaining agreements) or independent contractors (and hence prohibited by the competition laws when setting minimum compensation in the context of collective bargaining agreements). According to the ECJ, the substitute musicians fall outside the competition laws because they lack the independence typical of an independent contractor and are performing services equivalent to those of the employees for whom they are substituting.[21]

4. Bilateral Restraints of Competition

4.1 Elements of Violation

Article 101 of the TFEU contains three different provisions: a clause identifying what is prohibited (Art. 101(1)), a clause identifying the effects of violating the prohibition (Art. 101(2)), and a clause identifying the circumstances under which an otherwise prohibited practice is permitted (Art. 101(3)). The prohibition codified in Article 101(1) is typically broken down into three elements: (1) some form of collusion between undertakings; (2) the collusion must have the object or effect of restricting competition within the EU; and (3) an effect on trade between member states.

(a) Collusion

Article 101 is concerned with bilateral and multilateral restraints of competition. For that reason, its application requires some form of collusion between two or more undertakings. In the absence of some form of collusion, the conduct is not prohibited by Article 101 even if it has an appreciable anticompetitive effect.[22] This is an important point to emphasize. One should not assume that there is a violation of Article 101(1) just because there is a restraint of competition. A restraint of competition is only one of three requirements that must cumulatively be fulfilled. The threshold question is whether collusion exists. The specific types of collusion to which Article 101(1) applies are (1) agreements between undertakings, (2) concerted practices between undertakings, or (3) decisions of associations of undertakings.

(1) Agreements

The most obvious type of collusion is a formal agreement between undertakings. For example, a distribution agreement between a U.S. automobile manufacturer

---

21. Case C-413/13, FNV Kunsten Informatie en Media v. The Netherlands, 2014 E.C.R. I-___, at ¶42.
22. Joined Cases C-2/01 and C-3/01, Bundesverband der Arzneimittel-Importeure v. Bayer, 2004 E.C.R. I-64, 117 ¶141.

and one of its independent EU distributors would satisfy this requirement. However, the restraint of competition must arise out of that agreement. If, for example, a German automobile manufacturer enters into distribution agreements with its independent distributors, and these agreements do not determine the prices at which the distributors may resell the cars, the Commission may not rely on this agreement to satisfy the first requirement of Article 101(1) of the TFEU if it suspects the German automobile manufacturer and its dealers to be conspiring on resale prices.[23] In other words, there must be a connection between the agreement and the restraint of competition.

An enforceable formal agreement is not necessary. The decisive factor is whether there has been a concurrence of wills between the undertakings to conduct themselves in a way that restrains competition.[24] If there is no meeting of the minds, there is probably no agreement. For example, a manufacturer may unilaterally recommend the prices at which its distributors should resell the manufacturer's products. As long as the manufacturer does not engage in conduct to compel compliance with the recommendation, Article 101(1) does not apply.[25]

(2) Concerted Practices

The term concerted practice refers to "a form of coordination between undertakings which, without having reached the stage where an agreement properly so called has been concluded, knowingly substitutes practical cooperation between them for the risks of competition."[26] Assume, for example, that the Commission received complaints from various newspapers that the price of newsprint offered by the three competing suppliers of newsprint suspiciously and regularly increased within a few days of each other. In its investigation, the Commission is unable to find any evidence of an agreement between the undertakings. When it charts the price increases of those competitors over the preceding five years, however, the Commission finds that within one day after one of the industry leader announced its price increases, the other two companies followed suit. In itself, evidence of parallel conduct is insufficient to infer the existence of collusion.[27]

Additional conduct beyond the mere concerted behavior is necessary to support the inference because there may be other explanations for the parallel conduct.[28] In some industries, for example, the price structure of the competitors

---

23. *See, e.g.*, Case T-208/01, Volkswagen AG v. Comm'n, 2003 E.C.R. II-5141.
24. Case T-519/09, Toshiba Corp. v. Comm'n, 2014 E.C.R. I-___, at ¶34; Case T-44/07, Kaučuk a.s. v. Comm'n. 2011 E.C.R. II-4603, 4620 ¶48.
25. Case 161/84, Pronuptia de Paris GmbH v. Pronupti de Paris Irmgard Schillgallis, 1986 E.C.R. 353, 384 ¶25. *But see* Professional Videotape, Comm'n Decision of Nov. 20, 2007, Case COMP/38.432 (Nov. 20, 2007) at ¶102 where the Commission stated that "inchoate understandings" in the bargaining process prior to reaching a definitive agreement can consitute an agreement for purposes of Article 101(1) of the TFEU.
26. Case 48/69, Imperial Chemical Industries Ltd. v. Comm'n, 1972 E.C.R. 619, 655 ¶64.
27. Zinc Producer Group, 1984 O.J. (L 220) 27.
28. Professional Videotape, Comm'n Decision in Case COMP/38.432 (Nov. 20, 2007) at ¶106; *PO/Needles*, Comm'n Decision in Case F-1/38.338 (Oct. 26, 2004) at ¶239.

is transparent. Two gas stations located on opposite corners of an intersection clearly know the prices of each other. The mere fact that a price increase by one competitor is followed shortly thereafter by a price increase by the other does not mean that they colluded to raise prices. On the other hand, evidence that the sales managers of the suspect competitors regularly met in Switzerland a week before they announced price increases may be a sufficient plus factor. The basic question is factual: when is it fair to infer collusion when there is no direct evidence of an agreement?

The fact that the concerted practice may not have been implemented does not necessarily preclude the finding that the concerted practice existed. It is often an evidentiary issue. According to the General Court, the Commission may even base its conclusions on inferences arising from certain behavior provided there is no procompetitive explanation for such behavior.[29] The mere participation in cartel meetings may be sufficient even if the Commission is not able to show that the participants subsequently implemented what they allegedly agreed to at the meetings.[30] In order to avoid liability, the participant must publicly distance itself from the activities of the cartel.[31]

The classification as an agreement or concerted practice does not have any substantive relevance; both satisfy the collusion requirement.[32] As the Commission stated in *Citric Acid*:[33]

> The concepts of agreement and concerted practice are fluid and may overlap. Indeed, it may not even be possible realistically to make any such distinction, as an infringement may present simultaneously the characteristics of each form of prohibited conduct, while considered in isolation some of its manifestations could accurately be described as one rather than the other. It would however be artificial analytically to subdivide what is clearly a continuing common enterprise having one and the same overall objective into several discrete forms of infringement. A cartel may therefore be an agreement and a concerted practice at the same time. Article [101] lays down no specific category for a complex infringement of that type.

---

29. Case T-44/07, Kaučuk a.s. v. Comm'n. 2011 E.C.R. II-4603, 4621 ¶49; T-235/07, Bavaria NV v. Comm'n, 2011 E.C.R. II-3245, 3257 ¶41 *aff'd on appeal* Case C-445/11 P, Bavaria NV v. Comm'n, 2012 E.C.R. I-___.
30. Case T-53/03, BPB plc v. Comm'n, 2008 E.C.R. II-1333, 1382 ¶90; Case T-56/99, Marlines SA v. Comm'n, 2003 E.C.R. II-5225, 5252 ¶61.
31. Joined Cases C-189/02 P, C-202/02 P, C-205/02 P to C-208/02 P and C-213/02 P, Dansk Rørindustri A/S v. Comm'n, 2005 E.C.R. I-5488, 5540 ¶113; Case T-83/08, Denki Kagaku Kogyo KK v. Comm'n, 2012 E.C.R. II-___, at ¶52.
32. Case C-382/12 P, MasterCard Inc. v. Comm'n, 2014 E.C.R. I-___, at ¶63; Case T-18/03, CD-Contact Data GmbH v. Comm'n, 2009 E.C.R. II-1021, 1042 ¶48; Case T-99/04, AC-Treuhand AG v. Comm'n, 2008 E.C.R. II-1505, 1554 ¶118.
33. Citric Acid, 2002 O.J. (L 239) 18, 41 ¶143.

(3) Tacit Acquiescence

As indicated above, unilateral conduct does not fall under Article 101(1) of the TFEU. Thus, for example, a manufacturer may unilaterally declare a pricing or sales policy which has an anticompetitive effect but does not violate Article 101(1).[34] One should note, however, that tacit acquiescence may be considered as a meeting of the minds even though it may not arise to the level of an enforceable agreement under applicable contract law. As discussed above, a meeting of the minds may be considered collusion in the context of Article 101(1).[35]

One of the seminal cases on tacit acquiescence is *Sandoz v. Commission*.[36] Partly because of national regulations applicable to pharmaceutical products, prices for the same pharmaceutical products in the EU vary among member states. This creates an incentive for companies to purchase such products on the open market (i.e., not from the manufacturer) in a "low price" country and resell them in "high price" countries. These are often referred to as parallel imports. Manufacturers often want to prevent parallel imports for various reasons. However, a restriction on parallel imports amounts to a restriction of intra-brand competition and hence a restriction of competition in the context of Article 101(1).

In order to reduce parallel imports among member states, a pharmaceutical company, Sandoz, inserted into invoices which it sent to customers (i.e., wholesalers, pharmacies, and hospitals) the words "export prohibited." In an attempt to avoid the application of Article 101(1) of the TFEU, Sandoz intentionally avoided entering into agreements with its distributors not to export the products purchased from Sandoz. Nonetheless, the ECJ held that the "unilateral" policy adopted by Sandoz and the subsequent adherence by its distributors satisfied the collusion requirement of Article 101(1). The actual conduct of the distributors in relation to the clause, which they complied with de facto and without discussion, demonstrated their tacit acquiescence to that clause.

Distinguishing between permitted unilateral conduct and collusion in the form of tacit acquiescence is difficult. In *Bayer v. Commission*,[37] the General Court was faced with a fact pattern similar to the *Sandoz* case but came to a different conclusion. Bayer, the German pharmaceutical company, was concerned about parallel imports of a particular Bayer heart drug from Spain and France into the United Kingdom. Because prices for the particular heart drug were regulated in Spain and France, the prices in those countries were 40 percent lower than in the UK. Instead of entering into an agreement with its Spanish and French wholesalers not to export the drug to the UK, Bayer simply limited the quantity of drugs which wholesalers could purchase in Spain and France. The implicit

---

34. Case T-208/01, Volkswagen AG v. Comm'n, 2003 E.C.R. II-5141, 5155 ¶33.
35. T-235/07, Bavaria NV v. Comm'n, 2011 E.C.R. II-3245, 3255 ¶34 *aff'd on appeal* Case C-445/11 P, Bavaria NV v. Comm'n, 2012 E.C.R. I____.
36. Case C-277/87, Sandoz prodotti farmaceutici SpA v. Comm'n, 1990 E.C.R. I-45.
37. Case T-41/96, Bayer v. Comm'n, 2000 E.C.R. II-3383, 3410 ¶72 *aff'd on appeal* Cases C-2/01 and C-3/01, Bundesverband der Arzneimittel-Importeure v. Bayer, 2004 E.C.R. I-64.

objective was to limit the amount which those customers could export to the UK. The Commission, which decided that the practice violated Article 101(1) of the TFEU even though there was no express agreement between Bayer and its wholesalers to limit exports, imposed a significant fine on Bayer.[38]

In annulling the Commission's decision, the General Court held: "[T]he Commission cannot hold that apparently unilateral conduct on the part of a manufacturer, adopted in the context of the contractual relations which he maintains with his dealers, in reality forms the basis of an agreement between undertakings within the meaning of Article [101(1)] of the Treaty if it does not establish the existence of an acquiescence by the other partners, express or implied, in the attitude adopted by the manufacturer."[39] According to the General Court, the finding of an agreement in the context of Article 101(1) of the TFEU requires "a concurrence of wills between economic operators on the implementation of a policy, the pursuit of an objective, or the adoption of a given line of conduct on the market, irrespective of the manner in which the parties' intention to behave on the market in accordance with the terms of that agreement is expressed."[40] The General Court concluded that the Commission failed to show the required concurrence of wills.

On appeal, the ECJ confirmed the conclusion reached by the General Court and stated:

> To hold that an agreement prohibited by Article [101(1)] of the Treaty may be established simply on the basis of the expression of a unilateral policy aimed at preventing parallel imports would have the effect of confusing the scope of that provision with that of Article [102] of the Treaty. For an agreement within the meaning of Article [101(1)] of the Treaty to be capable of being regarded as having been concluded by tacit acceptance, it is necessary that the manifestation of the wish of one of the contracting parties to achieve an anti-competitive goal constitute an invitation to the other party, whether express or implied, to fulfill that goal jointly, and that applies all the more where, as in this case, such an agreement is not at first sight in the interests of the other party, namely the wholesalers.[41]

In *Opel Nederland BV v. Commission*,[42] the General Court came to yet a different conclusion. That case similarly involved an attempt by a manufacturer to limit parallel imports. Instead of expressly prohibiting its dealers from

---

38. 1996 O.J. (L 201) 1.
39. Case T-41/96, Bayer v. Comm'n, 2000 E.C.R. II-3383 *aff'd on appeal* Cases C-2/01 and C-3/01, Bundesverband der Arzneimittel-Importeure v. Bayer, 2004 E.C.R. I-64.
40. Case T-41/96, Bayer v. Comm'n, 2000 E.C.R. II-3383, 3444 ¶173.
41. Cases C-2/01 and C-3/01, Bundesverband der Arzneimittel-Importeure v. Bayer, 2004 E.C.R. I-64, 105 ¶¶101-102.
42. Case T-368/00, Opel Nederland BV v. Comm'n, 2003 E.C.R. II-4495 *aff'd on appeal* Case C-551/03 P, Opel Nederland BV v. Comm'n, 2006 E.C.R. I-3201.

exporting Opel cars to customers in the sales territory of other dealers, however, Opel instituted a bonus policy which created the incentive not to export to other member states. According to the announced Opel bonus campaign, annual bonuses were to be granted by Opel to reward dealers who sold a large volume of cars in that year. However, export sales (i.e., sales to customers outside that dealer's territory) were excluded from the calculation. The General Court held that this policy constituted a violation of Article 101(1) of the TFEU.[43]

(4) Intra-Undertaking Conspiracy

The concept of undertaking as used in competition law refers to an economic unit rather than individual companies.[44] An undertaking may encompass several legal entities that are pursuing the same economic interests. Consequently, agreements and concerted conduct between companies within the same undertaking do not fall within the scope of Article 101 of the TFEU.[45] For example, a distribution agreement between Nintendo and an independent distributor would violate Article 101(1) of the TFEU if it contained a provision whereby the distributor agreed not to sell the Nintendo games in other member states or below a certain price.[46] The same agreement between Nintendo and one of its subsidiaries or branches would not, however, violate Article 101(1) because it is not considered an agreement between independent undertakings.

Agreements between a joint venture entity and one of its parents present a challenge to the application of the general rule that agreements between undertakings under common control do not fall under Article 101(1). As discussed in greater detail below, a joint venture is an undertaking which is jointly controlled by two or more other independent undertakings. For example, companies A and B may each hold 50 percent of the outstanding voting securities of company C and each have equal representation on the board of directors of company C. The application of the general rule would mean that agreements between companies A and C or between companies B and C would fall outside the scope of Article 101 of the TFEU. In such cases, however, the Commission[47]

---

43. Case T-368/00, Opel Nederland BV v. Comm'n, 2003 E.C.R. II-4495, 4525 ¶98. The absense of collusion does not mean ipso facto that the practice is permitted under EU competition rules. If the undertaking holds a dominant position, the conduct which is legal under Article 101 because of the absence of collusion may be prohibited under Article 102 of the TFEU. See Joined Cases C-468/06 to C-478/06, Sot. Lelos kai Sia EE v. GlaxoSmithKlein AEVE Farmakeftikon, 2008 E.C.R. I-7139, 7188 ¶34.
44. Case C-407/08 P, Knauf Gips KG v. Comm'n, 2010 E.C.R. I-6415, 6443 ¶64; Case T-38/05, Agroexpansión SA v. Comm'n, 2011 E.C.R. II-7012, 7044 ¶100 aff'd on appeal C-668/11 P, Alliance One Int'l Inc. v Comm'n, 2013 E.C.R. I-____.
45. Case C-73/95 P, Viho v. Comm'n, 1996 E.C.R. I-5457, 5495 to 5496 ¶¶15 to 17; Case T-325/01, DaimlerChrysler v. Comm'n, 2005 E.C.R. II-3319, 3357 ¶85; Guidelines on the applicability of Art. 101(3) of the Treaty on the Functioning of the European Union to horizontal cooperation agreements, 2011 O.J. (C 11) 1, 5 ¶11 [hereinafter Horizontal Cooperation Guidelines].
46. PO Nintendo Distribution, 2003 O.J. (L 255) 33, 75 ¶245.
47. Ijsselcentrale, 1991 O.J. (L 28) 32; Gosme/Martell, 1991 O.J. (L 185) 23.

and General Court[48] have taken a more pragmatic approach to the application of the rule. In the case of a joint venture, the Commission and Court will examine whether the joint venture entity is merely a disguise for anticompetitive collusion between the parent companies. If so, the general rule is unlikely to dissuade the Commission from applying Article 101 of the TFEU.

(5) Agreements with Agents

As an agent is acting on behalf of a principal when promoting the sale of products or services, many aspects of the contractual relationship between the agent and the principal fall outside the scope of Article 101(1) of the TFEU.[49] Using the prior example, if Nintendo engages genuine sales agents to sell its electronic games throughout Europe, Nintendo may fix the prices at which these sales agents sell the games. If, instead, the sales agents were distributors, these same agreements would be prohibited by Article 101(1) as vertical resale price maintenance. The rationale is that in a principal/agent relationship, the agent does not have complete commercial autonomy and hence should not be treated as a separate economic entity.[50]

The fundamental requirement imposed by Article 101 is that the sales agent relationship be genuine. Two companies may not disguise a distribution agreement as a sales agent agreement and thereby avoid the application of Article 101. An important factor in determining the genuineness of the sales agent agreement is whether it is the agent or the principal who bears the financial and commercial risk.[51] If the agent bears the financial or commercial risk, it probably will not be treated as an agent for purposes of competition law. For example, if the sales agent is responsible for collecting on the invoices of the customers, the agent would probably not be considered an agent. Some additional important factors to consider are whether the agent is required to share in the costs related to the supply of the goods or services; investment by the agent in sales promotion; and responsibility for noncollectable accounts receivable.[52]

In *Daimler Chrysler v. Commission*, one issue was whether the German sales representatives of Daimler Chrysler were genuine sales agents. The implications of such a classification were significant. The Commission had imposed substantial fines on Daimler Chrysler based on the anticompetitive nature of the agreements with its dealers.[53] The evidence was clear that Daimler

---

48. Case T-145/89, Baustahlgewebe v. Comm'n, 1995 E.C.J. II-987 *on appeal* C-185/95, Baustahlgewebe v. Comm'n, 1998 E.C.R. I-8417.
49. Case C-217/05, Confederación Española de Empresarios de Estaciones de Servicio v. Compañía Española de Petróleos SA, 2006 E.C.R. I-11987, 12033 ¶43; Case T-56/99, Marlines SA v. Comm'n, 2003 E.C.R. II-5225, 5251 ¶60.
50. Case C-217/05, Confederación Española de Empresarios de Estaciones de Servicio v. Compañía Española de Petróleos SA, 2006 E.C.R. I-11987, 12033 ¶42.
51. Case C-279/06, CEPSA Estaciones de Servicio SA v. LV Tobar e Hijos SL, 2008 E.C.R. I-6681, 6732 ¶36; Case T-325/01, DaimlerChrysler v. Comm'n, 2005 E.C.R. II-3319, 3359 ¶88; Repsol CPP SA, 2004 O.J. (C 258) 7, 9 ¶16.
52. Guidelines on Vertical Restraints, 2010 O.J. (C 130) 1, 5 ¶16 [hereinafter Vertical Restraints Guidelines].
53. Mercedes-Benz, 2002 O.J. (L 257) 1.

Chrysler had conspired with certain of its dealers to restrict the flow of cars from Germany (where they were low-priced) to other member states. On appeal to the General Court, Daimler Chrysler argued that the conspiracy was based on genuine agreements with sales agents and therefore outside the scope of Article 101 of the TFEU.

In agreeing with Daimler Chrysler, the General Court pointed out that the sales agents could not sell the cars in their own name and the prices where set by Daimler Chrysler.[54] The fact that the sales agents had the authority to grant reductions did not alter their basic conclusion because the price reductions were taken out of the agent's sales commission.[55] Similarly, the requirement that the sales agent provide warranty services for the automobiles it sold did not dissuade the General Court even though sales agents do not typically provide after-sale services at their own cost. The reasoning of the General Court was that the sales agents received some compensation from Daimler Chrysler for approved repair work and any costs incurred by the agents were not appreciable when compared with the sales revenues of the agents.[56]

Not all aspects of the agency relationship are immune from the application of the competition rules. According to the ECJ, "only the obligations imposed on the [agent] concerning the sale of the goods to third parties on behalf of the principal, including the fixing of the retail price, fall outside the scope of Article [101 TFEU]."[57] The other aspects of the relationship—such as the exclusivity and noncompetition provisions—have to be examined under Article 101 of the TFEU.[58] The rationale supporting this distinction appears to be that the ECJ wants to prevent sales agency agreements (even if genuine) from being used as a means of "locking up the market."[59] For example, a manufacturer could exclusively engage a dominant sales representative in a member state and thereby effectively make access to this market more difficult for that manufacturer's competitors. Conversely, a dominant manufacturer may use exclusive sales agency agreements to segregate the markets of the member states. Consequently, the ECJ has taken the position that the exclusivity and noncompetition aspects could fall within the scope of Article 101(1) of the TFEU.

In the *eBooks* case, the Commission initiated an investigation into the contractual relationships that book publishers had with Apple, according to which they agreed not to sell their books to a third party at a price lower than

---

54. Case T-325/01, DaimlerChrysler v. Comm'n, 2005 E.C.R. II-3326.
55. *Id.* at 3363 ¶102.
56. *Id.* at 3365 ¶110-112.
57. Case C-279/06, CEPSA Estaciones de Servicio v. LV Tobar e Hijos, 2008 E.C.R. I-6716, 6733 ¶41.
58. Some national competition authorities have concluded that most favored customer clauses imposed by an agent on the principal may also violate competition law based on the theory that the agent is determining the strategy of the principal which is not characteristic of a genuine agency relationship. See Decision of the German Bundeskartellamt of March 5, 2014 *available at* http://www.bundeskartellamt.de/SharedDocs/Entscheidung/DE/Fallberichte/Kartellverbot/2013/B9-66-10.pdf?__blob=publicationFile&v=3.
59. *Id.*

the price at which they sold those books to Apple.[60] To avoid the application of Article 101 TFEU, a group of publishers agreed with Apple to switch from a wholesale model to an agency relationship in which Apple would serve as their sales agent but with the same most-favored customer obligations. Although the case was ultimately settled by the publishers and Apple who agreed to terminate the agency agreements, the Commission was careful to point out that it was not challenging the agency agreements themselves, but rather the coordination among the publishers to set up the system.[61]

(6) *Decision of Association*

In addition to agreements and concerted practices, the third and last form of collusion falling under Article 101(1) of the TFEU is decisions of associations. Trade associations are often comprised of undertakings—often competing undertakings. A decision of that association—for example, in the form of adopting association statutes or a code of conduct—may have the same effect of reducing competition as a horizontal agreement directly between the undertakings.[62] For example, the code of conduct of an association which recommends that the members should not charge prices below an "ethical level" has an effect similar to an agreement between competitors to fix prices.[63] The term decision is interpreted broadly to include any measure adopted by that association even if it is not binding on its members.[64]

In *Belgian Architects Association*, the Commission considered that the pay scale adopted by the Belgian Architects Association violated Article 101 of the TFEU.[65] Even the decision of an association composed of associations of undertakings falls under Article 101(1) of the TFEU. For example, the measures adopted by the Union of European Football Associations (UEFA), an association of 52 national soccer associations, fulfill the first element of Article 101(1) of the TFEU.[66]

Although decisions of associations are different than collusion facilitated by an association, the result is the same. In *Dutch Beer Market*, for example,

---

60. Communication of the Commission published pursuant to Article 27(4) of Council Regulation (EC) No. 1/2003 in Case COMP/39.847/E-Books, 2012 O.J. (C 283) 7.
61. *Id.*
62. Case C-136/12, Consiglio nationale dei geologi v. Autorità garante della concorrenza e del mercato, 2013 E.C.R. I-___, at ¶45; Case T-193/02, Piau v. Comm'n, 2005 E.C.R. II-209, 239 ¶72. As discussed in Chapter II, the decisions of a private association may be considered "state measures" if the association is fulfilling a public-interest function mandated by a member state. Case C-1/12, Ordem dos Técnicos Oficiais de Contas v. Autoridade da Concorrência, 2013 E.C.R. I-___, at ¶54. The competition rules do not apply to such association decisions. *Id.*
63. Case C-136/12, Consiglio nationale dei geologi v. Autorità garante della concorrenza e del mercato, 2013 E.C.R. I-___, at ¶46; Labco/ONP, Comm'n Decision of 8 December 2010 *summary available at* 2011 O.J. (C 92) 16.
64. Case T-325/01, Daimler Chrysler v. Comm'n, 2005 E.C.R. II-3326, 3399-3400 ¶210.
65. Comm'n, 2004 Annual Report on Competition Policy (2005) at 37 ¶77.
66. UEFA Broadcasting Regulations, 2001 O.J. (L 171) 22.

four beer breweries were members of the Centraal Brouwerij Kantoor.[67] In the context of this Dutch association, these four competitors conspired to fix the price of beer. The anticompetitive conduct was not in the form of a decision of the association, but rather in the form of collusion facilitated by the association.

(b) Effect on Trade Between Member States

As discussed in Chapter I, EU law co-exists with the law of the member states. Hence, there may be areas of overlap where both the EU and the member states have laws applicable to the same types of conduct. Competition law is an example of this overlap. The EU and each of the member states have their own competition law regimes. In order to delineate the scope of the EU and member state competition law regimes, Article 101(1) of the TFEU requires that the agreement or concerted practice have an effect on trade between member states.[68] The abstract standard employed by the ECJ is whether it is possible to foresee with a sufficient degree of probability, on the basis of a set of objective factors of law or of fact, that they have an influence, direct or indirect, actual or potential, on the pattern of trade between member states in such a way as to cause concern that they might hinder the attainment of a single market between member states.[69]

The Commission has identified three elements in the analysis which must be cumulatively fulfilled. The first element is concerned with trade between member states. It requires that there is an impact on cross-border economic activity involving at least two member states.[70] The most obvious example of an effect on trade between member states is an agreement between two undertakings from different member states not to sell their competing products in the member state in which the other is located. Such conduct—when it directly involves restraints on exports or imports or undertakings from different member states—is

---

67. Dutch Beer Market, 2007 O.J. (C 122) 1.
68. Case T-29/05, Deltafina SpA v. Comm'n, 2010 E.C.R. II-4088, 4142 ¶166; Case T-168/01, GlaxoSmithKline Sevices Unlimited v. Comm'n, 2006 E.C.R. II-2981, 2998 ¶55 *aff'd on appeal* Joined cases C-501/06 P, C-513/06 P, C-515/06 P and C-519/06 P, GlaxoSmithKline Services Unlimited v. Comm'n, 2009 E.C.R. I-9291.
69. Case C-425/07 P, AEPI Elliniki Etaireia pros Prostasian tis Pnevmatikis Idioktisias AE v. Comm'n, 2009 E.C.R. I-3226, 3244 ¶51; Case C-407/04P, Dalmine SpA v. Comm'n, 2007 E.C.R. I-901, 931 ¶90.
70. Comm'n Guidelines on the effect on trade concept contained in Articles 81 and 82 of the Treaty, 2004 O.J. (C 101) 81, 83 ¶21 [hereinafter Interstate Commerce Guidelines]. Although the Interstate Commerce Guidelines, as well as other guidelines and notices of the Commission, are binding on the Commission, Joined Cases T-67/00, T-68/00, T-71/00 and T-78/00, JFE Engineering Corp v. Comm'n, 2004 E.C.R. II-2514, 2694 ¶537 *aff'd on appeal* Joined cases C-403/04 P and C-405/04 P, Sumitomo Metal Industries Ltd. v. Comm'n, 2007 E.C.R. I-785, the binding effect of notices and guidelines on the courts of the member states is an open issue. In *Filigranbetondecken*, a German court considered the Interstate Commerce Guidelines not to be binding. Decision of the Oberlandesgericht Düsseldorf of June 10, 2005, VI – 2 Kart 12/04, *reported in* Wirtschaft und Wettbewerb 62 (2006).

considered by the Commission as an agreement by its very nature capable of affecting trade between member states.[71]

However, the commerce that is being restrained does not necessarily have to be interstate commerce in order for the interstate trade requirement to be fulfilled. In other words, an indirect effect on trade between member states is sufficient.[72] In indirect effect cases, the Commission must consider a combination of factors which, when considered individually, are not necessarily decisive.[73] Generally, an anticompetitive practice extending to the whole of a member state will have an effect on trade between member states as it will alter the trade flows between that member state and other member states.[74] For example a price cartel between sugar companies in the UK for the sale of sugar in the UK, was found to violate Article 101 as it has an indirect effect on imports.[75] Similarly, a conspiracy between Austrian banks for banking fees on transactions within Austria was nonetheless considered to have an effect on trade between member states because it had the potential effect of persuading foreign banks to enter the market.[76]

Even a restriction on competition between a single member state such as the United States and a non-member state may affect trade between member states.[77] The rationale employed by the Commission to reach such conduct is that the restraint may subsequently have an impact on the flow of goods from or into that particular member state from or into other member states.[78]

The second element of the interstate trade analysis is the concept of potential effect. The standard is whether the agreement may have an influence "direct or

---

71. Interstate Commerce Guidelines at 87 ¶53.
72. Case C-359/01 P, British Sugar v. Comm'n, 2004 E.C.R. I-4933, 4972 ¶27; Case 42/84, Remia v. Comm'n, 1985 E.C.R. 2545, 2572 ¶22.
73. Joined Cases C-295/04 – 298/04, Manfredi v. Lloyd Adriatico Assicurazioni SpA, 2006 E.C.R. I-6641, 6656 ¶43.
74. C-125/07 P, Erste Group Bank AG v. Comm'n, 2009 E.C.R. I-8821, 8844 ¶38; Case T-325/01, Daimler Chrysler v. Comm'n, 2005 E.C.R. II- 3326, 3400 ¶212.
75. Case C-359/01 P, British Sugar v. Comm'n, 2004 E.C.R. I-4933, 4972 ¶27; see also Case T-325/01, DaimlerChrysler v. Comm'n, 2005 E.C.R. II-3326, 3400 ¶212; Joined Cases T-202/98, T-204/98 and T-207/98, Tate & Lyle plc v. Comm'n, 2001 E.C.R. II-2035, 2065 ¶79.
76. Lombard Club, 2004 O.J. (L 56) 1, 60 ¶442 aff'd Joined cases C-125/07 P, C-133/07 P, C-135/07 P and C-137/07 P, Erste Group Bank AG v. Comm'n, 2009 E.C.R. I-8821. See also Case C-238/05, Asnef-Equifax, Servicios de Información sobre Solvencia y Crédito, SL v. Asociación de Usuarios de Servicios Bancarios, 2006 E.C.R. I-11145, 11157 ¶37.
77. See, e.g., Gas Insullated Switchgear, 2008 O.J. (C 5) 7; Franco-Japanese Ballbearing Agreement, 1974 O.J. (L 343) 19.
78. Interstate Commerce Guidelines at 93 ¶101. See also Gas Insulated Switchgear, 2008 O.J. (C 5) 7 (agreement between European and Japanese producers that each would not sell into the market of the others).

indirect, actual or potential, on the pattern of trade between Member States."[79] The possibility that an agreement at least potentially have an effect on trade between member states illustrates the broad scope of effect on trade between member states requirement. Moreover, according to the ECJ and General Court, it is not necessary that the conduct in question should, in fact, have substantially affected trade between member states: it is sufficient to establish that the conduct is capable of having such an effect.[80]

The requisite effect does not necessarily have to be negative. According to the ECJ, "the fact that an agreement or practice encourages an increase in the volume of trade between Member States does not preclude the possibility that that agreement or practice may affect trade."[81] One need only compare the actual situation to the hypothetical situation if the conduct had not occurred. If the flow of goods or services is merely different compared to what it would be in absence of the conduct, this requirement is fulfilled.[82]

The third element of the interstate trade analysis is the appreciability requirement: the effect or potential effect on trade between member states must be appreciable.[83] The starting point for the appreciability analysis is the market position of the parties involved. The Commission has stated that it will not initiate proceedings if (i) the aggregate market share of the parties on any relevant market within the EU affected by the conduct does not exceed 5 percent and (ii) the aggregate annual EU sales of the undertakings concerned (i.e., the corporate groups and not just the specific legal entities involved) do not exceed €40 million for horizontal agreements or for vertical agreements the annual EU sales of the supplier in the products concerned do not exceed €40 million.[84]

---

79. Case C-238/05, Asnef-Equifax, Servicios de Información sobre Solvencia y Crédito, SL v. Asociación de Usuarios de Servicios Bancarios, 2006 E.C.R. I-11125, 11159 ¶43; Case 42/84, Remia v. Comm'n, 1985 E.C.R. 2545, 2572 ¶22; Joined Cases C-89/85, C-104/85, C-114/85, C-116/85, C-117/85 and C-125/85 to C-129/85, Åhlström Osakeyhtiö v. Comm'n, 1993 E.C.R. I-1307, 1617 ¶143.
80. C-125/07 P, Erste Group Bank AG v. Comm'n, 2009 E.C.R. I-8821, 8846 ¶46; Case T-29/05, Deltafina SpA v. Comm'n, 2010 E.C.R. II-4088, 4143 ¶169.
81. Case C-238/05, Asnef-Equifax, Servicios de Información sobre Solvencia y Crédito, SL v. Asociación de Usuarios de Servicios Bancarios, 2006 E.C.R. I-11125, 11158 ¶38.
82. Lombard Club, 2004 O.J. (L 56) 1, 59 ¶439 *aff'd* Joined cases C-125/07 P, C-133/07 P, C-135/07 P and C-137/07 P, Erste Group Bank AG v. Comm'n, 2009 E.C.R. I-8681.
83. C-125/07 P, Erste Group Bank AG v. Comm'n, 2009 E.C.R. I-8821, 8844 ¶36; Comm'n Guidelines on the effect on trade concept contained in Articles 81 and 82 of the Treaty, 2004 O.J. (C 101) 81, 85 ¶44. The general principle of the law of legitimate expectations requires the Commission to apply the Guidelines on the effect on trade concept contained in Articles 101 and 102 of the TFEU. Case C-439/11P, Ziegler SA v. Comm'n, 2013 E.C.R. I-____, at ¶60.
84. Comm'n Guidelines on the effect on trade concept contained in Articles 81 and 82 of the Treaty, 2004 O.J. (C 101) 81, 86 ¶52. In practice, it is unlikely that the Commission will challenge a vertical agreement if the market shares of the parties do not exceed 15 percent and the agreement does not contain any hard-core rrestrictions. Vertical Restraints Guidelines at 4 ¶9.

A restriction on imports into the EU can even have an effect on trade between member states. In *Toshiba Corp. v. Commission*, Japanese and European manufacturers agreed not to sell power transformers into each other's territory. According to the ECJ, even this restriction had the requisite effect on interstate trade.[85]

The determination of appreciability in the context of applying the interstate trade requirement of Article 101 of the TFEU is independent from the requirement that the restraint on competition itself must be appreciable (which is discussed below).[86] In the context of determining whether the restraint of competition is appreciable, the focus is on the competition immediately affected. In the context of the interstate trade requirement, the focus is not only on the commerce directly involved in the restraint, but also on any commerce incidentally affected by the conduct. This distinction may be important in individual cases. For example, if two Irish sugar refineries operating and selling entirely within Ireland agree to set the minimum price for their processed sugar, the commerce directly affected is the sale by them of processed sugar in Ireland.

As discussed below, that restraint of competition must be appreciable regardless of whether it has an appreciable effect on trade between member states. In the context of determining a possible effect on trade between member states, however, one needs to identify an effect on trade between member states and determine whether that effect is appreciable (as opposed to the impact of the restraint of competition). Using the Irish sugar example, the effect on trade between member states may be that the inflated prices which the Irish customers of the sugar refineries pay reduce the ability of those customers to sell the packaged sugar to retailers in other member states. It is this indirect effect on trade between member states which must be appreciable (unless, of course, the direct effect of the conduct on trade between member states is appreciable).

(c) Object or Effect of the Restraint of Competition Within the Common Market

(1) The Concept of Restraint of Competition

The third and final element of a violation of Article 101(1) is that the collusion has as its object or effect a restraint of competition within the EU. The term "competition" can generally be understood to mean the commercial rivalry that exists between two undertakings for particular business.[87] Using this

---

85. Case T-519/09, Toshiba Corp. v. Comm'n, 2014 E.C.R. I-____, at ¶241.
86. Case T-199/08, Ziegler SA v. Comm'n, 2011 E.C.R. II-3514, 3528 ¶44 *aff'd on appeal* Case C-439/11 P, Ziegler SA v. Comm'n, 2013 E.C.R. I-____.
87. In 2003, the Competition Directorate of the Commission published a glossary of common terms used in European competition law. In that glossary, the term competition was defined as: "A situation in a market in which sellers of a product or service independently strive for the patronage of buyers in order to achieve a particular business objective, e.g., profits, sales and/or market share. Competitive rivalry between firms may take place in terms of price, quality, service or combinations of these and other factors which customers may value." http://europa.eu.int/comm/competition/general_info/c_en.html.

definition, a restraint of competition can be equated to the restriction of the commercial rivalry between two undertakings. However, this highly abstract definition is of little practical use. All competition law regimes are faced with the fundamental challenge of applying the inherently vague concept "restraint of competition" to different forms of commercial interaction. In the EU, a restraint of competition was traditionally equated by the Commission[88] and the EU courts[89] with a restraint of the commercial freedom of market actors. The general thought was that competition would be the natural result of securing the commercial freedom of the market actors. Hence, the task of competition law was to make sure that the market actors maintained their commercial freedom. Potential redeeming factors (such as the possibility that the overall effect of the agreement is to increase efficiency) were not traditionally considered in the context of determining whether a particular agreement violates Article 101(1) of the TFEU, but rather only when determining whether to grant an exemption under Article 101(3).

The practical implications of adhering to such a broad interpretation of a restraint of trade caused the EU to shift the analysis closer to that of the United States.[90] This shift is due to the recognition that not every agreement that restricts commercial freedom equates to a restriction on competition.[91] The purpose of an agreement is to regulate (i.e., restrain) the conduct of at least one of the parties. Hence, a strict application of the traditional EU approach to restraints of competition resulted in an excessive number of procompetitive agreements falling under Article 101(1) of the TFEU because they had the effect of limiting the commercial freedom of the parties. However, the purpose of competition law is to prevent only the restraints of competition which "reduce the welfare of the final consumer of the products in question."[92] Both the ECJ and the General Court have indicated that the traditional concept of restraint

---

88. *See, e.g.*, BP/Kellogg, 1985 O.J. (L 369) 1, 3, ¶15; Visa Int'l, 2002 O.J. (L 318) 17, 28 ¶64; UIP, 1989 O.J. (L 226) 25, 30 ¶40; Comm'n, 1993 Annual Report on Competition Policy (1994) at 49 ¶160; Horizontal Cooperation Guidelines at 8 ¶27.
89. *See, e.g.*, Case T-65/98, Van den Bergh Foods Ltd v. Comm'n, 2003 E.C.R. II-4662, 4698 ¶98 *aff'd on appeal* Case C-552/03 P, Unilever Bestfoods (Ireland) Ltd. v. Comm'n, 2006 E.C.R. I-9094; Case C-306/96, Javico Int'l and Javico AG v. Yves Saint Laurent Parfums SA, 1998 E.C.R. 1997, 2002 ¶13; Case 86/82, Hasselblad v. Comm'n, 1984 E.C.R. 883, 910 ¶51; Case 107/82, AEG v. Comm'n, 1983 E.C.R. 3151, 3201 ¶60.
90. A. Fiebig, *Modernization of European Competition Law as a Form of Convergence*, 19 Temple Int'l & Comp. L.J. 63 (2005).
91. Case T-168/01, GlaxoSmithKline Services Unlimited v. Comm'n, 2006 E.C.R. II-2981, 3014 ¶118 *aff'd on appeal* Joined cases C-501/06 P, C-513/06 P, C-515/06 P and C-519/06 P, GlaxoSmithKline Services Unlimited v. Comm'n, 2009 E.C.R. I-9291.
92. Case T-168/01, GlaxoSmithKline Services Unlimited v. Comm'n, 2006 E.C.R. II-2981, 3014 ¶118 *aff'd on appeal* Joined cases C-501/06 P, C-513/06 P, C-515/06 P and C-519/06 P, GlaxoSmithKline Services Unlimited v. Comm'n, 2009 E.C.R. I-9291.

of competition as a restriction of the commercial freedom of a market actor is no longer appropriate.[93]

In *Wouters v. Nederlandse Orde van Advocaten*, for example, the fundamental issue was whether a rule adopted by the Dutch bar prohibiting multidisciplinary partnerships between attorneys and accountants was contrary to the EU competition rules because it restricted the ability of lawyers and accountants to engage in certain commercial conduct.[94] According to the ECJ, "not every agreement between undertakings or any decision of an association of undertakings which restricts the freedom of action of the parties or of one of them necessarily falls within the prohibition laid down in Article 101(1) of the Treaty. For the purposes of application of that provision to a particular case, account must first of all be taken of the overall context in which the decision of the association of undertakings was taken or produces its effects."[95]

This departure from the traditional inflexible approach of the definition of restraint of competition in the context of Article 101(1) represents a significant shift in the jurisprudence of the EU courts. As part of the modernization of EU competition law in 2002, the Commission introduced a system for applying Article 101 of the TFEU that relies to a greater extent on a more comprehensive economic analysis of the impact of the agreement rather than a narrow focus on the effect of the agreement on commercial freedom. Although there is still no comprehensive definition of a restraint of competition that could be adequately applied in each case, competition lawyers rely on categories to determine when a particular agreement is permissible under Article 101. These categories are discussed below.

---

93. Case T-99/04, AC–Treuhand AG v. Comm'n, 2008 E.C.R. II-1505, 1515 ¶26; Case C-519/04 P, Meca-Medina v. Comm'n, 2006 E.C.R. I-7007, 7023 ¶42; Case C-309/99, Wouters v. Nederlandse Orde van Advocaten, 2002 E.C.R. I-1653, 1688 ¶97; Case T-168/01, GlaxoSmithKline Services Unlimited v. Comm'n, 2006 E.C.R. II-2981, 3029 ¶171. But the Commission and EU courts expressly refuse to apply a US-style rule of reason in the context of Article 101(1) of the TFEU. Case T-111/08, MasterCard, Inc. v. Comm'n, 2012 E.C.R. II-____, at ¶182 *aff'd on appeal* Case C-382/12 P, MasterCard, Inc. v. Comm'n, 2014 E.C.R. I-____. The reasoning provided by the General Court is that the application of a rule of reason in the context of Article 101(1) would devoid the Article 101(3) exception of any meaning. Case T-328/03, O_2 (Germany) GmbH & Co v. Comm'n, 2006 E.C.R. II-1234, 1254 ¶69; Case T-65/98, Van den Bergh Foods Ltd v. Comm'n, 2003 E.C.R. II-4662, 4701 ¶106 *aff'd on appeal* Case C-552/03 P, Unilever Bestfoods (Ireland) Ltd. v. Comm'n, 2006 E.C.R. I-9094; Case T-112/99, Metropole television v. Comm'n, 2001 E.C.R. II-2464, 2489 ¶77.
94. Although the competition rules codified in Articles 101 and 102 of the TFEU are directed at private undertakings and not at state actions as the Dutch law in this case, Article 10 of the TFEU, when read in conjunction with Articles 101 and 102, prohibits the member states from adopting legislation that would render the competition laws ineffective.
95. Case C-309/99, Wouters v. Nederlandse Orde van Advocaten, 2002 E.C.R. I-1653, 1688 ¶97. *See also* Case C-136/12, Consiglio nationale dei geologi v. Autorità garante della concorrenza e del mercato, 2013 E.C.R. I-____, at ¶53; Case C-1/12, Ordem dos Técnicos Oficiais de Contas v. Autoridade da Concorrência, 2013 E.C.R. I-____, at ¶93; Case T-461/07, Visa Europe Ltd v. Comm'n, 2011 E.C.R. II-1740, 1760 ¶67; Case T-99/04, AC–Treuhand AG v. Comm'n, 2008 E.C.R. II-1505, 1558 ¶126.

(2) *Object or Effect*

The agreement, decision or concerted practice must have as its object *or* effect the prevention, restriction or distortion of competition. An intent to restrain competition is not required.[96] If the effect is present, the Commission does not have to show that the parties had the objective of restraining competition.[97] However, where the Commission relies on the effects of the conduct, it must "take into consideration the actual context in which it is situated, in particular the economic and legal context in which the undertaking operate, the nature of the goods or services affected, as well as the real conditions of the functioning and the structure of the market or markets in question."[98] Conversely, if the conduct is considered to has as its object a restraint of competition, the actual effect of the conduct becomes irrelevant.[99] The distinction between object and effect is reminiscent of the per se/rule of reason dichotomy in the United States in that certain types of agreements inherently restrain competition in an unreasonable manner and are therefore prohibited per se without a closer examination of the actual effects in the particular case.[100]

The recognition of a category of "by object" restrictions has three important implications. First, the prohibition of an agreement "by object" presents the possibility that agreements which are never implemented violate Article 101(1). Merely entering into an anti-competitive agreement is prohibited if it has as its object a restraint of competition even if the anti-competitive clause was never implemented.[101]

---

96. Cases T-202/98, and 204/98 and 207/98, Tate & Tate v. Comm'n, 2001 E.C.R. II-2035, 2062 ¶72.
97. Case C-67/13 P, Groupement des cartes bancaires v. Comm'n, 2014 E.C.R. I-____, at ¶4.
98. Case C-1/12, Ordem dos Técnicos Oficiais de Contas v. Autoridade da Concorrência, 2013 E.C.R. I-____, at ¶70.
99. Case C-286/13 P, Dole Food Company Inc. v. Commission, 2015 E.C.R. I-____ at ¶¶113-114; Case C-67/13 P, Groupement des cartes bancaires v. Comm'n, 2014 E.C.R. I-____, at ¶49; Case C-226/11, Expedia Inc. v. Autorité de la concurrence, 2012 E.C.R. I-____, at ¶35; Joined cases C-501/06 P, C-513/06 P, C-515/06 P and C-519/06 P, GlaxoSmithKline Services Unlimited v. Comm'n, 2009 E.C.R. I-9347, 9399 ¶58; Case C-209/07, Competition Authority v. Beef Industry Development Society Ltd., 2008 E.C.R. I-8674, 8682 ¶16; Case T-519/09, Toshiba Corp. v. Comm'n, 2014 E.C.R. I-____, at ¶227; Joined cases T-122/07 to T-124/07, Siemens AG Österreich v. Comm'n, 2011 E.C.R. II-806, 832 ¶75.
100. Compare Nat'l Soc'y of Prof'l Eng'rs v. U.S., 435 U.S. 679, 692 (1978) ("Agreements whose nature and necessary effect are so plainly anticompetitive that no elaborate study of the industry is needed to establish their illegality...are illegal per se.") to Case C-286/13 P, Dole Food Company Inc. v. Commission, 2015 E.C.R. I-____ at ¶114 ("[C]ertain types of coordination between undertakings can be regarded, by their very nature, as being harmful to the proper functioning of normal competition.").
101. Case T-67/01, JCB Service v. Comm'n, 2004 E.C.R. II-56, 96 ¶117 *aff'd on appeal* Case C-167/04 P, JCB Service v. Comm'n, 2006 E.C.R. I-8972; Case 246/86, SC Belasco v. Comm'n, 1989 E.C.R. 2117, 2186 ¶15; Case C-277/87, Sandoz prodotti farmaceutici SpA v. Comm'n, 1990 E.C.R. I-45, 79 ¶13.

In *Dansk Rørindustri A/S v. Commission*, for example, the defendant argued that it should not be fined for violating Article 101(1) of the TFEU because even though it participated in some of the cartel meetings to fix the prices of heating pipes, it never implemented the anti-competitive practices allegedly agreed to at those meetings.[102] According to the ECJ, this is irrelevant in determining a violation of Article 101(1):[103]

> For the purposes of applying Article [101](1) of the Treaty, it is sufficient that the object of an agreement should be to restrict, prevent or distort competition irrespective of the actual effects of that agreement. Consequently, in the case of agreements reached at meetings of competing undertakings, that provision is infringed where those meetings have such an object and are thus intended to organise artificially the operation of the market. In such a case, the liability of a particular undertaking in respect of the infringement is properly established where it participated in those meetings with knowledge of their object, even if it did not proceed to implement any of the measures agreed at those meetings. The greater or lesser degree of regular participation by the undertaking in the meetings and of completeness of its implementation of the measures agreed is relevant not to the establishment of its liability but rather to the extent of that liability and thus to the severity of the penalty.

The second implication of recognizing "by object" restrictions is that it relieves the Commission and any private plaintiffs from the necessity of showing that the conduct actually had a negative effect on competition.[104] Similar to the per se rule in the United States, this is particularly handy when the Commission lacks the evidence or economic theory to prove that particular conduct is anti-competitive. All that is required is that the Commission show that the conduct is of the type which has been condemned as anti-competitive by object.

Finally, in addition to relieving the Commission of the obligation to prove that the conduct actually had a negative effect on competition, the classification of a restraint as being "by object" has the significant practical consequence that the agreement is unlikely to fulfill the requirements for an exemption under Art. 101(3) TFEU.[105] Nor can the "by object" restraint, according to the Commission, benefit from the de minimis safe harbor discussed below.[106]

---

102. Joined Cases C-189/02 P, C-202/02 P, C-205/02 P to C-208/02 P and C-213/02 P, Dansk Rørindustri A/S v. Comm'n, 2005 E.C.R. I-5488.
103. *Id.* at 5548 ¶145.
104. Case C-286/13 P, Dole Food Company Inc. v. Commission, 2015 E.C.R. I-____ at ¶¶113-114; Case C-67/13 P, Groupement des cartes bancaires v. Comm'n, 2014 E.C.R. I-____, at ¶49; Case C-226/11, Expedia Inc. v. Autorité de la concurrence, 2012 E.C.R. I-____, at ¶35.
105. Comm'n Staff Working Document, SWD (2014) 198 final (June 25, 2014) at 4.
106. *Id.*

Similar to the situation in the United States regarding the per se rule, there is no EU catalog of types of conduct which can be condemned based upon their object without looking at the effect, and the outcome of the case can depend on the categorization of the restraint at issue.[107] The ECJ has only been willing to provide general guidance: "[I]n order to determine whether an agreement between undertakings or a decision by an association of undertakings reveals a sufficient degree of harm to competition that it may be considered a restriction of competition 'by object' within the meaning of Article [101](1) [of the TFEU], regard must be had to the content of its provisions, its objectives and the economic and legal context of which it forms a part. When determining that context, it is also necessary to take into consideration the nature of the goods or services affected, as well as the real conditions of the functioning and structure of the market or markets in question."[108] Based on the case law, it is safe to say that naked horizontal price fixing[109] and exchange of pricing information between competitors[110] of such conduct which will be deemed a restraint of competition by object. Two other examples of "classical 'by object' restrictions"[111] identified by the Commission are output limitations[112] and division of markets.[113]

(3) Appreciability

The broad interpretation of restraint of competition under Article 101(1) of the TFEU, which was adopted early by the Commission and endorsed by the EU courts, has resulted in a number of agreements being caught by Article 101(1) even though their overall effect may be procompetitive. The EU competition law regime has developed several ways to address this concern. Largely in recognition of the contradiction, the ECJ early in the development of EU competition law introduced the requirement that "an agreement falls outside the prohibition in Article [101] when it has only an insignificant effect on the markets, taking into account the weak position which the persons concerned have on the market of the product in question."[114] As the rule is now phrased, Article 101(1) only applies to appreciable restraints of competition.[115]

---

107. *See, e.g.*, Case C-67/13 P, Groupement des cartes bancaires v. Comm'n, 2014 E.C.R. I-____, at ¶53; In re Sulfuric Acid Antitrust Litig., 600 F.3d 813 (7th Cir. 2010).
108. Case C-67/13 P, Groupement des cartes bancaires v. Comm'n, 2014 E.C.R. I-____, at ¶53.
109. *Id.* at ¶51.
110. Case C-286/13 P, Dole Food Company Inc. v. Commission, 2015 E.C.R. I-____ at ¶122.
111. Comm'n Staff Working Document, SWD (2014) 198 final (June 25, 2014) at 5.
112. *See, e.g.*, C-209/07, Competition Authority v. Beef Industry Development Society Ltd., 2008 E.C.R. I-8637.
113. *See, e.g.*, Joined cases C-501/06 P, C-513/06 P, C-515/06 P and C-519/06 P, GlaxoSmithKline Services Unlimited v. Comm'n, 2009 E.C.R. I-9291.
114. Case 5/69, Völk v. Vervaecke, 1969 E.C.R. 295, 302 ¶6.
115. Case C-439/11 P, Ziegler SA v. Comm'n, 2013 E.C.R. I-____, at ¶92; Case C-238/05, Asnef-Equifax, Servicios de Información sobre Solvencia y Crédito, SL v. Asociación de Usuarios de Servicios Bancarios, 2006 E.C.R. I-11125, 11160 ¶50.

The determination of whether the restraint of competition is appreciable must be made on a case-by-case basis and separate from the determination whether the effect on trade between member states itself is appreciable, as discussed above. Although the EU courts have not provided much guidance, the Commission has attempted to quantify the requirement in its De Minimis Notice.[116] The Commission's position is that agreements between actual or potential competitors (except for hard-core restraints) will not generally restrain competition appreciably if their combined market share on any of the relevant markets is less than 10 percent. For agreements between noncompetitors, the Commission uses a combined market share of 15 percent on any of the relevant markets as guidance. If it is difficult to classify the agreement as horizontal or vertical, the 10 percent threshold applies.

The legal effect of the De Minimis Notice is that the Commission will not initiate competition law proceedings on its own initiative or upon application.[117] In addition, the Commission will not impose fines if undertakings act in good faith reliance on the thresholds. Moreover, the EU courts may employ these Commission thresholds in determining the appreciability of a restraint.[118] This does not mean, however, that two small competitors may agree to fix prices and avoid the application of Article 101 TFEU. The de minimis exception does not apply to "hard-core" restraints[119] or to restrictions by object.[120] This includes

---

116. Comm'n Notice on agreements of minor importance which do not appreciably restrict competition under Article 101(1) of the Treaty on the Functioning of the European Union, 2014 O.J. (C 291) 1 [hereinafter De Minimis Notice].
117. *Id.* at 2 ¶5. The general legal effect of notices and guidelines issued by the Commission is that they constitute binding obligations on the Commission to observe them. Case C-439/11P, Ziegler SA v. Comm'n, 2013 E.C.R. I-____, at ¶60; Case T-119/02, Royal Philips Electronics NV v. Comm'n, 2003 E.C.R. II-1442, 1515 ¶242; Joined Cases T-67/00, T-68/00, T-71/00 and T-78/00, JFE Engineering Corp v. Comm'n, 2004 E.C.R. II-2514, 2694 ¶537 *aff'd on appeal* Joined cases C-403/04 P and C-405/04 P, Sumitomo Metal Industries Ltd. v. Comm'n, 2007 E.C.R. I-785. If the Commission wants to depart from the notice or guidelines, it must provide reasons why this departure conforms to the principle of equal treatment. Joined Cases C-189/02 P, C-202/02 P, C-205/02 P to C-208/02 P and C-213/02 P, Dansk Rørindustri A/S v. Comm'n, 2005 E.C.R. I-5488, 5565 ¶209. However, notices and guidelines issued by the Commssion are not binding on the member states. Case C-226/11, Expedia Inc. v. Autorité de la concurrence, 2012 E.C.R. I-__, at ¶29.
118. *See, e.g.*, Case T-44/00, Mannesmannröhren-Werke AG v. Comm'n, 2004 E.C.R. II-2233, 2287 ¶205 *aff'd on appeal* Case C-411/04 P, Salzgitter Mannesmann GmbH v. Commission, 2007 E.C.R. I-990.
119. Case T-36/05, Coats Holdings Ltd. v. Comm'n, 2007 E.C.R. II-110 (summary), at ¶162 (full version of case reported in the electronic reports of cases ECLI:EU:T:2007:268) *aff'd on appeal* Case C-468/07 P, Coats Holdings Ltd. v. Comm'n, 2008 E.C.R. I-127 (ECLI:EU:C:2008:503); Luxembourg Brewers, 2002 O.J. (L 253) 21, 37 ¶84.
120. De Minimis Notice at ¶13; Comm'n Staff Working Document, SWD (2014) 198 final (June 25, 2014) at 4.

horizontal and vertical price fixing, horizontal agreements to limit production or sales, and horizontal agreements to divide territories within the EU.[121]

4.2 Legal Effect of Infringing Article 101(1)

According to Article 101(2) of the TFEU, all agreements or decisions prohibited by Article 101(1) are automatically null and void. The nullity begins when the agreement is reached (*ab initio*) and not only after the Commission or the national authority makes its decision that the agreement violates Article 101(1) of the TFEU.[122] For example, if a manufacturer agrees with its distributors to fix the prices at which the distributors resell the manufacturer's product, those agreements are null and void from the date when the parties enter into them, even if the Commission does not discover their existence until several years later.

To merely declare an anticompetitive agreement null and void is only half the story. The parties to the agreement and even third parties may have acted in reliance on the validity of the agreement or have been negatively affected in some way. The rule is that the legal implications of the automatic nullity are determined by national law and not EU law.[123] For example, the rights of the manufacturer in the immediately preceding price-fixing example to collect any unpaid amounts from the distributors that may be owed under the illegal distribution agreements would be determined by the applicable national contracts law.

In *In re Courage*, a UK beer supplier leased pubs it owned to independent businesses on the condition that the pub operators purchase their requirements of beer from the supplier. In a contract dispute, the supplier filed suit against one of the pub operators in England to collect on outstanding bills for beer supplied by the supplier to the pub operator. The pub operator counterclaimed for damages based on the argument that the agreement violated Article 101(1) of the TFEU because the prices that it had to pay for the beer were substantially above the prices offered to customers of the beer supplier who were not tenants of the beer supplier. According to English law, a party to an illegal contract may not collect damages from the other party to such contract, as the plaintiff in such a case has unclean hands.

In its judgment, the ECJ stated that: "The principle of automatic nullity can be relied on by anyone, and the courts are bound by it once the conditions for the application of Article [101(1)] are met and so long as the agreement concerned does not justify the grant of an exemption under Article [101(3)] of

---

121. Since *Royal Philips Electronics NV v. Comm'n*, it is questionable whether the exception also applies to vertical absolute territorial protection. In that case, the General Court held that "even an agreement imposing absolute territorial protection may escape the prohibition contained in Article 101(1) if it affects the market only insignificantly." Case T-119/02, Royal Philips Electronics NV v. Comm'n, 2003 E.C.R. II-1442, 1507 ¶218.
122. Case 48/72, Brasserie de Haecht v. Wilkin, 1973 E.C.R. 77.
123. Joined Cases C-295/04 – 298/04, Manfredi v. Lloyd Adriatico Assicurazioni SpA, 2006 E.C.R. I-6641, 6661 ¶62.

the Treaty."[124] Accordingly, the ECJ held that the general rule is that a party to a contract which violates Article 101 of the TFEU can rely on the violation of Article 101(1) to obtain relief from the other contracting party. However, the converse is also true: "[EU] law does not preclude a rule of national law barring a party to a contract liable to restrict or distort competition from relying on his own unlawful actions to obtain damages where it is established that that party bears significant responsibility for the distortion of competition."[125] The case illustrates the deference the ECJ gives to national law in determining the contractual implications of agreements which violate Article 101.

4.3 Exemptions

(a) Individual Exemptions

As discussed above, the application of Article 101(1) of the TFEU has traditionally focused on the negative effects of agreements. The redeeming characteristics of the conduct are not considered when applying Article 101(1). In refusing to recognize a rule of reason approach to Article 101(1), the General Court held in *Métropole télévision v. Commission* that: "It is only in the precise framework of [Article 101(3)] that the pro and anti-competitive aspects of a restriction may be weighed."[126] Any redeeming characteristics based on noneconomic consideration can only be raised in the context of Article 101(3) of the TFEU.[127]

According to Article 101(3), Article 101(1) may be declared inapplicable to conduct violating Article 101(1) but which (i) contributes to improving the production or distribution of goods or to promoting technical or economic progress, (ii) while allowing consumers a fair share of the resulting benefit, provided (iii) that it does not impose on the undertakings concerned restrictions which are not indispensable to the attainment of these objectives or (iv) afford such undertakings the possibility of eliminating competition in respect of a substantial part of the relevant products or services in question.

The Commission enjoys a large degree of discretion in applying these four requirements. According to the ECJ, judicial review of Commission decisions "must necessarily be confined to verifying whether the rules on procedure and on the statement of reasons have been complied with, whether the facts have been accurately stated and whether there has been any manifest error of assessment or misuse of powers."[128] The undertakings seeking to benefit from the exception,

---

124. Case C-453/99, *In re* Courage, 2001 E.C.R. I-6297, 6322 ¶22.
125. *Id.* at 6327 ¶36. The English court subsequently awarded damages to the pub operator based on its counterclaim. Crehan v. Inntrepreneur Pub Company, 2003 EWHC 1510, 2003 WL 21491852.
126. Case T-112/99, Métropole télévision v. Comm'n, 2001 E.C.R. II-2464, 2488 ¶74.
127. Case C-209/07, Competition Authority v. Beef Industry Development Society Ltd., 2008 E.C.R. I-8674, 8683 ¶21.
128. Joined cases C-501/06 P, C-513/06 P, C-515/06 P, and C-519/06 P, GlaxoSmithKline Services Unlimited v. Comm'n, 2009 E.C.R. I-9374, 9406 ¶85.

and not the Commission, bear the burden of showing that the requirements of Article 101(3) of the TFEU are fulfilled in the particular case.[129]

(1) Economic Benefit

The economic benefit requirement means that the agreement must contribute to improving the production or distribution of products or services or to promoting technical or economic progress. It is at this point in the analysis that the efficiencies of the agreement—which in the United States are taken into account when applying the prohibition—are considered.[130] In general, efficiencies in the context of Article 101 of the TFEU are the benefits made possible by the coordination of commercial behavior. A distinction is made between cost efficiencies and efficiencies that create value in the form of new or improved products.[131]

Cost efficiencies refer to cost reductions made possible by the coordinated interaction. The achievement of economies of scale and scope are perhaps the most common cost efficiency gains. The agreement may also result in synergies by combining the complementary strengths of the parties to the agreement. Alternatively, the development of new production technologies may result in a more efficient process. Examples of agreements capable of producing efficiencies in the form of new or improved goods or services are research and development agreements, license agreements, and agreements providing for joint production of new or improved goods or services. As each case is different, there is no exhaustive list of efficient agreements. A case-by-case analysis must be made.

(2) Consumer Benefit

The economic benefits discussed above as the first requirement of Article 101(3) of the TFEU must flow not only to the parties to the agreement but also to consumers. The concept of "consumers" encompasses all users of the products covered by the agreement, including wholesalers, retailers, and final consumers.[132] In other words, consumers within the meaning of Article 101(3) are the customers of the parties to the agreement and subsequent purchasers. The net effect of the agreement (after weighing the benefits against the detriments) must at least be neutral from the point of view of consumers within each relevant market.[133] It is not required that consumers receive a share of each and every efficiency gain identified under the first condition. It suffices that sufficient benefits are passed on to compensate for the negative effects of the restrictive

---

129. *Id.* at 9424 ¶162.
130. *See, e.g.*, Case T-168/01, GlaxoSmithKline Services Unlimited v. Comm'n, 2006 E.C.R. II-2981, 3050 ¶247 *aff'd on appeal* Joined cases C-501/06 P, C-513/06 P, C-515/06 P and C-519/06 P, GlaxoSmithKline Services Unlimited v. Comm'n, 2009 E.C.R. I-9374.
131. Comm'n Guidelines on the Application of Article 81(3) of the Treaty, 2004 O.J. (C 101) 97, 105 ¶59.
132. Case 382/12 P, Case C-382/12 P, MasterCard Inc. v. Comm'n, 2014 E.C.R. I-___, at ¶236; Comm'n Guidelines on the Application of Article 81(3) of the Treaty, 2004 O.J. (C 101) 97, 109 ¶84.
133. Case C-382/12 P, MasterCard Inc. v. Comm'n, 2014 E.C.R. I-___, at ¶234.

agreement. Moreover, it is not necessary that all customers benefit from the practice as the relevant effect is the overall effect and not the effect on specific customers.

In *Asnef-Equifax, Servicios de Información sobre Solvencia y Crédito, SL v. Asociación de Usuarios de Servicios Bancarios*, a group of banks established a scheme to exchange information on the credit histories of their customers and potential customers. Although the information-sharing scheme had the negative effect that some customers who may otherwise receive credit would be turned down, the ECJ held "it is the beneficial nature of the effect on all consumers in the relevant markets that must be taken into consideration, not the effect on each member of that category of consumers."[134]

(3) Indispensability

The third requirement for an exemption under Article 101(3) of the TFEU is that the restriction of competition is necessary to achieve the redeeming efficiencies. The application of this requirement proceeds in two steps. First, the restrictive agreement itself must be necessary in order to achieve the efficiencies.[135] Second, the individual restrictions of competition that flow from the agreement must also be necessary for the attainment of the efficiencies.[136] If there are less restrictive means to achieve similar benefits, the claimed efficiencies cannot be used to justify the restrictions of competition (i.e., they are not indispensable).

(4) Substantial Competition

The last requirement for an exemption under Article 101(3) of the TFEU is that the agreement must not eliminate competition for a substantial part of the products in question. In other words, an agreement cannot benefit from the exemption if it involves a dominant undertaking or one that will become dominant as a consequence of an agreement. If the agreement has already been implemented, the Commission may rely on the actual market conduct of the parties to make its assessment. For example, substantial price increases following conclusion of an agreement serve as an indication that the parties are not subject to any real competitive pressure, and that competition has been eliminated with regard to a substantial part of the products concerned.

To a certain extent, this requirement overlaps with the consumer benefit requirement of Article 101(3) of the TFEU. As discussed above, in order to qualify for an exemption, not only must there be benefits stemming from the agreement or concerted practice, but consumers must share in that benefit. One important factor in determining whether consumers will benefit is the existence of sufficient competition which forces the undertakings concerned to pass on those benefits to their customers. Hence, if the agreement forecloses substantial competition, it will not fulfill the last requirement of Article 101(3) and probably not the second requirement of Article 101(3).

---

134. Case C-238/05, Asnef-Equifax, Servicios de Información sobre Solvencia y Crédito, SL v. Asociación de Usuarios de Servicios Bancarios, 2006 E.C.R. I-11125, 11166 ¶70.
135. Comm'n Guidelines on the Application of Article 81(3) of the Treaty, 2004 O.J. (C 101) 97, 107 ¶73.
136. *Id.*

(b) Block Exemptions

The exemption requirements codified in Article 101(3) of the TFEU are abstract and difficult to apply with certainty. In an effort to provide some legal certainty to the application of these general rules to specific types of agreements, the Commission has adopted a series of regulations known as block exemptions. These regulations attempt to set more specific parameters for determining when certain types or "blocks" of agreements will fulfill the requirements of Article 101(3). They generally provide that if a particular agreement meets the requirements set forth in the particular regulation, the agreement automatically fulfills the requirements of Article 101(3). The significance of the block exemptions relates to the legal certainty which they attempt to provide. They do not expand the exemption codified in Article 101(3) of the TFEU. Instead, they attempt to specifically identify when particular types of agreements benefit from the exemption.

There are three categories of block exemptions: horizontal, vertical, and sectorial. The two horizontal block exemptions—so-called because they apply to horizontal relationships—are the Specialization Block Exemption[137] and the Research & Development Block Exemption.[138] The two vertical block exemptions—so-called because they apply to vertical relationships—are the Technology Transfer Block Exemption[139] and the Vertical Restraints Block Exemption.[140] In addition there are several sectorial block exemptions which apply specifically to certain industries.[141] Each block exemption is unique in its construction and wording. Rather than discuss each of these block exemptions individually, they are discussed below in the context of the type of agreements to which they apply.

---

137. Commission Regulation (EU) No. 1218/2010 on the application of Article 101(3) of the Treaty on the Functioning of the European Union to certain categories of specialization agreements, 2010 O.J. (L 335) 43.
138. Commission Regulation (EU) No. 1217/2010 on the application of Article 101(3) of the Treaty on the Functioning of the European Union to certain categories of research and development agreements, 2010 O.J. (L 335) 36.
139. Commission Regulation No. 316/2014 of 21 March 2014 on the application of Article 101(3) of the Treaty on the Functioning of the European Union to categories of technology transfer agreements, 2014 O.J. (L 93) 17 [hereinafter Technology Transfer Block Exemption].
140. Commission Regulation (EU) No. 330/2010 of 20 April 2010 on the application of Art. 101(3) of the Treaty on the Fuctioning of the European Union to categories of vertical agreements and concerted practices, 2010 O.J. (L 102) 1.
141. Commission Regulation (EC) No. 246/2009 of 26 February 2009 on the application of Art. 81(3) of the Treaty to certain categories of agreements, decisions, and concerted practices between liner shipping companies, 2009 O.J. (L 79) 1; Commission Regulation (EU) No. 461/2010 of 27 May 2010 on the application of Article 101(3) of the Treaty on the Functioning of the European Union to categories of vertical agreements and concerted practices in the motor vehicle sector, 2010 O.J. (L 129) 52; Commission Regulation (EU) No. 267/2010 of 24 March 2010 on the application of Art. 81(3) of the Treaty to certain categories of agreements, decisions, and concerted practices in the insurance sector, 2010 O.J. (L 83) 1.

4.4 Ancillary Restraints

Contracts between companies tend to contain many provisions which are ancillary or designed to support the main objective or objectives of the agreement. It is possible that an otherwise legitimate contract contains specific clauses which are themselves restrictive of competition. For example, two firms might agree to cooperate by sharing research and development results for the purpose of achieving an inovation which neither could achieve on its own. It would not be uncommon in such a scenario for the parties to include clauses in the agreement which restricted the commercial freedom of the other partner.

According to the EU ancillary restraints doctrine, if a given operation or activity is not covered by the prohibition rule laid down in Article 101(1) TFEU, then ancillary restrictions are also not prohibited by Article 101 proovided "that restriction is objectively necessary to the implementation of that operation or that activity and proportionate to the objectives of one or the other."[142] The restrictions imposed in the context of a franchise system are good examples. In order to maintain uniformity within the franchise system, franchisors typically impose restrictions on the franchisees related to advertising, the design of the stores, and the use of the trademark. According to the ECJ, standard franchise systems do not violate Article 101(1) TFEU nor do the individual restrictions placed on the franchisees if they are necessary to achieve the legitimate objective of the franchise system.[143]

In *Gøttrup-Klim e.a. Grovvareforeninger v. Dansk Landbrugs Grovvareselskab AmbA*, for example, a provision included in a joint purchasing organization's documents which prohibited the members of the joint purchasing organization from cooperating with any other competing joint purchasing organization was held to be ancillary to the legitimate purpose of the joint purchasing organization as it was necessary to fulfill the basic objectives.[144]

The cases tend to revolve around which restrictions are "objectively necessary." Determining whether a particular clause is ancillary to a legitimate objective must be made on a case-by-case basis. The test is, however, a difficult one. According to the ECJ, the legitimate objective must be "impossible to carry out in the absence of the restriction in question."[145]

4.5 Types of Restraints

The preceding discussion of Article 101 of the TFEU is admittedly abstract. It provides only general guidance for the application of the competition rules in specific cases. In order to ease and facilitate the application of the competition rules, the Commission, courts, and practitioners rely on categories or types of agreements. The categorization of an agreement often (but not always) moves one closer to being able to determine the legality of the agreement as there is

---

142. Case C-382/12 P, MasterCard Inc. v. Comm'n, 2014 E.C.R. I-____, at ¶89.
143. Case 161/84, Pronuptia de Paris GmbH v. Comm'n, 1986 E.C.R. 374, 381 ¶15.
144. Case 250/92, Gøttrup-Klim e.a. Grovvareforeninger v. Dansk Landbrugs Grovvareselskab AmbA, 1994 E.C.R. 5671, 5687 ¶34.
145. Case C-382/12 P, MasterCard Inc. v. Comm'n, 2014 E.C.R. I-____, at ¶91.

commonly a Commission decision, guidelines, or judicial precedence applicable to that particular type of agreement.

The following discussion presents the various categories of agreements commonly used in the EU to facilitate the application of competition law. It is by no means exhaustive. The basic distinction used in Europe is between horizontal restraints and vertical restraints. As discussed above, horizontal restraints are those between actual or potential competitors. Vertical restraints are those between undertakings active at different levels of the value chain.

(a) *Horizontal Hard-core Restraints*

Several categories of horizontal agreements always violate Article 101(1) of the TFEU. These are referred to as "hard-core" restraints. The concept of a hard-core restraint of competition is analogous to per se restraints in U.S. antitrust law.

(1) Price Restraints

Agreements between competitors that have as their object or effect price fixing are prohibited by Article 101(1) and do not qualify for an exemption. A horizontal agreement to set minimum prices is perhaps the most egregious violation of Article 101 TFEU. The *Lombard Club* proceeding provides an example.[146] In that case, the leading Austrian banks regularly met to discuss the interest rates that the banks would charge on certain loans. Between January 1994 and June 1998, the banks met over 300 times. When the Commission conducted a "dawn raid"[147] at the offices of the banks, the cartel became apparent. In one of the documents discovered by the Commission, the host of one of the illicit meetings welcomed the other participants with the following words:

> The exchange of experience between banks in relation to interest rates has repeatedly proved to be a useful means of avoiding uncontrolled price competition. In this vein, today's meeting [...] should likewise ensure a focused and reasonable approach of all banks with regard to pricing. The way in which interest rates are currently being set shows very clearly that it is again necessary for us to sit down together and counteract problematic price developments[...] [I] hope, in the interests of your institutions, that constructive solutions will be found.

The motivation for the cartel cannot serve as a justification. In *Citric Acid*, for example, a group of European citric acid manufacturers formed a

---

146. Press Release IP/02/844 (June 11, 2002).
147. A "dawn raid" refers to the unannounced on-site investigations which the Commission is permitted to conduct under Council Regulation (EC) No. 1/2003 of 16 December 2002 on the implementation of the rules on competition laid down in Articles 81 and 82 of the Treaty, 2003 O.J. (L 1) 1, art. 20. Commission officials, with local law enforcement personnel, appear at the offices of the suspected company and review and copy the company's relevant files and computers.

cartel in part to counter what they perceived as unfair cheap imports from China. Even after recognizing the possible unfairness of the cheap imports, the Commission imposed significant fines on the cartel participants for violating the EU competition laws.[148]

Although price fixing is most common between sellers, price fixing between buyers is also a hard-core restraint of competition. In the *Raw Tobacco* investigation, for example, a group of Spanish tobacco processors entered into an agreement to fix the maximum price they would pay for raw tobacco. The Commission imposed significant fines on the tobacco processors for violating Article 101 of the TFEU.[149]

(2) Non-Price Terms of Sale

Competitors compete not only on the basis of price. Agreements which do not directly influence price may also violate Article 101(1) of the TFEU. For example, competitors may agree on the terms and conditions according to which they offer their goods or services (e.g., length of product warranties). Such an agreement would restrict the competition between them and preclude the customer from obtaining preferential terms and conditions of sale.[150] They are consequently considered hard-core restraints of competition.

(3) Market Division

Collusion between competitors to divide markets geographically or by customer is another example of a hard-core restraint of competition under Article 101 of the TFEU. In *Toshiba Corp. v. Commission*, Japanese and European power transformer manufacturers agreed to geographically divide the markets.[151] The European manufacturers agreed not to sell into Japan and the Japanese manufacturers agreed not to sell into Europe.

The *Methylglucamine* case is an example of a customer market division. In that case, pharmaceutical manufacturers Aventis and Merck conspired to allocate customers for methylglucamine, a chemical which is combined with other chemicals and injected into X-ray patients (the methylglucamine slows the process down by which the body expels the X-ray chemicals).[152] In that case, the undertakings—which together held almost 100 percent of the market for methylglucamine—agreed not to solicit each other's customers. If a customer of one of them requested a quote from the other, they agreed to respond to the quote with their standard list prices (which were typically higher than the rate they were actually charging). Hence, there was no incentive for customers to change suppliers. At the end of each year, the firms met to determine whether the customers had stayed with their supplier. Merck eventually came forward and revealed the cartel under the Commission's leniency program and was not fined. Aventis was fined €2.85 million.[153]

---

148. Citric Acid, 2002 O.J. (L 239) 18.
149. Comm'n, 2004 Annual Report on Competition Policy (2005) at 32 ¶57.
150. *See, e.g.*, La Cimenterie, 1972 O.J. (L 303) 24.
151. Case T-519/09, Toshiba Corp. v. Comm'n, 2014 E.C.R. I-____.
152. Methylglucamine, 2004 O.J. (L 38) 18.
153. *Id.* at 46.

(4) Collective Boycotts

A conspiracy between competitors not to do business with a third party is another example of a hard-core restraint of competition, regardless of whether the third party is a competitor, supplier, or a customer. In *LR af 1998 A/S v. Commission*, a group of pipe manufacturers for heating systems established a cartel to allocate customers and set prices in responding to public bids by contractors installing the heating systems.[154] The one competitor who refused to join the conspiracy threatened to jeopardize the success of the cartel by submitting bids below the cartel price. As the firms were not always in the position to fulfill the requirements of the public bid by themselves, they sometimes subcontracted certain portions of the work to other companies in the industry. In order to hinder the ability of the maverick competitor in responding to bids for larger projects, the members of the cartel agreed to boycott the maverick by not assisting it in projects won by the maverick. The conspiracy resulted in significant fines being imposed on the members of the conspiracy.

A similar boycott was integral to the ability of the cartel members in *Sorbates* to achieve their objectives.[155] Sorbates is a chemical preservative used in foods and beverages to prevent bacteria and mold. The German sorbates manufacturer Hoechst AG and a group of Japanese producers agreed to establish minimum prices for sorbates in the EU. As the price of sorbates was consequently higher than the market price would have been without the cartel, it became an attractive market for potential entrants. To prevent potential market entrants, the cartel members agreed not to supply critical technology to these companies.

(5) Limitation of Output

There are various ways competitors may artificially increase the prices they can demand for their products without a corresponding increase in benefit to the customers. As discussed above, an agreement between them on minimum prices is one way to achieve this objective. As there is generally an inverse relationship between prices and quantity—prices generally increase when the available quantity of a product decreases—competitors may artificially increase prices by agreeing to limit their output of a certain product. Such horizontal collusion is considered a hard-core restraint of competition in EU competition law.[156]

(6) Information Exchanges

The legality of the exchange of information among competitors or potential competitors depends on the context and the nature of the information exchanged. Although neither the ECJ nor the Commission has adopted a formal test for the

---

154. Case T-23/99, LR af 1998 A/S v. Comm'n, 2002 E.C.R. II-1705.
155. Sorbates, 2005 O.J. (L 182) 20.
156. *See, e.g.*, Zinc Producer Group, 1984 O.J. (L 212) 13. In certain circumstances, however, the Commission has been willing to permit agreements to limit output in response to a critical and sustained situation of overcapacity in the industry. *See* A. Fiebig, Crisis Cartels and the Triumph of Industrial Policy Over Competition Law in Europe, 25 Brooklyn J. Int'l L. 607 (1999).

legality of information exchanges, three aspects of the information exchange are typically examined:

- Existence of an agreement or concerted practice
- Type of information exchanged
- Purpose of the exchange.

As discussed above, the threshold question for the applicability of Article 101 of the TFEU is the existence of an agreement or concerted practice. If an undertaking receives strategic information about another competitor through a common customer, that exchange of information is not likely to violate Article 101(a) of the TFEU unless there is an agreement or concerted practice between the undertakings.[157] However, the Commission has taken the position—supported by the General Court[158] and the ECJ[159]—that the (mere) direct exchange of strategic information between competitors is sufficient to support a finding of a concerted practice.[160] This is based on an assumption that the only reason competitors would exchange such information is for anticompetitive purposes.[161] Consequently, the Commission or a private plaintiff does not have to show an actual anticompetitive effect.[162]

The requirement of an agreement or concerted practice also means that a unilateral release of strategic information by an undertaking does not violate Article 101(1) of the TFEU.[163] This may occur, for example, when an airline publicly announces its intent to raise its prices. The fact that the competitors of the airline receive this information does not mean that the release of information is illegal under Article 101(1) even though an exchange of the same information directly with the competitor on a unilateral or bilateral basis would violate Article 101(1).[164]

The second aspect of the information exchange examined by the Commission is the type of information exchanged. As a general rule, the exchange of genuinely public information is compatible with Article 101

---

157. Horizontal Cooperation Guidelines at 13 ¶60.
158. Case T-588/08, Dole Food Company, Inc. v. Comm'n, 2013 E.C.R. II-____, at ¶¶541-544 aff'd on appeal Case C-286/13 P, Dole Food Company Inc. v. Commission, 2015 E.C.R. I-____.
159. Case C-455/11 P, Solvay SA v. Comm'n, 2013 E.C.R. I-____, at ¶40. (The exchange of information between competitors in an oligopolistic market "suffices to prove the existence of a concerted practice.")
160. Horizontal Cooperation Guidelines at 14 ¶62.
161. Case T-588/08, Dole Food Company, Inc. v. Comm'n, 2013 E.C.R. II-____, at ¶¶541 aff'd on appeal Case C-286/13 P, Dole Food Company Inc. v. Commission, 2015 E.C.R. I-____.
162. Case C-286/13 P, Dole Food Company Inc. v. Commission, 2015 E.C.R. I-____ at ¶¶113-114.
163. Horizontal Cooperation Guidelines at 14 ¶63.
164. Case T-25/95, Cimenteries v. Comm'n, 2000 E.C.R. II-491, 958 ¶1849 (unilateral release of information to a competitor violates Article 101(1) of the TFEU if the competitor accepts it) aff'd on appeal Joined cases C-204/00 P, C-205/00 P, C-211/00 P, C-213/00 P, C-217/00 P and C-219/00 P, Aalborg Portland A/S v. Comm'n, 2004 E.C.R. I-123.

of the TFEU.[165] Conversely, the exchange of "strategic data" between the undertakings is inherently suspect. Although the Commission has not issued an exhaustive list of what constitutes strategic data, it has identified pricing information, customer lists, production costs, quantities, sales, capacities, qualities, marketing plans, risks, investments, technologies, and research and development efforts as potentially strategic.[166] Nonetheless, the exchange of such data may be legitimate and consequently permitted under Article 101 if it is properly aggregated[167] and historical[168] in nature. In each case, however, the purpose of the exchange should be examined.

The most significant threat to competition presented by the exchange of information among competitors is that the information is used to facilitate or monitor cartels. The creation of a cartel almost always requires the exchange of strategic information among the cartel members. The Commission is well aware that the subsequent implementation of the cartel also often depends on the exchange of information among the cartel members.[169] This is because cartels will seldom achieve their objectives if there is a lack of discipline among their members. The exchange of information directly or indirectly among the cartel members allows the cartel to determine if any members are not adhering to the agreement. The exchange of information for this purpose constitutes a violation of Article 101(1) of the TFEU.[170]

Finally, the characteristics of the particular market on which the information is exchanged are relevant to determining the legality of the exchange. In general, the greater the degree of market concentration and transparency, the more suspect the information exchange. According to the Commission, an anticompetitive purpose is more likely "in markets which are sufficiently transparent, concentrated, non-complex, stable and symmetric."[171] This is because it is much easier to achieve an anticompetitive effect through an exchange of information in markets bearing such characteristics.

---

165. Horizontal Cooperation Guidelines at 20 ¶92.
166. Id. at 19 ¶86. See also Case T-587/08, Fresh Del Monte Produce, Inc. v. Comm'n, 2013 E.C.R. II-____, at ¶¶310-325; Waste Management Products, 2012 O.J. (C 335) 4.
167. Data is sufficiently aggregated when it makes it impossible or "sufficiently difficult" for the recipient to identify a specific undertaking to which the data relates. Horizontal Cooperation Guidelines at 19 ¶89.
168. The older the data, the less likely that it is useful to a competitor in predicting future commercial behavior and hence the more likely its exchange is compatible with Article 101 of the TFEU. Horizontal Cooperation Guidelines at 20 ¶90. In general, data which is over one year old is considered historical by the Commission. UK Agricultural Tractor Registration Exchange, 1992 O.J. (L 68) 19, 29 ¶50; Wirtschaftsvereinigung Stahl, 1998 O.J. (L 1) 10, 19 ¶52.
169. Horizontal Cooperation Guidelines at 15 ¶67.
170. Refrigeration Compressors, Comm'n Decision of 7 December 2011, summary of decision available at 2012 O.J. (C 122) 6; DRAMs, Comm'n Decision of 19 May 2010, summary of decision available at 2011 O.J. (C 180) 15; Professional Videotape, Comm'n Decision in Case COMP/38.432 (Nov. 20, 2007) at ¶108.
171. Horizontal Cooperation Guidelines at 17 ¶77.

(b) Horizontal Cooperation

Although horizontal agreements have traditionally been the focus of competition regulators, globalization and the reduced significance of barriers to market entry have necessitated a renewed look at the prohibitive policy against cooperation between competitors. Collusion between competitors may lead to significant efficiencies which benefit not only the firms involved, but also the consumers. By cooperating, firms may be able to reduce risk, save costs, and introduce new products. For that reason, not all forms of horizontal agreements are prohibited.

(1) R&D Cooperation

The concept of research and development (R&D) cooperation captures a wide array of agreements ranging from outsourcing to the joint improvement of existing technologies and cooperation concerning the research, development, and marketing of completely new products. The R&D cooperation may take the form of a joint venture or (merely) a contractual relationship. There is no exhaustive list of forms of R&D cooperation.

According to the Commission, R&D cooperation between competitors or potential competitors may restrict competition by lessening the competition between the cooperating undertakings at the R&D stage.[172] This potentially leads to less innovation than if each of the undertakings independently engaged in the R&D efforts. R&D cooperation may also have a negative effect on competition by facilitating coordination of the commercial conduct of the undertakings outside the narrow scope of the R&D cooperation.

In analyzing R&D cooperation under Article 101 of the TFEU, the Commission distinguishes between pure R&D agreements and more comprehensive R&D cooperation agreements.[173] Pure R&D cooperation agreements are strictly limited to R&D and do not extend to the exploitation of the results. According to the Commission, exploitation of the results means the production or distribution of the products or the application of the resulting technologies or the assignment or licensing of intellectual property rights or the communication of know-how required for such manufacture.[174] Each of the parties is able to independently exploit the results of the R&D cooperation. According to the Commission, pure R&D agreements "will only rarely give rise to restrictive effects on competition within the meaning of Article 101(1)."[175]

The Commission gives greater scrutiny to more comprehensive R&D cooperation agreements.[176] Such agreements typically involve an agreement on

---

172. *Id.* at 28 ¶127.
173. *Id.* at 30 ¶137.
174. Commission Regulation (EU) No. 1217/2010 of 14 December 2010 on the application of Article 101(3) of the Treaty on the Functioning of the European Union to certain categories of research and development agreements, 2010 O.J. (L 335) 36, 39 art. 1(1)(g).
175. Horizontal Cooperation Guidelines at 29 ¶132.
176. *Id.* at 30 ¶137.

the exploitation of results, licensing, production, or even marketing.[177] In general, the more restrictions imposed on the parties as to the use of the R&D results and the higher the market shares of the undertakings involved, the more likely the R&D cooperation will violate Article 101 of the TFEU. The Commission is of the opinion that the potential negative effects are only likely to arise when the parties to the cooperation have significant market power. As a general rule, research and development agreements will present anticompetitive concerns only if the combined market share of the parties exceeds 25 percent.[178]

An important consideration in assessing R&D cooperation agreements between competitors or potential competitors is whether the undertakings are able to carry out the necessary research and development independently.[179] This might be the case, for example, if the firms combine complementary skills, technologies, and other resources which they each already have. The ability of a firm to conduct its own research and development must be assessed realistically. In other words, just because there is a remote theoretical possibility that the firms could individually achieve the same result does not mean that the Commission will prohibit cooperation. The decisive question is whether each party independently has the necessary assets, know-how, and other resources. For example, cooperation between two automobile producers to exchange research and development on hybrid engine technologies for the purpose of allowing them to enhance the quality of their product offerings may be characterized as a form of horizontal R&D cooperation.[180]

In addition to examining the context and the necessity of the R&D cooperation, the Commission will also consider the content of the agreement. The R&D Block Exemption identifies specific clauses which are prohibited by Article 101 even if the aggregate market share of the parties is less than 25 percent.[181]

(2) Production Cooperation

Production cooperation agreements involve two or more competitors or potential competitors at the production stage. Similar to R&D cooperation agreements, production cooperation may involve different levels of integration between the undertakings, ranging from the creation of a joint venture to a (mere) contractual relationship. Three types of production cooperation recognized by the Commission are joint production agreements, unilateral specialization, and reciprocal specializations.[182]

---

177. *Id.*
178. *Id.* at 29 ¶133; R&D Block Exemption at art. 4
179. Horizontal Cooperation Guidelines at 29 ¶130.
180. Norihiko Shirouzu & Jathon Sapsford, GM, Toyota Weigh a Bid to Share Hybrid Expertise, THE WALL STREET JOURNAL, p. A2 col. 3 (May 9, 2005).
181. R&D Block Exemption at arts. 5&6.
182. Commission Regulation (EU) No. 1218/2010 of 14 December 2010 on the application of Article 101(3) of the Treaty on the Functioning of the European Union to certain categories of specialisation agreements, 2010 O.J. (L 335) 43, 45 art. 1(1)(d) [hereinafter Specialization Block Exemption].

In a joint production agreement, two or more undertakings agree to produce a product or products jointly. Unilateral specialization exists if the undertakings agree that instead of producing a product jointly as in a joint production agreement, one of them will cease producing a product and procure that product from the other undertaking.[183] For example, two cellular phone manufacturers may find that, in view of the economies of scale in manufacturing the liquid crystal display screens that are used in their telephones, it makes more sense if just one of them produces the screens and sells them to the other one, rather than each of them producing screens. They might therefore enter into an agreement according to which one agrees to close its screen manufacturing facility and secure its supply from the competitor.

Reciprocal specialization refers to the situation where each of the competing undertakings agrees to cease production of different products and procure those products from the other undertaking. Using the previous example of the mobile phone manufacturers, the agreement would be considered reciprocal specialization if the party responsible for producing the screens agreed in return to cease production of the battery packs and secure its supply of battery packs from the other party.

Although production cooperation may yield efficiencies for the undertakings involved, the Commission is conscious that production cooperation between competitors or potential competitors can reduce competition.[184] Even if the undertakings market the products independently, cooperation at the production stage may lead to an alignment of the prices or output of the respective undertakings. Production cooperation may also have a foreclosure effect on third parties.[185] This is particularly the case where the undertakings involved face competition in a downstream market from competitors who are dependent on products in the upstream market where the cooperation between competitors takes place. According to the Commission, "by gaining enough market power, parties engaging in joint production in an upstream market may be able to raise the price of a key component for a market downstream. Thereby, they could use the joint production to raise the costs of their rivals downstream and, ultimately, force them off the market."[186]

Similar to the analysis of R&D cooperation, the market power of the undertakings involved in the production cooperation and the restrictions imposed on the undertakings in the agreement are important aspects of determining the compatibility of the cooperation with Article 101 of the TFEU. There is no absolute market share threshold that indicates that a production agreement creates some degree or market power and thus falls under Article 101(1) of the TFEU. However, agreements concerning unilateral or reciprocal specialization, as well as joint production, will generally be permitted if they are concluded between parties with a combined market share not exceeding 20 percent in

---

183. *Id.*
184. Horizontal Cooperation Guidelines at 36 ¶157.
185. *Id.* at 37 ¶165.
186. *Id.* at 36 ¶159.

the relevant markets.[187] If the parties' combined market share is higher than 20 percent, the likely impact of the production agreement on the market must be specifically analyzed. In this analysis, market concentration as well as market shares will be significant factors. The higher the level of concentration on the market, the more likely that the horizontal production cooperation will have a negative effect on competition.

Similar to R&D cooperation, the content of the agreement serving as the basis for the production cooperation is relevant in determining its conformity with Article 101 of the TFEU. The agreement upon which the production cooperation is based must not contain any hard-core restrictions even if the aggregate market share of the undertakings involved is below 20 percent.[188] The term "hard core" in this context refers to clauses in the agreement fixing the prices of the products when they are sold to third parties.[189] The other types of hard-core restrictions are clauses in the agreement which allocate markets or customers or limit the output or sales of the undertakings involved.[190]

(3) Purchasing Cooperation

Purchasing cooperation refers to agreements between competitors or potential competitors according to which they agree to purchase certain inputs jointly (or as a collective in the case of a group of undertakings). This can occur in the context of a joint venture or by contract. Joint purchasing commonly allows the cooperating undertakings to secure the inputs at lower prices or on more favorable terms because of the collective buying power they possess vis-à-vis suppliers.

An example of a procompetitive joint purchasing arrangement is the alliance between General Motors Corp. and Fiat SpA by which both parties agreed to cooperate in purchasing car components and parts.[191] After an analysis and consultation of interested third parties, the Commission took the view that although Fiat and General Motors coordinated their activities in the production of powertrains and in the purchasing of components and parts, the alliance benefited consumers. Components and parts accounted for a considerable share of the cost of a new car, and the increase in the two companies' bargaining power had the potential for substantial savings that would be passed on to the consumers. The Commission, therefore, concluded that the requirements for an exemption under Article 101(3) of the TFEU were met.

---

187. *Id.* at 38 ¶169; Specialization Block Exemption at art. 3.
188. Commission Regulation (EU) No. 1218/2010 of 14 December 2010 on the application of Article 101(3) of the Treaty on the Functioning of the European Union to certain categories of specialisation agreements, 2010 O.J. (L 335) 43, 46 art. 4.
189. Contractual clauses which fix the prices charged to immediate customers in the context of joint distribution are permitted. Specialization Block Exemption 46 art. 4.
190. The undertakings are allowed to agree on the amount of products in the context of specialization or the setting of the capacity and production volume in the context of joint production or the setting of sales targets in the context of joint distribution. Specialization Block Exemption at art. 4.
191. IP/00/932 (Aug. 16, 2000).

The Commission is aware, however, that purchasing cooperation between actual or potential competitors can, in certain circumstances, have anticompetitive effects.[192] Whether the purchasing cooperation violates Article 101 of the TFEU depends on the context in which it occurs, the content of the agreement, and the market power of the undertakings concerned. The structure of the market is important because it is an indication that the benefits resulting from the cooperation will be passed on to the customers.

If the cooperating undertakings in the aggregate enjoy a significant degree of market power on the *selling* market, the Commission considers it less likely that the lower purchase prices achieved by the joint purchasing arrangement will be passed on to the consumers.[193] Conversely, a significant degree of market power on the *purchasing* market could lead to a reduction in quality and innovation because of the ability of the cooperating undertakings to force suppliers to reduce the range or quality of products they produce.[194] In general, the purchasing cooperation between competitors or potential competitors is not prohibited if the combined market share of the parties on each of the purchasing market and the selling market is below 15 percent.[195] One should note, however, that the Commission is even willing to approve purchasing cooperation where the cooperating competitors have significant market power.[196] In the *Covisint* case, for example, a joint venture between automobile manufacturers with significant market shares, the Commission concluded that there was no violation of Article 101(1) of the TFEU.[197]

In addition, the agreement establishing the purchasing cooperation must not contain restrictions which are dispensable for attaining the legitimate objectives. For example, a clause restricting any of the parties involved in the purchasing cooperation in its reselling activities would likely be deemed dispensable to the cooperation.[198]

(4) Commercialization

Cooperation between actual or potential competitors in the selling, distribution, or promotion of their products is referred to as commercialization. A distribution agreement, for example, is a type of commercialization cooperation.[199] Absent the inclusion of hard-core restraints of competition, commercialization

---

192. Horizontal Cooperation Guidelines at 45 ¶200.
193. *Id.* at 45 ¶204.
194. *Id.* at 45 ¶203.
195. *Id.* at 46 ¶208.
196. *Id.* at 46 ¶209.
197. IP/01/1155 (Aug. 1, 2001).
198. Bitumen/NL, Comm'n Decision of Sept. 13, 2006, Case COMP/F/38.456 ¶167.
199. The Vertical Restraints Block Exemption applies to distribution agreements involving competitors provided that they are nonreciprocal and the parties are only competitors at the distribution level (and not at the manufacturing level). Commission Regulation (EU) No. 330/2010 of 20 April 2010 on the application of Article 101(3) of the Treaty on the Functioning of the European Union to categories of vertical agreements and concerted practices, 2010 OJ. (L 102) 1 at art. 2(4) [hereinafter Vertical Restraints Block Exemption].

agreements between competitors will only violate Article 101 of the TFEU if the parties have sufficient market power. According to the Commission, it is unlikely that market power exists if the parties to the commercialization agreement have an aggregate market share of less than 15 percent.[200] If the aggregate market share of the parties is 15 percent or greater, the commercialization cooperation is not automatically prohibited. Rather, the particular facts of the case must be examined in detail to identify the efficiencies and whether these efficiencies will be passed on to consumers.

(5) Standardization

The term "standardization" generally refers to the process of developing uniform technical specifications for a particular product made by different companies.[201] Standardization can cover various aspects of the products such as grades, dimensions or interoperability. The standard USB port, for example, is based on the USB peripheral device standard originally developed by seven companies as a way to connect computers to telephones.

Standardization of products may be coordinated by the various standardization bodies at the EU or national levels working with the private undertakings. In the EU, for example, the three main standards organizations are the European Committee for Standardization (CEN), the European Committee for Electrotechnical Standardization (CENELEC), and the European Telecommunications Standards Institute (ETSI). Standardization may also occur through the private efforts of cooperating undertakings. Such undertakings may develop a standard on their own. For example, the USB standard was the result of the coordinated efforts of DEC, NEC, Intel, IBM, Compaq, Microsoft, and Nortel.

The European Commission recognizes that standardization cooperation among undertakings is generally beneficial for the consumers. For example, it may be beneficial for consumers if the manufacturers of computers cooperate to set a standard for the ports that they include on their computers. This may make it easier for a computer user to switch between different computers because the cable connections/ports are standardized. There are, however, potentially anticompetitive effects that standardization can have. Standardization may have the effect of reducing price competition between the cooperating undertakings by making their products more uniform.[202] Second, the standardization may result in standards that make it more difficult for alternative technologies to enter the market even if those alternative technologies are preferred by the consumers.[203] Standardization may also restrict competition by allowing the cooperating undertakings to exclude certain other undertakings.

---

200. Horizontal Cooperation Guidelines at 51 ¶240.
201. As used in this context, "standardization" is limited to the standardization of the technical characteristics of the product as the standardization of the commercial aspects of the sale of the products—for example price, terms of sale, etc.—is not considered legitimate standardization under the competition laws.
202. *Id.* at 57 ¶265.
203. *Id.* at 57 ¶266.

According to the European Commission[204] and the General Court,[205] standardization cooperation does not violate Article 101(1) of the TFEU if the procedure for adopting the standard and access to the standard are nondiscriminatory, open, and transparent. This also applies to standards adopted by the recognized standardization bodies even though company representatives may be involved in these standards bodies. If, for example, the standard is created by CEN, CENELEC, or ETSI, and the procedures for those organizations were followed, it is likely that there will be no violation of Article 101(1) of the TFEU.[206]

High market shares held by the parties involved in the standardization do not necessarily mean that the standardization cooperation is prohibited.[207] This is based on the recognition that it is often necessary to effectively implement a standard to have a significant portion of the relevant industry involved. Each case must be examined on its own basis. However, the higher the market shares, the greater the possibility that the standard will foreclose competition. In such cases, it is even more important that third parties have nondiscriminatory and open access to the standard.

The permissibility of standards cooperation creates the risk that a particular standard, while not legally binding, becomes the de facto industry standard. The risk to competition is heightened in this case if the de facto standard is protected by proprietary rights, such as patent rights. The existence of a de facto standard does not establish an ipso facto violation of Article 101 of the TFEU provided that access to the standard is possible for third parties on fair, reasonable, and nondiscriminatory terms.[208]

(c) Vertical Restraints

(1) Resale Price Maintenance

It is often the case that a manufacturer of a product will want to control the price at which its product is resold by the manufacturer's distributors to third parties. If a supplier of products or services agrees with the buyer of those products or services that the buyer will not resell them below a certain price level, the agreement on minimum resale prices is considered a hard-core restraint of competition.[209] The prohibition on resale price maintenance also applies to indirect measures to achieve the same objective. For example, the supplier may set the price mark-up to be charged by the reseller. Another possibility is that the supplier and reseller fix the maximum level of discount the reseller can grant from a prescribed price level or prohibit the buyer from offering special discounts or clearance sales. A less obvious form of resale price maintenance is making the grant of rebates or reimbursement of promotional costs by the supplier subject to the observance of a given price level. These forms of indirect

---

204. *Id.* at 59 ¶280.
205. Case T-432/05, EMC Development AB v. Comm'n, 2010 E.C.R. II-1633, 1654 ¶65.
206. *Id.* at 1653 ¶61.
207. Horizontal Cooperation Guidelines at 66 ¶324.
208. Case T-432/05, EMC Development AB v. Comm'n, 2010 E.C.R. II-1633, 1653 ¶61.
209. JCB, 2002 O.J. (L 69) 1, 35.

resale price maintenance are hard-core restraints and prohibited by Article 101 of the TFEU.[210]

The qualification of vertical resale price maintenance as a hard-core restraint does not mean that the agreement cannot benefit from an exception. According to the Commission, the qualification as hard core (only) gives rise to a presumption that the agreement violated Article 101(1) TFEU and "is unlikely to fulfill the conditions of Article 101(3) TFEU."[211] In order to rebut the presumption in such cases, however, the parties to the agreement must show that the efficiencies justify the restriction on competition. Resale price maintenance may be justified where a manufacturer introduces a new product and the protection from price competition is necessary to incentivize the distributors to appropriately promote the new product.[212]

Vertical agreements imposing a maximum resale price are not considered hard-core restraints of competition.[213] The legality of maximum resale price maintenance depends on the circumstances. Maximum resale price maintenance does not violate Article 101 of the TFEU if both the supplier's and the buyer's market shares are 30 percent or less.[214]

Many consumer products have a minimum suggested resale price (sometimes even printed on the product packaging). The general rule in the EU is that a supplier may suggest or recommend list prices.[215] The rationale behind this policy is that there is no agreement or conspiracy as required by Article 101 of the TFEU. But when a supplier goes beyond mere communication of the recommended resale price and employs coercive tactics that interfere with the distributor's pricing independence, and the distributor follows the

---

210. Vertical Restraints Guidelines at 12 ¶48; Nathan-Bricolux, 2001 O.J. (L 54) 1, 12 ¶87. Not all member states agree with the Commission's critical position on vertical resale price maintenance. The Swedish Konkurrensverket, for example, refused to act on a complaint alleging resale price maintenance even though the complaint included clear evidence that it occurred. According to the Konkurrensverket, "the probability of any major harm to competition and consumers in the present case is not significant enough for the Competition Authority to prioritise a continued investigation. Decision of the Swedish Konkurrensverket in case no. 559/2013 (Oct. 30, 2014). The Chairman of the Dutch Autoriteit Consument & Markt has also incidcated that agency does not give high priority to vertical intrabrand retraint cases because they can be beneficial to the consumer. Speech of Chris Fonteijn on Vertical Agreements at Vereniging voor Mededingingsrecht Meeting November 25th 2014 *available at* https://www.acm.nl/en/publications/publication/13606/Speech-of-Chris-Fonteijn-on-vertical-agreements-at-VvM-seminar/.
211. *Id.* at 45 ¶223.
212. *Id.*
213. Vertical Restraints Block Exemption at art. 4(a); Nathan-Bricolux, 2001 O.J. (L 54) 1, 12 ¶87.
214. Vertical Restraints Guidelines at 46 ¶226. Of course, if the prices being suggested are minimum resale prices and the supplier exerts pressure on the distributor to observe the suggested minimum resale prices, it would be treated as an agreement to set the minimum resale prices.
215. Case T-67/01, JCB Service v. Comm'n, 2004 E.C.R. II-56, 99 ¶126 *aff'd on appeal* Case C-167/04 P, JCB Service v. Comm'n, 2006 E.C.R. I-8972.

recommendation, the Commission will likely find a violation of Article 101.[216] The higher the market share of the recommending supplier, the more likely the Commission will infer an agreement to abide by the recommended prices, the assumption being that the resellers are more likely to acquiesce to recommended prices when the supplier has a significant market share.

(2) *Exclusive Distribution and Division of Markets*

As a general rule, agreements or concerted practices that have as their direct or indirect object the territorial or customer restriction of sales by the buyer are generally prohibited as hard-core restraints.[217] The division of markets may be achieved in various ways. For example, the distributor may be prohibited from selling to certain customers or to customers in certain territories. If the distributor receives an order from these customers, it may be required to refer the order to the distributor assigned to that customer or territory. The division of markets or customers may also be achieved by indirect means.

In the *Nintendo* proceedings, for example, Nintendo sought to take advantage of price differences between member states by reducing the flow of its video games from the UK to other European countries where the same video games were significantly more expensive.[218] Nintendo and its distributors reduced supplies (and in some instances even refused) to supply those customers which were engaged in "re-export" from a country where the market price for the video games was low to countries where the market price for the games was high. The Commission consequently imposed fines in the aggregate amount of €167.8 million on Nintendo and its distributors.[219]

The mechanisms employed by firms to divide markets are often much more subtle. In one instance, an Italian manufacturer of coffee machines extended its product warranty service only to customers in the member states in which that customer had purchased her product and only if the product was purchased

---

216. Vertical Restraints Guidelines at 46 ¶226.
217. Vertical Restraints Block Exemption at art. 4(b). Case T-450/05, Automobiles Peugeot SA v. Comm'n, 2009 E.C.R. II-2539, 2553 ¶46; Case T-36/05, Coats Holdings Ltd. v. Comm'n, 2007 E.C.R. II-110 (summary), at ¶161 (full version of case reported in the electronic reports of cases ECLI:EU:T:2007:268) *aff'd on appeal* Case C-468/07 P, Coats Holdings Ltd. v. Comm'n, 2008 E.C.R. I-127 (ECLI:EU:C:2008:503). *But see* Case T-168/01, GlaxoSmithKline Services Unlimited v. Comm'n, 2006 E.C.R. II-2981, 3028 ¶167 in which the General Court suggested that restrictions on parallel trade may not constitute restrictions of competition in certain cases. The decision of the General Court was upheld by the ECJ on appeal Joined cases C-501/06 P, C-513/06 P, C-515/06 P, and C-519/06 P, GlaxoSmithKline Services Unlimited v. Comm'n, 2009 E.C.R. I-9291.
218. PO Nintendo Distribution, 2003 O.J. (L 255) 33.
219. In Case T-41/96, Bayer v. Comm'n, 2000 E.C.R. II-3383 (subsequently affirmed by the ECJ in Cases C-2/01 and 3/01, 2004 E.C.R. I-64) the General Court held that the unilateral reduction in products supplied to distributors did not violate Article 101(1) of the TFEU because of the absence of a conspiracy. In the *Nintendo* case, however, the reduction or elimination of products supplied was clearly part of an agreed strategy between Nintendo and its distributors. See Comm'n, Competition Policy Newsletter (Spring 2003) 50.

from an official dealer. The company changed this policy after the Commission initiated an investigation.[220] In the *Peugeot* proceedings, the Commission fined Peugeot €49.5 million for hindering its Dutch dealers from selling to customers in other member states.[221] The price of Peugeot cars in the Netherlands was significantly lower than in Germany and France. Hence, German and French customers sought to purchase cars from Dutch dealers. To discourage this practice, Peugeot refused to grant sales volume bonuses to Dutch dealers for cars sold to non-Dutch citizens and reduced the number of cars sold to dealers who engaged in export sales. The Commission concluded, and the General Court agreed,[222] that this amounted to an illegal division of markets.

These examples illustrate that indirect means employed by a seller to segregate markets are prohibited even if it is the seller's own product that is being restricted (referred to as an intra-brand restraint of competition). This is once again illustrated by the Commission's decision in the *Konica* proceedings.[223] To protect its distributors, Konica announced a policy whereby it would, largely at the insistence of its specialty dealers in Germany, buy up cheap imports into Germany from the UK. It also reimbursed the specialty dealers for any cheap imports that the specialty dealers bought up. Although there was no direct prohibition imposed by Konica on its non-German distributors, the conduct of Konica was deemed to violate Article 101 of the TFEU.

As markets have become more integrated, the Commission and courts have exhibited a willingness to relax the traditional prohibition on the division of markets in several ways. First, the courts have been less willing to recognize the existence of an agreement or concerted practice (a prerequisite for the application of the prohibition codified in Article 101 of the TFEU). In *Bayer v. Commission*, for example, the ECJ held that a manufacturer's unilateral refusal to supply customers in a particular member state did not constitute an agreement or concerted practice, and hence did not violate Article 101, even though the refusal had the effect of limiting parallel imports from one member state into another.[224]

Second, the courts have given greater scrutiny to the requirement imposed by Article 101(1) of the TFEU that the conduct has an appreciable effect on trade between member states. At issue in *Javico v. Yves Saint Laurent Parfums SA* was whether a contractual provision, imposed by Yves Saint Laurent Parfums on its distributors in Russia and the Ukraine preventing them from reimporting

---

220. Comm'n Press Release IP/00/684 (June 29, 2000).
221. Peugeot Nederland NV, 2006 O.J. (L 173) 20.
222. Case T-450/05, Automobiles Peugeot SA v. Comm'n, 2009 E.C.R. II-2539, 2569 ¶113.
223. 1988 O.J. (L 78) 34.
224. Joined Cases C-2/01 and C-3/01, Bundesverband der Arzneimittel-Importeure v. Bayer, 2004 E.C.R. I-64. The same conduct may, however, constitute a violation of Article 102 of the TFEU if it is without justification. *See* Joined Cases C-468/06 to C-478/06, Sot. Lelos kai Sia EE v. GlaxoSmithKline AEVE Farmakeftikon, 2008 E.C.R. I-7174, 7188 ¶34.

the products back into the EU, violated Article 101 of the TFEU.[225] The ECJ held that the hard-core rule which generally applies to restrictions on parallel imports does not apply to prohibitions of parallel imports from outside the EU as such agreements do not necessarily have an appreciable anticompetitive effect in the EU.[226] Rather, according to the ECJ, a more comprehensive analysis must be undertaken to determine the actual effect of the agreement. In *Royal Philips Electronics NV v. Commission*, the General Court expanded this rule to any absolute territorial protection even if it does not involve a third country.[227]

Third, the Commission has been willing to recognize several exceptions to the prohibition on territorial and customer restrictions. The Commission is of the opinion that it is permissible for a manufacturer to restrict a wholesaler from selling to end users.[228] If, for example, a U.S. television manufacturer sold televisions to an EU wholesaler, the U.S. manufacturer could prevent the wholesaler from selling the televisions at retail (i.e., require the wholesaler to sell only to stores). In addition, it is permissible to restrict an appointed distributor in a selective distribution system (i.e., a distribution network in which the participating distributors are admitted on the basis of certain objective characteristics justified by the nature of the product) from selling, at any level of trade, to unauthorized distributors in markets where such a system is operated.[229]

If, for example, a U.S. high-end computer manufacturer establishes a sales network in which it sells only to authorized distributors who have the requisite technical staff and facilities to adequately support the manufacturer's products, the manufacturer may prohibit those distributors from selling to unauthorized distributors. It is also permissible to restrict a buyer of components supplied for incorporation from reselling them to competitors of the supplier.[230] For example, if a Latvian company supplies rear view mirrors to Fiat, the Italian automobile manufacturer, the Latvian company may insert a clause in the supply agreement preventing Fiat from selling those rear view mirrors to a competitor of the Latvian company.

Finally, the Commission has been willing to recognize that customer or territorial restraints in legitimate exclusive distribution agreements are permissible under Article 101 of the TFEU. An exclusive distribution agreement is one in which a supplier agrees to sell exclusively to one distributor in a particular territory. Such agreements may contain the additional restriction discussed in the immediately preceding section whereby the distributor is prohibited from selling outside its territory (i.e., prohibition on parallel imports). In the EU, agreements according to which the supplier agrees to sell a certain

---

225. Case C-306/96, Javico Int'l v. Yves Saint Laurent Parfums SA, 1998 E.C.R. I-1997.
226. *Id.* at 2003 ¶ 15.
227. Case T-119/02, Royal Philips Electronics NV v. Comm'n, 2003 E.C.R. II-1442, 1507 ¶218. *See also* Case T-67/01, JCB Service v. Comm'n, 2004 E.C.R. II-56, 86 ¶85 *aff'd on appeal* Case C-167/04 P, JCB Service v. Comm'n, 2006 E.C.R. I-8972.
228. Vertical Restraints Block Exemption at art. 4(b)(ii).
229. *Id.* at art. 4(b)(iii).
230. *Id.* at art. 4(b)(iv).

product or products only to a specific distributor in a designated territory qualify for an exemption under the Vertical Restraints Block Exemption if the market share of each of the supplier and the buyer (on the buying market for those products) is less than 30 percent and the agreement does not contain any hard-core restrictions.[231] In the event that the market share of the supplier or the buyer is above the 30 percent level, the permissibility of the exclusive distribution agreement depends on the factual circumstances. According to the Commission, there is no presumption of illegality if the 30 percent threshold is exceeded.[232]

The exclusive distribution agreement may not prohibit the distributor from making passive sales outside its territory or to customer groups not reserved to the distributor.[233] The term "passive selling" means responding to unsolicited requests from individual customers.[234] By contrast, the term "active selling" means "actively approaching individual customers by for instance direct mail, including the sending of unsolicited e-mails, or visits; or actively approaching a specific customer group or customers in a specific territory through advertisement in media, on the internet or other promotions specifically targeted at that customer group or targeted at customers in that territory."[235] It is permissible for a supplier to restrict a distributor from actively selling into the territory of another exclusive distributor or to groups of customers reserved to another distributor or to the supplier. However, restrictions on passive selling are prohibited and will not qualify for an exemption under Article 101(3) of the TFEU.[236] There is no exclusive list of activities which constitute active or passive selling.[237]

The permissive rule on restrictions of active selling only applies to exclusive territories. It does not apply to a prohibition on active sales into a territory which is not exclusive. For example, a French manufacturer which sells products in Spain, and has also granted a nonexclusive distribution right for Spain to a Spanish distributor (this is often referred to as dual distribution), may not prevent its exclusive Portuguese distributor from actively selling in Spain. In addition, the exclusive distributor on which the prohibition of active selling is imposed must also be protected against active selling into its territory.[238] For example, if a Greek manufacturer grants an exclusive distributorship for Poland to a Polish distributor, and prohibits that Polish distributor from actively selling the products

---

231. *Id.* at art. 3(1).
232. Vertical Restraints Guidelines at 7 ¶23.
233. Case T-119/02, Royal Philips Electronics NV v. Comm'n, 2003 E.C.R. II-1442, 1508 ¶219; Vertical Restraints Block Exemption at art. 4(b)(i).
234. Vertical Restraints Guidelines at 13 ¶51.
235. *Id.*
236. *See, e.g.*, PO Nintendo Distribution, 2003 O.J. (L 255) 33, 77 ¶266; Nathan-Bricolux, 2001 O.J. (L 54) 1, 14 ¶108; Case T-67/01, JCB Service v. Comm'n, 2004 E.C.R. II-56, 86 ¶85 *aff'd on appeal* Case C-167/04 P, JCB Service v. Comm'n, 2006 E.C.R. I-8972.
237. The application of the distinction between active and passive sales to Internet commercial activity is discussed in greater detail in Chapter XII.
238. *Id.*

outside Poland, it must also prohibit its exclusive Slovakian distributor from actively selling in Poland.

(3) Exclusive Dealing

In an exclusive dealing agreement (sometimes referred to as single sourcing or single branding), the distributor is required by a supplier to purchase a specific type of product only from that supplier. Exclusive dealing arrangements have the potential effect of foreclosing other suppliers' access to distribution outlets for their products because the distributor can only purchase from one supplier.

Exclusive dealing agreements are generally permissible under EU competition law if (1) neither the distributor nor the supplier has a market share in excess of 30 percent and (2) the obligation imposed on the distributor not to sell competing brands does not extend beyond five years.[239] If the 30 percent market share threshold is exceeded, the exclusive dealing arrangement is not necessarily prohibited, but closely scrutinized.[240] In *Van den Bergh Foods Ltd. v. Commission*, for example, the General Court held that a subsidiary of Unilever plc which manufactured and sold ice cream products in Ireland violated Article 101(1) of the TFEU by supplying freezers to the retail outlets free of charge or at a nominal rent on the condition that they were used exclusively for Unilever ice creams.[241] Because of the high market share of Unilever in Ireland, the exclusivity provision illegally foreclosed competition from other ice cream companies, such as Mars.

(4) Exclusive Supply

In an exclusive supply agreement, the manufacturer is prohibited from selling the same products to other distributors except the distributor with which it has the exclusive supply agreement. The Commission is primarily concerned with the foreclosure effect that exclusive supply agreements have on competing distributors. If, for example, the manufacturer is supplying a dominant product, the inability of other distributors to purchase this product may impact their competitiveness.

If the supplier's and the distributor's market shares are each below 30 percent, the exclusive supply agreement falls under the Vertical Restraints Block Exemption.[242] The agreement is not automatically prohibited if the 30 percent threshold is exceeded. In such cases, the companies would need to examine the effect of the agreement in the particular circumstances. In addition to the market shares of the supplier and the distributor, other important factors examined by the Commission are the duration of the agreement (over five years generally not acceptable if the 30 percent market share threshold is exceeded) and the barriers to market entry at the supplier's level.[243]

---

239. Vertical Restraints Guidelines at 13 ¶52.
240. The relevant factors considered by the Commission are discussed in the Vertical Restraints Guidelines at 25 ¶¶111, 132-150.
241. Case T-65/98, Van den Bergh Foods Ltd. v. Comm'n, 2003 E.C.R. II-4662, 4711 ¶135 *aff'd on appeal* Case C-552/03 P, Unilever Bestfoods (Ireland) Ltd. v. Comm'n, 2006 E.C.R. I-9094.
242. Vertical Restraints Guidelines 40 ¶193.
243. *Id.* at 41 ¶195.

(5) Noncompete Agreements

As a distributor is intimately knowledgeable about the supplier's products and the customers in the distributor's market, the supplier will often want to prevent the distributor from competing with the supplier during the term of the distribution agreement as well as for a period of time after its termination. Noncompete obligations during the term of the agreement are exempted by the Vertical Restraints Block Exemption if their duration does not exceed five years and their respective market shares do not exceed 30 percent.[244] A distribution agreement which does not provide for a specific termination date is considered to exceed five years. "Rolling" noncompete obligations that are tacitly renewable beyond a period of five years also fall outside the scope of the Vertical Restraints Block Exemption. However, noncompete obligations are covered by the Vertical Restraints Block Exemption when their duration is limited to five years or less, or when renewal beyond five years requires explicit consent of both parties and no obstacles exist that hinder the buyer from effectively terminating the noncompete obligation at the end of the five-year period.

In contrast to noncompete obligations during the term of the agreement, post-termination noncompete obligations are only valid for one year after the date of termination. Moreover, the obligation must be indispensable to protect know-how transferred by the supplier to the buyer and limited to the point of sale from which the buyer has operated during the contract period.[245]

(6) Selective Distribution

Manufacturers of branded goods, to which a significant amount of goodwill has been attached, may not want their products being sold by distributors or discount retail chains which could damage the reputation or image of the manufacturer or the product. In such circumstances, the manufacturer may want to "selectively" set up its distribution network by only selling to those distributors who are in the position to uphold the goodwill of the brand. If the product is highly technical and requires qualified sales personnel at the point of sale, a manufacturer may want to restrict the class of entities that is selling its products. The luxury goods company Christian Dior, for example, established a selective distribution network and included the following restriction in its standard distribution agreement: "In order to maintain the repute and prestige of the trade mark the licensee agrees not to sell to wholesalers, buyers' collectives, discount stores, mail order companies, door-to-door sales companies or companies selling within private houses without prior written agreement from [Christian Dior], and must make all necessary provision to ensure that that rule is complied with by its distributors or retailers."[246]

For competition law purposes, a "selective distribution system" is defined as a distribution system where the supplier undertakes to sell the contract goods or services, either directly or indirectly, only to distributors selected on the basis of specified criteria and where these distributors undertake not to sell such

---

244. Vertical Restraints Block Exemption at art. 5(1).
245. *Id.* at art. 5(3).
246. Case C-59/08, Copad SA v. Christian Dior couture SA, 2009 E.C.R. I-3421, at ¶8.

goods or services to unauthorized distributors within the territory reserved by the supplier to operate that system.[247]

There are two types of selective distribution agreements differentiated based on the criteria used to select the distributors.[248] A qualitative selective distribution system uses qualitative criteria to select the distributors. Criteria are qualitative if they relate to the ability of the distributor to appropriately distribute the products in light of the product characteristics which justify the selective distribution system. A quantitative selective distribution system, on the other hand, limits the number of distributors in quantitative terms. The limitation by an automobile manufacturer of the number of dealers in a particular geographic area based on the number of inhabitants in each area would, for example, be considered a quantitative criterion.[249]

According to the Commission, a purely qualitative selective distribution system will not violate Article 101(1) TFEU if three conditions are fulfilled.[250] The first of these is that the nature of the product must justify selective distribution. According to the Commission, for qualitative selective distribution, the nature of the product must require that only distributors with certain qualifications sell the product. As the legitimate purpose of a selective distribution system is typically to help solve a free-rider problem between the distributors or to help create a brand image, the nature of the product in the particular case is very relevant in the eyes of the Commission.

According to the Commission, the case is strongest for new products, complex products, products whose qualities are difficult to judge before consumption (so-called experience products) or whose qualities are difficult to judge even after consumption (so-called credence products).[251] The ECJ has held that consumer electronics, computers, cameras, jewelry, and pharmaceutical products may justify a qualitative selective distribution system. On the other hand, tobacco, windsurfing equipment, furniture, and bananas do not. The requirement that the distributor sell only products of that particular manufacturer would probably not be considered a qualitative criterion.[252]

The second requirement for qualitative selective distribution systems to fall outside of Article 101(1) of the TFEU is that the qualitative criteria must be objectively applied in a nondiscriminatory manner. If, for example, the manufacturer refuses to authorize a distributor who is willing to distribute the manufacturers' products and who meets all of the qualitative criteria, the selective distribution system may violate Article 101(1).

Finally, the qualitative criteria must not go beyond what is necessary to achieve the legitimate objective of the selective distribution system.[253]

---

247. Vertical Restraints Block Exemption at art. 1(1)(e).
248. Vertical Restraints Guidelines at 36 ¶175.
249. *Id.* at 36 ¶187. *See, e.g.,* Case C-158/11, Auto 24 SARL v. Jaguar Land Rover France SAS, 2012 E.C.R. I-____.
250. Vertical Restraints Guidelines at 36 ¶175.
251. *Id.* at 36 ¶177.
252. *Id.* at 36 ¶186.
253. *Id.* at 36 ¶175.

As with qualitative distribution systems, quantitative selective distribution systems will not violate Article 101(1) TFEU if certain conditions are fulfilled. Similar to qualitative selective distribution systems, the first of these requirements is that the nature of the product must necessitate the use of quantitative criteria. For example, the nature of the product requires a limitation of the number of distributors selling that product in a particular area. In addition, the quantitative criteria must not go beyond what is necessary to achieve the legitimate objective of the selective distribution system. According to the ECJ, however, a quantitative selective distribution system in the automobile industry does not have to be applied in an objective and nondiscriminatory manner.[254]

Selective distribution systems that do not fulfill all of the above requirements are not necessarily prohibited, but subject to a closer scrutiny. Such selective distribution systems are exempt under Article 101(3) of the TFEU if (1) the 30 percent market share threshold is not exceeded, (2) the distributors are allowed to sell the product to each other and to end users,[255] and (3) the distributors are not prevented from selling the brands of particular (as opposed to all) competing suppliers.[256] If the 30 percent market share threshold is exceeded, the Commission will closely examine the circumstances surrounding the selective distribution system. The higher the market share of the supplier, the greater impact the reduction of intra-brand competition will have on inter-brand competition. Hence, the market share of the supplier is the starting point of the examination of the selective distribution system. The anticompetitive effect of a high supplier market share can be mitigated, however, if the distributors are permitted to sell competing brands.[257]

It is important to remember that the general rules on hard-core restraints of trade continue to apply to selective distribution systems even if the particular system fulfills the three requirements discussed above. The example of B&W Loudspeakers serves to illustrate this point. B&W Loudspeakers Ltd. is a British manufacturer of high-end loudspeakers for hi-fi and home cinema systems. Instead of selling its products to any distributor who was willing to carry them, B&W established a selective distribution system. As part of that system, B&W prohibited its dealers from engaging in (i) "bait pricing" (i.e., offering a certain product at a very attractive price with the aim of attracting customers to the sales outlet), (ii) cross supplies between authorized dealers and (iii) sales through the Internet. The Commission took the position that although the selective distribution system was justified under the circumstances, these additional restrictions violated Article 101(1) of the TFEU and did not qualify

---

254. Case C-158/11, Auto 24 SARL v. Jaguar Land Rover France SAS, 2012 E.C.R. I-____, at ¶35.
255. Vertical Restraints Guidelines at 36 ¶176.
256. Vertical Restraints Block Exemption at art. 5(1)(c).
257. The Commission is more concerned with restrictions imposed on the distributor not to sell the brands of particular competing suppliers than with restrictions not to sell any competing brands. Vertical Restraints Block Exemption at art. 5(1)(c); Vertical Restraints Guidelines at, 37 ¶182.

for an exemption.[258] In a different case, the UK Office of Fair Trade (OFT) (currently the Competition and Markets Commission) oobjected to a clause in Nike's standard distribution agreement that appeared to limit the ability of Nike distributors from discounting old lines of shoes.[259] The particular clause stated "Nike in season product should not be displayed alongside discounted out of season products." In addition, the agreement required the distributors to offer old-line products on a separate webpage. At the insistence of the OFT, Nike modified these clauses to clarify that the distributors were free to grant discounts on old-line products.

(7) Tying

A manufacturer may not be the market leader in each of the product markets in which it is active. Consequently, there may be an incentive to condition the sale of a "leading" product on the willingness of the buyer to also purchase another product. The maker of a leading printer may, for example, require its distributors to also purchase that manufacturer's ink toner cartridges.

As discussed below, this practice of tying one product to the purchase of another product may constitute an abuse of a dominant position prohibited under Article 102 of the TFEU. Tying can also constitute a violation of Article 101 of the TFEU even if the supplier does not enjoy a dominant position in the tied product or tying product market. As a general rule, however, tying agreements qualify for an exemption provided that the market share of the supplier in the tied product market as well as the tying product market are each below 30 percent.[260] Above this 30 percent threshold, the parties need to consider the application of Article 102 of the TFEU and other factors, such as the market shares of the nearest competitors, barriers to market entry, and countervailing buyer power.[261]

(8) Rebate and Discount Schemes

From the perspective of the consumer, rebates and discounts are generally welcome. Accordingly, they generally are permitted under Article 101 of the TFEU. Problems arise under Article 101, however, when they are used in an anticompetitive way by undertakings with market power greater than 30 percent (but less than a dominant position to which Article 102 of the TFEU applies). The general rule is that rebate and discount schemes employed by firms with market shares in excess of 30 percent are prohibited unless they are justified by costs and objectively applied. In other words, there must be a legitimate business reason for offering the rebate or discount and the program must be available on similar terms to all customers. For example, a pure volume discount scheme whereby customers receive a rebate at the end of the year calculated on the

---

258. Press Release, Commission clears B&W Loudspeakers distribution system after company deletes hardcore violations, IP/02/916 (24 June 2002).
259. CE/1706/02, Nike (Oct. 15, 2003), *reported in* the Gazette of the UK Office of Fair Trading (January 2004).
260. Vertical Restraints Guidelines at 44 ¶218.
261. *Id.* at 44 ¶220.

basis of the volume of products they purchased during that year will generally be permitted. However, a rebate scheme whereby distributors or wholesalers are rewarded disproportionately for their non-online sales may be prohibited if it is used to prevent online selling.[262]

(9) License Agreements

A license refers to the right granted by the owner of intellectual property to a third party which allows that third party to use that intellectual property. EU competition law distinguishes between pure license agreements and hybrid license agreements. A pure license agreement is one which has as its primary purpose the grant of a license. Hybrid licenses are those in which the license is related to the resale of goods but not the primary purpose of the agreement. In such cases, the license is only an ancillary aspect of the agreement. For example, distribution agreements containing licensing provisions will typically be considered hybrid license agreements even though the license may be an important—and even essential—component of the agreement.

The primary significance of the distinction between pure and hybrid licenses is that the type of license agreement determines which block exemption applies—and consequently the analytical paradigm used to determine the permissibility of the agreement under EU competition law. The Vertical Restraints Block Exemption generally applies to the licensing of intellectual property if the license grant is directly related to the resale of the goods and not the primary objective of the agreement, i.e., hybrid licenses.[263] Pure license agreements, on the other hand, generally fall under the Technology Transfer Block Exemption.[264]

There are two important limitations on the scope of the Technology Transfer Block Exemption. First, the exemption only applies to technology transfer agreements between two parties.[265] This means, for example, that patent pools and multiparty licensing arrangements do not fall under the Technology Transfer Block Exemption. The Commission has stated, however, that there is a safe harbor for technology pools "irrespective of the market position of the parties" if the following conditions are met:

- participation in the technology pool creation process is open to all interested technology rights owners;
- sufficient safeguards are adopted to ensure that only essential technologies are pooled;

---

262. *See, e.g.*, Dornbracht, Decision of the Oberlandesgericht Düsseldorf VI-U (Kart) 11/13 (Nov. 13, 2013) *aff'd on appeal* German Supreme Court, KRZ 88/13 (Oct. 7, 2014); Bosch Siemens Hausgeräte GmbH, Decision of the German Bundeskartellamt in case B7-11/13 (Dec. 23, 2013).
263. Vertical Restraints Block Exemption at art. 2(3).
264. Commission Regulation No. 316/2014 of 21 March 2014 on the application of Article 101(3) of the Treaty on the Functioning of the European Union to categories of technology transfer agreements, 2014 O.J. (L 93) 17.
265. This requirement arises out of the definition of "technology transfer agreement" in the Technology Transfer Block Exemption at art. 1(1)(c).

- sufficient safeguards are adopted to ensure that exchange of sensitive information (such as pricing and output data) is restricted to what is necessary for the creation and operation of the pool;
- the pooled technologies are licensed into the pool on a nonexclusive basis;
- the pooled technologies are licensed out to all potential licensees on fair and reasonable terms;
- the parties contributing technology to the pool and the licensees are free to challenge the validity and the essentiality of the pooled technologies, and;
- the parties contributing technology to the pool and the licensee remain free to develop competing products and technology.[266]

Second, in contrast to the Vertical Restraints Block Exemption, the Technology Transfer Block Exemption only applies to licensing of specific types of intellectual property: the primary objective of the agreement must be the license of patents, utility models, design rights, topographies of semiconductor products, supplementary protection certificates for medicinal products, plant breeders' certificates, know-how or software copyrights. The licensing of other types of intellectual property, such as trademarks and copyright, are only covered by the Technology Transfer Block Exemption if they are directly related to the production or sale of contract products.[267]

The primary objective requirement does not mean that no other issues may be addressed by the parties in the technology transfer agreement for it to benefit from the Block Exemption. As long as the license of patents, know-how, or software copyrights is the primary objective of the agreement, the agreement still may fall within the scope of the exemption.[268] For example, other intellectual property rights (such as trademarks) may be part of a technology transfer license. The primary objective requirement means that the Technology Transfer Block Exemption does not apply if the license is merely an ancillary component of the agreement. In other words, it only applies to pure license agreements.

For example, if Sony were to enter into a distribution agreement with a distributor for the sale of electronic game consoles and grant a license to the distributor to use certain Sony know-how, that agreement would not fall under the Technology Transfer Block Exemption as the license is merely an ancillary (albeit important) component of the distribution agreement. The Vertical Restraints Block Exemption potentially applies in such cases. If, however, Sony were to engage another company to produce the electronic game consoles and grant a patent or know-how license to that company for this purpose, that patent or know-how license agreement would probably fall within the scope of the Technology Transfer Block Exemption.

---

266. Guidelines on the Application of Article 101 of the Treaty on the Functioning of the European Union to technology transfer agreements, 2014 O.J. (C 89) 3, 48 ¶261 [hereinafter Technology Transfer Guidelines].
267. *Id.* at ¶47.
268. Technology Transfer Block Exemption at art. 2(3).

Assuming that the particular agreement falls within the scope of the Technology Transfer Block Exemption, the agreement is permissible under Article 101 of the TFEU if four basic requirements are fulfilled. First, the intellectual property being licensed must be valid. The exemption does not apply (or will cease to apply) if the intellectual property has expired, lapsed, or been declared invalid.[269] Second, the parties must not have market power as measured by market share. If the parties are competitors, the market share cannot exceed 20 percent of the relevant technology and product market.[270] If the parties are not competitors, that market share threshold increases to 30 percent.[271]

Third, the agreement must not contain any "hard-core restrictions."[272] A distinction should be made between horizontal hard-core restrictions and vertical hard-core restrictions. Horizontal hard-core restrictions in the context of the Technology Transfer Block Exemption are those that restrict a party's ability to determine its prices when selling products to third parties, limit the output of at least one of the parties,[273] allocate markets or customers,[274] or restrict the licensee's ability to exploit its own technology or the ability of any of the parties to the agreement to carry out research and development (unless such restriction on R&D is necessary to prevent the disclosure of the licensed know-how to third parties).

---

269. *Id.* at art. 2(2).
270. *Id.* at art. 3(1).
271. *Id.* at art. 3(2).
272. *Id.* at art. 4.
273. Limitations imposed on the licensee in a nonreciprocal agreement or imposed on only one of the licensees in a reciprocal agreement which limit the licensee's output of the specific products are not considered hard-core restrictions. For example, if a computer manufacturer grants a third party a patent to make certain computer components, the manufacturer may impose a limit on the volume of those components produced by the third party.
274. The following types of restrictions, although they may have the effect of market allocation, are permitted: (i) The obligation on the licensee to produce with the licensed technology only within one or more technical fields of use or one or more product markets, (ii) the obligation on the licensor and/or the licensee, in a nonreciprocal agreement, not to produce with the licensed technology within one or more technical fields of use or one or more product markets or one or more exclusive territories reserved for the other party, (iii) the obligation on the licensor not to license the technology to another licensee in a particular territory, (iv) the restriction, in a nonreciprocal agreement, of active and/or passive sales by the licensee and/or the licensor into the exclusive territory or to the exclusive customer group reserved for the other party, (v) the restriction, in a nonreciprocal agreement, of active sales by the licensee into the exclusive territory or to the exclusive customer group allocated by the licensor to another licensee provided the latter was not a competing undertaking of the licensor at the time of the conclusion of its own license, (vi) the obligation on the licensee to produce the contract products only for its own use provided that the licensee is not restricted in selling the contract products actively and passively as spare parts for its own products, and (vii) the obligation on the licensee, in a nonreciprocal agreement, to produce the contract products only for a particular customer, where the license was granted in order to create an alternative source of supply for that customer. *Id.* at art. 4(1)(c).

Vertical hard-core restrictions in the context of the Technology Transfer Block Exemption are those that restrict a party's ability to determine its prices when selling products to third parties,[275] restrict the territory into which the licensee may passively sell the contract products,[276] or restrict active or passive sales to end-users by a licensee which is a member of a selective distribution system and which operates at the retail level.

The fourth and final requirement for the application of the Technology Transfer Block Exemption is that the agreement must permit the production of products using the licensed technology.[277] This requirement would preclude, for example, a brand name pharmaceutical manufacturer from securing an exclusive license from a generic manufacturer with the intention of simply precluding the introduction of that generic drug and no intent of ever introducing it on the market.

If the particular agreement does not fall within the scope of the Technology Transfer Block Exemption, it is not automatically prohibited.[278] It simply means that it must be individually assessed to determine whether it constitutes a restraint of competition and, if so, whether the individual requirements of Article 101(3) are fulfilled. For example, grant-back and no challenge clauses are expressly precluded from the scope of the Block Exemption, but are not automatically prohibited as hard-core restraints.[279]

Grant-back clauses are commonly found in license agreements and require the licensee to "grant back" to the licensor the right to use the improvements made by the licensee to the licensed technology. Such clauses generally do not raise competition law concerns if they are nonexclusive (i.e., the licensee

---

275. This does not include maximum sale prices or recommending a sale price, provided that it does not amount to a fixed or minimum sale price as a result of pressure from, or incentives offered by, any of the parties. *Id.* at art. 4(2)(a).
276. The following types of territorial restrictions are not considered hard core: (i) the restriction of passive sales into an exclusive territory or to an exclusive customer group reserved for the licensor, (ii) the restriction of passive sales into an exclusive territory or to an exclusive customer group allocated by the licensor to another licensee during the first two years that this other licensee is selling the contract products in that territory or to that customer group, (iii) the obligation to produce the contract products only for its own use provided that the licensee is not restricted in selling the contract products actively and passively as spare parts for its own products, (iv) the obligation to produce the contract products only for a particular customer, where the license was granted in order to create an alternative source of supply for that customer, (v) the restriction of sales to end-users by a licensee operating at the wholesale level of trade, (vi) the restriction of sales to unauthorised distributors by the members of a selective distribution system. *Id.* at art. 4(2)(b).
277. This requirement arises out of the definition of "technology transfer agreement." *Id.* at art. 1(1)(c).
278. There is no presumption that technology transfer agreements falling outside the block exemption are caught by Article 101(1) or fail to satisfy the conditions of Article 101(3).
279. *Id.* at art. 5(1).
    As discussed above, although technology pools do not fall within the Block Exemption, they are not automatically prohibited.

retains the right to also use the improvement). If, however, the grant back is exclusive (i.e., the licensor is the only party that can use the improvement made by the licensee), competition issues may arise depending on the market shares and relationship of the parties and the compensation given to the licensee.[280]

No challenge clauses in license agreements prohibit the licensee from challenging the validity or ownership of the intellectual property being licensed.[281] Similar to grant-back clauses, these types of provisions fall outside the scope of the Technology Transfer Block Exemption but are not automatically prohibited as hard-core restraints.[282] In general, no challenge clauses are prohibited by Article 101 of the TFEU because they protect intellectual property that is otherwise not deserving of protection. According to the Commission: "Invalid intellectual property stifles innovation rather than promoting it."[283] Consequently, an agreement limiting the ability of the licensee to challenge the technology may be anticompetitive. In recognition of the difficulty of protecting know-how, however, the Commission is willing to recognize the necessity of no-challenge clauses relating specifically to know-how "where the recovery of the licensed know-how is likely to be impossible or very difficult once it is disclosed."[284]

(d) Vertical Agreements with Horizontal Implications

(1) Contract Manufacturing

The strong reliance on taxonomies to determine the fate of an agreement raises a number of issues for agreements that are difficult to characterize. In a contract manufacturing scenario, a company (commonly a distributor) engages a manufacturer to produce a product in accordance with specifications provided by that company to be sold by the company under its own brand name. For example, Bayer may outsource the production of its aspirin to a third party but sell those aspirin under the Bayer name. Although both parties technically are engaged in the sale of the same product (Bayer and the third party both sell aspirin), this relationship would be deemed vertical.[285] Contract manufacturing agreements qualify for an exemption under the Vertical Restraints Block Exemption if the company buying the product is not itself active at the manufacturing level and the respective market shares of the parties do not exceed 30 percent.

(2) Dual Distribution

Dual distribution describes the situation where the manufacturer of a product is also active at the distribution level along with its independent distributors (and therefore in competition with its distributors). If, for example, the U.S. manufacturer of earth-moving equipment, Caterpillar, decided to become active in the distribution of its tractors parallel to its independent distributors, one would

---

280. Technology Transfer Guidelines at 27 ¶130.
281. *Id.* at 28 ¶134.
282. Technology Transfer Block Exemption at art. 5(1)(b).
283. Technology Transfer Guidelines at 28 ¶134.
284. *Id.* at 29 ¶140.
285. Vertical Restraints Guidelines at 8 ¶27.

refer to this system as dual distribution. Although distribution agreements are typically classified as vertical, in a dual distribution context there is a horizontal relationship between the manufacturer and the distributors at the distribution market. Consequently, dual distribution does not fit nicely into the horizontal and vertical categories discussed above. Nonetheless, agreements between a manufacturer and a distributor fall under the Vertical Restraints Block Exemption even if the manufacturer is also active at the distribution level, and hence in competition with the independent distributor.[286] The supplier must not have a market share in excess of 30 percent, and the independent distributor must not be a manufacturer of competing goods or part of a corporate group that manufacturers competing goods.[287]

4.6 Joint Ventures

One topic that has not been addressed so far concerns joint ventures. This is because joint ventures do not fit neatly into the paradigm on which the preceding discussion relies. On the one hand, joint ventures could be considered a bilateral restraint of competition to which Article 101 of the TFEU would apply. On the other hand, they often result in a structural change in competitive relationships to which the Merger Control Regulation would more appropriately apply. Whether a joint venture falls under Article 101 of the TFEU or the Merger Control Regulation depends on whether it qualifies as a concentrative joint venture or a nonconcentrative joint venture. The basic rule is that Article 101 applies to nonconcentrative joint ventures and to the cooperative aspects of concentrative joint ventures. The Merger Control Regulation applies to the concentrative aspects of concentrative joint ventures.

(a) Definition of Joint Venture

In EU competition law, a joint venture is an undertaking jointly controlled by two or more economically independent undertakings. This definition contains three elements. First, the joint venture must be an undertaking. As discussed above, an undertaking is "any entity engaged in an economic activity, regardless of its legal status and the way in which it is financed."[288]

The second requirement is that the undertaking be jointly controlled. The concept of control over an undertaking is discussed below more thoroughly in the context of structural restraints of competition. Joint control exists where two or more undertakings or persons have the possibility of exercising decisive influence over the joint venture entity.[289] Decisive influence means

---

286. Vertical Restraints Block Exemption at art. 2(4)(a). As dual distribution is a form of nonexclusive distribution, the manufacturer may not prohibit the distributor from actively selling outside its territory.
287. Vertical Restraints Guidelines at 8 ¶27.
288. Case C-264/01, C-306/01, C-354/01 & C-355/01, AOK Bundesverband v. Ichthyol-Gesellschaft Cordes, 2004 E.C.R. I-2493, 2542 ¶46; Case C-309/99, J.C.J. Wouters, J.W. Savelbergh, Price Waterhouse Belastingadviseurs BV v. Algemene Raad van de Nederlandse Orde van Advocaten, 2002 E.C.R. I-1653, 1676 ¶46.
289. Comm'n Consolidated Jurisdictional Notice, 2008 O.J. (C 95) 1, 23 ¶91.

the contractual, legal, or de facto ability to block the strategic decisions of the undertaking. The clearest form of joint control exists where the shareholders hold equal shares in the undertaking (absent an agreement between them which gives one of the shareholders control). Ownership parity is, however, not the decisive criterion. It is necessary to examine the decision-making bodies of the entity. For example, two companies may each own 50 percent of another company, and yet for purposes of EU competition law, joint control would not exist if one of those owners had control over the board of directors of the company. The issue of whether there is joint control must be made on a case-by-case basis.

The third and final element of the definition of a joint venture is that the parents must be independent from each other. If, for example, the R&D division and the manufacturing division of the same undertaking agree to set up an undertaking to explore more efficient ways of commercialization of inventions, this is not a joint venture for purposes of EU competition law because they are both part of the same corporate group.

(b) Concentrative and Nonconcentrative Joint Ventures

The discussion of Article 101 of the TFEU above focused on agreements which do not entail the change of control over a particular undertaking. Indeed, a change in control is not one of the requirements for the application of Article 101. Hence, joint ventures would initially appear to fit more appropriately in the discussion of structural restraints of competition discussed below. And yet, joint ventures do not fit neatly within that paradigm because they do not involve the complete integration of the parent entities which remain under separate control. For example, when Robert Bosch GmbH and Samsung set up a joint venture to develop and produce batteries for hybrid automobiles, the creation of this joint venture did not mean that the two companies had a unified commercial purpose outside the joint venture.[290] The joint venture parents continue to operate as separate undertakings.

To deal with the unique character of joint ventures, the EU distinguishes between concentrative joint ventures and nonconcentrative joint ventures. A concentrative joint venture is a jointly controlled undertaking (i.e., joint venture) that performs, on a lasting basis, all the functions of an autonomous economic entity.[291] To qualify as a concentrative joint venture, the autonomous economic entity requirement mandates that the joint venture have a management dedicated to its day-to-day operations and access to sufficient resources (including finance, staff, and assets) in order to conduct business.[292] In the joint venture between Bosch and Samsung discussed above, the parents created a separate legal entity with adequate financial and personnel resources for the joint venture entity to independently develop, manufacture, and sell batteries for hybrid automobiles.

---

290. Case M. 5227, Robert Bosch/Samsung/JV (Aug. 18, 2008).
291. Merger Control Regulation at art. 3(4).
292. Celanese/Degussa/JV, 2004 O.J. (L 38) 47, 48 ¶10.

Nonconcentrative joint ventures, on the other hand, are joint ventures that assume only a specific function for the parents and are not independent commercial actors.[293] This is typically the case where two undertakings set up a joint venture to complete only a small task in the value chain exclusively for the parents. For example, a distribution joint venture established by a motorcycle manufacturer and an automotive manufacturer to sell motorcycles and cars exclusively may be deemed a nonconcentrative joint venture as it would probably be acting at the instruction of its parents and not as an autonomous economic actor on the market. As a rule, all joint ventures that do not qualify as concentrative are considered nonconcentrative.

(c) Legal Analysis Applied to Joint Ventures

The classification of joint ventures as concentrative or nonconcentrative is important because it determines the legal analysis to be applied. Nonconcentrative joint ventures are analyzed under Article 101 of the TFEU. They typically are considered a restraint of competition within the meaning of Article 101(1) if the parents are actual or potential competitors. The general disposition of the Commission is that competitors should not cooperate with each other. If, however, the parties to the nonconcentrative joint venture can show that their cooperation affords them the ability to achieve a legitimate commercial objective which they would not otherwise be able to achieve by themselves or by less restrictive means, the joint venture may be in conformity with Article 101 of the TFEU.

Concentrative joint ventures are treated as potential structural restraints of competition and consequently analyzed under the Merger Control Regulation as discussed later in this Chapter. However, the possibility that the parents of the concentrative joint venture coordinate their behavior outside the joint venture is not a concentrative effect, but rather a cooperative effect. Consequently, any cooperative effects of concentrative joint ventures are assessed under Article 101 of the TFEU but within the same procedure under the Merger Control Regulation.[294] As discussed below in the context of the Merger Control Regulation, the assumption is that while a concentrative joint venture eliminates competition between the parents in the field of the joint venture, the parents otherwise remain separate economic actors. Hence, coordination of their conduct in other sectors remains possible. In *Bertelsmann/Mondadori/BOL Italia*, for example, Bertelsmann and Mondadori combined their on-line CD and DVD sales businesses in Italy into a separate Italian company in which they each held a 50 percent interest.[295] As Bertelsmann and Mondadori were both active in the book publishing market, the Commission examined whether the joint venture would facilitate coordination outside the context of the joint venture (and concluded that such coordination was not likely).[296]

---

293. Comm'n Consolidated Jurisdictional Notice, 2008 O.J. (C 95) 1, 24 ¶94. *See, e.g.*, Continental/United/Lufthansa/Air Canada, 2013 O.J. (C 201) 8.
294. Merger Control Regulation at art. 2(4).
295. Case Comp/JV.51, Bertelsmann/Mondadori/BOL Italia (Sept. 1, 2000).
296. *Id.* at ¶25.

Although concentrative joint ventures are treated as concentrations under the Merger Control Regulation, the cooperative effects of concentrative joint ventures are examined under Article 101 of the TFEU. This means that the cooperative effects of s concentrative joint venture are examined by the Commission when the transaction creating the concentrative joint venture is notified to the Commission under the Merger Control Regulation. The analysis under Article 101 does not occur in a separate proceeding.

As discussed later in this Chapter, concentrative joint ventures which have a Union dimension must be notified to the Commission under the Merger Control Regulation prior to their consummation. Once the transaction is notified, the parties must await the approval of the Commission to proceed with the transaction. During that time, the Commission will examine the potential structural effect the notified transaction will have on competition, applying the substantive standards set forth in the Merger Control Regulation. If the concentrative joint venture also has a cooperative effect, the Commission will examine whether that effect violated Article 101 of the TFEU. If the transaction meets the substantive test under the Merger Control Regulation, and there is no violation of Article 101 of the TFEU, the Commission will approve the transaction.

It is worth noting that the joint creation of an undertaking by two or more independent undertakings does not necessarily constitute a concentrative or a nonconcentrative joint venture. As discussed above, the threshold requirement for a joint venture (concentrative and nonconcentrative) is the existence of an undertaking jointly controlled by two or more independent undertakings. It may be that two or more independent undertakings decide to establish a new entity which none of them controls. In this case, no joint venture exists. In *Indentrus*, for example, a group of seven banks including ABN-AMRO, Citibank, Deutsche Bank, and Chase Manhattan, agreed to set up an Illinois limited liability company to provide certification services related to e-commerce transactions.[297] As the Illinois limited liability company was not controlled by any of the shareholders (no one shareholder held more than 10 percent), it did not qualify as a joint venture.[298] The cooperation was examined under Article 101 of the TFEU, and the Commission concluded that there was no violation of Article 101(1).

Conversely, the creation of a separate legal entity is not necessary in order to be considered a nonconcentrative joint venture. In *Continental/United/ Lufthansa/Air Canada*, four airlines entered into a joint venture agreement to cooperate on certain trans-Atlantic routes without creating a separate legal entity. This nonequity joint venture was analyzed by the Commission as a nonconcentrative joint venture.[299]

---

297. Comm'n Decision of 31 July 2001, Indentrus, 2001 O.J. (L 249) 12.
298. *Id.* at ¶23.
299. Continental/United/Lufthansa/Air Canada, 2013 O.J. (C 201) 8.

4.7 Noneconomic Considerations in the Application of Article 101

The application of the EU competition law does not occur in a vacuum. Any application must account for the economic, political, and legal context in which the law is situated. The guiding economic principle of the EU is that of "a highly competitive social market economy."[300] The reference to a social market economy means that the allocation of resources by the market is not to be accepted in all circumstances. In some circumstances, state intervention in the market is necessary to achieve results that market forces would not otherwise yield.

The prohibition on restraints of competition in Article 101 of the TFEU is just one legal norm among many codified in the TFEU. The fundamental purpose of the TFEU is to govern the integration of the member states in those fields that have been ceded to the EU. It is possible that the implementation of the various competencies in particular cases leads to conflicting results. What happens, for example, when the result of a competition law case is the loss of employment, but the protection of employment is one of the policy objectives of the TFEU? The TFEU does not contain rules addressing the resolution of a conflict in the application between two primary legal norms. Hence, the protection of competition may have to yield to other policies with which the EU has been entrusted.

(a) Social Policies

Although it is difficult to quantify, social concerns have influenced the application of the EU competition rules. In the *Maatschappij Drijvende Bokken* case, for example, the ECJ was presented with the issue of whether a labor collective could be considered a cartel.[301] In a strict sense, employees are engaged in an economic activity; they sell their services to their employer. Hence, they could be considered undertakings and consequently the labor union could be considered a cartel. In the *Maatschappij Drijvende Bokken* case, however, the ECJ implicitly recognized the social policy implications of classifying the collective as a cartel and held that Article 101 did not apply even though the conduct at issue had a direct effect on competition.

The promotion of a high level of employment, the guarantee of adequate social protection, environmental and consumer protection are all requirements that the EU institutions are mandated to observe when acting.[302] The pragmatic necessity of allowing social policy to influence the application of competition law presents a juridical challenge to the paradigm currently used to apply Article 101 of the TFEU. The prohibition codified in Article 101(1) of the TFEU is interpreted very broadly with the understanding that a balancing of the procompetitive and anticompetitive characteristics of the conduct in question

---

300. EU Treaty at art. 3(3).
301. Case C-222/98, Maatschappij Drijvende Bokken, 2000 E.C.R. I-7111.
302. TFEU at arts. 7 to 14.

would be undertaken only in the context of applying the exemption codified in Article 101(3) of the TFEU. However, there may be anticompetitive conduct which does not meet all of the requirements of Article 101(3) but, from a social policy or political perspective, should not be prohibited. This forces the ECJ to adopt a pragmatic approach in applying Article 101. Using labor law again as an example, the ECJ has recognized that although collective bargaining agreements between employer federations and labor unions restrain competition, they simply do not fall under Article 101(1).[303]

(b) Cultural and Linguistic Diversity

The protection or promotion of cultural and linguistic diversity is recognized by the European Commission as having an influence on the application of competition law. In Germany, book publishers adopted a system referred to in German as "Sammelrevers" to allow the German publishers to fix the resale price of books.[304] Book stores were not able to sell books below the manufacturer's set price. In other words, the law legalized vertical resale price fixing for books. Thus, a particular book in Germany costs the same regardless of where it is purchased. As long as retail book buying was primarily a local activity, this system did not draw the attention of the Commission, and it was expressly exempted at the time under German competition law. The basic rationale behind allowing such activity was to preserve cultural heritage.[305] By precluding competition between retailers, the assumption was that the retailers would have a greater incentive to carry a wide range of books—even those that did not have high sales volumes. Once the Internet made the purchase of books easier, the issue arose whether the system violated Article 101(1) of the TFEU. After the book publishers association agreed not to fix the resale price of books for sale outside Germany, the Commission took the position that there was no effect on trade between member states and consequently outside the ambit of Article 101 of the TFEU.[306] It is not necessarily consistent with the Commission's otherwise broad interpretation of the interstate trade requirement or its position on vertical price fixing. As is generally recognized, this case illustrates the willingness of the Commission to take into account national claims of cultural and linguistic diversity.[307]

---

303. Case C-438/05, Int'l Transport Workers' Federation v. Viking Line ABP, 2007 E.C.R. I-10806, 10827 ¶49; Joined Cases C-115/97, C-116/97 and C-117/97, Brentjens' Handelsonderneming BV v. Stichting Bedrijfspensioenfonds voor de Handel in Bouwmaterialen, 1999 E.C.R. I-6025, 6048 ¶¶56-57.
304. The system established by the publishers was subsequently codified into statute. Gesetz über die Preisbindung für Bücher of 2 September 2002, BGBl. Teil I/2002, S. 3448.
305. Decision of the German Bundesgerichtshof in case no. KVR 1/77 (Mar. 13, 1979) *reported at* 32 Neue Juristische Wochenschrift 1411 (1979).
306. IP/02/461.
307. *See, e.g.*, Hanns Peter Nehl & Jan Nuijten, Commission Ends Competition Proceedings regarding German Book Price Fixing, 2002 (2) Competition Policy Newsletter 35 (2002).

(c) Environment

Article 11 of the TFEU specifically provides that: "Environmental protection requirements must be integrated into the definition and implementation of the Union policies..." One such Union policy is competition policy. The Commission is consequently required to consider environmental protection when making a decision based on the competition laws. Although environmental considerations appear in some Commission decisions, it is difficult to quantify their impact. The obvious point in the analysis for them to be considered would be in determining whether the requirements of Article 101(3) of the TFEU are fulfilled.[308] The Commission has even approved agreements initiated by trade associations according to which the major European manufacturers of appliances agreed to stop producing and importing large appliances that were not energy efficient.[309] In most other contexts, a horizontal agreement between competitors to limit production would be prohibited as a hard-core restraint competition.

(d) Fundamental Rights

As discussed in Chapter I, fundamental rights (as international law) form part of the law of the EU legal system. Fundamental rights may limit the application of EU competition law in several ways. Firms are increasingly relying on fundamental rights to contest the decisions and conduct of the Commission.[310] Because the enforcement of competition law may entail the imposition of significant sanctions, and the Commission is charged with investigative powers, there is the potential for the violation of fundamental rights of the defendants.

In *Coats Holdings Ltd. v. Commission*, for example, the General Court held that the fundamental human right of the presumption of innocence required the Commission to "show precise and consistent evidence in order to establish the existence of [a cartel]."[311] In *Solvay SA v. Commission*, the ECJ held that the Commission violated the fundamental rights of Solvay by not providing Solvay with access to certain documents in the Commission's files.[312] In *Mannesmannröhren Werke AG v. Commission*, the issue was whether the German tube manufacturer Mannesmann could refuse to answer interrogatories of the Commission on the grounds that it enjoyed a fundamental right against self-incrimination.[313] In that case, the Commission was investigating an alleged cartel involving Mannesmann in the seamless tube market. In holding that

---

308. *See* Eco-Emballages, 2001 O.J. (L 233) 45; Grüner Punkt, 1997 O.J. (C 100) 4.
309. CECED Water Heaters, 2001 O.J. (C 250) 4; CECED Dishwashers, 2001 O.J. (C 250) 2.
310. *See, e.g.*, Case C-109/10 P, Solvay SA v. Comm'n, 2011 E.C.R. I-10413, 10431 ¶53; Case C-411/04 P, Salzgitter Mannesmann GmbH v. Comm'n, 2007 E.C.R. I-990, 1004 ¶40; Joined Cases C-204/00 P, C-205/00 P, C-211/00 P, C-213/00 P, C-217/00 P and C-219/00 P, Aalborg Portland A/S v. Comm'n, 2004 E.C.R. I-123, 441 ¶64.
311. Case T-36/05, Coats Holdings Ltd. v. Comm'n, 2007 E.C.R. II-110 (summary), at ¶70 (full version of case reported in the electronic reports of cases ECLI:EU:T:2007:268) *aff'd on appeal* Case C-468/07 P, Coats Holdings Ltd. v. Comm'n, 2008 E.C.R. I-127 (ECLI:EU:C:2008:503).
312. Case C-109/10 P, Solvay SA v. Comm'n, 2011 E.C.R. I-10413, 10434 ¶65.
313. Case T-112/98, Mannesmannröhren Werke AG v. Comm'n, 2001 E.C.R. II-732.

Mannesmann did not have to answer the questions which would implicate it in the cartel, the General Court recognized the role of fundamental rights as a limitation on the application of the competition rules:

> Fundamental rights form an integral part of the general principles of Community law whose observance is ensured by the Community judicature... For that purpose, the Court of Justice and the Court of First Instance draw inspiration from the constitutional traditions common to the Member States and from the guidelines supplied by international treaties for the protection of human rights on which the Member States have collaborated and to which they are signatories.[314]

5. Unilateral Restraints of Competition

Article 102 of the TFEU prohibits the abuse of a dominant position which has an effect on trade between member states. All three elements—dominance, abuse, and effect on trade between member states—must be present to trigger the application of Article 102.

5.1 Dominance

Article 102 of the TFEU is concerned with the anticompetitive exercise of market power. Consequently, the threshold requirement for the application of Article 102 is the existence of a dominant position. The term dominant position is abstractly defined as "a position of economic strength enjoyed by an undertaking which enables it to prevent effective competition being maintained on the relevant market by giving it the power to behave to an appreciable extent independently of its competitors, customers and ultimately of its customers."[315]

(a) Importance of Market Share

According to the General Court[316] and the Commission,[317] extremely large market shares are in themselves evidence of the existence of a dominant position. A market share of under 25 percent, on the other hand, is generally not considered

---

314. *Id.* at 754 ¶60.
315. Case C-52/09, Konkurrensverksket v. TeliaSonera Sverige AB, 2011 E.C.R. I-564, 575 ¶23.
316. Case T-336/07, Telefónica, SA v. Comm'n, 2012 E.C.R. II-___, at ¶149 *aff'd on appeal* Case C-295/12 P, Telefónica, SA v. Comm'n, 2014 E.C.R. I-___; Case T-321/05, AstraZeneca AB v. Comm'n, 2010 E.C.R. II-2805, 2919 ¶242 *aff'd on appeal* C-457/10 P, AstraZeneca AB v. Comm'n, 2010 E.C.R. I-___; Case T-66/01, Imperial Chemical Industries Ltd v. Comm'n, 2010 E.C.R. II-2645, 2718 ¶256.
317. NDC Health/IMS Health, 2002 O.J. (L 59) 18, 25 ¶59; Michelin, 2002 O.J. (L 143) 1, 28 ¶174.

indicative of dominance.[318] A market share of greater than 50 percent creates a presumption of dominance.[319] A market share of above 70 percent "is, in itself, a clear indication of the existence of a dominant position."[320] Although the discussion of dominance tends to focus on market shares, it is important to remember that the prohibition contained in Article 102 of the TFEU is concerned with market power, of which market share is just one indication.

(1) Two Dimensions of Relevant Market

Determining the market share of an undertaking requires defining the relevant market. A relevant market for purposes of competition law has two dimensions: product and geographic. A market share cannot be quantified unless both of these dimensions are defined. A relevant product market includes products or services that are regarded as interchangeable or substitutable by the consumer by reason of the products' characteristics, their prices, and their intended use.[321] The relevant geographic market comprises the area in which the undertakings concerned are involved in the supply and demand of products or services, in which the conditions of competition are sufficiently homogenous, and which can be distinguished from neighboring areas because the conditions of competition are appreciably different in those areas.[322]

(2) Basic Principles for Product Market Definition

Even though it is critical to the application of competition law, defining the relevant market is an imprecise science which depends on subjective impressions as much as objective evidence. It is a factual determination for which the EU courts give the Commission broad discretion.[323] This challenge is even greater in an area such as the EU which comprises many different cultures. For example, whether whiskey forms the relevant product market, or whether there are separate product markets for Scotch whisky, U.S. whiskey, and Irish whiskey, depends inter alia on the subjective sensibilities of the particular culture forming the relevant geographic market.

In *Guinness/Grand Metropolitan*,[324] the Commission concluded that in certain countries of the EU (Spain and Ireland), each of these types of whiskey

---

318. Guidelines on the assessment of horizontal mergers under the Council Regulation on the control of concentrations between undertakings, 2004 O.J. (C 31) 5, 7 ¶18.
319. Case T-336/07, Telefónica, SA v. Comm'n, 2012 E.C.R. II-___, at ¶150 *aff'd on appeal* Case C-295/12 P, Telefónica, SA v. Comm'n, 2014 E.C.R. I-___; Case T-66/01, Imperial Chemical Industries Ltd v. Comm'n, 2010 E.C.R. II-2645, 2718 ¶256; Case T-340/03, France Télécom SA v. Comm'n, 2007 E.C.R. II-117, 148 ¶100 *aff'd on appeal* Case C-202/07 P, France Télécom SA v. Comm'n, 2009 E.C.R. I-2369.
320. Case T-336/07, Telefónica, SA v. Comm'n, 2012 E.C.R. II-___, at ¶150 *aff'd on appeal* Case C-295/12 P, Telefónica, SA v. Comm'n, 2014 E.C.R. I-___.
321. Comm'n Notice on the definition of relevant market for the purposes of European Community competition law, 1997 O.J. (C 372) 5, 5-6 ¶7 [hereinafter Market Definition Notice].
322. *Id.* at 6 ¶¶8-9.
323. Case T-301/04, ClearstreamBanking AG v. Comm'n, 2009 E.C.R. II-3155, at ¶47.
324. Guinness/Grand Metropolitan, 1998 O.J. (L 288) 24; *see also* Case M. 3779, Pernod Ricard/Allied Domecq (June 24, 2005) ¶11.

formed its own product market. In the other member states, however, the consumers were—in the view of the Commission—not so discerning. Although empirical evidence and consumer surveys assist the Commission in making this assessment, it is ultimately the judgment of the individual commissioners and the members of the Competition Directorate who controls the outcome. Further adding to the uncertainty is the rule that the Commission is not bound by the market definitions it has adopted in earlier cases.[325]

The Commission has adopted a notice on market definition which provides some guidance as to the basic principles used in defining the market. The commonly cited definition of the relevant product market (i.e., products which are regarded as interchangeable or substitutable by the consumer by reason of the products' characteristics, their prices, and their intended use)[326] is of only limited practical use because in some circumstances, functionally interchangeable products (or even the same products) can be considered to constitute different product markets. For example, the Commission takes the position that beer sold in bars and restaurants forms a separate product market from beer sold at retail outlets, even though it may be the same beer.[327] The Commission also generally takes the position that automotive parts form two different product markets depending on whether they are sold as replacement or as original equipment.[328]

(i) Demand Substitution

In an effort to provide some legal certainty to undertakings, the Commission has developed certain analytical and evidentiary tools to identify the dimensions of the relevant market. In most cases, the initial inquiry relates to the cross-elasticity of demand for the particular product vis-à-vis other products. Cross-elasticity of demand refers to the willingness of customers to switch between products or services. According to the General Court: "The concept of the relevant market in fact implies that there can be effective competition between the products which form part of it and this presupposes that there is a sufficient degree of interchangeability between all the products forming part of the same market in so far as a specific use of such products is concerned."[329]

Absolute cross-elasticity of demand is not required. In other words, the products do not have to be interchangeable for all of their respective uses.[330] There must only be a sufficient degree of interchangeability. Conversely, just because two products are interchangeable in some applications does not necessarily mean that they belong to the same market. In *France Télécom SA v. Commission*, the

---

325. Case T-151/05, Nederlandse Vakbond Varkenshouders v. Comm'n, 2009 E.C.R. II-1227, 1273 ¶136; Case T-301/04, ClearstreamBanking AG v. Comm'n, 2009 E.C.R. II-3164, 3182 ¶55.
326. Market Definition Notice at 6 ¶7.
327. M.4999, Heineken/Scottish & Newcastle (April 3, 2008) ¶12.
328. Case M. 3081, Michelin/Viborg (March 7, 2003); Michelin, 2002 O.J. (L 143) 1; Case M. 2939, JCI/Bosch-VB JV (Oct. 18, 2002).
329. Case T-340/03, France Télécom SA v. Comm'n, 2007 E.C.R. II-117, 142 ¶80 *aff'd on appeal* Case C-202/07 P, France Télécom SA v. Comm'n, 2009 E.C.R. I-2369.
330. Case T-301/04, ClearstreamBanking AG v. Comm'n, 2009 E.C.R. II-3164, 3186 ¶64.

issue was whether high-speed Internet access and low-speed Internet access were part of the same product market. Wanadoo Interactive SA, a subsidiary of France Télécom, in attempting to avoid being deemed to have a dominant position, argued that high-speed Internet access and low-speed Internet access belonged to the same product market. In concluding that they formed two separate markets, the Commission pointed out that although low-speed Internet access and high-speed Internet access can often be used for the same applications, there are a number of important applications—such as downloading video files or playing online games—for which the two services are not interchangeable.[331]

In considering the cross-elasticity of demand, the Commission and courts rely on the hypothetical monopolist test.[332] According to this test, two products belong to the same market if, given a hypothetical, small (e.g., 5-10 percent), and nontransitory (i.e., permanent) change in relative prices, a sufficient number of purchasers of the product would switch to another product so that any price increase would be unprofitable.

A practical example of this test can be provided by its application to the juice industry. Suppose Company A, which produces grapefruit juice, has an 80 percent market share in the market for grapefruit juice. However, if the market were to be defined as all citrus juices, the market share of Company A would only be 15 percent on the citrus juice market. The application of the hypothetical monopolist test would ask whether consumers of grapefruit juice would switch to other citrus juices when confronted with a permanent price increase of 5 percent to 10 percent for grapefruit juice. If a sufficient number of consumers would switch to other citrus juices to such an extent that a price increase for grapefruit juice would not be profitable due to the resulting loss of sales, then the market would comprise at least grapefruit juice and other citrus juices. The process would have to be extended in addition to other available beverages until a set of products is identified for which a price rise would not induce a sufficient substitution in demand. This is an area where economists (and empirical studies) are relied on extensively, as the results of the hypothetical monopolist test can determine the outcome of the case.

The hypothetical monopolist test accepted by the Commission has also found acceptance in the EU courts. As discussed above, the initial issue in *France Télécom SA v. Commission* was whether high-speed Internet access and low-speed Internet access were part of the same product market. To test the elasticity of demand, the Commission conducted a survey of Internet users and found that 80 percent of subscribers would not switch from high-speed Internet access to low-speed Internet access in response to a price increase for high-speed Internet access of between 5 percent and 10 percent.[333] The General Court concluded that this provided a strong indication that high-speed Internet access and low-speed Internet access belonged to separate product markets.

---

331. Case T-340/03, France Télécom SA v. Comm'n, 2007 E.C.R. II-117, 145 ¶88 *aff'd on appeal* Case C-202/07 P, France Télécom SA v. Comm'n, 2009 E.C.R. I-2369.
332. Market Definition Notice at 7 ¶17.
333. Case T-340/03, France Télécom SA v. Comm'n, 2007 E.C.R. II-117, 145 ¶90 *aff'd on appeal* Case C-202/07 P, France Télécom SA v. Comm'n, 2009 E.C.R. I-2369.

Reliance on the hypothetical monopolist test is not always appropriate. Its application is based on the fundamental precondition that there is some degree of functional interchangeability between the products. In the words of the Commission, the products tested must be "reasonable alternative[s] for each other in economic and technical terms."[334] In some instances, customers would not readily switch between products or services regardless of how much the price increases. For example, customers for artificial hips are unlikely to switch to other orthopedic products such as artificial knees in the event of an increase in the price of artificial hips.[335] The two products are simply not functionally interchangeable. Nonetheless, the lack of functional interchangeability does not necessarily justify the conclusion that the products belong to different markets.[336] Additional factors, such as elasticity of supply, must be considered.

(ii) Supply Substitution

Supply-side substitutability refers to the ability of suppliers to switch production between products. A high degree of substitutability exists if suppliers, in response to a small but permanent change in relative prices, are able to switch production between the products in a relatively short time without incurring significant additional costs or risks. The greater the cross-elasticity of supply, the more likely the products belong to the same market. For example, the different sizes of liquid crystal display computer screens probably all belong to the same market because they are all easily designed and produced in the same plant with minor adjustments.[337] In another case, the Commission concluded that private label tuna and branded label tuna belong to the same product market because of the high degree of supply side elasticity.[338] The manufacturers could readily switch from making branded label tuna to private label tuna.

The most important factors in determining whether there is a sufficient level of cross-elasticity of supply to suggest that two products belong to the same product market are the costs and time delays associated with switching from the production of one product to the other.[339] Cross-elasticity of supply is more likely to play a role in industries covering an array of different qualities or grades of a particular product or similar products as opposed to entirely different products.[340] The lower the costs and the shorter the time associated

---

334. CVC/Lenzing, 2004 O.J. (L 82) 20, 26 ¶32.
335. Case M. 3146, Centerpulse/Smith & Nephew (May 27, 2003).
336. *See, e.g.*, M.4781, Norddeutsche Affinerie/Cumerio (Jan. 23, 2008) ¶70 (Two products formed the same market even though there was no demand-side substitutability between them from the perspective of the end user.).
337. *See* Case M. 3459, Epson/Sanyo/JV (Sept. 22, 2004) ¶7.
338. Case M. 7010, Bolton/Tri-Marine/JV (Dec. 9, 2013) ¶35.
339. Market Definition Notice at 8 ¶23; Case M. 6360, NYNAS/Shell/Harburg Refinery (Sept. 2, 2013) at ¶33.
340. In contrast to markets for goods, supply side substitutability does not typically play a significant role in determining the relevant dimensions of markets for services. There will typically be very high supply side elasticity in service markets. See, e.g., Case M. 7458, IBM/INF Business of Deutsche Lufthansa (Dec. 15, 2014) ¶27.

with switching, the more likely that the products are in competition with each other. This is a factual determination that must be made in each case.

One of the issues in *Norddeutsche Affinerie/Cumerio* was whether two copper shapes (billets (circular sections) and cakes (rectangular sections)) formed part of the same product market.[341] Although the two shapes were both used for further processing into semi-finished copper products, the Commission concluded that there was "no demand-side substitutability between billets and cakes."[342] Whereas billets were processed into copper tubes and bars, cakes were typically processed into copper sheets or foil. However, the Commission went on to examine supply-side substitutability and found that billets and cakes were typically produced on the same equipment. In addition, the costs of switching from one product to another were relatively low. All that a manufacturer of one product had to do to was change some molds and parts on the equipment.[343] This was sufficient for the Commission to conclude that cakes and billets belonged to the same product market even though there was no demand-side substitutability between them.[344]

It is important to recognize that factors relating to the producers themselves are not the only factors that the Commission considers relevant in assessing supply-side substitutability. Factors outside the control of the producers, such as market characteristics, may also be relevant. In *Glatfelter/Crompton Assets*, for example, the customers of various types of fiber material used in coffee filtration and tea bags had certification requirements for each product depending on their application (e.g., coffee pods vs. tea bags). The Commission considered this relevant because it imposed additional burdens on the producer wanting to switch from the production of one type of fiber material to the other.[345]

(iii) Evidence Used to Define Markets

In addition to the analytical tools of cross-elasticity of demand and supply, the Commission commonly relies on less speculative evidence to define the relevant markets. The Commission sometimes relies on past incidents of substitution to identify the competitive relationship between products or services. If, for example, the price for one product increased or decreased suddenly, perhaps due to an unexpected increase in the costs of raw materials to produce the product, the reaction of the customers to such development would be used to identify the elasticity of demand (provided that the reaction could not be explained by reference to other considerations). The reaction of customers to the introduction of a new product may also serve as objective evidence of whether certain products belong to the same market.

At least as a starting point, the Commission often relies on the market definitions which are customarily used in the particular industry. The promotional literature of the companies active in the industry or the trade associations or trade journals often serve as evidence as to how the market participants

---

341. Case M. 4781, Norddeutsche Affinerie/Cumerio (Jan. 23, 2008).
342. *Id.* ¶70.
343. *Id.* ¶78.
344. *Id.* at ¶85.
345. Case M. 4215, Glatfelter/Crompton Assets (Dec. 20, 2006) ¶43.

characterize the market. In addition, marketing studies commissioned by the undertakings often identify products and undertakings which are perceived as competitors. The Commission can then test this industry characterization in its further investigation. The Commission seldom will rely exclusively on industry characterization to define the relevant market.

Just as a low degree of demand elasticity may not always preclude a finding that two products belong to the same market (particularly when supply elasticity is high), a high degree of cross-elasticity of demand may not be sufficient to support a finding that the products in question belong to the same market. According to the Commission, there are a number of barriers to substitution and switching and costs that may suggest that two demand substitutes do not belong to one single product market:[346]

- regulatory barriers or other forms of state intervention
- constraints arising in downstream markets
- need to incur specific capital investment or loss in current output in order to switch to alternative inputs
- the location of customers
- specific investment in production process
- learning and human capital investment
- retooling costs or other investments, and
- uncertainty about quality and reputation of unknown suppliers.

Past decisions of the Commission or the EU courts defining a relevant market cannot necessarily be relied on in future cases as the Commission and EU courts are not bound by their earlier market definitions.[347] This is because each case must be assessed on its own merits. The dimensions of a relevant market may—and often do—change over time. Nonetheless, prior decisions of the Commission and courts will for practical purposes provide a strong starting point for a market definition analysis.

(3) *Basic Principles for Defining Geographic Dimension*

Determining the geographic dimension of the relevant market is often more difficult than identifying the relevant product market. There is no exhaustive catalog of evidence the Commission considers relevant to determine the geographic dimension. Two factors on which the Commission and courts often rely are price differences and transportation costs. Significant price differences for the same product in two separate areas suggest separate geographic markets.[348] If, for example, the price for a package of chewing gum in one geographic area

---

346. Market Definition Notice at 11 ¶42.
347. Case T-151/05, Nederlandse Vakbond Varkenshouders v. Comm'n, 2009 E.C.R. II-1227, 1273 ¶136; Case T-301/04, ClearstreamBanking AG v. Comm'n, 2009 E.C.R. II-3164, 3182 ¶55.
348. Case M. 6360, NYNAS/Shell/Harburg Refinery (Sept. 2, 2013) ¶199 ("[T]he Commission relies not only on price level differences but also on the dynamics and co-movement of prices to conclude on the relevant market definition.").

is significantly more expensive than in another area, it is unlikely that these two areas comprise part of the same geographic market for chewing gum.

In addition, high transportation costs (measured as a proportion of the price at which the product is sold) suggest a limitation on the geographic dimension of the market. For example, the relevant market for glass containers for food products may be limited in geographical scope because the costs of transporting glass containers across a long distance would be prohibitively expensive.[349] Similarly, the relevant market for cement may be limited to a small geographic area because of the prohibitive costs of transporting the product over large distances.[350] In *Flextronics/Nortel*, the Commission suggested that the relevant geographic market for ready-mix concrete was probably only 20 kilometers from the concrete plant where it was mixed.[351] Conversely, the low costs associated with the transport of coffee filters and tea bags (below 10 percent of the end price) suggest a much broader geographic market.[352]

The basic demand characteristics of the product will also be examined to determine the geographic dimension of the relevant market. The nature of demand for the relevant product may in itself determine the scope of the geographic market. Factors such as national preferences or preferences for national brands, language, culture and lifestyle, and the need for a local presence may serve to limit the geographic scope of competition. In contrast to the United States, language differences also are a common factor in the EU when defining the geographic dimension of the relevant market. For example, the Commission has held that the geographic dimension of the market for television programs should be delineated along linguistic borders.[353]

An examination of the geographic pattern of purchases by the customers is also often helpful in determining the geographic dimension of the relevant market.[354] The fact that customers purchase from companies located throughout the EU on similar terms, or the customers determine their suppliers through public tenders in which companies from throughout the EU submit bids, suggests that the geographic market will be usually considered to be at least EU-wide.[355]

In *Nederlandse Vakbond Varkenshouders v. Commission*, for example, the issue was whether the Dutch and German markets for pigs formed part of the same geographic market. As evidence that they formed part of the

---

349. Case M. 3397, Owens-Illinois/BSN Glasspack (June 9, 2004) ¶19 (The transportation costs associated with the glass containers limited the scope of the geographic market to a 400-500 km radius of the manufacturing plant.)
350. Case M. 7009, Holcim/Cemex West (June 5, 2014) ¶63; Case M. 6360, NYNAS/Shell/Harburg Refinery (Sept. 2, 2013) ¶207; Case M. 3415, CRH/SEMAPA/SECIL JV (May 28, 2004) ¶16.
351. Case M. 3583, Flextronics/Nortel (Oct. 28, 2004) ¶21.
352. Case M. 4215, Glatfelter/Crompton Assets (Dec. 20, 2006) ¶56.
353. Case M. 7360, 21st Century Fox/Apollo/JV, (Oct. 9, 2014) ¶48.
354. Case M. 7061, Huntsman Corp./Rockwood Holdings (Sept. 10, 2014) summary at 2015 O.J. (C 67) 7, 10 ¶25.
355. Case M. 4941, Henkel/Adhesives & Electronic Business (Feb. 15, 2008) ¶55.

same geographic market, the General Court referred to the close relationship between price fluctuations in one country and the flow of exports.[356] When prices increased in Germany, the statistics showed a corresponding increase in exports from the Netherlands to Germany. Conversely, the absence of cross-border sales of the same product suggests that the geographic dimension of the relevant market is national.[357]

(b) Additional Factors Beyond Market Share

Although market share is given primary importance when determining whether an undertaking occupies a position of dominance on a relevant market, it is not the end of the analysis. There are a number of secondary considerations which may serve to mitigate or reinforce the implications drawn from a high market share.

(1) Relative Market Share

As discussed above, the starting point in identifying the existence of a dominant position is market share. However, absolute market share may not itself facilitate an accurate assessment of the strength of the undertaking. For example, the market power of an undertaking with a market share of 40 percent will likely differ depending on whether its next largest competitor has a market share of 35 percent or 5 percent. In other words, market share as an indicia of market power is relative to the number and strength of competitors.[358] In *British Airways v. Commission*, British Airways had a market share of approximately 40 percent but was considered dominant in part because the next largest competitor, Virgin Airlines, had a market share of only 5 percent.[359] In, *France Télécom SA v. Commission*, the fact that the market share of France Télécom was eight times that of the nearest competitor was evidence that France Télécom had a dominant position.[360]

The greater the difference between the undertaking's market share and that of its nearest rivals, the less relevant the other factors for assessing market power become. In *Van den Bergh Foods Ltd v. Commission*, for example, a subsidiary of Unilever held a market share in the market for single wrapped items of impulse ice cream (the kind of ice cream one purchases, for example,

---

356. Case T-151/05, Nederlandse Vakbond Varkenshouders v. Comm'n, 2009 E.C.R. II-1227, 1267 ¶106.
357. Summary of Comm'n Decision of 16 May 2012 declaring a concentration compatible with the internal market and the functioning of the European Economic Area (EEA) Agreement (Case M. 6286—Südzucker/ED & F MAN), 2014 O.J. (C 160) 11, 13 ¶27.
358. Case T-321/05, AstraZeneca AB v. Comm'n, 2010 E.C.R. II-2805, 2935 ¶289 *aff'd on appeal* C-457/10 P, AstraZeneca AB v. Comm'n, 2010 E.C.R. I-____; Case 27/76, United Brands v. Comm'n, 1978 E.C.R. 209, 276 ¶58.
359. Case T-219/99, British Airways v. Comm'n, 2003 E.C.R. II-5925, 5977 ¶210 *aff'd on appeal* Case C-95/04 P, British Airways v. Comm'n, 2007 E.C.R. I-2331.
360. Case T-340/03, France Télécom SA v. Comm'n, 2007 E.C.R. II-107, 150 ¶109 *aff'd on appeal* Case C-202/07 P, France Télécom SA v. Comm'n, 2009 E.C.R. I-2369.

in a vending machine) in Ireland of 89 percent.[361] Despite the fact that the other main competitors, Mars and Nestle, had significant financial and other resources to pose a real competitive threat to Unilever in Ireland, the General Court concluded that Unilever nonetheless held a dominant position. In that case, the market share gap between Unilever and these two competitors was simply too large to preclude the finding of dominance in that case even in light of the strength of Mars and Nestle.

(2) Vertical Integration

The degree of vertical integration is also a potentially relevant factor in assessing the market power of the undertaking. As discussed above, the typical value chain is composed of various vertically related steps from the supply of the raw materials to the sale to the end-user. In some industries, it may be a significant advantage to be active at more than one of these levels. For example, a manufacturer of aluminum parts for automobiles may be in a significantly stronger position than its competitors if it also is active in the upstream market of molten aluminum. Similarly, the manufacturer of retail products may find it easier to compete if it has its own established distribution network throughout Europe.

The influence of vertical integration on the dominance assessment must be made on a case-by-case basis. The aluminum parts manufacturer discussed above may receive no benefit from being vertically integrated in the upstream market if its competitors can easily secure molten aluminum from third-party suppliers. Each case requires a close examination.

(3) Market Entry

As discussed above, the abstract definition of a dominant position used by the EU courts and the Commission is "a position of economic strength enjoyed by an undertaking which enables it to prevent effective competition being maintained on the relevant market by giving it the power to behave to an appreciable extent independently of its competitors, customers and ultimately of its customers."[362] Pressure from competitors is clearly one of the considerations that prevent undertakings from acting independently. An undertaking will generally be less inclined to increase its prices if it is exposed to sufficient competition. However, a similar pressure may be exerted by potential market entrants. An undertaking may be prevented by market forces from increasing its prices because to do so would attract other undertakings into the market. In *Continental/Phoenix*, for example, the acquisition of Phoenix AG by Continental AG would have given Continental a market share of over 55 percent in the market for air springs for rail vehicles.[363] The Commission did not consider this a problem because "there

---

361. Case T-65/98, Van den Bergh Foods Ltd v. Comm'n, 2003 E.C.R. II-4662, 4719 ¶155 *aff'd on appeal* Case C-552/03 P, Unilever Bestfoods (Ireland) Ltd. v. Comm'n, 2006 E.C.R. I-9094.
362. Case 85/76, Hoffmann-La Roche v. Comm'n, 1979 E.C.R. 461, 520 ¶38.
363. 2006 O.J. (L 353) 7, 10 ¶26.

are enough potential competitors in the market who could prevent the parties from raising prices independently."[364]

Potential competition is relevant as a constraint if the potential entry can be considered likely, timely, and sufficient.[365] The likely criterion requires that potential entry be profitable for the entrant. An undertaking is unlikely to enter a new market if it is not able to realize a profit by doing so. The less effort required by the potential market entrant, the greater the likelihood of entry. The second criterion, timeliness, concerns the amount of time it would take for the potential market entrant to actually enter the market. It is incomplete to end the analysis with the first criterion because even if there is a strong likelihood of entry, that will be ineffectual as a constraint if it would take many years for the potential entrant to actually become a viable competitor on the market. As a general rule, the Commission considers that entry is timely only if it will occur within two years.[366] The third criterion requires that the entry be sufficient to deter the anticompetitive conduct.[367] In general, the entry of a large firm with significant financial and commercial resources is more likely to prove to be a sufficient entrant than a start-up firm with merely a good product.

(4) *Intellectual Property Rights as Evidence of Dominance*

As discussed in greater detail in Chapter X, intellectual property rights grant the holder exclusive rights over her invention, idea, or mark. The mere ownership of intellectual property rights does not ipso facto give the owner a dominant position for purposes of EU competition law.[368] Although the Coca Cola Company may hold the rights to the trademark "Coca Cola," the trademark does not necessarily give it dominance on the product market for soft drinks. While the computer manufacturer Dell may hold the exclusive right to sell Dell laptop computers, it probably does not hold a dominant position in the market for laptop computers as Dell laptop computers probably do not constitute a separate product market. Intellectual property rights by themselves only confer a monopoly for purposes of competition law if the dimensions of the relevant market are commensurate with the particular intellectual property right.[369]

Moreover, an intellectual property right is limited in its geographical scope. The holder of a trademark in France cannot rely on the French trademark to prevent a third party from legitimately selling a product under the same name in Ireland on the basis of the French trademark. The intellectual property right in this case does not permit the inference of market dominance if the geographic

---

364. *Id.*
365. Article 102 Guidelines at ¶16; Horizontal Merger Guidelines at ¶68; Case T-461/07, Visa Europe Ltd v. Comm'n, 2011 E.C.R. II-1740, 1788 ¶172.
366. Horizontal Merger Guidelines at ¶74.
367. *Id.*
368. Case T-321/05, AstraZeneca AB v. Comm'n, 2010 E.C.R. II-2830, 2928 ¶270 *aff'd on appeal* C-457/10 P, AstraZeneca AB v. Comm'n, 2010 E.C.R. I-____.
369. *See, e.g.*, Case 24/67, Parke Davis v. Probe, 1968 E.C.R. I-55, 72.

market is the entire EU. Although the holder of an intellectual property right may have a dominant position by virtue of those rights, this is not necessarily the case. It is a factual analysis that requires a case-by-case determination of the relevant market.

Although the Commission and EU courts have been reluctant to equate a patent with a dominant position in the context of Article 102 of the TFEU, the Commission has stated that a patent, if it achieves the status as a standard essential patent, may be considered its own "relevant technology market."[370] One could therefore argue that the holder of a standard essential patent is in a dominant position.[371] A patent becomes standard essential if it acquires two characteristics: it is essential to have access to the patent in order to produce a particular product and it cannot be designed around.[372]

(5) Role of Profits and Prices

It is a common assumption that dominant firms enjoy high profit margins and can maintain high prices due to the absence of pricing pressure from significant competitors. Conversely, firms in highly competitive markets generally exhibit low or no profit margins as their prices are close to their marginal costs. Consequently, there is an obvious temptation to use the existence of high profits as circumstantial evidence of a dominant position, and the absence of profits as evidence of a lack of dominance.

The ECJ has held that reference to profit margins is an inappropriate indicator of market dominance. In *United Brands v. Commission*, United Brands argued that the fact that it was incurring losses should be used as evidence that it did not enjoy a dominant position.[373] In dismissing the reference to losses as an indication of the absence of dominance, the ECJ cautioned that profits are a poor indicator of dominance or lack of dominance: "An undertaking's economic strength is not measured by its profitability; a reduced profit margin or even losses for a time are not incompatible with a dominant position, just as large profits may be compatible with a situation where there is effective competition."[374]

In contrast to profits, both the Commission and the General Court have used the ability of an undertaking to charge high prices over an extended period of time for a particular product as evidence that the undertaking is in a dominant position. The issue in *AstraZeneca AB v. Commission* was whether AstraZeneca

---

370. Case M. 7202, Lenovo/Motorola Mobility (June 26, 2014) ¶23; Case C-3/39.985, Motorola Mobility (April 29, 2014); Case M. 6381, Google/Motorola (Feb. 13, 2012) ¶51.
371. This was the conclusion reached by the Commission in Case C-3/39.985, Motorola Mobility (April 29, 2014) at ¶225.
372. Case M. 7202, Lenovo/Motorola Mobility (June 26, 2014) ¶23; Case M. 7047, Microsoft/Nokia (Dec. 4, 2013) ¶186.
373. Case 27/76, United Brands v. Comm'n, 1978 E.C.R. 209, 284 ¶125.
374. *Id.* at 284 ¶126. As discussed below, however, the ECJ has recognized that profit margin may be indicative of an abuse of a dominant position. *Id.* at 301 ¶251.

AB abused its dominant position in the market for a certain drug by making misleading statements to the national patent offices in Europe about those drugs. In order to establish that AstraZeneca had a dominant position, the Commission relied inter alia on the ability of AstraZeneca to charge prices higher than those charged by its competitors.[375] The General Court confirmed the Commission's approach. According to the General Court, "the fact that AZ was able to maintain a much higher market share than those of its competitors while charging prices higher than those charged for other PPIs is a relevant factor showing that AZ's behaviour was not, to an appreciable extent, subject to competitive constraints from its competitors, its customers and, ultimately, consumers."[376]

5.2 Collective Dominance

Article 102 of the TFEU applies to two different types of dominance: single firm dominance and collective dominance. The discussion up to this point has been primarily concerned with a situation of single firm dominance. However, Article 102 expressly applies to abuse of a dominant position "by one or more undertakings." Unfortunately, the TFEU does not indicate when two or more undertakings can be considered to hold a position of collective dominance. A literal interpretation of Article 102 precludes the possibility that each of the two or more undertakings must hold its own dominant position. The undertakings must together abuse "a dominant position."

There are two basic constellations in which collective dominance has been deemed to exist. The first of these is where connecting factors exist between firms in a concentrated market. This is illustrated in the *Compagnie Maritime Belge* case where common membership in a shipping liner conference was deemed to be a sufficient connecting factor.[377] The members of this shipping liner group then collectively engaged in exclusionary practices against competitors who were not in the group and who were undercutting their prices. The ECJ applied Article 102 of the TFEU to their conduct, even though none of the members individually held a dominant position.

The other constellation in which a finding of collective dominance may be deemed to exist is in an oligopolistic market. An oligopolistic market is one characterized by few competitors – typically less than five. In such markets, it is possible that the oligopolists tacitly coordinate their behavior even without

---

375. AstraZeneca, Comm'n Decision of 15 June 2005 relating to a proceeding under Article 82 of the EC Treaty and Article 54 of the EEA Agreement, ¶546 ("AZ's higher prices constitute evidence of its market power in relation to its competitors on the PPI market.")
376. Case T-321/05, AstraZeneca AB v. Comm'n, 2010 E.C.R. II-2830, 2924 ¶261 *aff'd on appeal* C-457/10 P, AstraZeneca AB v. Comm'n, 2010 E.C.R. I-___.
377. Case C-395/96, Compagnie Maritime Belge, 2000 E.C.R. I-1365. The Commission could not pursue the undertakings under Article 101 TFEU because the conduct qualified for an exemption under Article 101(3) TFEU. Although the members of the group also engaged in collusion in the sense of Article 101, a finding of collusion in the sense of Article 101 is not necessary for a finding of collective dominance.

any connecting factors or agreement between them. For example, if there are only four gas stations in an isolated town in Poland, one of those gas stations could unilaterally increase its prices with the hope or intention that the other competitors also increase their prices. The incentive for them is that they could all increase their revenues because the price level would be higher than it would be in a non-oligopolistic market.[378]

In recognition of this possibility, the General Court has held that a position of collective dominance may exist, even in the absence of connecting factors, if three conditions are fulfilled.[379] First, the market must be transparent. In other words, each member of the dominant oligopoly must have the ability to know and be able to monitor how the other oligopolists are behaving in order to monitor whether or not they are adopting the common policy.[380] In a transparent market, the prices charged by the competing firms and their price increases are readily available information.

For example, the airline industry is considered a transparent industry because each competitor can easily identify and monitor the prices charged by each of its competitors. Commodity markets for which there often exists an index price are typically considered vulnerable to oligopolistic dominance, assuming the appropriate market structure is present.[381] In this respect, important factors that play a role are highly homogeneous products, fairly stable demand, and relatively homogeneous firms (the cost structures of the competitors need to be similar). In *Sony/BMG*, for example, one reason why the Commission decided that there was not a situation of collective dominance in the recorded music markets was because the heterogeneity of the content of records reduced the transparency of the market.[382]

Second, the situation of tacit coordination must be sustainable. The sustainability requirement requires a prognostic assessment of the reaction of competitors, potential competitors, and customers to the tacit coordination. Consider the following report which appeared in the Wall Street Journal:[383]

---

378. This supra-competitive equilibrium—sometimes referred to as a Cournot equilibrium—is more likely to occur in industries with limited product differentiation. For a general discussion of oligopoly theory, see J.W. Friedman, Oligopoly Theory (1993); George Stigler, *A Theory of Oligopoly*, 1994 J.POL. ECON. 44.
379. Case T-212/03, MyTravel Group plc v. Comm'n, 2008 E.C.R. II-2034, 2062 ¶78; Case T-193/02, Piau v. Comm'n, 2005 E.C.R. II-209, 251 ¶111 *appeal dismissed* Case C-171/05 P, Piau v. Comm'n, 2006 E.C.R. I-37.
380. Case T-342/99, Airtours PLC v. Comm'n, 2002 E.C.R. II-2585, 2613 ¶62; Sony/BMG, 2005 O.J. (L 62) 30, 31 ¶13.
381. Conversely, the absense of an index for a particular product suggests a lack of transparency. Case M. 3276, Anglo American/Kumba Resources, Dec. 3, 2003 ¶24.
382. Sony/BMG, 2005 O.J. (L 62) 30, 33 ¶21.
383. THE WALL STREET JOURNAL, Sept. 28, 2004, p.D4, col. 6.

> **American Airlines Halts Fare Increase**
>
> FORTH WORTH, Texas – American Airlines reversed its $5 one-way fare increase in most North American markets after various major competitors failed to match on a broad basis.
>
> The AMR Corp. unit, which raised fares Thursday to help weather higher jet-fuel prices, reversed yesterday morning "to remain competitive," a spokeswoman said.
>
> American did retain the fare boost in a small number of markets where it competes with smaller carriers that fully matched and held their increases. Those carriers include Air Canada, Frontier, Spirit, and Midwest Airlines.
>
> Larger airlines that had fully or partially matched American's fare boost – including Delta, UAL's United, Continental, Northwest, America West and ATA – later reversed on either all or most of their routes. So American was forced to largely pull back, continuing a recent string of failed attempts by major carriers to raise fares.

In this particular circumstance, the attempt by American Airlines to increase prices apparently was not successful because of the maverick competitors who did not follow the price increase. Hence, the ability to sustain supra-competitive prices requires that there are no mavericks (i.e., competitors who do not abide by or conform to the tacit coordination). Each member of the dominant oligopoly must be aware that highly competitive action on its part designed to increase its market share would provoke identical action by the others, so that it would derive no benefit from its initiative.[384]

Third, tacit coordination will result in supra-competitive prices only if market entry can be adequately deterred. In the above example, even if the other major airline carriers would have followed the lead of American Airlines, the same result would have been experienced if potential competitors could easily enter the market. Supra-competitive prices make market entry attractive. Therefore, the existence of barriers to market entry is a condition for the application of the collective dominance doctrine.

5.3   Substantial Part of the Union

Article 102 of the TFEU also requires that the dominant position cover a substantial part of the EU. The ECJ has exhibited a great deal of pragmatism in applying this requirement. Even the southern part of Germany has been

---

384. Case T-102/96, Gencor v. Comm'n, 1999 E.C.R. II-759, 838 ¶276; Case T-342/99, Airtours PLC v. Comm'n, 2002 E.C.R. II-2592, 2613 ¶62.

considered by the ECJ to constitute a substantial part of the EU.[385] In *Bodson*, less than 10 percent of the communes in France were considered a substantial part of the EU.[386]

5.4 Abusive Conduct

Article 102 of the TFEU does not prohibit the mere existence of market power. According to the ECJ, "a finding of a dominant position is not in itself a ground of criticism of the undertaking concerned."[387] It requires additional anticompetitive conduct by the dominant undertaking. In the EU, this additional conduct is called abuse.[388] Although Article 102 of the TFEU contains a list of abusive practices, this list is not exhaustive.[389] The abstract definition of abuse adopted by the EU courts is conduct which "is such as to influence the structure of a market where, as a result of the very presence of the undertaking in question, the degree of competition is weakened and which, through recourse to methods different from those which condition normal competition in products or services on the basis of the transactions of commercial operators, has the effect of hindering the maintenance of the degree of competition still existing in the market or the growth of that competition."[390] This abstract definition provided by the EU courts is of limited practical use. Practitioners in this area rely on categories of abusive conduct which assist in identifying violations of Article 102 of the TFEU.

(a) Excessive Pricing

Although the imposition of excessive prices is perhaps the most obvious form of abuse, it is one of the most difficult to identify and sanction. The challenge is determining when a particular price is excessive. According to the ECJ, a price is excessive if it "has no reasonable relation to the economic value of the product supplied."[391] However, the absence of a consensus on the meaning of economic value means that this abstract standard is difficult to apply. It is easier to identify abuse where the customer does not receive any value compared to the situation where the customer receives some bargained-for value.

If, for example, a dominant undertaking imposes fees on its customers regardless of whether the customer wants the service corresponding to the fee,

---

385. Joined Cases 40/73, Suiker Unie v. Comm'n, 1975 E.C.R. 1663.
386. Case 30/87, Bodson v. SA Pompes funèbres des régions libérées, 1988 E.C.R. 2507, 2514 ¶24.
387. Case C-52/09, Konkurrensverket v. TeliaSonera Sverige AB, 2011 E.C.R. I-564, 575 ¶24.
388. Although intent is not an element of the offense, it can be used in supporting a finding of abuse. Case T-321/05, AstraZeneca AB v. Comm'n, 2010 E.C.R. II-2830, 2963 ¶351 *aff'd on appeal* C-457/10 P, AstraZeneca AB v. Comm'n, 2010 E.C.R. I-____.
389. Case C-52/09, Konkurrensverket v. TeliaSonera Sverige AB, 2011 E.C.R. I-564, 576 ¶26.
390. Case 85/76, Hoffmann-LaRoche, 1979 E.C.R. 461, 541 ¶91.
391. Case C-385/07 P, Der Grüne Punkt - Duales System Deutschland GmbH v. Comm'n, 2009 E.C.R. I-6219, 6261 ¶142.

the conduct of the dominant undertaking will likely be deemed abusive.[392] In most cases, however, there is a negotiated selling price and the Commission has to quantify the economic value the customer is receiving.

There are two methods employed by the Commission and courts in past cases to show that a price is excessive. In *United Brands v. Commission*, the ECJ suggested that "a comparison between the selling price of the product in question and its cost of production, which would disclose the amount of the profit margin" might be an appropriate method to determine whether the price was excessive.[393] This approach is problematic for three reasons. First, there may be procompetitive explanations as to why an undertaking has a large profit margin. For example, the undertaking may simply be more efficient than its competitors in the production of its goods or the provision of its services. As the profit margin is the difference between the costs of production and the price of the product, an undertaking may be able to increase its profit margin by increasing efficiency even without having to increase prices. Second, it is difficult to accurately capture and quantify all the costs in producing a product or providing a service.

In the *Scandlines* and the *Sundbusserne* investigations, for example, the Commission received complaints from ferry operators that the Port of Helsingborg in Sweden was charging excessive prices for certain routes. After an extensive investigation, the Commission concluded that it did not have sufficient evidence to show that the prices were excessive and expressly recognized that it is very difficult to show that prices are excessive.[394] Third, reliance on profit margin as an indication of excessive pricing is a difficult and vague standard to apply because the Commission and courts, even if they are in a position to accurately determine the profit margin, are required to distinguish between a reasonable and an unreasonable profit margin.[395]

The second method that has been endorsed by the courts is to compare the allegedly excessive prices to prices for the same products in neighboring markets or for closely competitive products in the same market.[396] If, for example, a Swedish latex paint manufacturer charges €50 for a liter of paint in Sweden where there are only two competitors, but sells that same paint in Finland for

---

392. *Id.* at 6261 ¶143.
393. Case 27/76, United Brands v. Comm'n, 1978 E.C.R. 209, 301 ¶251.
394. Comm'n, 2004 Annual Report on Competition Policy (2005) at 27 ¶46. Moreover, the Commission has the burden of proof in showing that the price is excessive. Case 27/76, United Brands v. Comm'n, 1978 E.C.R. 209, 303 ¶264.
395. *See, e.g.*, Attheraces Ltd. v. British Horseracing Board Ltd, [2007] All ER (D) 26; [2007] EWCA Civ. 38 (Feb. 2, 2007) in which the English Court of Appeal overturned the lower court's finding of excessive pricing because the cost-plus method employed by the lower court did not identify what profit margin was reasonable.
396. Case C-351/12, OSA v. Léčebné lázně Mariánské Lázně a.s., 2014 E.C.R. I-____, at ¶87; T-306/05, Scippacercola v. Comm'n, 2008 E.C.R. II-4 (summary), at ¶104 (full version of case reported in the electronic reports of cases ECLI:EU:T:2008:9) *aff'd on appeal* Case C-159/08 P, Scippacercola v. Comm'n, 2009 E.C.R. I-46 (summary) (full version of case reported in the electronic reports of cases ECLI:EU:C:2009:188); Case 27/76, United Brands v. Comm'n, 1978 E.C.R. 209, 301 ¶252.

€10, absent other reasons for the difference in prices the Commission may use this as an inference that the prices in Sweden are excessive. If the dominant undertaking is not active in other competitive markets, the comparison may be made to similar products charged by other undertakings in neighboring competitive markets.

Despite the attractiveness of this method, it is also difficult to apply because it requires the Commission to engage in a detailed factual analysis and to account for any extraneous differences that might legitimately explain the price differential. Neither the EU courts nor the Commission has identified specific price differences which would be presumptively indicative of abuse. In *United Brands v. Commission*, the ECJ held that a price differential of 7 percent is not prima facie evidence that the price is excessive.[397]

If the excessive prices are being charged by the dominant undertaking to a downstream rival who is not active in the upstream market, it is referred to as a margin squeeze. Margin squeeze occurs when a vertically integrated undertaking (i.e., active in related upstream and downstream markets) charges excessive prices for the upstream product to its competitors in the downstream market.[398] For example, if a computer manufacturer also manufactures the chips used in the computers it makes and then charges an excessive price to other computer manufacturers for the chips, this could be a margin squeeze because it affects the ability of the nonintegrated computer manufacturer in its competition with the integrated computer manufacturer.

The decisive consideration in margin squeeze cases is whether the spread between the price of the product at the wholesale level (where the undertaking is dominant) and the price at the retail level is fair.[399] The undertaking may or may not be dominant at the retail level.[400] A spread is unfair when it is negative (i.e., the wholesale price charged to the competitor is less than the price the dominant firm is charging its downstream customers) or is insufficient to cover the dominant firm's product-specific costs so that a competitor as equally efficient as the dominant firm is prevented from competing with the dominant undertaking in the downstream market.[401] As the spread is the decisive criterion, it is not required for a finding of unfairness that the wholesale prices are themselves abuses of a dominant position.[402] The ECJ recognizes that the reliance on

---

397. Case 27/76, United Brands v. Comm'n, 1978 E.C.R. 209, 303 ¶266.
398. Case C-295/12 P, Telefónica, SA v. Comm'n, 2014 E.C.R. I-___, at ¶124.
399. C-280/08 P, Deutsche Telekom AG v. Comm'n, 2011 E.C.R. I-9601, 9673 ¶167; Deutsche Bahn, 2013 O.J. (C 237) 28, 29 ¶5. Contrary to the essential facilities doctrine discussed below in the context of refusals to deal, it is not necessary to show that the upstream product is indispensable for the downstream competitor to compete in the downstream market. Case C-52/09, Konkurrensverket v. TeliaSonera Sverige AB, 2011 E.C.R. I-564, 587 ¶72.
400. Case C-52/09, Konkurrensverket v. TeliaSonera Sverige AB, 2011 E.C.R. I-564, 597 ¶114.
401. *Id.*; C-280/08 P, Deutsche Telekom AG v. Comm'n, 2011 E.C.R. I-9601, 9673 ¶169; Case C-52/09, Konkurrensverket v. TeliaSonera Sverige AB, 2011 E.C.R. I-564, 587 ¶73.
402. C-280/08 P, Deutsche Telekom AG v. Comm'n, 2011 E.C.R. I-9601, 9678 ¶183.

the spread could have the consequence that the customers in the downstream market pay more for the product or service because the dominant undertaking may increase this price to reduce the spread.[403] According to the ECJ, however, the long-term benefits of protecting the nondominant competitor outweigh any short-term disadvantages suffered by the downstream customers.[404]

(b) Imposition of Unfair Terms

Although the imposition of unfair terms is an example of abuse expressly identified in Article 102 of the TFEU, it is extremely difficult to decipher specific rules, given the subjective nature of the standard. There is no uniform definition of what qualifies as unfair.

(c) Tying and Bundling

Although tying and bundling are analyzed similarly from a competition law perspective, they refer to different commercial practices. Basic tying exists where a supplier of two or more products or services conditions the sale of the dominant product (referred to as the "tying product") on the willingness of the buyer to purchase the nondominant product or service (referred to as the "tied product"). In this tying scenario, the customer has the choice of purchasing just the tying product or purchasing both the tying product and the tied product—but not the tying product by itself.[405] Typically, an undertaking is able to impose this condition only when it is dominant in the market for the tying product. The customer will agree to also purchase the tied product because it wants or needs the tying product.

The commercial practice of bundling refers to the situation in which the seller only sells the two products together. Bundling is distinguished from tying in that the customer only has one choice; to purchase both products together. As discussed above, in a tying fact pattern the customer can always purchase the tied product by itself. A particular form of bundling, referred to as mixed bundling, occurs when the seller gives its customers a choice of purchasing the bundle (selected by the seller) or a bundle of the individual products selected by the customer, but the customer receives a discount as an incentive for purchasing a mixed bundle. For example, a beverage manufacturer might require its customers to either purchase a specific bundle of beverage types from it or purchase a bundle of beverage types selected by the customer at a discount.

The practice of tying or bundling, when engaged in by a dominant undertaking, is considered anticompetitive because it allows the dominant undertaking to foreclose competition on the market where it is not dominant by forcing products or services on customers who do not want them or may be able to purchase them from other suppliers at a better quality or price. For

---

403. *Id.*
404. *Id.*
405. A further distinction is sometimes made between contractual tying and technical tying. The term "contractual tying" refers to the situation in which the dominant firm agrees with its customer that the customer will purchase both products. The term "technical tying" refers to the situation in which the dominant undertaking builds the tied product into the tying product and sells them together.

example, the seller of a dominant cola drink may force its customers to purchase other less tasty beverages sold by that dominant cola producer because those customers need to have the dominant cola drink in their assortment.

Tying and bundling will constitute an abuse of a dominant position if the following four conditions are present: (1) the tying and tied products are two separate markets; (2) the undertaking concerned is dominant in the tying product market; (3) the undertaking concerned does not give customers a choice to obtain the tying product without the tied product; and (4) the practice in question forecloses competition.[406] In *Microsoft v. Commission*, for example, the General Court concluded that Microsoft abused its dominant position in the market for client PC operating systems (the tying market) by requiring that customers who wanted to purchase these products must also purchase from Microsoft the streaming media player software (the tied product) where it was not dominant.[407] According to the Commission and the General Court, Microsoft did not give its customers the opportunity to purchase the products separately. In the view of the Commission and General Court, this had the effect of foreclosing competition on the market for streaming media player software.

The Commission's investigation of Coca-Cola also provides a good example. Coca-Cola had employed the commercial practice of conditioning its sale on the agreement of the purchaser to also purchase other beverages from Coca-Cola. Because purchasers felt that they needed to be able to offer Coca-Cola to their customers, they may have agreed to purchase other products from Coca-Cola even though they would not have purchased those products in the absence of the tie. After the Commission challenged this practice, Coca-Cola agreed not to tie the sale of its dominant brand to the agreement of the customer to buy other nondominant brands.[408]

In *De Post/La Poste*, the Commission decided that the Belgian postal operator De Post/La Poste abused its dominant position by making a preferential tariff in the general letter mail service market (where it was dominant) subject to the acceptance of a supplementary contract covering a new business-to-business (B2B) mail service (where it was not dominant).[409] According to the Commission, this strategy was adopted in order to foreclose competition on the B2B market where De Post/La Post was attempting to drive out a UK company that had recently entered the B2B market in Belgium.

Tying applies even if the tying product is intellectual property. In Rio Tinto Alcan, for example, the holder of aluminum smelting technology tied its willingness to license the technology to the purchase of its specialty cranes used in aluminum smelting plants. The Commission concluded that this was an abuse of a dominant position in violation of Article 102 of the TFEU.[410]

---

406. Case T-201/04, Microsoft Corp. v. Comm'n, 2007 E.C.R. II-3601, 3880 ¶859.
407. *Id.* 3946 ¶1088.
408. Press Release, Commission close to settle antitrust probe into Coca-Cola practices in Europe, IP/04/1247 (Oct. 19, 2004). Coca-Cola, 2005 (L 253) 21.
409. De Post-La Poste, 2002 O.J. (L 61) 32.
410. Rio Tinto Alcan, 2013 O.J. (C 89) 5.

(d) Discrimination

Perhaps the easiest form of exclusionary abuse to identify is discrimination. The discrimination does not necessarily have to be on the basis of nationality.[411] The general rule in the EU is that once an undertaking occupies a position of dominance, it cannot discriminate in its terms of doing business without objective justification.[412] Increased profit is not a legitimate justification in this context. However, not all discriminatory acts by a dominant undertaking are prohibited. An undertaking may have legitimate business reasons for engaging in discriminatory behavior. For example, a dominant undertaking may extend preferential treatment to loyal customers or customers purchasing large quantities. Volume discounts are permissible as long as they are available to all customers purchasing that volume.[413] According to the ECJ:

> [I]t should be noted that it is of the very essence of a system of quantity discounts that larger purchasers of a product or users of a service enjoy lower average unit prices or—which amounts to the same—higher average reductions than those offered to smaller purchasers of that product or users of that service. It should also be noted that even where there is a linear progression in quantity discounts up to a maximum discount, initially the average discount rises (or the average price falls) mathematically in a proportion greater than the increase in purchases and subsequently in a proportion smaller than the increase in purchases, before tending to stabilize at or near the maximum discount rate. The mere fact that the result of quantity discounts is that some customers enjoy in respect of specific quantities a proportionally higher average reduction than others in relation to the difference in their respective volumes of purchase is inherent in this type of system, but it cannot be inferred from that alone that the system is discriminatory.[414]

The justification for discriminatory prices based on volume is typically given less credence by the ECJ when services (as opposed to products) are being sold.[415] This is because the connection between production volume and marginal costs for services is different than for services.

(e) Predatory Pricing

The most prominent type of exclusionary abuse is perhaps predatory pricing. Its prominence is due to the fact that it is passionately debated. One of the benefits of competition is that it assists in keeping prices low for the consumers. Because

---

411. Case C-163/99, Portugal v. Comm'n, 2001 E.C.R. I-2613, 2655 ¶46.
412. Clearstream, 2009 O.J. (C 165) 7, 10 ¶30 *aff'd on appeal* Case T-301/04, ClearstreamBanking AG v. Comm'n, 2009 E.C.R. II-3164, 3220 ¶194.
413. Case C-163/99, Portugal v. Comm'n, 2001 E.C.R. I-2613, 2657 ¶50.
414. *Id.* at 2657 ¶51.
415. Case T-301/04, ClearstreamBanking AG v. Comm'n, 2009 E.C.R. II-3164, 3221 ¶187.

predatory pricing refers to low pricing, its prohibition would seem inconsistent with the competition laws. The threat presented by predatory pricing is that it forces weaker competitors out of the market. There is a general consensus that predatory pricing by a dominant competitor should be prohibited in certain circumstances. However, the debate is over those circumstances.

The seminal predatory pricing case in the EU is *Akzo Chemie v. Commission.*[416] In that case, the ECJ held that prices below average variable costs are considered per se abuse within the context of Article 102 of the TFEU.[417] The average variable cost of a firm is derived by dividing the total variable cost by the firm's output in the same period of time.[418] For example, if a company's total variable costs for producing 100 tons of steel are €1 million, the average variable cost for a ton of steel is €10,000. Under the rule established in *Akzo*, predatory pricing would exist if the steel company then sold the steel for €7,500 per ton. The inference which forms the basis of the rule set forth in *Akzo* is that a firm would only sell below average variable costs (referred to by the Commission as a "sacrifice")[419] if it were engaged in an exclusionary strategy aimed to drive out its competitors.[420]

Prices by a dominant undertaking which are above average variable costs but below average total costs constitute abuse if it is shown that they are part of a plan for eliminating a competitor.[421] In other words, the inference applied to pricing below average variable cost is no longer appropriate because a firm may have fixed costs that explain why it is incurring (at least a short-term) loss. Although evidence of a predatory plan is necessary if the prices are above average variable costs but below average total costs, the ability of the dominant

---

416. Case 62/86, AKZO Chemie v. Comm'n, 1991 E.C.R. I-3439.
417. *Id.* at ¶71. *See also* Case C-209/10, Post Danmark A/S v. Konkurrencerådet, 2012 E.C.R. I-___, at ¶27; Case T-203/01, Michelin v. Comm'n, 2003 E.C.R. II-4082, 4161 ¶242. When determining prices charged by the dominant undertaking, account must be taken of any discounts or rebates offered by the dominant undertakings. *See* Case T-203/01, Manufacture française des pneumatiques Michelin v. Comm'n, 2003 E.C.R. II-4082, 4162 ¶244. For example, if an undertaking charges its customers €10 per widget and then gives them a €1 per widget discount at the end of the year based on the number of widgets, the relevant price is €9.
418. The Commission uses the term "average avoidable cost." Commission Guidance on the enforcement priorities in applying Article 82 of the EC Treaty to abusive exclusionary conduct by dominant undertakings, 2009 O.J. (C 45) 7, 11 ¶26 [hereinafter Article 102 Guidelines].
419. Article 102 Guidelines at ¶64.
420. Case 62/86, Akzo Chemie v. Comm'n, 1991 E.C.R. I-3439, 3455 ¶71.
421. *Id.* at ¶71; Case T-340/03, France Télécom SA v. Comm'n, 2007 E.C.R. II-117, 157 ¶130 *aff'd on appeal* Case C-202/07 P, France Télécom SA v. Comm'n, 2009 E.C.R. I-2403, 2414 ¶36; Case T-203/01, Michelin v. Comm'n, 2003 E.C.R. II-4082, 4161 ¶242. When determining prices charged by the dominant undertaking, account must be taken of any discounts or rebates offered by the dominant undertaking. See Case T-203/01, Michelin v. Comm'n, 2003 E.C.R. II-4082, 4161 ¶244. For example, if an undertaking charges its customers €10 per widget and then gives them a €1 per widget discount at the end of the year based on the number of widgets, the relevant price for determining whether there is predation is €9.

undertaking to recoup the losses it suffers as part of its predatory pricing strategy is not an element of the offence.[422]

For example, if a dominant manufacturer of bottled water, in an attempt to drive its remaining competitors from the market, sells its water at a price below average total costs but still above average variable costs, that undertaking is considered to be engaged in predatory pricing regardless of whether—having achieved its objective of driving the competitors from the market—it could recoup the losses it incurred from pricing below average total costs. In fact, if the barriers to market entry are low, it is unlikely that the bottled water manufacturer would be able to recoup all of its losses because as soon as it raised its prices to a supra-competitive level, it would attract competitors back into the market. This possibility, however, is not relevant in the predatory pricing analysis under the current interpretation of Article 102 of the TFEU.

(f) Vexatious Litigation and Petitions for Regulatory Action

The initiation of legal or administrative proceedings by a dominant undertaking may be used to dissuade other undertakings from entering the market or punish undertakings already in the market. This tends to be less of a problem in Europe where lawyers are generally prohibited from working on the basis of contingency fees, and the loser in the litigation is responsible for the legal fees of the prevailing party. Nonetheless, the ECJ has recognized the possibility that vexatious litigation can constitute abuse in "exceptional circumstances."[423] According to the Commission, the initiation of legal proceedings may constitute abuse if the action (i) cannot reasonably be considered as an attempt to establish the rights of the undertaking concerned and can therefore only serve to harass the opposite party and (ii) it is conceived in the framework of a plan whose goal is to eliminate competition.[424] These requirements are difficult to fulfill. It is, therefore, not surprising that there have been no successful vexatious litigation cases at the EU level based on Article 102 of the TFEU.

Regarding the petitioning activities of a dominant undertaking, one should distinguish between petitioning at the EU level and at the member state level. Petitioning the government—be it the EU or the member states—for the purpose of inducing the government to adopts laws or regulations can have an anticompetitive effect. At the member state level, a prohibition on petitioning activities is not necessary because the TFEU already provides adequate measures to address anticompetitive state measures. According to the ECJ, the TFEU prohibits the member states from adopting measures, "whether legislative or

---

422. Case C-333/94 P, Tetra Pak v. Comm'n, 1996 E.C.R. I-5987, 6013 ¶44; Case T-340/03, France Télécom SA v. Comm'n, 2007 E.C.R. II-117, 183 ¶228 *aff'd on appeal* Case C-202/07 P, France Télécom SA v. Comm'n, 2009 E.C.R. I-2403, 2414 ¶36.
423. Case T-111/96, ITT Promedia v. Comm'n, 1998 E.C.R. II-2937, 2961 ¶60.
424. The Commission argued for these criteria in Case T-111/96, ITT Promedia v. Comm'n, 1998 E.C.R. II-2937, 2960 ¶55. Although the General Court applied the criteria, it expressly refused to rule on whether the criteria correctly reflected the state of the law. Case T-111/96, ITT Promedia v. Comm'n, 1998 E.C.R. II-2937, 2961 ¶58.

regulatory, which may render ineffective the competition rules applicable to undertakings."[425] If petitioning by a dominant firm results in legislation that has an anticompetitive effect, the Commission can challenge the legislation as a violation of the TFEU.

Petitioning activities by a dominant undertaking may result in the adoption of legislation by the EU institutions, which has an anticompetitive effect. As discussed in greater detail in Chapter IV, a dominant firm may petition the Commission to initiate a trade investigation resulting in the imposition of duties on the goods imported into the EU by that dominant undertaking's competitors. Although the ECJ has not explicitly held that such petitioning activity can never violate Article 102 of the TFEU, it is unlikely that such a claim would be successful. In *Industrie des Poudres Spheriques v. Commission*,[426] for example, a dominant firm in the European metals market supported dumping proceedings against metals into the EU by foreign competitors from Russia and China. One of the minor competitors that benefited from the lower prices claimed that this was an abuse within the meaning of Article 102. The General Court held that the participation of a company in anti-dumping proceedings could not amount to abusive conduct:

> [I]t must be pointed out that recourse to a remedy in law and, in particular, participation by an undertaking in an investigation conducted by the [EU] institutions, cannot be deemed, of itself, to be contrary to Article [102] of the Treaty. In the present case, the anti-dumping procedure aims to re-establish undistorted competition in the market in the interest of the [EU] and is reflected in a thorough investigation conducted by the Community institutions during which the interested parties are heard and which may lead to the adoption of a binding [EU] measure. To assert that mere recourse to such a procedure is, of itself, contrary to Article [102] of the Treaty amounts to denying undertakings the right to avail themselves of legal instruments established in the interest of the [EU].[427]

(g) Refusal to Deal

A basic principle of competition law is that a company has no affirmative duty to do business with other market actors.[428] In a market economy, the decision as to when to do business is left to the entrepreneurs. In most instances, the decision not to do business is based on legitimate reasons. However, the unqualified right to refuse to do business can be used by a firm with market power to preclude competition. Assume, for example, that a vertically integrated manufacturer

---

425. Case C-437/09, AG2R Prévoyance v. Beaudout Père et Fils SARL, 2011 E.C.R. I-1003, 1020 ¶37; Case C-446/05, *In re* Doulamis, 2008 E.C.R. I-1404, 1411 ¶20.
426. Case T-5/97, Industrie des poudres sphériques v. Comm'n, 2000 E.C.R. II-3755.
427. *Id.* at 3818 ¶213.
428. Article 102 Guidelines at ¶75.

of chemical products held a dominant position in the upstream market for raw materials necessary to make those chemicals. It may be reasonable (in a profit-maximizing sense) for the vertically integrated undertaking to refuse to sell raw materials to its nonvertically integrated competitors in the downstream chemicals market. However, the inaccessibility to the raw materials will likely undermine the competitiveness of those nonvertically integrated undertakings.[429]

According to the Commission and EU courts, an undertaking which maintains a dominant position for a particular product or service abuses that position when it refuses access to that product or service to third parties without a legitimate reason.[430] The requisite refusal does not need to be overt. According to the Commission, a constructive refusal by a dominant undertaking is sufficient to fulfill this criterion.[431] For example, the dominant undertaking might impose unreasonable price or commercial terms rather than simply refusing to accept the order.[432] Although this is not a naked refusal to deal, it has the same effect and is considered a constructive refusal.

There is no exhaustive catalog of what constitutes a legitimate business reason for refusing to deal. The mere desire to avoid assisting a competitor—which may be completely understandable from a commercial perspective—is not in itself a sufficient reason for a refusal by a dominant undertaking.[433] If, however, the dominant manufacturer is exposed to capacity constraints so that the provisions of raw materials to a downstream competitor would jeopardize its ability to manufacture downstream products for its own customers, it may have a legitimate business reason for refusing to deal. Another example of a legitimate reason is if the customer's order is "out of the ordinary."[434] For example, an order may be considered out of the ordinary if the customer is ordering a product in extraordinarily large quantities for the purpose of exporting to a different member state where the prices for the product may be higher due to price regulations.[435]

(h) Refusal to License

As discussed in Chapter X, intellectual property rights are rights granted by statute to individuals or firms who contribute to society in a certain way

---

429. Joined cases 6/73 and 7/73, Commercial Solvents v. Comm'n, 1974 E.C.R. 223, 250 ¶25.
430. Joined Cases C-468/06 to C-478/06, Sot. Lelos kai Sia EE v. GlaxoSmithKlein AEVE Farmakeftikon, 2008 E.C.R. I-7174, 7188 ¶34; Clearstream, 2009 O.J. (C 165) 7, 9 ¶22 aff'd on appeal Case T-301/04, ClearstreamBanking AG v. Comm'n, 2009 E.C.R. II-3164; Port of Rødby, 1994 O.J. (L 55) 52, 55 ¶12. This is sometimes referred to as the "essential facilities doctrine." Case T-419/03, Altstoff Recycling Austria AG v. Comm'n, 2011 E.C.R. II-979, 1016 ¶104.
431. Article 102 Guidelines at ¶79.
432. IBM Maintenance Services, Comm'n Decision of 13 December 2011, summary available at 2012 O.J. (C 18) 6.
433. GVG/FS, 2004 O.J. (L 11) 17, 34 ¶121.
434. Joined Cases C-468/06 to C-478/06, Sot. Lelos kai Sia EE v. GlaxoSmithKlein AEVE Farmakeftikon, 2008 E.C.R. I-7174, 7190 ¶40.
435. *Id.* at 7198 ¶71.

(for example by inventing something) as a reward for making the investment necessary to realize that contribution. However, intellectual property rights do not grant the holder the guaranty that she will benefit commercially from the right; they represent only a promise by the state to preclude others from using that intellectual property right without the proprietor's permission. Whether the proprietor realizes a profit depends on the market and the initiative of the holder of the rights. Moreover, intellectual property law does not impose an affirmative duty to license the intellectual property to others. Nonetheless, the application of competition law may require the holder of an intellectual property right to license it to a third party, even if the third party is a competitor.

The refusal to license an intellectual property right can violate Article 102 of the TFEU if the holder of the right is in a dominant position.[436] As intellectual property presents a special case, there must also be exceptional circumstances in order to hold the intellectual property holder responsible.[437] Although there is no exhaustive list of exceptional circumstances, the following three requirements must be fulfilled:[438]

- The refusal relates to a product or service which is indispensable to the exercise of a particular activity on a neighboring market; and
- The refusal is of such kind as to exclude any effective competition on that neighboring market; and
- The refusal prevents the emergence of a new product for which there is potentially a demand.

The first condition requires that the product or service in which the undertaking is dominant be indispensable for other undertakings to compete in a neighboring market. If the other undertakings have reasonable access to securing the refused input from other sources or creating it themselves, the refusal will not be deemed to violate Article 102 of the TFEU.[439] In *Bronner v. Mediaprint*, a dominant Austrian media company refused to grant access to a competing newspaper to the distribution network (home delivery service) which the dominant media company had established. The smaller newspaper

---

436. Case C-418/01, IMS Health GmbH & Co. v. NDC Health GmbH & Co., 2004 E.C.R. I-5039, 5081 ¶35; Case T-201/04, Microsoft Corp. v. Comm'n, 2007 E.C.R. II-3601, 3726 ¶331. Décision n° 14-D-09 du 4 septembre 2014 sur les pratiques mises en oeuvre par les sociétés Nestlé, Nestec, Nestlé Nespresso, Nespresso France et Nestlé Entreprises dans le secteur des machines à café expresso, *available at* http://www.autoritedelaconcurrence.fr/pdf/avis/14d09.pdf.
437. The additional requirement of exceptional circumstances arises out of the recogition that intellectual property rights are fundamental rights. The tension between competition law and intellectual property rights is discussed at length in Case AT.39985, Mototola GPRS (April 29, 2014) at ¶¶497-534.
438. Case C-418/01, IMS Health GmbH & Co. v. NDC Health GmbH & Co., 2004 E.C.R. I-5039, 5082 ¶38; Case T-201/04, Microsoft Corp. v. Comm'n, 2007 E.C.R. II-3601, 3726 ¶332.
439. GVG/FS, 2004 O.J. (L 11) 17, 36 ¶133.

publisher maintained that it was unable to compete with the dominant media company. The ECJ held that the refusal by the dominant media company only constituted abuse if access to the distribution network was essential to the ability of the newspaper publisher to compete.[440] As the ECJ considered that it was not technically, economically, or legally impossible for the smaller publisher to establish its own network or cooperate with other companies to do so,[441] it concluded that the refusal to deal did not violate Article 102.

In *Tierce Ladbroke v. Commission*, French racehorse societies refused to license television broadcast rights to Belgian off-track betting parlors. The General Court held that access to this right was not indispensable for the Belgian betting parlors to conduct business.[442]

The second condition for a finding of exceptional circumstances is that the refusal is of such kind as to exclude all effective competition on the neighboring market. According to the General Court, the Commission is only required to show that the refusal "is liable to, or is likely to" eliminate all effective competition on the market of the product or service being refused.[443]

The third condition requires that the party seeking access to the intellectual property intend to introduce a new product. In *Magill*, for example, Magill TV Guide Ltd. sought to introduce a new comprehensive TV guide in the United Kingdom.[444] RTE, one of the television broadcasters, refused to allow Magill to use the listings of its program. Although RTE did not offer a comprehensive TV guide covering all programs, it did offer a guide for its own programs. The ECJ held that RTE's "refusal to provide basic information by relying on national copyright provisions thus prevented the appearance of a new product, a comprehensive weekly guide to television programs, which [RTE] did not offer and for which there was a potential consumer demand. Such refusal constitutes abuse [under Article 102 of the TFEU.]"[445] If, however, the party seeking the license intends to merely duplicate the goods or services offered by the owner of the intellectual property, it will probably not be an abuse if the owner refuses to license the intellectual property.[446]

The enforcement of patent rights by the holder of a standard essential patent has been considered "exceptional circumstances" allowing the Commission to find the abuse of a dominant position.[447] The holder of intellectual property (particularly patents) which has become part of an industry standard is in a particularly strong position. Manufacturers who intend to produce products

---

440. Case C-7/97, Oscar Bronner GmbH & Co. KG v. Mediaprint Zeitungs–und Zeitschriftenverlag GmbH & Co. KG, 1998 E.C.R. I-7791, 7831 ¶41.
441. *Id.* at 7831 ¶44.
442. Case T-504/93, Tierce Ladbroke v. Comm'n, 1997 E.C.R. II-923, 969 ¶130.
443. Case T-301/04, ClearstreamBanking AG v. Comm'n, 2009 E.C.R. II-3164, 3211 ¶148.
444. Joined Cases C-241/91 P and C-242/91 P, RTE and ITP v. Comm'n, 1995 E.C.R. I-743.
445. *Id.* at ¶54
446. Case C-418/01, IMS Health GmbH & Co. v. NDC Health GmbH & Co., 2004 E.C.R. I-5039, 5085 ¶49.
447. Case AT.39985, Mototola GPRS (April 29, 2014) at ¶281.

conforming to the established standards need to engineer around the patent or procure a license from the owner of the patent. If a license from the holder of the parent is essential to produce the standardized product because it cannot be engineered around, it is considered a standard essential patent.[448] Such standard essential patents are frequently considered their own relevant market and therefore give the patent holder a dominant position.[449]

In recognition of the potential abuse of a standard essential patent, most standard-setting bodies require their members to agree to license their technology on fair, reasonable, and nondiscriminatory terms (often referred to as "FRAND" terms) as a condition for considering such intellectual property to be included in the standard. In many cases, the licensing of the intellectual property on FRAND terms will address the competition law issues. For example, the Dutch electronics producer, Koninklijke Philips Electronics N.V., held a patent on some basic technology which was essential to be able to produce CDs meeting the industry standard. Philips was required to license the technology to third parties on fair and reasonable terms.[450]

The challenge in such cases is determining what terms are fair and reasonable. According to the Commission, this is a factual issue to be decided in each case by the national courts and competition agencies.[451] In the *Motorola/Apple* case, the Commission took the position that the inclusion of a "no-challenge" clause (according to which the licensee is required to agree not to challenge the validity of the technology) is unfair.[452]

If these three conditions are fulfilled, abuse is deemed to occur unless the dominant undertaking can show an objective justification for the conduct.[453] Similar to refusal to deal cases, the absence of a legitimate business reason suggests that the refusal is unjustified. In the context of refusal to deal, capacity constraints of a dominant manufacturer may be a legitimate reason not to provide materials to a downstream competitor. In the context of a refusal to license, however, capacity considerations will seldom serve as a justification. For example, it would be difficult for a software company to claim that capacity constraints presented a legitimate reason for its refusal to license its operating system software to a third party. Moreover, ownership of intellectual property rights is in itself not an objective justification by a dominant undertaking to refuse to license those rights.[454]

---

448. Case M. 7202, Lenovo/Motorola Mobility (June 26, 2014) ¶23; Case AT.39985, Mototola GPRS (April 29, 2014) at ¶213; Case M. 6381, Google/Motorola (Feb. 13, 2012) ¶51.
449. Case AT.39985, Mototola GPRS (April 29, 2014) ¶225.
450. Decision of the German Bundesgerichtshof in case no. KZR 39/06 (May 6, 2009) ("Orange-Book-Standard") *reported at* GRUR 2009, 694.
451. European Comm'n Memo/14322 (April 29, 2014).
452. European Comm'n Press Release IP/14/489 (April 29, 2014).
453. Case C-209/10, Post Danmark A/S v. Konkurrencerådet, 2012 E.C.R. I-___, at ¶40; Case T-201/04, Microsoft Corp. v. Comm'n, 2007 E.C.R. II-3601, 3726 ¶333; Case AT.39985, Mototola GPRS (April 29, 2014) ¶421.
454. Case T-201/04, Microsoft Corp. v. Comm'n, 2007 E.C.R. II-3601, 3831 ¶690; Case AT.39985, Mototola GPRS (April 29, 2014) ¶423.

(i) Exclusive Dealing

A dominant undertaking is often in a position to dictate the terms of sale to its customers. Exclusionary abuse occurs when, for example, the dominant undertaking imposes on its distributors the prohibition from selling the products or services of the competitors of the dominant undertaking. In the *Choice Point* proceedings, for example, the Commission required the Israeli software producer, Choice Point, to refrain from pressuring its distributors into agreeing not to sell firewall software products of Choice Point's competitors.[455]

Although exclusive dealing is slightly different from tying, these tactics are often used together by dominant suppliers. In the Coca-Cola investigation, for example, Coca-Cola imposed exclusive dealing obligations on its customers. Coca-Cola would only sell to that customer if the customer agreed not to sell competing soft drinks. This was the exclusive dealing component. The tying component was that Coke required its customers to purchase other sodas from Coca-Cola which were not as popular as Coke. Because many customers felt that they needed to be able to offer Coke in their product assortment (Coke being the dominant product), they accepted the terms imposed by Coca-Cola. After the Commission intervened, Coca-Cola agreed to refrain from imposing such requirements on its customers.[456]

The exclusivity requirement does not have to be written into the agreement. It is sufficient that the conduct of the dominant undertaking creates the incentive of customers to do business with it. In *Tomra Systems ASA v. Commission*, for example, the dominant supplier specifically avoided including an exclusivity clause in its agreements with its distributors. Instead, it included (merely) a clause designating the dominant undertaking as the "preferred supplier". The General Court concluded even if the distributors were not contractually required to purchase products from the dominant undertaking, it was sufficient that the dominant supplier created the incentive to do so.[457]

(j) Rebate and Discount Schemes

The use of rebates or discounts can be an effective and legitimate marketing strategy for companies. Moreover, rebates or discounts offered by a supplier create the possibility of lower prices for consumers. For example, a manufacturer of bicycles may offer a rebate or discount to its distributors if the distributor agrees to purchase all of its bicycles from that manufacturer. Assuming that this distributor and its retailers are exposed to competition from other brands of bicycles, they would be forced to pass on those cost savings to the consumers.

---

455. Nicholas Banasevic, Commission Accepts Formal Undertaking from Choice Point Regarding its Distribution Practices, 2002 Competition Policy Newsletter 40 (June 2002).
456. Coca-Cola, 2005 O.J. (L 253) 21; Press Release, Commission close to settle antitrust probe into Coca-Cola practices in Europe, IP/04/1247 (Oct. 19, 2004).
457. Case T-155/06, Tomra Systems ASA v. Comm'n, 2010 E.C.R. II-4361, 4395 ¶59 *aff'd on appeal* Case C- 549/10 P, Tomra Systems ASA v. Comm'n, 2012 E.C.R. I-____.

The Commission, however, has traditionally been very skeptical of rebates and discount schemes offered by dominant undertakings because they can be used as a means to exclude competition.[458] For example, a dominant seller of a product may preclude competition from other suppliers of that same product by offering customers rebates if they purchase exclusively from the dominant seller. Coca-Cola was required by the Commission to refrain from offering a rebate to customers if the customers purchased Coca-Cola's weaker products (such as Sprite and Vanilla Coke) together with its stronger brands (such as Coke and Fanta).[459]

Rebates or discount schemes may be employed downstream or upstream. Using the earlier example, if the bicycle manufacturer enjoys a position of dominance, the rebate scheme which gives incentives to the distributor to only sell the bicycles of that manufacturer—referred to as a fidelity rebate—has the effect of precluding other bicycle manufacturers from using that distributor to sell their bicycles. This is an example of a downstream discount scheme. However, that same bicycle manufacturer may employ an upstream discount scheme vis-à-vis its suppliers. For example, it may reward a discount to its supplier of bicycle seats if that bicycle seat supplier agrees to only supply seats to that specific bicycle manufacturer. This is considered an "upstream" discount scheme because the bicycle seat manufacturer is considered to be upstream from the bicycle manufacturer in the supply chain.

The test employed by the ECJ is whether the rebates "tend to prevent customers of the dominant undertaking from obtaining their supplies from competing producers."[460] The rebate or discount scheme must be capable of foreclosure in order to be considered abuse under Article 102 of the TFEU.[461] If, even after the rebate, the price is above the long-run average incremental costs of the dominant company, there is a low likelihood of foreclosure.[462] If, however, the rebate makes the dominant company's costs below average avoidable costs, the Commission will likely consider that the rebate is capable of foreclosure.[463]

The general rule is that rebate and discount schemes capable of foreclosure will amount to an abuse of a dominant position unless they are objectively applied and economically justified. The first requirement—that the scheme be objectively applied—means that the rebate or discount is equally available

---

458. Article 102 Guidelines at ¶37.
459. Press Release, Commission close to settle antitrust probe into Coca-Cola practices in Europe, IP/04/1247 (Oct. 19, 2004).
460. Case C- 549/10 P, Tomra Systems ASA v. Comm'n, 2012 E.C.R. I-____, at ¶72.
461. The Commission does not have to show that the rebate scheme actually had an exclusionary effect. It need only show that the rebate scheme "tends to restrict competition or that the conduct is capable of having that effect." *Id.* at ¶68.
462. Article 102 Guidelines at ¶43. The long-run average incremental cost is the average of all costs incurred by a company to produce a particular product. It is important to note that the ECJ has held that the Commission does not need to show that the prices were below cost in order to establish an abusive exclusionary rebate scheme. Case C- 549/10 P, Tomra Systems ASA v. Comm'n, 2012 E.C.R. I-____, at ¶72.
463. Article 102 Guidelines at ¶44.

to all business partners who meet the criteria of the scheme. If, for example, an upstream or downstream business partner meets the criteria of the scheme, the dominant undertaking may not discriminate between that business partner and the other business partners. The discount or rebate must be available to all of them.[464]

The more difficult determination in assessing rebate schemes is whether they are economically justified. There must be a legitimate business reason for offering the rebate or discount. For example, a pure volume rebate scheme where customers receive a rebate at the end of the year calculated on the basis of the volume of products purchased by that customer may be permitted even when employed by a dominant supplier.[465] In such cases, the rebate or discount is considered to reflect the economies of scale cost savings incurred by the dominant supplier.[466] However, rebates which are employed merely to secure the loyalty of the supplier or customer—so-called fidelity rebates—are prohibited when employed by a dominant undertaking even if the system is not applied in a discriminatory manner.[467] Similarly, retroactive rebates (i.e., a rebate based on all purchases made and not just those exceeding the threshold) are closely scrutinized by the Commission and courts because it is assumed that the benefits to the seller only begin to accrue after the threshold is achieved, and the only reason for the retroactive rebate is to bind the customer to the seller.[468]

The identification of an economic justification is a factual determination which depends on the context in which the rebate or discount takes place.[469] In the *Soda Ash-Solvay* case, the Commission decided that Solvay's granting of a "group rebate" of 1.5 percent to Saint-Gobain, if Saint-Gobain designated Solvay as its preferred European supplier, was abusive conduct in the context of Article 102 of the TFEU.[470] The fact that it was the individual Saint-Gobain

---

464. A discount scheme that is applied equally to all business partners may still be considered abusive if it is not economically justified. Case T-66/01, Imperial Chemical Industries Ltd v. Comm'n, 2010 E.C.R. II-2645, 2733 ¶309.
465. Case T-286/09, Intel Corp. v. Comm'n, 2014 E.C.R. II-____, at ¶75; Case T-66/01, Imperial Chemical Industries Ltd v. Comm'n, 2010 E.C.R. II-2645, 2729 ¶298.
466. The rebate must be closely tied to the volume purchased. The granting of a rebate by a dominant supplier in exchange for a general obligation to purchase all requirements from the dominant supplier does not meet the requirement because it is not tied to specific volumes purchased. Case T-155/06, Tomra Systems ASA v. Comm'n, 2010 E.C.R. II-4370, 4431 ¶210 *aff'd on appeal* Case C- 549/10 P, Tomra Systems ASA v. Comm'n, 2012 E.C.R. I-____, at ¶68.
467. Case C- 549/10 P, Tomra Systems ASA v. Comm'n, 2012 E.C.R. I-____, at ¶70; Case T-66/01, Imperial Chemical Industries Ltd v. Comm'n, 2010 E.C.R. II-2645, 2728 ¶296; Case T-219/99, British Airways v. Comm'n, 2003 E.C.R. II-5925, 5987 ¶248 *aff'd on appeal* Case C-95/04 P, British Airways v. Comm'n, 2007 E.C.R. I-2331.
468. Case C- 549/10 P, Tomra Systems ASA v. Comm'n, 2012 E.C.R. I-____, at ¶75.
469. Article 102 Guidelines at ¶46. The fact that the rebate might have even been requested by the customer does not mean that the rebate is consistent with Article 102 of the TFEU. Case T-66/01, Imperial Chemical Industries Ltd v. Comm'n, 2010 E.C.R. II-2645, 2732 ¶305.
470. Soda Ash-Solvay, 2003 O.J. (L 10) 10, 26 ¶162.

subsidiaries in the respective countries that were purchasing from Solvay was held out by the Commission as evidence that the group rebate was not tied to any cost saving attributed to global sourcing from a specific provider.

As the economic justification for volume rebates or discounts is typically the economies of scale that the supplier realizes by being able to sell more products, the use of rebates in service industries is generally difficult to justify. In general, the marginal costs of a supplier to manufacture and sell a product decrease with the amount of products manufactured and sold by that manufacturer. For example, the per bicycle cost of producing just 10 bicycles (i.e., total costs divided by 10) will generally be greater than the per bicycle cost of producing 100 bicycles (i.e., total costs divided by 100). This is because the fixed costs of the manufacturer can be spread out over 100 bicycles instead of just 10 bicycles. In most service industries, however, the fixed costs are relatively low. This makes it more difficult to justify volume discounts.

In *British Airways v. Commission*, for example, the General Court held that the performance rewards granted by British Airways (BA) to travel agents in the UK for sales of BA flights were not economically justified because they were not tied to efficiency gains or costs savings realized by BA.[471] In that case, the travel agents were paid a flat commission of 7 percent on sales of BA flights. If they achieved a certain target, they were rewarded with an additional variable percentage commission based not only on the additional flights sold after the target was met, but on all the flights. Hence, the costs incurred by BA in selling a seat after the target was met were higher than that same seat sold prior to hitting the target. The General Court considered that this scheme did not bear a direct relationship with any costs savings incurred by BA.[472]

Conditional rebate schemes are generally prohibited when employed by dominant undertakings. In a conditional rebate scheme, the dominant undertaking informs its customers that the customers can only receive the rebate on the condition that the customers purchase directly from the dominant undertaking. For example, the U.S. chip manufacturer, Intel, offered a rebate to the customers of certain Intel central processing units (Intel had a 70 percent worldwide market share on this market) only if the customer agreed not to purchase competing central processing units from Intel's main competitor (Advanced Micro Devices). The Commission concluded that this conduct constituted an abuse of a dominant position under Article 102 of the TFEU.[473]

In affirming the Commission's decision, the General Court held "such exclusivity rebates, when applied by an undertaking in a dominant position, are incompatible with the objective of undistorted competition within the common market, because they are not based—save in exceptional circumstances—on an economic transaction which justifies this burden or benefit but are designed to remove or restrict the purchaser's freedom to choose his sources of supply and to deny other producers access to the market. Such rebates are designed,

---

471. Case T-219/99, British Airways v. Comm'n, 2003 E.C.R. II-5925, 5995 ¶284 *aff'd on appeal* Case C-95/04 P, British Airways v. Comm'n, 2007 E.C.R. I-2331.
472. *Id.* at 5997 ¶290.
473. Intel, 2009 O.J. (L 227) 13.

through the grant of a financial advantage, to prevent customers from obtaining their supplies from competing producers."[474]

5.5 Effect on Trade Between Member States

Although the application of Article 102 of the TFEU requires an effect on trade between member states, this requirement has traditionally not prevented the application of Article 102 of the TFEU if all of the other elements are fulfilled. As discussed above, Article 102 only applies if the dominant position covers a substantial part of the EU. Even a dominant position limited to one member state will typically have an effect on trade between member states as competitors from other member states are often affected by the abusive conduct.[475] Moreover, an actual effect is not required. According to the General Court: "for the purposes of establishing a violation of Article [102 TFEU], it is not necessary to demonstrate that the abuse in question had a concrete effect on the markets concerned. It is sufficient in that respect to demonstrate that the abusive conduct of the undertaking in a dominant position tends to restrict competition, or, in other words, that the conduct is capable of having, or likely to have, such an effect."[476]

5.6 Relationship Between Articles 101 and 102

As discussed above, the application of Article 101 of the TFEU requires an agreement, concerted practice, or a decision of an association. In the absence of an agreement, concerted practice, or decisions, the Commission is limited to applying Article 102 of the TFEU.[477] Therefore, the potential for the parallel application of Article 101 and Article 102 in cases where there is no conspiracy is precluded. However, the existence of an agreement or concerted practice does not necessarily preclude the application of Article 102. Indeed, certain violations of Article 102 involve an agreement or concerted practice.[478] For example, when a dominant manufacturer imposes discriminatory terms on its distributors in the context of the distribution agreement, there is the possibility for the parallel application of Article 101 and Article 102. Similarly, an agreement between two competitors which violates Article 101(1) may be sufficient to allow the Commission to find that the competitors hold a position of collective dominance under Article 102.[479] The issue of which legal norm applies to such

---

474. Case T-286/09, Intel Corp. v. Comm'n, 2014 E.C.R. II-____, at ¶77.
475. Comm'n Guidelines on the effect on trade concept contained in Articles 81 and 82 of the Treaty, 2004 O.J. (C 101) 81, 92 ¶93. *But see* Case C-393/08, Sbarigia v. Azienda USL RM/A, 2010 E.C.R. I-6360, 6372 ¶32.
476. Case T-66/01, Imperial Chemical Industries Ltd v. Comm'n, 2010 E.C.R. II-2645, 2743 ¶335; Case T-219/99, British Airways plc v. Comm'n, 2003 E.C.R. II-5925, 5997 ¶293, *aff'd on appeal* Case C-95/04 P, British Airways v. Comm'n, 2007 E.C.R. I-2331.
477. Cases C-2/01 and C-3/01, Bundesverband der Arzneimittel-Importeure v. Bayer, 2004 E.C.R. I-64, 105 ¶102.
478. *See, e.g.*, Case C-395/96, Compagnie Maritime Belge, 2000 E.C.R. I-1365.
479. *In re* Flat Glass, 1989 O.J. (L 33) 44, 65 ¶79.

circumstances is important because, unlike violations of Article 101(1) of the TFEU, there are no exemption possibilities for violations of Article 102 of the TFEU.[480]

The starting point for the analysis is that Article 101 and Article 102 of the TFEU are directed at different types of restraints of competition. Article 101 is directed at bilateral or multilateral agreements that have been entered into willingly by the parties. Article 102 is directed at abuses of a dominant position that may or may not involve an agreement. If there is an agreement, it is often deemed to be "imposed" by the dominant firm on the other party. In *Duales System,* for example, Duales System Deutschland abused its dominant position by imposing a fee on its customers for certain services regardless of whether the client used those services.[481] Although an agreement existed between Duales System and its customers, the conduct was determined to be in violation of Article 102 of the TFEU and not examined under Article 101.

In certain cases in which Article 102 is applicable, the agreement may have been entered into willingly by the parties. Hence, reliance on the "imposition theory" may be inappropriate. As discussed above, two or more firms may be considered to be in a position of collective dominance for purposes of Article 102 of the TFEU if there is an agreement between them. The lack of a clear delineation of the respective scopes of application of Article 101 and Article 102 in cases involving dominant undertakings and agreements or concerted conduct gives the Commission a degree of discretion as to the legal norm which it applies to the particular facts (Article 101 or 102).

The exercise of this discretion is often influenced by strategic considerations relating to the evidence available to the Commission to prove its case. One reason why the Commission does not proceed on the basis of Article 101 of the TFEU in collective dominance cases is that it would have to show that the agreement or concerted practice is anticompetitive. In the context of Article 102, however, the agreement is merely used as a connecting factor between the undertakings, which allows the Commission to aggregate their respective market shares. The abuse does not necessarily have to have anything to do with the agreement. Conversely, if the Commission has sufficient evidence of an anticompetitive agreement, but considers that it will be difficult to prove dominance, the Commission will seek to rely on Article 101 of the TFEU.[482]

---

480. However, a dominant firm is allowed to justify its conduct by showing that "its conduct is objectively necessary or that the exclusionary effect produced may be counterbalanced, outweighed even, by advantages in terms of efficiency that also benefits consumers. Case C-209/10, Post Danmark A/S v. Konkurrencerådet, 2012 E.C.R. I-___, at ¶41.
481. Case C-385/07 P, Der Grüne Punkt - Duales System Deutschland GmbH v. Comm'n, 2009 E.C.R. I-6219, 6261 ¶143.
482. *See, e.g.,* Cases C-2/01 and C-3/01, Bundesverband der Arzneimittel-Importeure v. Bayer, 2004 E.C.R. I-64, 105 ¶¶101-102.

6. State Action

All societies recognize that there is a legitimate role for the state in the economy. Differences exist only in the scope and extent of the involvement of the state in the economy. Although the EU competition rules are designed to protect competition, the state can distort competition in a myriad of ways. For example, the state distorts competition when it exercises its sovereignty to impose duties on imports of products. The state also distorts competition when it grants the state-owned postal service the exclusive right to deliver mail in that state. The challenge to applying the competition rules to the member states is reaching a proper balance between the legitimate role of the state and a necessary distortion of competition to achieve those goals. The contours between permissible and prohibited state action are often vague, and perhaps intentionally so, as ambiguity facilitates pragmatism.

6.1 State as Sovereign Actor

The administration of state functions requires the state to engage in commerce. For example, the tax authorities in a particular state may need sharp pencils to fulfill their tasks. Unless the state owns a pencil manufacturer, the state will have to procure these pencils on the market. Conversely, a state might sell services. For example, a state might sell passports to its citizens. A member state can distort competition when it engages in commerce either as a buyer or seller. Using the example of the state selling passports, the state could be perceived as abusing its dominant position as issuer of passports by charging excessive prices for the passports. As discussed above, however, Articles 101 and 102 of TFEU apply only to undertakings. As long as the state is engaged in the exercise of public powers, and not activities of an economic nature, it is not considered an undertaking under Articles 101 and 102.[483] Therefore, a member state would not be violating Article 102 by charging an otherwise abusive price for passports. The same applies to Article 101. In *Consorizio Aziende Metano v. Comune di Cingia de Botti*, for example, the ECJ held that a contract between a local government and a private company to operate and monitor the local methane gas network was not a contract between undertakings for purposes on the competition laws.[484] The basic idea is that the state is not engaging in economic activity when it is fulfilling a public function expected of the state.[485]

Not all conduct of the state falls outside the scope of the EU competition rules. If the state is acting in a commercial capacity, its conduct may violate the competition laws. Whether the state is to be considered an undertaking

---

483. C-138/11, Compass-Datenbank GmbH v. Austria, 2012 E.C.R. I-____, at ¶36.
484. Case C-231/03, Consorizio Aziende Metano v. Comune di Cingia de Botti, 2005 E.C.R. I-7310, 7315 ¶12.
485. The term "state" in this context refers to any central, regional or local government or even an international agency. It refers generally any governmental unit as long as that governmental unit is entrusted with public authorities.

necessitates an examination of the nature of the particular activity at issue.[486] The state conduct only falls outside the scope of the competition laws if it is fulfilling a public interest function and not a commercial or economic function.[487] In *Selex Sistemi Integrati SpA v. Commission*, for example, the General Court held that Eurocontrol, an organization established by international treaty to develop a uniform system of air traffic management in Europe, was not an undertaking when it adopted technical standards but was an undertaking when it assisted the member states for remuneration in the selection process of private undertakings participating in public tenders.[488]

6.2 Public and Privileged Undertakings

6.2.1. Definition of Public and Privileged Undertakings

The term "public undertaking" in EU competition law jurisprudence means an undertaking which the state indirectly or directly exercises a dominant influence by virtue of its ownership of it, its financial participation in that undertaking, or the rules which govern it.[489] If, for example, the state holds a majority interest in a company, that company will be considered a public undertaking.[490] Even without a majority shareholding, the state may exercise a dominant influence if it can appoint more than half of the members of the undertaking's administrative, managerial or supervisory body.

An undertaking is considered a "privileged undertaking" in EU competition law jurisprudence when it has received special rights from the state to perform a public function such as waste disposal.[491] In contrast to public undertakings, privileged undertakings are not owned by the state.

6.2.2. Limits Placed on Member States

Member states are prohibited from enacting or maintaining "any measure" contrary to the competition rules codified in Articles 101 and 102 TFEU (Article 106(1) TFEU). The mere fact that a member state holds a controlling interest in a public undertaking or that it grants special rights to a privileged undertaking is not in itself prohibited by the TFEU even though it may give

---

486. Case C-49/07, Motosykletistiki Omospondia Ellados v. Dimosio, 2008 E.C.R. I-4892, 4902 ¶25.
487. C-138/11, Compass-Datenbank GmbH v. Austria, 2012 E.C.R. I-___, at ¶36.
488. Case T-155/04, Selex Sistemi Integrati SpA v. Comm'n, 2006 E.C.R. II- 4803, 4831 & 4840 ¶69 & ¶92 *aff'd on appeal* Case C-113/07 P, Selex Sistemi Integrati SpA v. Comm'n, 2009 E.C.R. I-___.
489. Comm'n Directive 2006/111/EC of 16 November 2006 on the transparency of financial relations between member states and public undertakings as well as financial transparency within certain undertakings, 2006 O.J. (L 318) 17, art. 2(b).
490. *See, e.g.*, Case C-553/12 P, Commission v. Mytilianios AE, 2014 E.C.R. I-___, at ¶56; Case C-340/99, TNT Traco SpA v. Poste Italiane SpA, 2001 E.C.R. I-4109, 4158 ¶39.
491. Eco-Emballages, 2001 O.J. (L 233) 37, 45 ¶70.

the private undertaking a position of dominance.[492] The granting of the special right is only prohibited if in the exercise of those rights, the undertaking cannot avoid violating the competition laws[493] or gives rise to the risk of a violation.[494] In *Motosykletistiki Omospondia Ellados v. Dimosio*, for example, the Greek Transportation Minister granted to a private non-profit motorcycling association the exclusive right to consent to applications to organize motorcycle competitions in Greece. According to the ECJ, "Articles [102] TFEU and Article [106(1)] TFEU are violated where a measure imputable to a Member State, and in particular a measure by which a Member State confers special or exclusive rights within the meaning of Article [106(1)] TFEU, gives rise to a risk of an abuse of a dominant position."[495] In this particular case, the ECJ held that the rights granted to the motorcycling association violated Article 106(1) of the TFEU because it "could lead [the association] entrusted with giving that consent to distort competition by favouring events which it organizes or those in whose organization it participates."[496]

A member state is deemed to grant special or exclusive rights where the member state confers protection on a limited number of undertakings and this substantially affects the ability of other undertakings in the same geographic market from exercising the same economic activity.[497] When the rights have been granted to other undertakings upon application to the member state, the ECJ has held that no special or exclusive rights have been granted.[498]

6.2.3. Limits Placed on Public and Private Undertakings

The mere fact that a public or private undertaking has received special rights from the state does not inoculate it from the application of Articles 101 and 102

---

492. Case C-351/12, OSA v. Léčebné lázně Mariánské Lázně a.s., 2014 E.C.R. I-___, at ¶83; Case C-437/09, AG2R Prévoyance v. Beaudout Père et Fils SARL, 2011 E.C.R. I-1003, 1028 ¶68.
493. *Id*.; Case C-250/06, United Pan-Europe Communications Belgium v. État belge, 2007 E.C.R. I-11135, at ¶17; Case C-340/99, TNT Traco v. Poste Italiane, 2001 E.C.R. I-4109, at ¶44.
494. Case C-49/07, Motosykletistiki Omospondia Ellados v. Dimosio, 2008 E.C.R. I-4892, 4908 ¶50. The Commission does not have to prove an actual anticompetitive effect. "All that is necessary is for the Commission to identify a potential or actual anti-competitive consequence liable to result from the State measure at issue. Such an infringement may thus be established where the State measures at issue affect the structure of the market by creating unequal conditions of competition between companies, by allowing the public undertaking or the undertaking which was granted special or exclusive rights to maintain (for example by hindering new entrants to the market), strengthen or extend its dominant position over another market, thereby restricting competition, without it being necessary to prove the existence of actual abuse." Case C-553/12 P, Commission v. Mytilianios AE, 2014 E.C.R. I-___, at ¶46.
495. Case C-49/07, Motosykletistiki Omospondia Ellados v. Dimosio, 2008 E.C.R. I-4892, 4908 ¶50.
496. *Id.* at 4908 ¶52.
497. Case 327/12, Ministero dello Sviluppo economico v. SOA Nazionale Construttori, 2013 E.C.R. I-___, at ¶41.
498. *Id.* at ¶41.

TFEU. The competition rules codified in Articles 101 and 102 continue to apply to the undertakings themselves directly (106(2) TFEU). If, however, the private undertaking with special rights is fulfilling a service of general economic interest on behalf of the state, it is not subject to the competition laws if the application of the competition laws obstructs the ability of those undertakings to perform the public interest tasks assigned to them.[499] Although the EU courts have not provides an exhaustive definition of "services of general economic interest", the Commissioner responsible for competition has defined it as "activities that would not be produced by market forces alone or at least not in a form that would be available to all. We are talking about postal services, energy, transport, telecommunications, social services, cultural services and other services."[500] In *Calì e Figli,* for example, the Port of Genoa (Italy) granted exclusive rights to a private environmental surveillance company.[501] The company was hired to monitor certain Italian ports for pollution spills. After the company was accused of abusing its dominant position, the ECJ held that the company's activities were of a general economic interest and therefore immune from the competition laws.[502]

Conversely, if the task entrusted to the private undertaking is a commercial task – and not a public interest task – its conduct falls under the competition laws. In *J.C.J. Wouters v. Algemene Raad van de Nederlandse Orde van Advocaten*, for example, the ECJ concluded that a national bar association of lawyers was not fulfilling a public function and was therefore subject to competition rules:[503]

> According to the case-law of the Court, the Treaty rules on competition do not apply to activity which, by its nature, its aim and the rules to which it is subject does not belong to the sphere of economic activity, or which is connected with the exercise of the powers of a public authority. When it adopts a regulation [regulating the partnership of accountants and lawyers], a professional body such as the Bar of the Netherlands is neither fulfilling a social function based on the principle of solidarity, unlike certain social security bodies, nor exercising powers which are typically those of a public authority. It acts as the regulatory body of a profession, the practice of which constitutes an economic activity (citations omitted).

---

499. TFEU at art. 106(2). The burdeon of proof of showing such obstruction is on the member state which granted the authority. Case T-556/08, Slovenská pošta v. Commission, ECLI:EU:T:2015:189 at ¶358.
500. J. Aluminia, Reform of the State aid rules for services of general economic interest, (Dec. 20, 2011) Speech/11/901.
501. Case C-343/95, Diego Calì & Figli Srl v. Servizi ecologici porto di Genova SpA, 1997 E.C.R. I-1547.
502. *Id.* at 1589 ¶23.
503. Case C-309/99, J.C.J. Wouters v. Algemene Raad van de Nederlandse Orde van Advocaten, 2002 E.C.R. I-1653, 1678-79 ¶¶57-59.

6.3 State Compulsion

In certain cases, the laws or the government of a member state may compel companies to engage in conduct which violates Article 101 or 102 of the TFEU. For example, a member state may require Japanese automobile manufacturers to agree to limit the quantity of automobiles that they import into that member state.[504] In such cases, one must distinguish between the responsibility of the state and the responsibility of the undertakings.

Anticompetitive conduct of private undertakings does not violate Article 101 or 102 of the TFEU if it is either required by the state or the state creates a legal framework that eliminates the possibility of competitive behavior.[505] If a national law merely encourages, or makes it easier for undertakings to engage in autonomous anticompetitive conduct, those undertakings remain subject to Article 101 and 102 of the TFEU.[506] In the *French Beef* case, for example, the French Minister for Agriculture strongly encouraged French farmers and slaughterhouses to agree not to import beef from other member states in the context of the mad cow crisis but stopped short of imposing legal requirements on them. The Commission concluded that the conduct of the French government did not require the anticompetitive conduct of the private undertakings as it left room for autonomous conduct of the farmers and slaughterhouses.[507]

The anticompetitive conduct must arise solely from the state compulsion. The mere approval by the state of certain anticompetitive conduct does not absolve the parties of liability. In *Deutsche Telekom AG v. Commission*, for example, the dominant German telecom company, Deutsche Telecom, tried to argue that it could not be held responsible for the allegedly abusive rates it was charging as these rates were reviewed by and approved by the German Federal Ministry of Post and Telecommunications. The ECJ held, however, that this approval did not absolve Deutsche Telecom of liability under Article 102 of the TFEU as the legislation gave Deutsche Telecom some discretion over the rates.[508]

---

504. *See, e.g.*, Case T-154/98, Asia Motor France v. Comm'n, 2000 E.C.R. II-3453; Comm'n Decision (74/634/EEC) 29 November 1974 relating to proceedings under Art. 85 of the Treaty establishing the EEC (IV/27.095—Franco-Japanese ballbearings agreement).
505. Case C-52/09, Konkurrensverket v. TeliaSonera Sverige AB, 2011 E.C.R. I-564, 582 ¶49; Case C-207/01, Altair Chimica SpA v. ENEL Distribuzione SpA, 2003 E.C.R I-8894, 8908 ¶30; Case C-198/01, Consorzio Industrie Fiammiferi v. Autorità Garante della Concorrenza e del Mercato, 2003 E.C.R. I-8079, 8095 ¶53.
506. Case 327/12, Ministero dello Svikuppo economico v. SOA Nazionale Construttori, 2013 E.C.R. I-____, at ¶38; Case C-52/09, Konkurrenzsversket v. TeliaSonera Sverige AB, 2011 E.C.R. I-564, 582 ¶50; Case C-280/08 P, Deutsche Telecom AG v. Comm'n, 2010 E.C.R. I-9601, 9640 ¶82; Case C-209/07, Competition Authority v. Beef Industry Development Society Ltd., 2008 E.C.R. I-8674, 8689 ¶40. According to the Commission's Guidelines on the method of setting fines imposed pursuant to Article 23(2)(a) of Regulation No. 1/2003, 2006 O.J. (C 210) 2, 4 ¶29, however, the fact that the state encouraged the anticompetitive conduct is a mitigating factor in determining the fines imposed on the undertakings.
507. French Beef, 2003 O.J. (L 209) 12, 36 ¶153.
508. C-280/08 P, Deutsche Telekom AG v. Comm'n, 2011 E.C.R. I-9601, 9641 ¶86.

The inapplicability of Article 101 of the TFEU in compulsion cases is based on the notion that conduct compelled by the state is not autonomous conduct as required by Article 101.[509] As discussed above, one of the elements of a violation of Article 101 is collusion. The existence of collusion assumes the autonomy of the parties to collude. Compelled collusion is insufficient to fulfill this requirement of Article 101.[510] However, if firms agree first, and then the state adopts their agreement as law, Article 101 is applicable.[511]

The finding of compulsion by the state relieves the undertakings themselves of responsibility.[512] However, it does not redeem the conduct of the member state. Article 4(3) of the EU Treaty prohibits member states from maintaining measures that compel private undertakings to engage in anticompetitive conduct.[513] It is the member state and not the undertakings that are liable in such cases.[514] In *Commission v. Italy*, for example, Italian law required customs officers to adopt a uniform rate for their services.[515] Consequently, the law precluded price competition between the customs officers. The ECJ held that Italy and not the customs officers were in violation of Article 4(3) of the EU Treaty together with Article 101 of the TFEU.

A member state violates Article 4(3) of the EU Treaty only if it actually compels the illegal conduct.[516] As stated above, if a national law merely encourages, or makes it easier for undertakings to engage in, anticompetitive conduct, those undertakings and not the member state are responsible for the violation.[517] In *Federico Cipolla v. Rosaria Fazari*, for example, the Italian National Legal Council was created by law and entrusted with establishing and maintaining a scale of legal fees that lawyers in Italy could charge for certain services. When a lawyer tried to charge his client fees based on this scale,

---

509. Case C-207/01, Altair Chimica SpA v. ENEL Distribuzione SpA, 2003 E.C.R. I- 8894, 8908 ¶30; Case C-198/01, Consorzio Industrie Fiammiferi v. Autorità Garante della Concorrenza e del Mercato, 2003 E.C.R. I-8079, 8095 ¶53.
510. The member states may achieve the same effect as a cartel even without compelling collusion between competitors. For example, the member state may attempt to establish minimum prices for certain products. Absent collusion between the competitors, the undertaking selling the products at the fixed price would, of course, not be liable for a violation of Article 101 of the TFEU. Case 231/83, Cullet v. Leclere, 1985 E.C.R. 305.
511. Case 136/86, BNIC v. Aubert, 1987 E.C.R. 3801; Case C-35/96, Comm'n v. Italy, 1998 E.C.R. I-3851.
512. Case C-198/01, Consorzio Industrie Fiammiferi v. Autorità Garante della Concorrenza e del Mercato, 2003 E.C.R. I-8079, 8095 ¶53 (Undertakings cannot be penalized for anticompetitive conduct which is required by the laws of a member state.).
513. Case C-437/09, AG2R Prévoyance v. Beaudout Père et Fils SARL, 2011 E.C.R. I-1003, 1020 ¶37; Case C-446/05, *In re* Doulamis, 2008 E.C.R. I-1404, 1411 ¶20.
514. Case C-35/99, Arduino v. Compagnia Assicuratrice, 2002 E.C.R. I-1561, 1572 ¶35.
515. Case C-35/96, Comm'n v. Italy, 1998 E.C.R. I-3851.
516. Case T-169/08, Dimosa Epicheirisi Ilektrismou AE v. Comm'n, 2012 E.C.R. II-10821, at ¶94.
517. Case C-446/05, *In re* Doulamis, 2008 E.C.R. I-1404, 1411 ¶22; Case C-198/01, Consorzio Industrie Fiammiferi v. Autorità Garante della Concorrenza e del Mercato, 2003 E.C.R. I-8079, 8096 ¶56.

the client argued that the establishment of the scale was anticompetitive and consequently infringed Article 4(3) of the EU Treaty in combination with Article 101 of the TFEU. The ECJ held, however, that Article 4(3) was not infringed because the scale was not binding on lawyers.[518]

A member state may also infringe the free movement rules by compelling certain anticompetitive conduct which results in a restriction on the flow of goods or services between member states. For example, a member state may violate the free movement rules by imposing a limit on the amount of Japanese automobiles that can be sold in that member state.[519] However, it is generally easier for the Commission to address such restrictions under the competition rules than under the free movement rules.

7. Jurisdictional Issues

7.1 Relationship Between EU and National Competition Law

As discussed in Chapter I, the EU is a legal system in which the institutions only have the authorities that have been ceded to them by the member states in the treaties. The authority to regulate trade with third countries is an example of an authority that the member states have ceded to the EU. As this Chapter illustrates, competition law is another authority that the member states have ceded to the EU institutions. In contrast to trade law, however, the member states have not completely relinquished their authority to legislate in the field of competition law. Consequently, there are two parallel systems of competition law in Europe potentially applicable to anticompetitive conduct: EU and national. In this respect, the system is quite similar to the U.S. system with federal and state antitrust law. Although the European Commission and courts do not have the authority to apply national competition law, the competition authorities and the courts of the member states have the authority to apply Article 101 and Article 102 of the TFEU in specific cases.[520]

The parallel application of national and EU competition law by the national authorities to the same facts presents the possibility of inconsistent results. For example, a particular commercial practice may be permissible under EU law but prohibited under national law. The decisive factor in determining the priority of

---

518. Joined Cases C-94/04 and C-202/04, Federico Cipolla v. Rosaria Fazari, 2006 E.C.R. I-11455, 11471 ¶50.
519. *See, e.g.*, Case T-154/98, Asia Motor France v. Comm'n, 2000 E.C.R. II-3453; Comm'n Decision (74/634/EEC) 29 November 1974 relating to proceedings under Art. 85 of the Treaty establishing the EEC (IV/27.095—Franco-Japanese ballbearings agreement).
520. Council Regulation (EC) No. 1/2003 of 16 December 2002 on the implementation of the rules on competition laid down in Art. 81 and 82 of the Treaty, 2003 O.J. (L 1) 1, art. 5 and 6. The relationship between the European Merger Control Regulation and national competition law is governed by the Merger Control Regulation as discussed above.

EU law and national law in a particular case is whether the conduct has an effect on trade between member states. If there is no effect on trade between member states, national competition agencies and courts may apply national competition law. In such cases, EU competition law does not even apply. If, however, there is an effect on trade between member states, the national competition authorities and courts are obligated to apply EU competition law.[521] This does not prevent them from also applying their national competition laws.[522] If, for example, two Belgian glass manufacturers agree to fix the minimum price for their products sold in Belgium and the Netherlands, the Belgian *Conseil de la Concurrence* may apply Belgian law to the conduct, but they must also apply EU competition law.

In cases in which both national law and EU competition law are applicable to the same case, their parallel application could provide a different result. For example, EU competition law may permit conduct which is prohibited by national competition law. The basic rules in such cases differ depending on whether the conduct is a bilateral restraint or a multilateral restraint. In cases of bilateral restraints, the basic rule is that the results of the application of Article 101 of the TFEU prevail over the application of national competition law.[523] If the conduct is permissible under Article 101, national competition cannot prohibit the conduct.[524] If the conduct is prohibited by Article 101, national competition law cannot be applied to permit it.[525] In other words, conduct which has an effect on trade between member states only has to clear the hurdle of Article 101.

This principle does not apply, however, to unilateral restraints of competition. The member states may apply stricter national competition laws to unilateral anticompetitive conduct which may be consistent with Article 102 of the TFEU. The *Walmart* case[526] illustrates the application of this rule. The German Act Against Restraints of Competition prohibited below-cost pricing by companies with a superior market position. In this case, the German Cartel Office decided that Walmart was offering milk at below-cost prices. On appeal to the German Supreme Court, Walmart argued that its conduct was consistent with Article

---

521. Council Regulation (EC) No. 1/2003 of 16 December 2002 on the implementation of the rules on competition laid down in Articles 81 and 82 of the Treaty, 2003 O.J. (L 1) 1 at art. 3(1) [hereinafter Regulation 2003/1].
522. *Id.*
523. *Id.* at art. 3(2). This rule only applies to preempt the application of national competition rules. It does not prevent the parallel application of national laws which pursue a different objective. For example, national rules regulating unfair trade may still be applied by the member states even though the conduct is consistent with Article 101 of the TFEU.
524. *Id.* at art. 3(2).
525. Case T-67/01, JCB Service v. Comm'n, 2004 E.C.R. II-56, 89 ¶93 *aff'd on appeal* Case C-167/04 P, JCB Service v. Comm'n, 2006 E.C.R. I-8972.
526. Decision of the German Bundesgerichtshof in case no. KVR 5/02 (Nov. 12, 2002) *reported at* 53 Wirtschaft und Wettbewerb 386 (2003).

102 of the TFEU and therefore could not be prohibited by national law.[527] The German Supreme Court held that "national and European competition law have parallel application as long as no conflict exists such as a national prohibition of conduct expressly exempted under European law."[528] The Supreme Court concluded that the German Cartel Office could therefore prohibit the conduct under German law.

There is, of course, presecutorial discretion involved. The decentralization efforts of the European Commission in the field of competition law has given greater import to national competition law regulators. Given limited resources, these agencies have to conduct some triage on the cases which they encounter. The necessity of prosecutorial discretion creates the possibility for inconsistent enforcement efforts and a certain degree of divergence among the member states in their respective competition policies. For example, both the Dutch Autoriteit Consument & Markt and the Swedish Konkurrensverket have expressed skepticism towards the Commission hard line approach on vertical price restraints[529] and publicly stated that they will not give enforcement priority to such cases absent market power because intrabrand restraints may be beneficial to consumders.[530]

7.2 Parallel Application of EU Law

As the Commission and the national competition agencies each have the authority to apply Articles 101 and 102 (and indeed the national authorities have an affirmative obligation to apply EU competition law when the anticompetitive conduct has an effect on interstate trade),[531] the potential for inconsistent results in the application of the same legal norm arises. In the event that the Commission has made a decision in a particular case, the member states are precluded from taking an inconsistent subsequent decision. However, if the Commission has not ruled on a particular practice, the national authorities and courts have the power to issue negative decisions (i.e., that Article 101 or 102 has been violated).[532] According to the ECJ, however, the national authorities and courts cannot declare the practice compatible with Article 101 or 102 as this

---

527. The doctrine of predatory pricing under Art. 102 of the TFEU, as discussed above, has slightly different elements than under German law.
528. *Id.* at 394.
529. The Commission's policy is set forth in Vertical Restraints Guidelines at 12 ¶48.
530. Speech of Chris Fonteijn on Vertical Agreements at Vereniging voor Mededingingsrecht Meeting November 25th 2014 *available at* https://www.acm.nl/en/publications/publication/13606/Speech-of-Chris-Fonteijn-on-vertical-agreements-at-VvM-seminar/; Decision of the Swedish Konkurrensverket in case no. 559/2013 (Oct. 30, 2014).
531. Regulation 2003/1 at art. 3(1); Case C-17/10, Toshiba Corporation v. Comm'n, 2012 E.C.R. I-___, at ¶91.
532. Regulation 2003/1 at art. 5.

"might prevent the Commission from finding subsequently that the practice in question amounts to a breach of those provisions of EU law."[533]

7.3 Extraterritorial Application of EU Competition Law

The topic of the extraterritorial application of competition laws refers to the application of EU law to conduct occurring outside the EU. If, for example, two insurance companies in the United States agree to fix minimum prices for their products in Slovenia, EU competition law may be applied to the insurance companies even though they are outside the EU and the prohibited conduct (price fixing) occurred outside the EU.

The permissibility of the extraterritorial application of competition law under international law was initially unclear. The exercise of jurisdiction was historically commensurate with the geographic territory of the particular country or nationality. The territoriality principle strictly applied is, however, not suitable for delineating the application of competition laws as the illegal conduct can take place entirely outside the territory in which the anticompetitive effect is realized. The strict application of the territoriality principle would allow companies to engage in anticompetitive practices without punishment as long as they were not active in the state in which their conduct had an effect. In the preceding hypothetical case involving two U.S. insurance companies, for example, a strict application of the territoriality principle would prevent the EU from sanctioning the anticompetitive conduct even though it had repercussions in the EU.

In 1927, the International Court of Justice suggested in the *Lotus* case that a state's jurisdiction may not always be limited to its territory: "far from laying down a general prohibition to the effect that States may not extend the application of their laws and the jurisdiction of their courts to persons, property and acts outside their territory, [international law] leaves them in this respect a wide measure of discretion which is only limited in certain cases by prohibitive rules; as regards other cases, every state remains free to adopt the principles which it regards as best and most suitable."[534] In 1945, Judge Learned Hand even went so far as to observe: "It is settled case law that any state may impose liabilities, even upon persons not within its allegiance, for conduct outside its borders that has consequences within its borders which the state reprehends."[535]

---

533. Case C-375/09, Prezes Urzędu Ochrony Konkurencji i Konsumentów v. Tele2 Polska sp. z o.o., 2011 E.C.R. I-3055, 3093 ¶28. *See also* Case C-344/98, Masterfoods Ltd. v. HB Ice Cream, 2000 E.C.R. I-11369, 11428 ¶48 ("Despite that division of powers, and in order to fulfil the role assigned to it by the Treaty, the Commission cannot be bound by a decision given by a national court in application of Articles [101](1) and [102] of the Treaty. The Commission is therefore entitled to adopt at any time individual decisions under Articles [101] and [102] of the Treaty, even where an agreement or practice has already been the subject of a decision by a national court and the decision contemplated by the Commission conflicts with that national court's decision.").
534. SS 'Lotus' (France v. Turkey) (1927) PCIJ, Series A, No. 10 (Sept. 7, 1927).
535. United States v. Aluminum Co. of America, 148 F.2d 416, 443 (2d Cir. 1945).

Although the U.S. did not have any reservations about applying its domestic law to conduct occurring outside its territory but having an effect in the United States, the EU was initially reluctant to adopt the effects test. Instead, the EU attempted to adhere to the strict territoriality principle by relying on the economic unit theory. As discussed above, an "undertaking" is defined as an economic unit and not necessarily a specific company.[536] If a non-EU company engaged in illegal conduct outside the EU, but had affiliated companies in the EU, the undertaking was deemed to be present in the EU because these legal entities were considered to all be part of the same economic unit.[537] Hence, the economic unit approach ostensibly allowed the EU to observe the territoriality principle.

As an anticompetitive practice may be engaged in by companies entirely outside the EU and which have no EU subsidiaries or affiliates, the reliance on the economic unit approach proved to be inadequate. In *Åhlstrom Osukeyhtiö v. Commission* (often referred to as the "Woodpulp" case), the ECJ introduced a new concept designed to address this shortcoming.[538] In that case, a group of wood pulp producers from outside the EU agreed to fix the prices for the sale of their wood pulp in the EU. Instead of relying on the economic unit theory, the ECJ held that the conduct was "implemented" in the EU since the products were sold there even though the objectionable conduct—the cartel agreement—took place outside the EU.[539] As subsequently applied, the rule means that the Commission will have jurisdiction if the undertaking sells products or services into the EU.[540] If the other elements of a violation of Article 101 or Article 102 of the TFEU are fulfilled, the Commission will have the authority under international law as interpreted by the ECJ to apply EU competition law even if the conduct occurred entirely outside the EU. Indeed, there are no cases in which international law prevented the application of EU competition law to conduct that had the requisite anticompetitive effect in the EU.

8. Liability for Violations of the Competition Rules

8.1 Parent Company Liability

As discussed earlier in this Chapter, EU competition law applies to "undertakings." The concept of undertaking does not necessarily correspond to a specific legal entity. For example, a parent corporation and its subsidiaries may comprise one undertaking for purposes of EU competition law.[541] This is why, for example, agreements between a parent company and its subsidiaries do not qualify as

---

536. Case C-407/08 P, Knauf Gips KG v. Comm'n, 2010 E.C.R. I-6415, 6443 ¶64; Case T-325/01, DaimlerChrysler v. Comm'n, 2005 E.C.R. II-3326, 3358 ¶85.
537. Case 48/69, Imperial Chemical Industries Ltd. v. Comm'n, 1972 E.C.R. 619, 664; Joined cases 6 and 7/73, Commercial Solvents v. Comm'n, 1974 E.C.R. 223, 255.
538. Joined cases 89, 104, 114, 116-117 and 125-129, 185, Åhlstrom Osukeyhtiö v. Comm'n,1988 E.C.R. 5193.
539. *Id.* at 5243 ¶17.
540. Amino Acids, 2001 O.J. (L 152) 24.
541. Case C-508/11 P, Eni SpA v. Comm'n, 2013 E.C.R. I-____, at ¶47.

"agreements between undertakings" for purposes of EU competition law. This presents an issue regarding the imposition of liability because, as stated by the ECJ, "the violation of EU competition law must be imputed unequivocally to a legal person on whom fines can be imposed."[542] Consequently, EU competition law needed to address the question of whether one legal entity may be held liable for the competition law violations committed by another legal entity within the same undertaking.[543]

The rule developed by the EU courts is that the mere status of being a controlled subsidiary is not in itself sufficient to "pierce the corporate veil."[544] The parent must either exercise decisive influence over the commercial decisions of the subsidiary[545] or be aware of and approve the illegal activity.[546] However, there is a rebuttable presumption that a parent company has a decisive influence over its wholly owned subsidiaries and can be held responsible for the violations committed by its subsidiaries.[547] The burden of proof is on the parent company to show that the subsidiary acts independently on the market.[548] The

---

542. Case C-97/08 P, Akzo Nobel NV v. Comm'n, 2009 E.C.R. I-8266, 8287 ¶57.
543. The issue is of significant practical import as the fines for violations of the competition laws are calculated based on the sales volumes of the liable undertaking and not just the sales volumes of the legal entities involved in the illegal conduct. *See, e.g.*, Case C-508/11 P, Eni SpA v. Comm'n, 2013 E.C.R. I-___, at ¶109. According to Article 23(2) of Regulation 1/2003, the fines can be up to 10 percent of the undertaking's worldwide sales. There is often a significant difference between 10 percent of the worldwide sales of a subsidiary as opposed to its parent company. The fact that the parent company is also exposed to fines or liability in the United States for the same conduct does not preclude the European Commission from imposing fines. C-499/11 P, The Dow Chemical Company v. Comm'n, 2013 E.C.R. I-___, at ¶52.
544. Case C-286/98, Stora Kopparsbergs Bergslag AB v. Comm'n, 2000 E.C.R. I-9925. *See also* Joined Cases C-189/02 P, C-202/02 P, C-205/02 P to C-208/02 P and C-213/02 P, Dansk Rørindustri A/S v. Comm'n, 2005 E.C.R. I-5488, 5541 ¶117. In Case T-386/06, Pegler Ltd. v. Comm'n, 2011 E.C.R. II-1267, at ¶103, however, the General Court held, without mentioning the decisive influence requirement, that the "Commission has the power to impute liability for unlawful conduct to the parent company, to the subsidiary, or to the parent company jointly and severally with its subsidiary."
545. Case C-286/98, Stora Kopparsbergs Bergslag AB v. Comm'n, 2000 E.C.R. I-9925, 9956 ¶80; Case T-185/06, L'Aire liquide v. Comm'n, 2011 E.C.R. II-2809, at ¶21. The ECJ has specifically refused to promulgate a list of factors indicative of decisive influence. Case C-440/11 P, Comm'n v. Stichting Administratiekontoor Portielje, 2013 E.C.R. I-___, at ¶60.
546. Case T-259/02 – T-264/02 & T-271/02, Raiffeisen Zentralbank Österrich AG v. Comm'n, 2006 E.C.R. II-5200, 5308 ¶330.
547. Joined Cases C-93/13 P and C-123/13 P, Commission v. Versalis SpA, 2015 E.C.R. I-___ at ¶40; Case C-238/12 P, FLSmidth & Co. A/S v. Comm'n, 2014 E.C.R. I-___, at ¶25; Case C-97/08 P, Akzo Nobel NV v. Comm'n, 2009 E.C.R. I-8266, 8288 ¶60. Although it is difficult to rebut the presumption, in *L'Aire liquide v. Comm'n*, the defendants were successful in rebutting in showing that the Commission had failed to properly consider all of the factors raised by the defendants. Case T-185/06, L'Aire liquide v. Comm'n, 2011 E.C.R. II-2812, 2836 ¶83.
548. Case C-58/12 P, Groupe Gascogne SA v. Comm'n, 2013 E.C.R. I-___, at ¶38.

presumption, and hence the liability, applies not only to the direct owner of the entity which engaged in the anticompetitive conduct, but also to its ultimate parent entity.[549] The fact that the parent company is not aware of or participate in the anticompetitive conduct of the subsidiary does not preclude the imposition of liability on the parent undertaking.[550]

The vicarious liability of a parent company even applies to anticompetitive conduct engaged in by a joint venture.[551] As discussed in greater detail below, a joint venture is a legal entity which is jointly controlled by two or more other undertakings. Joint control refers to the ability of at least two other undertakings to exercise decisive influence over the conduct of the joint venture entity.[552]

In *The Dow Chemical Company v. Commission*, The Dow Chemical Company and E.I. du Pont de Nemours and Company established a joint venture in the form of a Delaware limited liability company in which they each held 50 percent. After it was discovered that the joint venture company was involved in a price-fixing cartel in violation of Article 101 of the TFEU, the issue arose whether the Commission could impose fines on the Dow Chemical. According to the General Court, the parent companies of a joint venture incur the same joint and several liability for conduct of a joint venture as they do for wholly owned subsidiaries.[553]

The General Court has suggested that merely fulfilling the requirements of joint control within the meaning of the Merger Control Regulation is insufficient to hold the parents liable for competition law violations of the joint venture entity. According to the General Court, the Commission must prove that the parent companies not only had the ability to control the joint venture, but also that they actually exercised this ability.[554]

---

549. Case T-65/06, FLSmidth & Co. A/S v. Comm'n, 2012 E.C.R. II-____, at ¶27 *aff'd on appeal* Case C-238/12 P, FLSmidth & Co. A/S v. Comm'n, 2014 E.C.R. I-____; Case T-38/05, Agroexpansión SA v. Comm'n, 2011 E.C.R. II-7012, 7046 ¶108 *aff'd on appeal* C-668/11 P, Alliance One Int'l Inc. v. Comm'n, 2013 E.C.R. I-____; Case T-42/07, The Dow Chemical Company v. Comm'n, 2011 E.C.R. II-4538, 4562 ¶74 *aff'd on appeal* Case C-499/11 P, The Dow Chemical Company v. Comm'n, 2013 E.C.R. I-____.
550. Joined cases C-628/10 P and C-14/11 P, Alliance One Int'l Inc. v. Comm'n, 2012 E.C.R. I-____, at ¶102; Case T-77/08, The Dow Chemical Company v. Comm'n, 2012 E.C.R. II-____, at ¶106.
551. Joined cases C-628/10 P and C-14/11 P, Alliance One Int'l Inc. v. Comm'n, 2012 E.C.R. I-____, at ¶103. Case T-541/08 Jasol v. Comm'n, 2014 E.C.R. II-____, at ¶37. The liability associated with anticompetitive conduct of the joint venture may be attributed to both joint venture partners or one of them jointly and severally. Case T-541/08, Sasol v. Commission, 2014 E.C.R. II-____, at ¶167; Case T-314/01, Coöperatieve Verkoop-en Productievereniging van Aardappelmeel en Derivaten Avebe BA v. Comm'n, 2006 E.C.R. II-3085, 3131 ¶138.
552. Comm'n Consolidated Jurisdictional Notice under Council Regulation (EC) No. 139/2004 on the control of concentrations between undertakings, 2008 O.J. (C 95) 1, 18 ¶63.
553. Case T-77/08, The Dow Chemical Company v. Comm'n, 2012 E.C.R. II-____, at ¶89.
554. Case T-541/08, Sasol v. Commission, 2014 E.C.R. II-____, at ¶43.

8.2 Successor Liability

In some cases, violations of the competition rules are discovered long after they have actually occurred. The entity which engaged in the anticompetitive activity may no longer exist or its shares or assets may have been sold to a different owner. Further complicating matters is the state of the law regarding parent company liability. If, for example, a subsidiary was involved in anticompetitive conduct, and then the shares of the subsidiary are sold to a third party, the general rule of corporate law is that the liabilities of that subsidiary stay with that subsidiary (unless, of course, the parties allocate responsibility for the liabilities between them). As discussed above, however, the parent company may be responsible for the anticompetitive conduct of its subsidiaries. The question therefore arises whether the liabilities of the subsidiary for the anticompetitive conduct stay with the subsidiary or whether the selling parent company retains some or all liability.

The general rule is that liability for competition law violations remains with the legal or natural person managing the business at the time of the violation even if that natural or legal person is no longer managing the business.[555] This means, for example, that the liability stays with the seller of the assets of a business if it still exists at the time the liability is imposed.[556] By way of exception to the general rule, there may be circumstances in which the successor is liable (at least partially) for the violations committed by the previous entity.[557] If, for example, the successor was also a participant in the anticompetitive conduct,[558] agrees to assume the liability,[559] or continues to carry on the violations after the closing of the acquisition,[560] liability is apportioned between the buyer and the seller. In addition, the successor may be held liable for the violations of its predecessor under the economic continuity test. According to this test, liability associated with a competition law violation may be imposed on a successor to the business if the legal person operating the business at the time of the violations ceases to exist after the violation has occurred and a different legal person is operating the

---

555. Case C-444/11 P, Team Relocation, NV v. Comm'n, 2013 E.C.R. I-___, at ¶164; Case C-352/09 P, ThyssenKrupp Nirosta GmbH v. Comm'n, 2011 E.C.R. I-2410, 2454 ¶143. The personal liability of the managers and directors of the business involved in the anti-competitive conduct is an issue for national law. See, e.g., Dornbracht, Decision of the Oberlandesgericht Düsseldorf VI-U (Kart) 11/13 (Nov. 13, 2013) *aff'd on appeal* German Supreme Court, KRZ 88/13 (Oct. 7, 2014).
556. C-125/07 P, Erste Group Bank AG v. Comm'n, 2009 E.C.R. I-8821, 8854 ¶78; C-286/98, Stora Kopparsbergs Bergslag AB v. Comm'n, 2000 E.C.R. I-9945, 9978 ¶37.
557. Successor liability may even be imposed where the entity which actually engaged in the anticompetitive conduct still exists. Case C-511/11 P, Versalis SpA v. Comm'n, 2013 E.C.R. I-___, at ¶52; Case T-386/06, Pegler Ltd. v. Comm'n, 2011 E.C.R. II-1270, 1284 ¶55.
558. Case C-280/06, Autorità Garante della Conosrenza e del Mercado v. Ente tabicchi italiani, 2007 E.C.R. I-10893 at ¶39.
559. Case C-352/09 P, ThyssenKrupp Nirosta GmbH v. Comm'n, 2011 E.C.R. I-2410, 2456 ¶150.
560. Methylglucamine, 2004 O.J. (L 38) 18, 39 ¶207.

business[561] and the imposition of successor liability will avoid compromising the effectiveness of the competition rules.[562]

9. Private Enforcement

The enforcement of EU competition law in Europe has traditionally been left to public competition law agencies. At the EU level, this has been primarily the European Commission; although, as discussed above, the competition law authorities of the member states also have the authority to apply EU competition law. Private enforcement is a relatively new phenomenon in Europe as the state (rather than private individuals) has been perceived as being the more appropriate enforcer. In recognition of the imperfections of a purely public enforcement approach, the EU is now promoting greater private enforcement.

The nature of the EU legal system, however, makes the realization of this objective dependent on the member states. The EU judicial system is not established to address claims for damages brought by individuals as a result of a violation of EU competition law. Such claims must be brought in and are dependent upon the national courts in the respective member states. Raising a claim in a national court based on a violation of EU competition law is possible because the competition provisions in the TFEU are directly applicable in the member states.[563] However, whether parties injured by conduct in violation of Article 101 or 102 of the TFEU have a private claim for damages against the parties alleged to have engaged in the anti-competitive conduct is a matter of national law. EU law only makes such anticompetitive conduct illegal. The private law consequences of such illegality are left to the member states. However, the member states are required by EU law to adopt the procedural rules to facilitate private damages claims asserted by injured parties.[564] This means, for example, that in a case where the national authorities have conducted an investigation, the member states cannot maintain laws that flatly preclude access to the file for private litigants potentially injured by the anticompetitive conduct.[565]

In *In re Courage*, English common law precluded the plaintiff, who was a party to an agreement infringing Article 101 of the TFEU, from claiming damages against the other party.[566] The ECJ held that national law could not absolutely preclude a party to an agreement infringing Article 101 of the TFEU

---

561. Joined cases C-93/13 P and C-123/13 P, Commission v. Versalis SpA, 2015 E.C.R. I-____ at ¶53; Case C-280/06, Autorità Garante della Conosrenza e del Mercado v. Ente tabicchi italiani, 2007 E.C.R. I-10925, 10942 ¶40; T-161/05, Hoechst GmbH v. Comm'n, 2009 E.C.R. II-3567, 3579 ¶50.
562. Cases T-117/07 and 121/07, Areva SA v. Comm'n, 2011 E.C.R. II-649, 672 ¶66 *aff'd on appeal* Joined cases C-247/11/P and 253/11/P, Alstom SA v. Comm'n, 2014 E.C.R. I-____.
563. Case C-557/12, Kone AG v. ÖBB-Infrastruktur AG 2014, E.C.R. I-____, at ¶20.
564. *Id.* at ¶24; Case C-536/11, Bundeswettbewerbsbehörde v. Donau Chemie AG, 2013 E.C.R. I-____, at ¶25.
565. *Id.* at ¶39.
566. Case C-453/99, *In re* Courage, 2001 E.C.R. I-6297, 6327 ¶28.

from claiming damages against the other party. According to the ECJ: "Indeed, the existence of such a right strengthens the working of the [EU] competition rules and discourages agreements or practices, which are frequently covert, which are liable to restrict or distort competition. From that point of view, actions for damages before the national courts can make a significant contribution to the maintenance of effective competition in the [EU]."[567] However, the Court said that as an exception, a national rule (such as the doctrine of unjust enrichment in this case) may be relied on to preclude the claim as long as it is applied without discrimination and does not preclude all claims based on breach of EU law.[568]

As the private enforcement of EU competition law is dependent upon the national legal systems which themselves are generally unfamiliar with private actions based on competition law violations, there has been significant disparities among the member states. In an effort to harmonize the member state laws on private actions, the EU has adopted a directive which requires all member states to "ensure that any natural or legal person who has suffered harm caused by an infringement of competition law is able to claim and to obtain full compensation for that harm."[569] The member states have until December 27, 2016 to makes the appropriate adjustments to their domestic laws in line with the Private Actions Directive.

The private enforcement system envisaged by the Private Actions Directive differs from the private enforcement system in the United States in several important ways. First, the fact pleading thresholds in the EU member states tend to be higher than the liberal notice pleading thresholds of the U.S. Federal Rules of Civil Procedure. In the United States, the Federal Rules of Civil Procedure only require the plaintiff to make "a short and plain statement of the claim showing that the pleader is entitled to relief."[570] The plaintiff does not have to provide any evidence beyond plausible allegations.[571] In the EU, on the other hand, the plaintiff is required to include detailed factual assertions in the complaint initiating the litigation. Although the Private Actions Directive does not establish harmonized pleadings rules, the plaintiff only gets to the discovery phase of the litigation if it "has presented a reasoned justification containing available facts and evidence sufficient to support the plausibility of its claim for damages."[572]

Second, the discovery rights of plaintiffs in EU private litigation are significantly less than private plaintiffs in the United States. In the U.S., a plaintiff "may obtain discovery regarding any matter, not privileged, that is relevant to the claim."[573] Courts in the U.S. generally do not want to become

---

567. *Id.* at 6326 ¶27.
568. *Id.* at 6327 ¶31.
569. Directive 2014/104/EU of the European Parliament and of the Council of 26 November 2014 on certain rules governing actions for damages under national law for infringements of the competition law provisions of the member states and of the European Union, 2014 O.J. (L 349) 1 at art. 3(1) [hereinafter Private Actions Directive].
570. Federal Rules of Civil Procedure Rule 8(a)(2).
571. Bell Atlantic Corp. v. Twombly, 550 U.S. 544 (2007).
572. Private Actions Directive at art. 4.
573. Federal Rules of Civil Procedure Rule 26(b).

involved in the discovery process and tend to err on the side of allowing discovery requests. Consequently, discovery often becomes a tactical tool in the litigation process rather than simply a mean by which the parties can substantiate their claims. In a effort to avoid the perceived abuses of discovery experienced in the U.S. system, the Private Actions Directive requires the courts of the member states to exercise an active role in the discovery process and subject discovery requests to a proportionality test.[574] In making this assessment, the national courts must consider the extent to which the claim is supported by available facts and evidence justifying the request to disclose, the scope and cost of disclosure, and whether the evidence the disclosure of which is sought contains confidential information.

Third, the claim for damages under the Private Actions Directive is limited to compensatory damages, i.e., actual loss and loss of profit plus interest.[575] Based upon its understanding of the U.S. legal system, the EU was particularly careful to preclude punitive and multiple damages. The thinking was that these types of damages lead to "overcompensation" for the plaintiff and could possibly distort the motives of the plaintiffs or their attorneys.[576]

Finally, financing private litigation in the EU will likely continue to differ from that in the United States. Contingency fees are generally prohibited in the EU member states because of the apparent conflict of interest which they may create. Moreover, there is a general rule in civil law systems that the loser pays the legal fees of the prevailing party.[577] Consequently, the plaintiffs in the EU are required to fund the litigation. Although the Commission has encouraged the member states to adopt "collective redress mechanisms at national level for both injunctive and compensatory relief,"[578] U.S. style opt-out class actions are not available in EU litigation. To address the dissuasive effect this has on potential private plaintiffs, independent companies have been aggregating the individual claims for competition law violations and bringing their own actions as assignees of these claims.[579]

The promotion of private enforcement by the Commission will increase the incidence of parallel private enforcement proceedings not only among the member states but also with jurisdictions outside the EU. There are no supranational rules allocating jurisdiction when parallel private enforcement actions are brought in one of the EU member states and in a jurisdiction or

---

574. Private Actions Directive at art. 5.
575. *Id.* at art. 3(2).
576. *Id.*
577. See, e.g., Directive 2004/48/EC of the European Parliament and of the Council of 29 April 2004 on the enforcement of intellectual property rights, 2007 O.J. (L 154) 45.
578. Commission Recommendation of 11 June 2013 on common principles for injunctive and compensatory collective redress mechanisms in the member states concerning violations of rights granted under Union Law, 2013 O.J. (L 201) 60. The Private Actions Directive does not require the member states to recognize class actions.
579. Decision of the German Bundesgerichtshof in case KZR 42/08 (April 7, 2009).

jurisdictions outside the United States.[580] As between and among EU member states, however, the Brussels I Regulation applies.[581] Under Brussels I, an private enforcement action based on competition law violations may be brought where the defendant is incorporated[582] or where the harmful event occurred.[583] Once a private enforcement action is filed in a member state which has jurisdiction under Brussels I, the other member state courts must decline to exercise jurisdiction over any subsequently filed actions based on the same conduct and involving the same parties.[584]

10. Structural Restraints of Competition: EU Merger Control

This Chapter has so far addressed bilateral restraints of competition and unilateral restraints of competition. Structural restraints make up the third type of restraint of competition. In contrast to bilateral and unilateral restraints, structural restraints are regulated by secondary legislation and not the TFEU. The European Merger Control Regulation requires parties to certain transactions which are of a particular size to secure the approval of the European Commission prior to the consummation of the transaction. The EU Merger Control Regulation, similar to the U.S. Hart-Scott-Rodino Antitrust Improvements Act of 1976,[585] represents an attempt to identify which transactions could have a structural impact on competition such that they should be reviewed in advance by the appropriate competition regulators. The necessity for ex ante review of the transaction is a recognition that it is extremely difficult for the regulators to "unwind" mergers and acquisitions once they have been consummated.

Initially, there was no provision in EU law specifically applicable to structural restraints of competition. The Commission attempted to challenge such transactions by relying on Article 102 of the TFEU.[586] If a merger created

---

580. Arguably the international law concept of comity would apply is such cases. See, e.g. Timberlane Lumber Co. v. Bank of America, 549 F.2d 597 (1976). In reality, however, the concept of comity has proven of little restraint to courts where the conduct has an anti-competitive effect in its jurisdiction.
581. Council Regulation (EC) No. 44/2001 of 22 December 2000 on jurisdiction and the recognition and enforcement of judgments in civil and commercial matters, 2001 O.J. (L 12) 1 [hereinafter Brussels I Regulation]. Although the Brussels I Regulation does not explicitly state that it also applies to competition law matters, there is a general consensus that it does. SanDisk Corp. v. Koninklijke Philips Electronics, [2007] EWHC 332 (Ch). The applicable law in such multijurisdictional cases is determined pursuant to Regulation (EC) No. 864/2007 of the European Parliament and the Council of 11 July 2007 on the law applicable to non-contractual obligations, 2007 O.J. (L 199) 40.
582. Brussels I Regulation at art. 2(1).
583. *Id.* at art. 5(3).
584. *Id.* at art. 27(2).
585. The Hart-Scott-Rodino Act is codified as part of Section 7A of the Clayton Act. 15 U.S.C § 18a.
586. Case 6/72, Continental Can Company v. Comm'n, 1972 E.C.R. 157.

a dominant firm, it was characterized as an abuse of a dominant position. This approach was inadequate because the Commission was not able to prevent the transaction prior to its consummation. Once the firms were merged, it was extremely difficult for the Commission to "unscramble the eggs." The weaknesses of the reliance on Article 102 of the TFEU to address concentrations led to the adoption of Council Regulation 4064/89 in 1989.[587] The initial Merger Control Regulation was 15 years later replaced by Regulation 139/2004.[588]

The Merger Control Regulation prohibits concentrations with an EU dimension that would create or strengthen a dominant position in the EU. The application of the European Merger Control Regulation proceeds in two steps. The first step, referred to here as the procedural analysis, addresses the issue of whether the Merger Control Regulation is applicable to the particular transaction. Assuming its applicability, the second step, referred to here as the substantive analysis, addresses the issue of whether the transaction should be prohibited because of its potential effects on competition. The adjective "potential" is important. The European Merger Control Regulation is preventative in nature; it attempts to identify which transactions *could* have a negative effect on competition. The fact is that merger control regimes allow—and indeed require—the regulators to engage in a certain amount of speculation about the future impact of a proposed transaction. This exposes the regulators to criticism and probably results in some cases being prohibited which should be allowed (false positives) and some cases being allowed which should be prohibited (false negatives). This is perhaps an inevitable inefficiency of merger control regimes.

10.1 Procedural Analysis Under the Merger Control Regulation

The procedural analysis under the European Merger Control Regulation involves determining whether the particular transaction qualifies as a concentration with an EU dimension.[589] This determination has two important implications. First, it triggers a premerger notification obligation for the undertakings concerned. The failure to notify the transaction to the Commission and wait for clearance can result in significant fines being imposed on the undertakings concerned.[590] Second, it delineates the jurisdiction of the Commission to apply the substantive test to the transaction. Contrary to the U.S. premerger control law, the Commission's authority to prohibit a merger depends on whether the transaction is required to be notified to the Commission. Consequently, the applicability of the Merger Control Regulation plays a much more important role in securing approval of transaction than does the applicability of the Hart-

---

587. Council Regulation (EEC) No. 4064/89 of 21 December 1989 on the control of concentrations between undertakings O.J. 1989 (L 395) 1.
588. Council Regulation No. 139/2004 of 20 January 2004 on the control of concentrations between undertakings, 2004 O.J. (L 24) 1 [hereinafter Merger Control Regulation].
589. Merger Control Regulation at art. 1(1).
590. In M.4994, Electrabel/CNR (June 10, 2009), the Commission imposed a fine of €20 million on Electrabel for acquiring control of Compagnie Nationale du Rhône without notifying the transaction to the Commission in advance.

Scott-Rodino Antitrust Improvements Act,[591] the application or nonapplication of which does not prevent the U.S. Department of Justice or Federal Trade Commission from challenging the transaction.

(a) Concentration

(1) Types of Concentrations

The first requirement—that the transaction qualifies as a concentration—illustrates that the Merger Control Regulation is concerned with transactions that bring about a change in the structure of the market (as opposed to "behavioral restraints" where the parties remain independent legal entities). The EU takes a much more formal approach than does § 7 of the U.S. Clayton Act. A concentration under the European Merger Control Regulation exists only in two circumstances. The first circumstance is a merger of two or more previously independent undertakings or parts of undertakings.[592] Mergers come in several forms, all of which constitute concentrations under the Merger Control Regulation. Perhaps the most common form of merger is where one or more independent undertakings are merged into another undertaking with the latter retaining its identity and the former losing its identity. Another form of merger exists where two or more undertakings amalgamate into a new undertaking and cease to exist as separate legal entities.

The second circumstance in which a concentration is deemed to occur under the Merger Control Regulation is an acquisition of direct or indirect control of the whole or parts of another independent undertaking.[593] The majority of transactions falling under the Merger Control Regulation are of this category. The means by which control is attained is generally irrelevant. According to the Merger Control Regulation it can occur "by purchase of securities or assets, by contract or by *any other means*."[594] In this respect, the EU Merger Control Regulation takes a much more formalistic approach that does § 7 of the U.S. Clayton Act which does not require a change of control.

In both constellations, merger or acquisition of control, the transaction must be between two or more independent undertakings. The requirement of independent undertakings precludes the application of the Merger Control Regulation to a merger or change of control between two undertakings belonging to the same corporate group, for example, a company reorganization. As competition law generally assumes that undertakings under common ownership do not compete with one another, a concentration between such undertakings cannot have a negative effect on competition. Hence, such transactions fall outside the scope of the Merger Control Regulation.[595] If, for example, Google engages in an internal restructuring whereby it merges its wholly owned

---

591. 15 U.S.C. § 18a.
592. Merger Control Regulation at art. 3(1)(a). The fact that one of the undertakings is state-owned does not preclude the application of the Merger Control Regulation. *See, e.g.*, M.7318, Rosneft/Morgan Stanley Global Oil Merchanting Unit (Sept. 3, 2014) ¶2; M.4934, Kazmunaigaz/Rompetrol (Nov. 19, 2007) ¶1.
593. Merger Control Regulation at Article 3(1)(b).
594. *Id.* at art. 3(1)(b) [emphasis added].
595. Comm'n Consolidated Notice, 2008 O.J. (C 95) 1, 15 ¶51.

subsidiary Google Austria into Google Germany, this transaction—although perhaps legally a merger under applicable corporate law—would not be considered a concentration for purposes of the Merger Control Regulation.

(2) The Concept of Control

The concept of change of control is critical not just to the application of the Merger Control Regulation but also to competition law in general. For example, an agreement between two legal entities under common control falls outside the scope of Article 101 of the TFEU. Control is also important in the context of Article 102 of the TFEU. When determining whether an undertaking occupies a dominant position, for example, the market shares of all of the undertakings belonging to the same group are aggregated. As will be discussed below, the concept of control will arise in the context of determining whether the particular transaction falls under the Merger Control Regulation and in determining the market shares of the undertakings concerned.[596] This is one point where the EU Merger Control Regulation departs significantly from § 7 of the U.S. Clayton Act which does not require a change of control.

Control over an undertaking is generally determined by reference to the right to take or influence types of decisions concerning the business. A majority shareholder of a large corporation may legally control that entity and its various subsidiaries, but not be in a position to control every decision or even the day-to-day operations of the business. Control, for purposes of the Merger Control Regulation, does not necessarily require the power to exercise decisive influence on the day-to-day running of an undertaking. The crucial element is the ability to exercise decisive influence over the strategic business decisions of the undertaking.

Strategic decisions relate to such things as the appointment of senior management, financial planning and adoption of the budget, the approval of the business plan and major investments.[597] If the equity holders are not directly involved in the business, the right to appoint senior management tends to be the primary factor the Commission examines. The assumption is that the individuals who are members of the management organs will not disregard the wishes of the shareholders who have control over their positions.[598]

Many transactions involve the acquisition of only certain assets of another undertaking rather than all of the assets. Moreover, many asset transactions involve the acquisition of only intangible assets such as intellectual property. The Merger Control Regulation covers the acquisition of parts of undertakings provided that those assets constitute a business with a market presence to which sales revenue can be clearly attributed.[599] This same standard applies if only

---

596. The concept of "control" in the context of competition law may differ from control concepts used in other areas of law such as tax law. Comm'n Consolidated Notice, 2008 O.J. (C 95) 1, 9 ¶23.
597. *See, e.g.*, Celanese/Degussa/JV, 2004 O.J. (L 38) 47, 48 ¶9. Commission Notice on the concept of concentration under Council Regulation 4064/89 on the control of concentrations between undertakings, 1998 O.J. (C 66) 5.
598. Haniel/Cementbouw/JV, 2003 O.J. (L 282) 1, 4 ¶17.
599. Merger Regulation at art. 3(1)(b); Comm'n Consolidated Notice, 2008 O.J. (C 95) 1, 9 ¶24.

intangible assets are being acquired. Whether those assets constitute a business with a market presence to which sales revenues can be clearly attributed must be determined on a case-by-case basis and depends on the nature of the industry in which the target is active.[600] In *Otto/Primondo*, for example, the Otto Group acquired certain trademarks and customer lists of Primondo.[601] Because both of these companies were active in the home shopping business, the trademarks and customer lists were considered to constitute a business.

The acquisition of licenses (as opposed to ownership of the intellectual property) is treated somewhat differently. The transfer of licenses is only considered a change of control of an undertaking for purposes of the Merger Control Regulation if (1) the licenses are exclusive at least in a certain territory and (2) the transfer of such licenses will transfer the sales-generating activity.[602]

(3) Legal, Contractual and De Facto Control

There are three types of control: legal, contractual and de facto. Legal control is the most obvious form of control. It occurs when one undertaking acquires control over another undertaking on the basis of an equity interest or on the basis of a contract giving it the authority to manage the activities of the company and determine its business policy. For example, the German sugar producer Südzucker acquired a 24.99 percent interested in ED&F Man, one of Südzucker's competitors. This was sufficient to give Südzucker control over ED&F because the subscription agreement and the articles of association of ED&F gave Südzucker special veto rights over strategic decisions such as annual budget, business plan, and appointment of directors.[603]

The acquisition of an equity interest is not always necessary for a finding of legal control. Legal control may also exist based on the rights acquired by contract.[604] In *Bosch/Rexroth*, for example, Bosch entered into a business leasing agreement with Rexroth according to which Bosch secured the exclusive rights to operate the business of Rexroth without acquiring an equity interest in Rexroth.[605] The shareholders of Rexroth agreed to vote their shares in accordance with the instructions of Bosch. The compensation received by Bosch for managing the business was independent of the profitability of the business. Nonetheless, the transaction was considered an acquisition of legal control of Rexroth by Bosch.

---

600. Case M. 6360, NYNAS/Shell/Harburg Refinery (Sept. 2, 2013) ¶¶7-8.
601. Case M. 5721, Otto/Primondo Assets, (Feb. 16, 2010).
602. Comm'n Consolidated Notice, 2008 O.J. (C 95) 1, 9 ¶24.
603. Case No. M.6286, Südzucker/ED & F Man, May 16, 2012, 2014 O.J. (C 160) 11, 11 ¶5 (summary of decision). The Commission has proposed extending its jurisdiction under the Merger Control Regulation to minority interests even when the acquisition of those interests do not give the holder control. Commission, White Paper: Towards more effective EU merger control, COM (2014) 449 final (July 9, 2014).
604. Case M.3940, Lufthansa/Eurowings (Dec. 22, 2005) ¶6.
605. Bosch/Rexroth, 2004 O.J. (L 43) 1, 2 ¶11.

A similar situation existed in *Lehman Brothers/SCG/Starwood/LeMeridian*.[606] In this merger case, two U.S. companies, Lehman Brothers and Starwood Capital Group, created a new legal entity in Europe in which they each held a 50 percent interest. The newly created entity was then to acquire 23 Le Meridian hotels and contract with Starwood Hotels and Resorts Worldwide (independent of Starwood Capital Group) to manage the hotels. Although Starwood Hotels and Resorts Worldwide did not have an equity interest in the newly formed company which owned the hotels, the Commission concluded that the management contracts entered into with Starwood Hotels and Resorts Worldwide gave it joint control with Lehman Brothers and Starwood Capital Group.

Control may be acquired for purposes of the Merger Control Regulation even if the acquirer does not secure legal or contractual control over the target. If, because of the factual circumstances, the acquiring undertaking is able to exercise a decisive influence over the business of the target even without acquiring legal control, de facto control is deemed to exist. De facto control exists when the circumstances give the authority to manage the activities of the company and determine its business policy even though these rights are not secured by legal rights emanating from a majority shareholding or from a contract with the company or other shareholders.[607]

In *Konica/Minolta*, for example, Konica held only 38 percent of Sekonic (a manufacturer of light meters for cameras whose shares were publicly traded on the Tokyo Stock Exchange).[608] Although Konica did not have any contractual rights to control Sekonic, the Commission concluded that Konica held de facto control over Sekonic. It based its reasoning on the fact that the rest of the shares were widely dispersed (no other shareholder held more than 5 percent) and many of the other shareholders were passive investors who did not normally show up at shareholder meetings. Consequently, although Konica held only a 38 percent equity interest, a review of past shareholders meetings revealed that it held a de facto voting interest of around 58 percent. Consequently, it was considered to have de facto control of Sekonic.

The decisive consideration in de facto control cases is the disposition of the other shareholders. If the remaining shareholders are widely dispersed and only passive investors, the holder of a substantial minority interest may nonetheless have de facto control over the undertaking. Widely dispersed means that none of them individually holds a significant percentage. Passive investors are shareholders who are not likely to participate in the shareholders' meetings or coordinate their votes with other shareholders so as to give them greater influence. The Commission commonly looks to shareholder participation in previous years to make this determination.[609]

---

606. Case No. M.3858, Lehman Brothers/SCG/Starwood/LeMeridian, July 20, 2005.
607. T-332/09, Electrabel v. Comm'n, 2012 E.C.R. II-___, at ¶81; Comm'n Consolidated Notice, 2008 O.J. (C 95) 1, 17 ¶59.
608. Case M. 3091, Konica/Minolta (July 11, 2003).
609. *See, e.g.*, Case M. 4994, Electrabel/CNR (June 10, 2009) at ¶15 *aff'd on appeal* T-332/09, Electrabel v. Comm'n, 2012 E.C.R. II-___; Case M. 3330, RTL/M6 (Mar. 12, 2004) ¶8.

In the *Tchibo/Beiersdorf* decision, Tchibo (a German coffee company) increased its shareholding in Beiersdorf (a German personal hygiene product manufacturer) from 30.36 percent to 49.96 percent.[610] The Commission concluded that this increase gave Tchibo sole control over Beiersdorf as the annual shareholders' meetings were typically attended by shareholders representing only 78 percent of the outstanding voting shares.

On the other hand, the existence of other large shareholders may suggest that the largest minority shareholder does not have control over the undertaking. In *SAPA/Remi Claeys Aluminum*, the U.S. aluminum producer Alcoa did not have control over the Swedish company Elkem despite the fact that it held 46.53 percent interest in that company.[611] The decisive factor was the size of the second (39.44 percent interest) and third (7.88 percent interest) largest shareholders. Together, they served as a counterweight to the exercise of influence by Alcoa.

Common minority protection rights do not generally arise to the level of granting a minority shareholder de facto control. For example, the company laws of many member states provide for the protection of minority shareholders in order to protect their financial interests. This normal protection of the rights of minority shareholders is typically related to decisions on changes to the company's governing documents, an increase, or a decrease in the capital or liquidation.[612] The fact that a minority shareholder has these rights does not generally confer control. A veto right, for example, which prevents the sale or winding-up of the company does not confer control on the minority shareholders.[613] Minority shareholdings not arising to control fall outside the scope of the Merger Control Regulation. Consequently, Article 101 and 102 of the TFEU potentially apply.[614]

(4) Sole and Joint Control

The taxonomy of EU merger control practice differentiates between the acquisition of sole control and the acquisition of joint control. The distinction is important because it determines the product markets examined by the Commission in the substantive structural analysis. For example, it is presumed that the parents in a joint venture in a particular product market will not compete with one another in that same market as a result of the joint venture. Both sole control and joint control can be either on a legal, contractual or de facto basis.

Sole control is normally acquired on a legal basis where an undertaking acquires a majority of the voting rights of a company. It is not in itself significant

---

610. Case M. 3329, Tchibo/Beiersdorf (Dec. 16, 2003).
611. Case M. 3170, SAPA/Remi/Orkla (June 17, 2003).
612. The rights of minority shareholders under EU company law are discussed in Chapter V.
613. Case M. 062, Eridania/ISI (July 30, 1991).
614. *See, e.g.*, Cases 142 & 156/84, British-American Tobacco Company Ltd. v. Comm'n, 1987 E.C.R. 4566, 4577 ¶37; EEC Commission Intervenes Against Anti-Competitive Agreement for Acquisition of Shares in Competing Company (Hudson's Bay), IP/88/810 (Dec. 15, 1988).

that the acquired shareholding is 50 percent of the share capital plus one share[615] or that it is 100 percent of the share capital.[616] However, an interest below 50 percent can still be the basis for sole control as illustrated by *General Motors/ Daewoo Motors*.[617] In that case, General Motors, Suzuki Motor Corporation, and the Daewoo Creditors Committee set up an entity to purchase certain assets of Daewoo Motors. GM held only 42 percent of the entity, Suzuki 15 percent, and the Daewoo Creditors Committee 33 percent. However, GM had the right to appoint 5 of the 10 members of the board of directors where a minimum of six votes were necessary to take a decision. The fact that GM had the ability to create deadlock led the Commission to conclude that GM had sole control. In other words, GM had to approve any strategic decision of the entity even though it could not unilaterally take the strategic decisions.

Even though a company may not be able to unilaterally decide the strategic decisions of the entity which it partially owns, it may still be deemed to control that entity. In *Belgacom/BICS/MTN*, for example, Belgacom, Swisscom and MTN (Dubai) Limited owned 57.6 percent, 22.4 percent, and 20 percent respectively of BICS, a global telecommunication company. The strategic decisions of BICS were to be taken by its board of directors. However, board decisions on strategic issues required the vote of at least one Belgacon director and one Swisscom director or the vote of one Belgacom director and one MTN director. The Commission concluded that this structure gave Belgacom "negative sole control" of BICS as no strategic decisions could be taken without the consent of Belgacom (even though Belgacom could not take those decisions itself).[618]

In addition, two or more undertakings may acquire joint control over another undertaking. Joint control exists where two or more undertakings or persons have the possibility of exercising decisive influence over another undertaking.[619] Decisive influence in this sense normally means at least the power to block actions that determine the strategic commercial behavior of an undertaking. Unlike sole control, which confers the power upon a specific shareholder to determine the strategic decisions of an undertaking, joint control is characterized by the possibility of a deadlock situation resulting from the power of two or more parent companies to block strategic decisions.[620]

The clearest form of joint control exists where the shareholders hold equal shares in the undertaking (absent an agreement between them which gives one of the shareholders control). In *Kesko/ICA/JV*,[621] for example, Kesko (a Finnish grocery store chain) and ICA AB (a Swedish grocery store chain) agreed to transfer their respective businesses in Estonia, Latvia, and Lithuania to a newly formed entity in which they each held a 50 percent interest and equal representation on the board of directors. Neither of the shareholders was granted additional rights to unilaterally decide the strategic decisions affecting

---

615. Case M. 296, Crédit Lyonnais/BFG Bank, (Jan. 11, 1993).
616. Case M. 299, Sara Lee/BP Food Division, (Feb. 8, 1993).
617. Case M. 2832, General Motors/Daewoo Motors, (July 22, 2002).
618. Case M. 5584, Belgacom/BICS/MTN, (Oct. 26, 2009) ¶11.
619. Comm'n Consolidated Notice, 2008 O.J. (C 91) 1 ¶63.
620. *Id.* at 17 ¶62.
621. Case M. 3464, Kesko/ICA/JV, (Nov. 15, 2004).

the joint venture. In *AMSSC/BE Group/JV*,[622] Luxembourg steel conglomerate ArcelorMittal and Swedish BE Sverige established a joint venture to which they each contributed their respective distribution activities for flat carbon steel. Each parent company held a 50 percent interest in the joint venture and absolute equality in voting power and representation on the board of the joint venture.

Joint control may, however, exist even where there is no equality between the equity interests of the parent undertakings. This is the case where minority shareholders have additional rights which allow them to veto the strategic decisions of the undertaking.[623] These veto rights may be set out in the statute of the joint venture or conferred by agreement of the parent undertakings. The veto rights themselves may operate by means of a specific quorum required for decisions taken at the shareholders' meeting by the board of directors to the extent that the parent companies are represented on this board.

The additional rights may be set out in the statute of the joint venture or conferred by agreement of the parent undertakings. The veto rights themselves may operate by means of a specific quorum including the minority shareholder vote required for decisions taken at the shareholders' meeting or by the board of directors. In *John Wood Group/Siemens/JV*, for example, John Wood Group held 51 percent of the joint venture entity and Siemens held the remaining 49 percent. Nonetheless, there was joint control over the entity because the governing documents required the affirmative vote of a board representative from both John Wood Group and Siemens for the strategic decisions.[624]

It is also possible that strategic decisions are subject to approval by a corporate body, e.g., board of directors, where the minority shareholders are represented and form part of the quorum needed for such decisions. For example, Sony and Time Warner each held a 37 percent interest in CDnow, an online retailer of music and videos. Pursuant to a "Governance Agreement" they entered into, the consent of both Time Warner and Sony was required for any strategic decisions taken by CDnow. In those circumstances, the Commission concluded that Time Warner and Sony jointly controlled CDnow.[625]

In another case, three separate companies, Cintra, Abertis, and Itinere established a Spanish company to distribute electronic toll passes. Abertis held 50 percent of the voting shares of the JV entity and Centra and Itinere each held 25 percent. Although Abertis, with its 50 percent, was able to appoint four of the eight board members of the JV, and Cintra and Itinere just two members each, certain strategic decisions relating to the strategic plan, budget, and appointment of directors required a supermajority of 76 percent or seven of the eight members of the board.[626] An additional factor influencing the Commission's decision that the JV entity was jointly controlled was the fact that each of the shareholders had the right to appoint one of the members of the senior management of the JV entity.[627]

---

622. Case M. 5072, AMSSC/BE Group/JV (April 10, 2008) ¶6.
623. Comm'n Consolidated Notice, 2008 O.J. (C 95) 1, 18 ¶65.
624. Case M. 7083, John Wood Group/Siemens/JV (April 24, 2014) ¶7.
625. Case Comp/JV.25, Time Warner/Sony/Cdnow (Nov. 19, 1999).
626. Comp M.7075, Cintra/Abertis/Itinere (Feb. 18, 2014) ¶¶8-10.
627. *Id.* at ¶11.

(5) Concentrative Joint Venture

A joint venture is an undertaking which is jointly controlled by two or more other undertakings. The concept of joint control is discussed above. Because the Merger Control Regulation is concerned only with concentrations, it applies only to transactions bringing about a lasting change in the structure of the undertakings concerned. It is therefore necessary to distinguish between joint ventures that bring about a lasting change in the structure of the undertakings concerned (i.e., concentrative joint ventures) and those joint ventures that do not bring about a lasting change (i.e., nonconcentrative joint ventures). The significance of the distinction is that only concentrative joint ventures can be considered concentrations. Nonconcentrative joint ventures are reviewed under Article 101 of the TFEU.

The basic requirement for a jointly controlled entity to qualify as a concentrative joint venture is that it must perform, on a lasting basis, all the functions of an autonomous economic entity.[628] Although there is no exhaustive catalog of factors used to determine whether an undertaking qualifies as an autonomous economic entity, the two most important criteria are whether the undertaking has adequate management dedicated to its daily operations and access to sufficient financial resources to conduct its business as an independent competitor.[629]

In the *Airbus/SITA* decision, for example, Airbus and SITA Information Network Computing agreed to establish a jointly controlled entity to develop and sell aircraft connectivity services such as Internet access and in-seat telephony.[630] Airbus was a manufacturer of aircraft, and SITA was a provider of information technology systems. As the joint venture was provided with its own facilities, resources, and personnel, and would eventually sell its product to independent commercial airlines (and not just to Airbus), it was deemed an autonomous economic entity and hence a concentrative joint venture.

If, however, the joint venture entity is merely assuming one of the functions within the business activities of its parents, it is not likely to qualify as a concentrative joint venture.[631] For example, if two mobile telephone manufacturers set up a joint venture entity to which they contribute their respective manufacturing operations, and the joint venture entity sells these jointly manufactured phones only to its parent companies, the joint venture entity is unlikely to be considered an autonomous economic entity as it is merely completing one business activity for its parent companies. The ability to sell to third parties is an important indication of autonomy. If the joint venture entity sells at least 50 percent of its output to third parties, this is an indication that it is an autonomous economic entity.[632]

---

628. Merger Control Regulation at art. 3(4).
629. Consolidated Jurisdictional Notice at 24 ¶94. *See, e.g.,* Celanese/Degussa/JV, 2004 O.J. (L 38) 47, 48 ¶10.
630. Case M. 3657, Airbus/SITA/JV (Dec. 15, 2004).
631. Consolidated Jurisdictional Notice at 24 ¶95.
632. *Id.* at 25 ¶98.

The presence of the parent companies in upstream or downstream markets of the joint venture suggests a lack of commercial autonomy.[633] However, the fact that the joint venture relies almost entirely on sales to its parent companies or purchases from them only for an initial start-up period does not normally affect the concentrative character of the joint venture because it may be necessary for the success of the joint venture to have a source of supply or a customer during its start-up phase.[634] As a general rule, a period of three years will be the maximum duration for the start-up period.

Finally, the contemplated duration is an important consideration in determining whether the joint venture is an autonomous economic entity. The rule is that the parents must intend that the joint venture operate on a lasting basis. The Commission will commonly infer that the joint venture is set up on a lasting basis if the parents commit sufficient managerial and financial resources to allow it to act as an autonomous economic entity.[635] The Commission has not committed to a minimum duration, but it has considered three years to be too short.[636]

(6) *Concentrations Involving the Same Parties*

Merger law is about the aggregation of market power by change of control transactions which alter the structure of the competitive relationships in the market. As discussed above, only transactions between two or more independent undertakings fall under the Merger Control Regulation. The requirement of independence precludes the application of the Merger Control Regulation to a merger or change of control between two undertakings belonging to the same corporate group.[637] The basic idea is that if one company already controls another company, there is a unity of commercial interest between those entities.

Joint ventures, however, present an exception to this rule. A joint venture is an undertaking controlled by two or more other independent undertakings. Consequently, if one of the joint venture partners buys out the other joint venture partners, there is a change from joint control of an undertaking to sole control of an undertaking. Such a transaction will generally have no adverse effect on competition because the entity acquiring sole control is already deemed to have control.[638] As the *MAN Roland/Omnigraph* case illustrates, however, the Commission applies the notions of concentration and EU dimension rigidly and requires changes from joint control to sole control to be notified under the Merger Control Regulation even though the undertaking acquiring control already has

---

633. *Id.* at 24 ¶97. If the parents are active in upstream product markets which happen to be in different geographic markets in which the JV is active, the chance of coordination is less likely than if the upstream markets cover the same geographic market in which the JV is active. Case Comp/M.5399, Mubdala/Rolls-Royce/JV (Feb. 16, 2009) at ¶38.
634. Case M. 7083, John Wood Group/Siemens/JV (April 24, 2014) ¶9.
635. Consolidated Jurisdictional Notice at 26 ¶103.
636. Comp/M.3858, Lehman Brothers/Starwood/Le Meridian (July 20, 2005).
637. Consolidated Jurisdictional Notice at 15 ¶51.
638. *See, e.g.*, Case M. 3388, Ford Motor Company/Polar Motor Group (April 30, 2004) ¶6; Case M. 3330, RTL/M6 (Mar. 12, 2004) ¶17; Case M. 3385, Cargill/BCA (April 1, 2004) ¶16.

joint control. In that case, MAN Roland acquired 44 percent of an entity in which it already held 56 percent. Nonetheless, the transaction had to be notified under the Merger Control Regulation. The Commission then concluded that "the transaction will have no significant impact on competition."[639]

The Commission is inconsistent on whether a reduction of the number of joint controlling parents constitutes a concentration. In its Consolidated Notice, it stated that such transactions "will normally not lead to a notifiable transaction."[640] In *Norske Skog/Abitibi/Papco*,[641] however, three independent undertakings each held 33.3 percent of the joint venture. When one of the parents sold its shares to the other two shareholders, thereby resulting in a change of joint control by three undertakings to joint control by two undertakings, the Commission nonetheless scrutinized the transaction under the Merger Control Regulation.

The breakup of a joint venture, and the return to each of the joint venture partners of the assets which each partner had respectively contributed may constitute a concentration for purposes of the Merger Control Regulation.[642] In *Philips/Lucent Technologies* Philips and Lucent established a joint venture into which they merged their respective consumer telephone businesses.[643] Philips held 60 percent and Lucent 40 percent of the joint venture, but Lucent was granted certain rights which gave it joint control of the joint venture. Several years later, parties announced the unwinding of the joint venture. This too was treated as a concentration even though there was no negative effect on competition.[644]

Even the change in the nature of control over an already controlled entity may constitute a change in control for purposes of the Merger Control Regulation. In *Kraft Foods/United Biscuits*, for example, Kraft Foods already exercised control over United Biscuits, but did not hold all of the shares. When it subsequently acquired the remaining shares, the Commission took the position that this transaction resulted in a "change in the quality of control... and therefore constitutes a concentration."[645]

(7) *Concentrations Involving Related Parties*

More difficult cases involve businesses which are not part of the same group, but which are related such that there is some degree of unity of interest. This includes, in particular, distributors, agents and franchisees. The creation of a distribution relationship, agency relationship of franchise relationship does not generally constitute a concentration for purposes of the Merger Control Regulation. For

---

639. Case M. 1448, MAN Roland/Omnigraph (May 5, 1999) ¶13. *See also* Consolidated Jurisdictional Notice at 23 ¶89.
640. Consolidated Jurisdictional Notice at 23 ¶90.
641. Case M. 2493, Norske Skog/Abitibi/Papco (July 31, 2001).
642. *See also* Case No. M.3294, Exxon/Mobil-BEB (Nov. 20, 2003); Case No. M.3291, Preem/Skandinaviska Raffineradi (Dec. 1, 2003) (acquisition of 25 percent interest by 75 percent shareholder constituted a change of control).
643. Case M. 966, Philips/Lucent Technologies (Aug. 20, 1997).
644. Case M. 1358, Philips/Lucent Technologies II (Jan. 6, 1999).
645. Case M. 4343, Kraft Foods/United Biscuits, (Aug. 25, 2006) ¶3.

example, the acquisition by a manufacturer of one of its distributors may be a concentration for purposes of the Merger Control Regulation.

(b) EU Dimension

(1) Thresholds

Not all concentrations fall under the Merger Control Regulation. As discussed above, the Commission may scrutinize only those concentrations with an EU dimension. The Merger Control Regulation relies on sales volumes to determine which transactions should be notified in advance. The Merger Control Regulation provides two tests to determine which concentrations have an EU dimension. However, to understand the application of the thresholds, a brief explanation of the concept undertakings concerned is necessary because the thresholds are based on the sales of the undertakings concerned.

Although there is no definition of "undertaking concerned," the basic idea behind the concept is to capture those parties to the transaction whose market shares are relevant for the substantive analysis. In the case of a merger, the undertakings concerned are the merging undertakings. If, for example, Company A merges into Company B, with Company B being the surviving entity, the undertakings concerned are Company A and Company B. In the case of an acquisition, the buying undertaking is considered an undertaking concerned. On the seller's side, however, only the acquired entity is considered an undertaking concerned and not the seller. Therefore, if Microsoft Corporation were selling one of its subsidiaries to a third party, the sales of the subsidiary—and not Microsoft Corporation as a whole—are relevant.[646]

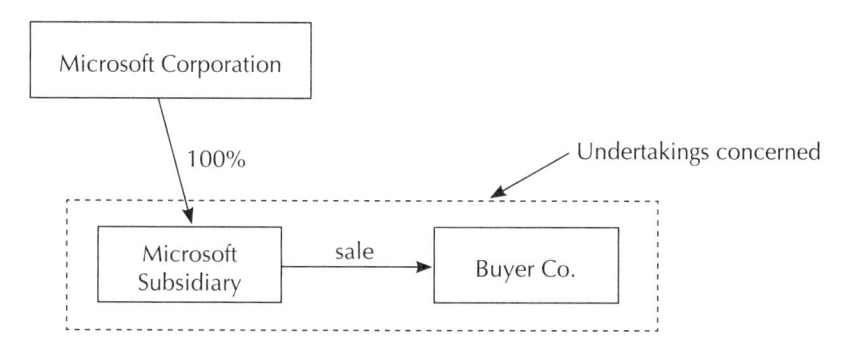

If two undertakings create a new joint venture, they are each undertakings concerned. If the joint venture entity already exists, then there are three undertakings concerned: the two joint venture parents and the joint venture itself.[647]

---

646. *See* Case T- 282/02, Cementbouw Handel & Industries v. Comm'n, 2006 E.C.R. II-331, 371 ¶116 *aff'd on appeal* Case C-202/06 P, Cementbouw Handel & Industries v. Comm'n, 2007 E.C.R. I-12129.
647. Consolidated Jurisdictional Notice at 32 ¶140.

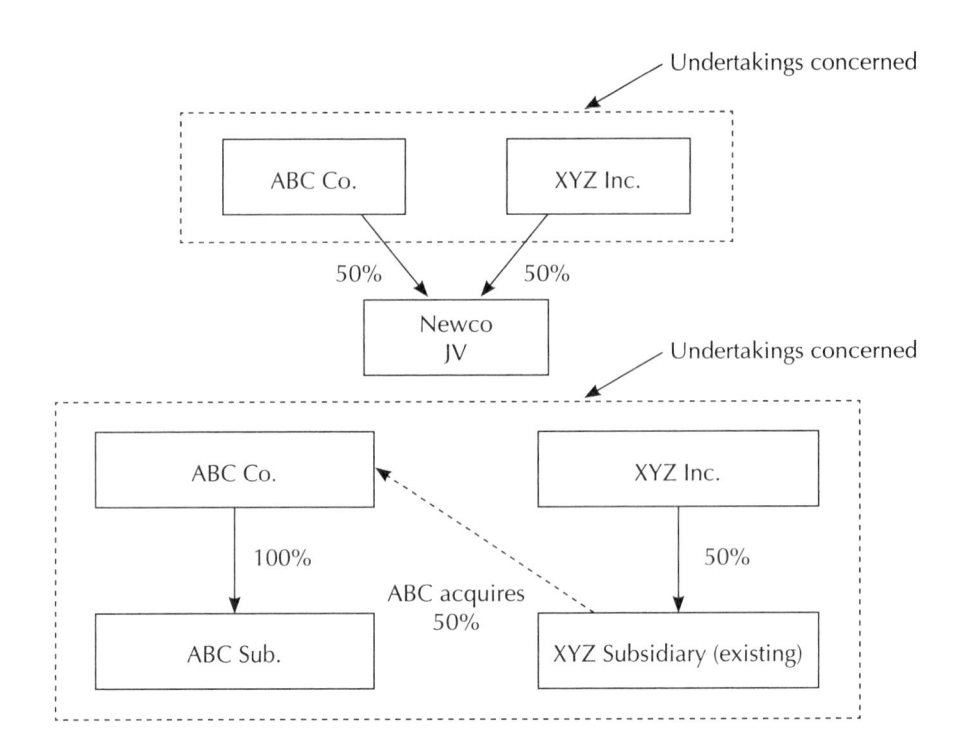

```
                    ┌─────────────────────────────────────┐  ← Undertakings concerned
                    │  ┌──────────┐      ┌──────────┐    │
                    │  │ ABC Co.  │      │ XYZ Inc. │    │
                    │  └────┬─────┘      └────┬─────┘    │
                    └───────┼─────────────────┼──────────┘
                         50%│                 │50%
                            ▼                 ▼
                          ┌──────────┐
                          │  Newco   │              ← Undertakings concerned
                          │   JV     │
                          └──────────┘
  ┌─────────────────────────────────────────────────────────┐
  │   ┌──────────┐                       ┌──────────┐       │
  │   │ ABC Co.  │◄─ ─ ─ ─ ─ ─ ─ ─ ─ ─ ─│ XYZ Inc. │       │
  │   └────┬─────┘                       └────┬─────┘       │
  │     100%│                                 │50%          │
  │         │         ABC acquires            │             │
  │         ▼              50%                ▼             │
  │   ┌──────────┐                  ┌────────────────────┐  │
  │   │ ABC Sub. │                  │ XYZ Subsidiary     │  │
  │   └──────────┘                  │ (existing)         │  │
  │                                 └────────────────────┘  │
  └─────────────────────────────────────────────────────────┘
```

One should note in this context that once the undertakings concerned are identified, it is the sales revenues not only of the immediate legal entities involved in the transaction, but also any legal entities that belong to the same group.[648] For example, if the Irish subsidiary of the Japanese company Sony Corporation were to acquire another company, the sales of the entities Sony corporate group—i.e., all entities controlled by the parent company—would be considered as sales of that undertaking concerned. The fact that the other members of the Sony group have nothing to do with the particular transaction, or may not even be in the same market, is irrelevant for the application of the thresholds. This is consistent with the basic assumption of competition law that legal entities which are part of the same corporate group do not compete with one another.

It is important to recognize that the criteria used to attribute sales to the undertaking concerned are not the same as the criteria used to determine control in the context of determining whether the transaction qualifies as a concentration. For the purposes of aggregating sales, the sales of the following undertakings will be considered sales of the undertaking concerned: (a) undertakings in which the undertaking concerned owns more than half the equity capital or business assets, and (b) undertakings in which the undertaking concerned has the power to exercise more than half the voting rights or has the power to appoint more than half of the members of the governing organ of the company or has the right to manage the undertakings affairs will be considered sales of the undertaking

---

648. If the undertaking concerned is state-owned, however, it is considered its own ultimate parent entity. The sales volumes of the state are not taken into account. M.4934, Kazmunaigaz/ Rompetrol (Nov. 19, 2007) ¶5. Consolidated Jurisdictional Notice at 43 ¶192.

concerned.[649] In most cases, the sales of a controlled undertaking will be aggregated. If, however, the control is de facto control, the sales of the de facto controlled undertaking will only be aggregated if one of the circumstances listed in Article 5(4) of the Merger Control Regulation exists.[650]

As mentioned above, the concept of undertakings concerned is used to apply the thresholds which comprise the tests to determine whether a particular concentration has an EU dimension. There are two separate tests codified in the Merger Control Regulation. According to the "initial test" (Article 1(2) Merger Control Regulation), a concentration has an EU dimension if all three of the following criteria are met:[651]

- The undertakings concerned have combined worldwide sales of €5 billion.
- At least two of the undertakings concerned each have sales in the EU of €250 million.
- The undertakings concerned each do not achieve more than two-thirds of their respective EU-wide sales in one and the same member state.

Aggregate sales within the meaning of the Merger Control Regulation make up the amounts derived by the undertakings concerned in the preceding financial year from the sale of products and the provision of services falling within the undertakings' ordinary activities after deduction of sales rebates and of value-added tax and other taxes directly related to sales.[652] Intra-group sales are not included.[653] For example, if one affiliate within a corporate group has sales to another affiliate in that same group, those sales are not included in determining whether the thresholds are fulfilled. The location of the sales is generally determined by the location of the purchaser of the goods or services from which the sales revenues are derived.[654] If, for example, a U.S. company sells widgets to a customer in Latvia, the revenues from this sale are considered Latvian.

If the concentration does not fulfill the thresholds of the "initial test," there is a second test to be applied. The "supplementary test" has four requirements, all of which must be fulfilled in order for the concentration to have an EU dimension:[655]

- The combined aggregate worldwide sales of all the undertakings concerned must be more than €2.5 billion.
- In each of at least three member states, the combined aggregate sales of all the undertakings concerned must be more than € 100 million.

---

649. Merger Control Regulation at art. 5(4).
650. Consolidated Jurisdictional Notice at 41 ¶184.
651. In order to convert sales into euros, the average exchange rate for the 12 months concerned is used. This rate is available on the website of the European Commission, http://europa.eu.int/comm/competition/mergers/others/exchange_rates.html.
652. Merger Control Regulation at art. 5(1).
653. Consolidated Jurisdictional Notice at 37 ¶167.
654. Merger Control Regulation at art. 5(1).
655. *Id.*

- In each of these three member states (i.e., the member states identified under the second prong of the test), the sales of each of at least two of the undertakings concerned must be more than €25 million.

- The aggregate EU-wide sales of at least two of the undertakings concerned must be more than €100 million.

- The undertakings concerned each do not achieve more than two-thirds of their respective EU-wide sales in one and the same member state.

The initial test and the supplemental test are mutually exclusive and not cumulative. In other words, if either test is met, the concentration has an EU dimension. The *Emerson Electric/Motorola* case provides an example of a concentration that does not meet the initial test but only meets the supplemental test.[656] In that case, Emerson Electric, Co., a U.S. conglomerate, acquired all of the assets of Motorola's embedded computing division. As that division did not have sales in the EU exceeding €250 million,[657] the transition did not have an EU dimension under the initial test even though the parties had combined worldwide sales exceeding €5 billion. However, the transaction had an EU dimension under the supplementary test as their combined sales exceeded €100 million in three member states, in each of those member states they each had sales of €25 million, and they each had sales in the EU exceeding €100 million.

(2) Concentrations Without an EU Dimension

In the event that a transaction qualifies as a concentration, but fails to meet the EU dimension requirements, the Commission does not have exclusive jurisdiction over the transaction.[658] The merger control regimes of the member states are potentially applicable to such transactions. However, there are two circumstances in which the Commission may assume jurisdiction over a concentration without an EU dimension: (1) referrals by a member state to the Commission and (2) referrals by the parties to the Commission.

A member state (or member states) may request the Commission to review a concentration without an EU dimension. The only requirements for a member state referral are that there is (1) a concentration, (2) the concentration has an effect on trade between member states and (3) threatens to significantly restrict competition within the member state making the request.[659] The decision to assume jurisdiction over a concentration without an EU dimension is within the discretion of the Commission. If the Commission decides to assume jurisdiction

---

656. Case M. 4933, Emerson Electric/Motorola (Nov. 20, 2007).
657. As discussed above, on the seller's side, only the sales of the business being sold (and not the sales of the entire seller group) are included in the assessment.
658. *See* Case T-282/02, Cementbouw Handel & Industrie v. Comm'n, 2006 E.C.R. II-331, 370 ¶114. Similarly, the Commission does not have exclusive jurisdictions over transactions which do not constitute concentrations. For example, a member state may require notification of minority investments which do not arise to the acquisition of control or do not constitute full function joint ventures. *See, e.g.*, § 37(3) of the German Gesetz gegen Wettbewerbsbeschränkungen *available at* http://www.gesetze-im-internet.de/gwb/BJNR252110998.html.
659. Merger Control Regulation at art. 22(1).

over the concentration, all member states are precluded from reviewing it under their respective national competition law regimes.[660]

According to the Commission, there are two categories of cases in which it will exercise its discretion to accept a referral from a member state.[661] The first is where the transaction gives rise to serious competition concerns in one or more markets whose geographic dimension is broader than national.[662] The second category of cases is where the transaction involves relevant markets encompassing several member states. The greater the number of member states impacted by the concentration, the more likely it is that the Commission will assume jurisdiction. In *Coca-Cola Hellenic Bottling Company/Lanitis Bros.*, for example, the only affected market was Cyprus, and the Commission refused to assume jurisdiction.[663] In *Procter & Gamble/Sara Lee Air Care*, by way of contrast, the Commission assumed jurisdiction because the transaction had an effect on 10 different member states.[664]

The second circumstance in which a concentration without an EU dimension may fall under the jurisdiction of the Commission is when the transaction falls within the competition laws of at least three member states and the parties have requested the Commission to assume jurisdiction.[665] In *Calyon/Société Générale/Newedge*, for example, the creation of a joint venture by Credit Agricole and Société Générale did not have an EU dimension because more than two-thirds of their respective sales were in France.[666] However, the transaction would have had to have been notified in 16 member states. Consequently, the parties made a request to the Commission under Article 4(5) of the Merger Control Regulation. As no member states objected, the Commission assumed jurisdiction over the transaction even though it did not have an EU dimension.

The possibility for the parties to request the Commission to assume jurisdiction is a recognition that the fundamental purpose of the Merger Control Regulation is to relieve undertakings of the burden of multiple premerger filings. This referral option available to the parties creates the potential that the parties tactically apply to the Commission because they anticipate an adverse decision at the member state level. However, the possibility of "forum shopping" is mitigated somewhat by the rule that the parties cannot wait to see how the member states will decide the case before making the request to the Commission. The request to the Commission must be made prior to any notification to the

---

660. *Id.* at art. 24(4).
661. Case M. 4124, Coca-Cola Hellenic Bottling Company/Lanitis Bros. (Feb. 24, 2006) ¶20.
662. Comm'n Notice on Case Referral in respect of concentration, 2005 O.J. (C 56) 2, 4 ¶27. *See, e.g.*, Case M. 4215, Glatfelter Crompton Assets (Dec. 20, 2006) ¶12.
663. Case M. 4124, Coca-Cola Hellenic Bottling Company/Lanitis Bros. (Feb. 24, 2006) ¶23.
664. Case M. 5828, Procter & Gamble/Sara Lee Air Care (March 31, 2010) at ¶16.
665. Merger Control Regulation at art. 4(5). The request for referral is made to the Commission on Form RS prior to the formal notification of the transaction. The request is then transmitted by the Commission to the member states. Comm'n Notice on Case Referral in Respect of Concentrations, 2005 O.J. (C 56) 2, at ¶49.
666. Case M. 4912, Calyon/Société Générale/Newedge (Dec. 19, 2007).

member states. In addition, the Commission will only assume jurisdiction in such cases if none of those member states object to the Commission asserting jurisdiction over the transaction.

(c) Review Procedure

As discussed above, the purpose of the European Merger Control Regulation is to allow the Commission to review the transaction ex ante to determine whether, if consummated, it would threaten competition. Hence, the Merger Control Regulation requires all concentrations with an EU dimension to be notified to the Commission prior to their implementation.[667] Once the notification is received, the Commission has basically three options. First, it may decide that the transaction does not fall under the Merger Control Regulation because it does not qualify as a concentration with an EU dimension.[668] Alternatively, it may review the transaction and determine that it does not raise any serious threat to competition (the substantive standard applied to the transaction is discussed below).[669] Conversely, it may consider that the transaction does present a threat to competition and decide to initiate a second phase investigation.[670]

Each of these three decisions needs to be taken within 25 working days after the notification is submitted to the Commission.[671] During that period, the parties are prohibited from consummating the transaction. In addition, the Commission may grant a referral to a member state[672] or entertain commitments (i.e., proposals from the parties to alter the transaction to alleviate concerns raised by the Commission) from the parties.[673] For example, the parties may offer to sell off a particular branch of the business to a third party. If the Commission receives a request from a member state or the parties submit commitments, the period in which the Commission has to respond increases to 35 working days.[674] The duration of the second phase is 90 working days. Although seemingly technical, these time periods are often of significant practical importance.

(d) Relationship Between the Merger Control Regulation and Articles 101 and 102

There are two reasons why a particular transaction may not fall under the Merger Control Regulation: either the transaction does not qualify as a concentration

---

667. Merger Control Regulation at art. 4(1). The Commission has imposed fines on companies which have failed to observe the waiting period even where the concerntration did not raise substantive issues. Case C-84/13 P, Electrabel v. Comm'n, 2014 E.C.R. I-____; Case M. 7184, Marine Harvest/Morpol (July 23, 2014). The Commission has the authority to use onsite investigations to determine whether the merging parties have "jumped the gun" and taken measures to intergrate prior to the expiration of the waiting period. Case M. 4734, INEOS/Kerling (Jan. 30, 2008).
668. Merger Control Regulation at art. 6(1)(a).
669. *Id.* at art. 6(1)(b).
670. *Id.* at art. 6(1)(c).
671. *Id.* at art. 10(1).
672. *Id.* at art. 9.
673. *Id.* at art. 6(2).
674. *Id.* at art. 10(1).

or it does not have an EU dimension. If the reason for the inapplicability of the Merger Control Regulation is that the transaction does not qualify as a concentration, clearly Articles 101 and 102 potentially apply, as do the national competition laws.[675] For example, Article 101 of the TFEU would apply to the acquisition of a minority interest which does not qualify as the acquisition of control.[676]

If the transaction qualifies as a concentration, but it does not have an EU dimension, Articles 101 and 102 of the TFEU apply only theoretically.[677] As the Commission considers the application of Articles 101 and 102 to concentrations to be inappropriate,[678] the Merger Control Regulation makes the application of these Treaty provisions to such facts difficult by declaring the regulations which give the Commission its investigative and enforcement authority for Articles 101 and 102 inapplicable to concentrations.[679] Consequently, although Articles 101 and 102 remain theoretically applicable, for practical purposes they are not enforceable by the Commission.[680]

The second fundamental issue relating to the relationship between the Merger Control Regulation and Articles 101 and 102 arises in transactions that do fall under the Merger Control Regulation. Whereas the Merger Control

---

675. T-411/07 R, Air Lingus Group plc v. Comm'n, 2008 E.C.R. II-417, 450 ¶103. In the case of *Covisint*, the B2B platform created jointly by DaimlerChrysler, Ford, and GM, the creation of the platform did not qualify as a concentration under the Merger Control Regulation. European Comm'n Press Release, Commission Clears the Creation of the Covisint Automotive Internet Marketplace (July 21, 2001). However, it was reviewed as a concentration by the German Cartel Office. Decision of the Bundeskartellamt of Sept. 25, 2000 (B5-34100-U40/00).
676. *See* Cases 142 & 156/84, Philip Morris/Rothmans, 1987 E.C.R. 4566, 4577 ¶37; EEC Commission Intervenes Against Anti-Competitive Agreement for Acquisition of Shares in Competing Company (Hudson's Bay), IP/88/810 (Dec. 15, 1988); Olivetti/Digital, 1994 O.J. (L 309) 24 (the standard is whether it leads to the coordination of the competitive behavior of the parties).
677. In addition, the merger laws of the member states may also apply. As discussed above, it is possible for the member states to refer concentrations to the Commission even if they do not have an EU dimension.
678. This does not mean that Article 102 of the TFEU is irrelevant to the application of the Merger Control Regulation. As discussed above, the Merger Control Regulation is designed to prohibit distortions of competition through the accumulation of market power before the distortion occurs. One could argue that this distortion is adequately policed by Article 102 which prohibits such distortion. Indeed, the Commission—in approving a transaction under the Merger Control Regulation—has recognized that the potential application of Article 102 is sufficient to police the competitive risk arising out of the merger. Case M. 7202, Lenovo/Motorola Mobility (June 26, 2014) ¶45. This reasoning could be employed to challenge the necessity of a merger control regime.
679. Merger Control Regulation at art. 21(1).
680. It might not be long berfore this ambiguity is legislatively addressed. The EU Commission has issued a White Paper proposing that the Commission have the authority to examine under the Merger Control Regulation the acquisition of non-controlling interests. Commission, White Paper: Towards more effective EU merger control, COM(2014) 449 final (July 9, 2014).

Regulation is in the form of a regulation, Articles 101 and 102 of the TFEU form part of primary EU law. As discussed in Chapter I, in the hierarchy of legal norms, primary EU law (i.e., the Treaties) take precedence over secondary law. Therefore, Articles 101 and 102 potentially apply to concentrations (even those with an EU dimension). The Merger Control Regulation addresses this potential conflict by declaring the regulations which give the Commission its investigative and enforcement authority for Articles 101 and 102 inapplicable to concentrations.[681] The legal situation is similar to concentrations without an EU dimension. Although Articles 101 and 102 theoretically remain applicable, for practicable purposes they are not enforceable by the Commission.[682]

The third aspect of the relationship between Article 101 of the TFEU and the Merger Control Regulation concerns joint ventures. As discussed above, concentrative joint ventures qualify as concentrations in the context of the Merger Control Regulation. The creation of a concentrative joint venture may lead to the coordination of the competitive behavior of undertakings that remain independent. For example, if two pharmaceutical companies create a joint venture to develop and produce a new drug, their efforts in this specific area may easily spill over into other areas involving related drugs. In such cases, Article 101 would appear to be the most appropriate legal norm to apply to this cooperation between the two parent companies. However, Article 2(4) of the Merger Control Regulation provides that those cooperative effects will be assessed within the same procedure as the concentration using the substantive standards developed under Article 101. The benefit for the parties is that separate analysis and procedure under Article 101 is not necessary. This is illustrated in *Bertelsmann/Planeta*. In that case, Bertelsmann (the German media conglomerate) and Planeta Corporacion (the Spanish publishing house) established a joint venture to distribute books online in Spain. As both parent companies remained independent competitors in the upstream market for publishing books in Spain in the context of the merger review procedure, the Commission examined whether the joint venture would facilitate the coordination of their competitive behavior on this upstream market.[683]

(e) Role of National Law

The European Merger Control Regulation was actually adopted to relieve firms from the burden of regulatory compliance. The law accomplishes this task by giving the Commission exclusive jurisdiction over concentrations with an EU dimension.[684] The member states are precluded from applying their own merger control laws to the transaction. This has immense practical implications for undertakings. Instead of having to secure permission from a number of national regulators, the parties to the transaction can seek clearance from the Commission

---

681. *Id.*
682. This does not preclude the possibility that the application of Article 101 or 102 of the TFEU to concentrations be raised in the context of private litigation in national courts.
683. Case M. 5838, Bertelsmann/Planeta (Aug. 23, 2010) ¶25.
684. Merger Control Regulation at art. 21(2).

and be on their way. As an exception to the rule that the Commission has exclusive jurisdiction over concentrations with an EU dimension, it is possible for the Commission to refer a case to a member state.

(1) Referral to a Member State

Even if a concentration has an EU dimension, the Commission may refer a concentration to a member state for review under national competition law. The Commission's authority to refer a case to a member state depends on whether the geographic dimension of the relevant markets is limited to that member state and the concentration threatens to significantly affect competition only within that member state.[685] In *Blackstone/NHP*, for example, the U.S. Blackstone Group notified the EU Commission of its planned acquisition of the UK company NHP plc.[686] As Blackstone is a large group, and NHP had significant sales in the UK, the concentration had an EU dimension under the initial test of the Merger Control Regulation. As NHP, the target company, was primarily active in the UK in the market for nursing homes for the elderly, the UK Office of Fair Trading submitted an application for a referral under Article 9 of the Merger Control Regulation. The Commission concluded that the market for care for the elderly was a distinct market, and that elderly people generally sought care within a short radius of their home. Although the transaction technically had an EU dimension, the Commission decided that it was appropriate to refer the case to the UK Office of Fair Trading.[687]

The *Hochtief/Holzman* case illustrates how the national authorities may use this referral possibility to thwart forum shopping.[688] The largest German contractor, Holzmann, was owned 20 percent by Hochtief, 15 percent by the Deutsche Bank, and the rest other minority shareholders. Holzmann proposed to increase its shareholding to 35 percent. Under German competition law, this was a concentration. Under EU law, however, no concentration occurred because there was no change of control. As the Merger Control Regulation did not apply, Germany was able to apply its law on concentrations.

Once the German Cartel Office indicated that it would take a negative position in the case, Hochtief and Deutsche Bank entered into a pooling agreement regarding their voting rights incident to their respective shareholdings. This pooling agreement had the effect of triggering a change of control. Consequently, the transaction qualified as a concentration with an EU dimension.[689] The German Cartel Office submitted an application for referral under Article 9 of the Merger Control Regulation. Once the Commission was about to refer the case back to the German Cartel Office, the parties abandoned the merger.

---

685. Merger Control Regulation at art. 9(2). The finding of a threat to competition is based on a preliminary review and without prejudice to the final assessment. Comm'n Notice on Case Referral in respect of concentrations, 2005 O.J. (C 56) 2, 6 ¶17. In other words, the fact that a case is referred to a member state does not necessarily mean the transaction will be prohibited.
686. Case M. 3669, Blackstone/NHP (Feb. 1, 2005).
687. *Id.* at ¶36.
688. Case M. 892, Hochtief/Deutsche Bank/Holzmann, 1997 O.J. (C 127) 10.
689. *Id.*

(2) Legitimate Interests of the Member States

The strict application of the rule that the Commission has exclusive jurisdiction over concentrations with an EU dimension requires the relinquishment of control by the member states over important sectors of the national economies. For example, a member state may have a particular interest when two electricity suppliers in that country merge. The Merger Control Regulation provides that the member states may take "appropriate measures" to protect legitimate interests (e.g., public security and plurality of the media) which are not taken into account by the Merger Control Regulation. Of course, the inclusion of this possibility in the Merger Control Regulation is subject to abuse.

In *Portugal v. Commission*, the Portuguese Government tried to rely on this exception in blocking the joint acquisition by a Spanish and German cement manufacturer of the dominant Portuguese cement manufacturer even though the transaction qualified as a concentration with an EU dimension. The Commission decided, and the ECJ confirmed, that Portugal had no legitimate interest in preventing the transaction.[690]

(3) Transactions Qualifying as Concentrations Under National Law

As addressed above, the European Merger Control Regulation is only applicable to concentrations. The concept of concentration requires a change of control.[691] The respective member states, however, might use a different standard for triggering the application of their respective laws applicable to structural restraints of competition. Therefore, a transaction may fall under the merger control rules of a member state without falling under the European Merger Control Regulation even if the thresholds for establishing an EU dimension are fulfilled. The UK, for example, uses a "material influence" standard which creates the possibility that the acquisition of minority shareholdings falls under the UK merger control law but not the EU Merger Control Regulation.[692] In such cases, EU law does not preempt the application of national law. Conversely, a transaction which qualifies as a concentration under national law does not necessarily qualify as a concentration under the Merger Control Regulation.[693]

(f) Extraterritorial Application

The European Merger Control Regulation has two important legal consequences. First, it requires all concentrations with an EU dimension to be notified to the Commission in advance. The Merger Control Regulation does not contain a specific limitation on its extraterritorial reach. The two tests for EU dimension identified above are the only tests relied on by the Commission for determining which concentrations it exerts jurisdiction over. The actual location of the

---

690. Case C-42/01, Portugal v. Comm'n, 2004 E.C.R. I-6079.
691. Merger Control Regulation at art. 3(1)(b).
692. *See, e.g.*, Coca-Cola Company/Fresh Trading Company, Decision of the OFT (ME/4091/09) dated June 11, 2009, in which the acquisition of 15-20 percent of a company was considered a concentration for purposes of UK law.
693. Case T-411/07, Aer Lingus v. Comm'n, 2010 E.C.R. II-3695, 3707 ¶27.

entities therefore becomes irrelevant for the jurisdictional application of the Merger Control Regulation. For example, the acquisition of a U.S. company by a U.S. company from a U.S. company must be notified to the Commission under the Merger Control Regulation if it qualifies as a concentration with an EU dimension regardless of the effect on competition in the EU.[694] The acquisition of the U.S. chewing gum company Wrigley by the U.S. candy company Mars had to be notified to the Commission.[695] In *Daimler/Beiqi Foton Motor Co.*, a joint venture to manufacture and sell trucks in China had to be notified to the Commission.[696] In *Diageo/Heineken/Olfitra*, Heineken, Diageo, and Olfitra established a joint venture to produce and sell beer in Namibia.[697] Nonetheless, the transaction had to be notified to the Commission.

The second important legal consequence of the Merger Control Regulation is its prohibition of anticompetitive concentrations. Here again, the location of the concentration is irrelevant. Theoretically, of course, the Commission is constrained by the limitations which international law imposes on the extraterritorial application of laws. In practice, however, if the thresholds for an EU dimension are fulfilled, the EU courts are likely to hold that the extension of jurisdiction in a particular case conforms with international law. The Commission's authority under international law to scrutinize such concentrations occurring outside the EU was first addressed by the General Court in *Gencor v. Commission*.[698] The case involved the acquisition of joint control of platinum mining operations in South Africa by a South African company and an English company. In response to the argument that public international law prevented the Commission from prohibiting the transaction, the General Court held that public international law only requires that the proposed concentration have a foreseeable, substantial, and immediate effect in the EU.[699] The court concluded that the Commission had jurisdiction under international law in this case.

The General Court in *Gencor* did not address the separate question of the requirements of public international law for exercising jurisdiction over concentrations with an EU dimension but without an effect in the EU. In other words, can the Commission impose sanctions on parties for failure to notify a concentration with an EU dimension if that transaction has no anticompetitive effect in the EU? This issue has not been specifically addressed by the Commission or the courts. The likely response of the EU courts would be that the thresholds provided by the Merger Control Regulation establish enough of a potential effect in the EU to satisfy public international law.

---

694. *See, e.g.*, Case M. 7061, Huntsman Corp./Rockwood Holdings (Sept. 10, 2014) summary at 2015 O.J. (C 67) 7; Case M. 5588, General Motors/Delphi Steering II (Aug. 12, 2009); Case M. 4933, Emerson Electric/Motorola (Nov. 20, 2007).
695. Case M. 5188, Mars/Wrigley (July 28, 2008).
696. Case M. 6073, Daimler/Beiqi Foton Motor Co. (Feb. 14, 2011).
697. Case M. 3176, Diageo/Heineken/Olfitra (July 10, 2003).
698. Case T-102/96, Gencor v. Comm'n, 1999 E.C.R. II-759.
699. *Id.* at ¶92.

10.2 Substantive Analysis

(a) Compatibility with the EU

The substantive standard applied by the Commission in reviewing concentrations with an EU dimension is whether the concentration would significantly impede effective competition in the EU, in particular as a result of the creation or strengthening of a dominant position. Although the creation or strengthening of a dominant position may simultaneously impede competition significantly, the creation and strengthening are treated as two separate elements that must be cumulatively fulfilled.[700] Hence, the creation or strengthening of a dominant position may (theoretically) be permissible if it does not significantly impede competition in the EU.[701] Nonetheless, the focus is clearly on whether the concentration creates or strengthens a dominant position.

The abstract definition of a dominant position in the context of the Merger Control Regulation is the same as that used in the application of Article 102 of the TFEU: a position of strength that allows the undertaking to act independently of its competitors, customers, and consumers.[702] In making this determination, particular emphasis is given to the market shares of the parties involved.[703] Consequently, the application of the Merger Control Regulation necessarily involves defining the markets relevant to the transaction. The principles used to define the relevant market are essentially the same as those used to define the market for the purpose of applying Article 102.

(b) Relevant Effects

In applying the substantive standard, the Commission attempts to identify what effects the concentration would have on the relevant markets. As this is a prospective assessment, it is often more challenging than applying Article 101 and 102 of the TFEU. In most cases, the Commission will examine the unilateral effects, the coordinated effects, and the conglomerate effects of the proposed concentration.

(1) Noncoordinated (Unilateral) Effects

There is an inherent tension between buyers and sellers of goods and services. A seller is primarily interested in making as much profit for as long a time as possible. The buyer, however, is interested in securing high quality goods that

---

700. Case T-210/01, General Electric Company v. Comm'n, 2005 E.C.R. II-5596, 5623 ¶87; Case T-87/05, Energias de Portugal v. Comm'n, 2005 E.C.R. II-3753, 3772 ¶45.
701. Case T-5/02, Tetra Laval v. Comm'n, 2002 E.C.R. II-4389, 4432 ¶120 *aff'd on appeal* Joined cases C-12/03 P-DEP and C-13/03 P-DEP, Tetra Laval v. Comm'n, 2010 E.C.R. I-67.
702. Case T-282/02, Cementbouw v. Comm'n, 2006 E.C.R. II-331, 397 ¶195 *aff'd* Case C-202/06 P, Cementbouw Handel & Industries v. Comm'n, 2007 E.C.R. I-12129; Case T-210/01, General Electric Company v. Comm'n, 2005 E.C.R. II-5596, 5633 ¶114; Case T-87/05, Energias de Portugal v. Comm'n, 2005 E.C.R. II-3753, 3772 ¶48.
703. Case T-282/02, Cementbouw v. Comm'n, 2006 E.C.R. II-331, 399 ¶201 *aff'd on appeal* Case C-202/06 P, Cementbouw Handel & Industries v. Comm'n, 2007 E.C.R. I-12129.

meet its requirements at the lowest possible prices. Competition between firms is what motivates them to produce quality goods or provide quality services at low prices. If that competition is removed, reduced, or restricted, the seller will be in a better position to realize a higher profit by increasing prices (without having to increase quality). Although this is a gross oversimplification of the competitive process, it serves as a basic assumption for the regulators.

A concentration may have the effect of eliminating competitive constraints between firms, thereby enhancing the ability of the resulting firm to unilaterally raise prices. Competition restrains competitors from charging whatever price they want for their goods or services. For example, the reason Ford cannot charge whatever price it wants for its automobiles is the competition from the other automobile manufacturers. If you remove this competition, Ford could act unilaterally. If this results from a concentration, a unilateral effect or, in European parlance, a noncoordinated effect is deemed to occur. Whether a concentration has an anticompetitive effect depends on a number of factors, such as the market shares of the parties.

(i) Market Shares

Despite the Commission's pronouncement that market share is merely a "first indication" of market dominance,[704] the combined market share (sometimes referred to as the "aggregate market share") of the merging parties typically plays a critical if not determinative role in the application of the substantive standard under the Merger Control Regulation.[705] It is important to note that the market shares required for a finding of a dominant position in the context of Article 102 of the TFEU discussed above are generally lower than the market shares required by the Commission to prohibit a concentration under the Merger Control Regulation. Although the Commission has not formally adopted this policy, one possible explanation for this difference is that in the context of the application of Article 102, anticompetitive conduct (i.e., abuse) is already present or at least alleged to have existed. The finding of dominance is then of secondary importance. The Merger Control Regulation, however, is prospective: the Commission is required to make a judgment on the potential future effects of a concentration rather than on past conduct as is the case with Article 102.

In using the market shares to assess the impact of the concentration, the Commission assumes that the post-merger combined market share of the

---

704. Guidelines on the assessment of horizontal mergers under the Council Regulation on the control of concentrations between undertakings, 2004 O.J. (C 31) 5, 7 ¶14 [hereinafter Horizontal Mergers Guidelines]; Guidelines on the assessment of non-horizontal mergers under the Council Regulation on the control of concentrations between undertakings, 2008 O.J. (C 256) 6, 9 ¶23 [hereinafter Non-Horizontal Mergers Guidelines]; Case M. 6360, NYNAS/Shell/Harburg Refinery (Sept. 2, 2013) ¶365.
705. Case T-342/07, Ryanair Holdings plc v. Comm'n, 2010 E.C.R. II-3470, 3486 ¶41; Case M. 7052, Lloyds Development Capital/PostNL/TNT Post UK (Jan. 30, 2014) ¶15.

merging parties is the sum of their pre-merger market shares.[706] There is a general understanding that an aggregate market share below 25 percent will not be considered indicative of dominance in the context of the Merger Control Regulation.[707] An aggregate market share between 25 percent and 50 percent in itself is not indicative of dominance, but requires consideration of additional factors.[708] On the other hand, a market share above 50 percent typically creates a rebuttable presumption of market dominance.[709]

As illustrated by the Commission's decision in *Heineken/BBAG*, however, even a high aggregate market share does not necessarily lead to the conclusion that the merger will result in the creation or strengthening of a dominant position if the increase is small.[710] In that case, although the merger of the two competitors resulted in a combined market share of over 80 percent in Greece, the Commission did not decide to initiate a second stage investigation of the transaction. The Commission relied on the fact that the merger would increase Heineken's position only to a de minimis extent. In *Novartis/Hexal*, the acquisition of Hexal by Novartis gave Novartis a 70 percent to 75 percent market share in Germany for a particular osteoporosis drug.[711] There was only one other competitor. Nonetheless, the Commission concluded that the concentration did not present any competitive concerns in this market because the market share of Hexal was less than 5 percent.

In *Tchibo/Beiersdorf*, the Commission confirmed that "an increase of less than 2% cannot lead to the creation or strengthening of a dominant position."[712] In that case, Beiersdorf had a market share in Austria for first-aid bandages of between 40 percent and 50 percent. Tchibo had a market share of less than 5 percent. In *Carlsberg/Holsten*, the proposed acquisition of the Germany

---

706. Case M. 6360, NYNAS/Shell/Harburg Refinery (Sept. 2, 2013) ¶373. It is the market share of the corporate group and not just the specific party to the transaction which is relevant. In Ryanair/Aer Lingus, the Commission even aggregated the market shares of a franchisee which was an independent undertaking. The explanation given by the Commission was that the franchisee was "closely linked to and dependent on [the franchisor] through the franchise agreement." Case M. 6663, Ryanair/Aer Lingus III (Feb. 27, 2013) ¶449.
707. Horizontal Mergers Guidelines at 7 ¶18.
708. Case T-282/06, Sun Chemical Group BV v. Comm'n, 2007 E.C.R. II-2153, 2207 ¶135.
709. Case T-342/07, Ryanair Holdings plc v. Comm'n, 2010 E.C.R. II-3470, 3486 ¶41; Case T-177/04, easyJet Airline Co. Ltd. v. Comm'n, 2006 E.C.R. II-1940, 1996 ¶174 ("almost 50%" creates a presumption of dominance); Case M. 6663, Ryanair/Aer Lingus III (Feb. 27, 2013) ¶¶462-66; Summary of Comm'n Decision of 7 November 2012 declaring a concentration compatible with the internal market and the functioning of the EEA Agreement (Outokumpu/Inoxum), 2013 O.J. (C 312) 11, 14 ¶34; Case M. 3558, Cytec/UCB-Surface Specialties, (Dec. 17, 2004) ¶¶23 & 32.
710. Case M. 3195, Heineken/BBAG, (July 18, 2003).
711. Case M. 3751, Novartis/Hexal, (May 27, 2005).
712. Case M. 7351, Henkel/Spotless Group (Sept. 25, 2014) ¶53; Case M. 3329, Tchibo/Beiersdorf, (Dec. 16, 2003) ¶17. *See also* Case M. 6214, Seagate/HDD Business of Samsung, (Oct. 19, 2011) *reported at* 2012 O.J. (C 154) 8, 11 ¶36.

beer brewer Holsten by the Danish beer brewer gave the combined entity a postmerger market share of between 60 percent and 70 percent in Denmark.[713] Nonetheless, the concentration was approved by the Commission as Holsten had a premerger market share in Denmark of less than 5 percent.

There is no objective standard for determining market dominance in all cases. The European Commission often relies on the Herfindahl-Hirschman Index (HHI) which is the sum of the sum of the squares of the market shares of all firms in the relevant market.[714] For example, a market with five competitors each holding a 20 percent market share is characterized as having an HHI of 2,000 ($20^2 + 20^2 + 20^2 + 20^2 + 20^2 = 2,000$). If two of these competitors were to merge, the postmerger HHI would increase to 2,800.[715] The delta in such a transaction (*i.e.*, the difference between the pre-merger HHI and the post-merger HHI) would be 800.

The Commission generally assumes that a horizontal merger in a market with a postmerger HHI of under 1,000 will not create significant competitive concerns.[716] Similarly, there is a general assumption that unless special circumstances exist, a concentration in a market with a postmerger HHI that is above 1,000 but below 2,000 will not be prohibited if the delta is below 250.[717] If the postmerger HHI is above 2,000, the concentration still will not create competitive concerns absent special circumstances, as long as the delta is below 150.[718]

It is important to remember that reliance on these general standards, particularly for horizontal mergers, may be limited in particular cases. The Commission has been careful to qualify the reliance on the HHI by stating that it may not apply in special circumstances. Examples of special circumstances are: one of the undertakings concerned has a premerger market share of 50 percent or more; the merger involves a potential entrant or a recent entrant with a small market share; one of the undertakings concerned is an important innovator whose strength is not adequately reflected in its market share; one of the firms is a maverick competitor;[719] or there are indications of coordination

---

713. Case M. 3372, Carlsberg/Holsten (Mar. 16, 2004)
714. *See, e.g.*, Case M. 7351, Henkel/Spotless Group (Sept. 25, 2014) ¶20.
715. This is based on the assumption that the merged entity would not lose any market share as a result of the merger, an assumption that does not always conform to reality.
716. Horizontal Merger Guidelines at 7 ¶19.
717. *See, e.g.*, Case M. 3493, Yamanouchi/Fujisawa, (Aug. 18, 2004) ¶14.
718. The reliance on the delta in the context of the HHI is separate from the de minimis increase standard that the Commission has applied in other cases. *See, e.g.*, Case M. 3506, Fox Paine/Advanta (Aug. 20, 2004) ¶32.
719. The term "maverick" as employed in this context refers to an undertaking which is not likely to conform its behavior to the other competitors in a highly concentrated market. As discussed below, the existence of maverick firms reduces the possibility of undertakings in a concentrated market to coordinate their behavior in an anticompetitive manner without actually entering into a conspiracy to do so. For example, in a market with only three competitors, if one of these competitors unilaterally raises its prices, it is unlikely that one of the other competitors will also raise its prices unless it is certain that the third competitor will also raise its prices.

in the market between the competitors.[720] Moreover, the nature of the industry might play an important role in assessing the weight to be given to market shares. In a dynamic market, for example, the market shares of the various competitors might fluctuate. Therefore, a high market share might not be as indicative of market dominance compared to a market where the market shares are stable over a long period of time.[721]

In addition to the market shares of the parties to the horizontal merger, the size and number of other competitors are relevant considerations.[722] The larger the discrepancy between the market shares of the merging parties and those of the next largest competitor, the more likely a finding of dominance based on noncoordinated effects.[723] Conversely, the presence of a large number of smaller competitors or a smaller number of strong competitors could present a significant competitive threat even if the merged entity will have a market share above the dominance threshold.[724]

For nonhorizontal mergers (i.e., vertical and conglomerate mergers), the Commission generally assumes that a vertical merger does not present concerns where the postmerger market share of the new entity in each of the markets concerned is below 30 percent and the HHI in each of these markets is below 2,000.[725] The delta is not relevant because there is no aggregation of market shares. Although these values do not constitute a presumption of legality of a safe harbor for merging firms, the Commission will not extensively investigate such mergers unless "special circumstances" exist, such as the merger involves a company that is likely to expand significantly in the near future, there are significant cross-shareholdings or cross-directorships among the market participants, one of the merging firms is a firm with a high likelihood of disrupting coordinated conduct, or there is evidence of past or ongoing coordination in the industry.[726]

(ii) Product Differentiation

In addition to market shares, in the context of a horizontal merger the Commission also examines the level of product differentiation between the products. A relevant market for purposes of competition law does not have to include only identical products. It may encompass differentiated products. For example, the market for downhill snow skis may encompass racing skis, freestyle skis, and carver skis, even though these are different types of skis. The degree of product differentiation *within* a relevant market is another factor the Commission takes into account in determining whether the concentration

---

720. Horizontal Merger Guidelines at 7 ¶20.
721. Case M. 6281, Microsoft/Skype (Oct. 7, 2011) ¶78.
722. M.7318, Rosneft/Morgan Stanley Global Oil Merchanting Unit (Sept. 3, 2014) ¶28.
723. Case T-282/02, Cementbouw v. Comm'n, 2006 E.C.R. II-331, 399 ¶201 *aff'd on appeal* Case C-202/06 P, Cementbouw Handel & Industries v. Comm'n, 2007 E.C.R. I-12,129; Bosch/Rexroth, 2004 O.J. (L 43) 1, 7 ¶62.
724. Case M. 6773, Canon/IRIS (Feb. 18, 2013) ¶63; Case M. 3401, Danish Crown/Flagship Foods (June 17, 2004) ¶11.
725. Nonhorizontal Mergers Guidelines at 9 ¶25.
726. *Id.* at 9 ¶26.

will strengthen or create a dominant position. Using the example of downhill snow skis, if there is a high degree of product differentiation between the types of downhill skis, the merger of two downhill ski manufactures may not present a significant competitive threat if one of the merging parties sells primarily one type of downhill ski and the other merging party sells primarily a different type of downhill ski, even though their combined market share on the market for downhill skis is well over 50 percent.[727]

Product differentiation (sometimes referred to as the closeness of substitutes) in the context of the review of horizontal concentrations involves two separate sets of relationships: (1) the relationship both between the products offered by the merging firms themselves (as in the downhill ski case discussed above) as well as (2) between the products of the merging firms on the one hand and the remaining competitors on the other. The basic principle the Commission recognizes is that there is greater competition between products with less differentiation.[728] For example, a merger between BMW and Audi would probably be treated differently than a merger between BMW and General Motors. Although they all belong to the market for passenger automobiles, there is generally less product differentiation between BMW automobiles and Audi automobiles (i.e., they are close competitors).

This principle, when applied to the relationship between the merging parties, means that the Commission generally infers that a low level of differentiation between the products of the merging firms (i.e., their products are very similar) is an indication that the merged entity will be able to increase prices postmerger.[729] In *Hutchison 3G Austria/Orange Austria*, for example, evidence that consumers of mobile phone services readily switched between the merging firms (i.e., a high diversion ratio) showed that the merging companies were close competitors and that the transaction would have an anticompetitive effect.[730] Conversely, if the products of the merging firms are not close substitutes, the inference is that there will be a weaker impact on competition arising from the merger.[731]

The principle is also applied to the relationship of the products involved in the merger to the products of third parties that form part of the relevant market. A low level of differentiation between the products of the merging firms and the products of the remaining competitors is an indication that intense competition will exist postmerger.[732] In such cases, customers may more easily switch

---

727. Case M. 3765, Amer/Salomon (Oct. 12, 2005) ¶62.
728. Case M. 7061, Huntsman Corp./Rockwood Holdings (Sept. 10, 2014) summary at 2015 O.J. (C 67) 7, 11 ¶31; Case M. 6796, Aegean/Olympic II, (Oct. 9, 2013) summary at 2015 O.J. (C 25) 7, 11 ¶41.
729. Horizontal Mergers Guidelines at ¶28; Case M. 7400, Federal-Mogul Corporation/TRW Engine Components (Dec. 15, 2014) ¶34; Case M. 6286, Südzucker/ED & F MAN, 2014 O.J. (C 160) 11, 15 ¶38; Case M. 7360, 21st Century Fox/Apollo/JV, (Oct. 9, 2014) ¶59; Case M. 6458, Universal Music Group/EMI Music, 2013 O.J. (C 220) 15, 18 ¶36; Case M. 6266, J&J/Synthes, 2013 O.J. (C 206) 11, 15 ¶43.
730. Case M. 6497, Hutchison 3G Austria/Orange Austria, 2013 O.J. (C 224) 12, 15 ¶38.
731. Case M. 6281, Microsoft/Skype (Oct. 7, 2011) ¶197; Case M. 4910, Motorola/Vertex (Dec. 21, 2007) ¶45.
732. Case M. 6281, Microsoft/Skype (Oct. 7, 2011) ¶198.

between the products of the merged entity and its competitors if the merged entity attempts to raise prices.

(iii) Level of Capacity Usage

Firms in many industries are limited as to their production capacity. For example, a steel mill may be limited as to the amount of tons it can produce in a given time period. Conversely, because of slow demand for its product, it may be producing at a level less than it could. The difference between what a firm is producing and what it could produce is its excess capacity. The existence or lack of excess capacity on the market is used by the Commission as an indication of the potential effect of a horizontal merger.

The existence of excess capacity may serve to mitigate the inference that high market shares are evidence of market dominance. Even a combined market share of 70 percent or greater may not be indicative of a dominant position if significant excess capacity exists in the product market.[733] The assumption of the Commission in such cases is that the competitors of the merged firms could easily increase output if the merged firms attempted to raise prices postmerger.[734] Assume, for example, there is significant excess capacity in the steel market. In other words, the steel manufacturers have the ability to produce substantially more than the market can currently absorb. Even if the two leading manufacturers with a combined market share of over 75 percent merge, they may not be able to increase their prices because the other competitors would simply increase their output by utilizing their excess capacity. Hence, the existence of excess capacity in the industry is used as an inference of strong competition.[735]

If, conversely, the industry is characterized by full (or nearly full) capacity, the Commission assumes that there is greater incentive for the merged entity to indirectly increase prices.[736] The assumption is that the merged entity may be able to increase the price by reducing output as it knows that the other

---

733. *See, e.g.*, Case M. 4215, Glatfelter/Crompton Assets (Dec. 20, 2006) ¶80; Celanese/Degussa/JV, 2004 O.J. (L 38) 47, 55 ¶55; Case M. 3347, Schneider Electric/MGE-UPS (Feb. 5, 2004) ¶40. *But see* Summary of Commission Decision of 7 November 2012 declaring a concentration compatible with the internal market and the functioning of the EEA Agreement (Outokumpu/Inoxum), 2013 O.J. (C 312) 11, 14 ¶38 where the Commission concluded that the remaining excess capacity in the industry was not sufficient to counteract the loss of competition due to the merger of the largest and second largest competitors. The remaining competitors, according to the Commission, would not have sufficient incentive to increase production in order to make a price increase by the merged firms unprofitable. Summary of Commission Decision of 7 November 2012 declaring a concentration compatible with the internal market and the functioning of the EEA Agreement (Outokumpu/Inoxum), 2013 O.J. (C 312) 11, 16 ¶60.
734. Case M. 7009, Holcim/Cemex West (June 5, 2014) ¶298; Case M. 6773, Canon/IRIS (Feb. 18, 2013) ¶50.
735. *See, e.g.*, Case M. 6773, Canon/IRIS (Feb. 18, 2013) ¶50; Boeing/Hughes, 2004 O.J. (L 63) 53, 61 ¶74; Case M. 3401, Danish Crown/Flagship Foods (June 17, 2004) ¶11.
736. Horizontal Mergers Guidelines at ¶32.

competitors may not be in a position to satisfy the demand from customers of the merged entity who may seek alternative sources of supply.[737]

(iv) Potential Competition: Barriers to Market Entry

Similar to excess capacity, potential market entry by undertakings not already in the market serves as a constraint on the ability of merging firms to raise prices after the merger.[738] For example, if two stainless steel manufacturers in Germany merge, the ability of the resulting entity to increase prices in Germany would be limited because of the low barriers to market entry that exist in this market.[739] If the merged entity tried to increase its postmerger prices, it would attract market entry from potential market entrants in surrounding markets. In *Motorola/Vertex*, Motorola proposed acquiring the Japanese company Vertex Standard.[740] Both Motorola and Vertex were active in the market for land mobile two-way radios (for example, the radios used by police and fire-fighters). In approving the acquisition, the Commission concluded:[741]

> There do not appear to be significant barriers that prevent manufacturers that already sell LMR terminals in Europe from increasing their output. Moreover, the parties submit that a number of manufacturers that currently sell Professional LMR terminals for wide-area networks, such as Matsushita, Hitachi, Mitsubishi and Toshiba, could easily enter the market for Professional LMR terminals for local/on-site networks or increase their presence in this market if, for whatever reason, it were to become less competitive. These companies have substantial resources, know-how and brand recognition that would allow them to become significant players in Professional LMR terminals for local/on-site networks. The same applies to certain Consumer LMR terminals manufacturers, such as Uniden, which once sold Professional LMR terminals for local/on-site networks and thus could easily re-enter this market; Giant, the world's leading supplier of Consumer LMR terminals; and Midland and Cobra, the world's second and third largest suppliers of Consumer LMR terminals.

The standard that the Commission applies in determining whether potential competition is relevant as a constraint in a particular case is that the potential entry must be likely, timely, and sufficient.[742] The mere theoretical possibility of an entrant is not sufficient.[743] The Commission will undertake a retrospective

---

737. Case M. 6286, Südzucker/ED & F Man (May 16, 2012), 2014 O.J. (C 160) 11, 16 ¶43 (summary of decision).
738. Case M. 6773, Canon/IRIS (Feb. 18, 2013) ¶54.
739. Case M. 7138, Thyssen Krupp/ACCIAI Speciali Terni/Outokumpu VDM, (Feb. 12, 2014) ¶25.
740. Comp/M.4910, Motorola/Vertex (Dec. 21, 2007).
741. *Id.* at ¶39.
742. Horizontal Merger Guidelines at ¶68.
743. Case T-342/07, Ryanair Holdings plc v. Comm'n, 2010 E.C.R. II-3470, 3561 ¶239.

examination of the market in order to identify what entry has occurred and infer from this the ease of market entry.[744]

The likely criterion requires that potential entry be profitable for the entrant.[745] A firm is unlikely to enter a new market if it is not able to realize a profit by doing so. The less effort required by the potential market entrant to enter the market, the greater the likelihood of entry. For example, market entry is more likely in the lawn mowing business than it is in the shipbuilding business because of differences in the costs associated with entry.

The second criterion, timeliness, concerns the amount of time it would take for the potential market entrant to actually enter the market. It is incomplete to stop the analysis at the first criterion because even if there is a strong likelihood of entry, that specter of entry will be ineffectual as a constraint if it would take many years for the potential entrant to actually become a competitor in the market. As a general rule, entry is timely only if it will occur within two years.[746]

Not all potential market entrants may be able to constrain the market conduct of a dominant competitor even if their entry is likely and timely. The entry must also be sufficient to deter the anticompetitive conduct.[747] Whether the entry is sufficient depends on the facts of the particular case. In general, the entry of a large firm with significant financial and commercial resources (for example, an already established sales network and brand name) is more likely to prove to be a sufficient entrant than a start-up firm with merely a good product.

(v) Size of Customers

One defense to a concentration resulting in a large postmerger market share for the merged entity is the countervailing power argument, i.e., that the strength of the purchasers of the product or service will prevent the seller from exercising its market power.[748] For example, the Commission is not likely to be concerned with a merger of two automobile parts suppliers because their customers, the automobile manufacturers, already exert sufficient buying power to counteract the market strength of the suppliers.[749] One source of countervailing power is the ability of the customer to easily switch suppliers or to enter the market of the supplier and make the product internally.

The countervailing power argument will not be sufficient to mitigate a finding of dominance if only a portion of the customers of the merged entity enjoy countervailing power.[750] Although the larger customers are often able to protect themselves against an otherwise dominant supplier, there is no

---

744. Case M. 6663, Ryanair/Aer Lingus III (Feb. 27, 2013) ¶¶651-60.
745. *Id.* at ¶639.
746. Horizontal Merger Guidelines at ¶74; Case T-342/07, Ryanair Holdings plc v. Comm'n, 2010 E.C.R. II-3470, 3584 ¶294.
747. Horizontal Merger Guidelines at ¶75.
748. Case M. 4910, *Motorola/Vertex*, (Dec. 21, 2007); Case M. 3789, Johnson Controls/Bosch/Delphi SLI, (June 29, 2005) ¶18; Celanese/Degussa/JV, 2004 O.J. (L 38) 47, 64 ¶111; Case M. 3506, Fox Paine/Advanta, (Aug. 20, 2004) ¶37.
749. *See, e.g.*, Comp M.3486, Magna/New Venture Gear (Sept. 24, 2004) at ¶50.
750. Horizontal Mergers Guidelines at ¶67; Case M. 190, Nestlé/Perrier (July 22, 1992) ¶80.

spill-over effect that would protect the smaller customers. In *Allied Signal/ Honeywell*, Honeywell, a U.S. manufacturer of various household and industrial products, planned to merge into Allied Signal, a U.S. manufacturer of aerospace, automotive, and electronics products.[751] The undertakings were competitors on the market for airborne collision- avoidance system processors used in airplanes. The combined market shares of the merged entity would have been in the neighborhood of 75 percent (the only other competitor was Rockwell Collins). In their defense, the parties argued that they would not be able to take advantage of this dominant position by raising prices because of the market power of their customers, i.e., the airline manufacturers. In rejecting this argument, the Commission pointed out that there are many smaller airlines that purchase the processors as replacement parts who would not be in the position to adequately defend themselves against a potential price increase.[752]

(vi) Foreclosure

The primary anticompetitive effect in the context of nonhorizontal mergers is market foreclosure. There are several types of foreclosure. The term "input foreclosure" describes the situation in which the merger reduces access to inputs for the competitors or potential competitors of the merged entity.[753] Assume, for example, that TreeCo Oy, a hypothetical Swedish tree farm, proposes acquiring LumberCo Oy, a hypothetical Finnish lumber company. Assume, further, that TreeCo is one of only two tree farms in Scandinavia, but that LumberCo has plenty of competitors in the lumber market (most of which purchase their wood from TreeCo). After the merger, TreeCo will have little incentive to offer the same conditions to these competitors in the lumber market as it offers to its newly acquired subsidiary. This will make it more difficult for competitors to compete and for potential competitors to enter the market. Consequently, the Commission examines (1) whether the merged entity would have the ability to substantially foreclose access to inputs, (2) whether it would have the incentive to do so, and (3) whether such foreclosure would have a significant detrimental effect on downstream competition.[754]

Customer foreclosure, on the other hand, exists when a vertical merger forecloses access to a sufficient customer base to its actual or potential competitors in the upstream market.[755] In other words, it is a reduction of competition in the downstream market by reducing the number of customers of companies active in the upstream market. If for example, a rubber band manufacturer merges with a rubber company, the rubber band manufacturer is unlikely to purchase rubber from competitors of the rubber company with which it is merging. The competing rubber companies will have one less customer in the downstream

---

751. 2001 O.J. (L 152) 1,11 ¶73.
752. Celanese/Degussa/JV, 2004 O.J. (L 38) 47, 55 ¶55; Case M. 3347, Schneider Electric/ MGE-UPS, (Feb. 5, 2004) ¶40.
753. Guidelines on the assessment of non-horizontal mergers under the Council Regulation on the control of concentrations between undertakings, 2008 O.J. (C 265) 6, 10 ¶31 [hereinafter Vertical Mergers Guidelines].
754. *Id.* at 10 ¶32.
755. *Id.* at 16 ¶58.

market. The foreclosure may also occur if one of the parties holds intellectual property rights required by upstream or downstream competitors. One of the issues in *Lenovo/Motorola Mobility* was whether the acquisition of Motorola Mobility by Lenovo would foreclose access to intellectual property in the smart phone market.[756] As Motorola Mobility was active in the smart phone market and Lenovo - which was active only in the tablet market - owned patents necessary for competitors of Motorola Mobility, one could argue that Lenovo post-merger would have an incentive to foreclose access to these patents once it acquired Motorola Mobility. However, in approving the concentration, the Commission mentioned that this foreclosure was unlikely to occur because Lenovo would be considered to be violating Article 102 of the TFEU if it refused to license its patent rights to competitors of Motorola Mobility.[757]

Similar to its examination of input foreclosure, the Commission examines (1) whether the merged entity would have the ability to foreclose access by reducing its purchases from its upstream competitors, (2) whether it would have the incentive to do so, and (3) whether a foreclosure strategy would have a significant detrimental effect on the downstream market.[758]

The threshold requirement is market power.[759] Without sufficient market power, a firm cannot foreclose upstream or downstream competition. Neither the Commission nor the EU courts have identified a market share level that would presumptively give the firm sufficient market power to engage in foreclosure. The determination will depend on the particular facts of the case and the nature of the markets involved.

(vii) Evidence

As the discussion above illustrates, determining market dominance is an imprecise science. The primary source of information on the relevant markets is the parties themselves. When submitting a notification, the parties are required to define the relevant markets and their respective positions on those markets as well as the structure of the markets.[760] In most cases, the characterization presented by the parties establishes the parameters in which the Commission examines the transaction. The Commission is not generally in a position to discount the characterization presented by the parties who are actually active in the relevant markets. Nonetheless, the Commission will often rely on external sources of evidence to at least confirm the characterization and information provided by the parties.

The primary source of external evidence are other firms active in the same or related markets. In the notification, the parties are required to identify their competitors and their customers. Once it has received the notification, the Commission will commonly contact these firms to confirm the facts presented by

---

756. Case M. 7202, Lenovo/Motorola Mobility (June 26, 2014).
757. Vertical Mergers Guidelines at 13 ¶45.
758. *Id.* at 16 ¶59.
759. Case M. 7052, Lloyds Development Capital/PostNL/TNT Post UK (Jan. 30, 2014) ¶17.
760. The undertakings are requierd to submit a specific form of notification as set forth in Commission Regulation (EC) No. 802/2004, 2004 O.J. (L 133) 1.

the parties.[761] The responses by third parties - particularly customers - is often a revealing and sometimes determinative source of information.[762] In addition, the Commission may rely on the results of investigations conducted by the national authorities in earlier cases involving the same market. This is particularly the case when the markets are national in their geographic dimension.[763]

The Commission may also try to conduct its own investigation into the markets based on information in its files and available on the Internet or trade publications. In *Group 4 Falck/Securicor*, Falck, the Danish security services provider, and Securicor, the British security services provider, proposed to merge their businesses. The Commission came across a press release of Falck issued several years earlier which boldly declared that it had a market share of 35 percent. It was difficult for the company to then claim in this transaction that it was an insignificant player in the market.[764]

(2) Coordinated Effects

The discussion of structural restraints of competition until now has focused on the loss of the competitive relationship between the parties to the concentration (noncoordinated or unilateral effects). However, the particular concentration may also have an anticompetitive effect involving firms not party to the concentration. As discussed above in the context of Article 102 of the TFEU, oligopoly theory suggests that in certain industries and in certain market conditions, it may be more rational for a firm to conform its behavior to that of the other firms rather than to compete.

In order to understand how this occurs, it is helpful to start with the realization that firms generally try to secure the highest prices possible for their products or services. Although an agreement between competitors to increase their prices would achieve this objective, such conduct is prohibited by Article 101 of the TFEU. In an oligopoly, however, firms can achieve this same objective by tacitly coordinating their prices—even without any collusion between them. Using the example presented in the discussion of Article 102, if there are only four gas stations in an isolated town in Poland, one of those gas stations could unilaterally increase its prices with the hope or intention that the other competitors also increase their prices. The incentive for them is that they could all increase their profits because the price level would be higher than it would be in a nonoligopolistic market.

From a regulatory perspective, Articles 101 and 102 may not always be the most effective instruments to address this situation. Both of these legal norms are remedial in nature; they apply only once the collusion or the abuse has occurred.

---

761. *See, e.g.*, Case M. 4215, Glatfelter/Crompton Assets (Dec. 20, 2006) ¶3.
762. Case M. 7351, Henkel/Spotless Group (Sept. 25, 2014) ¶50; Case M. 6360, NYNAS/Shell/Harburg Refinery (Sept. 2, 2013) ¶¶59-67. Although the Commission will also solicit the views of the competitors of the merging firms when defining the relevant market, it typically does so in conjunction with and in order to confirm the views of the customers. *See, e.g.*, Case M. 6360, NYNAS/Shell/Harburg Refinery (Sept. 2, 2013) ¶¶106-112.
763. *See, e.g.*, Case M. 3396, Group 4 Falck/Securicor (May 28, 2004) ¶109.
764. *Id.* at ¶110.

The merger laws, however, are preventative in nature; the Commission reviews the transaction before it is implemented. Consequently, the Merger Control Regulation affords the Commission the opportunity to prevent the creation of an anticompetitive oligopolistic market structure.

In addition, addressing the oligopoly problem in the context of the Merger Control Regulation avoids the evidentiary challenges that the Commission must overcome in the context of applying Articles 101 and 102 of the TFEU. In the context of Article 101, for example, the Commission has the burden of proving the existence of collusion. This is often a difficult task.[765] Moreover, the collusion that occurs in the context of an oligopoly may be less than is required by Article 101. As supra-competitive price may be the natural result of an oligopoly without collusion, it falls outside the scope of Article 101.

The Merger Control Regulation may be applied to prohibit a concentration if the concentration will lead to a market structure that would create the incentive or likelihood of tacit coordination between the competitors, provided four conditions are fulfilled.[766] First, the merger must lead to an oligopolistic market structure. The market structure required for the application of the doctrine is unclear. The merger of two competitors resulting in a combined market share in excess of 70 percent would likely attract the close scrutiny of the Commission.[767] However, as a general rule, the existence of three or four competitors of equal strength would probably not permit the conclusion that the structure of the market would facilitate tacit coordination.[768]

In *Price Waterhouse/Coopers & Lybrand*, two of the leading accounting firms proposed to merge.[769] In one of the affected markets, the market for auditing and accounting services for large clients (which the Commission considered a relevant product market), the merger would have meant the reduction from six to five competitors. The Commission recognized that the post-merger market would have many of the characteristics to facilitate tacit coordination: stagnant demand, price inelasticity of demand, structural links between the competitors (in the form of professional associations and common regulatory oversight). However, given the number of competitors remaining in the market, the Commission concluded that the likelihood of collusion was remote: "From a general viewpoint, collective dominance involving more than three or four suppliers is unlikely simply because of the complexity of the interrelationships involved, and the consequent temptation to deviate."[770]

The mere existence of an oligopolistic structure is not sufficient to support the inference that the merger will lead to tacit coordination between the competitors. An additional requirement is that the market characteristics must

---

765. *See, e.g.*, Joined Cases C-2/01 P and C-3/01 P, Bundesverband der Arzneimittel-Importeure eV v. Comm'n, 2004 E.C.R. I-64 (concluding that the Commission did not adequately prove collusion).
766. Horizontal Merger Guidelines at ¶39; Nonhorizontal Merger Guidelines at ¶79.
767. *See, e.g.*, DSM/Roche Vitamins, 2004 O.J. (L 82) 73, 82 ¶74.
768. Price Waterhouse/Coopers & Lybrand, 1999 O.J. (L 50) 27, 42 ¶103.
769. *Id.*
770. *Id.* at 42 ¶103. *See also* Linde/AGA, 2002 O.J. (L 120) 1 ¶45 *et seq.*

be such so as to allow the competitors to be able to monitor to a sufficient degree whether the terms of coordination are being adhered to.[771] In other words, the market must be transparent. As the Commission recognizes, if each of the competitors was not able to monitor the conduct of the other competitors, tacit coordination would be difficult if not impossible.[772] In *Norddeutsche Affinerie/ Cumerio*, for example, one of the competitors held a minority interest in the other main competitor. The Commission concluded that as a result of this minority shareholding (13.75 percent), that minority shareholder could sufficiently monitor the activities of the competitor.[773]

The third requirement is that the coordination must be sustainable.[774] Tacit coordination is typically precarious and can be threatened endogenously as well as exogenously. Even in an oligopoly, there is often an incentive to "cheat" on the tacit coordination by lowering prices. By doing so, a maverick competitor can increase its market share. According to the Commission, "coordination is not sustainable unless the consequences of deviation are sufficiently severe to convince coordinating companies that it is in their best interest to adhere to the terms of the coordination."[775] Consequently, the Commission requires the existence of a credible deterrent mechanism to impose discipline on a maverick.[776] This necessitates a close examination of the facts of each case. In *Norddeutsche Affinerie/Cumerio*, for example, the spare production capacity of one of the competitors was identified as an adequate deterrent mechanism.[777] This is because the competitor with spare capacity would be in a position to easily and quickly match any attempts by competitors to depart from the tacit coordination by increasing their sales volumes.

The tacit coordination can also be threatened endogenously by companies that are not a part of the coordination, such as customers, potential competitors, and nonparticipating competitors. For example, a customer with significant buying power may be able to dissuade coordination by playing the competitors off each other. Competitors in an oligopolistic market may also be dissuaded from coordinating their behavior by potential competitors. Tacit coordination in an oligopolistic market tends to create supra-competitive profits for the participating firms. Markets characterized by supra-competitive profits often attract market entry from companies not already in that market. Consequently, barriers to market entry and spare capacity play an important role in the assessment.

---

771. Case T-342/99, Airtours PLC v. Comm'n, 2002 E.C.R. II-2592, 2613 ¶62; M.7009, Holcim/Cemex West (June 5, 2014) ¶134.
772. M.7009, Holcim/Cemex West (June 5, 2014) ¶132; Case M. 5950, Munksjo/Arjowiggins (Feb. 21, 2011) ¶92.
773. Case M. 4781, Norddeutsche Affinerie/Cumerio (Jan. 23, 2008) ¶186.
774. Case T-342/99, Airtours PLC v. Comm'n, 2002 E.C.R. II-2592, 2613 ¶62.
775. Case M. 4781, Norddeutsche Affinerie/Cumerio (Jan. 23, 2008) ¶188.
776. Case M. 5950, Munksjo/Arjowiggins (Feb. 21, 2011) ¶92.
777. Case M. 4781, Norddeutsche Affinerie/Cumerio (Jan. 23, 2008) ¶188.

(3) Conglomerate Effects

Concentrations between undertakings which are not active in either horizontally or vertically related markets are often referred to as conglomerate mergers.[778] For example, the acquisition of Wrigley by Mars was considered a conglomerate merger because gum (Wrigley) and chocolate (Mars) are neither horizontally nor vertically related markets.[779] As the Commission recognizes,[780] conglomerate mergers generally present the least risk to competition because they do not result in the aggregation of market shares. Nonetheless, the Commission does examine the conglomerate effects of such mergers.

(i) Tying and Bundling

Conglomerate mergers may allow the merged entity to leverage its power in one market to achieve a result in another market that could not otherwise be achieved through competition. Although leveraging may manifest itself in numerous constellations, the Commission is primarily interested in the ability of the merged entity to engage in tying or bundling.[781] As discussed above in the context of Article 102 of the TFEU, the practice of tying refers to the practice where the seller conditions the sale of a product or service where the seller is dominant on the purchase of a product or service where the seller is not dominant.[782]

Tying is potentially relevant in the context of mergers because a merger may give an undertaking the opportunity to engage in anticompetitive tying. In *Intel/McAfee*, for example, the Commission concluded that the acquisition of McAfee, Inc. (a manufacturer of security software to protect against viruses being transmitted through the Internet) by Intel Corporation (central processing units (i.e., chips) for computers) would allow Intel to make the sale of its chips (market share between 80 percent and 90 percent) conditional on the willingness of the chip customer to also purchase security software from the combined Intel.[783]

The practice of bundling is another form of leveraging. The Commission distinguishes between pure bundling and mixed bundling. The term "pure

---

778. Nonhorizontal Mergers Guidelines, at 6 ¶5.
779. Case M. 5188, Mars/Wrigley (July 28, 2008).
780. Case M. 6281, Microsoft/Skype (Oct. 7, 2011) ¶141; Case M. 5984, Intel/McAfee, (Jan. 26, 2011) ¶121; Nonhorizontal Mergers Guidelines, at ¶92.
781. *See, e.g.*, Case M. 6381, Google/Motorola Mobility (Feb. 13, 2012) ¶165.
782. Non-Horizontal Mergers Guidelines, at 22 ¶97. Although the Commission recognizes that the anticompetitive effects associated with commercial conduct creating foreclosure can be addressed by the application of Article 102 of the TFEU, Case M. 5984, Intel/McAfee (Jan. 26, 2011) ¶127, it also examines the potential foreclosure effect in the context of applying the Merger Control Regulation because the Commission is aware of the possibility that reliance solely on Article 102 TFEU may be an ineffective means to restore competition once it is foreclosed. *Id.* at ¶207. However, in the context of applying the Merger Control Regulation, the Commission does consider whether the potential application of Article 102 will serve as an effective deterrent against possible exclusionary practices. Case M. 5984, Intel/McAfee, (Jan. 26, 2011) ¶265.
783. *Id.* at ¶221.

bundling" refers to the practice of selling various products only as a bundle. In contrast to tying, the nondominant product in the bundle is not sold separately. Using the *Intel/McAfee* case as an example, if postmerger Intel were to have only sold its chips with the McAfee security software loaded on those chips, this would be considered bundling. Customers in this hypothetical case of pure bundling would not have the option of purchasing the Intel chips or the McAfee software individually. The term "mixed bundling" falls between tying and pure bundling. In the context of mixed bundling, the individual products are available individually, but their cumulative price is higher than the bundled price.[784]

The likelihood that the merger will facilitate tying or bundling (pure or mixed) must be assessed on a case-by-case basis. The Commission examines (1) whether the undertaking will have the ability post-merger to adopt a leveraging strategy, (2) whether the undertaking will have the incentive to do so and (3) whether there will likely be an overall adverse effect on consumers.[785] In order to have the ability to leverage, the merged entity must have significant market power in at least one of the markets. The requisite market power is less than dominance.[786] In the absence of market power, the merged entity would lack the ability to control its customers.

In addition, the products will generally have to be complementary in order to give the firm the ability to leverage.[787] It is unlikely that the acquisition of a shoe manufacturer by a cement company would allow the cement company to leverage its position in the cement market into the shoe market even if it had a significant market position in the cement market.

Even though an undertaking may have the ability to engage in tying or bundling, it might lack the incentive to do so because of the negative effects it might incur by adopting such a strategy. In many instances, when a dominant firm attempts to leverage its market power by requiring customers to purchase products or services they would not otherwise purchase, not all customers will continue to purchase the tied or bundled products from that dominant undertaking. If the losses to the dominant firm are greater than the gains, the dominant firm will have no incentive to engage in the strategy of foreclosure. Although the prospective nature of this effect makes it difficult to quantify, the Commission does consider the "critical loss" associated with leveraging strategies to be relevant.[788]

---

784. Non-Horizontal Mergers Guidelines, at 22 ¶96.
785. *Id.* at 22 ¶94; Case M. 6381, Google/Motorola Mobility (Feb. 13, 2012) ¶¶167-178. It is important to note that these effects must be merger-specific. If, for example, the acquiring entity already has the ability or incentive to foreclose competition through tying or biundling, the Commission will not oppose the merger on these grounds. Case M. 6381, Google/Motorola Mobility (Feb. 13, 2012) ¶¶172-178; Case M. 6281, Microsoft/Skype (Oct. 7, 2011) ¶142.
786. Nonhorizontal Mergers Guidelines at 22 ¶99.
787. *Id.* at 22 ¶100.
788. Case M. 5984, Intel/McAfee (Jan. 26, 2011) ¶¶273-276.

In leveraging cases, the Commission also looks at the likely effect of the merger on competition and consumers.[789] This is the context in which the Commission examines the efficiencies of the possibility of tying or bundling.[790] For example, the ability of the merged entity to achieve economies of scope by offering two products together might be beneficial to the merging entities as well as to customers. The efficiencies are then examined in the context of barriers to market entry (which enhance the ability of the merged entity to foreclose competition) and countervailing buyer power (which prevents the merged entity from using its market power to force an unwanted product on customers.).

The Commission's treatment of the acquisition of Wrigley by Mars provides a good illustration of how these considerations are applied.[791] In that case, the candy manufacturer Mars proposed acquiring control of the chewing gum company Wrigley. The Commission assumed that the relevant markets were those of chocolate confectionary, gum, and sugar confectionary. As Mars was primarily active in the chocolate confectionary market and Wrigley primarily in the gum and sugar confectionary markets, the Commission concluded that the transaction would not result in any impermissible horizontal effect.

In examining the conglomerate effects, however, the Commission expressed concern that Mars had a 20 percent to 30 percent market share in chocolate confectionary in the UK and Wrigley had a market share between 80 percent and 90 percent for gum in the UK. Because of these significant market shares, the issue was, therefore, whether Mars would be able to leverage the strong position Wrigley enjoyed in the gum market to distort competition in the chocolate confectionary market. In concluding that the risk of leverage was low, the Commission placed particular weight on its assessment of the market that chocolate and gum were not complementary products: "According to most retailers, gum and chocolate are neither bought together, nor bought by the same customers, nor used together."[792] Consequently, the potential conglomerate effects of the merger were not sufficient to prevent its approval.

(ii) Portfolio Effect

The leverage discussed above assumes that the merged entity has market power in one market and is leveraging that power in another market. It is possible, however, that a conglomerate merger distort competition without such market power. If, for example, the merged entity is able to offer a broader portfolio of products because of the merger, it might be able to secure a preferential position with its customers to the detriment of its competitors who are not able to offer such a portfolio.[793] Although this ability is often beneficial to the consumer, it forces the "single product" competitors from the market or forces them to expand their product lines.

---

789. Case M. 6281, Microsoft/Skype (Oct. 7, 2011) ¶142.
790. Nonhorizontal Mergers Guidelines, at 25 ¶115.
791. Case M. 5188, Mars/Wrigley (July 28, 2008).
792. *Id.* at ¶34.
793. *See* Case M. 1355, Newell/Rubbermaid (Jan. 13, 1999); Allied Signal/Honeywell, 2001 O.J. (L 152) 1 ¶118.

The Commission's approach to the portfolio effect of conglomerate mergers is illustrated in its *Guinness/Grand Metropolitan* decision.[794] In this case, Guinness and Grand Metropolitan agreed to merge their respective alcohol distribution businesses. The major brands of the parties were Johnnie Walker Red Label, Dewar's, White Horse, Bell's, Haig, VAT 69 (Guinness) and J&B (GrandMet) in Scotch whisky; Smirnoff (GrandMet) in vodka; Metaxa (GrandMet) in brandy; Gordon's (Guinness) in gin; Ouzo 12 (GrandMet) in ouzo; and Baileys, Malibu, and Archer's (GrandMet) in liqueurs and fruit schnapps. The Commission decided that each individual spirit (whiskey, vodka, gin, rum, brandy, the various liqueurs) constituted a separate market (as opposed to "spirits" in general). According to the Commission, the merger would have an impermissible portfolio effect because the expansion of the product range of the merged entity would give it a preferred position with customers. In other words, customers (supermarkets, night clubs, bars, liquor stores) would prefer to deal with one distributor, the new entity, because of the strength of certain of its brands.

(4) Failing Firm Defense

The acquisition of shares or assets of a failing or failed company by a competitor may not lead to the creation or strengthening of a dominant position if the failing company would have otherwise existed the market and the acquiring company would have absorbed the market share of the failing company anyway. Consequently, both the ECJ and the Commission recognize the failing company defense as a justification for an otherwise impermissible agglomeration of market shares.[795] The justification is based on the lack of causation between the market structure and the transaction.[796] If the acquiring company would have absorbed the market share of the failing firm anyway, the transaction is not necessarily creating a concentrated market structure that would have otherwise been created.

The application of the failing firm defense is illustrated in the seminal case of *France v. Commission*.[797] In that case, Kali and Salz AG, a German potash and rock salt company, proposed acquiring control of one of its German competitors Mitteldeutsche Kali AG. The concentration would have given Kali and Salz a monopoly on the German market for potash. Nonetheless, the Commission and the ECJ came to the conclusion that the transaction would not be the cause of the creation of the monopoly as Mittledeutsche Kali would be forced out of the market in a relatively short time if the transaction did not take place.[798]

---

794. 1998 O.J. (L 288) 24.
795. Case M. 6796, Aegean/Olympic II, (Oct. 9, 2013) summary at 2015 O.J. (C 25) 7, 14-15 ¶¶67-78.
796. Horizontal Guidelines at ¶89; Case M. 6796, Aegean/Olympic II, (Oct. 9, 2013) summary at 2015 O.J. (C 25) 7, 15 ¶¶79; Case M. 6360, NYNAS/Shell/Harburg Refinery (Sept. 2, 2013) ¶¶307-310; BASF/Eurodiol/Pantochim, 2002 O.J.(L 132) 45, 61 ¶136; REWE/Meinl, 1999 O.J. (L 274) 1, 10 ¶62; Bertelsmannn/Kirch/Premiere, 1999 O.J. (L 53) 1, 14 ¶70.
797. Case C-68/94, France v. Comm'n, 1998 E.C.R. I-1375 (1998).
798. *Id.*

The failing firm defense only applies if the participating undertakings can show that three criteria are fulfilled.[799] First, the doctrine only applies if the acquired undertaking as a legal entity and as a going concern (i.e., its assets) will in the near future be forced out of the market if not taken over by another undertaking.[800] In *BASF/Pantochem/Eurodial*, for example, the two Belgian chemical companies, Pantochim SA and Eurodial SA, had initiated bankruptcy proceedings and the bankruptcy administrator made it clear that those two companies would not survive if BASF AG, a German competitor, did not acquire them.[801]

In *Deloitte & Touche/Andersen (UK)*, for example, the Commission concluded that it was inevitable that Andersen UK would exit the market if not acquired by Deloitte & Touche.[802] In *REWE/Meinl*, however, the Commission was not convinced that Meinl would have been forced out of the market in the near future: "[M]erely proving that ... Meinl suffers from major competitive disadvantages vis-à-vis other, much larger, competitors does not suffice to show why Meinl's food-retailing business activities must in any circumstances be terminated."[803] It is clear that the merging parties need to show more than just lack of profitability.[804]

Second, there must be no less anticompetitive alternative purchaser. For example, if another competitor, perhaps with a lower market share than the contemplated acquirer, is a potential purchaser, the acquirer could not rely on the failing firm defense. In *France v. Commission*,[805] for example, there was only one other competitor active in the relevant geographic market. Moreover, no other competitors exhibited a willingness to acquire the failing company. If there are other plausible acquirers, the undertakings concerned will likely have to show that negotiations were conducted with these other potential buyers in good faith and they failed.[806] In *Bertelsmann/Kirch/Premiere*, the Commission stated that the "mere reference to [the failing company's] lack of success in identifying a partner is insufficient to prove that there is no less anticompetitive alternative available."[807]

---

799. The merging parties carry the burden of proof. REWE/Meinl, 1999 O.J. (L 274) 1, 10 ¶64.
800. In *BASF/Eurodiol/Pantochim*, the Commission treated the exit of the company and the exit of its assets as two separate requirements. BASF/Eurodiol/Pantochim, 2002 O.J. (L 132) 45, 61 ¶142. They are, however, treated here as one requirement as they both require that the company has failed and will inevitably exit the market (i.e., the business will either be sold or liquidated).
801. BASF/Pantochem/Eurodial, 2002 O.J. (L 132) 45, 62 ¶144.
802. Case M. 2810, Deloitte & Touche/Andersen (UK) (July 1, 2002) ¶49.
803. REWE/Meinl, 1999 O.J. (L 274) 1, 11 ¶66.
804. Bertelsmann/Kirch/Premiere, 1999 O.J. (L 53) 1, 15 ¶72.
805. Case C-68/94, France v. Comm'n, 1998 E.C.R. I-1375 (1998).
806. REWE/Meinl, 1999 O.J. (L 274) 1, 11 ¶68.
807. Bertelsmann/Kirch/Premiere, 1999 O.J. (L 53) 1, 15 ¶75.

Third, the deterioration of the competitive structure through the merger must be no worse than in the absence of the merger.[808] In other words, the acquiring firm would absorb the market share of the failing firm regardless of whether the merger took place. This requirement is necessary to establish the lack of causality. In *France v. Commission*, for example, Kali and Salz AG was allowed to establish a monopoly in Germany by acquiring Mitteldeutsche Kali AG because Kali and Salz AG would have absorbed the market share anyway if Mitteldeutsche Kali AG would have failed and exited the market. In a market with only two competitors, meeting the absorption requirement is relatively easy but not always inevitable. Determining whether the acquiring undertaking would have absorbed the market share of the failing undertaking requires consideration of additional factors, such as the ease of market entry.

For example, if barriers to market entry are low, it is less likely that the absorption of market share inference would be accurate because the new market entrant might absorb part of the market share of the failing firm. Moreover, the assumption might not apply in markets with three or more competitors. In other words, additional factors must be considered to arrive at this conclusion (i.e., the level of capacity utilization, elasticity of supply, the structure of the market, the size and strength of competitors, elasticity of demand). The necessarily speculative character of the three conditions for the failing firm defense makes its application difficult and case-specific. The Commission has repeatedly refused to apply the defense.[809]

(5) Efficiency Justifications

(i) Concept of Efficiency

In certain cases, the potential negative effects of a concentration may be offset by the efficiencies resulting from the transaction. The types of efficiencies are similar to those discussed above in the context of applying Article 101(3) of the TFEU. One category of efficiencies relates to the cost savings that may consequently lead to lower prices or other benefits to consumers.[810] The other category of efficiencies are those resulting from new or improved products or services. For example, the combination of resources may allow the merged entity to offer a product that it was not able to offer prior to the concentration. In analyzing the cost efficiencies, the Commission distinguishes between cost efficiencies that lead to reductions in variable or marginal costs and cost efficiencies that lead to reduction of fixed costs. The Commission gives greater weight to reductions in variable costs, as these are more likely to benefit consumers.[811] For example, a transaction that allows a company to close a manufacturing plant (i.e., reduction of fixed costs) would be weighted differently than a transaction that allows two companies to combine their technology to produce a cheaper widget.

---

808. BASF/Eurodiol/Pantochim, 2002 O.J. (L 132) 45, 61 ¶143.
809. *See, e.g.*, Saint Gobain/Wacker Chemie, 1997 O.J. (L 247) 1; Bertelsmannn/Kirch/Premiere, 1999 O.J. (L 53) 1; REWE/Meinl, 1999 O.J. (L 274) 1.
810. Horizontal Mergers Guidelines at ¶80.
811. *Id.* at ¶80.

The parties claiming the efficiencies are responsible for offering proof of their likely realization. In substantiating their claims, parties often rely on expert reports of economists showing the type and size of efficiency gains, and on the extent to which consumers are likely to benefit. In addition, and sometimes more persuasive, the Commission will review internal documents that were used by the management to decide on the merger, statements from the management to the owners and financial markets about the expected efficiencies, historical examples of efficiencies and consumer benefit, and pre-merger external experts' studies on the type and size of efficiency gains, and on the extent to which consumers are likely to benefit.[812]

(ii) **Requirements**

Efficiencies are only considered in the substantive analysis if they benefit consumers, are merger-specific, and are verifiable.[813] Although the potential benefits to consumers may arise in an unlimited number of constellations, the most commonly advanced consumer benefit is reduced prices. Cost savings in production or distribution may give the merged entity the ability and incentive to charge lower prices following the merger.[814] Cost reductions that result from anticompetitive reductions in output cannot be considered as efficiencies benefiting consumers.[815] For example, the argument that a particular merger will increase efficiency by allowing the merged entity to close a factory and thereby reduce prices to consumers would be given less credence.

Second, the claimed efficiencies must be merger-specific. According to the Commission and General Court, an efficiency is merger-specific if it is a direct consequence of the merger and cannot be achieved by less anticompetitive alternatives.[816] For example, if the claimed efficiencies could be achieved by permissive cooperation (short of a concentration) or by a realistic unilateral investment of one of the undertakings concerned, they will not deemed merger specific.

Finally, the Commission requires that the efficiencies are verifiable.[817] In other words, they must be likely to materialize and substantial enough to counteract the potential negative effects of the concentration. The Commission will likely disregard efficiency claims that are based on pure speculation. In meeting the verifiability requirement, it is often useful to engage an expert to assist in the description of the efficiencies as presented to the Commission. According to the General Court, the verifiability requirement does not require that such documentation existed prior to or independent of the merger. The undertakings concerned may submit studies verifying their efficiency claims

---

812. *Id.* at ¶88.
813. *Id.* at ¶78.
814. *Id.* at ¶80.
815. Case T-342/07, Ryanair Holdings plc v. Comm'n, 2010 E.C.R. II-3470, 3640 ¶435.
816. Horizontal Mergers Guidelines at ¶85; Case T-342/07, Ryanair Holdings plc v. Comm'n, 2010 E.C.R. II-3470, 3631 ¶410.
817. Horizontal Mergers Guidelines at ¶86.

even if those studies were conducted specifically for securing the approval of the Commission.[818]

(c) Influence of Noncompetition Concerns

As discussed above, the fundamental purpose of the Merger Control Regulation is to prohibit the creation or strengthening of a dominant position in the EU. In making this determination, the obvious consideration is the effect which the transaction may have on competition in the EU. However, the Merger Control Regulation is not to be applied in a vacuum. It operates in the context of legal, political, and social constraints that may have an influence on its application. Leaving aside the potential political and social influences on the subjective decision-making process of the individual members of the Commission and bureaucrats involved in reviewing the transaction, EU law requires the Commission to consider noncompetition concerns in applying the Merger Control Regulation. This legal requirement arises from the structure of the EU legal system and the express wording of the Merger Control Regulation.

As discussed in Chapter I, the EU legal system is based on a hierarchy of laws. International law and primary EU law take precedence over secondary EU law. As the Merger Control Regulation is secondary law, its application must take into account and accommodate the requirements of international law and primary EU law. This would include, for example, fundamental rights and principles[819] as well as environmental law and labor law.[820] Article 2 of the EU Treaty, for example, specifically states that the task of the EU is to include "a high level of employment and of social protection," protection of the environment, and "social cohesion." In applying the Merger Control Regulation, the Commission is required to consider the enumerated tasks of the EU. In fact, the Merger Control Regulation expressly grants to employee representatives the right to be heard in the process of reviewing a concentration.[821]

(d) Ancillary Restraints

The merger or acquisition of a business or the formation of a joint venture almost always occur in a complex contractual framework. Contracts are created to regulate the present and future conduct of the parties and to allocate the risks associated with the operation of the business. For example, in most cases the buyer of a business probably will want to prevent the seller from competing with the buyer in the future, as the seller has detailed knowledge of the business it sold. Similarly, the buyer probably will want to preclude the seller from subsequently hiring employees of the business. These are just two

---

818. Case T-342/07, Ryanair Holdings plc v. Comm'n, 2010 E.C.R. II-3470, 3631 ¶410.
819. Merger Control Regulation at recital 36. This constraint typically arises in a procedural context related to the due process rights of the parties. Case C-299/95, Kremzow v. Austria, 1997 E.C.R. I-2637, 2645 ¶14; Case T-23/99, LR af 1998 A/S v. Comm'n, 2002 E.C.R. II-1705, 1786 ¶217; Case T-112/98 Mannesmannröhren-Werke v. Comm'n, 2001 E.C.R. II-732, 764 ¶60.
820. *See, e.g.*, TFEU at art. 127(z); TFEU at art. 158; TFEU at art. 174.
821. Merger Control Regulation at art.18(4).

of the "ancillary" provisions that are commonly included in the transaction documents. As these ancillary provisions may have an impact on competition, they are not always automatically cleared with the concentration. The analysis of any ancillary restraints constitutes an additional step in the substantive review of the concentration.

(1) Ancillary Restraints Doctrine

As discussed above, the substantive review of concentrations under the Merger Control Regulation focuses on the effect that the transaction will have on the competitive structure of the relevant markets. The effect of the specific provisions in the transaction documents is a secondary (but relevant) issue. According to the ancillary restraints doctrine as applied in the context of structural restraints of competition, these clauses are permitted as part of the concentration if the concentration itself is permitted, and the particular clause is directly related and necessary to the implementation of the concentration.[822]

The application of the ancillary restraints doctrine is based on the distinction between the "main" provisions (i.e., those which legally effectuate the change in ownership over the assets or shares) and the ancillary provisions (i.e., all other provisions which are not main provisions). The rule is that if the ancillary provision constitutes a restraint of competition, it follows the fate of the concentration provided it is directly related to and necessary for implementing the concentration. Otherwise, the restriction is examined separately under Article 101 of the TFEU. It is important to emphasize that the failure to qualify as ancillary does not mean the agreement or contractual provision is prohibited. It only means that it needs to be reviewed under Article 101.

A restraint is directly related to the implementation of the concentration if it is economically related to the main transaction and intended to allow a smooth transition to the changed company structure after the concentration.[823] For example, if the seller of the business agrees not to compete for a reasonable time with the business which it sold, this would probably be deemed directly related to the main transaction. However, an agreement according to which the seller agrees with the buyer that the seller will not only refrain from competing with the business sold, but also with any other line of business of the buyer would probably not be deemed directly related to the main transaction. Also, if the agreement was entered into at a later time, it is probably not ancillary. If, for example, a year after the transaction has closed, the buyer and the seller agree that the seller will not solicit employees of the buyer, this agreement would not be deemed ancillary.

The necessity requirement means that in the absence of those contractual provisions of agreements, the concentration could not be implemented or could only be implemented under considerably more uncertain conditions, at substantially higher cost, over an appreciably longer period, or with considerably

---

822. Merger Control Regulation at arts. 6(1)(b) and 8(1).
823. Commission Notice on restrictions directly related and necessary to concentrations, 2005 O.J. (C 56) 24, 26 ¶12 [hereinafter Ancillary Restraints Notice].

greater difficulty.[824] The necessity requirement is one of objective necessity. For example, in *UBS Capital/Heiploeg Shellfish International*, the buyer and seller agreed in the share purchase agreement that the seller would refrain from inducing customers of the target company to cancel their business with the target company after the closing of the transaction.[825] The share purchase agreement also included a typical confidentiality and nondisclosure clause.

The Commission decided that these clauses were not ancillary because the concerns of the parties which the clauses claimed to address were adequately addressed by national competition law governing unfair competition.[826] In other words, the mere fact that they appeared necessary to the parties was not sufficient to qualify them as ancillary. Because they are not deemed ancillary, they are examined under Article 101 of the TFEU rather than following the fate of the concentration. In *Lufthansa/Menzies/Sigma*, the Commission decided that a noncompete clause which prevented the parent companies from competing with the joint venture was not necessary because in order to qualify as a concentrative joint venture in the first place, as the parties claimed, the parents had to withdraw from the market of the joint venture.[827] Here again, the standard applied was one of objective necessity rather than subjective necessity.

(2) Specific Ancillary Restraints

The most common type of ancillary restraint in the context of mergers and acquisitions is a clause that prevents the seller from competing with the buyer after the transaction. Noncompete clauses are generally permissible as they serve to ensure that the buyer is receiving the full value of the business.[828] Noncompetition clauses are not deemed necessary in the context of the ancillary restraints doctrine if the buyer is purchasing only physical assets (such as land, buildings, or machinery) and not an ongoing business. The rationale is that the buyer is not in need of any protection in such cases. Similarly, if the buyer is only acquiring industrial and commercial property rights, a noncompete clause will probably not be necessary, according to the Commission. The rationale behind this position is that the buyer, once it has purchased those rights, could rely on those rights anyway to take action against violations by the seller. Hence, a noncompete clause is not necessary to protect the buyer.

The noncompete clause must have a reasonable temporal and geographic scope. In an acquisition, the seller can generally be prohibited from competing with the business sold for up to three years. In *Siemens/Areva*, for example, the Commission objected to a noncompete clause of eight years' duration and

---

824. *Id.* at ¶13. This characterization is slightly less stringent than the impossibility standard applied by the ECJ in Case C-382/12 P, MasterCard Inc. v. Commission, 2014 E.C.R. I-___, at ¶91 in the context of applying Article 101 of the TFEU.
825. Case M. 2078, UBS Capital/Heiploeg Shellfish Int'l (Aug. 21, 2000).
826. *Id.* at ¶26.
827. Case M. 1387, Lufthansa/Menzies/Sigma (Jan. 13, 1999).
828. Ancillary Restraints Notice at ¶20.

subsequently agreed with Areva to reduce the period to three years.[829] If only goodwill is being acquired, then the maximum duration is two years. The geographical scope of a noncompete clause must be limited to the area in which the business sold offered the relevant products or services before the transaction. If, for example, the company which was sold was only doing business in Latvia, a noncompete clause covering the entire EU would not be ancillary to the concentration.

In some circumstances, the seller of a business may want to retain some intellectual property for use in its other businesses. For example, when Google sold Motorola Mobility, it retained many patents used in the business it was selling. The alternative was to sell the intellectual property and take a license back. License agreements for intellectual property are generally considered directly related to and necessary for the transaction even if they are unlimited in duration. However, license agreements between the parent companies of a joint venture are not considered ancillary.

In many transactions, the seller of a business is prohibited from soliciting customers or employees of the business that was sold or from using any confidential information relating to that business. Nonsolicitation and confidentiality clauses are generally evaluated in the same way as noncompete clauses as they can have the same effect on competition as noncompete clauses. However, the Commission is generally more willing to recognize the legitimate value of confidentiality obligations.

In *Siemens/Areva*, for example, Siemens and Areva entered into a confidentiality agreement that prevented Siemens for a period of up to 11 years from using any confidential information related to a joint venture after the acquisition by Areva of Siemens' interest in the joint venture.[830] The broad scope of the confidentiality obligation would have impeded Siemens's ability to compete in the field of the joint venture (civil nuclear technology) as well as related fields. After the Commission intervened, Areva agreed to reduce this period to three years for certain confidential information while keeping in place the 11-year confidentiality obligation for certain highly sensitive information.[831]

In certain cases, the seller of a business may be selling a part of a business upon which the other parts of its business relies. In other words, the company may be outsourcing a portion of the business. It will, therefore, need to continue to receive the supply. For example, if Apple Computer were to outsource the production of the headphones for its iPod by selling the headphone manufacturing portion of the business to a third party, it would probably enter into a long-term supply agreement with that third party requiring the third party to continue selling headphones to Apple. Conversely, if the overall business is dependent on sales to the part of the business being sold, then a purchase agreement may be necessary to secure the continued demand. For example, if Coca-Cola were

---

829. Siemens/Areva, 2012 O.J. (C 280) 8.
830. *Id.* at 9 ¶16.
831. *Id.* at 11 ¶10.

to sell a bottling and distribution business responsible for all of the Scandinavian countries, Coca-Cola would probably require a purchase agreement according to which the third-party buyer would continue purchasing Coca-Cola products. The general rule is that supply or purchase obligations are permissible (i.e., ancillary) if they are nonexclusive and based on limited quantities to be supplied. Exclusive supply or purchase obligations are not considered necessary for the transaction. If, for example, Coca-Cola were to require the buyer to buy only Coke products, the agreement would not be deemed ancillary. Because supply or purchase obligations in the context of the change of control over a business are generally transitional arrangements, the general rule regarding their permissible duration is that they should be limited to three years.

CHAPTER **IV**

Regulation of External Trade

As discussed in Chapter II, the European Treaties establish an internal market in which goods and services flow freely between member states. However, the European Union (EU) is more than just a free trade area. The member states have granted the EU the exclusive competence for the common commercial policy (Article 3(1)(e) TFEU). This means that the EU, and not the member states, is responsible for external trade policy.[1] The legal instruments that facilitate the realization of the external trade policy are the customs laws and the external trade instruments.

1. Customs Law

1.1 The Customs Union

Customs law commonly refers to the rules and regulations that determine the tariffs on goods imported into the EU or the quantity of goods imported into the EU. As discussed in Chapter III, the EU is a customs union. This means that the individual member states have relinquished their authority to impose tariffs on goods imported from third countries in favor of a common tariff imposed upon the goods by the EU.[2] Consequently, the duties to be paid by importers on a particular good will be the same regardless of whether that good is imported into the EU *via* Greece or *via* Sweden or *via* any other member state. Customs law is made up of the legislation and case law applicable to the imposition of customs duties on the import and export of goods into and from the EU.

Customs duties are the charges imposed on goods imported into the EU. Customs duties are only imposed on the importation of non-Union goods. As discussed in Chapter II, Union goods benefit from the free movement of goods principle in the Treaty on the Functioning of the European Union (TFEU). The term "Union goods" refers to goods that are (i) wholly obtained in the EU and not incorporating goods imported from third countries, or (ii) goods imported from third countries which have been released for free circulation in a member

---

1. As discussed below, the member states still play an important role in the implementation of the external trade rules. For example, the member states are responsible for collecting customs duties on goods imported into the EU.
2. The prohibition on the imposition of duties by individual member states on imports from third countries is not express, but rather implied by the establishment of a common commercial policy. Case C-125/94, Aprile SrL v. Administrazione delle Finanze dello Stato, 1995 E.C.R. I-2939, 2950 ¶34.

state, or (iii) goods that have been obtained or produced in the EU from goods obtained wholly in the EU or from goods released for free circulation in the EU.[3] The interpretation of non-Union goods includes all goods that are not Union goods and Union goods that have been exported from the EU.

Another important element of European customs law is the tariff quotas imposed on goods imported from third countries. Parallel but complementary to the system of customs duties, the EU has established a system of quotas for certain goods.[4] A quota is simply a quantitative limitation of the amount of a particular good imported. For example, the EU established a quota for the amount of bananas that could be imported into the EU from countries which were not signatories to the Lome Convention (primarily comprised of former colonies of the EU member states).[5] Customs duties, in contrast, do not impose a direct "cap" on the amount of goods that may be imported.

There are two types of quotas: absolute quotas and tariff duty quotas. Absolute quotas are those described immediately above. They limit the quantity of a particular good that may be imported into the EU. For example, a hypothetical quota limiting the total amount of bananas imported into the EU at 1 million tons annually would be considered an absolute quota. A tariff rate quota, however, is more of a stepped-rate system. For example, the EU may allow the import of the first 1 million tons of bananas at 2 percent duty, but anything over that is charged a duty of 50 percent. There is no absolute cap on the importation, but rather an increase in the duty rate applied to imports above the stated limit.

1.2 Purpose of Customs Duties

Customs duties and quotas serve several functions. For example, they serve as a source of income for the EU. The amounts collected by the member states when goods from third countries are imported into their territory are remitted to the EU. In addition, customs duties serve to protect domestic industry from competition from goods imported from third countries. Finally, customs duties may be employed to persuade third countries to adopt a certain policy.

1.3 Common Customs Tariff

Customs law practitioners spend a significant portion of their time classifying goods into the classification system established in the Common Customs

---

3. Regulation (EC) No. 450/2008 of the European Parliament and of the Council of 23 April 2008 laying down the Community Customs Code, 2008 O.J. (L 145) 1 at art. 4(18).
4. Council Regulation (EC) No. 717/2008 of 17 July 2008 establishing a Community procedure for administering quantitative quotas, 2008 O.J. (L 198) 1 [hereinafter Trade Quotas Regulation].
5. Council Regulation 404/93 of 13 February 1993 on the Common Organization of the Market in Bananas, 1993 O.J. (L 47) 1. The restriction on imports was eventually found to violate the General Agreement on Tariffs and Trade (GATT) principle of national treatment, World Trade Organization (WTO) Panel Report, European Communities—Regime for the Importation, Sale and Distribution of Bananas, WT/DS27/R/ECU (May 22, 1997).

Tariff (CCT). As discussed in greater detail below, the classification of a certain product under a particular number in the CCT will determine the amount of duties the importer must pay on those goods. Because of the amount of money involved, it is not uncommon to encounter European Court of Justice (ECJ) cases involving nothing more than a classification issue, such as whether mozzarella cheese imported into the EU should be classified as ripened cheese or unripened cheese.[6]

The term Common Customs Tariff merely refers to the notion that the EU imposes one level of tariffs on goods imported to or exported from the EU regardless of the specific member state from or to which the goods are imported or exported. The term encompasses all of the various laws that have been enacted in order to facilitate the application of the common external tariff. The CCT is composed of two fundamental components: the Combined Nomenclature and the specific duty rates applied to each product.

(a) Combined Nomenclature

Not all goods imported into the EU pay the same customs duty. The amount of the duty depends on the type of good and the origin of the good. The imposition of differential customs duties requires establishing a system that classifies products by category. As there could be a significant difference in the amount of customs duties owed based on how the goods are classified, the process of classification becomes an extremely important issue for businesses.

The EU coding system is based on a regulation referred to as the Combined Nomenclature.[7] The Combined Nomenclature is itself based on the Harmonized Commodity Description and Coding System (HCDCS) established by the World Customs Organization (WCO).[8] The WCO is an international organization with over 175 signatories, including the EU. One of its tasks is to establish and maintain the HCDCS and provide general rules and explanatory notes (the Harmonized System of Explanatory Notes) which assist customs administrations around the world in applying their customs codes in a uniform manner. By signing the Convention on the Harmonized Commodity Description and Coding System,[9] the EU agreed to maintain a nomenclature corresponding to that of the HCDCS.

In addition to the HCDCS, the EU has adopted general rules and Combined Nomenclature of Explanatory Notes which provide guidance to the customs authorities of the member states and to importers and exporters.[10] Both the general rules and the explanatory note are almost identical to those of the WCO.

---

6. *See, e.g.*, Case C-196/05, Sachsenmilch AG v. Oberfinanzdirektion Nürnberg, 2006 E.C.R. I-5161.
7. Council Regulation (EEC) No. 2658/87 of 23 July 1987 on the tariff and statistical nomenclature and on the Common Customs Tariff, 1987 O.J. (L 256) 1.
8. Council Decision 87/369/EEC of 7 April 1987, 1987 O.J. (L 198) 1.
9. International Convention on the Harmonized Commodity Description and Coding System, done June 14, 1983 (entered into force Jan. 1, 1988), *available at* http:// www.wcoomd.org/ie/En/Conventions/conventions.html.
10. Explanatory Notes to the Combined Nomenclature of the European Union, 2015 O.J. (C 76) 1.

Although the Combined Nomenclature of Explanatory Notes closely follows the Notes to the HCDCS, the latter are not legally binding on the EU.[11]

The Combined Nomenclature is broken down into HS chapters (two-digit codes), HS headings (four-digit codes), HS subheadings (six-digit codes) and CN subheadings (eight-digit codes).[12] The CN subheadings are simply a more detailed breakdown of the six-digit subheadings provided in the Combined Nomenclature. In some instances, the six-digit breakdown is as detailed as it gets (in which case the CN subheading is '00'). Products under the Combined Nomenclature are divided into 21 chapters, over 1,000 headings and over 10,000 CN subheadings.

The treatment of musical instruments provides a good illustration of how the classification system works. Chapter 92 of the Combined Nomenclature covers "musical instruments; parts and accessories." This chapter is divided into several headings covering *inter alia* pianos (heading 9201); string musical instruments (heading 9202); keyboard instruments (heading 9203); accordions (heading 9204); wind musical instruments (heading 9205); and percussion musical instruments (heading 9206). Each of these headings is further broken down into subheadings to reflect the fact that there may be different types of this same instrument imported or exported. For example, the heading for string musical instruments is broken down into violins (subheading 9202 10 10), other string musical instruments played with a bow (subheading 9202 10 90), harps (subheading 9202 90 10), guitars (subheading 9202 90 30) and other not played with a bow (subheading 9202 90 90).

It is important to recognize that the Combined Nomenclature is a constantly evolving catalog. New products are continually being introduced into commerce which do not fit nicely in the existing categories. If there are differences in how the customs authorities of the member states are categorizing a particular product, the European Commission may adopt a regulation clarifying the classification for a particular good. For example, the relatively recent introduction of projectors attached to laptops to project data onto a screen (used, for example, to give a PowerPoint presentation) presented a challenge for the customs authorities in categorizing the product under the Combined Nomenclature. To clarify the situation, the Commission adopted a regulation that classified the projector as a video projector (as opposed to a data processing machine).[13]

(b) *Duty Rates*

The second fundamental component of the CCT is the duty rates which have been assigned to each code entry. These are annexed to the Combined Nomenclature. There are two types of duties: autonomous rate of duty and conventional rate

---

11. Case C-311/04, Algemene Scheeps Agentuur Dordrecht v. Inspecteur der Belqstingdienst, 2006 E.C.R. I-625, 637 ¶27; Case T-243/01, Sony Computer Entertainment Europe Ltd. v. Comm'n, 2003 E.C.R II-4195, 4239 ¶116.
12. Council Regulation (EEC) No. 2658/87 of 23 July 1987 on the tariff and statistical nomenclature and on the Common Customs Tariff, 1987 O.J. (L 256) 1 at art. 3.
13. Commission Regulation (EC) No. 1849/2004 of 21 October 2004 concerning the classification of certain goods in the Combined Nomenclature, 2004 O.J. (L 323) 3.

of duty.[14] The autonomous rate of duty is the rate which the EU unilaterally decided upon. The conventional rate of duty is the rate that has been agreed to by the EU and one or more of its trading partners. This is the most commonly applicable rate. For example, the tariff concessions which the EU made as part of the General Agreement on Tariffs and Trade (GATT) or association agreements would be considered conventional rates of duty. The application of the conventional rate of duty is much more common than the autonomous rate because of the numerous concessions the EU has made.

A duty rate, be it autonomous or conventional, may be expressed as a percentage or a fixed amount. An ad valorem duty is a rate of duty which is calculated based on the value of the good. For example, an ad valorem duty may set the rate of duty for violins imported from the United States at 3.2 percent of the value of the violin. A fixed rate duty is a flat rate based on quantity or volume of the product being imported. For example, a duty of €1 per liter of imported wine would be a fixed rate duty.

(c) TARIC System

The Combined Nomenclature and its Annexes are constantly changing to adapt to new and different products. Each year, the Commission publishes a regulation that contains the Combined Nomenclature, including any changes that have been made by the European Council or the European Commission. The TARIC system (acronym for Tarif Intégré Communautaire) is an informational instrument used by the customs authorities and traders to facilitate the application of the Combined Nomenclature and the rates of duty.[15] Once the importer has identified the code under which its products are classified and the country of origin, it can use the TARIC system to determine the precise level of duty to be applied to that particular product.

1.4 The Union Customs Code

The Common Customs Code is a compilation of the most important customs rules used to apply the Combined Nomenclature and the duty rates. As there are many more types of products than there are categories in the Combined Nomenclature, the application of the CCT depends on specific rules, interpretive devices, and procedures. These are contained in the Union Customs Code[16] and its Implementing Regulation.[17] These two legislative acts, the former

---

14. The same distinction also applies to autonomous quotas and conventional quotas.
15. Integrated Tariff of the European Communities, 2003 O.J. (C 103) 1. Art. 2 of Council Regulation (EEC) No. 2658/87 of 23 July 1987 on the tariff and statistical nomenclature and on the Common Customs Tariff, 1987 O.J. (L 256) 1.
16. Regulation (EC) No. 450/2008 of the European Parliament and of the Council of 23 April 2008 laying down the Community Customs Code, 2008 O.J. (L 145) 1 [hereinafter Union Customs Code].
17. Commission Regulation (EEC) No. 2454/93 of 2 July 1993 laying down provisions for the implementation of Council Regulations (EEC) No. 2913/92 establishing the Community Code, 1993 O.J. (L 253) 1 [hereinafter Customs Code Implementing Regulation].

being adopted by the Council and the latter by the Commission, are the primary sources of EU customs law.

1.5 Determining the Amount of the Duty

(a) Administration of the Common Customs Tariff

Although the specific rates of duty are fixed by the Council (Art. 31 TFEU), the member states have the responsibility of administering the customs laws for goods imported into their territory. This means, for example, that the member states are charged with collecting the duty when goods are imported from nonmember states into the EU through their country. Because of the importance of the Rotterdam port, the Netherlands historically has collected more customs duties than any other member state. These funds are then remitted to the EU for inclusion in the EU budget.

(b) Declaration

The first step in the process is for the importer to submit a customs declaration to the customs authorities in the member state into which the goods will be imported.[18] In the declaration, the importer identifies the goods and the tariff code under which the importer considers the goods to fall. The customs authorities periodically will conduct an audit to determine if the goods have been properly declared.

As each member state has its own customs authorities, and the classification in the declaration is determined by the importers, there is the potential for different classifications of the same goods. In *Sunshine Deutschland Handelsgesellschaft mbH v. Hauptzollamt Kiel*, for example, a German importer of pumpkin seeds classified the seeds under a heading that required it to pay a duty of 3 percent.[19] Sunshine Deutschland later discovered that the Dutch customs authorities had classified pumpkin seeds of a competitor under a different heading which carried no duties and Sunshine Deutschland applied for a refund. The ECJ held that the Dutch customs authority was correct, and that Sunshine Deutschland was incorrectly classifying its pumpkin seeds (to its own detriment).

The challenge of classification is eased somewhat for the importer by the possibility of requesting binding tariff information (often referred to as BTI) from the customs authorities of the member states.[20] This process essentially involves the importer asking the relevant customs authority in advance how to classify a particular product. Thousands of BTIs are issued each year by the customs authorities of the member states.

---

18. A customs declaration may be made by any person who is able to present the goods in question or to have them presented to the competent customs authority, together with all the documents that are required to be produced for the application of the rules governing the customs procedure in respect of which the goods were declared.
19. Case C-229/06, Sunshine Deutschland Handelsgesellschaft mbH v. Hauptzollamt Kiel, 2007 E.C.R. I-3251.
20. Union Customs Code at art. 20.

The conclusion reached by a member state is binding on all of the other member states.[21] However, the customs authorities may revoke a BTI if it becomes apparent that the original classification was wrong at the time or wrong based on subsequent knowledge.[22] The importer may challenge the classification made in the BTI by bringing a claim in the national court where the customs authority is located.[23] In order to monitor the uniformity of the binding information provided by the member states, the customs authorities are required to inform the Commission of any binding information which they issue. If the BTI is inconsistent with other binding tariff information, the Commission has the authority to issue a decision revoking the binding tariff information.[24] Although the importer is entitled to rely on the binding information, if the EU changes the classifications used in the CCT, the conclusion reached in the binding information may no longer be valid.[25]

(c) *Classification*

As discussed above, the Union Customs Code relies on a tariff system that identifies tariffs for categories of products. One of the fundamental challenges is, therefore, to classify specific goods into the appropriate category. In many instances, the classification of goods is unambiguous; the particular goods can be classified according to a specific heading in the Combined Nomenclature. However, for new products or products which could technically fit into two or more categories, the challenges are greater. In *BVBA Van Landeghem v. Belgium*, for example, the issue was whether pick-up trucks fell under the heading "motor cars and other motor vehicles principally designed for the transport of persons" or "motor vehicles for the transport of goods."[26] In reality, one may purchase pick-up trucks for both the transport of goods or for the transport of persons. The ECJ concluded, however, that the pick-up trucks were to be classified as "motor cars and other motor vehicles principally designed for the transport of persons."[27] Another case which illustrates the challenges associated with classification in customs law is *Canon Deutschland GmbH v. Hauptzollamt Duisburg*.[28] Canon imported into the EU camcorders that could easily have been classified under two CN codes. The only difference between the two codes was that the code with the lower customs duty did not contemplate video cameras with the ability to record images other than those taken with the camera or television.

---

21. Implementing Regulation at art. 11.
22. Case C-133/02 and C-134/02, Timmermanns Transport & Logistics BV v. Inspecteur der Belastingdienst Douanedistrict Roosendaal, 2004 E.C.R. I-1125, 1156 ¶25.
23. Joined cases C-288/09 & 289/09, British Sky Broadcasting Group plc v. The Commissioners for Her Majesty's Revenue & Customs, 2011 E.C.R. I-2854, 2889 ¶96.
24. *See, e.g.*, Commission Decision of 30 September 2003 concerning the validity of certain binding tariff information, 2003 O.J. (L 262) 27.
25. Case C-315/96, Lopex Export GmbH v. Hauptzollamt Hamburg-Jonas, 1998 E.C.R. I-317, 342 ¶28.
26. Case C-486/06, BVBA Van Landeghem v. Belgium, 2007 E.C.R. I-10661.
27. *Id.* at 10663 ¶43.
28. Joined Cases C-208/06 and 209/06, Canon Deutschland GmbH v. Hauptzollamt Duisburg, 2007 E.C.R. I-7965.

For example, camcorders with a DV-in capability able to record images from a computer fell under the code with the higher customs duty. In this particular case, the DV-in function of the camcorders was only possible if the customer manipulated the camcorder. Canon did not promote the DV-in function. The ECJ was forced to adopt a pragmatic solution. It held that the camcorders fell under the code with the higher duty if the activation of the DV-in function may easily be made by a user without special skills and without the camcorder being subjected to modification of its hardware.[29]

The general rule in classifying goods is that the decisive criterion for the classification is the wording of the relevant heading of the Combined Nomenclature and the notes to the relevant sections or chapters.[30] If the heading and the notes are not clear, reference is made to the general rules and the Explanatory Notes provided in the Customs Cooperation Council (CCC).[31] For example, the Explanatory Notes define "yogurt" under heading 04031011 as "products which are obtained by the lactic fermentation of *Streptococcus thermophilus* and *Lactobacillus delbrueckii* subsp. *bulgaricus* exclusively." Although limited space and the large number of Explanatory Notes that relate to specific categories of products prohibit an exhaustive discussion of that interpretive aid, a brief discussion of the six general rules assists in understanding the complexities of the classification component of EU customs law.

The first general rule (Rule 1) is that the titles of sections, chapters, and subchapters are for reference only. Classification is made on the basis of headings and section or chapter notes (and not on the titles). The classification of the product is determined by its objective characteristics as defined in the wording of the relevant heading of the CCT and the notes to the sections and chapters.[32] However, as illustrated by *Wiener v. Hauptzollamt Emmerich*,[33] sometimes the objective characteristics of the product are not sufficient to classify the product, and other factors must be relied on. The issue in that case was whether particular garments were to be classified as pajamas or dresses. The ECJ concluded that the goods were to be classified on the basis of the intended use. Although the garments could be used as dresses, they were intended to be used as pajamas.[34]

---

29. *Id.* at 7979 ¶43.
30. Case C-396/02, DFDS BV v. Inspecteur der Belastingdienst—Douanedistrict Rotterdam, 2004 E.C.R. I-8439, 8465 ¶27.
31. Explanatory Notes to the Combined Nomenclature of the European Communities, 2006 O.J. (C 50) 1. The Explanatory Notes are merely interpretive aids and not legally binding. Case C-380/12, X BV v. Staatssecretaris van Financiën, 2014 E.C.R. I-___, at ¶48; Case C-376/07, Staatssecretaris van Financiën v. Kamino International Logistics BV, 2009 E.C.R. I-1196, 1213 ¶28; Case C-500/04, Proxxon GmbH v. Oberfinanzdirektion Köln, 2006 E.C.R. I-1547, 1557 ¶22.
32. Case C-130/02, Krings GmbH v. Oberfinanzdirecktion Nürnberg, 2004 E.C.R. I-2121, 2136 ¶28; Case C-276/00, Turbon International GmbH v. Oberfinanzdirektion Koblenz, 2002 E.C.R. I-1389, 1419 ¶21.
33. Case 338/95, Wiener v. Hauptzollamt Emmerich, 1997 E.C.R. I-6495.
34. *Id.* at 6524 ¶15.

Rule 2 has two components. First, it addresses the classification of incomplete, unfinished, unassembled, or disassembled goods. Any reference in a heading to a product refers to the finished product as well as the incomplete or unfinished product if the incomplete or unfinished product has the essential character of the complete or finished product. The same rule also applies to an unassembled or disassembled product.

For example, many products are shipped in an unassembled or disassembled state because of packing limitations. The HS explanatory note to Rule 2(a) explains that unassembled or disassembled means products the components of which are to be assembled either by means of simple fixing devices (e.g., screws, nuts, or bolts) or by riveting or welding, provided that only simple assembly operations are involved. What is meant by simple assembly operations is determined on a case-by-case basis.

In *Develop Dr. Eisbein GmbH & Co. v. Hauptzollamt Stuttgart-West*,[35] a German company (Eisbein) tried to avoid paying an antidumping duty on photocopiers imported from Japan by importing the photocopiers in unassembled kits containing 200 parts. In its customs declaration, Eisbein classified the goods as unassembled parts for photocopiers. The German customs authorities, however, concluded that based on Rule 2(a), the kits should be classified as photocopiers. Eisbein argued that the assembly of the copiers using the kits involved more than a "simple assembly operation." The ECJ held that the importation of all parts of a completely unassembled product must be considered a complete product regardless of the effort needed to assemble the product, as the wording of Rule 2(a) does not refer to the assembly technique.

The second component of Rule 2 concerns mixtures. The basic rule is that any reference in a heading to a material or substance is to be interpreted to include a reference to mixtures or combinations of that material or substance with other materials or substances. Any reference to goods of a given material or substance is to be interpreted to include a reference to goods consisting wholly or partly of such material or substance (Rule 2(b)). Goods consisting of more than one material or substance are classified according to the principles of Rule 3.

Rule 3 addresses the situation when goods are classifiable under two or more headings.[36] In *Pacific World Limited v. The Commissioners for Her Majesty's Revenue & Customs*, plastic false finger nail sets fell both under heading 3304 (beauty or make-up preparations) and 3926 (other articles of plastic).[37] On the other hand, the ECJ held in *BVBA Van Landeghem v. Belgium* that pickup trucks could not reasonably be classified under both "motor cars and other motor vehicles principally designed for the transport of persons" and "motor vehicles for the transport of goods" and therefore Rule 3 was not applicable.[38] According

---

35. Case C-35/93, Develop Dr. Eisbein GmbH & Co. v. Hauptzollamt Stuttgart-West, 1994 E.C.R. I-2655.
36. Joined Cases C-362/07 and C-363/07, Kip Europe SA v. Administration des douanes, 2008 E.C.R. I-9520, 9539 ¶39.
37. C-215/10, Pacific World Limited v. The Commissioners for Her Majesty's Revenue & Customs, 2011 E.C.R. I-7257, 7269 ¶32.
38. Case C-486/06, BVBA Van Landeghem v. Belgium, 2007 E.C.R. I-10663, 10682 ¶42.

to Rule 3(a), if an article falls under two or more headings, the heading that provides the more specific description applies instead of the heading with a more general description (Rule 3(a)).[39] However, Rule 3(a) only provides assistance if there is a heading for the goods that provides a specific description under which the goods may be categorized.[40] For example, in *Vau De Sport GmbH & Co. KG v. Oberfinanzdirektion Koblenz*, the ECJ refused the application of Rule 3(a) because there was no specific tariff heading for back-pack-type baby carriers (neither the heading for baby carriages or backpacks specifically contemplated this good).[41]

According to Rule 3(b), if (a) a good falls under two or more headings and none of them provides a specific description of the goods at issue, or (b) the article is a mixture, a composite good consisting of different materials or made up of different components,[42] or (c) a good offered in sets for retail sale,[43] the article is classified as if it consisted of the material or component which gives it its essential character. According to the ECJ, the essential character of a product composed of various materials is that material which makes it necessary to determine whether the product would retain its characteristic properties if one of the other constituents were removed from it.[44]

In *Turbon International GmbH v. Oberfinanzdirektion Koblenz*, for example, the ECJ held that ink cartridges without an integrated print head should be classified as ink (and not parts for printers) because it is the ink that gives the cartridges their essential character.[45] In *Vau De Sport GmbH & Co. KG v. Oberfinanzdirektion Koblenz*, the ECJ considered that it was the fabric, and not

---

39. *See, e.g.*, Case C-183/06, RUMA GmbH v. Oberfinanzdirektion Nürnberg, 2007 E.C.R. I-1561, 1576 ¶35.
40. Case C-288/99, Vau De Sport GmbH & Co. KG v. Oberfinanzdirektion Koblenz, 2001 E.C.R. I-3683, 3727 ¶23.
41. *Id.*
42. To qualify as a composite good, the component parts of the goods should not be generally sold as individual parts.
43. Goods qualify as "sets" if they consist of at least two different articles which are prima facie classifiable in different headings, consist of articles placed together to meet a particular need, or carry out a specific activity and be placed in a manner suitable for sale directly to users without repackaging. The combination of a radio receiver, record player, and speakers, for example, would be considered as sets (i.e., music centers) when intended for sale as a package. Case 163/84, Hauptzollamt Hannover v. Telefunken Fernseh und Rundfunk GmbH, 1985 E.C.R. 3299. However, ladies' underwear made up of a brassiere and briefs is not considered a set. Case C-80/96, Quelle Schickedanz AG & Co. v. Oberfinanzdirektion Frankfurt am Main, 1998 E.C.R. I-123. The difference between these two cases is that the individual parts of the music center each contribute to the basic function of the music center even though they could be purchased as individual units. The individual parts of women's underwear serve different functions, even though they may be sold together.
44. Case C-173/08, Kloosterboer Services BV v. Inspecteur van de Belastingdienst/ Douane Rotterdam, 2009 E.C.R. I-5349, 5364 ¶32; Case C-150/08, Siebrand BV v. Staatssecretaris van Financiën, 2009 E.C.R. I-3943, 3958 ¶32.
45. Case C-250/05, Turbon International GmbH v. Oberfinanzdirektion Koblenz, 2006 E.C.R. I-10558, 10567 ¶21.

the aluminum frame, that gave the baby carrier its essential function as "the fabric parts sewn together are by themselves sufficient to enable a child to be carried by an adult."[46] Therefore, the carrier was classified as a textile article.

In *Sony v. Commission*, when Sony introduced PlayStation2, the UK Customs and Excise Department classified it as a video game player (CN code 9504 10 00), the imports of which were subject to an ad valorem duty of 2.2 percent. Sony, however, argued that the PlayStation2, with its microprocessor, a DVD player, and Internet connectivity should be classified as a computer (under code 8451 50 90) for which no duties should have been imposed. The General Court held that the Commission had incorrectly classified the Sony PlayStation2 as a video game because that was the function of the product which established its essential character. Instead, it was the computer unit which gave the PlayStation2 its essential character.[47]

According to Rule 4, products that cannot be classified in accordance with Rules 1 through 3 are to be classified under the heading appropriate to the goods to which they are most akin. In other words, if there is not a perfect fit, the product is to be classified under the closest code.

Rule 5 deals with certain products which, although they could be considered separate goods, are considered part of the product which they closely complement. This includes, for example, camera cases, musical instrument cases, gun cases, and similar cases specifically shaped or fitted to contain a specific product or set of products. Packing materials and packing containers presented with the products are to be classified with the goods if they are of a kind normally used for packing such goods. However, this provision is not binding when such packing materials or packing containers are clearly suitable for repetitive use. For example, the ECJ has held that ink and the plastic ink cartridges were to be classified under two different codes, despite the fact that the ink was imported in the ink-jet cartridges.[48] In *Schmid v. Hauptzollamt Stuttgart-West*, however, the ECJ held that beer barrels, bottles, and plastic crates are to be considered packing and not treated separately from the beer for customs purposes even though they were suitable for multiple use.[49]

(d) Origin

The country from which the goods are imported into the EU plays a significant role in the application of trade law because for most imported products, the level of duty differs depending on the country of origin. For example, shoes imported into the EU from China may have a different rate of duty than the same shoes imported from India. The EU has entered into several agreements with third countries and established preferential trade regimes for certain countries. For

---

46. Case C-288/99, Vau De Sport GmbH & Co. KG v. Oberfinanzdirektion Koblenz, 2001 E.C.R. I-3683, 3728 ¶26.
47. Case T-243/01, Sony Computer Entertainment Europe Ltd. v. Comm'n, 2003 E.C.R. II-4195, 4242 ¶127.
48. Case C-276/00, Turbon International GmbH v. Oberfinanzdirektion Koblenz, 2002 E.C.R. I-1389, 1422 ¶33.
49. Case 357/87, Schmid v. Hauptzollamt Stuttgart-West, 1988 E.C.R. 6257, 6260 ¶9.

example, in an effort to support developing countries, the EU has established a Generalized System of Preferences which lowers the customs duties for products imported from certain developing countries.[50] These regimes contain specific rules for determining the origin of products referred to as preferential rules of origin. The standard rules of origin (applicable when there exists no agreement or preferential regime) contained in the Union Customs Code are referred to as nonpreferential rules of origin.[51]

A distinction should be made between goods obtained entirely in one country and goods obtained in more than one country. Goods obtained wholly in one country generally means goods that are produced in one country exclusively from raw materials from that country.[52] As not all goods are "produced" (for example, a company may import fish into the EU), the Customs Code contains special rules. Mineral products extracted from its soil or from its seabed are considered to originate in the country where they are extracted; for vegetable products, it depends on where they are harvested; for products from live animals, it depends on where they are raised; for fish taken from the sea outside a country's territorial waters, it depends on where its vessels are registered.

Goods that have been produced in more than one country are deemed to originate in the country where they underwent their last, substantial, economically justified processing or working in a business equipped for that purpose and resulting in the manufacture of a new product or representing an important stage of manufacture.[53] This is determined primarily in technical terms (as opposed to value terms).[54] The relevant question is where the product underwent its decisive stage of production "during which the use to which the component parts are to be put becomes definite"?[55]

The case of *Brother International v. Hauptzollamt* illustrates some of the complexities of applying this rule to assembly operations.[56] The basic issue in that case was whether the electronic typewriters imported by Brother from Taiwan into Germany originated in Taiwan. The parts for the typewriters were manufactured in Japan and sent to Taiwan for assembly. The German customs authority argued that Brother's factory in Taiwan was a "screwdriver factory" which did no more than unpack and assemble separate parts and consequently did not constitute a substantial process or operation. The ECJ held that the mere assembly of previously manufactured parts originating in a country different

---

50. Council Regulation (EC) No. 980/2005 of 27 June 2005 applying a scheme of generalised tariff preferences, 2005 O.J. (L 169) 1.
51. Union Customs Code at arts. 35-39.
52. *Id.* at art. 36(1).
53. *Id.* at art. 36(2).
54. In exceptional circumstances, the value added by particular operations may be taken into account. Case C-372/06, Asda Stores Ltd. v. Commissioners of Her Majesty's Revenue and Customs, 2007 E.C.R. I-11228, 11251 ¶37.
55. Joined Cases C-447/05 and C-448/05, Thomson Multimedia Sales Europe v. Administration des douanes et droits indirects, 2007 E.C.R. I-2049, 2062 ¶26.
56. Case C-26/88, Brother International GmbH v. Hauptzollamt Giessen, 1989 E.C.R. 4253.

from that in which they were assembled may be sufficient to confer on the resulting product the origin of the country in which assembly took place. This depends on whether the assembly represents the decisive production stage during which the use to which the component parts are to be put becomes definite and the goods in question are given their specific qualities.[57] If the application of that criterion is not conclusive, it is necessary to examine whether all the assembly operations in question result in an appreciable increase in the commercial, ex-factory value of the finished product. Although the value added by the assembly can be a relevant criterion,[58] a value added of less than 10 percent "cannot in any event be regarded as sufficient to confer on the finished product the origin of the country of assembly."[59]

To determine whether the subsequent processing of goods in another country was decisive, the ECJ has recognized that a change in tariff heading or subheading resulting from the processing is a relevant (albeit not decisive or exclusive) factor.[60] Conversely, the fact that the processing did not cause a change in the heading or subheading classification of the goods does not automatically mean that the processing is insignificant.[61] The following operations are considered as insufficient working or processing to confer the status of originating products:

- Activities affecting only the presentation of the goods[62]
- Operations dividing up, packaging, grinding, or sieving[63]
- Operations to ensure the preservation of products in good condition during transport and storage (ventilation, spreading out, drying, chilling, placing in salt, sulfur dioxide or other aqueous solutions, removal of damaged parts, and like operations)
- Simple operations consisting of removal of dust, sifting or screening, sorting, classifying, matching (including the making-up of sets of articles), washing, painting, cutting up
- Changes of packing and breaking-up and assembly of packages
- Simple placing in bottles, flasks, bags, cases, boxes, fixing on cards or boards, etc., and all other simple packaging operations
- Affixing marks, labels, and other like distinguishing signs on products or their packaging.

---

57. *Id.* at 4281 ¶25.
58. Case C-260/08, HEKO Industrieerzeugnisse, 2009 E.C.R. I-11573, 11583 ¶31.
59. *Id.* 11581 ¶23.
60. *Id.* 11584 ¶35.
61. Case C-373/08, Hoesch Metals and Alloys GmbH v. Hauptzollamt Aachen, 2010 E.C.R. I-954, 975 ¶52.
62. Case C-260/08, HEKO Industrieerzeugnisse, 2009 E.C.R. I-11573, 11583 ¶29; Case C-93/83, Zentrag v. Hauptzollamt Bochum, 1984 E.C.R. 1095,1106 ¶13.
63. Case C-373/08, Hoesch Metals and Alloys GmbH v. Hauptzollamt Aachen, 2010 E.C.R. I-954, 974 ¶49.

- Simple mixing of products, whether or not of different kinds, where one or more components of the mixture do not meet the conditions laid down in this section to enable them to be considered as originating in a beneficiary country or in the EU.
- Simple assembly of parts to constitute a complete product.

Accessories, spare parts, or tools delivered with any piece of equipment, machine, apparatus, or vehicle which form part of its standard equipment shall be deemed to have the same origin as that piece of equipment, machine, apparatus, or vehicle.[64]

The theoretical treatment of this issue is often easier than the practical application of the rules. Products are manufactured and sold in almost limitless constellations. Hence, importers are often unable to accurately determine the classification of the particular product. In an effort to bring some clarity to the process, the EU customs rules allow an importer to apply for a certificate of origin from the customs authority of a member state. This is similar to the binding tariff information which is often used by importers in the classification of their products under a tariff code.

(e) Value

As discussed above, there are generally two types of duty rates: ad valorem and fixed rate. Most duties are based on the value of a product being imported (i.e., ad valorum). Hence, determining the value of the product is a necessary task in most cases in determining the amount of duty to be paid.

The general rule is that the customs value of imported goods (i.e., the number upon which the customs duties are based) is the transaction value. The definition of "transaction value" is the price actually paid or payable for the goods when sold for export to the EU.[65] The price actually paid or payable includes all payments made or to be made by the buyer to the seller as a condition of sale of the imported goods. It would also include payments made by the buyer to a third party in satisfaction of an obligation of the seller. The payment need not necessarily take the form of a transfer of money. Payment may be made by way of letters of credit or negotiable instrument and may be made directly or indirectly.

For example, if A sells 1,000 cans of paint to B for €25,000, the transaction value of a can of paint is €25 regardless of whether B pays A immediately in cash or by delivery of a promissory note to be paid at a later date. In *Kyocera Electronics Europe GmbH v. Hauptzollamt Krefeld*, the issue was whether interest paid by the EU importer to the foreign seller should be included in the customs value.[66] In that case, a Japanese company sold electronics products to a distributor in the EU. In an agreement separate from the sale agreement, the buyer agreed to pay the purchase price at a later date together with interest. The ECJ held that "interest ...does not form part of the customs value of imported

---

64. Implementing Regulation at art. 41.
65. Union Customs Code at art. 41(1).
66. Case C-152/01, Kyocera Electronics Europe GmbH v. Hauptzollamt Krefeld, 2003 E.C.R. I-13833.

goods ... but is payment for a service provided to the buyer on the purchase of those goods, the service in the case in the main proceedings consisting in granting deferral of payment to that buyer."[67]

In *Dollond & Aitchison Ltd. v. Commissioners of Customs & Excise*, the issue was whether the payment for examination, consultation, and after-care services associated with the sale of contact lenses should be included in the transaction value of the contact lenses.[68] A Jersey Islands company sold contact lenses to customers in the UK. The customers paid a monthly fee and received a supply of disposable lenses. The subscription fee also included the examination, consultation, and after-care services provided by the importer's network of opticians in the UK. The importer, of course, in an effort to reduce the amount of customs duty payable, argued that the transaction value should only include the price of the contact lenses (since there are no duties on services). The ECJ, however, held that the goods and services are part of a single transaction and should be treated together for purposes of determining the transaction value.

As the actual price paid or payable may not accurately reflect the value of the goods imported into the EU, the actual price paid or payable may be adjusted by the customs authorities. For example, the buyer in the EU may absorb certain costs customarily paid by the seller or provide services customarily provided by the seller. One incentive for structuring the transaction this way is that it lowers the transaction value and hence the amount of duties to be paid. If X agrees to purchase 100 bottles of drinking water from Y for €100, Y might agree to reduce that price to €95 if X provides the containers for transport. Although the price payable is €95, the actual value is closer to €100. The Union Customs Code therefore requires certain adjustments to be made to the price paid or payable if it is to be used as the transaction value.

Typical adjustments include any sales commission and brokerage costs, the costs of containers, and the cost of packaging. For example, if the price paid for the goods does not include the cost of packaging, the transaction value will be increased to take account of reasonable packaging costs. Transport and insurance costs and loading and handling charges are also to be added unless they are already included in the price. If the buyer provides to the seller materials, components, or parts which are incorporated into the good or tools, dies, molds, or similar items, the value of these must be added to the price unless the seller has paid for these separately. This is illustrated in *Compaq Computer International Corporation v. Inspecteur der Belastingdienst*.[69] In that case, Compaq US agreed to pay Microsoft US $31 for each Compaq computer sold with Microsoft software installed on it. Compaq US purchased computers from a Taiwanese manufacturer, and provided the Microsoft software to this manufacturer free of charge for installation on the computers. When the computers were imported into the EU by Compaq US to Compaq Netherlands, Compaq sought to use the

---

67. *Id.* at 13853 ¶36.
68. Case C-491/04, Dollond & Aitchison Ltd. v. Commissioners of Customs and Excise, 2006 E.C.R. I-2129.
69. Case C-306/04, Compaq Computer International Corporation v. Inspecteur der Belastingdienst, 2006 E.C.R. I-10991.

price paid by Compaq US to the Taiwanese manufacturer as the customs value (which, of course, did not reflect the value of the Microsoft software installed on those computers). The ECJ held that the transaction price had to be increased to reflect the value of the Microsoft software.

If the buyer must pay any royalty or license fees as a condition of sale of the goods, these must be added to the price if not already included in the price. Finally, if the goods are to be resold and the seller will receive a part of the proceeds of the resale, the amount of these proceeds needs to be added to the price. Here again, the basic idea is that in the absence of this right to receive proceeds on the resale, the price of the goods would be higher. For example, assume A offers to sell B 100 bicycles for €175 per bicycle. B is not sure that she can resell all of the bicycles at a price above €175. Therefore, A and B agree that B will purchase the bicycles for €150, but A will also receive 10 percent of the price at which B can sell the bicycles. Assuming that B resells each of the bicycles at €200, the subsequent €20 to be paid by B to A must be added to the initial sales price between A and B to determine the transaction value for customs purposes.

The use of the transaction value as the customs value is conditional on the reliability of the transaction price as an indicator of the actual value of the goods. There are four circumstances in which the transaction price is not reliable. First, the transaction value is not reliable if there are restrictions as to the disposal or use of the goods by the buyer (other than restrictions imposed or required by a law or by the public authorities in the EU), if the transaction value limits the geographical area in which the goods may be resold, or if it does not substantially affect the value of the goods. Second, the sale or price must not be subject to some condition or consideration for which a value cannot be determined with respect to the goods being valued. Third, no part of the proceeds of any subsequent resale, disposal, or use of the goods by the buyer will accrue directly or indirectly to the seller, unless an appropriate adjustment can be made.

Finally, the buyer and seller must not be related (unless the relationship did not influence the transaction value).[70] A Buyer and seller are considered to be related if they are officers or directors of each other's business, they are members of the same family, they are part of the same corporate group, they are business partners, they are employer and employee or if any person holds at least 5 percent of the outstanding voting stock in each of them.[71] If the transaction value is not reliable because the buyer and seller are related, the customs value will be constructed by using specific rules applicable to related party transactions. Although the transaction value between related parties is only to be disregarded when the relationship had an influence on the transaction value, there is a general presumption that the value on transactions between related parties is not a reliable indication of the objective value of the goods. The declarant can overcome the presumption that the transaction value between a related buyer and seller is not a reliable indicator of the value of the goods if the declarant can demonstrate

---

70. Union Customs Code at art. 70(3)(d).
71. Customs Code Implementing Regulation at art. 143.

that such value closely approximates the transaction value in sales of identical or similar goods sold to non-related buyers in the UE.

If the transaction value is not a reliable determinate of the customs value, the customs value is the transaction value of identical goods sold for export to the EU and exported at or about the same time as the goods being valued.[72] If the customs value cannot be determined using this method, the transaction value of similar goods sold for export to the EU and exported at or about the same time as the goods being valued is to serve as the customs value.[73] If neither of these two methods proves fruitful, the next method is the value based on the unit price at which the imported goods for identical or similar imported goods are sold within the EU in the greatest aggregate quantity to persons not related to the sellers.[74]

If none of these methods works, the customs authority will use a computed value, consisting of the sum of:

- The cost or value of materials and fabrication or other processing employed in producing the imported goods,
- An amount for profit and general expenses equal to that usually reflected in sales of goods of the same class or kind as the goods being valued which are made by producers in the country of exportation for export to the UE, and
- The cost of value of transport and insurance of the imported goods, and loading and handling charges associated with the transport of the imported goods to the EU.[75]

The commission is primarily responsible for defining the substantive rules and procedures applicable to applying the Common Customs Tariff. The Council is involved only in adopting the Union Customs Code. Although the member states do not have a legislative function, they are responsible for the application and interpretation of the rules, the collection of the duties, and their subsequent remission to the EU. The authorities of the member states in this area are enumerated in the Union Customs Code and the Customs Code Implementing Regulation.

(f) Quotas

As mentioned above, the imposition of quantitative quotas on products imported into or exported from Europe is a part of EU customs law. The Council has the right to limit the quantity or volume of a particular product imported into or exported from the EU but must do so in conformity with the GATT rules.[76] As discussed briefly above, there are two types of quotas. A quota may set an absolute cap on the quantity or volume of products imported into the EU (absolute quotas) or may increase the duty rate applicable to imports of

---

72. Union Customs Code art. 74(2)(a).
73. *Id.* at art. 74(2)(b).
74. *Id.* at art. 742(2)(c).
75. *Id.* at art. 74(2)(d).
76. Cases C-93/02 P and C-94/02 P, Biret Int'l SA v. Council, 2003 E.C.R. I-10497.

a particular product once a specified quota is reached (tariff rate quota). For example, a quota stating that only 1 million widgets may be imported into the EU in a year would be an absolute quota. If the quota stated that the customs duty for the first 1 million widgets imported into the EU would be 1 percent, but the duty for any widgets over 1 million would be 10 percent, it would be a tariff rate quota.

In contrast to the imposition of duties which are not tied to a specific quantity or volume, the establishment of a quantitative quota raises the question of allocation: who gets to import or export how much? Where only duties are imposed, this issue does not arise.

The Commission is responsible for establishing the allocation of quotas.[77] The regulation introducing the quota will identify the method of allocation. There are three common methods of allocation.[78] The first is based on traditional trade flows. The quota is allocated among the traders who can adequately demonstrate that they have exported the particular product during a specified reference period. A certain portion is set aside for nontraditional importers or exporters. The second method of allocation is based on the first come, first served principle. In other words, import or export licenses are allocated based on when the application for the license was submitted. The third method is referred to as the simultaneous examination procedure. Once all of the applications for licenses have been submitted, they are forwarded to the Commission (the members states collect the applications) and the Commission allocates the quotas in proportion to the quantities requested.

Once a license is issued to an importer or exporter, that license is valid throughout the EU regardless of the place of import or export. Import and export licenses may not be loaned or transferred by the person in whose name the license was issued.[79]

1.6 Relief from Customs Duties

The general rule is that non-Union goods are subject to customs duties (if any) when imported into the EU. The application of this rule in specific cases is not always easy because of the myriad of constellations in which a product may find its way to or into the EU. What happens, for example, if a product is merely shipped through the EU from one nonmember state to a customer in another nonmember state? Does the manufacturer or customer have to pay EU customs duties on those goods? The Union Customs Code contains specific rules applicable to different constellations that differ from the "simple" case of a product manufactured in a non-EU country and then exported to and sold in the EU.

(a) External Transit

Union goods are goods that have been released into free circulation in the EU. Non-Union goods are goods that have not been released into free circulation.

---

77. Trade Quotas Regulation at art. 13(1).
78. *Id.* at art. 2(2).
79. *Id.* at art. 18.

This is a fairly obvious point, but it is important to remember the EU terminology. The external transit procedure applies to the movement of non-Union goods from one point to another within the customs territory of the EU.[80] The "external" component of the phrase applies to the goods (it designates that the goods must be non-Union goods) and not to the location of the transport. For example, the external transit procedure applies when non-Union goods are transported from the UK to Ireland. But it may also apply when a Russian manufacturer ships goods to a customer in Macedonia via Poland, Hungary, and Slovenia.

The basic purpose of the external transit procedure is to allow goods to be transported within the EU until they are ready to be released into free circulation or to get them to a customer outside the EU without having to pay customs duties in the EU. The manufacturer can either submit an application for authorization under the external transit procedure or rely on a TIR carnet (a system of external transit established by the Transports Internationaux Routiers Treaty under the auspices of the United Nations Economic Commission for Europe in November 1975).[81] As the movement of goods from one member state to another member state is entirely within a customs union, the TIR carnet would not be the appropriate mechanism. Instead, the manufacturer would probably rely on the external transit procedure.

(b) Customs Warehousing

In practice, when goods are exported to the EU from a third country, the customs authorities in the member state to which the goods are sent do not require the customs duties to be paid before the goods are taken off the ship and physically enter the EU. It is possible that the goods physically enter the EU while retaining their non-Union status. They may be placed in a customs warehouse in the EU until the owner wants to introduce them into free circulation or re-export them.[82] The customs warehousing procedure requires that the warehouse be approved by and under the supervision of the customs authorities in the member state where goods are stored. In some instances, the customs authorities of the member state may operate a warehouse themselves. In other cases, the owner of the goods may use a commercial public warehouse not operated by the customs authorities. In this case, the commercial warehouse must have already received proper authorization to operate as a customs warehouse.

(c) Inward Processing

Many products are made from various raw materials. For example, a chair may be made out of wood, leather, nails, and glue. If a chair manufacturer in the EU imports these raw materials, it would normally have to pay customs duties on them. If, however, the chair manufacturer subsequently exports the chairs rather than selling them in the EU, the raw materials are not technically being consumed in the EU. In recognition of this possibility, the Union Customs

---

80. Union Customs Code at art. 144.
81. The EU is a member of the TIR Convention, Council Regulation (EEC) No. 2112/78 of 25 July 1978, 1978 O.J. (L 252) 1.
82. Union Customs Code at art. 148.

Code contains an inward processing procedure that allows non-Union goods to be imported into the EU without having to pay customs duties if they are used in processing operations and intended for re-export from the EU in the form of compensating products.[83] This includes goods that are assembled into other goods and exported as well as raw materials that are physically processed into a new product.

(d) *Processing under Customs Control*

If the goods are imported into the EU and used in the EU in operations that alter their state, EU customs duties are not imposed on the imported goods but rather on the goods resulting from the processing.[84] For example, a fruit drink manufacturer in the EU may import sugar to be added to the fruit drinks which it processes in the EU.[85] The applicable rate of duty is that for fruit drinks and not for sugar. Of course, this exception for processing under customs control—for which authorization from the national customs authorities is required[86]—is only attractive for importers if the rate of duties on the processed product is less than the duties on the imported inputs. In the fruit drink example, the processing exception is probably attractive given the high duty rates imposed on sugar imports into the EU.

(e) *Outward Processing*

The converse of the processing under customs control is the situation where Union goods are exported from the EU, processed, and then reimported back into the EU. The outward processing procedure applies to this constellation. It allows EU goods to be exported temporarily from the customs territory of the EU in order to undergo processing operations and the products resulting from those operations to be released for free circulation with total or partial relief from import duties.[87]

(f) *Temporary Importation*

If the non-Union goods enter the EU for only a brief period, are used there, and then are exported from the EU back to the nonmember state in essentially the same state as they were imported, neither the inward processing nor the processing under customs control procedures applies. For example, a manufacturer of heavy equipment in Los Angeles may have a customer in Paris. In order to install the equipment at the customer's factory in Paris, the U.S. manufacturer has to send technicians and tools to France. The temporary importation of the tools will generally not require the payment of customs duties if the temporary importation procedure is followed.[88] The basic requirement is that the imported products be exported in substantially the same state as they

---

83. *Id.* at arts. 142 and 168.
84. *Id.* at art. 168.
85. *See, e.g.*, Case C-11/05, Friesland Coberco Dairy Foods BV v. Inspecteur van de Belastingdienst, 2006 E.C.R. I-4285.
86. Union Customs Code at art. 136.
87. *Id.* at arts. 48 and 171.
88. *Id.* at art. 162.

were imported. There is a specific authorization procedure under which one applies for an Admission Temporaire/Temporary Admission (ATA) carnet.

(g) Internal Transit

Whereas the external transit procedure deals with non-Union goods passing through the EU, the internal transit procedure deals with Union goods passing through countries outside the EU. Most products have to be transported from the manufacturer to the customer. As the EU is not made up of contiguous countries, products manufactured in one member state may have to pass through a nonmember state for delivery to the customer in another member state. For example, a shipment of olives from Greece to Denmark on a truck may have to pass through several nonmember states. Just because the Union good leaves the territory of the EU does not mean that it loses its status as a Union good. The Customs Code provides for an internal transit procedure that allows the goods to retain their customs status as Union goods.[89]

2. Common Commercial Policy

As discussed in Chapter I, the Treaty of Rome established a common market. This is an area characterized by the absence of tariff barriers to trade between the member states as well as the free movement of labor and capital. Another important characteristic of the common market is the relinquishment by the individual member states of their autonomy to adopt individual commercial policies vis-à-vis nonmember states (i.e., external trade). In the EU, this area of law is considered part of the common commercial policy.[90]

From a legal perspective, there are two important implications of having a common commercial policy. First, the EU as a subject of international law can enter into international trade agreements and assume obligations with other nations. Second, the EU has the authority to adopt measures to achieve the objectives of the common commercial policy.

2.1 International Regimes

(a) General Background of the World Trade Organization

It was originally intended that the post-war international economic order would consist of three institutions: the World Bank, the International Monetary Fund (IMF) and an International Trade Organization (ITO). The World Bank and the IMF were successfully established in 1944. Due to opposition from the United States, the instrument which was supposed to establish the ITO, the Havana Charter, was never ratified. However, the need for an international body to administer global trading rules was still widely recognized. Part IV of the Havana Charter relating to trade policy was accepted by 23 states.

---

89. *Id.* at art. 145.
90. The Common Commercial Policy is codified in Art. 206-207 of the TFEU.

These provisions, known as the General Agreement on Tariffs and Trade, came into force on January 1, 1948.[91] The EU is a member of GATT.[92]

The fundamental objective of GATT is the progressive liberalization of world trade. There are several basic principles upon which the GATT regime is based. Perhaps the most important of these is the principle of nondiscrimination. This principle is implemented in the form of the most-favored-nation status. Other important principles codified in the GATT are: more favorable treatment for developing countries; elimination of quantitative restrictions and prohibition of export subsidies; tariffs as the only legal instrument of protection; and transparency of national trade legislation.

(b) *The Uruguay Round*

The Uruguay Round refers to the negotiations which were launched in Punta del Este, Uruguay, in 1986. The central agreement, to which the EU is a party,[93] is an expansive document with over 600 pages of text and 25,000 pages of schedules. In addition, there were 16 separate multilateral agreements reached as part of the Uruguay Round:

- Agriculture
- Sanitary and Phytosanitary Measures
- Textiles and Clothing
- Technical Barriers to Trade
- Trade-related Investment Measures
- Anti-Dumping
- Customs Valuation
- Preshipment Inspections
- Rules of Origin
- Import Licensing Procedures
- Subsidies and Countervailing Measures
- Safeguards
- General Agreement of Trade in Services
- Trade-related Intellectual Property
- Dispute Settlement
- Trade Policy Review Mechanism

Some of these agreements simply built on or refined existing agreements, whereas others extended the application of GATT to new sectors. All aspects

---

91. General Agreement on Tariffs and Trade, Oct. 30, 1947, 61 Stat. A-11, T.I.A.S. 1700, 55 U.N.T.S. 194 [hereinafter GATT].
92. 1994 O.J. (L 336) 3.
93. Council Decision 94/800/EC of 22 December 1994 concerning the conclusion on behalf of the European Community, as regards matters within its competence, of the agreements reached in the Uruguay Round multilateral negotiations (1986-1994), 1994 O.J. (L 336) 1.

of agricultural policy were brought into GATT. The field of application of the GATT was extended to include new sectors such as the agreements on Trade-Related Aspects of Intellectual Property Rights (commonly referred to as TRIPS), on General Agreement on Trade in Services (commonly referred to as GATS), on public procurement markets, and on trade-related investment measures (commonly referred to as TRIMS). The Uruguay Round also resulted in the revision of the GATT trade protection measures, particularly anti-dumping and anti-subsidy measures, measures based on the safeguard clause, customs valuation, preshipment inspection, rules of origin, and export licenses.

(c) Creation of the WTO

In response to the perceived inability of the GATT to act as an effective guarantor of the rules, the states participating in the Uruguay Round agreed to create a new international organization to oversee world trade. The World Trade Organization (WTO) started its activities in 1995 under the administrative umbrella of the United Nations. The WTO framework substantially differs from the GATT: it established the administration of a unified package of agreements to which all members are committed, it introduced new areas into the multilateral trading system, and it established a new dispute settlement procedure.

(d) Settlement of Disputes

The effectiveness of a supranational legal regime depends largely on its enforcement. The WTO is only indirectly involved in enforcing the rules. The WTO relies on its members to initiate disputes and impose sanctions. The WTO members are permitted to impose sanctions in the form of the suspension of concessions or obligations but only after the Dispute Settlement Mechanism (DSM) has been complied with.

The details of the DSM, as a forum for settling trade disputes between the signatories to the GATT, are set out in the Understanding on Rules and Procedures Governing the Settlement of Disputes.[94] If a WTO member considers that another member is not complying with its obligations, it may request consultations with the alleged offending member. If the WTO members are unable to resolve their dispute within 60 days through consultation, or the alleged offending member refuses to enter into consultations within 30 days, the complaining member may request the establishment of a panel.[95]

The Dispute Settlement Body (DSB), the permanent organ of the DSM, then establishes a panel of three "well-qualified governmental and/or non-governmental individuals."[96] If the parties to the dispute cannot agree on the panelists within 20 days after the panel is established, the Director General of the WTO makes the ultimate decision.[97] After hearing the parties, the panel then

---

94. Understanding on Rules and Procedures Governing the Settlement of Disputes, Apr. 1, 1994, Marrakesh Agreement Establishing the World Trade Organization, Annex 1C, 33 I.L.M. 112 (1994) [hereinafter DSU].
95. DSU at art. 4(7).
96. DSU at art. 8(1). The Secretariat of the DSB maintains a list of individuals meeting the qualifications of a panelist.
97. DSU at art. 8(7).

adopts a report which is presented to the DSB for adoption or refusal. However, either party may appeal the decision of the panel to the Appellate Body,[98] in which case the decision of the DSB on the panel report is suspended. Within 60 days, the Appellate Body will issue its report on the case. The conclusions reached by the Appellate Body are considered those of the DSB unless the DSB affirmatively decides not to adopt the report.[99]

The members are expected to comply with the DSB's decisions within a "reasonable period of time."[100] In the EU, the Commission has the authority to repeal or amend the disputed measure once the DSB issues a negative report on that measure.[101] If the WTO member fails to comply within a reasonable time, that member is obligated to enter into negotiations with the member that initiated the dispute settlement procedures.[102] If the members cannot agree to a resolution within 20 days after the end of the reasonable period of time, the complaining party may impose sanctions in the form of the suspension of concessions or other obligations.[103] As discussed above, there are two duty rates for each product classified in the Union Customs Code: the autonomous rate of duty and the conventional rate of duty. The autonomous rate of duty does not reflect the concessions which the EU has made in trade agreements. Consequently, it is higher than the conventional rate.

As a member of the WTO, the EU is obligated to grant the conventional rate of duty to imports from other WTO countries. Noncompliance with a decision of the DSB allows a WTO country to suspend the application of the concessions it has made in the context of the WTO to the noncomplying country. As membership in the WTO secures mutual beneficial trade treatment to the members, the suspension of these concessions may impose a substantial stimulus for compliance. For example, in response to the failure of the United States to conform its dumping and subsidy law to the WTO rules as decided by the Appellate Body and the DSB,[104] the EU suspended tariff concessions

---

98. The Appellate Body is a standing body of the DSM composed of seven individuals. Three of these individuals will be assigned to a specific case. DSU at art. 17(1).
99. DSU at art. 17(14).
100. DSU at art. 21(3).
101. Regulation (EU) 2015/476 of the European Parliament and of the Council of 11 March 2015 on the measures that the Union may take following a report adopted by the WTO Dispute Settlement Body concerning anti-dumping and anti-subsidy matters, 2015 O.J. (L 83) 6.
102. DSU at art. 22(2).
103. DSU at art. 22(1). *See, e.g.*, Council Regulation (EC) No. 2193/2003 establishing additional customs duties on imports of certain products originating in the United States of America, 2003 O.J. (L 328) 3.
104. The particular law that was challenged was the Continued Dumping and Subsidy Offset Act of October 28, 2000 (often referred to as the Byrd Amendment). The offending part of the law allowed the U.S. government to distribute the anti-dumping and anti-subsidies duties collected by the U.S. government to the U.S. companies that brought the cases.

and even increased duties on certain products exported from the United States to the EU.[105]

In many instances, the WTO member will comply with the decision of the DSB without the imposition of sanctions.[106] In the Dynamic Random Access Memories (DRAMs) investigation, the EU imposed countervailing duties of 33 percent on imports of DRAMs from South Korea.[107] As discussed in greater detail below, countervailing duties are imposed when foreign imports have benefited from illegal subsidies. The basic idea is that the countervailing duties offset the subsidies and place the domestic industry on a level playing field. In this particular case, however, South Korea initiated a WTO dispute resolution panel to contest the conformity of the EU legislation with the WTO Agreement on Subsidies and Countervailing Measures. The panel upheld several of South Korea's claims. The DSB subsequently adopted the findings of the dispute resolution panel.[108] The EU then amended the legislation to bring it into conformity with the Agreement on Subsidies and Countervailing Measures.[109]

Political considerations, of course, do not always allow for prompt compliance. In many cases, countries will need to be prodded into compliance. As the U.S. Steel Tariffs case illustrates, an indirect enforcement mechanism may be just as effective as if the WTO were given direct enforcement powers. Section 201 of the U.S. Trade Act of 1974 permits the President to grant temporary relief in the form of safeguard tariffs to domestic industries that are found to be seriously injured by an increase in imports of goods which are like or competitive with the products produced by those industries. After a report of the U.S. International Trade Commission that certain steel products were being imported into the United States in quantities that could cause serious injury to the domestic industry,[110] President Bush imposed tariffs ranging from 8 percent to 30 percent on certain steel products such as flat-rolled steel, rebar, stainless

---

105. Council Regulation (EC) No. 673/2005 of 25 April 2005 establishing additional customs duties on imports of certain products originating in the United States of America, 2005 O.J. (L 110) 1.
106. *See, e.g.*, Notice regarding the anti-dumping measures in force on imports of certain iron or steel fasteners originating in the People's Republic of China, following the recommendations and rulings adopted by the Dispute Settlement Body of the World Trade Organisation on 28 July 2011 in the EC—Fasteners dispute (DS397), 2012 O.J. (C 66) 29.
107. Council Regulation (EC) No. 1480/2003 of 11 August 2003 imposing a definitive countervailing duty and collecting definitively the provisional duty imposed on imports of certain electronic microcircuits known as DRAMs (dynamic random access memories) originating in the Republic of Korea, 2003 O.J. (L 212) 1.
108. European Communities—Countervailing Measures on Dynamic Random Access Memory Chips from Korea—(WT/DS299)—Report of the Panel, WT/DS299/R.
109. Council Regulation (EC) No. 2116/2005 of 20 December 2005 amending Regulation (EC) No. 1480/2003 imposing a definitive countervailing duty and collecting definitively the provisional duty imposed on imports of certain electronic microcircuits known as DRAMs (dynamic random access memories) originating in the Republic of Korea, 2006 O.J. (L 340) 7.
110. 66 Fed. Reg. 35267 (July 3, 2001).

steel bar, and welded pipe imported into the United States.[111] The EU, along with several other countries (Brazil, China, Japan, Korea, New Zealand, Norway, and Switzerland) claimed that the U.S. steel tariffs violated the Agreement on Safeguards, the GATT, and Article XVI of the WTO Agreement.

The inability of the United States and the EU to settle their dispute through mandatory consultations led the DSB to create a panel on June 3, 2002.[112] The panel subsequently issued a report which concluded that the U.S. steel tariffs violated the WTO Agreement on Safeguards. The Unites States then appealed the panel report to the WTO Appellate Body. In November 2003, the WTO Appellate Body upheld most of the findings reached by the panel. Political pressure and the threat of retaliation measures by the EU caused President Bush to terminate the safeguard measures.[113] Once the United States withdrew its safeguard measures, the EU did the same.[114] This example illustrates how the WTO dispute resolution system works without the WTO itself having enforcement authority.

(e) Relationship Between the WTO Agreements and EU Law

The Agreement Establishing the WTO states that the ancillary multilateral agreements identified above are integrated into it.[115] The signatories are required to conform their laws, regulations, and administrative practices with each of these multilateral agreements.[116] As a signatory to the WTO Agreement,[117] the EU is therefore obligated to transpose the WTO multilateral agreements into the EU legal system. The various EU trade law instruments discussed below represent the EU's attempt to comply with this obligation. Although EU trade law is based on EU legislation (and not directly on the WTO Agreements), the EU trade instruments discussed below closely resemble the text of the WTO Agreements.

As the text of the EU trade laws is not identical to the WTO multilateral agreements and is subject to interpretation and application by bodies which are not immune to political influences, there is the potential for conflict between the WTO agreements and EU trade law. The general rule commanded by international law is that in cases of conflict, the WTO Agreements take precedence over EU trade law. Consequently, the EU trade instruments must be

---

111. Presidential Proclamation 7529.
112. Separate panels were created for the other complaining countries.
113. According to Section 204 of the Trade Act of 1974.
114. Commission Regulation No. 2142/2003 of 5 December 2003 terminating the definitive safeguard measures in relation to certain steel products imposed by Commission Regulation No. 1694/2002, 2003 O.J. (L 321) 1.
115. Art. 2(2) of the Agreement Establishing the World Trade Organization in Final Act Embodying the Results of the Uruguay Round of Multilateral Trade Negotiations, Apr. 15, 1994, 33 I.L.M. 1125, 1144-1154 (1994) [hereinafter WTO Agreement].
116. WTO Agreement at art. 16(4).
117. Council Decision 94/800/EC of 22 December 1994 concerning the conclusion on behalf of the European Community, as regards matters within its competence, of the agreements reached in the Uruguay Round multilateral negotiations (1986-1994), 1994 O.J. (L 336) 1.

interpreted and applied by the EU institutions and member states in conformity with the international trade laws.[118]

The impact of the primacy of WTO law over EU law has been tempered by the pragmatic limitation of the ECJ on its jurisdiction to adjudicate such issues. According to Article 263 of the TFEU, the ECJ has jurisdiction to review the legality of acts adopted by the EU institutions relating to an infringement of the TFEU or of any rule of law relating to its application. Nonetheless, the ECJ has repeatedly stated that it does not have general subject matter jurisdiction to review the legality of EU legislation for its conformity with WTO law.[119] Instead, the ECJ has taken the position that it only has jurisdiction to adjudicate the conflict between WTO and EU law in two instances: (1) where the EU has intended to implement a particular obligation assumed in the context of the WTO or (2) where the EU legislation expressly refers to the precise provision of WTO law.[120]

In *Petrotub and Republica v Council*, for example, the conformity of the EU Anti-Dumping Regulation with the WTO Anti-Dumping Code was contested.[121] The specific issue was whether the method of comparison of the export price and the normal price under the EU Anti-Dumping Regulation (as discussed below, a finding of dumping requires a comparison of the export price of the products with the normal price) conformed to the WTO Anti-Dumping Code.[122] As a threshold issue, however, the ECJ had to determine whether it (as a court of limited jurisdiction) had jurisdiction in this case to review the conformity of EU legislation with the WTO Anti-Dumping Code. As the EU Anti-Dumping Regulation was intended to implement the WTO Anti-Dumping Code, the ECJ concluded that it had jurisdiction in this case.[123] The jurisdiction of the EU courts to review the Anti-Dumping and the Anti-Subsidy Regulations for conformity with the corresponding WTO Agreement has been subsequently confirmed.[124]

2.2 EU Trade Instruments

As discussed above, the member states have ceded authority for external trade to the EU. The laws and policy decisions made under this authority are generally referred to as the common commercial policy. The TFEU provisions governing the common commercial policy (Articles 206 and 207) not only grant the EU the authority to conclude trade treaties with third countries (such as the

---

118. Case C-76/00 P, Petrotub International SA v. Council, 2003 E.C.R. I-118, 142 ¶57.
119. Case C-351/04, Ikea Wholesale Ltd. v. Commissioners of Customs & Excise, 2007 E.C.R. I-7771, 7784 ¶29; Case C-76/00 P, Petrotub and Republica v. Council, 2003 E.C.R. I-118, 141 ¶53; Case T-118/10, Acron OAO v. Council, 2013 E.C.R. I-___, at ¶63.
120. Case C-361/11, Hewlett-Packard Europe BV v. Inspecteur van de Belastingsdienst, 2013 E.C.R. I-___, at ¶57; Case C-351/04, Ikea Wholesale Ltd. v. Commissioners of Customs & Excise, 2007 E.C.R. I-7771, 7784 ¶29.
121. Case C-76/00 P, Petrotub and Republica v. Council, 2003 E.C.R. I-118, 141 ¶53.
122. Agreement on Implementation of Article VI of the General Agreement on Tariffs and Trade 1994, 1994 O.J. (L 336) 103.
123. Case C-76/00 P, Petrotub and Republica v. Council, 2003 E.C.R. I-118 142 ¶56.
124. Case T-45/06, Reliance Industries Ltd. v. Council, 2008 E.C.R. II-2404, 2437 ¶91.

WTO agreements), but also grant the EU the authority to adopt measures to implement the common commercial policy (Art. 207 TFEU). There are four main instruments of EU legislation adopted on the basis of this authority. They are often referred to as "trade instruments" or "trade measures":[125]

- Anti-Dumping Regulation[126]
- Anti-Subsidy/Countervailing Measures Regulation[127]
- Safeguards Regulation[128]
- Trade Barriers Regulation[129]

2.3 Anti-Dumping

The term "dumping" generally refers to selling a product at a price below the cost of making the product. In general, anti-dumping laws are designed to prevent the perceived damage that dumping by a foreign importer may cause to the domestic industry. The laws accomplish this objective by imposing anti-dumping duties which have the effect of increasing the prices for the products concerned above a level at which they would be sold if the anti-dumping duties were not imposed.[130] Hence, businesses established in the EU may achieve results (i.e., artificially high prices) via the anti-dumping laws, which they may not otherwise achieve in a competitive market (i.e., the type of market which the competition laws discussed in Chapter III were designed to protect). For example, if the Council imposes anti-dumping duties of 10 percent on bicycles imported into the EU from China, the market price for bicycles in the EU may increase by a percentage somewhere between 0 percent and 10 percent. If, however, the European bicycle producers got together and agreed that they

---

125. The first three (the Anti-Dumping Regulation, Anti-Subsidy Regulation, and Safeguards Regulation) are referred to as trade defense instruments whereas the fourth (the Trade Barriers Regulation) is referred to as a trade barriers instrument to illustrate that it is proactive (employed to open markets) rather than defensive.
126. Council Regulation (EC) No. 1225/2009 of 30 November 2009 on protection against dumped imports from countries not members of the European Community, 2009 O.J. (L 343) 51 [hereinafter Anti-Dumping Regulation].
127. Council Regulation (EC) No. 597/2009 of 11 June 2009 on protection against subsidised imports from countries not members of the European Community, 2009 O.J. (L 188) 93 [hereinafter Anti-Subsidy Regulation].
128. Council Regulation (EC) No. 260/2009 of 26 February 2009 on the common rules for imports, 2009 O.J. (L 84) 1 [hereinafter Safeguards Regulation].
129. Council Regulation (EC) No. 3286/94 of 22 December 1994 laying down Community procedures in the field of the common commercial policy, 1994 O.J. (L 349) 71 [hereinafter Trade Barriers Regulation].
130. The policymakers clearly recognize this effect on prices but justify it on the basis that they are restoring fair competition. *See, e.g.*, Council Regulation (EC) No. 716/2006 of 5 May 2006 imposing a definitive anti-dumping duty on imports of dead-burned (sintered) magnesia originating in the People's Republic of China, 2006 O.J. (L 125) 1, 16 ¶115; Council Regulation (EC) No. 397/2004 of 2 March 2004 imposing a definitive anti-dumping duty on imports of cotton-type bed linen originating in Pakistan, 2004 O.J. (L 66) 1, 12 ¶121. The EU is not unique in this respect.

would all raise their prices between 0 percent and 10 percent, their conduct would be strictly prohibited under Article 101 of the TFEU.

The policy justification for the anti-dumping law is that it establishes a level playing field on which EU companies can compete with their non-EU competitors. The EU Anti-Dumping Regulation is the instrument by which the level playing field policy is implemented. In general, the law proceeds in two steps: (1) it identifies the elements of dumping and (2) it identifies when and how the EU may impose anti-dumping duties. The imposition of the anti-dumping duties is thought to be a remedial measure to offset the potential damage of low-priced products. The general rule is that the EU may impose anti-dumping duties if dumping has caused or threatens to cause material injury to a Union industry.

(a) Existence of Dumping

In the EU, the term dumping describes the situation where the price at which the product is sold on the EU market (i.e., the export price) is less than a comparable price for the like product in the exporting country (i.e., the normal value). The term dumping is often mistakenly used to describe the selling of products below market price. For example, if a U.S. steel manufacturer sells steel in the EU at below the prices being offered by the EU steel producers, this would colloquially be referred to as dumping because the U.S. producers are undercutting the EU producers. As will become clear in the discussion below, merely selling products below market prices is not technically dumping. This is because in the context of EU anti-dumping law, the comparison of the export price is made to the normal value and not the market price. However, the relationship between the export price and the market price is relevant at a later stage of the analysis (but not at the dumping determination stage). As discussed in greater detail below, anti-dumping measures are only allowed if the dumping causes injury to the Union industry. It is at the injury determination stage (and not at the dumping determination stage) that price undercutting becomes relevant.[131]

(1) Product Concerned

The term "product concerned" is used to refer to the products allegedly being dumped in the EU and whose manufacturers are suffering injury allegedly caused by the dumping. EU legislation does not formally define the concept of product concerned. According to the General Court: "For the purposes of defining the product concerned, the institutions may take account of a number of factors, such as the physical, technical and chemical characteristics of the products; their use; their interchangeability; consumer perception of the products; distribution

---

131. Council Regulation (EC) No. 1136/2006 of 24 July 2006 imposing a definitive anti-dumping duty and collecting definitively the provisional duty imposed on imports of lever arch mechanisms originating in the People's Republic of China, 2006 O.J. (L 205) 1, 7 ¶64; Commission Regulation (EC) No. 1620/2006 of 30 October 2006 imposing a provisional anti-dumping duty on imports of ironing boards originating in the People's Republic of China and Ukraine, 2006 O.J. (L 300) 13, 27 ¶92, *aff'd by* Council Regulation (EC) No. 452/2007, 2007 O.J. (L 109) 12.

channels; the manufacturing process; costs of production; and quality."[132] Both the Council and the Commission have avoided clarifying whether the term product concerned used in the context of anti-dumping law is different from the concept of "relevant product" used in the context of EU competition law as discussed in Chapter III.[133]

The criteria used by the Commission in defining the relevant market for purposes of competition law do not appear to be meaningfully different from the criteria used in determining the product concerned in the context of anti-dumping proceedings. The relevant product market for purposes of competition law includes products that are regarded as interchangeable or substitutable by the consumer by reason of the products' characteristics, their prices, and their intended use.[134] In determining the product concerned for purposes of anti-dumping law, the Commission and the Council similarly focus on functional interchangeability. Nevertheless, the results of the analyses may differ. One of the issues in the *Aluminum Wheels Originating in the People's Republic of China* case was whether automobile wheels manufactured for the OEM market (i.e., sold directly to original equipment manufacturers) and the same wheels sold to the aftermarket (i.e., as replacement wheels) constituted the product concerned or were two separate products.[135] In the context of EU competition law, the Commission has tended to consider the OEM and the aftermarket two separate product markets.[136] In this case, however, the Council, after analyzing the functional interchangeability and the supply side elasticity of OEM and aftermarket wheels concluded that they "are considered to form one single product market."[137]

---

132. Case T-369/08, European Wine Rope Importers Association v. Commission, 2010 E.C.R. II-6283, 6324 ¶82.
133. However, the General Court has recognized that the existence of competition between two products suggests that they are both products concerned for purposes of EU anti-dumping law. Case T-369/08, European Wine Rope Importers Association v. Comm'n, 2010 E.C.R. II-6283, 6325 ¶88. Moreover, in determining whether the Union industry has suffered injury caused by the anti-dumping, the Commission and Council look at the effect of the imported products on the market shares of the companies comprising the Union industry. In order to derive market shares, the Commission and Council consistently use the definition of products concerned to refer to the relevant market. *See, e.g.*, Commission Regulation (EU) No. 118/2011 of 10 February 2011 imposing a provisional anti-dumping duty on imports of certain ring binder mechanisms originating in Thailand, 2011 O.J. (L 37) 2, 6 ¶44.
134. Commission Notice on the definition of relevant market for the purposes of Community competition law, 1997 O.J. (C 372) 5, 6 ¶7.
135. Council Implementing Regulation (EU) No. 964/2010 of 25 October 2010 imposing a definitive anti-dumping duty and collecting definitively the provisional duty imposed on imports of certain aluminum road wheels originating in the People's Republic of China, 2010 O.J. (L 282) 1, 2 ¶11.
136. Commission Decision of 26 October 2004 declaring a concentration compatible with the common market and the functioning of the European Economic Area (EEA) Agreement (Case No COMP/M.3436—Continental/Phoenix), 2006 O.J. (L 353) 7, 8 ¶6.
137. Council Implementing Regulation (EU) No. 964/2010 of 25 October 2010 imposing a definitive anti-dumping duty and collecting definitively the provisional duty imposed on imports of certain aluminum road wheels originating in the People's Republic of China, 2010 O.J. (L 282) 1, 3 ¶29.

(2) Like Product

As discussed above, dumping exists where the export price of a product to the EU is less than a comparable price for the like product in the exporting country. The term "like product" means a product which is alike in all respects to the product concerned, or in the absence of such a product, another product which, although not alike in all respects, has characteristics closely resembling those of the product under consideration.[138]

(3) Export Price

Determining the export price is relatively simple in most cases; it is the price at which the product is sold to an unrelated buyer in the EU (i.e., the actual export price). For example, if a company in China sells its ring binders to a distributor in the EU, the export price would in most instances be the sale price paid by the EU distributor.[139] In some circumstances, however, reliance on the export price may not provide an accurate basis to compare to the normal value and make the assessment of whether dumping exists. There are two basic reasons why the sales price may not be used. First, there may not be an export price. Second, the export price may be unreliable. The reliability of the export price is commonly at issue. This is because the dumping margin is determined by the difference between the export price and the normal price. There is consequently the tendency to artificially inflate the export price to bring it more into line with the normal price (i.e. reduce the dumping margin).

The Commission, which conducts the investigation, may treat the export price as unreliable in two instances. First, the export price may be unreliable if there is an association between the exporter and the importer or a third party.[140] An association exists, for example, when the exporter and importer are affiliates under common control.[141] Although the Commission and Council will entertain arguments why the prices to a related importer should be used, "the mere fact of association between the exporter and the importer is enough to enable the Commission to treat the actual export prices as unreliable."[142]

Second, the export price may be deemed unreliable if there is a compensatory arrangement between the exporter and the importer or a

---

138. Anti-Dumping Regulation at art. 1(4).
139. *See* Council Regulation (EC) No. 2074/2004 of 29 November 2004 imposing a definitive anti-dumping duty on imports of certain ring binder mechanisms originating in the People's Republic of China, 2004 O.J. (L 359) 11, 14 ¶30.
140. *See, e.g.*, Commission Regulation (EC) No. 390/2007 of 11 April 2007 imposing a provisional anti-dumping duty on imports of peroxosulphates (persulphates) originating in the United States of America, the People's Republic of China, and Taiwan, 2007 O.J. (L 97) 6, 10 ¶44; Council Regulation (EC) No. 258/2005 of 14 February 2005 amending the anti-dumping measures imposed by Regulation (EC) No. 348/2000 on imports of certain seamless pipes and tubes of iron or nonalloy steel originating in Croatia and Ukraine, 2005 O.J. (L 46) 7, 14 ¶46.
141. Case T-466/12, RFA International LP v. Comm'n, ECLI:EU:T:2015:151 at ¶39.
142. Commission Implementing Regulation (EU) 2015/84 of 21 January 2015 imposing a definitive anti-dumping duty and collecting definitively the provisional duty imposed on imports of monosodium glutamate originating in Indonesia, 2015 O.J. (L 15) 54, 55 ¶15.

third party.[143] For example, in an attempt to artificially increase the export price and hence avoid anti-dumping duties, an exporter may agree with the importer in the EU that the importer will pay a high price for the products but will receive a rebate to compensate the importer for the high prices. In these circumstances, i.e. where the actual export price is unreliable, or where there is no export price, the Commission may "construct" an export price.

The constructed export price is based on the price at which the imported products are first resold to an independent buyer in the EU with a deduction being made for costs incurred between import and resale including a reasonable margin for selling, general and administrative costs, and profits.[144] If the goods imported are not resold to an independent buyer, or they are not resold in the condition imported, the EU may use "any reasonable basis" to construct the export price.

(4) Normal Value

(i) Sales Price as Normal Value

The existence of dumping requires a comparison of the export price and the normal value. If the export price is lower than the normal value, dumping is deemed to exist. Determining the normal value is usually more difficult than determining the export price. The general rule is that the normal value is the price paid or payable in the ordinary course of trade by independent customers of the exporter in the exporting country.[145] For example, the normal value of U.S. automobiles imported from the United States to Portugal would be the price at which the U.S. manufacturer is selling that same type of automobile in the United States.

There are generally two situations in which the prices for the product in the exporting country are not used as the normal value. First, there may be no sales or an insufficient volume of sales of a like product in the exporting country. In the *Bicycles Originating in Vietnam* investigation, for example, one Vietnamese producer had no sales of bicycles in Vietnam, as it exported its entire production.[146] Consequently, normal value had to be determined on a constructed basis.

In determining a sufficient sales volume, a threshold of 5 percent is used: if the domestic sales of the exporting producer are less than 5 percent of the total sales volume of the product to the EU, then domestic sales will not be used for

---

143. Anti-Dumping Regulation at art. 2(9).
144. Because there is an incentive to increase the export price in order to reduce the dumping margin, these costs are deducted from the price if they are reflected in the price paid by the EU buyer. In other words, an exporter cannot artificially increase the export price by shifting costs to the buyer which the seller normally would bear.
145. Anti-Dumping Regulation at art. 2(1). The courts give the Council and Commission broad discretion in determining the normal value. Case T-459/07, Hangzhou Duralamp Electronics Co., Ltd. v. Council, 2013 E.C.R. II-4015, at ¶147.
146. Council Regulation (EC) No. 1095/2005 of 12 July 2005 imposing a definitive anti-dumping duty on imports of bicycles originating in Vietnam, and amending Regulation (EC) No. 1524/2000 imposing a definitive anti-dumping duty on imports of bicycles originating in the People's Republic of China, 2005 O.J. (L 183) 1, 13 ¶76.

normal value.[147] If the sales of the like product intended for consumption in the exporting country constitute 5 percent or more of the domestic sales of the exporter, the volume will generally be deemed sufficient.[148] If, for example, the case involved the alleged dumping of Norwegian salmon, and the Norwegian sales of salmon are 10 million tons, and the EU sales of Norwegian salmon are 100 million tons, the value of the Norwegian sales would be considered reliable as the normal value.[149] If the sales volumes of Norwegian salmon are only 1 million tons, they would not be used to determine normal value.[150] This 5 percent threshold is only a general rule. In the *Polyethlene Terephthate* case, 10 percent was deemed to be an insufficient volume for purposes of determining the normal value.[151]

The second situation in which the prices for the product in the exporting country are not used as the normal value is where the sales in the exporting country are not in the ordinary course. Although there is no codified definition of "ordinary course", the ECJ has defined it as being compatible with "commercial practice for sales of the like product in that market and at the relevant time".[152] A common example of sales outside the ordinary course are sales between affiliated companies.[153] The ordinary course rule applies even if the sales in the exporting country are above the 5 percent threshold discussed above. In cases where there is an insufficient volume of sales in the exporting country or the sales are not in the ordinary course, the anti-dumping rules allow the EU to construct the normal value because the sales by the company in its home company are not reliable as an indicator of normal value.

If the exporter does not sell the product in the exporting country, the normal value may be established by the sales of other sellers of the like product in the exporting country. The legal issues concerning the first scenario—the absence of sales of a like product in the exporting country—typically revolve around whether a similar product (of either the exporter or other sellers in the exporting country) could be considered a like product. As discussed above, the term like product means a product which is alike in all respects to the product concerned, or in the absence of such a product, another product which, although not alike in all respects, has characteristics closely resembling those of the product under consideration.[154] This tends to be a factual issue which must be decided on a case-

---

147. *See, e.g.*, Council Regulation No. 1212/2005 of 25 July 2005 imposing a definitive anti-dumping duty on imports of certain castings originating in the People's Republic of China, 2005 O.J. (L 199) 1, 8 ¶48.
148. Anti-Dumping Regulation at art. 2(2). Only profitable sales in the exporting country will be considered.
149. *See, e.g.*, Commission Regulation (EC) No. 628/2005 of 22 April 2005 imposing a provisional anti-dumping duty on imports of farmed salmon originating in Norway, 2005 O.J. (L 104) 5, 8 ¶21.
150. *See, e.g.*, Disodium Carbonate, 1995 O.J. (L 83) 8.
151. Commission Regulation (EC) No. 306/2004 of 19 February 2004 imposing a provisional anti-dumping duty on imports of polyethlene terephthalate originating in Australia, the People's Republic of China, and Pakistan, 2004 O.J. (L 52) 5, 7 ¶24.
152. Case C-393/13 P, Council v. Alumina d.o.o., 2014 E.C.R. I-____, at ¶23.
153. *Id.* at ¶28.
154. Anti-Dumping Regulation at art. 1(4).

by-case basis.[155] The Commission typically looks at the physical and technical characteristics and the uses of the products to make this determination.

For example, in the *Camera Systems Originating in Japan* case, the Council concluded that cameras sold in Japan and those sold in the EU were a like product for purposes of determining the normal value in anti-dumping proceedings against imports of such products from Japan. The Council noted that the cameras sold in Japan had the same technical characteristics and uses as those sold in the EU.[156]

Significant quality differences may preclude the finding that the products are like products. However, the quality differences must be significant. The general rule appears to be that if the products still directly compete with each other, they will be considered like products even though there may be differences in quality. In the *Synthetic Fibre Ropes Originating in India* proceedings, the Council rejected arguments that the rope produced in the EU should not be considered like products to the Indian ropes.[157] Despite the fact that the rope was of a different quality, they had the same physical, technical, and chemical characteristics and competed with each other.[158] In *Okoumé Plywood Originating in the People's Republic of China*, quality differences in the plywood—lower quality glue and thinner layers of wood used—were insufficient to preclude the finding of a like product because there was evidence that the Chinese plywood and the European plywood competed against each other.[159]

Even if there are sales of a like product in the exporting country, the prices in the exporting country may be disregarded in determining the normal value if such sales are outside the ordinary course. There are three common situations in which the prices in the exporting country are considered to be outside the ordinary course of trade. To fully understand these three situations, it helps to remember that the EU rules try to take account of the tendency of exporters to lower the normal value (and hence decrease the dumping margin).

First, sales to an associated company are not generally in the ordinary course of trade.[160] If, for example, Walmart USA were to sell products to its European subsidiary, Walmart France, the price charged to Walmart France would not be

---

155. *See, e.g.*, Cases T-33/98 and T-34/98, Petrotub SA v. Republica SA, 1999 E.C.R. II-3837.
156. Council Regulation (EC) No. 2042/2000 of 26 September 2000 imposing a definitive anti-dumping duty on imports of television camera systems in Japan, 2000 O.J. (L 244) 38, 39 ¶ 18.
157. Council Regulation (EC) No. 1736/2004 of 4 October 2004 imposing a definitive anti-dumping duty on imports of synthetic fibre ropes originating in India, 2004 O.J. (L 311) 1, 2 ¶ 12.
158. *Id.* at 2 ¶ 14.
159. Council Regulation (EC) No. 1942/2004 of 2 November 2004 imposing a definitive anti-dumping duty and collecting definitively the provisional anti-dumping duty imposed on imports of okoumé plywood originating in the People's Republic of China, 2004 O.J. (L 336) 4, 6 ¶ 17. However, the quality difference was taken into account by the Council in determining injury. The Council increased by 10 percent the EU frontier price charged by the Chinese producers. *Id.* at 8 ¶ 41
160. Anti-Dumping Regulation at art. 2(1).

considered a reliable indicator of the normal value because Walmart France is associated with the seller. The assumption is that sales to associated companies are not on an arms-length basis.

Second, if there is an association or a compensatory arrangement between the parties on the domestic market, those sales may not be considered to be in the ordinary course of trade (and hence may not be used to establish normal value) unless the prices are unaffected by the relationship.[161] For example, it would be inappropriate to rely on sales prices between a parent and subsidiary on the domestic market to extrapolate the normal value of the product as one assumes that such sales are not in the ordinary course.

Finally, in certain circumstances, sales of the like product in the domestic market of the exporting country, or export sales from the exporting country to a third country, at prices below unit production costs (fixed and variable) plus selling, general, and administrative costs may be treated as not being in the ordinary course of trade by reason of price, and may be disregarded in determining normal value.[162] The basic requirements for disregarding such sales are that they are made within an extended period (generally one year) in substantial quantities, and are at prices that do not provide for the recovery of all costs within a reasonable period of time.[163]

The application of these rules often proves difficult because each case is different. The importer will typically want to use a low normal value because this will reduce the difference between the export price and the normal value (i.e. the dumping margin). In *NutraSweet v. Council*, the issue was whether U.S. aspartame, an artificial sweetener, was being dumped by NutraSweet in the EU.[164] Because the European patent for aspartame had expired, prices in Europe were lower than in the United States. NutraSweet consequently argued that the patent protection in the United States meant that the actual prices in the U.S. market were unreliable, and that a normal value should therefore be constructed. The Council nonetheless used the actual price in the United States as the normal value. The ECJ held that the existence of the patent did not mean that sales in a market where no protection existed were outside the ordinary course.

(ii) Constructing Normal Value

If the sales price in the exporting country is an unreliable indicator of the normal value, or there are no sales of the like product in the exporting country, the normal value must be constructed. The constructed normal value is calculated

---

161. *Id. See, e.g.*, Case C-76/00, Petrotub v. Republica SA, 2003 E.C.R. I-79, 147 ¶84.
162. *See, e.g.*, Commission Regulation (EC) No. 988/2004 of 17 May 2004 imposing provisional anti-dumping duties on imports of okoumé plywood originating in the People's Republic of China, 2004 O.J. (L 181) 5, 10 ¶44.
163. Anti-Dumping Regulation at art. 2(4). Sales below unit cost are considered to be made in substantial quantities within such a period when it is established that the weighted average selling price is below the weighted average unit cost, or that the volume of sales below unit cost is not less than 20 percent of sales being used to determine normal value.
164. Cases C-76/98 and C-77/98, Ajnomoto and NutraSweet v. Council, 2001 E.C.R. I-3223.

in one of two ways. First, the calculation may be based on the cost of production in the country of origin plus a reasonable amount for selling, general, and administrative costs (often referred to as SG&A costs) and a reasonable profit margin.[165] In the alternative, the normal value may be calculated on the basis of the export prices, in the ordinary course of trade, to an appropriate third country, provided that those prices are representative. For example, if the sales of bicycles in China are an unreliable indicator of the normal value of Chinese bicycles imported into the EU because those sales on the domestic market are below unit production costs, the Council may rely on the prices at which those bicycles are exported to the United States to construct the normal value.

The two alternatives discussed immediately above for constructing normal value only apply if the allegedly dumped products are exported from a country with a market economy. There are special rules for constructing normal value of imports from nonmarket economy countries.[166] The justification for this differential treatment is the assumption that the price of a product in a nonmarket economy is not an accurate reflection of the real market value of the product.[167] The standard used to determine whether a country has a market economy is whether "the decisions of firms regarding prices, costs and inputs must be made in response to market signals reflecting supply and demand, and without significant state interference."[168]

The basic rule is that for imports from a nonmarket economy country, normal value is determined on one of the follow three bases:[169]

(1) the price or constructed value in a third country which has a market economy;

(2) the price from such a third country to other countries (including the EU); or

(3) on any other reasonable basis.

In determining the appropriate analog country for purposes of applying these three alternatives, the threshold issue is whether there are sufficient sales of a like product on the domestic market of that country to facilitate a fair comparison. In the *Footwear Originating in China and Vietnam* investigation, for example, India and Thailand were ruled out as analog countries because too few domestic producers cooperated with the Commission to allow the Commission to make

---

165. Anti-Dumping Regulation at art. 2(3). In determining a reasonable profit margin, the Commission often relies on the profit margin on domestic sales. *See, e.g.*, Council Regulation (EC) No. 964/2003 of 2 June 2003 imposing definitive anti-dumping duties on imports of tube or pipe fittings originating in China and Thailand, 2003 O.J. (L 139) 1, 3 ¶20.
166. Anti-Dumping Regulation at art. 2(7). Examples of nonmarket economy countries are Albania, Armenia, Azerbaijan, Belarus, Georgia, North Korea, Kyrgyzstan, Moldavia, Mongolia, Tajikistan, Turkmenistan, Uzbekistan.
167. Case C-338/10, Grünwald Logistik Service GmbH v. Hauptzollamt Hamburg, 2012 E.C.R. I-___, at ¶20 (reported in the electronic reports of cases ECLI:EU:C:2012:158).
168. Case T-35/01, Shanghai Teraoka Electronics Co. Ltd. v. Council, 2004 E.C.R. II-3663, 3693 ¶55.
169. Anti-Dumping Regulation at art. 2(7)(a).

a fair comparison.¹⁷⁰ The domestic sales of the cooperating producers in the analog country should be at least 5 percent of the export sales to the EU which are the subject of the anti-dumping investigation.¹⁷¹

Companies from the Peoples Republic of China, Vietnam, Kazakhstan, or a nonmarket-economy country which is a member of the WTO at the date the investigation is initiated can still receive market economy treatment if they can show that market conditions exist in that country and market for the products concerned.¹⁷² The company applying for market economy treatment must show, in particular the following:¹⁷³

- decisions of firms regarding prices, costs, and inputs, including, for instance, raw materials, cost of technology and labor, output, sales, and investment, are made in response to market signals reflecting supply and demand, and without significant State interference in this regard, and costs of major inputs substantially reflect market values,
- firms have one clear set of basic accounting records that are independently audited in line with international accounting standards and are applied for all purposes,
- the production costs and financial situation of firms are not subject to significant distortions carried over from the former nonmarket economy system, in particular in relation to depreciation of assets, other write-offs, barter trade, and payment via compensation of debts,
- the firms concerned are subject to bankruptcy and property laws which guarantee legal certainty and stability for the operation of firms, and
- exchange rate conversions are carried out at the market rate.

The first factor—absence of state interference in prices, costs and inputs—requires the actual interference of the state (not just the possibility) and this interference must be significant. In *Council v. Zhejiang Xinan Chemical Industrial Group Co. Ltd.*, a Chinese company listed on the Shanghai Stock Exchange contested the Council's conclusion that the company was not entitled to market economy conditions. According to the Council, the Chinese state exercised significant interference in the pricing decisions of the Chinese company by virtue of the fact that the Chinese state held the largest block of shares (even though the majority of shares were held by private individuals and

---

170. Commission Regulation (EC) No. 553/2006 of 23 March 2006 imposing a provisional anti-dumping duty on imports of certain footwear with uppers of leather originating in the People's Republic of China and Vietnam, 2006 O.J. (L 98) 3, 20-22 ¶103-124.
171. Council Regulation (EC) No. 1942/2004 of 2 November 2004 imposing a definitive anti-dumping duty and collecting definitively the provisional anti-dumping duty imposed on imports of okoumé plywood originating in the People's Republic of China, 2004 O.J. (L 336) 4, 7 ¶30.
172. Anti-Dumping Regulation at art. 2(7)(b).
173. *Id.* at art. 2(7)(c). The producer claiming market economy treatment bears the burden of proving that these conditions are met. Case C-249/10 P, Brosmann Footwear (HK) Ltd. v. Council, 2012 E.C.R. I-___, at ¶32 (reported in the electronic reports of cases ECLI:EU:C:2012:53).

traded on the Shanghai Stock Exchange) and therefore controlled the company.[174] This control was further exhibited by the fact that the majority of the board of directors was appointed by the Chinese state and the majority of the board was either state officials or employed by state-owned companies.

The ECJ, however, rejected the inference that state control necessarily means state interference for purposes of the market economy treatment (MET). The purpose of the rule is to allow the foreign companies from nonmarket economies to show that their pricing decisions are made based on purely commercial considerations.[175] According to the ECJ, the mere fact that a company from a nonmarket economy is controlled by the state does not mean in every case that its pricing decisions are not made in response to market forces independent of the state: "In the present case, it must be found that State control, such as that found by the institutions ... is not, by its nature, incompatible with market economy conditions. In addition, although the fact that the distribution of the shares enabling State shareholders—even though minority shareholders—to control *de facto* the general meeting of Xinanchem's shareholders, and thereby appoint the board of directors, does give the State a certain influence over that company, it does not, however, follow that the State actually interferes—still less significantly—in the company's decisions regarding prices, costs and inputs. Nor does such interference automatically follow either from the fact that some of the directors of that company are connected to it by employment contracts or by a contract for the supply of services."[176]

Consequently, the Commission and Council must examine in each case not only whether the state can control the company, but also whether the state's actual involvement in the company's affairs are incompatible with a market economy. According to the ECJ, "the EU institutions have a wide power of appraisal when assessing factual situations of a legal and political nature in the country concerned in order to determine whether an exporter can be granted MET."[177]

(b) Comparison

The determination of the export price and the normal value is merely the means by which the EU is able to identify the dumping margin. Once the export price and normal value are determined, the finding of dumping requires a comparison of the export price to the normal value. If the export price of the products concerned is below the normal value, dumping is deemed to exist.[178] However,

---

174. Council Regulation 1683/2004, 2004 O.J. (L 303) 1 at recital 13.
175. Case C-337/09 P, Council v. Zhejiang Xinan Chemical Industrial Group Co. Ltd., 2012 E.C.R. I-___, at ¶66 (reported in the electronic reports of cases ECLI:EU:C:2012:471).
176. *Id.* at ¶78.
177. Case T-443/11, Gold East Paper (Jiangsu) Co. Ltd. v. Council, 2014 E.C.R. II-___, at ¶122.
178. According to the Council, it is not necessary to compare the prices of all of the exported products. Council Implementing Regulation (EU) No. 964/2010 of 25 October 2010 imposing a definitive anti-dumping duty and collecting definitively the provisional duty imposed on imports of certain aluminum road wheels originating in the People's Republic of China, 2010 O.J. (L 282) 1, 7 ¶58. Only a reasonable percentage is required.

the Commission must terminate the investigation if the dumping margin is less than 2 percent (expressed as a percentage of the export price).[179] For example, if the Commission's investigation reveals that the dumping margin is €10 but the per unit export price is €1000, the Commission is required to terminate the investigation.

There are a number of detailed rules to ensure that the comparison yields an accurate assessment. Using our earlier example, would it be fair to compare the U.S. price for a U.S.-produced automobile to the price for the same automobile in Portugal without taking into account the extra costs incurred by the seller in transporting that automobile to the buyer? To address such challenges in making an accurate comparison, the Anti-Dumping Regulation contains detailed adjustment rules.

The general rule is that the comparison must be made at the same level of trade and in respect of sales made at as nearly as possible the same time and with due account taken of other differences that affect price comparability.[180] The same level of trade requirement means, for example, that sales by a manufacturer to a distributor or wholesaler are not compared to sales at the retail level.[181] It is generally assumed that wholesale prices are lower than retail prices and consequently should not be used as a comparison.

In making the comparison, the Commission may account for other factors which affect prices and price comparability. Some of the common factors for which adjustment can be made are:[182]

- physical characteristics,
- import charges and indirect taxes,
- discounts,
- rebates and volume discounts,

---

179. Anti-Dumping Regulation at art. 9(3). *See, e.g.*, Commission Decision of 17 March 2008 terminating the anti-dumping proceeding concerning imports of polyvinyl alcohol originating in the People's Republic of China and Taiwan and releasing the amounts secured by way of the provisional duties imposed, 2008 O.J. (L 75) 66, 69 ¶32; Commission Decision of 3 April 2007 terminating the anti-dumping proceeding concerning imports of pentaerythritol originating in the People's Republic of China, Russia, Turkey, Ukraine, and the United States of America, 2007 O.J. (L 94) 55, 59 ¶43.
180. Anti-Dumping Regulation at art. 2(10)(d).
181. Council Regulation (EC) No. 172/2008 of 25 February 2008 imposing a definitive anti-dumping duty and collecting definitively the provisional duty imposed on imports of ferro-silicon originating in the People's Republic of China, Egypt, Kazakhstan, the former Yugoslav Republic of Macedonia, and Russia, 2008 O.J. (L 55) 6, 10 ¶50; Commission Regulation (EC) No. 145/2005 of 28 January 2005 imposing a provisional anti-dumping duty on imports of barium carbonate originating in the People's Republic of China, 2005 O.J. (L 24) 4, 12 ¶63.
182. According to the ECJ and General Court, the party seeking to make these adjustments carries the burden of proving that the adjustments are justified under the circumstances. Case 255/84, Nachi Fujikoshi v. Council, 1987 E.C.R. 1861, 1893 ¶33; Case T-6/12, Godrej Industries Ltd. v. Council, 2013 E.C.R. II-____, at ¶25.

- transportation,
- insurance,
- handling and loading,
- ancillary costs incurred for conveying the product concerned from the premises of the exporter to an independent buyer,
- after-sales costs of providing warranties,
- technical assistance and services, and
- commissions paid in respect of the sales under consideration, and currency conversions.

In the *Ironing Boards Originating in China and Ukraine proceedings,* for example, the Commission took account of the fact that ironing boards coming from China were not equipped with electric sockets whereas the ironing boards coming from Turkey (the analog country on which the comparison was based) were typically equipped with electric sockets.[183]

(c) Material Injury to Union Industry

As indicated above, the Anti-Dumping Regulation addresses two basic issues: it sets forth the elements of dumping and determines when and how the EU may react. As discussed above, dumping exists if the export price is below the normal value. However, a finding of dumping is not in itself sufficient for the EU to adopt anti-dumping measures against the dumped imports. Anti-dumping measures can only be taken where dumping causes material injury (or threatens to cause material injury) to the Union industry. When determining injury, the Commission and Council will consider the volume of dumped imports, the effect of dumped imports on the EU market for the like product, and the consequent impact on the Union industry.[184] Intent is irrelevant in the analysis.[185] In other words, dumping duties may be imposed even though the foreign companies engaged in dumping had no intent to injure the Union industry or even engage in dumping.

If the products are coming from more than one country, the Commission may assess the cumulative impact of the imports from these countries if certain conditions are met. For example, allegedly dumped bicycles may be coming from China, India, and Vietnam all at the same time. In assessing the impact of these imports, the Commission and Council do not have to assess each country separately. If (1) the margin of dumping established in relation to the imports from each country is more than 2 percent, (2) the volume of imports from each

---

183. Commission Regulation (EC) No. 1620/2006 of 30 October 2006 imposing a provisional anti-dumping duty on imports of ironing boards originating in the People's Republic of China and Ukraine, 2006 O.J. (L 300) 13, 22 ¶62.
184. Anti-Dumping Regulation at art. 3(2). According to the ECJ, the Commission and the Council "enjoy a broad discretion by reason of the complexity of the economic, political and legal situations which they have to examine" when determining injury. Case T-443/11, Gold East Paper (Jiangsu) Co. Ltd. v. Council, 2014 E.C.R. II-___, at ¶182.
185. Case T-274/02, Ritek Corp. and Prodisc Technology Inc. v. Council, 2006 E.C.R. II-4310, 4328 ¶57.

country is not negligible and (3) a cumulative assessment of the effects of the imports is appropriate in light of the conditions of competition between imported products and the conditions of competition between the imported products and the like Union product, the Commission and Council can aggregate the impact from each of the countries.[186]

Common themes that arise in determining injury are loss of market share, reduced prices for EU producers, lower profits, and increased excess capacity.[187] For example, in the *Graphite Electrode Systems Originating in India* investigation, the Commission concluded that injury existed because, among other things, the volume of dumped graphite electrode systems from India increased 76 percent, EU market share of the imports increased 3.4 percent, and EU production of graphite electrodes decreased 1 percent all during the time when the Indian graphite electrodes were being dumped in the EU.[188]

Although an increased market share held by the imports is an important determinant in supporting the finding of injury, the converse is not necessarily true: a loss of market share held by the imports does not preclude a finding of injury. In such cases, the Council will look at the profitability of the Union industry. In *Granular Polytetrafluoroethylene Originating in Russian and China* the Commission's investigation revealed that the market share of the EU producers had actually increased and the market share of imports from Russia and China decreased.[189] Nonetheless, the Commission concluded that the Union industry was injured because its profitability had decreased.[190]

It is not necessary that the Union industry be suffering a loss because of the dumped imports as profitability is but one consideration in the analysis. In the *Trichloroisocyanuric Acid Originating in China and the United States* case, several of the Chinese exporters argued that there was no material injury because

---

186. Anti-Dumping Regulation at art. 3(4).
187. *See, e.g.*, Council Regulation (EC) No. 1420/2007 of 4 December 2007 imposing a definitive anti-dumping duty on imports of silico-manganese originating in the People's Republic of China and Kazakhstan and terminating the proceeding on imports of silico-manganese originating in Ukraine, 2007 O.J. (L 317) 5, 23 ¶124; Council Regulation (EC) No. 1467/2004 of 13 August 2004 imposing a definitive anti-dumping duty and collecting definitively the provisional duty imposed on imports of polyethylene terephthalate originating in Australia and the People's Republic of China, terminating the anti-dumping proceeding concerning imports of polyethylene terephthalate originating in Pakistan and releasing the amounts secured by way of the provisional duties imposed, 2004 O.J. (L 271) 1, 8 ¶76; Council Regulation (EC) No. 397/2004 of 2 March 2004 imposing a definitive anti-dumping duty on imports of cotton-type bed linen originating in Pakistan, 2004 O.J. (L 66) 1, 10 ¶101.
188. Commission Regulation (EC) No. 1009/2004 of 19 May 2004 imposing a provisional anti-dumping duty on imports of certain graphite electrode systems originating in India, 2004 O.J. (L 183) 61, 72 ¶69 (Graphite electrodes are produced from petroleum coke and used in the steel industry in electric arc furnaces to carry current.)
189. Commission Regulation (EC) No. 862/2005 of 7 June 2005 imposing provisional anti-dumping duties on imports of granular polytetrafluoroethylene originating in Russia and the People's Republic of China, 2005 O.J. (L 144) 11, 26 ¶103.
190. *Id.* at 28 ¶119.

the Union industry was actually profitable.[191] However, the Council pointed out that profitability in itself is not decisive. What is relevant is the profitability in comparison to the situation in the absence of the dumping. As the profits achieved by the Union industry had declined 50 percent, the Council held that there was material injury even though the industry was still profitable.[192]

Even if the dumping did not result in a reduction of the price for the products in the EU, the Council and Commission may still conclude that the Union industry was injured. In *Crown Equipment (Suzhou) Co. Ltd. v. Council*, for example, the importation of hand pallet trucks from China to the EU did not lead to a reduction of the prices for hand pallet trucks in the EU.[193] Nonetheless, the General Court agreed with the Council that "because of the considerable undercutting of the prices of the Union industry by Chinese imports (by between 43% and 78%) and the increase in market share of the Chinese imports" there was an injury in the EU.[194]

In many instances, the presence of low-cost products in the EU can be explained by the fact that the imported products, although of the same type as products produced by the Union industry, are of different quality. This is often the case with products imported from developing countries. In determining the existence of injury, the Commission has been willing to recognize the differences in quality.[195] Although it will not justify the dumping, the Commission has been willing to increase the export price to adjust for the difference in quality. In the *Okoumé Plywood Originating in the People's Republic of China* proceedings, the Council

---

191. Council Regulation (EC) No. 1631/2005 imposing a definitive anti-dumping duty and collecting definitively the provisional duty imposed on imports of trichloroisocyanuric acid originating in the People's Republic of China and the United States of America, 2005 O.J. (L 261) 1, 6 ¶59.
192. *Id.* See also Council Regulation (EC) No. 1420/2007 of 4 December 2007 imposing definitive anti-dumping duty on imports of silico-manganese originating in the People's Republic of China and Kazakhstan and terminating the proceeding on imports of silico-manganese originating in Ukraine, 2007 O.J. (L 317) 5, 23 ¶124; Council Regulation (EC) No. 1659/2005 of 6 October 2005 imposing a definitive anti-dumping duty and collecting definitively the provisional duty imposed on imports of certain magnesia bricks originating in the People's Republic of China, 2005 O.J. (L 267) 1, 6 ¶54.
193. Case T-643/11, Crown Equipment (Suzhou) Co. Ltd. v. Council, 2014 E.C.R. II-___, at ¶171.
194. *Id.* at ¶171.
195. As mentioned above, the quality of the products is a factor to be considered when comparing the export price to the normal value of like products. As long as the products directly compete with one another, the Council has been willing to use them in the comparison even though there may be a quality difference between them. Council Regulation (EC) No. 1736/2004 of 4 October 2004 imposing a definitive anti-dumping duty on imports of synthetic fibre ropes originating in India, 2004 O.J. (L 311) 1, 2 ¶12. Nonetheless, as illustrated by the *Okoumé Plywood* proceedings, this quality difference may be compensated for in the injury assessment even if the products are considered like products for purposes of the comparison. Council Regulation (EC) No. 1942/2004 of 2 November 2004 imposing a definitive anti-dumping duty and collecting definitively the provisional anti-dumping duty imposed on imports of okoumé plywood originating in the People's Republic of China, 2004 O.J. (L 336) 4, 8 ¶41.

increased the export price 10 percent to account for the lower quality of plywood being imported into the EU from China.[196]

The findings of dumping and material injury are in themselves insufficient to support the imposition of anti-dumping duties. There must also be a causal link between the injury and the dumped imports. According to the General Court, "the Council and the Commission are under an obligation to consider whether the injury on which they intend to base their conclusions actually derives from dumped imports and must disregard any injury deriving from other factors."[197] The Commission and Council first examine whether the injury occurred during the investigation period. If so, they will often infer a causal link between the dumping and the injury.[198]

If the Commission or Council finds a temporal coincidence between the dumping and the injury, and infers causation from that, it will then look at other factors that might have caused the injury and negate the inference of causation. This is referred to as the nonattribution analysis.[199] The test is not whether the other factors could have had an influence on the injury or contributed to the injury, but rather whether these other factors are sufficient to break the causal connection which the Commission and Council consider to exist.[200]

Although the Anti-Dumping Regulation identifies several potentially relevant additional factors, this list is not exclusive.[201] The Commission and

---

196. *Id.*
197. Case T-443/11, Gold East Paper (Jiangsu) Co. Ltd. V. Council, 2014 E.C.R. II-____, at ¶322.
198. *See, e.g.*, Commission Implementing Regulation (EU) 2015/84 of 21 January 2015 imposing a definitive anti-dumping duty and collecting definitively the provisional duty imposed on imports of monosodium glutamate originating in Indonesia, 2015 O.J. (L 15) 54, 62 ¶66; Commission Regulation (EU) No. 138/2011 of 16 February 2011 imposing a provisional anti-dumping duty on imports of certain open mesh fabrics of glass fibres originating in the People's Republic of China, 2011 O.J. (L 43) 9, 19 ¶91; Council Regulation (EC) No. 703/2009 of 27 July 2009 imposing a definitive anti-dumping duty and collecting definitively the provisional duty imposed on imports of wire rod originating in the People's Republic of China and terminating the proceeding concerning imports of wire rod originating in the Republic of Moldova and Turkey, 2009 O.J. (L 203) 1, 10 ¶¶84-88; Council Regulation (EC) No. 261/2008 of 17 March 2008 imposing a definitive anti-dumping duty on imports of certain compressors originating in the People's Republic of China, 2008 O.J. (L 81) 1, 15 ¶114.
199. Case T-394/13, Photo USA Electronic Graphic, Inc. v. Council, 2014 E.C.R. II-____, at ¶65; Case T-6/12, Godrej Industries Ltd. v. Council, 2013 E.C.R. II-____, at ¶62.
200. Case C-10/12 P, Transnational Company AO v. Council, 2013 E.C.R. I-____, at ¶24; Council Implementing Regulation (EU) No. 157/2013 of 18 February 2013 imposing a definitive anti-dumping duty on imports of bioethanol originating in the United States of America, 2013 O.J. (L 49) 10, 25 ¶148.
201. According to Article 3(7) of the Anti-Dumping Regulation, additional factors that may be considered include the volume and prices of imports not sold at dumping prices, contraction in demand or changes in the patterns of consumption, restrictive trade practices of, and competition between, third country and EU producers, developments in technology, and the export performance and productivity of the EU industry. According to the ECJ, legislative changes do not constitute additional factors which may be included in the analysis because their impact—if any—is indirect. Case C-638/11 P, Council of the European Union v. Gul Ahmed Textile Mills Ltd., 2013 E.C.R. I-____, at ¶31.

Council commonly examine imports from third countries, increases in prices of raw materials, the conduct of the EU producers including violations of the competition rules.[202] If there is no temporal coincidence between the injury and the occurrence of dumping, or there are other causes of the injury (such as significant imports from other countries not subject of the investigation), the causal link between the dumping and the injury will not exist.

In *Styrene-butadiene thermoplastic rubber originating in Korea and Russia*, the investigation showed that dumping indeed existed.[203] However, the Council terminated the proceedings because there was only a partial coincidence in time between the deterioration of the Union industry and the alleged dumping,[204] and the volume of nondumped imports of the same product increased by 56 percent during the same period (which represented 2.4 times the volume of dumped imports during the investigation period).[205] Similarly, in the *cathode-ray colour television tubes proceedings*, the Commission found that imports from China and Thailand were being dumped into the EU.[206] Although the EU producers had suffered significant losses in the preceding years, the Commission found that their situation was the result of a shift in consumer demand to flat-screen televisions and not the result of dumping by the foreign manufacturers of television tubes.[207]

Although there is no codified de minimis exception, the injury to the EU industry must be material.[208] If the dumped imports represent only an insignificant market share in the EU, it is unlikely that a causal link will be

---

202. *See, e.g.*, Case T-394/13, Photo USA Electronic Graphic, Inc. v. Council, 2014 E.C.R. II-____, at ¶73; Council Implementing Regulation (EU) No. 157/2013 of 18 February 2013 imposing a definitive anti-dumping duty on imports of bioethanol originating in the United States of America, 2013 O.J. (L 49) 10, 24-25 ¶¶133-145; Council Regulation (EC) No. 91/2009 of 26 January 2009 imposing a definitive anti-dumping duty on imports of certain iron or steel fasteners originating in the People's Republic of China, 2009 O.J. (L 29) 1, 22 ¶¶172-179.
203. Council Regulation (EC) No. 1372/2005 of 19 August 2005 terminating the anti-dumping proceeding concerning imports of styrene-butadiene-styrene thermoplastic rubber originating in the Republic of Korea and Russia, terminating the interim review of the anti-dumping measures applicable to imports of styrene-butadiene-styrene thermoplastic rubber originating in Taiwan and repealing these measures, 2005 O.J. (L 223) 27.
204. *Id.* at 38 ¶101.
205. *Id.* at 39 ¶110.
206. Commission Decision of 15 November 2006 terminating the anti-dumping proceeding concerning imports of cathode-ray color television picture tubes originating in the People's Republic of China, the Republic of Korea, Malaysia, and Thailand, 2006 O.J. (L 316) 18.
207. *Id.* at 33 ¶110; *see also* Commission Decision of 3 April 2007 terminating the anti-dumping proceeding concerning imports of pentaerythritol originating in the People's Republic of China, Russia, Turkey, Ukraine, and the United States of America, 2007 O.J. (L 94) 55, 67 ¶123 (Even though dumping occurred, the Commission terminated the investigation because it could not rule out that other factors may have led to the injury to the Union producers).
208. Case C-13/12 P, Chelyabinsk Electrometallurgical Integrated Plant OAO v. Council, 2013 E.C.R. I-____, at ¶58.

found to exist.[209] For example, in determining whether bed linens from India being dumped in the EU were causing material injury to a Union industry, the Council concluded that even assuming the existence of a material injury being suffered by EU bed linen manufacturers, the fact that the imports from India represented less than 1 percent of all bed linens sold in the EU was conclusive evidence that no causal link existed.[210] In the anti-dumping proceedings against Chile for salmon exported to the EU, the Council concluded that in view of the finding that non-Chilean imports representing a market share of 30 percent in the EU were sold at low prices, "it is difficult to see how the imports from Chile when taken in isolation could have had a material impact on the Union industry."[211]

The injury must be suffered by a Union industry. Although the mere fact that the dumping may be causing injury to one or two companies in the EU is insufficient by itself to fulfill the injury requirement,[212] the material injury need not be suffered by all of the companies making up the Union industry. It is sufficient that there is an injury to the undertakings comprising the Union industry which supported the initiation of the anti-dumping proceedings.[213] In determining what constitutes the Union industry, the Commission and Council have broad discretion.[214] The concept covers EU producers whose output constitutes at least a major proportion of the total EU production of the like products. To be considered part of the companies comprising the Union industry, an EU company must not only support the complaint but also cooperate with

---

209. Commission Decision of 17 March 2008 terminating the anti-dumping proceeding concerning imports of polyvinyl alcohol originating in the People's Republic of China and Taiwan and releasing the amounts secured by way of the provisional duties imposed, 2008 O.J. (L 75) 66, 74 ¶78. This criterion is in addition to the requirement discussed above that the dumping margin itself must be at least 2 percent expressed as a percentage of the export price. Art. 9(3) Anti-Dumping Regulation.
210. Council Regulation (EC) No. 2239/2003 of 17 December 2003 terminating the partial interim review and the expiry review concerning the anti-dumping measures imposed by Regulation (EC) No. 2398/97 on imports of cotton-type bedlinen originating in India, 2003 O.J. (L 333) 3, 7 ¶38; see also Commission Decision of 20 October 2005 terminating the anti-dumping proceeding concerning imports of certain iron or steel ropes and cables originating in the Republic of Korea, 2005 O.J. (L 276) 62, 67 ¶45.
211. Council Regulation (EC) No. 930/2003 of 26 May 2003 terminating the anti-dumping and anti-subsidy proceedings concerning imports of farmed Atlantic salmon originating in Norway and the anti-dumping proceeding concerning imports of farmed Atlantic salmon originating in Chile and the Faeroe Islands, 2003 O.J. (L 133) 1, 28 ¶214.
212. Council Regulation (EC) No. 172/2008 of 25 February 2008 imposing a definitive anti-dumping duty and collecting definitively the provisional duty imposed on imports of ferro-silicon originating in the People's Republic of China, Egypt, Kazakhstan, the former Yugoslav Republic of Macedonia, and Russia, 2008 O.J. (L 55) 6, 12 ¶64 (The injury assessment is conducted only at the aggregate industry level and not at the individual company level even if the alleged dumping has a disparate impact on the individual companies in the industry.).
213. Case C-13/12 P, Chelyabinsk Electrometallurgical Integrated Plant OAO v. Council, 2013 E.C.R. I-____, at ¶60.
214. Case T-469/07, Philips Lighting Poland S.A. v. Council, 2013 E.C.R. II-____, at ¶92.

the Commission in the investigation. Cooperation generally requires that the company responds to the questionnaire which the Commission typically sends out and provides the Commission with documentation and data.[215]

Two tests must be met to substantiate a finding that the complaining and cooperating firms constitute a major proportion of the Union industry.[216] First, the cooperating Union producers must account for at least 25 percent of the total EU production.[217] For example, if there are four EU producers of widgets, and one of them representing 80 percent of the EU production does not support the complaint, an anti-dumping investigation cannot be initiated. Conversely, it is possible that one Union producer constitutes a major proportion of the Union industry.[218]

Second, EU producers representing 50 percent or more of the total EU production do not oppose the initiation of the investigation. For example, if there are five EU producers of widgets each with 20 percent of the EU production, and two of them file an anti-dumping complaint (thereby fulfilling the first requirement of major proportion), there is still no injury to a major proportion

---

215. Council Implementing Regulation (EU) No. 54/2010 of 19 January 2010 imposing a definitive anti-dumping duty on imports of ethanolamines originating in the United States of America, 2010 O.J. (L 17) 1, 9 ¶53.

216. Anti-Dumping Regulation at art. 5(4). In determining whether the major proportion thresholds are met, only the EC producers cooperating in the investigation are included. Council Regulation (EC) No. 1472/2006 of 5 October 2006 imposing a definitive anti-dumping duty and collecting definitively the provisional duty imposed on imports of certain footwear with uppers of leather originating in the People's Republic of China and Vietnam, 2006 O.J. (L 275) 1, 17 ¶156; Council Regulation (EC) No. 1136/2006 of 24 July 2006 imposing a definitive anti-dumping duty and collecting definitively the provisional duty imposed on imports of lever arch mechanisms originating in the People's Republic of China, 2006 O.J. (L 205) 1, 3 ¶29. These tests are applied when the investigation opens. If, during the investigation, the support for the investigation subsides so that the percentages employed in these tests are no longer met, the Commission is not required to terminate the investigation. Case T-469/07, Philips Lighting Poland S.A. v. Council, 2013 E.C.R. II-____, at ¶84.

217. To be included as a cooperating Union producer for this calculation, the Union producer does not have to be one of the producers submitting the complaint. For example, if there are five Union producers of a product, and only two submit the complaint, but the other three later cooperate with the Commission in the investigation, the output of all five Union producers will be taken into account for purposes of testing this requirement. Commission Decision of 3 April 2007 terminating the anti-dumping proceeding concerning imports of pentaerythritol originating in the People's Republic of China, Russia, Turkey, Ukraine, and the United States of America, 2007 O.J. (L 94) 55, 62 ¶81. If a Union producer also imports a significant volume of the product, the entire production of that Union producer will not be included in the calculation. Council Regulation (EC) No. 261/2008 of 17 March 2008 imposing a definitive anti-dumping duty on imports of certain compressors originating in the People's Republic of China, 2008 O.J. (L 81) 1, 7 ¶64.

218. Notice of initiation of an anti-dumping proceeding concerning imports of vinyl acetate originating in the United States of America, 2010 O.J. (C 327) 23.

of the Union industry if the other three producers oppose the anti-dumping duties.

In determining these thresholds, the captive production of the EU producers is excluded.[219] The term "captive production" refers to the output of the product at issue which is sold or otherwise transferred within the same corporate group. If, for example, a company produces steel and sells that steel to an affiliate which processes the steel into rods, the volumes of steel sold to the affiliate are not included in determining whether the thresholds are exceeded.

The reliance on production rather than number of firms means that anti-dumping investigations can be initiated by one EU company if that company represents 50 percent or more of the EU production.[220] In *Trichloroisocyanuric Acid Originating in China and the United States*, for example, the complaint was submitted by only one EU producer.[221] The Chinese producers argued that if there are more than two EU producers, a complaint cannot be submitted by only one of them. According to the Council, however, the degree of support for a complaint is not measured by the number of companies supporting the complaint, but rather by the production volume represented by the complaining company.[222] As the single complaining company in this case represented over 50 percent of the EU production, the Council rejected the arguments of the Chinese producers.

The ultimate ownership of the firms constituting the Union industry is not necessarily decisive in determining whether a particular company can be considered part of the Union industry. In one instance, the complaining firms

---

219. Council Regulation (EC) No. 703/2009 of 27 July 2009 imposing a definitive anti-dumping duty and collecting definitively the provisional duty imposed on imports of wire rod originating in the People's Republic of China and terminating the proceeding concerning imports of wire rod originating in the Republic of Moldova and Turkey, 2009 O.J. (L 203) 1, 5 ¶54.
220. *See, e.g.*, Commission Regulation (EU) No. 118/2011 of 10 February 2011 imposing a provisional anti-dumping duty on imports of certain ring binder mechanisms originating in Thailand, 2011 O.J. (L 37) 2, 4 ¶31; Council Regulation (EC) No. 654/2008 of 29 April 2008 imposing a definitive anti-dumping duty on imports of coumarin originating in the People's Republic of China, as extended to imports of coumarin consigned from India, Thailand, Indonesia and Malaysia, whether declared as originating in India, Thailand, Indonesia and Malaysia or not following an expiry review pursuant to Article 11(2) of Regulation (EC) No. 384/96, 2008 O.J. (L 183) 1, 9, ¶75; Commission Regulation (EC) No. 488/2008 of 2 June 2008 imposing a provisional anti-dumping duty on imports of citric acid originating in the People's Republic of China, 2008 O.J. (L 143) 13, 18 ¶55; Council Regulation (EC) No. 1331/2007 of 13 November 2007 imposing a definitive anti-dumping duty on imports of dicyandiamide originating in the People's Republic of China, 2007 O.J. (L 296) 1, 5 ¶47.
221. Council Regulation (EC) No. 1631/2005 imposing a definitive anti-dumping duty and collecting definitively the provisional duty imposed on imports of trichloroisocyanuric acid originating in the People's Republic of China and the United States of America, 2005 O.J. (L 261) 1.
222. *Id.* at 5 ¶44.

were all owned by a privately held company in the Dominican Republic.[223] Nonetheless, the Council imposed anti-dumping duties on the Chinese importers in that case. Given the protectionist nature of anti-dumping duties, it is the location of the manufacturing facilities injured by the dumped products (rather than the location of the ultimate parent entity) that will be considered rather than ultimate ownership.[224] If, however, the owners of the complaining company are from the country from which the dumped goods are being exported, the arguments of the EU producers controlled by owners from these countries will be given little credence.[225]

If the EU producers are related to the exporters of the products in question, the output of those EU producers is excluded from the Union industry when applying the two major proportion thresholds discussed above.[226] Two companies are related if one is controlled by the other or they are under common control of a third party or there is some other relationship between them which causes them not to treat each other at arm's length.[227] For example, in the *Ethanolamines Originating in the United States* proceedings, the Council excluded the output of Union Carbide Belgium from the Union industry because this entity was controlled by Union Carbide Corp. in the United States, and Union Carbide Corp. exported *ethanolamines* (chemical used in fertilizers and other applications).[228] The basic idea behind this rule is that the interests of the related companies may not be commensurate with those of the independent Union industry. In effect, the application of the rule gives more influence to the independent EU producers because only their output will be used to determine injury to the Union industry.

In addition, the Commission and Council may exclude the output of EU producers who themselves import the allegedly dumped product.[229] In *Ring binder Mechanisms Originating in Thailand*, for example, only one of the two EU ring binder mechanism producers supported the initiation of the investigation. However, the Commission excluded the one EU producer which did not support

---

223. Council Regulation (EC) No. 1905/2003 of 27 October 2003 imposing a definitive anti-dumping duty and collecting definitively the provisional duty imposed on imports of furfuryl alcohol in the People's Republic of China, 2003 O.J. (L 283) 1, 3 ¶26.
224. Council Regulation (EC) No. 1683/2004 of 24 September 2004 imposing a definitive anti-dumping duty on imports of glyphosate originating in the People's Republic of China, 2004 O.J. (L 303) 1, 6 ¶52 ("[T]he manufacturing operations, the technological and capital investment for the manufacturing operations and the sales operations take place in the [Union].")
225. Council Regulation (EC) No. 85/2006 of 17 January 2006 imposing a definitive anti-dumping duty and collecting definitively the provisional duty imposed on imports of farmed salmon originating in Norway, 2006 O.J. (L 15) 1, 6 ¶37.
226. Anti-Dumping Regulation at art. 4(1)(a).
227. *Id.* at art. 4(2).
228. Council Regulation (EC) No. 1603/2000 of July 2000 imposing a definitive anti-dumping duty on imports of ethanolamines originating in the United States of America, 2000 O.J. (L 185) 1, 3 ¶25.
229. Anti-Dumping Regulation at art. 4(1)(a).

the initiation of the investigation from the definition of Union industry because that producer also imported ring binder mechanisms from Thailand.[230] The decision to exclude certain EU producers who import the allegedly dumped products lies in the discretion of the Commission and Council.[231] In practice, as long as the imports merely supplement the EU production of the producer, the Commission and Council tend not to exclude EU producers on the basis that they import the allegedly dumped product.[232] If, however, the company has its "core of activities" outside the EU, it will not be considered part of the Union industry.[233]

(d) Union Interest

Anti-dumping measures will only be taken where it is in the interest of the Union to do so. The concept of Union interest is not defined in the Anti-Dumping Regulation, and the ECJ typically gives the Council broad discretion in applying the Union interest test. In making this assessment, the Council typically examines the interests of the complaining industry, the interests of related importers and firms operating in the EU, and the users of the particular product. In most instances, the complaining Union industry, which may be just one company,[234] will be the beneficiary of the anti-dumping duties. The imposition of the duties will either increase the market price of the product in the EU, or increase the market share of the Union industry on that market.[235] By protecting the domestic industry, the anti-dumping duties have the potential of

---

230. Commission Regulation (EU) No. 118/2011 of 10 February 2011 imposing a provisional anti-dumping duty on imports of certain ring binder mechanisms originating in Thailand, 2011 O.J. (L 37) 2, 4 ¶31.
231. Case T-164/94, Ferchimex SA v. Council, 1995 E.C.R. II-2685, 2721 ¶114.
232. Commission Regulation (EC) No. 1620/2006 of 30 October 2006 imposing a provisional anti-dumping duty on imports of ironing boards originating in the People's Republic of China and Ukraine, 2006 O.J. (L 300) 13, 24 ¶75; Council Regulation (EC) No. 1531/2002 of 14 August 2002 imposing a definitive anti-dumping duty on imports of color television receivers originating in the People's Republic of China, the Republic of Korea, Malaysia, and Thailand and terminating the proceeding regarding imports of colour television receivers originating in Singapore, 2002 O.J. (L 231) 1, 11 ¶109.
233. Commission Decision of 20 October 2006 terminating the anti-dumping proceeding concerning imports of recordable digital versatile discs (DVD+/-R) originating in the People's Republic of China, Hong Kong, and Taiwan, 2006 O.J. (L 293) 7, 11 ¶1.
234. *See, e.g.*, Council Regulation (EC) No. 1193/2008 of 1 December 2008 imposing a definitive anti-dumping duty and collecting definitively the provisional duties imposed on imports of citric acid originating in the People's Republic of China, 2008 O.J. (L 323) 1, 1 ¶2.
235. One possible result of the initiation of an anti-dumping investigation may be that the exporter increases the price of the products in its domestic market in order to decrease the dumping margin. This effect is, however, not relevant for the European courts. Case T-235/08, Acron OAO v. Council, 2013 E.C.R. II-___, at ¶51; Case T-459/08, EuroChem Mineral and Chemical Company OAO v. Council, 2013 E.C.R. II-___, at ¶72.

protecting employment (at least in the short term)[236] within the EU—an effect that is not irrelevant in anti-dumping cases.[237]

On the other hand, the imposition of the anti-dumping duties will commonly have a negative effect on the purchasers of the product as well as on downstream users. In most cases, customers of the dumped product will be forced to pay a higher price for the product than they would in the absence of the anti-dumping duties.[238] In assessing the effect of dumping, the Commission issues questionnaires to EU traders in the same industry and even to users of the product. The purpose of these questionnaires is to enable the Commission to assess the impact of the dumping. In many cases, there is no response or a relatively low response rate—a fact from which the Commission and Council

---

236. Although the protection accorded to the domestic industry by anti-dumping duties will promote employment in the short term, the effect on employment in the long term could be negative. By artificially keeping individuals employed in an industry which may be inefficient or obsolete, the anti-dumping duties are preventing the redirection of those employees to industries in which that country has a competitive advantage.

237. *See, e.g.*, Commission Regulation (EC) No. 1620/2006 of 30 October 2006 imposing a provisional anti-dumping duty on imports of ironing boards originating in the People's Republic of China and Ukraine, 2006 O.J. (L 300) 13, 31 ¶109; Commission Regulation (EC) No. 1551/2006 of 17 October 2006 imposing a provisional anti-dumping duty on imports of certain frozen strawberries originating in the People's Republic of China, 2006 O.J. (L287) 3, 22 ¶117; Council Regulation (EC) No. 2042/2000 of 26 September 2000 imposing a definitive anti-dumping duty on imports of television camera systems in Japan, 2000 O.J. (L 244) 38, 46 ¶79; Commission Regulation (EC) No. 1009/2004 of 19 May 2004 imposing a provisional anti-dumping duty on imports of certain graphite electrode systems originating in India, 2004 O.J. (L 183) 61, 73 ¶70.

238. *See, e.g.*, Commission Regulation (EC) No. 1551/2006 of 17 October 2006 imposing a provisional anti-dumping duty on imports of certain frozen strawberries originating in the People's Republic of China, 2006 O.J. (L287) 3, 23 ¶118 *aff'd by* Council Regulation (EC) No. 407/2007, 2007 O.J. (L 100) 1; Commission Regulation (EC) No. 134/2006 of 26 January 2006 imposing a provisional anti-dumping duty on imports of lever arch mechanisms originating in the People's Republic of China, 2006 O.J. (L 23) 13, 30 ¶128 ("As regards possible cost increases, it cannot be excluded that this would take place immediately after the imposition of [anti-dumping] measures."); Council Regulation (EC) No. 1631/2005 imposing a definitive anti-dumping duty and collecting definitively the provisional duty imposed on imports of trichloroisocyanuric acid originating in the People's Republic of China and the United States of America, 2005 O.J. (L 261) 1, 9 ¶93 (A price increase resulting in each consumer paying an additional €10 per year was insignificant, according to the Council.). In fact, if the prices do not go up, the competitors may request the initiation of an "anti-absorption reinvestigation" under Article 12 of the Anti-Dumping Regulation. If the importers are considered to have absorbed the anti-dumping duties, the Council may increase the anti-dumping duties until the prices of the imported products increase. *See, e.g.*, Council Regulation (EC) No. 236/2004 of 10 February 2004 amending Regulation (EC) No. 1339/2002 imposing a definitive anti-dumping duty and collecting definitively the provisional duty imposed on imports of sulphanilic acid originating in the People's Republic of China and India, 2004 O.J. (L 40) 17.

will infer that the anti-dumping measures will have little or no impact on the downstream industries.[239]

In the *Tube and Pipe Fittings* decision, the fact that only three out of 23 users of the pipe fittings responded to the Commission's questionnaire caused the Commission to infer that pipe fittings represented only a small part of the production costs of these users. Consequently, the imposition of anti-dumping duties would, according to the Commission, not have a significant effect on these companies.[240] In the *Camera Systems* investigation, the fact that only 15 out of 60 users responded to the Commission's questionnaire was "in itself an indication that this sector did not suffer any substantial negative effect on its economic situation as a result of the anti-dumping measures."[241] In *Synthetic Fibre Ropes Originating in India*," when none of the end-users responded, the Council inferred that they were not negatively affected.[242]

There is an obvious deficiency in this process. The incremental costs imposed on the downstream users are seldom sufficient to prompt them into investing the time and effort in preparing a response. For example, is it likely that grocery store owners would concern themselves with potential anti-dumping duties imposed on hand pallet trucks that they use in their storeroom or warehouses? Is it likely that bicyclists or bicycle consumer groups will spend the time and money to complain to the Commission about contemplated anti-dumping duties on bicycle seats from China?[243] Nonetheless, the Council will infer that the

---

239. Commission Regulation (EU) No. 138/2011 of 16 February 2011 imposing a provisional anti-dumping duty on imports of certain open-mesh fabrics of glass fibres originating in the People's Republic of China, 2011 O.J. (L 43) 9, 19 ¶108; Council Regulation (EC) No. 649/2008 of 8 July 2008 imposing a definitive anti-dumping duty on imports of powdered activated carbon originating in the People's Republic of China, 2008 O.J. (L 181) 1, 11 ¶89; Council Regulation (EC) No. 172/2008 of 25 February 2008 imposing a definitive anti-dumping duty and collecting definitively the provisional duty imposed on imports of ferro-silicon originating in the People's Republic of China, Egypt, Kazakhstan, the former Yugoslav Republic of Macedonia, and Russia, 2008 O.J. (L 55) 6, 16 ¶113.

240. Council Regulation (EC) No. 964/2003 of 2 June 2003 imposing definitive anti-dumping duties on imports of certain tube or pipe-fittings, of iron or steel, originating in the People's Republic of China and Thailand, and those consigned from Taiwan, whether declared as originating in Taiwan or not, 2003 O.J. (L 139) 1, 10 ¶89. *See also* Council Regulation (EC) No. 778/2005 of 23 May 2005 imposing a definitive anti-dumping duty on imports of magnesium oxide originating in the People's Republic of China, 2005 O.J. (L 131) 1, 15 ¶84 (None of the downstream users responded.)

241. Council Regulation (EC) No. 2042/2000 of 26 September 2000 imposing a definitive anti-dumping duty on imports of television camera systems in Japan, 2000 O.J. (L 244) 38, 46 ¶84.

242. Council Regulation (EC) No. 1736/2004 of 4 October 2004 imposing a definitive anti-dumping duty on imports of synthetic fibre ropes originating in India, 2004 O.J. (L 311) 1, 8 ¶81.

243. *See, e.g.*, Commission Regulation (EC) No. 1999/2006 of 20 December 2006 imposing a provisional anti-dumping duty on imports of certain bicycle saddles originating in the People's Republic of China, 2006 O.J. (L 379) 11, 32 ¶134 in which the Commission disregarded the impact on bicyclists because of an absence of objections by consumer organizations.

contemplated anti-dumping duties will not have a negative effect on this group if they fail to answer the Commission's questionnaire. Consider, for example, the Council's response in *Hand Pallet Truck Originating in China*:[244]

> Two exporting producers and certain importers claimed that the increase in the price of Chinese hand pallet trucks following the imposition of measures is having an immediate and disproportionate effect on hundreds of thousands of shops, stores and factories using hand pallet trucks in the [Union]. However, it is noted that no such [Union] user of hand pallet trucks has submitted any comments on the findings set out in the provisional Regulation. Since this claim has not been supported by any evidence, it should be rejected.

If the Commission finds the other elements of dumping to be present, i.e., dumping, injury, and causality, it generally presumes that the imposition of anti-dumping duties would be in the Union interest unless the targets of the investigation can prove otherwise. Although there is a negative impact (in the form of higher prices) on downstream users and consumers, this does not tend to dissuade the Council from imposing duties unless those negative effects are greater than the short-term benefits to the complaining Union industry.[245]

Even if the downstream industries formally express their objections to the imposition of anti-dumping duties, their concerns are seldom sufficiently persuasive to dissuade the Commission and Council from imposing the duties.[246] The Commission and the Council typically examine whether the incremental costs imposed on the downstream users will outweigh the interests of the complaining Union industry.[247] For example, in the *Glyphosate Originating in*

---

244. Council Regulation (EC) No. 1174/2005 of 18 July 2005 imposing a definitive anti-dumping duty and collecting definitively the provisional duty imposed on imports of hand pallet trucks and their essential parts originating in the People's Republic of China, 2005 O.J. (L189) 1, 12 ¶78.
245. Council Regulation (EC) No. 1095/2005 of 12 July 2005 imposing a definitive anti-dumping duty on imports of bicycles originating in Vietnam, and amending Regulation (EC) No. 1524/2000 imposing a definitive anti-dumping duty on imports of bicycles originating in the People's Republic of China, 2005 O.J. (L 183) 1, 33 ¶190.
246. Attempts by the negatively affected parties to argue that their fundamental right to be heard are violated by the failure of the Council and Commission to give credence to their arguments have been unsuccessful. *See, e.g.*, Case T-643/11, Crown Equipment (Suzhou) Co. Ltd. v. Council, 2014 E.C.R. II-____, at ¶44.
247. *But see* Council Regulation (EC) No. 1205/2007 of 15 October 2007 imposing anti-dumping duties on imports of integrated electronic compact fluorescent lamps (CFL-i) originating in the People's Republic of China following an expiry review pursuant to Article 11(2) of Council Regulation (EC) No. 384/96 and extending to imports of the same product consigned from the Socialist Republic of Vietnam, the Islamic Republic of Pakistan, and the Republic of the Philippines, 2007 O.J. (L 272) 1, 15 ¶115. In this case, the Council concluded that the extension of anti-dumping duties to certain environment-friendly lamps was not in the Union interest due to the impact it would have on consumers. This case is an exception and can probably be explained by the facts that the reduced sales of the lamps resulting from price increases were not consistent with the EU's environmental policy.

China proceedings, the Council concluded that the increase in costs imposed on farmers in the EU (i.e., the end-users of glyphosate) due to the imposition of anti-dumping duties did not outweigh the other Union interests because it would only reduce the profit margin of the farmers 0.1 percent.[248] In *Lever Arch Mechanisms* Originating in China, a cost increase of 2 percent to 3 percent for the downstream uses which would result from the imposition of anti-dumping duties was considered insignificant.[249]

In many cases, the product which is the target of the anti-dumping proceedings will constitute an insignificant portion of the production costs of the downstream industry. In these cases, the Commission and the Council apply an undefined de minimis standard and dismiss the concerns of the downstream industries. In *Aluminum Wheel Originating in China*, for example, the Commission concluded that because an anti-dumping duty of 20 percent on aluminum automobile wheels would only increase the price of the automobile 0.2 percent, the interests of the customers did not outweigh the interests of the Union industry.[250] In *Citric Acid Originating in China*, despite opposition from the EU food industry—where citric acid is used as an ingredient—to the proposed imposition of anti-dumping duties on citric acid being imported from China, the Council concluded that citric acid represented only an insignificant portion (less than 20 percent) of the production costs of the food industry.[251]

In *Potassium Chloride Originating in Belarus and Russia*, the Commission and Council used essentially the same logic even though the product concerned, potash, represented 15 percent to 30 percent of the cost of the final product (fertilizer used by farmers).[252] Despite protestations by European fertilizer manufacturers that the increased costs of potash, which would necessarily result from the imposition of anti-dumping on potash from Belarus and Russia, would have adverse consequences for them by increasing their prices, the Commission and Council concluded that this effect was minimal and did not outweigh the interest of the complaining Union industry.

In *Polyester Filament Fabric Originating in China*, several EU clothing producers argued that the imposition of anti-dumping duties on the Chinese

---

248. Council Regulation (EC) No. 1683/2004 of 24 September 2004 imposing a definitive anti-dumping duty on imports of glyphosate originating in the People's Republic of China, 2004 O.J. (L 303) 1, 16 ¶114.
249. Council Regulation (EC) No. 1136/2006 of 24 July 2006 imposing a definitive anti-dumping duty and collecting definitively the provisional duty imposed on imports of lever arch mechanisms originating in the People's Republic of China, 2006 O.J. (L 205) 1, 10 ¶95.
250. Commission Regulation (EU) No. 404/2010 of 10 May 2010 imposing a provisional anti-dumping duty on imports of certain aluminium wheels originating in the People's Republic of China, 2010 O.J. (L 117) 64, 80 ¶165.
251. Council Regulation (EC) No. 1193/2008 of 1 December 2008 imposing a definitive anti-dumping duty and collecting definitively the provisional duties imposed on imports of citric acid originating in the People's Republic of China, 2008 O.J. (L 323) 1, 11 ¶85.
252. Council Regulation (EC) No. 1050/2006 of 11 July 2006 imposing a definitive anti-dumping duty on imports of potassium chloride originating in Belarus and Russia, 2006 O.J. (L 191) 1, 18 ¶148.

fabrics which they used to produce clothing would effectively force them to shift production outside the EU market because they could not compete with the low-cost clothes imported from China.[253] In other words, their competitors outside the EU would be able to purchase low-cost Chinese fabric and sell clothes in the EU at lower prices. The Commission dismissed these concerns by stating that "the non-imposition of anti-dumping measures would not address this particular issue."[254]

Even if the downstream price increase resulting from the imposition of anti-dumping duties on upstream products forces the downstream industry to incur losses, the interests of the complaining industry may prevail. In *Frozen Strawberries Originating in the People's Republic of China*, the Council imposed anti-dumping duties on the imported frozen strawberries even though—as recognized by the Council—the duties would reduce the profit margins of some of the EU jam producers so dramatically that they would suffer losses.[255] The Council reasoned that the losses did not outweigh the damage of the continued dumping to which the Polish strawberry industry was exposed.[256]

The Council often overlooks the interests of importers from countries that are not the target of the anti-dumping investigation.[257] As anti-dumping proceedings are typically directed at imports from specific countries, the imposition of duties will not only benefit the particular complaining European industry but, because the duties will increase the market price for the products concerned, importers from other countries outside the EU will benefit. For example, the imposition of anti-dumping duties on DVDs from Taiwan may benefit importers of DVDs from Brazil into the EU because it will allow the Brazilians to sell more of their product or increase their selling price (assuming that there are no other restrictions placed on the imports from Brazil).

---

253. Commission Regulation (EC) No. 1487/2005 of 12 September 2005 imposing a definitive anti-dumping duty and collecting definitively the provisional duty imposed on imports of certain finished polyester filament fabrics originating in the People's Republic of China, 2005 O.J. (L 240) 1, 12 ¶87.
254. *Id.* at 12 ¶90.
255. Council Regulation (EC) No. 407/2007 of 16 April 2007 imposing definitive anti-dumping measures and releasing the provisional duty imposed on imports of certain frozen strawberries originating in the People's Republic of China, 2007 O.J. (L 100) 1, 9 ¶74.
256. Council Regulation (EC) No. 407/2007 of 16 April 2007 imposing definitive anti-dumping measures and releasing the provisional duty imposed on imports of certain frozen strawberries originating in the People's Republic of China, 2007 O.J. (L 100) 1, 10 ¶85.
257. *See, e.g.*, Council Regulation (EC) No. 172/2008 of 25 February 2008 imposing a definitive anti-dumping duty and collecting definitively the provisional duty imposed on imports of ferro-silicon originating in the People's Republic of China, Egypt, Kazakhstan, the former Yugoslav Republic of Macedonia, and Russia, 2008 O.J. (L 55) 6, 16 ¶107; Council Regulation (EC) No. 1472/2006 of 5 October 2006 imposing a definitive anti-dumping duty and collecting definitively the provisional duty imposed on imports of certain footwear with uppers of leather originating in the People's Republic of China and Vietnam, 2006 O.J. (L 275) 1, 31 ¶251.

Even if such spillover effects are present, the focus of the inquiry remains on the Union industry and whether a sufficient portion of the EU will benefit. This applies even where the benefit to the non-EU importers exceeds the benefit to the Union industry.[258] If, however, the Union industry is only a small portion of the overall European market, the other importers may even be the primary beneficiaries of the duties. The Union interest in this situation may not be sufficient to justify the imposition of the duties. For example, in the *Atlantic Fisheries Anti-Dumping* proceedings, the Council concluded that since the Union industry constituted only a small percentage of the European market for salmon (less than 5 percent), there was insufficient Union interest to impose anti-dumping duties.[259]

(e) *Procedure*

(1) *Initiation of Anti-Dumping Proceedings*

Anti-dumping proceedings are initiated by a complaint to the Commission or a member state (which then forwards the complaint to the Commission). In exceptional circumstances, the Commission can initiate an investigation on its own initiative.[260] The complaint may be submitted by any natural or legal person, or any association not having legal personality, acting on behalf of the Union industry.[261] As discussed above, in order to qualify as the Union industry, the output of the complaining EU producers must constitute a major proportion of the total EU production of the products in question. The output only constitutes a major proportion if (1) it represents at least 25 percent of the total EU production and (2) EU producers representing 50 percent or more of the total EU production do not oppose the initiation of the investigation.[262] The major proportion requirement relates only to the initiation of the investigation. If

---

258. Council Regulation (EC) No. 172/2008 of 25 February 2008 imposing a definitive anti-dumping duty and collecting definitively the provisional duty imposed on imports of ferro-silicon originating in the People's Republic of China, Egypt, Kazakhstan, the former Yugoslav Republic of Macedonia, and Russia, 2008 O.J. (L 55) 6, 16 ¶107.
259. Council Regulation (EC) No. 930/2003 of 26 May 2003 terminating the anti-dumping and anti-subsidy proceedings concerning imports of farmed Atlantic salmon originating in Norway and the anti-dumping proceeding concerning imports of farmed Atlantic salmon originating in Chile and the Faeroe Islands, 2003 O.J. (L 133) 1, 31 ¶238.
260. Anti-Dumping Regulation at art. 5(6).
261. *Id.* at art. 5. In order to be included in the "Union industry" it is not necessary that a particular company is actually being injured or threatens to be injured from the alleged dumping. Commission Regulation (EC) No. 994/2007 of 28 August 2007 imposing a provisional anti-dumping duty on imports of ferro-silicon originating in the people's Republic of China, Egypt, Kazakhstan, the former Yugoslav Republic of Macedonia, and Russia, 2007 O.J. (L 223) 1, 9 ¶80.
262. In order to be included in the Union industry calculation, the company must be willing to cooperate with the Commission in its investigation. The output of Union producers who support the filing of a complaint but fail to cooperate with the Commission are not included when calculating these thresholds. Case T-401/06, Brosmann Footware (HK) Ltd. v. Council, 2010 E.C.R. II-678, 713 ¶105 *aff'd on appeal* Case C-249/10 P, Brosmann Footware (HK) Ltd. v. Council, 2012 E.C.R. I-___.

the 25 percent and 50 percent thresholds are fulfilled at the time the investigation is initiated, the subsequent reduction of the EU production to levels below these thresholds does not require the Commission to terminate the investigation.[263]

In most instances, the complaint is filed by a trade association on behalf of the EU producers. For example, in *Strawberries Originating in the People's Republic of China*, the Polish Freezing Industry Union (which only represented Polish producers) was successful in convincing the Commission to initiate an investigation and ultimately impose duties on imports from China despite opposition from many EU downstream users.[264] However, it is not necessary that the complaint be issued by the representative industry association. An individual company may submit a complaint and trigger an investigation if that company accounts for at least 25 percent of the EU production.[265] It is important to note, however, that only the EU producers cooperating in the investigation are included.[266] This is determined both when the Commission decides to initiate the investigation and when the Council imposes the anti-dumping duties. For example, if a company supports the initiation of proceedings and then fails to cooperate with the Commission in its investigation, it will not be included in the Union industry when determining whether the Union industry was injured.[267]

---

263. Case T-469/07, Philips Lighting Poland S.A. v. Council, 2013 E.C.R. II-____, at ¶84; Case T-249/06, Interpipe Nikopolsky Seamless Tubes Plant Niko Tube ZAT v. Council, 2009 E.C.R. II-390, 453 ¶139 *aff'd on appeal* Joined cases C-191/09 P and C-200/09 P, Interpipe Nikopolsky Seamless Tubes Plant Niko Tube ZAT v. Council, 2012 E.C.R. I-____ (reported in the electronic reports of cases ECLI:EU:C:2012:78).
264. Commission Regulation (EC) No. 1551/2006 of 17 October 2006 imposing a provisional anti-dumping duty on imports of certain frozen strawberries originating in the People's Republic of China, 2006 O.J. (L 287) 3, 3 ¶2.
265. *See, e.g.*, Commission Regulation (EU) No. 118/2011 of 10 February 2011 imposing a provisional anti-dumping duty on imports of certain ring binder mechanisms originating in Thailand, 2011 O.J. (L 37) 2, 4 ¶31; Notice of initiation of an anti-dumping proceeding concerning imports of vinyl acetate originating in the United States of America, 2010 O.J. (C 327) 23; Commission Regulation (EC) No. 488/2008 of 2 June 2008 imposing a provisional anti-dumping duty on imports of citric acid originating in the People's Republic of China, 2008 O.J. (L 143) 13, 18 ¶55; Commission Regulation (EC) No. 1069/2007 of 17 September 2007 imposing a provisional anti-dumping duty on imports of polyvinyl alcohol originating in the People's Republic of China, 2007 O.J. (L 243) 23, 23 ¶2.
266. Council Regulation (EC) No. 1472/2006 of 5 October 2006 imposing a definitive anti-dumping duty and collecting definitively the provisional duty imposed on imports of certain footwear with uppers of leather originating in the People's Republic of China and Vietnam, 2006 O.J. (L 275) 1, 17 ¶156; Council Regulation (EC) No. 1136/2006 of 24 July 2006 imposing a definitive anti-dumping duty and collecting definitively the provisional duty imposed on imports of lever arch mechanisms originating in the People's Republic of China, 2006 O.J. (L 205) 1, 3 ¶29.
267. Council Regulation (EC) No. 1472/2006 of 5 October 2006 imposing a definitive anti-dumping duty and collecting definitively the provisional duty imposed on imports of certain footwear with uppers of leather originating in the People's Republic of China and Vietnam, 2006 O.J. (L 275) 1, 17 ¶156.

If the complaint is supported by the Union industry, the Commission then determines whether there is sufficient evidence to justify initiating an investigation. There is a de minimis safe harbor. If the imports constitute less than 1 percent market share in the EU, the Commission will not initiate an investigation. The Commission has 45 days after filing the complaint to determine if there is sufficient evidence to justify initiating a proceeding.

(2) Investigation

The Commission is responsible for conducting anti-dumping investigations. The two primary methods by which the Commission collects data are site visits and questionnaires. Commission representatives from the Trade Directorate will visit the alleged dumping firms and review relevant financial and production data. In addition, they will send questionnaires to interested parties. The Commission may also request member states to carry out all necessary checks and inspections, particularly among importers, traders, and EU producers. As a general rule, an investigation should be concluded within one year. In exceptional circumstances, the Commission can take up to 15 months to complete an investigation.

Confidentiality during and after the investigation is generally a concern not only of the companies directly involved, but also all companies that cooperate with the Commission. The willingness of companies to cooperate in the investigation is influenced by the level of confidentiality accorded to the information they provide. This requires a difficult balancing of the rights of defense of the companies negatively affected by the investigation against the confidentiality interests of the cooperating parties. The general rule is that the affected parties have a right to review the information submitted to the Commission. However, the Commission may refuse to disclose information which is confidential or which is provided on a confidential basis.[268] In one case, for example, the General Court held that customers of the companies which initiated the investigation may legitimately request that their identities not be disclosed in order to protect them from retributive commercial conduct of their suppliers.[269]

(3) Imposition of Duties

The complaint can be withdrawn at any time. If it is withdrawn, the proceeding is terminated unless such termination would not be in the Union interest.[270] Similarly, if the Commission finds that dumping does not exist, or it accepts undertakings offered by the companies involved in the investigation,[271] the Commission will terminate the investigation. However, if the Commission finds that all of the elements of dumping are fulfilled, it makes a proposal to the Council to impose anti-dumping duties. If supported by the facts, and the Union

---

268. Anti-Dumping Regulation at art. 19(1).
269. Case T-274/07, Zhejiang Harmonic Hardware Products Co. Ltd. v. Council, 2012 E.C.R. II-377, at ¶61.
270. Anti-Dumping Regulation at art. 9.
271. According to Article 8 of the Anti-Dumping Regulation, the Commission has the authority to negotiate with and accept undertakings offered by the companies under investigation.

interest calls for intervention, the Council imposes a definitive anti-dumping duty.[272] Anti-dumping duties are not compensatory in nature, but rather a protective measure to offset or deter future dumping.[273] The anti-dumping duty remains in force only as long as necessary to counteract the dumping which is causing injury.[274] However, a definitive anti-dumping measure automatically expires five years from its imposition, unless it is determined in a review that the expiration would be likely to lead to a continuation or recurrence of dumping and injury.[275]

(f) Consequences

Assuming that dumping and injury exist, and there is a Union interest in imposing anti-dumping duties, the Council may adopt a regulation imposing definitive anti-dumping duties.[276] The collection of these duties then becomes a matter of customs law as discussed above. When the products are then exported to the EU, the importer must pay the duties (including the anti-dumping duties) before those goods are released into circulation in the EU.[277] Anti-dumping duties are generally imposed on the specific products coming from a particular country or countries which are subject of the investigation. A company may, however, be treated individually if undertakings that it may offer are accepted by the Commission or if it is granted individual treatment.[278]

---

272. Anti-Dumping Regulation at art. 9(4).
273. Case T-138/02, Nanjing Metalink International Co. Ltd v. Council, 2006 E.C.R. II-4351, 4372 ¶60.
274. Anti-Dumping Regulation at art. 11(1).
275. An anti-dumping duty may be extended even if the Union industry is no longer suffering an injury, provided that there is a likelihood that the injury will reoccur in the future if the anti-dumping duties are repealed. *See, e.g.*, Council Regulation (EC) No. 442/2007 of 19 April 2007 imposing a definitive anti-dumping duty on imports of ammonium nitrate originating in Ukraine following an expiry review pursuant to Article 11(2) of Regulation (EC) No. 384/96, 2007 O.J. (L 106) 1, 16 ¶99. However, the mere possibility that dumping and injury *might* continue or recur is insufficient to extend the anti-dumping duties. Case T-158/10, The Dow Chemical Company v. Council, 2012 E.C.R. II-___, at ¶22 (reported in the electronic reports of cases ECLI:EU:T:2012:218).
276. Anti-Dumping Regulation at art. 9(4).
277. As anti-dumping duties are typically imposed based on Combined Nomenclature (CN) code and country of origin, all goods falling under that CN code originating in that country will be subject to the anti-dumping duties even if they are slightly different than the products that were the subject of the anti-dumping investigation. The standard enunciated by the ECJ is whether the new products bear the same characteristics as the products subject of the investigation. Case C-595/11, Steinel Vertrieb GmbH v. Hauptzollamt Bielefeld, 2013 E.C.R. I-___, at ¶42. According to the ECJ, some relevant factors are whether the products have the same physical and technical characteristics, the same basic end use, the same prices level, and whether they compete with each other. *Id.* at ¶42. In *Steinel Vertrieb GmbH v. Hauptzollamt Bielefeld*, the ECJ remanded the issue—whether lamps with a twilight switch and lamps without a twilight switch (being introduced to the market several years later) -bore the same characteristics.
278. Anti-Dumping Regulation at art. 9(5).

The companies affected by the anti-dumping duties can, of course, appeal the decision of the Council to the ECJ. However, the ECJ is reluctant to second-guess the conclusions reached by the Council. According to the ECJ, "in the sphere of the common commercial policy and, most particularly, in the realm of measures to protect trade, the institutions of the European Union enjoy a broad discretion by reason of the complexity of the economic, political and legal situations which they have to examine."[279] The ECJ will generally restrict its analysis to "verifying whether relevant procedural rules have been complied with, whether the facts on which the contested choice is based have been accurately stated, and whether there has been a manifest error in the appraisal of those facts or a misuse of powers."[280]

(g) Circumvention

As the imposition of anti-dumping duties is product and country specific, there is an obvious incentive for an importer to try to circumvent the impact of those duties by importing the product through another country. For example, if anti-dumping duties are imposed on imports of shoes from China, the Chinese toy manufacturer may want to shift production (or a part of the production) to Macao so that the toys are exported from Macao to the EU.[281]

There are two ways by which the law addresses this incentive to circumvent the anti-dumping duties. First, as discussed above, EU customs law contains detailed rules that can be applied to determine the origin of a product. One of the purposes of the rules of origin is to prevent importers from disguising the country from which their products are really being exported. When a product is imported into the EU, its origin must be determined and declared. This applies equally to products on which an anti-dumping duty has been imposed. In practice, the determination of whether an anti-dumping duty is owed can only be made after the product's origin has been determined.

Second, the Anti-Dumping Regulation contains rules specifically applicable to circumvention.[282] In cases of circumvention, the Council may extend the anti-dumping duties to imports from third countries. A finding of circumvention has two elements (note that the intent of the parties is not relevant). First, there must be a change in the pattern of trade between third countries and the EU which stems from a practice, process, or work for which there is insufficient due cause

---

279. Case C-13/12 P, Chelyabinsk Electrometallurgical Integrated Plant 040 v. Council, 2013 E.C.R. I-____, at ¶61.
280. Case C-351/04, Ikea Wholesale Ltd. v. Commissioners of Customs & Excise, 2007 E.C.R. I-7771, 7787 ¶41.
281. *See, e.g.*, Commission Regulation (EC) No. 1028/2007 of 5 September 2007 initiating an investigation concerning the possible circumvention of anti-dumping measures imposed by Council Regulation (EC) No. 1472/2006, 2007 O.J. (L 234) 3.
282. Anti-Dumping Regulation at art. 13(1). The member states "or any interested party" may request that the Commission initiate a circumvention regulation. *Id.* at art. 13(3). The support of the Union industry is not required. Even a single EU competitor might be able to persuade the Commission to open an investigation. *See, e.g.*, Commission Implementing Regulation (EU) 2015/395 of 10 March 2015 initiating an investigation concerning the possible circumvention of anti-dumping measures, 2015 O.J. (L 66) 4.

or economic justification other than the imposition of the duty. According to the ECJ, the EU institutions enjoy "a broad margin of discretion" in determining what constitutes circumvention.[283] This condition is be met, for example, if immediately after the Council imposed anti-dumping duties on shoes imported from Australia, there was a dramatic increase in the importation of shoes from New Zealand and a corresponding decrease in imports from Australia.

The second element of circumvention requires that there be evidence that the remedial effects of the anti-dumping duty are being undermined.[284] Similar to the first element, the EU courts give the Council and Commission broad discretion in weighing the evidence. According to the ECJ, the mere coincidence in time between the imposition of anti-dumping duties and the change in the pattern of trade between third countries and the EU constitutes significant evidence of circumvention.[285]

In *Simon, Evers & Co GmbH v. Hauptzollamt Hamburg-Hafen*, the Council imposed anti-dumping duties on hand pallet trucks coming from China. Shortly after the imposition of the duties, imports of hand pallet trucks from Thailand increased dramatically. The Council's inference that this constituted circumvention of the anti-dumping duties was affirmed by the ECJ on appeal.[286] It is interesting to note that the ECJ held that the Council, in determining whether circumvention exists, may make a negative presumption against noncooperating importers.[287]

In *Electronic Fluorescent Lamps*, the Council had imposed anti-dumping duties on imports of electronic fluorescent lamps originating in China.[288] During the investigation, one of the Chinese producers quietly transferred some equipment and machinery to a related company in Pakistan. The Chinese producer then shipped the parts to the Pakistan facility for assembly and export to the EU. After the imposition of anti-dumping duties, exports from China decreased 50 percent and imports from Pakistan increased over 100 percent. Consequently, the Council extended the anti-dumping duties to Pakistan based on the conclusion that Pakistan was engaged in circumvention.[289]

---

283. Case C-21/13, Simon, Evers & Co GmbH v. Hauptzollamt Hamburg-Hafen, 2014 E.C.R. I-____, at ¶48.
284. Anti-Dumping Regulation at art. 13(1).
285. Case C-21/13, Simon, Evers & Co GmbH v. Hauptzollamt Hamburg-Hafen, 2014 E.C.R. I-____, at ¶52.
286. *Id.* at ¶57.
287. *Id.* at ¶36.
288. Council Regulation (EC) No. 1470/2001 of 16 July 2001 imposing a definitive anti-dumping duty and collecting definitively the provisional duty imposed on imports of integrated electronic compact fluorescent lamps (CFL-i) originating in the People's Republic of China, 2001 O.J. (L 195) 8.
289. Council Regulation (EC) No. 866/2005 of 6 June 2005 extending the definitive anti-dumping measures imposed by Regulation (EC) No 1470/2001 on imports of integrated electronic compact fluorescent lamps (CFL-i) originating in the People's Republic of China to imports of the same product consigned from the Socialist Republic of Vietnam, the Islamic Republic of Pakistan, and the Republic of the Philippines, 2005 O.J. (L 145) 1.

Because establishing assembly operations in another country is a tempting way to circumvent anti-dumping duties, the Anti-Dumping Regulation contains rules specifically applicable to assembly operations.[290] There is a presumption that an assembly operation in the EU or a third country is considered to circumvent anti-dumping duties if three conditions are fulfilled. First, the assembled parts must constitute 60 percent or more of the total value of the parts of the assembled product. For example, if anti-dumping duties are imposed on cellular telephones from Canada, circumvention will only be presumed to exist for cellular phones assembled in the United States and exported to the EU if the value of the Canadian manufactured parts that go into those U.S. assembled phones exceed 60 percent of the total aggregate value of all the parts making up the phones.

There is one exception to this rule: if the local value which is added to the parts is greater than 25 percent of the manufacturing cost, no circumvention will be presumed to exist (even if the value of the assembled parts constitutes more than 60 percent of the total value of the parts of the assembled product). The idea behind this exception is that the alleged assembly operations are really closer to a manufacturing operation, as evidenced by the fact that there is some real local value being added. Assume, for example, all the parts of a flat screen television are being manufactured in the United States, but assembled in Mexico. As the parts are quite standard, their aggregate value is only €100, but the overall manufacturing cost is €1000. Consequently, the local value added is greater than 25 percent of the total manufacturing cost (90 percent of the total manufacturing costs are local), and there is no circumvention.

Second, the assembly operation must have started (or at least substantially increased) since, or just prior to, the initiation of the anti-dumping investigation. Third, the parts concerned must be from the country subject to the anti-dumping measures. For example, if anti-dumping duties are imposed on bicycles from China, a bicycle assembly plant in Korea cannot be considered indicative of circumvention if the bicycles assembled in Korea are from parts manufactured in Japan. Finally, the remedial effects of the anti-dumping duty are being undermined in terms of the prices and/or quantities of the assembled like product and there is evidence of dumping in relation to the normal values previously established for the like or similar products. For example, if the parts assembled in the other country are not being dumped in the EU, there is no reason to extend the anti-dumping duties to them even though the other elements of circumvention exist.

2.4 Countervailing Measures

The ancillary domestic political benefits associated with increased exports by domestic industry (even if artificially induced) create the incentive for domestic governments to subsidize domestic industry. For example, subsidies may persuade a local producer that employs a large number of local workers to open or keep its business in that country rather than moving abroad. The WTO Agreement on Subsidies and Countervailing Measures allows a country

---

290. Anti-Dumping Regulation at art. 13(2).

to increase duties (i.e., take countervailing measures) to offset illegally granted subsidies. This Agreement has been transposed into the EU trade regime in the form of Council Regulation (EC) No. 597/2009 on protection against subsidized imports from countries not members of the EU.[291] The general rule codified in the Anti-Subsidy Regulation is that the Council may impose a countervailing duty for the purpose of offsetting any subsidy granted for the production, export, or transport of any product whose release for free circulation in the EU causes injury.

(a) Elements

Four elements need to be fulfilled before countervailing duties are imposed: specific subsidy, injury, causation, and Union interest. The first of these is the existence of a specific subsidy. The term "subsidy" broadly includes any financial contribution given by a foreign government.[292] The use of the terms financial contribution and government in this context should be interpreted broadly. Just about any benefit will be considered a financial contribution. Government loans to a company that was not otherwise able to receive financing on the open market will be considered a financial contribution. Even the failure of a state to collect fees or taxes otherwise due constitutes a subsidy. A common subsidy resulting in the imposition of countervailable duties is a tax exemption or credit granted by a foreign country to its manufacturers for income related to exports.[293]

The financial contribution can also be indirect. For example, by placing a limit on the maximum interest rate that banks could charge exporters was considered a subsidy because the exporters were able to obtain better rates (even though from private banks) than they otherwise would have been able to obtain in the absence of the limitation.[294]

The notion of government includes not only government agencies, but also public bodies. A public body is defined as "an institution authorised to act on behalf of a community as a government entity, as distinct from a private body

---

291. 2009 O.J. (L 188) 93.
292. A formal definition of subsidy is provided in Article 3 of the Anti-Subsidy Regulation.
293. *See, e.g.*, Case T-556/10, Novatex Ltd. v. Council, 2011 E.C.R. II-____ (reported in the electronic reports of cases ECLI:EU:T:2012:537); Case T-300/03, Moser Baer India Ltd. v. Council, 2006 E.C.R. II-3911 *aff'd on appeal* Case C-535/06 P, Moser Baer India Ltd. v. Council, 2009 E.C.R. I-7051; Council Regulation (EC) No. 598/2009 of 7 July 2009 imposing a definitive countervailing duty and collecting definitively the provisional duty on imports of biodiesel originating in the United States of America, 2009 O.J. (L 179) 1, 6 ¶51; Council Regulation (EC) No. 713/2005 of 10 May 2005 imposing a definitive countervailing duty on imports of certain broad spectrum antibiotics originating in India, 2005 O.J. (L 121) 1, 21 ¶117.
294. Council Regulation (EC) No. 193/2007 of 22 February 2007 imposing a definitive countervailing duty on imports of polyethylene terephthalate (PET) originating in India following an expiry review pursuant to Article 18 of Regulation (EC) No. 2026/97, 2007 O.J. (L 59) 34, 38 ¶43.

which is presumed to act in the interests of its owners."[295] In determining whether the entity granting the financial contribution is a public body, the Council considers whether the body pursues public policy objectives, and the government exercises some degree of control going beyond ownership.[296] For example, the Reserve Bank of India is considered part of the government because it sets monetary policy, which is a public policy objective.[297]

This broad notion of the term subsidy without any qualification would encompass general assistance such as the maintenance of roads that may be considered a subsidy to an industry heavily reliant on road transport. For this reason, the Anti-Subsidy Regulation requires the subsidy to be specific.[298] The specificity requirement precludes countervailing duties for such general benefits to society offered by a foreign state which may also (incidentally) benefit companies. For example, a national unemployment insurance scheme may benefit companies because it relieves them of providing a benefit to their employees which they may otherwise be expected to provide. The specificity requirement means that such general benefits do not justify the imposition of countervailing measures. Specific subsidies are export subsidies, or subsidies limited to a company, an industry, or a group of companies or industries. An investment by a foreign country in a failing entity, for example, will be considered a subsidy if a normal market investor would not have made the investment on the same terms.[299] The subsidy does not, however, have to be directed toward a particular company to be considered specific. An income tax exemption on profits from export sales of recordable CDs is an example of a specific subsidy as it benefits specific companies in a particular industry.[300]

The second element that needs to be fulfilled before countervailing duties are imposed is that the import sales must either have caused or threaten to cause damage or injury to a substantial part of the industry within the EU.[301] Both the

---

295. Council Regulation (EC) No. 1480/2003 of 11 August 2003 imposing a definitive countervailing duty on electronic microcircuits known as DRAMS (dynamic random access memory) originating in the Republic of Korea, 2003 O.J. (L 212) 1, 2 ¶13.
296. A private body, i.e., one in which the state does not hold an equity interest, will generally only be deemed a public body if it distributes the financial contribution at the direction of the state. Art. 2(1)(a)(iv) Basic Regulation.
297. Council Regulation (EC) No. 193/2007 of 22 February 2007 imposing a definitive countervailing duty on imports of polyethylene terephthalate (PET) originating in India following an expiry review pursuant to Article 18 of Regulation (EC) No. 2026/97, 2007 O.J. (L 59) 34, 38 ¶45.
298. Anti-Subsidy Regulation at art. 4(1).
299. *See, e.g.*, Council Regulation 708/2003 of 23 April 2003 imposing a provisional countervailing duty on imports of certain electronic microcircuits known as DRAMs originating in the Republic of Korea, 2003 O.J. (L 102) 7.
300. *See, e.g.*, Council Regulation No. 960/2003 of 2 June 2003 imposing a definitive countervailing duty on imports of recordable compact discs originating in India, 2003 O.J. (L 138) 1.
301. Anti-Subsidy Regulation at art. 8(5).

Anti-Subsidy Regulation[302] and the EU courts give the EU institutions broad discretion in determining whether injury exists.[303] Examples of evidence of injury in this context are similar to the evidence relied on in the context of anti-dumping investigations: loss of market share, reduced prices for producers, and resulting pressure on production, sales, profits, or productivity.[304] In the *Graphite electrodes Originating in India* proceedings, an increase in market share of 3.4 percent of the subsidized imports was evidence of injury.[305] Profitability is probably the most important factor. "Stainless Steel Bars Originating in India," for example, concluded that the Union industry suffered injury as a result of a subsidy even though the market share of the Union industry (which remained at 81 percent) had not decreased. The Commission's conclusion was based on the recognition that the profitability of the Union industry decreased significantly.[306]

The third element is causation: the subsidized imports must be the cause of the injury to the Union industry. Similar to the causation analysis under the Anti-Dumping Regulation, causation in subsidy investigations is generally examined in two steps. First, the Commission and Council examine whether the injury occurred during the investigation period. If so, the Commission and Council will infer the existence of causation between the subsidies and the injury to the Union industry.[307] In the second step, the Commission and Council examine

---

302. The Anti-Subsidy Regulation (Article 8) identifies a broad range of factors to be considered, but leaves it to the discretion of the Council and Commission to assess these factors in the specific cases.
303. See, e.g., Case C-373/08, Hoesch Metals and Alloys GmbH v. Hauptzollamt Aachen, 2010 E.C.R. I-954, 975 ¶61 ("in the sphere of the common commercial policy and, most particularly, in the realm of measures to protect trade, the Community institutions enjoy a broad discretion by reason of the complexity of the economic, political and legal situations which they have to examine.").
304. Council Regulation (EC) No. 598/2009 of 7 July 2009 imposing a definitive countervailing duty and collecting definitively the provisional duty on imports of biodiesel originating in the United States of America, 2009 O.J. (L 179) 1, 15 ¶130; Council Regulation No. 74/2004 of 13 January 2004 imposing a definitive countervailing duty on imports of cotton-type bed linen originating in India, 2004 O.J. (L 12) 1, 21 ¶171.
305. Commission Regulation (EC) No. 1008/2004 of 19 May 2004 imposing a provisional anti-subsidy duty on imports of certain graphite electrodes systems originating in India, 2004 O.J. (L 183) 35, 52 ¶113.
306. Commission Regulation (EU) No. 1261/2010 of 22 December 2010 imposing a provisional countervailing duty on imports of certain stainless steel bars originating in India, 2010 O.J. (L 343) 57, 70 ¶120.
307. Commission Regulation (EU) No. 1261/2010 of 22 December 2010 imposing a provisional countervailing duty on imports of certain stainless steel bars originating in India, 2010 O.J. (L 343) 57, 72 ¶136; Commission Regulation (EC) No. 194/2009 of 11 March 2009 imposing a provisional countervailing duty on imports of biodiesel originating in the United States of America, 2009 O.J. (L 67) 50, 77 ¶243; Council Regulation (EC) No. 598/2009 of 7 July 2009 imposing a definitive countervailing duty and collecting definitively the provisional duty on imports of biodiesel originating in the United States of America, 2009 O.J. (L 179) 1, 15 ¶132.

whether factors exist that break the causal connection.[308] In *Mukand v. Council*, for example, the General Court held that the Council, in imposing countervailing duties on stainless steel bars imported from India, failed to take into account the effect on the Union industry of a price cartel in which the Union industry was involved.[309] The injury suffered by the Union industry allegedly as a result of the subsidized imports could have been caused by the anti-competitive practices of the injured firms. Consequently, the General Court annulled the Council's decision imposing countervailing duties.[310]

In making this determination, the Commission and Council are required to consider other factors that may have caused the injury.[311] There is no exhaustive catalog of factors which the Commission and Council are required to consider. One obvious relevant consideration is the effect or contribution of nonsubsidized imports to the injury of the EU industry. In *Stainless Steel Fasteners and Parts Thereof Originating in India*, the Commission concluded that certain Indian producers of stainless steel fasteners had received subsidies and that the EU industry had suffered injury at the same time as these subsidized fasteners were being imported into the EU from India.[312] Because, however, the portion of imports that was actually subsidized was only 13 percent of the overall imports of steel fasteners being imported from India, the Commission terminated the investigation: "In view of the finding that exports by the largest Indian exporting producer, which represented 87 percent of the Indian exports to the Union in the [investigation period], were not subsidized, it is considered that a causal link between the subsidized imports, accounting for a mere 13 percent of the total quantity exported from India, and the injury suffered by the Union industry cannot be sufficiently established."[313]

The Commission and Council do not typically recognize that the injury may be caused by the inefficiency of the industry itself. In a case involving imports of recordable compact discs from India, the Indian producers argued that the injury suffered by the EU producers of recordable compact discs could be

---

308. Commission Regulation (EU) No. 115/2012 of 9 February 2012 imposing a provisional countervailing duty on imports of certain stainless steel fasteners and parts thereof originating in India, 2012 O.J. (L 38) 6, 24 ¶174.
309. Case T-58/99, Mukand v. Council, 2001 E.C.R. II-2521.
310. *Id.* at 2544 ¶57. *But see* Case T-462/04, HEG Ltd. v. Council, 2008 E.C.R. II-3691, 3729 ¶122, where the General Court concluded that a cartel existing simultaneous with the subsidization did not cause the injury allegedly suffered due to the subsidization.
311. Anti-Subsidy Regulation at art. 8(6); C-398/05, AGST Draht- und Biegetechnik GmbH v. Hauptzollamt Aachen, 2008 E.C.R. I-1059, 1070 ¶35. The Commission and Council are given "broad discretion" in considering these other factors. Case T-444/11, Gold East Paper (Jiangsu) Co. Ltd. Council, 2014 E.C.R. II-____, at ¶225. Case C-535/06 P, Moser Baer India Ltd. v. Council, 2009 E.C.R. I-7094, 7130 ¶85.
312. Commission Decision of 23 May 2012 terminating the anti-subsidy proceeding concerning imports of certain stainless steel fasteners and parts thereof originating in India, 2012 O.J. (L 134) 31, 34 ¶46.
313. *Id.* at 34 ¶46.

attributed to the high cost of production and high labor costs in the EU.[314] The Council dismissed this argument by reasoning that "the production process is the same in the EU and in India especially since the Indian producer uses European machinery and also some raw materials imported from the Union."[315] As to the labor costs, the Council found that the production of recordable compact discs is not labor-intensive. Unfortunately, the Council failed to go one step further and examine whether, given similar production and labor costs, the inability of the Union industry to match the prices of the Indian producers could be explained by the inefficiency of the European industry.

It is not sufficient to break the causation to show that external factors could have equally caused the injury. If, even in the absence of the external factors, the injury would have occurred and been material, the causal connection is not broken regardless of the significance of the other factors.[316] In the *Cotton-type Bedlinen* case, for example, the Indian producers of bed linen at whom the investigation was directed argued that the injury alleged to have been caused by the Indian subsidies was at least partially due to the dumping of the same product by Pakistani producers. The Council, which had already initiated an anti-dumping investigation against bed linen originating in Pakistan, recognized that it was a source of the injury. However, "this is not to deny that Indian imports equally caused material injury by themselves."[317]

(b) Union Interest

If the first three elements exist, the issue then becomes whether the imposition of countervailing duties is in the interests of the Union.[318] The question is framed not whether Union interests support the imposition of countervailing duties, but rather whether "compelling reasons" exist not to impose countervailing duties.[319] There is no exhaustive list of legitimate compelling reasons. In making this assessment, the interests of the Union industry, other EU producers and suppliers, importers, and consumers are considered. It is not necessary that the entire

---

314. Council Regulation No. 960/2003 of 2 June 2003 imposing a definitive countervailing duty on imports of recordable compact discs originating in India, 2003 O.J. (L 138) 1, 22, ¶136.
315. *Id.*
316. Case C-535/06 P, Moser Baer India Ltd. v. Council, 2009 E.C.R. I-7094, 7129 ¶81.
317. Council Regulation No. 74/2004 of 13 January 2004 imposing a definitive countervailing duty on imports of cotton-type bed linen originating in India, 2004 O.J. (L 12) 1, 23 ¶184.
318. Anti-Subsidy Regulation at art. 31.
319. Council Implementing Regulation (EU) No. 1239/2013 of 2 December 2013 imposing a definitive countervailing duty on imports of crystalline silicon photovoltaic modules and key components (i.e., cells) originating in or consigned from the People's Republic of China, 2013 O.J. (L 325) 66, 198 ¶833; Council Implementing Regulation (EU) No. 215/2013 of 11 March 2013 imposing a countervailing duty on imports of certain organic coated steel products originating in the People's Republic of China, 2013 O.J. (L 73) 16, 94 ¶558; Commission Regulation (EC) No. 194/2009 of 11 March 2009 imposing a provisional countervailing duty on imports of biodiesel originating in the United States of America, 2009 O.J. (L 67) 50, 78 ¶246.

industry in the EU which is alleged to be incurring the injury, i.e., the competitors of the foreign producers, support the imposition of countervailing duties.[320] In the *Cotton-type Bedlinen* case, the support of EU producers comprising only 45 percent of the EU production was sufficient to support a finding that the imposition of countervailing duties was in the Union interest.[321]

Consumers make up the group most often negatively affected by the imposition of countervailing duties, as the economic effect of the imposition of duties is to increase the prices of the products concerned. Consequently, the end-users are the ones who incur the greatest economic injury. Nonetheless, the interests of the consumers are so diffused and the impact upon them individually so minor, that their interests become secondary to those of the Union industry.[322] In the r*ecordable c*ompact d*iscs* case, the Council dismissed the concerns expressed by the largest consumer protection organization in Europe that the countervailing duty would increase prices to consumers. The projected price increase of 3 cents per CD was not sufficiently significant in the eyes of the Council.[323] In the *Graphite Electrode Systems Originating in India* proceedings, one of the arguments was that the imposition of countervailing duties would be counter to the Union interest because it would raise the costs of the EU users of the electrode systems (i.e., electric arc furnaces for steel production). The Commission, in conducting the investigation and imposing provisional duties, dismissed the significance of this concern by stating that the price increases would be passed on to downstream customers.[324] Similar to anti-dumping duties, impact on the downstream consumers does not generally prevent the imposition of countervailing duties.

---

320. Anti-subsidy proceedings are typically initiated in response to a complaint of a European industry association comprising some or all of the European competitors of the foreign producers who are allegedly the recipients of the subsidies. *See, e.g.*, Notice of initiation of an anti-subsidy proceeding concerning imports of coated fine paper originating in the People's Republic of China, 2010 O.J. (C 99) 30 (Commission investigation initiated in response to a complaint of the European association of fine paper manufacturers).
321. Council Regulation No. 74/2004 of 13 January 2004 imposing a definitive countervailing duty on imports of cotton-type bed linen originating in India, 2004 O.J. (L 12) 1, 16 ¶138.
322. *See, e.g.*, Council Implementing Regulation (EU) No. 861/2013 of 2 September 2013 imposing a definitive countervailing duty and collecting definitively the provisional duty imposed on imports of certain stainless steel wires originating in India, 2013 O.J. (L 240) 1, 11 ¶¶93-101; Council Implementing Regulation (EU) No. 857/2010 of 27 September 2010 imposing a definitive countervailing duty and collecting definitively the provisional duty imposed on imports of certain polyethylene terephthalate originating in Iran, Pakistan, and the United Arab Emirates, 2010 O.J. (L 254) 10, 26 ¶159.
323. Council Regulation No. 74/2004 of 13 January 2004 imposing a definitive countervailing duty on imports of cotton-type bed linen originating in India, 2004 O.J. (L 12) 1, 24 ¶161.
324. Commission Regulation (EC) No. 1008/2004 of 19 May 2004 imposing a provisional anti-dumping duty on imports of certain graphite electrode systems originating in India, 2004 O.J. (L 183) 35, 58 ¶151.

In cases where there will be a clear price increase imposed on consumers, the Commission can justify the imposition of countervailing duties as being in the interests of consumers by hypothesizing that the extended effect of the low prices will ultimately have a negative effect on consumers by driving the Union industry out of business.[325] This approach is at best incomplete. To draw this conclusion, it would be necessary to examine the ease of market entry. If there were low barriers to getting back into the market, the effects on the consumer of the Union industry being driven from the market are less than if the barriers are high. Moreover, it is unclear why competition from Union industry is different than competition between foreign competitors in the absence of EU competitors. Although there may be cases where this assumption is correct, one cannot simply assume that a market lacking EU competitors is less competitive than a market including EU competitors.

General public policy concerns unrelated to trade are not considered. In *Biodiesel Originating in the United States*, for example, one of the parties argued that the imposition of countervailing subsidies on imports of biodiesel fuel originating in the United States would be contrary to environmental policy as it would reduce the reliance on this environmentally friendly fuel by increasing prices in the EU. According to the Commission, however, "general considerations on environmental protection and supply of mineral diesel cannot be taken into account in the analysis."[326]

(c) *Consequences*

If all of the elements are met, a countervailing subsidy may be imposed on the product that has been subsidized.[327] The amount of the countervailing subsidy is determined by the benefit conferred on the subsidy recipient.[328] These duties are imposed independent of the normal customs duties that are imposed on the products.[329]

---

325. Commission Regulation (EC) No. 194/2009 of 11 March 2009 imposing a provisional countervailing duty on imports of biodiesel originating in the United States of America, 2009 O.J. (L 67) 50, 79 ¶261. ("If, however, no measures were to be imposed, the future of the Union industry would be at stake. Its disappearance would severely reduce competition on the [EU] market."), *aff'd by* Council Regulation (EC) No. 598/2009 of 7 July 2009 imposing a definitive countervailing duty and collecting definitively the provisional duty on imports of biodiesel originating in the United States of America, 2009 O.J. (L 179) 1, 18 ¶171.
326. Commission Regulation (EC) No. 194/2009 of 11 March 2009 imposing a provisional countervailing duty on imports of biodiesel originating in the United States of America, 2009 O.J. (L 67) 50, 79 ¶260, *aff'd by* Council Regulation (EC) No. 598/2009 of 7 July 2009 imposing a definitive countervailing duty and collecting definitively the provisional duty on imports of biodiesel originating in the United States of America, 2009 O.J. (L 179) 1, 18 ¶171.
327. Anti-Subsidy Regulation at art. 1(1).
328. *Id.* at art. 5.
329. *Id.* at art. 24(1).

2.5 Safeguard Measures

The third EU trade barrier instrument is safeguard measures. The term "safeguard measures" refers to the measures the Commission may take to prevent large quantities of a product being imported into the EU which would cause injury to EU producers, even though those imports may not be dumped or subsidized. The GATT specifically allows members to take "protective action" if imports into that country (or area in the case of the EU) threaten to cause serious injury to domestic producers.[330] Based on this exception, the EU adopted the Safeguards Regulation. In order to "safeguard the interests of the Union," the Safeguards Regulation allows the Commission to adopt appropriate measures to prevent a product being imported into the EU in such greatly increased quantities or on such terms or conditions as to cause serious injury to EU producers of like or directly competing products.[331]

(a) Elements

The precondition for the Council's action is that a product is imported into the EU in greatly increased quantities or on such terms or conditions as to cause (or threaten to cause) serious injury to EU producers and the interests of the EU so require. The term "serious injury" means a significant overall impairment in the position of EU producers. This analysis is similar to the injury analysis under the Anti-Dumping Regulation and the Anti-Subsidy Regulation. A loss of market share or excess capacity will constitute injury. However, the EU has exhibited greater reluctance to rely on safeguard measures and has consequently interpreted this requirement more narrowly than in the context of the Anti-Dumping Regulation or the Anti-Subsidy Regulation. The injury must be significant and imminent.

In the *U.S. Steel Products* case, the Commission concluded that a decline in market share from 96 percent to 89 percent for the EU producers of rebar was not a significant enough overall impairment of their position to justify adopting safeguard measures against an increase in imports from the United States.[332] If the importing country is a member of the WTO, serious injury will not be imminent if that country's share of EU imports of the product concerned does not exceed 3 percent.[333]

The Commission does not rely on the Safeguards Regulation frequently. One exception is the imposition of safeguard measures against steel imports of Eastern European and Asian steel from the United States. The imposition by the United States of safeguard measures on steel had caused a redirection of the

---

330. GATT at art. XIX(1)(a). A separate Agreement on Safeguards was concluded to regulate the conditions under which such "protective actions" may be implemented.
331. Safeguards Regulation at art. 17.
332. Commission Regulation No. 142/2003 of 27 January 2003 terminating the safeguard proceedings relating to certain steel products and providing for the refund of certain duties, 2003 O.J. (L 23) 9, 15 ¶28.
333. Safeguards Regulation at art. 19.

flow of imports from the United States to Europe.[334] In response, the European producers claimed a serious threat of injury due to the trade diversion. The Commission subsequently adopted safeguard measures in the form of quotas on certain steel products for a duration equal to that of the U.S. safeguard measures.[335]

(b) *Procedure*

The safeguards procedure starts by a member state informing the Commission of import trends that appear to justify the imposition of safeguard measures. Within eight days, the Commission is required to consult with the Advisory Committee composed of representatives from the member states.[336] Based on these consultations, the Commission may initiate an investigation if it deems there is sufficient evidence of a serious injury. The Commission then has nine months to conduct the investigation.[337] During that time, the Commission may impose provisional safeguard measures if, after an initial assessment, serious injury is threatened and irreparable damage is likely.[338]

If the Commission decides to terminate the investigation, it must inform the Advisory Committee. Otherwise, it may adopt safeguard measures. The Safeguards Regulation gives the Commission discretion to determine the appropriate safeguard measures. The Commission has the authority to make the importation of the goods subject to import authorization on the terms established by the Commission.[339] As safeguard measures are justified by increased quantities that threaten to cause injury to a Union industry, quotas are most commonly employed as safeguard measures.

2.6 Trade Barriers

The Anti-Dumping Regulation, Anti-Subsidy Regulation, and Safeguards Regulation are designed to protect Union industry against potentially harmful imports. Their purpose is not necessarily to secure access to foreign markets for European industry. Hence, they are commonly referred to as trade defense instruments. The purpose of the Trade Barriers Regulation,[340] on the other hand, is to provide a mechanism for EU firms and industries to act against trade barriers affecting their access to third country markets. In the *On-line Gambling* case, for example, the Commission launched an investigation of U.S. online gambling laws under the Trade Barriers Regulation to give EU online gambling

---

334. Those measures consisted of a staged increase in duty on imports into the United States of 13 percent in the first year, 10 percent in the second year and 7 percent in the third year.
335. Commission Regulation No. 1694/2002 of 27 September 2002 imposing definitive safeguard measures against imports of certain steel products, 2002 O.J. (L 261) 1.
336. Safeguards Regulation at art. 3.
337. *Id.* at art. 7.
338. *See, e.g.*, Commission Regulation (EC) No. 1447/2004 of 13 August 2004 imposing provisional safeguard measures against imports of farmed salmon, 2004 O.J. (L 267) 3.
339. Safeguards Regulation at art. 16.
340. Council Regulation (EC) No. 3286/94 of 22 December 1994 laying down Community procedures in the field of the common commercial policy, 1994 O.J. (L 349) 71.

companies access to the U.S. market.[341] As discussed below, the Trade Barriers Regulation is the method by which Union industry prompts the Commission to call for WTO dispute resolution proceedings (private parties are not able to initiate WTO dispute resolution proceedings directly). In contrast to the trade defense measures, the application of the Trade Barriers Regulation does not result in the imposition of remedial measures by the EU.

(a) Elements

(1) Obstacle to Trade

The WTO Dispute Settlement Procedure begins when a member initiates proceedings. How a member decides to initiate proceedings is a matter for internal law. The Trade Barriers Regulation allows the EU to commence an action under the WTO Dispute Settlement Procedure if the Commission finds that another WTO member has implemented and continued to maintain an obstacle to trade. The term "obstacle to trade" is defined as any trade practice adopted or maintained by a third country in respect of which international trade rules establish a right of action.[342] For example, if a third country adopts a law which violates the GATT rules, this may be viewed as an obstacle to trade in the context of the Trade Measures Regulation. This is illustrated in the Commission's *U.S. Anti-Dumping Act Decision* in which U.S. anti-dumping laws were at issue.[343] In that case, the Commission concluded that various aspects of the U.S. Antidumping Act of 1916 were inconsistent with the WTO Anti-Dumping Agreement, inter alia the possibility of the United States imposing anti-dumping duties during the formal investigation without having to undertake even an initial investigation or the possibility in the United States of a private party bringing an anti-dumping action.

Additional cases that received significant media attention are the Commission's Decision of December 11, 1998, in which the U.S. Copyright Act was found to be an obstacle to trade, in violation of the Berne Convention and the Agreement on Trade-Related Aspects of Intellectual Property Rights (TRIPs) Agreement,[344] and the Commission's Decision of October 20, 2000, where the U.S. rules of origin for textiles were found to violate the WTO Agreement on Rules of Origin.[345] In addition to these multilateral agreements, the term

---

341. Commission Notice of initiation of an examination procedure concerning obstacles to trade within the meaning of Council Regulation (EC) No. 3286/94 consisting of the U.S. ban on foreign Internet gambling and its enforcement, 2008 O.J. (C 65) 5.
342. Trade Measures Regulation at art. 2(1).
343. Commission Decision of 16 April 1998 under the provisions of Council Regulation (EC) No. 3286/94 of 22 December 1994 concerning the failure of the United States of America to repeal its Antidumping Act of 1916, 1998 O.J. (L 126) 36.
344. Commission Decision of 11 December 1998 under the provisions of Council Regulation (EC) No. 3286/94 concerning section 110(5) of the Copyright Act of the United States of America, 1998 O.J. (L 346) 60.
345. Commission Decision of 20 October 2000 terminating the examination procedure concerning changes made by the United States of America in their rules of origin for textiles and apparel products, 2000 O.J. (L 278) 35.

"international trade rules" includes bilateral trade agreements to which the EU is a party.[346] A trade practice that may have a negative impact on trade from the EU does not constitute an obstacle to trade within the meaning of the regulation unless it infringes an international trade rule.[347]

(2) Adverse Effect

The obstacle to trade must have an effect on the market of the EU or even the market of a third country. Formally, there is no requirement that there be an adverse effect specifically within the EU. An adverse effect on a third country may be sufficient. However, the standing and Union interest requirements discussed below mean that in most cases there will be an adverse effect in the EU.

(3) Standing

If an obstacle to trade exists, a complaint may be brought by a Union industry, an EU enterprise, or a member state. There are, however, different standing requirements for each complainant. A Union industry may lodge a complaint with the Commission if that industry has suffered injury in the EU.[348] In the *Scotch Whisky* investigation, the complaint was lodged by the Scotch Whisky Association composed of Scottish whisky distillers, brokers, and exporters.[349] In the *U.S. Anti-Dumping Act Decision* discussed above, the complaint was filed by the European Confederation of Iron and Steel Industries. In that instance, the Commission considered that the initiation of anti-dumping proceedings in the United States against members of this industry association could have a significant adverse impact on them, and indeed an anti-dumping action had been filed in the United States.[350]

Because trade practices of foreign countries may injure individual companies without injuring the entire industry, the Trade Barriers Regulation allows an individual company—referred to in the Regulation as a Union enterprise—organized under the laws of one of the member states the right to file a complaint if it has suffered adverse trade effects as a result of obstacles to trade that have

---

346. *See, e.g.*, Commission Decision of 23 January 2001 terminating the examination procedure concerning measures affecting the trade of cognac in Brazil, 2001 O.J. (L 35) 53.
347. *See, e.g.*, Commission Decision of 9 July 2002 terminating the examination procedures concerning obstacles to trade, within the meaning of Council Regulation (EC) No. 3286/94, consisting of trade practices maintained by the United States of America in relation to imports of prepared mustard, 2002 O.J. (L 195) 72, in which the Commission concluded that the selective suspension of concessions for some member states but not others did not violate international trade rules.
348. Trade Barriers Regulation at art. 3(1).
349. Notice of initiation of an examination procedure concerning obstacles to trade within the meaning of Council Regulation (EC) No. 3286, consisting of measures imposed and practices followed by the Eastern Republic of Uruguay affecting trade in Scotch whisky, 2004 O.J. (C 261) 3.
350. Commission Decision of 16 April 1998 under the provisions of Council Regulation (EC) No. 3286/94 of 22 December 1994 concerning the failure of the United States of America to repeal its Antidumping Act of 1916, 1998 O.J. (L 126) 36, 37 ¶16.

an effect on the market of a third country.[351] This has become the most common way of initiating a complaint. For a Union enterprise to have standing to initiate a complaint, the obstacle to trade must cause adverse trade effects in a third country and on the economy of the EU, a region in the EU, or a sector of the economy in the EU.[352] This will generally be the case where the complaining industry can show losses of profit, market share, sales prices, or employment because of the obstacle to trade.[353] However, there must be a causal connection between the obstacle to trade and the adverse trade effects. The mere fact that an EU exporter is suffering adverse trade effects in a foreign market is insufficient if those trade effects are not attributable to an obstacle to trade that violates international trade rules.[354]

The third group of potential complainants is the member states.[355] Each of the member states has the right to ask the Commission to initiate trade barriers procedures under the Trade Barriers Regulation. It is incumbent on that member state to supply the Commission with sufficient evidence to support its request. The Commission is not required to initiate an investigation. If, however, it decides not to do so, it must provide the member state with a reasoned decision explaining its conclusion.

(4) Union Interest

Finally, the Commission will consider whether the initiation of the WTO Dispute Settlement Procedure is in the Union interest.[356] As with the other EU trade instruments, the finding of Union interest will seldom have persuasive impact on the final determination if all of the other elements are present. In the Commission's *U.S. Anti-Dumping Act decision*, it was in the Union's interest to ensure that the United States complied with its WTO obligations.[357]

---

351. Trade Barriers Regulation at art. 4. To qualify as a Union enterprise, a company or firm must be formed in accordance with the law of a member state and have its registered office, central administration, or principal place of business within the Union and be directly concerned by the production of goods or the provision of services which are the subject of the obstacle to trade.
352. Trade Barriers Regulation at arts. 2(4) and 4.
353. Commission Decision 2002/818/EC under the provisions of Council Regulation (EC) No. 3286/94 concerning trade practices maintained by Korea affecting trade in commercial vessels, 2002 O.J. (L 281) 15, 16 ¶13.
354. *See, e.g.*, Commission Decision of 9 July 2002 terminating the examination procedures concerning obstacles to trade, within the meaning of Council Regulation (EC) No. 3286/94, consisting of trade practices maintained by the United States of America in relation to imports of prepared mustard, 2002 O.J. (L 195) 72.
355. Trade Barriers Regulation at art. 6.
356. Commission Decision of 16 April 1998 under the provisions of Council Regulation (EC) No. 3286/94 of 22 December 1994 concerning the failure of the United States of America to repeal its Antidumping Act of 1916, 1998 O.J. (L 126) 36, 38 ¶22.
357. Commission Decision of 16 April 1998 under the provisions of Council Regulation (EC) No. 3286/94 of 22 December 1994 concerning the failure of the United States of America to repeal its Antidumping Act of 1916, 1998 O.J. (L 126) 36, 38 ¶22.

(b) Remedies

Upon receipt of a complaint, the Commission must decide (usually within 45 days) whether to initiate the examination procedure. If the examination substantiates the claim that an obstacle to trade exists contrary to international rules, and that injury or adverse trade effects have been inflicted on a Union industry or company, the EU may take action at an international level, bringing a case under the WTO Dispute Settlement Procedure or other appropriate international mechanism. For example, in the *U.S. Anti-Dumping Act* decision, the Commission concluded that the appropriate result would be to initiate WTO dispute settlement proceedings involving the United States.[358] The WTO Panel subsequently ruled in favor of the EU.

In many instances, the country which is the target of the examination may take unilateral action to remove the obstacle or come to an agreement with the Commission without resort to the WTO Dispute Settlement Procedure. In the *U.S. Textiles* case, for example, after initiating trade measure proceedings against the United States, the Commission came to an agreement with the United States that the United States would amend its import rules for textiles to the satisfaction of the complaining European industry.[359] In the *Columbia Motor Vehicle* case, the trade practice complained of was a higher sales tax for imported vehicles into Columbia.[360] After initiation of an investigation under the Trade Barriers Regulation, Columbia and the Commission agreed that the sales tax differential would be eliminated by July 1, 2005, and the Commission suspended the proceedings.

If the Commission decides to initiate a WTO Dispute Settlement Procedure and is successful, but the country concerned refuses to alleviate the obstacle, the Commission can propose to retaliate through measures that target trade from the country concerned. Possible measures available to the Commission include suspension or withdrawal of trade concessions, increase in customs duties for imports into the EU, imposition of quotas or other measures to modify import or export questions, or other forms of retaliation.

2.7 Relationship Between Trade Measures

As discussed above, each of the trade instruments provides for some form of remedial action. In the case of the Anti-Dumping Regulation, the Anti-Subsidy Regulation, and the Safeguard Regulation, duties may be imposed to address the injury. Because the requirements of each of these trade instruments overlap in certain respects, they potentially apply to the same facts. However, the

---

358. Commission Decision of 16 April 1998 under the provisions of Council Regulation (EC) No. 3286/94 of 22 December 1994 concerning the failure of the United States of America to repeal its Antidumping Act of 1916, 1998 O.J. (L 126) 36.
359. Commission Decision of 20 October 2000 terminating the examination procedure concerning changes made by the United States of America in its rules of origin for textiles and apparel products, 2000 O.J. (L 278) 35.
360. Commission Decision of 20 May 2003 on suspending the examination procedure concerning obstacles to trade, consisting of trade practices maintained by the Republic of Colombia in relation to imports of motor vehicles, 2003 O.J. (L 143) 33.

imposition of duties under any of the regulations may alleviate the injury or the threat of injury for the other regulations. To avoid the unnecessary parallel application of remedies, the Council has adopted a regulation that allows the Council to suspend, amend, or repeal duties imposed by one trade instrument if caught by another trade instrument.[361] Although parallel investigations under different trade instruments are possible, the Council has the authority to preclude the overlapping application of trade remedies.

2.8 Relationship Between Trade Law and Competition Law

(a) Parallel Application

EU trade law and competition law are considered to be complementary and not preclusive. In other words, the initiation of an anti-dumping investigation by the Commission does not necessarily preclude the initiation of competition law proceedings against the same undertaking. Moreover, both trade law and competition law may apply to the very same practices. For example, if a non-EU company imports its products into the EU at prices that are below the price at which it is offering those products in its domestic market, it may be engaging in dumping (under the Anti-Dumping Regulation) as well as predatory pricing (under Article 102 of the TFEU).

Although the imposition of trade sanctions under the EU trade laws generally has an anti-competitive effect (in the sense that it gives EU procedures protection from competitors which they would not otherwise have), the EU competition rules do not apply to the imposition of trade sanctions because the competition rules codified in the TFEU do not apply to the Council and the Commission. Hence, the competition rules do not preclude the imposition of trade sanctions even if such sanctions are anti-competitive.

(b) Trade Law and Competitive Strategy

The effects of the imposition of sanctions under the trade laws make them an attractive weapon for domestic competitors. For example, if an undertaking in the EU is not able to compete with the products being imported into the EU by a foreign competitor, the EU undertaking can protect itself by convincing the EU to impose trade sanctions (typically in the form of anti-dumping duties). In certain circumstances, several EU competitors may find it beneficial to jointly attempt to convince the EU to impose trade sanctions against their foreign competitors. As discussed above, a complaint may be filed by one or more EU producers as long as its or their output constitutes more than 25 percent of the

---

361. Council Regulation (EU) No. 2015/477 of 11 March 2015 on measures that the Union may take in relation to the combined effect of anti-dumping or anti-subsidy measures with safeguard measures, 2015 O.J. (L 83) 11. The Trade Barriers Regulation (Article 15) expressly addresses this overlap by precluding the application of that regulation in cases where the other trade instruments apply. Council Regulation (EC) No. 3286/94 of 22 December 1994 laying down Community procedures in the field of the common commercial policy, 1994 O.J. (L 349) 71.

EU production of that product.[362] The cooperation between EU competitors to achieve this objective raises the possibility of the application of Article 101 of the TFEU.

The general rule is that undertakings may legitimately conspire for the purpose of initiating complaints to the Commission leading to trade sanctions.[363] Although, as discussed in Chapter III, the competition rules may be applied by the initiation of vexatious litigation,[364] it is unlikely that this vexatious litigation theory would be extended to investigations under the trade laws. The difference is that in trade law proceedings, the Commission takes the decision whether to initiate the investigation. In private litigation, the proceedings begin with the complaint and there is no objective filter to determine whether the proceedings are in the public interest. In the EU, the Commission has never imposed sanctions against a company for initiating trade measures.

This is not meant to suggest that anti-competitive conduct is irrelevant in applying the trade laws. As discussed above, the application of the trade measures requires an actual or threatened injury to a Union industry and a causal link between the dumping and the injury allegedly suffered by the Union industry. For example, the Union industry may be suffering injury because of the costs of maintaining excess capacity. The excess capacity may be the result of a conspiracy to increase prices, thereby resulting in a lower demand for the industry's products and not because of dumping. The imposition of duties on imports in such circumstances would merely have the effect of facilitating and reinforcing the conspiracy. It is often argued in the context of trade proceedings that the injury alleged to be suffered by the Union industry is the result of anti-competitive behavior of the Union industry.[365] Although the Council is required to take this argument into account when adopting trade remedies,[366] it seldom has a determinative effect where political considerations support the imposition of trade measures.

---

362. Anti-Dumping Regulation at art. 5.
363. Case T-5/97, Industrie des poudres sphériques v. Comm'n, 2000 E.C.R. II-3755.
364. The Commission's position is set forth in Case T-111/96, ITT Promedia v. Comm'n, 1998 E.C.R. II-2937,2960 ¶55. Legal proceedings are considered vexatious if they (i) cannot reasonably be considered as an attempt to establish the rights of the undertaking concerned and can therefore only serve to harass the opposite party and (ii) are conceived in the framework of a plan whose goal is to eliminate competition.
365. *See, e.g.*, Case T-58/99, Mukand v. Council, 2001 E.C.R. II-2521; Council Regulation (EC) No. 2074/2004 of 29 November 2004 imposing a definitive anti-dumping duty on imports of certain ring binder mechanisms originating in the People's Republic of China, 2004 O.J. (L 359) 11, 21 ¶95.
366. Case T-300/03, Moser Baer India Ltd. v. Council, 2006 E.C.R. II-3918, 3987 ¶260 *aff'd on appeal* Case C-535/06 P, Moser Baer India Ltd. v. Council, 2009 E.C.R. I-7051.

CHAPTER **V**

Company Law

1. Introduction

Company law refers to the rules applicable to how companies are established, governed, and operated. Similar to the United States, company law in the European Union (EU) is not centralized. There is no uniform EU company law. Instead, EU company law is derived from three sources: the TFEU, secondary EU law, and national law.

The TFEU serves as a source of company law in two respects. First, all of the secondary legislation that provides the main body of EU company law is based on a provision of the TFEU. As discussed in Chapter I, the principle of limited powers means that the EU legal system has only those authorities which the member states have ceded to it in the TFEU. What this means in practice is that each piece of legislation adopted by the EU must be based on a TFEU provision enabling the EU to adopt such legislation. For example, the Eleventh Company Law Directive, which applies to disclosure requirements in respect of branches opened in a member state, is based on the authority granted to the European Council and the European Commission in Article 50 of the TFEU to abolish restrictions on the ability of companies to establish branch offices in other member states.[1]

The second respect in which the TFEU serves as a source of company law is more direct. As discussed in Chapter II, the TFEU contains directly applicable provisions which secure the right of companies to do business in all member states. According to Article 49 of the TFEU, for example, a member state cannot restrict an EU citizen from establishing a company in that member state. Moreover, the member states are required to recognize legal entities established in other member states. As discussed in greater detail below, these directly applicable rights make up an important component of EU company law.

In addition to the TFEU, secondary EU law offers another source of EU company law. The provisions of the TFEU are necessarily general. By itself, the TFEU would at best be a clumsy source of harmonizing EU company law as it would necessitate a very active European Court of Justice (ECJ).

---

1. Eleventh Council Directive 89/666/EEC of 21 December 1989 concerning disclosure requirements in respect of branches opened in a member state by certain types of company governed by the law of another state, 1989 O.J. (L 395) 36 [hereinafter Eleventh Company Law Directive].

In recognition of this limitation, the TFEU gives the Council and the Commission the authority to adopt secondary legislation harmonizing the company of the member states. As discussed above, in reliance on this authority, the EU has adopted a series of directives which form the corpus of European company law. The Shareholders Rights Directive, for example, attempts to harmonize the formalities of calling and holding general meetings of shareholders of companies listed on a regulated market in the EU.[2] The Takeover Directive attempts to harmonize the laws of the member states protecting minority shareholders in the event of a takeover bid.[3] These directives, and the other directives comprising EU company and securities law, are addressed in greater detail below.

The third source of EU company law is the member states. As discussed above, EU company law is based primarily on directives. This means that each member state retains its own company and securities laws and even stock markets. There is no EU company code, no EU stock market, and no EU securities regulator. EU company law relies primarily—and is in fact dependent—on the laws of the member states. Consequently, reference to EU company and securities law includes not only EU primary and secondary law, but also the respective company and securities laws of the 28 member states. Out of respect for the limitation of time and space, the discussion below will focus only on the EU primary and secondary laws comprising EU company and securities law.

2. Pan-European Corporate Forms

2.1 Societas Europeae

EU company law remains largely national law. There are only two forms of pan-European legal entities: the *Societas Europeae* (SE) and the European Economic Interest Grouping. Even these forms of legal entities fall short of a true EU company. The closest substitute for a true pan-European company form is the SE. As will become evident in the discussion below, there are two characteristics of the SE which distinguish it from a company as commonly perceived. First, the SE can only be formed in limited circumstances. As discussed below, two individuals with a business plan are not able to form an SE. Although there are requirements for any form of company, the SE is even more limited in its availability to businesses. Second, the SE lacks a uniform legal basis. The SE Regulation only regulates certain aspects of the SE.[4] As discussed in greater detail below, the SE relies on the laws of the member states

---

2. Directive 2007/36/EC of the European Parliament and of the Council of 11 July 2007 on the exercise of certain rights of shareholders in listed companies, 2007 O.J. (L 184) 17 [hereinafter Shareholders Rights Directive].
3. Directive 2004/25/EC of the European Parliament and of the Council of 21 April 2004 on takeover bids, 2004 O.J. (L 142) 12 [hereinafter Takeover Directive].
4. Council Regulation (EC) No. 2157/2001 of 8 October 2001 on the Statute for a European company, 2001 O.J. (L 294) 1.

to effectuate its existence and regulate its operation. For example, the duties of the managers of an SE are regulated by national law and not the SE Regulation.[5] The SE Regulation is intentionally incomplete in its regulation of the various aspects of SEs. However, in the hierarchy of laws applicable to SEs, the SE Regulation enjoys primary application.[6] If an issue is not regulated by the SE Regulation (or only partially regulated), national company law applies.[7]

(a) Formation

Setting up an SE is not an alternative to establishing a new company, but rather an option only available to existing companies. In other words, a person wanting to establish a business in the EU cannot incorporate as an SE. There are only four ways of forming an SE: a merger of public companies, a holding company, a subsidiary, or a conversion.

(1) Merger of Public Companies

An SE may be created by a merger of public companies.[8] There are three basic requirements for creating an SE by merger. First, the merging companies must be established in the EU. A U.S. company and a European company may not merge to form an SE. Second, the merging companies must be public companies. For example, an Italian *società per azioni* and a German *Aktiengesellschaft* may merge to form an SE. A merger of private limited liability companies such as the French *société à responsabilité limitée*, the Italian *società a responsabilità limitata*, or the German *Gesellschaft mit beschränkter Haftung*, into an SE is not possible. The types of national public companies that may merge to form an SE are as follows:

Austria:	Aktiengesellschaft
Belgium:	la société anonyme//de naamloze vennootschap
Bulgaria:	акционерно дружество
Croatia:	dioničko društvo
Czech Republic:	akciová společnost
Denmark:	Aktieselskaber
Estonia:	Aktsiaselts
Finland:	julkinen osakeyhtiö//publikt aktiebolag
France:	la société anonyme
Germany:	die Aktiengesellschaft
Greece:	ανώνυμη εταιρία
Cyprus:	Δημόσια Εταιρεία περιορισμένης ευθύνης με μετοχές, Δημόσια Εταιρεία περιορισμένης ευθύνης με εγγύηση
Latvia:	Akciju sabiedrība
Lithuania:	akcinės bendrovės

---

5. SE Regulation, art. 39(1).
6. *Id.* at art. 9(1)(a).
7. *Id.* at art. 9(1)(c).
8. *Id.* at art. 2(1)

Ireland:	Public companies limited by shares public companies limited by guarantee having a share capital
Italy:	società per azioni
Hungary:	Részvénytársaság
Malta:	kumpaniji pubblići/public limited liability companies
Luxembourg:	la société anonyme
Netherlands:	de naamloze vennootschap
Poland:	spólka akcyjna
Portugal:	a sociedade anónima de responsabilidade limitada
Romania:	societate pe acțiuni
Slovenia:	delniška družba
Slovakia:	akciová spoločnos
Spain:	la sociedad anónima
Sweden:	publikt aktiebolag
United Kingdom:	public companies limited by shares public companies limited by guarantee having a share capital

The third requirement for creating an SE by merger is that the public companies are from two different member states. In other words, two Swedish *publikt aktiebolags* may not merge to form an SE. As only two of the merging companies need to be from different member states, it is possible for three public companies to create an SE by merger as long as there is diversity between at least two of them. For example, an Estonian *Aktsiaselts* a Swedish *publikt aktiebolag,* and a Polish *spólka akcyjna* may merge to form an SE.

The merger itself can be effectuated in several ways. The two public companies may establish an SE into which they both merge, with the SE being the surviving company (Type A below). Or one of the public companies may merge into the other company which then is converted to an SE (Type B below).

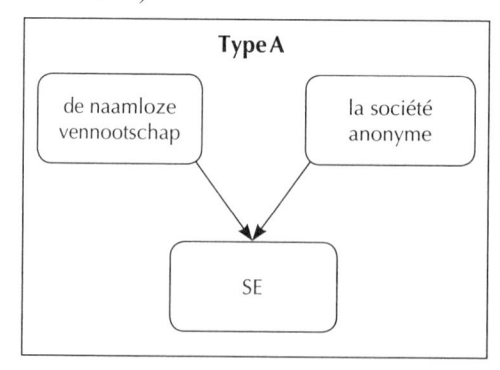

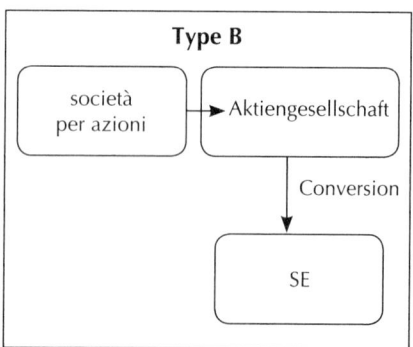

Type A: de naamloze vennootschap + la société anonyme → SE

Type B: società per azioni → Aktiengesellschaft → (Conversion) SE

The SE Regulation does not contain an exhaustive treatment of the various aspects of the creation of an SE by merger. The default rule is that those issues which are not covered by the SE Regulation are governed by the provisions of the law of the member state to which it is subject.[9] For example, national law

---

9. *Id.* at art. 18.

applies to such issues as the protection of the interests of creditors and minority shareholders of the merging companies and holders of bonds of the merging companies.[10]

The first step in the process of creating an SE by merger of public companies is for the management of the respective companies to prepare a plan of merger. The plan includes the essential elements relating to the merger, such as the share-exchange ratio, the amount of any compensation for the shares being relinquished by the shareholders, the date from which the holding of shares in the SE will entitle the holders to share in the profits, and any special conditions affecting that entitlement. In this respect, the merger plan for an SE resembles the typical plan of merger under U.S. corporate law. The merger plan also includes the proposed bylaws of the SE.

A notice of planned merger is then published in the public company registers of the respective member states involved in the merger.[11] For example, if an Italian *società per azioni* and an Austrian *Aktiengesellschaft* were planning to merge into an SE, a notice would have to be filed in Italy and in Austria. The notice must include such essential information as the name and registered office of the merging companies, a description of how the creditors and minority shareholders can exercise their rights, and the name and registered office proposed for the SE. The shareholders of each of the merging companies must then approve the draft terms of merger.[12]

In each member state concerned, the court, notary, or other competent authority under national law then issues a certificate attesting to the completion of the premerger acts and formalities.[13] The formation of the SE takes effect on the date on which the SE is registered. The completion of the merger is then publicized in the respective member states in accordance with national law.[14]

The legal effects of the merger into an SE are similar to mergers in general. Similar to the United States, the assets and liabilities of the merging companies are automatically transferred to the surviving SE entity and the merging companies cease to exist.[15] The shareholders of the merging companies become shareholders of the surviving SE.

(2) SE as Holding Company

An SE may also be formed as a holding company by public or private limited companies.[16] The basic requirement for this method of establishing an SE is that at least two of the forming companies are from different member states or each have had a subsidiary or branch in another member state for at least two years.

The creation of an SE via a holding company differs from the creation of an SE by merger in two important respects. First, even private companies may

---

10. *Id.* at art. 24.
11. *Id.* at art. 21
12. *Id.* at art. 23(1)
13. *Id.* at art. 25(2)
14. *Id.* at art. 28
15. *Id.* at art. 29
16. *Id.* at art. 2(2)

establish a holding SE. For example, a Danish *anpartselskaber* and a Spanish *la sociedad de responsabilidad limitada* may establish a holding SE. Each of the companies transfers at least 50 percent of their respective shares to the SE in exchange for shares in the SE.

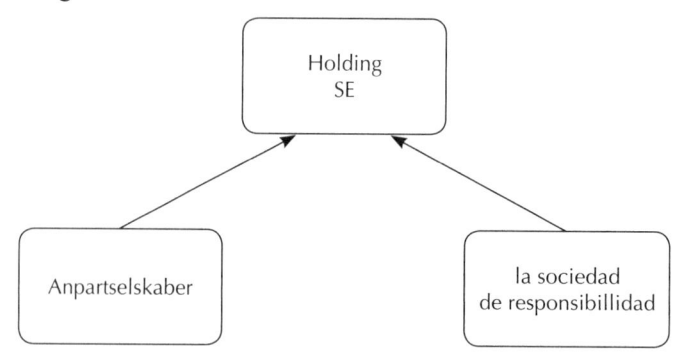

```
                    ┌──────────┐
                    │ Holding  │
                    │    SE    │
                    └──────────┘
                     ↗        ↖
        ┌──────────────┐    ┌──────────────────┐
        │Anpartselskaber│    │   la sociedad    │
        │              │    │de responsibillidad│
        └──────────────┘    └──────────────────┘
```

Second, in contrast to the creation of an SE by merger as discussed above, the creation of an SE by way of holding company does not result in the cessation of existence for the companies forming the SE. Each of the companies—the Danish *Aktieselskaber* and the Portuguese *sociedade anónima de responsabilidade limitada* in the diagram above—continue to exist after the SE's creation. In the context of a merger to form an SE, however the merging entities do not survive the merger.[17]

The management or administrative organs of the companies are required to draft terms for the formation of the holding SE. The draft terms include a report explaining and justifying the legal and economic aspects of the formation and indicating the implications for the shareholders and for the employees of the adoption of a holding SE.[18]

The draft terms for the formation of the holding SE are publicized in the manner required by national law at least one month before the date of the shareholder meeting called to make a decision on the issue.[19] One or more approved experts, independent of the companies promoting the operation, must examine the draft terms of formation and draw up a written report for the shareholders of each company.[20] By agreement between the companies, a single expert report may be drawn up for the shareholders of all the companies in accordance with national law.[21] The report must state whether the proposed share-exchange ratio is fair and reasonable, the methods used to arrive at the valuation, and whether such methods are adequate in the particular circumstances.

---

17. *Id.* at art. 32(1).
18. *Id.* at art. 32(1).
19. *Id.* at art. 32(3).
20. *Id.* at art. 32(4).
21. Of course, the national law must comply with the terms of the Directive 2011/35/EU of the European Parliament and of the Council of 5 April 2011 concerning mergers of public limited liability companies, O.J. 2011 (L 110) 1 [hereinafter Domestic Mergers Directive], which harmonizes the laws of the member states applicable to domestic mergers.

The formation of the holding SE must be approved by the shareholders of each company.[22] The shareholders of the companies have a period of three months in which to inform the promoting companies whether they intend to contribute their shares to the formation of the holding SE.[23] That period begins on the date upon which the terms for the formation of the holding SE have been finalized.

(3) Jointly Owned Subsidiary

The third manner of forming an SE is as a subsidiary of companies from at least two different member states.[24] This possibility is available to any form of legal entity, including partnerships, and not just public and private limited companies. Similar to the holding SE, the basic requirement for this method of establishing an SE is that at least two of the forming companies are from different member states or have had a subsidiary or branch in another member state for at least two years. The formation is accomplished by each of the parent companies subscribing for shares in the SE.

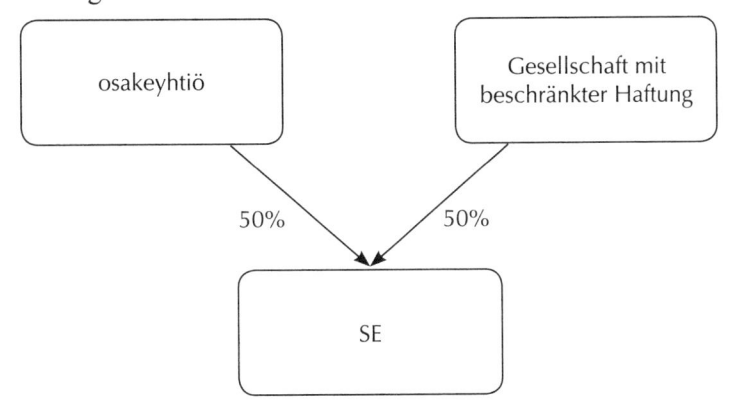

```
┌─────────────────┐              ┌─────────────────────┐
│   osakeyhtiö    │              │  Gesellschaft mit   │
│                 │              │ beschränkter Haftung│
└─────────────────┘              └─────────────────────┘
              \      50%      50%      /
               \                      /
                ▼                    ▼
                ┌─────────────────┐
                │       SE        │
                └─────────────────┘
```

(4) Conversion

An SE may also be formed by a public company converting into an SE.[25] There are three requirements for this method of establishing an SE. First, the company must be a public company. The various forms of public companies in the member states are discussed above. Second, the public company must be established in a member state. A U.S. corporation, for example, could not convert into an SE. Third, the public company must have had a subsidiary in another member state. This requirement satisfies the cross-border element of an SE.

The procedure for such a conversion is governed by EU and national law. Management first prepares a report on the legal and economic effects of the contemplated conversion, as well as the consequences for shareholders and employees. The company must engage an approved independent expert to confirm that the net assets of the company are at least equivalent to the company's capital plus those reserves that must not be distributed under applicable law or

---

22. SE Regulation at art. 32(6).
23. *Id.* at art. 33(1).
24. *Id.* at art. 2(3).
25. *Id.* at art. 2(4).

the company's governing documents—a point which must be certified by an external expert prior to the conversion.[26] The draft terms of conversion are then publicized pursuant to applicable member state law at least one month before the requisite shareholders' meeting. The shareholders' meeting of the company must then approve the draft terms of conversion together with the governing documents of the SE.[27] The decision of the shareholders is taken pursuant to national law.[28] Upon resolution of the shareholders' meeting and registration in the appropriate company register, the conversion is complete and the SE comes into existence. By operation of law, the rights and obligations of the company existing at the date of the registration are transferred to the SE.

(5) Subsidiary of SE

There is technically a fifth way to form an SE. Once an SE is established in one of the four manners discussed above, that SE may establish a subsidiary in the form of an SE.[29] If, for example, a Danish *anpartselskaber* and a Spanish *la sociedad de responsabilidad limitada* establish a holding SE, that holding SE may establish its own subsidiary in the form of an SE in any of the member states.

(b) Registration

There is no central company registration for an SE. Each SE is registered in a member state in the same register as companies established under national law. However, the registration of each SE is also published in the EU's Official Journal.

(c) Capital

The minimum capital required to form an SE is €120,000.[30] If the laws of a member state require companies exercising certain types of activity to have more capital, those laws will apply if the SE has its registered office in that member state. The maintenance and changes to the capital of an SE, together with its shares, bonds, and other similar securities, is regulated by the national law where the SE is registered.[31] That member state is required to apply the same laws to the SE as it applies to public limited liability companies.

---

26. *Id.* at art. 37(7).
27. *Id.*
28. *Id.* The national law applicable to the shareholders' meeting must comply with the terms of the Domestic Mergers Directive. According to Article 7 of the Domestic Mergers Directive, a merger requires the affirmative vote of not less than two-thirds of the shareholder votes attaching either to the shares or to the subscribed capital represented unless the laws of the member state involved provide that a simple majority of the votes is sufficient when at least half of the subscribed capital is represented at the shareholders' meeting. If there is more than one class of shares, the decision concerning a merger requires a separate vote by each class of shareholders.
29. SE Regulation at art. 3(2).
30. *Id.* at art. 4(2).
31. *Id.* at art. 5.

(d) Structure

(1) Shareholders

The shareholders of an SE exercise ultimate control of the SE. In Europe, the body representing the shareholders is the general meeting of the shareholders.[32] The general meeting decides on matters for which it is given exclusive responsibility by the SE Regulation or the national laws of the member state where the SE has its registered office.[33] The organization and conduct of general meetings, together with voting procedures, are governed by the law applicable to public limited liability companies in the member state in which the SE's registered office is situated.[34]

An SE must hold a general shareholders' meeting at least once each calendar year within six months after the end of its fiscal year. The law of the member state in which the SE's registered office is situated may require more frequent meetings.[35] General shareholders' meetings may be convened at any time by the management, administrative, or supervisory organ of the company or any other company organ in accordance with the national law applicable to public limited liability companies in the member state in which the SE's registered office is situated.[36] One or more shareholders who together hold at least 10 percent of an SE's subscribed capital may request the SE to convene a general shareholders' meeting. The SE's statutes or national legislation may provide for a smaller proportion under the same conditions as those applicable to public limited liability companies.[37]

The general rule is that decisions of the general shareholders' meeting are taken by a majority vote.[38] The SE Regulation or applicable national law may require a supermajority vote for certain issues. For example, the SE Regulation requires that the amendment of an SE's statutes requires a decision by the general shareholders' meeting taken by a two-thirds majority unless the law applicable to public limited liability companies in the member state in which an SE's registered office is situated requires a larger majority.[39] Where an SE has two or more classes of shares, a separate vote by each class of shareholders whose class rights are affected by a decision is necessary.[40]

(2) Managing Bodies

The shareholders have two options concerning the structure of the management of the SE. They can either establish a two-tier system with a supervisory organ and a management organ or a one-tier system with an administrative organ. This decision is codified in the statutes of the SE at the time of its formation.

---

32. *Id.* at art. 38
33. *Id.* at art. 52.
34. *Id.* at art. 53.
35. *Id.* at art. 54(1).
36. *Id.* at art. 54(2).
37. *Id.* at art. 55(1).
38. *Id.* at art. 57.
39. *Id.* at art. 59(1).
40. *Id.* at art. 60.

The inclusion of these two possible structures in the SE Regulation reflects the political compromise that was necessitated by the fact that some member states have traditionally relied on two-tier systems whereas other member states have one-tier systems.

Two-Tier System

The two-tier system is quite similar to the structure of U.S. corporations. The supervisory organ operates similar to a U.S. board of directors. The number of seats on the supervisory board is determined by the statute of the SE. Its members are appointed by the shareholders. The supervisory organ elects a chairman from among its members.[41] The supervisory organ is basically responsible for supervising the management organ and electing its members.[42] It is not directly involved in the management of the SE.

The management organ in a two-tier system is responsible for managing the SE.[43] The number of members of the management organ and its rules are set forth in the SE's statutes. The member or members of the management organ are appointed and removed by the supervisory organ. A member state may provide that a managing director or managing directors will be responsible for the current management under the same conditions as for public limited liability companies that have registered offices within that member state's territory.

Membership in both the management organ and the supervisory organ of the same SE is not allowed.[44] The supervisory organ may, however, nominate one of its members to temporarily act as a member of the management organ in the event of a vacancy. During such a period, the functions of the person concerned as a member of the supervisory organ are suspended.

The management organ is required to report to the supervisory organ at least once every three months on the progress and foreseeable development of the SE's business.[45] In addition, the management organ must promptly inform the supervisory organ of any events likely to have a material effect on the SE.

One-Tier System

In a one-tier system, the supervisory and management functions are performed by one organ: the administrative organ. The number of members of the administrative organ or the rules for determining it are set forth in the SE's statutes.[46] The members of the administrative organ are elected by the shareholders. The administrative organ elects a chairman from among its members.[47] The administrative organ also manages the SE.[48] A member state may provide that a managing director or managing directors be responsible for

---

41. *Id.* at art. 42.
42. *Id.* at art. 40.
43. *Id.* at art. 39.
44. *Id.* at art. 40(3).
45. *Id.* at art. 41(1).
46. *Id.* at art. 43(2).
47. *Id.* at art. 45.
48. *Id.* at art. 43(1).

the day-to-day management under the same conditions as for public limited liability companies that have registered offices within that member state. The administrative organ must meet at least once every three months at intervals laid down by the SE's statutes to discuss the progress and foreseeable development of the SE's business.[49]

(3) Rules Common to the One-Tier and Two-Tier Systems

The duration of the terms of office of the members of the SE's governing bodies is to be established in the SE's statutes. However, the duration may not exceed six years (but with the possibility of a one-time reappointment).[50] An SE's statutes may permit a company or other legal entity to be a member of one of its governing bodies provided that the law applicable to public limited liability companies in the member state in which the SE's registered office is situated does not provide otherwise.[51] That company or other legal entity is required to designate a natural person to exercise its functions as a member of the particular body.

The qualifications of the members are set forth in the SE's statutes and the national law applicable to public limited liability companies. If the law of the member state in which the SE's registered office is situated prevents a person from serving on a governing organ of a public limited liability company in that member state, that person may not serve on the corresponding organ of an SE.[52] An SE's statutes may impose special conditions of eligibility for members representing the shareholders.

The rules relating to voting procedures and quorums are typically contained in the SE's governing documents. If the SE's statutes are silent on the issue, decisions are made by a majority of the members present or represented at the particular meeting.[53] The chairman of the particular organ has the decisive vote in the event of a tie. For a quorum, at least half of the members of the organ must be present or represented.

The statute of the SE identifies the categories of transactions that require authorization of the management organ by the supervisory organ in the two-tier system or an express decision by the administrative organ in the one-tier system.[54] A member state may, however, provide that in the two-tier system the supervisory organ may itself make certain categories of transactions subject to authorization.

(e) Fiduciary Duties

The SE Regulation does not contain specific rules concerning the fiduciary duties of the members of an SE's governing bodies. Instead, it relies on the law of the member state in which the SE has its registered office. The general rule is that the members of an SE's management, supervisory, and administrative bodies

---

49. *Id.* at art. 44(1).
50. *Id.* at art. 46(1).
51. *Id.* at art. 47(1).
52. *Id.* at art. 47(2).
53. *Id.* at art. 50(1).
54. *Id.* at art. 48.

are liable for loss or damage sustained by the SE following any breach on their part of the legal, statutory, or other obligations inherent in their duties in the same way as a member of a corresponding organ of a public limited liability company in the member state where the SE is registered.[55]

(f) Termination

The winding-up, liquidation, insolvency, and suspension of payments of an SE are generally governed by national law.[56]

(g) Conversion from an SE

As discussed above, it is possible to convert a public limited liability company to an SE. Once an SE is created—by any available means—it can be converted (back) into a public limited liability company governed by the law of the member state in which its registered office is situated.[57] Prior to converting, however, the SE must wait for two years after its registration or until the first two sets of annual financial statements have been approved.

(h) Employee Participation

SEs are required to involve employees in the SE's decisions.[58] The first stage of employee participation is when the SE is being established. During that period, representatives of the companies involved are required to meet with a special negotiating body representing the interests of the employees. The rules for electing the members of the special negotiating body are codified in national law. The primary task of the special negotiating body is to negotiate the terms of an agreement with the company representatives as to the involvement of the employees in the affairs of the SE and its subsidiaries.[59] The special negotiating body may request experts, e.g., trade union representatives, to provide advice and participate in the negotiations.[60]

The special negotiating body has a relatively short life span. During the negotiations between the special negotiating body and representatives of the companies involved, the parties are to agree on the composition and role of the representative body. Once established, the representative body, which is composed of and represents employees from not only the SE but also its EU subsidiaries, essentially takes over the role of representing the employees vis-à-vis the management of the SE. The agreement between the participating companies and the special negotiating body is to address such issues as the composition, number of members and allocation of seats on the representative body, the functions and the procedure for the information and consultation of

---

55. *Id.* at art. 51.
56. *Id.* at art. 63.
57. *Id.* at art. 66(1).
58. *Id.* at art. 23(2).
59. Article 3(3) Council Directive 2001/86/EC of 8 October 2001 supplementing the Statute for a European company with regard to the involvement of employees, 2001 O.J. (L 294) 22.
60. *Id.* at art. 4(2).

the representative body by management, and the financial and material resources to be allocated to the representative body.[61]

If the special negotiating body and the company representatives cannot reach an agreement within six months (which may be extended up to one year by mutual agreement),[62] certain standard rules (attached as an annex to the SE Directive) apply by default to the structure and role of the representative body. An SE may not be registered unless an agreement has been reached with the special negotiating body or the six-month period has elapsed with no agreement. The relevant standard rules are the applicable national rules of the member state in which the registered office of the SE is to be situated. Each member state is required to adopt standard rules commensurate with the guidelines established by the Council in an annex to the Directive.[63]

According to the standard rules set forth in the annex, the representative body is to be composed of employees of the SE (and its subsidiaries) elected or appointed by the employees. The members of the representative body must be elected in proportion to the number of employees employed in each member state by the SE and its subsidiaries. A 10 percent rule is applied to ensure proportionate representation on the representative body among the employees working in various member states. One seat is allocated per portion of employees employed in that member state which equals 10 percent, or a fraction thereof, of the number of employees employed by the SE and subsidiaries in all the member states taken together. For example, if an SE and its subsidiaries has 1,000 employees in the EU spread out among Slovakia (340), Poland (290), Hungary (220), Lithuania (85), and Malta (65), the employees in Slovakia would be ensured four seats, Poland three seats, Hungary three seats, and Lithuania and Malta each one seat.

The representative body has the right to be informed and consulted on the progress of the business of the SE and its prospects. It meets at least once a year with the responsible body of the SE. At the meeting with the representative body, the SE management is required to inform the representative body of the structure, economic and financial situation of the business, the situation and anticipated trend of employment, investments, substantial changes concerning organization, transfers of production, mergers or closures of businesses, and collective redundancies. Between such meetings, the management has the obligation to inform the representative body of exceptional events which could affect the interests of the employees. At its request, the representative body has the right to meet the management of the SE to be informed and consulted on measures significantly affecting employees' interests. The representative body informs the employees of the SE and its subsidiaries of the content and outcome of the meetings with management.

---

61. Council Directive 2001/86/EC of 8 October 2001 supplementing the Statute for a European company with regard to the involvement of employees, 2001 O.J. (L 294) 22 at art. 3(5).
62. *Id.* at art. 5(2).
63. *Id.* at art. 7(1).

The SE must pay the costs of the representative body. These costs include the cost of organizing meetings and providing interpretation facilities and the accommodation and traveling expenses of members of the representative body.

2.2 European Economic Interest Grouping

Prior to the introduction of the SE, the only form of pan-European company was the European Economic Interest Grouping (EEIG). The original idea behind the EEIG, which is based on Council Regulation (EEC) No 2137/85,[64] was to stimulate cross-border cooperation between legal entities within the EU. It represents a modest attempt at creating a pan-European company form in view of the realization that political hurdles at the time prevented the introduction of a true pan-European company.

As a form of doing business, an EEIG has legal personality and can hold title to assets, enter into legal transactions, and assume liabilities.[65] However, the EEIG is not independent from its members in a commercial sense. Although it can engage in economic activity, that activity must be related to the economic activities of its members and cannot be anything more than ancillary to the economic activities of its members.[66] The EEIG may not hold shares or interests in any of its members or be a member of another EEIG.[67]

(a) Establishment

An EEIG is formed by a written agreement between the members. The legal entity is then registered at the national level (and not at the EU level) in the member state where it has its main address as determined in the EEIG formation agreement. Although the members may make cash or in-kind contributions to the EEIG (no minimum capital is required), it cannot accept equity investments from the public. It may, however, secure loans from third parties.

An EEIG may be formed by companies that have been formed in accordance with the law of a member state and that have their registered or statutory office and central administration in the EU. For example, a U.S. company could not be a member of an EEIG. Natural persons may also form an EEIG, but only if they already carry on an industrial, commercial, craft, or agricultural activity or if they provide professional or other services in the EU. For example, a group of lawyers from several member states may form an EEIG. However, two natural persons who are not already commercially active could not form a start-up venture in the form of an EEIG to sell books over the Internet. As indicated above, the activities of the EEIG must be merely ancillary to those of the members. It is therefore necessary that the members themselves have independent activities.

---

64. Council Regulation (EEC) No. 2137/85 of 25 July 1985 on the European Economic Interest Grouping, 1985 O.J. (L 199) 1.
65. *Id.* at art. 1(2).
66. *Id.* at art. 3(1).
67. An EEIG may hold shares or interests in other companies but only on behalf of its members and if the holding of such shares are necessary for the achievement of the EEIG's purpose.

EEIGs are not available on a purely domestic basis. The formation of an EEIG must include a cross-border element. At a minimum, the members must have their respective central administrations in different member states (single member EEIGs are not permitted). This requirement would preclude, for example, VW and BMW from forming an EEIG as they each have their central administration in Germany. If the EEIG is being formed by natural persons, the cross-border requirement is that they carry on their principal activities in different member states. The cross-border requirement does not require complete diversity of the members. It is sufficient that at least two of the members are from different member states.

Although EEIG membership interests are transferable to third parties, a transfer of membership interests in an EEIG requires the unanimous consent of the other members.[68] Similarly, the admission of new members requires the unanimous consent of the existing members.[69] A member of the EEIG may offer the EEIG interest as security to a third party, but only with the unanimous consent of the other members or a provision in the EEIG formation agreement that specifically permits the member to encumber the EEIG interest.

(b) Management

The EEIG has a bifurcated governance structure: the members (acting as a body) and managers. The members, similar to shareholders in a regular company, are responsible for the strategic decisions of the EEIG. In general, each member has one vote unless the formation agreement provides otherwise. The only limitation in this respect is that no one member may hold a majority of the votes.[70] The quorum and voting majorities needed for the EEIG to take a decision are regulated in the EEIG formation agreement. However, unanimity is required by law to:

- change the purpose of the EEIG;
- change the number of votes allotted to each member or the conditions for the taking of decisions;
- extend the duration of the EEIG beyond any period fixed in the formation agreement;
- change the contribution by every member or by some members to the EEIG's financing; or
- amend the EEIG formation agreement unless otherwise provided by that agreement.

Whereas the important strategic decisions are taken by the members, they must appoint at least one natural person as manager to take the day-to-day decisions affecting the EEIG.[71] Additional management positions can be agreed to by the members in the EEIG formation agreement.[72] The authorities of the

---

68. *Id.* at art. 23.
69. *Id.* at art. 26.
70. *Id.* at art. 17.
71. *Id.* at art. 19.
72. *Id.* at art. 16.

manager(s) are set forth in the EEIG formation agreement. As an agent of the EEIG, the manager has the authority to bind the EEIG vis-à-vis third parties. The fiduciary duties of the manager are determined by national law.

(c) Liability

Perhaps the most significant characteristic of an EEIG which prevents its broad use relates to the liability of the EEIG members for the EEIG's debts. In contrast to most forms of companies under national law, the members of an EEIG have unlimited joint and several liability for the debts and other liabilities of the EEIG.[73] For example, if a Belgian company, a Dutch company, and a Luxembourg company set up an EEIG, and the EEIG incurs debts (as discussed above, the EEIG has legal personality and consequently may incur debts), the creditors of the EEIG can pursue any one (or all) of the members for the entire amount owed by the EEIG (assuming that the EEIG is not in a position to satisfy the debt). Hence, EEIGs are typically not used in situations where significant liability could be incurred. For example, EEIGs are commonly used by interest groups in a particular industry to promote their common interests. Some examples are the European Alliance for Artisan and Traditional Raw Milk Products E.E.I.G., the European Consortium for Agricultural Research in the Tropics, the Organisation of European Cancer Institutes, and the European Federation for Cosmetic Ingredients.

The joint and several liability extends even after a member exits the EEIG. Once that member ceases to be a member of the EEIG, the member remains liable for the debts and other liabilities arising out of the activities of the EEIG before that member's withdrawal.[74] This liability exposure extends for five years after the publication of the member's withdrawal from the EEIG.[75] Moreover, when a new member joins the EEIG, that new member is liable not only for the EEIG's debts and other liabilities after the date of membership, but also for the debts and liabilities arising out of the EEIG's activities prior to that date.[76]

(d) Taxation

For purposes of profits and taxes, the EEIG is treated as a flow-through entity (similar to a partnership). In other words, the EEIG is not a taxable entity. The profits of the EEIG (if any) are deemed to be the profits of the members and are apportioned among them equally unless they agreed otherwise in the EEIG formation agreement.[77]

2.3 National Company Law

With the exceptions of the SE and the EEIG, there is no pan-European form of company. Company law in Europe continues to be primarily national law. Even the SE Regulation, as discussed above, relies heavily on the company laws of

---

73. *Id.* at art. 24.
74. *Id.* at art. 34.
75. *Id.* at art. 37.
76. The new member may, however, preclude such liability by including a clause in the contract for the formation of the grouping or in the instrument of admission from the payment of debts and other liabilities which originated before the admission of the new member.
77. *Id.* at art. 21.

the respective member states. However, as discussed below, many aspects of company law—although national—have been harmonized by EU directives.

3. Freedom of Establishment and Its Implications for European Company Law

The freedom of establishment, as codified in Articles 49 and 54 of the TFEU and discussed in detail in Chapter II, generally prohibits restrictions on the freedom of establishment of nationals of a member state in the territory of another member state. Two important principles for EU company law arise from this prohibition: mutual recognition and equal treatment. The principle of mutual recognition requires the member states to recognize legal entities formed in accordance with the laws of the other member states. For example, Sweden must recognize a company that was formed in accordance with the laws of Greece even if the requirements for forming a company in Greece are different than those in Sweden. The principle of mutual recognition even applies where the ultimate ownership of the legal entity is located outside the EU. For example, if a U.S. company establishes a subsidiary in the Czech Republic pursuant to Czech law, Estonia must recognize that Czech company even though it is ultimately owned by a U.S. shareholder.

The prohibition on restrictions on the freedom of establishment extends beyond the principle of mutual recognition. Not only must the member states recognize legal entities established in other member states, but they must also treat those legal entities the same way as they treat their own nationals.[78] This is the principle of equal treatment. Any difference in treatment will violate the prohibition on restrictions of the right of establishment unless it qualifies for an exception. *In re Sevic Systems* involved a German company law that only recognized mergers between German legal entities.[79] In this case, a Luxembourg company wanted to merge into a German company. The German commercial registry, where the merger would have had to be notified in order to complete the merger under German law, refused the registration because German law only recognized mergers between German companies. The ECJ held that this difference in treatment constituted a restriction on the right of establishment.[80] Germany was forced to recognize the merger. Hence, one of the most important implications of the freedom of establishment for EU company law is that even in the absence of a unified company law regime, it allows legal entities to do business throughout the EU.

The principles of mutual recognition and equal treatment combined with differences in national company laws among the member states create an

---

78. Case T-168/01, GlaxoSmithKline Services Unlimited v. Comm'n, 2006 E.C.R. II-2981, 3039 ¶204; Case C-496/01, Comm'n v. France, 2004 E.C.R. I-2377, 2396 ¶58.
79. Case C-411/03, *In re* Sevic Systems AG, 2005 E.C.R. I-10825.
80. *Id.* at 10833 ¶23. Germany has subsequently changed its law to conform to the Cross-Border Mergers Directive.

incentive for forum shopping. For example, a U.S. company planning to establish operations in the EU could establish a subsidiary in any member state and then benefit (through that subsidiary) from the mutual recognition and equal treatment principles. It is only natural for businesses or investors to "shop" for the most advantageous member state in which to establish a business. If, for example, a group of college students in Germany would like to establish an online company to do business in Germany, but they lack the financial resources to pay the mandatory minimum share capital required by German company law, they may decide to shop around for a member state that imposes lower minimum paid-in capital requirements. Once they are established in that member state, the strict application of the freedom of establishment would require Germany to recognize them as a legal entity.

There are two important judicially created limitations to this broad interpretation of the prohibition on restrictions on the freedom of establishment. First, member states retain the authority to determine the minimum connecting factors that companies must have with their member states in order to retain their corporate registration in that member state. In *In re Cartesio Oktató és Szolgáltato bt*, Hungarian corporate law prohibited Hungarian companies from changing their seat to another member state while retaining their status as a Hungarian corporate entity.[81] In that case, a Hungarian company tried to change its headquarters from Hungary to Italy. When the Hungarian Commercial Registry refused to register the change of headquarters, the Hungarian company argued that the Hungarian law violated Article 54 of the TFEU. The ECJ held that member states have the power to determine the connecting factor required of a company if it is to be regarded as incorporated under the law of that member state and if the company is to be subsequently able to maintain that status.[82] As applied to the particular facts of the case, Hungary was permitted to impose the registered seat or headquarters on a company as the connecting factor to Hungary for companies established under Hungarian law.

The second limitation is the abuse exception to the freedom of establishment.[83] According to this exception, "a national measure restricting freedom of establishment may be justified where it specifically relates to wholly artificial arrangements aimed at circumventing the application of the legislation of the member state concerned."[84] The abuse exception has an objective and a subjective element.[85] The objective component requires that the objective circumstances

---

81. Case C-210/06, *In re* Cartesio Oktató és Szolgáltato bt, 2008 E.C.R. I-9641.
82. *Id.* at ¶110.
83. Case C-446/03, Marks & Spencer, 2005 E.C.R. I-10,886, 10884 ¶57; Case C-324/00, Lankhorst-Hohorst v. Finanzamt Steinfurt, 2002 E.C.R. I-11,802, 11814 ¶37. The abuse exception is a general principle of EU law that prevents EU law from being used in an abusive or fraudulent manner. Case C-373/97, Dionysios Diamantis v. Elliniko Dimosio, 2000 E.C.R. I-1723, 1734 ¶33.
84. Case C-524/04, Test Claimants in the Thin Cap Group Litigation v. Commissioners of Inland Revenue, 2007 E.C.R. I-2157, 2189 ¶72.
85. Joined cases C-58/13 and 59/13, Torresi v. Consiglio dell'Ordine degli Avvocati di Macerata, 2014 E.C.R. I-___, at ¶45.

indicate that despite formal observance of the conditions of the EU rules, the purpose of those rules is not achieved. The subjective component requires an intent to obtain an improper advantage.

Although the abuse exception is also applicable in the area of company law, member states have experienced only limited success in using it to justify national measures which restrict the freedom of establishment. As long as the particular exercise of the right of establishment involves "genuine economic activities," a member state cannot rely on the abuse exception even if the purpose of the establishment was to reduce the tax burden of the company.[86] Merely shopping for the most advantageous jurisdiction and then establishing operations there does not rise to the level of abuse required for the application of the abuse exception.

A series of ECJ decisions illustrate the court's narrow application of the abuse exception. In *Centros v. Erhvervs- og Selskabsstyrelsen*,[87] several individuals in Denmark wanted to do business in Denmark, but did not want to pay the minimum capital of DKK200,000 required by Danish law to establish a company in Denmark. Instead, they incorporated the company in the UK, which did not require a minimum paid-in capital, and then sought to register in Denmark a branch office of the UK company. The Danish agency responsible for registering branch offices refused to register the branch in this case on the grounds that it was merely a mechanism to avoid compliance with the minimum paid-in capital requirements set forth in Danish law. The ECJ held that something more than the intent to shop for the most advantageous company laws was needed to support an abuse exception to the freedom of establishment: "[T]he fact that a company does not conduct any business in the Member State in which it has registered office and pursues its activities only in the Member State where its branch is established is not sufficient to prove the existence of abuse or fraudulent conduct which would entitle the latter Member State to deny that company the benefit of the provisions of EU law relating to the right of establishment."[88]

In *Überseering BV v. Nordic Construction Company Baumanagement GmbH*,[89] a Dutch company had purchased a piece of land in Germany and engaged a German contractor to build on the land. When the German contractor allegedly failed to complete the tasks properly, the Dutch company brought suit in Germany. According to the German rules of civil procedure, however, the Dutch company could only bring an action in Germany if it had legal capacity as determined by reference to the law applicable in the place where its actual center of administration is established (and not necessarily its state of incorporation). As the Dutch company (Überseering BV) had its center of administration in Germany, but did not have legal capacity in Germany because

---

86. Case C-196/04, Cadbury Schweppes plc v. Commissioners of Inland Revenue, 2006 E.C.R. I-8031, 8047 ¶51.
87. Case C-212/97, Centros v. Erhvervs- og Selskabsstyrelsen, 1999 E.C.R. I-1484.
88. *Id.* at 1494 ¶29.
89. Case C-208/00, Überseering BV v. Nordic Construction Company Baumanagement GmbH, 2002 E.C.R. I-9943.

it was not registered there, the German court held that Überseering BV could not pursue its claim in Germany.

In the proceedings before the ECJ, Germany sought to justify the restriction by arguing that the German rule of civil procedure served overriding requirements relating to the general interest by enhancing legal certainty and creditor protection. According to Germany, there is an assumption held by the general public that a company doing business in Germany has met the minimum requirements of German law (e.g., minimum capital requirements). Companies with their primary operations in Germany could essentially defraud suppliers, customers, and creditors by incorporating in another member state and conduct business in Germany. Following its holding in *Centros*, the ECJ held that Articles 49 and 54 of the TFEU require Germany to allow the Dutch company to be a party to legal proceedings regardless of its actual center of administration.[90] The potential for abuse in this case, according to the ECJ, does not outweigh the freedom of establishment.[91]

A member state also tried to rely on the abuse exception in *Kamer van Koophandel en Fabrieken voor Amsterdam v. Inspire Art Ltd*[92] but experienced the same result. In that case, a Dutch art dealer set up a UK company under favorable UK company laws (compared to Dutch laws) and subsequently registered a branch office in the Netherlands. The sole purpose of the UK company was to market and sell art in the Netherlands. The Dutch authorities, however, designated the UK company as a "foreign company" (as opposed to a branch) which triggered the application of additional formalities, such as the filing of the articles of association and the inclusion on all company documents of a reference to the registered office, principal place of business, and registration number. Moreover, foreign companies had to meet the minimum capital requirements that Dutch companies were required to observe. In characterizing the Dutch law as a restriction on the freedom of establishment, the ECJ repeated the general rule that forming a company in a particular member state for the sole purpose of taking advantage of its favorable company laws cannot, in itself, constitute an abuse of the freedom of establishment: "[I]t is immaterial, having regard to the application of the rules on freedom of establishment, that the company was formed in one Member State only for the purpose of establishing itself in a second Member State, where its main, or indeed entire, business is to be conducted. ... [T]he fact that the company was formed in a particular Member State for the sole purpose of enjoying the benefit of more favourable legislation does not constitute abuse even if that company conducts its activities entirely or mainly in that second State."[93]

---

90. *Id.* at 9974 ¶93.
91. *Id.*
92. Case C-167/01, Kamer van Koophandel en Fabrieken voor Amsterdam v. Inspire Art Ltd, 2003 E.C.R. I-10195.
93. *Id.* at 10223 ¶¶95-96.

4. Company Law

4.1 Applicable Legislation

The *Centros, Überseering,* and *Inspire Art* cases discussed above illustrate some of the challenges caused by the lack of a unified or completely harmonized company law in Europe. As long as there remain differences in the company laws of the member states, there will be forum shopping and hence competition between the member states. In recognition of the limited ability of Article 54 of the TFEU to smooth over the differences between member states, Article 50 of the TFEU empowers the Council to adopt legislation designed to harmonize various aspects of company law among the member states. The various directives that have been adopted by the Council on this basis make up the main corpus of EU company law.[94] The areas of harmonization are discussed in the following sections.

In addition, the member states are required to observe the free movement principles discussed in Chapter II. This can have important practical significance in the field of company law—even though company law is still primarily national law. In *In re VALE Építési kft,* Hungarian company law prevented an Italian company from transferring its seat from Italy to Hungary.[95] According to the ECJ, the freedom of establishment codified in the TFEU prohibits Hungary from maintaining such a law.[96] This can have important implications for domestic company law. German law, for example, only recognized conversions of companies if both companies were registered in Germany.[97] In light of the ECJ's decision in *In re VALE Építési kft,* however, the Appeals Court in Nürnberg held that the conversion of a Luxembourg Sarl into a German GmbH should be recognized by the German courts.[98]

4.2 Taxonomy of European Companies

As EU company law remains largely national law, there are a large number of different company forms. In other words, the forms of companies available in Malta are different from the forms of companies available in Poland. As discussed above, there are only two pan-European forms of companies. To complicate matters even further, European company law is based primarily on directives which apply only to certain types of companies. For example, whereas the Second Company Law Directive requiring such things as a minimum

---

94. A list of the directives can be accessed at http://ec.europa.eu/internal_market/company/official/index_en.htm.
95. Case C-378/10, *In re* VALE Építési kft, 2012 E.C.R. I-____ (reported in the electronic reports of cases ECLI:EU:C:2012:440).
96. *Id.* at ¶62.
97. Section 190 Umwandlungsgesetz.
98. Decision of the Oberlandesgericht Nürnberg in case no. 12 W 520/13 (June 19, 2013).

capitalization applies only to public limited liability companies,[99] the Limited Liability Company Directive requiring such things as compulsory disclosure of certain documents applies to all companies with limited liability.[100]

Although an exhaustive discussion of the various company forms recognized by the member states is beyond the scope of this work, there are some basic categories which are useful to discuss because they are employed by EU law. The first important distinction to be made is between legal entities with limited liability and those without limited liability. A company has limited liability if the owners of that company are not liable for the debts of the company. The reason that member states limit the liability of certain forms of companies is to stimulate commerce by allowing for the accumulation of capital without the risk of liability exceeding that capital contribution. EU company law deals primarily with legal entities that enjoy limited liability. Legal entities without limited liability, such as partnerships and foundations, remain almost exclusively within the purview of member state law.

In addition to companies with limited liability and those without limited liability, there is a third group of legal entities which are referred to in European nomenclature as social economy enterprises. This includes cooperatives, mutual societies, foundations, and social enterprises. These forms of legal entity are distinguished from companies in that their primary purpose is not a return on capital to the owners, but rather to promote specific causes or interests. They are often organized around industries or professions. For example, cooperatives are common in the agricultural industry, mutual societies in the insurance industry, associations in the trade industry, and foundations in philanthropic endeavors. With the exception of the Statute for a European Co-Operative Society,[101] there are no pan-European forms of social economy enterprises.

---

99. Directive 2012/30/EU of the European Parliament and of the Council of 25 October 2012 on coordination of safeguards which, for the protection of the interests of members and others, are required by member states of companies within the meaning of the second paragraph of Article 54 of the Treaty on the Functioning of the European Union, in respect of the formation of public limited liability companies and the maintenance and alteration of their capital, with a view to making such safeguards equivalent, 2012 O.J. (L 315) 74 at art. 1(1) [hereinafter Public Company Capitalization Directive].
100. Directive 2009/101/EC of the European Parliament and of the Council of 16 September 2009 on coordination of safeguards which, for the protection of the interests of members and third parties, are required by member states of companies within the meaning of the second paragraph of Article 48 of the Treaty, with a view to making such safeguards equivalent, 2009 O.J. (L 258) 11 [hereinafter Limited Liability Company Directive].
101. Council Regulation (EC) No. 1435/2003 of 22 July 2003 on the Statute for a European Cooperative Society, 2003 O.J. (L 207) 24.

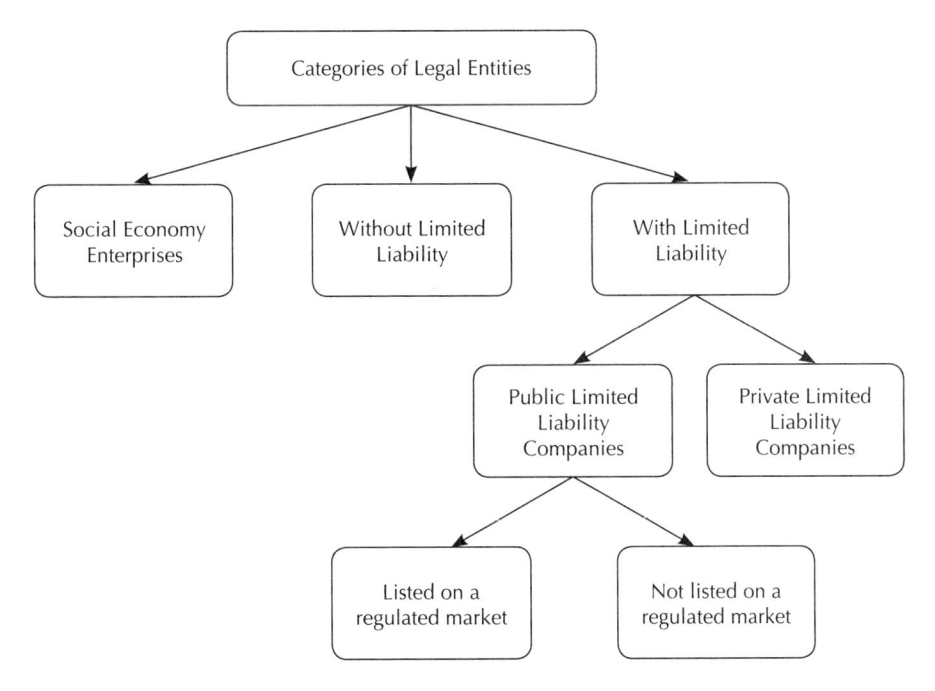

```
                    ┌─────────────────────────┐
                    │ Categories of Legal Entities │
                    └─────────────────────────┘
           ┌────────────────┼────────────────┐
           ▼                ▼                ▼
  ┌──────────────┐  ┌──────────────┐  ┌──────────────┐
  │ Social Economy│  │Without Limited│  │ With Limited │
  │  Enterprises  │  │   Liability   │  │   Liability  │
  └──────────────┘  └──────────────┘  └──────────────┘
                                    ┌─────────┴─────────┐
                                    ▼                   ▼
                          ┌──────────────┐    ┌──────────────┐
                          │Public Limited│    │Private Limited│
                          │  Liability   │    │   Liability   │
                          │  Companies   │    │   Companies   │
                          └──────────────┘    └──────────────┘
                         ┌────────┴────────┐
                         ▼                 ▼
                  ┌──────────────┐  ┌──────────────┐
                  │  Listed on a │  │Not listed on a│
                  │regulated market│ │regulated market│
                  └──────────────┘  └──────────────┘
```

The second important distinction to be made is between public and private limited liability companies. There is no abstract definition of "private limited liability company" or "public limited liability company" in EU company law. Instead, the concepts are defined by reference to annexes to the respective company law directives listing the specific forms of companies that are considered private limited liabilities and public limited liability companies. For example, Annex I to the Twelfth Company Law Directive lists the types of companies in each member state that are considered "private limited liability companies" for purposes of that Directive,[102] and the SE Regulations lists the types of legal entities in the member states which are considered public limited liability companies for purposes of that legislation.[103]

The distinction between private and public limited liability companies is important because it delineates the scope of application of the respective European company law directives. For example, the Second,[104] and Sixth[105] Company Law Directives, as well as the Takeover Directive and the Domestic Mergers Directive, apply only to public limited liability companies. The Limited

---

102. Directive 2009/102/EC of the European Parliament and of the Council of 16 September 2009 in the area of company law on single-member private limited liability companies, 2009 O.J. (L 258) 20.
103. SE Regulation at Annex I.
104. Public Company Capitalization Directive at art. 1(1).
105. Sixth Council Directive 82/891/EEC of 17 December 1982 based on Article 54(3)(g) of TFEU, concerning the division of public limited liability companies, 1982 O.J. (L 378) 47.

Liability Company Directive, the Accounting Directive,[106] and the Cross-Border Mergers Directive[107] apply to all forms of limited liability companies. The Twelfth Company Law Directive applies only to private limited liability companies.[108] The ECJ has been reluctant to extend the protections accorded by one directive beyond the scope of such directive. For example, the ECJ refused to recognize a general principle of minority shareholder protection for private companies based on the argument that the directives only establish minority protection for shareholders in public companies.[109]

The third important distinction in EU company law taxonomy involves public limited liability companies. In the European nomenclature, the term "public limited liability company" encompasses companies whose shares are listed on a stock market (referred to in EU parlance as a regulated market).[110] This includes, for example, the Dutch *Naamloze vennootschap*, the Belgian *Société Anonyme,* and the Danish *Aktieselskap.* Reference to a public company in the United States implies that the shares of that company's stock are listed on a stock market. In Europe, however, the shares of a public limited liability company do not necessarily have to be listed on a regulated market and may even be owned by one shareholder in some member states. In Germany, for example, the shares of an *Aktiengesellschaft* do not necessarily have to be listed on a stock market. In most instances, however, the public limited liability structure is used when the owners intend to have the shares freely traded on a regulated market. Otherwise, the extra burdens placed on a public limited liability company would prompt the owners to do business as a private limited liability company. As discussed below, certain of the EU company law directives only apply to public limited liability companies whose shares are publicly listed.[111] Other directives apply to all forms of public limited liability companies regardless of whether their shares are publicly listed.[112]

There are two categories of private limited liability companies in Europe. The first category, private limited partnerships, requires that the liability of at least one of the owners of the company is not limited to the capital contributed by that owner to the legal entity. Several prominent examples would be the German *Kommanditgesellschaft auf Aktien*, the French *Société en commandite*

---

106. Directive 2013/34/EU of the European Parliament and of the Council of 26 June 2013 on the annual financial statements, consolidated financial statements, and related reports of certain types of undertakings, amending Directive 2006/43/EC of the European Parliament and of the Council repealing Council Directives 78/660/EEC and 83/349/EEC, 2013 O.J. (L 182) 18 [hereinafter Accounting Directive].
107. Directive 2005/56/EC of the European Parliament and of the Council of 26 October 2005 on cross-border mergers of limited liability companies, 2005 O.J. (L 310) 1.
108. Directive 2009/102/EC of the European Parliament and of the Council of 16 September 2009 in the area of company law on single-member private limited liability companies, 2009 O.J. (L 258) 20.
109. Case C-101/08, Audiolux SA v. Groupe Bruxelles Lambert SA, 2009 E.C.R. I-9864, 9884 ¶52.
110. The concept of "regulated market" is discussed below.
111. *See, e.g.*, Takeover Directive; Shareholders Rights Directive.
112. *See, e.g.*, Public Company Capitalization Directive.

par action, and the Italian *Società in accomandita per azioni.* The other corporate forms, which do not qualify as public limited liability companies, are referred to as private limited companies. This would include, for example, the Romanian *societate cu răspundere limitată,* the Polish *Spólka z ograniczona odpowiedzialnoścą* and the Czech *Společnost s ručením omezeným.*

4.3 Shareholder Meetings of Public Limited Liability Companies Listed on a Regulated Market

In European company law, the term "general meeting of shareholders" refers to both an event and to a decision-making body of the company. In one sense, the general meeting of shareholders refers to the meeting of the shareholders. There can be annual meetings (commonly referred to as the annual general meeting) or meetings during the year (commonly referred to as special general meetings). As the event of holding a general meeting can result in decisions of the company, the general meeting of shareholders is also a decision-making organ of the company. Only the formalities of calling and holding general meetings of shareholders of companies listed on a regulated market in the EU have been harmonized by EU legislation.[113] The formalities of general meetings of companies not listed on a regulated market in the EU have not been harmonized. Consequently, the discussion here is limited to companies whose shares are listed on a regulated market in Europe.

(a) Notice of General Meeting of the Shareholders

(1) Notice Period

Companies whose shares are listed on a regulated market in the EU are required to issue the notice of a general meeting at least 21 days prior to the date of the meeting.[114] There are three important exceptions to this rule. First, the rule does not apply to notices of shareholder meetings necessary to effectuate takeovers falling under the Takeovers Directive. As discussed above, the Takeovers Directive permits a general meeting of shareholders in certain circumstances "to be called at short notice" but no less than two weeks prior to the meeting.[115] In these instances, the 21-day rule does not apply. Second, member states may allow a notice period of less than 21 days (but not less than 14 days) for special general meetings if (1) the meeting is not an annual meeting, (2) the shorter notice period is approved by a two-thirds majority shareholders vote, and (3) the company offers to the shareholders the ability to vote by electronic means.[116] The third exception to the 21-day notice period rule applies where a general meeting is properly called, but there is a lack of quorum. In such cases, the member states are free to derogate from the 21-day rule for the second or subsequent general meeting provided no new item is put on the agenda and that

---

113. See Shareholders Rights Directive.
114. *Id.* at art. 5(1).
115. Takeover Directive at arts. 9(4) and 11(4).
116. Shareholders Rights Directive at art. 5(1).

at least 10 days elapse between the first general meeting lacking a quorum and the subsequent general meeting.[117]

(2) Means of Issuing Notice

There is no one legal standard for the proper means of issuing notices of shareholder meetings. The member states are only required to ensure that the notice of the general meeting is issued via such media "as may reasonably be relied upon for the effective dissemination of information to the public throughout the EU."[118] EuropeanIssuers, a not-for-profit association representing European issuers, has published nonbinding Market Standards for General Meetings which represents an attempt at harmonizing some of the procedural aspects of holding general meetings.

(3) Content of Notice

The notice of a general meeting must contain the agenda, the record date,[119] and the time and place of the general meeting. The notice must also contain a description of the procedures that shareholders must comply with to be able to participate and to cast their vote in the general meeting.[120] This includes, at a minimum, information concerning the rights available to shareholders and the deadlines by which those rights may be exercised,[121] the procedure for voting by proxy, and, where applicable, the procedures for casting votes by correspondence or by electronic means. The notice must also indicate where and how the full, unabridged text of the relevant documents and draft resolutions may be obtained and indicate the address of the Internet site on which the information is available.

In addition to the notice of the meeting sent to the individual shareholders, for the 21 days prior to the general meeting the company must make available to its shareholders on its website at least the following information:[122]

- the notice;
- the total number of shares and voting rights (including separate totals for each class of shares where the company's capital is divided into two or more classes of shares);
- the documents to be submitted to the general meeting;

---

117. *Id.*
118. *Id.* at art. 5(2).
119. The term "record date" refers to the date prior to the general meeting on which the rights of a shareholder to participate in the shareholders' meeting is determined. Article 7(2) Shareholders Rights Directive. Only those natural or legal persons who are shareholders on that date have the right to participate and vote in the general meeting.
120. Shareholders Rights Directive at art. 5(3)(b).
121. The notice may confine itself to stating only the deadlines by which those rights may be exercised, provided the notice contains a reference to more detailed information concerning those rights being made available on the company's Internet site.
122. Where the forms cannot be made available on the Internet for technical reasons, the company is required to indicate on its Internet site how the forms can be obtained on paper. In this case, the company is required to send the forms by postal services and free of charge to every requesting shareholder.

- a draft resolution or, where no resolution is proposed to be adopted, a comment from a competent body within the company for each item on the proposed agenda of the general meeting;
- the forms to be used to vote by proxy and to vote by correspondence.

(b) *Agenda of the General Meeting*

As identified above, the agenda for the general meeting must be sent out with the notice of the general meeting. Shareholders (individually or collectively) have the right to put items on the agenda of the general meeting provided that each item proposed by a shareholder is accompanied by a justification or a draft resolution to be adopted at the general meeting.[123] To avoid having to send out the agenda twice, shareholder comments are commonly solicited sufficiently prior to sending out the notice of the general meeting. The company than can identify a cutoff time by which the shareholders need to submit items for the agenda. The relevant time period by which shareholders may exercise the right to add an item to the agenda is a matter for national company law.[124]

If the company sends out the agenda and there are subsequent modifications, it is required to make available a revised agenda in the same manner as the previous agenda in advance of the applicable record date or, if no record date applies, sufficiently in advance of the date of the general meeting so as to enable other shareholders to appoint a proxy or, where applicable, to vote by correspondence.

(c) *Participation and Voting at the General Meeting*

The ability to participate in and vote at a general meeting of the shareholders is determined on the record date. The record date must be set by the company not more than 30 days before the date of the general meeting to which it applies. The one exception to this rule is where a company is able to identify the names and addresses of their shareholders from a current register of shareholders on the day of the general meeting.[125]

Companies are permitted (but not required) to offer to their shareholders the possibility to participate in the general meeting by electronic means.[126] This would include real-time transmission of the general meeting over the Internet or participation via real-time two-way teleconference. It could also include

---

123. Shareholders Rights Directive at art. 6(1). Member states may limit this right to shareholders holding at least 5 percent or more of the company's share capital or to annual meetings as long as the shareholders otherwise have the right to call a general meeting that is not an annual meeting.
124. Shareholders Rights Directive art. 6(3).
125. *Id.* at art. 7(2) Shareholders Rights Directive. Member states need not apply this rule to companies that are able to identify the names and addresses of their shareholders from a current register of shareholders on the day of the general meeting.
126. Shareholders Rights Directive at art. 8(1). The use of electronic means for the purpose of enabling shareholders to participate in the general meeting may be made subject only to such requirements and constraints as are necessary to ensure the identification of shareholders and the security of the electronic communication, and only to the extent that they are proportionate to achieving those objectives. *Id.* at art. 8(2).

a mechanism for casting votes, whether before or during the general meeting, without the need to appoint a proxy holder who is physically present at the meeting. These alternatives facilitate participation of shareholders from other member states who might not otherwise participate because of the prohibitive costs.

During the general meeting, each shareholder has the right to ask questions related to items on the agenda, and the company has the corresponding obligation to answer those questions (subject to appropriate confidentiality and business secret limitations).[127] As anyone who has participated in a shareholders' meeting will attest to, this rule has the potential to extend the general meeting to an unbearable duration. Consequently, EU law allows companies to provide one overall answer to questions having the same content. In addition, an answer to a specific shareholder question may be deemed to be given if the relevant information is available on the company's website in a question and answer format. Companies often rely on these alternatives in order to streamline the general meeting of shareholders.

(d) Proxy Voting

The general rule on proxy voting is that each shareholder must have the right to appoint any other natural or legal person as a proxy holder to attend and vote at a general meeting in that shareholder's name.[128] The only requirement that company may impose on the eligibility of the proxy holder is that he or she possess legal capacity. Member states may limit the appointment of a proxy holder to a single meeting or to such meetings as may be held during a specified period.[129] A person acting as a proxy holder may hold a proxy from more than one shareholder and may cast votes for a certain shareholder differently from votes cast for another shareholder. Companies cannot restrict the exercise of shareholder rights through proxy holders for any purpose other than to address potential conflicts of interest between the proxy holder and the shareholder.[130]

(e) Voting by Correspondence

Companies may offer their shareholders the possibility of voting by correspondence in advance of the general meeting. Voting by correspondence may be made subject only to such requirements and constraints as are necessary to ensure the identification of shareholders and only to the extent that they are proportionate to achieving that objective.[131]

---

127. *Id.* at art. 9(1).
128. *Id.* at art. 10(1).
129. *Id.* at art. 10(2).
130. There is no exhaustive list of situations in which a conflict of interest may arise. Some common situations giving rise to a conflict of interest are when the proxy holder is a direct or indirect controlling shareholder of the company, is a member of the administrative, management, or supervisory organ of the company, or is an employee or an auditor of the company.
131. Shareholders Rights Directive at art. 12.

(f) Voting Results

The general meeting of shareholders makes decisions in the form of resolutions. Each resolution of the general meeting must identify at least the number of shares for which votes have been validly cast, the proportion of the share capital represented by those votes, the total number of votes validly cast as well as the number of votes cast in favor of and against each resolution, and, where applicable, the number of abstentions. However, member states may provide or allow companies to provide that if no shareholder requests a full account of the voting, it is sufficient to establish the voting results only to the extent needed to ensure that the required majority is reached for each resolution.[132] The results of votes of the general meeting of shareholders must be published on the company's website no later than 15 days after the general meeting.

4.4 Minimum Number of Shareholders for Limited Liability Companies

The Twelfth Company Law Directive requires the member states to recognize private limited liability companies even if they have only one shareholder.[133] It is up to each member state to decide if it wants to allow for single shareholder public limited liability companies.[134] In either case, the fact that the limited liability company is owned by only one entity must be notified to the commercial register and made known to the public.[135]

4.5 Capitalization of Public Limited Liability Companies

The EU rules governing capitalization issues apply only to public limited liability companies.[136] There is no harmonization at the EU level of the rules regarding the capitalization of private limited liability companies. Each member state has its own rules (subject, of course, to the free movement principles discussed in Chapter II). The capitalization rules can generally be divided into rules governing the initial capitalization or share subscription and rules governing subsequent changes to the capital of the company. These rules are designed to protect creditors (involuntary and voluntary) and minority shareholders.

(a) Initial Capitalization and Subscribed Capital

Public limited liability companies must have a minimum capitalization of €25,000 when they are established.[137] There is no minimum threshold set by the EU for private limited liability companies. Hence, the minimum amounts required to establish a private limited liability company vary among member

---

132. *Id.* at art. 14(1).
133. Twelfth Council Company Law Directive of 21 December 1989 on single-member private limited-liability companies, 1989 O.J. (L 395) 40.
134. *Id.* at art. 6.
135. *Id.* at art. 3.
136. Public Company Capitalization Directive at art. 1(1).
137. *Id.* at art. 6(1).

states. This, of course, creates the potential for forum shopping by incorporators when deciding where to establish their private limited liability company. Incorporators with limited access to capital may decide to establish their private limited liability company in a member state with low or even no minimum capital requirements. This was basically what happened in the *Centros*[138] and *Inspire Art*[139] cases discussed above.

The shares of the public limited liability company must be issued at no lower than their nominal or par value.[140] Shares issued for consideration must be paid up at the time of incorporation at not less than 25 percent of their nominal value.[141] The member states may derogate from this rule to the extent necessary for the adoption of employee stock participation programs.[142] For example, a company may set aside shares for its employees without those shares having to be paid for.

In-kind contributions to the subscribed capital of public limited liability companies are generally permissible to reach the €25,000 threshold, but the noncash asset being contributed must be "capable of economic assessment."[143] However, a promise to perform work or supply services to the company is expressly precluded from qualifying as an acceptable in-kind contribution.[144] If the shares are issued upon incorporation for an in-kind contribution, that consideration must be fully transferred to the company within five years.[145] The public limited liability company must secure a report from an independent expert assessing the value of the in-kind contribution.[146] This report must be disclosed to the commercial register and the public.[147]

There are three important exceptions to the requirement of an independent valuation report for in-kind contributions.[148] First, if the in-kind contribution is

---

138. Case C-212/97, Centros v. Erhvervs- og Selskabsstyrelsen, 1999 E.C.R. I-1484.
139. Case C-167/01, Kamer van Koophandel en Fabrieken voor Amsterdam v. Inspire Art Ltd, 2003 E.C.R. I-10195.
140. Public Company Capitalization Directive at art. 8.
141. *Id.* at art. 9(1).
142. *Id.* at art. 45.
143. *Id.* at art. 7.
144. This does not prevent the member states from allowing companies to issue financial instruments such as Genussscheine (in Germany), strumenti finanziari partecipatiri (in Italy) or titres participaatits (in Belgium) in exchange for work or services contributed to the company. These alternative instruments are not considered voting equity in the company.
145. *Id.* at art. 9(2).
146. *Id.* at art. 10(1).
147. *Id.* at art. 10(2).
148. In the event one of these exceptions applies, the company must publish certain information about the in-kind contribution. *Id.* at art. 12(1).

in the form of transferable securities[149] or money market instruments,[150] member states may relieve the public limited liability companies from having to secure the report as long as the transferable securities or money market instruments are contributed at their weighted average price at which they have been trading on a regulated market.[151] Second, the member states may relieve the public company from securing an independent valuation if the in-kind contribution is in the form of assets which have already been subject to an independent fair value opinion in the immediately preceding six months and the valuation was performed in accordance with generally accepted valuation standards in that member state.[152] Third, an exception to the general requirement to have an independent valuation report for in-kind contributions is available if the assets being contributed have been valued in the previous fiscal year in a company's audited accounts in accordance with Directive 2006/43/EC.[153] For example, if Siemens AG, a German public limited liability company, wants to establish a public limited liability company in Denmark and contribute the assets of one of its Danish subsidiaries, an independent fair value report is not necessary if those Danish assets were already valued in Siemens's annual audited financial in the past year. In the event the company benefits from one of these exceptions, it still must disclose the details of the in-kind contribution.[154]

The in-kind contribution valuation and disclosure rules are designed to prevent certain subscribers from contributing assets at inflated values and thereby diluting the per share value of the other subscribers (particularly the shareholders who contributed cash). As the in-kind contribution valuation and disclosure rules obviously do not apply to cash contributions, it would be possible to avoid the application of such rules if certain subscribers, instead of making the in-kind contribution, contributed cash for their shares, and then, once the company was established, caused the company to purchase the assets from these shareholders at prices exceeding their fair value. To address this possibility, the same valuation and disclosure obligations apply if, within two years after incorporation, the company acquires assets from the original subscriber for consideration of 10 percent or more of the subscribed capital.[155]

---

149. According to Article 4(1)(18) of Directive 2004/39/EC of the European Parliament and of the Council of 21 April 2004 on markets in financial instruments amending Council Directives 85/611/EEC and 93/6/EEC and Directive 2000/12/EC of the European Parliament and of the Council and repealing Council Directive 93/22/EEC, 2004 O.J. (L 145) 1, the term "transferable securities" means "those classes of securities which are negotiable on the capital market, with the exception of instruments of payment."
150. According to Article 4(1)(19) of Directive 2004/39/EC, the term "money-market instruments" means "those classes of instruments which are normally dealt in on the money market, such as treasury bills, certificates of deposit and commercial papers and excluding instruments of payment."
151. Public Company Capitalization Directive at art. 11(1). The period of time during which the weighted average price is determined is up to the respective member states.
152. *Id.* at art. 11(2).
153. *Id.* at art. 11(3).
154. *Id.* at art. 12(1).
155. *Id.* at art. 13.

(b) Share Buybacks

Share buybacks are sometimes viewed with caution as they can be used to defraud investors and creditors. For example, the controlling shareholders of a company heavily in debt could get some cash out of the company by forcing the company to buy back part or all of their shares. Share buybacks may also be used by company management to thwart a hostile takeover. However, share buybacks may be also used for benevolent purposes such as returning cash to stockholders after a significant disposition, use of the shares in employee stock plans,[156] or increasing earnings per share by reducing the number of outstanding shares. Moreover, a share buyback has the advantage over the issuance of a dividend because it gives the shareholders the option to sell their shares back to the company or hold on to their shares and not take the payout.

In recognition of the possible positive uses of share buyback programs, EU law allows (but does not require) the member states to permit certain types of companies to buy their shares back from their shareholders.[157] If a member state does permit share buybacks, EU company law sets forth minimum requirements which the member states must impose on the company: The buyback can only be of fully paid-up shares, it must be approved at a general meeting of the shareholders, and the acquisition may not result in the company's net assets falling below the amount of the subscribed capital.[158] In addition, the company must indicate in its subsequent annual report the reasons for the share buyback, the number and value of the shares bought back, the consideration paid for the shares, and the number and value of all shares bought back and the proportion of subscribed capital which they represent.[159]

If the shares are being bought back specifically for an employee stock plan or it becomes necessary to prevent serious and imminent harm to the company, for example to prevent a free fall of the company's shares listed on a public market, the requirement of a general meeting of shareholders can be dispensed with.[160] The member states have the autonomy to impose additional requirements on the company involved in the share buyback.[161]

EU company law also imposes limitations on what a company may do with the shares it has bought back from its shareholders. The voting rights associated with those shares are suspended.[162] Moreover, if those shares appear as an asset in the company's balance sheet, then the company must also create a reserve in the same amount.

---

156. *See, e.g.*, Case C-42/95, Siemens v. Nold, 1996 E.C.R. I-6017.
157. It should be noted in this context that public companies are not permitted to subscribe to their own shares. Public Company Capitalization Directive at art. 20. The difference between a share buyback and share subscription is that in a share buyback, the company is purchasing shares from third parties rather than itself as in a share subscription.
158. *Id.* at art. 21(1).
159. *Id.* at art. 24(2).
160. *Id.* at art. 21(2) & (3).
161. *Id.* at art. 21(1).
162. *Id.* at art. 24(1).

If the company loans money or otherwise advances funds to a third party for the purpose of buying shares in the company, the transaction must take place "at fair market conditions."[163] The management organ of the company must prepare and deliver to the shareholders a report explaining the third-party transaction and the risks to the company. Also, the transaction must be approved by the shareholders of the company. These requirements do not apply to banks and financial institutions or when the shares are being purchased for the company's employees.[164]

A company could technically avoid the restrictions on share buybacks by using a controlled affiliate to acquire the shares. For example, a parent company could cause its subsidiary to acquire shares in the parent company. In the event that a company which is directly or indirectly controlled by a public limited liability company buys shares in the public limited liability company, the transaction is treated as a share buyback by the public limited liability company and subject to the same restrictions discussed above.[165] Although this rule only applies to public limited liability companies established in the EU, the location of the controlled company is irrelevant. For example, the rule applies if the U.S. subsidiary of a Spanish *Sociedad Anonima* were to acquire shares in the Spanish *Sociedad Anonima*.[166]

For publicly listed companies, a share buyback program has the potential of affecting the price of those shares on the exchange where they are listed. When a company trades in its own shares, it could be considered a form of market abuse. As discussed below in the context of market abuse, EU company law provides a safe harbor for buyback programs provided the company follows the necessary procedures.[167]

(c) Increases in Share Capital

Access to additional capital is often a prerequisite for the company's growth. EU company law generally permits companies to increase their share capital but, in order to protect the rights of the creditors and shareholders,[168] places limitations as to the procedures used to accomplish that share capital increase. The shareholders must approve all share capital increases of public companies. If there are several classes of shares, the affirmative vote of each of the classes affected by the share capital increase is necessary. The company statutes or instrument of incorporation may authorize the appropriate company body to increase the share capital increases up to a certain amount.[169] This is analogous

---

163. *Id.* at art. 25(2).
164. *Id.* at art. 25(6).
165. *Id.* at art. 28(1) "Control" in this context means holding a majority of the voting rights or enjoying rights allowing it to exercise a dominant influence on the affiliate.
166. Public Company Capitalization Directive at art. 28(1).
167. Commission Regulation (EC) No. 2273/2003 of 22 December 2003 implementing Directive 2003/6/EC of the European Parliament and of the Council as regards exemptions for buyback programmes and stabilisation of financial instruments, 2003 O.J. (L 336) 33.
168. Case C-373/97, Diamantis v. Elliniko Dimosio, 2000 E.C.R. I-1723, 1734 ¶32.
169. Public Company Capitalization Directive at art. 29(2).

to authorized but unissued shares in the United States. In such cases, shareholder approval is not needed.

The consideration for the shares can be paid in cash or in-kind. For example, a company contemplating the acquisition of another company may increase its share capital to use the shares in an in-kind exchange for the shares of the acquired company. In the event of an in-kind payment, the company must engage an independent expert to report on the value of the in-kind consideration. The consideration must be transferred to the company within five years.[170]

If the shares are to be issued for cash, the existing shareholders[171] have preemptive rights to participate in the share capital increase. The basic rationale is that the shareholders should have the right to avoid the dilutive effect which a share capital increase will have on their shareholdings. The shares must be preemptively offered to the existing shareholders in proportion to their respective shareholdings.[172] This general rule applies even if the company has several classes of shares and one class of shares is being increased. In such cases, however, the member states may limit the preemption rights to the specific class of shares being increased.[173] The preemptive requirement means that the shares must be offered to the existing shareholders and convertible bondholders prior to the offering to the new shareholders. It cannot be done simultaneously.[174]

In *Siemens v. Nold*, the issue arose as to whether a member state can extend preemptive rights to share increases in exchange for in-kind consideration, for example, if a company issues additional shares to acquire shares in other companies.[175] In this particular case, the shareholders of the German company Siemens authorized the Siemens board to issue additional shares to acquire other companies. As this was an in-kind exchange, Siemens took the position that the preemptive rights mandated by EU company law did not apply. German law, however, granted preemptive rights in the event shares were issued for cash or in-kind. The ECJ concluded that EU company law "left Member States at liberty to provide or not to provide for a right of pre-emption [in the event of capital increases by consideration in-kind]."[176]

(d) Reduction of Share Capital

Just as a company may increase its share capital, it may decide to decrease its share capital. This is expressly permitted under EU company law provided the share capital is not reduced below the statutory minimum.[177] A reduction in

---

170. *Id.* at art. 31.
171. According to the ECJ in Case C-338/06, Comm'n v. Spain, 2008 E.C.R. I-10169, 10187 ¶46, this right held by existing shareholders also extends to holders of bonds convertible into shares.
172. Public Company Capitalization Directive at art. 33(1).
173. *Id.* at art. 33(2)(b).
174. Case C-338/06, Comm'n v. Spain, 2008 E.C.R. I-10169, 10186 ¶39.
175. Case C-42/95, Siemens v. Nold, 1996 E.C.R. I-6017.
176. *Id.* at 6035 ¶18.
177. Public Company Capitalization Directive at art. 38. As discussed above, public limited liability companies must have and maintain a minimum capitalization of €25,000. *Id.* at art. 6(1).

share capital requires the affirmative vote of two-thirds of the votes attaching to the shares at a meeting held for that purpose.[178] This applies to each class of voting shares affected by the reduction.[179] The member states have the option of adopting an exception to this two-thirds majority rule. If at least half of the share capital is present at the meeting called for the purpose of voting on a reduction in share capital, a simple majority may suffice.[180]

In addition to the shareholders, another group that could be negatively affected by a reduction in share capital is the creditors. Their decision to extend credit to the company is typically based (at least partially) on the capitalization of the company. In the event of a capital reduction, the creditors have the right to require the company to provide them with additional security for their claims which will become due after the capital reduction.[181] The procedures applicable to the exercise of this right by the creditors are regulated by national law.

4.6 Distributions to Shareholders of Public Limited Liability Companies

Distributions and dividend payments to shareholders are generally permitted. However, a public limited liability company cannot make a year-end cash or in-kind distribution (including dividend payments and interest payments) to its shareholders if, at the time of or following such distribution, the assets of the company are less than the amount of the subscribed capital plus the reserves which cannot be distributed pursuant to applicable member state law as shown on the company's year-end accounts (adjusted for profits and losses to the actual date of the distribution).[182] For distributions made during the year (referred to as interim distributions), the company must prepare interim accounts showing that the funds available for distribution are sufficient.[183] These financial calculations must be made in accordance with the accounting rules set forth in the Accounting Directive.

4.7 Disclosure Requirements for Limited Liability Companies

EU company law attempts to establish a minimum level of transparency by imposing requirements on member states that companies (both public and private) registered in their respective territories make certain information available to the public. As discussed in the context of securities law, there are additional obligations imposed specifically on companies whose shares are listed on a regulated market in the EU. However, the publication requirements discussed here apply regardless of whether or not the limited liability company is listed on a regulated market.

---

178. *Id.* at art. 34.
179. *Id.* at art. 35.
180. *Id.* at art. 34.
181. *Id.* at art. 36.
182. *Id.* at art. 17(1).
183. *Id.* at art. 17(5).

Each member state is required to maintain a companies registration system covering all limited liability companies (both public and private) registered in that member state.[184] The names of the registration agencies in the respective member states are different as are the specific national rules applicable to them. At a minimum, however, the central registry must maintain a file for each company containing the following information disclosed by the companies:[185]

- Incorporation and governing documents (and all amendments);[186]
- The appointment, termination of office, and particulars of the persons who are authorized to act on behalf of the company;
- The amount of the capital subscribed;
- The accounting documents for each fiscal year;
- Any transfer of the seat of the company;
- The voluntary or involuntary dissolution, termination, or liquidation or any declaration of nullity of the company.

The information must be filed with and retained by the commercial register of the member state of incorporation and made available to the public in the national gazette and upon request.[187] The disclosure is made in one of the languages permitted by that member state. The company may also make a disclosure in any of the official languages of the EU, but this option is voluntary and does not supersede the obligation to disclose the information in the language mandated by the member state where the company is incorporated.[188] Once published in the national gazette, the public is presumed to have constructive knowledge of the information.[189] The specific person within the company responsible for these disclosures, as well as liability for failure to disclose, is determined by member state law.[190]

4.8 Financial Statement and Annual Report of Limited Liability Companies

As discussed above, limited liability companies must disclose in the national register the annual accounting documents and the amount of the subscribed capital. In addition, the company must publish annual accounts consisting of a balance sheet, profit and loss account, and the notes.[191] Although the specific laws governing the annual accounts and consolidation are national laws, the EU

---

184. Limited Liability Company Directive at art. 3(1).
185. *Id.* at art. 2(1).
186. The content of the incorporation and governing documents for public limited liability companies is prescribed in Articles 2 and 3 of the Public Company Capitalization Directive. EU law does not prescribe the content of the incorporation or governing documents of private limited liability companies.
187. Limited Liability Company Directive at art. 3(5).
188. *Id.* at art. 4(2).
189. *Id.* at art. 3(6).
190. *Id.* at art. 6.
191. See Accounting Directive.

Accounting Directive harmonizes these laws by setting forth the basic accounting principles that must be followed in preparing the financial statements.

4.9 Branch Offices of Limited Liability Companies

The concept of a "branch" in company law refers to establishment by a legal entity of an office or business (which is not a separate legal entity) in a different jurisdiction. For example, an Estonian company may do business in Latvia by setting up a branch office rather than establishing a separate subsidiary in Latvia. The right of establishment codified in Article 49 of the TFEU covers not only the establishment of a separate legal entity in another member state, i.e., a subsidiary, but also a branch.[192] This alternative form of doing business is particularly attractive to small and mid-size companies as the establishment of the branch requires less formalities and capital than the creation of a separate legal entity. The obvious disadvantage is that the liabilities of the branch office, in contrast to the liabilities of a subsidiary, inure to the legal entity for which that office serves as a branch.

The freedom to do business in the form of a branch office under Article 49 of the TFEU is not absolute. In other words, a company established in one member state may not simply open a branch office, lease office space, hire employees, and start selling products in another member state. Member states may require companies from other member states to register their branch offices and make certain disclosures. Although this is technically a restriction on the freedom of establishment, it is justified as such registration and disclosure serve to protect the public.

(a) Branch Offices of EU Companies

When a company which is already established in a member state opens a branch office in another member state, it must register that branch office with the central register, commercial register, or companies register of the other member state.[193] This registration requires the company to disclose certain information about itself so that individuals and other companies doing business with the branch are able to confirm the legitimacy of the company. At a minimum, the branch registration must include the following documents and particulars:[194]

- the name and legal form of the company and the name of the branch (if that is different from the name of the company) as well as the address and a description of the activities of the branch;
- identification of the register in which the company is registered, together with the company's registration number;

---

192. Case C-414/06, Lidl Belgium GmbH & Co. KG v. Finanzamt Heilbronn, 2008 E.C.R. I-3617, 3625 ¶18.
193. Eleventh Company Law Directive. For credit and financial institutions, *see* Council Directive of 13 February 1989 on the obligations of branches established in a member state of credit institutions and financial institutions having their head offices outside that member state regarding the publication of annual accounting documents, 1989 O.J. (L 44) 40 at art. 1(1).
194. *Id.* at art. 2(1).

- the appointment, termination of office, and particulars of the persons who are authorized to act on behalf of the company in dealings with third parties and in legal proceedings (as a branch does not have its own legal personality, these same individuals will be able to act on behalf of the branch);
- the accounting documents of the company (together with a certified translation if required by the law of the branch's host member state);
- the winding-up, liquidation, or insolvency of the company; and
- the closing of the branch.

In addition to these compulsory disclosures, the member state where the branch is located may require the disclosure of the following additional information:[195]

- the signatures of the persons who are authorized to act on behalf of the company;
- the incorporation and governing documents of the company (together with a certified translation if required by the law of the branch's host member state).[196]
- an attestation from the commercial register where the company was incorporated confirming the existence of the company; and
- a listing of the liens on the company's property situated in the member state where the branch is located.

All documents and information disclosed relating to the branch are retained by the commercial register. The documents and information are available to the public. The correspondence and order forms used by the branch must identify the register where the branch is registered.

(b) Branch Offices of Non-EU Companies

Even companies established outside the EU can open a branch office in the EU. Similar registration and disclosure obligations as for branch offices of EU companies apply. In most instances, the laws of the member states will require that the documents disclosed be translated into the local official language.[197] One requirement which often presents a cost burden for non-EU companies opening up branch offices in the EU is that the member state where the branch office is located may require that the accounting documents relating to the activities of the branch be drawn up in accordance with or in a manner equivalent to the standard codified in the Accounting Directive. As accounting principles often vary between countries, the non-EU company intending to establish the branch in the EU may have to maintain a separate set of accounts for the branch to conform to EU accounting principles.

---

195. *Id.* at art. 2(2).
196. *Id.* at art. 4.
197. *Id.* at art. 9(2).

4.10 Shareholder and Manager Liability

(a) Pre-Incorporation Liability of Shareholders and Managers

Prior to the date of incorporation, the (future) incorporators are personally liable for the acts of the company unless the company assumes those obligations. If, for example, the future general manager of the company signs a lease agreement for the office space in which the company will have its main offices, that general manager will be liable as though he or she had signed the lease in his or her own name. In recognition of the fact that certain pre-incorporation acts are often necessary, once it is incorporated, the company may agree to assume the pre-incorporation liabilities which the incorporators may have incurred prior to the date of incorporation.[198] Hence, it is quite common that a declaration or resolution to this effect be adopted by the company simultaneously with or immediately after its incorporation.

(b) Post-Incorporation Liability of Shareholders and Managers

The liability of the shareholders for debts of the company in which they hold an interest is governed by national law.[199] Similar to the United States, the general rule in Europe is that the shareholders are not liable for the debts of the company beyond the extent of their respective capital contributions. In contrast to the United States, it is generally more difficult in Europe to pierce the corporate veil. Member state laws generally require a showing of fraud before they are willing to pierce the corporate veil.

Concerning the liability of the directors and managers of the company, an important distinction needs to be made between their personal liability to the company (internal liability) and their personal liability to third parties (external liability). Internal liability rules have not been harmonized by EU law. Hence, member state law will apply exclusively to such issues. Although an exhaustive treatment of the national laws applicable to internal liability is beyond the scope of this Chapter, the general rule is that the directors and managers will not be held personally liable to the company if they acted within the scope of their duties as set forth in the company's governing documents and applicable law.

In contrast to internal liability issues, the national laws applicable to the liability of the company's directors and managers vis-à-vis third persons are harmonized by EU law. External liability has two aspects: (1) when is the company itself liable for the acts of its directors and managers and (2) when are the company's directors and managers personally liable for their acts to the company or to third parties.

---

198. Limited Liability Company Directive at art. 8.
199. Case C-81/09, Idrima Tipou AE v. Ipourgos Tipou kai Meson Mayikis Enimerosis, 2010 E.C.R. I-10206, 10221 ¶39.

The general rule is that the company is bound by acts of its organs even if those acts are not within the registered purpose of the company.[200] For example, if the object of the company is the manufacture and sale of pistons, and the general manager starts a software development division, the obligations incurred vis-à-vis third parties in the software business are binding on the company even though they may exceed the object of the company as set forth in its governing documents. There is a presumption that the persons disclosed in the commercial register as being authorized to act on behalf of the company are indeed authorized even if these persons have not been correctly appointed.[201]

However, member states may provide that the company shall not be bound where such acts are outside the purpose of the company if it proves that the third party knew that the act was outside the purpose or could not in view of the circumstances have been unaware of it.

4.11 Corporate Governance

The rights and duties of the governing organs of the various European legal entities remain within the scope of national legislation. Although the Fifth Company Law Directive was intended to harmonize the member state laws in this regard,[202] it was never adopted. The Commission has, however, adopted two influential recommendations on remuneration for directors of listed companies and the role of nonexecutive directors in listed companies.[203] Although the recommendations are not binding on the member states, some of the member states have adopted legislation implementing many of the suggestions made by the Commission in these recommendations.

(a) Remuneration of Directors

The member states are encouraged to require each company listed on a regulated market in that member state to disclose a statement of the company's remuneration policy for the directors. The remuneration statement should include the variable and nonvariable components of the directors' remuneration, performance criteria, information on the linkage between remuneration and performance, a summary of any annual bonus scheme and other noncash benefits, and a description of the pension or early retirement schemes set up for directors. The member states are also encouraged to make the remuneration policy an agenda item at the annual shareholders' meeting. The remuneration of the individual directors should be disclosed in the company's annual report. The member states are invited to require shareholder approval of share-based remuneration schemes for the directors, such as stock option plans.

---

200. Limited Liability Company Directive at art. 10(1).
201. *Id.* at art. 9.
202. 1972 O.J. (C 131) 49.
203. Commission Recommendation of 14 December 2004 fostering an appropriate regime for the remuneration of directors of listed companies, 2004 O.J. (L 385) 55; Commission Recommendation of 15 February 2005 on the role of non-executive or supervisory directors of listed companies and on the committees of the (supervisory) board, 2005 O.J. (L 52) 51; Commission Recommendation complementing Recommendations 2004/913/EC and 2005/162/EC as regards the regime for the remuneration of directors of listed companies, 2009 O.J. (L 120) 28.

(b) Role of External Directors

The member states are encouraged by the Commission to adopt either legislation or codes of conduct applicable to nonexecutive directors of companies listed on a regulated market in their country. The term "nonexecutive director" refers to any member of the board who is not engaged in the daily management of the company. The qualifications of the nonexecutive directors should be determined by the board. The organization of the board and the balance between executive directors and nonexecutive directors is up to the company. However, the board should be organized to make sure the nonexecutive directors play an effective role.

Directors—even external directors—are likely to be considered "workers" under EU law if they receive remuneration for their services, are under the supervision of another corporate body, and can be removed from their position.[204] This means that such directors benefit from the broad protections mandated by EU primary and secondary law applicable to workers.

(c) Annual Corporate Governance Statement

Although the member states are not required to follow the Commission's recommendations on remuneration of directors or the role of external directors, they are required to make companies listed on a regulated market in their country publish an annual corporate governance statement.[205] The corporate governance statement, which may be included in the annual report or in a separate report published together with the annual report, must contain a reference to the corporate governance code to which the company is subject or may have voluntarily decided to apply and all relevant information about the corporate governance practices of the company above and beyond the legal requirement the company is otherwise required to apply. In addition, the statement must provide a description of the main features of the company's internal control and financial risk management systems and the composition and operation of the administrative, management, and supervisory bodies and committees. The obligation to publish an annual corporate governance statement is imposed on all companies (not just companies listed on a regulated market). However, the member states may exempt companies not listed on a regulated market from the obligation.[206]

4.12 Mergers

(a) Domestic Mergers

For purposes of company law, the term "merger" refers to a transaction where one legal entity merges into another legal entity and ceases to maintain its own legal personality. A basic distinction is made in EU company law between domestic mergers (i.e., mergers between companies from the same member state) and international mergers (i.e., mergers between companies from different member states). Prior to the adoption of the Domestic Mergers Directive, mergers—even

---

204. C-232/09, Danosa v. LKB Līzings SIA, 2010 E.C.R. I-11405, 11457 ¶51.
205. Accounting Directive at art. 20.
206. *Id.* at art. 20(4).

domestic mergers—were not recognized by all member states. Moreover, the merger laws of the various member states which did recognize mergers were significantly different. In order to harmonize the laws of the member states and provide some minimum level of protection for shareholders and creditors of the merging entities, the Council adopted the Domestic Mergers Directive which requires all the member states to recognize certain types of mergers and harmonizes the procedures required to implement these mergers.

(1) Recognition of Domestic Mergers

The Domestic Mergers Directive requires the member states to recognize (i) mergers (ii) between public limited liability companies (iii) in one member state. In order to fall under the Domestic Mergers Directive, the transaction must be structured as a merger. The concept of merger as used in the Domestic Mergers Directive encompasses three types of mergers: merger by acquisition, merger by the formation of a new company and merger of a subsidiary into a parent. A merger by acquisition describes the situation where one or more legal entities (referred to as the merging company or companies) transfer all their assets and liabilities to another existing company (referred to as the acquiring company) in exchange for shares in the acquiring company or a combination of cash and shares.[207] A merger by acquisition is depicted in the diagram below. Company A merges with and into Company B, and the shareholders of Company A receive shares or cash and shares in Company B. Company A is then dissolved.

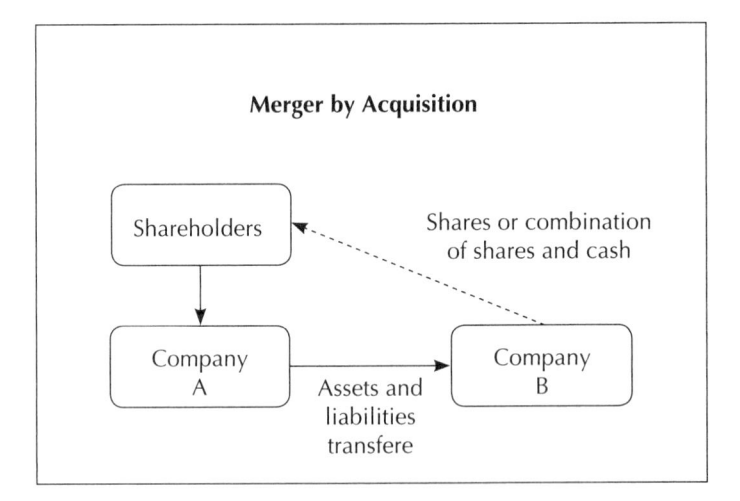

Merger by Acquisition

Shareholders → Company A → (Assets and liabilities transfere) → Company B
Shareholders ←----- Shares or combination of shares and cash ----- Company B

The second merger constellation, referred to in EU company law as a merger by formation of a new company, is where two or more companies (referred to as the merging companies) transfer all their assets and liabilities to a newly formed entity (referred to as the acquiring company) and the merging companies are dissolved as legal entities. The surviving entity is the acquiring company. The shareholders of the merging companies receive shares or a combination

---

207. The cash component of the merger consideration may not exceed 10 percent of the nominal value, or, in the absence of a nominal value, of the accounting par value of the shares. Domestic Mergers Directive at art. 4(1).

of cash and shares in the acquiring company.[208] A merger by formation of a new company is depicted in the diagram below. Company A and Company B establish Newco. Company A and Company B each merge with and into Newco. The shareholders of Company A and Company B each receive shares in Newco, or a combination of shares and cash. Company A and Company B are then dissolved.

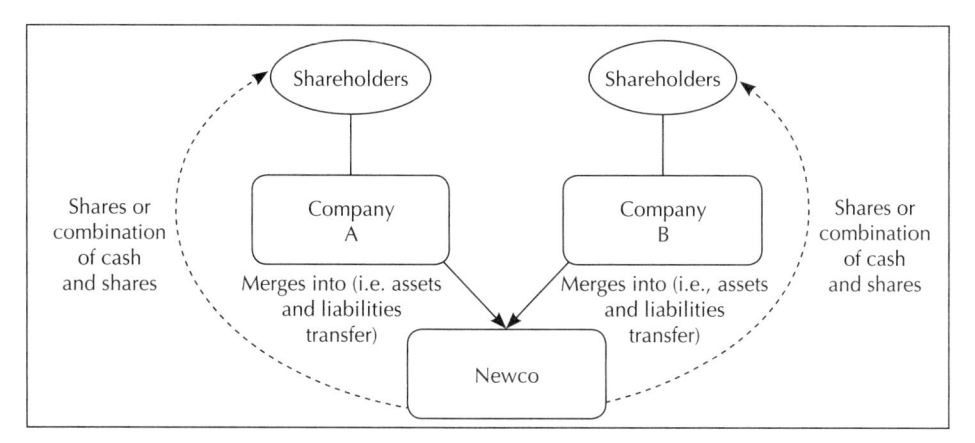

The third type of merger falling within the scope of the Domestic Mergers Directive is where a wholly owned subsidiary merges into its parent company by transferring all of its assets and liabilities to the parent.[209] The subsidiary is then dissolved. In this constellation, the shareholder of the merged entity does not need to receive shares in the surviving entity because it is the surviving entity. Hence, it would not qualify as a merger by acquisition (which requires the issuance of shares to the shareholder of the merged entity). A subsidiary-parent merger is depicted in the diagram below. Subsidiary A, a wholly owned subsidiary of Company A, merges with and into Company A. At that point, Subsidiary A is dissolved and ceases to exist.

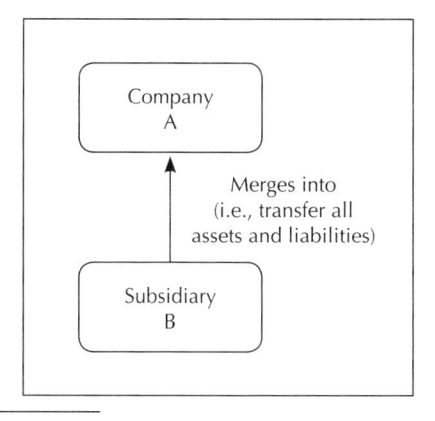

---

208. The cash component may not exceed 10 percent of the value of the shares of the newly formed entity.
209. Domestic Mergers Directive at art. 24. As there is no issuance of shares to the shareholders of the merged entity, the provisions of the Domestic Mergers Directive applicable to the issuance of shares in other types of mergers do not apply in the case of a subsidiary into parent merger.

Second, the Domestic Mergers Directive only applies to mergers of public limited liability companies.[210] Domestic mergers between private limited liability companies fall outside the scope of the Directive. For example, the merger of an Estonian *Osaühing* into another Estonian *Osaühing* or into an *Aktsiaselts* (Estonian public company) would fall outside the scope of the Domestic Mergers Directive. There has been no harmonization of the member state laws applicable to mergers between private limited liability companies.

Third, the scope of the Domestic Mergers Directive is limited to mergers between two public limited liability companies within one member state. For example, the merger of two Hungarian *részvénytársaság* would fall within the scope of the Directive. However, the merger between a Hungarian *részvénytársaság* and a Romanian *societate pe acțiuni* would not fall under the Directive even though both companies are public limited liability companies. As discussed below, the Cross-Border Mergers Directive (and not the Domestic Mergers Directive) would apply to the latter type of mergers.

(2) Implementation of Domestic Mergers

The Domestic Mergers Directive not only requires the member states to recognize mergers, it also harmonizes the basic steps member states must require for implementing domestic mergers. The first step in the implementation of a domestic merger is the preparation of the terms of merger by the boards of each of the merging companies. At a minimum, the terms of merger must contain the following information:[211]

- the type, name, and registered office of each of the merging companies;
- the share exchange ratio (and the amount of any cash payment), the terms relating to the allotment of shares in the acquiring company, and the date from which the holding of such shares entitles the holders to participate in profits and any special conditions affecting that entitlement;[212]
- the date from which the transactions of the company being acquired are to be treated for accounting purposes as being those of the acquiring company;
- the rights conferred by the acquiring company on the holders of shares to which special rights are attached and the holders of securities other than shares, or the measures proposed concerning them; and
- any special advantage granted to the independent experts and members of the merging companies' administrative, management, supervisory, or controlling bodies.

---

210. *Id.* at art. 1. The concept of "public limited liability company" is discussed above. A list of public company forms under national law is provided in Article 1 of the Domestic Mergers Directive.
211. Domestic Mergers Directive at art. 5(1).
212. If the merger is a subsidiary into a parent company, this information does not have to be included in the terms of merger as the acquiring company in that case is not issuing shares to itself. Domestic Mergers Directive at art. 24.

The terms of merger must then be published in the public register by the administrative or management bodies of the respective companies at least one month prior to the shareholders' meeting to approve the merger.[213] In addition to the terms of merger, the administrative or management bodies of each of the merging companies must prepare a report explaining the terms of the merger and setting out the legal and economic grounds for the merger, including the share exchange ratio.[214] Although the report does not have to be published in the public register, it (along with the terms of merger, the annual accounts and annual reports of the merging companies for the preceding three financial years, and an accounting statement) must be made available to the shareholders for inspection during the 30 days prior to the shareholders' meeting to approve the terms of merger.[215]

The administrative or management bodies of the respective companies must also inform the general shareholders' meeting of their company of any material changes in the assets or liabilities between the date of the draft terms of merger and the date on which the general meeting is to vote on the terms of merger.[216] Any civil liability of the administrative or management bodies relating to misconduct in preparing and implementing the merger is governed by the laws of the respective member states.[217]

Each of the companies is required to engage an independent expert to give a fairness opinion addressing the fairness of the exchange ratio used in the terms of merger.[218] In addition to its opinion as to the fairness and reasonableness of the exchange ratio, the independent expert report must indicate the method used to arrive at the share exchange ratio (and state whether such method is adequate in the case in question), indicate the values arrived at using each such method, and give an opinion on the relative importance attributed to such method in arriving at the value.

---

213. *Id.* at art. 6. The company is relieved of this obligation if, for a continuous period of at least one month prior to the date of the general meeting to decide on the merger, the company has made the draft terms of merger available on its website free of charge.
214. *Id.* at art. 9(1). Although the Domestic Mergers Directive contains an exception from the publication requirement if the shareholders agree, the requisite consent must be obtained from all holders of voting shares. *Id.* at art. 9(3). This exception is therefore seldom helpful.
215. *Id.* at art. 11(1). The company is relieved of this obligation if, for a continuous period of at least one month prior to the date of the general meeting to decide on the merger, the company has made the documents available on its website free of charge. *Id.* at art. 11(4).
216. *Id.* at art. 9(2).
217. *Id.* at art. 20.
218. *Id.* at art. 10(1). The fairness opinion is not necessary if all the shareholders agree to dispense with this requirement. *Id.* at art. 10(4). The member states may permit all the companies to rely on the same fairness opinion if the independent expert is appointed by the court or an administrative authority. *Id.* at art. 10(2). This can lead to considerable cost savings for the parties.

A general meeting of the shareholders of each of the merging companies must be called to approve the merger.[219] This meeting must take place at least 30 days after the publication of the terms of merger. In order to protect minority shareholders, a two-thirds majority of those present at a shareholders' meeting which has a quorum is necessary to approve the merger. The rules governing the procedure for holding the meeting and the quorum are governed by national law. If the company has more than one class of securities, each class of security affected by the merger must approve the merger by a two-thirds majority. The laws of the member states may require a simple-majority approval if at least half of the subscribed capital is represented at the shareholders' meeting called for the purpose of approving the merger.

In certain instances, the Domestic Mergers Directive alleviates the requirement of holding a general meeting of the shareholders to approve a merger. Similar to the short-form merger in the United States, if the parent company owns 90 percent or more (but not all) of the voting shares of the merging company, a general meeting of shareholders is not required.[220] In such short-form mergers, the shareholders of the acquiring company are entitled to inspect the disclosure documents at least one month before the date on which the meeting should otherwise have occurred. Moreover, a certain percentage of minority shareholders (as determined by national law) must be given the right to call a shareholders' meeting to approve the merger.[221] The minimum percentage is left to the individual member states to decide, but it cannot be more than 5 percent.

In addition, the acquiring company in a merger by acquisition is relieved of holding a general meeting of shareholders if (1) the terms of merger are published, (2) the shareholders of that company are given at least 30 days to inspect the documents and (3) a minimum percentage of shareholders has not exercised its right to require a meeting.[222] Here again, the minimum percentage is a matter for national company law, but it cannot be more than 5 percent.

(b) Cross-Border Mergers

As company law remains largely in the realm of the member states, the types of legal entities recognized in each of the member states differ. As discussed above, the only "pan-European" form of legal entity available in most instances is the SE. The differences in legal entities (and differences in their formation and governance structures) have traditionally made cross-border mergers and corporate reorganizations difficult. Moreover, the laws of some member states expressly precluded such mergers. The impediments to cross-border mergers were partially addressed by the SE Regulation. As discussed above, however, the SE as a form of legal entity is primarily used by large companies. Hence, the

---

219. *Id.* at art. 7(1).
220. *Id.* at art. 27.
221. *Id.* at art. 8(c).
222. *Id.* at art. 8. This exception is not available to mergers by the formation of a new company. *Id.* at art. 23(1).

Cross-Border Mergers Directive,[223] which applies to other forms of companies, was adopted to facilitate the merger of a broader range of companies across member states.

(1) Recognition of Cross-Border Mergers

The Cross-Border Mergers Directive requires member states to recognize (i) mergers (ii) between limited liability companies (iii) in a cross-border transaction. First, in order to fall under the Cross-Border Mergers Directive, the transaction must be structured as a merger. Similar to the Domestic Mergers Directive, the concept of "merger" includes mergers by acquisition, mergers by formation of a new company, and subsidiary into parent mergers.[224]

Second, the Cross-Border Mergers Directive is only applicable to mergers of limited liability companies.[225] The term "limited liability company," as discussed above, applies to both public and private limited liability companies. In this respect, the scope of the Cross-Border Mergers Directive differs from that of the Domestic Mergers Directive which applies only to mergers of public limited liability companies. Like the Cross-Border Mergers Directive, however, the Domestic Mergers Directive only applies to the merger of one company into another company. As discussed below, the transfer of assets and liabilities to two companies, and the subsequent issuance of shares to the shareholders of the merged entity, are referred to and treated as a "division" to which different legislation is applicable.[226]

The third requirement for the application of the Cross-Border Mergers Directive is that at least two of the limited liability companies involved in the merger must have been formed in accordance with the laws of two different member states. For example, a merger between two Maltese *kumpanija pubblika* would not fall under the Cross-Border Mergers Directive; neither would a merger between a Delaware (U.S.) corporation and a Polish *spóka akcyjna* as the cross-border element requires that the companies are from different EU member states. However, a merger between a Maltese *kumpanija pubblika* and a Polish *spóka akcyjna* could fall within the scope of the Cross-Border Mergers Directive as it meets the cross-border element.

(2) Implementation of Cross-Border Mergers

The basic purpose of the Cross-Border Mergers Directive is to harmonize the steps prescribed by national law to implement cross-border mergers. The steps and requirements to implement a cross-border merger are quite similar to domestic mergers. The first step in the implementation of a cross-border merger between limited liability companies is that the management of the respective

---

223. Directive 2005/56/EC of the European Parliament and of the Council on cross-border mergers, 2005 O.J. (L 310) 1 as most recently amended by [hereinafter Cross-Border Mergers Directive].
224. *Id.* at art. 2(2).
225. *Id.* at art. 1.
226. Sixth Council Directive of 17 December 1982 based on Article 54(3)(g) of the Treaty, concerning the division of public limited liability companies, 1982 O.J. (L 378) 47 [hereinafter Division of Companies Directive].

merging entities draws up the fundamental common terms of the contemplated merger. The Directive prescribes the specific information that, at a minimum, needs to be included in the common terms of merger.[227] At least one month prior to the shareholders' meeting to approve the merger, the management must publish the common terms of merger in the national gazette of each member state involved in the merger.[228]

In addition to the common terms, the management of each of the merging companies must draw up an impact report "explaining and justifying" the legal and economic aspects and implications of the contemplated merger.[229] In contrast to the common terms of merger, which must be made available to the general public through publication in the national gazette, the impact report must only be made available to the shareholders and employees of the respective companies. It is to be made available at least one month prior to the shareholders' meeting to approve the merger.[230]

In addition to the impact report, the companies are required to engage an independent expert to prepare a report addressing the fairness of the exchange ratio used in the common terms. In addition to its opinion as to the fairness and reasonableness of the share-exchange ratio, the report must (1) indicate the method used to arrive at the share-exchange ratio and state whether this method is adequate in the case in question, (2) indicate the values arrived at using each such method and (3) give an opinion on the relative importance attributed to the method in arriving at the value decided on.[231] The necessity of the independent expert report can be avoided if all of the shareholders of the merging entities agree.[232]

At least a month after the publishing of the impact report and the independent expert report, the shareholders of the respective companies must meet to approve the merger. As it is possible that the negotiations with the employees of the merging companies may not yet be concluded at the time of the shareholders' meeting, the approval of the shareholders may be made conditional upon subsequent review of these agreements with the employees.[233]

Assuming the shareholders of the respective companies approve the merger, the merging parties then are required to secure a pre-merger certificate from each of the member states involved.[234] The purpose of the pre-merger certificate is to certify that the companies have taken the required pre-merger steps to complete

---

227. Cross-Border Mergers Directive at art. 5.
228. *Id.* at art. 6(1). The merging parties are relieved of this obligation if they have published the merger terms on their websites for a continuous period of at least one month prior to the date of the general meeting.
229. *Id.* at art. 7.
230. The rights of employees in the event of a cross-border merger are discussed in Chapter IX. To avoid duplication, they are not discussed here. Nonetheless, it is critically important to be aware of the rights of the employees when contemplating a cross-border merger as negotiations with the employee representatives may be necessary.
231. Cross-Border Mergers Directive at art. 8(3).
232. *Id.* at art. 8(4).
233. *Id.* at art. 9(2).
234. *Id.* at art. 10(3).

the merger. This pre-merger certificate is different from and independent of the pre-merger clearance which the parties may need to secure under applicable competition law.[235]

As the implementation steps described above can be time-consuming and expensive, the Cross-Border Mergers Directive provides for a simplified procedure.[236] Limited liability companies which have only one shareholder may avoid several of the steps. For example, if Company A, the sole shareholder of Subsidiary A, wants to merge Subsidiary A into Subsidiary B, and Subsidiary B's shares are all held by Company B, the simplified procedure set forth in the Cross-Border Mergers Directive applies. The simplified procedure, for example, relieves the management from having to draw up a report for the shareholders.

4.13 Divisions of Companies

The concept of merger used in the Domestic Mergers Directive would not capture de facto mergers or the division of an entity into two or more other entities. If, for example, Company A were to transfer 50 percent of its assets and liabilities to Company B and the remaining 50 percent to Company C, with the shareholders of Company A receiving shares in Company B and Company C respectively, and Company A being dissolved, the transaction would not strictly be considered a merger for purposes of EU company law. As discussed above, the concept of merger is limited to the merger of one company into one other company. Instead, these types of transactions—which share some of the characteristics of mergers such as the transfer of all assets and liabilities, the issuance of shares, and the dissolution of the company—are referred to as "divisions" in EU company law parlance and are regulated by the Division of Companies Directive.[237]

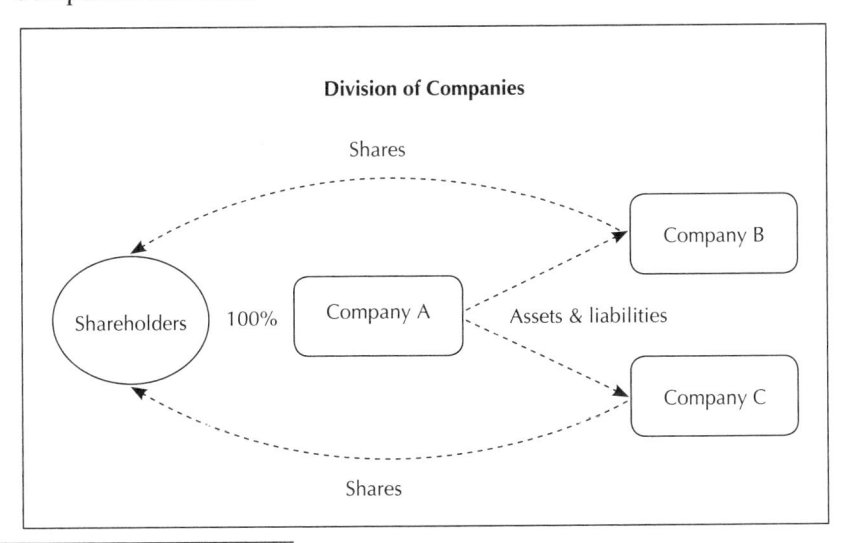

Division of Companies

Shareholders —100%— Company A

Shares → Company B
Assets & liabilities → Company B
Assets & liabilities → Company C
Shares → Company C

---

235. The competition law aspects of mergers are discussed in Chapter III.
236. Cross-Border Mergers Directive at art. 15(1).
237. Sixth Council Directive of 17 December 1982 based on Article 54(3)(g) of the Treaty, concerning the division of public limited liability companies, 1982 O.J. (L 378) 47 [hereinafter Division of Companies Directive].

(a) Recognition of Divisions

The Division of Companies Directive does not require all member states to recognize these types of business combinations. Instead, it applies only to those member states that recognize divisions between public limited liability companies: If a member state recognizes divisions, it must observe the terms of the Division of Companies Directive. Similar to the Domestic Mergers Directive, the Division of Companies Directive only applies to public limited liability companies in one member state.

Three basic types of divisions fall under the Directive: division by acquisition, division by the formation of new companies, and combination division. The differences among the three types of division are slight but important because not all provisions of the Division of Companies Directive apply equally to all types of divisions.

A division by acquisition is depicted above. One company (in the diagram Company A) transfers all of its assets and liabilities to more than one company (in the diagram Company B and Company C). In exchange for the transfer of the assets and liabilities, the shareholders of the company being divided (as Company A is referred to in EU company law) receive shares in each of the recipient companies (as Company B and Company C are referred to in EU company law).[238]

If each of Company B and Company C were to set up subsidiaries to serve as the recipient companies, the division would be considered a division by the formation of new companies.[239] This is the only difference in the structure between a division by acquisition and a division by the formation of new companies.

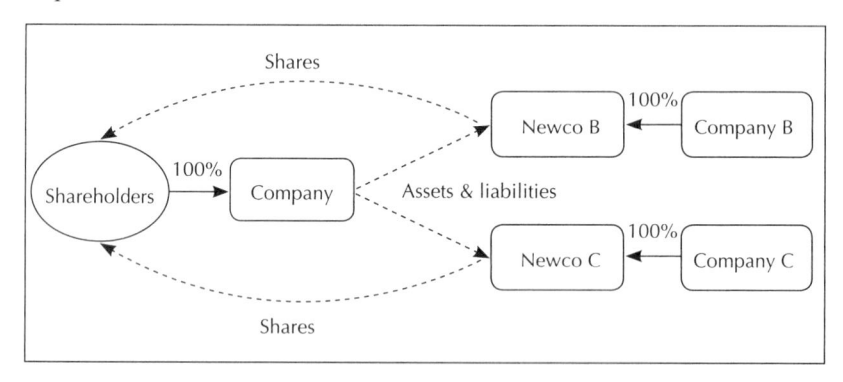

The third basic type of division falls between the two types of division just discussed and exhibits characteristics of both. A combination division exists if one of the recipient companies is set up specifically for receiving the assets

---

238. The Division of Companies Directive does not require that the shares in the recipient companies are allocated to the shareholders of the company being acquired in proportion to their rights in the capital of the company being divided. *Id.* at art. 5(2). In such cases, however, the member states may adopt legislation requiring the acquiring company to pay them the fair value of their shares in cash (as opposed to taking shares of the acquiring companies).
239. *Id.* at art. 21(1).

and liabilities of the company being divided and the other recipient company pre-exists.[240]

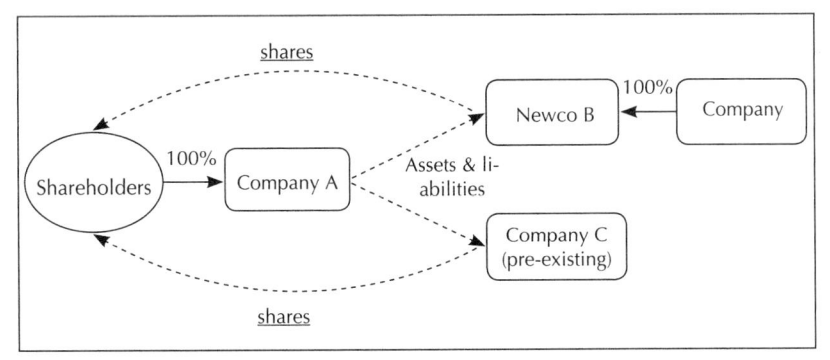

[Diagram: Shareholders own 100% of Company A. Company A transfers assets & liabilities to Newco B (100% owned by Company) and to Company C (pre-existing). Shareholders receive shares in both.]

(b) *Implementation of Divisions*

Similar to the Domestic Mergers Directive and the Cross-Border Mergers Directive, the Division of Companies Directive prescribes specific steps which the companies involved must follow in order to implement the division. The first step in the implementation of a division is the preparation of the terms of division by the administrative and management bodies of each of the companies. The required content of the terms of division is identical to the content of the terms of merger discussed above except that the terms of division must also include a description and allocation of the assets and liabilities to be transferred and a description of the allocation (and allocation methodology) of the shares in the recipient companies to the shareholders of the company being divided.[241] The administrative and management bodies must also prepare a report explaining the division and its legal and economic basis, the exchange ratio, and the criteria for determining the allocation of shares.[242]

The third main document necessary to effectuate the division is a report of an independent expert of each of the companies involved in the division.[243] The purpose of this independent expert report is to give a fairness opinion on the exchange ratio. These two reports—the report of the administrative or management bodies and the report of the independent expert—are not necessary if the shares of the new companies are allocated to the shareholders of the divided company in proportion to their rights in the capital of that company.[244]

The terms of division must then be published in the commercial register at least one month before the general meeting of shareholders called for the purpose of approving the division.[245] The report explaining the division and the report of the independent expert must be made available to the shareholders

---

240. *Id.* at art. 1(3).
241. *Id.* at art. 3(2)(h)&(i).
242. *Id.* at art. 7.
243. *Id.* at art. 8. The necessity of securing a report of an independent expert may be dispensed with if all the shareholders agree. *Id.* at art. 10(1).
244. *Id.* at art. 22(5).
245. *Id.* at art. 4.

at least one month prior to the shareholders' meeting together with the annual reports for each of the last three years and the accounting records.[246] These publication obligations do not apply if the companies involved in the division post the terms of division on their websites for a period of at least one month prior to the date of the general meeting to vote on the division.[247]

At the general shareholders' meeting, the shareholders of each of the companies involved in the division must approve the division. The required majority is the same as for domestic mergers: a two-thirds majority of those present at a meeting which has a quorum is necessary to approve the division. The rules governing the procedure for holding the shareholders' meeting and the quorum are governed by national law. If the company has more than one class of securities, each class of security affected by the merger must approve the division with the two-thirds majority. The laws of the member states may require simple majority approval if at least half of the subscribed capital is represented at the shareholders' meeting called for the purpose of approving the division.

As discussed above, there are certain instances in which a general meeting of shareholders can be dispensed with, without contradicting the objective of the law. The recipient company is relieved of holding a general meeting if the terms of division are published, the shareholders of that company are given at least 30 days to inspect the documents, and a minimum percentage of shareholders has not exercised its right to require a meeting.[248] The minimum percentage is a matter for national company law, but it cannot be more than 5 percent. In addition, the company being divided does not have to hold a general shareholders' meeting if the recipient companies comprise all of its shareholders and the publication formalities are observed.[249]

4.14 Takeovers

(a) Scope of EU Takeover Law

The takeover laws of the member states are partially harmonized by the EU Takeover Directive.[250] The basic objectives of the Takeover Directive are to promote takeovers, establish equivalent protection throughout the EU for minority shareholders of public companies in the event of a change in control, and ensure the transparency of the takeover procedure.[251] To qualify as a takeover bid in the context of the Takeover Directive, the bid must be a public offer by any other natural or legal person to acquire securities of the target (referred to

---

246. *Id.* at art. 9(1).
247. *Id.* at arts. 4 & 9(4).
248. *Id.* at art. 6.
249. *Id.* at art. 20.
250. Directive 2004/05 of the European Parliament and of the Council of 21 April 2004 on takeover bids, 2004 O.J. (L 142) 12.
251. EU law does not harmonize the law applicable for takeovers of private companies. Moreover, the protections accorded to minority shareholders under the Takeover Directive cannot be applied by analogy to takeovers of private companies. Case C-101/08, Audiolux SA v. Groupe Bruxelles Lambert SA, 2009 E.C.R. I-9864, at ¶64.

as the offeree company) giving that offeror control.[252] The reference to "other" legal person means, for example, that a share buyback program by the target itself cannot constitute a takeover bid in the context of the Takeover Directive. As discussed elsewhere in this chapter, share buybacks are governed by the Market Abuse Directive and the Buy-Back Implementation Regulation.

The Takeover Directive only applies if the bid will result in an acquisition of control. Whether a bid will give the offeror control is an issue for the national law of the member state where the target has its registered office.[253] In Italy, UK, Spain, Belgium, the Netherlands, and Germany, for example, control is defined as the acquisition of 30 percent or more of that company's outstanding voting securities.[254] The situations in which the shares must be aggregated for purposes of determining control are governed by member state law. For example, under Swedish law, the shares held by the offeror's subsidiaries or by a third party on behalf of the offeror are attributed to the offeror.[255] Although there are many similarities between the concept of "control" in the context of takeover law and the same concept used in the context of the Merger Control Regulation discussed in Chapter III, they are not necessarily the same. Consequently, not every change of control falling under the Merger Control Regulation will also fall under the Takeover Directive.

The Takeover Directive only applies to target companies whose securities are traded on a regulated market in the EU.[256] For example, the Takeover Directive would not apply to a takeover bid by a French company attempting to acquire control of a corporation listed only on the New York Stock Exchange. Nor would it apply to the acquisition by an Estonian public company of a Latvian family-held company (regardless of the size of the Latvian company). The notion of an EU-regulated market in this context is defined in Council Directive

---

252. Takeover Directive at art. 2(1)(a).
253. This assumes that the target's shares are also listed on a regulated market in that same member state. If the target's securities are not admitted to trading on a regulated market in the member state in which it has its registered office, the applicable takeover law is that of the member state on the regulated market of which the company's securities are admitted to trading. Takeover Directive at art. 2(b). If the target's securities are admitted to trading in several member states, the applicable law is that of the member state where the target's securities were first admitted to trading on a regulated market. Takeover Directive at art. 2(c). And if the target's securities were first admitted to trading on regulated markets in more than one member state simultaneously, the target may determine which laws apply. In each of these circumstances, of course, the company law of the member state where the company was registered continue to apply to the corporate issues (but not the takeover issues).
254. The nuances of identifying control and the exceptions are matters for national law. In Germany, for example, 30 percent may give a person control if a third party holds a significant percentage of the other shares or it is unlikely that the 30 percent shareholder will have a majority of the votes at the annual meeting (assuming that all the minority shareholders actually participate). Wertpapierübernahmegesetz Article 29.
255. Section 5 of the Swedish Act Concerning Public Takeover Bids.
256. Takeover Directive at art. 1(1). In this respect, the scope of the Takeover Directive is narrower than the scope of the Domestic Mergers Directive which applies to all public limited liability companies and not just listed public companies.

93/22[257] and covers the main stock exchanges in the member states. Not all of the securities of the target have to be listed on an EU-regulated market in order to trigger the application of the Takeover Directive. It is sufficient that some of the securities are listed in the EU.[258] If, for example, a U.S. corporation has shares listed on the New York Stock Exchange and the Cyprus Stock Exchange, a bid for control of the U.S. corporation would fall under the Takeover Directive because some of its shares are listed on a regulated market in the EU.

The takeover offer may be conditional and still fall under the Takeover Directive. For example, the offeror may condition its offer on its acquisition of a certain percentage of shares of the target company. As discussed below, in order to be able to squeeze out minority shareholders, the offeror is often prepared to complete the acquisition only if the requisite percentage level to squeeze out the minority shareholders is exceeded. Another frequent condition used to qualify an offer is that no other party has announced its intention to offer a competing bid. These types of conditional offers fall under the Takeover Directive.

(b) *Financing the Takeover*

The Takeover Directive does not regulate the means by which the acquiring entity can finance the takeover. In fact, the EU company law directives do not comprehensively regulate the financing of transactions. However, the rules on company capital contained in the Second Company Law Directive impose an indirect limitation on financing takeovers by using the target company's cash or shares. Although the Public Company Capitalization Directive allows the member states to permit the use of the target company's cash or shares to finance an acquisition, specific conditions are imposed on such financing mechanisms.[259]

A common example of this transaction is a leveraged buyout. In such cases, the management of the target company has the responsibility of ensuring that the transaction takes place "at fair market conditions." This means that the management body must closely scrutinize the terms and conduct due diligence on the credit standing of the acquiring company. The management body then must present a written report to the shareholders and secure the approval of the general meeting of the shareholders. Although these requirements were introduced to protect the company's shareholders and other creditors, it makes leveraged takeovers more difficult in the EU than in the United States.

(c) *Protection of Minority Shareholders*

In many instances, the offeror may not need or want to acquire 100 percent of the shares of the target. Indeed, the acquisition of 100 percent of the shares is often difficult to achieve. Instead, the offeror may only seek to acquire sufficient number of shares to give it control of the target. Once the offeror has control, the position of the remaining shareholders is typically weakened. If, for example,

---

257. Council Directive 93/22/EEC of 10 May 1993 on investment services in the securities field, 1993 O.J. (L 141) 27.
258. Takeover Directive at art. 1(1).
259. Public Company Capitalization Directive at art. 23. The limitations discussed here apply not only to the acquisition of control, but to any acquisition of shares, including minority investments.

an investor seeks to acquire 80 percent of the issued and outstanding voting shares of a public company, which prior to that time was not controlled by any one shareholder, the influence of the holders of the remaining 20 percent is significantly less than if the company were not controlled by one entity. The 80-percent shareholder can unilaterally determine the direction and future of the company.

The Takeover Directive protects minority shareholders in two ways. First, the Takeover Directive requires the offeror seeking to acquire control to make an offer (referred to as a mandatory bid) for all of the shares of the target (i.e., all classes of shares and not necessarily just the voting shares).[260] The mandatory bid must be addressed at the earliest opportunity (typically four weeks after control has been reached) to all the holders of the target's securities for all their holdings at an equitable price.[261] In general, the equitable price will be the highest price paid for the same securities by the offeror over a period of not less than six months and not more than 12 months before the bid.[262]

Assume, for example, XYZ S.A. acquires 10 percent of ABC OY (listed on the Helsinki Securities and Derivatives Exchange) in January for €2 per share. In July of that same year, XYZ S.A. intends to increase its shareholding by making a bid for an additional 45 percent of the shares of ABC OY. The equitable per share price which XYZ S.A. must offer to the other shareholders as part of the mandatory bid is €2 regardless of the development of the share price since January. If the offeror had purchased additional shares in March of that same year for €1 per share, the equitable price for the mandatory bid still remains €2. If the highest bid in the prescribed period was €2 at the time of the mandatory bid, and XYZ S.A. either purchases a few additional shares (short of control) before the offer closes, or XYZ S.A. purchases securities at a price higher than the offer price, XYZ S.A. would be required to increase its offer in the mandatory bid so that it is not less than the highest price paid for the securities earlier acquired.[263]

The form of consideration used by the offeror in the context of a mandatory bid may be securities, cash, or a combination of both.[264] However, if the consideration offered by the offeror does not consist of liquid securities admitted to trading on a regulated market, the offeror is required to also offer cash as an alternative. In addition, the offeror must offer cash consideration at least as

---

260. Takeover Directive at art. 5.
261. *Id.* art. 5(1).
262. The exact time period is determined by the laws of the member state in which the target has its registered office.
263. *Id.* at art. 5(4). The national supervisory authorities may draw up a list of circumstances in which the highest price may be adjusted either upwards or downwards to account for the situation where the purchase price is not a reliable indicator of the equitable price if, for example, the prior purchase price was affected by exceptional circumstances.
264. *Id.* at art. 5(5). Member states may provide that a cash consideration must be offered, at least as an alternative, in all cases.

an alternative if the offeror has used cash to purchase 5 percent or more of the voting securities of the target.

The second way in which the Takeover Directive protects minority shareholders is by requiring the member states to secure a sell-out right for the minority shareholders in certain circumstances even after the bid has been made.[265] The sell-out right is in addition to the mandatory bid requirement. A minority shareholder can require the offeror to purchase the minority shareholder's shares at a fair price if the offeror holds securities (or has contracted to acquire securities) representing 90 percent or more of the voting shares of the target.[266] The sell-out right expires three months after the expiration period of the initial tender offer made by the offeror. In other words, a shareholder may decline to sell its shares as part of the initial takeover bid and later force the offeror (assuming that the offeror acquired 90 percent of the voting shares) to buy its shares for a fair price.

(d) *Disclosure Requirements*

The takeover bid must be reported to the appropriate supervisory authority and made public "without delay."[267] The precise period of time is determined by member state law. The authority competent to supervise a bid and the authority to which the takeover bid must be reported is the authority of the member state in which the target has its registered office. If the target's securities are not admitted to trading on a regulated market in the same member state as its registered office, the appropriate supervisory authority is that in the member state where the target's securities are admitted to trading. For example, if a German company only has shares listed on an exchange in Ireland, the Irish authority will have the jurisdiction to supervise the bid. If the target's securities are admitted to trading in several member states, the supervisory authority is that of the member state where the target's securities were first admitted to trading on a regulated market.

The offeror must draw up and make public an offer document containing the information necessary to enable the holders of the target's securities "to reach a properly informed decision" on the takeover bid. Before the offer document is made public, the offeror must communicate it to the appropriate supervisory authority.[268] When it is made public, the boards of the offeror and the target must communicate it to their respective employees.

Where the tender offer is subject to the prior approval of the supervisory authority and has been approved, the other member states are required to recognize that offer (subject to any translation requirements). This relieves the offeror of having to seek approval in several member states. The party making the tender offer must provide the supervisory authorities of its member state at any time on request with all the information in its possession that is necessary

---

265. *Id.* at art. 16(1).
266. Member states may set a higher threshold that may not, however, be higher than 95 percent of the voting shares.
267. *Id.* at art. 6(1).
268. *Id.* at art. 6(5).

for the supervisory authority to discharge its functions.[269] The supervisory authorities in other member states may require the inclusion of additional information in the offer document but only if such information (i) is specific to the market of a member state or member states on which the target's securities are admitted to trading, (ii) relates to the formalities to be complied with to accept the bid and (iii) relates to the consideration due at the close of the bid as well as to the tax arrangements relevant to the target's shareholders.

The time allowed for the acceptance of a tender offer by the shareholders of the target may not be less than two weeks nor more than 10 weeks from the date of publication of the offer document.[270] Member states may provide that the period of 10 weeks may be extended on condition that the offeror gives at least two weeks' notice of its intention of closing the bid. Also, a member state may authorize a supervisory authority to grant a derogation from the 10-week period to allow the target to call a general meeting of shareholders to consider the bid.

(e) *Limitations of Defenses to Takeovers*

Takeover offers from third parties are not always welcomed by the directors and managers of a target company. The interests of the directors and managers may diverge from those of the shareholders. In other words, a takeover offer may be welcomed by the shareholders of a company (because they will realize a gain on their investment) while at the same time be disfavored by the directors or managers of that company (because, for example, they might lose their positions as directors). Hence, directors or managers may put defensive mechanisms in place that deter or frustrate takeover offers even if not in the interests of the shareholders. As company law in EU is primarily national law, the permissibility of takeover defenses in the EU is found in national law. However, the Takeover Directive attempts to harmonize the minimum level of protection for shareholders.

According to the board neutrality rule set forth in the Takeover Directive, the board of the target company must remain neutral once it receives the takeover bid. Before taking any action, other than seeking alternative bids, the board is required to secure shareholder approval if the action of the board may result in the frustration of the offer.[271] For example, the board could not adopt a poison pill such as issuing preferred stock that gives the shareholders the right to redeem their shares at a premium after the takeover. For those member states with a two-tiered board structure (a management board and a supervisory board) such as Germany, the neutrality rule applies to both tiers.

---

269. *Id.* at art. 6(5).
270. *Id.* at art. 7(1).
271. *Id.* at art. 9(2). Member states may require that such shareholder authorization be obtained at an earlier stage. For example, a member state may require that the board seek shareholder approval as soon as the board of the target becomes aware that the bid is imminent. At the shareholders' meeting to authorize the board's action, any restrictions on the voting rights of shareholders do not apply. *Id.* at art. 11(3). Moreover, multiple-vote securities carry only one vote each at that shareholders' meeting.

Once it receives the bid, the board of the target must draw up and make public a document setting out its opinion of the bid and the reasons on which it is based. These should include its views on the effects of implementation of the bid on all the company's interests and specifically employment, and on the offeror's strategic plans for the target and the likely repercussions on employment and the locations of the company's places of business as set out in the offer document. If the employee representative of the target issues a separate opinion on the effects of the bid on employment, that opinion must be appended to the document issued by the board.[272]

According to the breakthrough rule, any restrictions on the transfer of securities provided for in the target company's governing documents and any restrictions on the transfer of securities provided for in contractual agreements between the target and its shareholders, or in contractual agreements between the shareholders themselves, do not apply (i.e., are "broken through") vis-à-vis the offeror during the time allowed for acceptance of the bid.[273] If, for example, the articles of association of the target company require the shareholders to offer their securities to the target before they can be sold to a third party, that restriction is suspended during the term of the bid. Some member states, such as Germany, require the offeror in such circumstances where the rights of the shareholders are broken through to compensate those shareholders for the diminution of their rights.[274]

Both the neutrality rule and the breakthrough rule are optional for the member states.[275] In other words, member states are not required to transpose these provisions into national law. If a member state chooses not to adopt the rules, companies that have their registered offices within that member state still have the option of adopting the rules.[276] For example, if a company is listed on a regulated market in Germany (which has not adopted the board neutrality rule), that company can still adopt a rule that prohibits poison pills (even though the prohibition on poison pills is not mandated by the law of that member state).[277] Of course, if the member state does transpose the neutrality rule and the breakthrough rule, companies that have their registered offices within their territories no longer have the option: they must observe them. Whereas the majority of member states have adopted the board neutrality rule, very few have adopted the breakthrough rule.

The optional character of the neutrality and breakthrough rules has prevented the Takeover Directive from establishing a level playing field in the EU for takeovers. Companies often encounter different rules when they embark on a takeover in other member states. This situation is the result of a lack of political consensus among the member states. During the preparation of the Takeover Directive, certain member states were not convinced of the overall benefits to

---

272. *Id.* at art. 9(5).
273. *Id.* at art. 11(2).
274. § 33b(5) WpÜG.
275. Takeover Directive at art. 12(1).
276. *Id.* at art. 12(2).
277. § 33b(2) WpÜG.

shareholders by disarming the board of directors of the traditional tools which they had to thwart takeovers of companies in their jurisdictions.

(f) Post-Bid Squeeze-out Rights

As discussed above, the Takeover Directive protects minority shareholders by providing them with the right to force the offeror to buy its securities at a fair price (sell outright).[278] Of course, it is possible (and likely) that not all shareholders will want to sell their securities as part of the offer. This may result in a situation where the offeror acquires control but still less than 100 percent of the voting securities of the target. This is often an unacceptable result for many offerors. The continued existence of minority shareholders imposes additional administrative costs on companies that they would not have incurred if they acquired 100 percent of the target company's shares. The offeror could, of course, make the offer contingent on the acquisition of 100 percent of the shares. However, as there is a very low likelihood of all shareholders accepting the offer, this option is not practical. In order to avoid deterring public takeovers, the Takeover Directive permits the offeror to force the holders of the remaining securities to sell those securities to the offeror at a fair price (squeeze-out right).[279] The squeeze-out right is triggered if the offeror directly or indirectly holds securities representing 90 percent or more of the voting shares.[280]

The squeeze-out rights related to the takeover exist for a period of three months after the end of the time period set for the acceptance of the bid giving rise to the squeeze-out rights.[281] If, for example, an offeror makes a voluntary bid to acquire the shares of the target and the bid acceptance period terminates on December 31, the offeror—assuming it is able to acquire the requisite percentage of shares for squeeze-out rights under national law—has until March 31 to exercise those squeeze-out rights. Of course, this three-month rule does not preclude the application of national rules which grant squeeze-out rights outside the context of a takeover, such as German law which generally permits squeeze-outs (and not just in the context of a takeover). In most cases, however, the requisite procedures are different.

The price for the securities in the context of a squeeze-out or a sellout must be a fair price. As the fairness of a price is largely a subjective assessment,

---

278. Takeover Directive at art. 16(1).
279. *Id.* at art. 15(1).
280. Member states may set a higher threshold that may not, however, be higher than 95 percent of the capital carrying voting rights and 95 percent of the voting rights. The "indirectly holds" language creates the possibility that the applicable squeeze-out threshold be reached without actually owning the shares outright. The aggregation of shares for purposes of the squeeze-out might occur, for example, on the basis of a share loan agreement (Decision of the German Supreme Court in case no. ZR 302/06 (Mar. 16, 2009) reported in Betriebs-Berater (2009) 1025) or on the basis of irrevocable commitments to buy or sell the shares (Decision of the Oberlandesgericht Frankfurt of Dec. 9, 2008, reported in Betriebs-Berater (2009) 112).
281. Takeover Directive at art. 15(4). In most instances, the offeror will make the offer conditional upon acquisition of the necessary squeeze-out threshold and will announce at the time of its bid that it will exercise its squeeze-out right.

the Takeover Directive provides two presumptions of fairness depending on whether the squeeze-out right arose through a mandatory bid or a voluntary bid. As discussed above, the squeeze-out right arises when the offeror achieves a prescribed percentage of the target's voting shares. If this threshold is achieved as a result of a voluntary bid, the price offered in that voluntary bid is presumptively "fair" for purposes of a subsequent squeeze-out.[282] This presumption is valid for three months following the time allowed for acceptance of the voluntary bid.[283]

The presumption of fairness is slightly different in the context of exercising a squeeze-out right subsequent to a mandatory bid. Once control of a public company is acquired, the acquiring entity must present an offer (i.e., mandatory bid) to all of the other shareholders of the company to acquire their shares for an equitable price.[284] If, as a result of this mandatory bid, the offeror reaches the thresholds giving it squeeze-out rights, the presumptive "fair price" for purposes of the subsequent squeeze-out is the price offered in the mandatory bid (i.e., the equitable price).[285]

As discussed above, the equitable price in the context of a mandatory bid is the highest price paid for the same securities by the offeror over a period to be determined by the member states between six and 12 months prior to the bid. For example, if a wealthy Greek businessman acquires 45 percent of the voting securities of an Austrian *Aktiengesellschaft* publicly listed on the Vienna Stock Exchange, the businessman must make an offer to the other shareholders at a price no lower than the average price quoted for the securities over the preceding six months and no higher than 15 percent of the highest price paid by the offeror for any of the securities in the past 12 months.[286] If, as a result of this mandatory bid, the businessman acquires over 90 percent of the outstanding voting securities of the Austrian *Aktiengesellschaft*, he may exercise his squeeze-out rights, and the "fair price" for purposes of the squeeze-out is the price the businessman offered in the mandatory bid pursuant to Austrian law.

---

282. *Id.* at art. 15(5).
283. *Id.* at art. 15(4).
284. *Id.* at art. 5(1).
285. *Id.* at art. 15(5).
286. § 26 Austrian Übernahmegesetz. The law of the member state where the securities are listed applies (in this case Austria).

CHAPTER **VI**

Securities Law

Similar to European Union (EU) corporate law, EU securities law is still primarily based on EU harmonizing directives with the exception of insider trading and market manipulation. The reliance on directives means—just as with EU corporate law—that EU securities law has two levels: EU and member state. Although the national laws transposing EU directives should conform to the EU directives, there are inevitably differences between the member states. In recognition of the inefficiencies and ineffectiveness of policing insider trading and market manipulation, the EU has introduced a market abuse regulation which is directly applicable in the member states and not dependent on national laws transposing them into the respective member state legal systems.

1. Supervisory Authorities

There is no pan-EU regulatory body analogous to the U.S. Securities and Exchange Commission with jurisdiction over the securities exchanges located in the member states. The enforcement of the securities laws in the EU is left to the respective national supervisory authorities. These supervisory authorities are assisted at the EU level by the European Securities and Markets Authority (ESMA).[1] The ESMA advises the European Commission on securities issues, coordinates the national supervisory authorities, and promotes cooperation with securities regulators in third countries. However, the ESMA does not have any direct enforcement authorities.

2. Regulated Markets

The concept of "regulated market" in EU company and securities law is important because it is often used to delineate the scope of application of the respective laws. For example, the Takeover Directive only applies to target companies whose securities are traded on a regulated market in the EU.[2] Each member state is required to identify the regulated markets within its domestic jurisdiction

---

1. Regulation (EU) No. 1095/2010 of the European Parliament and of the Council of 24 November 2010 establishing a European Supervisory Authority (European Securities and Markets Authority), 2010 O.J. (L 331) 84. The ESMA is the successor to the Committee of European Securities Regulators.
2. Takeover Directive at art. 1(1).

and provide that list to the other member states and the Commission. The basic requirement to become a regulated market is that the competent authority of the home member state is satisfied that the particular market complies with the requirements set forth in the applicable directives and regulations. In practice, the concept of regulated market includes the main stock exchanges in the member states.[3] Although these are clearly the main stock exchanges active in the EU, the concept of regulated market does not include all of the European stock exchanges. For example, the Professional Securities Market (UK), Latibex (Spain), First North (Denmark), and the Alternative Investment Market (UK) are not considered regulated markets for purposes of EU securities law. This means that many of the requirements imposed on companies issuing shares on regulated markets do not apply to companies that are listed only on such nonregulated markets.

The lists of regulated markets drawn up by the member states and provided to the other member states and the Commission are not exhaustive. A market may be considered a regulated market even though it is not listed. In *In re Rareş Doralin Nilaş*, for example, one of the issues was whether the Romanian Rasdaq market was a regulated market for purposes of EU securities law even though it was not included on the list of regulated markets identified by Romania.[4] According to the European Court of Justice (ECJ), "the sole fact that it is not included on that list is not sufficient to exclude the market in question from being a regulated market."[5]

3. Obligation to Publish a Prospectus

The Prospectus Directive[6] imposes a requirement on the member states to require all issuers of securities to the public within the EU or in connection with the admission of securities to trading on a European regulated market to publish a prospectus, unless one of the enumerated exemptions[7] or one of the judicially created exceptions[8] applies. Each member state is required to identify a central competent authority with responsibility for receiving and reviewing prospectuses

---

3. The list of regulated markets in the EU is also available on the website of the ESMA. http://mifiddatabase.esma.europa.eu/Index.aspx?sectionlinks_id=23&language=0&pageName=REGULATED_MARKETS_Display&subsection_id=0.
4. Case C-248/11, *In re* Rareş Doralin Nilaş, 2012 E.C.R. I-___ (reported in the electronic reports of cases ECLI:EU:C:2012:166).
5. *Id.* at ¶54.
6. Directive 2003/71/EC of the European Parliament and of the Council of 4 November 2003 on the prospectus to be published when securities are offered to the public or admitted to trading and amending Directive 2001/34/EC, 2003 O.J. (L 345) 64 at art. 3 [hereinafter Prospectus Directive].
7. *Id.* at art. 3(1) and (3).
8. The ECJ has held, for example, that the Prospectus Directive does not apply to the sale of securities in the context of foreclosure proceedings. Case C-441/12, Almer Beheer BV v. Van den Dungen Vastgoed BV, 2014 E.C.R. I-___ .

and ensuring compliance with the national laws implementing the Prospectus Directive.[9] EU law also applies to the format and content of the prospectus.[10]

3.1 Definition and Types of Securities

The obligation to publish a prospectus only applies to public offerings and regulated market registrations of securities. The term "securities" means shares in companies, bonds, and other forms of securitized debt which are negotiable on a capital market and any other securities either giving the right to acquire any such transferable securities by subscription or exchange or giving rise to a cash settlement.[11] The transferability requirement means, for example, that the issuance of nonnegotiable promissory notes would not fall under the Prospectus Directive. The ESMA has also taken the position that nontransferable stock options offered as part of an employee stock option plan do not meet the transferability requirement and therefore do not fall under the Prospectus Directive.

To qualify as a security for purposes of the Prospectus Directive, the instrument must have a maturity of less than 12 months.[12] If, for example, securitized debt does not mature for over a year, it is not considered a security for purposes of the Prospectus Directive. Money market instruments are expressly excluded from the definition of securities.[13]

There are generally two types of securities: equity securities and nonequity securities. As discussed below, the distinction is important for the application of some of the exemptions and determining the home member state. As the term implies, "equity securities" includes shares and other transferable securities equivalent to shares in companies. It also includes any other type of transferable securities giving the right to acquire shares and other transferable securities equivalent to shares in companies as a consequence of their being converted or the rights conferred by their being exercised.[14]

Securities that do not qualify as equity securities are considered nonequity securities. Two common examples of securities treated as nonequity securities are debt instruments and depositary receipts. It is uncertain whether convertible debt (i.e., debt that can be converted into equity upon a particular event) qualifies as equity or nonequity. A strict wording of the definition of equitable securities codified in Section 2(1)(b) of the Prospectus Directive suggests that convertible debt is to be treated as a type of equity security because it gives the holder the right to acquire shares in a company. According to paragraph 12 of

---

9. Prospectus Directive at art. 21(1).
10. Commission Delegated Regulation (EU) No. 486/2012 of 30 March 2012 as regards the format and content of the prospectus, 2012 O.J. (L 150) 1.
11. The Prospectus Directive relies on the definition of securities codified in Article 1(4) of Council Directive 93/22/EEC of 10 May 1993 on investment services in the securities field, 1993 O.J. (L 141) 27.
12. Prospectus Directive at art. 2(1)(a).
13. *Id.* at art. 2(1)(a).
14. *Id.* at art. 2(1)(b).

the Preamble to the Prospectus Directive, however, "securities convertible at the option of the investor fall within the definition of non-equity securities." This inconsistency suggests that a further distinction needs to be made between debt which is automatically convertible (qualifying as an equity security) and convertible debt which is convertible at the option of the holder (qualifying as a nonequity security). However, the apparent contradiction could just as easily be attributed to poor drafting of the Prospectus Directive.

There are certain instruments which may qualify as securities under the abstract definition discussed above, but which are expressly precluded from the scope of the Prospectus Directive.[15] These include the following instruments:

- securities issued by nonprofit associations or by a member state or by one of a member state's regional or local authorities, by public international bodies of which one or more member states are members, by the European Central Bank, or by the central banks of the member states;
- securities guaranteed by a member state or by one of a member state's regional or local authorities;
- nonfungible shares of capital whose main purpose is to provide the holder with a right to occupy an apartment, or other form of immovable property or a part thereof and where the shares cannot be sold without this right being relinquished;
- securities included in an offer where the total consideration of the offer is less than €2,500,000 in the aggregate in the European Economic Area in a period of 12 months;
- certain nonequity securities issued in a continuous or repeated manner by credit institutions;
- nonequity securities issued in a continuous or repeated manner by credit institutions where the total consideration of the offer is less than €50,000,000 (calculated over a period of 12 months), provided that these securities are not subordinated, convertible, or exchangeable, do not give a right to subscribe to or acquire other types of securities, and are not linked to a derivative instrument.

3.2 Admission for Trading on a Regulated Market and Public Offers

Publishing a prospectus is necessary under EU law in two situations. The first situation is when the securities are to be admitted to trading on a regulated market.[16] The concept of "regulated market" includes the main stock exchanges in the member states as discussed above. If the securities are to be listed on a market not designated on this list—such as the UK Alternative Investment

---

15. *Id.* at art. 1(2).
16. *Id.* at art. 3(3).

Market—no prospectus needs to be prepared unless required by the rules of that exchange or the offering qualifies as a nonexempt public offering discussed below.

The second situation in which a prospectus is required is for public offerings (regardless of whether offered on a regulated market).[17] The concept of "offer to the public" is defined broadly. It means a communication to persons in any form and by any means, presenting sufficient information on the terms of the offer and the securities to be offered, so as to enable an investor to decide to purchase or subscribe to these securities.[18] According to the ESMA, it would not include the publication of the company's share price on its website unless this was combined with other factors constituting a solicitation.[19] Free offers (e.g., options granted to employees for no consideration) would not be considered to be a public offering.[20] Even the subsequent exercise of the option does not constitute a public offer according to the ESMA as "it is just the execution of a previous offer."[21]

An offer may be limited to the public in one member state. The issuer then only has to publish a prospectus in that member state. Nonetheless, this would not preclude residents from other member states from participating in the public offer. The fact that residents from other member states subscribe to the securities does not mean that the offeror has to publish a prospectus in that other member state.[22]

3.3 Non-EU Issuers

The location of the issuer does not determine the applicability of the obligation to publish a prospectus. As indicated above, the obligation to publish a prospectus arises in two circumstances: registration on a regulated market and public offerings. The applicability of the obligation to non-EU issuers is relatively clear in the case of a registration on a regulated market: if the regulated market is in the EU, the obligation applies regardless of the location of the issuer. Similarly, the location of the issuer is irrelevant in the case of a public offering of securities. As the purpose of the law is to protect investors, the decisive criterion is the location of the public to which the securities are issued. For example, if a corporation incorporated under the laws of Delaware (U.S.) wants to issue securities in the EU, it will have to publish a prospectus in accordance

---

17. *Id.* at art. 3(1).
18. *Id.* at art. 2(1)(d).
19. Committee of European Securities Regulators, FAQs 9th version (September 2009).
20. ESMA, Questions and Answers - Prospectuses (21st updated version Jan. 14, 2014) (ESMA/2014/35) at 12 *available at* http://www.esma.europa.eu/system/files/2014-esma-35_21st_version_qa_document_prospectus_related_issues.pdf.
21. Committee of European Securities Regulators, Common Positions Agreed by CESR Members, February 2007, CESR/07-110, at 6 *available at* http://www.esma.europa.eu/system/files/07_110.pdf.
22. ESMA, Questions and Answers - Prospectuses (21st version Jan. 14, 2014) (ESMA/2014/35) *available at* http://www.esma.europa.eu/system/files/2014-esma-35_21st_version_qa_document_prospectus_related_issues.pdf.

with EU law and the law of the home EU member state (assuming that the offering falls within the scope of the Prospectus Directive and no exemptions apply). For such non-EU issuers, the "home member state" is either the EU member state where the securities are intended to be offered for the first time or the member state where the first application for trading on a regulated market is made.[23] The issuer or the person seeking admission has the discretion to choose between these two options.

3.4 Exemptions

The concepts of "offer to the public" and "securities" are so broad that they threaten to burden even the most insignificant transactions with the costs of publishing a prospectus. For that reason, the Prospectus Directive requires the member states to adopt exceptions from the obligation to publish a prospectus in the context of a public offering as well as a registration with a regulated market.[24] Although many of the exemptions applicable to public offerings and registrations with a regulated market are similar, an exemption from the obligation to publish a prospectus in the context of a public offering does not necessarily relieve the issuer from the obligation to publish a prospectus if that issuer seeks admission to trading on a regulated market in the EU.[25]

(a) Exemptions for Public Offerings

(1) Qualified Investors Exemption

Public offerings of securities addressed solely to "qualified investors" are exempt from the obligation to publish a prospectus.[26] A natural person is a qualified investor if he or she requests classification as a qualified investor and meets at least two of the following criteria:

- The person has carried out transactions of a significant size on securities markets at an average frequency of at least 10 per calendar quarter over the previous four calendar quarters;

---

23. Prospectus Directive at art. 2(1)(m)(iii).
24. Issuers who benefit from one of the exemptions from publishing a prospectus are not necessarily precluded from issuing information and naming it a prospectus. The ESMA recommends, however, that the nonrequired prospectus include a statement that it has not been approved under the Prospectus Directive. Otherwise, there is the risk that such information will be considered misleading. Frequently asked questions regarding Prospectuses: Common positions agreed by CESR Members (Nov. 23, 2010) (CESR/10-1337) at FAQ 49, *available at* http://www.esma.europa.eu/system/files/10_1337.pdf.
25. Frequently asked questions regarding Prospectuses: Common positions agreed by CESR Members (Nov. 23, 2010) (CESR/10-1337) at FAQ 44, *available at* http://www.esma.europa.eu/system/files/10_1337.pdf.
26. Prospectus Directive at art. 3(2)(a). The term "qualified investor" in the Prospectus Directive differs from the scope of "professional clients" and "eligible counterparties" used in the Financial Instruments Directive (Directive 2004/39/EC of the European Parliament and of the Council of 21 April 2004 on markets in financial instruments amending Council Directives 85/611/EEC and 93/6/EEC and Directive 2000/12/EC of the European Parliament and of the Council and repealing Council Directive 93/22/EEC, 2004 O.J. (L 145) 1.

- The person's securities portfolio exceeds €500,000;
- The person works or has worked for at least one year in the financial sector in a professional position which requires knowledge of securities investment.

A legal entity will be considered a qualified investor if it exceeds at least two of the following three thresholds: (i) more than 250 employees on an average during the last financial year, (ii) a total balance sheet greater than €43,000,000 or (iii) annual net sales in the last fiscal year of more than €50,000,000.[27] Of course, the term qualified investors also includes legal entities that are authorized or regulated to operate in the financial markets, such as credit institutions, investment firms, other authorized or regulated financial institutions, insurance companies, collective investment schemes, pension funds, and commodity dealers, as well as entities whose corporate purpose is solely to invest in securities.[28]

As indicated above, offers of securities addressed solely to qualified investors do not need to be accompanied by a prospectus. The "solely" requirement means that if just one of the targeted investors is not a qualified investor, this exemption will not apply. For example, if the securities are being offered to 100 investors, and just one of them fails to qualify as a qualified investor, the exemption does not apply regardless of whether that one nonqualified investor actually purchases any of the offered securities.

(2) Small Offerings

The Prospectus Directive does not require the issuer to publish a prospectus in the event of a public offering if it qualifies as a "small offering." There are four different types of small offerings:[29]

- an offer of securities addressed to fewer than 150 natural or legal persons (excluding qualified investors) per member state;
- an offer of securities addressed to investors who each acquire securities for a total consideration of at least €100,000 for each separate offer;
- an offer of securities with a per unit denomination of €100,000 or higher;
- an offer of securities with a total consideration of less than €100,000 (calculated over a period of 12 months).

(3) Share Substitutions

If the shares offered in the public offering are issued in substitution for shares of the same class already issued, the offer is exempt from the requirements of

---

27. Prospectus Directive at art. 2(1)(e)(iii). A legal entity not exceeding two of these three thresholds is considered a "small and medium sized company." Such small and medium sized companies can also be considered qualified investors but they have to make a formal registration with and be recognized as qualified investors by the member state where they have their registered office.
28. *Id.* at art. 2(1)(e)(i).
29. *Id.* at art. 3(2)(b).

publishing a prospectus, provided that the issuing of such new shares does not involve any increase in the issued capital.[30]

(4) Mergers, Divisions, and Takeovers

Public offers of securities offered in connection with a takeover by means of an exchange offer or in connection with a merger or division are exempt from the Prospectus Directive as long as a document is available containing information that is regarded by the competent authority as being equivalent to that of the prospectus.[31]

(5) Share Dividends

A dividend to existing shareholders of shares of the same class as the shares in respect of which such dividends are paid does not require a prospectus if a document is made available containing information on the number and nature of the shares and the reasons for and details of the offer.[32]

(6) Employee Share Plans

If a company already has securities admitted to trading on a regulated market in the EU, it (or an affiliate) may offer securities to employees without needing to prepare a prospectus if either the company has its head office in the EU or the company is established outside the EU but has securities admitted to trading either on a regulated market in the EU or on a third country market which has been deemed equivalent by the Commission.[33] This exception is based on the recognition that employees will generally not require the same information as outside investors. Although the Prospectus Directive alleviates the requirement of publishing a prospectus, the issuer must still make a document available containing information on the number and nature of the securities and the reasons for and details of the offer.[34]

(b) Exemptions for Offerings on a Regulated Market

The general rule is that a prospectus must accompany the registration of securities on a regulated market in the EU. As mentioned above, however, there are exemptions which are unique to offerings of securities on a regulated market.

(1) Secondary Registrations

The subsequent registration of additional shares of the same class is generally exempt from the necessity of publishing another prospectus. These secondary registrations are, however, subject to certain limitations. If the shares are to be offered on the same regulated market where they are already admitted, the shares covered by the secondary offering or offerings in the last 12 months

---

30. *Id.* at art. 4(1)(a).
31. *Id.* at art. 4(1)(b) & (c).
32. *Id.* at art. 4(1)(d).
33. *Id.* at art. 4(1)(e). The equivalency concept is discussed below in this Chapter. If the company is established in the EU but has securities listed on a third country market, "adequate information" must be made available in a language customary in international finance (such as English). *Id.* at art. 4(1)(e).
34. *Id.* at art. 4(1)(e).

must be less than 10 percent of the number of shares of the same class already admitted to trading on that regulated market.[35] For example, if an issuer has already registered 100,000 shares on the Warsaw Stock Exchange, and then it wants to register additional shares of the same class, it does not have to publish a prospectus if the number of additional shares is less than 10,000.

(2) Prior Registrations

If the securities are already registered on a regulated market in the EU, and the issuer wants to register those same securities on a regulated market in another member state, the issuer does not have to publish another prospectus if the following conditions are met:[36]

- the securities (or securities of the same class) must have already been admitted to trading on the other regulated market for more than 18 months;
- the admission to trading on the other regulated market must have been accompanied by an approved prospectus made available to the public pursuant to applicable law;
- the issuer is in compliance with the requirements for trading on that other regulated market; and
- the issuer makes a summary document available to the public in a language accepted by the competent authority of the member state of the regulated market where admission is sought.[37]

(3) Securities Offered for No Consideration

The registration of securities being offered free of charge to existing shareholders does not have to be accompanied by a prospectus as long as a document is made available containing information on the number and nature of the shares and the reasons for and details of the offer.[38]

(4) Share Substitutions

If a company wants to issue shares in substitution for shares of the same class which it has already admitted to trading, it does not have to prepare a prospectus if the substitution is taking place on the same regulated market and if it does not involve any increase in the issued capital.[39] There are two basic requirements for this exception. First, the shares must be the same class as the shares already

---

35. *Id.* at art. 4(2)(a). In calculating whether this percentage threshold is met, the ESMA has clarified that shares admitted without a prospectus based on another exemption are not to be included. Frequently asked questions regarding Prospectuses: Common positions agreed by CESR Members (Nov. 23, 2010) (CESR/10-1337) at FAQ 31, *available at* http://www.esma.europa.eu/system/files/10_1337.pdf.
36. Prospectus Directive at art. 4(2)(h).
37. The publication must be made in the manner set out in Article 14(2) of the Prospectus Directive and the contents of the summary document must comply with Article 5(2) of the Prospectus Directive.
38. *Id.* at art. 4(2)(e).
39. *Id.* at art. 4(2)(b).

admitted to trading on the same regulated market. Second, a document must be available containing information on the number and nature of the shares and the reasons for and details of the offer.

(5) Mergers, Divisions, and Takeovers

Another context in which an issuer is relieved of the obligation to prepare a prospectus in connection with a registration on a regulated market in the EU exists when the securities are being offered in connection with a merger or a division.[40] Similarly, if the securities being registered are offered in connection with a takeover by means of an exchange offer, the issuer does not need to publish a prospectus.[41] In each of these cases (merger, division, or takeover), however, the issuer must make a document available containing information which is regarded by the competent authority as being equivalent to that of the prospectus required by the Prospectus Directive.

(6) Share Exchange or Conversion

The obligation to publish a prospectus does not apply to the admission to trading of shares on a regulated market if the shares are resulting from a conversion or exchange of securities which are of the same class as the shares already admitted to trading on the same regulated market.[42]

(7) Share Dividends

Similar to the exemption from public offerings, a prospectus is not necessary in the context of the admission to trading on a regulated market if the shares are being issued as dividends and they are of the same class as shares that have already been admitted to trading on the same regulated market.[43]

(8) Employee Share Plans

There is also an exception specifically for employee share plans in the context of the registration of shares on a regulated market. The obligation to publish a prospectus does not apply for securities offered, allotted, or to be allotted to existing or former directors or employees by their employer or an affiliated undertaking.[44] Similar to the other exceptions, the shares must be of the same class as the securities already admitted to trading on the same regulated market and a document must be available containing information on the number and nature of the securities and the reasons for and detail of the offer.

3.5 Approval and Publication of a Prospectus

If a public offering or registration with a regulated market does not qualify for an exemption, the issuer must publish a prospectus. The prospectus must be approved prior to its publication by the competent authority of the home member

---

40. *Id.* at art. 4(2)(d).
41. *Id.* at art. 4(2)(c).
42. *Id.* at art. 4(2)(g).
43. *Id.* at art. 4(2)(e).
44. *Id.* at art. 4(2)(f).

state.[45] The format and minimum information requirements of the prospectus are prescribed by the Prospectus Directive in broad terms and by Commission Regulation 809/2004 in more specific terms.[46] The procedure for registration and the acceptable languages are prescribed by national law.[47] The publication must occur at a reasonable time in advance of the public offer or admission to trading.[48] Although there are several means of meeting the publication requirement, the most common is by making the prospectus available on the issuer's website and the website of the financial intermediaries placing or selling the securities.[49] Prior to publication, however, the prospectus must be approved by the competent authority of the home member state.[50]

Although monitoring compliance with the prospectus requirements is relatively straightforward in cases where registration to a regulated market is sought (because registration is not permitted if the prospectus requirements are not completed), issuers in the EU also have an obligation to issue a prospectus in public offerings even if they are not a listed company. The supervising authorities in the member states rely on a number of monitoring devices such as media reports, whistle-blowing, complaints, and web spidering in order to identify issues of securities not accompanied by a required prospectus.

3.6 Home Member State and Host Member State

The notion of home member state is a critical element in the application of the Prospectus Directive. One of the fundamental objectives of the Prospectus Directive is to alleviate the burdens associated with drafting and publishing multiple prospectuses in the various member states where investors are being solicited. In order to fulfill this objective, the Directive codifies the rule that a prospectus approved by the home member state will serve as a "passport" for an offer to the public or admission to trading on a regulated market in any

---

45. *Id.* at art. 13(1). Each member state is required to identify a central authority competent for receiving and reviewing prospectuses. *Id.* at art. 21(1). The host member state is not allowed to intervene in the publication process in the home member state. ESMA, Questions and Answers—Prospectuses (21st updated version) Jan. 14, 2014) (ESMA/2014/35) at 10 *available at* http://www.esma.europa.eu/system/files/2014-esma-35_21st_version_qa_document_prospectus_related_issues.pdf.
46. Commission Regulation (EC) 809/2004 of 29 April 2004 implementing Directive 2003/71/EC of the European Parliament and of the Council as regards information contained in prospectuses as well as the format, incorporation by reference and publication of such prospectuses and dissemination of advertisements, 2004 O.J. (L 149) 1.
47. The ESMA publishes a summary list of the languages each member state accepts when acting as the home competent authority.
48. Prospectus Directive art. 14(1).
49. *Id.* at art. 14(2). According to the ECJ, the company cannot impose a fee for downloading or ordering the prospectus off the website or impose any other conditions such as agreeing to a disclaimer or registering more information with the company than is necessary to send the prospectus. Case C-359/12, Timmel v. Aviso Zeta AG, 2014 E.C.R. I-____, ____¶51.
50. Prospectus Directive at art. 13(1).

of the other member states.[51] The issuer merely needs to submit a notification with the competent authority of each host member state. This rule makes the determining the home member state a significant legal and practical issue.

(a) Home Member State for EU Issuers

For EU issuers of equity securities, the rule is that home member state is the member state where the issuer has its registered office.[52] Determining the home member state for nonequity securities of EU issuers is slightly more complicated. If the per unit denomination of the nonequity securities is less than €1000, the home member state is the member state where the issuer of the nonequity securities has its registered office.[53] If, however, the per unit denomination amounts to €1000 or more, the issuer of the nonequity securities can choose between (i) the member state where the issuer has its registered office, (ii) the member state where the nonequity securities were or are to be admitted to trading on a regulated market or (iii) where the securities are offered to the public. The EU issuer has the same three choices of home member state if the issuance is of nonequity securities giving the right to acquire any transferable securities or to receive a cash amount, as a consequence of their being converted or the rights conferred by their being exercised, provided that the issuer of the nonequity securities is not the issuer of the underlying securities or an entity belonging to the same group.

(b) Home Member State for Non-EU Issuers

It is possible that securities of an issuer established outside the EU be sold in the EU. The rules applicable to determining the home member state in such cases are slightly different than for EU issuers. If the securities of the non-EU issuer are offered to the public outside of a regulated market in the EU, the home member state is the member state where the securities are intended to be offered to the public for the first time. If the public offer by the non-EU issuer is to take place in conjunction with a registration on a regulated market in the EU, the issuer can chose the home member state: it is either the member state where the securities are intended to be offered to the public for the first time or the member state where the first application for admission to trading on a regulated market is made.[54] This is often the same member state.

If, for example, a corporation organized under the laws of the U.S. state of Delaware intends to make an initial public offering in the EU on the Frankfurt Stock Exchange, the home member state is Germany. If, however, the issuer is registering the shares on the Frankfurt Stock Exchange but offering the shares to the public in France, the issuer may choose between Germany and France as the home member state.

---

51. *Id.* at art. 17(1).
52. *Id.* at art. 2(1)(m)(i).
53. *Id.* at art. 2(1)(m)(iii).
54. *Id.* at art. 2(1)(m)(iii). The Commission has issued a guidance paper for issuers from outside the EU. http://ec.europa.eu/internal_market/securities/docs/prospectus/art-30-1_en.pdf.

Once the home member state for the non-EU issuer is selected, that member state remains the home member state for reporting requirements. Even if the non-EU issuer delists in the initial home member state, and registers in another member state, the member state that first qualified as the home member state remains the home member state.[55]

(c) Host Member State

The term "host member state" refers to the other member states where an offer to the public is made or admission to trading is sought outside the home member state.[56] If, for example, an Italian issuer with Italy being its home member state registers to have its shares traded on the Frankfurt and London stock exchanges, Germany and the UK would be host member states. The same rule applies to non-EU issuers. If, for example, a Delaware corporation with its home member state in the UK wants to list its shares on the Stockholm and Helsinki stock exchanges, Sweden and Finland would be host member states.

(d) Implications of Identifying the Home Member State

A prospectus cannot be distributed until it has been approved by the competent authority of the home member state. The determination of the home member state, therefore, will determine which regulatory authorities the issuer must deal with. Once the issuer has complied with the requirements imposed by the home member state, the approved prospectus serves as a passport for all of the other member states. The competent authorities of host member states are precluded from taking any approval or administrative procedures relating to prospectuses once approved by the home member state. To certify that the prospectus has been prepared in conformity with the Prospectus Directive, the issuer can request the competent authority of the home member state to send a certificate of approval to any host member states.

Because of the costs involved in translations, and in view of the fact that the EU is made up of territories with a multiplicity of languages, the required language of the prospectus is often an important practical consideration. If the admission to trading on a regulated market or public offer is to occur in only the home member state, the required language of the prospectus is determined by the law of that member state.[57] If, however, the admission to trading or offer is made in the home member state *and* one or more other member states, the prospectus must not only be prepared in a language accepted by the home member state, but also either (at the choice of the issuer) in a language accepted by each host member state or a language "customary in the sphere of international

---

55. Committee of European Securities Regulators, Frequently Asked Questions, 2nd Version October 2009, CESR/09-965.
56. Prospectus Directive at art. 2(1)(n).
57. *Id.* at art. 19(1). Special rules apply for admission to trading of nonequity securities. If the admission to trading involves nonequity securities with a per unit denominated value of €100,000 or more, the prospectus must be drawn up either (at the choice of the issuer) in a language accepted by the home and host member states or in a language customary in the sphere of international finance. *Id.* at art. 19(4).

finance" (e.g., English).[58] If the admission to trading or offer is only made in one or more member states outside the home member state (i.e., host member states) and not in the home member state, the prospectus must be prepared (at the choice of the issuer) in either a language accepted by the competent authorities of those member states or a language customary in the sphere of international finance.[59] In such circumstances, however, the competent authority of each host member state may require that a summary of the prospectus be translated into the official language or languages of that host member state.[60]

3.7 Precautionary Measures to Protect Investors

One potentially important limitation to the principle of mandatory recognition is that the competent authority of the host member state may take precautionary measures to protect investors. If the competent authority of the host member state considers that irregularities have been committed by the issuer or by the financial institutions in charge of the offer, that competent authority is first required to refer these findings to the competent authority of the home member state.[61] If, despite the measures taken by the competent authority of the home member state or because such measures prove inadequate, the issuer or the financial institution in charge of the public offer persists in breaching the relevant legal or regulatory provisions, the competent authority of the host member state, after informing the competent authority of the home member state, is required to take all appropriate measures to protect investors.[62] It is up to that member state to determine which measures are appropriate in the circumstances.

3.8 Third Country Prospectuses and Equivalency

The fact that an issuer has published a prospectus for a public offering or admission to trading outside the EU does not obviate the need for that issuer to publish a prospectus in accordance with the Prospectus Directive if it intends a public offering or admission to trading in the EU. However, an issuer with its registered office outside the EU may apply to its home member state to approve a prospectus which was prepared in conformity with the laws of that third country without having to prepare an entirely new prospectus for the EU.

---

58. *Id.* at art. 19(3). If the issuer decides to file the prospectus in the host member state or member states in a language customary in international finance which is not the official language of that member state, the host member state may only require that the summary be translated into its official language. According to the ESMA, the quality of the translation is the responsibility of the issuer. ESMA, Questions and Answers - Prospectus (21st version Jan. 14, 2014) (ESMA/2014/35) at 29. If the host competent authority has a concern with the translation, it can express those concerns through a special precautionary measure discussed below.
59. *Id.* at art. at art 19(2).
60. *Id.* at art. 19(2).
61. *Id.* at art. 23(1).
62. *Id.* at art. 23(2).

There are two minimum requirements for such approval by the home member state.[63] First, the third country prospectus must have been drawn up in accordance with international standards such as those adopted by the International Organization of Securities Commissions.[64] Second, the information requirements of the law of the third country must be equivalent to the requirements of the Prospectus Directive. Although the Commission has the authority to adopt general equivalency standards,[65] the ultimate decision of whether a particular country has met the equivalency standard is left to the member states.[66] As the recognition granted by that member state is not binding on the other member states, a third country issuer would potentially have to apply for recognition in each EU member state in which it intended to issue securities. One way for a third country issuer to avoid this burden is to register an EU prospectus with the home member state and then take advantage of the principle of mandatory recognition.

3.9 Enforcement and Liability

There is no pan-EU authority that monitors the application of the Prospectus Directive. This task is left to the supervisory authorities of the member states. Although the ESMA is active at a pan-European level, it does not have enforcement authority and its recommendations are nonbinding. In some of the member states, it is possible to ask for an interpretation or nonbinding advice in a given case. Other member states, such as the UK and Sweden, rely on a risk-based approach, leaving it up to the issuers and their advisors to determine the applicability of the exemptions.

Responsibility for the information given in a prospectus attaches at least to the issuer or its administrative, management, or supervisory bodies, the offeror, the person asking for the admission to trading on a regulated market, or the guarantor.[67] Most of the member states have expanded the scope of responsible persons beyond the groups of persons set forth in the Prospectus Directive. For example, France and Austria hold the company's auditors responsible. The persons responsible must be clearly identified in the prospectus by their names and functions or, in the case of legal persons, their names and registered offices. The prospectus must also contain a declaration that the information contained in the prospectus is accurate and that the prospectus makes no material omission. The type and severity of the sanctions imposed on the responsible persons is an

---

63. *Id.* at art. 20(1).
64. http://www.iosco.org/.
65. Prospectus Directive at art. 20(3).
66. The ESMA has issued a nonbinding framework setting forth the information that third country prospectuses should include in their "wrap." The term wrap in this context refers to the supplementary documentation to be submitted along with the third country prospectus to EU investors. ESMA, Framework for third country prospectuses under Article 20 of the Prospectus Directive, ESMA/2011/36 (Mar. 23, 2011) *available at* http://www.esma.europa.eu/system/files/11_36.pdf.
67. Prospectus Directive at art. 6(1).

issue for national law. The Prospectus Directive (merely) sets forth the minimum requirement that the sanctions are "effective, proportionate and dissuasive."[68]

4. Maintaining Market Transparency: Reporting Obligations

The sustained success of capital markets depends on public confidence in those markets. If the public does not have confidence in the fairness and transparency of the markets, it will be reluctant to invest its money in securities offered on those markets. The consequence is that firms will have a more difficult time using the regulated capital markets to raise capital. Access to information helps secure transparency and fairness. In recognition of this, EU law imposes regular disclosure requirements on issuers listed on regulated markets in the EU.[69] These reporting obligations are in addition to the reporting and disclosure obligations generally imposed on companies under company law as discussed. The general reporting obligations discussed in Chapter V apply regardless of whether the company is listed on a regulated market.

4.1 Periodic Reporting Requirements

The Transparency Directive requires issuers admitted to trading on a regulated market in the EU to publish semi-annual financial reports and an annual financial report.[70] Annual reports must be filed within four months after the end of the issuer's fiscal year. The semi-annual reports must be issued within three months after the end of the relevant six-month period. The annual reports must contain the audited financial statements, the management report, and a statement of a company representative that the financial statements are prepared in accordance with the applicable accepted accounting standards, give a fair and accurate representation of the issuer and its business, and a description of the principal risks and uncertainties facing the issuer.[71]

---

68. *Id.* at art. 25(1).
69. Directive 2004/109/EC of the European Parliament and of the Council of 15 December 2004 on the harmonization of transparency requirements in relation to information about issuers whose securities are admitted to trading on a regulated market and amending Directive 2001/34/EC, 2004 O.J. (L 390) 38 *as most recently amended by* Directive 2013/50, O.J. 2013 (L 294) 13 [hereinafter Transparency Directive] and Commission Directive 2007/14/EC of 8 March 2007 laying down detailed rules for the implementation of certain provisions of Directive 2004/109/EC on the harmonisation of transparency requirements in relation to information about issuers whose securities are admitted to trading on a regulated market, 2007 O.J. (L 69) 27 *as most recently amended by* Directive 2013/50/EU of the European Parliament and of the Council of 22 October 2013, 2013 O.J. (L 294) 13 [hereinafter Transparency Implementing Directive].
70. Transparency Directive at art. 4 & 5.
71. *Id.* at art. 4(2). The accounting used to compile the financial disclosure position of the annual reports is governed by the Fourth Council Directive of 25 July 1978 based on Article 54(3)(g) of the Treaty on the annual accounts of certain types of companies, 1978 O.J. (L 222) 11.

The semi-annual reports must similarly contain a condensed set of financial statements (not necessarily audited), an interim management report covering the first six months of the fiscal year, and a statement of a company representative.[72] They may contain additional information not specifically required by law (such as the CEO's statement and news regarding the issuer) provided that such additional information is not misleading.[73] The annual and semi-annual reports must be filed with the competent authority of the host member state and that of the home member state (assuming that they are different) and made publicly available (usually by posting them on the issuer's website). The filing formalities are prescribed by national laws of the home and host member states.

EU law no longer requires issuers to publish interim management statements. Abolishing the requirement to publish interim financial reports in addition to the annual and semi-annual reports was meant to relieve small and mid-sized businesses of burdensome and costly compliance costs. However, the home member state may require the issuer to publish financial information in addition to the annual and semi-annual reports provided that the requirement imposed by the member state does not constitute a "financial burden" on the issuer and the content of the financial information is proportionate to the factors that contribute to the investment decision of the investors.[74]

4.2 Changes in Major Shareholdings

Major shareholders are required to notify the issuer when they acquire shares in that issuer which puts them above certain thresholds. In addition, once a shareholder holds above 5 percent of the outstanding voting shares of an issuer, that shareholder is required to inform the issuer when he or she disposes of shares causing him or her to fall below a certain threshold. The thresholds for both (acquisition and disposition) are 5%, 10%, 15%, 20%, 25%, 30%, 50%, and 75% of the outstanding voting shares.[75] For example, if a shareholder holding 18 percent of an issuer's outstanding voting shares plans to acquire an additional 3 percent of the issuer's shares, that acquirer must notify the competent authority of the home member state because the additional 3 percent will put that shareholder over the 20 percent threshold. The notification to the issuer must occur within four business days.[76] The issuer then has up to three days to disclose the major shareholding to the public (although some member states have imposed shorter time periods).[77]

The purpose of the notification requirement is to inform the shareholders and the public of changes in shareholdings that could influence the management of

---

72. Transparency Directive at art. 5(2). For more detail on the content of the semi-annual report see Article 3 of Commission Directive 2007/14/EC, 2007 O.J. (L 69) 27.
73. Committee of European Securities Regulators, Frequently Asked Questions, 2nd Version October 2009, CESR/09-965 *available at* http://www.esma.europa.eu/system/files/09_965.pdf.
74. Transparency Directive at art. 3(1a).
75. *Id.* at art. 9(1).
76. *Id.* at art. 12(2).
77. *Id.* at art. 12(6).

the company.[78] It is therefore necessary to also apply the Directive to situations where a person indirectly acquires or increases (or decreases) its influence over the company short of actually acquiring ownership or disposing of shares. This commonly arises where the owner of the shares transfers the right to vote the shares to a third party.[79] If, for example, the owner of the shares lodges those shares as collateral with a third party and the parties agree that the third party will exercise the voting rights attached to the shares, for purposes of the thresholds the owner of the shares will be considered of having disposed of those shares and the third party will be considered having acquired the shares. Another example is if the owner and a third party enter into a voting rights agreement allowing the third party to vote those shares. If the acquirer enters into an agreement with a third party that requires the third party to concertedly exercise the voting rights held by that third party, the shares are aggregated for the purpose of determining the thresholds.[80] Even the change of control over a company that holds the interests would be covered. For example, if Company A holds a significant interest in Issuer X, and Company B acquires control over Company A, Company B would be required to notify its indirect holding in Issuer X even though there was no change in the shares held by Company A.[81]

4.3 Additional Disclosures

Securities are often qualified by certain rights or preferences. For example, an issuer may issue a specific class of shares with special preference rights which give the holders of such shares preference over other classes of shareholders in the event of liquidation or dividends. If an issuer makes any change in the rights attaching to the various classes of its shares, the issuer must make a public disclosure of such change without delay.[82]

4.4 Language

As publicly listed companies may have investors throughout the EU, the language in which the disclosure occurs is often important. If the securities are listed only on a regulated market in the home member state, the rule is relatively straightforward: disclosure can occur in any language accepted by the regulatory agency of that home member state.[83] For example, if the issuer

---

78. *Id.* at Preamble 18.
79. The circumstances in which there is deemed to be an indirect change of ownership over the shares are enumerated in Article 10 of the Transparency Directive.
80. *Id.* at art.10(a). In such an instance, the obligation to notify is on both parties. However, they may cooperate to file just one notification on behalf of each of them. Article 8 Transparency Implementing Directive.
81. Committee of European Securities Regulators, Frequently Asked Questions, 2nd Version October 2009, CESR/09-965 *available at* http://www.esma.europa.eu/system/files/09_965.pdf.
82. Transparency Directive at art. 16(1). The meaning of "without delay" is left up to the member states to determine.
83. *Id.* at art. 20(1).

only has securities listed on the Bratislava Stock Exchange, the disclosures may be made in Slovakian.

If an issuer has securities admitted to trading on a regulated market both in the home member state and in one or more host member states, the disclosures must be made not only in a language accepted by the home member state, but also either (at the discretion of the issuer) in a language accepted by the competent authorities of those host member states or in a language customary in the sphere of international finance.[84] If the issuer is not listed in its home member state, but only in one or more host member states, the disclosures must be either (at the discretion of the issuer) in a language accepted by host member states or in a language customary in the sphere of international finance.[85]

4.5 Home and Host Member States

Although both the Prospectus Directive and the Transparency Directive employ the concepts of home member state and host member state, they are slightly different. For purposes of the Transparency Directive, the home member state is generally the member state where the issuer is incorporated.[86] If the issuer is not incorporated in the EU, the issuer has some latitude in choosing a member state to be designated as its home member state: it can choose any member state where its securities have been admitted for trading on a regulated market. It must make that choice within three months after the issuer's shares are first admitted to trading on a regulated market in the EU.[87]

Similar to the Prospectus Directive, the host member state is where the issuer's securities are admitted to trading on a regulated market.[88] Whereas an issuer can only have one home member state, it might have multiple host member states. The host member state may be the same as the home member state, but not necessarily so. If a German company lists its shares only on the Frankfurt Stock Exchange, then the home member state and the host member state will be the same. If, however, that same German company decides to list its shares only on the London Stock Exchange, the home member state and the host member state will be different. For non-EU issuers, there will always be some overlap between the home member state and the host member state. For example, a Delaware company may have its shares admitted to trading in Frankfurt, Milan, and London. In such a case, it must designate one of these host member states (Germany, Italy, or the UK) as the home member state.

---

84. *Id.* at art. 20(2).
85. *Id.* at art. 20(3). Although the EU institutions have not issued a binding list of languages customary in the sphere of international finance, a list of the languages accepted by the member states for purposes of the summary is compiled by the ESMA (www.esma.europa.eu).
86. *Id.* at art. 2(1)(i).
87. *Id.* at art. 2(1)(iv).
88. *Id.* at art. 2(1)(j).

4.6 Home Member State Rule

The Transparency Directive sets forth a minimum level of protection which the member states have to achieve through their national laws and regulations. The member states are free to impose disclosure requirements on issuers and investors that are more stringent than or in addition to those stipulated by the Transparency Directive. Consequently, the reporting obligations imposed on companies in the EU differ among the member states.[89] For example, Article 9(1) of the Transparency Directive states that a shareholder acquiring voting shares in a listed company above certain thresholds must disclose those shareholdings. As discussed above, the thresholds codified in the Transparency Directive begin at 5 percent. Some member states, however, have established lower thresholds beginning at 2 percent (Italy and Portugal). In order to reduce the compliance costs associated with such divergence—which exists in various aspects of the Transparency Directive—the Transparency Directive introduced the home member state rule.

According to the home member state rule, the host member state may not impose disclosure requirements on an issuer from another member state which are more stringent than those laid down in the Transparency Directive.[90] If, for example, a home member state requires the issuer to continue to make its annual financial report available to the public for a period of 10 years—as is consistent with Article 4(1) of the Transparency Directive—a host member state may not require that company to make it available for 15 years.

4.7 Third-country Equivalence

In order to make the EU more attractive as a market for companies outside the EU to raise capital, the Transparency Directive relieves foreign issuers (i.e., issuers who have their registered office outside the EU) from some of the disclosure requirements.[91] The competent authority of the home member state in the EU may exempt the issuer from most of the disclosure requirements enumerated in the Transparency Directive if (i) the law of the third country has equivalent disclosure requirements or (ii) the issuer complies with requirements of the law of a third country that the competent authority of the home member state considers to be equivalent. The issue of equivalency requires a comparison of the particular disclosure rule in the Transparency Directive and the regulation of the third country. Detailed guidance can be found in the Transparency Implementing Directive.

For example, the Transparency Directive requires companies listed on a regulated market in the EU to publish an annual management report giving a

---

89. In addition, the member states have the discretion to determine the sanctions imposed for violations of the transparency obligations. Case C-174/12, Hirmann v. Immofinanz AG, 2013 E.C.R. I-___, at ¶40. Consequently, there is no uniformity among the member states as to the sanctions.
90. Transparency Directive at art. 20(3). But the home market state may impose more stringent requirements than those prescribed in the Transparency Directive at art. 3(1)(1).
91. *Id.* at art. 23(1).

fair and accurate representation of the issuer and its business and a description of the principal risks and uncertainties facing the issuer.[92] A third country will be deemed to have equivalent requirements if the third country requires an annual management report containing (i) a fair review of the development and performance of the issuer's business and of its position, together with a description of the principal risks and uncertainties that it faces, (ii) an indication of any important events that have occurred since the end of the issuer's fiscal year; and (iii) indications of the issuer's likely future development.[93]

The recognition of equivalence does not operate as a total exemption from compliance with EU securities law. The foreign issuer must still disclose to the EU home member state the information disclosed in the third country,[94] grant access to the public the same as EU issuers,[95] and provide translations as required by the home member state.[96] The foreign issuer does not have to create a parallel set of financial statements for the EU if the financial statements are prepared in accordance with International Financial Reporting Standards (IFRS) or the generally accepted accounting principles of the United States, Canada, China, North Korea, and Japan.[97] Financial statements prepared in accordance with the generally accepted accounting principles (GAAP) of other countries outside the EU may be regarded as equivalent if the third country authority has demonstrated a commitment to converging its standards to IFRS.[98]

5. Market Abuse

As mentioned above, the sustained success of capital markets depends on public confidence in the fair operation of the markets. The system is undermined when some players have access to more information than the others or are in

---

92. *Id.* at art. 4(2).
93. Transparency Implementing Directive at art. 13. Commission Regulation (EC) No. 1569/2007 of 21 December 2007 establishing a mechanism for the determination of equivalence of accounting standards applied by third country issuers of securities pursuant to Directives 2003/71/EC and 2004/109/EC of the European Parliament and of the Council, 2007 O.J. (L 340) 66.
94. Transparency Directive at art. 19.
95. *Id.* at art. 21.
96. *Id.* at art. 20.
97. Commission Implementing Decision of 11 April 2012 amending Decision 2008/961/EC on the use by third countries' issuers of securities of certain third country's national accounting standards and International Financial Reporting Standards to prepare their consolidated financial statements, 2012 O.J. (L 103) 49 at art. 1; Commission Decision of 4 December 2006 on the use by third country issuers of securities of information prepared under internationally accepted accounting standards, 2006 O.J. (L 343) 96 at art. 1. For additional information see http://ec.europa.eu/internal_market/accounting/third_countries/index_en.htm.
98. Article 1(c) Commission Decision of 4 December 2006 on the use by third country issuers of securities of information prepared under internationally accepted accounting standards, 2006 O.J. (L 343) 96 at art. 1(c).

a position to manipulate the market to their advantage. In an attempt to preserve the "integrity of financial markets and public confidence in securities and derivatives,"[99] EU legislation prohibits the improper use of inside information (such as insider trading and the unlawful disclosure of inside information) and market manipulation and imposes certain disclosure requirements to prevent market abuse. These market-distorting actions are collectively referred to as "market abuse" in the EU nomenclature.

5.1 Types of Market Abuse

(a) Improper Use of Inside Information

(1) Insider Dealing

The most prominent type of market abuse prohibited by the Market Abuse Regulation is insider dealing.[100] The purpose of this prohibition is to place all market participants on equal footing in respect to the information available to them when making an investment decision.[101] The concept of "insider dealing" covers the situation where an insider uses inside information to directly or indirectly acquire or dispose of financial instruments to which that information relates. It also covers the situation where the person uses the inside information for the account of a third party to directly or indirectly acquire or dispose of financial instruments to which that information relates.[102] An insider may also be deemed to have engaged in insider dealing by placing an order for a financial instrument without inside information, but subsequently cancelling or amending the order after receiving inside information about those financial instruments.[103]

The court may infer insider dealing from the close temporal connection between the receipt of the information and the placing of the trades. In *In re Andre Scerri*, for example, Scerri was accused of receiving inside information about a company in which he was heavily invested. He was allegedly informed by another investor by text and telephone call that the company was planning to issue new shares the following day. Within several minutes after receiving the information, he placed a trade to sell a significant number of his shares in the company. Although the UK authorities did not have concrete evidence of the context of the text message or the telephone call other than that they had occurred, the fact that he placed unusual trades shortly thereafter was sufficient circumstantial evidence to convict him of insider dealing.[104]

---

99. Preamble of Regulation (EU) No. 596/2014 of the European Parliament and of the Council of 16 April 2014 on market abuse, 2014 O.J. (L 173) 1 [hereinafter Market Abuse Regulation].
100. *Id.* at art. 14.
101. Case C-628/13, Lafonta v. Autorité des marchés financiers, 2015 E.C.R. I-___, at ¶21.
102. Market Abuse Regulation at art. 8.
103. *Id.* at art. 8(1).
104. *In re* Andre Scerri, Decision of the UK Upper Tribunal (Tax and Chancery Chamber) of May 21, 2010 *available at* http://www.tribunals.gov.uk/financeandtax/documents/decisions/andrewscerrioliver_v_fsa_0016.pdf.

(i) Insider

An insider is any person who possesses inside information by virtue of his or her: (a) being a member of the administrative, management, or supervisory bodies of the issuer or emission allowance market participant; (b) having a holding in the capital of the issuer or emission allowance market participant; (c) having access to the information through the exercise of an employment, profession, or duties; or (d) being involved in criminal activities.[105] Even a lawyer may be considered an insider. In one case in the UK, the general counsel of TTP Communications was informed confidentially that Motorola was planning to acquire TTP Communications. The general counsel informed his father-in-law of the anticipated acquisition. The father-in-law then purchased 153,824 shares of TTP Communications two days before the acquisition was announced. Both the general counsel and the father-in-law were found guilty of insider dealing.[106]

The prohibition of insider dealing also applies to any other person who possesses inside information while that person knows, or ought to have known, that it is inside information.[107] If, for example, the receptionist at the company headquarters becomes aware of confidential negotiations regarding the sale of the company, and then tells his wife, the receptionist's wife is considered an insider. In *In re Grøngaard and Bang*, the concept of insider was interpreted by the ECJ to include the employees' representative on the board of directors of a publicly listed Danish company.[108] As discussed in Chapter IX, the employees of European companies over a certain size have the right to be represented on the board of directors of the company through a representative elected by them. In *In re Grøngaard and Bang*, the representative of the employees who became aware of a pending merger involving the company was considered an insider.

An insider does not necessarily have to be a paid employee of the company. In the *Uberoi* case in the UK, an intern at a corporate brokerage firm working on takeovers and other price-sensitive deals was considered an insider and found guilty of insider dealing for passing on inside information to his father in relation to deals in three companies. His father then purchased shares in those companies and made substantial profits.[109] The UK's Financial Services Authority concluded that the intern was an insider.

---

105. Market Abuse Regulation at art. 8(4).
106. Decision of the UK Financial Services Authority of March 27, 2009 (FSA/PN/042/2009) *available at* http://www.fsa.gov.uk/pages/Library/Communication/PR/2009/042.shtml. Although the cases discussed here were decided prior to the adoption of the Market Abuse Regulation, the statutory definition of insider under the previous market abuse legislation—Directive 2003/6—was essentially the same. See Article 2(1) of Directive 2003/6/EC of the European Parliament and of the Council of 28 January 2003 on insider dealing and market manipulation, 2003 O.J. (L 96) 16.
107. Market Abuse Regulation at art. 8(4).
108. Case C-384/02, *In re* Grøngaard and Bang, 2005 E.C.R. I-9961, 9978 ¶54.
109. UK Financial Services Authority v. Uberoi, FSA/PN/149/2009 (November 4, 2009) available at http://www.fsa.gov.uk/pages/Library/Communication/PR/2009/149.shtml.

(ii) Inside Information

Not all information about a particular company qualifies as inside information. For example, knowledge that the company is planning to lease new office space may not necessarily constitute inside information for purposes of the Market Abuse Regulation. The term "inside information" covers "information of a precise nature, which has not been made public, relating, directly or indirectly, to one or more issuers or to one or more financial instruments, and which, if it were made public, would be likely to have a significant effect on the prices of those financial instruments or on the price of related derivative financial instruments."[110]

For information to qualify as inside information, it must be of a precise nature. Information is precise if it indicates a set of circumstances that exist or that may reasonably be expected to come into existence, or an event that has occurred or that may reasonably be expected to occur, provided that it is specific enough to enable a conclusion to be drawn as to the possible effect of that set of circumstances or event on the prices of the financial instruments.[111] According to the ECJ, in order to qualify as precise, it is not necessary that the information allows the insider to predict a change in the prices of the financial instruments concerned.[112] Moreover, the information does not have to be wholly accurate in order to constitute inside information.[113] In a case in the UK, the managing director of a UK oil and gas company which had a contract to drill two wells in Uganda passed on information to his father that the first well looked unlikely to yield any oil. Based on this information, and with the inferred knowledge that the drilling of the second well would be unnecessary, the father sold his shares just before the news was made public. The UK Financial Services Authority found the father and son guilty of insider dealing even though it was not 100 percent certain that the second well would be unnecessary.[114] Whether the information is sufficiently precise is determined on the basis of the information available at that time and not with the benefit of hindsight.[115]

The fact that the information relates to an intermediate step in a process does not preclude a finding that it is inside information.[116] In *Geltl v. Daimler AG*, for

---

110. Market Abuse Regulation at art. 7(1).
111. *Id.* at art. 7(2).
112. Case C-628/13, Lafonta v. Autorité des marchés financiers, 2015 E.C.R. I-____, at ¶38. The position taken by the ECJ in this case on the second prong of the preciseness requirement is contrary to the position taken by the UK Upper Tribunal in Hannam v. Financial Conduct Authority, [2014] UKUT 233 (May 27, 2014) *available at* http://www.tribunals.gov.uk/financeandtax/Documents/decisions/Hannam-v-FCA.pdf.
113. Hannam v. Financial Conduct Authority, [2014] UKUT 233 at ¶68 (May 27, 2014) *available at* http://www.tribunals.gov.uk/financeandtax/Documents/decisions/Hannam-v-FCA.pdf.
114. FSA Final Notice, *In re* Jeremy Burley (19 July 2010) *available at* http://www.fsa.gov.uk/pubs/final/jeremy_burley.pdf.
115. Committee of European Securities Regulators, Level 3 second set of CESR guidance and information on the common operation of the Directive to the market (July 2007) CESR/06-562b at § 1.5 *available at* http://www.esma.europa.eu/system/files/06_562b.pdf.
116. Market Abuse Regulation at art. 7(2).

example, the CEO of Daimler AG mentioned to the chairman of the supervisory board of Daimler that the CEO was prepared to resign at the end of the year. One of the shareholders claimed that this qualified as inside information. Daimler, on the other hand, argued that the statement of the CEO was merely an initial step in the resignation process. The ECJ held, however, that "in the case of a protracted process intended to bring about a particular circumstance or to generate a particular event, not only may that future circumstance or future event be regarded as precise information within the meaning of [the market abuse law], but also the intermediate steps of that process which are connected with bringing about that future circumstance or event."[117] The reason is, according to the ECJ, that individuals in possession of this intermediate information are in an advantageous position vis-à-vis people without the information.[118]

The second requirement for information to be considered inside information is that the information must not be public. For example, knowledge held by a company's general counsel of a significant pending acquisition would be inside information.[119] However, if a corporate insider working for a snow shovel company watches the evening weather report on television and learns that snow is forecast for the upcoming week, that knowledge is not considered to be inside information because it is public information (even though it might have an effect on the company's share price). The term "public" in this context should be interpreted in the broad sense of an indeterminable number of people. Information made available only to the shareholders at a shareholders' meeting would probably not be public information. However, if that same information were posted on the company's website accessible to the general public, it probably would be considered public.

The fact that the public might reasonably suspect (as opposed to knowing) that certain information is true does not mean that it is public information. In one case, the German Supreme Court had to decide whether the fact that a company had experienced a significant decrease in sales qualified as inside information prior to the announcement of the quarterly financial results. The defendant argued that it did not qualify as inside information because the public already expected the company to report significant sales decreases. The German Supreme Court held, however, that "the fact that the market may have a certain suspicion does not in itself make the fact public."[120]

---

117. Case C-19/11, Geltl v. Daimler AG, 2012 E.C.R. I-____ at ¶40 (reported in the electronic reports of cases ECLI:EU:C:2012:397).
118. *Id.* at ¶36.
119. Decision of the UK Financial Services Authority of March 27, 2009 (FSA/PN/042/2009) *available at* http://www.fsa.gov.uk/pages/Library/Communication/PR/2009/042.shtml. Although the cases discussed here were decided prior to the adoption of the Market Abuse Regulation, the statutory definition of inside information under the previous market abuse legislation—Directive 2003/6—was essentially the same. See Article 1(1) of Directive 2003/6/EC of the European Parliament and of the Council of 28 January 2003 on insider dealing and market manipulation, 2003 O.J. (L 96) 16.
120. Decision of the German Supreme Court in case no. 5 STR 224/09 (Jan. 10, 2010).

The third component of the definition of inside information is that it must be of a nature that if it were made public, it would likely have a significant effect on the prices of the financial instruments. Nonpublic information about the issuer does not qualify as inside information if it is not price-sensitive.[121] There are two components to this requirement. The "likely" component means more than merely possible; but according to the ECJ it does not require "high probability."[122] It is sufficient that there is a "realistic prospect" that the circumstance or event will occur.[123] Four important factors in assessing the likelihood of the significant effect of the disclosure are:[124]

- the anticipated magnitude of the matter or event in question in the context of the totality of the company's activity;
- the relevance of the information as regards the main determinants of the financial instrument's price;
- the reliability of the source; and
- market variables that affect the price of the financial instrument in question.[125]

In addition, even if a disclosure is likely to have an effect on share prices, it will only qualify as inside information if that effect is likely to be significant. If, for example, a senior manager of a publicly held software company was informed by her CFO that an individual who purchased €100 of software from the company in the past year decided to cancel the order, this inside knowledge is unlikely to have a significant effect on the company's share price. Similarly, knowledge of a company's 20 percent reduction in earnings compared with the prior year may not be of a nature that it will have a significant effect on prices if management has been repeatedly telling the public to expect an earnings reduction of 20 percent. Whether information is likely to have a significant

---

121. FSA Final Notice, *In re* Nicholas Kyprios (Mar. 13, 2012) at ¶7 *available at* http://www.fsa.gov.uk/static/pubs/final/nicholas-kyprios.pdf.
122. Case C-19/11, Geltl v. Daimler AG, 2012 E.C.R. I-____, at ¶46 (reported only in the electronic reports of cases ECLI:EU:C:2012:397). *See also* Hannam v. Financial Conduct Authority, [2014] UKUT 233 at ¶118 (May 27, 2014) *available at* http://www.tribunals.gov.uk/financeandtax/Documents/decisions/Hannam-v-FCA.pdf ("[W]e reject the 'more probable than not' conclusion. Our conclusion is that the Authority's approach is correct and that the word 'likely'…is properly to be construed as meaning that there is a real (in contrast with fanciful) prospect of that information having an effect on the price of qualifying instruments.").
123. Case C-19/11, Geltl v. Daimler AG, 2012 E.C.R. I-____ at ¶43 (reported only in the electronic reports of cases ECLI:EU:C:2012:397).
124. Committee of European Securities Regulators, Level 3 second set of CESR guidance and information on the common operation of the Directive to the market (July 2007) CESR/06-562b at § 1.13 *available at* http://www.esma.europa.eu/system/files/06_562b.pdf.
125. These variables could include prices, returns, volatilities, liquidity, price relationships among financial instruments, volume, supply, demand, etc.

effect is a determination to be made on a case-by-case basis. Three factors are regularly taken into account in assessing the significance of the effect:[126]

- the type of information is the same type of information which has in the past had a significant effect on prices;
- pre-existing analysts' research reports and opinions indicate that the type of information in question is price- sensitive; and
- the company itself has already treated similar events as inside information.

The effect of the subsequent publication of the inside information is not relevant in determining whether the release of the inside information would likely have a significant effect on the prices of the financial instruments as the determination is made a priori.[127]

(2) *Recommending or Inducing Insider Dealing*

In addition to insider dealing, the Market Abuse Regulation prohibits a person from recommending or inducing another person to engage in insider dealing.[128] This arises where an insider recommends to or induces another person to acquire or dispose of financial instruments to which that information relates or to cancel or amend an order. For example, if a financial broker acquires inside information that a specific company is about to announce losses far exceeding analysts' expectations, that broker cannot pass on that information to his clients who then sell their shares in that company prior to the announcement.[129]

In the *Bakaert* case in Belgium, a member of the board of directors of Bakaert NV, a Belgian company listed on the Belgian Stock Exchange, participated in a board meeting on November 20, 1992, during which a possible significant dividend was discussed.[130] Bakaert had recently sold its interest in a Japanese joint venture and was sitting on a significant amount of cash. The formal decision to declare a dividend of €2.48 per share was not taken by the Bakaert board of directors until December 18, 1992, and not publicly announced until December 21, 1992, after the securities markets had closed. However, earlier that day, another Belgian company, Batibo NV, had placed an order for 400 shares of Batibo. Within two days after the announcement of the dividend, the Bakaert shares rose to over €17 per share. The Belgian Banking and Finance Commission, the supervisory authority for the Belgian Stock Exchange, initiated an investigation and discovered that the majority shareholder and director of

---

126. Committee of European Securities Regulators, Level 3 second set of CESR guidance and information on the common operation of the Directive to the market (July 2007) CESR/06-562b at § 1.14 *available at* http://www.esma.europa.eu/system/files/06_562b.pdf.
127. Case C-45/08, Spector Photo Group NV v. Commissie voor het Bank-, Financie- en Assurantiewezen, 2009 E.C.R. I-12100, 12125 ¶69. *But see* Decision of German Supreme Court in case no. II ZB 7/09 (April 23, 2013) at ¶28 (the effect of the subsequent disclosure of the information on the share price is relevant).
128. Market Abuse Regulation at art. 14.
129. *See, e.g., In re* Rahul Shah, Final Notice RXS01352 UK Financial Conduct Authority (Nov. 13, 2013) *available at* http://www.fca.org.uk/static/documents/final-notices/shah.pdf.
130. Ghent Court of First Instance, Sept. 27, 1995, 9 Bank- en Financiewezen 535 (1995).

Batibo was the husband of one of the directors of Bakaert. The trial court found that this constituted insider dealing.[131]

(3) *Unlawful Disclosure of Inside Information*

The proper functioning of securities markets can be distorted if not all market participants have access to the same information.[132] For that reason, the Market Abuse Regulation also prohibits the unlawful disclosure of inside information.[133] An unlawful disclosure occurs when an insider in possession of inside information directly or indirectly discloses that information to another person. If, however, an insider discloses the inside information "in the normal exercise of employment, a profession or duties," it is not considered market abuse.[134] Whether a particular disclosure is within a person's employment, profession, or duties depends on the laws of the member states which delineate those relationships. The two requirements for a permitted disclosure identified by the ECJ are (1) a close link between the disclosure and the exercise of employment, profession, or duties, and (2) the disclosure is strictly necessary for the exercise of that employment, profession, or duties.[135] The mere fact that the disclosure by a banker of inside information promotes the interest of the banker's client does not mean that the disclosure is within the scope of that banker's employment or duties.[136]

In order to be able to more closely monitor such disclosures, issuers (and others working with or on their behalf such as investor relations consultants, lawyers, ratings agencies, credit institutes) are required to maintain a list of those persons working for them who have access to inside information.[137] This list of insiders includes not only employees but also any third parties providing goods or services to the company, such as consultants. The list of insiders must be provided upon request of the competent authority. Managerial-level employees must – even if they are not engaging in insider dealing – notify all

---

131. First Instance Criminal Court of Ghent Decision of Sept. 27, 1995, 9 Bank- en Financiewezen 535 (1995). The decision of the trial court was overturned on appeal for lack of sufficient evidence showing a link between the inside information and the trading. Ghent Court of Appeal, April 30, 1997, 11 Bank- en Financiewezen 414 (1997).
132. Case C-19/11, Geltl v. Daimler AG, 2012 E.C.R. I-____ at ¶33 (reported in the electronic reports of cases ECLI:EU:C:2012:397).
133. Market Abuse Regulation at art. 10.
134. *Id.* at art. 10(2).
135. Case C-384/02, *In re* Grøngaard and Bang, 2005 E.C.R. I-9961, 9977 ¶48. Although this case was decided prior to the adoption of the Market Abuse Regulation, the "in the normal exercise of employment, a profession or duties" carve-out under the previous market abuse legislation—Directive 2003/6—was the same. *See* Article 3(a) of Directive 2003/6/EC of the European Parliament and of the Council of 28 January 2003 on insider dealing and market manipulation, 2003 O.J. (L 96) 16.
136. FSA Final Notice, *In re* Ian Hannam (Feb. 27, 2012) at 4.17 *available at* http://www.fca.org.uk/static/pubs/final/ian-hannam.pdf *affirmed on appeal* Hannam v. Financial Conduct Authority, [2014] UKUT 233 (May 27, 2014) *available at* http://www.tribunals.gov.uk/financeandtax/Documents/decisions/Hannam-v-FCA.pdf.
137. Market Abuse Regulation at art. 18(1)(a).

trades of securities of the issuer for which they are employed.[138] The notification to the competent authorities must be made within three business days after the transaction date.

(4) Legitimate Conduct

As the prohibition on the use and disclosure of inside information—particularly when combined with the criminal sanctions discussed below— has the potential of dissuading market participants such as market makers and traders from engaging in legitimate market conduct,[139] the Market Abuse Regulation identifies certain circumstances in which it is inappropriate to make an inference of insider dealing based solely on the fact that the person is in possession of inside information.[140] In these instances, the insider has the benefit of a presumption of legitimacy which can be rebutted by a regulator in the EU by showing an "illegitimate reason for the orders."[141]

(i) Trades Made by Market Makers

A "market maker" is a person who holds himself or herself out on the financial markets on a continuous basis as being willing to deal on one's own account by buying and selling financial instruments against that person's proprietary capital.[142] The basic idea is that the Market Abuse Regulation should not punish a market maker for making a legitimate trade for someone even if the market maker qualifies as an insider.[143] For that reason, there is a presumption of legitimacy where a market maker (or a person authorized to act as a counterparty) acquires or disposes of financial instruments in the normal course of the exercise of its function as a market maker or as a counterparty for that financial instrument.[144]

(ii) Trades Made by Authorized Person

There may be individuals who are authorized to execute orders on behalf of third parties, but who are not market makers in the formal sense. The Market Abuse Regulation applies the same rationale to this group as it does to market makers. As long as the person authorized to execute orders on behalf of third parties makes the acquisition or disposal of financial instruments legitimately in the normal course of the exercise of that person's employment, profession, or duties, there is a rebuttable presumption that it does not constitute market abuse.[145]

---

138. *Id.* at art. 19(1). There is a €5000 minimum annual threshold for such notification requirements.
139. *Id.* at preamble 29.
140. *Id.* at art. 9.
141. *Id.* at art. 9(6).
142. Article 4(1)(7) Directive 2014/65/EU of the European Parliament and of the Council of 15 May 2014 on markets in financial instruments and amending Directive 2002/92/EC and Directive 2011/61/EU, 2014 O.J. (L 173) 349.
143. Market Abuse Regulation at preamble 30.
144. *Id.* at art. 9(2)(a).
145. *Id.* at art. 9(2)(b).

(iii) Trades Made in Good Faith

Another circumstance in which a strict application of the prohibition on insider dealing would unfairly punish an insider is where a person engages in a transaction in the discharge of an obligation that has become due in good faith and not to circumvent the prohibition against insider dealing. Such a person is protected by a rebuttable presumption of legitimacy if either the obligation results from an order placed or an agreement concluded before the person concerned possessed inside information or the transaction is carried out to satisfy a legal or regulatory obligation that arose, before the person concerned possessed inside information.[146]

(iv) Trades Made in Connection with Public Mergers and Acquisitions

One final scenario in which an insider may legitimately engage in a trade in the financial instruments for which she holds inside information relates to public mergers and acquisitions. It is not uncommon for a potential buyer of a company to secure possession of inside information in the due diligence or negotiations leading up to the takeover or merger. Technically, the subsequent acquisition of the company would be considered insider dealing. However, the Market Abuse Regulation specifically states that this will not constitute insider dealing as long as the information to which the acquirer has access is made public at the point of approval of the merger or acceptance of the offer by the shareholders of that company.[147]

(b) Market Manipulation

The other type of market abuse is referred to as market manipulation. An individual can cause distortions to securities markets even without access to inside information. As the possession of inside information is a requirement for insider dealing, such distorting activity would not be caught by the prohibition on insider dealing. For that reason, the Market Abuse Regulation also prohibits any person from engaging in market manipulation.[148]

(1) Types of Market Manipulation

There are various ways that the market can be manipulated. The Market Abuse Regulation attempts to describe several categories of actions that constitute market manipulation. These categories are necessarily abstract as it is not possible to legislate every type of market manipulation in detail.

(i) Misleading Signals

The first category of conduct constituting market manipulation is conduct which gives, or is likely to give, false or misleading signals as to the supply of, demand for, or price of a financial instrument or secures, or is likely to secure, the price of one or several financial instruments at an artificial level.[149] For example, the buying or selling of financial instruments at the opening or closing of the market which has or is likely to have the effect of misleading investors acting

---

146. *Id.* at art. 9(3).
147. *Id.* at art. 9(4).
148. *Id.* at art. 15.
149. *Id.* at art. 12(1)(a)(i).

on the basis of the prices displayed, including the opening or closing prices, is specifically identified as a form of market manipulation.[150]

In *Visser v. FSA*, the CEO of a hedge fund at the end of the fund's month-end valuation personally placed exorbitant bids on a small number of shares of Sandhaven plc listed on the UK's PLUS exchange in order to artificially inflate the value of Sandhaven's shares and consequently the value of the fund.[151] In another case, the UK Financial Services Authority imposed a fine of £350,000 on the CEO of Sibir Energy plc because the CEO made false announcements about the advances Sibir had made to Sibir's largest shareholder.[152] The purpose of the cash advances was to prevent the shareholder from selling off its shares in Sibir because of the financial difficulties the shareholder was experiencing. This conduct, according to the FSA, created a false market in that it created a misleading impression of the value of Sibir.

The realization of a profit or even a profit motive is not necessarily an element of the offense. In one case, the UK Financial Services Authority imposed a fine of £72,000 on a trader for giving false signals as to the demand for financial instruments by placing trades at home for commodity derivatives on behalf of clients who had not authorized the trades.[153] It later turned out that the trader had no recollection of placing the trades as he was heavily under the influence of alcohol at the time.

If, however, the person establishes that the transaction qualifies as an accepted market practice, it is not considered market manipulation.[154] It is ultimately up to the national regulators to determine what constitutes an accepted market practice, and a decision by one regulator is not binding on the other member states.[155] The Market Abuse Regulation only prescribes that the activity is "carried out for legitimate reasons."[156] Nonetheless, the Regulation contains a list of criteria to be used by the national regulators in identifying accepted market practices. According to the Regulation, the national regulators should consider:[157]

- whether the practice provides a substantial level of transparency;
- whether the practice ensures a high degree of safeguards to the operation of market forces and the proper interplay of the forces of supply and demand;

---

150. *Id.* at art. 12(2)(b).
151. Visser v. Financial Services Authority, Decision of Aug. 9, 2011 of the Upper Tribunal (Tax and Chancery Chamber) *available at* http://www.tribunals.gov.uk/financeandtax/Documents/decisions/VisserandFagbulu_v_FSA.pdf.
152. *In re* Cameron, Final Notice, UK Financial Services Authority (July 6, 2010) *available at* http://www.fsa.gov.uk/pubs/final/henry_cameron.pdf.
153. *In re* Perkins, Final Notice, UK Financial Services Authority (June 24, 2010) *available at* http://www.fsa.gov.uk/pubs/final/steven_perkins.pdf.
154. Market Abuse Regulation at art. 12(1)(a).
155. *Id.* at art. 13(2).
156. *Id.* at 13(1). The "safe harbor" for accepted market practices only applies to the first category of market manipulation otherwise prohibited by Article 12(1)(a) of the Market Abuse Regulation.
157. *Id.* at art. 13(2).

- whether the practice has a positive impact on liquidity and efficiency;
- whether the practice takes into account the trading mechanism of the relevant market and enables market participants to react properly and in a timely manner to the new market situation created by that practice;
- whether the practice does not directly or indirectly threaten the integrity of related markets in the relevant financial instrument within the EU;
- the outcome of any investigation of the relevant practice by any competent authority; and
- the structural characteristics of the relevant market.

Although the ultimate decision on an accepted market practice is left to the national regulators, they are required to follow a procedure involving the ESMA. Three months prior to approving the accepted market practice, the national regulator is required to notify the ESMA and the other national regulators of its intention to approve an accepted market practice.[158] The ESMA then reviews the proposed accepted market practice and issues an opinion assessing the compatibility of the accepted market practice with the criteria codified in the Market Abuse Regulation.[159] The national regulator may approve the accepted market practice contrary to the opinion of the ESMA, but the national regulator must publish its reasoning for diverging from the ESMA's opinion.

(ii) Fictitious Devices

The second type of market manipulation covers transactions or orders to trade which employ fictitious devices or any other form of deception or contrivance.[160] This would include, for example, "pump and dump" transactions, "trash and cash" transactions and "layering." In a pump and dump transaction, the person takes a long position in a security and then disseminates misleading but positive information about the company in an effort to artificially drive up the market price of the particular security.[161] In a trash and cash transaction, the person acquires a short position in securities and then disseminates negative misleading information in an attempt to drive down the market price for the securities. Layering occurs when a trader enters large orders to buy or sell shares, thereby influencing the prices for those shares. That trader then sells shares at the inflated price or buys shares at the deflated price and subsequently cancels the initial order that triggered the movement in price.[162]

---

158. *Id.* at art. 13(3).
159. The ESMA's opinions are posted on its website: http://www.esma.europa.eu/page/accepted-markets-practices.
160. Market Abuse Regulation at art.12(1)(b). Annex I of the Market Abuse Regulation contains a list of "indicators" suggesting the employment of a fictitious device.
161. Committee of European Securities Regulators, Level 3 first set of CESR guidance and information on the common operation of the Directive, CESR/04-505b, § 4.13.
162. See, e.g., *In re* Swift Trade Inc., [2013] EWCA Civ. 1662 *available at* http://www.bailii.org/ew/cases/EWCA/Civ/2013/1662.html.

(iii) Manipulative Dissemination of Information

The third type of market manipulation is giving false or misleading signals as to the supply, demand, or price of financial instruments by the dissemination of information.[163] The dissemination of the information includes any medium, including the Internet. This would include, for example, disseminating rumors and false or misleading news, where the person who made the dissemination knew, or ought to have known, that the information was false or misleading. One type of market manipulation specifically cited in the Market Abuse Regulation is taking advantage of occasional or regular access to the traditional or electronic media by voicing an opinion about a financial instrument while having previously taken positions on that financial instrument based on emission allowances. In this instance, the individual subsequently profits from the impact of the opinions voiced on the price of that instrument without having simultaneously disclosed the conflict of interest to the public in a proper and effective way.[164]

The information does not necessarily have to be false. Information can be manipulative by creating a false impression in the mind of the recipient because of the way it is presented.[165] For example, an issuer may state in a press release that the imminent adoption of a law by that member state will have the effect of increasing demand for a certain range of approved pharmaceutical products. If the issuer's pharmaceutical products are not yet approved, this true statement is misleading because it creates the impression that the law will have an impact on the sales of the issuer's products.

(iv) False or Misleading Information Relating to a Benchmark

The term "benchmark" refers to a public or published index or rate based on a formula or on the basis of the value of one or more underlying assets or prices and which is used to determine the value of a financial instrument.[166] As the prices of financial instruments are frequently tied to benchmarks, manipulating a benchmark can have serious implications on the functioning of the market. Therefore, specific provisions in relation to benchmarks are required to preserve the integrity of the markets and ensure that competent authorities can enforce a clear prohibition of the manipulation of benchmarks. The Market Abuse Regulation therefore prohibits transmitting false or misleading information or providing false or misleading inputs in relation to a benchmark where the person who made the transmission or provided the input knew or ought to have known that it was false or misleading.[167]

(2) Exceptions for Trading in Own Shares

There may be circumstances in which an issuer wants to legitimately trade in its own shares. For example, a company may want to buy back its own shares in order to use the shares to establish an employee stock incentive plan. Alternatively, a share buyback may be motivated by a need to prop up the

---

163. Market Abuse Regulation at art. 12(1)(c).
164. *Id.* at art. 12(2)(d).
165. *Id.* at preamble 47.
166. *Id.* at art. 3(1)(29).
167. *Id.* at art. 12(1)(d).

company's share price, and by increasing demand for those shares, it can often force up the market price. Or the company may want to use the share buyback as a means to pay out some of its earnings to the shareholders without having to issue a dividend (because a dividend may be taxed higher than capital gains).

In a share buyback, the sellers of the securities are the shareholders. As the company—and more particularly the managers of the company—are inherently in a better position than the sellers to assess the value of the securities, buying back the securities may constitute market abuse. For example, the company may be expecting a large order from a customer of which not all shareholders may be aware. If the company were then to buy back the shares of the shareholders who were not aware of the pending order, the company (i.e., the other shareholders) would unfairly benefit. In recognition of the fact that trading in a company's own shares may constitute market abuse under the Market Abuse Regulation, the law creates exemptions to allow issuers to trade in their own securities if part of a buyback program or necessary for stabilizing the securities.

(i) Buyback Program

An issuer may trade in its own securities if such trading is part of a share buyback program.[168] The share buyback program must have a legitimate purpose. There are three legitimate purposes identified by the Market Abuse Regulation: (1) to reduce the capital of an issuer; (2) to meet obligations arising from debt financial instruments that are exchangeable into equity instruments; or (3) to meet obligations arising from share option programs, or other allocations of shares, to employees or to members of the administrative, management, or supervisory bodies of the issuer or of an associate company.[169] This would, for example, preclude the use of a share buyback program for the purpose of subsequently exchanging shares as consideration in an acquisition.

(ii) Stabilization Program

The other context in which issuers are expressly allowed to trade in their own securities is as part of a share stabilization effort. For example, an issuer may be experiencing high volatility in its share price, which has the effect of deterring investors. By initiating a share stabilization program, the issuer can strategically intervene in the market to stabilize its share price. Such stabilization programs are exempted from the prohibition on insider trading and market manipulation, provided certain conditions are met. The stabilization must only be carried out for a limited period, the relevant information about the stabilization must be disclosed and notified to the competent authority, adequate limits with regard to price must be observed, and the trading complies with the conditions for stabilization laid down in the technical standards established by the ESMA.

---

168. *Id.* at art. 5.
169. *Id.* at art. 5(2).

5.2 Enforcement

(a) Enforcement Authorities

Although some of the authorities of the ESMA are comparable to those held by the Securities and Exchange Commission in the United States, the ESMA is not charged with the responsibility for enforcing the EU law on market abuse. Each member state has a single "competent authority" for the purpose of enforcing EU market abuse law.

(b) Sanctions

The member states generally have broad discretion in adopting sanctions to prevent market abuse. Regarding civil sanctions for insider dealing and market manipulation, the member states are required to adopt maximum fines of up to at least €5 million for natural persons and €15 million for legal persons.[170] In recognition of the weakness and disparity of sanctions among the member states,[171] EU law requires the member states to adopt minimum rules for criminal sanctions on insider dealing, unlawful disclosure of inside information, and market manipulation when committed intentionally.[172] Although EU law does not prescribe the specific criminal sentences to be imposed, the sanctions must be "effective, proportionate and dissuasive."[173] The maximum sentence prescribed by EU law is four years.[174] The obligation to impose criminal sanctions is triggered if the market abuse occurs entirely or partially in that member state or if committed by a national of that member state.[175]

(c) Notification and Disclosure Obligations

In order to maintain the transparency of the capital markets in the EU and to reduce the opportunity for market abuse, EU law imposes certain disclosure obligations on companies, corporate insiders, and financial professionals: disclosure of inside information, disclosure of insider transactions, and notification of suspicious transactions. These disclosure obligations are in addition to those regular securities law disclosure obligations based on the Transparency Directive discussed above. It is important to recall that these obligations apply to all issuers who have financial instruments listed on a regulated market in the EU. Hence, a U.S. issuer listed on the New York Stock Exchange may have to observe these disclosure requirements and maintain a list of insiders if it also has securities listed in the EU on a regulated market.

The basic obligation imposed on issuers is to inform the public "as soon as possible" of inside information which "directly concerns" that issuer.[176] The manner in which such disclosure occurs must enable the public to make a

---

170. *Id.* at art. 30(2)(i).
171. Directive 2014/57/EU of the European Parliament and of the Counsel of 16 April 2014 on criminal sanctions for market abuse, 2014 O.J. (L 173) 179 at recital 4.
172. *Id.* at art. 3(1).
173. *Id.* at art. 7(1).
174. *Id.* at art. 7(2).
175. *Id.* at art. 10(1).
176. *Id.* at art. 17(1).

"fast access and complete, correct and timely assessment of the information." If the Transparency Directive also requires the disclosure of such information, then the issuer is also required to follow the disclosure procedure promulgated by the Transparency Directive and the national legislation transposing the Transparency Directive. The information must be posted on the issuer's website for at least five years.[177]

It is often difficult to determine what events or information need to be disclosed and when disclosure should be made.[178] This must be done on a case-by-case basis. Some typical events requiring disclosure are mergers and acquisitions, reorganizations, changes to the financial reports, bankruptcy of a significant customer or debtor, significant lawsuits, termination of significant contracts, unexpected changes in the senior management, and employee strikes. In one case, the UK Financial Services Authority imposed a penalty of £500,000 on Photo-Me International plc, a company listed on the London Stock Exchange, for its delay in disclosing that its sales would not meet announced expectations.[179] In that case, Photo-Me announced that sales were expected to increase substantially in the ensuing six months due to new contracts for sales of mini photo labs which were currently under negotiation with large U.S. customers. When the likelihood of securing these contracts sank three months later, Photo-Me failed to publicly disclose this inside information and consequently violated the UK disclosure rules implementing the Market Abuse Directive.

The prompt disclosure of all inside information—even inside information which has a material impact on the issuer—is not always in the interests of the shareholders of the issuer. For example, the issuer may be negotiating an important acquisition and the disclosure of those negotiations threatens to cause the target company to discontinue negotiations. In recognition of this possibility, the Market Abuse Regulation allows an issuer to delay the disclosure if three conditions are fulfilled.[180] First, the immediate disclosure as otherwise required by the Regulation is likely to prejudice the legitimate interests of the issuer. Second, the issuer may delay the disclosure only if such delay is not likely to mislead the public. Finally, the issuer must be able to ensure the confidentiality of that information.

5.3 Geographic Scope of Prohibition on Market Abuse

The market abuse does not have to occur in the EU for it to be prohibited by the EU Market Abuse Regulation. The prohibition on market abuse applies to any market abuse (even if it takes place in a third country) and regardless of

---

177. *Id.*
178. *See, e.g.*, Case C-19/11, Geltl v. Daimler AG, 2012 E.C.R. I-____ (reported in the electronic reports of cases ECLI:EU:C:2012:397).
179. In re Photo-Me International plc, UK Financial Services Authority, Final Notice (June 21, 2010).
180. Market Abuse Regulation at art. 17(4).

whether or not the trade is conducted on a trading venue.[181] In *In re Swift Trade Inc.*, for example, the UK market abuse law was applied to a Canadian trader.[182] The only jurisdictional nexus prescribed by the Market Abuse Regulation[183] is that the market abuse concern financial instruments admitted to trading on a regulated market, multilateral trading facility, or an organized trading facility (or applied for) in the EU. For example, if a U.S. employee of a U.S. subsidiary of a German company listed on the Frankfurt Stock Exchange learns of inside information, and then has his broker in New York sell shares of the German company based on the inside information, the Market Abuse Regulation would still apply (subject, of course, to any personal jurisdiction challenges).

---

181. *Id.* at art. 2(3).
182. *In re* Swift Trade Inc., [2013] EWCA Civ. 1662 *available at* http://www.bailii.org/ew/cases/EWCA/Civ/2013/1662.html.
183. Market Abuse Regulation at art. 2(4).

CHAPTER **VII**

Insolvency Law

1. Introduction

EU legislation in the area of insolvency of companies is limited in scope, relatively new, and primarily limited to procedural issues. The Current Insolvency Regulation, which was adopted in 2000 and came into force on May 31, 2002,[1] and its successor legislation which applies as of June 26, 2017,[2] replaces the various bilateral treaties that existed between member states applicable to cross-border insolvencies.[3] These treaties, as well as the

---

1. Council Regulation (EUC) No. 1346/2000 of 29 May 2000 on insolvency proceedings O.J. 2000 (L 160) 1 [hereinafter Current Insolvency Regulation].
2. Regulation (EU) 2015/848 of the European Parliament and of the Council of 20 May 2015 on insolvency proceedings, 2015 O.J. (L 141) 19 [hereinafter New Insolvency Regulation]. As the New Insolvency Regulation does not apply until June 26, 2017, this Chapter is based on the Current Insolvency Regulation with cross references to the New Insolvency Regulation to the extent that the New Insolvency Regulation will introduce changes to the current law.
3. The Convention between Belgium and France on Jurisdiction and the Validity and Enforcement of Judgments, Arbitration Awards and Authentic Instruments, signed at Paris on 8 July 1899; The Convention between Belgium and Austria on Bankruptcy, Winding-up, Arrangements, Compositions and Suspension of Payments (with Additional Protocol of 13 June 1973), signed at Brussels on 16 July 1969; The Convention between Belgium and the Netherlands on Territorial Jurisdiction, Bankruptcy and the Validity and Enforcement of Judgments, Arbitration Awards and Authentic Instruments, signed at Brussels on 28 March 1925; The Treaty between Germany and Austria on Bankruptcy, Winding-up, Arrangements and Compositions, signed at Vienna on 25 May 1979; The Convention between France and Austria on Jurisdiction, Recognition and Enforcement of Judgments on Bankruptcy, signed at Vienna on 27 February 1979; The Convention between France and Italy on the Enforcement of Judgments in Civil and Commercial Matters, signed at Rome on 3 June 1930; The Convention between Italy and Austria on Bankruptcy, Winding-up, Arrangements and Compositions, signed at Rome on 12 July 1977; The Convention between the Kingdom of the Netherlands and the Federal Republic of Germany on the Mutual Recognition and Enforcement of Judgments and other Enforceable Instruments in Civil and Commercial Matters, signed at The Hague on 30 August 1962; The Convention between the United Kingdom and the Kingdom of Belgium providing for the Reciprocal Enforcement of Judgments in Civil and Commercial Matters, with Protocol, signed at Brussels on 2 May 1934; The Convention between Denmark, Finland, Norway, Sweden and Iceland on Bankruptcy, signed at Copenhagen on 7 November 1933; The European Convention on Certain International Aspects of Bankruptcy, signed at Istanbul on 5 June 1990.

Insolvency Regulation, address the jurisdictional issues related to bankruptcies of companies with assets and creditors in several countries.

Insolvency law, in very general terms, is about allocating between creditors of an insolvent entity or person rights to assets or proceeds from the sale of assets. Issues arise, however, when assets of the insolvent entity are located in several jurisdictions. For example, when a French company with assets in several member states institutes insolvency proceedings in France, the rights of creditors to the assets outside France are of primary concern. As the laws regulating the rights of creditors and claims to the assets differ among the member states, the threshold question in such a case concerns the legal effect of that French filing in the other member states. The Current Insolvency Regulation and the New Insolvency Regulation were adopted to address this issue. Their application is consequently limited to cases where a company or business has a presence in more than one member state. Neither the Current Insolvency Regulation nor the New Insolvency Regulation establishes a uniform insolvency code across the EU. Rather, they "merely" promulgate rules for allocating jurisdiction in cross-border insolvencies and determining the applicable law.[4] EU insolvency law has traditionally been and continues to fall within the authority of the member states.[5]

It is worth noting that the EU legislation in this field is in the form of a regulation. As discussed in Chapter I, a regulation is directly applicable in the member states without the member state having to take any additional step to transpose the regulation into national law. The Insolvency Regulations consequently preempt the application of the member state laws which may be otherwise applicable to resolve the same issues. This avoids the inefficiencies created by requiring the affected parties to review and apply the laws of the various jurisdictions affected by the insolvency. As, however, the Insolvency Regulations do not establish a uniform insolvency code, the national insolvency laws of the respective member states remain applicable to the substantive issues.

2. Scope of Insolvency Regulation

Both the Current Insolvency Regulation and the New Insolvency Regulation set forth rules allocating jurisdiction over collective insolvency proceedings which entail the partial or total divestment of a debtor and the appointment of

---

4. It should be noted in this context that the general rules for determining jurisdiction and the applicable law in civil matters—Regulation (EU) No. 1215/2012 of the European Parliament and of the Council of 12 December 2012 on jurisdiction and the recognition and enforcement of judgments in civil and commercial matters, 2012 O.J. (L 351) 1—expressly exclude insolvency proceedings. Consequently, the member states addressed the issue by entering into the conventions identified in note 3 above.
5. Current Insolvency Regulation at art. 4; New Insolvency Regulation at art. 7. Although the Commission has issued a recommendation addressing certain substantive issues, this is not binding on the member states. Commission Recommendation of 12 March 2014 on a new approach to business failure and insolvency, 2014 O.J. (L 74) 65.

a liquidator (the liquidator under the New Insolvency Regulation is referred to as the insolvency practitioner). As discussed above, the Insolvency Regulations only apply in cross-border insolvencies (i.e., the debtor has assets in more than one member state). The term insolvency is defined broadly. The Insolvency Regulations generally apply to all types of insolvency proceedings that involve the partial or total divestment of a debtor and the appointment of a liquidator.[6] There are, however, some sectoral exceptions codified in both the Current Insolvency Regulation and the New Insolvency Regulation. For example, insolvency proceedings concerning insurance companies, credit institutions, and investment firms and collective investment undertakings are governed by separate legislation and consequently do not fall under the Insolvency Regulations.[7] Once its application begins in 2017, the New Insolvency Regulation will also apply to debt-in-possession proceedings.[8]

3. Jurisdiction and Proper Forum for Insolvency Proceedings

As between the EU member states, the Current Insolvency Regulation and the New Insolvency Regulation designate the proper forum and the applicable law for filing insolvency proceedings.[9] The rule is that the courts of the member state where the debtor has its center of main interests (often referred to as the company's "COMI") have primary jurisdiction over the main insolvency proceedings.[10] If the center of main interests of the debtor is outside the EU, the Insolvency Regulations do not apply.[11] For example, if a U.S. company with its headquarters in New York files for bankruptcy protection, the rules codified in the Insolvency Regulations which preclude several member states from exercising jurisdiction over the insolvent company do not apply. The U.S.

---

6. As the member states use different terms for insolvency proceedings, both the Current Insolvency Regulation and the New Insolvency Regulation identify in an annexes what is meant by an insolvency proceeding.
7. Current Insolvency Regulation at art. 1(2); New Insolvency Regulation at art. 1(2). Insolvencies in the insurance industry are regulated by Directive 2001/17/EC of 19 March 2001 on the reorganization and winding up of insurance undertakings, 2001 O.J. (L 110) 28. Insolvencies in the banking industry are regulated by Directive 2001/24/EC of 4 April 2001 on the reorganization and winding up of credit institutions, 2001 O.J. (L 125) 15.
8. New Insolvency Regulation at art. 1(1)(c).
9. The allocation of jurisdiction within a particular member state is a matter of member state law. *See* Decision of the German Supreme Court in case no. (IX ER 39/06) (May 19, 2009), *reported at* Praxis des Internationalen Privat- und Verfahrensrechts (2009) at 15.
10. Current Insolvency Regulation at art. 3(1); New Insolvency Regulation at art. 3(1).
11. Current Insolvency Regulation at Preamble 14; New Insolvency Regulation at Preamble 25.

company in such a case would be faced with the potential application of the insolvency laws of the respective EU member states.[12]

The center of main interests is where the debtor conducts the administration of its interests on a regular basis.[13] For legal entities, the center of main interests is presumed to be the place of the registered office of the insolvent entity. Under the Current Insolvency Regulation, this presumption "can be rebutted only if factors which are both objective and ascertainable by third parties enable it to be established that an actual situation exists which is different from that which locating it at that registered office is deemed to reflect."[14] According to the European Court of Justice (ECJ), this would be the case, for example, if the company were a letterbox company with no activities in the jurisdiction of its registration. It is for the courts of the member states to determine the center of main interests in individual cases.[15] In order to prevent forum shopping by entities in the period prior to insolvency, the New Insolvency Regulation disallows such presumption if the registered office has been moved between member states in the 3 months prior to the insolvency filing.[16]

The term "main solvency proceeding" refers to the insolvency proceeding opened in the member state in which the debtor has its center of main interest.[17] It is possible, however, for a legal entity to be active in member states outside the member state where it has its center of main interests. The opening of insolvency proceedings in the member state where the debtor has its main interests does not necessarily preclude the other member states where the debtor has assets from opening an insolvency proceeding regarding the assets in those member states. However, in order for these member states to do so, the debtor must have an establishment in that member state.[18] All such proceedings are referred to as the secondary insolvency proceedings for purposes of EU insolvency law.

The jurisdiction granted to the member state where the debtor has its center of main interests includes ancillary proceedings related to the insolvency. The criterion used by the ECJ in determining which actions are ancillary is whether the action derives directly from the bankruptcy or winding-up and is closely connected with the insolvency proceedings.[19] In *Seagon v. Deko Marty Belgium NV*, for example, a German company transferred €50,000 to a German bank account of a Belgian company the day before the German company filed for bankruptcy. The insolvency trustee in Germany sought to

---

12. In general, U.S. insolvency proceedings are recognized by the member states. *See, e.g.*, Decision of the German Supreme Court in case no. X ZR 79/06 (Oct. 13, 2009) in which the German Supreme Court held that a U.S. Chapter 11 proceeding has a suspensory effect on legal proceedings in Germany.
13. Current Insolvency Regulation at Preamble 13; New Insolvency Regulation at art. 3(1).
14. C-341/04, *In re* Eurofood IFSC Ltd., 2006 E.C.R. I-3854, 3868 ¶34.
15. *Id.* at 3868 ¶35.
16. New Insolvency Regulation at art. 3(1).
17. Current Insolvency Regulation at art. 3(1); New Insolvency Regulation at art. 3(1).
18. Current Insolvency Regulation at art. 3(2); New Insolvency Regulation at art. 3(2).
19. Case C-339/07, Seagon v. Deko Marty Belgium NV, 2009 E.C.R. I-791, 799 ¶19. This is addressed in the New Insolvency Regulation at art. 6(1).

have the transfer of funds set aside. The issue was whether the German court where the main insolvency proceedings were filed also had jurisdiction over the claim for unwinding the transaction. The ECJ concluded that "the courts of the member state within the territory of which insolvency proceedings have been opened have jurisdiction to decide an action to set a transaction aside by virtue of insolvency that is brought against a person whose registered office is in another Member State."[20]

In cases of corporate groups, determining the center of main interests must be done for each legal entity within the group.[21] For example, if a Maltese company has subsidiaries in Estonia, Latvia, and Lithuania, and each of these entities is insolvent, they each need to determine where their respective centers of main interests are located. The center of main interests in not necessarily that of the parent company.[22] The *Daisytek* case illustrates, however, that they may all have the same center of main interests. In that case, the U.S. corporation, Daisytek International Corporation, filed for bankruptcy protection in the United States under Chapter 11 of the U.S. Bankruptcy Code. Daisytek International Corporation owned 100 percent of Daisytek-ISA Ltd., an English limited company, which served as a holding company for 15 other subsidiaries throughout Europe. Daisytek filed one solvency proceeding in the UK covering all of its European subsidiaries. The High Court in Leeds agreed that the UK was the center of main interests not only for the UK holding company, but also for all of its European subsidiaries.[23]

The main proceedings may take the form of either reorganizations or winding-up (i.e., liquidation) proceedings and generally include all of the assets of the debtor wherever located except those subject to the jurisdiction of a secondary proceeding. It is important to distinguish reorganizations from winding-up proceedings in the context of insolvency law. In a reorganization proceeding, the company continues to exist under protection from its creditors but with the perspective of the company eventually emerging from such protection. In a winding-up proceeding, the company's assets are liquidated and the operations sold or closed.

As indicated above, the opening of the main proceedings in the primary jurisdiction does not preclude the other member states from opening secondary insolvency proceedings under the Current Insolvency Regulation. However, there are three important limitations imposed on secondary proceedings. First, secondary proceedings under the Current Insolvency Regulation are

---

20. Case C-339/07, Seagon v. Deko Marty Belgium NV, 2009 E.C.R. I-791, 801 ¶28.
21. The New Insolvency Regulation (arts. 56-77) establishes a new framework for cooperation among insolvency practitioners and national courts in cases of group insolvencies.
22. C-341/04, *In re* Eurofood IFSC Ltd., 2006 E.C.R. I-3813, 3867 ¶30. According to the ECJ, there is not even a presumption that the center of main interests of a subsidiary is in the same member state where the parent company is established. As discussed in Chapter III, this is different from the presumptions used in competition law. Competition law assumes that a parent and its subsidiary are one economic unit. Case T-12/03, Itochu Corp. v. Comm'n, 2009 E.C.R. II-890, 906 ¶49.
23. *In re* Daisytek-ISA Ltd., [2003] BCC 562.

limited to winding-up proceedings.[24] This means that a reorganization is not allowed in a secondary insolvency, the idea being that there should only be one jurisdiction responsible for overseeing the reorganization. The opening of secondary proceedings may be requested by the liquidator (referred to as the insolvency practitioner in the New Insolvency Regulation) in the main proceedings or any other person or authority empowered to request the opening of insolvency proceedings under the law of the member state where the opening of secondary proceedings is requested.[25]

The second important limitation on secondary insolvency proceedings is that a member state may only open secondary insolvency proceedings if the debtor possesses an establishment within its territory.[26] The term "establishment" does not necessarily mean a subsidiary. It includes any place of operations where the debtor carries out a nontransitory economic activity with human means and goods.[27] According to the ECJ, "the presence alone of goods in isolation or bank accounts does not, in principle, satisfy the requirements for classification as an 'establishment.'"[28] The opening of the main insolvency proceedings in the member state in which the debtor has its center of main interests is generally considered to be universal, i.e., apply to assets owned by the debtor wherever located. The third limitation is that secondary proceedings apply only to assets located in that member state (whereas the main insolvency proceedings apply to all other assets).[29] For example, a Dutch court in a secondary insolvency proceeding may not rule on the disposition of assets located in Belgium.

The center of main interests is determined at the time the bankruptcy proceedings are filed. That determination applies regardless of whether the debtor changes its center of main interest after the insolvency filing. In *In re Staubitz-Schreiber*, for example, the German debtor with her center of main interests in Germany filed an application for opening insolvency proceedings in Germany.[30] Several months later she moved to Spain, and with it her center of main interests changed. However, the ECJ held that "the Regulation must be interpreted as meaning that the court of the Member State within the territory of which the centre of the debtor's main interests is situated at the time when the debtor lodges the request to open insolvency proceedings retains jurisdiction to open those proceedings if the debtor moves the centre of his main interests

---

24. Current Insolvency Regulation at art. 3(3). Under the New Insolvency Regulation, secondary proceedings are not limited to liquidation proceedings.
25. Current Insolvency Regulation at art. 29; New Insolvency Regulation at art. 37.
26. Current Insolvency Regulation at art. 3(2); New Insolvency Regulation at art. 3(2).
27. Under the New Insolvency Regulation, "establishment" is limited to "any place of operations where a debtor carries out or has carried out in the 3-month period prior to the request to open main insolvency proceedings a non-transitory economic activity with human means and assets."
28. Case C-327/13, Burgo Group SpA v. Illochroma SA, 2014 E.C.R. I-___, at ¶31.
29. Current Insolvency Regulation at art. 27; New Insolvency Regulation at art. 34.
30. For individuals, the center of main interest is presumptively the habitual residence of the insolvent individual. Current Insolvency Regulation at art. 3(1); New Insolvency Regulation at art. 3(1).

to the territory of another Member State after lodging the request but before the proceedings are opened."[31]

4. Applicable Law

The Current Insolvency Regulation and the New Insolvency Regulation not only determine the appropriate forum for insolvency proceedings but they also determine which member state's law is to be applied. The law applicable to main and secondary insolvency proceedings and their effects is that of the member state where such main or secondary proceedings are opened (*lex concursus*).[32] For example, if the main proceedings are opened in Portugal and secondary proceedings opened in Greece, the law of Portugal would apply to the main proceedings and the law of Greece to the secondary proceedings. This includes issues related to the opening of the proceedings, their conduct, and their completion. It also determines (subject to some exceptions) other issues such as set-off, proof of debts, the powers of the liquidators, and the distribution of assets. Hence, it is national insolvency law which continues to apply to the substantive issues. The Current Insolvency Regulation and the New Insolvency Regulation merely identify whose laws apply.

The application of the law of the forum may be inappropriate in particular cases to certain relationships affected by the insolvency. For example, if an insolvency proceeding were filed in Finland by a Finnish conglomerate, the effect of the insolvency on employee contracts for that conglomerate's German operations would probably be inappropriate. The Insolvency Regulations therefore contain certain exceptions to the general rule that the applicable law is that of the member state where the insolvency proceedings were filed. For example, the effects of insolvency proceedings on employment contracts and relationships are governed solely by the law of the member state applicable to the contract of employment.[33] In addition, issues relating to real property and *in rem* rights (e.g., mortgages, liens, and floating charges) will generally be governed by the law of the member state where such assets are located (which may or may not be where the insolvency proceedings are initiated).[34] Another exception is that the rights and obligations of parties to a payment or settlement system or to a financial market will be governed by the law of the member state applicable to that system or market.[35] The London Stock Exchange, International Financial Futures and Options Exchange, and the London Commodity Exchange are some of the recognized financial markets.

---

31. Case C-1/04, *In re* Staubitz-Schreiber, 2006 E.C.R. I-719, 729 ¶29.
32. Current Insolvency Regulation at art. 4(1); New Insolvency Regulation at art. 7(1).
33. Current Insolvency Regulation at art. 10; New Insolvency Regulation at art. 13(1).
34. Current Insolvency Regulation at art. 5(1); New Insolvency Regulation at art. 8(1). This exception does not apply, however, if the conduct at issue – for example, the payment of a pre-existing debt out of the bankruptcy estate – is subject to the law of another member state. Case C-557/13, Lutz v. Bäuerle, ECLI:EU:C:2015:227 at ¶41.
35. Current Insolvency Regulation at art. 9; New Insolvency Regulation at art. 12.

5. Automatic Mutual Recognition

One important aspect of both the Current Insolvency Regulation and the New Insolvency Regulation is that they require the member states to recognize both orders opening proceedings (main proceedings as well as secondary) and judgments of other member states handed down in connection with those proceedings.[36] As soon as a court in one member state where the debtor has its main interest issues a judgment to open proceedings under the laws of that member state, this precludes the other member states from opening main proceedings (but they may open secondary proceedings). The Current Insolvency Regulation does not define when a judgment to open proceedings is deemed to have been issued. As the member states all have different insolvency procedures, identifying the occurrence of this important event can sometimes be a challenge.[37] According to the ECJ:

> A 'decision to open insolvency proceedings' for the purposes of the Regulation must be regarded as including not only a decision which is formally described as an opening decision by the legislation of the Member State of the court that handed it down, but also a decision handed down following an application, based on the debtor's insolvency, seeking the opening of proceedings referred to in Annex A to the Regulation, where that decision involves divestment of the debtor and the appointment of a liquidator referred to in Annex C to the Regulation. Such divestment involves the debtor losing the powers of management which he has over his assets. In such a case, the two characteristic consequences of insolvency proceedings, namely the appointment of a liquidator referred to in Annex C and the divestment of the debtor, have taken effect, and thus all the elements constituting the definition of such proceedings, given in Article 1(1) of the Regulation, are present.[38]

In addition, the other member states are required to give the debtor and creditors the same protection as if the insolvency proceeding were opened in their country.[39] In other words, the judgment opening the proceedings produces the same effects in any other member state as under the law of the state of the opening of proceedings. This does not apply, however, to any member states where secondary insolvency proceedings are opened. If, for example, an Austrian court accepts an insolvency filing against an Austrian company with

---

36. Current Insolvency Regulation at art. 16; New Insolvency Regulation at art. 19.
37. The New Insolvency Regulation (art. 2(8)) tries to avoid this problem by defining the time of the opening of proceedings as "the time at which the judgment opening insolvency proceedings becomes effective, regardless of whether the judgment is final or not."
38. C-341/04, *In re* Eurofood IFSC Ltd., 2006 E.C.R. I-3854, 3874 ¶54.
39. Current Insolvency Regulation at art. 17; New Insolvency Regulation at art. 20.

assets in Italy, Italian creditors of that Austrian company cannot foreclose on the Italian assets if the insolvency law of Austria precludes them from doing so because of the opening of the insolvency proceedings in Austria. If, however, secondary proceedings are opened in Italy, the Italian insolvency law would apply to the assets located in Italy.

The general rule is that the decision to open insolvency proceedings by a member state court is not subject to challenge by the courts of the other member states.[40] Therefore, if a member state court decides that the company's center of main interests is in that member state, the courts in other member states must respect that decision even though they may have arrived at a different conclusion. The only exception is that a member state may refuse to recognize insolvency proceedings opened in another member state or to enforce a judgment handed down in the context of such proceedings if the effects of such recognition or enforcement would be manifestly contrary to that state's public policy.[41] If, for example, the member state where the insolvency proceedings were opened committed "a manifest breach of a rule of law regarded as essential in the legal order of the State in which enforcement is sought or of a right recognized as being fundamental within that legal order."[42]

6. Rights of Creditors

As soon as insolvency proceedings are opened in a member state, the court of that state having jurisdiction or the liquidator appointed by it has the obligation to immediately inform known creditors who have their habitual residences, domiciles, or registered offices in the other member states of the insolvency filing.[43] That notice must include time limits, the penalties laid down in regard to those time limits, the body or authority empowered to accept claims, any other measures laid down, and whether creditors whose claims are preferential or secured *in rem* need to lodge their claims.

Creditors, even those in other member states,[44] then have the right to file claims in accordance with the law of the member state of the main proceedings or secondary proceedings as the case may be.[45] There are specific rules for foreign creditors. According to the New Insolvency Regulation, once insolvency proceedings are opened in a member state, the insolvency practitioner appointed by the court or the court itself is required to "immediately inform" the known foreign creditors by providing those creditors individual notice containing the time deadlines, the consequences of not meeting the to those time deadlines, the

---

40. *Id.* at 3871 ¶42.
41. Insolvency Regulation at art. 33.
42. C-341/04, *In re* Eurofood IFSC Ltd., 2006 E.C.R. I-3854, 3876 ¶63.
43. Current Insolvency Regulation at art. 40; New Insolvency Regulation at art. 54.
44. Current Insolvency Regulation at art. 40; New Insolvency Regulation at art. 53.
45. Current Insolvency Regulation at art. 32; New Insolvency Regulation at art. 45.

body or authority to which claims are to be submitted.[46] The foreign creditor then can lodge its claim using the standard claims form used for EU creditors. If the foreign creditor does not want to use the standard form, it can file its claim using a different document as long as it contains the prescribed information.[47] Claims by foreign creditors may be lodged in any official language of the institutions of the Union.[48]

7. Reservation of Title

In many civil law countries, the seller of products may retain title to those products until they are fully paid for. This possibility, similar to a purchase money security interest in the United States (§ 9-103 UCC), gives the seller some security over products delivered in the event that the buyer is unable to pay for those products. For example, when a German supplier sells products to a customer, the German supplier and the customer can agree on a retention of title clause (*Eigentumsvorbehalt*) which allows the German supplier to get its products back in the event of nonpayment by or insolvency of the customer.[49]

EU commercial law requires that the member states recognize retention of title agreements.[50] Both the Current Insolvency Regulation and the New Insolvency Regulation expressly recognize this form of security. The opening of insolvency proceedings against the purchaser of an asset does not affect the seller's rights based on a reservation of title if, at the time of the opening of proceedings, the asset is situated within the territory of a member state other than the state of the main proceedings.[51] For example, if a debtor files for insolvency in Malta, but has assets in Greece which are subject to a retention of title right held by a Greek supplier, the Maltese insolvency administrator or court must recognize this right in the Maltese insolvency proceedings.

In most cases, the reservation of title issue will arise when the purchaser of the products is insolvent. This is illustrated in the case immediately above involving the Maltese debtor and a Greek creditor. It is possible, however, that a seller holding a reservation of title becomes insolvent. For example, in the case immediately above, the Greek supplier could have filed for insolvency protection and not the Maltese debtor. In such cases, the reservation of title is considered an asset of the seller. If it is the seller for whom insolvency proceedings are

---

46. New Insolvency Regulation at art. 54(1) & (2). As a general rule, the notice must be in the official language of the member state where the proceedings were opened or in another language which that member state has indicated it can accept (often this is English).
47. *Id.* at art. 55(4).
48. *Id.* at art. 55(5).
49. § 449 German Civil Code.
50. Article 4 of the Directive 2000/35/EC of the European Parliament and of the Council of 29 June 2000 on combating late payment in commercial transactions, 2000 O.J. (L 200) 35.
51. Current Insolvency Regulation at art. 7; New Insolvency Regulation at art. 10.

opened after delivery of the asset, the opening of such proceedings does not constitute grounds for rescinding or terminating the sale. Moreover, the filing of insolvency proceedings against the seller does not prevent the purchaser from acquiring title in accordance with their agreement.

8. Insolvency Forum Shopping

The choice of law rules codified in the Insolvency Regulation, combined with the lack of harmonization of the substantive insolvency rules among the member states, creates the possibility and even the incentive for forum shopping. There may be advantages of filing for insolvency in one member state as opposed to the other. This was illustrated in the *Schefenacker* insolvency case.[52] The German company, Schefenacker AG, experienced cash flow difficulties and considered applying for insolvency protection. However, it worked out a deal with its secured creditors to exchange debt (corporate bonds issued by the company) for equity in the company. German insolvency law, however, did not permit the debt-to-equity conversion. Consequently, to effectuate the agreement, the company had to migrate to the UK whose insolvency law permitted such debt-for-equity swaps in the context of insolvency proceedings.

Schefenacker AG first transformed from a German Aktiengesellschaft (stock corporation) into a German GmbH & Co. KG (limited partnership) in which the newly formed Schefenacker plc, an English company, served as the general partner. The other general partner and the limited partner in Schefenacker GmbH & Co. KG then withdrew from the partnership. Under German law, the partnership dissolved and all assets and liabilities transferred by operation of law to Schefenacker plc.[53]

Forum shopping to achieve the most advantageous results for the company is possible under the Current Insolvency Regulation. However, the insolvency courts in the EU are scrutinizing the center of main interests in such cases. As discussed above, the center of main interests is presumptively—but not conclusively—the place of the company's registered office. If creditors and other stakeholders can prove that the debtor conducts its regular administration in another member state, they may challenge this presumption. Therefore, merely migrating the company's place of incorporation may be insufficient.

In *Hans Brochier Holdings Ltd v. Exner*, for example, the German company Hans Brochier GmbH & Co. KG attempted to migrate its center of main interests from Germany to the UK using a similar procedure as employed by Schefenacker and discussed above. Within an hour after the newly formed Hans Brochier Holdings Ltd. opened insolvency proceedings in the UK, the employees of Brochier in Germany applied to a German court for the opening of insolvency proceedings in Germany. According to Article 16(1) of the Current Insolvency

---

52. "Schefenacker strebt Insolvenz nach britischem Recht an", reported at Handelsblatt, http://www.handelsblatt.com/unternehmen/industrie/unkonventioneller-rettungsversuch-schefenacker-strebt-insolvenz-nach-britischem-recht-an-seite-2/2728708-2.html.
53. § 738(1) German Civil Code.

Regulation, the German court should have refrained from opening insolvency proceedings. However, it considered the English insolvency proceedings invalid as contrary to German public policy.[54] Upon further contemplation, the English court agreed and held its initial decision invalid.[55]

These cases are less likely to arise under the New Insolvency Regulation. As mentioned above, the presumption that the member state where the registered office is located does not apply if the registered office has been moved to another member state within the 3-month period prior to the request for the opening of insolvency proceedings.[56] When the presumption does not apply, the court must identify where "the debtor conducts the administration of its interests on a regular basis and which is ascertainable by third parties."[57]

9. Insurance and Financial Industry Insolvencies

As discussed above, insurance companies, credit institutions, and investment firms holding funds or securities for third parties are excluded from the scope of the Insolvency Regulation. The rationale for these exclusions is that such corporate entities are subject to special arrangements and are subject to oversight by national supervisory authorities. There is separate legislation applicable to insurance companies and banks.[58] The basic principle is that only the competent authorities of the home member state are entitled to decide on the reorganization measures with respect to an insurance undertaking, including its branches in other member states.[59] Reorganization measures and winding up proceedings are governed by the laws, regulations, and procedures applicable in the home member state.

---

54. Decision of the Amtsgericht Nüremberg of August 15, 2006 reprinted in 10 Neue Zeitschrift für Insolvenzrecht 185 (2007). As discussed above, the only exception to the obligation to recognize a decision of another member state is public policy. Current Insolvency Regulation at art. 7; New Insolvency Regulation at art. 10.
55. Hans Brochier Holdings Ltd. v. Exner, [2006] EWHC 2594 (Ch).
56. New Insolvency Regulation at art. 3(1).
57. Id.
58. Directive 2003/138/EC of the European Parliament and of the Council of 25 November 2009 on the taking-up and pursuit of the business of Insurance and Reinsurance 2009 O.J. (L 335) 1; Directive 2002/83/EC of the European Parliament and of the Council of 5 November 2002 concerning life insurance, 2002 O.J. (L 345) 1.
59. The "home member state" means the member state in which an insurance undertaking has been authorized.

CHAPTER **VIII**

Sales Agency Law

1. Applicable Law

Developing and producing a product are only the preliminary steps to achieving commercial success with that product. As many manufacturers have experienced, even a superior product does not guarantee high sales volumes. Establishing an adequate distribution and sales network is often critical. As discussed in Chapter IV, the manufacturer of a product basically has three choices by which to bring its goods to market. It can set up subsidiaries or branch sales offices to market the products; it can sell the products to an independent distributor; or it can engage sales representatives to secure orders for the product. The latter of these three options is the subject of this Chapter.

Sales representatives are often individuals or small businesses operating from their residence. As the sales representative does not commonly take possession of the products, but merely arranges their sale, there is not a need for capital-intensive operations. On the other hand, the manufacturers on whose behalf the sales representatives act are often large companies. Once the sales representative does the groundwork and establishes an attractive portfolio of customers, there is often an incentive for the manufacturer to terminate the sales representative and deal with the customer directly. Based on a concern that these large companies will take advantage of their position vis-à-vis the sales representatives, member states enacted laws to protect them. The different levels of protection, and the fact that some member states accorded no protection, created a perceived barrier to trade between member states. In an attempt to harmonize these national laws, the Council adopted the Sales Representative Directive in 1986.[1]

2. Scope of Law

The Sales Representative Directive applies only to "commercial agents." A commercial agent is a natural or legal person who has continuing authority to negotiate the sale or purchase of goods on behalf of another person, the principal,

---

1. Council Directive 86/653/EEC of 18 December 1986 on the coordination of the laws of the member states relating to self-employed commercial agents, 1986 O.J. (L 382) 17 [hereinafter Sales Representative Directive].

or to negotiate and conclude such transactions on behalf of and in the name of that principal.[2] The requirement of goods means that a person selling services on behalf another person—for example, selling subscriptions to a particular cable television service—would not qualify as a commercial agent for purposes of the Sales Representative Directive.[3] The term commercial agent is often used synonymously with sales agent or sale representative.

In *Poseidon Chartering v. Marianne Zeeschip*, the definition of "continuing authority" was at issue.[4] It is clear that the definition of commercial agent in the Sales Representative Directive requires that the agent have continuing authority to act on behalf of the principal. In this case, the purported agent was engaged to charter a ship for the purported principal. The agent chartered a ship. The charter was subsequently extended by the purported principal on an annual basis from 1994 to 2000. When the relationship between the principal and agent came to an end, the agent claimed that it had rights under the Sales Representative Directive for an indemnification payment. The issue was whether the agent qualified as an agent under the Directive even though it was engaged for only one contract.

The European Court of Justice (ECJ) recognized that the number of transactions the intermediary concludes on behalf of the principal is normally an indication of whether the authority is continuing.[5] But the mere fact that an intermediary concludes only one contract does not preclude the finding that the authority was continuing. In the present case, the ECJ held, the intermediary was to be considered a commercial agent (even though it had concluded only one contract) if it had the authority to negotiate extensions of that contract (a factual issue which the ECJ left to the national court).[6]

The definition of commercial agent excludes (1) a person who, in her capacity as an officer of the principal, is empowered to enter into commitments binding on a company, (2) a partner who is lawfully authorized to enter into commitments binding on her partners, or (3) a receiver, a receiver and manager, a liquidator, or a trustee in bankruptcy. For example, if two individuals agree to set up a partnership to sell USB flash drives to college students, and one of the partners takes responsibility for promoting the product and securing customers, that partner cannot claim she is a commercial agent of the partnership under the Sales Representative Directive. Moreover, the Sales Representative Directive does not apply to commercial agents whose activities are unpaid, or commercial agents when they operate on commodity exchanges or in the commodity market.

Many member states require commercial agents to register with a central authority. In most instances, the purpose is to deter tax evasion on the commissions

---

2. Sales Representative Directive at art. 1(2). The parameters of the agency relationship for purposes of competition are discussed in detail in the Commission Guidelines on Vertical Restraints, 2010 O.J. (C 130) 1, 4 ¶¶12-21.
3. Crane v. Sky In-Home Service Ltd., [2007] EWHC 66 (Ch).
4. Case C-3/04, Poseidon Chartering v. Zeeschip, 2006 E.C.R. I-2518.
5. *Id.* at 2529 ¶25.
6. *Id.* at 2529 ¶26.

earned by commercial agents. Although such registration requirements conform to the Sales Representative Directive, the failure to register must not preclude the agent from the protections accorded by the Sales Representative Directive.[7] In other words, the commercial agent is entitled to the protections regardless of whether she registers in accordance with the national law.

3. Protections Offered

3.1 Right to Remuneration

A commercial agent is generally entitled to reasonable remuneration.[8] If the principal and agent have not agreed to an amount or national law does not provide for a specific amount, the amount of remuneration is determined by what is customary for commercial agents in the same industry in the place where the commercial agent carries on his activities. That determination is a factual issue in the discretion of the national courts. If there is no such customary practice, a commercial agent is entitled to reasonable remuneration, taking into account all the aspects of the transaction.

3.2 Right to Commission

The basic rule is that a commercial agent is entitled to commissions on commercial transactions concluded during the period covered by the sales representative contract,[9] and in some instances after the sales representative contract is terminated.[10] For transactions concluded during the period covered by the sales representative contract, the agent is entitled to a commission if the transaction has been concluded as a result of his action or has been concluded with a third party whom he has previously acquired as a customer for transactions of the same kind. Assume that Orange Computers (a large computer manufacturer) engages Dansk Computers, which has been active in this field for a number of years, as a sales agent in Denmark to sell computers manufactured by Orange Computers in that country. Dansk Computers has sold computers to the Copenhagen school system for a number of years. Once Orange Computers engages Dansk as a commercial agent, Dansk will have a claim for commission on sales of computers manufactured by Orange Computers to the Copenhagen school system even though Dansk did not necessarily go out and secure the school system as a customer specifically for Orange Computers.

In addition, if the agent is entrusted with a specific geographical area or group of customers, or has an exclusive right to a specific geographical area or group of customers, which is often the case, the agent is also entitled to commission

---

7. Case C-456/98, Centrosteel Srl v. Adipol GmbH, 2000 E.C.R. I-6007; Case C-215/97, Barbara Bellone v. Yokahama SpA, 1998 E.C.R. I-2191.
8. Sales Representative Directive at art. 6(1).
9. *Id.* at art. 7(1).
10. *Id.* at art. 8.

on transactions concluded during the period covered by the agency contract with customers belonging to that area or group.[11] Whereas the first right of commission discussed above relates to sales arranged by the commercial agent, this provision of the Directive extends the right to commissions to potentially include sales to customers which are not arranged by the agent. This raises the issue of whether the commercial agent has a claim for commission for all sales within his or her territory even if he or she had nothing to do with the sale. As the reliance on the Internet for marketing and securing supplies has replaced or at least reduced the traditional reliance on sales agents, the issue becomes more important. For example, customers commonly order directly from the manufacturer's website, thereby bypassing the sales agent.

The *Kontogeorgas v. Kartonpak* case illustrates that no action by the commercial agent is required in order for the agent to claim a commission if the customer is located in the area allocated to the agent.[12] In that case, Georgios Kontogeorgas entered into a sales agent agreement with Kartonpak giving him commission on sales in a certain part of Greece. Kartonpak was subsequently merged into Saint Ritsis. Kartonpak then began selling to Saint Ritsis customers in the territory of Kontogeorgas without paying him a commission because they were Saint Ritsis customers. The ECJ held, however, that the Sales Representative Directive requires the principal to pay Kontogeorgas a commission even though he had nothing to do with securing the customer for the principal.[13]

The commercial agent has a claim to a commission for transactions concluded after the agency contract has terminated only in narrow circumstances. If the transaction is mainly attributable to the commercial agent's efforts during the period covered by the contract with the commercial agent, and if the transaction was entered into within a reasonable period after that contract terminated, the agent may have a claim for a commission on those sales if, for example, the sales agent has been marketing to a specific customer for a long period of time and there is some indication that the customer is ready to purchase a large quantity of the product. The manufacturer, in that case, may want to allow the sales agency agreement to expire and make the sales to the customer directly to avoid having to pay the sales agent a commission.[14] This provision of the Sales Representative Directive is designed to protect the sales agent in this circumstance.

The other situation in which the agent can claim compensation for sales concluded after termination of the contract is if the order of the third party reached the principal or the commercial agent before the contract with the commercial agent terminated. For example, assume hypothetically that Sony engaged Guido Volare as its sales agent in Italy for one year. With only one week left on the contract, Sony received a large order for products from an Italian customer arranged by Guido. Sony would owe Guido a commission

---

11. *Id.* at art. 7(2).
12. Case C-104/95, Kontogeorgas v. Kartonpak, 1996 E.C.R. I-6643.
13. *Id.* at I-6666 ¶30.
14. Sales Representative Directive art. 8(a).

on that sale even if Sony delayed filling the order until after the sales agency relationship with Guido had ended.

3.3 Right to Compensation upon Termination

(a) Types of Compensation

Commercial agents tend to be individuals or smaller companies. In many instances, they promote and sell the products or services of a significantly larger company. The primary service provided by the commercial agent is establishing relationships with customers. Given this relationship and the nature of the commercial agent's services, there is the possibility that the principal might terminate the agency relationship once the principal has been introduced to the customer. In this way, the principal could avoid having to pay the agent a commission. In order to protect the sales agent in such circumstances, the Sales Representative Directive requires that the member states grant the commercial agent the right to receive either an indemnification payment or termination compensation.

(b) Termination

The fundamental requirement for both the indemnification payment and the termination payment is the termination of the agreement. In most cases, termination is not an issue. The Sales Representative Directive entitles the sales representative to receive a written agreement setting out the terms of the agency contract.[15] The agreement between the principal and agent will typically establish the conditions for termination. Where the contract is for an indefinite period, either party may terminate it by giving the other party notice. Termination, which is an issue for national contract law, generally means that the contract has come to an end either in accordance with its terms or by termination by one or both of the parties. Terminating the sales agent agreement by effluxion of time constitutes termination for purposes of the Sales Representative Directive. For example, if the agreement has a duration of three years, the expiration of the agreement after those three years is considered a termination.[16]

Not all terminations will trigger compensation rights. The general rule is that the commercial agent has a claim to indemnity payment or the termination compensation unless (1) the agent has terminated the agency contract or (2) the agent is terminated by the principal for cause.[17] For example, if the commercial agent is simply not performing under the terms of the agreement with the principal, a subsequent termination by the principal will not trigger

---

15. *Id.* at art. 13. As this is a compulsory provision, it cannot be waived by the sales representative.
16. Stuart Light v. Ty Europe Ltd, 2003 WL 21729331 (Ct of Appeal QB 2003); Tigana Ltd. v. Decoro Ltd., 2003 EWHC 23 (QB).
17. According to the ECJ, if the principal terminates the agent without cause, and then later finds out that it had sufficient cause to terminate the agent, the principal cannot claim termination for cause and avoid paying compensation to the agent. Case C-203/09, Volvo Car Germany GmbH v. Autohof Weidensdorf GmbH, 2010 E.C.R. I-10740, 10757 ¶39.

compensation rights. These are issues of fact which are left to the national courts to determine in each case. In *NPower Direct Ltd. v. South of Scotland Power Ltd.*, an electricity company engaged a sales agent to sell electricity to small and medium-sized companies in the UK.[18] After the price of electricity increased, and the relationship between the parties deteriorated, the sales agent ceased promoting the principal's electricity. Consequently, the principal terminated the agreement, and the agent claimed compensation. The English court held that the agent anticipatorily repudiated the agreement, and the termination by the principal was justified.

As discussed above, termination by the agent generally precludes the agent from claiming compensation. It is important to point out at this stage that there are exceptions to this rule. If the termination by the agent is justified by (1) circumstances attributable to the principal or (2) on grounds of age, infirmity, or illness of the agent in consequence of which the agent cannot reasonably be required to continue its activities, then the agent is not considered to have terminated the agreement.[19] If, for example, a commercial agent represents a manufacturer for a number of years and then is involved in an automobile accident in which she incurs injuries preventing her from working, the agent still has a claim for compensation even though she—and not the principal—fails to perform the agreement.

Less clear is the situation where the business of the principal is sold. In the event that the principal's shares are sold, then the agreement with the sale agent stays with the business (i.e., legal entity). If, however, the principal sells the assets of the business, but not the legal entity, it is not clear whether a termination has occurred. Assuming that the sale of the assets of the business does not breach the agreement with the sales agent, the contractual relationship could still exist (i.e., not terminate) as the legal entity which entered into the agreement continues to exist. The problem is, however, that the commercial agent will not have any products to sell. As most courts tend to favor the sales representative, one would expect that the transfer of all the assets of a business is deemed a constructive termination of the agency relationship if there is no business for the commercial agent to promote.

There must, of course, be a contractual relationship between the principal and the agent. If a manufacturer sells its products to a distributor or a wholesaler, and that distributor or wholesaler engages a sales agent to sell those products, the principal-agent relationship is between the distributor or wholesaler and the agent, and not between the manufacturer and the agent. In *Stuart Light v. Ty Europe Ltd*, the U.S. maker of beanie babies entered into a distribution agreement with a UK company.[20] The UK distributor hired individual sales agents to market the products in the UK. At the end of these agreements, the sales agents sought termination compensation from Ty Europe with which it did not have a contractual relationship. The UK court of appeals held that these subagents did not have a claim against the principal under UK law which transposed the Sales

---

18. NPower Direct Ltd. v. South of Scotland Power Ltd., [2005] EWHC 2123 (QB).
19. Sales Representative Directive at art. 18.
20. Stuart Light v. Ty Europe Ltd, 2003 WL 21729331 (Ct of Appeal QB 2003).

Agent Directive. The same would apply if the manufacturer engaged a sales representative who then engaged sub-agents to sell the products or services. The contractual relationship in this case would be between the agent and its sub-agents and not between the manufacturer and the sub-agents.

(c) Indemnification Payment

The commercial agent has a right to receive an indemnification payment if the agent has brought the principal new customers or has significantly increased the volume of business with existing customers and the principal continues to derive substantial benefits from the business with such customers.[21] In general, the amount of the indemnification payment will correspond to the value of the new customers brought in by the commercial agent and the business which the commercial agent was able to expand from the principal's existing customers.[22] According to the ECJ, the member states should only look to the benefits accruing to the principal and not to any other legal entities that might belong to the same corporate group.[23]

The Sales Representative Directive imposes only two general limitations on the indemnification payment. First, the maximum amount of the indemnification payment is equal to the agent's average annual commissions over the preceding five years. If the contract is less than five years in duration, the indemnity is calculated on the average for the period in question. Second, the payment amount must be equitable. The Directive leaves it up to the member states to decide what is equitable given the particular circumstances in the case. Consequently, there is significant disparity among the member states regarding the equitable cap placed on indemnification amounts.

(d) Termination Compensation

As an alternative,[24] the member states may choose to grant the agent a claim for termination compensation. In contrast to the indemnification payment, which is a fixed amount based on a formula, the amount of the termination compensation is determined by the damage incurred by the agent as a result of the termination.[25] This is measured by the amount of the commission which the agent would have received had the contract not been terminated (and assuming that the agent properly performed). The damage assessment may also include costs incurred by the agent in performing the contract and which he has not been able to amortize.

---

21. Sales Representative Directive at art. 17.
22. Case C-348/07, Turgay Semen v. Deutsche Tamoil GmbH, 2009 E.C.R. I-2355, 2363 ¶19.
23. *Id.* at 2365 ¶28.
24. The member state has the option of deciding the nature of the compensation, i.e., indemnification payment or termination compensation. *Id.* at 2363 ¶15. At the time the Directive was adopted, most member states already provided for indemnification rights of the agent. The UK, however, opposed the introduction of this right. As a compromise, the alternative of termination compensation was introduced.
25. Sales Representative Directive at art. 17(3).

3.4 Statute of Limitations

The commercial agent loses his entitlement to the indemnity payment or termination compensation if, within one year following termination of the contract, he has not notified the principal that he intends to pursue his entitlement.

3.5 Mandatory Character of Law

The relatively generous protection extended to commercial agents under the Sales Representative Directive raises the legal question of whether the principal and agent can agree in the contract establishing the relationship that the indemnity payment or the termination compensation will not apply in that particular case.[26] The general rule is that the Directive has mandatory character, and consequently the parties may not derogate from the indemnity or compensation provisions to the detriment of the commercial agent before the agency contract expires.[27] Therefore, a clause in a sales agent agreement according to which the sales agent waives his or her termination or indemnity rights is not enforceable.

One theoretically important condition to the application of this rule is that the waiver is detrimental to the commercial agent. If the waiver is actually beneficial to the commercial agent, there is a theoretical possibility that it will be recognized and enforced. In practice, however, it is difficult to prove the absence of detriment to the commercial agent. The mere possibility that the agreement waiving the indemnification claim could be beneficial to the commercial agent is not enough. As indicated by the ECJ in *Honyvem Informazioni Commerciali v. Mariella De Zotti*, a derogation from the Directive in the agreement is only possible if there is no possibility that the derogation will prove detrimental to the commercial agent.[28]

The general prohibition on derogations from the Directive applies regardless of whether the principal is a company established in the EU or outside the EU. For example, in *Ingmar GB Ltd. v. Eaton Leonard Technologies Inc.*, a U.S. company engaged a sales agent in the EU and the parties agreed that California law was applicable. The ECJ held, however, that the Directive is mandatory even in these circumstances for the protection of the commercial agent.[29] In a similar case, a Virginia company entered into a sales representative agreement with a sales representative in Germany. The agreement specified Virginia law as the governing law and Virginia as the exclusive forum for disputes. After the Virginia company terminated the German sales representative, the representative filed a lawsuit in Germany for compensation under the German law transposing

---

26. As discussed above, the level of remuneration (as opposed to indemnification and termination compensation) can be set by agreement of the principal and agent.
27. Sales Representative Directive at art. 19.
28. Case C-465/04, Honyvem Informazioni Commerciali v. Mariella De Zotti, 2006 E.C.R. I-2899, 2911 ¶27.
29. C-381/98, Ingmar GB Ltd v. Eaton Leonard Technologies Inc., 2000 E.C.R. I-9325, 9335 ¶26.

the Sales Representative Directive. The German Supreme Court affirmed the decision of the lower courts that the parties could not contract out of the mandatory German law protecting sales representatives in Germany.[30]

If, however, the sales agent is located outside the EU and the principal inside the EU, the result is not quite as clear. The ECJ has not yet addressed the issue. The fundamental purpose of the Directive is to protect commercial agents in the EU. Hence, the preclusion of termination compensation between a European principal and a U.S. sales agent may be permissible under the Directive. For example, a German court allowed a German company to contract out of the termination compensation in its contracts with sales agents in Columbia and Venezuela.[31]

---

30. Decision of the German Supreme Court in case no. VII ZR 25/12 (Sept. 5, 2012) available at http://www.rws-verlag.de/fileadmin/zbb-volltexte-2/7zb2512.pdf.
31. Decision of OLG Munich of Jan. 11, 2002, *reported in* 48 Recht der Internationalen Wirtschaft 319 (2002).

CHAPTER **IX**

Labor Law

As the relationship between employer and employee is a critical element in the success of a business, an understanding of EU labor law is an essential prerequisite of doing business in Europe. This is particularly applicable to businesses from the United States because the rights granted to employees in Europe are quite different from those granted in the United States.

1. Sources of Labor Law

Labor law, similar to most areas of EU business law, is based both on primary and secondary EU law. The provisions of primary law which apply to the employment context tend to be phrased generally and directed at the member states (as opposed to businesses directly). The specifics of EU labor law, however, are found in the myriad regulations and directives adopted by the EU institutions in reliance on the general provisions of the EU Treaties. The EU Treaties in general terms mandate equality between men and women and prohibit discrimination on the grounds of nationality, gender, racial or ethnic origin, religion or belief, disability, age, or sexual orientation.

Articles 46 and 157(3) of the Treaty on the Functioning of the European Union (TFEU) give the European Council the authority to legislate in the area of labor law. In reliance on these provisions of the TFEU, the Council has adopted myriad legislation which may be discussed under the heading "labor law." This secondary law regulates a number of different aspects of the employment relationship.[1] For example, the Working Time Directive[2] addresses

---

1. Directive 2004/38/EC of the Parliament and of the Council of 29 April 2004 on the right of citizens of the Union and their family members to move and reside freely within the territory of the member states, 2004 O.J. (L 158) 77; Regulation (EU) No. 492/2011 of the European Parliament and of the Council of 5 April 2011 on the freedom of workers within the Union, 2011 O.J. (L 141) 1 [hereinafter Workers Free Movement Directive]; Council Directive 77/486/EEC of 25 July 1977 on the education of the children of migrant workers, 1977 O.J. (L 199) 32.
2. Directive 2003/88/EC of the European Parliament and of the Council of 4 November 2003 concerning certain aspects of the organization of working time, 2003 O.J. (L 299) 9.

such issues as rest time,[3] breaks,[4] weekly rest periods,[5] maximum weekly hours,[6] and annual leave.[7] Because of space constraints, the focus in this Chapter is on the protection against discrimination, the rights of employees in the event of a transfer or merger of their employer, collective redundancies, protection of workers in the event of their employer's insolvency, and the rights of employees in the management of their employer's business.

2. Free Movement of Labor: Discrimination Based on Nationality

In the EU, the most obvious form of discrimination which is prohibited is discrimination based on nationality. As discussed above, the TFEU (Art. 45 TFEU) requires the member states to treat nationals of other member states equal to the treatment accorded to their own nationals.[8] According to the European Court of Justice (ECJ), the purpose of Article 45 of the TFEU "is to assist in the abolition of all obstacles to the establishment of a common market in which the nationals of the member states may move freely within the territory of those states in order to pursue their economic activities. ... [Article 45 is] intended to give workers established in the different countries of the EU free access to employment available in countries of the EU other than the one in which they are established, without regard to their nationality, by prohibiting any restriction on their movement within the EU, whether in the form of restrictions on access to the national territory or restrictions on free movement within a national territory, which would prevent them from effectively exercising that right."[9] This provision of the TFEU forms the basis of what is commonly referred to as the "free movement of labor" (sometimes referred to as the free movement of workers).

---

3. Every worker is entitled to a minimum daily rest period of 11 consecutive hours per 24-hour period. Working Time Directive at art. 3.
4. If the working day is longer than six hours, every worker is entitled to a rest break. *Id.* at art. 4.
5. Per each seven-day period, every worker is entitled to a minimum uninterrupted rest period of 24 hours. *Id.* at art. 5.
6. The average working time for each seven-day period, including overtime, may not exceed 48 hours. *Id.* at art. 6.
7. Every worker is entitled to paid annual leave of at least four weeks in accordance with the conditions for entitlement to, and granting of, such leave laid down by national legislation and/or practice. *Id.* at art. 7.
8. Case C-356/98, Arben Kaba v. Secretary of State for the Home Department, 2000 E.C.R. I-2623, 2676 ¶27; Case C-57/96, H. Meints v. Minister van Landbouw, Natuurbeheer en Visserij, 1997 E.C.R. I-6689.
9. Case 298/84, Iorio v. Azienda Autonoma delle Ferrovie dello Stato, 1986 E.C.R. 247, 254 ¶13.

2.1 State Measure

As discussed above, the prohibition of restrictions on the free movement of goods applies only to restrictions caused by state measures. In contrast, the TFEU provisions relating to the free movement of workers do not expressly limit their application to state measures. According to the ECJ, Article 45 of the TFEU applies not only to the actions of public authorities but also to collective private measures regulating employment.[10] In *URBSFA v. Bosman*,[11] for example, the ECJ applied Article 45 to the internal rules of a soccer association (Union Royale Belge des Sociétés de Football Association) which was not a state controlled entity. In that case, the rules of the soccer association made it more difficult for Jean-Marc Bosman to leave his Belgian team to play in France. Although neither the Belgian state nor a state measure was involved, the ECJ examined the rules under Article 45 of the TFEU and held that Article 45 applies to rules adopted by soccer associations.[12]

Angonese v. Cassa di Risparmio di Bolzano SpA, involved an Italian who had moved to Austria to study German. He then applied for a position with a private bank back in Italy. One of the requirements for the position was that the applicant must have a certificate of Italian/German bilingualism. As he did not have this certificate, he did not get the position and subsequently claimed that this requirement restricted his right of free movement under Article 45 of the TFEU. The fact that there was no state measure involved did not preclude the application of Article 45. The ECJ held that Article 45 "precludes an employer from requiring persons applying to take part in a recruitment competition to provide evidence of their linguistic knowledge exclusively by means of one particular diploma issued only in one particular province of a member state."[13]

The ECJ, however, has stopped short of clearly stating that Article 45 of the TFEU applies to private companies outside of the employment area. The unwillingness of the ECJ to clearly state that Article 45 also applies to private conduct may be explained by the recognition that the law was initially directed at restrictions imposed by member states.[14] Private restrictions were thought to be the subject matter of the competition law provisions of the TFEU. The adoption of such a clear delineation would have limited the ability of the ECJ to invalidate private restrictions which may restrict the free movement of labor but not rise to the level of a restraint of competition. The conduct of the employer in the *Angonese* case discussed above, for example, would probably not have

---

10. Case C-325/08, Olympique Lyonnaise SASP v. Bernard, 2010 E.C.R. I-2196, 2206 ¶31; Case C-94/07, Raccanelli v. Max-Planck-Gesellschaft, 2008 E.C.R. I-5942, 5954 ¶43.
11. Case C-415/93, Union Royale Belge des Sociétés de Football Association v. Bosman, 1995 E.C.R. I-4921.
12. *Id.* at 5066 ¶86.
13. Case C-281/98, Angonese v. Cassa di Risparmio di Bolzano SpA, 2000 E.C.R. I-4139.
14. Indeed, this was the position of the Commission in Case 36/74, Walrave and Koch v. UCL, 1974 E.C.R. 1405.

constituted an infringement of the competition rules codified in Articles 101 and 102 of the TFEU.

2.2 Interstate Commerce Requirement

Similar to the rules on the free movement of goods, the free movement of labor protections only apply if there is an effect on commerce between member states. The general rule is that Article 45 applies where the worker has her residence in one member state and seeks employment in another member state.[15] There must, however, be a connection to two or more member states. According to the ECJ: "It is settled case-law that [t]he provisions of the Treaty on freedom of movement for workers cannot ... be applied to situations which are wholly internal to a Member State, in other words, where there is no factor connecting them to any of the situations envisaged by EU law."[16] For example, in *Moser v. Land Baden-Württemberg*, Hans Moser, a German, claimed that a German state law preventing him from taking the post-graduate training necessary to become a teacher because of his membership in the German communist party was contrary to Article 45 of the TFEU.[17] The ECJ held that Article 45 of the TFEU did not apply in this case as the situation was "wholly internal to a member state." [18]

This strict application of the interstate commerce requirement is probably the exception and not the rule. It is commonly used by the ECJ to avoid having to upset the member states in politically sensitive cases. As illustrated by *F.C. Terhoeve v. Inspecteur van de Belastingdienst Particulieren*[19] and subsequent cases,[20] the circumstances must be exclusively limited to one member state in order to fall outside the prohibition. In that case, a Dutch national was allowed to rely on Article 45 of the TFEU to challenge a Dutch law which effectively required him to pay more taxes than other Dutch nationals because he had worked outside of the Netherlands.[21] Even though it was a Dutch law applying to a Dutch national, ostensibly a purely domestic situation, the interstate commerce requirement was fulfilled as the law had the effect of deterring Dutch nationals from seeking employment abroad.

---

15. Case C-527/06, Renneberg v. Staatssecretaris van Financiën, 2008 E.C.R. I-7766, 7778 ¶36.
16. Case 175/78, Regina v. Saunders, 1979 E.C.R. 1129, 1135 ¶11. *See also* Case C-208/05, ITC Innovative Technology Center GmbH v. Bundesagentur für Arbeit, 2007 E.C.R. I-181, 213 ¶29.
17. Case 180/83, Moser v. Land Baden-Württemberg, 1984 E.C.R. 2539.
18. *Id.* at 2548 ¶20.
19. Case C-18/95, Terhoeve v. Inspector van de Belastingdienst Particulieren, 1999 E.C.R. I-345.
20. Case C-104/06, Comm'n v. Sweden, 2007 E.C.R. I-671, 681 ¶20.
21. Case C-18/95, Terhoeve v. Inspector van de Belastingdienst Particulieren, 1999 E.C.R. I-345.

2.3 Beneficiaries of Prohibition

The free movement of labor principle codified in Article 45 only applies to the movement of workers. The TFEU does not provide a definition of the term "workers." According to the ECJ, the essential feature of worker is that for a certain period of time, a person performs services for and under the direction of another person (subordination element), in return for which he or she receives remuneration (payment element).[22] Subject to the public service exception codified in Article 45(4) of the TFEU and discussed below, even civil servants and other governmental employees are considered workers for purposes of the TFEU.[23]

The concept of worker should be distinguished from that of a self-employed person. The free movement rights of the self-employed persons are secured by Articles 56 and 63 of the TFEU discussed in Chapter II.[24] There is a fine line between workers and self-employed persons. The issue in *Aldona Malgorzata Jany v. Staatssecretaris*[25] was whether prostitutes are workers or self-employed persons. The ECJ held that they are self-employed because they are not working under the direction of an employer but rather simply providing services in exchange for remuneration.[26]

In determining whether a person is a worker or is self-employed, the ECJ will look beyond the nominal designation given by the parties or by national law to the relationship. For example, an employer cannot preclude the application of Article 45 of the TFEU by simply changing the title of its employment agreements to consultant agreements. The same applies to classifications under national law. In *Allonby v. Accrington & Rossendale College*, the fact that a college lecturer was designated by national law as a self-employed individual did not prevent the ECJ from characterizing that person as a worker for purposes of European labor law: "The formal classification of a self-employed person under national law does not change the fact that a person must be classified as a worker within the meaning of [Article 45 of the TFEU] if his independence is merely notional."[27]

The free movement of labor provisions apply also to part-time workers regardless of the form of remuneration. The form of remuneration is not decisive. In other words, it is not necessary that the individual work a traditional job where she is paid with cash. The question arose in *Steymann v. Staatssecretaris*

---

22. Case C-270/13, Haralambidis v. Casilli, 2014 E.C.R. I-___, at ¶29; Case C-228/07, Petersen v. Arbeitsmarktservice Niederösterreich, 2008 E.C.R. I-7022, 7041 ¶45; Case C-94/07, Raccanelli v. Max-Planck-Gesellschaft, 2008 E.C.R. I-5942, 5952 ¶34; Case C-138/02, Collins v. Secretary of State for Work and Pensions, 2004 E.C.R. 2703, 2743 ¶26.
23. Case C-392/05, Alevizos v. Ipourgos Ikonomikon, 2007 E.C.R. I-3535, 3561 ¶68 (NATO employee considered "worker").
24. *See, e.g.*, Case C-20/03, *In re* Burmanjer, 2005 E.C.R. I-4153, 4160 ¶19.
25. Case C-268/99, Aldona Malgorzata Jany v. Staatssecretaris, 2001 E.C.R. I-8615.
26. *Id.*
27. Case C-256/01, Allonby v. Accrington & Rossendale College, 2004 E.C.R. I-903, 932 ¶79.

van Justitie as to whether a person could be considered a worker in the sense of Article 45 of the TFEU even if he did not work for money.[28] In that case, a German plumber joined a religious commune in the Netherlands which provided food and shelter for its members in exchange for their work for the commune. The German was denied a residency permit by the Netherlands. The ECJ held that he nonetheless should be considered a "worker" because he did work for some remuneration even though it was not money.

A person does not necessarily have to be employed at the time in order to be considered a worker.[29] A contrary interpretation would mean that the free movement rights would only apply to employed individuals; an unemployed person or a person searching for his or her first employment would be precluded from the free movement of labor codified in Article 45 of the TFEU. Nonetheless, the scope of the rights accorded to an employed worker and an unemployed worker may legitimately differ. If member states were required to provide the same social benefits to all individuals regardless of whether they were employed or unemployed, there would be a disproportionate migration of individuals to the member states that provided the most generous social benefits. Hence, the ECJ distinguishes between employed and unemployed workers.[30] An unemployed person may benefit from the equal treatment principle only as regards access to employment. Employed individuals from other member states, on the other hand, may claim the same social and tax benefits as national workers. For example, an unemployed worker in Spain may migrate to Portugal and expect the same access to employment as Portuguese nationals. That Spaniard may not, however, claim access to the same social benefits as the Portuguese—such as unemployment compensation.

As discussed in Chapter II, the free movement of goods rules apply to goods originating in the EU or placed into free circulation in the EU regardless of whether the goods were manufactured inside or outside the Union. The free movement of labor protections are, however, much more limited. The general rule is that they apply only to citizens of an EU member state.[31] If, for example, the soccer player in the *Bosman* case discussed above had been a U.S.-American playing for the Belgian club, he would not have been able to rely on Article 45 of the TFEU to challenge the league rules even if he was lawfully working in Belgium.

One important exception to this rule relates to family members of the EU national. Of course, if the family members are also EU nationals, they can take advantage of the free movement of labor protections. If, however, the family members are not nationals of an EU member state, they can only take advantage of the free movement of workers protections if they pursue employment in the same member state as the family member who is an EU national. For example,

---

28. Case 196/87, Steymann v. Staatssecretaris van Justitie, 1988 E.C.R. 6159.
29. Case C-507/12, Prix v. Secretary of State for Work and Pensions, 2014 E.C.R. I-____, at ¶37; Case C-138/02, Collins v. Secretary of State for Work and Pensions, 2004 E.C.R. 2703, 2745 ¶30.
30. Case C-138/02, Collins v. Secretary of State for Work and Pensions, 2004 E.C.R. 2703, 2745 ¶31.
31. Case C-230/97, *In re* Ibiyinka Awoyemi, 1998 E.C.R. I-6795, 6806 ¶29.

if Susanne, a French national, and Fred, a U.S. national, were married and living in Portugal, Fred could only benefit from the free movement of labor protections in Portugal if his wife, Susanne, were working in Portugal. In such a case, Fred could not claim protection of Article 45 when seeking employment in Spain.[32]

2.4 Substantive Protection

Article 45 of the TFEU basically requires the member states to extend the same treatment to nationals of other member states as that member state extends to its own nationals.[33] Article 45(2) of the TFEU specifically prohibits "any discrimination based on nationality between workers of the Member States as regards employment, remuneration and other conditions of work and employment." The specific substantive protection extended to workers is embodied in other provisions of primary and secondary EU law and in the case law. As interpreted by the ECJ, Article 45 "precludes, first, overt discrimination by reason of nationality and all covert forms of discrimination which, by the application of other criteria of differentiation, lead in fact to the same result and second, provisions which preclude or deter a national of a Member State from leaving his country of origin to exercise his right to freedom of movement."[34] There are numerous directives and regulations which, together with primary EU law, form the basis of EU labor law.

Direct Discrimination. The most obvious form of discrimination prohibited by Article 45 is direct discrimination. This occurs when the law explicitly treats the individual differently than it treats its own nationals. For example, Sweden could not adopt a law that only allowed Swedish citizens to receive licenses to drive trucks in Sweden. This would be a form of direct discrimination based on nationality.

Indirect Discrimination. Article 45 of the TFEU prohibits "not only overt discrimination on grounds of nationality but also all covert forms of discrimination which, by the application of other criteria of differentiation, lead in fact to the same result."[35] According to the ECJ, indirect discrimination exists if the national law is applicable irrespective of nationality but affects nationals of other member states differently than nationals of that member state, or can more easily be satisfied by workers from the home member state, or there is a risk that they operate to the detriment of workers from other member states.[36]

---

32. *See, e.g.*, Case C-10/05, Mattern v. Ministre du Travail et de l'Emploi, 2006 E.C.R. I-3145.
33. Case C-356/98, Arben Kaba v. Secretary of State for the Home Department, 2000 E.C.R. I-2623, 2676 ¶27; Case C-57/96, H. Meints v. Minister van Landbouw, Natuurbeheer en Visserij, 1997 E.C.R. I-6689.
34. Case C-240/10, Schulz v. Finanzamt Stuttgart III, 2011 E.C.R. I-8557, 8569 ¶34.
35. Case C-228/07, Petersen v. Arbeitsmarktservice Niederösterreich, 2008 E.C.R. I-7022, 7042 ¶53.
36. *Id.* at 7034 ¶18; C-208/05, ITC Innovative Technology Center GmbH v. Bundesagentur für Arbeit, 2007 E.C.R. I-213, 225 ¶33. *See also* Directive 2006/54/EC of the European Parliament and of the Council of 5 July 2006 on the implementation of the principle of equal opportunities and equal treatment of men and women in matters of employment and occupation, 2006 O.J. (L 204) 23 art. 2(1)(b) [hereinafter Equal Opportunities Directive].

The issue in *O'Flynn v. Adjudication Officer*[37] was whether the extension by the UK of monetary support for burials to the family of a deceased worker in the UK on the condition that the funeral take place in the UK was contrary to the equal treatment rule. In this particular case, an Irish national died in the UK but was buried in Ireland. The ECJ held "[t]he Court has consistently held that the equal treatment rule laid down in Article [45] of the Treaty ... prohibits not only overt discrimination by reason of nationality but also all covert forms of discrimination which, by the application of other distinguishing criteria, lead in fact to the same result."[38] Although the law was indistinctly applicable to nationals of the UK and foreigners, it had a disparate effect on foreigners because the requirement could more easily be satisfied by domestic workers.

These cases illustrate that the intent of the state measure at issue does not determine its legality. Although an intentionally discriminatory state measure will infringe Article 45 of the TFEU, the absence of a discriminatory intent does not necessarily save the state measure. The determining factor is the effect of the state measure.

Deterring the Exercise of the Free Movement of Labor. The finding of direct or indirect discrimination implies the existence of the comparability of the situations which are treated differently. In its case law, the ECJ has expanded the concept of a restriction on the free movement of labor to include state measures that deter the movement of workers.[39] Comparability is not an issue in these cases. In *F.C. Terhoeve v. Inspecteur van de Belastingdienst Particulieren*,[40] for example, Terhoeve challenged a Dutch law that treated taxpayers differently depending on whether or not they were residing in the Netherlands. Terhoeve was a Dutch taxpayer but was sent by his employer to work in the UK. The ECJ held that the Dutch law had the effect of deterring persons from seeking employment in other member states and was therefore contrary to Article 45 of the TFEU. A similar case, *Öberg v. Försäkringskassan*, involved a Swedish law that required individuals to be Swedish residents in order to receive a parental benefit from Sweden for having a child.[41] The individual challenging the law in that case was a Swedish national working for the ECJ in Luxembourg. After he was denied the parental benefit in Sweden, he argued that the Swedish law violated Article 45 of the TFEU. The ECJ held that the Swedish law violated the free movement of persons because it served as a deterrent to individuals seeking employment in other member states.[42]

Access to Employment. The free movement of workers also protects the right to accept offers of employment actually made (Article 45(3)(a) TFEU).

---

37. Case 237/94, O'Flynn v. Adjudication Officer, 1996 E.C.R. I-2617.
38. *Id.* at 2637 ¶17.
39. Case C-325/08, Olympique Lyonnaise SASP v. Bernard, 2010 E.C.R. I-2196, 2207 ¶34; Case C-208/05, ITC Innovative Technology Center GmbH v. Bundesagentur für Arbeit, 2007 E.C.R. I-213, 225 ¶33; Case C-104/06, Comm'n v. Sweden, 2007 E.C.R. I-673, 682 ¶21.
40. Case C-18/95, F.C. Terhoeve v. Inspecteur van de Belastingdienst Particulieren, 1999 E.C.R. I-345.
41. Case C-185/04, Öberg v. Försäkringskassan, 2006 E.C.R. I-1455.
42. *Id.* at 1461 ¶15.

As secondary legislation makes clear, member states are required to ensure that jobs are open to workers of all nationalities.[43] If a member state through its employment offices offers assistance to its nationals in finding a job, that member state must offer the same assistance to nationals from other member states seeking employment.[44]

Entry and Residence. A worker has the right to stay in a member state for purposes of employment (Article 45(3)(c) TFEU) and even the right to stay in a member state after termination of employment (Article 45(3)(d) TFEU). This right also extends to the children of the worker. In *Echternach v. Moritz*,[45] the ECJ held that German children in the Netherlands whose parents had moved back to Germany but who wanted to stay in the Netherlands were entitled the same access to public education and financial support as Dutch children.

Relocation. The TFEU guarantees workers who are nationals of a member state the right to move freely within the EU for the purpose of employment (Article 45(3)(b) TFEU). For example, a national of a member state has the right to quit her job in one member state and seek employment with another employer in another member state. This is slightly different than the right to relocate based on a transfer of employment for the same employer. If an employee is relocated by her employer to another member state, Article 56 of the TFEU prohibits the member state to which she is transferred from preventing the transfer or imposing discriminatory requirements on her.[46] In other words, if a business decides to move to another member state, it has the right to bring its employees. The fact that the taxes in one member state may be different than the taxes in another member state does not violate Article 45 of the TFEU unless the criteria for the application of the tax somehow treats them differently. According to the ECJ, "the Treaty offers no guarantee to a citizen of the Union that transferring his activities to a Member State other than that in which he previously resided will be neutral as regards taxation. Given the relevant disparities in the tax legislation of the Member States, such a transfer may be to the citizen's advantage or not, according to the circumstances."[47]

Social Benefits. The right to move freely throughout the EU for purposes of employment necessarily raises the issue of access to welfare and social programs offered by that member state. For example, when a Polish worker goes to Germany to work and brings along her family, do the worker and the family enjoy access to the same welfare benefits as German workers? The general rule is that once hired, nationals from other member states must also enjoy the same extra-contractual benefits as domestic workers.[48] The rules on the extension of social security benefits to foreign workers are codified in Regulation 1408/71 on the application

---

43. Workers Free Movement Regulation.
44. *Id.* at art. 5.
45. 1989 E.C.R. 723.
46. Case C-113/89, Rush Portuguesa v. Office national d'immigration, 1990 E.C.R. I-1439, 1443 ¶12.
47. Case C-240/10, Schulz v. Finanzamt Stuttgart III, 2011 E.C.R. I-8557, 8571 ¶42.
48. Workers Free Movement Regulation. at art. 7.

of social security schemes to employed persons, to self-employed persons, and to members of their families moving within the EU.[49]

Family. Extending the protections to the families of the workers has presented a number of difficult legal and political issues. As an obvious extension of the right to pursue work in another member state, workers are granted the right to migrate with their families.[50]

2.5 Legitimate Limitations on the Free Movement of Workers

As discussed above, the ECJ requires that a restriction on the free movement of goods must be certain and direct in order to fall under the prohibitions of Articles 34 and 35 of the TFEU.[51] In *Graf v. Filzmoser Maschinenbau GmbH*, the ECJ introduced a similar requirement to the application of Article 45 of the TFEU.[52] The case involved an Austrian law mandating that compensation be paid to employees terminated in Austria. However, if the employee terminated the employment relationship, the termination compensation under the Austrian law did not have to be paid. An Austrian employee argued that this prevented him from terminating and seeking employment in Germany. The ECJ recognized that laws which are not discriminatory on their face (i.e., indistinctly applicable) may nonetheless violate Article 45.[53] In this case, however, the ECJ held that the discriminatory effect was "too uncertain and indirect a possibility for the legislation to be capable of being regarded as liable to hinder freedom of movement for workers."[54]

Article 45(3) of the TFEU indicates that certain free movement rights of workers may be limited on grounds of public policy, public security, or public health.[55] In *Las v. PSA Antwerp NV*, for example, a Belgian law requiring employment contracts to be in Dutch was justified on public policy grounds even though it restricted the movement of labor under Article 45 of the TFEU. According to the ECJ, "the objective of encouraging the use of Dutch, which is one of the official languages of the Kingdom of Belgium, constitutes a legitimate interest which, in principle, justifies a restriction on the obligations imposed by Article 45 TFEU."[56]

---

49. Regulation (EEC) No. 1408/71 of the Council of 14 June 1971 on the application of social security schemes to employed persons and their families moving within the Community, 1971 O.J. (L 149) 2.
50. Regulation 1612/68 at Art. 7
51. Case C-412/97, ED Srl v. Fenocchio, 1999 E.C.R. I-3845.
52. Case C-190/98, Graf v. Filzmoser Maschinenbau GmbH, 2000 E.C.R. I-513.
53. *Id.* at 523 ¶23.
54. *Id.* at 523 ¶24.
55. For secondary legislation in this area, *see* Directive 64/221 on the coordination of special measures concerning the movement and residence of foreign nationals which are justified on grounds of public policy, public security or public health, 1964 O.J. (L 56) 1. These same exceptions are available not only to the member states, but also to private companies. Case C-415/93, UBSFA v. Bosman, 1995 E.C.R. I-4921, 5066 ¶86.
56. Case C-202/11, Las v. PSA Antwerp NV, 2013 E.C.R. ____ at ¶27.

In certain instances, it may be appropriate for a member state to limit public service employment to its nationals. For example, Sweden may have a legitimate interest in requiring anyone employed by the Swedish Security Service to be a Swedish citizen. The free movement of persons rules enumerated in Article 45 do not apply to employment in the public service.[57] The term "public service" is not defined in the TFEU. According to the ECJ, "the concept of 'public service' ... covers posts which involve direct or indirect participation in the exercise of powers conferred by public law and duties designed to safeguard the general interests of the State or of other public authorities and this presumes on the part of those occupying them the existence of a special relationship of allegiance to the State and reciprocity of rights and duties which form the foundation of the bond of nationality."[58] Consequently, not every employee of the state is considered in the public service.[59] For example, there is no legitimate reason for a member state to discriminate in hiring workers for the state-owned telephone company.[60] In addition, the mere fact that a person is compensated by the state does not in itself justify the conclusion that the person is employed in the public service. In *Kranemann v. Land Nordrhein Westfalen*, for example, the ECJ held that a trainee lawyer working at a private firm was not an employee in the public service even though, as is customary for trainee lawyers in Germany prior to being admitted to the bar, the trainee was compensated by the state.[61]

The tasks to be performed by the person will determine whether position is in the public service. Only those positions that require a special allegiance to the state should be exempted from the free movement of persons rules. For example, it may be legitimate for a member state to impose nationality requirements on judicial appointments. On the other hand, postal service employees,[62] teachers,[63] and nurses[64] would not be considered public service employees for purposes of Article 45 of the TFEU.

3. Other Forms of Discrimination

As discussed above, Article 45 of the TFEU applies to discrimination based on nationality. The member states must treat nationals from other member states the same way they treat their own nationals. But discrimination, particularly in

---

57. TFEU at art. 45(4).
58. Case C-270/13, Haralambidis v. Casilli, 2014 E.C.R. ___ at ¶44.
59. Case 149/79, Comm'n v. Belgium, 1980 E.C.R. 3881, 3900 ¶11.
60. However, a member state may impose linguistic conditions on the employment. Art. 3(1) Regulation 1612/68 at art. 3(1). For example, a customer service operator for the Greek telephone company should be able to speak Greek fluently. A Belgian with no Greek language skills cannot claim discrimination if Greek language skills are a prerequisite for the position.
61. Case C-109/04, Kranemann v. Nordrhein Westfalen, 2005 E.C.R. I-2433, 2440 ¶21.
62. Case 173/94, Comm'n v. Belgium, 1996 E.C.R. I-3282.
63. Case 473/93, Comm'n v. Luxembourg, 1996 E.C.R. I-257.
64. Case 307/84, Comm'n v. France, 1986 E.C.R. 1725; Case C-37/93, Comm'n v. Belgium, 1993 E.C.R. I-6295.

the employment context, may take many forms. The most obvious example is gender discrimination. There are, however, many other forms of discrimination that occur in the employment context.[65] The focus here is on two of the more common forms of discrimination: gender and race. There are, of course, other forms of discrimination which are prohibited, but which go beyond the scope of this book.

3.1 Gender Discrimination

Article 157 of the TFEU requires the member states to "ensure the principle of equal pay for male and female workers for equal work or work of equal value." As interpreted by the ECJ, this requirement prohibits all discrimination on grounds of gender with regard to aspects of pay unless the disparate treatment is justified by a legitimate objective unrelated to gender.[66] The term "pay" includes not only the salary of the workers but also "any other consideration, whether in cash or in kind, which the worker receives directly or indirectly, in respect of his/her employment from his/her employer."[67] For example, an employer in calculating the period a person has been with the company for purposes of promotion or salary must include maternity days taken by women employees.[68] The concept of pay also includes payments made after termination of the employment period (such as severance payments) provided that the post-termination payments are related to the employment.[69]

The protection against discrimination secured by primary and secondary law extends beyond the equal pay requirement for men and women set forth in Article 157 of the TFEU.[70] It also prevents direct and indirect gender discrimination with regard to access to employment (including selection criteria, recruitment,

---

65. For example, the Equal Treatment Framework Directive discussed below prohibits discrimination based on gender, religion, disability, age, or sexual orientation.
66. Case C-173/13, Leone v. Garde des Sceaux, 2014 E.C.R. I-___, at ¶40; Case C-17/05, B.F. Cadman v. Health & Safety Executive, 2006 E.C.R. I-9608, 9622 ¶31; Case C-285/02, Edeltraud Elsner-Lakeberg v. Land Nordrhein-Westfalen, 2004 E.C.R. 5861, 5875 ¶12.
67. Equal Opportunities Directive at art. 2(1)(d).
68. Case C-284/02, Land Brandenburg v. Sass, 2004 E.C.R. I-11143. A woman on maternity leave is entitled to return to her job or to an equivalent position on terms and conditions which are no less favorable to her than when she began her maternity leave. Equal Opportunities at art. 15. Issues related to pregnant workers and maternity leave are specifically addressed in Directive 92/85/EEC on the Introduction of Measures to Encourage Improvements in the Safety and Health at Work of Pregnant Workers and Workers who have Recently Given Birth or are Breast-feeding, 1992 O.J. (L 348)1.
69. Case C-19/02, Hlozek v. Roche Austria Gesellschaft mbH, 2004 E.C.R. I-11523, 11541 ¶40.
70. Although this is a provision of the TFEU, it applies directly to the relationship between a company and its employees. Case C-284/02, Land Brandenburg v. Sass, 2004 E.C.R. I-11143, 11166 ¶25.

and promotion) and to vocational training as well as discrimination with regard to working conditions[71] and access to social security.[72]

Direct forms of gender discrimination are generally easier to identify than indirect forms of discrimination. An example of direct gender discrimination is one in which a person is treated less favorably than another is, has been, or would be treated in a comparable situation on the grounds of gender.[73] A measure involves indirect discrimination when, although worded in gender-neutral terms, it places that person at a particular disadvantage compared with other persons.[74] For example, a rule which works to the disadvantage of a much higher percentage of women than men is discriminatory.[75] The issue in *Katharina Rinke v. Ärztekammer Hamburg*[76] was whether a rule that training for part-time health care workers must include a certain number of periods of full-time training constituted indirect discrimination against females. In that case, the evidence showed that the percentage of women working part-time is much higher than that of men working on a part-time basis. The rule allegedly placed an unequal burden on women even though it was worded in gender-neutral terms. The ECJ recognized that the rule constituted a form of indirect discrimination against women.[77]

The practical effects of a measure—rather than the objective of the law—are sometimes used to illustrate the discriminatory effect of a state measure. In *Leone v. Garde des Sceaux*, a French pensions law awarded French civil servants certain benefits if they had children and took care of the children while they were working. One of the requirements, however, was that the civil servant had at some point taken a career break for at least two months to take care of the child. Although French law extended equal rights to both men and women to take such a two month break, the ECJ concluded that it was indirect discrimination against men because "in reality [the requirement was] liable to be met by a much lower proportion of male civil servants than female civil servants."[78]

---

71. Council Directive 2000/78/EC of 27 November 2000 establishing a general framework for equal treatment in employment and occupation, O.J 2000 (L 303) 16 at art. 1 [hereinafter Equal Treatment Framework Directive]; Equal Opportunities Directive at art. 14(1).
72. *Id.*
73. Equal Treatment Framework Directive at art. 2.
74. Equal Opportunities Directive at art. 2(1)(b). Case C-173/13, Leone v. Garde des Sceaux, 2014 E.C.R. I-____, at ¶41 ("[I]ndirect discrimination on grounds of sex arises where a national measure, albeit formulated in neutral terms, puts considerably more workers of one sex at a disadvantage than the other.").
75. Cases C-4/02 and C-5/02, Schönheit v. Stadt Frankfurt an Main, 2003 E.C.R. I-12575, 12634 ¶74; Case C-226/98, Jørgensen, 2000 E.C.R. I-2447, 2479 ¶29. *See also* Equal Treatment Framework Directive at art. 2(2).
76. Case C-25/02, Katharina Rinke v. Ärztekammer Hamburg, 2003 E.C.R. I- 8349.
77. However, the ECJ held that it was justified by objective factors unrelated to any discrimination on grounds of gender because it was reasonable for the legislature to take the view that that requirement enables health care workers to acquire the experience necessary to become effective health care workers. *Id.* at 8386 ¶40.
78. Case C-173/13, Leone v. Garde des Sceaux, 2014 E.C.R. I-____, at ¶51.

The discrimination does not fall under the prohibition if it is between persons in objectively different situations.[79] This is illustrated in *Hlozek v. Roche Austria Gesellschaft mbH*.[80] In that case, the ECJ recognized that it was generally more difficult for an elderly woman to secure employment than an elderly man. Consequently, an Austrian social welfare plan which provided a "bridging allowance" (for the period until they reached retirement) to women who were 50 when terminated by their employers was not prohibited by Article 157 of the TFEU even though men had to be 55 to receive the same bridging allowance.[81]

The application of the equal treatment principle does not mean that an employer is required to treat men and women identically in every situation. In other words, there is no absolute prohibition of gender discrimination. A member state may permit discrimination if the different treatment is objectively justified by a legitimate objective and the means of achieving that aim are appropriate and necessary.[82] In certain circumstances related to the nature of the work and the context in which the circumstances are carried out, for example, the employment of a female may be more appropriate.

Discrimination based on genuine "occupational requirements" may be permitted by national law.[83] In *B.F. Cadman v. Health & Safety Executive*, a female employee of the UK Health & Safety Executive argued that the fact that she was paid less than male colleagues performing the same tasks constituted gender discrimination.[84] However, the reason she was paid less was because she had less experience than her male colleagues. The ECJ held that a difference in pay, while constituting a form of discrimination, is justified by the legitimate objective of rewarding an employee who has more experience.[85]

3.2 Racial Discrimination

The Equal Treatment Framework Directive does not expressly prohibit racial or ethnic discrimination in the employment context. This deficit is corrected by the Racial and Ethnic Discrimination Directive.[86] Similar to the prohibition of gender discrimination, the prohibition of racial or ethnic discrimination is based on the principle of equal treatment.[87] Member states are required to take such measures as are necessary to prohibit direct and indirect racial and ethnic

---

79. Case C-19/02, Hlozek v. Roche Austria Gesellschaft mbH, 2004 E.C.R. I-11523, 11543 ¶45. *See also* Equal Opportunities Directive at art. 14(2).
80. Case C-19/02, Hlozek v. Roche Austria Gesellschaft mbH, 2004 E.C.R. I-11523.
81. *Id.* at 11545 ¶51.
82. Equal Treatment Framework Directive at art. 2(2)(b)(i); Equal Opportunities Directive at art. 14(2); Case C-173/13, Leone v. Garde des Sceaux, 2014 E.C.R. I-___, at ¶53.
83. Equal Treatment Framework Directive at art. 4(1).
84. Case C-17/05, B.F. Cadman v. Health & Safety Executive, 2006 E.C.R. I-9583.
85. *Id.* at 9623 ¶34.
86. Council Directive 2000/43/EC Implementing the Principle of Equal Treatment Between Persons Irrespective of Racial or Ethnic Origin, 2000 O.J. (L 180) 22 [hereinafter Racial and Ethnic Discrimination Directive].
87. *Id.* at art. 2.

discrimination and extend appropriate judicial recourse to persons who consider themselves wronged because of a violation of the principle of equal treatment. Once a claim has been asserted, the burden of proof is on the employer to prove that there has been no breach of the principle of equal treatment.[88]

Direct racial or ethnic discrimination is deemed to exist where one person is treated less favorably than another person in a comparable situation is treated and the different treatment is on grounds of racial or ethnic origin. Harassment (i.e., unwanted conduct related to racial or ethnic origin creating an intimidating, hostile, degrading, humiliating, or offensive environment) is considered a form of racial or ethnic discrimination. Indirect racial or ethnic discrimination occurs where a neutral provision, criterion, or practice would put persons of a racial or ethnic origin at a particular disadvantage compared with other persons, unless that provision, criterion, or practice is objectively justified by a legitimate aim and the means of achieving that aim are appropriate and necessary.

The prohibition on racial or ethnic discrimination applies to all persons, both in the public and private sectors, in relation to conditions for access to employment (including selection criteria and recruitment conditions), promotion, working conditions, dismissals and pay.[89] However, the prohibition is not absolute. Member states may provide that a difference in treatment based on racial or ethnic origin does not constitute discrimination if, by reason of the nature of the particular occupational activities concerned or of the context in which they are carried out, racial or ethnic origin constitutes a genuine occupational requirement (provided, of course, that the objective is legitimate and the requirement is proportionate). For example, a television program director or a stage director may use a racial or ethnic criterion in casting for a part that requires a particular racial or ethnic origin. In most cases, however, the use of racial or ethnic criteria will not be justified.

Technically, immigration laws would infringe the principle of equal treatment as set forth in the Directive as a form of ethnic discrimination. However, laws relating to the entry into and residence of third-country nationals on the territory of member states, and to any treatment which arises from the legal status of the third-country nationals, are not prohibited.[90] Moreover, the Directive does not apply to discrimination based on nationality.[91]

The Directive does not address affirmative action in significant detail. Based on the definition of discrimination, a policy which promotes one racial or ethnic group more favorably than individuals who do not belong to that racial or ethnic group would fall under the definition of discrimination. The Directive does not explicitly exclude affirmative action policies from the definition. Nor does it identify affirmative action as a form of discrimination. It merely provides that the principle of equal treatment will not prevent any member state

---

88. *Id.* at art. 8(1).
89. *Id.* at art. 3.
90. *Id.* at art. 3(2).
91. *Id.* at art. 3(2).

from maintaining or adopting specific measures to prevent or compensate for disadvantages linked to racial or ethnic origin.[92]

4. Protection in Event of Change of Employer

The acquisition of a business often results in loss of employment for many employees. In many instances, the acquiring company already has someone fulfilling the function of its counterpart at the acquired company. The acquiring business may even have the technology to achieve the objectives of the acquired business using a smaller workforce. In other cases, the redundancies result from the acquiring company's attempt to lower the labor costs of the acquired business. In recognition of and response to this common consequence, and the market segregating effects which different levels of protection among the member states would cause, the Council attempted to harmonize the laws of the member states relating to the rights of employees in the event of transfers of businesses by adopting the Transfer Directive.[93] As discussed in detail below, the Transfer Directive protects employees in two ways. First, when a business is transferred to another owner, the employment contracts and relationships which the selling company has with its employees automatically transfer to the buyer. Second, the transfer of the business cannot be used as the basis for terminating the employees.

4.1   Scope of Application

(a) Subject Matter

The Transfer Directive applies to the transfer of an undertaking, business, or part of a business to another employer as a result of a legal transfer or merger.[94] The concept of an "undertaking, business or part of a business" is meant to cover any organized grouping of resources which has the objective of pursuing an economic activity, whether or not that activity is central or ancillary to the transferor's operations.[95] Thus, it is not a requirement that the entity being transferred be a stand-alone business.

In *Christel Schmidt v. Spar-und Leihkasse*, for example, the ECJ held that the outsourcing of an activity of a company can qualify as a transfer of a business or undertaking, even if the activity in question is only conducted by

---

92. *Id.* at art. 5(1).
93. Council Directive 2001/23/EC on the approximation of the laws of the member states relating to the safeguarding of employees' rights in the event of transfers of undertakings, businesses or parts of undertakings or businesses, 2001 O.J. (L 83) 16 [hereinafter Transfer Directive] (repealed the Acquired Rights Directive 77/187). The Transfer Directive prescribes only the minimum protections to be given employees. The member states are able to expand the notion of a transfer as well as the rights accorded to employees. Case C-458/12, Amatori v. Telecom Italia SpA, 2014 E.C.R. I-__, at ¶40.
94. Transfer Directive at art. 1(1)(a).
95. *Id.* at art. 1(1)(b). Case C-458/12, Amatori v. Telecom Italia SpA, 2014 E.C.R. I-__, at ¶31.

a single person.[96] In that case, a cleaning person was hired by a local bank to clean the bank's offices. She was terminated when the bank decided to entrust the cleaning to an outside company which was already cleaning the bank's other offices. As the outside company refused to hire her, Spiegel bank offered to employ Schmidt for a monthly wage which was higher than she had previously been receiving. Schmidt, however, was not prepared to work on those terms, as she calculated that her hourly wage would, in fact, be lower as a result of the increase in the surface area to be cleaned.

The issue arose as to whether the transfer of a single person could constitute the transfer of an undertaking, business, or part of a business. According to the ECJ, the fact that the activity was performed, prior to the transfer, by a single employee is not sufficient to preclude the application of the Transfer Directive "since its application does not depend on the number of employees assigned to the part of the undertaking which is the subject of the transfer. It should be noted that one of the objectives of the directive, as clearly stated in the second recital in the preamble thereto, is to protect employees in the event of a change of employer, in particular to ensure that their rights are safeguarded. That protection extends to all staff and must therefore be guaranteed even where only one employee is affected by the transfer."[97]

The Transfer Directive also applies to not-for-profit businesses and public undertakings (i.e., companies owned by the state).[98] For example, the ECJ has held that the Directive applies to the privatization of a public company (i.e., transfer from public control to private control)[99] as well as the transfer of an outsourced business back to public administration.[100] However, an administrative reorganization of public administrative authorities, or the transfer of administrative functions between public administrative authorities, is not a transfer within the meaning of this Directive.

This is illustrated by *Henke v. Gemeinde Schierke.*[101] In this case, two small German cities thought that it would be more cost efficient to merge some of their administrative tasks. Consequently, Annette Henke, a secretary in the mayor's office of one of these cities, was laid off. In response to her argument that the Transfer Directive protected her job, the ECJ held that the Transfer Directive only applies to transfers of undertakings, businesses, or parts of businesses, and that municipalities did not fall under this definition.

---

96. Case C-392/92, Christel Schmidt v. Spar- und Leihkasse, 1994 E.C.R. I-1508, 1513 ¶15.
97. *Id.*
98. Transfer Directive at art. 1(1)(c).
99. Case C-343/98, Collino v. Telecom Italia, 2000 E.C.R. I-6659 (privatization of Telecom Italy).
100. Case C-151/09, Federación de Servicios Públicos de la UGT v. Ayuntamiento de La Línea de la Concepción, 2010 E.C.R. I-7617, 7628 ¶23.
101. Case C-298/94, Henke v. Gemeinde Schierke, 1996 E.C.R. I-4989.

A transfer of an undertaking commonly occurs in the parameters of the acquisition or merger of a business.[102] Business acquisitions are typically divided into asset transactions and stock transactions. In other words, when one company acquires another company, it typically acquires its assets or its stock. The Transfer Directive is not directed at stock acquisitions. In a stock acquisition, the acquired company is acquired as a legal entity. Its rights and liabilities remain with the same entity: only the name of the shareholder changes. Hence, employment relationships would not necessarily be affected. In asset acquisitions, however, the purchaser only takes certain assets and liabilities of the seller. As the legal entity is not transferred, any agreements which the transferor (assuming that the transferor is the seller)[103] is a party to (including employment agreements) would normally stay with that entity. In many instances, the transferor and transferee agree that the employee contracts will also be transferred to the acquiring company. However, this is not always the case. The acquiring entity may not want to accept all of the employees for the reasons stated above. For this reason, the Transfer Directive is primarily aimed at asset transactions.

When a business is comprised of a group of assets, it is relatively easy to determine when a transfer of an economic entity occurs. What happens, however, if the business is not made up of assets? In some cases, a company may only want to acquire the goodwill or intellectual property of another company. Or what happens if a company outsources a particular part of its business and then awards the contract to another supplier? Does the transfer of the business from the old outsourcing company to the new one constitute a transfer even though there is no agreement between them? These issues have been addressed on several occasions by the EU courts.

According to the ECJ, "the decisive criterion is whether the entity in question keeps its identity after being taken over by the new employer."[104] Although each case must be examined on its own merits, the ECJ has been quite clear

---

102. It is important to note that the ECJ takes a "sufficiently flexible interpretation" of the concept of a transfer. It does not even require the existence of an agreement between the buyer and the seller. Case C-108/10, Scattolon v. Ministero dell'Instruzione, 2011 E.C.R. I-7532, 7553 ¶63.
103. The terms transferor and transferee are not always synonymous with buyer and seller of a business. The term transferor refers to any natural or legal person who, by reason of a transfer, ceases to be the employer in respect of the undertaking, business, or part of the undertaking or business. The term transferee refers to any natural or legal person who, by reason of a transfer, becomes the employer in respect of the undertaking, business, or part of the undertaking or business. In most cases, the seller will be the transferor and the buyer will be the transferee. However, when a company outsources a particular aspect of its business to a third party, and then after awhile decides to use another outsourcing supplier for that particular aspect of the business, the initial third party is considered the transferor and the new outsourcing supplier is considered the transferee even though there is no sale of a business between them. *See, e.g.*, Case C-340/01, Alber v. Sodexho MM Catering GmbH, 2003 E.C.R. I-14023 (A transfer of an economic entity occurred when a hospital changed caterers).
104. Case C-458/12, Amatori v. Italia SpA, 2014 E.C.R. I-___ at ¶30.

that the "transfer of an undertaking, business or part of a business" does not necessarily require the transfer of physical assets.[105] This is illustrated in *Oy Liikenne Ab v. Pekka Liskojärvi*[106] and *Abler v. Sodexho MM Catering GmbH*.[107] In *Oy Liikenne,* Helsinki had outsourced bus services to a private contractor. The issue under the Transfer Directive arose when Helsinki changed contractors. The new contractor did not acquire any of the old contractor's assets. Due to the loss of the contract, the old contractor dismissed a number of employees. In response to the arguments of these employees that the Transfer Directive required the new contractor to assume their employment relationships, the ECJ held that the lack of a transfer of assets indicated that the business was not transferred to the new contractor, particularly in view of the fact that the assets were a fundamental part of the business.[108]

The facts in *Abler v. Sodexho MM Catering GmbH* were similar to those in *Oy Liikenne*. In *Abler,* a hospital changed caterers. In this case, however, the assets used by the old caterer and the new caterer belonged to the hospital. The ECJ concluded that the Transfer Directive did apply.[109] In both of these cases, the absence of a contractual link (i.e., sales contract for the business) between the transferor and the transferee was not the decisive factor. Instead, the important consideration, and distinguishing characteristic, seems to have been that the new business was using the assets of the old business.

The holding of the ECJ in *CLECE SA v. Valor* represents an attempt by the ECJ to limit this expansive interpretation of the notion of a transfer of a business. In *CLECE SA v. Valor*, a local Spanish government council outsourced the cleaning of its schools to a third party service company. When the council terminated the outsourcing agreement and decided to clean the schools with its own employees, an employee of the third party service company sued for unlawful termination. In arriving at a different conclusion than in the cases previously discussed, the ECJ stated:

> [T]he mere fact that the activity carried out by [the third party] and that carried out by the [council] are similar, even identical, does not lead to the conclusion that an economic entity has retained its identity. An entity cannot be reduced to the activity entrusted to it. Its identity emerges from several indissociable

---

105. Case C-108/10, Scattolon v. Ministero dell'Instruzione, 2011 E.C.R. I-7532, 7552 ¶49; Case C-151/09, Federación de Servicios Públicos de la UGT v. Ayuntamiento de La Línea de la Concepción, 2010 E.C.R. I-7617, 7629 ¶28. Decision of the German Bundesarbeitsgericht in case no 8 AZR 648/13 (Aug. 21, 2014) at ¶17 *reported at* Betriebs-Berater (2015) 115.
106. Case C-172/99, Oy Liikenne Ab v. Pekka Liskojärvi, 2001 E.C.R. I-745.
107. Case C-340/01, Abler v. Sodexho MM Catering GmbH, 2003 E.C.R. I-14023. Although both of these cases involved the application of Directive 77/187, the legislation which the Transfer Directive replaced, the wording of the provisions of the law at issue was the same.
108. Case C-172/99, Oy Liikenne Ab v. Pekka Liskojärvi, 2001 E.C.R. I-745, 774 ¶39.
109. Case C-340/01, Abler v. Sodexho MM Catering GmbH, 2003 E.C.R. I-14023, 14057 ¶36.

factors, such as its workforce, its management staff, the way in which its work is organized, its operating methods or indeed, where appropriate, the operational resources available to it (citations omitted). In particular, the identity of an economic entity, such as that forming the subject of the dispute in the main proceedings, which is essentially based on manpower, cannot be retained if the majority of its employees are not taken on by the alleged transferee.[110]

Acquisitions out of bankruptcy are treated somewhat differently. The Directive does not apply where the purpose of the proceedings is to liquidate the assets of the transferor but is applicable where their object was to secure the survival of the business.[111] Unless member states provide otherwise, it applies where the transferor is the subject of insolvency proceedings that have been instituted with a view to liquidation of the transferor's assets.[112] Member states are also given the option of relaxing some of the Directive's requirements for insolvent businesses (e.g., to provide that the outstanding debts in respect of transferring employees do not pass to the transferee).

(b) Territorial Scope

In most instances, the territorial scope of the Transfer Directive is not an issue. The business is acquired by another business and the work is continued at the same facility. Globalization, however, has reduced the significance of geographic boundaries. Companies frequently outsource portions of their businesses to other companies. Often these are not even located in the same country. For example, a company which traditionally operated a call center near its facility in the EU may decide that it is more efficient to outsource those same activities to a call center in India. This, of course, would constitute a transfer of part of a business.

The territorial scope of the Directive does not depend on the location of the headquarters or state of incorporation of the transferor or transferee. The Directive applies if the undertaking, business, or part of the undertaking or business to be transferred is situated within the EU.[113] This is because the Transfer Directive is primarily concerned with protecting workers in the EU. In *Holis Metal Industries Ltd. v. GMB*, for example, the UK's Employment Appeal Tribunal held that the Transfer Directive applied to the acquisition of a UK business by an Israeli business.[114] In that case, the Israeli business moved

---

110. Case C-463/09, CLECE SA v. Valor, 2011 E.C.R. I-122, 135 ¶41.
111. Transfer Directive at art. 5. As discussed below, employees are given some protection by Council Directive 80/987/EEC of 20 October 1980 on the approximation of the laws of the member states relating to the protection of employees in the event of the insolvency of their employer, 1980 O.J. (L 283) 23, in the event that their employer is liquidated.
112. Transfer Directive at art. 5.
113. *Id.* at art. 1(2).
114. Employment Appeal Tribunal, appeal No. UKEAT/0171/07/CEA (Dec. 12, 2007).

the jobs to Israel. The Tribunal held that the UK law transposing the Transfer Directive applied in this circumstance.

4.2 Rights of Employees in Event of Transfer

(a) *Employment Automatically Transferred*

The general rule is that the rights and obligations of the transferor (i.e., the employer)[115] arising from a contract of employment or from an employment relationship existing on the date of a transfer are automatically transferred to the transferee when the business is transferred.[116] In other words, a subrogation of rights and obligations occurs. The practical effect is that the acquirer of a business is obligated to take on the existing employees of the acquired business.[117] However, the implications of the automatic transfer go beyond the mere transfer of the employment relationship. The obligations which the transferring employer has under the existing employment agreements must be assumed by the transferee employer.[118] For example, if the employees were offered an early retirement option by the transferring employer, the transferee

---

115. The transferor is typically the legal entity which is the contractual employer of the employee. The issue in *Albon Catering BV v. FNV Bondgenoten* was whether the term "transferor" is necessarily limited to the contractual employer. In that case, the Dutch brewing company Heineken established a legal entity which served as the formal employer of the catering employees. These employees then were assigned to work in various businesses within the Heineken corporate group. The legal issue arose in this case because Heineken was outsourcing the catering business, but there was no transfer of the business of the formal employer. The ECJ held that the concept of transferor extends not only to the formal employer but also to a legal entity "responsible for the economic activity of the entity transferred and who, in that capacity, establishes working relations as employer with the staff of that entity, in some cases despite the absence of contractual relations with those employees." Case C-242/09, Albon Catering BV v. FNV Bondgenoten, 2010 E.C.R. I-10324, 10335 ¶28.
116. Transfer Directive at art. 3(1). Unless the particular member state has adopted legislation to the contrary, the automatic transfer does not apply to any transfer of an undertaking, business, or part of an undertaking or business where the transferor is the subject of bankruptcy proceedings or any analogous insolvency proceedings which have been instituted with a view to the liquidation of the assets of the transferor and are under the supervision of a competent public authority. Transfer Directive at art. 5(1).
117. This does not mean that the new employer must accept subsequent changes to the employee relationship if the employee, prior to the transfer, was under a collective bargaining agreement. Once the employee is transferred and the collective bargaining agreement is subsequently changed, the new employer does not have to accept the collective bargaining changes unless it is otherwise party to the collective bargaining agreement. Case C-426/11, Alemo-Herron v. Parkwood Leisure Ltd., 2013 E.C.R. I-____ at ¶22.
118. The same applies to any collective agreements to which the transferor is party at the time of the transfer. Transfer Directive at art. 3(3).

employer must assume those same obligations.[119] In other words, it is not just the employment relationship that is transferred.

To avoid the application of the rule, employers are often tempted to induce the employee to terminate his or her employment by substantially changing the employee's responsibilities. However, if the employer terminates the employment contract or the employment relationship because the transfer resulted in a substantial change in working conditions to the detriment of the employee, the employer is considered to have terminated the employment relationship.[120] For example, a reduction in the employee's salary[121] or a substantial change in the employee's responsibilities and title[122] would be deemed substantial changes in the working conditions of that employee. However, the Directive does not preclude the new employer from entering into a new employment agreement with an employee on different terms, even if less favorable to the employee.[123] But there is typically no incentive for the employee to agree to this new agreement because the employee has the right to employment on substantially the same terms. The compensatory claims of the employees in these circumstances are determined by applicable member state law.[124]

The Transfer Directive also accords protection to the representatives of the employees. If the undertaking, business, or part of an undertaking or business being transferred preserves its autonomy, the status and function of the representatives of the employees must also be preserved.[125] The phrase "preserves its autonomy" means that the organizational structure of the transferred employees does not change.[126] A change of indirect supervision over the employees does not mean that the entity has not preserved its autonomy. Instead, the relevant question is whether the direct supervision of the employees has changed. If the transferor keeps the same immediate managers, it is likely to be deemed as preserving its autonomy.[127]

In certain circumstances, there might be an incentive for an undertaking to terminate employees prior to the transfer of the undertaking. In many circumstances, an undertaking will be of greater value to a potential acquirer

---

119. Case C-4/01, Martin v. South Bank University, 2003 E.C.R. I-12859, 12901 ¶30. Although there is an exception in the Transfer Directive for old-age, invalidity, or survivors' benefits under supplementary company or intercompany pension schemes outside the statutory social security schemes in member states (Article 3(4)), the ECJ held in this case that early retirement benefits do not constitute "old-age, invalidity or survivors' benefits." *Id.* at 12902 ¶35.
120. Transfer Directive at art. 4(2).
121. Case C-425/02, Delahaye v. Ministre de la Fonction publique et de la Réforme administrative, 2004 E.C.R. I-10823, 10851 ¶33.
122. Case C-466/07, Klarenberg v. Ferrotron Technologies GmbH, 2009 E.C.R. I-819, 835 ¶52.
123. Case C-4/01, Martin v. South Bank University, 2003 E.C.R. I-12859, 12905 ¶43.
124. Case C-396/07, Mirja Juuri v. Fazer Amica Oy, 2008 E.C.R. I-8907, 8917 ¶29.
125. Transfer Directive at art. 6(1).
126. Case C-151/09, Federación de Servicios Públicos de la UGT v. Ayuntamiento de La Línea de la Concepción, 2010 E.C.R. I-7617, 7634 ¶46.
127. *Id.* at 7636 ¶56.

if the undertaking is not overly staffed. Consequently, an undertaking may terminate employees in anticipation of an acquisition. The Transfer Directive does not specifically address the situation of employee terminations prior to the transaction. If the termination is part of an agreement or even if the acquiring undertaking has been identified and the parties are in negotiations, the Transfer Directive will likely apply. If, however, the acquiring undertaking has not been identified (for example, in preparation for an auction of the undertaking), the result is not as clear. In *Spaceright Europe Ltd. v. Baillavoine*, the English Employment Appeal Tribunal held that the termination of an employee was unfair even though the acquirer was not identified at the time of the termination.[128] The critical fact, according to the Tribunal, was that the transfer of the undertaking was contemplated by the owners even though a purchaser had not been identified at the time of termination.

(b) *Right to Be Informed of the Transaction*

The Directive also protects employees by requiring the seller and the purchaser to inform and consult the employees or their representatives in the event of a transfer of undertakings.[129] The notice must be given to the employees prior to the consummation of the transaction. Similarly, the Cross-Border Merger Directive requires the merging companies to inform their respective employees prior to the merger.[130] The Transfer Directive does not specify a precise time, but merely states that notice must be given in good time.[131] Although the employee representatives cannot legally veto the transaction, they can make its consummation more difficult.

(c) *Right of Continued Employee Participation*

EU labor law is not completely harmonized even though it is based on numerous directives. As discussed in Chapter I, directives merely establish the guidelines that member states are required to transpose into national law. Hence, there are differences in the wording of the labor laws of the respective member states. In addition, many of the labor law directives only set the minimum level of protections for employees. The member states are free to grant employees greater protections. Consequently, differences remain in the level of protections accorded to employees by member state laws. For example, some member states grant employees the right to participate in the management of companies,

---

128. Spaceright Europe Ltd. v. Baillavoine, Employment Appeal Tribunal, appeal no. UKEAT/0339/10/sm (Feb. 1, 2011).
129. Transfer Directive at art. 7.
130. Cross-Border Merger Directive at art. 7.
131. Transfer Directive at art. 7(1).

going beyond any rights mandated by a European directive.[132] These differences create the incentive for employers to shift their businesses from member states with a high level of employee protection to member states with lower employee protection. To address the problems that arise because of the differences between member states, the Cross-Border Mergers Directive secures certain rights for employees of the merged entity.

In the event of a cross-border merger,[133] the rights of the employees to continue to participate in the management of the surviving entity are secured by the Cross-Border Merger Directive. If the acquiring company is located in a different member state than the merged company, the employee participation rules and regulations of the acquiring company's member state will generally apply.[134] For example, if a Belgian *société anonyme* were to merge into a Czech *spolecnost* with the Czech *spolecnost* being the acquiring company, the application of the general rule would mean that the Czech laws on employee participation would apply. This rule creates the incentive for companies to merge into "employer-friendly" countries.[135] For example, a German company could avoid the application of German employee participation rules by merging into a UK company. To remove this incentive, the Cross-Border Merger Directive limits the ability of the merging companies to reduce the rights of the employees of the merged company to participate in the acquiring company's management bodies.

---

132. The following EU directives require the member states to establish some form of employee participation: Council Directive 2001/23/EC of 12 March 2001 on the approximation of the laws of the member states relating to the safeguarding of employees' rights in the event of transfers of undertakings, businesses or parts of undertakings or businesses, 2001 O.J. (L 82) 16; Directive 2002/14/EC of the European Parliament and of the Council of 11 March 2002 establishing a general framework for informing and consulting employees in the European Community—Joint declaration of the European Parliament, the Council and the Commission on employee representation, 2002 O.J. (L 80) 29; Council Directive 2009/38/EC of the European Parliament and of the Council of 6 May 2009 on the establishment of a European Works Council or a procedure in Community-scale undertakings and Community-scale groups of undertakings for the purposes of informing and consulting employees, 2009 O.J. (L 122) 28 [hereinafter Works Council Directive].
133. The definition of cross-border merger is discussed in Chapter V.
134. Cross-Border Merger Directive at art. 16(1).
135. Because of political differences among the member states, the laws of the respective member states applicable to employee participation in the management of European companies have not been completely harmonized. Partial harmonization has been sought by the following directives: Directive 2002/14/EC of the European Parliament and of the Council of 11 March 2002 establishing a general framework for informing and consulting employees in the European Community—Joint declaration of the European Parliament, the Council and the Commission on employee representation, 2002 O.J. (L 80) 29; Council Directive 2009/38/EC of the European Parliament and of the Council of 6 May 2009 on the establishment of a European Works Council or a procedure in Community-scale undertakings and Community-scale groups of undertakings for the purposes of informing and consulting employees, 2009 O.J. (L 122) 28.

The Cross-Border Merger Directive provides that the general rule will not be applied in three situations.[136] First, the general rule does not apply if at least one of the merging companies has an average number of employees above 500 (over the previous six months) and is already operating under an employee participation system.

Second, the general rule will not apply if the law of the acquiring company's member state does not provide for at least the same level of employee participation the merging companies had in place at the time of the merger. The Cross-Border Merger Directive tries to establish an objective criterion to measure whether the level of protection before the merger is greater than what is mandated by the member state of the acquiring company. If the proportional representation of the employees in the management of the acquiring company as mandated by that entity's member state is less than the proportional representation of employees in management prior to the merger in any of the merging entities, then the general rule does not apply. If, for example, Company A (a French *sociéte á responsabilité limitée*) merges into Company B (a Dutch *naamloze vennootschap*), and the employee participation scheme established by Company A grants employees 20 percent of the seats on the board of directors, the Dutch rules on employee participation will not automatically apply if they grant the employees less than 20 percent of the seats on the board of directors of the surviving Company B.

The third situation in which the general rule does not apply is if the national law applicable to the acquiring company does not provide for employees of establishments of the acquiring company that are situated in other member states the same entitlement to exercise participation rights as is enjoyed by those employees employed in the member state where the acquiring company has its registered office. For example, if a Swedish *Aktiebolag* with facilities in Finland and Denmark is merging into a Slovenian *delniska druzba*, the employee participation rules of Slovenia will not apply if Slovenian law does not provide for employee participation rights of the employees at the facilities in Finland and Denmark as it does for the Slovenian employees.

If one of these three situations exists, the employee participation law of the acquiring company's member state does not apply. Instead, the national law on employee participation transposing the SE Directive[137] applies (even though an SE is not involved in the merger) by default unless the companies involved and the employee representatives can agree on a system of employee participation.[138] If, for example, the acquiring company in a cross-border merger is a Dutch company, and one of the three exceptions to the general rule applies, the employee participation rights codified in the *Wet van 17/3/2005 tot uitvoering van richtlijn NR. 2001/86/EG van de Raad van de Europese Unie van 8/10/2001 tot aanvulling van het statuut van de Europese vennootschap met betrekking tot de rol van de werknemers* would apply as this Dutch statute transposes the

---

136. Cross-Border Merger Directive at art. 16.
137. Council Directive 2001/86/EC of 8 October 2001 supplementing the Statute for a European company with regard to the involvement of employees, 2001 O.J. (L 294) 22.
138. Cross-Border Merger Directive at art. 16(3).

SE Directive unless the companies and the employee representatives agree otherwise.

There is a specific procedure mandated by the Cross-Border Merger Directive for informing and negotiating with the employees. The first step is that the companies involved in the cross-border merger must set up a special negotiating body for the purpose of agreeing on employee participation in the acquiring company.[139] The special negotiating body is comprised of employee representatives elected or appointed by the employees in accordance with national law. It must include at least one employee representative from each member state in which the companies involved in the merger have employees. Each member state has one employee representative on the special negotiating body for each 10 percent (or fraction thereof) of the total number of employees of the companies involved in the merger. If, for example, Company A, which has 100 employees (50 each in Spain and Portugal), merges into Company B which has 200 employees (170 in Latvia and 30 in Lithuania), the special negotiating body must include six representatives of the Latvian employees, two representatives from each of the Spanish and Portuguese employees and one for the Lithuanian employees.

The agreement on employee participation between the acquiring company and the special negotiating body requires the affirmative vote of an absolute majority of the members of the special negotiating body. However, if the level of employee participation established by the agreement is less than the employees had before, at least two-thirds of the members representing at least two-thirds of the employees must vote affirmatively.

If the merging entities and the employees are not able to reach an agreement within six months, the standard rules of employee participation set forth in an annex to the SE Directive apply. The merging companies can avoid establishing a special negotiating body and negotiating with the representatives of the employees by establishing a level of employee participation equal to the highest level of protection mandated by the member states of the merging entities.[140] For example, if an Austrian *Gesellschaft mit beschränkter Haftung* is merging into an Irish limited liability company, the merging parties may adopt employee participation rights commensurate with Austrian law as Austrian law gives employees greater protection than Irish law does.

5. Protection in Event of Collective Redundancy

In addition to other protections, the EU has attempted to provide protection for workers in cases where large numbers of employees are terminated together (similar to the U.S. Worker Adjustment and Retraining Notification Act). To

---

139. The companies involved in the merger can avoid this process by simply adopting employee participation rights commensurate with the strictest rules of the member state involved.
140. Cross-Border Merger Directive at art. 16(4)(a) together with Part 3 of Annex to Directive 2001/86.

this end, it has tried to harmonize the minimum protections offered by the laws of the member states. As the European legislation in this field is in the form of a directive,[141] much of the law relating to collective redundancies remains national law.

5.1   Qualification of Collective Redundancy

The Collective Redundancies Directive only applies to cases of collective redundancies. The term collective redundancy refers to mass dismissals effected by an employer[142] for reasons not specifically related to the individual workers concerned.[143] There are two basic components to the concept of collective redundancy. First, the redundancy component refers essentially to the termination of the employment relationship without the consent of the employee.[144] In *Commission v. Portugal*, the issue arose whether the express will of the employer to terminate the employment relationship is required for the finding of a redundancy. If, for example, the employment relationship ends because the company is dissolved, does a redundancy exist? Under Portuguese law, the ending of the employment relationship in such circumstances was considered merely the expiration of the employment relationship and not its termination by the employer. The ECJ held that the will of the employer is irrelevant. What is relevant is that the relationship came to an end against the will of the employee.[145] It should be noted, however, that the expiry of an employment contract entered into for a specific term is not considered a redundancy under the Collective Redundancies Directive.[146]

The second component of the definition of collective redundancy precludes application of the Collective Redundancies Directive in cases of individual terminations. In other words, a group of employees must be terminated in order to trigger the application of the Collective Redundancies Directive. The minimum number of redundancies required for a group layoff to qualify as a collective redundancy depends on the time frame involved (30 or 90 days) and size of the company.[147] A situation of collective redundancy occurs if within

---

141. Council Directive 98/59/EC of 20 July 1998 on the approximation of the laws of the member states relating to collective redundancies, 1998 O.J. (L 225) 16 [hereinafter Collective Redundancies Directive].
142. The term employer also covers nonprofit employers such as a labor union or church, Case C-32/02, Comm'n v. Italy, 2003 E.C.R. 12063, 12075 ¶26, but does not apply to government agencies or the military, Case C-583/10, United States v. Nolan, 2012 E.C.R. I-___, at ¶34 (reported only in the electronic reports of cases ECLI:EU:C:2012:638).
143. Collective Redundancies Directive at art. 1(1).
144. Joined Cases C-187/05 – 190/05, Agorastoudis v. Goodyear Hellas AVEE, 2006 E.C.R. I-7777, 7789 ¶28; Case C-55/02, Comm'n v. Portugal, 2004 E.C.R. I-9387, 9419 ¶50.
145. Case C-55/02, Comm'n v. Portugal, 2004 E.C.R. I-9387, 9421 ¶62.
146. Collective Redundancies Directive at art. 1(2).
147. The Collective Redundancies Directive only applies when the employer is a legal entity. Case C-323/08, Ovido Rodríguez Mayor v. Herencia yacente de Rafael de las Heras Davila, 2009 E.C.R. I-11650, 11673 ¶53.

a period of 30 days, at least 10 redundancies occur in "establishments"[148] normally employing more than 20 and less than 100 workers. For establishments normally employing at least 100 but less than 300 workers, the standard is at least 10 percent of the number of workers employed within a 30-day period. If the establishment normally employs 300 workers or more, the standard is at least 30 employees within a 30-day period. Finally, regardless of the size of the establishment, a collective redundancy will also be deemed to occur if, over a period of 90 days, at least 20 workers are laid off. The 30-day and 90-day time periods used in determining whether a collective redundancy exists begin on the date on which the employer declares its intention to terminate the employment relationship and not on the date on which the termination actually takes effect.[149]

5.2 Consultation Requirements in Event of Collective Redundancy

The legal effect of qualifying as a collective redundancy is that the employer must begin consultations with the workers' representatives "in good time" after the employer first begins contemplating collective redundancies.[150] The reference to employer is not strictly limited to the legal entity[151] which employs the employees, but includes any legal entities controlling that legal entity.[152] For example, the obligation to consult may arise when the parent company begins contemplating collective redundancies even though the actual employer has no idea of the plan. If the parent company owns several subsidiaries, and it begins contemplating terminations qualifying as collective redundancies generally for the group of companies, the obligation to consult employees does not arise until the particular subsidiary where the redundancies are to occur has been identified.[153]

The member states may adopt legislation which is more favorable to workers.[154] At a minimum, however, the consultations must address ways and means of avoiding collective redundancies or reducing the number of workers affected, and of mitigating the consequences by recourse to accompanying

---

148. The concept of establishment is not the same as undertaking or company. A branch or division of a company or even a factory—which itself does not have legal personality—may be considered an establishment. It merely needs to have a workforce and "a certain degree of permanence and stability." Case C-270/05, Athinaiki Chartopoiia AE v. L. Panagiotidis, 2007 E.C.R. I-1502, 1514 ¶27.
149. C-188/03, Junk v. Kühnel, 2005 E.C.R. I-903, 919 ¶39.
150. Collective Redundancies Directive at art. 2(1).
151. The member states may, however, adopt laws which extend these protections to employees in undertakings falling below the thresholds set forth in the Directive. Case C-323/08, Ovido Rodríguez Mayor v. Herencia yacente de Rafael de las Heras Davila, 2009 E.C.R. I-11650, 11666 ¶23
152. Case C-44/08, Akavan Erityisalojen Keskusliitto AEK v. Fujitsu Siemens Computers Oy, 2009 E.C.R I-8188, 8203 ¶43.
153. *Id.* at 8208 ¶63.
154. Collective Redundancies Directive at art. 5.

social measures aimed, inter alia, at aid for redeploying or retraining workers made redundant.

Because the Directive allows the member states to adopt legislation more favorable to workers, the consultation requirements in respect of redundancies are different for each member state. In the UK, if there are redundancies which result in more than 20 employees in an undertaking being made redundant over a 90-day period, there would be a consultation period of 90 days (where more than 100 were affected) or 30 days (where less than 100 were affected). In France, collective consultation obligations begin with a proposal to dismiss two to nine employees over 30 days, with a different time line for consultation where at least 10 employees within companies employing more than 50 employees are proposed to be dismissed over a 30-day period.

5.3 Notification of Collective Redundancies

In addition to initiating consultation with the employees, employers are required to notify the competent public authority of any projected collective redundancies.[155] The notification must contain all relevant information concerning the projected collective redundancies and the consultations with workers' representatives, and particularly the reasons for the redundancies, the number of workers to be made redundant, the number of workers normally employed, and the period over which the redundancies are to be effected. A copy of the notice is also sent by the employer to the workers' representatives who may send any comments to the competent public authority.

The notification to the public authorities may take place any time prior to the redundancies. However, the projected collective redundancies notified to the competent public authority must take effect not earlier than 30 days after the notification unless the 30-day period is reduced by the public authority.[156] For practical purposes, therefore, the notification should be submitted at least 30 days prior to the date on which the employer wants the redundancies to take effect. If the problems raised by the projected collective redundancies are not likely to be solved within the initial period, the public authority may extend the 30-day period to 60 days. Conversely, if a solution is found, the public authority may shorten the 30-day period.

6. Protection in Event of Insolvency of Employer

Various groups of legal entities and individuals suffer when a company becomes insolvent. Among the hardest hit are the employees. In addition to losing their jobs, many of them will have claims for earned wages against the insolvent entity. The free movement of persons in the EU means that a large number of individuals work in different member states. In an attempt to establish a minimum level of

---

155. *Id.* at art. 3.
156. *Id.* at art. 4(1). However, member states may grant the competent public authority the power to reduce the period provided for in the preceding subparagraph.

protection across the EU for employees in the event of bankruptcy, the Council adopted the Employer Insolvency Directive.[157]

6.1 Scope of Directive

The Directive applies to employees' claims arising from contracts of employment or employment relationships and existing against employers who are in a state of insolvency. An employer is considered to be in a state of insolvency if three conditions are fulfilled.[158] First, a request must have been made under the laws of a member state to open proceedings based on the employer's insolvency. Second, the proceedings must involve the partial or total divestment of the employer's assets and the appointment of a liquidator or a person performing a similar task. Third, the responsible authority in the member state has either decided to open the proceedings or has established that the business has been definitively closed down and that the available assets are insufficient to warrant opening the proceedings. The Directive applies not only if the responsible authority has ordered the liquidation of the insolvent company, but also where the insolvent company is ordered to continue operating under protection of the insolvency administrator.[159]

The Employer Insolvency Directive protects all the employees of the insolvent business. The term employee is defined by reference to the applicable laws of the member states.[160] The definition of "employee" must, however, be consistent with the social objective of the Directive[161] and include part-time employees, employees with a fixed term contract and temporary employees. The duration of employment is irrelevant.[162] Consequently, even an employee hired the day before the insolvency falls under the protections of the Employer Insolvency Directive. The fact that an employee may also be a minority shareholder at the time of insolvency does not necessarily preclude that person from the protections offered by the Directive.[163]

---

157. Directive 2008/94/EC of the European Parliament and of the Council of 22 October 2008 on the protection of employees in the event of the insolvency of their employer, 2008 O.J. (L 283) 36 [hereinafter Employer Insolvency Directive].
158. Employer Insolvency Directive at art. 2(1).
159. Case C-247/12, Mustafa v. Direktor na fond 'Garantirani vzemania na rabotnitsite i sluzhitelite' kam Natsionalnia osiguritelen institut, 2013 E.C.R. I-____, at ¶33.
160. Employer Insolvency Directive at art. 2(2). The protection also applies in narrow circumstances (*i.e.*, old age benefits) to former employees, Case C-398/11, Hogan v. Minister for Social and Family Affairs, 2013 E.C.R. I-____, at ¶27, and to employees who make be illegal aliens in that member state, Case C-311/13, Tümer v. Raad van bestuur van het Uitvoeringsinstituut werknemersverzekeringen, 2014 E.C.R. I-____, at ¶45.
161. *Id.* at ¶42.
162. Employer Insolvency Directive at art. 2(3).
163. Case C-201/01, Walcher v. Bundesamt für Soziales und Behindertenwesen Steiermark, 2003 E.C.R. I-8827. As discussed below, however, the fact that an employee may be the owner of the business may limit the protections to be claimed by that owner-employee. Employer Insolvency Directive at art. 12(c).

6.2 Protections for Employees

The fundamental obligation imposed by the Directive on the member states is the requirement that the member states take the measures necessary to ensure that they guarantee payment of employees' outstanding claims resulting from contracts of employment or employment relationships and relating to pay for the period prior to a given date. In other words, if a company becomes insolvent, the member states must have a mechanism in place to make sure that the claims of the employees are protected. This is accomplished by the required establishment of guarantee institutions in each member state.[164] These guarantee institutions assume the liabilities of the insolvent company to its employees.

The member states may set a limit on these liabilities provided such a limit is "socially compatible" with the objectives of the Employer Insolvency Directive.[165] There must, however, be a link between the limits imposed by the member state and the social objective. In *Van Ardennen v. Raad van bestuur van het Uitvoeringsinstituut werknemersverzekeringen*, the ECJ held that The Netherlands could not impose a requirement that the individual register as a "job seeker" as a condition to receiving his insolvency benefit.[166]

The general rule is that the guaranty institution of the member state where the insolvent company is located will have to make sure the employees are compensated. If the insolvent company is active in two or more member states, the member state responsible for meeting employees' outstanding claims is the member state in whose territory they work or habitually work.[167] The issue in *Svenska staten v. Holmqvist* was whether the insolvent company (a Swedish trucking company) was "active in the territory of at least two Member States." The Swedish Authority for Insolvencies argued that it was not obligated to compensate an employee of the Swedish insolvent company because the company was active in two or more member states and the employee's task was fulfilled primarily outside Sweden (his job was to transport goods from Sweden to Italy).

The ECJ held that although it is not required that a company have a branch or a fixed establishment for it to be considered to be "active" there, it must at least have a "stable economic presence" in that member state.[168] In the present case, the Swedish company did not have a stable economic presence outside Sweden. As the insolvent Swedish company was not active in two or more member states, Article 9 of the Employer Insolvency Directive did not apply and the Swedish guarantee institution was responsible for compensating the employee even if the truck driver was primarily working outside Sweden.

The typical scenario falling under the Directive is where an employer becomes insolvent and its employees have not been paid. However, there are a number of variations that present interesting issues. The fundamental requirement

---

164. Employer Insolvency Directive at art. 3.
165. *Id.* at art. 4(3).
166. Case C-435/10, Van Ardennen v. Raad van bestuur van het Uitvoeringsinstituut werknemersverzekeringen, 2011 E.C.R. I-11707, 11722 ¶39.
167. Employer Insolvency Directive at art. 9(1).
168. Case C-310/07, Svenska staten v. Holmqvist, 2008 E.C.R. I-7891, 7904 ¶36.

is that the employee claims result from contracts of employment or employment relationships and relate to pay for the period prior to a given date.

In *Valero v. Fondo de Garantia Salarial*, the issue was whether the Directive applied to the payments which an insolvent employer owed to a terminated employee.[169] Several years earlier, after a Spanish court held that the employee had been terminated unfairly, the employer and employee reached a settlement to be paid out over time. Before it was fully paid out, the employer filed for bankruptcy protection. The ECJ held that the issue of whether the settlement was to be considered "pay" for purposes of the Directive was an issue for the national court to decide, applying Spanish law.[170]

6.3 Exceptions

Member states may, by way of exception, exclude claims by certain categories of employees from the scope of the Directive, based on the existence of other forms of guarantee offering the employee protection equivalent to that resulting from the Directive.[171] Italy, for example, exempts employees covered by benefits that will be paid in the event that the company is hit by an economic crisis. The rationale for this exception is that it prevents the employee from getting double compensation.

In addition, the member states have the ability to limit or exclude the claims of the employee if (1) necessary to prevent abuse, (2) compensation to the employee would be unjustifiable because of "special links" between the employee and employer and (3) the employee alone or together with his or her close relatives was the owner of an essential part of the employer's undertaking or business and had considerable influence on its activities.[172] Although the Directive does not provide a look-back period, the consensus seems to be that the national laws look back for a period of six months prior to the date of the insolvency filing to determine whether the employee was an owner or partial owner of the insolvent business.[173]

In *Riksskatteverket v. Soghra Gharehveran,* the question arose whether a relative who himself or herself holds no interest in the insolvent company may be precluded from receiving compensation on the basis of the fact that a close relative (the husband in this case) held a controlling interest in the insolvent company.[174] Soghra Gharehveran was employed by Zarrinen AB, a company operating a restaurant for which she performed, as employee, certain accounting duties. All the shares in that company were held by her husband. After Zarrinen had been put into liquidation, Gharehveran lodged a claim for payment of her wages. That claim was rejected by the liquidator on the ground that she was

---

169. Case C-520/03, Valero v. Fondo de Garantia Salarial, 2004 E.C.R. I-12065.
170. *Id.* at 12082 ¶33.
171. Employer Insolvency Directive at art. 1(2).
172. *Id.* at art. 12.
173. Case C-30/10, Andersson v. Staten genom Kronofogdemyndigheten I Jönköping, 2011 E.C.R. I-513; Case C-441/99, Riksskatteverket v. Soghra Gharehveran, 2001 E.C.R. I-7687.
174. Case C-441/99, Riksskatteverket v. Soghra Gharehveran, 2001 E.C.R. I-7687.

a close relative of the person owning the liquidated company that had employed her. According to Swedish law, an employee who, on his own or together with a close relative, had owned an essential part of the undertaking and had considerable influence over its business in the six months preceding the petition in bankruptcy enjoys no preferential right as regards his or her pay. The ECJ held in this case that the wife was entitled to protection under the Directive because she herself had no interest in the company.

7. Employee Consultation

The relationship between employer and employee in Europe is often characterized as cooperative. This is partially the result of legal norms which have been implemented to secure rights for workers which they may not have secured through negotiation. One aspect of labor law in which this cooperative characteristic is particularly apparent relates to the rights of employees to be consulted by management in certain circumstances affecting the employees.

7.1 Applicable Law

The two primary legal norms that require that employees are informed and consulted about the major decisions of their employer are the Works Council Directive[175] and the Framework Consultation Directive.[176] In addition, the employees of European companies enjoy certain rights based on a separate directive addressed specifically to this form of legal entity.[177]

7.2 Scope of Works Council Directive

The Works Council Directive provides employees in Community-scale undertakings and Community-scale groups of undertakings with the right to information and consultation. A Union scale undertaking means any undertaking with (1) at least 1,000 employees within the EU, and (2) at least 150 employees in each of at least two member states.[178] An EU-scale group of undertakings

---

175. Works Council Directive and for the United Kingdom: Council Directive 97/74/EC of 15 December 1997 extending, to the United Kingdom of Great Britain and Northern Ireland, Directive 94/45/EC on the establishment of a European Works Council or a procedure in Community-scale undertakings and Community-scale groups of undertakings for the purposes of informing and consulting employees, 1998 O.J. (L 10) 22.
176. Directive 2002/14/EC of the European Parliament and of the Council of 11 March 2002 establishing a general framework for informing and consulting employees in the European Community, O.J. 2002 (L 80) 29 [hereinafter Framework Consultation Directive].
177. Council Directive 2001/86/EC of 8 October 2001 supplementing the Statute for a European company with regard to the involvement of employees, 2001 O.J. (L 294) 22.
178. Works Council Directive at art. 2(1)(c). The number of employees is based on the average number of employees, including part-time employees, employed during the previous two years.

means a group of undertakings[179] with (1) at least 1,000 employees within the European Community, (2) at least two group undertakings in different member states, and (3) at least one group undertaking with at least 150 employees in one member state and at least one other group undertaking with at least 150 employees in another member state. For ease of reference, the term "covered entity" is commonly used to refer to a Community-scale undertaking or an EU-scale group of undertakings.

7.3 Scope of Framework Consultation Directive

The Framework Consultation Directive, which grants employees certain information and consultation rights, gives the member states some discretion in determining the size of entities to which it applies. The member states may choose to apply it to undertakings employing at least 50 employees in any one member state or to establishments employing at least 20 employees in any one member state.[180] The difference between undertaking and establishment is not clear. Both would cover a division of a company even if that division were not a separate legal entity. One may presume, however, that the term "establishment" was meant to apply to business units which are not in themselves legal entities. The rights granted in the Framework Consultation Directive are in addition to those granted in the Works Council Directive.[181] As the Works Council Directive at a minimum applies only if the undertaking has at least 150 employees in one member state, the Framework Consultation Directive will apply to all undertakings to which the Works Council Directive applies. Thus, businesses that meet the thresholds of both Directives must legally observe two sets of requirements. In practice, however, compliance with the national laws implementing the Works Council Directive will typically fulfill the national laws implementing the Framework Consultation Directive.

7.4 Responsibility for the Establishment of a Works Council or an Employee Information and Consultation Procedure

The Works Council Directive requires every covered entity to have a works council or at least a procedure for informing and consulting employees.[182] The decision whether to establish a works council or a procedure for informing and consulting employees is not unilaterally made by the covered entity. Instead, it is the result of a negotiation procedure mandated by the Directive.

---

179. A "group of undertakings" includes all companies under "dominant influence" of another company and is not limited to companies that qualify as Community-scale undertakings. Works Council Directive at art. 3. There is a presumption of dominant influence if the undertaking holds a majority of the subscribed capital, controls a majority of shareholder votes, or can appoint more than half of the administrative, management, or supervisory body of the undertaking.
180. Framework Consultation Directive at art. 3(1).
181. *Id.* at art. 9(2).
182. Works Council Directive at art. 1(2).

The central management of the covered entity is responsible for negotiating in good faith with the special negotiating body representing the employees to either set up a works council or an information and consultation procedure for the employees.[183] The central management is the central management of the ultimate parent company and not necessarily the individual company involved.[184] If the central management is located outside of the EU, the responsibility falls on either the representative designated by national law or, in the absence of such a representative, the management of the establishment or group undertaking employing the greatest number of employees in any one member state.[185] For example, if a corporation incorporated in the U.S. state of Delaware has subsidiaries in each of Poland, Latvia, and Lithuania each with 500 employees, the Delaware corporation is required to designate one of these entities as being responsible for facilitating the establishment of the works council for the European operations.

The covered entity is required to supply the employees' representatives with the information necessary for opening negotiations.[186] This obligation extends to all group companies that control such information. In *Betriebsrat der Firma ADS Anker GmbH v. ADS Anker GmbH*, ADS Anker GmbH, a Germany company, refused to supply the employees with information requested by the employees' representatives. ADS Anker claimed that it was not able to accommodate the request because the requested information was not in its control: it was in the control of the parent company, Anker BV, established in the Netherlands.

The labor court in Germany (Arbeitsgericht Bielefeld) held that, since the German law transposing the Works Council Directive is a national law, its scope of application can cover only German territory and it does not impose an obligation on undertakings in the group which are established outside Germany to provide certain information to undertakings established in German territory. In a reference proceeding, the ECJ held in that case that the Directive imposes the obligation on all undertakings within the group to supply the information.[187] As applied to the case, the Dutch parent company was obligated to supply the German company with the information requested by the employees of the German company.

---

183. *Id.* at art. 4(1).
184. Case C-349/01, Betriebsrat der Firma ADS Anker GmbH v. ADS Anker GmbH, 2004 E.C.R. I-6803, 6839 ¶52.
185. Works Council Directive at art. 4(2). The central management resulting from the application of this rule is referred to as the "deemed central management." Case C-349/01, Betriebsrat der Firma ADS Anker GmbH v. ADS Anker GmbH, 2004 E.C.R. I-6803, 6839 ¶53.
186. Case C-440/00, Gesamtbetriebsrat der Kühne & Nagel AG & Co. KG v. Kühne & Nagel AG & Co. KG, 2004 E.C.R. I-787, 826 ¶49.
187. Case C-349/01, Betriebsrat der Firma ADS Anker GmbH v. ADS Anker GmbH, 2004 E.C.R. I-6803, 6839 ¶58.

7.5 Establishment of a Works Council or Information and Consultation Procedure

The central management of the company must initiate negotiations for the establishment of a works council or an information and consultation procedure either on its own initiative or at the written request of at least 100 employees in at least two undertakings or establishments in at least two different member states.[188] In either case, a special negotiating body must be established for the purpose of negotiating with the central management the scope, composition, functions, and term of office of the works council or the arrangements for implementing a procedure for the information and consultation of employees.[189] The composition of the special negotiating body itself is determined by the laws of the member states with the restriction that it must have a minimum of three and a maximum of 18 members.

The central management and the special negotiating body then enter into negotiations. The purpose of the negotiations is to either set up a works council or establish an information and consultation procedure between management and the employees.[190] If the negotiations between central management and the special negotiating body result in a works council, the resulting written agreement must cover:

- the composition of the works council;
- the number of members;
- the allocation of seats and the term of office;
- the functions and the procedure for information and consultation of the works council;
- the venue, frequency, and duration of meetings;
- the financial and material resources to be allocated to the works council; and
- the duration of the agreement and the procedure for its renegotiation.

If the negotiations do not result in the establishment of a works council, but rather an information and consultation procedure, the resulting written agreement must stipulate by what method the employees' representatives will have the right to meet to discuss the information conveyed to them.[191] The employees have the right to be informed about events or issues that significantly affect their interests. The decision as to what constitutes an event or issue significantly affecting the employees is a matter for national law. Under German and French law, for example, this includes relocation or closure of businesses or divisions, collective redundancies, fundamental changes in the organization

---

188. Works Council Directive at art. 5(1).
189. *Id.* at art. 5(2).
190. *Id.* at art. 6(3).
191. *Id.* at art. 6(3).

of the company, financial condition of the company, the merger or disposition of businesses, and the trend of employment.

The rights granted to employees under the Works Council Directive should be distinguished from codetermination rights granted to employees in some of the member states. The Works Council Directive does not grant the employees the right to participate in the decision-making process of the undertaking. Of course, the information and consultation rights agreed to with the special negotiating body will have an influence on the decisions of the management. However, this influence is indirect. National codetermination laws, however, give the employees a right of direct participation in management decisions. Under the codetermination laws of Germany, for example, the employees have the actual right to elect a certain number of the board of directors.[192] This is participation as opposed to mere consultation under the Works Council Directive. EU labor law does not mandate that the member states provide employees with codetermination rights.

7.6 Default Provisions: Inability to Reach Agreement

The Works Council Directive provides specific default provisions which apply if the special negotiating body and the central management are unable to reach an agreement after three years or if the central management simply refuses to negotiate or the special negotiating body decides to terminate negotiations.[193] In such instances, national law is applied to determine the consequences. The Works Council Directive requires the member states to provide for the establishment of a works council composed of employees of the covered entity. The "default works council" must have a minimum of three members and a maximum of 30 and is responsible for adopting its own rules of procedure. The works council has the right to meet with the central management once a year to be informed and consulted on the progress of the business of the undertaking and its prospects. At the meeting with the works council, the central management is required to discuss with the works council:

- the structure, economic and financial situation, the probable development of the business and of production and sales of the covered entity;
- the situation and probable trend of employment;
- investments;
- substantial organizational changes;
- the introduction of new working methods or production processes, transfers of production, mergers, cutbacks, or closures; and
- collective redundancies.

The works council also has the right to be informed of exceptional circumstances affecting the employees' interests. This would include, for example, relocations, the closure of establishments or undertakings, and collective redundancies.

---

192. Gesetzüber die Mitbestimmung der Arbeitnehmer.
193. *Id.* at art. 7(1).

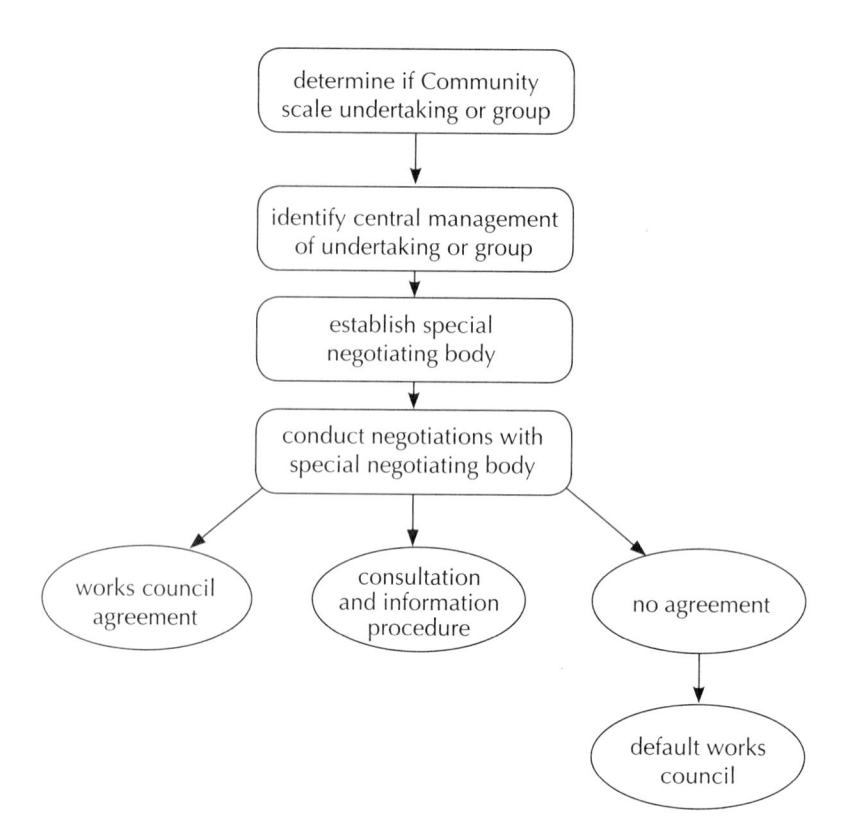

```
determine if Community
scale undertaking or group
          ↓
identify central management
of undertaking or group
          ↓
establish special
negotiating body
          ↓
conduct negotiations with
special negotiating body
     ↙        ↓        ↘
works      consultation    no agreement
council    and information       ↓
agreement  procedure       default works
                           council
```

7.7 Confidentiality

The consultation process does not necessarily require the management or the employees to divulge confidential information. The central management is not obliged to transmit information that would seriously harm the functioning of the undertakings concerned or would be prejudicial to them.[194] The contours of this right are governed by the law of the member states. The members of special negotiating bodies, the employee representatives, and the works councils (and any experts who assist them) are required to respect the confidentiality of all information that has been provided to them in confidence.[195]

7.8 Application to Non-EU Companies

The Works Council Directive even applies to companies based outside the EU. As discussed above, the application of the Directive—and hence the obligations imposed by the Directive—depends on whether an entity qualifies as a Union-scale undertaking or a Union-scale group of undertakings. The location of the headquarters or the central management of the undertaking is not determinative. Although the obligations set forth in the Directive are generally imposed on the central management, the Directive provides that the undertaking's agent in the EU bears responsibility.[196] If there is no agent, the management of the

---

194. *Id.* at art. 8(2).
195. *Id.* at art. 8(1).
196. *Id.* at art. 4(1).

establishment employing the greatest number of employees in one member state has the responsibility for setting up a works council or an information and consultation procedure.[197] For example, if a European subsidiary of a corporate group from outside the EU needs information from a non-EU affiliate in order to comply with the Directive as implemented by national law, the affiliate is obligated to provide that information if it is in possession of the information or in a position to acquire it.[198] The member states are required to make sure that the management of establishments in their country complies with the Directive.[199]

7.9 Consultation in Small and Medium-sized Companies

As discussed above, the Works Council Directive applies primarily to large businesses. The Framework Consultation Directive represents an attempt to impose more flexible consultation obligations on small and medium-sized businesses in recognition of the burdens imposed by compliance with the Works Council Directive. As discussed above, the Framework Consultation Directive gives the member states the discretion in determining the size of entities to which it applies. The member states may choose to apply it to undertakings employing at least 50 employees in any one member state or to establishments employing at least 20 employees in any one member state.[200] The Framework Consultation Directive imposes information and consultation obligations on covered entities. As the name implies, however, the Framework Consultation Directive only establishes a general framework, leaving responsibilities for the details to the member states.

The company must provide the employees with information on the recent and probable development of the undertaking's or the establishment's activities and economic situation. In addition, the employees must be informed on structure and probable development of employment within the undertaking or establishment, any anticipatory measures envisaged (in particular if there is a threat to employment), and decisions likely to lead to substantial changes in work organization or in contractual relations. The information must be shared with the employees at such time, in such fashion, and with such content as appropriate to enable the employees' representatives to conduct an adequate study and, where necessary, prepare for consultation.

---

197. *Id.* at art. 4(2). This is referred to by the ECJ as the "deemed central management." Case C-440/00, Gesamtbetriebsrat der Kühne & Nagel AG & Co. KG v. Kühne & Nagel AG & Co. KG, 2004 E.C.R. I-787, 826 ¶51.
198. *Id.* at 828 ¶59.
199. Works Council Directive at art. 11(1).
200. Framework Consultation Directive at art. 3(1).

CHAPTER **X**

Intellectual Property

1. Types of Intellectual Property Rights and Their Creation

The term "intellectual property" generally refers to the collection of property rights which the law recognizes in the creative work product of the human mind. In the European Union (EU), the term generally refers to trademarks, trade names, designs, copyrights, and any related right as provided for by national or EU law, geographical indications, patents, supplementary protection certificates for medicinal products, supplementary protection certificates for plant protection products, plant variety rights, topographies of semiconductor products and utility models.[1] Legislation at the EU level relating to trade secrets has been proposed but not adopted.[2]

Intellectual property rights, similar to all property rights, are creations of the law. For example, there is nothing legally inherent about the association between two golden arches and the McDonald's Corporation which allows McDonald's to preclude other fast food outlets from displaying golden arches outside their establishments. For various public policy reasons discussed below, however, legislatures have adopted laws granting the creators of such ideas property rights that reward them for their creative work product.

2. Trademark Protection

The term "trademark" refers to distinctive symbols or words of authenticity through which the products of particular manufacturers or the providers of

---

1. Regulation (EU) No. 608/2013 of the European Parliament and of the Council of 12 June 2013 concerning customs enforcement of intellectual property rights and repealing Council Regulation (EC) No. 1383/2003, 2013 O.J. (181) 15 at art. 2(1). The distinction is sometimes made between two categories of intellectual property rights (*i.e.*, trademarks, patents, and trade secrets) referred to as industrial property, and intellectual property rights of authors – *i.e.*, copyrights and related rights. There is no significance to this categorization for purposes of the discussion here but to alert the reader that he or she may encounter such terminology in the cases and literature.
2. Proposal for a Directive of the European Parliament and of the Council on the protection of undisclosed know-how and business information (trade secrets) against their unlawful acquisition, use and disclosure, COM/2013/0813 final *available at* http://eur-lex.europa.eu/legal-content/EN/TXT/?uri=celex:52013PC0813.

certain services can be distinguished from others. The essential function of a trademark is to guarantee the origin of the marked goods or services to the consumer or end user.[3]

2.1 Sources of Trademark Rights

There are essentially three sources of trademark rights for firms operating in the EU: international law, EU law, and national law.

(a) *International Trademark Regimes*

International law, as a source of trademark rights, is derived from international conventions. There are four important international conventions involving trademarks to which some or all of the EU member states are signatories:[4]

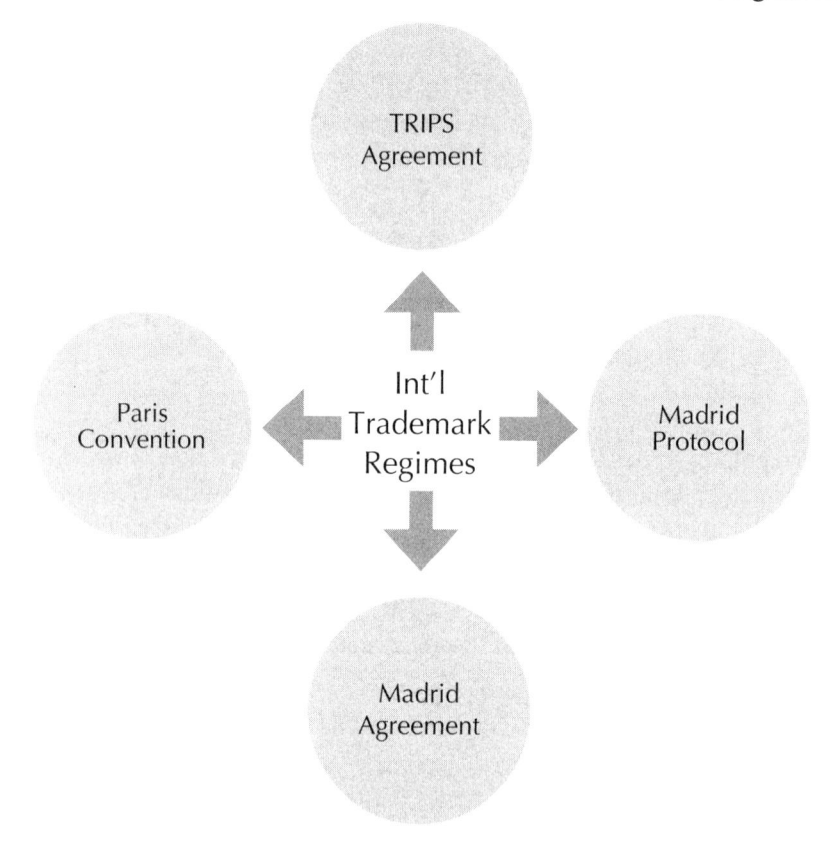

(1) Paris Convention

The Paris Convention is an international treaty which has been signed by over 160 countries including all of the EU member states. It applies not only to

---

3. Case C-661/11, Martin Y Paz Diffusion SA v. Depuydi, 2013 E.C.R. 1-___, at ¶58; Case C-304/06 P, Eurohypo AG v. OHIM, 2008 E.C.R. I-3316, 3333 ¶56.
4. The Madrid Agreement and the Madrid Protocol are two separate instruments with not necessarily overlapping signatories. Because many countries failed to sign the Madrid Agreement (including the United States and the UK), the Protocol was introduced to address the concerns of these reluctant countries. Although the text of these two international conventions is different, there is a common set of implementing rules.

marks, but also to designs and patents. The Convention does not establish a central system of trademark registration, but rather sets forth rules which the signatories are required to observe in the codification and application of their respective national trademark laws.

The two basic rules of the Paris Convention are national treatment and the rule of priority. According to the rule of national treatment, each party to the Convention is required to grant to nationals of other signatory countries the same rights it extends to its own nationals.[5] If, for example, a U.S. company applies for trademark protection in Portugal, Portugal is required to treat the U.S. company in the same way as it treats Portuguese companies. The rule also extends to natural and legal persons domiciled in a signatory country. Domicile for a company means that it has a real and effective establishment in that country.

The rule of national treatment does not guarantee that the outcome of the applications will be the same. As the substantive tests of the respective signatory countries are not affected by the Paris Convention, an application may be denied in the second country even though it is protected by the rule of national treatment. This is sometimes referred to as the principle of independence. Each country applies its own substantive and procedural requirements to the application. This is not always inconvenient for the applicant. The principle of independence also means that if a trademark application is terminated ex officio or by contest of a third party, any protection achieved in other signatory countries is not automatically terminated.

The rule of priority is based on the recognition that the Paris Convention does not replace the need for registration in the signatory countries. According to the rule, once a trademark is registered in a signatory state, the registrant then has six months to register in other signatory states.[6] The later applications are then considered to have been made on the date of the initial application. By giving the initial application priority, the Convention allows the applicant to decide the countries in which additional protection is necessary or desired. For example, if a German company files a trademark application in Germany, and one month later a U.S. company files an application in the U.S. for the same trademark, the Germany company can still file a registration in the United States and preempt the U.S. company.

The expiry of this six-month period does not, however, leave the applicant without remedies against third parties who apply for a preemptory trademark in a jurisdiction where the applicant has failed to register its trademark. The trademark applicant may have remedies under national unfair trade law. In *In re Akademiks*, for example, a U.S. company registered in 1999 the trademark "Akademiks" for use with clothing. Over a year later, another company registered the same trademark in Germany for precisely the same use. That company then tried to prevent the first applicant, who had not registered its trademark in Germany prior to the registration of the second company, from using the Akademiks trademark in Germany. The German Supreme Court held that although the

---

5. Paris Convention of 1883 at art. 2.
6. *Id.* at art. 4.

second company technically had the right to use the trademark in Germany, it would infringe German unfair trade law in this particular circumstance because the second applicant—although first to register in Germany—did not have a legitimate commercial intent in registering the mark.[7]

(2) TRIPS *Agreement*

The TRIPS Agreement, which has been signed by over 130 countries and came into force on January 1, 1995, is an international treaty concluded in the context of the World Trade Organization. Similar to the Paris Convention, the TRIPS Agreement applies to various forms of intellectual property. In addition to trademarks, geographical indications, patents, and designs (the same as the Paris Convention), it also applies to copyrights and related rights, industrial designs, topographies of integrated circuits, and industrial designs. Hence, there is some overlap with the Paris Convention as it applies to trademarks. The TRIPS Agreement addresses this overlap by incorporating the Paris Convention by reference. In effect, TRIPS requires its signatories to comply with the substantive rules codified in the Paris Convention.

The two basic principles of TRIPS are national treatment and most-favored nation treatment. The principle of national treatment is the same as under the Paris Convention: the signatory countries are required to extend the same protections to nationals of other signatory states as they do to their own nationals. The principle of most-favored nation treatment is, however, new. If a signatory country extends protections to a national of any other country (regardless of whether that third country is a TRIPS member), the signatory country must extend those same rights to nationals of all the other signatory countries. If, for example, the UK were to extend special rights to nationals of one of its former colonies which is not a TRIPS member, the UK would have to extend those same rights to nationals of all other TRIPS members.

(3) *Madrid Trademark System*

The EU and its member states participate in the Madrid trademark system which is based on the Madrid Agreement[8] and the Madrid Protocol.[9] These international treaties establish separate but similar systems which allow applicants to register their trademarks in a number of countries through one application filed in their home country but recognized in other countries. The system is administered by the World Intellectual Property Organization (WIPO).

The reason for two separate international treaties that say essentially the same thing has to do with politics. As the Madrid Agreement prohibits intergovernmental organizations (such as the EU) from becoming members, the individual member states and not the EU are members (referred to as contracting parties). Hence, instead of having one vote in the Assembly

---

7. *In re* Akademiks, Decision of the German Bundesgerichtshof in case no. I ZR 38/05 (Jan. 10, 2008) *reported at* 58 Recht der Internationalen Wirtschaft 392 (2008).
8. Madrid Agreement Concerning the International Registration of Marks, Apr. 14, 1891, 23 U.S.T. 1353.
9. Madrid Protocol for the International Registration of Marks, June 28, 1989, O.J. 2003 (L 296) 22.

(the governing organ), the Europeans had one vote for each European contracting party.[10] The United States objected to the disproportionate representation of the Europeans and refused to ratify the Madrid Agreement. The Madrid Protocol was subsequently introduced to address this political issue. It allowed the EU to become a member of the Protocol instead of its member states[11] and thereby assuaged the concerns of the United States The United States has since then signed and ratified the Madrid Protocol (but not the Madrid Agreement). The Madrid Agreement and Madrid Protocol essentially work the same way. An application under the Madrid Agreement or the Madrid Protocol may only be filed by a natural or legal person who is a national of or domiciled in a country that has signed and ratified the particular convention. For example, a U.S. company could not file an application under the Madrid Agreement because the U.S. has not ratified the Madrid Agreement.

As the initial step, trademark applicants must first apply for trademark protection in a contracting party.[12] These national applications are called "basic applications" and "basic registrations." It is important to note that there is no international registration independent of the national registration. In other words, an applicant cannot apply directly to the WIPO for trademark protection. For example, if a U.S. company wants to secure trademark protection in Sweden, Greece, and Latvia, it would first have to file a trademark application with the U.S. Patent and Trademark Office pursuant to U.S. trademark law. In the U.S. trademark application, there is a space for the applicant to designate the Madrid Protocol countries where it would like protection. As Sweden, Greece, and Latvia are each contracting parties to the Madrid Protocol, the U.S. company could indicate in its U.S. application that it is seeking protection in these three countries under the Madrid Protocol.

The home national trademark office then examines the application under national trademark law. If the basic application conforms to national law, and assuming that the applicant has indicated in its application it is seeking protection under the Madrid system, the home national trademark office registers the trademark and passes the application on to the International Bureau of the WIPO. The International Bureau records the application in the International Register and publishes it in the "WIPO Gazette of International Marks."

The International Bureau then forwards the application to the national trademark offices in the countries where the applicant has indicated that it wants trademark protection. The respective national trademark offices can then (within one year) reject the application but only on the grounds that would apply in the case of a mark filed for national registration. If no objections are raised, the trademark is considered registered in these countries and enjoys the same protections as a national mark registered in that country. If, however,

---

10. Madrid Agreement at art. 10(3)(a).
11. Council Decision of 27 October 2003 approving the accession of the European Community to the Protocol relating to the Madrid Agreement concerning the international registration of marks, adopted at Madrid on 27 June 1989, 2003 O.J. (L 296) 20.
12. A Union trademark registration will support a registration under the Madrid Agreement or Protocol. Trademark Regulation at art. 141.

the national trademark office—or the Office for Harmonization in the Internal Market (OHIM) in the context of an EU trademark—considers that the mark does not fulfill the requirements for registration, it can refuse to register the mark in that member state (or the EU) even though other states have granted protection to the mark.[13]

The legal effect of a registration under the Madrid Agreement or Madrid Protocol, which lasts for 20 years with the possibility of renewal, is that the protection of the mark in each contracting party is the same as if the mark had been registered directly with the office of that contracting party.[14] Using the example discussed above, once the U.S. company files a trademark application in the United States, and the steps required by the Madrid Protocol are taken, the U.S. company will have trademark protection in the United States, Sweden, Greece, and Latvia in this particular case. One of the main benefits to the U.S. company is that it only has to pay one fee (to the U.S. Patent & Trademark Office) and it avoids having to engage foreign trademark counsel in Sweden, Greece, and Latvia.[15] The costs will generally be considerably less than if the U.S. company had to file separately in each of the jurisdictions where protection was sought. Moreover, if the trademark owner ever wants to assign its rights to a third party, the owner does not have to register the assignment in each country in which it has protection. Instead, a single "request for the recordal of a change in ownership" can be filed with the WIPO International Bureau.

The most obvious disadvantage of reliance on the Madrid system is that a successful opposition to the home registration within five years after registration will result in termination of protection not only in the home country but also in each of the contracting countries where protection was applied for under the Madrid system.[16] For example, if a U.S. company registers a trademark in the United States and applies under the Madrid Protocol for protection in Hungary, the Czech Republic, and Germany, and the U.S. registration is successfully opposed by a U.S. competitor, the U.S. company loses its protection in Hungary, the Czech Republic, and Germany. If the U.S. company had filed individual trademark applications in the United States, Hungary, the Czech Republic, and Germany, and the U.S. competitor was successful only in the United States, the trademark owner would still enjoy protection in Hungary, the Czech Republic, and Germany.

Another disadvantage particular to the relationship between the United States and EU relates to the use requirement which is a part of the substantive trademark laws in the United States and Europe. As discussed in greater detail below, both the United States and the EU impose a use requirement for an applicant to achieve trademark protection. Under U.S. law, the applicant has to actually use the trademark in the claimed fields of protection in order

---

13. *See, e.g.,* T-291/12, Deutsche Bank AG v. OHIM, 2014 E.C.R. II-____, at ¶59.
14. Madrid Agreement at art. 4(1); Madrid Protocol at art. 4(1).
15. Generally, it is only necessary to engage local counsel in the jurisdictions outside the home jurisdiction if the international application is rejected or objected to in the foreign jurisdiction.
16. Madrid Agreement at art. 6; Madrid Protocol at art. 6.

to achieve trademark protection. In the EU, however, the applicant does not have to actually have used the trademark in order to secure registration. For this reason, U.S. trademark applications are often drafted much more narrowly than trademark applications in the EU. Hence, if a U.S. company uses a U.S. trademark application as its home application under the Madrid Protocol, and then seeks protection under the Madrid Protocol in the EU, it may be giving up a broader scope in the EU than if the U.S. company were to file separate applications in the EU.

(4) Relationship Between International Treaties and European Trademark Law

There are two important implications of these international conventions for European trademark law. First, to the extent that the particular convention or treaty establishes a separate or additional registration or trademark regime, it offers alternative or supplemental protection for a company seeking trademark protection in Europe. For example, a U.S. company doing business in Europe may file for trademark protection under the national trademark laws of one or more of the EU member states or file a registration under the Madrid Protocol based on its U.S. trademark.

The second important implication for European trademark law is that the codification and application of European trademark law is influenced and even limited by these conventions and treaties. For example, the European OHIM is required by the Paris Convention to grant nationals of non-EU states from states which are party to the Paris Convention the same rights as it grants to nationals of EU member states.

(b) National Trademark Regimes

In the Treaty on the Functioning of the European Union (TFEU), the member states do not cede authority over intellectual property to the EU. According to Article 345 of the TFEU, "the Treaties shall in no way prejudice the rules in the Member States governing the system of property ownership." Hence, an important source of trademark rights in the EU is the law of the member states. As a panoply of national trademark laws may hinder the economic integration of the member states by increasing the burdens of doing business in various member states, the EU adopted the Trademark Directive in 1988[17] to try to harmonize these laws.

Although the Trademark Directive brings the laws of the member states into line with one another, it does not obviate the need to file registrations in each of the member states in which a firm intends to do business and seek protection. Protection in one member state does not automatically confer protection in all member states. It is possible, however, for the applicant or a proprietor of a Union trademark (discussed below) to request the conversion of the Union trademark registration or its application into a national trademark application.

---

17. Directive 2008/95/EC of the European Parliament and of the Council of 22 October 2008 to approximate the laws of the member states relating to trade marks, 2008 O.J. (L 299) 25 [hereinafter Trademark Directive].

In practice, conversion becomes an option if a Union trademark application is rejected or has to be withdrawn because of a senior national conflicting mark. The conversion of a Union trademark is not available, however, where the rights in the Union trademark have been revoked for non-use. The same applies if the conversion seeks protection for a country in which protection for the Union trademark is refused on absolute or relative grounds.

2.2 Union Trademark

Another source of trademark protection in Europe is the Union trademark. The legal basis for the Union trademark is the Trademark Regulation.[18] Whereas the Trademark Directive serves to harmonize the trademark laws of the member states, the Trademark Regulation establishes a central system of trademark registration which obviates the need to file separate applications in each member state in which protection is sought. The Trademark Regulation does not replace or repeal the Trademark Directive.[19]

The Union trademark grants a uniform right, valid throughout the EU. The right allows the holder to prevent any other person from using the trademark for the same products or services and for similar products if there is a risk of confusion. As the Union trademark does not replace national trademarks, companies have the choice of applying for trademarks either from the national or the European OHIM depending on the scope of protection sought. The Union trademark replaces the necessity of applying for trademark protection in all member states. In certain circumstances, this may prove disadvantageous because if a Union trademark is challenged and loses once, it is invalid in all member states.[20] A system of 28 individual registrations in each of the member states would not be vulnerable to a "single shot" as is the reliance on a Union trademark. As the national trademark systems and the EU system are autonomous, it is possible to have a trademark validly registered in a member state but be rejected by the OHIM.[21]

The OHIM is responsible for administering the system. However, the OHIM is not directly involved in enforcing Union trademarks. The OHIM accepts and reviews trademark applications under the Trademark Regulation. It makes the initial determination of whether the application meets the requirements discussed below. Appeal of its decisions may be made to the General Court. If a trademark registration is accepted by the OHIM, the subsequent enforcement

---

18. Council Regulation (EC) No. 207/2009 of 26 February 2009 on the Community trademark, 2009 O.J. (L 78) 1 [hereinafter Trademark Regulation].
19. Although the Trademark Directive and the Trademark Regulation are independent sources of law, the European courts interpret the two laws the same way. Case 320/12, Malaysia Dairy Industries Pte. Ltd. v. Ankenævnet for Patenter og Varmærker, 2013 E.C.R. I-____, at ¶35.
20. Moreover, a finding of the OHIM as to the lack of distinctiveness of a mark for which protection is applied under the EU Trademark Regulation does not necessarily mean that any national registrations are invalid. Case C-98/11 P, Chocoladefabriken Lindt & Sprüngli AG v. OHIM, 2012 E.C.R. I-____ (summary), at ¶50.
21. T-291/12, Deutsche Bank AG v. OHIM, 2014 E.C.R. II-____, at ¶59.

of the rights associated with that trademark is the responsibility of the member states. For disputes concerning the infringement of Union trademarks, designated national trademark courts in the respective EU member states have exclusive jurisdiction.

(a) Registration Requirements of the Union Trademark

The Trademark Regulation contains specific requirements that a mark must fulfill before the OHIM will allow it to be registered. These are proprietorship, graphic representability, public policy, and distinctiveness. The basic procedure for registering a Union trademark is as follows: First, the applicant prepares an application containing the information required by Article 26 of the Trademark Regulation and in the Implementing Regulation.[22] The application can be filed with the OHIM. The OHIM then publishes the trademark in the "Union Trade Marks Bulletin" (to see if the public has any objections) and conducts an examination of the registration requirements and makes a decision. If successful, the trademark is recorded in the CTM Register, a database containing all trademarks registered with the OHIM. If unsuccessful, the applicant may appeal the decision to a Board of Appeal internal to the OHIM. If the applicant is still not satisfied with the result, the applicant can appeal the decision of the OHIM's Board of Appeal to the European General Court.

It is important to note that the registration requirements tested by the OHIM in each case (referred to as absolute grounds for refusal) are slightly different from the relative grounds for refusal. Once an applicant submits a trademark application to the OHIM, and it is published in the "Union Trade Marks Bulletin," a third party may file (within three months) a notice of opposition based on relative grounds for refusal.[23] For example, if the third party considers that the trademark will cause a likelihood of confusion with its trademark, it may file an opposition with the OHIM. Only then will the OHIM test for the likelihood of confusion.

(1) Graphic Representability

A Union trademark must consist of a sign capable of being represented graphically.[24] The obvious examples specifically enumerated in the Trademark Regulation are words, designs, letters, numerals, the shape of goods, or of their packaging. The term "graphically" does not mean visually. A trademark may consist of a sign which is not in itself capable of being perceived visually.[25] Sound signs and olfactory signs are the obvious examples. In *Shield Mark*

---

22. There is an official application form, but it is not mandatory.
23. The applicant may require that the party opposing the registration show that the earlier mark has been put to use in the EU in the prior 5 years. Trademark Regulation at art. 42. The level of use required in this context is not necessarily the same as is required to prevent revocation of a registered mark under Article 51(1)(c) of the Trademark Regulation or the level of use to make an otherwise indistinctive mark distinctive. Case T- 341/13, Groupe Léa Nature SA v. OHIM, 2014 E.C.R. II-____, at ¶35.
24. Trademark Regulation at art. 4.
25. Case C-273/00, Sieckmann v. Deutsches Patent- und Markenamt, 2002 E.C.R. I-11737, 11771 ¶55.

BV v. Joost Kist, the European Court of Justice (ECJ) held that sounds may be registered as trademarks provided that they are capable of being represented graphically and that their representation is "clear, precise, self-contained, easily accessible, intelligible, durable and objective."[26] In another case, the OHIM Board of Appeal held that the "smell of fresh cut grass" was registrable as a trademark for tennis balls.[27]

It should be emphasized that the distinctiveness of a particular trademark is not tested by the graphic representation but rather by the underlying mark. As discussed in detail below, one of the requirements for registering a Union trademark is that the mark is distinctive. That means that it is able to establish an association between the product or service and the particular company making or providing it. When testing the distinctiveness, the issue is not the distinctiveness of the graphic representation, but rather the underlying thing that the graphic represents. For example, when Metro Goldwyn Mayer used the sonogram of the roar of a lion to represent the sound mark of a roar of a lion for films, the OHIM did not test the distinctiveness of the sonogram, but rather the roar of a lion.[28]

(2) Public Policy

The mark must not be contrary to public policy or to accepted principles of morality or of such a nature as to deceive the public.[29] The OHIM may refuse the registration of a vulgar or sexually explicit term as contrary to public policy. For example, the terms "Bollox"[30] "Opium"[31] and "Hijoputa"[32] have been rejected under this standard. In addition, religiously or politically sensitive terms may also be refused registration under this standard. For example, the terms "Fidel Castro"[33] and "Bill Clinton"[34] have been refused as contrary to public policy. The application of the public policy standard is obviously subject to established social norms which may change over time.

It is not necessary that the mark evoke the same reaction throughout the Union. If the mark is contrary to the public policy of a significant proportion of the population of just one member state, this may be sufficient to preclude its patentability. In *Couture Tech Ltd. v. OHIM*, for example, the OHIM rejected the application for a mark consisting of a Soviet coat of arms as being contrary to the political sensitivities of a significant portion of Hungary.[35]

---

26. Case C-283/01, Shield Mark BV v. Joost Kist, 2003 E.C.R. I-14329, 14348 ¶55.
27. Decision R-156/1998 of the OHIM Board of Appeals, Venootschap Onder Firma Senta Aromatic Marketing Application, 1999 E.R.M.R. 429.
28. Decision of the OHIM Fourth Board of Appeal in case no. R 781/1999-4 (Aug. 25, 2003).
29. Trademark Regulation at art. 7(1)(f).
30. CMT Application Number 0099103 refused by letter of Nov. 27, 1998.
31. CMT Application Number 002481935 refused by letter of July 1, 2003.
32. Case T-417/10, Frederico Cortés del Valle López v. OHIM, 2012 E.C.R. II-____ (summary), at ¶26.
33. CMT Application Number 00921155 refused by letter of Sept. 24, 1999.
34. CMT Application Number 00956540 refused by letter of Aug. 25, 1999.
35. Case T-232/10, Couture Tech Ltd. v. OHIM, 2011 E.C.R. II-6472, 6489 ¶62.

(3) Distinctiveness

Because the essential function of a trademark is to guarantee the origin of the marked goods or services, it must have a distinctive character either by its intrinsic properties or through use. This requirement relates directly to the fundamental purpose of trademarks: to allow the buyer of the product or service to identify its source.[36] Lack of distinctiveness is an absolute ground for refusal, i.e., the OHIM will test this requirement on its own initiative. The basic idea is that a purely descriptive sign should be available for all undertakings in a particular industry to use and not reserved for just one company.[37]

Distinctiveness means that the mark must enable the targeted public to distinguish the goods or services from those of other undertakings, and to believe that all the goods or services identified by it are manufactured or provided under the control of the trademark owner.[38] The distinctiveness requirement ensures that the consumer who purchases the goods or services identified by the mark is in a position, when engaged in a subsequent purchase, to make the same choice, if her experience is a positive one. For example, consumers associate the graphic representation of golden arches with the particular products and services McDonald's promotes.[39]

Marks which are not distinctive are generally considered descriptive. Descriptive marks do not qualify for trademark protection. In other words, the mark must not consist exclusively of signs or indications which serve to designate the kind, quality, quantity, intended purpose, value, geographical origin, or the time of production of the goods or of rendering of the service, or other characteristics of the goods or service.[40] For example, the mark "Truewhite" for light bulbs,[41] "Insulate for Life"[42] for insulation materials, "Built to Last"[43] for clothing and footwear, "Golf USA"[44] for golf clothing and equipment, or "The Coffee Store"[45] for coffee shops are not distinctive because they are merely descriptive of the products or services to which they relate.

---

36. Case T-499/13, nMetric LLC v. OHIM, 2015 E.C.R. I-____ at ¶13.
37. Case C-273/05 P, OHIM v. v Celltech R&D Ltd., 2007 E.C.R. I-2912, 2936 ¶75; Case C-191/01 P, OHIM v. v Wm. Wrigley Jr. Company, 2003 E.C.R. I-12473, 12485 ¶31.
38. Case C-398/08, P Audi v. OHIM, 2010 E.C.R. I-535 (summary), at ¶23 (reported in the electronic reports of cases at ECLI:EU:C:2010:29); Joined cases C-456/01 P and C-457/01 P, Henkel KGaA v. OHIM, 2004 E.C.R. I-5115, 5130 ¶34.
39. Community Mark 62 521 (July 15, 1999).
40. Trademark Regulation at art. 7(1)(c).
41. Case T-208/10, Cree, Inc. v. OHIM, 2011 E.C.R. II-218 (summary), at ¶23.
42. Case T-157/08, Paroc Oy AB v. OHIM, 2011 E.C.R. II-137 (summary), at ¶53.
43. Case T-80/07, JanSport Apparel Corp. v. OHIM, 2009 E.C.R. II-152 (summary), at ¶28.
44. Case T-230/05, Golf USA, Inc. v. OHIM, 2007 E.C.R. II-23 (summary), at ¶45.
45. Case T-323/05, The Coffee Store GmbH v. OHIM, 2008 E.C.R. II-129 (summary), at ¶43.

The purpose of precluding such descriptive marks from registration is to insure that such signs or indications are available for other firms to use.[46]

A trademark is descriptive (and not distinctive) if there is a "sufficiently direct and specific association between the sign and the categories of goods or services in respect of which registration is sought."[47] A sign that describes the intended purpose of the goods, for example "ROBOTUNITS" for automated machinery, is not distinctive.[48] The neologism "PAPERLAB" for paper testing equipment,[49] as well as the expression "THE LEADERSHIP COMPANY"[50] for executive recruitment services or "BIOMILD"[51] for yogurt are considered descriptive and not registrable. A word that merely describes the quality of services, for example "BESTPARTNER" for insurance and financial services, is not distinctive.[52] Even the mark "NURSERYROOM" for infant products was denied registration because there was too close a connection between the products for which it was registered and the concept specifically represented by the word mark, i.e., a nursery room.[53]

Just because the mark is not descriptive does not necessarily mean that it is distinctive.[54] As mentioned above, the distinctiveness standard requires that the mark enables the targeted public to distinguish the goods or services from those of other undertakings. A mark can be nondescriptive and nondistinctive at the same time. In *Ashoka v. OHIM*, for example, the General Court upheld the OHIM's refusal to register the mark DREAM IT, DO IT! for certain consulting services.[55] Although the mark was not descriptive of the services the applicant was providing, the General Court held that "the trademark applied for would not be perceived, by the relevant English-speaking public, as an indication of the commercial origin of the services in question."[56]

Distinctiveness is determined through the eyes of the targeted customers of the trademarked product or service and not from the perspective of the applicant or the OHIM. For many products, the targeted customers will be the general public. However, this is not always the case, and the relevant public is an important consideration in the analysis. For example, a German metal products manufacturer attempted to register the trademark "SnPUR" for use on

---

46. Case T-289/02, Telepharmacy Solutions, Inc. v. OHIM, 2004 E.C.R. II-2851, 2872 ¶53; Case C-265/00, Campina Melkunie BV v. Belelux-Merkenbureau, 2004 E.C.R. I-1699, 1719 ¶35; Case T-16/02, Audi AG v. OHIM, 2003 E.C.R. II-5167, 5183 ¶29.
47. Case T-222/02, Heron Robotunits GmbH v. OHIM, 2003 E.C.R. II-4995, 5008 ¶38.
48. *Id.* at 5009 ¶42.
49. Case T-19/04, Metso Paper Automation Oy v. OHIM, 2005 E.C.R. II-2383.
50. Case T-43/14, Heidrick & Struggles International Inc. v. OHIM, 2014 E.C.R. II-____ (summary), at ¶28.
51. Case C-265/00, Campina Melkunie BV v. Benelux-Merkenbureau, 2004 E.C.R. I-1699.
52. Case T-270/02, MLP Finanzdienstleistungen AG v. OHIM, 2004 E.C.R. II-2839, 2848 ¶27.
53. Case T-173/03, Anne Geddes v. OHIM, 2004 E.C.R. II-4165.
54. Case T-499/13, nMetric LLC v. OHIM, 2015 E.C.R. I-____ at ¶22.
55. Case T-186/07, Ashoka v. OHIM, 2008 E.C.R. II-109.
56. *Id* at ¶38.

various metal products such as tubes and strips made from pure tin. Although it would not necessarily be obvious to the general public that the mark SnPUR is a combination of the chemical symbol for tin (Sn) and pure, the General Court held that in the eyes of the targeted public—specialists in metallurgy—the mark was descriptive and consequently not distinctive of the manufacturer's products.[57]

The targeted customers are not necessarily all customers in the EU. For example, the targeted customers may be located in only one country or speaking only one particular language. This is potentially significant because of different languages and customs in the various member states. For example, a particular word mark in Dutch may not be descriptive for a Polish customer, but it may be for a Dutch customer. In *Eurohypo AG v. OHIM*, the ECJ considered the mark "EUROHYPO" descriptive for financial services.[58] The relevant public in that case was the German-speaking consumer. In German, Hypothek means mortgage. As the trademark applicant was in that line of business, it was readily apparent that the mark "EUROHYPO" was descriptive. If, however, the relevant public were Swedish-speaking consumers, the outcome may have been different.

The objective characteristics of the particular product may also assist in defining the class of customers. In *Bang & Olufsen A/S v. OHIM*,[59] for example, the OHIM denied a three-dimensional trademark sought to be registered by Bang & Olufsen. The mark consisted of a shape of one of the Bang & Olufsen speakers. On appeal to the General Court, the court held that in view of the high-end nature of the goods at issue, the relevant customers are those who pay "a particularly high level of attention when purchasing such goods."[60]

If a term has become customary in common language or a particular industry, it cannot be registered as a trademark.[61] In *Alcon v. OHIM*, the mark "BSS" could not be registered for a particular medical solution because it was already being used in the medical profession as a generic term.[62] According to the General Court: "A sign which was at one time capable of acting as a trade mark may, by reason of the use thereof by third parties as a customary designation of a product, loses the capacity to perform the essential function of a trade mark, and in particular that of identifying the origin of the goods or services, thus enabling the consumer who acquired them to repeat the experience, if it proves to be positive, or to avoid it, if it proves to be negative, on the occasion of a subsequent acquisition."[63] However, the mere fact that a term may be customary in general does not mean that it is customary in the trade of the goods or services to which it relates. In *The International Music*

---

57. Joined cases T-367/02 to 369/02, Wieland-Werke AG v. OHIM, 2005 E.C.R. II-50, 59 ¶34.
58. Case C-304/06 P, Eurohypo AG v. OHIM, 2008 E.C.R. I-3316, 3336 ¶69
59. Case T-460/05, Bang & Olufsen A/S v. OHIM, 2007 E.C.R. II-4209.
60. *Id.* at 4220 ¶34.
61. Trademark Regulation at art. 7(1)(d).
62. Case T-237/01, Alcon v. OHIM, 2003 E.C.R. II-415.
63. *Id.* at 429 ¶48.

Company AG v. OHIM, a company registered the mark "past perfect" for use in connection with musical recordings. One of its competitors argued that the mark was customary and could not be registered. The General Court held that although the term past perfect may be common in general, it was not customary in the musical recording industry.[64]

On the other hand, a mark which initially is not distinctive may acquire distinctiveness through use.[65] The three diagonal stripes used by the sport shoe manufacturer Adidas, for example, may not have been distinctive when first introduced. However, after years of marketing and selling the shoes and other sporting apparel, the diagonal stripes have become distinctive.[66]

Four basic factors are relevant in determining whether a mark has become distinctive through use.[67] First, at least a significant proportion of the relevant public must identify the goods or services as originating from a particular firm because of the trademark. Second, the distinctive character acquired through the use must be demonstrated in the substantial part of the EU where it was previously devoid of any such character.[68] A single member state may constitute a substantial part.[69] Third, the commercial context of the mark and the undertaking must support the finding of distinctiveness. Relevant considerations are the market share held by the mark, the intensity, geographic scope and duration of the use, the proportion of the relevant class of persons who, because of the mark, identify goods as originating from a particular undertaking, consumer opinion polls, statements from trade and professional associations, and the amount invested by the firm in promoting the mark.[70] For example, it would be difficult for a firm with a low market share to prove distinctiveness through use, particularly where it has not made a substantial investment in promoting the brand.

---

64. Case T-133/06, The International Music Company AG v. OHIM, 2008 E.C.R. II-233, 250 ¶52
65. The term "use" in this context is different than the use required in order for a third party to oppose the registration trademark pursuant to Article 42 of the Trademark Regulation. Case T- 341/13, Groupe Léa Nature SA v. OHIM, 2014 E.C.R. II-____, at ¶35.
66. Case C-408/01, Adidas-Salomon AG v. Fitnessworld Trading Ltd., 2003 E.C.R. I-12537.
67. Case T-237/10, Louis Vuitton Malletier v. OHIM, 2011 E.C.R. II-449 (summary), at ¶87 (reported in the electronic reports of cases at ECLI:EU:T:2011:741) *aff'd on appeal* Case C-97/12 P, Louis Vuitton Malletier v. OHIM, 2014 E.C.R. I-____; Case T-269/06, Rautaruukki Oyj v. OHIM, 2008 E.C.R. II-273 (summary), at ¶44-47 (reported in the electronic reports of cases at ECLI:EU:T:2008:512).
68. Case T-91/99, Ford Motor v OHIM (OPTIONS), 2000 E.C.R. II-1925, 1937 ¶27.
69. Case T-237/10, Louis Vuitton Malletier v. OHIM, 2011 E.C.R. II-449 (summary), at ¶98 (reported in the electronic reports of cases at ECLI:EU:T:2011:741) *aff'd on appeal* Case C-97/12 P, Louis Vuitton Malletier v. OHIM, 2014 E.C.R. I-____.
70. Joined cases C-217/13 and 218/13, Oberbank AG v. Deutscher Sparkassen-und Giroverband, 2014 E.C.R. I-____, at ¶41; Case C-353/03, Société des produits Nestlé SA v. Mars UK Ltd, 2005 E.C.R. I-6149, 6174 ¶31. Financial investment in the promotion of the product—as opposed to the promotion of the mark—is not relevant. Case T-396/02, August Storck KG v. OHIM, 2004 E.C.R. II-3824, 3846 ¶64.

Fourth, the mark must have acquired distinctive character through use before the application for registration is filed.[71] As distinctiveness through use is a factual analysis in which the applicant has the burden of presenting evidence showing distinctiveness through use, the OHIM and EU courts have been reluctant to recognize distinctiveness through use.[72]

Whether a particular mark is distinctive must be determined on a case-by-case basis and in relation to the goods for which it has been registered. A trademark applicant is required to identify the specific goods or services for which the trademark is going to be used. These categories are defined in the Nice Agreement. Although the individual categories encompass several goods or services, the OHIM is required to examine distinctiveness for each good or service within the category claimed by the applicant.[73] A mark registered for several categories of goods may be distinctive for some categories but not others.[74] In addition, the greater the number of goods and services for which a trademark is sought to be registered, the more distinctive it must be. This is because the distortive effect a trademark has on competition is greater if protection is granted for a wider range of goods or services. Consequently, the ECJ and OHIM hold the mark to a higher level of distinctiveness if the applicant has applied for protection in a broad range of product categories.[75]

(4) Prior Distinctiveness Determinations

The OHIM has broad discretion in determining the distinctiveness of trademarks. The general rule is that each case is to be assessed individually. This has two important practical implications. First, the OHIM is not bound by decisions of the national trademark offices or the national courts or international registrations.[76] In *Sunrider Corporation v. OHIM*, the trade name "VITALITE" had been registered in all EU member states and the court only said that this

---

71. Case T-247/01, eCopy v OHIM (ECOPY), 2002 E.C.R. II-5304, 5320 ¶36
72. Case T-230/05, Golf USA, Inc. v. OHIM, 2007 E.C.R. II-23 (summary), at ¶85; Case T-16/02, Audi AG v. OHIM, 2003 E.C.R. II-5167, 5195 ¶68.
73. Case T-387/06 - 390/06, Inter-Ikea Systems BV v. OHIM, 2008 E.C.R. II-212 (summary), at ¶41.
74. Case T-237/10, Louis Vuitton Malletier v. OHIM, 2011 E.C.R. II-449 (summary), at ¶82 (reported in the electronic reports of cases at ECLI:EU:T:2011:741) *aff'd on appeal* Case C-97/12 P, Louis Vuitton Malletier v. OHIM, 2014 E.C.R. I-____.
75. Case C-104/01, Libertel Group BV v. Benelux-Merkenbureau, 2003 E.C.R. I-3822, 3841 ¶56; Decision of the OHIM First Board of Appeal in case no. R 467/2009-1 (Oct. 15 2009) at ¶39.
76. Case T-318/09, Audi AG v. OHIM, 2011 E.C.R. II-3843, 3850 ¶20; Case T-112/09, Icebreaker Ltd. V. OHIM, 2010 E.C.R. II-172 (summary), at ¶52. However, the OHIM is entitled to use the decision of a national trademark authority as evidence. Case T-108/08, Zino Davidoff SA v. OHIM, 2011 E.C.R. II-5585, at ¶23.

was one factor to be taken into account.[77] This applies not only to the EU member states, but also to determinations made by trademark offices outside the EU. The General Court has repeatedly held that a trademark which was successfully registered in the United States cannot necessarily be considered distinctive in the EU based on the fact that it was considered distinctive in the United States.[78]

The second important practical implication of the general rule that each case must be assessed individually is that the OHIM is not even bound by its own prior decisions.[79] For example, the registration of a similar mark by the OHIM is not relevant in proving the distinctiveness of a mark. In *Apollo Group, Inc. v. OHIM*, Apollo had applied for registration of the mark "Thinking Ahead" for training, education sporting, and cultural activities. To show the distinctiveness of this mark, Apollo pointed out that the OHIM had allowed registration of similar marks such as "Think Ahead. Stay Ahead" and "Think Ahead!" In holding that the "Thinking Ahead" trademark was descriptive, the General Court stated that the distinctiveness of a trademark "must be assessed solely on the basis of [the Trademark Regulation] as interpreted by the Union judicature, and not on the basis of an earlier decision-making practice of the [OHIM] Boards."[80]

(b) Types of Marks

Although the general standard of distinctiveness is the same for all types of marks (i.e., whether it is capable of identifying the product as originating from

---

77. Case T-24/00, Sunrider Corporation v. OHIM, 2001 E.C.R. II-449. *See also* Case C-529/07, Chocoladefabriken Lindt & Sprüngli AG v. Franz Hauswirth GmbH, 2009 E.C.R. I-4918, 4934 ¶53. But in Case T-393/02, Henkel KGaA v. OHIM, 2004 E.C.R. II-4117, 4131 ¶43, the fact that the shape had been recognized as being distinctive in 11 of the then 15 member states was an important factor in the General Court's holding that the bottle for liquid laundry detergent was distinctive. Similarly, the national trademark authorities are not bound by the decisions made by the trademark authorities of the other member states under their national regimes even of it is the exact same mark. Case C-218/01, *In re* Henkel KGaA, 2004 E.C.R. I-1725, 1759 ¶62; Case C-363/99, Koninkijke KPN Nederland v. Benelux-Merkenbureau, 2004 E.C.R. I-1619, 1671 ¶43.
78. Case T-499/13, nMetric LLC v. OHIM, 2015 E.C.R. I-____ at ¶47; Case T-208/10, Cree, Inc. v. OHIM, 2011 E.C.R. II-218 (summary), at ¶32.
79. Case T-384/13, Intermark Srl v. OHIM, 2015 E.C.R. II-____ ¶47; Case T-269/06, Rautaruukki Oyj v. OHIM, 2008 E.C.R. II-273 (summary), at ¶52 (reported only in the electronic reports of cases ECLI:EU:T:2008:512); Joined Cases T-324/01 & T-110/02, Axion v. OHIM, 2003 E.C.R. II-1897, 1943 ¶51. Although the General Court has recognized that the principles of equal treatment and sound administration require the OHIM to take into account the decisions already taken and at least to consider whether it should decide in the same way or not, the OHIM's interpretation of the Trademark Regulation ultimately prevails. Case T-712/13, Monster Energy Company v. OHIM, 2014 E.C.R. I-____, at ¶32.
80. Case T-473/08, Apollo Group, Inc. v. OHIM, 2010 E.C.R. II-215 (summary), at ¶41. *See also* Joined Cases T-146/02 – T-153/02, Deutsche SiSi-Werke GmbH & Co. Betriebs KG v. OHIM, 2004 E.C.R. II-447, 466 ¶55; Case T-128/01 DaimlerChrysler v. OHIM, 2003 E.C.R. II-701.

a particular undertaking),[81] it is more difficult to prove distinctiveness for some categories of trademarks. Hence, it is useful to discuss several different categories of marks.

(1) Words, Expressions, and Letters

Marks composed of words, expressions, or letters of the alphabet are perhaps the most common form of trademark. As with other trademarks, a word, expression, or letter must be distinctive to qualify for trademark protection. This is the most significant challenge for such marks. A word or letter mark is not distinctive if it merely describes the goods or services for which it is registered.[82] For example, a seller of artificial grass surfaces may not register a trademark "Looks Like Grass…Feels Like Grass…Plays Like Grass" as that phrase informs the public that the goods concerned have characteristics similar to natural grass rather than identifying the origin of the product.[83] Even the letters "TDI" (standing for Turbo Diesel Injection) were not distinctive for automobiles.[84] The purpose of this prohibition is to ensure that general words and expressions are freely available to all to use.[85] This is why it is often difficult to register words or expressions as trademarks, when they have something to do with the goods or services. For example, it would be unfair to allow an ice cream manufacturer to reserve the name "good ice cream" for its products only. Even the term "life" was deemed not have distinctive character in connection with foods and drink.[86]

Word marks created by combining two common words to form a new word are referred to as neologisms.[87] The mark "baby dry" used in connection with the sale of diapers is an example. The standard for neologisms is the same for other types of marks: they must be distinctive. The mere fact that each of the component words of a neologism are themselves descriptive does not necessarily mean that the neologism itself will be considered descriptive

---

81. Joined cases C-217/13 and 218/13, Oberbank AG v. Deutscher Sparkassen-und Giroverband, 2014 E.C.R. I-____, at ¶46.
82. Case T-23/07, BARCO-Marken-Import Matthiesen GmbH & Co. KG v. OHIM, 2009 E.C.R. II-887 (summary), at ¶56 (letter mark) (reported in the electronic reports of cases at ECLI:EU:T:2009:126); Case T-222/02, Heron Robotunits GmbH v. OHIM, 2003 E.C.R. II-4995, 5010 ¶46 (word mark).
83. Case T-216/02, Fieldturf, Inc. v. OHIM, 2004 E.C.R. II-1023, 1035 ¶30.
84. Case T-16/02, Audi AG v. OHIM, 2003 E.C.R. II-5167, 5186 ¶38.
85. Case C-191/01 P, OHIM v. Wm. Wrigley Jr. Company, 2003 E.C.R. I-12447, 12485 ¶31.
86. Case T-79/00, Rewe Zentral AG v. OHIM, 2002 E.C.R. II-705. If a word has several meanings, it is considered descriptive if at least one of those meanings designates a characteristic of the goods or services. Case T-28/10, Euro-Information v. OHIM, 2011 E.C.R. II-1541, 1558 ¶50. For example, although the word "spirit" has several meanings (some of which have nothing to do with alcoholic beverages), it was held to be descriptive for alcoholic beverages. Case T-207/13, *1872* Holdings vof v. OHIM, 2014 E.C.R. II-____, at ¶26.
87. The fact that the neologism is not referenced in dictionaries does not necessarily mean that it is distinctive. Case T-188/14, Grohe Multimedia AG v. OHIM, 2015 E.C.R. I-___ at ¶38.

(i.e., not registrable).[88] For example, just because the words "home" and "zone" may not be distinctive by themselves does not mean that the mark "Homzone" for telecommunications equipment is not distinctive.[89] In such cases, however, there must be a perceptible difference between that mark as a whole and the mere sum of its parts.[90] For example, the neologisms "Easycover" for monuments (such as gravestones),[91] "Foodlube" for industrial oils[92] and "CellTec" for pharmaceutical products[93] are not descriptive and hence registrable. In contrast, the marks "Color Edition" (for cosmetics),[94] "Pure Power" for engine parts,[95] "Companyline" (in connection with insurance services),[96] "Blue Soft" (for contact lenses),[97] "Truewhite" (for light bulbs),[98] "carcheck" (for automobile diagnostic software)[99] and "Telepharmacy Solutions" (for a telepharmacy business)[100] were considered descriptive of characteristics of the goods or services for which protection was sought. The fact that the neologism is not recognized as a word in dictionaries does not mean that it is distinctive.[101]

In order to meet the perceptible difference requirement, the neologism must create an impression which is sufficiently far removed from that produced by the mere combination of meanings lent by the elements of which it is composed, with the result that the word is more than the sum of its parts.[102] In *Procter & Gamble v. OHIM*, for example, the ECJ held that the mark "baby-dry" has distinctive character for diapers because of the unusual juxtaposition of the words.[103] In addition, a perceptible difference may exist if the word combination

---

88. Case C-92/10 P, Media-Saturn-Holding GmbH v. OHIM, 2011 E.C.R. I-2 (summary), at ¶36; Case T-248/11, International Engine Intellectual Property Company, LLC v. OHIM, 2013 E.C.R. II-____, at ¶28.
89. Case T-344/07, O2 (Germany) GmbH & Co v. OHIM, 2010 E.C.R. II-153 (summary), at ¶26.
90. Case C-408/08 P, Lancôme parfums et beauté & Cie SNC v. OHIM, 2010 E.C.R. I-1372, 1388 ¶62; Case T-117/06, DeTeMedien Deutsche Telekom Medien GmbH v. OHIM, 2007 E.C.R. II-174 (summary), at ¶31.
91. Case T-346/07, Duro Sweden AB v. OHIM, 2008 E.C.R. II-263 (summary), at ¶75.
92. Case T-200/08, Interflon BV v. OHIM, 2011 E.C.R. II-210 (summary), at ¶50.
93. Case C-273/05 P, OHIM v. Celltech R&D Ltd., 2007 E.C.R. I-2883.
94. Case C-408/08 P, Lancôme parfums et beauté & Cie SNC v. OHIM, 2010 E.C.R. I-1347.
95. Case T-248/11, International Engine Intellectual Property Company, LLC v. OHIM, 2013 E.C.R. II-____, at ¶47.
96. Case T-19/99, Deutsche Krankenversicherung v. OHIM, 2000 E.C.R. II-1 *aff'd on appeal* Case C-104/00 P, Deutsche Krankenversicherung v. OHIM, 2002 E.C.R. I-7561.
97. Case T-330/06, Novartis AG v. OHIM, 2008 E.C.R. II-85 (summary), at ¶54.
98. Case T-208/10, Cree, Inc. v. OHIM, 2011 E.C.R. II-218 (summary), at ¶23.
99. Case T-14/10, CheckMobile GmbH v. OHIM, 2011 E.C.R. II-76 (summary), at ¶28.
100. Case T-289/02, Telepharmacy Solutions, Inc. v. OHIM, 2004 E.C.R. II-2851, 2872 ¶53.
101. Case T-248/11, International Engine Intellectual Property Company, LLC v. OHIM, 2013 E.C.R. II-____, at ¶33; Case T-208/10, Cree, Inc. v. OHIM, 2011 E.C.R. II-218 (summary), at ¶25.
102. Case T-346/07, Duro Sweden AB v. OHIM, 2008 E.C.R. II-263 (summary), at ¶41.
103. Case C-383/99 P, Procter & Gamble v. OHIM, 2001 E.C.R. I-6251.

has become part of everyday language and has acquired its own meaning, with the result that it is independent of its components.[104]

The word or expression does not have to be exclusively descriptive for the registration to be denied. Even if a word or expression could have several meanings, and one of these meanings is descriptive, it is not eligible for a Union trademark.[105] This is illustrated in *OHIM v. Wm. Wrigley Jr. Company*.[106] In that case, the General Court had held that "Doublemint" was not merely descriptive because "the multiplicity of possible semantic combinations precludes the consumer from remembering one of them in particular."[107] The General Court pointed out that "double" could have various meanings, not all of which were descriptive. On appeal, however, the ECJ held that "[a] sign must therefore be refused registration ...if at least one of its possible meanings designates a characteristic of the goods or services concerned."[108]

Neologisms which are exclusively evocative of the products to which they relate are not descriptive. In *Dart Industries, Inc. v. OHIM*, for example, a U.S. company registered the mark "UltraPlus" for microwavable plasticware. The OHIM refused registration on the grounds that it was not distinctive. On appeal, the General Court held that:

> When an undertaking extols, indirectly and in an abstract manner, the excellence of its products by way of a sign such as UltraPlus, yet without directly and immediately informing the consumer of one of the qualities or specific characteristics of the ovenware, it is a case of evocation and not designation for the purposes of Article 7(1)(c) of Regulation No 40/94 (citations omitted). [109]

(2) Domain Names

Domain names are used on the Internet as addresses for particular websites. For example, the Internet website for Gucci is "Gucci.com." Their ownership is established by registration with a domain name registrar which is accredited by the Internet Corporation for Assigned Names and Numbers or by a national country code top-level domain (ccTLD) authority.[110] However, this registration

---

104. Joined Cases T-178/03 and 179/03, CeWe Color AG & Co. OHG v. OHIM, 2005 E.C.R. II-3107, 3117 ¶26.
105. Case C-265/00, Campina Melkunie BV v. Benelux Merkenbureau, 2004 E.C.R. I-1699, 1720 ¶38; Case C-363/99, Koninklijke KPN Nederland NV v. Benelux-Merkenbureau, 2004 E.C.R. I-1619, 1685 ¶97.
106. Case C-191/01 P, OHIM v. Wm. Wrigley Jr. Company, 2003 E.C.R. I-12447, 12485 ¶31.
107. Case T-193/99, Wm. Wrigley Jr. Company v. OHIM, 2001 E.C.R. II-417.
108. Case C-191/01 P, OHIM v. Wm. Wrigley Jr. Company, 2003 E.C.R. I-12447, 12485 ¶32.
109. Case T-360/00, Dart Industries, Inc. v. OHIM, 2002 E.C.R. II-3867, 3878 ¶27.
110. The Union has its own registration system for .eu top level domain names. Commission Regulation (EC) No. 874/2004 of 28 April 2004 laying down public policy rules concerning the implementation and functions of the .eu Top Level Domain and the principles governing registration, 2004 O.J. (L 164) 40.

does not accord trademark protection to the registrant of the domain name. That registrant must also apply for trademark protection. Domain names may be registered under the EU Trademark Regulation provided they meet the distinctiveness requirement applicable to all other marks.[111] In *DeTeMedien Deutsche Telekom Medien GmbH v. OHIM*, for example, DeTeMedien Deutsche Telekom tried to register as a trademark its domain name "suche.de" (which would be equivalent of someone registering "search.com" in the United States). The ECJ held that although there is no per se rule prohibiting the registration of domain names as trademarks, this particular domain name lacked the necessary degree of distinctiveness required by the Trademark Regulation.[112]

The registration of a domain name does not protect the registrant from trademark infringement claims even if the registration complies with the domain name registration procedures. Whether the use of the domain name infringes the trademark rights of the trademark proprietor is determined under trademark law. In addition, national unfair trade laws may be applicable if the domain registration implicates national trademark law.[113]

(3) *Slogans*

A slogan may be registered as a Union trademark provided that it is capable of distinguishing the goods or services of one firm from those of other firms.[114] For example, the slogan Wet Dust Can't Fly has been considered distinctive for carpet cleaning solutions.[115] Although the same distinctiveness standard is applied to slogans,[116] they are frequently considered descriptive. Slogans that simply inform potential consumers or clients as to the nature and the advantage or quality of the goods or services in relation to which they are used are, in general, lacking in any distinctive character. The same applies to advertising slogans. In *Delphi Technologies, Inc. v. OHIM*, for example, the slogan "Innovation for the Real World" for car parts was considered descriptive.[117] In *Sykes Enterprises v. OHIM*, the slogan "Real People, Real Solutions" was found not to be distinctive for computer hardware maintenance services.[118] Similarly, the slogans "Care to Care" for medical services and "Passion to Perform" for business management

---

111. Case T-117/06, DeTeMedien Deutsche Telekom Medien GmbH v. OHIM, 2007 E.C.R. II-174 (summary), at ¶35; Case T-281/02, Norma Lebensmittelfilialbetrieb v. OHIM, 2004 E.C.R. II-1917, 1927 ¶25.
112. Case T-117/06, DeTeMedien Deutsche Telekom Medien GmbH v. OHIM, 2007 E.C.R. II-174 (summary), at ¶37
113. British Telecommunications plc. v. One In A Million Ltd, [1998] EWCA Cov/1272; Euromarket Designs v. Peters and Crate & Barrel, [2001] F.S.R. 288.
114. Case T-68/13, Novartis AG v. OHIM, 2014 E.C.R. II-____, at ¶17.
115. Case T-133/13, Pro-Aqua International GmbH v. OHIM, 2015 E.C.R. II-____ at ¶51.
116. The General Court has refused to impose heightened requirements on slogans. Case T-133/13, Pro-Aqua International GmbH v. OHIM, 2015 E.C.R. II-____ at ¶43; Case T-11/14, Grundig Multimedial AG v. OHIM, 2015 E.C.R. II-____ at ¶19.
117. Case T-515/11, Delphi Technologies, Inc. v. OHIM, 2013 E.C.R. II-____.
118. Case T-130/01, Sykes Enterprises v. OHIM, 2002 E.C.R. II-5179.

and administration services were refused by the OHIM and General Court for nondistinctiveness.[119]

(4) Collective Marks

The term collective mark refers to a designation that is capable of distinguishing the goods or services of the members of the association which is the proprietor of the mark from those of nonmembers of the association.[120] Similar to "regular" trademarks, collective marks indicate commercial origin of goods or services. The difference is, however, that collective marks indicate origin in members of an association rather than origin in just one company. For example, the mark used by the Boy Scouts of America may be considered a collective mark. The registration of collective marks is available to associations of manufacturers, producers, suppliers of services, or traders that have the capacity in their own name to have rights and obligations of all kinds, to make contracts or accomplish other legal acts, and to sue and be sued, as well as legal persons governed by public law. The protection afforded by collective marks is much weaker than standard trademarks. The proprietor does not have the right to prohibit a third party from using in the course of trade such signs or indications, provided the third party uses them in accordance with honest practices in industrial or commercial matters; in particular, such a mark may not be invoked against a third party who is entitled to use a geographical name.

An applicant for a Union collective mark must submit regulations governing its use within the period prescribed. The regulations governing use specify the persons authorized to use the mark, the conditions of membership of the association and, where they exist, the conditions of use of the mark including sanctions. The regulations governing use of a collective mark must allow any person whose goods or services originate in the geographical area concerned to become a member of the association which is the proprietor of the collective mark.

(5) Shapes and Packaging

There is no per se rule against the registrability of marks consisting of the shape or packaging of the goods. In fact, both the Trademark Regulation[121] and the Trademark Directive[122] specifically cite "the shape of goods or of their packaging" as examples of marks that may be eligible for trademark protection.[123]

---

119. Case T-291/12, Deutsche Bank AG v. OHIM, 2014 E.C.R. II-____, at ¶22; Case T-68/13, Novartis AG v. OHIM, 2014 E.C.R. II-____, at ¶39.
120. Geographical Indications Regulation at art. 64(1).
121. Trademark Regulation at art. 4.
122. Trademark Directive at art. 2.
123. The packaging is treated as a shape only when the packaging is equivalent in the mind of the user with the shape of the product. A plastic water bottle, for example, is packaging that would be treated as a shape. "That is not the case either with nutcrackers or candlesticks. Although it is perfectly conceivable that, when they are sold, those goods will be placed in an appropriate box or case, and indeed may come with a protective cover, neither their nature nor trade practices will cause those who purchase and use them to regard them as indissociable from their packaging or wrapper." Case T-237/10, Louis Vuitton Malletier v. OHIM, 2011 E.C.R. II-449 (summary), at ¶41 (reported in the electronic reports of cases at ECLI:EU:T:2011:741) *aff'd on appeal* Case C-97/12P, Louis Vuitton Malletier v. OHIM, 2014 E.C.R. I-____, at ¶56.

The ECJ has repeatedly recognized that a shape may be registered as a trademark provided that it is capable of being represented graphically and capable of distinguishing the products or services of one undertaking from another undertaking.[124] The General Court has held that the shape of a particular bottle[125] and the shape of a toy puzzle cube[126] met these criteria.

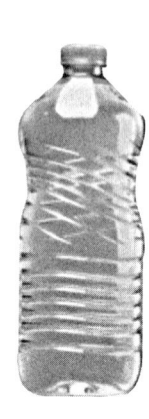

As a general rule, the criteria for assessing the distinctiveness of a shape or packaging of goods are the same as for other categories of trademarks.[127] However, there are two reasons why it is more difficult to register a shape or packaging as a trademark. First, the OHIM and the EU courts apply a heightened distinctiveness standard to shapes and packaging. In the context of applying the distinctiveness requirement, the ECJ and the General Court have held that distinctiveness requires the shape to depart from the norm or custom of the sector (as opposed to being a mere variant of the shape of the goods or the norm of the sector).[128] The reason for this requirement is that average consumers are not in the habit of making assumptions about the origin of products on the basis of their shape or the shape of their packaging in the absence of any graphic or word element and it could therefore prove more difficult to establish distinctiveness in relation to shape marks than in relation to a word or figurative mark.[129]

In *Procter & Gamble Company v. OHIM*, the ECJ held that the shape of a bar of soap could not be registered as it was not capable of distinguishing the soap of

---

124. Case C-48/09 P, Lego Juris A/S v. OHIM, 2010 E.C.R. I-8432, 8456 ¶39; Joined cases C-468/01 to C-472/01, Procter & Gamble Company v. OHIM, 2004 E.C.R. I-5141, 5162 ¶29; Joined cases C-456/01 P and C-457/01 P, Henkel KGaA v. OHIM, 2004 E.C.R. I-5115, 5130 ¶31. In addition, because shapes typically have less distinctiveness than figurative marks, they generally enjoy less protection than figurative marks in the context of opposition proceedings. Case T-479/08, Adidas AG v. OHIM, 2012 E.C.R. I-335 (summary), at ¶47.
125. Case T-305/02, Nestlé Waters France v. OHIM, 2003 E.C.R. II-5207.
126. Case T-450/09, Simba Toys GmbH & Co. KG v. OHIM, 2014 E.C.R. II-____.
127. Case C-344/10 P, Freixenet SA v. OHIM, 2011 E.C.R. I-10207, 10222 ¶45; Joined cases C-468/01 P to C-472/01 P, Procter & Gamble Company v. OHIM, 2004 E.C.R. I-5145, 5162 ¶29.
128. Case C-97/12 P, Louis Vuitton Malletier v. OHIM, 2014 E.C.R. I-____, at ¶51; Case T-178/11, Voss of Norway ASA v. OHIM, 2013 E.C.R. II-____, at ¶44.
129. Case C-344/10 P, Freixenet SA v. OHIM, 2011 E.C.R. I-10207, 10222 ¶46; Case C-238/06 P, Develey Holding GmbH & Co. Beteiligungs KG v. OHIM, 2007 E.C.R. I-9379, 9407 ¶80; Case C-24/05, August Storck KG v. OHIM, 2006 E.C.R. I-5693, 5706 ¶25.

Procter & Gamble from the soap of other undertakings.[130] In *Koninklijke Philips Electronics NV v. Remington Consumer Products Ltd.*, a graphic representation and configuration of the head of a three-headed rotary electric shaver which Philips had developed in 1966 was not sufficiently distinctive to be registrable.[131] In *Eurocermex SA v. OHIM*, for example, the shape of a Corona beer bottle with a lime in it was not distinctive for beer.[132]

The second reason why it is more difficult to register shapes and packaging as trademarks relates to the requirements codified in the Trademark Regulation specifically for shapes and packaging. Not only must the shape be distinctive, signs consisting exclusively of the shape of the goods cannot be registered as trademarks if (1) the shape results from the nature of the product, (2) the shape is necessary to obtain a technical result, or (3) the shape gives the goods substantial value.[133]

The reason for these three additional requirements imposed specifically on shapes is "to prevent trade mark protection from granting its proprietor a monopoly on functional characteristics of a product and to prevent the protection conferred by the trade mark from forming an obstacle preventing competitors from freely offering for sale products incorporating such functional characteristics in competition with the proprietor of the mark."[134] The OHIM is conscious of the fact that functional shapes are patentable, and to extend trademark protection to such shapes would provide a "back door" to grant permanent protection to functional shapes because trademark protection can be renewed whereas patent protection cannot be renewed.[135]

If the shape being registered results from the shape of the product, the shape is not eligible for registration as an EU trademark.[136] The more closely

---

130. Joined cases C-468/01 to C-472/01, The Procter & Gamble Company v. OHIM, 2004 E.C.R. I-5141.
131. Case C-299/99, Koninklijke Philips Electronics NV v. Remington Consumer Products Ltd., 2002 E.C.R. I-5475. Philips probably did not seek design protection because that form of intellectual property right is limited to 25 years. Although trademarks are limited in time, they can easily be renewed and often are.
132. Case C-286/04 P, Eurocermex SA v. OHIM, 2005 E.C.R. I-5797. *See also* Case T-12/04, Almdudler-Limonade v. OHIM, 2005 E.C.R. II-21 (three-dimensional shape of a bottle was not distinctive for soda).
133. Trademark Regulation at art. 7(1)(e); Trademark Directive at art. 3(1)(e).
134. Case T-270/06, Lego Juris A/S v. OHIM, 2008 E.C.R. II-3117, ___ ¶41 *aff'd on appeal* Case C-48/09 P, Lego Juris A/S v. OHIM, 2010 E.C.R. I-8432. *See also* Case C-205/13, Hauck GmbH & Co. KG v. Stokke A/S, 2014 E.C.R. I-___, at ¶18 ("The rationale…is to prevent trade mark protection from granting its proprietor a monopoly on technical solutions or functional characteristics of a product which a user is likely to seek in the products of competitors.").
135. Decision of the OHIM Second Board of Appeal in case no. R 747/2005-2 (Sept. 5, 2006) at ¶19.
136. Case T-450/09, Simba Toys GmbH & Co. KG v. OHIM, 2014 E.C.R. II-___, at ¶31.

the shape for which registration is sought resembles the shape of the product, the more likely the shape will be considered to result from the nature of the product.[137] For example, the shape of a head of a golf club results from the nature of the good itself:[138]

Second, a shape cannot be registered as a trademark if it is necessary to obtain a technical result.[139] The issue is not whether the design of the product is functional, but rather whether the function of the product is performed by the shape. For example, the function of a Lego toy building block is achieved by its shape.[140]

The fact that there may be other shapes that can be used to achieve that same technical result does not necessarily preclude a finding that the particular shape being registered is necessary to achieve the technical result.[141] The rationale behind this requirement is that trademark law should not confer exclusive rights for technical solutions.[142] Such protection is accorded by patents. Trademarks are used to identify the origin of products.

Finally, a shape cannot be registered as a trademark if it gives the goods substantial value.[143] Whether the shape gives the particular product substantial value is determined from the perspective of the customer. According to the General Court, a shape gives the product substantial value if the shape "determine[s] to a very large extent the consumer's choice. Where the shape thus gives substantial value to the goods at issue, it is irrelevant that other characteristics of those goods, such as their technical qualities, may also confer on them considerable value."[144] In *Bang & Olufsen A/S v. OHIM*, one of the issues was whether the shape of a speaker could be refused trademark protection because the shape gave the speaker substantial value.[145] In concluding that the shape gave the speaker substantial value, the General Court focused on the aesthetic value to the consumer and not necessarily that the design actually made the speaker perform better:

> In the present case…it must be noted that, for the goods at issue, the design is an element which will be very important in the consumer's choice even if the consumer also takes other characteristics of the goods at issue into account. Indeed, the shape for which registration was sought reveals

---

137. Decision of the OHIM First Board of Appeal in case no. R 467/2009-1 (Oct. 15, 2009) at ¶30; Decision of the OHIM Board of Appeal in case no. R 1462/2007-4 (Oct. 29, 2009) at ¶19.
138. Decision of the OHIM re CTM application no. 001436351 (Mar. 20, 2002).
139. Case T-164/11, Reddig GmbH v. OHIM, 2012 E.C.R. II-____, at ¶17.
140. Case C-48/09 P, Lego Juris A/S v. OHIM, 2010 E.C.R. I-8432.
141. Case T-270/06, Lego Juris A/S v. OHIM, 2008 E.C.R. II-3117, at ¶43 *aff'd on appeal* Case C-48/09 P, Lego Juris A/S v. OHIM, 2010 E.C.R. I-6975; Decision of the OHIM First Board of Appeal in case no. R 353/2006-1 (Nov. 30, 2010) at ¶27.
142. Case T-508/08, Bang & Olufsen v. OHIM, 2011 E.C.R. II-4209, 4229 ¶63.
143. Trademark Regulation at art. 7(1)(e)(iii).
144. Case T-450/09, Simba Toys GmbH & Co. KG v. OHIM, 2014 E.C.R. II-____, at ¶87.
145. Case T-460/05, Bang & Olufsen A/S v. OHIM, 2007 E.C.R. II-4209, 4223 ¶45.

a very specific design and [Bang & Olufsen] itself admits...
that that design is an essential element of its branding and
increases the appeal of the product at issue, that is to say, its
value. Furthermore, it is apparent from the evidence...namely
extracts from distributors' websites and on-line auction or
second-hand websites, that the aesthetic characteristics of
that shape are emphasized first and that the shape is perceived
as a kind of pure, slender, timeless sculpture for music
reproduction, which makes it an important selling point. It
does not therefore appear that, in the present case, the Board
of Appeal committed any error in holding that, independently
of the other characteristics of the goods at issue, the shape
in respect of which registration was sought gives substantial
value to the goods concerned.[146]

It is important to recognize that the three additional requirements imposed on shapes by Article 7(1)(e) of the Trademark Regulation are separate from the distinctiveness requirement. As discussed above, a mark which is not distinctive may become distinctive through use. The use exception, however, is not applicable if the lack of one of the three requirements codified in Article 7(1)(e) of the Trademark Regulation is not fulfilled. In *Lego Juris A/S v. OHIM*, for example, it was clear that the shape of the Lego block had acquired distinctiveness through use.[147] Lego was unsuccessful, however, because the issue was whether the shape of the block was necessary to obtain a technical result and not whether it was distinctive.

(6) Colors

Despite repeated declarations of the ECJ that there is no per se rule against colors or color combinations constituting trademarks,[148] it is extremely difficult to secure trademark protection for colors. The ECJ has stated that because colors are not inherently distinctive, "distinctiveness without any prior use is inconceivable save in exceptional circumstances."[149] Consumers are not accustomed to making an assumption about the origin of goods on the basis of their color or the color of their packaging, in the absence of a graphic or textual

---

146. *Id.*
147. Case C-48/09 P, Lego Juris A/S v. OHIM, 2010 E.C.R. I-8432, 8456 ¶40.
148. Joined cases C-217/13 and 218/13, Oberbank AG v. Deutscher Sparkassen- und Giroverband, 2014 E.C.R. I-____, at ¶36; Case C-447/02P, KWS Saat AG v. OHIM, 2004 E.C.R. I-10107, 10154 ¶78.
149. Case C-447/02P, KWS Saat AG v. OHIM, 2004 E.C.R. I-10107, 10154 ¶79; Case T-404/09, Deutsche Bahn AG v. OHIM, 2010 E.C.R. II-249 (summary), at ¶18 *aff'd on appeal* Case C-45/11 P, Deutsche Bahn AG v. OHIM, 2011 E.C.R. I-190; Case T-97/08, KUKA Roboter GmbH v. OHIM, 2010 E.C.R. II-5059, at ¶33.

element, because a color per se is not normally used as a means of identification of the source of the goods.[150]

According to the General Court, "the perception of the relevant section of the public is not necessarily the same in the case of a sign composed of a color or color combination *per se* as it is in the case of a word or figurative mark composed of a sign that bears no relation to the appearance of the goods that it identifies. While the public is accustomed to perceiving word or figurative marks as instantly identifying the commercial origin of the goods, the same is not necessarily true where the sign forms part of the look of the goods in respect of which registration of the sign is sought."[151] For example, the OHIM refused registration by Wrigley of its Juicy-Fruit yellow for chewing gum.[152] The combination of green and gray was also refused for lawn mowers and other lawn equipment.[153]

If, however, the relevant section of the public is a group of trade people who use color to differentiate products, or the relevant public has come to rely on colors to distinguish companies in a particular industry, the applicant's chances of gaining registration are improved. For example, the color green (Pantone number 348) was accepted by the OHIM for National Car Rental System, Inc.[154] According to the OHIM:

> In the car and van rental service, colors are particularly important distinctive signs since they can be perceived by the clients at first glance. The use of colors is specially emphasized in the relevant trade. It is a common experience that in the international airport parking areas, for instance, the rental services are mainly identified from a distance by their color signs even before the users can read the trade names. As in the example given by the appellant, it is well known that in the parallel situations where services must be recognized at the roadside, as in the case of filling stations, brands and services are perceived from a long distance firstly through

---

150. Decision of the OHIM Fourth Board of Appeal in case no. R 797/2008-4 (Apr. 21. 2009) at ¶28: The color red on a golf putter was considered not distinctive because "consumers will perceive the colour red, when applied to a golf club or parts thereof, merely as an inherent feature of the goods themselves and not as a reference to a commercial origin." Another reason for disfavoring the registrability of colors as trademarks: "the fact that the number of colours actually available is limited means that a small number of trademark registrations for certain services or goods could exhaust the entire range of the colours available." Decision of the OHIM First Board of Appeal in case R 467/2009-1 (Oct. 15, 2009) ¶37.
151. Case T-316/00, Viking-Umwelttechnik GmbH v. OHIM, 2002 E.C.R. II-3715, 3726 ¶27.
152. Decision of the OHIM Third Board of Appeal in case no. R 169/1998-3 (Jan. 22, 1999).
153. Case T-316/00, Viking-Umwelttechnik GmbH v. OHIM, 2002 E.C.R. II-3715, 3725 ¶23.
154. Decision of the OHIM Third Board of Appeal in case no. R 194/2000-3 (July 3, 2002).

the colors applied to the pump stations, surfaces of premises, decorations or flags installed on the roads.

(7) Olfactory Marks

The requirement discussed above that a trademark be capable of being represented graphically presents a difficulty for the recognition of smells as trademarks. There is no per se prohibition on the registration of olfactory marks. As the ECJ stated in *Sieckmann v. Deutsches Patent und Markenamt*, "a trade mark may consist of a sign which is not in itself capable of being perceived visually, provided that it can be represented graphically, particularly by means of images, lines or characters, and that the representation is clear, precise, self-contained, easily accessible, intelligible, durable and objective."[155] In that case, the applicant unsuccessfully tried to register the chemical formula for methyl cinnamate which provided the smell the trademark applicant sought to have protected. The ECJ held "few people would recognize in such a formula the odor in question. Such a formula is not sufficiently intelligible. In addition, as that Government and the Commission stated, a chemical formula does not represent the odor of a substance, but the substance as such, and nor is it sufficiently clear and precise."[156]

(8) Sounds

Sound marks confront the same challenge as olfactory marks—they are not visually perceptible. However, there is no per se rule against the registration of sounds as trademarks. A sound may be registered as a trademark provided it can be represented graphically, "particularly by means of images, lines or characters, and that its representation is clear, precise, self-contained, easily accessible, intelligible, durable and objective."[157] There are several ways to graphically represent sounds. Music, for example, can be represented by musical notes. Nonmusical sounds can be represented by words (such as "the sound of a Harley-Davidson motorcycle motor"), or diagrams such as oscillograms, sound spectrums, and sonograms. The issues related to whether these forms of representing sounds are adequate for purposes of EU trademark law were addressed by the General Court in *Shield Mark BV v. Joost Kist* and by the OHIM's Board of Appeal in response to the application of Metro-Goldwyn-Mayer for a trademark on the sound of a lion's roar.[158]

Shield Mark BV v. Joost Kist involved musical sounds represented in several ways by musical notes and a nonmusical sound represented by an onomatopoeia. In that case, Shield Mark had registered several sound marks in Belgium that it used as jingles in promoting its products. In particular, Shield Mark used several methods to register the first nine notes of Beethoven's *Für Elise*. In addition, the

---

155. Case C-273/00, Sieckmann v. Deutsches Patent- und Markenamt, 2002 E.C.R. I-11754, 11771 ¶55.
156. *Id.* at 11774 ¶69.
157. Case C-283/01, Shield Mark BV v. Joost Kist, 2003 E.C.R. I-14329, 14348 ¶55.
158. Decision of the OHIM Fourth Board of Appeal in case R 781/1999-4 (Aug. 25, 2003).

company registered the onomatopoeia"'"kekelekuuuuu" representing the sound of a cock's crow. The issue was whether the registration met the requirements of graphical representation.

The ECJ held that a written sequence of the notes was an insufficient graphic representation of the excerpt from *Für Elise*. However, the registration made by Shield Mark, which has the notes for *Für Elise* written in musical text with bars, was an adequate graphical representation. Regarding the onomatopoeia, the ECJ held that by itself an onomatopoeia is not an adequate graphical representation because it may be perceived differently by different people.

The decision by the OHIM Board of Appeal in the MGM Lion's Roar application was consistent with *Shield Mark BV v. Joost Kist* and elaborated on the graphic representations of nonmusical sounds which may be adequate to support a trademark application.[159] MGM had registered the sound of a lion's roar represented by a sonogram. After stating that oscillograms and sound spectrums will normally be inadequate graphic representations of sounds for purposes of a trademark application, the Board of Appeal recognized that a sonogram may be an adequate representation of a sound if it is combined with a time scale and frequency scale. As the MGM sonogram in this case was not accompanied by such a scale, the Board of Appeal rejected the application.

(9) Tastes

Similar to sounds and olfactory marks, one of the challenges of registering gustatory marks is the preclusion which such a trademark would give to its holder. One of the fundamental purposes of precluding marks that designate characteristics of the goods or services is that it may, by reserving access to that characteristic to one undertaking, give the holder of the trademark an unfair advantage. Eli Lilly and Company, the U.S. pharmaceutical company, sought to register the description "the taste of artificial strawberry flavour" as a gustatory mark for pharmaceutical products. In affirming the examiner's denial of registration, the Board of Appeal concluded that the restriction of availability of this taste to other pharmaceutical manufacturers would unfairly restrict competition.[160] Moreover, according to the Board of Appeal, the taste of strawberries is not able to distinguish Eli Lilly's product from those of other pharmaceutical companies: "[T]he taste is unlikely to be perceived by consumers as a trade mark; they are far more likely to assume that it is intended to disguise the unpleasant taste of the product."[161]

(10) Marks of Geographic Origin

Trademarks consisting of geographic origins are generally not registrable as trademarks. For example, the General Court has held that the trademark "Oldenburger" cannot be registered as a trademark for milk products because it is the name of a town in Germany where the products are made.[162] Similarly, the trademark "MunichFinancialServices" was refused registration for a financial

---

159. *Id.*
160. Decision of the OHIM Board of Appeal in case R120/2001-2 (Aug. 4, 2003) at ¶16.
161. *Id.*
162. Case T-295/01, Nordmilch eG v. OHIM, 2003 E.C.R. II-4365.

services company because of the association with the town in Bavaria.[163] The basic rationale supporting this prohibition is that no one company should be able to secure the use of a geographic designation to exclusively identify its products or services.

Not all marks that include a geographic reference are precluded from being registered.[164] Preclusion only exists if the relevant public will make an association between the products or services and the geographic place. As illustrated by *Windsurfing Chiemsee Produktions- und Vertriebs-GmbH v. Boots- und Segelzubehör Walter Huber*, a mark that includes a reference to a geographic place may be registrable if it has acquired distinctiveness through use in relation to the relevant products.[165] In this case, the ECJ said that "Chiemsee" (a lake in Germany) could be registered as a trademark for sports clothing as it acquired distinctiveness of character over the years. In other words, the relevant public would not necessarily associate the products with the place because the mark was independently known among the relevant public.

In *Peek & Cloppenburg v. OHIM*, the General Court similarly concluded that the relevant public would not assume an association between the mark and the geographic place.[166] In that case, the OHIM refused registration of the mark "Cloppenburg" by a German clothing retailer on the grounds that it was descriptive of the German city Cloppenburg where the retailer was based. According to the General Court, however, the rejection of a geographical origin as a mark requires that the relevant portion of the public make an association between the goods and the geographic place.[167] The General Court held that the OHIM was incorrect in this particular case because of the relative obscurity of the town in Germany.[168] As most consumers would not even be aware that the town existed, the likelihood of an association between the products and the town was small.

(11) Special Rights for Agricultural Products and Foodstuffs

As discussed above, trademarks that include reference to a geographic place may not be registered if there is an apparent association between the goods or services and the geographic place. For example, a Spanish vineyard would not be able to reserve the designation "Spanish wine" for itself by way of a trademark. And yet, certain geographic designations may serve a socially useful function precisely because they create such association. For example, the designation

---

163. Case T-316/03, Münchener Rückversicherung-Gesellschaft v. OHIM, 2005 E.C.R. II-1953, 1962 ¶32.
164. *See, e.g.,* Case T-499/04, Hammarplast AB v. OHIM, 2006 E.C.R. II-84.
165. Case C-109/97, Windsurfing Chiemsee Produktions- und Vertriebs-GmbH v. Boots- und Segelzubehör Walter Huber, 1999 E.C.R. I-9779. Previously, producers of goods whose geographical origin was important (e.g., champagne, cheese, and wine), relied on protection accorded by regulations on designation of origin. Under the laws of most member states, geographic signs were not registrable as trademarks.
166. Case T-379/03, Peek & Cloppenburg v. OHIM, 2005 E.C.R. II-4636.
167. *Id.* at 4647 ¶38.
168. *Id.* at 4649 ¶46.

"champagne" for sparkling wine serves to assist consumers in making sure that they are purchasing a product from the Champagne region of France.

In recognition of this potential benefit, the EU recognizes three types of special designation rights for agricultural products and foodstuffs:[169] geographic indications, indications of origin, and traditional specialties guaranteed.[170] In contrast to a trademark, these designations are not reserved or limited to use by one company. The source function of these special rights is not to indicate a specific company as the source, but rather a geographic area. Any company meeting the specifications can use the designation.

The terms designation of origin and geographic indication both refer to the use of a name of a region, specific place, or country to identify the origin of an agricultural product or foodstuff.[171] They differ, however, as to the significance of the link between the nature of the products and the geographic place. To qualify for a designation of origin (sometimes referred to as appellations of origin), there must also (1) be a link between the quality or characteristics of the agricultural product or foodstuff and the particular geographic environment of the region, place, or country and (2) the production, processing, and preparation of the product or foodstuff must take place in that region, place, or country.[172] For example, the "link" between Roquefort cheese and the particular region of France is as follows: "The distinctive characteristics of *Roquefort* are the result of close synergies between mankind and nature. They stem partly from the characteristics of the milk obtained from traditional breeds of sheep and fed according to tradition, and partly from the uniqueness of the natural caves in Roquefort-sur-Soulzon, which are formed wholly from the scree at the foothills of the calcareous cliffs in Combalou, where a miracle of nature conspires to give Roquefort its unique taste."[173] Additional examples include Prosciutto di Parma[174] and Comté cheese.[175]

A geographical indication, on the other hand, merely signifies that a product comes from a particular area (regardless of whether there is a certain quality the product possesses because it comes from the indicated geographic area). For

---

169. The types of agricultural products and foodstuffs eligible for registration are listed in Annexes I and II of Council Regulation (EC) No. 510/2006 of 20 March 2006 on the protection of geographical indications and designations of origin for agricultural products and foodstuffs, 2006 O.J. (L 93) 12 [hereinafter Geographical Indications Regulation]. In addition, the designation may be protected by national unfair trade laws of the member states. In *Fage UK Ltd. v. Chobani UK Ltd.*, for example, Chobani was found to have unfairly used the designation "Greek yogurt" in the UK where its competitor, Fage, had built up goodwill associated with the designation Greek yogurt even though the designation was not a protected designation. Fage UK Ltd. v. Chobani UK Ltd., [2013] EWHC 630 (Ch).
170. The TRIPS Agreement requires its members to provide protection for geographical indications which are recognized under the laws of the other TRIPS members.
171. The geographic area does not have to be in the EU.
172. Geographical Indications Regulation at art. 2(1)(a).
173. Commission Regulation (EC) No. 510/2006, 2006 O.J. (L 93) 1, 2.
174. Commission Regulation (EC) No. 101/2008, 2008 O.J. (L 31) 29.
175. Commission Regulation (EC) No. 1107/96, 1996 O.J. (L 148) 1.

example, "Schwäbische Spätzle" refers to a particular form of noodle which is popular in the Swabian region of Germany but is not necessarily linked to the particular attributes of that region.[176] There are two requirements: (1) the product comes from a particular geographic area which has a specific quality, reputation, or other characteristics attributable to that geographical origin and (2) the product or foodstuff is either produced, processed, or prepared in that area.[177] These requirements are sometimes referred to as indications of source. Prominent examples of geographical indications are the designations "Scottish Farmed Salmon",[178] "Nürnberg Bratwurst",[179] "Bayerisches Bier",[180] "Scotch Lamb"[181] and "Gouda Cheese."[182]

Whereas a geographical indication informs the consumer that the product bearing that indication comes from a particular place, region, or country, a designation of origin guarantees not only the product's geographical provenance, but also that the goods have been manufactured according to quality requirements or manufacturing standards prescribed by an act of public authority and thus that they have certain specific characteristics.[183] Traditionally, geographic indications were protected by national rules prohibiting unfair or misleading advertising. Designations of origin, on the other hand, were traditionally protected under specifically applicable national rules.

The fundamental requirement for registering a designation of origin or geographic indication is that there must be a direct link between the characteristics of the product and its geographical provenance.[184] This is a factual determination for which the European courts give the authorities of the member states much deference.[185] For example, the designation "Warsteiner" for beer merely suggests that it is from the German town of Warstein, without any necessary reflection of its quality. Consequently, it falls outside the scope of the Geographical Indications Regulation.[186] In *Bavaria NV v. Bayerischer Brauerverbund*, however, the ECJ held that there could be a link between Bavaria

---

176. Commission Implementing Regulation (EU) No. 186/2012 of 7 March 2012 entering a name in the register of protected designations of origin and protected geographical indications, 2012 O.J. (L 69) 3.
177. Geographical Indications Regulation at art. 2(1)(b).
178. Commission Regulation (EC) No. 1437/2004 of 11 August 2004, O.J. 2004 (L 265) 3.
179. Commission Regulation (EC) No. 1257/2003, 2003 O.J. (L 177) 3.
180. Case C-343/07, Bavaria NV v. Bayerischer Brauerverbund, 2009 E.C.R. I-5491.
181. Commission Regulation (EC) No. 1345/2004, 2004 O.J. (L 249) 14.
182. 2008 O.J. (C 61) 15.
183. Case C-3/91, Exportur SA v LOR SA and Confiserie du Tech SA, 1992 E.C.R. I-5553, 5557¶11; Case C-47/90, Etablissements Delhaize Freres et Compagnie Le Lion SA v. Promalvin SA, 1992 E.C.R. I-3704, 3709 ¶¶17-18.
184. Joined Cases C-321/94 – C-324/94, *In re* Jacque Pistre, 1997 E.C.R. I-2343, 2372 ¶35.
185. Case C-343/07, Bavaria NV v. Bayerischer Brauerverbund, 2009 E.C.R. I-5536, 5571 ¶93.
186. Case C-312/98, Schutzverband gegen Unwesen in der Wirtschaft v. Warsteiner Brauerei Haus Cramer GmbH & Co. KG, 2000 E.C.R. I-9187.

and Bavarian beer.[187] The application of France for the geographic indication "choucroute d'Alsace" for a type of cabbage from the Alsace region of France was similarly refused.[188] In that instance, France argued that the climate and the characteristics of the soil in the Alsace region resulted in a quality of cabbage with a unique character. The Commission rejected the application because the characteristics of Alsace which allegedly gave rise to the unique character of the cabbage were present in other regions.[189]

One additional limitation is that the registration of a designation of origin or geographic indication is not allowed for designations that have become generic.[190] In order to become generic, the link between the specific quality and the geographic location must have disappeared in the eyes of the relevant public.[191] For example, Greece is not allowed to register the term "Feta" as a designation of origin because the name had been used for a considerable amount of time in other member states to refer to a type of cheese.[192] Additional examples of names which have become generic are "pasta,"[193] "beer"[194] and "yogurt."[195] In contrast, the term "Parmesan" to refer to a type of cheese has not become generic.[196] According to the ECJ, when assessing the generic character of a name, it is necessary to take into account the places of production of the product concerned both inside and outside the member state that obtained the registration of the name at issue, the consumption of that product and how it is perceived by consumers inside and outside that member state, the existence of national legislation specifically relating to that product, and the way in which the name has been used in EU law.[197]

In order to secure protection, an application must be filed with the EU Commission by an association of producers or processors working with that agricultural product or foodstuff.[198] For example, a group of vineyards in Spain

---

187. Case C-343/07, Bavaria NV v. Bayerischer Brauerverbund, 2009 E.C.R. I-5536, 5573 ¶99.
188. Commission Decision of 12 January 2006 concerning an application for registration in the 'Register of protected designations of origin and protected geographical indications' provided for in Council Regulation (EEC) No. 2081/92, 2006 O.J. (L 10) 70.
189. *Id.* at 70 ¶4.
190. Geographical Indications Regulation at art. 3(1); Council Regulation (EC) No. 510/2006 of 20 March 2006 on the protection of geographical indications and designations of origin for agricultural products and foodstuffs, 2006 O.J. (L 93) 12.
191. Case C-343/07, Bavaria NV v. Bayerischer Brauerverbund, 2009 E.C.R. I-5536, 5575 ¶107.
192. Joined Cases C-289/96, C-293/86 and C-299/96, Denmark v. Comm'n, 1999 E.C.R. I-1541.
193. Case C-407/85, Gloken v. sUSL Centro Süd, 1988 E.C.R. 4233.
194. Case C-178/84, Comm'n v. Germany, 1987 E.C.R. 1227.
195. Case C-298/87, Smanor v. Comm'n, 1998 E.C.R. 4489.
196. Case C-132/05, Comm'n v. Germany, 2008 E.C.R. I-957.
197. Case C-343/07, Bavaria NV v. Bayerischer Brauerverbund, 2009 E.C.R. I-5536, 5573 ¶101.
198. Geographical Indications Regulation at art. 5; Geographical Indications Regulation at art. 2(1)(a).

could not apply for registration of the name "Champagne" to designate their sparkling wine as they are not located in the French region of Champagne. An individual natural person or legal entity may also file an application if it is the only producer in the geographical area willing to submit an application and the geographical area possesses characteristics that differ appreciably from those of neighboring areas or the characteristics of the product are different from those produced in neighboring areas.[199] Neither the applying association nor the geographical area need to be within the EU in order to apply for protection. For example, the Tea Board of India has registered the geographical indication "Darjeeling" for tea grown in the Indian district of Darjeeling.[200]

The application for registration must include a specification of the attributes of the product.[201] These specifications are designed to ensure the link between the characteristics of the product and its geographical provenance. In other words, a product may use the designation of origin or the geographic indication only if it fulfills all of the provided specifications. In *Consorzio del Prosciutto di Parma v. Asda Stores Ltd*, for example, the issue was whether ham had to be sliced in the region of Parma, Italy, for it to be considered Parma ham.[202] A UK company, which sold ham under the label Parma ham, argued that the slicing and packaging of the ham did not affect the quality of the Parma ham, and therefore it should be able to label its ham as Parma ham. The ECJ held that such a specification is permissible if it is shown that it is necessary and proportionate and capable of upholding the reputation of the designation of origin.[203] As Parma ham is consumed mainly in slices and the operations leading to that presentation are all designed to obtain in particular a specific flavor, color, and texture that consumers will appreciate, the ECJ held that the slicing and packaging of the ham constitute important operations that may harm the quality and hence the reputation of the designation of origin if they are carried out in conditions that result in a product not possessing the organoleptic qualities expected. The risk to the quality and authenticity of the product finally offered to consumers is consequently greater where it has been sliced and packaged outside the region of production than when that has been done within the region because of the lack of experts who have specialized knowledge of the characteristics of Parma ham.[204]

---

199. Commission Regulation (EC) No. 1898/2006 of 14 December 2006 laying down detailed rules of implementation of Council Regulation (EC) No. 510/2006 of 20 March 2006 on the protection of geographical indications and designations of origin for agricultural products and foodstuffs, 2006 O.J. (L 369) 1 at art. 2.
200. O.J. 2009 (C 246) 12.
201. Geographical Indications Regulation at art. 4. The procedures for applying for protection are governed by Commission Regulation (EC) No. 1898/2006 of 14 December 2006 laying down detailed rules of implementation of Council Regulation (EC) No. 510/2006 of 20 March 2006 on the protection of geographical indications and designations of origin for agricultural products and foodstuffs, 2006 O.J. (L 369) 1.
202. Case C-108/01, Consorzio del Prosciutto di Parma v. Asda Stores Ltd, 2003 E.C.R. I-5163.
203. *Id.* at 5185 ¶66.
204. *Id.* at 5187 ¶75.

The protection granted to designations of origin or geographical indications is similar to that of a trademark, but somewhat narrower. Registered designations are protected against any direct or indirect commercial use of a name registered in respect of products not covered by the registration insofar as those products are comparable to the products registered under that name or insofar as using the name exploits the reputation of the protected name.[205] They are also protected against any misuse, imitation, or evocation, even if the true origin of the product is indicated or even if the protected name is translated or accompanied by an expression such as "style," "type," "method," "as produced in," "imitation" or similar qualification. For example, a company from Bulgaria could not sell its cheese using the designation "Gouda" even if that company specifically stated on the packaging that the cheese was produced in Bulgaria. The right also prohibits any other false or misleading indication as to the provenance, origin, nature, or essential qualities of the product,[206] and any other practice liable to mislead the public as to the true origin of the product.[207]

Designations of origin and geographical indications generally take precedence over trademarks. Where a designation of origin or geographical indication is registered in accordance with the Geographical Indications Regulation, the subsequent application for registration of a trademark for the same type of products will be refused.[208] If the trademark was registered in good faith before the date on which application for registration of a designation of origin or geographical indication was made, that trademark is valid (assuming, of course, it meets the requirements for trademark registration discussed above). In *Consorzio per la tutela del formaggio Gorgonzola v. Käserei Champignon Hofmeister GmbH & Co. KG and Eduard Bracharz GmbH*, for example, the registered trademark "Cambozola" could be used even though it might have created confusion with the subsequently registered designation of origin Gorgonzola, provided that the earlier registration was made in good faith.[209]

There is a third designation possible for agricultural products and foodstuffs: traditional specialty guaranteed designations.[210] As discussed above, geographical indications and designations of origin relate a product to a particular geographic area. For traditional specialty guaranteed designations, however, there is no direct connection between the designation and the origin. Instead, a traditional specialty guaranteed designation indicates that the agricultural product or foodstuff has a particular technical character in its composition or

---

205. Geographical Indications Regulation at art. 13(1)(a).
206. *Id.* at art. 13(1)(c).
207. *Id.* at art. 13(1)(d).
208. Trademark Regulation at art. 14(1). *See, e.g.,* Joined Cases C-4/10 and C-27/10, Bureau national interprofessionel du Cognac v. Gust. Ranin Oy, 2011 E.C.R. I-6131; Case T-291/03, Consorzio per la tutela del formaggio Grana Padano v. OHIM, 2007 E.C.R. II-3081.
209. Case C-8787/97, Consorzio per la tutela del formaggio Gorgonzola v. Käserei Champignon Hofmeister GmbH & Co. KG and Eduard Bracharz GmbH, 1999 E.C.R. I-1301.
210. Council Regulation (EC) No. 509/2006 of 20 March 2006 on agricultural products and foodstuffs as traditional specialties guaranteed, 2006 O.J. (L 93) 1.

means of production. For example, the designation "Kriek-Lambic" for a beer that is the result of blending various lambics containing 10 percent and 25 percent fruit would meet this criterion.[211]

(c) Relative Grounds for Refusal

In contrast to absolute grounds for refusal, there are several grounds upon which a registration may be refused if an opposition is filed by a prior owner within three months of publication.[212] The OHIM will not test relative grounds for refusal on its own. The opposition procedure can only be initiated by the proprietor of an earlier registered trademark. The earlier trademark does not necessarily have to be a Union trademark. The earlier trademark may have been registered with one or more of the member state trademark offices[213] or may have been registered pursuant to an international convention to which the EU is a party.[214] For example, the proprietor of a U.S. registered trademark may initiate an opposition procedure in the EU if that trademark has also been registered under the Madrid Protocol as discussed above. An earlier trademark that has not been registered may also initiate an opposition procedure if that mark has become well-known in a member state.[215]

(1) Identical Marks

The proprietor of an earlier trademark may contest the subsequent registration of a trademark if that subsequent trademark is identical with the earlier trademark, and the goods or services for which registration is applied for are identical with the goods or services for which the earlier trademark is protected.[216] A similarity between the marks does not work for this relative ground for refusal.[217] The earlier trademark does not necessarily have to be a Union trademark. The concept of "earlier trademark" includes Union trademarks as well as trademarks registered in a member state, or trademarks registered under international arrangements which have effect in a member state, for example the Madrid Protocol discussed above.[218]

(2) Likelihood of Confusion

Another relative ground for refusal exists if, because of its identity with or similarity to an earlier trademark and the identity or similarity of the goods or

---

211. Commission Regulation (EC) No. 954/98 of 6 May 1998, 1998 O.J. (L 133) 10.
212. The lapsing of the three-month period in which to file an opposition does not automatically preclude a third party from challenging the mark. It is possible for a third party to initiate invalidity proceedings with the OHIM or to challenge the validity of the trademark in enforcement proceedings. Trademark Regulation at art. 52.
213. Case T-366/07, The Procter & Gamble Company v. OHIM, 2010 E.C.R. II-194 (summary), at ¶48.
214. Trademark Regulation at art. 8(2)(a)(iii).
215. *Id.* at art. 8(2)(c).
216. *Id.* at art. 8(1)(a).
217. OHIM Decision No. 2551/2002 of Aug. 28, 2002 ruling on opposition No. B 184 970 (McBagel trademark could not be opposed by McDonald's on these grounds because it was not identical to any trademarks which McDonald's already had.).
218. Case T-90/05, Omega SA v. OHIM, 2007 E.C.R. II-145 (summary), at ¶37.

services covered by the trademarks, there exists a likelihood of confusion on the part of the targeted public in the territory in which the earlier trademark is protected.[219] Likelihood of confusion exists if there is a risk that the public might believe that the goods or services in question come from the same undertaking.[220] For example, the trademark "McBagel" filed by an Irish company was successfully challenged by McDonald's on the basis that many consumers would assume that the McBagel came from McDonald's.[221]

As with distinctiveness, the likelihood of confusion is determined through the eyes of the targeted customers of the trademarked product or service and not from the perspective of the applicant or the OHIM. For example, when determining whether the use of the "Bud" trademark by the U.S. beer manufacturer Anheuser-Busch creates a likelihood of confusion with the earlier mark "Bit" registered by the German Bitburger Brewery, the targeted public is made up of German beer drinkers.[222]

The likelihood of confusion does not have to exist throughout the EU.[223] It is sufficient to oppose a registration if the likelihood exists in a significant part of the EU. For example, the likelihood of confusion may exist only among a particular linguistic group.[224] For word marks, however, the level of similarity may differ in those member states where the word marks are in the local language as opposed to those member states where the word marks have no independent meaning. In *Rewe-Zentral AG v. OHIM*, for example, the General Court concluded that the level of similarity between "Solfrutta" and "Frutisol" in Italy and Spain is higher than in those member states such as Hungary, Finland, and Lithuania where those terms have no independent meaning.[225]

The likelihood of confusion applies not only to Union marks which may create confusion, but also to national trademarks and trademarks registered under international arrangements.[226] In *Biofarma SA v. OHIM*, for example, a French company successfully argued that the trademark "ALREX" registered by Bausch & Lomb Pharmaceuticals for eye drops could not be registered as a Union trademark because there was a likelihood of confusion with the French mark "ARTEX" which was previously registered in France for a heart drug.[227]

---

219. Trademark Regulation at art. 8(1)(b). The likelihood of confusion does not have to exist throughout the EU. It is sufficient that the likelihood of confusion exists in a part of the EU. Case T-460/11, Scandic Distilleries SA v. OHIM, 2012 E.C.R. II-____, at ¶52.
220. Case T-41/12, LS Fashion, LLC v. OHIM, 2015 E.C.R. II-____ ¶50; Case T-394/10, Grebenshikova v. OHIM, 2013 E.C.R. II-____, at ¶15; Case T-54/12, K2 Sports Europe GmbH v. OHIM, 2013 E.C.R. II-____, at ¶18.
221. OHIM Decision in case no. 2551/2002 (Aug. 28, 2002) (ruling on opposition no. B 184 970).
222. Case T-350/04 to T-352/04, Bitburger Brauerei Th. Simon GmbH v. OHIM, 2006 E.C.R. II-4258, 4282 ¶69.
223. Case T-460/11, Scandic Distilleries SA v. OHIM, 2012 E.C.R. II-____, at ¶52.
224. Case C-514/06 P, Armacell Enterprise GmbH v. OHIM, 2008 E.C.R. I-128 (summary), at ¶56.
225. Case T-331/08, Rewe-Zentral AG v. OHIM, 2010 E.C.R. II-11 (summary), at ¶24.
226. Trademark Regulation at art. 8(2)(a)(ii).
227. Case T-154/03, Biofarma SA v. OHIM, 2005 E.C.R. II-4743.

The analysis of the likelihood of confusion has two components: (1) visual, phonetic, or conceptual similarity and (2) similarity of scope.[228] First, the marks must share some visual, phonetic, and conceptual similarity.[229] The marks do not have to be identical; it is sufficient that they are similar. For example, the "McBagel" trademark discussed above was not identical to any trademarks that McDonald's was already using.[230] The visual similarity of the marks refers to their appearance. The phonetic or aural similarity refers to how they are pronounced. In *Reckitt Benckiser v. OHIM*, for example, the registration of the mark "ALADIN" for cleaning supplies was determined to create a likelihood of confusion with the mark "ALADDIN," also for cleaning supplies.[231] In *Bitburger v. OHIM*, however, the phonetic similarity of the mark "Bud" (for beer) with "Bit" (also for beer) was not significant enough to create the likelihood of confusion in the minds of German beer drinkers.[232] Similarly, the General Court found that there was insignificant aural similarity between the following two marks (both of which were registered for use with furniture):[233]

A comparison of the conceptual similarities of the marks is more abstract. The basic question is whether the conceptual content of the two marks is similar. In *Picasso v. OHIM*, for example, the estate of Pablo Picasso challenged the registration of the mark "Picaro" which Daimler Chrysler wanted to use for a new model automobile.[234] The Picasso estate had already registered the mark "Picasso" for the very same use. The General Court held that there was a low risk of confusion given the fact that the word "Picasso" has a "clear and semantic content" for the public and the realization that buyers of automobiles customarily conduct a detailed inspection of automobiles prior to purchase and hence are unlikely to be confused:

> The reputation of the painter Pablo Picasso is such that it is not plausible to consider, in the absence of specific evidence to the contrary, that the sign PICASSO as a mark for motor vehicles may, in the perception of the average consumer,

---

228. Case T-54/12, K2 Sports Europe GmbH v. OHIM, 2013 E.C.R. II-___, at ¶19.
229. Case C-57/08 P, Gateway, Inc. v. OHIM, 2008 E.C.R. I-188 (summary), at ¶51.
230. Decision No. 2551/2002 of Aug. 28, 2002 ruling on opposition No. B 184 970.
231. Case T-126/03, Reckitt Benckiser v. OHIM, 2005 E.C.R. II-2861.
232. Case T-350/04 to T-352/04, Bitburger Brauerei Th. Simon GmbH v. OHIM, 2006 E.C.R. II-4258, 4290 ¶95.
233. Case T-112/06, Inter-Ikea Systems BV v. OHIM, 2008 E.C.R. II-6 (summary), at ¶66.
234. Case T-185/02, Picasso v. OHIM, 2004 E.C.R. II-1739, *aff'd on appeal* Case C-361/04 P, Picasso v. OHIM, 2005 E.C.R. I-660. A surname may be registrable as a trademark as long as it is distinctive. Case C-404/02, Nichols plc v. Registrar of Trademarks, 2004 E.C.R. I-8499 (the use of "Nichols" for vending machines).

override the name of the painter so that that consumer, confronted with the sign PICASSO in the context of the goods concerned, will henceforth disregard the meaning of the sign as the name of the painter and perceive it principally as a mark, among other marks, of motor vehicles. It follows that the conceptual differences separating the signs at issue are, in the present case, such as to counteract the visual and phonetic similarities...[235]

It should be mentioned at this point that trademarks have different levels of distinctiveness. In examining the absolute grounds for refusal, as discussed above, the OHIM tests whether the mark has a minimum level of distinctiveness to meet that particular requirement for registration. However, some marks may be very distinctive while others only slightly so. The golden arches of McDonald's are a good example. As arches have nothing really to do with hamburgers or fast food, they are considered highly distinctive. The shape of a hamburger, on the other hand, would be less distinctive as it is closer to being descriptive. In determining whether there is a likelihood of confusion, the degree of distinctiveness of the earlier registered mark is relevant. The less distinctive the earlier mark, the more difficult it is to successfully claim a likelihood of confusion.[236]

The second component in the analysis of the likelihood of confusion is the similarity of the goods or services that the trademark represents. As discussed above, when registering a trademark, the applicant is required to designate the fields of use in which that trademark will be applied. There is a likelihood of confusion only if the mark is identical or similar to the earlier mark *and* the goods or services which the trademark is used for are similar.[237] According to the General Court, "a low degree of similarity between the goods or services covered may be offset by a high degree of similarity between the marks, and vice versa."[238] Even identical marks can be used to represent different products or services. In *Commercy AG v. OHIM*, for example, the General Court found that the subsequent registration of the word mark "Easyhotel" did not create the likelihood of confusion with an earlier registered identical mark because the subsequent mark was registered for different goods and services.[239]

In *Alecansan SL v. OHIM* the issue was whether the U.S. company CompUSA could register its CompUSA trademark in view of the fact that another company had already registered essentially the same mark in Spain.[240] The only difference was that the category of goods was different. The U.S.

---

235. Case T-185/02, Picasso v. OHIM, 2004 E.C.R. II-1739, 1760 ¶¶57 & 58, *aff'd on appeal* Case C-361/04 P, Picasso v. OHIM, 2005 E.C.R. I-660, 672 ¶27.
236. *See, e.g.,* Case T-41/12, LS Fashion, LLC v. OHIM, 2015 E.C.R. II-___ ¶53; Case T-153/03, Inex SA v. OHIM, 2006 E.C.R. II-1680, 1696 ¶48.
237. Case C-106/03 P, Vedial SA v. OHIM, 2004 E.C.R. I-9573, 9606 ¶51.
238. Case T-41/12, LS Fashion, LLC v. OHIM, 2015 E.C.R. II-___ ¶
239. Case T-316/07, Commercy AG v. OHIM, 2009 E.C.R. II-43 (summary), at ¶43.
240. Case T-202/03, Alecansan v. OHIM, 2006 E.C.R. II-19 *aff'd on appeal* Case C-196/06 P, Alecansan v. OHIM, 2007 E.C.R. I-36.

company registered the mark for computer hardware and software and electronic products. The Spanish trademark was registered for transportation services and packaging of goods.

The General Court concluded that "although there is a high degree of similarity between the marks now in question, the two marks being almost identical, it is apparent from the foregoing considerations that the goods and services of the trademark applied for and the services covered by the earlier Spanish trademark are not similar. The applicant cannot, therefore, rely on the existence of a likelihood of confusion between the two marks because even the fact that the two marks are identical cannot compensate for the absence of similarity between the services and the goods in question."[241]

In determining whether a likelihood of confusion exists, there is an inverse relationship between the similarity of the marks and the similarity of their designated fields of use.[242] The greater the similarity in appearance, the greater the difference in fields of use needs to be in order to avoid a finding that the trademark will create a likelihood of confusion with a preexisting mark. This is illustrated in *Phillips-Van Heusen Corp. v. Office for Harmonisation in the Internal Market* where a German clothing manufacturer, Pash Textilvertrieb und Einzelhandel GmbH, challenged the registration of the mark "BASS" as a Union trademark which was filed by the U.S. clothing company, Phillips-Van Heusen Corp.[243] The BASS trademark was registered for goods falling within Class 25 of the Nice Agreement concerning the International Classification of Goods and Services for the Purposes of the Registration of Marks of 15 June 1957 "footwear and clothing." Pash had already registered a trademark in German consisting of the word mark PASH for goods falling within Classes 18 and 25 for the purposes of the Nice Agreement "Goods made of leather or of leather imitations and other plastic materials" and "clothing, also made of leather, belts for clothing, footwear, headgear." The General Court held that in view of the fact that the marks were not identical and the fields of use were different, there was no likelihood of confusion on behalf of the public.[244]

Although there is an inverse relationship between the similarity of the marks and the similarity of the designated fields of use, the similarity between the marks is generally given more weight. Moreover, exact identity of the fields of use will not suffice as a basis for likelihood of confusion. There must be some degree of aural, visual, or conceptual similarity between the trademarks themselves. In *Il Ponte Finanziaria SpA v. OHIM*, for example, the proprietor of the trademark "The Bridge" claimed that there was a likelihood of confusion with the subsequently registered mark "Bainbridge" as the two marks were both registered for exactly the same use (leather goods).[245] The ECJ held, however,

---

241. *Id.* at ¶51.
242. Case C-398/07 P, Waterford Wedgwood plc v. Assembled Investments (Proprietary) Ltd., 2009 E.C.R. I-75 (summary), at ¶31; Case C-171/06 P, T.I.M.E. ART v. OHIM, 2007 E.C.R. I-41 (summary), at ¶35.
243. Case T-292/01, Phillips-Van Heusen Corp. v. OHIM, 2003 E.C.R. II-4335, 4357 ¶45.
244. *Id.*
245. Case C-234/06 P, Il Ponte Finanziaria SpA v. OHIM, 2007 E.C.R. I-7367.

that even though the fields of use were identical, the two trademarks were not sufficiently similar in their aural, visual, or conceptual characteristics to create the likelihood of confusion.[246]

According to the Trademark Regulation, "the likelihood of confusion includes the likelihood of association between the sign and the trade mark."[247] This ambiguous wording has given rise to significant litigation over the issue of whether the likelihood of confusion requires a finding of the likelihood of association. The General Court has held that the likelihood of association is not an alternative to the confusion requirement discussed above.[248] In other words, it is not sufficient for the plaintiff to show that the subsequent mark creates a likelihood of association. The likelihood of association does not even give rise to a presumption of confusion.[249] Instead, it is a factor to be considered in the analysis.

(3) Unfair Advantage and Detriment

The owner of a trademark may be able to prevent the subsequent registration of another mark that takes unfair advantage or potentially causes detriment to the earlier mark even without showing the likelihood of confusion.[250] The Trademark Regulation recognizes this relative basis for refusal in order to protect trademarks that have achieved a high level of recognition. For example, it would be unfair to allow the registration of the following logo for real estate agents and appraisers by someone not related to Citibank as it would be taking advantage of the reputation Citibank has secured with its word mark "CITI" even though there is no likelihood of confusion.[251]

There are three fundamental requirements to a successful objection on the basis of unfair advantage or detriment.[252] First, the trademark applied for must be identical with or similar to the earlier trademark. The degree of similarity required under this similarity test differs slightly from the degree required under similarity test pursuant to Article 8(1)(b) of the Trademark Regulation. That provision of the Trademark Regulation, as discussed above, requires that the similarity between the marks creates a likelihood of confusion on the part of the relevant section of the public. The similarity test under Article 8(5) of the Trademark Regulation, however, does not require that high a degree of similarity.[253] It is sufficient for the degree of similarity between those marks to have the effect of stimulating a link between them in the eyes of the relevant

---

246. *Id.* at 7382 ¶48.
247. Trademark Regulation at art. 8(1).
248. Case T-158/05, Trek Bicycle Corp. v. OHIM, 2007 E.C.R. II-49 (summary), at ¶80.
249. Case C-425/98, Marca Mode CV v. Adidas, 2000 E.C.R. I-4861, 4893 ¶39.
250. Trademark Regulation at art. 8(5). It is not necessary that the detriment actually occur. The requirement is that "there is a serious risk that such injury will occur in the future." Case C-100/11 P, Helena Rubenstein SNC v. OHIM, 2012 E.C.R. I-____, at ¶93.
251. Case T-181/05, Citigroup, Inc. v. OHIM, 2008 E.C.R. II-673, 693 ¶64.
252. Case T-480/12, The Coca-Cola Company v. OHIM, 2014 E.C.R. II-____, at ¶25; Case T-525/11, Volvo Trademark Holding AB v. OHIM, 2014 E.C.R. II-____, at ¶18.
253. Joined Cases C-581/13 P and C-582/13 P, Intra-Presse SAS v. OHIM, 2014 E.C.R. I-____, at ¶72; Case C-102/07, adidas AG v. Marca Mode CV, 2008 E.C.R. I-2464, 2479 ¶40.

public.²⁵⁴ The requisite link may exist even though the relevant public is not confused about the marks.²⁵⁵ Whether a link exists is a factual determination that necessitates a close examination of the similarities of the marks and the goods and services they respectively cover. The relevant factors identified by the ECJ are:²⁵⁶

- the degree of similarity between the conflicting marks;
- the nature of the goods or services for which the conflicting marks were registered, including the degree of closeness or dissimilarity between those goods or services, and the relevant section of the public;
- the strength of the earlier mark's reputation;
- the degree of the earlier mark's distinctive character, whether inherent or acquired through use; and
- the existence of the likelihood of confusion on the part of the public.

Second, the earlier trademark must have a reputation in the EU (if a Union mark) or in the member state concerned (if a national mark). This means that the earlier mark must be known by a significant part of the public concerned by the goods or services covered by that trademark.²⁵⁷ If there is no reputation, it is difficult for the proprietor of the earlier trademark to claim that the new applicant is "free-riding" off its reputation or causing a detriment to its mark. As discussed above, the word mark "CITI" owned by Citibank has achieved a strong reputation in the EU to fulfill this requirement.²⁵⁸ Another example of a mark that has achieved a sufficiently strong reputation is "The Beatles." Thus, the owner of The Beatles trademark can prevent the registration of the mark Beatle for wheelchairs as taking unfair advantage of the repute of The Beatles' famous mark.²⁵⁹

The third requirement is the most difficult to apply: the use of the trademark would be detrimental to or take unfair advantage of the distinctive character or the repute of the earlier trademark. There are two types of detriment. Detriment to the distinctive character of a trademark exists when the earlier mark is no longer capable of arousing immediate association with the goods for which it is registered²⁶⁰ or at least that there is a change or serious likelihood of change in

---

254. Joined Cases C-581/13 P and C-582/13 P, Intra-Presse SAS v. OHIM, 2014 E.C.R. I-___, at ¶72; Case T-480/12, The Coca-Cola Company v. OHIM, 2014 E.C.R. II-___, at ¶32.
255. Case C-252/07, Intel Corporation, Inc. v. CPM United Kingdom Ltd., 2008 E.C.R. I-8852, 8864 ¶30; Case T-60/10, Jackson International Trading Co. v. OHIM, 2012 E.C.R. II-___, at ¶49.
256. Case C-252/07, Intel Corporation, Inc. v. CPM United Kingdom Ltd., 2008 E.C.R. I-673, at ¶42; Case T-480/12, The Coca-Cola Company v. OHIM, 2014 E.C.R. II-___, at ¶27.
257. Case T-369/10, You-Q BV v. OHIM, 2011 E.C.R. II-___, at ¶27; Case T-477/04, Aktieselskabet v. OHIM, 2007 E.C.R. II-399 (summary), at ¶48.
258. Case T-181/05, Citigroup, Inc. v. OHIM, 2008 E.C.R. II- 669.
259. Case T-369/10, You-Q BV v. OHIM, 2011 E.C.R. II-___, at ¶74.
260. Case T-47/06, Antarctica Srl v. OHIM, 2007 E.C.R. II-42 (summary), at ¶55.

the economic behavior of the consumer of the particular goods or services for which the mark was registered.[261] Detriment to the repute of an earlier trademark exists when the goods for which the mark is applied appeal to the public's senses in a way that diminishes the power of attraction of the earlier mark.[262] Unfair advantage requires evidence of free-riding on the coattails of a famous mark or an attempt to trade upon its reputation.[263] For example, the use as a keyword in Internet advertising by a competitor of a trademark owned by another competitor would be considered taking unfair advantage of the competitor's trademark.[264] The stronger the link the relevant public will make between the two marks, the greater the likelihood of unfair advantage.[265] In *Antarctica Srl v. OHIM*, for example, an Italian bicycle and ski paraphernalia manufacturer tried to register the mark "nasdaq." The Nasdaq Stock Market Inc., which had earlier registered the "NASDAQ" mark, objected on the grounds that the nasdaq mark used on bicycle and ski paraphernalia would take unfair advantage of the earlier registered NASDAQ mark. Even though there was little likelihood of confusion on the part of the customers because of the different industries, the General Court concluded that "taking account of the similarity of the marks at issue, the importance of the reputation and the highly distinctive character of the trade mark NASDAQ, it must be held that the intervener has established prima facie the existence of a future risk, which is not hypothetical, of unfair advantage being drawn by the applicant, by the use of the mark applied for, from the reputation of the trade mark NASDAQ."[266]

Each of these three requirements must be fulfilled in order for a successful opposition by the owner of the earlier mark. The mere fact that there is a similarity between the latter mark and the earlier mark is not prima facie evidence of unfair use or detriment.[267] In *Spa Monopole v. OHIM*, for example, Spa-Finders Travel Arrangements, a New York travel agency, sought to register the mark "Spa-Finders" for travel agency services and printed publications such as brochures.[268] Spa Monopole, a Belgian bottled water company, argued that Spa-Finders was free-riding on its earlier registered mark and would cause detriment to it. Although the General Court recognized the likelihood of association, it concluded that the evidence did not show that the use of the trademark by Spa Finders would cause detriment to Spa Monopole.

---

261. Case C-383/12 P, Environmental Manufacturing LLP v. OHIM, 2013 E.C.R. I-____, at ¶34.
262. Case T-67/04, Spa Monopole v. OHIM, 2005 E.C.R. II-1829, 1845 ¶46.
263. Case T-369/10, You-Q BV v. OHIM, 2011 E.C.R. II-____ (summary), at ¶63; Case T-67/04, Spa Monopole v. OHIM, 2005 E.C.R. II-1829, 1846 ¶51.
264. Case C-323/09, Interflora, Inc. v. Marks & Spencer plc, 2011 E.C.R. I-8664, 8694 ¶86.
265. Case T-21/07, L'Oréal SA v. Spa Monopole, 2009 E.C.R. II-31 (summary), at ¶39.
266. Case T-47/06, Antarctica Srl v. OHIM, 2007 E.C.R. II-42 (summary), at ¶61 *aff'd on appeal* C-320/07 P, Antarctica Srl v. OHIM, 2009 E.C.R. I-28.
267. Case T-570/10, Environmental Manufacturing LLP v. OHIM, 2012 E.C.R. II-____ (summary), at ¶36; Case T-67/04, Spa Monopole v. OHIM, 2005 E.C.R. II-1829, 1844 ¶44.
268. *Id.*

(4) Trademark Appropriation

Another relative ground for refusal of a trademark application is one in which the trademark has been illegitimately appropriated. Appropriation occurs if a person's agent or representative files a trademark application without the person's consent.[269] This assumes, of course, that the principal is the proper owner of the trademark.

2.3 Scope of Rights Conferred by a Union Trademark

The issue relating to the registrability of a mark should be distinguished from the issue as to the scope of the rights of the proprietor of the trademark. The rights of the trademark proprietor generally correspond to the relative grounds for refusal of registration discussed above. The rights of the trademark proprietor extend not only to preventing a third party from registering a similar mark but also to preventing a third party from using a similar mark. The basic right that the registration of a Union trademark confers on its proprietor is the right, for a period of 10 years beginning on the date of registration, to prevent a third party from using an identical or confusing mark or one that would be unfair or detrimental.[270] The use of a name as a company name is not "use" for purposes of trademark law because it is not used for distinguishing goods or services.[271]

Examples of use include offering the goods for sale, offering or supplying services using the trademark, importing or exporting the goods with the trademark, or using the sign on business letterhead or in advertising.[272] In contrast, a company filling cans or packages provided by a third party is not using the mark in the event that the mark on the can or package provided by the third party infringes another trademark.[273] Similarly, an online marketplace such as eBay does not "use" trademarks when it allows third parties to sell products on its web platform.[274]

As trademark protection is limited to the territory of the EU,[275] the use must be in the EU in order to be prohibited. In *Eli Lilly & Company v. 8pm Chemist Ltd.*, Eli Lilly claimed that the shipment of Eli Lilly pharmaceutical products from Turkey to the United States via England violated Eli Lilly's registered EU trademark. Individuals in the United States had ordered these pharmaceutical products to take advantage of lower prices for the same Eli Lilly pharmaceutical

---

269. Trademark Regulation at art. 8(3).
270. Trademark Regulation at art. 9.
271. Case C-17/06, Céline SARL v. Céline SA, 2007 E.C.R.I-7060, 7069 ¶21; Decision of the German Supreme Court (BGH) of Sept. 13, 2007 *reported at* 58 Recht der Internationalen Wirtschaft 242 (2008).
272. Case C-661/11, Martin Y Paz Diffusion SA v. Depuydt, 2013 E.C.R. I-____, at ¶62.
273. Case C-119/10, Frisdranken Industrie Winters BV v. Red Bull GmbH, 2011 E.C.R. II-13194, 13206 ¶34.
274. Case C-324/09, L'Oréal SA v. eBay International AG, 2011 E.C.R. I-6073, 6115 ¶105
275. Case C-235/09, DHL Express France SAS v. Chronopost SA, 2011 E.C.R. I-2825, 2844-46 ¶¶45-50.

products in Turkey. The court in this case held that there was no trademark infringement because the goods were not in free circulation in the UK.[276]

(a) *Identical Marks*

The obvious right enjoyed by the proprietor of the trademark is the right to prevent third parties from using any sign that is identical with the Union trademark in relation to goods or services that are identical with those for which the Union trademark is registered.[277] This corresponds to the right of the trademark proprietor to prevent registration of an identical trademark.[278] In *Google France SARL v. Louis Vuitton Malletier SA*, for example, certain Internet sellers of imitation Vuitton handbags used the keywords "Louis Vuitton" and other trademarks of Louis Vuitton Malletier SA to attract buyers to their websites. The keywords and the trademarks were identical. The ECJ held that this constituted use by a third party of a sign that is identical to a registered trademark.[279]

The use of the identical trademark cannot be prohibited merely because it is identical. The trademark proprietor must also show that the identical mark is liable to cause an adverse effect to one of the functions of the trademark.[280] Those functions include not only the essential function of the trademark (i.e., to guarantee to consumers the origin of the goods or services) but also any of its other functions, such as guaranteeing the quality of the goods or services.[281]

In *Die BergSpechte Outdoor Reisen und Alpinschule Edi Koblmüller GmbH v. Guni*, for example, an Austrian adventure travel tour organizer, trekking.at, used the terms "Bergspechte" and "Edi Kolbmüller"—which were part of the trademarks of a competing adventure tour organizer—as keywords in a Google referencing service. The use of these keywords resulted in the trekking.at website appearing as a sponsored link on the screen of Internet users entering Google searches with the words "Bergspechte" or "Edi Kolbmüller." The ECJ examined whether the use of the terms in the Internet referencing service caused an adverse effect to one of the functions of the trademark. According to the ECJ, the function of indicating origin is adversely affected when Internet users are shown, on the basis of a keyword identical with a mark, a third party's ad and the ad does not enable normally informed and reasonably attentive Internet users, or enables them only with difficulty, to ascertain whether the goods or services referred to by the ad originate from the proprietor of the trademark or

---

276. Eli Lilly & Company v. 8PM Chemist Ltd., [2008] EWCA Civ 24, Court of Appeal for England and Wales, Feb. 5, 2008.
277. Trademark Regulation at art. 9(1)(a).
278. Trademark Regulation at art. 8(1)(a).
279. Case C-236/08, Google France SARL v. Louis Vuitton Malletier SA, 2010 E.C.R. I-2467, 2508 ¶99.
280. Case C-323/09, Interflora, Inc. v. Marks & Spencer plc, 2011 E.C.R. I-8664, 8678 ¶34; Case C-278/08, Die BergSpechte Outdoor Reisen und Alpinschule Edi Koblmüller GmbH v. Guni, 2010 E.C.R. I-2520, 2531 ¶30.
281. Case C-65/12, Leidseplein Beheer BV v. Red Bull GmbH, 2014 E.C.R. I-____, at ¶30; Case C-278/08, Die BergSpechte Outdoor Reisen und Alpinschule Edi Koblmüller GmbH v. Guni, 2010 E.C.R. I-2520, 2531 ¶31.

an undertaking economically connected to it or, on the contrary, originate from a third party.[282] The ECJ remanded the case to the national court to make these factual determinations.

The right to prevent third parties from using any identical sign also applies to identical signs that are also registered Union trademarks.[283] This situation of dueling Union trademark is possible because the acceptance of a registration by the OHIM is not conclusive even if the OHIM has determined that the applicant has met all of the absolute criteria for registration. Consequently, an applicant may register a trademark that is identical to an earlier registered trademark. The Trademark Regulation allows the prior applicant to prevent the subsequent applicant from using that mark. The prior applicant is not necessarily required to have the subsequent registration declared invalid based on one of the bases of invalidity discussed below.[284]

(b) Likelihood of Confusion

The trademark holder may also prohibit a third party from using any sign where, because of its identity with or similarity to the Union trademark and the identity or similarity of the goods or services covered by the Union trademark and the sign, creates a likelihood of confusion on the part of the public.[285] The threshold question is whether the marks are identical or similar. The ECJ has held that even if the earlier mark is highly distinctive, if the marks are not similar, the distinctiveness of the earlier mark is not relevant.[286]

The "likelihood of confusion" standard means that there is a risk that the public might believe that the goods or services in question come from the same company or economically linked companies.[287] This corresponds to the right of

---

282. Case C-278/08, Die BergSpechte Outdoor Reisen und Alpinschule Edi Koblmüller GmbH v. Guni, 2010 E.C.R. I-2520, 2532 ¶35. *See also* Case C-324/09, L'Oréal SA v. eBay International AG, 2011 E.C.R. I-6073, 6113 ¶97.

283. Case C-561/11, Fédération Cynologique Internationale v Federación Canina Internacional de Perros de Pura Raza, 2013 E.C.R. I-____, at ¶33 ("First of all, it should be noted that Article 9(1) of the Regulation does not make any distinction on the basis of whether the third party is the proprietor of a Community trade mark or not. Thus, that provision grants the proprietor of a Community trade mark an exclusive right to prevent 'any third party', not having its consent, from using, in the course of trade, any signs liable to infringe its mark.")

284. Case C-561/11, Fédération Cynologique Internationale v Federación Canina Internacional de Perros de Pura Raza, 2013 E.C.R. I-____, at ¶52 ("Article 9(1) of the Regulation must be interpreted as meaning that the exclusive right of the proprietor of a [Union] trade mark to prohibit all third parties from using, in the course of trade, signs identical with or similar to its trade mark extends to a third-party proprietor of a later registered Community trade mark, without the need for that latter mark to have been declared invalid beforehand.").

285. Trademark Regulation at art. 9(1)(b).

286. Case C-558/12 P, OHIM v. riha WeserGold Getränke GmbH & Co KG, 2014 E.C.R. I-____, at ¶48.

287. Case C-51/09 P, Becker v. OHIM, 2010 E.C.R. I-5822, 5832 ¶31; Case C-278/08, Die BergSpechte Outdoor Reisen und Alpinschule Edi Koblmüller GmbH v. Guni, 2010 E.C.R. I-2520, 2533 ¶38.

the trademark proprietor to prevent the registration of a similar trademark that is likely to cause confusion among the public.[288] In both cases, the characteristics of the relevant public are important in determining whether a likelihood of confusion exists. For example, cigarette smokers tend to pay close attention to the brand name of cigarettes. Therefore, confusion may not be created when two cigarette manufacturers use similar brand names such as "POWER" and "TURKISH POWER."[289] If, however, the relevant public in that case were the general public, a likelihood of confusion may have existed because the general public "normally perceives a mark as a whole and does not proceed to analyse its various details."[290]

(c) Unfair Advantage

Finally, a trademark holder may prohibit a third party from using a sign which—without due cause—takes unfair advantage of *or* is detrimental to, the distinctive character or the repute of the Union trademark provided that the mark has a reputation in the EU.[291] The holder of a trademark with a reputation only has to show unfair advantage or detriment, but not both.[292] In either case, however, there must be a link between them.[293] This does not mean that the trademark owner has to show confusion.[294]

A mark has a reputation in the EU when it is known by a "significant part of the public concerned" in relation to the particular goods or services.[295] The relevant geographical area must comprise a "substantial part of the territory of the [Union]."[296] The General Court has expressly refused to identify a specific percentage of the public in which the trademark must have a reputation.[297] However, the ECJ has held that a single member state (in that case Austria) may comprise a substantial part of the EU.[298]

The right to prevent unfair advantage or detriment only extends to the use by a third party without due cause. There is no codified definition of due cause. In *Interflora Inc. v. Marks & Spencer plc*, the ECJ held that a third party has due cause to use a trademark in a keyword advertisement displayed on the Internet as long as the use of the trademark in that context does not dilute, tarnish, or

---

288. Trademark Regulation at art. 8(1)(b).
289. Case T-34/04, Plus Warenhandelsgesellschaft mbH v. OHIM, 2005 E.C.R. II-2401.
290. Case C-51/09 P, Becker v. OHIM, 2010 E.C.R. I-5822, 5832 ¶33.
291. Trademark Regulation at art. 9(1)(c).
292. C-65/12, Leidseplein Beheer BV v. Red Bull GmbH, 2014 E.C.R. I-____, at ¶40.
293. Case T-74/13, Compagnie des montres Longines, Francillon SA v. OHIM, 2015 E.C.R. II-____ at ¶123.
294. Case C-136/08 P, Japan Tobacco v. OHIM, 2009 E.C.R. II-70 (summary), at ¶25 (reported in the electronic reports of cases at ECLI:EU:C:2009:282).
295. Case C-301/07, PAGO International GmbH v. Tirolmilch registriete Genossenschaft mbH, 2009 E.C.R. I-9447, 9455 ¶24.
296. *Id.* at 9455 ¶27.
297. Case T-74/13, Compagnie des montres Longines, Francillon SA v. OHIM, 2015 E.C.R. II-____ at ¶87.
298. *Id.* at 9455 ¶29.

otherwise adversely affect the functions of the trademark.[299] However, the EU courts tend to consider it an affirmative defense: if the trademark proprietor proves unfair advantage or detriment, the burden shifts to the third party that it has due cause to use its mark in that particular way.[300]

(d) Limitations

The trademark rights of the proprietor are limited in several important ways. Of course, the trademark is limited to the field of use designated in the application. As discussed above, when registering the trademark, the applicant is required to identify a "class" of use. The classes are defined in the Nice Agreement on International Classification of Goods and Services for the Purpose of the Registration of Marks of 15 June 1997.

A trademark does not entitle the proprietor to prohibit a third party from using his own name or address[301] or indications concerning the kind, quality, quantity, intended purpose, value, geographical origin, the time of production of goods or of rendering of the service, or other characteristics of goods or services.[302] This is, however, subject to an important limitation: the third party must be acting in accordance with honest commercial practices.[303] For example, Gerry Apple could not free ride off the efforts of Apple Computer and start selling computers using the "Apple" trademark. Even though it is her name, she is likely using it only to take advantage of the goodwill Apple Computer has built up.

The proprietor of a trademark cannot prevent a third party from using that mark where it is necessary to inform the public of the nature of the products or the intended purpose of the services offered.[304] For example, a seller of spare parts may advertise that its products are compatible for use in a trademarked product.[305] A company that makes razor blades that are compatible with Gillette razors may use the Gillette trade name in advertising the compatibility of its razors with the Gillette handles.[306] The fundamental requirement is that the information conveyed to the public by the use of the trademark cannot be communicated without using the trademark.[307]

A disclaimer that the trademarked products do not originate from the proprietor of the trademark is not necessarily a defense to a trademark infringement claim. In *Arsenal Football Club v. Reed*,[308] Matthew Reed sold scarves with the Arsenal soccer team's name and logo. In an attempt to avoid

---

299. Case C-323/09, Interflora Inc. v. Marks & Spencer plc, 2011 E.C.R. I-8664, 8696 ¶91.
300. C-65/12, Leidseplein Beheer BV v. Red Bull GmbH, 2014 E.C.R. I-____, at ¶44.
301. Trademark Regulation at art. 12(a); Trademark Directive at art. 6(1)(a).
302. Trademark Regulation at art. 12(a); Trademark Directive at art. 6(1)(b).
303. Case C-17/06, Céline SARL v. Céline SA, 2007 E.C.R. I-7041, at ¶33.
304. Trademark Regulation at art. 12(a); Trademark Directive at art. 6(1)(c).
305. Case C-63/97, Bayerische Motorenwerke AG v. Deenik, 1999 E.C.R. I-905.
306. Case C-228/03, The Gillette Company v. LA-Laboratories Ltd. Oy, 2005 E.C.R. I-2337.
307. *Id.* at 2379 ¶35.
308. Case C-206/01, Arsenal Football Club v. Reed, 2002 E.C.R. I-10299.

infringing Arsenal's trademark, he attached a sign on his stall outside the stadium that read:

> The word or logo(s) on the goods offered for sale, are used solely to adorn the product and does not imply or indicate any affiliation or relationship with the manufacturers or distributors of any other product, only goods with official Arsenal merchandise tags are official Arsenal merchandise.

The ECJ held that this disclaimer did not eliminate the likelihood of confusion because "there is a clear possibility in the present case that some consumers, in particular if they come across the goods after they have been sold by Reed and taken away from the stall where the notice appears, may interpret the sign as designating Arsenal FC as the undertaking of origin of the goods."[309]

The trademark owner is also prevented from relying on its trademark rights to prohibit the use of its trademark in permissible comparative advertising under the Misleading and Comparative Advertising Directive. As discussed in greater detail in Chapter XI, comparative advertising refers to advertising that explicitly or by implication identifies another undertaking or goods or services offered by a competitor.[310] This could include use of the competitor's trademark. In *O2 Holdings Ltd. v. Hutchinson 3G UK Ltd.*, Hutchinson 3G ran a series of advertisements drawing comparisons between its services and those of its competitors.[311] In these advertisements, Hutchinson used depictions of bubbles that were quite similar to the bubbles that O2 had trademarked and was using. Hutchinson argued that the use of the bubbles in the comparative advertising did not infringe O2's trademark rights because its use complied with the requirements of the Misleading and Comparative Advertising Directive. The ECJ held that although this is technically "use" of a trademark, Hutchinson was permitted to use the trademark in comparative advertising as long as it met all the requirements of the Misleading and Comparative Advertising Directive and is not confusing.[312] If the comparative advertising clearly differentiates the two products—which is the purpose of comparative advertising—the likelihood of confusion will be low and therefore the use of the trademark is permitted.

(e) Property Rights

Although trademark rights are intangible, they are in many respects treated similarly to property rights in tangible objects. A Union trademark may be sold or otherwise conveyed or licensed to a third party on an exclusive or nonexclusive basis.[313] It may also be used, similar to tangible property, as security for the performance of an obligation or the payment of a debt.[314]

---

309. *Id.* at 10318 ¶57.
310. Misleading and Comparative Advertising Directive at art. 2(c).
311. Case C-533/06, O2 Holdings Ltd. v. Hutchinson 3G UK Ltd., 2008 E.C.R. I-4254.
312. *Id.* at 4274 ¶69.
313. Trademark Regulation at arts. 17(1) and 22(1). An agreement to transfer a Union trademark must be in writing. *Id.* at art. 17(3).
314. *Id.* at art. 19.

2.4 Duration

The rights conferred by a Union trademark last for a period of 10 years beginning on the date of registration with the OHIM.[315] This temporal limitation is of little practical relevance as the registration can be unilaterally extended for additional 10-year periods.

2.5 Cancellation

The filing and subsequent acceptance of a trademark application does not mean that the owner of the trademark achieves a "safe harbor" or absolute protection. As stated above, the protection accorded the trademark is limited in its duration. Moreover, the trademark application is subject to cancellation by revocation or invalidity. The cancellation of a trademark registration can occur as a result of a challenge brought by a third party[316] or a counterclaim brought by the defendant in infringement proceedings. For example, if the proprietor of a Union trademark brings an infringement proceeding against a third party, that third party may counterclaim that the registered trademark owned by the plaintiff in the case should be revoked or is invalid. The difference between revocation and invalidity relates to the point in time at which the rights in the trademark are deemed to exist. The revocation of a trademark means that the trademark is considered not to have effects as of the date of application for revocation (or if raised in the context of a counterclaim, then from the date of the counterclaim).[317] By contrast, if a trademark is considered invalid, it is considered not to have the protections accorded by the Trademark Regulation from the beginning.[318]

(a) Revocation

The rights of the proprietor of the trademark that has been registered with the OHIM may be revoked on application to the OHIM or in response to a counterclaim in infringement proceedings for three reasons: non-use, the mark has become a common name, or the mark is liable to mislead the public.[319]

(1) Non-Use

There is a general expectation that a registered mark will be used. A trademark can be revoked upon application to the OHIM by any third party if the owner of the trademark fails to put the trademark to genuine use in the Union for a

---

315. *Id.* at art. 46.
316. The application for revocation does not have to be filed by a third party with a direct interest in the case. It can be filed by a third party in the public interest. Case C-408/08 P, Lancôme parfums et beauté & Cie SNC v. OHIM, 2010 E.C.R. I-1371, 1383 ¶40.
317. Trademark Regulation at art. 55(1).
318. Trademark Regulation at art. 55(2).
319. *Id.* at art. 51.

continuous period of five years.[320] The public policy rationale behind the use requirement is that the use of a trademark is the quid pro quo for the grant of exclusivity by the state.[321] The five-year period does not necessarily have to start upon registration of the mark. For example, if the owner is using the mark for a year after registration, and then ceases using it for five consecutive years, that owner may no longer claim trademark protection.

The concept of "genuine use" is central in each of these scenarios. According to the General Court, "there is genuine use of a trade mark where the mark is used in accordance with its essential function, which is to guarantee the identity of the origin of the goods or services for which it is registered, in order to create or preserve an outlet for those goods or services; genuine use does not include token use for the sole purpose of preserving the rights conferred by the mark. Moreover, the condition of genuine use of the mark requires that that mark, as protected on the relevant territory, be used publicly and outwardly."[322] The "publicly and outwardly" requirement means that the internal use of a mark—for example, the use of the mark in internal company communications—does not qualify as genuine use.[323]

Whether a trademark has been put to genuine use is a question of fact which is not always easy to prove. Clearly, the use of the trademark for the sole purpose of preserving the rights, i.e., token use, does not qualify as genuine use.[324] The scale and frequency of the use are important factors. In examining the scale and frequency, the courts consider the commercial volume of the overall use, its duration, and its frequency.[325] Although the commercial success of the trademark is not necessary to prove genuine use,[326] the sales volume may be a relevant indication of genuine use.[327] If the owner of the prior trademark can show that he or she used the trademark on millions of Euros worth of products, it is unlikely that such use will be deemed merely token. In *Silberquelle GmbH v. Maselli-Strickmode GmbH*, prior use of a trademark on a product the trademark

---

320. *Id.* at art. 51(a). The use requirement applies to each category for which the trademarks are registered. If, for example, the trademark is registered from protection in two categories, but the owner fails to use the trademark in one category, the trademark protection can be revoked only for the category where non-use occurred. Case C-495/07, Silberquelle GmbH v. Maselli-Strickmode GmbH, 2009 E.C.R. I-152, 159 ¶19.
321. Case C-610/11 P, Centrotherm Systemtechnik GmbH v. OHIM, 2013 E.C.R. I-____, at ¶53.
322. Case T-132/12, Scooters India Ltd. v. OHIM, 2014 E.C.R. II-____, at ¶16.
323. Case T-514/10, Fruit of the Loom, Inc. v. OHIM, 2012 E.C.R. II-____, at ¶58.
324. Case C-234/06 P, Il Ponte Finanziaria SpA v. OHIM, 2007 E.C.R. I-7367, 7389 ¶72; Case T-308/06, Buffalo Milke Automotive Polishing v. OHIM, 2011 E.C.R. II-7887, 7903 ¶47; Case T-203/02, The Sunrider Corp. v. OHIM, 2004 E.C.R. II-2815, 2828 ¶39.
325. Joined cases T-495/12 to 497/12, European Drinks SA v. OHIM, 2014 E.C.R. II-____, at ¶26; Case T-514/10, Fruit of the Loom, Inc. v. OHIM, 2012 E.C.R. II-____, at ¶49.
326. Case T-41/12, LS Fashion, LLC v. OHIM, 2015 E.C.R. II-____ ¶20; Case T-278/13, Now Wireless Ltd. v OHIM, 2015 E.C.R. II-____ at ¶45; Case T-504/09, Völkl GmbH & Co. KG v. OHIM, 2011 E.C.R. II-8183, 8208 ¶77.
327. Case T-28/09, Park v. OHIM, 2011 E.C.R. II-1 (summary), at ¶85; Case T-131/06, Sonia Rykiel v. OHIM, 2008 E.C.R. II- 67 (summary), at ¶40.

owner gave away as a promotion and never sold was insufficient to constitute use under the Trademark Directive.[328]

Conversely, the negative inference of a low sales volume "may be offset by the fact that the use of the mark was extensive or very regular."[329] In *LS Fashion, LLC v. OHIM*, sales of only €600 were sufficient to establish genuine use in combination with other factors.[330] *The Sunrider Corp. v. OHIM*, €4,800 of sales of a fruit juice were sufficient to illustrate genuine use as the owner of the prior trademark could show that it had made efforts to market the product.[331]

The General Court has explicitly refused to identify a sales threshold for genuine use.[332] The requisite commercial volume depends on how extensively the mark was used.[333] If the trademark proprietor can show that the mark was used widely and regularly in the EU, the proprietor will not be required to show high commercial volumes. Conversely, if the proprietor cannot show that the mark was widely used, the proprietor will have to show significant commercial volumes. In cases where the sales referenced to prove genuine use are relatively low, the General Court examines whether the use was indicative of an attempt to maintain or create market share in the relevant market.[334] Relevant considerations may be the intensity of sales promotion and advertising efforts and the duration of those sales and efforts.[335]

In *Verein Radetzky-Orden v. Bundesvereinigung Kameradschaft 'Feldmarschall Radetzky'*, the question arose whether the use of a mark by a nonprofit association can constitute genuine use even though it was not used for a commercial purpose.[336] Although the ECJ held that a non-profit association couold register a mark which it intended to use only for non-profit purposes, the court distinguished between internal use and external use. In this particular case, the use of the mark exclusively for its own internal ceremonies and events did not constitute genuine use for purposes of the Trademark Directive.[337]

The burden is on the owner of the prior trademark to proffer evidence of its prior use.[338] In *Kabushiki Kaisha Fernandes v. OHIM*, the owner of the trademark "HIWATT," which was registered in Germany, France, and Italy, challenged the subsequent registration of HIWATT with the OHIM by a third

---

328. Case C-495/07, Silberquelle GmbH v. Maselli-Strickmode GmbH, 2009 E.C.R. I-152, 159 ¶20 (the product was given away to customers who purchased €600 of other merchandise.).
329. Case T-41/12, LS Fashion, LLC v. OHIM, 2015 E.C.R. II-___ ¶24.
330. *Id.* at ¶39.
331. Case T-203/02, The Sunrider Corp. v. OHIM, 2004 E.C.R. II-2811, 2830 ¶48.
332. Case T-504/09, Völkl GmbH & Co. KG v. OHIM, 2011 E.C.R. II-8183, 8209 ¶82.
333. Case T-524/12, Recaro Holding GmbH v. OHIM, 2013 E.C.R. II-___, at ¶20.
334. Case T-504/09, Völkl GmbH & Co. KG v. OHIM, 2011 E.C.R. II-8183, 8209 ¶82.
335. According to the General Court, the relevant sales and marketing efforts need not be to the end user. Evidence of promotional efforts to the industry at trade shows is relevant. Case T-524/12, Recaro Holding GmbH v. OHIM, 2013 E.C.R. II-___, at ¶26.
336. Case C-442/07, Verein Radetzky-Orden v. Bundesvereinigung Kameradschaft 'Feldmarschall Radetzky', 2008 E.C.R. I-9223.
337. *Id.* at 9241 ¶22.
338. Case C-610/11 P, Centrotherm Systemtechnik GmbH v. OHIM, 2013 E.C.R. I-___, at ¶62.

party.[339] Because the only evidence of prior use submitted by the owner of the prior registered trademark was a U.S. sales catalog showing that the speakers with the HIWATT trademark were being sold in the Unites States, the General Court rejected the challenge. In *Laboratories RTB v. OHIM*, the General Court held that the owner of the "AIR GIORGI" trademark did not adequately prove genuine prior use of that mark and consequently could not challenge the subsequent registration of the trademark "GIORGIO AIRE."[340] The General Court concluded that the handful of invoices and catalog references submitted by the owner of the AIR GIORGI mark were insufficient to show that it had consistently used the mark in the prior five years.[341]

It is not necessary that the genuine use occur in each member state. It is sufficient that it is used in only a part of the EU—even a single member state.[342] This is another advantage of the Union trademark over national trademarks. If a company registers national trademarks in each of the member states, that company would be required to put the trademark to genuine use in each of those member states in order to maintain trademark protection throughout the entire EU.

The use must relate to all of the goods or services for which it is registered. As discussed above, a trademark applicant is required to designate the specific types of goods or services relating to the trademark the applicant is registering. A trademark may be registered for several categories of goods or services. In the event that the applicant uses the trademark in relation to only certain of these goods or services, the trademark may be declared invalid for non-use relating to the other categories of goods or services for which it was registered but not used.[343]

(2) Generic

If the trademark has become the common name in the trade for a product or service in respect of which it is registered, it may be revoked upon application to the OHIM or in the context of an infringement proceeding.[344] The generic character of the trademark must have been a consequence of acts or inactivity of the proprietor. Although neither the Trademark Regulation nor the Trademark Directive identifies which acts or inactivity may be sufficient to revoke a trademark, the ECJ has stated that it "includes all those by which the proprietor of a trademark shows that he is not sufficiently vigilant as regards the preservation of the distinctive character of his trade mark."[345]

---

339. Case T-39/01, Kabushiki Kaisha Fernandes v. OHIM, 2002 E.C.R. II-5233.
340. Case T-156/01, Laboratories RTB v. OHIM, 2003 E.C.R. II-2792.
341. *Id.* at 2810 ¶47.
342. Case T-237/10, Louis Vuitton Malletier v. OHIM, 2011 E.C.R. II-449 (summary), at ¶98 (reported in the electronic reports of cases at ECLI:EU:T:2011:741) *aff'd on appeal* Case C-97/12P, Louis Vuitton Malletier v. OHIM, 2014 E.C.R. I-____.
343. Case T-278/13, New Wireless Ltd. v. OHIM, 2015 E.C.R. II - ____ at ¶24; Case T- 196/13, Nanu-Nana Joachim Hoepp GmbH & Co. KG v. OHIM, 2014 E.C.R. II-____, at ¶36.
344. Trademark Regulation at art. 51(1)(b).
345. C-409/12, Backaldrin Österreich The Kornspitz Company GmbH v. Pfahnl Backmittel GmbH, 2014 E.C.R. I-____, at ¶34.

(3) Misleading

A trademark may also be revoked by the OHIM if it is liable to mislead the public.[346] This refers, in particular, to the nature, quality, or geographical origin of the goods or services. In order to be revoked, however, the capacity of the mark to mislead the public must be in consequence of the use made of it by the trademark proprietor (or with the consent of the proprietor). Therefore, if a third party is using the mark in a misleading manner, the protection accorded to the proprietor will not necessarily be revoked.

(b) Invalidity

A registered Union trademark may be declared invalid either on application to the OHIM or on the basis of a counterclaim in infringement proceedings. The mark may be declared invalid in respect to all of the goods and services for which it was registered or only partially. There are several bases of invalidity.

(1) Contrary to Absolute Grounds for Refusal

A trademark can be declared invalid if it has been registered contrary to the absolute grounds for refusal.[347] As discussed above, the OHIM is supposed to test the absolute grounds for refusal when a trademark application is filed. The OHIM's acceptance of a registration is not conclusive even if the OHIM has determined that the applicant has met all of the absolute criteria for registration.[348] Even after a mark is registered with and accepted by the OHIM, a third party may apply to the OHIM to invalidate the trademark if it fails to meet the absolute grounds for refusal.[349] In *Mars v. OHIM*, for example, the U.S. confectionary producer Mars registered with the OHIM a three-dimensional rendering of its product. After the OHIM accepted the application and permitted the trademark, a competitor filed a claim for invalidity, arguing that the trademark lacked distinctiveness. The General Court agreed with the competitor and invalidated Mars's previously registered trademark.[350]

(2) Bad Faith

A trademark may also be declared invalid if the applicant, at the time of the application, was acting in bad faith.[351] For example, if a distributor knew that the manufacturer was using a particular mark, and then the distributor registered that mark before the manufacturer, that registration is likely to be considered

---

346. Trademark Regulation at art. 51(1)(c).
347. *Id.* at art. 52(1)(a).
348. Case C-561/11, Fédération Cynologique Internationale v Federación Canina Internacional de Perros de Pura Raza, 2013 E.C.R. I-____, at ¶33.
349. If, however, the mark has achieved a distinctive character between the time of registration and when it is subsequently challenged, it may not be declared invalid for lack of distinctive character. Trademark Regulation at art. 52(2).
350. Case T-28/08, Mars, Inc. v. OHIM, 2009 E.C.R. II-106 (summary), at ¶68.
351. Trademark Regulation at art. 52(1)(b). The party seeking a declaration that the trademark was registered in bad faith carries the burden of proof. Case T-327/12, Simca Europe Ltd. v. OHIM, 2014 E.C.R. II-____, at ¶35

to be in bad faith.[352] However, the fact that the applicant knew that the third party was already using the sign outside the EU or the particular member state for which registration is sought does not establish a prima facie case of bad faith.[353] The determination of bad faith is a factual determination that will differ in each case. The ECJ has identified the following factors that are "in particular" relevant:[354]

- Whether the applicant knows or on the basis of the facts must have known that a third party is using the same or similar sign or mark in another member state for the same or similar products (and that the two signs or marks at issue are confusingly similar);
- Whether the applicant has the intention of preventing that third party from continuing to use such a mark or sign;
- The degree of legal protection enjoyed by the third party's sign and by the sign for which registration is sought. If, for example, the applicant's mark already has a reputation in the Union, it is less likely that the applicant is acting in bad faith.

(3) Existence of Earlier Identical Mark

A Union trademark may be declared invalid on application to the OHIM or on the basis of a counterclaim in infringement proceedings where there is an earlier identical or similar registered trademark.[355] In *Intermarcas v. García*, for example, Intermarcas successfully registered the following mark with the OHIM for clothing:

ESTÚDIO CHOCOLATE

Two years later, Mr. García came across Intermarcas's mark and claimed that it created a likelihood of confusion with the following mark which he had registered two years prior to the registration of Intermarcas's mark for shirts:

---

352. This applies even if the manufacturer was using the mark outside the EU. Decision of the OHIM Board of Appeal in case R 529/2008-4 (Apr. 1, 2009) at ¶14.
353. Case C-320/12, Malaysia Dairy Industries Pte. Ltd. v. Ankenævnet for Patenter og Varmærker, 2013 E.C.R. I-___, at ¶36; Case T-506/13, Urb Rulmenti Suceava SA v. OHIM, 2014 E.C.R. II-___, at ¶47.
354. Case C-529/07, Chocoladefabriken Lindt & Sprüngli AG v. Franz Hauswirth GmbH, 2009 E.C.R. I-4918, 4934 ¶53. This list of factors is not exhaustive. Case T-33/11, Peeters Landbouwmachines BV v. OHIM, 2012 E.C.R. II-___, at ¶20. "Account may also be taken of the commercial logic underlying the filing of the application for registration of that sign as a [Union] trademark, and the chronology of events leading to that filing." Case T-506/13, Urb Rulmenti Suceava SA v. OHIM, 2014 E.C.R. II-___, at ¶47 (citations omitted).
355. Trademark Regulation at art. 53(1).

CH CHOCOLATE

The OHIM's Board of Appeal concluded that there was a likelihood of confusion and consequently the earlier trademark, even though successfully registered, was declared invalid.[356]

Even if the earlier trademark is not registered, the proprietor of that earlier nonregistered trademark can seek invalidity of the subsequently registered trademark.[357] In *Last Minute Network Ltd. v. OHIM*, for example, a company using the unregistered mark "lastminute.com" sought cancellation of the registered trademark "Last Minute Tour" which was registered with and accepted by the OHIM. The General Court held that even though the mark "lastminute.com" was not registered, it could be relied upon to invalidate the registered trademark.[358] The two fundamental requirements are that the nonregistered mark must have more than mere local significance and EU or national law recognize rights of the nonregistered trademark to prohibit the use of a subsequent trademark.

(4) Conflict with Other Prior Rights

A Union trademark may also be declared invalid on application to the OHIM or on the basis of a counterclaim in infringement proceedings where the use of the trademark may be prohibited pursuant to another earlier right under the Union legislation or national law governing its protection.[359] This includes, for example, a right to a name, a right of personal portrayal, a copyright, or an industrial property right.

2.6 Protection for Unregistered Trademarks and Trademarks of Local Significance

The rights attaching to a Union trademark can only be secured by registration under the Trademark Regulation.[360] However, neither the Trademark Regulation[361] nor the Trademark Directive[362] preempts the member states from

---

356. Intermarcas v. García, Decision of the OHIM Board of Appeal in case R 292/2008-1 (Sept. 17, 2008) at ¶17.
357. Trademark Regulation at art. 53(1)(c).
358. Joined Cases T-114/07 and T-115/07, Last Minute Network Ltd. v. OHIM, 2009 E.C.R. II-1921, 1948 ¶102.
359. Trademark Regulation at art. 53(2).
360. *Id.* at preamble ¶7.
361. *Id.* at preamble ¶6.
362. Trademark Directive at preamble ¶7.

recognizing unregistered trademarks.[363] The Trademark Regulation makes accommodation for this possibility by recognizing the unregistered trademark in two respects. First, registration of a mark may be opposed or declared invalid if all of the following four conditions are fulfilled:[364] (1) the unregistered mark is used in the course of trade; (2) it is of more than mere local significance; (3) it confers on its proprietor (under EU law or national law)[365] the right to prohibit the use of a subsequent trademark; (4) rights to the unregistered mark under national law were acquired prior to the date of application for registration of the EU mark.[366]

The standard of "use in the course of trade" is different from the standard of "genuine use" discussed below in the context of the revocation of a registered trademark.[367] Instead of genuine use, the standard is "must actually be used in a sufficiently significant manner in the course of trade. In order to ascertain whether that is the case, account must be taken of the duration and intensity of the use of that sign as a distinctive element vis-a-vis its addressees, namely purchasers and consumers as well as suppliers and competitors."[368] A mark is used in the course of trade "where that use occurs in the context of commercial activity with a view to economic advantage and not as a private matter."[369]

The requirement of "more than mere local significance" means not only that the geographic territory must be beyond local, but also that the sign actually be used in a substantial part of that territory.[370] According to the ECJ, "In order to ascertain whether that is the case, account must be taken of the duration and intensity of the use of that sign as a distinctive element vis-à-vis its addressees, namely purchasers and consumers as well as suppliers and competitors. In that regard, the use made of the sign in advertising and commercial correspondence is of particular relevance."[371]

The party making the assertion must not only show that the unregistered mark is recognized by that law, but also that the law allows that party to prohibit the subsequent registration of a similar mark by a third party. It is not necessary,

---

363. In the UK, for example, the law of passing off may protect the goodwill associated with a brand or mark from third parties taking advantage of the goodwill even though the brand or mark is not a registered trademark. Fage UK Ltd. v. Chobani UK Ltd., [2013] EWHC 630 (Ch).
364. Trademark Regulation at art. 8(4) and 53(1)(c).
365. Joined Cases T-225/06, T-255/06, T-257/06 and T-309/06, Budějovický Budvar, národní podnik v. OHIM, 2009 E.C.R. II-3563, 3587 ¶79.
366. Case T-435/05, Danjaq LLC v. OHIM, 2009 E.C.R. II-2100, 2115 ¶35.
367. Case C-96/09 P, Anheuser-Busch, Inc. v. Budějovický Budvar, národní podnik, 2011 E.C.R. I-2177, 2219 ¶142; Case T-430/08, Grain Millers, Inc. v. OHIM, 2010 E.C.R. II-145 (summary), at ¶26.
368. Case T-344/13, Out of the blue KG v. OHIM, 2014 E.C.R. II-___, at ¶23.
369. Case T-430/08, Grain Millers, Inc. v. OHIM, 2010 E.C.R. II-145 (summary), at ¶28.
370. Case C-96/09 P, Anheuser-Busch, Inc. v. Budějovický Budvar, národní podnik, 2011 E.C.R. I-2177, 2223 ¶159.
371. *Id.* at 2223 ¶160.

however, that the opponent actually have exercised its right to prohibit the use of the subsequent mark.[372]

The other way the Trademark Regulation recognizes unregistered trademarks is by giving the owner of the unregistered mark the right to oppose registration or challenge the validity of a Union trademark if that owner can show that the applicant was acting in bad faith when he filed the application.[373] In such cases, the owner of the unregistered mark must show that "the applicant for registration was acting in bad faith when it filed the application for registration of the trade mark."[374] In determining bad faith, "account must be taken of all the relevant factors specific to the particular case which obtained at the time of filing the application for registration of a sign as a [Union] trade mark, in particular: (i) the fact that the applicant knows or must know that a third party is using, in at least one Member State, an identical or similar sign for an identical or similar product or service capable of being confused with the sign for which registration is sought; (ii) the applicant's intention to prevent that third party from continuing to use such a sign; and (iii) the degree of legal protection enjoyed by the third party's sign and by the sign for which registration is sought."[375]

2.7 Advantages and Disadvantages of a Union Trademark

The existence of parallel trademark systems—the national systems and the Union trademark system—presents the practical issue of where a firm should register its trademark in a given circumstance. As discussed above, one fundamental advantage of the Union trademark is that it allows a single application to be filed and prosecuted in order to obtain protection in 28 member states. The single filing also alleviates the need to fulfill all the requirements of the trademark laws of the individual member states. For example, if a registration for a Union trademark is made, the trademark owner does not have to use the mark in all of the member states. Under a system of national registrations, however, the registrant would need to fulfill the use requirement in each of the member states. Moreover, the standard of distinctiveness applied by the OHIM may be different than that applied in the member states. With a Union trademark, the applicant only needs to meet one standard of distinctiveness.

As concerns the enforcement of trademark rights, the primary advantage of the Union trademark is that it eliminates the need for multiple country enforcement proceedings. A single infringement action can be brought to dispose of infringement throughout the EU. If, for example, a firm relied on

---

372. *Id.* at 2230 ¶191.
373. Art. 52(1)(b). The possibility of a mark being registered under the EU Trademark Regulation and the existence of an unregistered mark under national law arises because the EU trademark regime and the national laws on trademarks and unfair competition are autonomous regimes. See Case T-33/11, Peeters Landbouwmachines v. OHIM, 2012 E.C.R. II-____ ¶16 (reported in the electronic reports of cases ECLI:EU:T2012:77).
374. Case T-257/11, Pangyrus Ltd. v. OHIM, 2015 E.C.R. II-____ ¶63.
375. *Id.* at ¶66.

a network of national registrations, and then discovered that a competitor was using a confusingly similar trademark in five different member states, the firm would only have to initiate one infringement proceeding rather than five individual proceedings.

As mentioned above, the EU trademark system and the national systems continue to exist but are independent of each other. Although the Trademark Directive has served to harmonize the trademark systems of the member states with each other as well as with the Union trademark, the application of the rules remains largely dependent upon the perceptions of the individuals charged with their application. What may appear distinctive to a trademark officer at the OHIM may appear descriptive to a trademark office in Athens. A national trademark cannot be contested under the EU rules, and EU trademarks cannot be contested under the national rules.[376]

As recognized by the ECJ, "it is possible not only that, because of linguistic, cultural, social and economic differences, a trade mark which is devoid of distinctive character in one Member State is not so in another Member State, but also that a mark devoid of distinctive character at EU level is not so in a Member State."[377] As the registrability of a trademark depends on its distinctiveness, and distinctiveness is largely a subjective impression, an applicant may want to register the trademark in those jurisdictions where the individuals making the distinctiveness determination are more likely to agree with the applicant's arguments. For example, the color purple is probably not distinctive for chocolate to an English person. However, in Germany a good portion of the population will associate a purple label on a chocolate bar with Milka chocolate bars. Consequently, a color—which is ordinarily difficult to register as a trademark—may be considered registrable in Germany but not in other member states.[378]

The same consideration needs to be made when assessing the likelihood of confusion. As discussed above, the likelihood of confusion is a relative ground for refusal of a trademark registration. It is not necessary that the likelihood of confusion exists throughout the EU. For example, it is possible for someone to successfully challenge the Union trademark based on the grounds that it creates the likelihood of confusion even if the likelihood of confusion is only among a

---

376. Case C-196/11 P, Formula One Licensing BV v. OHIM, 2012 E.C.R. I-____, at ¶38. Similarly, the national trademark authorities are not bound by the decisions made by the trademark authorities of the other member states. Case C-218/01, *In re* Henkel KGaA, 2004 E.C.R. I-1725, 1759 ¶62.

377. Case C-238/06 P, Develey Holding GmbH & Co. Beteiligungs KG v. OHIM, 2007 E.C.R. I-9379, 9402 ¶58. The fact that a mark has been recognized as being distinctive by national trademark authorities is only one factor to be considered by the OHIM in determining whether a mark applied for under the EU Trademark Regulation is distinctive. Case C-98/11 P, Chocoladefabriken Lindt & Sprüngli AG v. OHIM, 2012 E.C.R. I-____, at ¶50.

378. Decision of the German Bundesgerichtshof of Oct. 7, 2004, I ZR 91/02, *reported at* 107 Gewerblicher Rechtsschutz und Urheberrecht 427(2005).

particular linguistic group within the EU or a member state.[379] Therefore, the Union trademark may be the inappropriate vehicle if this risk exists.

Moreover, the registration of a national trademark does not necessarily mean that the same mark is registrable at the EU level even though the legal requirements for registration are the same. In *Develey Holding GmbH & Co. Beteiligungs KG v. OHIM*,[380] for example, Develey had successfully registered a trademark in Germany for the shape of a bottle. However, the OHIM rejected the application based on the lack of distinctiveness. On appeal, both the General Court and the ECJ agreed with the OHIM and held that the shape was not distinctive even though the German Patent and Trademark Office came to a different conclusion. The inconsistent results are the unavoidable consequence of parallel systems.

However, the lack of interdependence between the national regimes and the EU regime may operate to the advantage of the applicant. It is possible for a firm to register a trademark at each of the national and EU levels. It then has the option to seek enforcement at the EU level or the national level in the event another firm is infringing on that trademark.

3. Patent Protection

The term "patent" refers to a grant of a right to preclude others from making, using, or selling an invention. Patent law grants an "exclusion right" for the purpose of encouraging new, nonobvious, and industrial applicable solutions to technical problems.[381] In the EU, patents are sometimes referred to as "industrial property rights" because they are traditionally associated with the process by which a product is manufactured. This is, however, no longer exclusively the case. As discussed below, patents protect inventions that have nothing to do with a manufacturing process.

There are generally three types of patents: utility patents, design patents, and plant patents. The most common type of patent—utility patents—protects four broad categories of inventions: products, machines, compositions of matter, and methods or processes. Design patents protect the aesthetic appearance of a product or a part of a product. Utility models provide more limited protection than a utility patent for inventions that may not rise to the level of invention required for utility patent protection. It is usually easier, and often quicker, to obtain utility model protection than a utility patent. However, the term of utility model protection is generally shorter than that of a utility patent. Plant patents protect asexually reproduced plants.

---

379. Case C-514/06 P, Armacell Enterprise GmbH v. OHIM, 2008 E.C.R. I-128 (summary), at ¶56.
380. Case C-238/06 P, Develey Holding GmbH & Co. Beteiligungs KG v. OHIM, 2007 E.C.R. I-9379, 9402 ¶58.
381. Judgment of the German Bundesgerichtshof in case no. X ZB 16/00 (Oct. 17, 2001), English translation available at EPO Official Journal (July 2002) at 345.

3.1 Source of Patent Rights

It is important to recall that patent rights, like intellectual property in general, are granted by the state in order to achieve specific policy objectives. The definition of patent provided above refers to a "grant of a right." There is no inherent or natural right that an inventor has to exclusively use his or her invention. Consequently, patent rights (i.e., the right to preclude others from making, using, or selling one's invention) are based on statutes. Although there are several international and regional patent law regimes, patent law remains primarily national.

(a) International Regimes

It is important to recognize that there is no comprehensive EU patent law regime. As discussed below, the European Patent Convention (which is often mistakenly considered part of EU primary law) exists independent of the EU. The source of patent rights in the EU is the national laws of the respective EU member states. Although there are several international and regional treaties and organizations dealing with patents to which the member states are signatories, these international regimes are not the source of patent rights.

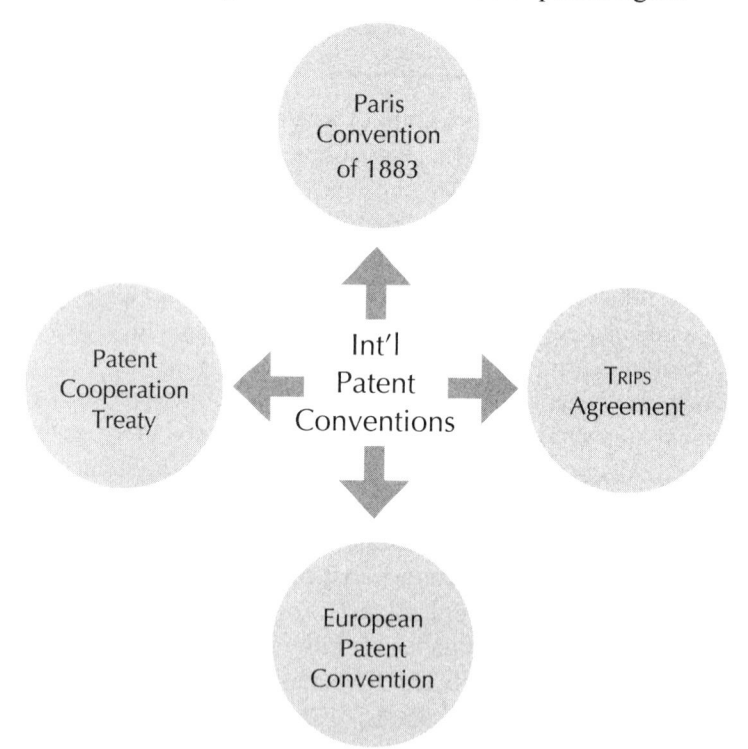

```
                    Paris
                  Convention
                   of 1883
                      ↑
    Patent          Int'l          TRIPS
  Cooperation  ←   Patent    →   Agreement
    Treaty        Conventions
                      ↓
                  European
                   Patent
                 Convention
```

Instead, these international conventions facilitate the process by which patent rights are secured under national law. The process by which an inventor secures patent protection is often a costly exercise. As patent law is national in nature, the costs increase dramatically when patent protection for the same invention is sought in multiple jurisdictions. The international regimes are aimed at reducing the burdens traditionally associated with the process of seeking patent protection in multiple jurisdictions.

(1) Paris Convention of 1883

As discussed above in the context of trademarks, all of the EU member states have signed the Paris Convention. It applies not only to trademarks and designs, but also to patents. However, it only codifies certain principles; it does not establish a centralized system of patent registration. The three important principles relating to patents codified in the Paris Convention of 1883 are that of national treatment, priority, and independence.

According to the principle of national treatment, nationals of countries that have signed and ratified the Convention enjoy the same rights regarding their patent applications in other countries that have signed and ratified the Convention as those other countries accord to their own nationals.[382] For example, if a French company files a patent application in Latvia, the Latvian Patent Office is required to treat that application the same way as it treats applications of Latvian companies because both France and Latvia are signatories to the Paris Convention.

Most countries do not allow patents to be registered for inventions which are already known or which have already been registered by another inventor. Consequently, it is often a race to the patent office if two or more inventors are working on similar inventions. As, however, patents are national in scope, it is possible that an inventor files for a patent in one country while another inventor files for a patent in another country. To reward the first inventor through the door, the rule of priority codified in the Patent Convention gives a patent applicant in one signatory country six months' priority to file subsequent applications (for the same patent) in other signatory countries.[383] For example, if a U.S. inventor files an application in the United States, he or she has up to six months to prepare and file an application for that same invention in Germany without having to worry that someone is going to beat him or her through the door at the German Patent Office.

Patent applications are processed and granted (or denied) by the national patent authorities. The signatories of the Patent Convention refused to relinquish this authority. Hence, the Paris Convention recognizes the principle of independence according to which the patent systems of the respective signatories remain independent of each other.[384] The signatory countries are not required to register a patent just because that same application was accepted in another signatory country. Consequently, a company may encounter a situation where it receives patent protection in one signatory country but not another. The national treatment rule only means that the signatory countries treat the applications the same way; it does not guarantee the outcome.

(2) Patent Cooperation Treaty

The Patent Cooperation Treaty is an international convention signed by over 130 countries, including all of the EU member states. As patents are national in character, separate patent applications had to traditionally be prepared and

---

382. Paris Convention of 1883 at art. 2(1).
383. *Id.* at art. 4.
384. *Id.* at art. 4bis.

filed in each country where protection was sought. As the applications and the standards for granting a patent are quite similar between countries, the process of separate applications is inefficient for the inventor as well as for the respective patent offices. In many instances, an inventor would have to incur the costs of filing in multiple jurisdictions just to determine whether his or her invention was patentable. The Patent Cooperation Treaty attempts to alleviate some of these burdens by establishing an international application, search, and preliminary examination system. It should be noted, however, that the Patent Cooperation Treaty does not establish a system for granting patents. The substantive examination is left up to the countries where protection is sought.

The Patent Cooperation Treaty operates in two phases. The first phase, the international phase, involves an international search and preliminary examination of the patent application. A patent application under the Patent Cooperation Treaty is filed with a national patent office in much the same way as a "purely" national patent. The difference is that the applicant may designate other Patent Cooperation Treaty countries in which it is seeking protection. The receiving national office collects the fees, accords a filing date to the application, and sends copies of the application to the WIPO and the appropriate international searching authority. The international searching authorities are national patent authorities that have been designated under the Patent Cooperation Treaty as authorized to conduct international searches under the Patent Cooperation Treaty.[385] Every application seeking to benefit from the Patent Cooperation Treaty must undergo an international search by an international searching authority. The international search examines whether prior art exists (the existence of prior art precludes the granting of the patent in all of the Patent Cooperation Treaty countries).

The international searching authority then issues a report as to its findings on the existence of prior art. The report is then sent to the applicant and the national patent offices designated by the applicant in its initial application. After receipt of the search report, and assuming it is favorable to the applicant, the applicant may request an international preliminary examination. Similar to the international search, there are specific national patent offices that have been selected by the Assembly of the Patent Cooperation Treaty Union to serve as international preliminary examination authorities. (They are the same offices as the international searching authorities with the exception of the Spanish Patent Office). The international preliminary examining authority examines the other requirements for a patent: whether the invention is novel, whether it involves an inventive step, and whether it is industrially applicable. The international preliminary examining authority then issues a report on its findings. This report is then sent to the patent offices in the countries designated by the applicant. Although the international search and preliminary examination are not binding on the national patent offices, they carry significant influence.

---

385. The following offices have been designated as international searching authorities: Australian Patent Office, Austrian Patent Office, Chinese Patent Office, European Patent Office, Japanese Patent Office, Russian Patent Office, Spanish Patent Office, Swedish Patent Office, and U.S. Patent Office.

At this point, the second phase—the national phase—of the Patent Cooperation Treaty system begins. As stated above, the Patent Cooperation Treaty does not establish a system for granting patents. Once the international search and the international preliminary examination processes are completed, it is then up to the applicant to decide whether to prosecute the patent at the national level. The obvious benefit of the Patent Cooperation Treaty process is that it gives the applicant an idea of whether her invention is patentable. If the reports of either the international searching authority or the international preliminary examination authority are negative, the applicant may decide to forgo patent prosecution at the national level and save the time and money associated with pursuing the application further. If, on the other hand, the reports are favorable to her, the applicant has a strong basis for claiming patent protection from the national office.

(3) TRIPS Agreement

Similar to the Paris Convention, the TRIPS Agreement does not establish a centralized registration. Instead, the TRIPS Agreement prescribes the minimum protections and sets forth specific principles which the signatories are obligated to observe in applying their respective patent laws. The two main principles are those applicable to trademarks and copyrights: national treatment and most-favored nation. The principle of national treatment requires each signatory country to treat nationals of other signatory states no less favorably than it treats its own nationals with regard to the protection of patents.[386] The most- favored nation principle requires the signatory countries to extend "any advantage, favor, privilege or immunity" to nationals of one signatory country to nationals of all the other signatory countries (subject to certain exceptions).[387]

The TRIPS Agreement also establishes the criteria for patentable subject matter. The signatory countries are required to make patents available for any inventions provided that they are new, involve an inventive step, and are capable of industrial application.[388] If, however, the exploitation of invention would threaten *ordre public* or morality (e.g., protect human, animal, or plant life or health or to avoid serious prejudice to the environment), they may deny patent protection. The protection accorded by a patent is the right to prevent third parties from making, using, offering for sale, selling, or importing for these purposes that product without the owner's consent.[389] This protection must last for at least 20 years from the filing date.[390]

(b) National

Although Article 118 of the TFEU authorizes the European Parliament and the Council to establish a patent law system similar to the EU trademark system, the member states have failed to reach the necessary political consensus to adopt appropriate legislation. With the exception of the EU patent with unitary

---

386. TRIPS Agreement at art. 3(1).
387. *Id.* at art. 4.
388. *Id.* at art. 27.
389. *Id.* at art. 28(1).
390. *Id.* at art. 33.

effect, EU patent law remains primarily national law.[391] The national structure of the patent system increases the possibility of inconsistent interpretations about the same patent.

In *Occlutech GmbH v. AGA Medical Corp.*, for example, a German court found a patent infringement whereas the Dutch and English courts concluded there was no infringement.[392] Such results have driven the debate over the introduction of an EU patent law. The legal and political debate over the introduction of a patent law system within the context of the EU has raged for many years. However, sufficient political consensus has not been achieved in order to adopt the appropriate legislation. In the absence of an independent international patent law system, patent law remains primarily in the purview of the individual EU member states. A discussion of the patent laws of each of the EU member states is beyond the scope of this book.

3.2 European Patents

There are two types of pan-European patent protection: bundle patents under the Convention on the Grant of European Patents[393] and unitary patents under Regulation (EU) No 1257/2012.[394] The Convention on the Grant of European Patents, signed in Munich in 1973, is an autonomous multinational patent regime comprising all of the 28 EU member states as well as Switzerland, Liechtenstein, Turkey, Monaco, Bulgaria, and Iceland.[395] It establishes a centralized patent system administered by the European Patent Office (EPO) independent of the patent regimes of the member countries. Patents granted by the EPO under the European Patent Convention are referred to in the EU as "European patents."[396] The EU unitary patent under Regulation 1257/2012, however, is limited to the EU member states and has its own patent court.[397] Patents granted under this procedure are referred to in Europe as "European patents with unitary effect."[398]

Although the substantive requirements for a European patent with unitary effect are the same as for European patents, the rights attached to a European

---

391. As discussed below, the European Patent Convention establishes a supra-national patent system, but this system is outside the EU (even though all of the member states are part of the European Patent Convention).
392. Occlutech GmbH v. AGA Medical Corp., [2009] EWHC 2013 (CH).
393. Convention on the Grant of European Patents, Oct. 5, 1973, available at 13 I.L.M. 268 (1974) [hereinafter European Patent Convention].
394. Regulation (EU) No. 1257/2012 of the European Parliament and of the Council of 17 December 2012 implementing enhanced cooperation in the area of the creation of unitary patent protection, 2012 O.J. (L 361) 1.
395. The EU itself is not a signatory to the European Patent Convention.
396. Regulation (EU) No. 1257/2012 of the European Parliament and of the Council of 17 December 2012 implementing enhanced cooperation in the area of the creation of unitary patent protection, 2012 O.J. (L 361) 1 at art. 2(b).
397. Agreement on a Unified Patent Court, 2013 O.J. (C 175) 1.
398. Regulation (EU) No. 1257/2012 of the European Parliament and of the Council of 17 December 2012 implementing enhanced cooperation in the area of the creation of unitary patent protection, 2012 O.J. (L 361) 1 at art. 2(c).

patent with unitary effect are different. A European patent "confers on its proprietor from the date on which the mention of its grant is published in the European Patent Bulletin, in each Contracting State in respect of which it is granted, the same rights as would be conferred by a national patent granted in that State."[399] Issues of infringement are addressed under national law.[400] In this sense, a successful application under the European Patent Convention gives the proprietor a "bundle" of rights. The EU patent with unitary effect, however, gives the proprietor uniform rights across all of the participating EU member states.[401] It can only be limited, transferred, or revoked or lapse in respect to all of the participating member states (as opposed to a European patent whose limitations, transferability, or revocation depend on the national patent laws of the respective signatory states to the European Patent Convention). Neither of these pan-European patent regimes replaces the patent regimes of the individual member states.

(a) Substantive Requirements for European Patent Convention and EU Patents

Inventions which are susceptible of industrial application, which are new, and which involve an inventive step are patentable provided that they are not excluded as such from patentability.[402] An invention is patentable under the European Patent Convention if it is patentable, qualifies as an invention which is new, involves an inventive step, and is susceptible of industrial application.[403] The requirements are the same regardless of whether the European Patent Convention application is filed with the EPO or a national patent office.

(1) Patentability

The basic substantive requirement for a patent is that the invention has technical character. The technical character requirement is sometimes interpreted as a requirement for a "technical teaching," i.e., an instruction addressed to a skilled person as to how to solve a particular technical problem using particular technical means.[404] Whether the invention contributes to technical advancement or is novel is not tested when determining patentability.[405]

---

399. European Patent Convention at art. 64(1).
400. *Id.* at art. 64(2).
401. Regulation (EU) No. 1257/2012 of the European Parliament and of the Council of 17 December 2012 implementing enhanced cooperation in the area of the creation of unitary patent protection, 2012 O.J. (L 361) 1 at art. 3(2). The EU patent with unitary effect is not recognized in all EU member states. Because Spain and Italy did not agree to the official languages, they refused to sign on to the EU patent.
402. European Patent Convention at art. 52(1).
403. *Id.*
404. OJ SE 4/2007.
405. G 3/08, OJ 2011, 10; T 388/04, Decision of the EPO Board of Appeal of Mar. 22, OJ 2007, 16.

(2) Nonpatentable Subject Matters

There are two basic categories of exceptions to patentability under the European Patent Convention. The first category of exceptions is made up of the specific subject matter or activities listed in Art. 52(2) of the European Patent Convention. According to this provision of the European Patent Convention, the following are not regarded as inventions because they lack a technical character:[406]

- discoveries, scientific theories, and mathematical methods;
- aesthetic creations;
- schemes, rules, and methods for performing mental acts, playing games or doing business, and programs for computers;
- presentations of information.

The second category of activities, while they may have a technical character, are simply not patentable based on public policy:[407]

- inventions contrary to *ordre public* or morality;
- plant or animal varieties or essentially biological processes for the production of plants or animals; and
- methods for treatment of the human or animal body by surgery or therapy and diagnostic methods practiced on the human or animal body.

It is generally thought that software is not patentable because, as indicated above, it falls under the exclusions listed under Article 52(2) of the European Patent Convention ("programs for computers"). The EPO, however, has indicated that computer programs are not necessarily precluded from patentability in all circumstances.[408] According to the European Patent Convention, programs for computers are only precluded from patentability "as such."[409] This as such qualification has been interpreted as evidence that the legislators did not want to exclude from patentability all programs for computers.[410] According to the EPO, the fact that only patent applications relating to programs for computers as such are excluded from patentability means that patentability may be allowed for patent applications relating to programs for computers where the latter

---

406. European Patent Convention at art. 52(2).
407. European Patent Convention at art. 53.
408. T-1173/97, IBM Computer Program, 1999 O.J. EPO 609.
409. European Patent Convention at art. 52(3): "Paragraph 2 shall exclude the patentability of the subject matter or activities referred to therein only to the extent to which a European patent application or European patent relates to such subject-matter or activities as such."
410. T-935/97, IBM Computer Program II (Feb. 4,1999); "The combination of the two provisions (Article 52(2) and (3) European Patent Convention) demonstrates that the legislators did not want to exclude from patentability all programs for computers. In other words the fact that only patent applications relating to programs for computers as such are excluded from patentability means that patentability may be allowed for patent applications relating to programs for computers where the latter are not considered to be programs for computers as such."

are not considered to be programs for computers as such.[411] In other words, computer programs need to have one additional attribute to software to give them a technical character. This additional attribute is sometimes referred to as "further technical effect." A computer program is functioning as a computer program as such when it performs the direct function of a computer program by modifying the computer's hardware, causing electrical currents to manipulate bit patterns. The ECO recognizes that although such modifications may be considered technical in character, they are an essential and common feature of computer programs. Software must have a further technical effect to be patentable. If, for example, the software is integrated into a product such as a car, and it serves to inform the car's owner of the need for a repair, this might be considered a further technical effect sufficient to give the software a technical character for purposes of patentability.

The second category of activities, while they may have a technical character, are simply not patentable based on public policy:[412]

- inventions contrary to *ordre public* or morality;
- plant or animal varieties or essentially biological processes for the production of plants or animals; and
- methods for treatment of the human or animal body by surgery or therapy and diagnostic methods practiced on the human or animal body.

(3) Inventive Step

The European Patent Convention requires that the invention embody an inventive step. An invention embodies an inventive step if, having regard to the state of the art, it is not obvious to a person skilled in the art. To determine whether the invention embodies an inventive step, the EPO generally applies the "problem and solution approach."[413] The threshold question is whether, in view of the prior art, a skilled person would have considered the invention an obvious solution to the technical problem. A person skilled in the art means more than just the average consumer. It is a practitioner who has average knowledge and abilities and is aware of what was common general knowledge in the relevant art concerned. That person is assumed to be aware of the totality of the prior art pertinent to the relevant area of technology and in particular of everything made available to the public.[414]

(4) Novelty

The European Patent Convention requires that a patentable invention be new. An invention is considered new if it does not form part of the state of the art. The standard of state of the art comprises everything made available to the public by means of a written or oral description, by use, or in any other way,

---

411. T-1173/97, IBM Computer Program, 1999 O.J. EPO 609.
412. European Patent Convention at art. 53.
413. EPO Guidelines G-VII, 5 - June 2012 version.
414. Decision of the EPO Board of Appeal in case no T 0333/09 (Aug. 6, 2013).

before the date of filing of the European Patent Convention patent application.[415] The term "public" may include even a single individual. For example, if the inventor sells just one sample of her invention prior to the date of filing, it is considered to have been made available to the public.[416] In one instance, the invention was incorporated by the inventor into another product which was to be used as a prototype. The buyer of the prototype was not even aware of the invention. Nonetheless, the invention was not considered new because of its use in the prototype.[417]

If an invention remains secret, there is generally not an issue with the novelty requirement. However, except for inventors working by themselves in the basement of their homes, it is difficult not to disclose an invention. In most instances, inventions are the result of a long process of research and development involving many people within a company. Hence, in order to maintain a workable patent system, not every disclosure to the public will negate the novelty of the invention.

If the invention has been disclosed to someone under an obligation of confidentiality, then a disclosure has not taken place. For example, if 20 researchers working for a drug company discover a new cure for cancer, the fact that they all know about the invention does not mean that there has been a disclosure to the public, provided that they are all under a duty to retain the secrecy of the invention. Although the obligation of confidentiality need not be written, there must be evidence of an agreement or fiduciary obligation. In one case, a patent applicant had provided details on the invention to one of his business partners. The business partner was supposed to conduct the final development of the invention. While it was developing the invention, the business partner then passed the technical drawings on to one of his customers without the knowledge of the patent applicant. Although the applicant argued that there was a tacit agreement between it and the business partner, the EPO's Board of Appeal held that there was no evidence of a confidentiality agreement and therefore there was a public disclosure.[418]

There are two instances in which a prior disclosure of the invention is not to be taken into consideration as part of the state of the art. First, if the disclosure resulted from an evident abuse in relation to the applicant or his legal predecessor, the abusive disclosure does not constitute a public disclosure precluding patentability.[419] An abuse occurs, for example, when a third party who had not been authorized to communicate to other persons the information received goes ahead and discloses it.[420] According to the EPO Board of Appeal

---

415. European Patent Convention at art. 56.
416. Decision of the EPO Board of Appeal in case no. T 482/89 (Dec. 11, 1990), O.J. 1992, 646 (alimentation électrique).
417. Decision of the EPO Board of Appeal in case no. T 1022/99 (Apr. 10, 2001).
418. Decision of the EPO Board of Appeal in case no. T 173/83 (July 1, 1985), O.J. 1987, 465 (antioxidant).
419. European Patent Convention at art. 55.
420. Decision of the EPO Board of Appeal in case no. T 173/83 (July 1, 1985), O.J. 1987, 465 (antioxidant).

"[T]here would be abuse not only when there is the intention to harm, but also when a third party, knowing full well that it is not permitted to do so, acts in such a way as to risk causing harm to the inventor, or when this third party fails to honor the declaration of mutual trust linking him to the inventor."[421] However, an inadvertent disclosure to the public would not constitute evident abuse.[422]

Second, if the patent applicant or her legal predecessor had displayed the invention at an official international exhibition, a public disclosure is not deemed to have occurred.[423] For example, if an engineer is working on a new fuel source for automobiles that does not cause harm to the environment, and presents his findings to a group of engineers at the annual meeting of the Swedish Association of Concerned Engineers, the presentation is not deemed a public disclosure, and the invention may still be deemed new.

Merely the theoretical possibility of having access to information is sufficient to deem the invention available to the public.[424] For example, if the inventor is a scientist and disclosed the invention at a public lecture to which no one came, there would be a disclosure to the public. If the invention appeared on the publicly accessible Internet and no one accessed the particular website, the theoretical possibility that a member of the public could have accessed the website means that it was made available to the public.

(5) Industrial Application

Not all novel inventions deserve patent protection. The European Patent Convention requires that the invention is susceptible of industrial application.[425] An invention is considered as susceptible of industrial application if it can be made or used in any kind of industry, including agriculture.[426] This is a very broad standard. Methods for treating the human or animal body by surgery or therapy[427] and diagnostic methods practiced on the human or animal body are per se not be regarded as inventions which are susceptible of industrial application. For example, chemotherapy is not susceptible of industrial application.[428]

(b) Process for Securing a European Patent

Applicants who wish to obtain protection under the European Patent Convention have the choice of making an application either to the EPO (located in Munich

---

421. *Id.*
422. Decision of the EPO Board of Appeal in case no. T 585/92 (Feb. 9, 1995), O.J. 1996, 129 (deodorant detergent).
423. European Patent Convention at art. 55.
424. Decision of the EPO Board of Appeal in case no. T 444/88 (May 9, 1990).
425. European Patent Convention at art. 57.
426. *Id.* Decision of the EPO Board of Appeal in case no. T 144/83 (Mar. 27, 1986), O.J. 1986, 301 (appetite suppressant).
427. The first definition of the term was given in Decision of the EPO Board of Appeal in case no. T 144/83, O.J. 1986, 301 (appetite suppressant). According to this decision, therapy relates to the treatment of a disease in general or to a curative treatment in the narrow sense as well as the alleviation of the symptoms of pain and suffering.
428. Decision of the EPO Board of Appeal in case no. G 0005/83 (Dec. 5, 1984), O.J. EPO 1985, at 64.

with branches in The Hague and Berlin) or to a national patent office. A patent application must be submitted to the EPO in English, French, or German. Nationals of states with official languages other than English, French, or German may submit an application in their language and at a later stage a translation into English, French, or German. In the application, the applicant designates the signatory countries in which he or she is seeking protection. Once the patent application is submitted to it, the EPO processes the application, conducts a search of prior art, publishes the application, and grants patents for the designated states for an initial period of 20 years. The rights given to the patent holder are defined by the national laws of the respective countries designated by the applicant in his application. It is often said that an applicant under the European Patent Convention receives a "bundle" of rights which simply means that he receives patent protection in the designated countries.

The only subsequent involvement of the EPO is the opposition procedure. Third parties may challenge the grant of a patent by initiating an opposition procedure. Once the patent is granted, the issues of validity and infringement are matters for national law and national courts (although there is a certain degree of harmonization that occurred under the European Patent Convention). As the opposition procedure and national infringement procedure are independent, it is possible that a third party initiate parallel opposition procedures. A European patent holder has the same rights as a national patent holder.

(c) *Process for Securing a European Patent with Unitary Effect*

As indicated above, the European patent gives the proprietor a bundle of national patent rights. The applicant designates the signatory states in which it wants protection. The EU patent with unitary effect, on the other hand, gives the proprietor uniform EU-wide protection based on the EU Patent Regulation.[429] The process for securing a European patent with unitary effect is substantially the same as the process for securing a European patent. During the process, the applicant may request unitary effect.[430] If such a request is not made, the applicant is deemed to have applied for just a European patent under the European Patent Convention. There is a separate Register for Unitary Patent Protection maintained by the EPO as part of the European Patent Register under the European Patent Convention. If the application meets all of the substantive requirements, it is then registered in the Register for Unitary Patent Protection.

---

429. Regulation (EU) No. 1257/2012 of the European Parliament and of the Council of 17 December 2012 implementing enhanced cooperation in the area of the creation of unitary patent protection, 2012 O.J. (L 361) 1.
430. Only European patents that have been granted for all of the participating member states with the same claims may apply for unitary protection. art. 3 Regulation (EU) No. 1257/2012 of the European Parliament and of the Council of 17 December 2012 implementing enhanced cooperation in the area of the creation of unitary patent protection, 2012 O.J. (L 361) 1.

(d) Advantages and Disadvantages

The obvious advantage of a European patent (including a European patent with unitary effect) over a national patent is that it alleviates the need to submit multiple applications to each patent office in the signatory countries where the applicant seeks protection. An inventor can file one application and achieve patent protection in a number of countries. Moreover, the application can be filed and prosecuted in English, saving translation expenses until it is known whether a patent will issue. Once the European patent is issued, then the patent holder is required to submit within three months translations into the official languages of the signatory countries where protection is sought.[431] If the EPO rejects the patent application, the applicant does not have to incur these translation costs.

On the other hand, the decision of patentability for all of the designated countries rides on the determination of the EPO examiner. The standards in the EPO may be more stringent than in certain of its member countries. Moreover, the costs associated with filing an application under the European Patent Convention are relatively high. Patent practitioners often advise against making an application under the European Patent Convention unless more than three national applications would otherwise be filed. But even if there are more than three countries where protection is sought, revocation of the European patent means the revocation of the protection for all of the countries. If there is an opposition in the first nine months after the patent application is filed, the resulting revocation means the loss of patent protection in all of the member states designated by the patent applicant. Once revoked at the EPO level, a contrary decision at the national level cannot revive the patent. It is not uncommon for third parties to bring parallel opposition proceedings at the EPO and the national level.

3.3 Biotechnology Patents

Subject to *ordre public* discussed above, biotechnological inventions are patentable under the European Patent Convention if they concern: (a) biological material which is isolated from its natural environment or produced by means of a technical process even if it previously occurred in nature; (b) plants or animals if the technical feasibility of the invention is not confined to a particular plant or animal variety; or (c) a microbiological or other technical process, or a product obtained by means of such a process other than a plant or animal

---

431. European Patent Convention at art. 65(1). A European patent with unitary effect can be submitted in English, French, or German. If applied for in French or German, the applicant is required to submit a full translation of the specification of the European patent into English. If applied for in English, a full translation of the specification of the European patent into any other official language of the Union is required. Council Regulation (EU) No. 1260/2012 of 17 December 2012 implementing enhanced cooperation in the area of the creation of unitary patent protection with regard to the applicable translation arrangements, 2012 O.J. (L 361) 89 at art. 6.

variety.[432] Although there is no EU patent, the EU Biotechnology Patent Directive[433] requires member states to permit biotechnology patents subject to certain limits. In order to avoid divergent interpretations between the European Patent Convention and the patent laws of the EU member states, the European Patent Convention mandates that the EU Biotechnology Patent Directive be used as an interpretation tool.[434]

(a) *Patentability*

(1) Biotechnology

Although the Biotechnology Patent Directive does not create a new category of rights for biotechnological inventions, it requires the member states to protect biotechnological inventions under national patent law.[435] As the Biotechnology Directive does not provide a definition of a biotechnological invention, it is left to the member states to make that determination. Reference to the European Patent Convention provides some assistance in this respect. The Implementing Regulation of the European Patent Convention defines "biotechnological inventions" as inventions that concern a product consisting of or containing biological material (i.e., material containing genetic information and capable of reproducing itself or being reproduced in a biological system) or a process by means of which biological material is produced, processed, or used.[436] This definition captures not only genetic engineering (for example, the manipulation of existing gene sequences), but also the creation or manipulation of a new organic form from existing organic forms. For example, Harvard College has applied for and received a patent for transgenic animals which are animals such as lab mice in which there has been a deliberate modification of their genome.[437]

As long as the invention is new, involves an inventive step, and is susceptible of industrial application, the member states must provide patent protection even if the invention concerns a product consisting of or containing biological material (i.e., any material containing genetic information and capable of reproducing

---

432. Implementing Regulations to the Convention on the Grant of European Patents of 5 October 1973 as adopted by decision of the Administrative Council of the European Patent Organisation of 7 December 2006 at Rule 27.
433. Directive 98/44/EC of the European Parliament and of the Council of 6 July 1998 on the legal protection of biotechnological inventions, O.J. 1998 (L 213) 13 [hereinafter Biotechnology Patent Directive].
434. Implementing Regulations to the Convention on the Grant of European Patents of 5 October 1973 as adopted by decision of the Administrative Council of the European Patent Organisation of 7 December 2006 at Rule 26.
435. Biotechnology Patent Directive at art. 1(1).
436. Implementing Regulations to the Convention on the Grant of European Patents of 5 October 1973 as adopted by decision of the Administrative Council of the European Patent Organisation of 7 December 2006 at Rule 26(2).
437. European Patent No. 0169672. This patent application survived opposition by various opponents on a number of grounds. Decision of the EPO Opposition Division of 7 Nov. 2001, EPO Official Journal 10/2003, 473.

itself or being reproduced in a biological system) or a process by means of which biological material is produced, processed, or used.[438]

The Directive does not require the member states to protect the mere discovery of biological material. For example, the mere discovery of a DNA sequence without any application of that sequence is probably not patentable.[439] However, the mere fact that a biological material previously occurred in nature does not preclude its patentability as long as it is isolated from its natural environment or produced by means of a technical process.[440]

(2) Plant and Animal Varieties

Plant and animal varieties and biological processes for the production of plants or animals are not patentable.[441] However, inventions that concern plants or animals may be patentable if the technical feasibility of the invention is not confined to a particular plant or animal variety.

(3) Human Cloning

Given the uncertainty of its applications, human cloning is not patentable. The human body, at the various stages of its formation and development, and the simple discovery of one of its elements, including the sequence or partial sequence of a gene, cannot constitute a patentable invention.[442] However, an element isolated from the human body or otherwise produced by means of a technical process, including the sequence or partial sequence of a gene, may constitute a patentable invention, even if the structure of that element is identical to that of a natural element.[443]

(4) Public Policy Limitation

Biotechnological inventions are not patentable if their commercial exploitation would be contrary to *ordre public,* or public morals. According to the ECJ, the intent of this limitation is "to exclude any possibility where respect for human dignity could thereby be affected.[444] However, the member states may not use the mere fact that a particular exploitation is contrary to their laws as conclusive proof that the exploitation is contrary to public policy.[445] Nonetheless, certain processes are to be considered *per se* contrary to public policy. This includes processes for cloning human beings and for modifying the germ line genetic

---

438. Biotechnology Patent Directive at art. 3(1).
439. *Id.* at recital 23; Case C-428/08, Monsanto Technology LLC v. Cefetra BV, 2010 E.C.R. I-6790, 6805 ¶50.
440. Biotechnology Patent Directive at art. 3(2).
441. *Id.* at art. 4.
442. *Id.* at art. 5(1).
443. *Id.* at art. 5(2).
444. Case C-34/10, Brüstle v. Greenpeace, 2011 E.C.R. I-9849, 9871 ¶34.
445. Biotechnology Patent Directive at art. 6(1).

identity of human beings.[446] The use of human embryos for commercial purposes[447] is also considered per se contrary to public policy.[448]

The public policy limitation on the patentability of biotechnological inventions expresses a concern not only for humans, but also for animals. Processes for modifying the genetic identity of animals which are likely to cause them suffering without any substantial medical benefit to man or animal, and also animals resulting from such processes, are not patentable because they are contrary to *ordre public*.[449]

(b) Scope of Protection

If biological material is patentable (referred to as first-generation material), the patent protection also extends to any biological material derived from that biological material through propagation or multiplication in an identical or divergent form and possessing those same characteristics (referred to as second generation material).[450] Material is considered "biological material" if it contains genetic information and is capable of reproducing itself or being reproduced in a biological system.[451] In cases where the patent is a process that enables biological material to be produced, the patent protection extends to biological material directly obtained through that process *and* to any other biological material derived from the directly obtained biological material through propagation or multiplication in an identical or divergent form and possessing those same characteristics.[452]

The protection conferred by a patent on a product containing or consisting of genetic information extends to all material (except human bodies) in which the product is incorporated and in which the genetic information is contained and performs its function.[453] If, for example, genetic material is used in a soy plant, and the soy plant is made into soy meal, patent protection continues to extend to the genetic material as long as that genetic material continues to perform its function in the soy meal as it did in the soy plant.[454]

---

446. *Id.* at art. 6(2).
447. The term "commercial purpose" encompasses scientific uses which may result in a commercial use. Case C-34/10, Brüstle v. Greenpeace, 2011 E.C.R. I-9849, 9874 ¶46.
448. For purposes of EU law, a human embryo is any human ovum which is fertilized if that fertilization is such as to commence the process of a development of a human being. The term also covers nonfertilized human ova into which a cell nucleus from a mature human cell has been transplanted or whose division and development have been stimulated by parthenogenesis. Case C-34/10, Brüstle v. Greenpeace, 2011 E.C.R. I-9849, 9872 ¶¶35-36.
449. Biotechnology Directive at art. 6(2).
450. *Id.* at art. 8(1).
451. *Id.* at art. 2(a).
452. *Id.* at art. 8(2).
453. *Id.* at art. 9.
454. Case C-428/08, Monsanto Technology LLC v. Cefetra BV, 2010 E.C.R. I-6790, 6806 ¶50.

If the patent holder places the biological material on the market in the EU, the holder cannot prevent the propagation or multiplication of that biological material where the multiplication or propagation necessarily results from the application for which the biological material was marketed, provided that the material obtained is not subsequently used for other propagation or multiplication.[455]

3.4 Utility Model Patents

Obtaining a patent is often a long and costly process for an inventor. In most cases, the inventor will need to engage a patent lawyer to research prior art, and prepare and file the application. As an alternative to a "regular" patent, there is a lesser form of patent protection called utility model.

There is no EU legislation applicable to utility model patents. Protection for utility models, if any, comes from the laws of the member states. Most of the industrial property regimes of the member states grant protection to utility models.[456] However, there are important differences among the member states. For example, some member states limit protection of utility models to products whereas other member states accord protection to both products and processes. The European Commission proposed a directive to harmonize the laws of the member states, but the proposal was never adopted by the Parliament and Council.[457] Nonetheless, the Proposed Utility Model Directive provides a useful tool for illustrating the basic contours of utility model patents in Europe.

The requirements for utility model protection are similar to those of patents. An invention is deserving of utility model protection only if it is new, represents an inventive step, and is commercially useful.[458] As under the European Patent Convention, the Proposed Utility Model Directive does not attempt to identify the term "invention." Instead, it provides a list of things that cannot qualify as an invention. Scientific theories, mathematical models, aesthetic creations, schemes, rules, and methods for performing mental acts, playing games, or doing business as well as presentations of information do not qualify as inventions and therefore cannot receive utility model protection. Inventions contrary to public policy, relating to biological material, chemical or pharmaceutical substances or processes, and inventions involving computer programs are excluded from utility model protection even though they may constitute inventions.

The novelty requirement for utility models is similar to that of patents. According to the Proposed Utility Model Directive, the term "state of the art" encompasses everything made available to the public before the date of

---

455. Biotechnology Patent Directive at art. 10.
456. Some of the European countries that provide utility model protection are Austria, Belgium, Czech Republic, Denmark, Estonia, Finland, France, Germany, Greece, Hungary, Ireland, Italy, Netherlands, Poland, Portugal, Slovakia, and Spain.
457. Proposal for a European Parliament and Council Directive approximating the legal arrangements for the protection of inventions by utility model, O.J. 1998 (C 36) 13 [hereinafter Proposed Utility Model Directive].
458. *See, e.g., Id.* at art. 1(3); German Gebrauchsmustergesetz, BGBl. I, S. 1455 at art. 1(1).

which the application for utility model protection is submitted. Some member states—such as Belgium, France, and the Netherlands—require global novelty. Spain, however, applies only a local novelty requirement; the invention must only be new for Spain.

For a "regular" patent, an invention is commonly considered as involving an inventive step if, having regard to the state of the art, it is not obvious to a person skilled in the art.[459] For a utility model, however, an invention embodies an inventive step if, compared with the state of the art, it exhibits either particular effectiveness or a practical or industrial advantage.[460] Hence, the utility model applicant does not have to show that the invention was not obvious to a person skilled in the art.

The industrial application requirement is defined broadly. As with a patent, the Proposed Utility Model Directive provides that an invention is susceptible to industrial application if it can be made or used in any kind of industry. Some member states require the invention to take a three-dimensional form (Finland, Greece, Italy, Portugal, Spain). This would preclude, for example, processes from enjoying utility model protection, such as in Germany.

To secure protection of a utility model, the invention must be registered with the national patent office. One fundamental difference between a utility model and a regular patent application is that there is no examination of the requirements for protection once the utility model application is filed. As discussed above, when an inventor submits a patent application, the patent agent conducts an examination of whether the requirements for protection are fulfilled. In the case of a utility model, protection effectively begins upon registration. The national patent office does not examine the requirements set forth above. This is not to say, however, that the applicant gets a free ride in the case of a utility model application. The issue of fulfilling the requirements arises in an infringement proceeding or if contested by a third party.

The scope of protection accorded by registered utility models is similar to that of patents. According to the Proposed Utility Model Directive, the proprietor of a registered utility model has the right to prevent third parties from making, using, offering for sale, selling, or importing the product.[461] If the member states recognize utility models for processes,[462] the right conferred is generally the right to prevent third parties from using the process and from selling products obtained from this process.[463] As the innovation involved in such models is typically less than that involved in patentable technology, duration of utility model patents is generally more limited than traditional patents. For example, utility model protection in Germany is only 10 years, whereas patent protection is for 20 years. In contrast, protection accorded to utility models in Portugal is unlimited in duration.

---

459. European Patent Convention at art. 57.
460. Proposed Utility Model Directive at art. 6.
461. *Id.* at art. 20(1).
462. Some member states such as Germany do not extend utility model protection to processes.
463. *Id.* at art. 20(2).

In view of the similarities of the registration requirements and the scope of protection between patents and utility models, the decision as to which type of protection to seek is practical rather than legal. Utility model protection should be considered by businesses as an alternative to patent protection. It is generally quicker and less costly to apply for. Therefore, in some cases a utility model may be more appropriate for short-lived novelty items. If an applicant cannot accept the legal uncertainty associated with the utility model, some member states, and including the Proposed Utility Model Directive, allow companies to apply for both patent protection and utility model protection for the same invention.

As discussed above, the national patent offices do not test utility models upon registration. In certain instances, where the inventor is not certain whether it meets the requirements, it might nonetheless be able to achieve a deterrent effect via registration of a utility model. The onus for contesting the fulfillment of the requirements then shifts to the third party. This deterrent effect may even be stronger against smaller competitors who could not fund the litigation to challenge a utility model or to defend an infringement claim by the utility model proprietor.

Utility models are not recognized in all member states (for example, UK, Sweden, and Luxembourg), and important trading partners such as the United States do not recognize utility models. If worldwide protection is sought, a patent application will probably be more appropriate.

4. Copyright Protection

A copyright is an intangible right granted to the author or originator of certain literary or artistic expressions for a limited period to prevent others from making copies of the production for publication or sale. In contrast to a patent, which protects the application of an idea, and in contrast to a trademark, which protects a symbol or device that indicates the provider of the particular services or goods, it is commonly said that a copyright protects the expression of an idea.

In a strict sense, the term copyright refers to literary and artistic works, such as novels, musical works, drawings, paintings, photographs, and architectural designs. However, there are certain expressions of an idea which are protected not as copyright but rather as neighboring rights (sometimes referred to as related rights). The concept of neighboring rights includes fixation of performances (for example, a video of a ballet performance), phonograms made by phonogram producers, fixations of films, and fixations of broadcasts (for example, an audio tape of a football game). The distinction between copyrights and neighboring rights is important because, as discussed in greater detail below, there are different rights which attach to each.

4.1 Source of Rights

(a) *International Conventions*

Several international conventions apply to copyrights in the EU. The Berne Convention for the Protection of Literary and Artistic Works,[464] which does not have a centralized system of registering copyrights, rests on three basic principles that are similar to the basic principles codified in other intellectual property international conventions. First, the principle of national treatment requires the signatory countries to extend the same protections to nationals of other signatory countries as it does to its own nationals.[465] Second, the principle of automatic protection prohibits the signatory countries from imposing procedural conditions to copyright protection. For example, a signatory country could not require an author to register her copyright prior to receiving copyright protection. Third, the principle of independence of protection means that the rights granted in one Berne Convention member country are independent of the rights granted in other member countries.[466] Hence, if protection is terminated in one member country, that does not mean it is lost in the other member countries.

Another important international convention in the field of copyright is the TRIPS Agreement[467] to which the EU acceded in 1995.[468] As discussed above in the context of trademarks, the TRIPS Agreement applies to various forms of intellectual property, including copyrights. The basic principles—national treatment and most-favored nation treatment—apply to the application of copyright law. For example, the national treatment principle requires the TRIPS signatories to apply their copyright law to nationals of other TRIPS members as they do to their own nationals.

---

464. Berne Convention for the Protection of Literary and Artistic Works, Sept. 9, 1886, completed at Paris on May 4, 1896, revised at Berlin on Nov. 13, 1908, completed at Paris on May 4, 1896, revised at Berlin on Nov. 13, 1908, completed at Berne on Mar. 20, 1914, revised at Rome on June 2, 1928, at Brussels on June 26, 1948, at Stockholm on July 14, 1967, and at Paris on July 24, 1971, 1161 U.N.T.S. 3 [hereinafter Berne Convention]. The phrase "literary and artistic works" is defined as "every production in the literary, scientific and artistic domain." Berne Convention at art. 2(1).
465. *Id.* at art. 5(1).
466. *Id.* at art. 5(2).
467. Agreement on Trade-Related Aspects of Intellectual Property Rights, Apr. 15, 1994, pmbl., Marrakesh Agreement Establishing the World Trade Organization, Annex 1C, 33 I.L.M. 1197 (1994).
468. Council Decision of 22 December 1994 concerning the conclusion on behalf of the European Community, as regards matters within its competence, of the agreements reached in the Uruguay Round multilateral negotiations (1986-1994), O.J. 1994 (L 336) 1.

The WIPO Copyright Treaty,[469] to which the EU acceded in 2000,[470] is a "special agreement" within the meaning of the Berne Convention.[471] All of the substantive provisions of the Berne Convention are incorporated by reference into the WIPO Copyright Treaty.[472] The most significant effect of the WIPO Copyright Treaty is to extend the Berne Convention rights to digital reproduction and transmission. Authors have the exclusive right to communicate their works or authorize the communication of their works by wire or wireless means.[473]

The WIPO Performances and Phonograms Treaty[474] generally applies to performers (e.g., actors, singers, musicians, dancers, etc.) and producers of phonograms. Similar to other international conventions on intellectual property, the WIPO Performances and Phonograms Treaty codifies the principle of national treatment. Each signatory country is required to give nationals of other signatory countries the treatment it accords to its own nationals with regard to performances.

On a more specific level, the Treaty requires the signatory countries to grant performers (for a period of 50 years)[475] the right of reproduction, the right of distribution, rental rights, and certain moral rights. The right of reproduction gives the performers the exclusive right to authorize the direct or indirect reproduction of their performances fixed in phonograms, in any manner or form[476] Performers are also granted a right of distribution. This is the exclusive right to authorize making available to the public the original and copies of their performances fixed in phonograms through sale or other transfer of ownership.[477] The rental rights granted to performers is the exclusive right of authorizing the commercial rental to the public of the original and copies of their performances fixed in phonograms.[478] Finally, performers are granted moral rights in their performances. Even after a performer transfers his or her rights, the performer retains the right to claim to be identified as the performer of his or her performances and to object to any distortion, mutilation, or other modification of his or her performances that would be prejudicial to his or her reputation.[479]

---

469. World Intellectual Property Organization Copyright Treaty, adopted by Diplomatic Conference at Geneva, Dec. 20, 1996, 36 I.L.M. 65 (1997).
470. Council Decision of 16 March 2000 on the approval on behalf of the European Community of the WIPO Copyright Treaty and the WIPO Performances and Phonograms Treaty [Not published in the Official Journal].
471. The Berne Convention (Article 20) expressly allows the signatories to enter into special agreements among themselves to grant authors more extensive rights than those in the Berne Convention.
472. WIPO Copyright Treaty at art. 1(4).
473. *Id.* at art. 8.
474. WIPO Performances and Phonograms Treaty, adopted by Diplomatic Conference at Geneva, Dec. 20, 1996, 36 I.L.M. 67.
475. WIPO Copyright Treaty at art. 17(1).
476. *Id.* at art. 7.
477. *Id.* at art. 8(1).
478. *Id.* at art. 9.
479. *Id.* at art. 5(1).

The rights of producers of phonograms are similar to the rights of performers with the exception that the producers do not have moral rights. Similar to the rights of performers, the rights of producers generally last for 50 years. The right of reproduction as applied to producers of phonograms means that the producers have the exclusive right of authorizing the direct or indirect reproduction of their phonograms, in any manner or form.[480] The right of distribution is the exclusive right of authorizing the making available to the public of the original and copies of their phonograms through sale or other transfer of ownership.[481] And, finally, the right of rental gives producers the right to authorize the commercial rental to the public of the original and copies of their phonograms, even after distribution of them, by or pursuant to, authorization by the producer.[482]

(b) EU Copyright Law

The member states retain the authority to legislate in the field of copyright and neighboring rights. There is no EU copyright regulation. The EU legislation relating to copyright exists out of a patchwork of directives designed to harmonize certain aspects of copyright and related rights throughout the member states. The following directives constitute EU copyright law:

- Copyright Term Directive
- Rental Rights Directive
- Computer Software Directive
- Satellite and Cable Directive
- Database Directive
- Information Society Directive
- Resale Right Directive

The various European directives that comprise the field of European copyright law were adopted or amended to conform to the international treaties discussed above.[483]

4.2 Reproduction Rights

Each member state is required to provide copyright holders with a reproduction right. Reproduction right means the exclusive right to authorize or prohibit, direct or indirect, temporary or permanent reproduction by any means and in any form, in whole or in part.[484] This applies not only to copyrights involving the information society,[485] but also to certain aspects of the rights of authors

---

480. *Id.* at art. 11.
481. *Id.* at art. 12.
482. *Id.* at art. 13(1).
483. Council Decision of 16 March 2000 on the approval, on behalf of the European Community, of the WIPO Copyright Treaty and the WIPO Performances and Phonograms Treaty, 2000 O.J. (L 89) 6.
484. Information Society Directive at art 2.
485. The term "information society" generally refers to electronic means of communication, *i.e.*, the Internet.

generally. The right of reproduction applies to authors in respect of their works (i.e., traditional copyright) as well as neighboring rights (i.e., to performers in respect to fixations of their performances; to phonogram producers in respect to their phonograms; to producers of the first fixations of films, in respect to the original and copies of their films; and to broadcasting organizations in respect to fixations of their broadcasts, whether those broadcasts are transmitted by wire or over the air, including by cable or satellite).[486] In *Infopaq International A/S v. Danske Dagblades Forening*, the issue was whether the reproduction of only 11 words from a newspaper article constituted a part of the work.[487] The ECJ held that not every reproduction of a part of a work violates the rights of the copyright owner. The standard for determining whether the reproduction is to be prohibited is whether the part reproduced constitutes the expression of the intellectual creation of the author of the work.[488] In the present case, the ECJ deferred to the national court to determine whether the 11 words from the newspaper article constituted an intellectual creation of the author.

The right to prevent third parties from reproducing a work or fixation is not absolute. There are specific exceptions, some of which are mandatory for the member states and others optional. As the concept of reproduction is extremely broad and covers any copying process, there is a mandatory exception for temporary acts of reproduction that meet the following five criteria: (1) the act is temporary, (2) it is transient or incidental, (3) it is an integral and essential part of a technological process, (4) the sole purpose of that process is to enable a transmission in a network between third parties by an intermediary of a lawful use[489] of a work or protected subject matter and (5) the act has no independent economic significance.[490]

The application of these requirements is illustrated in *Public Relations Consultants Ass'n Ltd. v. Newspaper Licensing Agency Ltd.* which raised the question whether the on-screen copying which occurs when a person views a website and the caching of that copy on the computer's hard drive benefits from one of the exceptions. In concluding that these reproductions fulfill the requirements for the exception, the ECJ reasoned that these copies were temporary because they are automatically deleted "after a certain time.[491] Regarding the second requirement, a reproduction is transient" if its duration is limited to what is necessary for that process to work proper and deleted without human intervention.[492]. As the on-line copy and the cached copy are automatically deleted after they were used, the ECJ considered the reproduction

---

486. Information Society Directive at art. 2.
487. Case C-5/08, Infopaq International A/S v. Danske Dagblades Forening, 2009 E.C.R. I-6624.
488. *Id.* at 6642 ¶39.
489. The lawful use can be based on contract or statute. Case C-403/08, Football Association Premier League v. QC Leisure, 2011 E.C.R. I-9159, 9232 ¶168.
490. Information Society Directive at art. 5(1).
491. Case C-360/13, Public Relations Consultants Ass'n Ltd. v. Newspaper Licensing Agency Ltd., 2014 E.C.R. ___, at ¶26.
492. *Id.* at ¶40.

to be transient. The requirement of being integral and essential part of a technological process has two prongs.[493] Under the first prong, the reproduction "must be carried out entirely in the context of a technological process". Under the second prong, the technological process must not be able to function properly without the reproduction.[494] Because the on-screen copying and the caching were necessary to use the Internet, the ECJ in *Public Relations Consultants* concluded that these types of copying fulfilled the two prongs.[495]

Although the temporary copying of data on routers and servers or caching would not infringe the author's reproduction rights. However, if the reproduction involves copying on a paper medium, it is unlikely to fulfill this exception because it is more than temporary or incidental. In *Infopaq International A/S v. Danske Dagblades Forening*, the ECJ held that in order to qualify as transient, the reproduction must be created and deleted without human intervention.[496] In that case, a media monitoring service reviewed Danish newspapers for clients and provided them with summaries. Because these summaries were printed out, the ECJ concluded that they were not temporary acts or reproductions.[497]

The member states, at their option, may provide for exceptions or limitations to the reproduction right in the following cases:[498]

- reproductions on paper or any similar medium (e.g., photocopying or printing from a computer, with the exception of copying sheet music) provided that the rightholders receive fair compensation;[499]
- reproductions on any medium made by a natural person for noncommercial,

---

493. *Id.* at ¶28.
494. Case C-5/08, Infopaq International A.S. v. Danske Dagblades Forening, 2009 E.C.R. I-6624, 6647 ¶61.
495. *Id.* at 6641 ¶33.
496. *Id.* at 6648 ¶64.
497. Id. at 6649 ¶70.
498. Information Society Directive at art. 5(2) and (3). Although these exceptions are optional, they are exhaustive. The member states may not provide for any additional exceptions. Where the member states may provide for an exception or limitation to the right of reproduction pursuant to Article 5(2) and (3), they may provide similarly for an exception or limitation to the right of distribution as referred to in Article 4 to the extent justified by the purpose of the authorized act of reproduction. *Id.* at art. 5(4).
499. Although the Information Society Directive does not identify who owes the "fair compensation," the ECJ has given the member states broad discretion in instituting procedures to make sure the rightholders are adequately compensated. Joined Cases C-457/11 to 460/11, Verwertungsgesellschaft Wort v. Kyocera, 2013 E.C.R. I-___, at ¶76. The fair compensation requirement is satisfied, for example, if the member states impose a "private copying levy" on manufacturers of digital reproduction equipment to compensate copyright holders for private copying. Case C-462/09, Stichting de Thuiskopie v. Opus Supplies Deutschland, 2011 E.C.R. I-5349, 5363 ¶36; Case C-467/08, Padawan v. Sociedad General de Autores y Editores de España, 2010 E.C.R. I-10098, 10122 ¶46. It is unnecessary to show that the private individuals actually used the equipment to copy the protected data. Case C-463/12, Copydan Båndkopi v. Nokia Danmark A/S, 2015 E.C.R. I-___ at ¶24.

- private use provided that the rightholders receive fair compensation;
- reproduction made by publicly accessible and noncommercial libraries, educational establishments, or museums;
- ephemeral recordings of works made by broadcasting organizations by means of their own facilities and for their own broadcasts;
- reproductions of broadcasts made by social institutions pursuing noncommercial purposes (e.g., hospitals or prisons), provided that the rightholders receive fair compensation[500];
- for the sole purpose of illustration for teaching or scientific research;
- use for the noncommercial benefit of people with a disability;
- reproduction by the press, communication to the public, or making available of published articles on current economic, political, or religious topics;
- quotations for purposes such as criticism or review, provided that they relate to a work or other subject-matter which has already been lawfully made available to the public;
- use for the purposes of public security or to ensure the proper performance or reporting of administrative, parliamentary or judicial proceedings;
- use of political speeches as well as extracts of public lectures or similar works;
- use during religious celebrations or official celebrations organized by a public authority;
- use of works, such as works of architecture or sculpture, made to be located permanently in public places;
- incidental inclusion of a work or other subject-matter in other material;
- use for the purpose of advertising the public exhibition or sale of artistic works, to the extent necessary to promote the event, excluding any other commercial use;
- use for the purpose of caricature or parody;
- use in connection with the demonstration or repair of equipment;
- use of an artistic work in the form of a building or a drawing or plan of a building for the purposes of reconstructing the building;
- use by communication or making available, for the purpose of research or private study, to individual members of the public by dedicated terminals on the premises of libraries or educational establishments; and
- use in certain other cases of minor importance where exceptions or limitations already exist under national law.

---

500. Information Society Directive at art. 5(3).

4.3 Right of Communication to the Public

A copyright holder also enjoys the exclusive right to authorize or prohibit any communication to the public of its works.[501] The ECJ applies a two-prong analysis in making this determination.[502] The first prong of the test is whether the conduct constitutes an act of communication. The term "communication," which is to be interpreted broadly,[503] means "any transmission of the protected works, irrespective of the technical means or process used."[504] Offering on-demand transmissions of programs,[505] showing television programs throughout a spa on closed circuit television,[506] as well as the use of a hyperlink on a website to a copyrighted work,[507] have been held to constitute acts of communication. On the other hand, a live performance is not a communication because the public is present at the place where the communication originates and there is consequently no transmission.[508]

Second, the communication must be to the public. The term "public" presupposes an indeterminate large number of potential recipients.[509] Showing a DVD to a small group of friends at home would not be a communication to the public.[510] If that same person were to show the same DVD at an open viewing in the local park, it would likely be considered a communication to the public. In *Sociedad General de Autores y Editores de España v. Rafael Hoteles SA*, the issue was whether showing television programs in a hotel lobby and in the rooms was a communication to the public.[511] The ECJ held that the fact that the broadcast may occur in a private place, such as the hotel or even the individual rooms, did not preclude the finding that a communication to the public exists.[512] According to the ECJ, the right of communication to the public covers making works available to the public in such a way that the public may access them from a place and at a time individually chosen by them.[513]

---

501. *Id.* at art. 3(1).
502. Case C-466/12, Svenson v. Retriever Sverige AB, 2014 E.C.R. I-___, at ¶16.
503. *Id.* at ¶17.
504. Case C-351/12, OSA v. Léčebné lázně Mariánské Lázně a.s., 2014 E.C.R. I-___, at ¶25; Case C-403/08, Football Association Premier League v. QC Leisure, 2011 E.C.R. I-9159, 9238 ¶193.
505. Case C-279/13, C More Entertainment AB v. Sandberg, ECLI:EU:C:2015:199 at ¶26.
506. Case C-351/12, OSA v. Léčebné lázně Mariánské Lázně a.s., 2014 E.C.R. I-___, at ¶33.
507. Case C-466/12, Svenson v. Retriever Sverige AB, 2014 E.C.R. I-___, at ¶20.
508. Case C-283/10, Circul Globus București v. Uniunea Compozitorilor şi Muzicologilor din România, 2011 E.C.R. I-12033, 12048 ¶36. The member states may, however, grant the copyright holder greater protections than the protections established in the Copyright Directive. Case C-279/13, C More Entertainment AB v. Sandberg, ECLI:EU:C:2015:199 at ¶36.
509. Case C-466/12, Svenson v. Retriever Sverige AB, 2014 E.C.R. I-___, at ¶21.
510. Case C-89/04, Mediakabel v. Commissariaatvoor de Media, 2005 E.C.R. I-4909, 4924 ¶30; Case C-192/04, Lagardère Active Broadcast v Société pour la perception de la rémunération equitable, 2005 E.C.R. I-7218, 7231 ¶31.
511. Case C-306/05, Sociedad General de Autores y Editores de España v. Rafael Hoteles SA, 2006 E.C.R. I-11543.
512. *Id.* at 11561 ¶51.
513. *Id.*

In addition, the term "public" refers only to a group of people different from the group of people contemplated by the author when the author authorized the communication to the original public.[514] For example, a hyperlink on a website to a copyright protected work available on another website is not a communication to the public because the copyright protected work, once published on the Internet, had as its contemplated audience the same set of people.[515] If, however, access to the copyright protected work is protected in some way to restrict access to a limited number of people, a hyperlink to the copyright protected work which bypasses this restriction would be a communication to the public.[516]

4.4 Distribution Rights

In addition to reproduction rights and public communication rights, authors have the exclusive right to authorize or prohibit any form of distribution to the public by sale or otherwise of originals or copies of their works.[517] The concept of "distribution to the public" is not defined in the Copyright Directive. The ECJ and General Court rely on the WIPO Copyright Treaty and the WIPO Performances and Phonograms Treaty for guidance in determining what constitutes distribution.[518] As discussed above, the exclusive right to prohibit communication to the public would forbid a person from buying a DVD and showing it to the public. The right of distribution is slightly different; it prohibits that person from copying the DVD and selling it (as opposed to merely showing it) to the public. As stated by the ECJ in *Peek & Cloppenburg v. Cassina SpA*, the concept of distribution requires a transfer of ownership of the object.[519] In that case, the German department store Peek & Cloppenburg used Le Corbusier chairs in its stores for its customers to rest in. The chairs were made legally in Italy and purchased by Peek & Cloppenburg. The plaintiff in the case claimed that the use of the chairs by Peek & Cloppenburg violated its German copyrights. The ECJ held that the use of the chairs by Peek & Cloppenburg did not constitute "distribution to the public" because there was no transfer of ownership.

This right of distribution also attaches to neighboring rights. Member states are required to grant performers, phonogram producers, film producers, and broadcasting organizations the exclusive right to make available to the public (by sale or otherwise) fixations of their performances, phonograms, films, and broadcast.[520]

4.5 Duration of Copyright Protection

The duration of the copyright protection in the EU depends on the nature of the work. The rights of an author of a literary or artistic work is limited to the life of

---

514. Case C-466/12, Svenson v. Retriever Sverige AB, 2014 E.C.R. I-___, at ¶24; Case C-403/08, Football Association Premier League v. QC Leisure, 2011 E.C.R. I-9159, 9239 ¶197.
515. Case C-466/12, Svenson v. Retriever Sverige AB, 2014 E.C.R. I-___, at ¶25.
516. *Id.* at ¶31.
517. Information Society Directive at art. 4(1).
518. Case C-5/11, *In re* Donner, 2012 E.C.R. I-___, at ¶23; Case C-456/06, Peek & Cloppenburg v. Cassina SpA, 2008 E.C.R. I-2750, 2762 ¶30.
519. *Id.*
520. Rental Rights Directive at art. 9(1).

the author (or the last surviving author in the event of works of joint authorship) plus 70 years.[521] For neighboring rights, the term is generally shorter. The rights of performers and producers of phonograms expire 50 years after the date of the performance or fixation.[522] The rights of broadcasting organizations expire 50 years after the first transmission of a broadcast, whether this broadcast is transmitted by wire or over the air, including by cable or satellite. However, the term of protection of cinematographic or audiovisual works expires 70 years after the death of the last of the principal director, author of the screenplay, author of the dialogue, or composer of the music.[523]

The duration of the rights of works originating in third states may be shorter but can never be longer. As discussed above, the EU and its member states are signatories to several international conventions that require them to recognize intellectual property rights originating in certain third countries. If the country of origin of a work (i.e., the country where the work was first published) is not an EU member state, and the author of the work is not a national of the EU member state, the term of protection granted by the member states expires on the date of expiration of the protection granted in the country of origin of the work, but may not exceed the term laid down in the Term Directive.[524] Regarding neighboring rights, if the holder is not a national of one of the EU member states, the duration of the protection expires no later than the date of expiry of the protection granted in the country of which the rightholder is a national but may not exceed the term provided for in the Term Directive for the particular right.[525]

4.6 Database Protection

Similar to copyright law, EU database law is primarily within the realm of national law; databases are not addressed in the TFEU or in an EU regulation. Instead, the EU Database Directive attempts to harmonize the laws of the member states as they apply to databases. A database, according to the Database Directive, is a collection of data or other materials arranged in a systematic or methodological way and which is individually accessible by electronic or other means. For example, an index of all English language articles written on EU intellectual property law in the last five years is a database.

The Database Directive represents a recognition that collections of works or data may have a value in and of themselves independent of the value of the individual works that are collected and are worthy of copyright protection. For example, a telephone book is valuable to society as a collection of telephone numbers independent of the value of the individual telephone numbers that comprise the collection. Although collections of data may be socially beneficial, their compilation often requires significant effort. From a public policy perspective, therefore, certain protections should be accorded to those

---

521. Term Directive at art. 1(1).
522. Id. at art. 3.
523. Id. at art. 2(2).
524. Id. at art. 7(1).
525. Id. at art. 7(2).

individuals who invest time and resources in deriving such compilations in order to encourage this conduct.

Prior to the adoption of the Database Directive in 1992, the legal protections and the requirements to secure legal protection for databases differed among the member states. One fundamental difference was the level of originality that needed to be met for a compilation to qualify for protection under national copyright law. Some member states considered that compilations were original only if they embodied an element of intellectual creation (sometimes referred to as "droit d'auteur member states"). Other member states merely required that the compilation necessitated considerable skill, labor, and judgment in gathering the data or checking its accuracy (sometimes referred to as "sweat-of-the-brow member states"). For example, a compilation of television programs for the upcoming week would have qualified for copyright protection in the latter jurisdictions, but not the former as it is lacking the necessary intellectual element. The fundamental objective of the Database Directive is to harmonize the legal protection accorded to databases under the national copyright laws of the member states.

(a) *Definition of Database*

The Database Directive requires the member states to grant copyright protection to databases. A database is a collection of independent works, data, or other materials organized in a systematic or methodical way and individually accessible by electronic or other means.[526] It includes literary, artistic, musical, or other collections of works or collections of other material such as texts, sound, images, numbers, facts, and data. A recording or an audiovisual, cinematographic, literary, or musical work as such does not fall within the scope of the Directive; a database is a collection of these things. A database does not have to be in electronic format. The Directive also covers nonelectronic databases.

It is important to recall that the status or ownership of the data making up the database is not relevant. Even publicly available data may be compiled to form a protected database. In *Apis-Hristovich EOOD v. Lakorda AD*, for example, the database consisted of Bulgarian codified laws and cases that were readily available on the Internet and at most libraries.[527] This is because the focus is on the work that goes into creating the database and rewarding the compiler for such work.

(b) *Types of Protection*

The Database Directive is a compromise between the droit d'auteur member states and the sweat-of-the-brow member states. As mentioned above, certain member states require an intellectual creation before they recognize a compilation to be original. Other member states simply require a certain level of effort to qualify as original. The Directive recognizes that the strict requirement of intellectual creation may be too narrow as it would not protect compilations that were created as a result of a substantial investment, for example TV guides.

---

526. Database Directive at art. 1(2).
527. Case C-545/07, Apis-Hristovich EOOD v. Lakorda AD, 2009 E.C.R. I-1621.

Consequently, the drafters of the Database Directive decided to establish two separate types of protection for databases to appease both camps.

The Directive provides for copyright protection for databases that constitute the author's own intellectual creation by reason of its selection and arrangement. However, even if the creation does not represent an intellectual creation, the creator of a database may secure what is referred to as a sui generis right for the database maker. The basic requirement for the sui generis right is that there has been a substantial investment in either obtaining, verifying, or presenting the contents to prevent extraction or reutilization of the whole or of a substantial part of the contents of that database. From a legal perspective, the difference is as follows: the database protection accorded to compilations representing an intellectual creation is copyright protection; the protection accorded to sweat-of-the-brow compilations is something less than copyright protection (as discussed below).

(1) Copyright Protection

A database is eligible for copyright protection if it constitutes the author's own intellectual creation by reason of its selection and arrangement.[528] The rights of the database creator are similar to traditional copyright discussed above. The database creator has the exclusive right to carry out or to authorize temporary or permanent reproduction of the database by any means and in any form, in whole or in part. The author also has the right to prevent translations, adaptations, arrangements, and any other alterations of the database and any form of distribution to the public of the database or of copies. This would include, for example, the search of an electronic online database which necessarily involves the temporary creation of a copy in the user's computer. The copyright protection of databases does not extend to the contents of the database.[529]

The requirement that the database constitute the intellectual creation of the author is often referred to as the originality requirement. The author must go beyond merely compiling the data. He or she must have actually put some thought into which data are included and the way it is compiled (sometimes referred to as the "personal touch" of the database author).[530] A telephone book, for example, may not be considered original because it represents a collection of facts, compiled without any of the creativity required for copyright protection.[531] A German court held that a listing of top music hits ranked by sales figures and by times played on radio stations did not represent an intellectual creation.[532] Nonetheless, such works may qualify for sui generis protection as discussed below because such protection does not require originality.

---

528. Database Directive at art. 3(1).
529. Database Directive at art. 3(2).
530. Case C-604/10, Football Dataco Ltd. v. Yahoo! Ltd., 2012 E.C.R. I-____, at ¶38.
531. This was the position taken by the U.S. Supreme Court in Feist Publications, Inc. v. Rural Telephone Service Co., 499 U.S. 340 (1991).
532. Decision of the Oberlandesgericht Munich in case no. 6 U 5487/01 (Oct. 10, 2002) reported at 56 Neue Juristische Wochenschrift 675 (2003).

The copyright protection for database authors is not absolute. A user of a database may (without the consent of the database creator) reproduce, adapt or alter the database if it is necessary for the purposes of access to the contents of the databases and normal use of the contents.[533] In addition, the member states are permitted to limit the copyright protection for databases in the case of reproduction for private (*i.e.*, non-commercial) purposes of a nonelectronic database or for the sole purpose of illustration for teaching or scientific research, as long as the source is indicated and to the extent justified by the noncommercial purpose to be achieved. In addition, member states may limit the rights of the author's use for the purposes of public security or for the purposes of an administrative or judicial procedure or for other exceptions to copyright, which are traditionally authorized under national law.

(2) Sui Generis Right/Database Right

The copyright protection for databases discussed above requires that the database be an intellectual creation by reason of its selection and arrangement. The Database Directive provides for an additional type of protection for databases—a sui generis right—that is not necessarily the result of an author's intellectual creation but nonetheless represents a significant effort of the database maker.[534] The purpose of protecting the effort of compiling and organizing data—and not necessarily the intellectual creation itself—is based on the recognition that the "exponential growth in the amount of information generated and processed annually in all sectors of activity" due to the widespread use of computers has created a need for compiling and organizing the data.[535]

The maker of a database (the term "maker" is not defined) is accorded protection if there has been qualitatively or quantitatively a substantial investment in either obtaining, verifying, or presenting the contents of the database.[536] The investment in the creation of the data compiled in the database should be distinguished from the investment in the creation of the database itself. For example, the work going into compiling an index of law journal articles

---

533. Database Directive at art. 6(1).
534. The requirements for copyright protection of a database are separate and distinct from the requirements of the sui generis right. Consequently, the fact that a database does not qualify for protection under one type of protection does not necessarily mean that it does not qualify for the other type of protection. Case C-604/10, Football Dataco Ltd. v. Yahoo! Ltd., 2012 E.C.R. I-____, at ¶28. The distinction between the copyright and the sui generis right is illustrated in Football Dataco Ltd. v. Brittens Pools Ltd., [2010] EWHC 841 (Ch) of the English High Court. In that case, the English Football League, which organized soccer matches in England and Scotland, argued that the annual match schedules it published were protected by the database copyright and the sui generis right. The High Court held, however, that only the database copyright applied because the match schedule was actually the creation of the Football League (and not just the collection of data from third parties which is characteristic of the sui generis right). Identifying who should play whom and on what date and time was a complex process, the end result of which was an intellectual creation of the Football League.
535. Case C-604/10, Football Dataco Ltd. v. Yahoo! Ltd., 2012 E.C.R. I-____, at ¶34.
536. Database Directive at art. 7(1).

on European labor law (to which the sui generis right might apply) should be distinguished from the work put into writing the articles (to which the sui generis right would not apply). The existence of a substantial investment in creating the data does not necessarily mean that the substantial investment requirement for database protection is fulfilled.[537]

In *Fixtures Marketing Ltd. v. Svenska Spel AB*, for example, the English professional football league claimed that the game schedules for its member teams deserved database protection.[538] One of the narrow issues was whether the league had made a substantial investment in creating the list of games, or whether the list of games and times was merely incidental to the games themselves. The ECJ drew a distinction between the investment that goes into creating the data comprising the database (i.e., the games) and the effort that goes into creating the database itself (i.e., the schedule): "[T]he resources used for the creation as such of works or materials included in the database, in this case on a CD, cannot be deemed equivalent to investment in the obtaining of the contents of that database and cannot, therefore, be taken into account in assessing whether the investment in the creation of the database was substantial."[539]

In other words, the company claiming database protection cannot extrapolate the substantial investment in the creation of the data to fulfill the first requirement of sui generis database protection. In that case, the ECJ concluded that the efforts of the league in scheduling the games could not be used to satisfy the substantial investment requirement as they were independent of each other. The requirement of an investment in obtaining the contents of a database "must be understood to refer to the resources used to seek out existing independent materials and collect them in the database. It does not cover the resources used for the creation of materials which make up the contents of a database."[540]

The sui generis right which the maker of the database has is the right to prevent extraction or reutilization of the whole or of a substantial part of the contents of that database. According to the ECJ, the concept of extraction means the permanent or temporary transfer of all or a substantial part of the contents of a database to another medium by any means or in any form.[541] For example, in *Directmedia Publishing GmbH v. Universität Freiburg*, the ECJ held that a company engaged in "extraction" by consulting a list of "The 1,100 Most Important Poems in German Literature between 1730 and 1900" compiled by the University of Freiburg in Germany.[542] Although the company did not

---

537. Case C-203/02, The British Horseracing Board Ltd. v. William Hill Organization Ltd., 2004 E.C.R. I-10415, 10476 ¶31 ("The purpose of the protection by the *sui generis* right provided for by the directive is to promote the establishment of storage and processing systems for existing information and not the creation of materials capable of being collected subsequently in a database.").
538. Case C-338/02, Fixtures Marketing Ltd. v. Svenska Spel AB, 2004 E.C.R. I-12173.
539. *Id.* at ¶26.
540. *Id.* at ¶33.
541. Case C-545/07, Apis-Hristovich EOOD v. Lakorda AD, 2009 E.C.R. I-1631, 1646 ¶41; Case C-304/07, Directmedia Publishing GmbH v. Universität Freiburg, 2008 E.C.R. I-7587, 7599 ¶34.
542. *Id.* at 7605 ¶60.

copy the list verbatim, 856 of the poems it compiled on its CD "1,000 Poems Everyone Must Have" were the same as on the list compiled by the University of Freiburg.

Reutilization means any form of making available to the public all or a substantial part of the contents of a database by the distribution of copies, by renting, by online, or other forms of transmission.[543] An off-track betting parlor reutilizes the horse race information of a horse race organizer when it makes the data available on its Internet site in order to allow its clients to bet on horse races.[544] A company reutilizes top-of-the-charts music lists published in a newspaper if it merely takes those lists and compiles the data in another format, such as a CD-ROM or book.[545]

Mere consultation of a database does not amount to extraction or reutilization.[546] For example, if an author posts a database online, that online database may be freely consulted by third parties without the necessity of securing the consent of the database author.[547] Of course, the maker of the database may legitimately restrict access to the database (for example, requiring a password to access the database). However, once she makes the database public, she cannot then prevent third parties from consulting that database as long as the consultation does not involve extraction and reutilization.[548]

The challenge is to distinguish between permitted consultation and prohibited reutilization. For example, does a dedicated meta search engine (which makes use of search engines on other websites) merely consult the data on the other websites or is it reutilizing them? That was essentially the issue in *Innoweb BV v. Wegener ICT Media BV*.[549] In that case, the ECJ used the element of deprivation of investment to distinguish between consultation and reutilization: if the use of the data is without the consent of the database maker and deprives the database maker of "revenue which should have enabled him to redeem the cost of the investment" in making the database, then it is considered reutilization.[550]

---

543. Case C-545/07, Apis-Hristovich EOOD v. Lakorda AD, 2009 E.C.R. I-1631, 1648 ¶49.
544. *See, e.g.*, Case C-203/02, The British Horseracing Board Ltd. v. William Hill Organization Ltd., 2004 E.C.R. I-10415, 10485 ¶65.
545. Decision of the German Bundesgerichtshof in case no. I ZR 290/02 (July 21, 2005), English translation at 37 IIC Int'l Rev. Industrial Property 489 (2006).
546. Case C-202/12, Innoweb BV v. Wegener ICT Media BV, 2013 E.C.R. I-___, at ¶46; Case C-203/02, The British Horseracing Board Ltd. v. William Hill Organization Ltd., 2004 E.C.R. I-10415, 10482 ¶54.
547. Case C-304/07, Directmedia Publishing GmbH v. Universität Freiburg, 2008 E.C.R. I-7587, 7604 ¶53.
548. Case C-203/02, The British Horseracing Board Ltd. v. William Hill Organization Ltd., 2004 E.C.R. I-10415, 10483 ¶58. The concept of exhaustion of an intellectual property right is discussed below.
549. Case C-202/12, Innoweb BV v. Wegener ICT Media BV, 2013 E.C.R. I-____.
550. *Id.* at ¶37.

The sui generis right only protects against the extraction or reutilization of a substantial part of the contents of the database.[551] Whether data comprises a substantial part of the database is a relative assessment. A comparison must be made between the amount of data extracted or reutilized as a proportion of the overall data contained in the database.[552]

The Database Directive allows the member states to permit users of a database to extract (but not reutilize) a substantial part of its contents for private purposes as illustration for teaching or scientific research (as long as the source is indicated and to the extent justified by the noncommercial purpose to be achieved). In addition, the member states may permit the extraction or reutilization for purposes of public security or an administrative or judicial procedure.

(c) Scope of Protection

It is important for U.S. businesses to note that the protection offered by the Database Directive does not extend to nationals or companies established outside of the EU unless the country in question offers comparable protection to EU nationals. As the United States does not currently have sui generis protection for databases or compilations,[553] U.S. companies cannot take advantage of the protections offered by the Database Directive unless they are established in the EU.[554]

The term of copyright protection for databases is 70 years, i.e., the same as for traditional copyright. In recognition of the fact that the database right is less deserving than intellectual property which represents an original work—and not just the substantial investment of the maker—the term for database right protection is limited to 15 years.

4.7 Protection of Computer Programs

In a sense, computer software is merely a set of instructions used by a computer to instruct it to perform certain functions. As such, computer software challenges the traditional notions of patent and copyright law. It can arguably be protected by patent as well as copyright, but at the same time does not fit nicely into either category. The EPO has taken the position that software that does not produce a technical result is not patentable (for example, when it is merely a mathematical method prescribing how to operate on numbers). It is only patentable if the mathematical method is used in a technical process and the process is carried out on a physical entity by some technical means that produce a change in that entity.[555]

---

551. Database Directive at art. 8(1).
552. Case C-545/07, Apis-Hristovich EOOD v. Lakorda AD, 2009 E.C.R. I-1631, 1651 ¶59.
553. The U.S. requires some form of originality. *See* Feist v. Rural Telephone Services, 499 U.S. 340, 345 (1991).
554. For a discussion of the concept of establishment in the EU, see Chapter II.
555. Case T 208/84, *In re* Vicom, OJ EPO 1987, 14 (July 15, 1986).

(a) Requirements for Protection

The Computer Software Directive[556] requires the member states to extend copyright protection to computer programs as literary works. The basic requirement for copyright protection for a computer program is that it is original.[557] In other words, the computer program must be the author's own intellectual creation. The author can be the natural person or group of natural persons who created the program. Although legal entities do not in themselves have the intellectual capacity necessary to generate an intellectual creation, the law of the member state may permit a legal person to be designated as the rightholder. For example, if a computer program is created by an employee in the execution of his duties or following the instructions given by his employer, the employer exclusively is entitled to exercise all economic rights in the program so created, unless otherwise provided by contract.[558]

(b) Scope of Rights

The protection mandated by the Computer Software Directive applies to "the expression in any form of a computer program" including preparatory design material.[559] Copyright protection includes the graphic user interface.[560] However, the ideas and principles that underlie the computer program are not protected[561] nor are user interfaces.[562] The basic rationale is that "to accept that the functionality of a computer program can be protected by copyright would amount to making it possible to monopolise ideas, to the detriment of technological progress and industrial development."[563]

The rights attaching to computer software are similar to the rights attaching to a database. The rightholder has the exclusive right to do or to authorize the permanent or temporary reproduction of a computer program by any means and in any form, in part or in whole (except for making of a back-up copy).[564] Insofar as loading, displaying, running, transmitting, or storing of the computer program necessitate such reproduction, such acts are subject to authorization by the rightholder. The rightholder also can prevent the translation, adaptation, arrangement, and any other alteration of the computer program and any form of distribution to the public (including rental of the computer program).

---

556. Council Directive 91/250/EC on the legal protection of computer programs, 1991 O.J. (L 122) 42 [hereinafter Computer Software Directive].
557. *Id.* at art. 1(3); Case C-355/12, Nintendo Co. Ltd v. PC Box Srl, 2014 E.C.R. I-___, at ¶21.
558. Computer Software Directive at art. 2(3).
559. *Id.* at art. 1(1).
560. Case C-406/10, SAS Institute Inc. v. World Programming Ltd., 2012 E.C.R. I-___, at ¶38.
561. Computer Software Directive at art. 1(2).
562. Case C-393/09, Bezpečnostní softwarová asociace – Svaz softwarové ochrany v. Ministerstvo kultury, 2010 E.C.R. I-13990, 14004 ¶41.
563. Case C-406/10, SAS Institute Inc. v. World Programming Ltd., 2012 E.C.R. I-___, at ¶40.
564. Computer Software Directive at art. 4.

However, the lawful acquirer of a computer program has the implied right to reproduce, adapt, arrange, or alter the software provided that it is necessary for the use of the computer program in accordance with its intended purpose and provided that he or she has not agreed with the seller of the software to the contrary.[565] In addition, a person having a right to use a copy of a computer program is entitled, without the authorization of the rightholder, to observe, study, or test the functioning of the program to determine the ideas and principles that underlie any element of the program if he does so while performing any of the acts of loading, displaying, running, transmitting, or storing the program which he is entitled to do.

The interoperability of software is often critical. This is particularly the case when the software is purchased from different suppliers. A person who has licensed the software or has rights to use it may reproduce the code and translation of its form if it is indispensable to obtain the information necessary to achieve the interoperability of an independently created computer program with other programs if the information necessary to achieve interoperability has not previously been readily available to the person.[566] Nonetheless, the reproduction in such cases must only be used to achieve the interoperability of the independently created computer program and may not be given to third parties.

(c) Term

The protection accorded to computer programs extends for the life of the author and for 50 years after his or her death or after the death of the last surviving author in the case of joint works. If the author is a legal person, the term of protection is 50 years from the time that the computer program is first lawfully made available to the public.[567]

4.8 Rental and Lending Rights

The possibility of a third party purchasing a copyrighted work and subsequently renting it to third parties for a fee (without the copyright holder receiving compensation) diminishes the value of the copyright. The amount of copyrighted work sold would be reduced because people would rent the work rather than buy it. The owner of the copyright would otherwise be prevented from relying on his or her copyright to prevent the rental because, as discussed below, a copyright is exhausted once the owner places the copyrighted product in commerce in the European Economic Area (EEA). The rights of the copyright holder were practically limited to preventing the subsequent copying.[568]

To address this diminution of a copyright's value, the EU has given the author a rental and lending right. The Rental Rights Directive requires the member states to provide a right to authorize or prohibit the rental and lending of

---

565. *Id.* at art. 5(1).
566. *Id.* at art. 6(1).
567. *Id.* at art. 8(1).
568. As mentioned below, only the right of distribution is exhausted upon first sale.

originals and copies of copyrighted works, including films and recorded music.[569] The rental rights are not exhausted by any sale or other act of distribution of originals and copies of copyrighted works.

Where an author or performer has transferred or assigned his rental right concerning a phonogram or an original or copy of a film to a phonogram or film producer, that author or performer retains the right to obtain an equitable remuneration for the rental. The right to obtain an equitable remuneration for rental cannot be waived by authors or performers.

The owner of the exclusive right to authorize or prohibit rental and lending depends on the type of work being rented. For recorded music or film, the producer holds the right. For recorded performances, the performer holds the right. In all other works, the author holds the right.

4.9 Rights of Performers and Broadcasters

Performances and broadcasts are fleeting. In other words, once a performance is completed, it no longer exists except in the mind of the audience. The performances of the great pantomime Marcel Marceau, which were not recorded on a fixed medium, are lost forever. The same applies to a broadcast. Once a broadcast is over, it no longer exists unless recorded on a fixed medium. To reward performers and broadcasters for the intellectual and creative investment they put into their performances and broadcasts, performers[570] and broadcasters[571] have the exclusive right to authorize or prohibit the fixation of their performances and broadcasts.

In addition, performers have the right to prohibit reproductions of such fixations as discussed above[572] as well as the right to prohibit broadcasting by wireless means and the communication to the public of their performances, except where the performance is itself already a broadcast performance or is made from a fixation.[573] Broadcasting organizations have the exclusive right to authorize or prohibit the rebroadcasting of their broadcasts by wireless means, as well as the communication to the public of their broadcasts if such communication is made in places accessible to the public against payment of an entrance fee.[574]

Member states may provide for limitations to the rights of performers and broadcasters for private use; use of short excerpts in connection with the reporting of current events; ephemeral fixation by a broadcasting organization

---

569. Directive 2006/115/EC of the European Parliament and of the Council of 12 December 2006 on rental right and lending right and on certain rights related to copyright in the field of intellectual property, 2006 O.J. (L 376) 28.
570. *Id.* at art. 7(1).
571. *Id.* at art. 7(2).
572. Information Society Directive at art. 2(b).
573. Rental Rights Directive at art. 8(1).
574. *Id.* at art. 8(3). According to the ECJ, the concept of "communication to the public" in the context of the Rental Rights Directive is different than the same concept used in the Copyright Directive which is discussed above. Case C-351/12, OSA v. Léčebné lázně Mariánské Lázně a.s., 2014 E.C.R. I-____, at ¶35.

by means of its own facilities and for its own broadcasts; and use solely for the purposes of teaching or scientific research.[575]

4.10 Artists' Resale Rights

For practical (and most often legal) purposes, once an artist sells his artwork, he generally loses control over subsequent sales of that artwork. He also does not typically share in any monetary benefits resulting from such subsequent sale. For example, a photographer may hold a gallery exhibition of a series of her photographs. A buyer of one of those photographs may display it on his wall for a number of years and then decide to sell it. When that buyer subsequently sells that photograph, the photographer is typically not involved in the transaction and receives no direct financial benefit from it (unless, of course, an appropriate agreement was reached between the photographer and the initial buyer). In some cases, the subsequent sellers are able to realize significant profits from the subsequent sale of the artwork. Rarely does the artist benefit financially from these subsequent transactions.

The Artists Resale Rights Directive is based on the recognition that the artist is not in a position to adequately negotiate favorable terms of sale, but should nonetheless receive some financial participation in subsequent sales of his or her artwork. To ensure that the artist receives some financial benefit from the subsequent sale of his or her artwork, the Artists Resale Rights Directive requires the member states to adopt laws giving the artist a nonwaivable right to a royalty for subsequent sales of his/her work.[576] This right, similar to a copyright, lasts for 70 years and is transferred to the artist's heirs upon the artist's death.[577]

The general rule is that the royalty must be paid by the seller of the work. National law may, however, permit the buyer and the seller to agree in the contract for the sale of the work of art that the buyer is responsible for the royalty payment to the artist.[578] The right attaches to works selling above €3,000. The highest rate of royalty is 4 percent. The right extends to artists of third states (e.g., the United States), provided that the country where the artist is a national also recognizes artists resale rights. As the United States does not recognize artists' resale rights, this precludes artists from the United States claiming the right in the EU even if their artwork is sold there.

---

575. Rental Rights Directive at art. 10(1).
576. Directive 2001/84/EC of 27 September 2001 on the resale right for the benefit of the author of an original work or art, 2001 O.J. (L 272) 32 [hereinafter Artists Resale Rights Directive].
577. *Id.* at art. 8(1). According to the ECJ, it is up to each member state to decide whether this transfer at death is limited to statutory heirs or to testamentary heirs. Case C-518/08, Fundación Gala-Salvador Dalí v. Société des auteurs dans les arts graphiques et plastiques, 2010 E.C.R. I-3111, 3127 ¶36.
578. Case C-41/14, Christie's France SNC v. Syndicar national des antiquarires, 2015 E.C.R. I-____ ¶32.

5. Design Rights

The term "design" generally refers to the outwardly visible appearance of a product. The uniqueness of a design often results from its lines, contours, colors, shape, texture, or materials. For example, the shape of a Porsche Carrera car is very distinctive. When an automobile consumer is looking at a car, and sees a car in the shape of a Porsche Carrera, he will probably associate that car with Porsche without even having to look at the label.

Designs could technically be protected by copyright, trademark, or patent law. In fact, many companies have both trademark and design protection for the same design. However, designs often do not meet the requirements for trademark protection.[579] As designs often relate to the packaging of a product or its function, it is difficult for a design to benefit from trademark protection unless it has become distinctive through use.[580] For example, B&W Loudspeakers Ltd applied for a trademark on the design of one of its speakers. The OHIM Board of Appeal held that "the relevant consumer..., when noticing the particular shape of the loudspeaker ...will perceive it, in the first place, as at least serving some functional purpose but will not, without previously having been told to

---

579. There is a close similarity between design protection and trademark protection for shapes. As discussed above, trademark protection for shapes is possible under the Trademark Regulation. In fact, it is possible to secure trademark and design protection for the same image. However, the requirements for trademark protection and design protection are different. One fundamental requirement of trademark protection is that the shape be distinctive. Design protection, however, requires only that the design is new and has individual character. It is not necessary that the design have the ability to distinguish that company's products and create an association between the product and the company. In addition, the distinctiveness of a trademark will be examined by OHIM upon registration. The novelty and individual character of a design are not examined upon registration. It may be advantageous for a company to register a design under the Design Regulation and use the 25 years of protection to establish distinctiveness—i.e., that the public associates that design with the company. The term of trademark protection is generally longer as it can be renewed. Because of this, owners of new graphic trademarks, such as corporate logos, should consider Union design protection to supplement trademark protection. The reason is that trademark protection is based on a likelihood of public confusion as to the product origin, which in turn may depend on whether the parties' respective goods or services are similar or related. Union design rights may be infringed even if there is no likelihood of confusion of source because the parties' goods are totally unrelated and would not be expected to come from a common source. This duration allows the owner of a Union design to build up the necessary distinctiveness to later secure trademark protection.
580. Case C-136/02P, Mag Instrument, Inc. v. OHIM, 2004 E.C.R. I-9165 (three dimensional shape of a flashlight not distinctive for flashlights); Joined Cases T-146/02 – T-153/02, Deutsche SiSi-Werke GmbH & Co. Betriebs KG v. OHIM, 2004 E.C.R. II-447 (three-dimensional shape of a pouch used as packaging for certain beverages not distinctive and hence nonregistrable as a trademark.); Decision of the OHIM Board of Appeals in case R0402/2004 (Nov. 3, 2004) (shape of a bottle not sufficiently distinctive); Decision of the OHIM Board of Appeal in case R 64/2004-1 (Oct. 5, 2004) (shape of a chocolate bar not sufficiently distinctive).

do so, understand or recognize it as a trademark identifying the undertaking marketing the good."[581]

5.1 Source of Law

In the EU, designs are protected under national law as well as under EU law. The national laws of the member states are harmonized by the Design Directive.[582] In addition, it is possible to register a design with the OHIM, giving the registrant EU-wide design rights. The EU design rights system is established by the Design Regulation[583] which grants protection to designs provided that the design is new and has individual character.[584]

Several international conventions apply to designs. The Paris Convention for the Protection of Industrial Property simply requires its signatories to protect industrial designs.[585] There are no additional constraints on the signatories. Although the EU is not a signatory, most of the EU member states have acceded to this Convention.

As discussed above, the TRIPS Agreement to which the EU has acceded covers various types of intellectual property, including designs. The signatories are required to provide for the protection of independently created industrial designs that are new or original.[586] The owner of a protected industrial design has the right (for a period of at least 10 years) to prevent third parties from making, selling, or importing articles bearing or embodying a design which is a copy, or substantially a copy, of the protected design, when such acts are undertaken for commercial purposes.[587]

The Geneva Act of the Hague Agreement for the International Registration of Industrial Designs[588] establishes an international system which confers national protection by filing a single application with the WIPO. Within this application, the states in which protection is sought must be designated. For example, the applicant may designate protection in the United States and in the EU. A registration under the Geneva Act is treated the same as a registration under the Trademark Regulation.[589]

---

581. Decision of the OHIM Fourth Board of Appeal in case R 0811/2002-4, (Jan. 5, 2004) at ¶12.
582. Directive 98/71/EC of the European Parliament and of the Council of 13 October 1998 on the legal protection of designs, 1998 O.J. (L 289) 28.
583. Council Regulation No. 6/2002 on Community Designs, 2002 O.J. (L 3) 1 [hereinafter Design Regulation].
584. The design must not be contrary to public policy or morals. Design Regulation at art. 9.
585. TRIPS at art. 5*quinquies*.
586. *Id.* at art. 25(1).
587. *Id.* at art. 26(1).
588. The Hague Agreement, which originated in 1925, has several versions. The version to which the EU has acceded is the Geneva Act. Council Decision of 18 December 2006 approving the accession of the European Community to the Geneva Act on the Hague Agreement concerning the international registration of industrial designs, adopted in Geneva on 2 July 1999, 2006 O.J. (L 386) 28.
589. Design Regulation at art. 106d.

5.2 Requirements for European Design Protection

As mentioned above, it is possible to register a design with the OHIM in accordance with the Design Regulation. Only designs that are new and have individual character may be registered, provided they are not contrary to public morals or solely dictated by function.

(a) Concept of a Design

The concept of a design refers to the outward appearance of a product resulting from the lines, contours, colors, shape, texture, materials, or ornamentation.[590] However, it is the appearance and not the color, shape, texture, or material that is protected. For example, the design of a glass bottle does not protect the glass but rather the design of the glass.

The appearance must be that of a product. A "product" means any industrial or handicraft item, including packaging, get-up, graphic symbols, or typographic typescales.[591] The concept of product would not include, for example, computer programs. It does not have to be an end product. Parts of a product composed of multiple components are also considered products for purposes of the Design Regulation.

The concept of product includes component parts such as the bumper of a car provided that the component part is visible.[592] It should be noted, however, that the protection accorded to component parts is less than other designs. A third party is allowed to produce and sell these parts specifically for repair of an original product without infringing the registered Union design. This means, for example, that an automobile manufacturer may rely on design rights to prevent its competitors from using the same design on their competing automobiles, but may not prevent spare parts manufacturers from selling replacement parts for that automobile.

(b) Newness of Design

A design must be new. A design is considered to be new if no identical design has been previously made available to the public.[593] The identical requirement does not mean absolutely identical. If the designs differ only in immaterial details, they will still be considered identical.[594] This is a factual determination to be made

---

590. *Id.* at art. 3(a).
591. *Id.* at art. 3(b).
592. *Id.* at art. 4(2). A design which is incorporated in a complex product meets the newness requirement only if the component part, once it has been incorporated into the complex product, remains visible during normal and those visible features fulfill in themselves the requirements as to novelty and individual character. A complex product is one which is composed of multiple components and those components can be disassembled and reassembled. T-494/12, Biscuits Poult SAS v. OHIM, 2014 E.C.R. II-____, at ¶27 (a cookie is not a complex product because its component parts cannot be disassembled and reassembled).
593. Design Regulation at art. 5(1).
594. *Id.* at art. 5(2).

on a case-by-case basis. The General Court uses a perceptibility standard.[595] In *EHEIM Möbel GmbH v. Grandtra Group Europe Sp. Zo.o.*, for example, a Polish company registered a design for the following stadium seat:

A German company challenged the registration. One of the arguments advanced by the German company was that the design was not novel. A design fulfills the newness requirement only if it has not previously been made available to the public. Several years earlier, the German company had registered the following design for stadium seats:

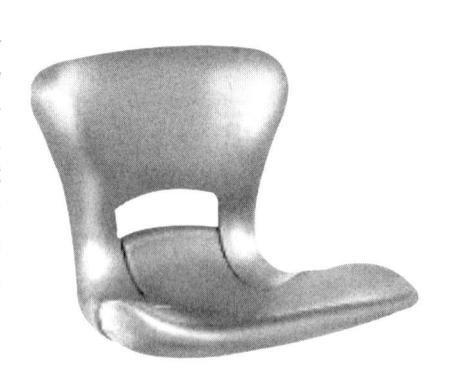

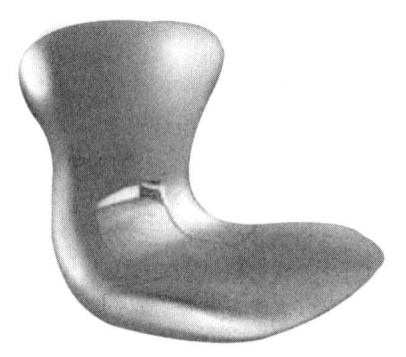

The only perceptible difference between the two designs was that the design of the German company was in black and white and the design of the Polish company was in blue. Nonetheless, the OHIM concluded that the two designs were not identical within the meaning of the Design Regulation because "the feature of colour is not an immaterial detail."[596] Consequently, the subsequently registered design met the newness requirement.[597]

For a design to fulfill the newness requirement, it must have not previously been made available to the public. There are two ways in which a design may be made available to the public. First, a design is made available to the public once it is registered and subsequently published. Second, a design may be made available to the public without its having been registered if it is exhibited, used in trade, or otherwise disclosed in such a way that, in the normal course of business, these events could reasonably have become known to the circles specialized in the sector concerned within the EU.[598] In *Sphere Time v. OHIM*, for example, a shipment of the goods from Hong Kong to the Netherlands prior to the design's registration date precluded the registrant from enforcing that design.[599]

---

595. Case T-41/14, Argo Development and Manufacturing Ltd. v. OHIM, 2015 E.C.R. II-____, at ¶27.
596. EHEIM Möbel GmbH v. Grandtra Group Europe Sp. Zo.o., Decision of the OHIM of Mar. 7, 2011.
597. As discussed below, however, the subsequently registered design lacked the requisite individual character.
598. Design Regulation at art. 7.
599. Case T-68/10, Sphere Time v. OHIM, 2011 E.C.R. II-2779, 2790 ¶30.

The exhibition, use, or disclosure itself does not have to occur in the EU.[600] The critical issue is whether the design has become known to the circles specialized in the sector concerned operating within the EU. This means that designs exhibited outside Europe—for example, the presentation of a new car design at a car show in the United States—could preclude the subsequent registration of the design in the EU if it is reasonable to expect that car designers from the EU would be present at the trade show.

It is important to point out, however, that there is a one-year grace period for the owner of the design after disclosure. Once the design is made available to the public, the owner of the design has 12 months in which to register.[601] If, for example, Ford were to introduce to European designers its new design for a particular line of automobiles at a trade show in Detroit, Ford would still have one year to register that design in the EU and still claim it was new.

It is, of course, difficult to maintain the absolute secrecy of a design for a long period of time. In many cases, a number of employees and outside marketing consultants will contribute to the creation of the new design. The fact that these individuals are aware of the design—even for an extended period of time exceeding one year—does not necessarily preclude the finding that the design is new for purposes of the Design Regulation. If the design becomes available to a legal or natural person under a confidentiality agreement, it will not be considered to have been made available to the public for purposes of the novelty requirement codified in the Design Regulation.

(c) Individual Character

In addition to being new, a Union design must have individual character. A design is considered to have individual character if the overall impression it produces on the informed user differs from the overall impression produced on such a user by any design that has previously been made available to the public.[602] As design protection concerns the appearance of the product, the internal design of the product is not relevant in the analysis unless it can be observed by the user.[603]

The "user" is the person who uses the product into which the design is incorporated.[604] The qualification as an informed user means that the user is

---

600. Case C-479/12, H. Gautzsch Großhandel GmbH & Co. KG v. Münchener Boulevard Möbel Joseph Duna GmbH, 2014 E.C.R. I-____, at ¶33.
601. Design Regulation at art. 7(2)(b).
602. Case T-41/14, Argo Development and Manufacturing Ltd. v. OHIM, 2015 E.C.R. II-____, at ¶27. The comparison to previous designs must look at the previous designs individually, and not at the various elements of previous designs. Case C-345/13, Karen Millen Fashions Ltd. v. Dunnes Stores, 2014 E.C.R. I-____, at ¶35. For example, a design does not lack individual character just because it shares some elements with various past designs. The comparison must be made to each past design individually.
603. Case T-357/12, Sachi Premium-Outdoor Furniture v. OHIM, 2014 E.C.R. II-____, at ¶56.
604. Case T-68/11, Kastenholz v. OHIM, 2013 E.C.R. II-____, at ¶58; Case T-337/12, El Hogar Perfecto del Siglo XXI v. OHIM, 2013 E.C.R. II-____, at ¶23.

more than the average consumer but not necessarily an expert.[605] At a minimum, the informed user must have a basic familiarity with the designs used in the particular industry at issue and show a relatively high degree of attention to the design when she uses them.[606] The "informed" element requires that "without being a designer or a technical expert, the user knows the various designs which exist in the sector concerned, possesses a certain degree of knowledge with regard to the features which those designs normally include, and, as a result of his interest in the products concerned, shows a relatively high degree of attention when he uses them."[607]

Although similar, the individual character requirement needs to be distinguished from the newness requirement.[608] As discussed above, the newness requirement examines whether any identical designs have been previously made available to the public. The individual character requirement does not examine the specific characteristics of the design, but rather the overall impression the design has on an informed user. A design may be new and yet not have individual character. As discussed above, for example, in *EHEIM Möbel GmbH v. Grandtra Group Europe Sp. Zo.o.*, the OHIM concluded that a stadium seat was new despite the fact that the design for a similar seat had previously been registered as an EU design.[609]

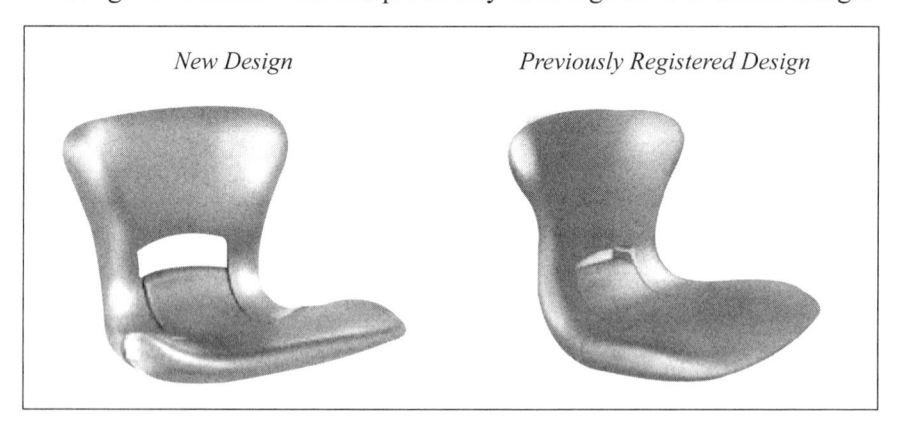

New Design *Previously Registered Design*

According to the OHIM, the subsequently registered design was new because it was in blue (instead of in black and white as the previously registered design). In this particular case, however the previously registered design did not meet the individual character requirement because the overall impression of the two chairs was the same from the perspective of an informed user: "the informed user is aware that chairs are produced in all kinds of colours. The overall impressions of the [newly registered design] and the

---

605. Case C-281/10 P, PepsiCo, Inc. v. Grupo Promer Mon Graphic SA, 2011 E.C.R. I-10178, 10195 ¶53; Case T-68/11, Kastenholz v. OHIM, 2013 E.C.R. II-____, at ¶59.
606. Case T-68/10, Sphere Time v. OHIM, 2011 E.C.R. II-2779, 2796 ¶51.
607. Case C-281/10 P, PepsiCo, Inc. v. Grupo Promer Mon Graphic SA, 2011 E.C.R. I-10178, 10197 ¶59.
608. Case T-357/12, Sachi Premium-Outdoor Furniture v. OHIM, 2014 E.C.R. II-____, at ¶29.
609. EHEIM Möbel GmbH v. Grandtra Group Europe Sp. Zo.o., Decision of the OHIM of Mar. 7, 2011.

prior design are determined by the shape and the contours of the chairs. Since these features are the same for both designs, the overall impressions produced on an informed user by the prior design and the [subsequent design], respectively, are the same."[610]

In *Apple Inc. v. XOYA Limited & Co. KG*, a German company tried to register a design for an MP3 player which looked remarkably similar to a design previously registered by Apple.

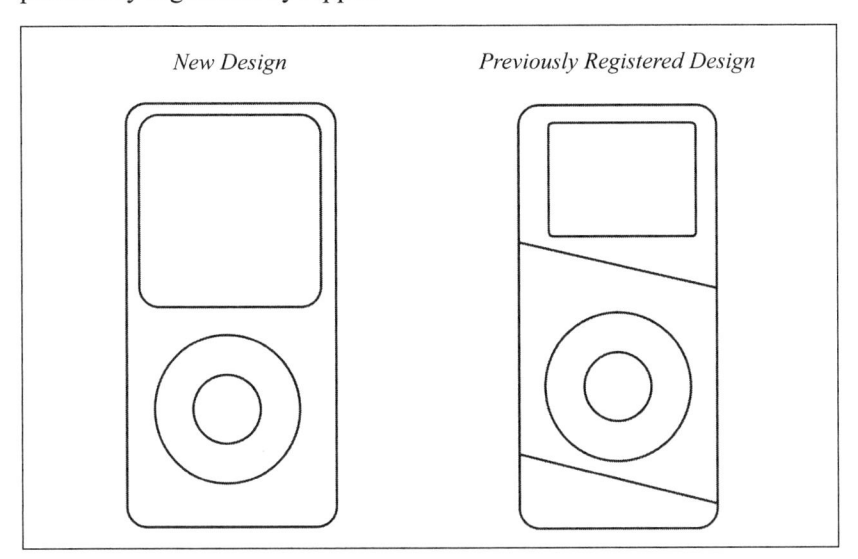

The OHIM concluded that the subsequently registered design was new as the two designs were not identical.[611] However, the subsequently registered design lacked individual character. According to the OHIM: "The contested design and the [Apple design] each have a basic rectangular shape, a square display in the upper region of the device and a circular operating element. The informed user will focus on these dominant common features of the Union design. The non-identical proportions of the displays on the other hand are noticeable only when making a direct comparison of both devices, and are not capable of making a different overall impression on the informed user. The contested design therefore lacks the necessary individual character."[612]

Another important consideration is the degree of the designer's freedom in developing the design at issue. The greater the freedom the designer has when developing a design, the less likely that minor differences between the design and any earlier designs will be sufficient to produce a different overall impression on the user.[613] In other words, if the designer has broad latitude

---

610. *Id.* at 16.
611. Apple Inc. v. XOYA Limited & Co. KG, OHIM Decision of May 26, 2008, ¶18. *See also* Decision of the Third Board of Appeal of October 19, 2009 in case R 1080/2008-3 ¶18.
612. *Id.* at ¶21.
613. Case T-41/14, Argo Development and Manufacturing Ltd. v. OHIM, 2015 E.C.R. II-____ ¶¶37-48; Case T-337/12, El Hogar Perfecto del Siglo XXI v. OHIM, 2013 E.C.R. II-____, at ¶31; Case T-11/08, Kwang Yang Motor v. OHIM, 2011 E.C.R. II-266, at ¶26.

in designing the product, minor differences are less likely to give the product individual character.[614] Conversely, if the designer has narrow latitude in designing the product, minor differences are more likely to give the product individual character.

As illustrated in *EHEIM Möbel GmbH v. Grandtra Group Europe Sp. Zo.o.*, in making the comparison to any prior designs, the presentation of the design in the application is important. Only features presented in the application are included in the comparison. For example, if the design is represented in the application by merely an outline of the design without any color, then that same colorless design will be used when determining if the overall impression it produces on the informed user differs from the overall impression produced on such a user by any design that has previously been made available to the public.[615] Hence, the incentive to draft an application broadly to preclude future designers from copying the design is tempered by the risk that design that is broadly presented in the application will not differ from an earlier design. For example, if the design of the iPod depicted above were presented in the application in bright red, the chances of its differing from previous designs is greater. However, such a narrow presentation would result in narrower protection against future designs.

An additional requirement is imposed if the design is for a component part of another product. A product which constitutes a component part of a complex product must be visible during normal use of the product in addition to being novel and having individual character.[616] For example, the design of a heat exchanger which is inside of a boiler was held not to be protected under the Design Regulation.[617]

(d) Contrary to Public Morals

The design must not be contrary to public policy or to accepted principles of morality.[618] Merely being in poor taste is (unfortunately) not a ground for the OHIM to refuse registrability. However, a design containing a racist message would not be registrable as it is contrary to public morals.

(e) Not Dictated by Function

A design may not subsist in features of appearance of a product which are solely dictated by the product's technical function.[619] For example, the design of a table tennis ball is dictated by its function.[620] The fact that the technical function may be achieved through more than one design (commonly referred to as the multiplicity of forms theory) does not necessarily mean that the

---

614. Case T-339/12, Gandia Blasco, SA v. OHIM, 2014 E.C.R. II-____, at ¶18.
615. The Procter & Gamble Company v. Reckitt Benckiser (UK) Ltd., [2006] EWHC 3154 (Ch) ¶48 (Dec. 13, 2006).
616. Case T-616/13, Aic S.A. v. OHIM, 2015 E.C.R. II-____ ¶11.
617. *Id.* at ¶35.
618. Design Regulation at art. 9.
619. *Id.* at art. 8(1).
620. The Procter & Gamble Company v. Reckitt Benckiser (UK) Ltd., [2006] EWHC 3154 (Ch) ¶28 (Dec. 13, 2006).

particular design is not solely dictated by function. According to the OHIM's Board of Appeals: "This would mean that both solutions could be the subject of a design registration, possibly held by the same person, which would have the consequence that no one else would be able to manufacture a competing product capable of performing the same technical function."[621] Instead, "a product's configuration [is] solely dictated by its technical function if every feature of the design [is] determined by technical considerations."[622]

5.3 Registration

Designs are registered with the OHIM in a similar way to an EU trademark. Once registered, the application is published in the *Union Design Bulletin* and a certificate of registration issued. Although the OHIM does not examine the newness of the design or its individual character, the examiner can refuse the application where he or she finds that the subject matter of the application does not correspond to the definition of a design as discussed above or is contrary to public morality.[623] However, the examiner does not examine the newness of the design. Instead, the newness and individual character of a design are only examined in the context of a challenge by a third party.[624] A third party has the right to challenge a registered Union design by filing with the OHIM an application for a declaration of invalidity.[625]

5.4 Scope of Protection

The fundamental protection accorded to the owner of a registered Union design is that the owner has the exclusive right to use the design and to prevent any third party from using it.[626] The term "use" includes the making, offering, putting on the market, importing, exporting, or using a product in which the design is incorporated or to which it is applied, or stocking such a product for those purposes. Acts that constitute infringement are unauthorized manufacture, supply, use, import, export, or other dealing. Intent to infringe is not required. The infringers may not even be aware of the registered design.

The design rights are held by the designer or his successor in interest.[627] If two or more persons have jointly developed a design, they hold the right jointly. If the designer is an employee, and the design was developed in the scope

---

621. Decision of the OHIM Board of Appeals in case no. R 690/2007-3 (of Oct. 22, 2009) at ¶30.
622. *Id.* at ¶31.
623. Design Regulation at art. 47(1).
624. This is one of the fundamental differences between the registration of designs in the EU and in the United States, where the examiner undertakes an independent review of the novelty of the design as part of the application process.
625. Design Regulation at art. 52(1).
626. *Id.* at art. 19(1).
627. *Id.* at art. 14(1). The issue of the ownership of the design is not decided by the OHIM, but rather by the national courts of the member states. Decision of the OHIM Third Board of Appeal in case no. R 64/2007-3 (Feb. 11, 2008) at ¶17.

of the employment, then the rights to the design are held by the employer.[628] However, if a company outsources or consigns the development of the design to a third party, the company is not the designer (but rather the person to which it was outsourced or consigned). To prevent this from happening, it is common for companies to include provisions in their design development agreements according to which the actual designer assigns his or her rights to the company. According to the ECJ, a "successor in interest" includes a company to which the rights were assigned on the basis of a contract.[629]

5.5 Duration

The protection accorded to registered designs lasts for five years as of the date of the filing of the application. However, the right holder may have the term of protection renewed for one or more periods of five years each, up to a total term of 25 years from the date of filing.[630] In certain cases, a company may introduce a design which is not distinctive and therefore cannot qualify for trademark protection. Assume, for example, a startup chair manufacturing company intends to introduce a new line of chairs. The shape of the chair might not be sufficiently distinctive to distinguish that company's chairs from those of its competitors. Hence, it could not secure trademark protection. It could, however, secure design protection (assuming it was new and had individual character). It would then have at least five (and potentially 25) years to achieve distinctiveness through use. It could then apply for trademark protection for that same shape.

5.6 Invalidity of Registered Designs

As discussed above, the OHIM does not examine the newness of a design when it is registered. The validity of a registered design can be subsequently challenged by a third party in a claim brought by a third party or as part of a defense to an infringement claim brought against the third party by the owner of the design. For example, if the company which registered the design seeks to prevent another party from using a similar design, it may initiate legal proceedings in a member state under national law against the third party.[631] There are several bases for declaring a registered design invalid.

(a) Failure to Meet Requirements

As discussed above, a design must meet specific requirements in order to gain protection under the Design Regulation. As the OHIM does not examine newness and individual character upon registration, designs may be registered that do not meet these requirements. Such designs are, however, subject to being challenged by third parties. A Union design may be declared invalid if

---

628. Design Regulation at art. 14(3).
629. Case C-32/08, Fundación Española para la Innovación de la Artesanía v. Cul de Sac Espacio Creativo SL, 2009 E.C.R. I-5611, at ¶71.
630. Design Regulation at art. 12.
631. Each member state has specific courts with jurisdiction to hear design-related cases. Design Regulation at art. 80(1). These courts have the authority to decide infringement issues and even to declare an EU registration invalid. *Id.* at art. 81.

the design does not correspond to the definition of design or failure to meet the requirements discussed above.[632]

(b) Conflict with Other Design

A design may be declared invalid if it conflicts with a prior design which has been made available to the public either after the date the application of the Union design is filed or, if a priority is claimed for the Union design, the date of priority of the Union design.[633] The prior design must already be a registered Union design or registered as a design in at least one member state. The possibility of two designs both being registered with the OHIM arises because the OHIM does not test the substantive requirements for a design when the design is registered. The subsequently registered design remains valid until it has been declared invalid by the OHIM or a court with jurisdiction.[634]

(c) Unauthorized Incorporation of a Protected Sign

A registered design may not incorporate a distinctive sign which is protected by EU or member state law, such as a trademark.[635] The sign that is incorporated into the design does not have to be identical to a protected sign. It is sufficient that the sign is similar to a protected design.[636] In *Hrudka v. Ajeto, Spol. S.R.O.*,[637] for example, Ajeto, Spol. S.R.O. registered the following design as a Union design:

PRAGUE DRINKING TEAM
CZECH REPUBLIC

Jiří Hrudka contested the design registration, claiming that it incorporated the following national trademark registered in the Czech Republic:

PRAHA DRINKING TEAM
ČESKÁ REPUBLIKA

---

632. *Id.* at art. 25(1).
633. *Id.* at art. 25(1)(d).
634. Case C-488/10, Celaya Emparanza y Galdos Internacional SA v. Proyectos Integrales de Balizamiento SL, 2012 E.C.R. I-____, at ¶51.
635. Design Regulation at art. 25(1)(e).
636. Case T-55/12, Su-Shan Chen v. OHIM, 2013 E.C.R. II-____, at ¶31; Case T-608/11, Beifa Group Co. Ltd. v. OHIM, 2013 E.C.R. II-____, at ¶82.
637. Decision of the OHIM of Sept. 6, 2010 (Design number 000915095-0001).

According to the OHIM, a registered design is deemed to use a sign which is identical or similar to the sign of the earlier trademark where the following two conditions are met: (1) the design contains a feature which is perceived as a sign and (2) that sign is identical or similar to the sign of the trademark.[638] In invalidating the design registration, the OHIM stated:

> In the present case, the [design] comprises the term "PRAGUE DRINKING TEAM CZECH REPUBLIC" which is very similar to the earlier trade mark word element, the only difference being the translation of the Czech capital city and country's name from Czech into English. Furthermore, the figurative elements used in both signs are also very similar since a glass of beer and a Czech national flag are included in both signs. Therefore, the [design] contains a feature which could be perceived as a sign identical or similar to the sign of the earlier trade mark.[639]

(d) Unauthorized Incorporation of a Protected Copyright

Similar to the restrictions on the use of a trademark in a registered Union design, a registered design may be declared invalid if it constitutes an unauthorized use of a work protected under the copyright law of a member state.[640]

5.7 Possible Disadvantage of Registered Designs

As designs registered with the OHIM, like trademarks registered with the OHIM, have a unitary character (i.e., they are valid throughout the EU without the need for separate registrations in the individual member states), they are exposed to the same disadvantages. A third party needs only to be successful once in its challenge to the validity of the registration. A design that is registered at the national level in each of the member states would have to be challenged in each of the member states. Moreover, the owner of the OHIM-registered design right can only transfer ownership of the whole right. If that owner instead had a bundle of national design rights, and it wanted to transfer the rights to specific member states, it could do so.

5.8 Unregistered Designs

It is not necessary to register a design with the OHIM to secure protection. Even unregistered designs enjoy some protection under the Design Regulation. However, the protection accorded to unregistered designs is slightly different than for registered designs. An unregistered Union design confers the right to prevent third parties from using the design only if the contested use results from copying the protected design. For example, if the design results from an independent work by a designer who may be reasonably thought not to be

---

638. *Id.* at ¶16.
639. *Id.* at ¶¶17-18.
640. Design Regulation at art. 25(1)(f).

familiar with the design made available to the public by the holder, the holder of an unregistered design cannot prevent that person from using it.[641]

The unregistered design must fulfill the same newness and individuality requirements as apply to registered designs. An unregistered design is considered to be new if no identical design has been made available to the public before the date on which the design for which protection is claimed has first been made available to the public. Similar to a registered design, an unregistered design has individual character if the overall impression it produces on the informed user differs from the overall impression produced on such a user by any design which has previously been made available to the public.[642]

In addition to having a broader scope of protection, registered designs have other advantages over unregistered designs. The protection accorded to unregistered designs only lasts for three years beginning on the date the unregistered design was made public in the EU (as opposed to a maximum of 25 years for registered designs).[643] If, for example, the unregistered design is used or made public only in China, the protection in the EU has not started (and the owner of the unregistered design cannot preclude others in the EU from using it).[644] Another benefit of registering a design is that registration and subsequent publication establishes public disclosure and hence would preclude a third party from meeting the novelty requirement discussed above.

6. Limitations on Intellectual Property Rights

Intellectual property rights serve the social purpose of stimulating creativity. They achieve this objective by granting certain exclusive rights to the individual who derived the idea. However, there are a number of important limitations which the European legal system places on intellectual property rights.

6.1 General Principles of the Treaties

Intellectual property rights in the EU are limited by the general principles set forth in the treaties. This is illustrated in *Phil Collins v. Imtrat* which involved the conflict between a national intellectual property right and the fundamental

---

641. Design Regulation at art. 19(2). As opposed to a registered design, however, the person opposing the unregistered design carries the burden of proof. Case C-479/12, H. Gautzsch Großhandel GmbH & Co. KG v. Münchener Boulevard Möbel Joseph Duna GmbH, 2014 E.C.R. I-____, at ¶41.
642. Case C-345/13, Karen Millen Fashions Ltd. v. Dunnes Stores, 2014 E.C.R. I-____, at ¶25.
643. Design Regulation at art. 11. Whether a design is made available to the public is a question of fact. Case C-479/12, H. Gautzsch Großhandel GmbH & Co. KG v. Münchener Boulevard Möbel Joseph Duna GmbH, 2014 E.C.R. I-___, at ¶29.
644. Decision of the German Bundesgerichtshof in case no. I ZR 126/06 (Oct. 9, 2008) *reported in* 111 Gewerblicher Rechtsschutz und Urheberrecht 79 (2009).

prohibition against discrimination set forth in the TFEU.[645] In this case, Imtrat was trying to sell in Germany CD recordings of a concert Phil Collins gave in the United States which was recorded without his permission. Although German copyright law gave performers the right to prohibit the distribution of unauthorized recordings of their work, this protection only applied to German nationals. Non-Germans could only rely on the law if the performance took place in Germany. The ECJ essentially held that a member state may not apply its intellectual property law in such a way that it discriminates against nationals from other member states as in the present case. Hence, the German copyright law had to extend the same rights to other EU nationals as it does to Germans.

6.2 Relationship between IP Rights and Free Movement of Goods Principle

Intellectual property rights are negative in nature: they are a promise that the state will prevent others from encroaching on those rights. They are not "affirmative" in nature because they do not entitle the proprietor to use, create, or copy anything. Because they rely on state protection, they are also territorial in nature. In other words, they extend only to the geographic area under the sovereignty of the state which granted the rights. This means, for example, that the proprietor of a trademark in Spain can prohibit an unauthorized person from selling products under that trademark even if the third party is the lawful owner of the trademark in another country.

As discussed in Chapter III, Article 34 of the TFEU prohibits state measures which have an effect equivalent to quantitative restrictions on trade between member states. Laws and regulations such as intellectual property rights may be considered state measures. Consequently, reliance on these state measures by an intellectual property right holder may trigger the application of the prohibition on the free movement of goods codified in Article 34 of the TFEU.

If, for example, a pharmaceutical company with a UK trademark for a particular drug relies on that trademark to prevent the importation of a drug by another manufacturer under the same name, this would restrict the free movement of goods between member states. As discussed in Chapter III, however, Article 36 of the TFEU provides that the prohibition contained in Article 34 does not apply to "the protection of industrial and commercial property." Moreover, Article 345 of the TFEU specifically provides that the Treaty cannot prejudice the national rules on intellectual property rights. Consequently, the EU is limited by the TFEU in its application of the free movement of goods rule to restrictions involving intellectual property rights.

The application of Articles 36 and 345 of the TFEU created an obstacle to the integration efforts of the EU institutions. A company with intellectual property rights in several member states could effectively prevent the sale of its

---

645. Joined cases C-92/92 & C-326/92, Collins v. Imtrat, 1993 E.C.R. I-5145. Another case in which the TFEU was applied to limit national copyright laws is Case C-360/00, *Land Hessen v. G. Ricordi & Co.*, 2002 E.C.R. I-5089, with facts similar to *Collins v. Imtrat*.

products from one member state to another member state where it enjoyed such protection. To circumvent this potentially segregating effect, the ECJ relied on the distinction between the existence of an intellectual property right and the exercise of that right.[646] The distinction played a critical role in *Centrafarm BV v. Sterling Drug, Inc.*[647] In that case, Centrafarm purchased Sterling drugs in the UK and Germany (where they were relatively inexpensive) and resold them in the Netherlands (where they were more expensive). As Sterling Drug had a Dutch patent on the drugs, it sought to prevent these sales in the Netherlands. The issue was then whether Dutch law infringed Art. 34 of the TFEU because it restricted the trade of goods between member states.

On the one hand, the ECJ recognized the need to integrate the markets of the member states (note the early date of the case). On the other hand, Articles 30 and 345 of the TFEU restrict the ability of the EU institutions from encroaching on the intellectual property regimes maintained by the member states. In order to reconcile these provisions, the ECJ held that the TFEU could be applied to limit the exercise of an intellectual property right, but not its existence. The basic idea was that the TFEU prevented the EU from encroaching on the essential function (i.e., existence) of intellectual property rights granted by the member states. However, the TFEU did not prevent the EU institutions from limiting the "exercise" of the intellectual property right unless the exercise related to the essential function of the intellectual property right.[648] For example, it belongs to the essential function of a trademark that the proprietor may prevent the resale of a trademarked product which has been altered in a way (e.g., packaged) so as to impair the guarantee of origin function served by the trademark.[649]

Even the exercise of an intellectual property right may be prohibited by Article 34 of the TFEU if it is merely a disguised restriction on trade between member states.[650] Whether the exercise of a particular intellectual property right constitutes a disguised restriction on trade between member states arises frequently in the context of repackaging pharmaceutical products. The "repackaging cases" are discussed in greater detail below.

6.3 Exhaustion of Rights Doctrine

The introduction of the exercise/existence distinction facilitated the introduction of the exhaustion of rights doctrine, as the doctrine is applied to limit the exercise of intellectual property rights granted by the member states. Similar to the first sale doctrine in the United States,[651] this doctrine sets forth the basic principle that once the intellectual property right holder has exercised its right by placing

---

646. Case 78/70, Deutsche Grammophon GmbH v. Metro SB Großmärkte GmbH & Co., 1971 E.C.R. 487.
647. Case 15/74, Centrafarm BV v. Sterling Drug, Inc., 1974 E.C.R. I-1147.
648. Case C-421/04, Matratzen Concord AG v. Hukla Germany SA, 2006 E.C.R. I-2322, 2331 ¶28.
649. Case C-348/04, Boehringer Ingelheim v. Swingward Ltd., 2007 E.C.R. I-3430, 3448 ¶14.
650. *Id.* at 3448 ¶16.
651. Kirtsaeng v. John Wiley & Sons, Inc., 133 S.Ct. 1351 (2013).

the goods on the market, it has "exhausted" the right as it relates to subsequent sales of that product. The owner of that right can no longer rely on the right to preclude the subsequent sale of the goods.[652]

The exhaustion doctrine has essentially two elements. First, the goods must be placed into commerce in the EEA. Second, the introduction of the goods into commerce must have been by the owner or with the consent of the owner of the intellectual property right. The consent may be express or implied.[653]

(a) Sale in the EEA

Intellectual property rights are exhausted only upon the first sale in the EEA. This requirement has two components. First, there must be a sale. If, for example, the proprietor of the intellectual property gives the product away for free as a promotion, this would not exhaust its intellectual property rights in those products.[654] In *UsedSoft GmbH v. Oracle International Corp.*, the ECJ held that a "sale" of software occurs for purposes of the Computer Software Directive even when the software is licensed.[655] The mere importation into the EEA—and even the subsequent customs clearance—does not equate to a sale for the purposes of the exhaustion doctrine.[656] Moreover, the term sale does not include the rental or lending of the product. As discussed above, the Rental Rights Directive provides for a right to rent a copyrighted work.

In *Foreningen af Danske Videogramdistributer v. Laserdisken*,[657] a Danish company was importing video disks from the UK into Denmark where it would rent them. According to Danish law, renting a copyrighted work required the consent of the copyright holder. In this case, however, Laserdisken argued that the right of the copyright holder had been exhausted because it had consented to the renting of the video disks in the UK. The ECJ held that the rental rights of the copyright owner were not exhausted upon first rental in the EEA. To conclude otherwise would make the rental right "meaningless" because the owner would not receive any commercial benefits from subsequent rentals.[658] In other words, the owner in this case would only benefit from the rental of the first video disk.

---

652. *See, e.g.*, Information Society Directive at art. 4(2) and 9(2); Design Regulation at art. 21.
653. Case C-244/00, Van Doren + Q.GmbH v. Lifestyle sports + Sportswear Handelsgesellschaft mbH, 2003 E.C.R. I-3051, 3090 ¶34.
654. Case C-419/13, Art & Allposters International BV v. Stichting Pictoright, 2015 E.C.R. I-____ ¶31; Case C-324/09, L'Oréal SA v. eBay International AG, 2011 E.C.R. I-6073, 6106 ¶71.
655. Case C-128/11, UsedSoft GmbH v. Oracle International Corp., 2012 E.C.R. I-____, at ¶48.
656. Case C-16/03, Peak Holding AB v. Axolin-Elinor AB, 2004 E.C.R. I-11313, 11344 ¶44.
657. Case C-61/97, Foreningen af Danske Videogramdistributer v. Laserdisken, 1998 E.C.R. I-5171.
658. *Id.* at ¶18.

Second, the sale must be in the EEA.[659] The general rule is that the location of the sale is the location of the buyer. Therefore, if a company in Poland purchases products from a U.S. manufacturer, the European manufacturer's intellectual property rights relating to those specific products are exhausted. The issue in *Peak Holding AB v. Axolin-Elinor AB* was whether there is a sale in the EEA if the manufacturer prohibits its European distributor from reselling the product in the EEA, and the distributor, in breach of this contractual obligation, nonetheless resells the products in the EEA.[660] The ECJ held that this contractual prohibition does not prevent the exhaustion doctrine from applying to the particular goods (although the manufacturer may have a breach of contract claim against the distributor).[661]

The *Silhouette International Schmied v. Hartlauer Handelsgesellschaft*[662] case raises the interesting question of whether the right is exhausted when an owner in the EU introduces goods into commerce outside the EU, but those same goods are subsequently resold back into the EU. The Austrian eyeglasses manufacturer, Silhouette, sold a large number of eyeglasses to a Bulgarian wholesaler with the agreement that it would sell only in Bulgaria and in the former Soviet Republics. Nonetheless, Hartlauer was able to purchase the eyeglasses in Bulgaria and start selling them in Austria. At the time, some countries in the EU (including Austria) had been actively applying a principle of international exhaustion (i.e., the first sale anywhere in the world exhausts the intellectual property rights). In such countries, brand owners were unable to prevent branded goods put on the market elsewhere in the world from being resold in the EU. As applied to the *Silhouette* facts, international exhaustion would have prevented Silhouette from relying on its trademark to prevent the reimportation of its glasses.

According to the Trademark Directive (Art. 7), the proprietor of a trademark is not able to prevent the use of the trademark in relation to goods which have already been placed on the market in the EU. The issue was whether this case was limited to placing the goods on the market in the EU (EU exhaustion) or also outside the EU (international exhaustion), and whether—assuming the exhaustion was limited to the EU—the Trademark Directive prevented the member states from adopting more expansive exhaustion doctrine. The ECJ refused to adopt the principle of international exhaustion and held that the Directive embodied a complete harmonization and consequently precluded diverging national laws.

Silhouette International Schmied v. Hartlauer Handelsgesellschaft involved the exhaustion of trademark rights. As trademarks are commonly attached to physical objects, the territorial limitation of the exhaustion principle is relatively straightforward. Intellectual property rights embodied in intangible products

---

659. Case C-479/04, Laserdisken ApS v. Kulturministeriet, 2006 E.C.R. I-8113, 8120 ¶21.
660. Case C-16/03, Peak Holding AB v. Axolin-Elinor AB, 2004 E.C.R. I-11331.
661. *Id.* at 11347 ¶56.
662. Case C-355/96, Silhouette International Schmied v. Hartlauer Handelsgesellschaft, 1998 E.C.R. I-4799.

present a different issue. *Micro Leader Business v. Commission*[663] involved the application of the exhaustion principle to software. The issue was whether Microsoft could prohibit its French retailers from buying French versions of a certain software in Canada and selling it in France even though Microsoft was not selling the same software in France. The General Court held that there was no exhaustion in this case. Microsoft could rely on its intellectual property rights to prohibit the sale in France.[664]

(b) *Consent of IP Owner*

The second element of the exhaustion doctrine is the consent requirement: the first sale in the EEA must have been with the consent of the owner of the intellectual property. Generally, the consent required must be express. The ECJ will recognize implied consent only where the facts unequivocally show an intent by the trademark holder to release his or her rights. In *Levi-Strauss v. Tesco*,[665] Levi-Strauss sold Levis jeans in the United States, Canada, and Mexico. Someone in Europe noticed the high prices for the "501 jeans" in Europe and started buying them retail in the United States and exporting them for sale in the EU. Levi-Strauss claimed that the importer in the EU was infringing Levi's EU trademark. In its defense, the importer argued that Levi-Strauss implicitly consented by not prohibiting its U.S. retailers from selling for export. The ECJ refused to recognize implied consent in this case. It considered that the onus lay on the trader wishing to import the goods to demonstrate unequivocal consent by the proprietor of the trademark. Implied consent cannot be inferred from: (1) mere silence from the trademark proprietor; (2) the trademark proprietor's failure to communicate his opposition to marketing of such goods within the EEA (3) a lack of any warning or prohibition on the goods or contractual reservations from the proprietor regarding resale within the EEA or (4) the fact that, according to the law governing the contract, the property right transferred includes, in the absence of any reservations, an unlimited right of resale or a right to market the goods subsequently within the EEA.

In *Roche v. Kent Pharmaceuticals*, an English case decided by the English Court of Appeal, Roche USA, a subsidiary of Roche Germany, had sold certain medical diagnostic devices to a customer in Latin America.[666] The products were stamped with a "CE" marking which signified that they complied with EU regulations and could be sold there. The Court of Appeal held, however, that the mere fact that the goods displayed a CE marking did not establish express consent to the products being sold in Europe. Hence, the sale of the products to the Latin American customer did not exhaust the trademark rights in the EU held by the proprietor.

In *Vorschaubilder II*, however, the German Supreme Court was willing to imply the consent of a copyright holder. That case involved a photographer who gave consent to certain individuals to post some of his photographs on the

---

663. Case T-198/98, Micro Leader Business v. Comm'n, 1999 E.C.R. II-3989.
664. *Id.*
665. Joined cases C-414/99 – 416/99, Levi Strauss v. Tesco, 2001 E.C.R. I-8691.
666. Roche v. Kent Pharmaceuticals, [2006] EWCA Civ 1775 (2006).

Internet. When Google posted these images as thumbnails together with links to third party websites, the photographer claimed Google had infringed his copyright. The German Supreme Court, however, held that the consent of the photographer was to be implied once he posted these on the Internet.[667]

The consent must also be specific. *Sebago, Inc. and Ancienne Maison Dubois v. GB-Unic* addresses the issue of whether the consent given to specific goods applies to all goods of the same type.[668] In that case, a Belgian supermarket chain was selling Docksides shoes manufactured by Sebago in El Salvador. Sebago claimed that the supermarket chain was infringing its Belgian trademark by advertising the shoes for sale in Belgium. The supermarket argued that although Sebago did not give its consent to placing these specific shoes on the market in the EU, it did sell identical shoes in Europe, and hence exhausted its trademark rights. The ECJ held that the consent must relate to the specific goods. Otherwise, the trademark rights are not exhausted.

The consent must also be freely given. A compulsory license granted by the proprietor of an intellectual property right would not necessarily mean that the proprietor had consented to the sale of the goods. In *Pharmon BV v. Hoechst AG*, the German pharmaceutical manufacturer Hoechst held a patent in Germany, the Netherlands, and the UK for a particular pharmaceutical product called Frusemide. (Frusemide is a type of diuretic that is used for treating edema (fluid retention) caused by heart failure and certain lung, liver, and kidney disorders).[669] Under UK law at the time, a compulsory license could be granted for certain medicines and medical devices to any interested person unless there were good reasons for refusing the application. A UK company applied for and received a nonassignable, nonexclusive compulsory license for the drug in the UK from the UK Patent Office. Under the terms of the license, the licensee was prohibited from exporting the product. Although Hoechst did not agree to the license, the law did not require the patent holder's agreement. The law was based on the rationale that such compulsory patents serve to reduce the costs of pharmaceutical products by increasing competition. A third party, intending to market the product in the UK and in the Netherlands, argued that this license exhausted the rights of Hoechst in the drug. The ECJ held that the patentee in such circumstances should not be considered to have consented to the sale of its product.[670]

Granting a license to distribute the product or service in question may already exhaust the rights of the owner of the intellectual property unless the license agreement limits the exploitation rights of the licensee. In *Copad SA v. Christian Dior couture SA*, for example, a distributor of Christian Dior sold Dior trademarked products to a discount store in violation of the distribution agreement that distributor had with Christian Dior. In an attempt to protect the

---

667. Decision of the German Bundesgerichtshof in case no. Az. 1 ZR 140/10 (Oct. 19, 2011) reported in 65 Neue Juristische Wochenschrift 1886 (2012).
668. Case C-173/98, Sebago, Inc. and Ancienne Maison Dubois v. GB-Unic, 1999 E.C.R. I-4103.
669. Case 19/84, Pharmon BV v Hoechst AG, 1985 E.C.R. 2281.
670. *Id.* at 2298 ¶25.

image of Christian Dior products, the distribution agreement expressly prohibited sales to mail order companies and discount stores. The ECJ held that the sales by the distributor to the discount store did not exhaust the trademark rights of Christian Dior.[671] Consequently, Christian Dior was able to rely on its trademark rights to prohibit the discount store from selling the products.[672]

(c) Exhaustion in the Context of Various Intellectual Property Rights

Although the exhaustion doctrine is most commonly associated with trademarks, it generally applies to all forms of intellectual property. It is important to remember, however, that only the distribution right relating to that particular product or physical manifestation of the intellectual property right is exhausted. Neither the underlying intellectual property right nor the reproduction right is exhausted. For example, just because a patent holder sells a product which was made using his patent does not mean that the underlying patent right is exhausted. Nor does it mean that the purchaser of that product can copy or reproduce that product. Only the distribution right to that product is exhausted.

Patents. Patents protect the right to exclude others from making, using, or selling one's invention. Once the product is placed on the market, the distribution rights to that product are exhausted.[673] The holder of the patent right cannot control the further sale of that product on the basis of her patent right.[674]

Design Right. Once a product into which a protectable design is incorporated is sold by the holder of the design right, the rights conferred by a Union design are exhausted.[675]

Copyrights. Copyright and neighboring rights are exhausted once the tangible object embodying those rights is sold in the EU.[676] For example, if music is reduced to a DVD, its subsequent sale exhausts the musician's rights in that tangible medium (i.e., the DVD). The introduction of nontangible formats presents a conceptual challenge to the application of the exhaustion rule. For example, the distribution of software via the Internet does not require the reduction of the software to a tangible format. According to the Computer Software Directive, the first sale of a computer program exhausts the copyright in that program. Although the Directive does not explicitly require the sale

---

671. Case C-59/08, Copad SA v. Christian Dior couture SA, 2009 E.C.R. I-3439, 3454 ¶51.
672. *See also* Case C-140/10, Greenstar-Kanzi Europe NV v. Jean Hustin, 2011 E.C.R. I-10092, 10106 ¶43 (stating that the limitation in the license agreement must relate directly to the essential features of the Union intellectual property right).
673. Regulation (EU) No. 1257/2012 of the European Parliament and of the Council of 17 December 2012 implementing enhanced cooperation in the area of the creation of unitary patent protection, 2012 O.J. (L 361) 1 at art. 6.
674. However, the patent holder may exercise some control over the further sale of the products based on a contract with the buyer. The terms of the contract must comply with competition law as discussed in Chapter III.
675. Design Regulation at art. 21.
676. Information Society Directive at art. 4(2).

in a tangible medium, the ECJ has held that exhaustion occurs even when the software is downloaded from the Internet.[677] It should be recalled, however, that the sale only exhausts the distribution rights of the copyright or the neighboring right to that product, and the copyright holder still retains the reproduction right.[678] If one purchases software over the Internet, for example, one cannot copy that software for a friend without the copyright holder's consent. The reproduction of the copyright is only permissible if it is necessary for the lawful holder of the right to use the right.[679]

If the product is sold in the EU but subsequently altered, then the copyright holder's rights are not necessarily exhausted vis-a-vis the altered product. In *Art & Allposters International BV v. Stichting Pictoright*, a company in the Netherlands acquired posters which were protected by copyright. It then transposed those posters onto canvasses with the resulting image substantially the same. The General Court held that the rights of the copyright holder were not exhausted with respect to these reproductions on canvass: "What is important is whether the altered object itself, taken as a whole, is, physically, the object that was placed onto the market with the consent of the rightholder."[680] If not, then the right is not exhausted.

Database. The first sale in the EU of tangible medium containing a protected database by the rightholder or with his consent exhausts the right to control resale of that tangible medium within the EU.[681] This rule does not apply to online distribution because it is not "incorporated in a material medium."[682] In other words, the holder of the database right retains those rights even if she sells a copy of the database over the Internet.

Plant variety rights. The protections given to plant varieties under the Plant Variety Regulation are exhausted once the plant variety has been disposed of to others by the holder or with her consent, in any part of the Union.[683]

(d) Repackaging Limitation on the Exhaustion Doctrine

The application of the exhaustion doctrine means that the intellectual property owner no longer can control the subsequent sale of that product based on the intellectual property right. However, in situations where the product is altered or manipulated in some way, the proprietor of the intellectual property may be able to prevent or limit the subsequent resale if the alteration or manipulation is

---

677. Case C-128/11, UsedSoft GmbH v. Oracle International Corp., 2012 E.C.R. I-____, at ¶59.
678. Computer Software Directive at art. 4.
679. Case C-128/11, UsedSoft GmbH v. Oracle International Corp., 2012 E.C.R. I-____, at ¶81.
680. Case C-419/13, Art & Allposters International BV v. Stichting Pictoright, 2015 E.C.R. I-____ ¶45.
681. Database Directive at art. 5.
682. *Id.* at recital 33.
683. Council Regulation (EC) No. 2100/94 of 27 July 1994 on Community plant variety rights, 1994 O.J. (L 227) 1 at art. 16; Case C-140/10, Greenstar-Kanzi Europe NV v. Jean Hustin, 2011 E.C.R. I-10092, 10104 ¶31.

contrary to the objective of the intellectual property right. For example, one of the purposes of a trademark is to allow a purchaser to identify the quality of the product he or she is purchasing. If the condition of the product has been changed or impaired since it has been put on the market, the owner of the trademark may still be able to rely on her trademark rights to prevent the subsequent sale of the product.[684] The idea is that interference with the condition of the product means that the purpose (i.e., subject matter) of the mark (as an indication of origin) is obviated.[685]

The issue arises frequently in cases where an undertaking purchases pharmaceutical products in a low-cost member state and resells them in a high-cost member state. In most instances, the regulatory requirements of the high-cost member state necessitate the repackaging of the pharmaceutical products being brought in from another member state. But even taking into account the costs associated with the repackaging, the often significant price differences between the member states make this a financially rewarding enterprise. In such cases, the issue commonly arises whether the pharmaceutical manufacturer holding the trademark right has legitimate reasons for asserting those rights even though it has otherwise exhausted those rights by selling the products in another member state.[686]

The general rule is that the proprietor of the trademark may legitimately oppose the subsequent resale of the repackaged pharmaceutical product unless the importer can fulfill five requirements:[687]

- reliance on the trademark rights by the trademark proprietor would contribute to the artificial partitioning of the markets between member states;
- the new label does not affect the original condition of the product inside the packaging;
- the packaging clearly states who repackaged the product and the name of the manufacturer;
- the presentation of the repackaged product is not such as to be liable to damage the reputation of the trademark and of its proprietor; thus, the label must not be defective, of poor quality, or untidy; and
- the importer gives notice to the trademark proprietor before the repackaged product is put on sale, and, on demand, supplies him with a specimen of that product.

A trademark proprietor's opposition to repackaging pharmaceutical products contributes to artificial partitioning of the markets between member states

---

684. Case C-324/09, L'Oréal SA v. eBay International AG, 2011 E.C.R. I-6073, 6109 ¶83.
685. Case C-427/93, Bristol-Myers v. Paranova, 1996 E.C.R. I-3457.
686. Trademark Directive at art. 7(2).
687. Cases C-400/09 & 207/10, Orifarm A/S v. Merck Sharp & Dohme Corp., 2011 E.C.R. I-7080, 7094 ¶27; Case C-348/04, Boehringer Ingelheim KG v. Swingward Ltd, 2007 E.C.R. I-3430, 3454 ¶32.

where the repackaging is necessary in order to enable the particular product to be marketed in the importing state.[688] The change brought about by any repackaging of a trademarked pharmaceutical product—creating by its very nature the risk of interference with the original condition of the product—may be prohibited by the trademark proprietor unless the repackaging is necessary in order to enable the marketing of the products imported in parallel and the legitimate interests of the proprietor are also safeguarded.[689] To qualify as necessary, products purchased by the parallel importer cannot be placed on the market in the member state of importation in their original packaging by reason of national rules or practices relating to packaging, or where sickness insurance rules make reimbursement of medical expenses depend on a certain packaging or where well-established medical prescription practices are based, inter alia, on standard sizes recommended by professional groups and sickness insurance institutions. In that regard, it is sufficient for there to be an impediment in respect of one type of packaging used by the trademark proprietor in the member state of importation.[690] In contrast, the trademark proprietor may not oppose the repackaging if it is based solely on the parallel importer's attempt to secure a commercial advantage.

6.4 Counterfeit Goods from Outside the EU

As intellectual property rights are territorial, a product produced outside of the EU may be legally produced and sold in that non-EU country without infringing intellectual property rights in the EU. However, EU intellectual property law becomes relevant when those foreign-produced goods (sometimes referred to as grey market goods) are imported into the EU. The customs authorities in the EU have the right to seize and destroy goods which are suspected of infringing an intellectual property right in the EU.[691] The process is initiated when the holder of the intellectual property right submits an application.[692] That application is submitted to the member state or member states where the customs authorities

---

688. *Id.* at 3449 ¶18.
689. *Id.* at 3449 ¶19.
690. *See* Case C-427/93, Bristol-Myers v. Paranova, 1996 E.C.R. I-3457, 3534 ¶¶53 and 54.
691. Regulation (EU) No. 608/2013 of the European Parliament and of the Council of 12 June 2013 concerning customs enforcement of intellectual property rights and repealing Council Regulation (EC) No. 1383/2003, 2013 O.J. (L 181) 15 [hereinafter Counterfeit Goods Regulation]. The term "intellectual property right" covers an EU or national trademark registered in one of the member states; an EU design or a design under member state law; a copyright or any related right as provided for by member state or EU law; a geographical indication; a patent as provided for by member state or EU law; an EU supplementary protection certificate for medicinal products; an EU or member state plant variety right; a topography of semiconductor product as provided for by member state or EU law; a utility model in so far as it is protected as an intellectual property right by member state or EU law; a trade name in so far as it is protected as an exclusive intellectual property right by member state or EU law.
692. *Id.* at art. 3. In addition to the holder of the intellectual property right, other bodies authorized by law may initiate the process leading to the seizure of the goods.

are being requested to take action.[693] If those customs authorities identify goods suspected of infringing an intellectual property right,[694] they will suspend the release of the goods or detain them.[695] The customs authorities are required to notify the person importing the goods of the detention of the goods within one working day. It is possible for the declarant to secure the release of goods if three conditions are fulfilled: the declarant or the holder of the goods has provided a guarantee in an amount sufficient to protect the interests of the holder of the decision, the authority competent to determine whether an intellectual property right has been infringed has not authorized precautionary measures, and all customs formalities have been completed.[696]

Grey market goods suspected of infringing an intellectual property right in the EU may be destroyed under customs control without the consent of the declarant or without there being any need to determine whether an intellectual property right has been infringed if the holder of the decision has confirmed in writing to the customs authorities that an intellectual property right has been infringed or has agreed to the destruction of the goods.[697] The customs authorities must release the goods if the holder of the decision has not provided the customs authorities with a written confirmation that an intellectual property right has been infringed. If the customer's authorities have been informed about the initiation of infringement proceedings, they do not have to release the goods. However, if they have not been informed within 10 days, they must release the goods.[698]

The submission of an application is not without risk to the party submitting the application. The applicant is liable to the holder of the goods or the declarant

---

693. The form of application is set forth in an implementing regulation. Commission Implementing Regulation (EU) No. 1352/2013 of 4 December 2013 establishing the forms provided for in Regulation (EU) No. 608/2013 of the European Parliament and of the Council concerning customs enforcement of intellectual property rights, 2013 O.J. (L 341) 10.
694. The term "goods suspected of infringing an intellectual property right" means goods with regard to which there are reasonable indications that, in the member state where those goods are found, they are prima facie: (a) goods which are the subject of an act infringing an intellectual property right in that member state; (b) devices, products or components which are primarily designed, produced or adapted for the purpose of enabling or facilitating the circumvention of any technology, device or component that, in the normal course of its operation, prevents or restricts acts in respect of works which are not authorized by the holder of any copyright or any right related to copyright and which relate to an act infringing those rights in that member state; (c) any mould or matrix which is specifically designed or adapted for the manufacture of goods infringing an intellectual property right, if such moulds or matrices relate to an act infringing an intellectual property right in that member state. Counterfeit Goods Regulation at art. 2(7).
695. *Id.* at art. 17(1).
696. *Id.* at art. 24(2).
697. *Id.* at art. 23(1). The holder has 10 working days after receiving notice.
698. *Id.* at art. 23.

for damages if the procedure is discontinued because the goods in question are subsequently found not to infringe an intellectual property right.[699]

6.5 Relationship Between Competition Law and Intellectual Property

The relationship between competition law and intellectual property rights is tenuous because the objectives pursued by intellectual property laws are achieved by precluding competition. In a very general sense, intellectual property rights preclude third parties from copying or using certain ideas, inventions, signs, or designs of individuals. Although intellectual property rights are enshrined in the Charter of Fundamental Rights (Article 17(2)), the ECJ has clearly stated that these rights are not absolute.[700]

Competition law potentially limits intellectual property rights in three fundamental ways. First, the application of the competition law may limit the ability of the holder of the right to license or transfer the right. For example, two competitors may be prohibited in certain circumstances from granting exclusive licenses to one another. Alternatively, the competition laws may prohibit a dominant undertaking from acquiring intellectual property rights from a potential competitor which may threaten its dominance.

Second, competition law may determine when the holder of an intellectual property right must license that right to a third party. According to the ECJ, an undertaking may be compelled to license intellectual property in exceptional circumstances.[701] An example of exceptional circumstances, as illustrated by *RTE and ITP v. Commission*, would be if the holder of a copyright prevented the introduction of a new product by refusing to license its intellectual property.[702]

Third, competition law limits intellectual property rights by determining the terms on which the holder of the right may license that right to third parties. As discussed in greater detail in Chapter III, for example, the Technology Transfer Block Exemption prohibits the licensor from restricting the territory into which the licensee may passively sell the contract products, or restricting the licensee from producing the products using the licensed technology.[703]

The interrelationship of competition law and intellectual property is a public policy compromise between the general consensus of the social benefits of granting protection to inventors, authors, artists, or others, and the necessity to maintain an adequate level of competition to ensure the proper functioning of

---

699. *Id.* at art. 28(1).
700. Case C-70/10, Scarlet Extended SA v. Société belge des auteurs, compositeurs et éditeurs, 2011 E.C.R. I-12006, 12025 ¶43.
701. Case C-418/01, IMS Health GmbH & Co. v. NDC Health GmbH & Co. KG, 2004 E.C.R. I-5039, 5081 ¶35; Case T-201/04, Microsoft Corp. v. Comm'n, 2007 E.C.R. II-3619, 3831 ¶690.
702. Case C-241/91, RTE and ITP v. Comm'n, 1995 E.C.R. I-743. For a more detailed discussion of the refusal to license cases, *see* Chapter III.
703. Commission Regulation (EU) No. 316/2014 of 21 March 2014 on the application of Article 101(3) of the Treaty on the Functioning of the European Union to categories of technology transfer agreements, 2014 O.J. (L 93) 17.

the market economy. As that balance is fluid, and arises in an almost unlimited number of constellations, it is often difficult to identify in the case law. This relationship is discussed in greater detail in Chapter III.

CHAPTER **XI**

The Regulation of Electronic Commerce

1. The Challenge of E-Commerce

The spread of e-commerce has created a broad range of legal issues, only some of which can be addressed here. In many instances, existing laws may be applied to new business practices. In other instances, new business practices or technology require the introduction of new legal norms. The possibility to sign contracts electronically is an example.

In the context of the European Union (EU), the spread of e-commerce has reduced the significance of national borders, both from a commercial and from a legal perspective. For example, many of the member states have laws regulating the use of sales promotions by companies selling product or services within their borders (e.g., sales below costs prohibition in France and the maximum 33 percent discount rule in Belgium). As discussed in Chapter II, these national laws are permitted under Article 34 of the Treaty on the Functioning of the European Union (TFEU).[1] By reducing the barriers to trade across borders, e-commerce highlighted the impact these laws have.

Most of the EU legislation in this area is in the form of directives. Although this has given the member states greater flexibility in regulating e-commerce, it has created more legal uncertainty for companies doing business internationally. As one example, the laws of the member states and the judicial decisions have been inconsistent on the issue of liability of Internet users for illegal file sharing. The German Supreme Court, for example, held that an individual who has an Internet connection which has been used by another person without his consent for illegal file sharing can be held vicariously liable.[2] The courts in other member states may take an entirely different approach.

---

1. *See* Case C-268/91, Keck and Mithouard, 1993 E.C.R. I-6097.
2. Decision of the German Bundesgerichtshof in case no. I ZR 121/08 (May 12, 2010) *reported at* 63 Neue Juristische Wochenschrift 2061 (2010).

2. Contract Formation Issues

The Electronic Signatures Directive has harmonized the rules applicable to the use of electronic signatures in commercial relations and judicial form. It imposes the basic requirement on the member states to ensure that advanced electronic signatures satisfy the legal requirements of a signature in the same manner as a handwritten signature and are admissible as evidence in legal proceedings.[3] An "advanced electronic signature" is an advanced electronic signature which is uniquely linked to the signatory, is capable of identifying the signatory, is created by means that remain under the sole control of the signatory, and is linked to the data in such a way that any change is detectable.[4] Electronic signatures are generally based on so-called asymmetric cryptosystems, using a private and a public key. Only the originator can generate the digital signature, but anyone can verify the message with the public key.

To legally qualify as an advanced electronic signature, it must be treated in the same manner as a handwritten signature and be admissible in judicial proceedings. To be recognized as a valid signature, however, the electronic signature must be based on a qualified certificate.[5] The Directive envisages the creation of certification service providers (CSPs)[6] who would issue such certificates and the electronic signature must be created by a "secure-signature-creation device." The definition of a secure-signature-creation device is in Annex III of the Directive.

What is particularly important for U.S. businesses is that the Electronic Signatures Directive also requires the member states to recognize certificates of third-country CSPs under certain conditions.[7] If the third-country CSP fulfills the requirements set forth in the Directive and has been accredited in the member state, the member states are required to recognize the electronic signature. In the alternative, a certificate issued by a third country may be guaranteed by a CSP in the EU. Finally, the certificate or the provider may be recognized by international agreement with the EU or international organizations.

3. Consumer Protection

As discussed in Chapter XII, the term consumer protection covers a broad range of legislation. Consumer protection in the area of e-commerce involves two categories of legislation. The first category is made up of general consumer protection legislation generally (but not specifically) applicable to

---

3. Directive 1999/93 on a Community framework for electronic signatures, 2000 O.J. (L13) 12 [hereinafter: Electronic Signatures Directive]. Compare Electronic Signatures in Global and National Commerce Act, 15 U.S.C. §§7001-7031.
4. Electronic Signatures Directive at art. 2(2).
5. *Id.* at art. 5.
6. The requirements for CSPs are identified in Annex II to the Directive.
7. Electronic Signatures Directive at art. 7.

e-commerce. This would include, for example, the Unfair Terms Directive,[8] Consumer Guarantees Directive,[9] Distance Marketing of Consumer Financial Services Directive,[10] Consumer Interest Injunctions Directive,[11] Product Safety Directive,[12] Consumer Product Pricing Directive,[13] Defective Products Directive,[14] Misleading and Comparative Advertising Directive,[15] and Consumer Credit Directive.[16] As this legislation does not specifically preclude its application to commerce conducted electronically, it could be also considered e-commerce legislation. For example, although the Unfair Commercial Practices Directive and the Distance Selling Directive were not specifically intended to apply to consumer transactions over the Internet, the obligations imposed on the seller by those legislative acts would apply to the seller using e-commerce. As another example, a choice of law clause in an Internet seller's standard terms and conditions may be considered unfair under the Unfair Commercial Practices Directive.[17] Similarly, the Distance Selling Directive may apply to transactions concluded using the online auction site eBay.[18]

The second category of legislation consists of e-commerce laws that contain consumer protection elements. The E-Commerce Directive, for example,

---

8. Council Directive 93/13/EEC of 5 April 1993 on unfair terms in consumer contracts, 1993 O.J. (L 95) 29.
9. Directive 1999/44/EC of the European Parliament and of the Council of 25 May 1999 on certain aspects of the sale of consumer goods and associated guarantees, 1999 O.J. (L 171) 12.
10. Directive 2002/65/EC of the European Parliament and of the Council of 23 September 2002 concerning the distance marketing of consumer financial services and amending Council Directive 90/619/EEC and Directives 97/7/EC and 98/27/EC, 2002 O.J. (L 271) 16.
11. Directive 98/27/EC of the European Parliament and of the Council of 19 May 1998 on injunctions for the protection of consumers' interests, O.J. 1998 (L 166) 51.
12. Directive 2001/95/E of the European Parliament and of the Council of 3 December 2001 on general product safety, 2002 O.J. (L 11) 4.
13. Directive 98/6/EC of the European Parliament and of the Council of 16 February 1998 on consumer protection in the indication of the prices of products offered to consumers, 1988 O.J. (L 80) 27.
14. Council Directive 85/374/EEC of 25 July 1985 on the approximation of the laws, regulations and administrative provisions of the member states concerning liability for defective products, 1985 O.J. (L 210) 29.
15. Council Directive 84/450/EEC of 10 September 1984 relating to the approximation of the laws, regulations and administrative provisions of the member states concerning misleading advertising, 1984 O.J. (L 250) 17.
16. Directive 87/102/EEC of 22 December 1986 for the approximation of the laws, regulations and administrative provisions of the member states concerning consumer credit, O.J. 1987 (L 42) 48.
17. Case C-137/08, VB Pénzügyi Lízing Zrt. v. Schneider, 2010 E.C.R. I-10888, 10904 ¶46.
18. Decision of German Bundesgerichtshof in case no. VIII ZR 375/03 (Nov. 3, 2004) *reported at* 58 Neue Juristische Wochenschrift 53 (2005).

does not apply specifically or exclusively to consumer transactions.[19] As discussed below, it applies generally to several business practices which may happen to involve e-commerce.[20] Nonetheless, it also applies to commercial transactions with consumers and consumer protection is one of the objectives of the Directive.[21] Consequently, there is a certain degree of overlap with the practice-specific directives.

In applying these two categories of legal norms, it is important to remember the principle of *lex specialis derogat legi generali*. This principle, which is playing an increasingly important role in the EU because of the large volume of legislation, requires that in the event of parallel application of two legal norms to the same facts, the law that was specifically intended to apply to the facts takes precedence over any general law that may apply differently. The E-Commerce Directive is not intended to limit the application of the consumer protection legislation.[22]

As the Distance Selling Directive, and indeed other consumer protection legislation, does not distinguish between transactions using electronic means of communication and other types of communication, the requirements imposed by that Directive on sellers need to be observed by companies involved in e-commerce transactions with consumers. The following discussion relates only to the additional requirements imposed by legislation specifically applicable to e-commerce. For example, a consumer purchasing a product over the Internet has at least seven working days in which to withdraw from the contract without penalty and without giving any reason. Although this right is not mentioned in the E-Commerce Directive, it is mentioned in the Distance Selling Directive.[23]

The E-Commerce Directive applies generally to any service normally provided for remuneration, at a distance (i.e., the service is provided without the parties being simultaneously present), by electronic means, and at the

---

19. The concept of "consumer" used in the E-Commerce Directive is the same as that used in the general consumer protection legislation, i.e., any natural person who is acting for purposes which are outside his or her trade, business, or profession. Directive 2000/31/EC of the European Parliament and of the Council of 8 June 2000 on certain legal aspects of information society services, in particular electronic commerce, in the Internal Market, 2000 O.J. (L 178) 1 at art. 2(e). [hereinafter E-Commerce Directive].
20. The E-Commerce Directive applies to the establishment of service providers in other member states, commercial communications, electronic contracts, the liability of intermediaries, codes of conduct, out-of-court dispute settlement, court actions, and cooperation between member states. *Id.* at art. 1(2).
21. *Id.* at recital 10.
22. *Id.* at recital 11.
23. Distance Selling Directive at art. 6(1). *See, e.g.*, Decision of German Bundesgerichtshof in case no. VIII ZR 375/03 (Nov. 3, 2004) *reported at* 58 Neue Juristische Wochenschrift 53 (2005).

individual request of a recipient of services.[24] Such services are referred to as "information society services." "Electronic means" denotes that the service is sent initially and received at its destination by means of electronic equipment for the processing (including digital compression) and storage of data, and entirely transmitted, conveyed, and received by wire, by radio, by optical means, or by other electromagnetic means. The term "services" should not be understood in contradistinction to goods. As is made clear in the preamble to the E-Commerce Directive, the term services includes "a wide range of economic activities which take place on-line."[25] This would include selling goods via the Internet.

Information society services are not solely restricted to services giving rise to online contracting but also, insofar as they represent an economic activity, extend to services that are not remunerated by those who receive them, such as those offering online information or commercial communications, or those providing tools allowing for search, access, and retrieval of data. Information society services also include services consisting of the transmission of information via a communication network, providing access to a communication network, or hosting information provided by a recipient of the service. Television and radio broadcasting are not information society services because they are not provided at individual request. However, video-on-demand or the provision of commercial communications by electronic mail are information society services, as they are transmitted point-to-point. The use of electronic mail or equivalent individual communications, by natural persons acting outside their trade, business, or profession—including their use for the conclusion of contracts between such persons—is not an information society service.[26]

3.1 Commercial Transactions Involving Consumers

(a) Contract Formation

The E-Commerce Directive requires all the member states to ensure that their respective legal systems permit contracts to be concluded by electronic means.[27] Therefore, if a member state has a law which requires a writing for certain types of contracts, that member state is required to change the law to allow such

---

24. E-Commerce Directive art. 2(a) in reference to Article 1(a) Directive 98/34/EC of the European Parliament and of the Council of 22 June 1998 laying down a procedure for the provision of information in the field of technical standards and regulations, 1998 O.J. (L 204) 37.
25. E-Commerce Directive at recital 18.
26. *Id.* If information society services are being provided together with services not qualifying as information society services (i.e., cannot be performed at a distance or electronically), the E-Commerce Directive does not apply if the two types of services are inseparable (i.e., cannot be provided independently). Case C-108/09, Ker-Optika bt v. ÀNTSZ Dél-dunántúli Regionális Intézete, 2010 E.C.R. I-12213, 12256 ¶34.
27. E-Commerce Directive at art. 9(1).

contracts to be concluded electronically. The E-Commerce Directive does not apply to online lotteries and contests.[28]

(1) Information To Be Provided

Similar to the Distance Selling Directive, the E-Commerce Directive imposes a basic obligation on the service provider, i.e., the natural or legal person providing the service, to also provide the buyer with a minimum amount of information prior to ordering the service. At a minimum, the service provider must provide information on the different technical steps to follow to conclude the contract, whether or not the concluded contract will be filed by the service provider and whether it will be accessible, the technical means for identifying and correcting input errors, and the languages offered for conclusion of the contract.[29]

There are two exceptions to this requirement. If the contract is concluded exclusively by the exchange of e-mail or equivalent individual communications, then the information does not have to be provided.[30] For example, if a customer finds the e-mail address of a business and places an order by sending an e-mail, and the supplier accepts the order by e-mail, then the supplier does not need to provide the otherwise required information. Unfortunately there is no definition of "equivalent individual communications." Second, the supplier does not have to provide the information if the supplier and the customer have agreed that it will not be provided. If, however, the customer is a consumer, such an agreement is not valid for purposes of waiving the information obligation.

(2) Placing Orders

Placing orders via electronic means presents new issues as to acceptance of the order. For example, if one submits an order electronically, it is often difficult to determine whether the order has been received and processed. To avoid this problem, for contracts concluded by electronic means, the service provider is required to acknowledge the receipt of the customer's order without delay and by electronic means.[31] This does not apply to contracts concluded by individual e-mail between the buyer and seller.[32] The order and the acknowledgment of receipt are deemed to be received when the parties to whom they are addressed are able to access them.

(3) Right to Withdraw

The statutorily imposed ability to withdraw from a contract may be inappropriate in certain circumstances and lead to the unwillingness of the seller to supply a

---

28. Decision of the German Bundesgerichtshof in case no. I ZR 317/01 (Apr. 1, 2004) *reported at* 57 Neue Juristische Wochenschrift 2158 (2004).
29. E-Commerce Directive at art. 10(1).
30. *Id.* at art. 10(4).
31. *Id.* at art. 11(1). The E-Commerce Directive does not identify when a contract is concluded. Earlier drafts contained the rule that a contract is concluded only when the customer received confirmation from the online trader, the trader electronically acknowledged receipt of the customer's acceptance, and the customer confirmed receipt of the trader's confirmation.
32. *Id.* at art. 11(3).

particular product or service. In recognition of this fact, the Distance Selling Directive identifies certain types of contracts for which the mandatory right of withdrawal is not required (but the parties may agree otherwise). For example, if the contract requires performance of a service, once the service has begun with the consumer's agreement, the consumer is no longer allowed to withdraw from the contract.

Additional examples include the following: contracts for the supply of goods or services, the price of which is dependent on fluctuations in the financial market which cannot be controlled by the supplier; contracts for the supply of goods made to the consumer's specifications or clearly personalized or which, by reason of their nature, cannot be returned or are liable to deteriorate or expire rapidly; contracts for the supply of audio or video recordings or computer software which were unsealed by the consumer; and contracts for the supply of newspapers, periodicals, and magazines.

(b) Contract Content

The E-Commerce Directive does not regulate the content of the contract. In *Ker-Optika bt v. ÀNTSZ Dél-dunántúli Regionális Intézete*, for example, the issue was whether the selling of contact lenses over the Internet fell under the E-Commerce Directive. The European Court of Justice (ECJ) held that although the conditions under which a contract is to be considered concluded over the Internet fall under the E-Commerce Directive, the terms and conditions of that same agreement fall outside the E-Commerce Directive.[33]

3.2 Promoting and Soliciting to Consumers on the Internet

The limits on comparative advertising in the EU are tighter than those in the United States. Although each member state has its own laws regulating misleading and comparative advertising, these laws are harmonized by the Misleading and Comparative Advertising Directive.[34] "Advertising" in this context means the making of a representation in any form in connection with a trade, business, craft, or profession in order to promote the supply of goods, services, or property. It encompasses not only traditional forms of advertising, such as in newspapers and magazines, but also advertising on the Internet. In *Belgian Electronic Sorting Technology NV v. Peelaers*, the ECJ went so far as to hold that the use of metatags is a form of advertising within the meaning of the Misleading and Comparative Advertising Directive.[35]

---

33. Case C-108/09, Ker-Optika bt v. ÀNTSZ Dél-dunántúli Regionális Intézete, 2010 E.C.R. I-12213, 12255 ¶30.
34. Directive 2006/114/EC of the European Parliament and of the Council of 12 December 2006 concerning misleading advertising and comparative advertising, 2006 O.J. (L 376) 21 [hereinafter Misleading and Comparative Advertising Directive].
35. Case C-657/11, Belgian Electronic Sorting Technology NV v. Peelaers, 2013 E.C.R. I-____, at ¶457.

The general rule set forth in the Misleading and Comparative Advertising Directive is that comparative advertising should be permitted if it meets the following conditions:

- it is not "misleading";
- it compares goods or services meeting the same needs or intended for the same purpose;
- it objectively compares one or more material, relevant, verifiable, and representative features of those goods and services, which may include price;
- it does not create confusion in the marketplace between the advertiser and a competitor or between the advertiser's trademarks, trade names, other distinguishing marks, goods, or services and those of a competitor;
- it does not discredit or denigrate the trademarks, trade names, other distinguishing marks, goods, services, activities, or circumstances of a competitor;
- for products with designation of origin, it relates in each case to products with the same designation;
- it does not take unfair advantage of the reputation of a trademark, trade name, or other distinguishing marks of a competitor or of the designation of origin of competing products;
- it does not present goods or services as imitations or replicas of goods or services bearing a protected trademark or trade name.

The issues tend to fall into one of two categories: (1) Does the conduct constitute comparative advertising; and (2) if so, is the comparative advertising used properly. In *Toshiba Europe GmbH v. Katun Germany GmbH*,[36] the ECJ addressed the basic issue of what constitutes comparative advertising. A company (Katun) began to manufacture and sell spare parts which fit Toshiba photocopiers. Toshiba, which sold its own spare parts for its copiers, objected to the reference to Toshiba photocopiers made in the marketing materials of the other company. In order for the customer to order the proper spare part, Katun identified the specific Toshiba model number. The materials also suggested that its spare parts were sold at a lower price ("these quality products are clearly a more profitable alternative for businesses"). Toshiba claimed that this amounted to unfair comparative advertising.[37] The ECJ held that, in order for there to be comparative advertising within the meaning of the Directive, it is sufficient for a representation to be made in any form that refers, even by implication, to a competitor or to the goods or services he offers. The application of this

---

36. Case C-112/99, Toshiba Europe GmbH v. Katun Germany, 2001 E.C.R. I-7945.
37. The reason that Toshiba did not pursue the case under a trademark infringement theory is because the use of another person's trademark may be legitimate where it is necessary to inform the public of the nature of the products or the intended purpose of the services offered. Case C-63/97, BMW v. Deenik, 1999 E.C.R. I-905.

rule to the facts led to the conclusion that the conduct of Katun amounted to comparative advertising.

The use of a competitor's logo or trademark for purposes of comparative advertising is legitimate provided all of the other conditions of permissible comparative advertising are met. Misleading advertising means any advertising which in any way, including its presentation, deceives or is likely to deceive the persons to whom it is addressed or whom it reaches and which, by reason of its deceptive nature, is likely to affect their economic behavior or which, for those reasons, injures or is likely to injure a competitor. In *Pippig Augenoptik GmbH v. Hartlauer Handelsgesellschaft mbH*, the ECJ held that price comparisons are not per se misleading even if the compared products are of a different quality (in this case eyeglasses).[38]

One of the disadvantages of much consumer protection legislation in the EU is that it allows the member state to adopt stricter measures if that member state desires. The Directive on Comparative Advertising is somewhat unique in this respect. Because the Directive on Comparative Advertising is intended to exhaustively harmonize the conditions in which comparative advertising should be permitted, stricter national laws are prohibited.[39] Consequently, if an advertiser meets the fairness requirements discussed above, a member state cannot prohibit the comparative advertising.

4. Applicable Law

Consumer protection in the EU, and the regulation of e-commerce, are based on directives given effect through national laws. The E-Commerce Directive does not establish rules of private international law (i.e., conflicts rules).[40] National private international rules together with the Brussels Convention determine which member state's laws apply. It does, however, set forth the general principle that the appropriate national law implementing the E-Commerce applicable to a service provider is that where the service provider is established.[41]

---

38. Case C-44/01, Pippig Augenoptik GmbH v. Hartlauer Handelsgesellschaft mbH, 2003 E.C.R. I-3095, 3156 ¶80.
39. *Id.* at 3146 ¶44.
40. E-Commerce Directive at art. 1(4).
41. *Id.* at art. 3 & recital 19. The place at which a service provider is established should be determined in conformity with the case-law of the ECJ according to which the concept of establishment involves the actual pursuit of an economic activity through a fixed establishment for an indefinite period; this requirement is also fulfilled where a company is constituted for a given period; the place of establishment of a company providing services via an Internet website is not the place at which the technology supporting its website is located or the place at which its website is accessible but the place where it pursues its economic activity; in cases where a provider has several places of establishment it is important to determine from which place of establishment the service concerned is provided; in cases where it is difficult to determine from which of several places of establishment a given service is provided, this is the place where the provider has the centre of his activities relating to this particular service.

The significance of this rule should not be overestimated. First, it applies only to the laws transposing the E-Commerce Directive which are applicable based on the location of the service provider. Second, there are significant exceptions to the rule.[42] These exceptions include, for example, copyright or industrial property rights, the freedom of the parties to choose the law applicable to their contract, contractual obligations concerning consumer contacts, and formal validity of contracts creating or transferring rights in real estate where such contracts are subject to mandatory formal requirements of the law of the member state where the real estate is situated. Finally, it does not apply if the service provider is located in a third country which is not a member of the EU.[43]

The E-Commerce Directive only applies if the service provider, i.e., the provider of the information society service, is established in the EU.[44] If, for example, the service provider is established in the United States, national law would apply, and the member states are not required to apply laws conforming to the E-Commerce Directive.

5. Competition Law

The EU consumer protection legislation and the e-commerce legislation do not apply to the competition law issues presented by e-commerce. Resolution of these issues relies on the application of the existing legal norms applicable in the field of competition law. As there is no competition law legislation specifically applicable to e-commerce, Articles 101 and 102 of the TFEU remain the primary bases of the legal analysis.

5.1 Horizontal Issues

For many industries, the spread of e-commerce has altered the traditional ways of doing business. This applies not only to the selling activities of a business but also to the way a firm interacts with its suppliers and competitors. In many instances, the application of the traditional analyses will suffice. In the eBooks case, for example, a group of e-book publishers allegedly conspired to switch their respective relationships with Apple from a wholesale model to an agency model. Using traditional concepts of concerted practices, the European Commission challenged the agreements with Apple as horizontal conspiracies with the object of raising the prices of e-books in the EU. The Commission ultimately agreed to close the proceedings in response to commitments by the publishers to terminate the agency agreements with Apple.[45]

Two horizontal issues which have been addressed by the European Commission in the competition law context somewhat unique to e-commerce are B2B (business-to-business) exchanges and standardization.

---

42. *Id.* at art. 3(3) E-Commerce Directive.
43. *Id.* at recital 58.
44. *Id.*
45. Communication from the Commission in Case Comp/39.847/E-BOOKS, 2013 O.J. (C 112) 9.

(a) B2B Exchanges

A B2B exchange is an Internet trading platform used to procure or sell products or services or to exchange information usually between actors in a certain product or service market or industry. The basic functions are to exchange information and sell products and services.

There are three basic types of B2B exchanges. One type, match-maker exchanges, serves to match individual buyers with potential sellers and individual sellers with potential buyers. In contrast, seller-managed exchanges are created by sellers of products or services to combine their products or product lines to sell in larger volumes to buyers who use the exchange to purchase products. Buyer-managed exchanges are just the opposite: they combine buyers of the same or related products for the purpose of securing better procurement terms. An example is Covisint, the B2B buyer-managed exchanged established by Ford, DaimlerChrysler, General Motors, Renault, and Nissan to procure parts for automobiles.[46]

The Commission recognizes that B2B exchanges can offer substantial cost savings and alternative distribution or procurement channels.[47] If membership in the exchange is open and the membership criteria applied in an objective manner, the B2B exchange will not violate Art. 101(1).[48] However, there are three competitive effects that may arise from a B2B exchange involving competitors or potential competitors. The Commission may be concerned about the potential exclusionary effect of a B2B exchange. If access to an exchange becomes an important element in a firm's ability to compete in a particular industry, the exclusion of certain competitors could negatively affect competition in that industry by placing these competitors at a disadvantage.

The B2B exchange may also have an exclusivity effect vis-à-vis other exchanges. As a condition to inclusion in a B2B exchange, the participants may be precluded from joining other exchanges or buying or selling to firms participating in other exchanges.

Finally, the Commission may examine the collusion-enhancing effect of a B2B exchange. As membership in a B2B exchange is often comprised of competing firms, the information exchanged or even the participation may serve to facilitate collusion between competitors. Use of a "neutramediary" is recommended.

(b) Standardization

As discussed in Chapter III, the term "standardization" refers to the process of developing technical specifications for a particular product which are then

---

46. *Covisint*, IP/01/1155 (Aug. 1, 2001).
47. *See, e.g.*, Press Release, Commission clears GF-X air freight trading platform between several European airlines, IP/02/1560 (Oct. 28, 2002).
48. *See, e.g.*, Press Release, Commission clears electronic multi-bank trading platform for foreign exchange products, IP/02/943 (June 27, 2002); Press Release, Commission clears the creation of Eutilia and Endorsia electronic marketplaces, IP/01/1775 (Dec. 10, 2001); Press Release, Commission clears GF-X air freight trading platform between several European airlines, IP/02/1560 (Oct. 28, 2002).

accepted as the industry norm. This process is particularly prevalent and important in electronic commerce. It is hard to imagine a world without interoperability. Standardization creates efficiencies for companies that are often enjoyed by consumers.[49] For example, standardization is essential to achieve the compatibility of software with other software and other hardware.

As standardization often involves cooperation between competitors, the application of Article 101 of the TFEU is potentially applicable. If the procedure for the adoption of the standard and access to the standard is nondiscriminatory, open, and transparent, the standardization cooperation does not violate Article 101(1).[50] For example, a number of competing banks cooperated to establish a standardized system for authenticating electronic signatures.[51] As entry into the group (a joint venture) was open to all qualified banks (i.e., those meeting certain objective capital requirements), the participants were free to participate in other systems, and there were competing authentication systems, the Commission concluded that the cooperation (in the form of a Delaware limited liability company) did not violate Article 101 of the TFEU.[52]

5.2 Vertical Issues

The increased use of the Internet as a means of buying and selling products or even services has presented a challenge to traditional forms of distribution. In some respects, the existing rules continue to apply to Internet sales. For example, traditional hardcore restraints such as resale price maintenance and absolute territorial protection remain prohibited regardless of whether the sales occur over the Internet or through traditional channels.[53] However, the increased reliance on the Internet has forced the Commission to rethink its position in certain respects. It is relatively easy for a potential buyer to compare the prices of similar or even the same product sold by different distributors or retailers. This, of course, leads to greater inter-brand and even intra-brand competition. Consequently, the use of the Internet makes it difficult for manufacturers to benefit from high price levels in certain member states as products from member states where prices are low will easily find their way to member states where prices for those same products are higher.

As discussed in Chapter IV, although a supplier may prohibit its distributors from engaging in active sales outside the supplier's territory or to specific customer groups reserved to the supplier or to another distributor, it may not prohibit passive selling. As discussed in Chapter III, by contrast, passive selling means responding to unsolicited requests from individual customers.[54] According to the Commission, the maintenance of a website by a distributor is

---

49. Commission Communication on the role of European standardization in the framework of European policies and legislation, Com (2004) 674 final.
50. Case T-432/05, EMC Development AB v. Comm'n, 2010 E.C.R. II-1633, 1654 ¶65 aff'd on appeal C-367/10 P, EMC Development AB v. Comm'n, 2011 E.C.R. I-46.
51. IP/01/1165 (Aug. 1, 2001).
52. Identrus, 2001 O.J. (L 249) 12.
53. Vertical Restraints Block Exemption, 2010 O.J. (L 102) 1 at art. 4.
54. Guidelines on Vertical Restraints, 2010 O.J. (C 130) 1, 13 ¶51.

a form of passive selling. Consequently, a prohibition blanket ban on Internet sales in a distribution agreement (i.e., a prohibition on distributors from selling or advertising on the Internet) violates Article 101(1) of the TFEU.[55]

For example, the Commission required B&W Loudspeakers Ltd, a UK-based company which makes high-quality loudspeakers for hi-fi and home cinema sound reproduction systems, to remove a clause in its distribution contracts that prohibited Internet sales by its dealers.[56] In another case, the Commission required Triumph (the motorcycle manufacturer) to make sure that its dealers in Belgium and Holland removed text on their websites that indicated that they do not sell to UK customers.[57]

In its Guidelines on Vertical Restraints, the Commission has identified several practices it considers hardcore restrictions of Internet passive selling:[58]

- Requiring the distributor to prohibit customers located outside that distributor's territory from viewing the distributor's website
- Requiring the distributor to automatically reroute customers from outside that distributor's territory.
- Prohibiting a distributor from concluding transactions over the Internet once the customer's credit card data reveal an address that is not within the distributor's territory
- Agreeing with the distributor that it will limit its proportion of overall sales made over the Internet.
- Charging a higher price to the distributor for products intended to be resold by the distributor online than for products intended to be resold offline.

A supplier is not entirely unable to limit its distributor's activities on the Internet. As discussed in Chapter III, a supplier may prohibit its distributor from actively selling outside of its territory or to certain customer groups. As applied to Internet sales, this would mean, for example, that the supplier may prohibit online advertising specifically addressed to certain customers.[59] This would also include paying a search engine or online advertisement provider to have advertisements (banner or search ads) displayed specifically to users in a particular territory. The line between active and passive selling must be drawn on a case-by-case basis. A German supplier may be able to prohibit its French distributor from registering a website with a .de domain name or advertising on a German website as this constitutes active selling.[60] If, however, the French

---

55. *Id.* at 13 ¶52 ("In principle, every distributor must be allowed to use the internet to sell products."); Press Release, Commission clears B&W Loudspeakers distribution system after company deletes hard-core violations, IP/02/916 (June 24, 2002).
56. Press Release, Commission clears B&W Loudspeakers distribution system after company deletes hard-core violations, IP/02/916 (June 24, 2002).
57. Commission, Competition Policy Newsletter (Feb. 2001) at 34.
58. Guidelines on Vertical Restraints, 2010 O.J. (C 130) 1, 13 ¶52.
59. *Id.* at 14 ¶53.
60. These examples were cited by then Commissioner Mario Monte in his speech on May 21, 2001 at the German Bundeskartellamt, "Competition in the New Economy" SPEECH/01/232.

distributor merely provided a German language version of its website, this would amount to passive selling.

The Commission recognizes that manufacturers may need to have traditional "bricks-and-mortar" distributors. The existence of Internet distributors undermines the ability of the manufacturer to support its bricks-and-mortar distributors because the Internet distributors, who do not have the overhead costs of the bricks-and-mortar stores, can underprice the bricks-and-mortar stores while at the same time free-riding on the benefits of the bricks-and-mortar stores. For example, a potential customer for a new computer may go to her nearest electronics store to receive advice on the best computer for her needs and to physically experience the various options. After she receives guidance from the employees of the store and finds the computer that best suits her, she then goes home and orders that computer from an Internet seller for a lower price. The Internet seller can often offer a lower price because it does not have to maintain a qualified sales staff, pay rent for the retail location, and maintain an inventory on site.

In recognition of the legitimate need to prohibit the free-rider problem, the Commission allows some restrictions on Internet sales. Although a supplier cannot impose a blanket ban on Internet sales, the supplier may appropriately compensate its off-line distributors for their legitimate sales efforts. For example, a supplier may require its distributors to have one or more physical shops or showrooms as a condition for becoming a member of the supplier's distribution system. The supplier may also require the distributor to observe certain quality standards when using the Internet to sell the supplier's products.[61] The supplier may require that its distributors use third-party platforms to distribute the contract products only in accordance with the standards and conditions agreed between the supplier and its distributors for the distributors' use of the Internet. For instance, where the distributor's website is hosted by a third-party platform, the supplier may require that customers do not visit the distributor's website through a site carrying the name or logo of the third-party platform.

In general, a supplier may not discriminate in pricing between offline and online distributors.[62] There are, however, certain exceptions to this rule. A supplier may agree to pay the offline distributor a fixed fee to support that distributor's sales efforts.[63] The compensation should be directly related to the distributor's efforts. For example, if online sales result in greater costs for the supplier than do offline sales, the supplier may legitimately charge a higher price to the online distributor to compensate for these extra costs.[64] This often arises because the online supplier is not in a position to service the products, and this task is left to the supplier.

---

61. Guidelines on Vertical Restraints, 2010 O.J. (C 130) 1, 14 ¶54.
62. This practice is known as dual pricing. *Id.* at 16 ¶64. *See, e.g.*, Decision of the Oberlandesgericht Düsseldorf in case no. VI-U (Kart) 11/13 (Nov. 13, 2013) *aff'd on appeal* German Supreme Court, KRZ 88/13 (Oct. 7, 2014); Bosch Siemens Hausgeräte GmbH, Decision of the German Bundeskartellamt in case B7-11/13 (Dec. 23, 2013).
63. Guidelines on Vertical Restraints, 2010 O.J. (C 130) 1, 13 ¶52.
64. *Id.* at 16 ¶64.

6. Intellectual Property Protection and E-Commerce

6.1 Database Protection

A database is a "collection of works or material arranged, stored and accessed by electric means."[65] The idea is that the choice or arrangement of the material, rather than the material itself, is the intellectual creation of the author, who should retain the exclusive sui generis right to carry out or authorize its reproduction, processing, translation, and distribution (Art. 7). The material within the database will continue to be protected by existing copyright laws. This right will accrue for 15 years following the date that the database is made public.

6.2 Trademarks

(a) Cybersquatting

E-commerce may implicate trademark law in various ways. As domain names and trademarks are registered with different agencies, it is possible that a trademark is subsequently registered as a domain name or a domain name is subsequently registered as a trademark. In fact, there are individuals who monitor the online trademark registration databases. Once a trademark is registered, they check to see if a corresponding domain name has been registered. If not, they file a registration of the domain name in the hope that the owner of the trademark will purchase the domain name from them. This practice is colloquially referred to as cybersquatting or domain-grabbing and is the reason why companies should register the matching domain name in all generic top level domains (gTLDs) and in the country code top level domains for each EU country (ccTLDs).

There is no EU legislation that applies specifically to cyber-squatting. The practice is generally prohibited as unfair trade or infringement of trademark rights under the laws of the member states. In *British Telecommunications v. One In a Million*, for example, a court in England held that the subsequent registration of the domain name "www.marksandspencer.com" constituted illegal passing off under English law.[66] According to the court, an Internet user would likely assume that the website was that of the well-known department store Marks and Spencer. In another case, the German Federal Supreme Court ruled that the use of the domain "shell.de" by a private individual for private purposes constitutes an infringement of the name "Shell" belonging to the well-known oil company Deutsche Shell GmbH. The court held that in this specific case, the "first come, first serve" principle could not be applied and if a company enjoys outstanding publicity and fame, the company's interests take priority.[67]

---

65. Council Directive 96/9/EEC of March 11, 1996 on the legal protection of databases, 1996 O.J. (L 77) 20.
66. British Telecommunications v. One In a Million, [1998] 4 All ER 476.
67. Decision of the German Bundesgerichtshof in case I ZR 138/99 (Nov. 22, 2001), *reported at* 38 Neue Juristische Wochenschrift 2031 (2002).

Cybersquatting has become less of a problem since the adoption of the Uniform Dispute Resolution Procedure (UDRP) by ICANN (Internet Corporation for Assigned Names and Numbers) in 1999. The UDRP has been adopted by all registrars of gTLDS (e.g., *.com, .net, .org*) which now make it a term of their service agreements with domain name registrants that the UDRP will apply to any domain name registration disputes. A complaint may be filed with ICANN concerning a gTLD if the domain name registered is identical or confusingly similar to a trademark or service mark in which the complainant has rights, the domain name registrant has no rights or legitimate interests in respect of the domain name in question, and the domain name has been registered and is being used in bad faith.

(b) *Keyword Searches*

The practice of cybersquatting in not the only issue related to trademark law and e-commerce. As discussed in Chapter X, a trademark allows the owner to prevent others from using that mark without the owner's permission. This raises the issue of whether the use of a trademark as a keyword on the Internet constitutes "use" for purposes of trademark law. A keyword is a word, term, or phrase used by websites to assist Internet search machines in navigating users to their website. For example, a clothing company called Hemd might register the keywords "Hemd shirts" with a search engine such as Google. This increases the chances that an Internet user entering the same or similar terms in the same search engine will come across that company's website. In addition, the entry of a particular keyword may trigger an ad appearing on the user's computer screen. Most search engines allow the company to even reserve a keyword or give it priority for a fee.

The ECJ has held that the selection of keyword by a company to use in a search engine constitutes "use in the course of trade" by that company and therefore could violate the rights of the owner of a similar trademark if such a use is liable to cause a detriment to the trademark's functions.[68] In relation to keyword advertising, the relevant functions are the function of indicating the origin of the goods or services and the function of advertising.[69] Regarding the origin function, the trademark is adversely affected if the ad which is shown as a result of the user entering the keyword does not allow "informed and reasonably attentive internet users, or enables them only with difficulty, to ascertain whether the goods or services referred to by the ad originate from the proprietor of the trademark or an undertaking economically linked to it or, on the contrary, originate from a third party."[70] Regarding the advertising function, the ECJ has held that the use of a keyword in an Internet search engine

---

68. Case C-558/08, Portakabin Ltd. v. Primakabin BV, 2010 E.C.R. I-6967, 6980 ¶27; Case C-236/08, Google France SARL v. Louis Vuitton Malletier SA, 2010 E.C.R. I-2467, 2508 ¶99.
69. Case C-558/08, Portakabin Ltd. v. Primakabin BV, 2010 E.C.R. I-6967, 6981 ¶31; Case C-236/08, Google France SARL v. Louis Vuitton Malletier SA, 2010 E.C.R. I-2467, 2503 ¶81.
70. Case C-558/08, Portakabin Ltd. v. Primakabin BV, 2010 E.C.R. I-6967, 6982 ¶34.

to direct Internet users to a website is not liable to have an adverse effect on the advertising function of the trademark.[71]

In *Google France SARL v. Louis Vuitton Malletier SA,* certain Internet sellers of imitation Vuitton handbags used the keywords "Louis Vuitton" and other trademarks of Louis Vuitton Malletier SA to attract buyers to their websites. The ECJ held that this constituted use by a third party of a sign which is identical to a registered trademark.[72] In *L'Oréal SA v. eBay International AG*, the issue was whether the host of an Internet website—in this case eBay—used marks when it allowed third parties to sell products using the trademarks owned by the trademark proprietor. The ECJ concluded "that the use of signs identical with or similar to trade marks in offers for sale displayed on an online marketplace is made by the sellers who are customers of the operator of that marketplace and not by that operator itself."[73]

6.3 Copyright

The Information Society Directive[74] is the EU's first successful attempt at extending copyright law to the information society. The legislation is designed to implement the World Intellectual Property Organization (WIPO) Copyright Treaty[75] and the WIPO Performances and Phonograms Treaty.[76] As discussed above, the term information society generally refers to electronic means of communication, i.e., the Internet. Despite its name, the Information Society Directive is not limited to copyright issues involving electronic means of communication. The aspects of the Directive not relating specifically to the Internet were discussed in Chapter X.

(a) Reproduction Rights

The right of reproduction introduced by the Information Society Directive and discussed in Chapter X applies also to reproduction via electronic means. Thus, the member states are required to provide for the exclusive right to authorize or prohibit direct or indirect, temporary or permanent, reproduction by any means and in any form, in whole or in part.[77] The exceptions and limitations to the assertion of reproduction rights are discussed in greater detail in Chapter X.

As EU copyright law is in the form of a directive, the law of the member states and the related case law would need to be consulted to determine whether

---

71. *Id.* at 6981 ¶31; Case C-278/08, Die BergSpechte Outdoor Reisen und Alpinschule Edi Koblmüller GmbH v. Guni, 2010 E.C.R. I-2520, 2532 ¶33.
72. Case C-236/08, Google France SARL v. Louis Vuitton Malletier SA, 2010 E.C.R. I-2467, 2508 ¶99.
73. Case C-324/09, L'Oréal SA v. eBay International AG, 2011 E.C.R. I-6073, 6115 ¶103.
74. Directive 2001/29/EC of the European Parliament and of the Council of 22 May 2001 on the harmonisation of certain aspects of copyright and related rights in the information society, 2001 O.J. (L 167) 10.
75. World Intellectual Property Organization Copyright Treaty, art. 14(1), adopted by Diplomatic Conference at Geneva, Dec. 20, 1996, 36 I.L.M. 65 (1997).
76. World Intellectual Property Organization Performances and Phonograms Treaty, adopted by Diplomatic Conference at Geneva, Dec. 20, 1996, 36 I.L.M. 67.
77. Information Society Directive at art. 2.

a particular e-commerce activity implicates copyright law. Google has borne the brunt of many claims of copyright infringement. In the *Vorschaubilder* case, for example, the German Supreme Court held that Google did not violate the copyright of an artist by displaying the artist's work as thumbnails within Google's image search function whenever her name was entered as a term in Google's image search function.[78] In coming to this conclusion, the court pointed out that, although the artist had not expressly given Google permission to use the images, she had made the content of her website accessible to search engines and had not made use of the possibility of preventing the images from inclusion in these search engines.

(b) Distribution Rights

The source of distribution rights differs depending on whether the underlying right is a copyright or a neighboring right. Authors, in respect of the original of their works or of copies thereof, have the exclusive right to authorize or prohibit any form of distribution to the public by sale or otherwise.[79]

The Information Society Directive does not establish distribution rights for neighboring rights such as fixations of performances, phonograms, fixation of broadcasts, and films. Distribution rights for neighboring rights are provided for in the Rental Rights Directive as discussed in Chapter IX.[80]

(c) Right of Communication to the Public

The wide use of the Internet creates an additional means by which authors can make their works available to the public. For example, the authors of an article may make its contents available on the Internet in electronic format. The Information Society Directive provides authors with the exclusive right to authorize or prohibit any communication to the public of their works by wire or wireless means.[81] The "wire or wireless" qualification means that the public is not present at the place where the communication originates.[82] Hence, it would include not only communications by the Internet but also interactive television.

Member states may provide for exceptions or limitations to communication rights in the following cases:[83]

- illustration for teaching or scientific research
- use for the noncommercial benefit of people with a disability
- reproduction by the press
- quotations for purposes such as criticism or review
- use for the purposes of public security

---

78. Decision of the German Bundesgerichtshof in case no. I ZR 69/08 (April 23, 2010) *reported at* 46 Neue Juristische Wochenschrift 2731 (2010).
79. Information Society Directive at art. 4(1).
80. Rental Rights Directive at art. 9.
81. Information Society Directive at art. 3(1).
82. *Id.* at recital 23.
83. *Id.* at art. 5(3).

- use necessary to ensure the proper performance or reporting of administrative, parliamentary, or judicial proceedings
- use of political speeches as well as extracts of public lectures or similar works
- use during religious celebrations or official celebrations organized by a public authority
- use of works, such as works of architecture or sculpture, made to be located permanently in public places
- incidental inclusion of a work or other subject matter in other material
- use for the purpose of advertising the public exhibition or sale of artistic works, to the extent necessary to promote the event, excluding any other commercial use
- use for the purpose of caricature or parody
- use in connection with the demonstration or repair of equipment; use of an artistic work in the form of a building or a drawing or plan of a building for the purposes of reconstructing the building
- use by communication or making available, for the purpose of research or private study, to individual members of the public by dedicated terminals on the premises of libraries and educational establishments
- use in certain other cases of minor importance where exceptions or limitations already exist under national law.

(d) Prevention of Circumvention

Protecting copyrights has become more important with the advent of the Internet because of the ease at which copyrighted material is obtained and illegitimately reproduced. Holders of copyrights have introduced technological measures that assist in the prevention or deterrence of such illegitimate exploitation of their works. Encryption, scrambling, and password protection are examples of these technological measures. However, technological protective measures are vulnerable to technological means of circumvention. For example, manufacturers of DVDs commonly embed the DVD with encryption software which prevents copying the DVD. Nonetheless, decryption devices have been developed to circumvent this technological protective measure.

To enhance the effectiveness of the technological measures employed to protect copyrighted works, member states are required to provide adequate legal protection against the circumvention of such technological measures.[84] "Technological measures" means any technology, device, or component that, in the normal course of its operation, is designed to prevent or restrict acts, in respect of works or other subject matter, which are not authorized by the rightholder of any copyright or any right related to copyright.

---

84. *Id.* at art. 6(1).

(e) Remedies

The member states are required to provide appropriate sanctions and remedies for copyright infringements.[85] This means that the copyright holder should have a claim for damages or injunctive relief. As the assertion of rights and the collection of damages from private users may be practically difficult, the member states are allowed to impose a private copying levy on the manufacturers of the equipment which make the private copying possible.[86] This levy is then used to compensate the coyright holder. The claim for injunctive relief also applies against intermediaries whose services are used by a third party to violate a copyright or related right.[87] According to the ECJ, the term "intermediary" includes "any person who carries a third party's infringement of a protected work or other subject matter in a network."[88] For example, an Internet service provider (ISP) is considered an intermediary.[89] Consequently, an ISP can be enjoined from allowing a third party to post content that violates the copyright of another person.[90] This does not mean that the ISP must actively monitor all traffic that goes through its servers.[91] As recognized by the ECJ, the monitoring obligations imposed on the ISP must be reasonable under the circumstances.[92]

The ability of the copyright holder to secure damages from the ISP is more restricted. The general rule is that an ISP is exempt from liability unless it has knowledge of the infringement and still does not act expeditiously to terminate the infringement.[93] Whether the ISP acts expeditiously in particular circumstances is left to the national courts.[94]

(f) Obligations Concerning Rights-Management Information

The holders of copyrights and related rights in electronic format often embed their work with an identification or code that allows them to monitor or perhaps deter illegitimate exploitation. For example, the producer of software may encode the software to inform users that the work is protected. This is referred to as rights management. Hence, the term "rights-management information"

---

85. Directive 2001/29/EC of the European Parliament and of the Council of 22 May 2001 on the harmonisation of certain aspects of copyright and related rights in the information society, 2001 O.J. (L 167) 10 at art. 8(1).
86. Case C-463/12, Copydan Båndkopi v. Nokia Danmark A/S, 2015 E.C.R. I-___ at ¶23.
87. *Id.* at art. 8(3).
88. Case C-314/12, UPC Telekabel Wien GmbH v. Constantin Film Verleih GmbH, 2014 E.C.R. I-___, at ¶30.
89. Case C-557/07, LSG v. Gesellschaft zur Wahrnehmung von Leistungsschutzrechten, 2009 E.C.R. I-1230, 1252 ¶44.
90. Case C-314/12, UPC Telekabel Wien GmbH v. Constantin Film Verleih GmbH, 2014 E.C.R. I-___, at ¶64.
91. E-Commerce Directive at art. 15.
92. Case C-70/10, Scarlet Extended v. SABAM, 2011 E.C.R. I-12006, 12026 ¶47.
93. E-Commerce Directive at art. 14.
94. *See, e.g.*, Alone in the Dark, Decision of the German Bundesgerichtshof in case no. I ZR 18/11 (July 12, 2012) *reported at* 66 Neue Juristische Wochenschrift 784 (2013) (a period of two weeks after the ISP became aware was not expeditious).

formally means any information provided by rightholders that identifies the work or other subject matter referred to in the Information Society Directive, the author or any other rightholder, or information about the terms and conditions of use of the work or other subject matter, and any numbers or codes that represent this information. Member states are required to provide for adequate legal protection against any person who knowingly removes or alters any electronic rights-management information.[95]

6.4 Specific Practices

(a) Linking

A link is text or an image on an Internet website which, when clicked, takes the user to another electronic address (Universal Resource Locator or URL) which is represented by that link. There are several forms of linking encountered on the Internet. A simple link is an element (source anchor) in an electronic document that links to another place (destination anchor) in the same document or to an entirely different document posted on the Internet. The term deep link refers to a link that does not take the user to the home page of another site but into part of the site beyond the home page.

Links can be beneficial for the owner of the linking site as well as the linked site. For example, the use of links may increase the sales opportunities for a commercial website. That website may reward the owner of the website for sales consummated by links from that website. However, the use of links may not be welcomed by the owner of the linked website. Deep links may bypass certain notices or advertising which that proprietor wishes the user to see before going deeper into the website. Circumventing the home page reduces its reach and can, in turn, mean that the provider of the material referred to loses income from advertising. As a rule, advertisers who place banners on a particular website pay a fee based on the number of hits recorded by each website.

Another issue could be that the link is set up in such a way that it creates the appearance that the content is part of the linking site rather than the linked site. This can occur in particular with so-called framing, where another's material is imported into the graphic and visual framework of the initial page, thus giving it a new frame. However, this also blanks out material that is contained within the actual framework of the imported material.

There are no European rules regulating the practice of linking. The issues have been addressed by the member states. Even though a website owner may not like to be associated with another site, the general rule in the member states is that no copyright infringement by linking or framing is likely to occur, so long as copyright material from the linked site is not reproduced by the linking site on or in conjunction with the link (such as a title or an extract from the linked site). The basic rationale is that linking is not a reproduction of the protected material, but merely a reference to this information.[96] However, if the link is

---

95. Information Society Directive at art. 7(1).
96. Decision of the German Bundesgerichtshof in case no. I ZR 259/00 (of July 17, 2003) *reported at* 56 Neue Juristische Wochenschrift 3406 (2003).

done in a way to make users think the two sites are connected, as is much more likely to be the case with framing, there could be a case for a passing-off or unfair competition action.

(b) Framing

The practice of framing refers to the appearance of several independently controllable web pages or sections on the same computer screen. A nonframed website will typically have only one HTML file. A framed website, however, has one HTML file with the other "framed" HTML files for each section embedded in the master HTML file. Thus, when the Internet user visits the master HTML file, the framed sections will appear as a frame.

Framing is often a useful tool for the Internet user. For example, it may allow the user to view a document's table of contents while remaining in the body of the document. However, the framed page may not even be owned by the same person who owns the master HTML file in which the frame file is embedded. When it appears as a framed web page, its appearance may be different than its owner intended.

The practice of framing is not specifically regulated by EU legislation. As it involves the copying of an HTML file, it could implicate copyright law. The national courts have not been consistent in their treatment of framing. Some courts have taken the position that framing constitutes a duplication, which requires the permission of the owner of the framed webpage. Other courts have taken the position that anyone who puts content on the Internet must assume that it will be linked to by third parties.

(c) Caching

The term "cache" refers to the area on a computer's hard drive which a web browser uses to store pages that were recently downloaded.[97] The cache is necessary to allow a user to quickly return to the stored page, as it can be retrieved from the cache rather than from the Internet server. As caching involves copying data, it raises potential copyright issues. As discussed in Chapter X, national copyright law prohibits the reproduction of the works of others. In recognition of the essential nature of caching in effectively using the Internet, however, the ECJ has held that it qualifies as a permitted temporary act of reproduction under the Information Society Directive.[98]

(d) Meta Tagging

Internet users commonly rely on search engines to identify material available on the Internet relevant to their particular interests or needs. Search engines commonly rely on headers that indicate the type of information or subject matter discussed in a particular document together with proprietary algorithms that serve to rank the pages in order of relevance to a particular search. The HTML tags that are placed in the header of a document are called meta tags. The Internet user typically does not see the header or the meta tag.

---

97. E-Commerce Directive at art. 13(1).
98. Case C-360/13, Public Relations Consultants Ass'n Ltd v. Newspaper Licensing Agency Ltd., 2014 E.C.R. I-____.

As meta tags serve to direct Internet users to websites, and it is a common objective of many websites to stimulate traffic (i.e., the number of visitors to their website), meta tags may be employed in a misleading fashion for commercial objectives. A word that has nothing to do with the content of a document or website may be inserted in the header to increase the likelihood that that website will be included in lists produced by searches for the name of a competitor by the search engine browser. For example, the seller of suggestive jeans may use the name "Playboy" in its meta tag, assuming that a person who is searching for Playboy is a potential customer of the suggestive jeans.

The misleading use of meta tags is not directly regulated by EU legislation. The regulation of the practice is addressed primarily by the unfair trading laws and the trademark laws of the member states. For example, an appeals court in Munich held that under German trademark law, the use of a trademarked name in a meta tag violates the trademark rights of the trademark holder because it creates confusion on the part of the Internet user.[99] In that case, the manufacturer of electronic products using the name Hanseatic sued an electronics repair insurance service for use of the Hanseatic name in the meta tag of the repair service. The repair service sold insurance for the repair of Hanseatic products. The problem was, however, that the manufacturer also offered an extended warranty service for an additional cost on its Hanseatic products. The court said that the use of the name in the meta tag created the impression that Hanseatic products could be purchased on the website.

7. Regulation of Commercial Practices Involving the Internet

7.1 Cookies, Apps, and Other Devices Related to Behavioral Advertising

Cookies are placed by providers in the browsers of users who have accessed the website. They enable the provider to collect data concerning which websites the user contacts and how frequently. The provider can call up the collected data and thus generate a profile of the user to which he can then specifically adjust his advertising.

In legal terms, cookies primarily intervene in the user's information self-determination rights, i.e., the right to control data concerning one's own person and one's own activities and only to notify such to others knowingly. The use of cookies, therefore, falls within the scope of the infringement of personality rights. However, cookies involve a competition-law dimension alongside this tort element: the data obtained using cookies can generate a considerable competitive advantage by enabling the specific adjustment of measures by the

---

99. Decision of the OLG München in case no. 6 U 4123/99 (Apr. 6, 2000) *reported at* 2000 Wettbewerb in Recht und Praxis 775.

provider and thus increasing his chances of concluding an agreement with the potential customer addressed in this way.

The use of cookies or other forms of tracking devices, such as spyware and malware, are not outright prohibited under EU law. However, the user must consent to the installation of a cookie or any other devices stored on that user's computer or used to gain access to the information stored on that user's computer.[100] This applies regardless of whether the data collected qualifies as "personal data."[101]

In order to give a valid consent, the user must have been provided with clear and comprehensive information about the purposes of the processing, this information must be provided to the user prior to the granting of consent, and the consent must be unambiguous and freely given.[102] The user must also have the right to revoke the consent at any time. The traditional method of obtaining the user's consent—automatically installing the cookie unless the user affirmatively opts out—is not a valid consent even though the user can set his or her browser to prohibit the installation of cookies and to delete them.[103] The user must affirmatively consent to each cookie installed on his or her computer. The fact that the user has set his or her browser setting to accept all cookies is not sufficient to be deemed a valid consent. Once the consent is obtained, however, it is valid for subsequent collections of data from the cookie for up to one year.[104]

The user's consent for the installation of cookies is not required in two circumstances: (1) the cookie is used for the sole purpose of carrying out or facilitating the transmission of a communication over an electronic communications network, or (2) its use is strictly necessary in order to provide an information society service explicitly requested by the subscriber or user.[105] A cookie is the used for the sole purpose of carrying out or facilitating the transmission of a communication over an electronic communications network only when the transmission is not possible without the cookie.[106] The mere fact

---

100. Directive 2002/58/EC of the European Parliament and of the Council of 12 July 2002 concerning the processing of personal data and the protection of privacy in the electronic communications sector, 2002 O.J. (L 201) 37 at art. 5(3) [hereinafter ePrivacy Directive]. Although the Data Privacy Directive could also be applied to the collection of data through cookies, the provisions of the Data Privacy Directive only apply if not regulated in the ePrivacy Directive. For example, the provisions of the Data Privacy Directive regulating data quality, confidentiality, security, and transfer continue to apply to cookies and other means of collecting data through the browser of the user. *See* Article 29 Working Party, Opinion 2/2010 on Behavioural Advertising, WP171 (June 22, 2010) at 10.
101. Article. 29 Working Party, Opinion 2/2010 on Behavioural Advertising, WP171 (June 22, 2010) at 9.
102. Article 29 Working Party, Working Document 02/2013 providing guidance on obtaining consent for cookies, WP208 (Oct. 2, 2013).
103. Article 29 Working Party, Opinion 2/2010 on Behavioural Advertising, WP171 (June 22, 2010) at 13.
104. *Id.*
105. ePrivacy Directive at art. 5(3).
106. Article 29 Working Party, Opinion 02/2012 on Cookie Consent Exemption, WP194 (June 7, 2012) at 3.

that the cookie facilitates the transmission is not sufficient. The use of a cookie is strictly necessary to provide an information society service, according to the Commission, only if the user has explicitly requested the information society service and the cookie is strictly needed to enable the information society service (i.e., the information society service will not work without the cookie).[107]

In contrast to cookies, apps installed on a smart phone are able to access significantly more data. Once an app is installed on a smart phone, it often allows access to data stored on the device including, for example, the user's address book. Although the exchange of data through the installation of an app can provide useful services to the smart phone owner, it raises privacy concerns above and beyond those raised in the context of cookies. The party that installs the app is considered to be a "controller" for purposes of EU data privacy law.[108] This triggers the application of the EU Data Privacy Directive and the ePrivacy Directive. According to Article 5(3) of the ePrivacy Directive, the user must consent to the storing of information, or the gaining of access to information already stored, in the terminal equipment of a subscriber or user.[109] In contrast to the Data Privacy Directive, this consent requirement applies not only to personal data, but also, according to the Article 29 Working Group, to any information stored on the device.[110]

The consent must be free, specific, and informed (as defined in Article 2(h) of the Data Privacy Directive). According to the Article 29 Working Group, consent is "freely given" if the user has the choice to accept or refuse the processing of her personal data. The user is "informed" if she had sufficient information at her disposal to form an accurate decision to grant consent. Finally, the consent must be specific. This means that it must relate to the processing of a particular data item or a limited category of data processing. In the opinion of the Article 29 Working Group, simply clicking an install button is not valid consent because it is not sufficiently specific. The safer approach, from the perspective of the Working Group, is to secure a consent for each type of data the app intends to access.[111]

The practice of device fingerprinting in treated similar to cookies. The practice refers to placing of a tracking device on a specific computer to track the on-line activity of that user. As such, it closely resembles cookies. Device fingerprints, however, function even where the user has turned off or not accepted cookies. Similar to cookies, the ePrivacy Directive requires that the user consent

---

107. *Id.*
108. Article 29 Working Party, Opinion 02/2013 on apps on smart devices, WP 202 (Feb. 27, 2013).
109. Although the ePrivacy Directive generally applies only to providers of publicly available electronic communication services and networks, Article 5(3) applies also to private entities that place on or read information from smart devices. According to the Article 29 Working Group, the consent requirement applies to services offered in the EU regardless of the location of the service provider. Article 29 Working Party, Opinion 02/2013 on apps on smart devices, WP 202 (Feb. 27, 2013).
110. *Id.*
111. *Id.*

to device fingerprinting.[112] The consent must be free, specific, and informed (as defined in Article 2(h) of the Data Privacy Directive).

7.2 Regulation of Unsolicited E-mails

The practice of sending unsolicited e-mail messages (i.e., spam) is prevalent because of the relatively low costs involved. The "spammers" typically collect addresses from vendors or from newsgroups. From the perspective of the advertisers, a mass e-mail offers a cost-effective way to reach a large number of recipients. From the recipient's perspective, however, unsolicited e-mails present a burden. Not only do they distract employees but, if they contain a large amount of text, they may unnecessarily overload mail servers. Additionally, spamming blocks the capacities of the points of further distribution, preventing them from being available for other purposes.

There is no absolute prohibition in the EU on sending out unsolicited e-mails. Although the practice of sending unsolicited e-mails could fall under several directives,[113] the ePrivacy Directive specifically regulates unsolicited e-mails. The general rule is that unsolicited e-mails are prohibited as a direct marketing tool without the consent of the subscribers.[114] It is not enough to allow the recipient the right to opt out of receiving the unsolicited e-mails. The recipients actually have to opt in to receive the e-mail.[115] Moreover, the sender of the unsolicited e-mail must also consult regularly and respect the opt-out registers in which individuals not wishing to receive such commercial communications can register themselves.[116]

The opt in may occur by the recipient specifically and expressly giving its consent to receiving subsequent unsolicited e-mails. If the sender of the unsolicited e-mail has obtained the electronic contact details of the customer in an earlier distance sale, the seller may then use these electronic contact details for direct marketing of its similar products provided (1) the customer has been given the possibility to refuse to receive e-mail and (2) the customer has not objected.[117] If sending the unsolicited e-mail is permitted, the e-mail must be clearly and unambiguously identified as a commercial communication.[118]

---

112. Opinion 9/2014 on the application of Directive 2002/58/EC to device fingerprinting, 14/EN WP 224 (Nov. 25, 2014). Consent is not required in the limited circumstances where the fingerprinting is "strictly necessary" to provide the services requested by the subscriber or for the sole purpose of carrying out the transmission of an electronic communication over an electronic communications network.
113. The Distance Selling Directive (Article 11) prohibits unsolicited commercial communications by telephone (automatic calling machine) or by fax without the consent of the customer. It could, by analogy, be extended to e-mail communications.
114. ePrivacy Directive at art. 13(1).
115. The opt-in rule applies not only to e-mail but also to other forms of marketing such as telemarketing and faxes. Article 29 Data Protection Working Party Opinion 5/3004 (Feb. 27, 2004) 11601/EN.
116. E-Commerce Directive at art. 7(2).
117. ePrivacy Directive at art. 13(2).
118. E-Commerce Directive at art. 7(1).

8. Data Privacy

8.1 Applicable Legal Norms

The issue of privacy in general, and the privacy of personal data in particular, has been a topic of legal concern in Europe for a number of years. The topic of the protection of personal data has attracted increased attention in the last decade due to the heightened difficulty individuals experienced in controlling the flow of data. The wide use of the Internet may be the primary cause of this loss of control.

The right of privacy is secured by the constitutions of most of the member states and is a fundamental principle of European law.[119] According to Article 16 of the TFEU: "Everyone has the right to the protection of personal data concerning them."[120] In addition, several member states have had laws in place for decades that specifically protect the privacy of personal data. At the EU level, there are several secondary laws that protect data privacy.[121] Primary among these is the so-called EU Data Privacy Directive.[122]

---

119. European Convention for the Protection of Human Rights and Fundamental Freedoms, 213 U.N.T.S. 222 *entered into force* Sept. 3, 1953; Council of Europe Convention of 28 January 1981 for the Protection of Individuals with Regard to Automatic Processing of Personal Data at art. 8.
120. According to the ECJ, "the right to protection of personal data is not, however, an absolute right, but must be considered in its relation to its function in society." Case C-92/09, Volker and Markus Schecke GbR v. Land Hessen, 2010 E.C.R. I-11117, 11143 ¶48.
121. Commission Regulation (EU) No 611/2013 of 24 June 2013 on the measures applicable to notification of personal data breaches under Directive 2002/58/EC of the European Parliament and of the Council on privacy and electronic communications, 2013 O.J. (L 173) 2; Directive 95/46/EC of the European Parliament and of the Council of 24 October 1995 on the protection of individuals with regard to the processing of personal data and on the free movement of such data, 1995 O.J. (L 281) 31; ePrivacy Directive; Regulation (EC) 45/2001 of the European Parliament and of the Council of 18 December 2000 on the protection of individuals with regard to the processing of personal data by the Community institutions and bodies and on the free movement of such data, 2001 O.J. (L 8) 1; Directive 97/66/EC of the European Parliament and of the Council of 15 December 1997 concerning the processing of personal data and the protection of privacy in the telecommunications sector, 1998 O.J. (L 24) 1.
122. Directive 95/46/EC of the European Parliament and of the Council of 24 October 1995 on the protection of individuals with regard to the processing of personal data and on the free movement of such data, 1995 O.J. (L 281) 31. Another EU data privacy law which is applicable to businesses in Europe is Regulation (EC) No 45/2001 of the European Parliament and the Council of 18 December 2000 on the protection of individuals with regard to the processing of personal data by the Community institutions and bodies and on the free movement of such data, 2001 O.J. (L 8) 1. This regulation applies, for example, to personal data collected by the Community institutions when conducting an investigation of a business. *See, e.g.*, Case C-28/08P, Comm'n v. The Bavarian Lager Co. Ltd., 2010 E.C.R. I-6055.

8.2 Scope of the Data Privacy Directive

There are two important limitations to the scope of the EU Data Privacy Directive. First, it only applies to personal data i.e., any information relating to an identified or identifiable natural person. Second, it only applies to the processing of personal data.

(a) *Personal Data*

The concept of "personal data" includes four elements.[123] First, it applies to "any information." It is not necessary that the information be true or accurate. Moreover, it includes subjective information. For example, the subjective assessment of a supervisor about the abilities of an employee is "information" for purposes of the Data Privacy Directive. The transfer of that information to a third party would implicate the provisions of the national law implementing the Data Privacy Directive. Even biometric data (such as fingerprints, facial structures, voice patterns, behavioral characteristics, etc.) would qualify as information.

Second, the information must "relate to" a person. In most instances, this is relatively easy to determine. For example, information compiled in a doctor's office on a person's health will relate to that person. In certain circumstances, however, the information will only indirectly relate to a person. For example, the information that 100 tablets of a particular drug are contained in a bottle is information that directly relates to an object and not a person. If, however, there is a connection between that bottle and the patient for whom it is destined, then that same information (that there are 100 tablets in the bottle) is considered to relate to the person.

Third, the individual to whom the information relates must be "identified or identifiable." This means that the information must be sufficiently specific to be able to distinguish the person from all others. The easy case is if the information contains the name of the person, her address, or any numerical reference specific to that individual. Even if the person is not specifically identified, if the recipient of the information already contains sufficient knowledge to ascertain the identity of the person once the information is transferred to that recipient, then the person is identifiable. For example, if the CEO of a small company knows the street addresses of all of the employees, when the local newspaper announces that an employee of the company living on Main Street was just caught shoplifting, then this is identifiable information even though the person's name is not mentioned.

It is possible to anonymize data so that it falls outside the scope of the Data Privacy Directive. This is, however, a difficult task. According to the Article 29 Data Protection Working Party, in order to be anonymous, "the data must be stripped of sufficient elements such that the data subject can no longer be identified."[124] To assist firms in achieving the appropriate level of

---

123. Article 29 Data Protection Working Party, Opinion 4/2007 on the concept of personal data (June 20, 2007).
124. Article 29 Data Protection Working Party, Opinion 05/2014 on Anonymisation Techniques, 0829/14/EN (Apr. 10, 2014) at 5.

anonymization, the Working Group has identified several possible anonymization techniques.[125]

E-mail addresses can be identifiable (at least to the Internet access provider) even if the owner of the address is not identified in the address. In a case brought by the German Consumer Protection Society against Apple, the German Landgericht inferred that Apple's collection of data from consumers on its website was not anonymized because it was subsequently used to provide individualized product and service announcements to the consumers.[126] The German court assumed that in order to provide these individualized communications, the data Apple was collecting could not be adequately anonymized.

Finally, the Data Privacy Directive only applies to "natural persons." This element precludes protection for data relating to companies.[127] Nonetheless, some member states (such as Austria, Italy, and Luxembourg) extend the protection to legal persons. This is possible because the Data Privacy Directive only sets a minimum standard, leaving the member states to adopt stricter standards.

It is important to recall that the concept of personal data is not limited to confidential information. The fact that personal data is public does not necessarily mean it falls outside the protections offered by the Data Privacy Directive. The term "personal data" even applies to data that is readily available to the public.[128] In *Tietosuojavaltuutettu v. Satakunnan Markkinapörssi Oy*, for example, a Finnish person collected personal income data on Finnish individuals from public records made publicly available by the Finnish tax authorities. Despite the fact that the data was already public, the ECJ concluded that it qualified as personal data under the Data Privacy Directive.[129]

(b) Data Processing

The Data Privacy Directive applies only to the "processing" of personal data.[130] The extremely broad definition of this term hardly limits the Directive's scope of application. Processing means any operation performed on personal data, e.g., collection, storing, alteration, consultation, use, transfer, etc. For example,

---

125. *Id.* at Annex.
126. Bundesverband der Verbraucherzentralen und Verbraucherverbände v. Apple Sales International, in Decision of the Landgericht Berlin case no. 15 O 92/12 (Apr. 30, 2013) *reported at* 67 Neue Juristische Wochenschrift 2605 (2013).
127. Data which belongs to a company, however, may still be considered personal data for purposes of the Data Privacy Directive. In Case C-342/12, Worten – Equipamentos para o Lar SA v. Autoridade para as Condições de Trabalho, 2013 E.C.R. I-____, at ¶21, for example, information collected by the company about the working hours of its employees was considered personal data. Moreover, some member states—Austria, Italy, and Luxembourg—extend the protection to legal persons even though they are not required to under the Data Privacy Directive.
128. Working Group Opinion 7/2003 on the re-use of public sector information and the protection of personal data, 10936/03/EN (Dec. 12, 2003) at 4.
129. Case C-73/07, Tietosuojavaltuutettu v. Satakunnan Markkinapörssi Oy, 2009 E.C.R. I-7094, 7121 ¶48.
130. Data Privacy Directive at art. 3.

a company processes data when it collects data from consumers visiting that company's website.[131] Even a company's transfer of data to the government in accordance with the law constitutes processing for purposes of the Data Privacy Directive.[132] According to the ECJ, processing is to be interpreted so broadly that it even covers the retrieval by a search engine such as Google of information already available on the Internet.[133] Even the capturing of video data via a security camera on a private residence constitutes the processing of personal data if the trespasser can be identified in video.[134]

The transfer of data in a purely private (noncommercial) context may not fall under the Directive as, for example, sending a private letter.[135] The rule is that a natural person may process personal data in the course of a purely personal or household activity.[136] However, the "purely" requirement is interpreted strictly. In *In re Bodil Lindqvist,* the ECJ held that the exception did not apply to a woman who posted personal data (names, addresses, and telephone numbers) about some of her colleagues on her personal website.[137] To qualify for the exception, the activities must be carried out only within the private or family life of individuals.

One common misconception is that the Directive only applies to electronic personal data. Although the Directive applies to data that is processed by automated means (e.g., computers), it also applies to data not processed by automated means but which is part of a filing system.[138] For example, the personnel files a company retains on its employees would be personal data for purposes of the Data Privacy Directive.

8.3   Relationship to National Law

(a) Preemption

Although the Data Privacy Directive establishes minimum measures the member states must implement to protect the privacy of personal data, it does not preempt national law. In this respect, it is similar to the U.S. Gramm-Leach-Bliley Act.[139] The fact that the Data Privacy Directive does not preempt national data privacy laws is often viewed as one of the Directive's greatest shortcomings.

---

131. Case C-131/12, Google Spain SL v. AEPD, 2014 E.C.R. I-____, at ¶26; Bundesverband der Verbraucherzentralen und Verbraucherverbände v. Apple Sales International, Decision of the Landgericht Berlin in case no. 15 O 92/12 (April 30, 2013) *reported at* 67 Neue Juristische Wochenschrift 2605 (2013).
132. Case C-342/12, Worten – Equipamentos para o Lar SA v. Autoridade para as Condições de Trabalho, 2013 E.C.R. I-____, at ¶20.
133. Case C-131/12, Google Spain SL v. AEPD, 2014 E.C.R. I-____, at ¶28.
134. Case C-212/13, František Ryneš v. Úřad pro ochranu osobních údajů, 2014 E.C.R. I-____, at ¶22.
135. Data Privacy Directive at recital 12.
136. *Id.* at art. 3(2).
137. Case C-101/01, *In re* Bodil Lindqvist, 2003 E.C.R. I-12971, 13013 ¶46.
138. Data Privacy Directive at art. 3(1).
139. The GLB Act sets a floor for data protection and does not preempt more stringent state law, 81 BNA Antitrust & Trade Reg. Rep 30 (July 13, 2001).

For internationally active firms, compliance with the basic principles in the Directive does not result in legal certainty. A multinational company active in all of the member states must comply with the national laws applicable in each of those states. In certain federalist states (e.g., Germany), the task is further complicated by the fact that each of the states making up that member state have their own data privacy authority responsible for the interpretation and application of the law. As illustrated in *In re Lindqvist*, however, the right of the member state to provide greater protection to personal data than that provided in the Directive is limited by the freedom of movement of personal data.[140] In other words, although the member states may adopt more stringent data protection laws, they must not disproportionately restrict the movement of that data within the EU.

(b) Applicable Law

The Data Privacy Directive does not contain conflict of laws rules which determine the applicable law for a particular situation. Instead, it requires the member states to apply their national law provisions if the processing is carried out in the context of the activities of an establishment of the controller on the territory of the member state.[141] The controller is the party that determines the purpose and means of the data processing. If the controller happens to be established in several member states, that controller must take the necessary measures to ensure that each of these establishments complies with the obligations laid down by the applicable national law.[142]

Similar to other concepts codified in the Data Privacy Directive, determining where processing is carried out in the context of the activities of an establishment is interpreted broadly in favor of the data subject. In *Google Spain SL and Google Inc. v. Agencia Española de Protección de Datos*, for example, the issue was whether Spain could apply its data privacy laws to Google, even though Google's establishment in Spain was limited to advertising and sales and not data processing (the search operator was outside Spain). The ECJ held, however, that the processing is carried out in the context of the activities of an establishment in Spain because these advertising and sales activities were "inextricably linked" to the search operations.[143]

If the controller is not established in the EU—for example, a U.S. company with no subsidiary or branch in the EU—the national data privacy law will be applied in accordance with the member state's conflicts rules.[144] If the controller is not established in the EU but, for purposes of processing personal data makes use of equipment situated in the EU, the law of the member state where the equipment is located applies, unless the equipment is used only for purposes of transit through the EU.

---

140. Case C-101/01, *In re* Bodil Lindqvist, 2003 E.C.R. I-12971, 13027 ¶99.
141. Data Privacy Directive at art. 4.
142. *Id.*
143. Case C-131/12, Google Spain SL v. Agencia Española de Protección de Datos, 2014 E.C.R. I-____, at ¶56.
144. Data Privacy Directive at art. 4.

8.4 Registration

The Data Privacy Directive establishes a system of notification for processing operations. National data protection authorities are required to keep a public register indicating details of the data controllers and of the particular processing involved. As the definition of "processing" covers almost any use of the data, the scope of this requirement can be extremely broad. Some member states have adopted practical solution to address the burden that registration would place on businesses as well as on the agencies charged with oversight over the registers. The Netherlands, for example, has adopted exemptions from the notification requirement for innocuous forms of data processing. Germany, on the other hand, relieves the data controller from the obligation of notifying if the data controller has appointed a data protection officer.[145]

8.5 Public Enforcement

The Directive gives the member states the responsibility of enforcing personal data protection law. Each member state has established a national data protection office which has assumed primary responsibility for the enforcement of the respective national laws implementing the Directive. There is no EU institution charged with the responsibility of enforcing data privacy laws. Although there is a European Data Privacy Supervisor and European Data Protection Officers, their role is to monitor the protection of data by the European institutions.[146] However, Art. 29 of the Directive establishes a Working Group (commonly referred to as the Article 29 Working Group).

The federalist approach to the enforcement of data privacy, combined with the ease at which data flows across national borders, has prompted the Working Group to take a more active role in enforcement than provided for in Art. 30 of the Data Privacy Directive. For example, when Microsoft introduced its "Passport" authentication service which allows Internet users to log into multiple password-protected websites by centrally registering with Passport, Microsoft worked out a solution with the Working Group rather than with each individual member state.[147] As the Working Group is comprised of representatives from the member states, a more active role for the Working Group is a convenient alternative, even though it legally does not have the authority to preempt the data privacy authorities of the member states.

---

145. German Bundesdatenschutzgesetz at § 4d(2).
146. Regulation (EC) No.45/2001 of the European Parliament and of the Council of 18 December 2000 on the protection of individuals with regard to the processing of personal data by the Community institutions and bodies and on the free movement of such data, 2001 O.J. (L 8) 1; Decision No 1247/2002/EC of the European Parliament, of the Council and of the Commission of 1 July 2002 on the regulations and general conditions governing performance of the European Data Protection Supervisor's duties, 2002 O.J. (L 183) 1.
147. Microsoft's experience is reported by Peter Fleischer, Microsoft Director of Regulatory Affairs, in P. Fleischer, Microsoft: Working with Privacy Regulators, Privacy Laws & Business International Newsletter 34 (Oct./Nov. 2003).

The Directive requires each of the member states to set up a notification system for data controllers in their respective jurisdictions.[148] In other words, national law requires data controllers to notify the national data protection authority in their jurisdiction of their data processing activities. Some member states have gone beyond this and imposed an authorization requirement according to which the controller must not only notify its activities, but also wait for an authorization. Although the imposition of an authorization requirement is not expressly provided for in the Directive, the Commission has accepted the practice.[149] However, the member states may not require authorization of processing which has been approved by the Commission.

8.6 Private Enforcement

The Directive also relies on private enforcement to induce compliance. The member states are required to provide for the right of a person to receive compensation from the data controller for the damages suffered as a result of an unlawful processing operation.[150] The compensation to be paid by the controller is granted irrespective of the controller's fault, but there is an exculpatory provision if the controller proves he is not responsible for the event giving rise to the damage. The Directive does not specify the type or amount of compensation which is to be granted.

The term "controller" means the natural or legal person, public authority, agency, or any other body which alone or jointly with others determines the purposes and means of processing personal data. Although the identification of the controller is important because most of the responsibilities under the Directive are imposed on the controller, determining the controller is not always an easy task. It is relatively clear that a company that purchases personal information from a third party which has independently collected that information is not the controller. What if, however, a company engages a third party to provide it with personal data, leaving it to the third party to determine how the data is collected? The process by which clinical trials are conducted on new drugs provides a good illustration. Drug companies commonly outsource the clinical trials required to support the application for approval of a new drug. The company conducting the clinical trial has broad autonomy in selecting the participants in the clinical trial. The drug company is primarily interested in the results of the trials. In this situation, it is unclear which entity would be considered the data controller.

The determination of the data controller is left up to the member states. One of the central issues in Google Spain SL and Google Inc. v. Agencia Española de Protección de Datos was whether Google could be considered a "data controller regarding personal data published by a third party. The case was brought by a Spanish citizen against a daily newspaper and Google.

---

148. Data Privacy Directive at art. 18. The minimum content of the notification is set forth in Article 19 of the Data Privacy Directive.
149. Report from the Commission, First Report on the Implementation of the Data Privacy Directive, COM (2003) 265 final at 18.
150. Data Privacy Directive at art. 23.

The newspaper had posted on its website an announcement mentioning the plaintiff by name in connection with a foreclosure on the plaintiff's real estate for debts he owed. The ECJ held that Google was a data controller for purposes of the Data Privacy Directive.[151]

When collecting personal data, the Directive requires the controller to provide the person to whom the personal data relates (i.e., the "data subject") with basic information that would make the data subject aware that his or her personal data is being collected.[152] The information that must be provided includes the identity of the controller, the purposes for which the data is being collected, recipients of the data, and the ability of the data subject not to provide the data. These obligations are imposed on the controller even if the personal data is not being collected directly from the data subject.[153]

The Directive gives the data subject broad rights of access. The data subject has the right to require the controller to provide him or her with confirmation as to whether or not data relating to the subject is being processed along with information as to the purposes of the processing, the categories of data concerned, and the recipients or categories of recipients to whom the data is disclosed.[154] In Google Spain SL v. Agencia Española de Protección de Datos, the data subject plaintiff was able to force Google to de-list a link to a newspaper article which contained personal data on the data subject.[155]

In addition, the data subject has the right to require the data controller to inform him or her of the particular data being processed and the source of the data. The data controller can charge a reasonable fee for granting the data subject access, but the fee must be reasonably proportionate to the costs incurred by the controller in providing such access.[156] The duration of time the controller must store the data is left to the discretion of the member states, subject to the requirement that the duration represents a fair balance between the interests of the data subject and the burden on the controller to maintain the data.[157]

8.7 Five Processing Principles

The Data Privacy Directive requires the member states to transpose their laws to ensure compliance with five basic principles and prohibit the processing of

---

151. Case C-131/12, Google Spain SL v. Agencia Española de Protección de Datos, 2014 E.C.R. I-____.
152. Data Privacy Directive at art. 10.
153. *Id.* at art. 11(1).
154. *Id.* at art. 12(a). The data subject also has the authority to require the data processor to correct or erase incorrect data. Case C-131/12, Google Spain SL v. Agencia Española de Protección de Datos, 2014 E.C.R. I-____, at ¶77.
155. *Id.* at ¶28. The Article 29 Working Group has subsequently issued Guidelines on complying with this case. Guidelines on the Implementation of the Court of Justice of the European Union Judgment on Google Spain SL v. Agencia Española de Protección de Datos, 14/EN/WP225 (Nov. 26, 2014).
156. The ECJ ultimately held that the member states could impose a fee provided that it was not excessive. Case C- 486/12, *In re* X, 2013 E.C.R. I-____, at ¶22.
157. C-553/07, College van burgemeester en wethouders van Rotterdam v. M.E.E. Rijkeboer, 2009 E.C.R. I-3919, 3937 ¶64.

personal data except in certain enumerated circumstances.[158] Unfortunately, however, these principles are formulated in very general terms. Data must be processed fairly and lawfully.[159] It should be collected for specified purposes and used accordingly. The purpose of the processing should be explicit and legitimate. Data should be adequate, relevant, and not excessive in relation to the purpose for which it is processed. Data should be accurate and kept up to date. Data controllers are required to take any reasonable step to ensure the rectification or removal of inaccurate data. Finally, data should be kept in a form that permits identification of individuals for no longer than necessary. The responsibility for compliance is imposed on the data controller.[160]

8.8 Permitted Processing

Compliance with these five general principles is difficult because they are formulated in very broad terms. However, the Directive identifies specific instances in which the processing of data is permitted. Personal data can be processed if the data subject has unambiguously given his or her consent. Consent requires that it is freely and specifically given after being adequately informed.[161]

The processing of personal data is also permitted when done by a natural person in the course of a purely personal or household activity.[162] This exception, like all of the exceptions, is interpreted very narrowly. The requirement of purely personal or household activity is difficult to overcome. In *František Ryneš v. Úřad pro ochranu osobních údajů*, for example, a homeowner in the Czech Republic had been the subject of attacks on him and his family. So he installed a video surveillance camera on his home. This allowed him and the police to identify the criminals. One of the criminals argued that the video surveillance camera was illegal because it captured not only criminals on his property, but also people who might be walking by on the sidewalk. The General Court, remarkably, concluded that this was data processing under the Data Privacy Directive. "To the extent that video surveillance such as that at issue in the main proceedings covers, even partially, a public space and is accordingly directed outwards from the private setting of the person processing the data in that manner, it cannot be regarded as an activity which is a purely 'personal or household' activity."[163]

Another instance of processing expressly permitted under the Directive is data processing that is necessary for the performance of a contract or in order to enter into a contract requested by the data subject. This would include, for example, processing data for billing purposes or processing data relating to an

---

158. Data Privacy Directive at art. 5. The eligibility and responsibilities of the data protection officer are set forth in German law.
159. *Id.* at art. 6(1)(a).
160. *Id.* at art. 6(2).
161. *Id.* at art. 2(h).
162. *Id.* at art. 3(2).
163. Case C-212/13, František Ryneš v. Úřad pro ochranu osobních údajů, 2014 E.C.R. I-____, at ¶33.

applicant for a job or for a loan. In addition, processing is expressly permitted if it is required by law. Transferring personal data in accordance with a court order would be an example of permissible data processing.

Processing of data is also permitted if it is necessary to protect a vital interest of the data subject or processing is necessary in the performance of tasks carried out in the public interest or by official authorities (such as the government, the tax authorities, the police etc.) where this is necessary for accomplishing their tasks. In *Worten – Equipamentos para o Lar SA v. Autoridade para as Condições de Trabalho*, for example, a company was permitted to collect data on the working hours of its employees and transfer that information to the government authorities responsible for monitoring the working hours of employees.[164]

Finally, data can be processed whenever the controller or a third party has a legitimate interest in doing so and this interest is not overridden by the interest of protecting the fundamental rights of the data subject.[165] This requires balancing the legitimate business interests of the data controllers against the privacy of the data subjects.[166] The sensitivity of the data will often play a role in this balancing process.

In addition to the cases of expressly permitted data processing, member states may provide for exemptions or derogations for the processing of personal data carried out solely for journalistic purposes or the purpose of artistic or literary expression only if it is necessary to reconcile the right to privacy with the rules governing freedom of expression.[167] Journalistic activities are those having the sole object of disclosing to the public information, opinions, or ideas, irrespective of the medium used to transmit them.[168]

8.9 The Prohibition as Related to Transfers of Data Outside the EU

The Data Privacy Directive requires the member states to prohibit the transfer of personal data to all nonmember states that do not offer an adequate level of protection.[169] This prohibition applies even to the transfer of data within a corporate group. For example, the transfer of personal data by a European subsidiary to its parent company in the United States would be prohibited unless one of the exceptions applies. The rationale for this general prohibition is the recognition that the protections accorded by the Directive would be seriously undermined if the personal data could be transferred to a third country which did not have laws

---

164. Case C-342/12, Worten – Equipamentos para o Lar SA v. Autoridade para as Condições de Trabalho, 2013 E.C.R. I-____, at ¶34.
165. Data Privacy Directive at art. 7(f).
166. The Article 29 Data Protection Working Party has issued a helpful opinion on balancing the legitimate interests of the data controller against the interest of the data subject. Opinion 06/2014 on the notion of legitimate interests of the data controller under Article 7 of the Directive 95/46/EC, 844/14/EN (April 9, 2014).
167. Data Privacy Directive at art. 9.
168. Case C-73/07, Tietosuojavaltuutettu v. Satakunnan Markkinapörssi Oy, 2009 E.C.R. I-7094, 7124 ¶61.
169. Data Privacy Directive at art. 25(1).

protecting such data or offered a level of protection below that of the EU. The authority to determine which states offer adequate protection is reserved to the European Commission.[170] Currently, the Commission has identified Switzerland, Hungary, Argentina, Canada, Guernsey, and the U.S. safe harbor program as providing an adequate level of protection.[171] The legal significance of a decision that a third country has adequate protection is that the member states may no longer prohibit transfers of personal data to those countries.[172]

8.10 Compliance Alternatives for Transfers of Data Outside the EU to Countries Without Adequate Protection

As the Commission has not identified the United States as providing adequate protection to personal data, transfers of personal data from Europe to the United States are generally prohibited. Unfortunately, the Directive does not define what is meant by a transfer. For example, if a person merely places personal data about another person on her personal web page, does this constitute a transfer to the United States if that web page can be accessed by individuals in third countries including the United States? That was one of the issues in *In re Lindqvist*.[173]

In that case, the ECJ held that when an individual transfers data to her hosting provider in the European Economic Area (EEA) for posting on her home page, that transfer to the hosting provider is not considered a transfer to a third country even if the home page is accessible to individuals outside the EEA. The court did not rule on whether the subsequent posting of the data by the hosting provider constituted a transfer of data to a third country. However, the court's reasoning seems to suggest that posting data on a website accessible to individuals in third countries (i.e., a passive transfer) should not be considered a transfer of data to a third country. According to the ECJ, to hold otherwise would mean that unless the Commission designated all third countries to have adequate protection, any posting of personal data on the Internet would violate the prohibition in the Directive, as data posted on the Internet is readily accessible by individuals throughout the world.[174]

---

170. *Id.* at art. 25(6).
171. Commission Decision of 21 November 2003 on the adequate protection of personal data in Guernsey, 2003 O. J. (L 308) 27; Commission Decision of 30 June 2003 pursuant to Directive 95/46/EC of the European Parliament and of the Council on the adequate protection of personal data in Argentina, 2003 O. J. (L 168) 19; Commission Decision 2000/519/EC of 26.7.2000, 2000 O. J. (L 215) 4 (Hungary); Commission Decision 2000/518/EC of 26.7.2000, 2000 O. J. (L 215) 1. (Switzerland); Commission Decision 2000/520/EC of 26.7.2000, 2000 O. J. (L 215) 7 (U.S. Safe Harbor); Commission Decision 2002/2/EC of 20.12.2001 on the adequate protection of personal data provided by the Canadian Personal Information Protection and Electronic Documents Act, 2002 O. J. (L 2) 13 (Canada).
172. Data Privacy Directive at art. 25(6) second sentence.
173. Case C-101/01, *In re* Bodil Lindqvist, 2003 E.C.R. I-12971.
174. *Id.* at 13020 ¶69.

This case raises the question of whether a transfer of data within a corporate group, for example, posting on the parent company's intranet website, would be considered a transfer of data for purposes of the Data Privacy Directive. The holding in *In re Lindqvist* is probably limited to the facts of the case, as its logical extension would allow companies to avoid the application of the Directive in many instances.

The prohibition on transfers of personal data to third countries which have not been designated by the Commission as providing adequate protection does not mean, however, that there are no means by which personal data can be transferred out of Europe to the United States. In general, there are three options for U.S. entities receiving personal data from Europe: (1) seek adequacy determination; (2) join the U.S. safe harbor; or (3) comply with one of the exceptions. In each instance, the data controller is required to register with the national data protection authority.[175]

(a) First Option: Adequacy Determination by Member States

The first option is to secure an adequacy determination by the member states. Each member state has the authority to approve a transfer of data to a third country that does not ensure an adequate level of protection if the data controller has established adequate safeguards to protect the rights of the data subject.[176] This will typically require the controller to have appropriate contractual clauses in place regarding the onward transfer of the data. For companies doing business in a limited number of member states, this may be a viable option. However, securing such a decision by several member states would be a daunting and time-consuming effort.

There is an alternative to securing an adequacy determination for each type of transfer within corporate groups. As explained above, the prohibition on the transfer of personal data from the EU to a third country extends even to transfers within a corporate group. Hence, the application of the prohibition would paralyze many multinational companies who send data to and from the EU on a regular basis to their European operations. In fact, many of them share the same computer server. One practical solution is for these multinational companies to adopt binding corporate rules applicable to all the members of their corporate group. Accenture, for example, adopted binding corporate rules for the legal entities within its corporate group. It then applied for and received authorization from the UK Information Commissioner to transfer personal data

---

175. Data Privacy Directive at art. 18(1). For subsequent transfers of the data after the data has left the EU, the Article 29 Working Group has published sample contractual clauses. Working Document 01/2014 on Draft Ad Hoc Contractual Clauses EU Data Processor to non-EU Sub-processor, 757/14/EN WP214 (Mar. 21, 2014).
176. Data Privacy Directive at art. 26(2). Obviously, a member state determination is not required if the country outside the EU to which the data is transferred already provides adequate protection as determined by the Commission.

from Europe to its parent company in the United States.[177] Hyatt Hotels, another corporate group that transfers a significant amount of data between its affiliates worldwide, similarly adopted binding corporate rules that were approved by the UK Information Commissioner.[178]

In order to get its binding corporate rules approved, one of the legal entities within the group[179] submits an application to a national data protection authority which it proposes to be the lead data protection authority. As a general rule, the binding corporate rules should be submitted in the language of the proposed national data protection authority and in English. In its application, the entity needs to explain why the particular data protection authority it proposed is most appropriate. The primary criterion is the location of the group's EU headquarters.[180] Other potentially relevant factors according to the Article 29 Working Party are the location of the company within the group with delegated data protection responsibilities, the location of the company that is best placed to deal with the application and to enforce the binding corporate rules in the group, the place where most decisions in terms of the purposes and the means of the processing are taken, and the member state within the EU from which most transfers outside the EEA will take place.[181]

The national data protection authority to which the application is sent has the discretion to decide whether it is in fact the most appropriate data protection authority. If that data protection authority decides that it should be the lead data protection authority, the other national data protection authorities have two weeks to object. If another data protection authority objects, then the data protection authorities must work out a solution between or among themselves.

Although there are no standard forms of binding corporate rules approved by the Article 29 Working Party, it has issued a "framework" establishing how acceptable binding corporate rules might look.[182] The content of the application and the issues that need to be addressed in the binding corporate rules are prescribed in a working document issued by the Working Party.[183] In addition, the Working Party has published a chart describing the elements it expects to

---

177. Press Release of the UK Information Commissioner's Office of May 1, 2009, "Accenture and Atmel given authorization by the ICO to transfer personal information outside Europe based on binding corporate rules."
178. Press Release of the UK Information Commissioner's Office of Sept. 23, 2009, "Hyatt to transfer personal information outside Europe based on binding corporate rules."
179. For corporate groups with headquarters outside the EU, the most appropriate entity to do this is the European headquarters.
180. Article 29 Working Party, Working Document Setting Forth a Co-Operation Procedure for Issuing Common Opinions on Adequate Safeguards Resulting From "Binding Corporate Rules," WP 107 (Apr. 14, 2005) § 2.1.
181. *Id.* at § 2.2.
182. Article 29 Working Party, Working Document Setting up a framework for the structure of Binding Corporate Rules, WP 154 (June 24, 2008).
183. Article 29 Working Party, Working Document Establishing a Model Checklist Application for Approval of Binding Corporate Rules, WP 108 (Apr. 14, 2005).

see in binding corporate rules.[184] The rules must be binding both within the corporate group (i.e., enforceable against the members of the corporate group) and vis-à-vis third parties (i.e., third-party beneficiaries). Individuals covered by the scope of the binding corporate rules must be able to enforce compliance with the rules both via the data protection authorities and the courts within the jurisdiction of the member of the group at the origin of the transfer or the EU headquarters or the European member of the group with delegated data protection responsibilities. The binding corporate rules must also provide for the use of either internal auditors, external auditors, or a combination of both. Regarding the specific personal data being collected and transferred, the binding corporate rules should identify:

- the nature of the data;
- the purposes for which the data is processed;
- the extent of the transfers within the group that are covered by the rules;
- any group members in the EU from which personal data may be transferred; and
- any group members outside the EEA to which personal data may be transferred.

(b) Second Option: Reliance on Standard Contractual Clauses

An alternative to seeking an adequacy determination of a member state is to comply with a blanket adequacy decision of the Commission. In recognition of the impracticability of large businesses securing approval for each type of transfer of personal data outside the EU, the Data Privacy Directive allows the Commission to adopt standard contractual clauses that businesses may use to achieve compliance with the Data Privacy Directive.[185] The Commission has relied on this authority to adopt two sets of contractual clauses that serve as alternative compliance options.[186] The standard contractual clauses are designed as part of a contract between the data exporter in the EU and the data

---

184. Article 29 Working Party, Working Document setting up a table with the elements and principles to be found in Binding Corporate Rules WP 153 (June 24, 2008) .
185. Data Privacy Directive at art. 26(4).
186. Decision 2001/497/EC of 15 June 2001 under the Directive 95/46/EC, 2001 O.J. (L 181) 19, *as amended by* Commission Decision of 27 December 2004, 2004 O. J. (L 385) 74; and Commission Decision of 5 February 2010 on standard contractual clauses for the transfer of personal data to processors established in third countries under Directive 95/46/EC of the European Parliament and the Council, 2010 O. J. (L 39) 5. Although there are situations in which either set of standard contractual clauses could apply, they are mutually exclusive in the sense that firms may not combine portions of one with portions of the other. *See* preamble ¶3 of Commission Decision of 27 December 2004, 2004 O. J. (L 385) 74.

importer outside the EU. Among other things, contractual clauses require the data importer to maintain adequate technical and organizational procedures to protect the personal data from disclosure and process the data only within certain parameters. Although the data exporter can transfer the data back to the EU, it may not transfer the data to a third country that does not provide adequate protection to personal data.

The appropriateness of this option for businesses will depend on the particular circumstances, in particular the regulatory compliance disposition of the particular business. It is commonly relied upon by firms who want to avoid having to provide a declaration to the U.S. Department of Commerce as required under the safe harbor discussed below. The obvious benefit of this compliance option is that the member states are required to recognize the transfers in accordance with the standard clauses as conforming with the adequacy requirements under the Data Privacy Directive.[187] In other words, the proper implementation on compliance with the approved standard contractual clauses will obviate the need for an adequacy determination from each member state from which the data is being exported.[188]

One aspect of relying on standard contractual terms as a method of compliance is that some member states require notification and authorization. The Commission tolerates this "oversight" by the national data protection authorities as long as it is limited to verifying the conformity of the standard contractual terms employed by the company with those adopted by the EU Commission. In order to ease the burden of having to secure approval from a multitude of member states and to avoid divergent results in the authorization process, the Article 29 Working Party has adopted a procedure which allows a company to procure an authorization from a lead data protection authority and have that decision recognized in other member states.[189]

(c) Third Option: Safe Harbor

Another compliance option for the transfer of personal data to the United States is the safe harbor alternative agreed to by the United States and the EU. The Data Privacy Directive allows the Commission to negotiate agreements with third countries.[190] As a result of the inability of the EU to fail to designate the United States as providing adequate protection under the Data Privacy Directive, the U.S. Department of Commerce and the Commission negotiated an agreement whereby companies could transfer personal data from the EU to

---

187. Data Privacy Directive at art. 26(4).
188. The member states are not precluded from approving other contractual solutions.
189. Working Document Setting Forth a Co-Operation Procedure for Issuing Common Opinions on Contractual Clauses Considered as compliant with the EC Model Clauses 14/EN WP 226 (Nov. 26, 2014); Working Document Establishing a Model Checklist Application for Approval of Binding Corporate Rules, 05/EN WP 108 (Apr. 14, 2005).
190. Data Privacy Directive at art. 25(b).

the United States, provided that such transfer complied with certain safe harbor requirements.[191]

Compliance with the safe harbor requires data controllers to take two basic steps. They must first adopt, implement, and enforce a policy in accordance with the seven safe harbor principles. They must then publicly declare such policy by filing a statement to that effect with the U.S. Department of Commerce. The seven safe harbor principles are:

- **Notice.** Individuals must be informed about the purposes for which the data is collected and how to contact the company with any inquiries or complaints, the types of third parties to which it discloses the information, and the choices and means the company offers individuals for limiting its use and disclosure.

- **Choice.** Individuals must have the opportunity to affirmatively choose (i.e., opt out) whether their personal information is (a) to be disclosed to a third party or (b) to be used for a purpose that is incompatible with the purpose(s) for which it was originally collected. Individuals must be provided with clear and conspicuous, readily available, and affordable mechanisms to exercise their choice.

- **Onward Transfer.** To disclose information to a third party, companies must apply the Notice and Choice Principles. Where an organization wishes to transfer information to a third party, it may do so if it first either ascertains that the third party subscribes to the Principles or is subject to the Directive or another adequacy finding or enters into a written agreement with such third party requiring that the third party provide at least the same level of privacy protection as is required by the relevant Principles.[192]

- **Security.** Companies creating, maintaining, using, or disseminating personal information must take reasonable precautions to protect it

---

191. Only U.S. companies subject to the jurisdiction of the Federal Trade Commission (FTC) and U.S. air carriers subject to the jurisdiction of the U.S. Dept. of Transportation are eligible to participate in the safe harbor. This would preclude, for example, financial institutions which are regulated by the U.S. Treasury Department and not the FTC. The Commission was willing to find that the U.S. had "adequate safeguards" because the FTC had authority under Article 5 of the FTC Act (unfair and deceptive practices) to impose sanctions for breaches. Therefore, the safe harbor is only available for those entities falling within the jurisdiction of the FTC. One express exception to the FTC's authority under Section 5 are "banks, savings and loan institutions described in 15 U.S.C. § 57a(f)(3)" and federal credit unions described in 15 U.S.C. § 57a(f)(4). The Commission has taken the position, even after the adoption of the Gramm-Leach-Bliley Act, that the regulations applicable to the financial services industry do not provide adequate safeguards under the Directive. But this exception does not apply to the securities sector. Brokers, dealers, and others in the securities industries are subject to the concurrent jurisdiction of the Securities and Exchange Commission and the FTC and therefore the safe harbor may be relied on by actors in the securities industries.
192. The Article 29 Working Group has published standard contractual terms to use with non-EU sub-processors. Working Document 01/2014 on Draft Ad Hoc Contractual Clauses EU Data Processor to non-EU Sub-processor, 757/14/EN WP214 (Mar. 21, 2014).

from loss, misuse and unauthorized access, disclosure, alteration, and destruction.

- **Data Integrity.** Personal data must be relevant for the purposes for which it is to be used. A company may not process personal information in a way that is incompatible with the purposes for which it has been collected or subsequently authorized by the individual.
- **Access.** Individuals must have access to personal information about them that a company holds and be able to correct, amend, or delete that information where it is inaccurate, except where the burden or expense of providing access would be disproportionate to the risks to the individual's privacy in the case in question, or where the rights of persons other than the individual would be violated. Expense and burden are important factors and should be taken into account but they are not controlling in determining whether providing access is reasonable. The sensitivity of the data is also important in considering whether access should be provided.
- **Enforcement.** Effective privacy protection must include mechanisms for assuring compliance with the Principles, recourse for individuals affected by noncompliance with the Principles, and consequences for the organization when the Principles are not followed.

The enforcement principle is often where many companies fail to meet the requirements of the safe harbor. It requires that the company establish and maintain procedures for verifying that the representations it makes about its data privacy compliance are true, establish and maintain independent recourse mechanisms by which each individual's complaints and disputes are investigated and resolved, and provide remedies for failure to comply with the principles.

In order to meet the verification component of the enforcement principle, a company may rely on a self-assessment or a third-party assessment program. Under the self-assessment approach, verification would indicate that an organization's published safe harbor privacy policy is accurate, comprehensive, prominently displayed, completely implemented, accessible, and in conformance to the safe harbor principles. It would also need to indicate that appropriate employee training is in place and that internal procedures for periodically conducting objective reviews of compliance are in place.

A company statement verifying the self-assessment is signed by a corporate officer or other authorized representative of the organization at least once a year. As an alternative to self-assessment, a company can engage a third party to verify compliance. There are a number of private data privacy verification services that will comply with the safe harbor privacy principle on enforcement. Where the organization has chosen outside compliance review, the review needs to demonstrate that its privacy policy conforms to the safe harbor privacy principles, that it is being complied with, and that customers are informed of the mechanisms through which they may pursue complaints.

The independent recourse component of the enforcement principle is commonly fulfilled by engaging a private organization like TRUSTe or WebTrust. These services have mechanisms that allow for the filing of complaints by individuals. Alternatively, a company when certifying under the safe harbor may select the EU Data Protection Panel as its independent recourse mechanism. This mechanism offers a complaint procedure to individuals who feel aggrieved by an alleged violation of the principles. The Panel is then responsible for investigating and resolving the dispute.

The second fundamental step which a company must take to benefit from the safe harbor is to publicly declare compliance. This involves a relatively simple filing with the U.S. Department of Commerce. In the filing, the company certifies compliance with the safe harbor principles discussed above. To continue to benefit from the protection, companies need to recertify every 12 months. The U.S. Federal Trade Commission (FTC) has the authority to prosecute companies that fail to comply with the declaration. For example, the FTC pursued claims against Google after Google launched its social network "Google Buzz," declared compliance with the safe harbor principles, but failed to observe them.[193]

(d) Fourth Option: Compliance with a Derogation

If the country to which personal data is to be transferred is considered not to have an adequate level of protection, the member states are required to permit transfers in certain circumstances.[194] Whereas the adequacy determination of the member states discussed above is within the discretion of the member states, the member states are required to permit transfers of data to third countries when they comply with one of these derogations.

Perhaps the most obvious of these is to secure the unambiguous consent of the data subject.[195] The challenge in many cases is to determine when the consent of the data subject is unambiguous. As the Directive does not defined "unambiguous consent," it is left up to the courts of the member states to interpret. The national data protection authorities and the national courts have been inclined to find that the data subject has given its unambiguous consent in very narrow circumstances.[196]

According to the UK Information Commissioner's Office, consent is only ambiguous if the person knows and understands what he or she is agreeing to,

---

193. In re Google, Inc., FTC File No. 102 3136 (Mar. 30, 2011). The FTC has also secured settlement with a number of companies alleged to have breached §5 of the FTC for failing to observe the safe harbor principles. In re Charles River Laboratories International, Inc., FTC, File No. 142 3022 (Jan. 21, 2014); In re DataMotion, Inc., FTC, File No. 142 3023 (Jan. 21, 2014); In re DDC Laboratories, Inc., FTC, File No. 142 3024 (Jan. 21, 2014); In re Level 3 Communications, LLC, FTC, File No. 142 3028 (Jan. 21, 2014); In re Reynolds Consumer Products, Inc., FTC, File No. 142 3030 (Jan. 21, 2014); In re Receivable Management Services Corp., FTC, File No. 142 3031 (Jan. 21, 2014); In re Apperian, Inc., FTC, File No. 142 3017 (Jan. 21, 2014); In re Baker Tilly Virchow Krause, LLP, FTC, File No. 142 3019 (Jan. 21, 2014); In re BitTorrent, Inc., FTC, File No. 142 3020 (Jan. 21, 2014).
194. Data Privacy Directive at art. 26(1).
195. *Id.* at art. 26(1)(a).
196. Bundesverband der Verbraucherzentralen und Verbraucherverbände v. Apple Sales International, Decision of the Landgericht Berlin in case no. 15 O 92/12 (Apr. 30, 2013) *reported at* 67 Neue Juristische Wochenschrift 2605 (2013).

the consent is explicitly and freely given, the person has been informed of the reason for the transfer of the data, and is made aware of any particular risks to the personal data that may be caused by the transfer. Given the uncertainty over whether a consent is unambiguous, this compliance option is primarily used in specific cases of one-off data transfer.

The transfer of personal data is also permitted if it is necessary for the performance of a contract between the data subject and the controller[197] or is necessary for the conclusion or performance of a contract between the data subject and a third party.[198] For example, if a person in the EU orders widgets from a U.S. supplier, and then sends the U.S. supplier her address, this transfer is necessary for the performance of the contract.

If the transfer is necessary or legally required on public interest grounds or is necessary or for the establishment, exercise, or defense of legal claims, it qualifies for a derogation.[199] This exception was utilized in the *Madoff* case to transfer personal data from the UK to the United States. In that case, the liquidator of the bankrupt Bernard L. Madoff Investments Securities LLC in the United States sought to transfer personal data in the possession of UK companies to the United States for the purpose of the U.S. bankruptcy proceeding. The High Court in London (Justice Lewison) held that the transfer qualified for a derogation "as necessary for reasons of substantial public interest."[200]

If it is necessary to protect the vital interests of the data subject,[201] personal data can be transferred out of the EU to a country such as the United States which has not been deemed to have an adequate level of protection. For example, if a Swedish citizen, who is on vacation in Miami, suffers from a serious illness and is unable to consent to the transfer, the emergency transfer of his or her personal medical data from Sweden to the United States would fall under this exception.

Finally, a transfer of personal data from a public registrar is permissible under the Data Privacy Directive.[202] For example, a transfer of the public real estate records for a specific person showing the property that he or she owns would probably not violate the Directive.

8.11 Security Obligations

Security is a critical element in e-commerce and data privacy. The Data Privacy Directive addresses security of personal data by placing the obligation on the data controller to implement appropriate technical and organizational measures to protect personal data from unauthorized access.[203] However, the data controller may not be the only point of access to data. For example, an e-mail communication even to someone within the same company electronically

---

197. Data Privacy Directive at art. 26(1)(b).
198. *Id.* at art. 26(1)(c).
199. *Id.* at art. 26(1)(d).
200. In the Matter of Bernard L Madoff Investment Securities LLC [2009] EWHC 442 (Ch).
201. Data Privacy Directive at art. 26(1)(e).
202. *Id.* at art. 26(1)(f).
203. *Id.* at art. 17.

travels outside the company before it lands on the recipient's computer. Extensive reliance on electronic communication services places such service providers in an important position. To address this potential loophole, the EU adopted the ePrivacy Directive.

The ePrivacy Directive imposes security obligations on providers of publicly available electronic communications services.[204] An electronic communication service is a service consisting wholly or mainly in the conveyance of signals on electronic communications networks, including telecommunications services and transmission services in networks used for broadcasting.[205] It does not encompass information society services as discussed above. The basic distinction is that information society services use electronic communications to sell products or services, whereas electronic communication services involve the sale of the electronic services themselves (for example, Internet service providers).

The ePrivacy Directive imposes two basic obligations on the member states: security and confidentiality. The provider of a publicly available electronic communications service is required to take appropriate technical and organizational measures to safeguard security of its services.[206] A proportionality standard is applied to determine whether the measures are appropriate: the measures must be appropriate when weighed against the risk presented and having regard to the state of the art and the cost of their implementation. In case of a particular risk of a breach of the network's security, the provider of a publicly available electronic communications service must inform the subscribers concerning such risk and, where the risk lies outside the scope of the measures to be taken by the service provider, of any possible remedies, including an indication of the likely costs involved.[207]

In addition to the security obligation, the ePrivacy Directive requires the member states to adopt laws ensuring the confidentiality of electronic communications.[208] This includes, for example, a prohibition on tapping into or intercepting communications without the consent of the users concerned. As an exception to this rule, the member states may limit the confidentiality obligation to safeguard national security, defense, and public security and to prevent, investigate, detect, and prosecute criminal offenses.[209]

In *Productores de Música de España v. Telefónica de España SAU*, the ECJ held that the member states may also limit the confidentiality obligation in certain civil cases.[210] In that case, a Spanish nonprofit organization of music producers and publishers brought an action against Telefónica, a Spanish Internet

---

204. ePrivacy Directive at art. 4.
205. This definition is adopted by reference to Article 2(c) of Directive 2002/21/EC of the European Parliament and of the Council of 7 March 2002 on a common regulatory framework for electronic communications networks and services, 2002 O. J. (L 108) 33.
206. ePrivacy Directive at art. 4(1).
207. *Id.* at art. 4(2).
208. *Id.* at art. 5(1).
209. *Id.* at art. 15(1).
210. Case C-275/06, Productores de Música de España v. Telefónica de España SAU, 2008 E.C.R.I-309.

access provider, to disclose the names and addresses of certain of Telefónica's customers. The Spanish nonprofit organization suspected that those customers were illegally downloading music from the Internet. The applicable Spanish law which transposed the EU ePrivacy Directive did not have an express exception for civil proceedings, only criminal proceedings. Nonetheless, the Spanish court of first instance ordered Telefónica to disclose the names and addresses. On appeal, the Spanish appeals court decided to stay the proceedings and ask the ECJ for a preliminary ruling on the issue. The ECJ held that the ePrivacy Directive neither prevented nor required the member states to extend the exception to civil proceedings.[211]

8.12 Data Breaches

Data breaches must be notified by providers of publicly available electronic communications services to the competent national data protection authority without undue delay. The general rule is that this must be done within 24 hours after the breach has been discovered.[212] The ePrivacy Directive defines a data breach as a breach of security leading to the accidental or unlawful destruction, loss, altercation, unauthorized disclosure of or access to personal data.[213] One important exception to this rule is that the provider of electronic communications services does not have to notify the data subjects if the provider is able to implement appropriate technological protection measures to render the data unintelligible to any person who is not authorized to access it.[214] The Article 29 Working Group has issued an opinion on when the data subjects should be notified.[215]

8.13 U.S. Compliance Codes and EU Data Privacy

The implementation of uniform global compliances codes has created some conflict with EU data privacy rules. The compliance programs of many U.S. multinational companies often include an internal whistleblower component which allows employees of the company to anonymously and confidentially report observed violations of the company's policies. This obligation has raised two important issues in the EU. First, the imposition of the obligation to inform company management of certain conduct may violate the labor laws applicable in the member state where the employees are located. The courts of

---

211. *Id.* at 341-42 ¶¶54-55.
212. Commission Regulation (EU) No 611/2013 of 24 June 2013 on the measures applicable to the notification of personal data breaches under Directive 2002/58/EC of the European Parliament and of the Council on privacy and electronic communications, 2013 O.J. (L 173) 2.
213. ePrivacy Directive at art. 2.
214. *Id.* at art. 4(3); Commission Regulation (EU) No 611/2013 of 24 June 2013 on the measures applicable to the notification of personal data breaches under Directive 2002/58/EC of the European Parliament and of the Council on privacy and electronic communications, 2013 O.J. (L 173) 2 at art. 4(1).
215. Opinion 03/2014 on Personal Data Breach Notification, 693/14/EN WP 213 (Mar. 25, 2014).

Germany and France, for example, have held that the implementation of U.S. style whistleblower policies must be approved by the works councils operating in each facility.[216]

The other issue often raised by the implementation of undifferentiated compliance policies related to data privacy. In many instances, the whistleblower policy of a U.S. multinational company requires the employees to report alleged violations to the Chief Compliance Officer, the General Counsel or a designated hotline. As the information being reported is typically personal data, the transfer from the EU employee to the U.S. would violated the EU data privacy laws. In recognition of the legitimacy of such policies, however, the Article 29 Working Group has issued an opinion on the characteristics of U.S. whistleblower policies should have in order to conform to EU data privacy laws.[217]

8.14 U.S. Discovery and EU Data Privacy

The simultaneous compliance with U.S. discovery requests and EU data privacy law has presented a challenge for U.S. companies with operations in Europe s well as European companies doing business in the United States. U.S. civil procedure law permits parties to litigation in the United States to request information directly from the other party. Although the Federal Rules of Civil Procedure impose a relevancy standard,[218] there is very little judicial oversight of the discovery process. Moreover, U.S. courts very rarely allow the location of the requested information to influence compliance with discovery requests where it has jurisdiction over the entities involved in the lawsuit.

The broad discovery permitted in the United States often requires the transfer of personal data from Europe to the United States. The collection of the personal data would be considered "processing" for purposes of EU data protection law. According to the Article 29 Working Party,[219] the most likely derogation is under Article 7(f): data can be processed whenever the controller or a third party has a legitimate interest in doing so and this interest is not overridden by the interest of protecting the fundamental rights of the

---

216. McDonald's Decision No 2005-110 of the French Commission nationale de l'informatique et des libertés dated May 26, 2005; Wal-Mart Decision 5 BV 20/05 of German Federal Labor Court Wuppertal dated June 15, 2005 *reported at* 24 Der Bertrieb 1800 (2005).
217. Opinion 1/2006 on the application of EU data protection rules to internal whistleblowing schemes in the fields of accounting, internal accounting controls, auditing matters, fight against bribery, banking and financial crime, 00195/06/EN WP 117 (Feb. 1, 2006). Although the opinions of the Article 29 Working Group are not binding on the member states, they are persuasive evidence of how the EU Commission would interpret the law.
218. Federal Rules of Civil Procedure Rule 26(b).
219. Article 29 Data Protection Working Party, Working Document 1/2009 on pre-trial discovery for cross border civil litigation (Feb. 11, 2009). The "compliance with a legal obligation" is unlikely to apply because, according to the Article 29 Working Party, "an obligation imposed by a foreign legal statute or regulation may not qualify as a legal obligation by virtue of which data processing in the EU would be made legitimate." *Id.* at 9.

data subject. The subsequent transfer of the data from Europe to the United States would require compliance with one of the compliance options discussed above. The three possible options mentioned by the Article 29 Working Party are instances in which the recipient of the personal data has subscribed to the safe harbor scheme, has contracted with the EU company transferring the data, or has adopted binding corporate rules.[220]

The strict application of the data protection rules in the EU member states often collides with the liberal discovery rules of the U.S. judicial system. European companies may be asked to produce information or documents in the context of U.S. litigation which is considered personal data under the EU data privacy rules.[221] The International Section of the American Bar Association has urged U.S. courts to carefully consider foreign data privacy laws before compelling discovery.[222] U.S. courts have exhibited relatively little sympathy for the difficult position in which this conflict places European companies. In *AccessData v. ALSTE Technologies GmbH*, for example, the court held that a German company involved in U.S. civil litigation as a defendant was required to disclose information about its customers even though the information constituted personal information under the Data Privacy Directive.[223] In *In re Activision Blizzard, Inc. Stockholders Litigation*, the court required the production of the evidence located in France despite protestations of the defendant that such disclosure would violate French data protection law.[224] According to the court, the defendant's concerns could be adequately addressed by the parties agreeing to keep the data confidential.

---

220. *Id.*
221. *See, e.g., In re* Activision Blizzard Inc. Stockholders Litig., 86 A.3d 531 (De. Ch. Feb. 21, 2014).
222. ABA Section of International Law Resolution 103 (Feb. 2012).
223. AccessData v. ALSTE Technologies GmbH, 2010 U.S. Dist. LEXIS 4566 (D. Utah Jan. 21, 2010). *See also* Strauss v. Credit Lyonnais, S.A., 242 F.R.D. 199 (E.D.N. Y. 2007).
224. *See, e.g., In re* Activision Blizzard Inc. Stockholders Litig., 86 A.3d 531 (De. Ch. Feb. 21, 2014).

CHAPTER **XII**

Consumer Protection

Although Article 185 of the Treaty on the Functioning of the European Union (TFEU) grants the European Union (EU) the authority to legislate in the area of consumer protection, it does not define the term consumer protection. As examples of consumer protection, Article 185(1) of the TFEU identifies protecting the health, safety, and economic interest of consumers, their right to information and education about products and services, and the right to organize themselves to safeguard their interests. The legislation adopted by the EU in reliance on Article 185 defines "consumer" as any natural person who buys a product for purposes that do not fall within the sphere of his or her commercial or professional activity.[1]

A legal entity is generally not a consumer in the context of the consumer protection legislation, even if it is the end-user of a consumer product. In *Cape Snc v. Idealservice Srl*[2], Idealservice supplied automatic drink dispensers to two companies that used the dispensers for their staff. These two companies then brought actions against Idealservice, claiming that the jurisdiction clause in the supply contract was unfair. As the Directive 93/13/EEC on Unfair Terms in Consumer Contracts[3] only applies to contracts with consumers, Idealservice claimed that the consumer protection legislation was not applicable because the customers were not consumers. The European Court of Justice (ECJ) held that for purposes of the Directive on Unfair Terms, a legal entity which concludes a contract with a seller or supplier cannot be regarded as a consumer within the meaning of the Directive.

1. Consumer Protection Legislation

Although there is no clear definition of EU consumer protection law, it is generally applied to include the following legislation:

---

1. Directive 1999/44/EC of 25 May 1999 on certain aspects of the sale of consumer goods and associated guarantees, O.J. 1999 (L 171) 12 at art. 1(2)(a); Directive 2000/31/EC of the European Parliament and of the Council of June 2000 on certain legal aspects of information society services, O.J. 2000 (L 178) 1 art. 2(e).
2. Joined Cases C-541/99 and C-542/99, Cape Snc v. Idealservice Srl, 2001 E.C.R. I-9057.
3. 1993 O.J. (L 95) 29.

- Consumer Rights Directive[4]
- Unfair Commercial Practices Directive[5]
- Unfair Terms Directive[6]
- Consumer Guarantees Directive[7]
- Distance Marketing of Consumer Financial Services Directive[8]
- Consumer Interest Injunctions Directive[9]
- Product Safety Directive[10]
- Consumer Product Pricing Directive[11]
- Defective Products Directive[12]
- Misleading and Comparative Advertising Directive[13]
- Consumer Credit Directive[14]
- Universal Service Directive[15]

---

4. Directive 2011/83/EU of the European Parliament and of the Council of 25 October 2011 on consumer rights, 2011 O.J. (L 304) 64.
5. Directive 2005/29/EC of the European Parliament and of the Council of 11 May 2005 concerning unfair business-to-consumer commercial practices, 2005 O.J. (L 149) 22.
6. Council Directive 93/13/EEC of 5 April 1993 on unfair terms in consumer contracts, 1993 O.J. (L 95) 29 [hereinafter Unfair Terms Directive].
7. Directive 1999/44/EC of the European Parliament and of the Council of 25 May 1999 on certain aspects of the sale of consumer goods and associated guarantees, 1999 O.J. (L 171) 12.
8. Directive 2002/65/EC of the European Parliament and of the Council of 23 September 2002 concerning the distance marketing of consumer financial services and amending Council Directive 90/619/EEC and Directives 97/7/EC and 98/27/EC, 2002 O.J. (L 271) 16.
9. Directive 98/27/EC of the European Parliament and of the Council of 19 May 1998 on injunctions for the protection of consumers' interests, OJ 1998 (L 166) 51.
10. Directive 2001/95/EC of the European Parliament and of the Council of 3 December 2001 on general product safety, 2002 O.J. (L 11) 4.
11. Directive 98/6/EC of the European Parliament and of the Council of 16 February 1998 on consumer protection in the indication of the prices of products offered to consumers, 1998 O.J. (L 80) 27.
12. Directive 85/374/EEC of 25 July 1985 on the approximation of the laws, regulations and administrative provisions of the member states concerning liability for defective products, 1985 O.J. (L 210) 29.
13. Directive 2006/114/EC of the European Parliament and of the Council of 12 December 2006 concerning misleading advertising and comparative advertising, 2006 O.J. (L 376) 21 [hereinafter Misleading and Comparative Advertising Directive].
14. Directive 87/102/EEC of 22 December 1986 for the approximation of the laws, regulations and administrative provisions of the member states concerning consumer credit, 1987 O.J. (L 42) 48.
15. Directive 2002/22/EC of the European Parliament and of the Council of 7 March 2002 on universal service and users' rights relating to electronic communications networks and services, 2002 O.J. (L 108) 51.

- Late Payment Directive[16]
- Foodstuffs Advertising Directive[17]
- Timeshare Directive[18]
- Medical Products Advertising Directive[19]
- Toy Safety Directive[20]
- Package Vacation Directive[21]

There are a number of laws which protect consumers without having their main or sole purpose being consumer protection. For example, the E-Commerce Directive may apply to distance selling to consumers although its application is not limited to consumer sales. Consequently, there may be a certain degree of overlap with the practice-specific directives. To the extent that the application of two legal norms to the same business practice creates a conflict, the principle *lex specialis derogat legi generali* requires giving preference to the practice-specific legal norm.

2. Enforcement of Consumer Protection

Although the EU has broad authority to adopt legislation in the field of consumer protection, it has not assumed primary responsibility for enforcing the consumer protection laws. Enforcement remains within the authority of the member states. As cross-border consumer sales have increased dramatically due to the increased reliance on the Internet, the need for coordination of the consumer protection efforts of the consumer protection agencies of the respective member states becomes more important. The European Council has adopted rules for coordination of these national consumer protection agencies in cases of "intra-Community infringements," i.e., conduct that harms consumers in other member

---

16. Directive 2000/35/EC of the European Parliament and of the Council of 29 June 2000 on combating late payment in commercial transactions, O.J. 2000 (L 200) 35.
17. Directive 2000/13/EC of the European Parliament and the Council of 20 March 2000 on the approximation of the laws of the member states relating to the labeling, presentation and advertising of foodstuff, O.J. 2000 (L 109) 29.
18. Directive 2008/122/EC of the European Parliament and of the Council of 14 January 2009 on the protection of consumers in respect of certain aspects of timeshare, long-term holiday product, resale and exchange contracts, O.J. 2009 (L 33) 10.
19. Directive 2001/83/EC of the European Parliament and of the Council of 6 November 2001 on the Community code relating to medicinal products for human use, O.J. 2001 (L 311) 67.
20. Directive 2009/48/EC of the European Parliament and of the Council of 18 June 2009 on the safety of toys, O.J. 2009 (L 170) 1.
21. Council Directive 90/314/EEC of 13 June 1990 on package travel, package holidays and package tours, 1990 O.J. (L 158) 59.

states.[22] This Regulation addresses such issues as exchange of information between national consumer protection agencies, requests for enforcement procedures, and coordination of parallel enforcement efforts.

Consumer protection laws are difficult to enforce even at a local or member state level. It is difficult for the regulators to monitor individual cases of consumer fraud. Moreover, the interests of consumers are often so diverse, and the individual impact of misleading advertising so minimal on an individual level, that individual consumers rarely have the incentive to initiate proceedings against businesses suspected of engaging in such conduct. In recognition of this fact, there are private consumer advocate organizations that exist in many member states. The basic function of these organizations is to monitor compliance with the consumer protection laws. These organizations are critical to the proper enforcement of EU consumer law as they often have the resources and influence to pursue consumer fraud claims.

In recognition of their special role, they are recognized by the EU consumer protection legislation as having standing to bring claims under the respective statutes. For example, the Misleading and Comparative Advertising Directive (in Article 5(1)) specifically allows not only individuals, but also organizations to take legal action against such advertising or initiate proceedings with the appropriate administrative tribunal.

3. Consumer Sales

3.1 Scope of Rules

(a) Consumers and Traders

The EU consumer protection directives extend only to commercial practices between a trader (or in some directives referred to as a supplier[23] or seller[24]) and a consumer.[25] The legal concept "trader" is defined as a natural or legal

---

22. Regulation (EC) No. 2006/2004 of the European Parliament and of the Council of 27 October 2004 on cooperation between national authorities responsible for the enforcement of consumer protection laws, O.J. 2004 (L 364) 1, art. 3(b). Valuable information about the application of the various EU consumer law directives including national case law can be found at http://www.eu-consumer-law.org/index.html.
23. Unfair Terms Directive at art. 2(c).
24. Consumer Guarantees Directive at art. 1(2)(c). The Unfair Terms Directive (Article 2(c)) uses the terms supplier and seller synonymously. The E-Commerce Directive uses the term "service provider" which is broader than the notion of trader. A service provider is any natural or legal person providing an information society service. E-Commerce Directive at art. 2(b).
25. Unfair Commercial Practices Directive at art. 2(b); Consumer Rights Directive at art. 2(2); Consumer Guarantees Directive at art. 1(2)(a); Consumer Product Pricing Directive at art. 2(e). The E-Commerce Directive is not limited to consumer transactions.

person who is involved in a trade, business, craft, or profession.[26] There are two important limitations to this definition. First, a natural or legal person engaged in commercial activity is not always a "trader." That person is only a trader when she or he is engaged in a trade, business, craft, or profession and the conduct in question is related to that trade, business, craft, or profession. A baker, for example, is a trader when selling bread, but not a trader when selling her old sofa on Ebay. However, even individuals selling on Ebay may be considered traders in certain circumstances. According to the Commission, "hidden" traders are individuals who sell to consumers but as a business. They do not have a formal business, but essentially function as one. The Commission considers these individuals traders.[27]

On the other side of the transaction must be a consumer. The legal concept "consumer" encompasses only natural persons who are acting outside their business, trade, or profession.[28] There is no requirement that the natural person acquiring the goods or services actually consume the goods or services. In contrast to the definition of trader, a legal entity cannot be a consumer.[29] The sale of a product or service to a business would not be covered by the consumer protection directives even if the buying business was the end-user of the product.[30] For example, a misleading claim made by a truck manufacturer when selling a truck to a business would not fall under the Unfair Commercial Practices Directive because this is a business-to-business transaction. If, however, that same statement were made to an individual person purchasing the truck for his or her own use, the practice would fall under the Unfair Commercial Practices Directive.

In addition, the natural person must be acting outside his or her trade or profession in order to be considered a consumer. A baker, for example, is not a consumer when purchasing yeast for use in her bakery. However, she is a consumer when purchasing flour to make a cake at home for her child's birthday. In the case of dual purpose contracts, where the contract is concluded for purposes partly within and partly outside the person's trade, the person is still considered a consumer as long as the trade purpose is so limited as not to be predominant in the overall context of the contract.[31] If, for example, a person were purchasing an automobile for personal use as well as for use in his consulting business, the national court would have to determine whether the use of the automobile in his business were predominant.

---

26. Unfair Commercial Practices Directive at art. 2(b); Consumer Rights Directive at art. 2(2); Unfair Terms Directive at art. 2; Consumer Product Pricing Directive at art. 2(d).
27. Commission, Guidance on the Implementation/Application of Directive 2005/29/EC on Unfair Commercial Practices, SEC (2009) 1666 (Dec. 3, 2009) at 15.
28. Unfair Commercial Practices Directive, at art. 2(a); Consumer Rights Directive at art. 2(1); Unfair Terms Directive at art. 2(b); Consumer Guarantees Directive at art. 1(2)(a); Consumer Product Pricing Directive at art. 2(e); E-Commerce Directive at art. 2(e).
29. Joined cases C-541/99 & C-542/99, Cape Snc v. Idealservice Srl, 2001 E.C.R. I-9057, 9064 ¶16.
30. *Id.*
31. Consumer Rights Directive at recital 17.

(b) Goods and Services

The general EU consumer protection directives apply to transactions for the sale of goods (some directives refer to "products"[32]) as well as for services.[33] The Unfair Terms Directive, for example, covers residential leases[34] and mortgages.[35] There are, however, some directives that apply to specific service industries such as the Distance Marketing of Consumer Financial Services Directive,[36] Universal Service Directive,[37] Foodstuffs Advertising Directive,[38] Timeshare Directive,[39] Medical Products Advertising Directive,[40] Package Vacation Directive,[41] and the Consumer Credit Directive.[42]

The term "goods" or "products" in the consumer protection context generally refers to tangible movable items.[43] The definition employed in the Unfair Commercial Practices Directive is slightly broader. It includes not only movable items but also immovable items and services.[44] The treatment of software and digital content (such as computer programs, applications, games, music, videos, or texts) is not consistent among the consumer protection directives. If the software or digital content is reduced to a tangible medium such as a DVD,

---

32. Unfair Commercial Practices Directive at art. 2(c).
33. Consumer Rights Directive at art. 2(3); Consumer Guarantees Directive at art. 1(2)(b).
34. Case C-488/11, Brusse v. Jahani BV, 2013 E.C.R. I-____, at ¶32.
35. Case C-34/13, Kušionová v. SMART Capital a.s., 2014 E.C.R. I-____, at ¶45.
36. Directive 2002/65/EC of the European Parliament and of the Council of 23 September 2002 concerning the distance marketing of consumer financial services and amending Council Directive 90/619/EEC and Directives 97/7/EC and 98/27/EC, 2002 O.J. (L 271) 16.
37. Directive 2002/22/EC of the European Parliament and of the Council of 7 March 2002 on universal service and users' rights relating to electronic communications networks and services, 2002 O.J. (L 108) 51.
38. Directive 2000/13/EC of the European Parliament and the Council of 20 March 2000 on the approximation of the laws of the member states relating to the labeling, presentation and advertising of foodstuff, 2000 O.J. (L 109) 29.
39. Directive 94/47/EC of the European Parliament and the Council of 26 October 1994 on the protection of purchasers in respect of certain aspects of contracts relating to the purchase of the right to use immovable properties on a timeshare basis, 1994 O.J. (L 280) 83.
40. Council Directive 92/28/EEC of 31 March 1992 on the advertising of medicinal products for human use, 1992 O.J. (L 297) 8.
41. Council Directive 90/314/EEC of 13 June 1990 on package travel, package holidays and package tours, 1990 O.J. (L 158) 59.
42. Council Directive 87/102/EEC of 22 December 1986 for the approximation of the laws, regulations and administrative provisions of the member states concerning consumer credit, 1986 O.J. (L 133) 66.
43. Consumer Guarantees Directive at art. 1(2)(b); Consumer Rights Directive at art. 2(3) (For purposes of the Consumer Rights Directive, water, gas and electricity are considered "goods" if they are put up for sale in a limited volume or a set quantity. Excluded from the concept of goods under the Consumer Rights Directive is tangible personal property sold by way of execution or otherwise by authority of law.).
44. Unfair Commercial Practices Directive at art. 2(c). Case C-435/11, *CHS* Tour Services GmbH v. Team4 Travel GmbH, 2013 E.C.R. I-____, at ¶27.

it is likely to be considered a good or a product.[45] Software and digital content which is not sold on a tangible medium is treated differently in the consumer protection directives. For practical purposes, it is necessary to review the specific legislation at issue to determine if it is applicable in a particular case or transaction.

(c) Online Consumer Transactions

With exception of the E-Commerce Directive, the consumer protection directives generally do not distinguish between online consumer sales and traditional forms of consumer sales. As discussed in detail below, however, certain directives give additional protections to consumers in commercial transactions that are not solicited or concluded in person. These protections would apply to online consumer transactions just as they would apply to telephone solicitations.

(d) Importance of National Law

It is important to recall the nature of directives—particularly in the field of consumer law—as it can have an important impact on the application of the rules in particular cases. As discussed in Chapter I, directives require the member states to amend their national laws to conform to the rules codified in the particular directive. This characteristic of directives, together with the broad nature of the language used in directives, means that there are often differences in the laws of the member states on a certain issue. In addition, most of the consumer protection directives expressly grant the member states the authority to diverge from the rules established in the particular directive.

For example, the Consumer Rights Directive expressly allows the member states to not apply the law to transactions below a certain threshold.[46] This increases the differences between the consumer protection laws applicable at the member state level. From a practical perspective, therefore, it is imperative to examine the particular member state law implementing the directives to determine the rights and obligations of the parties in particular cases.

3.2 Soliciting Consumer Sales

(a) Unfair Commercial Practices

The Unfair Commercial Practices Directive prohibits commercial practices by traders if those practices are unfair to consumers. The prohibition on unfair commercial practices extends only to commercial practices that are directly connected with the promotion, sale, or supply of a product or service. The concept of commercial practice includes any act, omission, course of conduct or representations, and commercial communication including advertising and marketing, by a trader.[47]

The commercial practice at issue must be directly related to the promotion, sale, or supply of a good or service. For example, if a drug company were to

---

45. Consumer Rights Directive recital 19.
46. *Id.* at art. 3(4).
47. Case C-206/11, Köck v. Schutzverband gegen unlauteren Wettbewerb, 2013 E.C.R. I-____, at ¶26.

falsely claim in its advertisements to consumers that its product cures a particular illness, this would be directly related to the sale of the product. If, however, the false claims were made to the regulatory body responsible for approving the drug, the conduct would be only indirectly related to the promotion, sale, or supply of the product to the consumer. Similarly, a false claim made in an offering prospectus by a company trying to attract investors in its business would not qualify as an unfair commercial practice under this Directive because it is only indirectly related to the sale of that company's goods or services.[48]

There are two requirements for a commercial practice to be considered unfair.[49] First, the practice must be contrary to the requirements of professional diligence. This standard is defined as the special skill and care a trader may reasonably be expected to exercise toward consumers, commensurate with honest market practice and/or the general principle of good faith in the trader's field of activity.[50]

Second, the practice must materially distort or be likely to materially distort the economic behavior of the average consumer whom it reaches or to whom it is addressed.[51] If the practice is addressed to a particular group of consumers, then the relevant economic behavior is that of the average member of the group. To materially distort the economic behavior of consumers means using a commercial practice to appreciably impair the consumer's ability to make an informed decision and consequently, causing the consumer to take a transactional decision that he or she would not have taken otherwise. In other words, if the allegedly unfair practice would not have an influence on the consumer's decision, it does not qualify as an unfair commercial practice. In recognition of the abstract character of these elements of an unfair commercial practice, the Unfair Commercial Practices Directive divides unfair practices into three categories: (1) per se unfair practices, (2) misleading practices, and (3) aggressive practices.

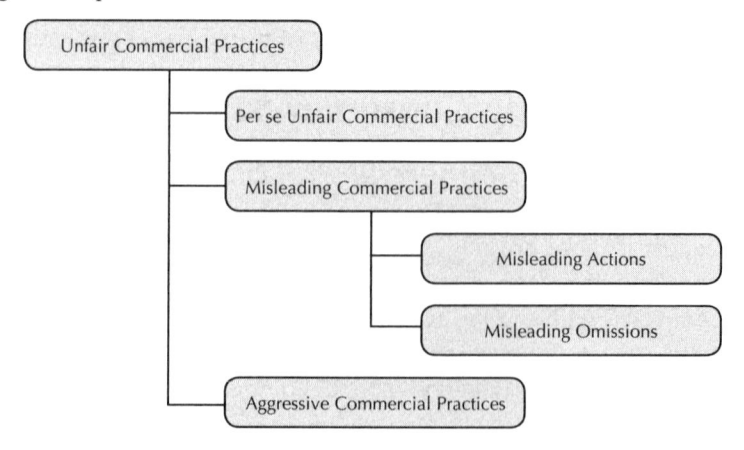

```
Unfair Commercial Practices
├── Per se Unfair Commercial Practices
├── Misleading Commercial Practices
│   ├── Misleading Actions
│   └── Misleading Omissions
└── Aggressive Commercial Practices
```

---

48. Consumer Rights Directive at recital 7.
49. *Id.* at art. 5(2).
50. *Id.* at art. 2(h).
51. *Id.* at art. 5(2)(b).

The abstract description of the elements of an unfair commercial practice, along with the equally abstract definitions used in the Unfair Commercial Practices Directive, make it difficult to determine in specific cases whether a commercial practice is permitted or prohibited (particularly in a heterogeneous polity such as the EU). What a judge or regulator in one member state may consider unfair may be the accepted norm in another member state. In an effort to provide businesses operating in Europe with greater legal certainty, the Unfair Commercial Practices Directive contains an annex with an exhaustive list of practices which are per se prohibited.[52] That list includes inter alia the following:

- Displaying a trust mark, quality mark, or equivalent without having obtained the necessary authorization.

- Claiming that a trader or a product has been approved, endorsed, or authorized by a public or private body when that trader has not been approved.

- Making an invitation to purchase products at a specified price without disclosing the existence of any reasonable grounds the trader may have for believing that the trader will not be able to offer for supply (or to procure another trader to supply) those products or equivalent products at that price for a period that is, and in quantities that are, reasonable having regard to the product, the scale of advertising of the product, and the price offered. This is referred to as bait advertising.

- Making an invitation to purchase products at a specified price and then refusing to show the advertised item to consumers or refusing to take orders for it or deliver it within a reasonable time or demonstrating a defective sample of it, with the intention of promoting a different product. This is referred to as bait and switch.

- Falsely stating that a product will only be available for a very limited time in order to elicit an immediate decision and deprive consumers of sufficient opportunity or time to make an informed choice.

- Falsely claiming that a product is able to cure illnesses, dysfunction, or malformations.

- Including in marketing material an invoice or similar document seeking payment which gives the consumer the impression that he or she has already ordered the marketed product when he or she has not.

- Creating the false impression that after-sales service in relation to a product is available in a member state other than the one in which the product is sold.

---

52. This is not an exhaustive list of all practices that may be considered unfair, but only those that are per se unfair (i.e., without an examination of its unfairness in the particular circumstances). Case C-421/12, Comm'n v. Belgium, 2014 E.C.R. I-____, at ¶56; Case C-206/11, Köck v. Schutzverband gegen unlauteren Wettbewerb, 2013 E.C.R. I-____, at ¶35; Case C-540/08, Mediaprint Zeitungs- und Zeitschriftenverlag GmbH & Co. KG v. Österreich-Zeitungsverlag GmbH, 2010 E.C.R. I-10909, at ¶34. According to the ECJ, there is no de minimis exception to the per se prohibition of these terms. C-428/11, Purely Creative Ltd. v. Office of Fair Trading, 2012 E.C.R. I-____, at ¶57.

The list attached to the Directive as Annex I is an exhaustive list of commercial practices that may be considered per se unlawful by the member states.[53] In all other cases, the member states must examine the particular facts of the case and may not expand the list of per se prohibited practices.[54] In *VTB-VAB NV v. Total Belgium NV*, for example, Belgian law prohibited companies from offering deals that tied two separate products together. A Belgian gas station was accused of violating this law by offering customers who purchased 25 liters of fuel a free three-week breakdown service. The ECJ held, however, that the practice of combining products did not fall under the list of per se prohibited commercial practices. Consequently, the Belgian law violated the Directive.[55] According to the ECJ, "Member States may not adopt stricter rules than those provided for in the Directive, even in order to achieve a higher level of consumer protection."[56]

In *Mediaprint Zeitungs- und Zeitschriftenverlag GmbH & co. KG v. Österreich-Zeitungsverlag GmbH*, the ECJ similarly annulled an Austrian law which prohibited granting customers bonuses as part of a sales promotions. In that case, an Austrian newspaper, in an effort to attract readers, initiated a campaign to have readers elect the "footballer of the year." The newspaper would then randomly select one of the individuals who submitted a ballot for the "footballer of the year" to have dinner with the winning footballer. The ECJ held that since this practice was not listed in the list of per se unfair practices, it was not automatically prohibited by the Unfair Commercial Practices Directive.[57]

The use of standard terms in consumer contracts is not per se unfair under the Unfair Commercial Practices Directive. Such standard agreements will, however, typically attract a higher level of scrutiny. In *VB Pénzügyi Lízing Zrt. v. Schneider*, for example, the ECJ held that a choice of forum clause in the standard terms of a leasing company may be considered unfair if it is not individually negotiated and requires the consumer to litigate any disputes related to the contract outside the consumer's home member state and in the jurisdiction of the commercial seller.[58] This is because, according to the ECJ, the consumer is forced to agree to terms on which he or she is unable to have any influence.[59]

---

53. Case C-421/12, Comm'n v. Belgium, 2014 E.C.R. I-____, at ¶55; Case C-515/12, 4finance UAB v. Valstybiné vartotoju teisiu apsaugos tarnyba, 2014 E.C.R. 2014 E.C.R. I-____, at ¶31; Joined cases C-261/07 & 299/07, VTB-VAB NV v. Total Belgium NV, 2009 E.C.R. I-2993, 3022 ¶62.
54. Case C-540/08, Mediaprint Zeitungs- und Zeitschriftenverlag GmbH & co. KG v. Österreich-Zeitungsverlag GmbH, 2010 E.C.R. I-10957, 10974 ¶35.
55. Joined cases C-261/07 & 299/07, VTB-VAB NV v. Total Belgium NV, 2009 E.C.R. I-2993, 3022 ¶61.
56. *Id.* at 3020 ¶52.
57. Case C-540/08, Mediaprint Zeitungs- und Zeitschriftenverlag GmbH & co. KG v. Österreich-Zeitungsverlag GmbH, 2010 E.C.R. I-10957, 10974 ¶35.
58. Case C-137/08, VB Pénzügyi Lízing Zrt. v. Schneider, 2010 E.C.R. I-10888, 10903 ¶42.
59. *Id.* at 10904 ¶46.

It is important to recall that the law on unfair commercial practices is based on a directive. This means that outside the catalog of per se unfair practices, the application of the standard is left to the courts of the member states. Consequently, the same commercial practice which is deemed unfair in one member state may be considered fair in another member state. In *Lenovo France v. M.X.*, for example, a consumer claimed that it was unfair for Lenovo to sell its computers with preinstalled software. The French Supreme Court concluded that the sale of these two products together - computer and software - was not unfair because a computer is otherwise inoperable without software.[60] One could imagine, however, a court in a different member state coming to a different conclusion. Consequently, the EU laws on unfair commercial practices provide only limited relief for companies operating across the EU.

(b) Misleading Commercial Practices

In addition to the category of per se unfair commercial practices, the Unfair Commercial Practices Directive establishes a category of misleading commercial practices. This category is further subdivided into misleading actions and misleading omissions.

(1) Misleading Actions

There are four types of misleading actions that are prohibited by the Unfair Commercial Practices Directive: false practices, deceptive practices, practices which cause confusion, and misleading code compliance.

False practices. The clear case of a misleading commercial practice is one that contains false information and causes or is likely to cause the consumer to take a transactional decision that she would not have otherwise taken.[61] For example, claiming that the product is a "green" product when such claims cannot be verified is misleading.[62] Environmental claims, according to the Commission, must be stated in a specific and unambiguous manner and there must be scientific evidence to support the claim.[63]

Deceptive practices. A commercial practice does not have to be false to qualify as misleading. Many commercial practices are not necessarily false, but are designed to mislead consumers. Consequently, the Unfair Commercial Practices Directive classifies a commercial practice as misleading, even if not false, if it in any way deceives or is likely to deceive the average consumer in relation to one or more of the following respects and causes or is likely to cause the consumer to take a transactional decision that she would not have otherwise taken:[64]

---

60. Decision of the French cour de cassation in case no. 12-25748 (Feb. 5, 2014).
61. Unfair Commercial Practices Directive at art. 6(1). The term "transactional decision" means any decision taken by a consumer concerning whether, how and on what terms to purchase, make payment in whole or in part for, retain or dispose of a product or to exercise a contractual right in relation to the product, whether the consumer decides to act or to refrain from acting. *Id.* at art. 2(k). Even the decision to enter the store to buy an item is a transactional decision. C-281/12, Trento Sviluppo srl v. Autorità Garante della Concorrenza e del Mercato, 2013 E.C.R. I-____, at ¶36.
62. Commission, Guidance on the Implementation /Application of Directive 2005/29/EC on Unfair Commercial Practices, SEC (2009) 1666 (Dec. 3, 2009) at 38.
63. *Id.* at 41.
64. Unfair Commercial Practices Directive at art. 6(1).

- the existence or nature of the product or service;
- the main characteristics of the product or service, such as its availability, benefits, risks, execution, composition, accessories, after-sale customer assistance and complaint handling, method and date of manufacture or provision, delivery, fitness for purpose, usage, quantity, specification, geographical or commercial origin or the results to be expressed from its use, or the results and material features of tests or checks carried out on the product;
- the extent of the trader's commitments, the motives for the commercial practice, and the nature of the sale process, any statement or symbol in relation to direct or indirect sponsorship or approval of the trader or the product or service;
- the price or the manner in which the price is calculated, or the existence of a specific price advantage. Increasing prices 20 percent immediately prior to introducing a "20% rebate" campaign is an example of this.[65] Another example would be the use by a trader of unreasonably high recommended prices to create the impression that the products being sold to the customer are at a substantial discount.[66]
- the need for a service, part, replacement, or repair;
- the nature, attributes, and rights of the trader or his or her agent, such as the trader's identity and assets, qualifications, status, approval, affiliation, or connection and ownership of industrial, commercial, or intellectual property rights or awards and distinctions;
- the consumer's rights or the risks the consumer may face.

Practices that cause confusion. In addition, a practice involving the marketing of a product, including comparative advertising that creates confusion with any products, trademarks, trade names, or other distinguishing marks of a competitor is considered misleading.[67] For example, if a car dealer used the Porsche trade name to promote the sale of her automobile without the authorization of Porsche, that dealer may be engaging in a misleading commercial practice. As discussed in Chapter X, this same practice may also infringe the trademark rights of the proprietor of the trademark who has the right under the Trademark Regulation to prohibit a third party from using any sign where, because of its identity with or similarity to the Union trademark and the identity or similarity of the goods or services covered by the Community trademark and the sign, creates a likelihood of confusion on the part of the public.[68]

---

65. Decision of the German Bundesgerichtshof in case no. I ZR 122/06 (Nov. 20, 2008) *reported at* 62 Neue Juristische Wochenschrift 2541 2009.
66. Commission, Guidance on the Implementation /Application of Directive 2005/29/EC on Unfair Commercial Practices, SEC (2009) 1666 (Dec. 3, 2009) at 34.
67. Unfair Commercial Practices Directive at art. 6(2).
68. Council Regulation (EC) No. 207/2009 of 26 February 2009 on the Community trademark, 2009 O.J. (L 78) 1 art. 9(1)(b).

The practice does not necessarily have to constitute an infringement of third-party intellectual property to be considered an unfair commercial practice. According to the Commission, "copycat packaging" (i.e., the practice of designing a product's packaging to give it the general look and feel of a competing product but stopping short of using the trademarks of the competitor) can constitute a misleading commercial practice.[69]

Misleading code compliance. Misleading commercial actions may arise in connection with codes of conduct or company policies. If the company represents that it complies with such a code, then its subsequent non-compliance may be considered a misleading commercial action.[70] The commitment must be firm and not merely aspirational and must be capable of being verified. It would be an unfair commercial practice if, for example, an online seller of over-the-counter medical products adopts a code of conduct declaring that it protects the privacy of its customers and does not disclose any confidential information to third parties, but then sells personal data about its employees to a marketing firm.

Causation. In each of the four categories of misleading commercial practices discussed above, the misleading action must cause or be likely to cause the consumer to make a transactional decision that he or she would not have otherwise made. If the trader can prove that the consumer would have purchased the product anyway, then the practice may not be misleading.

(2) Misleading Omissions

As the omission of an important fact may be just as misleading to a consumer as the affirmative assertion of a claim, the second category of misleading commercial practices is misleading omissions.

Omission. A trader commits misleading commercial practice if that trader omits or conceals material information that the average consumer needs to take an informed transactional decision.[71] In *Perenicová v. SOS finance spol. s.r.o.*, for example, a consumer loan business failed to include certain fees imposed on the consumer related to the loan. The ECJ concluded that the failure to provide this information was a misleading commercial practice.[72] For commercial "invitations to purchase," the Directive identifies the following types of information that are considered "material:"[73]

---

69. Commission, Guidance on the Implementation /Application of Directive 2005/29/EC on Unfair Commercial Practices, SEC (2009) 1666 (Dec. 3, 2009) at 36.
70. Unfair Commercial Practices Directive at art. 6(2).
71. Unfair Commercial Practices Directive at art. 7(1) and art. 7(2).
72. Case C-453/10, Perenicová v. SOS finance spol. s.r.o., 2012 E.C.R. I-___, at ¶41.
73. Inclusion of this information does not result in a "safe harbor" for the trader. The member states may impose different information requirements based on the type of product or service provided. These categories of information do not have to be in every communication between a trader and a customer or in every advertisement. Unfair Commercial Practices Directive at recital 14. It is sufficient that they are in the document that sets forth the terms of the transaction.

- the main characteristics of the product to an extent appropriate to the medium and the product;[74]
- the address and the identity of the trader;
- the price, inclusive of taxes, or where the names of the product means that the price cannot reasonably be calculated in advance, the manner in which the price is calculated, as well as, where appropriate, all additional freight, delivery, or postal charges or, where these charges cannot reasonably be calculated in advance, the fact that such additional charges may be payable;[75]
- the arrangements for payment, delivery, performance, and the complaint handling policy, if they depart from the requirements of professional diligence;
- for products and transactions involving a right of withdrawal or cancellation, the existence of such a right.

To qualify as an "invitation to purchase," it is not necessary that the communication include an offer or the actual opportunity to purchase the product as long as it contains information "sufficient for the consumer to be able to make a transactional decision."[76] In the event that the communication does not constitute an invitation to purchase, the nonexhaustive list of material information contained in Annex II of the Directive applies.[77]

Ambiguous. A misleading omission also exists even if the trader does provide material information to the consumer, but does so in an unclear, unintelligible, ambiguous, or untimely manner.[78]

Commercial Intent. A trader engages in a misleading omission if the trader fails to identify the commercial intent of the commercial practice unless it is already apparent from the context.[79]

Causality. Similar to misleading actions, each case of a misleading omission requires that the omission causes or is likely to cause the average consumer to make a transactional decision that he or she would not have made otherwise.

---

74. The degree of detail required in order to meet this requirement will depend on the particular medium used for the communication (radio, television, paper, or electronic), Case C-122/10, Konsumentombudsmannen v. Ving Sverige AB, 2011 E.C.R. I-3933, 3950 ¶45. If space does not permit a complete description of the characteristics, it is possible to include in the communication a reference to a website where the characteristics are discussed in greater detail. *Id.* at 3953 ¶56.
75. In the event that there may be different prices for different versions of the same product, it may be appropriate in certain circumstances to include just the entry-level price for the product. *Id.* at 3956 ¶69. The price terms in consumer contracts are also governed by the Consumer Product Pricing Directive.
76. Case C-122/10, Konsumentombudsmannen v. Ving Sverige AB, 2011 E.C.R. I-3933, 3947 ¶33.
77. Unfair Commercial Practices Directive at art. 7(5).
78. *Id.* at art. 7(2).
79. *Id.*

(c) Aggressive Commercial Practices

In addition to misleading actions and misleading omissions, aggressive commercial practices are also considered unfair and consequently prohibited. This category of unfair commercial practices is intended to apply to the situation where the trader perhaps truthfully discloses all material information but uses aggressive tactics to persuade the consumer to buy the product or service. A commercial practice is considered aggressive if, by harassment, coercion—including the use of physical force—or undue influence, it significantly impairs or is likely to significantly impair the average consumer's freedom of choice or conduct with regard to the product and thereby causes her or is likely to cause her to make a transactional decision that she would not have made otherwise.[80] The following are examples of aggressive commercial practices:

- Creating the impression that the consumer cannot leave the premises until a contract is formed.

- Conducting personal visits to the consumer's home and ignoring the consumer's request to leave or not to return except in circumstances and to the extent justified, under national law, to enforce a contractual obligation.

- Explicitly informing a consumer that if she does not buy the product or service, the trader's job or livelihood will be in jeopardy.

3.3 Concluding Consumer Contracts

(a) Types of Consumer Sales

EU consumer protection law distinguishes between distance sales, off-premises sales, and on-premises sales. The significance of this distinction is that legal norms and obligations of the trader and the rights of the consumer differ depending on the type of sale.

(1) Distance Sales

The term "distance selling" generally refers to a sale of goods or services where the buyer and seller are not physically present in the same location. A "distance contract" under the Consumer Rights Directive is any contract concerning goods or services concluded between a trader and a consumer under an organized distance sales or service-provision scheme run by the supplier without the physical presence of the supplier and the consumer and which makes exclusive use of one or more means of distance communication up to and including the moment at which the contract is concluded.[81] For example, the German Supreme Court has held that an agreement reached between a buyer and seller on eBay qualifies as a distance sale.[82] Although selling over the Internet is the obvious example

---

80. *Id.* at art. 8.
81. Consumer Rights Directive at art. 2(7).
82. Decision of the German Bundesgerichtshof in case no. VIII ZR 375/03 (Nov. 3, 2004) reported at 68 Neue Juristische Wochenschrift 53 (2005). The scope of the Consumer Rights Directive may not be as broad as it initially appears.

of a distance sale, the term is not necessarily limited to e-commerce.[83] It also includes selling by unaddressed printed matter, press advertising with order form, catalogue, telephone, radio, e-mail, facsimile machine (fax), or television.

The Directive on Consumer Rights excludes certain types of contracts from its scope even if they otherwise qualify as distance contracts. Contracts relating to insurance[84] or financial services[85] are excluded from the scope of the Consumer Rights Directive as are contracts concluded by means of automatic vending machines or automated commercial premises, contracts concluded with telecommunications operators through the use of public pay phones, contracts concluded for the construction and sale of immovable property or relating to other immovable property rights, and contracts concluded at an auction. In addition, business-to-business (B2B) commerce would not generally fall under the consumer protection directives if none of the parties to the transactions is considered a consumer. As discussed above, the term consumer only refers to natural persons who are acting for purposes that are outside their trade, business, or profession.[86]

The critical factor in determining whether a sale is a distance sale is the location of the consumer and the trader at the time the contract for the sale of goods or services is entered into. For example, if a consumer visits the premises of the trader, but then leaves the premises and subsequently negotiates and concludes the contract at a distance, that transaction is considered a distance sale.[87] If that same consumer were to stay at the premises and enter into a contract for the sale of the goods or services, the transaction would not be considered a distance sale. Reliance on the location of the parties at the time the contract is entered into also means that a contract initiated by means of

---

83. Distance selling also includes "information society services" as defined in the E-Commerce Directive. As discussed in greater depth in Chapter XI, the term information society services refers to any service normally provided for remuneration, at a distance (i.e., the service is provided without the parties being simultaneously present), by electronic means, and at the individual request of a recipient of services. E-Commerce Directive at art. 2(a) in reference to Directive 98/34/EC of the European Parliament and of the Council of 22 June 1998 laying down a procedure for the provision of information in the field of technical standards and regulations, 1998 O.J. (L 204) 37 at art. 1(a). This would include, for example, selling goods on the Internet. E-Commerce Directive at recital ¶18.
84. Case C-166/11, Alonso v. Nationale Nederlanden Vida Cia De Seguros y Reaseguros SAE, 2012 E.C.R. I-___.
85. There is a separate directive that applies specifically to the distance selling of financial services. Directive 2002/65/EC of the European Parliament and of the Council on 23 September 2002 concerning the distance marketing of consumer financial services, 2002 O.J. (L 271) 16.
86. As discussed above, however, the Commission considers individuals who act in a commercial capacity to be "hidden" traders. Commission Guidance on the Implementation/ Application of Directive 2005/29/EC on Unfair Commercial Practices, SEC (2009) 1666 (Dec. 3, 2009) at 15.
87. Directive 2011/83/EU of the European Parliament and of the Council of 25 October 2011 on consumer rights, 2011 O.J. (L 304) 64 at recital ¶20.

distance communication, but finally concluded at the business premises of the trader, is not considered a distance sale.[88]

(2) Off-Premises Sales

In general, an off-premises sale is one which is concluded between a consumer and a trader outside the premises of the trader but in the simultaneous physical presence of the trader and the consumer.[89] In contrast to distance sales, however, the physical location of the trader and the consumer at the time the contract is entered into is not necessarily the determining characteristic. If the consumer and trader meet outside the business premises of the trader, and the consumer makes an offer to the trader at that time, a contract which is concluded later when the consumer and trader are not together would still be considered an off-premises contract.

An off-premises sale can even occur when the consumer was personally and individually addressed in a place that is not the business premises of the trader but later concluded on the business premises of the trader or through any means of distance communication.[90] However, the concept of off-premises sale does not cover situations in which the trader first comes to the consumer's home strictly with a view to taking measurements or giving an estimate without any commitment of the consumer and where the contract is then concluded only at a later point in time on the business premises of the trader or via means of distance communication on the basis of the trader's estimate.[91] In those cases, the contract is not to be considered as having been concluded immediately after the trader has addressed the consumer if the consumer has had time to consider the estimate of the trader before concluding the contract.

(3) On-Premises Sales

If a contract for the sale of goods or services by a trader to a consumer does not qualify as a distance sale or an off-premises sale, it is generally considered an on-premises sale. Although the EU consumer protection directives do not use the term "on-premises" sale,[92] it is used here because certain directives apply only to distance and off-premises contracts whereas other consumer protection directives apply to all contracts between a trader and a consumer, i.e., to distance contracts, off-premises contracts, and all other contracts between consumers and traders (on-premises contracts).

---

88. *Id.* The German Supreme Court has held, however, that a distance sale occurs when a consumer orders a cellular telephone via telephone even though the consumer signs the contract when the telephone is delivered by a commercial messenger service. Decision of the German Bundesgerichtshof in case no. III ZR 380/03 (Oct. 21, 2004) reported at 57 Neue Juristische Wochenschrift 3699 (2004).
89. Consumer Rights Directive at art. 2(8)(a).
90. *Id.* at art. 2(8)(c).
91. *Id.* at recital 21.
92. The Directive simply refers to "contracts other than a distance or off-premises contract." *Id.* at recital ¶34.

(b) Pre-Contractual Information Obligations

(1) Distance Sales

If the transaction qualifies as a distance contract, the trader is required to provide the customer with the following information "in a clear and comprehensible manner."[93] This does not mean, however, that the Consumer Rights Directive dictates the contents of the substantive agreement between the consumer and the trader. As recognized in the legislation, despite these pre-contractual information obligations, "the contracting parties should be able to expressly agree to change the content of the contract subsequently concluded."[94] The minimum information to be provided to the consumer in the context of a distance sale is:[95]

- the identity of the trader;
- the main characteristics of the goods or services, to the extent appropriate to the medium and to the goods or services;
- the geographical address at which the trader is established and the trader's telephone number, fax number, and e-mail address;
- the total price of the goods or services inclusive of taxes, as well as all additional freight, delivery, or postal charges and any other costs or, where those charges cannot reasonably be calculated in advance, the fact that such additional charges may be payable;
- the cost (if any) of using the means of distance communication for the conclusion of the contract where that cost is calculated other than at the basic rate;[96]
- the arrangements and timing for payment, delivery, performance, and, where applicable, the trader's complaint-handling policy;
- the conditions, time limit, costs, and procedures for exercising any right of withdrawal;[97]
- a reminder of the existence of a legal guarantee of conformity for goods;
- where applicable, the existence and the conditions of after-sale customer assistance, after-sale services, and commercial guarantees;

---

93. *Id.* at art. 6.
94. *Id.* at recital ¶35.
95. Consumer Rights Directive at art. 6(1); Unfair Commercial Practices Directive at art. 6(1).
96. The failure by the trader to provide this information on the costs means that the consumer does not have to pay for them.
97. The Consumer Rights Directive contains model instructions for withdrawal that traders can use to comply with the information requirements related to the withdrawal rights of the consumer. The benefit for the trader of using these model instructions is that the trader will be deemed to have fulfilled the information requirements if it has supplied these instructions to the consumer. If the trader is not required to provide the consumer with the right of withdrawal because of the applicability of one of the exceptions, the trader must nonetheless inform the consumer that he or she will not benefit from a right of withdrawal.

- the existence of relevant codes of conduct, and how copies of them can be obtained by the consumer;
- the duration of the contract and the minimum duration of the consumer's obligations under the contract;
- the existence and the conditions of deposits or other financial guarantees (if any) to be paid or provided by the consumer at the request of the trader;
- the functionality of any digital content included as part of the transaction and any relevant interoperability of digital content with hardware and software that the trader is aware of or can reasonably be expected to have been aware of;
- the possibility of having recourse to an out-of-court complaint and redress mechanism to which the trader is subject, and the methods for having access to it.

Member states may not impose any additional precontractual information requirements on the trader.[98] The method by which the information must be provided to the consumer depends on the circumstances. The rule codified in the Consumer Rights Directive is that the information must be made available "in a way appropriate to the means of distance communication used in plain and intelligible language."[99] For distance contracts, this obligation is likely fulfilled if the trader provides a toll-free number or a hyperlink to a web page where the information is available.[100] The particular languages in which this information is to be provided is left up to the individual member states. The trader has the obligation to make sure that the consumer, when placing his order, explicitly acknowledges that the order implies an obligation to pay. If, for example, the transaction occurs over the Internet, the trader must include a step or click with an unambiguous formulation indicating that placing the order entails an obligation to pay the trader.[101]

With this requirement, the drafters of the legislation intended to ensure that the consumer is able to determine the moment at which she assumes the obligation to pay the trader.[102] In addition, the website must state at the latest at the beginning of the ordering process whether any delivery restrictions apply and which means of payment are accepted.[103]

The trader is also required to provide the consumer with the confirmation of the contract and this confirmation must be on a durable medium within a reasonable time after the conclusion of the distance contract (at the latest at the time the goods are delivered or before the performance of the service begins.)[104]

---

98. Consumer Rights Directive at art. 7.
99. *Id.* at art. 8(1).
100. *Id.* at recital ¶36.
101. The consequence of not providing this step is that the consumer is not bound by the order. *Id.* at art. 8(2).
102. *Id.* at recital 39.
103. *Id.* at art. 8(3).
104. *Id.* at art. 8.

That confirmation must include the required information discussed above (unless the trader has already provided that information to the consumer on a durable medium prior to the conclusion of the distance contract).

If the distance contract is to be concluded by electronic means, and involves "information society services," the E-Commerce Directive requires the seller to also provide the buyer with the different technical steps to follow to conclude the contract, the means for identifying and correcting input errors prior to placing the order, and the languages offered for conclusion of the contract.[105] If the customer is a business (e.g., B2B transactions), the E-Commerce Directive allows the parties to contract out of these requirements.[106] Moreover, the requirements imposed by the E-Commerce Directive do not apply to "contracts concluded exclusively by exchange of electronic mail or by equivalent individual communications."[107] The E-Commerce Directive also requires the service provider to acknowledge the receipt of the customer's order without delay and by electronic means.[108] The order and the acknowledgment of receipt are deemed to be received when the parties to whom they are addressed are able to access them. The following information must also be given in writing: arrangements for exercising the right of withdrawal; place to which the consumer may address complaints; information relating to after-sales service; and conditions under which the contract may be rescinded.[109]

(2) Off-Premises Sales

The information requirements for traders in the context of off-premises transactions are the same as those for distance contracts. In the context of off-premises contracts, however, the trader is required to provide the information and a copy of the signed contract to the consumer on paper or, if the consumer agrees, on another durable medium.[110]

(3) On-Premises Sales

The information requirements imposed on traders in the context of on-premises sales are slightly different than in the context of distance sales and off-premises sales. The following information must be provided to the consumer in the context of an on-premises sale:[111]

- the identity of the trader;
- the main characteristics of the goods or services, to the extent appropriate to the medium and to the goods or services;
- the total price of the goods or services inclusive of taxes, as well as all additional freight, delivery, or postal charges and any other costs or,

---

105. E-Commerce Directive at art. 10(1).
106. *Id.* at art. 10(1).
107. *Id.* at art. 10(4). As discussed above, the Consumer Rights Directive does not apply to B2B sales as a consumer is not a party to the transaction.
108. *Id.* at art. 11(1).
109. *Id.* at art. 5.
110. Consumer Rights Directive at art. 7.
111. *Id.* at art. 5(1); Unfair Commercial Practices Directive at art. 7.

where those charges cannot reasonably be calculated in advance, the fact that such additional charges may be payable;

- the arrangements for payment, delivery, performance, the time by which the trader undertakes to deliver the goods or to perform the services and, where applicable, the trader's complaint-handling policy;
- a reminder of the existence of a legal guarantee of conformity for goods;
- where applicable, the existence and the conditions of after-sale customer assistance, after-sale services, and commercial guarantees;
- the functionality of any digital content included as part of the transaction and any relevant interoperability of digital content with hardware and software that the trader is aware of or can reasonably be expected to have been aware of.

(c) Right to Withdraw from Contract

(1) Distance Sales

The Consumer Rights Directive requires the trader in the context of a distance sale to give the consumer at least 14 calendar days in which to withdraw from the contract without penalty and without giving any reason.[112] The purpose of granting this withdrawal right is because the consumer has not in most instances had the opportunity to inspect and test the products prior to committing to purchase them.[113] If the consumer has been provided with the required information, the 14-day period for exercise of the right to withdraw begins on the day the consumer receives the goods.[114] If, however, the consumer has not been provided with the required information, the withdrawal period expires 12 months from the end of the initial withdrawal period.[115]

In order to exercise his or her right of withdrawal, the consumer must merely make an "unequivocal statement setting out his decision to withdraw from the contract."[116] The Consumer Rights Directive contains a model withdrawal form (in Annex I(B)) which consumers may use to exercise their withdrawal right. The trader is then required "without delay" to send an acknowledgement of receipt of such a withdrawal to the consumer on a durable medium.[117]

If the consumer properly exercises his or her right of withdrawal within the prescribed time limit, the obligations of the parties are terminated.[118] Unless the trader has otherwise offered to collect the goods, the consumer is required to send back or deliver the goods within 14 days after the date on which the

---

112. Consumer Rights Directive at art. 9(1). The critical point in time is the date on which the withdrawal is sent by the consumer and not the date on which it is received by the trader. *Id.* at art. 11(2).
113. *Id.* at recital ¶37.
114. *Id.* at art. 10(2).
115. *Id.* at art. 10(1).
116. *Id.* at art. 11(1)(b).
117. *Id.* at art. 11(3).
118. *Id.* at art. 12.

consumer communicated his or her decision to withdraw from the contract.[119] The consumer must bear the direct cost of returning the goods unless the trader has agreed to bear them or the trader failed to inform the consumer that the consumer has to bear them.[120]

Within 14 days after being informed of the consumer's decision to exercise his or her right of withdrawal, the trader is required to reimburse the consumer for all payments received from the consumer using the same means of payment as the consumer used for the initial transaction.[121] If, however, the trader has not received the goods back or has not received evidence that the goods have been sent back, the trader may withhold the reimbursement.[122]

The member states may require the consumer to pay fair compensation for the use of the product between the time of receipt of the goods and the exercise of the withdrawal rights.[123] In *Messner v. Krüger*, for example, the consumer purchased a used computer in December on the Internet. When the monitor broke the following August, the consumer tried to exercise his right of withdrawal. The seller argued that he could deduct from the purchase price the benefit the consumer received prior to the exercise of the right of withdrawal. The ECJ agreed and held that the Consumer Rights Directive allows the member states to require consumers to pay fair compensation for the use of the products prior to their exercise of their right of withdrawal.[124]

The statutorily imposed ability to withdraw from a contract may be inappropriate in certain circumstances and lead to the unwillingness of the seller to supply a particular product or service. In recognition of this fact, the Consumer Rights Directive identifies certain types of contracts for which the mandatory right of withdrawal is not required (but the parties may agree on a withdrawal right).[125] For example, if the contract requires performance of a service, once the trader has started performing the service, the consumer is no longer allowed to withdraw from the contract. Additional examples include:[126]

- the supply of goods or services for which the price is dependent on fluctuations in the financial market which cannot be controlled by the trader and which may occur within the withdrawal period;
- the supply of goods made to the consumer's specifications;
- the supply of goods which are liable to deteriorate or expire rapidly;
- the supply of sealed goods which are not suitable for return due to health protection or hygiene reasons and were unsealed after delivery;
- the supply of goods which are, after delivery, according to their nature, inseparably mixed with other items;

---

119. *Id.* art. 14(1).
120. *Id.*
121. *Id.* at art. 13(1).
122. *Id.* at art. 13(3).
123. *Id.* at art. 14(3).
124. Case C-489/07, Messner v. Krüger, 2009 E.C.R. I-7356, 7368 ¶26.
125. Consumer Rights Directive at art. 16.
126. *Id.*

- the supply of alcoholic beverages, the price of which has been agreed upon at the time of the conclusion of the sales contract, the delivery of which can only take place after 30 days and the actual value of which is dependent on fluctuations in the market which cannot be controlled by the trader;
- contracts where the consumer has specifically requested a visit from the trader for the purpose of carrying out urgent repairs or maintenance;
- the supply of sealed audio or sealed video recordings or sealed computer software which were unsealed after delivery;
- the supply of a newspaper, periodical, or magazine with the exception of subscription contracts for the supply of such publications;
- contracts concluded at a public auction;
- the provision of accommodation other than for residential purpose, transport of goods, car rental services, catering, or services related to leisure activities if the contract provides for a specific date or period of performance; and
- the supply of digital content which is not supplied on a tangible medium if the performance has started with the consumer's prior express consent and his acknowledgment that he loses his right of withdrawal once the performance has started.

(2) Off-Premises Sales

The right of withdrawal in the context of off-premises contracts is the same as for distance sales. The rationale for extending this right to off-premises sales is "because of the potential surprise element and/or psychological pressure" to which the EU feels consumers are exposed in off-premises sales.[127] One slight difference between distance sales and off-premises sales is that where the goods have been delivered to the consumer's home at the time of the conclusion of the off-premises contract, the trader is required to collect the goods at the trader's own expense if, by their nature, those goods cannot normally be returned by post.[128] For example, if the consumer purchases a new washing machine in an off-premises sale, the trader is required to pick up the goods if the consumer properly exercises its withdrawal right rather than require the consumer to bring the washing machine back to the trader's premises.

(3) On-Premises Sales

The withdrawal rights extended to consumers in the Consumer Rights Directive do not extend to on-premises sales. However, as the EU legislation has not preempted action by the member states, national laws may extend withdrawal rights to consumers in on-premises sales provided that such laws are commensurate with the free movement principles discussed in Chapter II.

---

127. *Id.* at recital 37.
128. Consumer Rights Directive at art. 14(1). As discussed above, the general rule is that the consumer is required to bear the costs of returning the goods. *Id.* at art. 14(1).

3.4 Content of Consumer Contracts

(a) Unfair Terms in Consumer Contracts

Whereas the Consumer Rights Directive and the E-Commerce Directive address contract formation issues, the Unfair Terms Directive addresses the content of the agreement.[129] The basic assumption is that the consumer is generally is a weak position vis-à-vis commercial sellers.[130] The general rule codified in the Consumer Rights Directive is that unfair terms used in a contract concluded with a consumer by a trader are *not binding* on the consumer.[131] A term is unfair if it is contrary to good faith and causes a significant imbalance in the parties' rights and obligations to the detriment of the consumer.[132] The consequence of being considered unfair is that the unfair component of the contract is not binding on the consumer.[133]

If the unfair term can be deleted from the contract and the contract still contains all the elements of an enforceable contract under applicable national law, the contract may be enforced without the unfair term. However, the courts cannot amend the contract by modifying the unfair term to make it fair. In *Banco Español de Crédito SA v. Camino*, the national court concluded that an interest rate of 29 percent on late payments on a consumer loan was unfair. However, according to the ECJ, the national court could not adjust that rate to make it fair: "[T]he national courts are required only to exclude the application of an unfair contractual term in order that it does not produce binding effects with regard to the consumer, without being authorized to revise its content. That contract must continue in existence, in principle, without any amendment other than that resulting from the deletion of the unfair terms."[134]

The Unfair Terms Directive does not apply to the main subject matter of the contract or the price of the goods or services.[135] The ECJ has been characteristically coy about providing a useful definition of what constitutes the main subject matter of the contract. According to the ECJ, the contractual

---

129. Another difference is that the Unfair Terms Directive applies to agreements between consumers and sellers or suppliers, and not just traders. A seller or supplier is any natural or legal person who is acting in the scope of his or her trade, business or profession. Unfair Terms Directive at art. 2. For example, an engagement letter between an attorney and a client falls under the Unfair Terms Directive. Case C-537/13, Šiba v. Devėnas, 2015 E.C.R. I-____ ¶24.
130. Case C-470/12, Pohotovost's s.r.o. v. Vašuta, 2014 E.C.R. I-____, at ¶39; Case C-488/11, Brusse v. Jahani BV, 2013 E.C.R. I-____, at ¶32; C-472/11, Banif Plus Bank Zrt v. Csaba Csipai, 2013 E.C.R. I-____, at ¶19.
131. Unfair Terms Directive at art. 6.
132. The concept of "significant imbalance" is relative. The ECJ compares the position of the consumer with the contractual term at issue to the position of the consumer under national law had the contractual term not been included in the contract. Case C-226/12, Constructora Principado SA v. Álvarez, 2014 E.C.R. I-____, at ¶21.
133. Case C-453/10, Perenicová v. SOS finance spol. s.r.o., 2012 E.C.R. I-____, at ¶31.
134. Case C-618/10, Banco Español de Crédito SA v. Camino, 2012 E.C.R. I-____, at ¶65.
135. Unfair Terms Directive at art. 4(2).

terms that form the main subject matter of the contract are "those that lay down the essential obligations of the contract and, as such, characterise it."[136] The application of this abstract definition is typically left to the courts of the member states. The fact that a particular term has been individually negotiated with the consumer does not necessarily mean that it forms part of the main subject matter of the contract.[137]

The application of the Unfair Terms Directive rests on a distinction between individually negotiated contracts and nonindividually negotiated contracts.[138] The term individually negotiated refers to contract terms in which the consumer has had the opportunity to influence the substance of the terms.[139] If the consumer has not had a chance to influence and negotiate the terms of the contract, it is considered a nonindividually negotiated contract. Standard contract terms—the small print on the back of many invoices—are an example. A contractual term that has not been individually negotiated is presumptively unfair if it causes a significant imbalance in the rights and obligations of the parties to the detriment of the consumer.[140] An individually negotiated contract, on the other hand, must be assessed on a case-by-case basis taking into account the context in which it was concluded and the specific terms of the contract.[141] As the standard of unfairness is abstract, there are a number of terms used in consumer contracts that are considered per se unfair. The following are some examples provided in the Unfair Terms Directive:[142]

- terms which have the object or effect of excluding or limiting the legal liability of a seller or supplier in the event of the death of a consumer or personal injury to the latter resulting from an act or omission of that seller or supplier;

- terms which have the object or effect of inappropriately excluding or limiting the legal rights of the consumer vis-à-vis the seller or supplier or another party in the event of total or partial nonperformance or inadequate performance by the seller or supplier of any of the contractual obligations, including the option of offsetting a debt owed to the seller or supplier against any claim which the consumer may have against him;

---

136. Case C-26/13, Kásler v. OTP Jelzálogbank Zrt, 2014 E.C.R. I-____, at ¶49.
137. Id. at ____, at ¶47.
138. The Directive only applies to the terms in the contract. If applicable national law imposes certain default terms or gap-filling terms, the Directive does not apply to those terms. Case C-280/13, Barclays Bank SA v. García, 2014 E.C.R. I-____, at ¶40.
139. Unfair Terms Directive at art. 3(2).
140. Id. at art. 3(1).
141. In determining whether a particular provision of a consumer contract is unfair, all the terms of the contract must be considered as they relate to that particular provision. In other words, the focus is not just on the particular provision in isolation. Case 472/11, Nemzeti Fogyasztóvédelmi Hatóság v. Invitel Távözési Zrt, 2012 E.C.R. I-____, at ¶11.
142. The list of examples of per se unfair terms provided in the Unfair Terms Directive is not exhaustive. Case 472/11, Nemzeti Fogyasztóvédelmi Hatóság v. Invitel Távözési Zrt, 2012 E.C.R. I-____, at ¶25.

- terms which have the object or effect of making an agreement binding on the consumer whereas provision of services by the seller or supplier is subject to a condition whose realization depends on his own will alone;
- terms which have the object or effect of permitting the seller or supplier to retain sums paid by the consumer where the latter decides not to conclude or perform the contract, without providing for the consumer to receive compensation of an equivalent amount from the seller or supplier where the latter is the party canceling the contract;
- terms which have the object or effect of requiring any consumer who fails to fulfill his obligation to pay a disproportionately high sum in compensation;
- terms which have the object or effect of authorizing the seller or supplier to dissolve the contract on a discretionary basis where the same facility is not granted to the consumer, or permitting the seller or supplier to retain the sums paid for services not yet supplied by him where it is the seller or supplier himself who dissolves the contract;
- terms which have the object or effect of enabling the seller or supplier to terminate a contract of indeterminate duration without reasonable notice except where there are serious grounds for doing so;
- terms which have the object or effect of automatically extending a contract of fixed duration where the consumer does not indicate otherwise, when the deadline fixed for the consumer to express this desire not to extend the contract is unreasonably early;
- terms which have the object or effect of irrevocably binding the consumer to terms with which he had no real opportunity of becoming acquainted before the conclusion of the contract;
- terms which have the object or effect of enabling the seller or supplier to alter the terms of the contract unilaterally without a valid reason which is specified in the contract;
- terms which have the object or effect of enabling the seller or supplier to alter unilaterally without a valid reason any characteristics of the product or service to be provided;
- terms which have the object or effect of providing for the price of goods to be determined at the time of delivery or allowing a seller of goods or supplier of services to increase their price without in both cases giving the consumer the corresponding right to cancel the contract if the final price is too high in relation to the price agreed when the contract was concluded;
- terms which have the object or effect of giving the seller or supplier the right to determine whether the goods or services supplied are in conformity with the contract, or giving him the exclusive right to interpret any term of the contract;

- terms which have the object or effect of limiting the seller's or supplier's obligation to respect commitments undertaken by his agents or making his commitments subject to compliance with a particular formality;
- terms which have the object or effect of obliging the consumer to fulfill all his obligations where the seller or supplier does not perform his;
- terms which have the object or effect of giving the seller or supplier the possibility of transferring his rights and obligations under the contract, where this may serve to reduce the guarantees for the consumer, without the latter's agreement;
- terms which have the object or effect of excluding or hindering the consumer's right to take legal action or exercise any other legal remedy, particularly by requiring the consumer to take disputes exclusively to arbitration not covered by legal provisions, unduly restricting the evidence available to him or imposing on him a burden of proof which, according to the applicable law, should lie with another party to the contract.

It is for the national courts to assess the fairness of the terms of the contract.[143] In determining whether a particular clause of the contract is unfair, the ECJ has instructed the national courts to compare the rights of the consumer under the terms of the contract to the rights the consumer would have under applicable national law if the contract terms were not applicable.[144] The greater the discrepancy, the more likely that the terms will be considered unfair.

One of the characteristics of the Unfair Terms Directive that makes it of limited use from the perspective of firms doing business is that it only sets a minimum standard. The Unfair Terms Directive does not preclude member states from retaining or adopting provisions with a view to ensuring more extensive protection, with regard to misleading advertising, for consumers, persons carrying on a trade, business, craft, or profession, and the general public. But this does not apply to comparative advertising as far as the comparison is concerned.

The prohibition on unfair contract terms in consumer contracts places a significant burden on many businesses in the retail sector. In the United States, for example, businesses rely on standard contract terms in their daily activities. The law in the United States is more lenient toward businesses. The lower level of protection accorded to consumers in the United States creates the possibility of including a choice of law provision in a consumer contract by which the parties agree that U.S. law will apply. The Unfair Terms Directive anticipates this development and precludes the inclusion of such choice of law terms if their application is to deprive the European consumer of the protections of

---

143. Case C-280/13, Barclays Bank SA v. García, 2014 E.C.R. I-____, at ¶34; Case C-472/10, Nemzeti Fogyasztóvédelmi Hatóság v. Invitel Távközlési Zrt, 2012 E.C.R. I-____, at ¶22.
144. Case 415/11, Aziz v. Caixa d'Estalvis de Catalunya, Tarragona i Manresa, 2013 E.C.R. I-____, at ¶68 ("Such a comparative analysis will enable the national court to evaluate whether and, as the case may be, to what extent, the contract places the consumer in a legal situation less favourable than that provided for by the national law in force.").

the Directive.[145] As illustrated by *Oceano Group Editorial v. Rocio Murcian Quintero*, even an intra-EU choice of law clause requiring application of a member state's law granting consumers the minimum protection required by the Directive or the jurisdiction of the seller would be unenforceable as such clause would be deemed unfair to the consumer.[146]

(b) Price Terms in Consumer Contracts

The presentation of prices on consumer products is addressed in the Consumer Product Pricing Directive. The Directive requires that the selling price of a product and the unit price must be unambiguous, easily identifiable, and clearly legible. In contrast to the United States, the selling price must include the value-added tax (VAT) and all other taxes. The Consumer Product Pricing Directive applies for distance and off-premises sales as well as on-premises sales.

The Directive gives the member states some discretion to decide not to apply the general rule to products in certain circumstances. For example, a member state may decide not to apply the Directive to products supplied in the course of the provision of a service, sales by auction, and sales of works of art and antiques.[147] For products sold in bulk (i.e., products that are not pre-packaged and are measured in the presence of the consumer), only the unit price must be indicated. Any advertisement which mentions the selling price of products must also indicate the unit price.[148] In addition, the Consumer Product Pricing Directive includes a brand exception. Member states may waive the obligation to indicate the unit price of products for which such indication would not be useful because of the products' nature or purpose or would be liable to create confusion.

4. Misleading and Comparative Advertising

The laws of the member states applicable to misleading and comparative advertising are harmonized by the Misleading and Comparative Advertising Directive. In this context, the term "advertising" means the making of a representation in any form in connection with a trade, business, craft, or profession in order to promote the supply of goods or services, including immovable property, rights, and obligations.[149] It would therefore include not only traditional forms of advertising such as in newspapers and magazines but also advertising on the Internet. In *Belgian Electronic Sorting Technology NV v. Peelaers*, for example, the ECJ held that the use of metatags is a form of advertising within the meaning of the Misleading and Comparative Advertising Directive.[150]

---

145. Unfair Terms Directive at art. 6(2).
146. Joined cases C-240/98 to C-244/98, Oceano Group Editorial v. Rocio Murciano Quintero, 2000 E.C.R. I-4941, 4973 ¶24.
147. Consumer Product Pricing Directive at art. 3(2).
148. *Id.* at art. 3(4).
149. *Id.* at art. 2(a).
150. Case C-657/11, Belgian Electronic Sorting Technology NV v. Peelaers, 2013 E.C.R. I-____, at ¶457.

The Misleading and Comparative Advertising Directive requires the member states to implement adequate and effective means to combat misleading advertising and to permit legitimate forms of comparative advertising. The member states must give persons or organizations having a legitimate interest in prohibiting misleading advertising or regulating comparative advertising a legal claim or administrative complaint against such advertising. The Directive sets a minimum level of protection as the member states may adopt stricter laws applicable to misleading and comparative advertising.[151]

(a) Misleading Advertising

Advertising is misleading when it in any way deceives or is likely to deceive the persons to whom it is addressed or whom it reaches and which, by reason of its deceptive nature, is likely to affect their economic behavior or which, for those reasons, injures or is likely to injure a competitor.[152] In determining whether a particular advertisement is misleading, the standard used is that of an average consumer who is reasonably well informed.[153] Each case must be examined on its own merits.

For example, a company selling products on the Internet with the slogan "Factory Direct! No Middleman! Guaranteed Lowest Price" engaged in misleading advertising according to a German court because the price at which it sold the goods included its profit margin. According to the German court in that case, the slogan misled the consumer by suggesting that the consumer was getting the same price as the wholesaler.[154] In another case, the German Supreme Court held that an advertisement containing the slogan "20% off everything" was misleading because the store making the advertisement had increased the prices for some of its products shortly before the start of the 20 percent off promotion.[155]

The advertisement does not have to contain an untrue statement to be considered misleading. The omission of a material fact which, had it been contained in the advertisement would have deterred the purchaser, may be misleading.[156]

(b) Comparative Advertising

One specific type of advertising addressed by the Misleading and Comparative Advertising Directive is comparative advertising. Misleading advertising and

---

151. Misleading and Comparative Advertising Directive at art. 8(1).
152. *Id.* at art. 2(b).
153. Case C-220/98, Estee Lauder Cosmetics v. Lancaster Group GmbH, 2000 E.C.R. I-117, 146 ¶27.
154. Decision of the German Bundesgerichtshof in case no. I ZR 96/02 (Jan. 20, 2005) *reported at* 2005 Wettbewerb in Recht und Praxis 474 (2005).
155. Decision of the German Bundesgerichtshof in case no. I ZR 122/06 (Nov. 20, 2008) *reported at* 62 Neue Juristische Wochenschrift 2541 (2009).
156. Case C-356/04, Lidl Belgium GmbH & Co. KG v. Etablissementen Franz Colruyt NV, 2006 E.C.R. I-8524, 8552 ¶80.

unlawful comparative advertising are two separate prohibitions.[157] As the Comparative Advertising Directive exhaustively harmonizes the comparative advertising laws of the member states, the member states may not impose stricter prohibitions on comparative advertising than are set forth in the Directive.[158]

(1) Scope of Directive

The term comparative advertising includes (1) any advertising, (2) which explicitly or by implication identifies another undertaking or goods or services offered by another undertaking and (3) that other undertaking is a competitor.[159] An advertisement is comparative in nature if it *explicitly or implicitly* identifies competing products or services.[160] Cases involving explicit reference to other products or services represent the easy cases. The more difficult cases are those where the comparison is implicit. In *Längerfrische Vollmich*, the Austrian Supreme Court held that the words "longer-fresh milk" on a milk carton constituted comparative advertising even though competitors or competing products were not explicitly mentioned.[161] According to the Court: "The designation 'longer fresh' contains the allegation that the milk qualified in this way remains fresh longer than other milk."[162]

In *Toshiba Europe GmbH v. Katun Germany GmbH*,[163] the ECJ also addressed the issue of whether an implicit reference to a product constitutes comparative advertising. A German company (Katun) began to manufacture and sell spare parts which fit Toshiba photocopiers. Toshiba, which sold its own spare parts for its copiers, objected to the reference to Toshiba photocopiers made in the marketing materials of the other company. To enable the customer to order the proper spare part, Katun identified the specific Toshiba model and part number. The materials also suggested that its spare parts were sold at a lower price ("these quality products are clearly a more profitable alternative for businesses"). Toshiba claimed that this amounted to unfair comparative advertising.[164] The ECJ held that in order for there to be comparative advertising within the meaning of the Directive, it is sufficient for a representation to be made

---

157. Case C-52/13, Posteshop SpA v. Autorità Garante della Concorrenza e del Mercato, 2014 E.C.R. I-___, at ¶26.
158. Case C-159/09, Lidl SNC v. Vieryon Distribution SA, 2010 E.C.R. I-11782, 11792 ¶22.
159. Misleading and Comparative Advertising Directive at art. 2(c).
160. Case C-533/06, O2 Holdings Ltd. v. Hutchinson 3G UK Ltd., 2008 E.C.R. I-4254, 4268 ¶43.
161. Decision of the Austrian Oberster Gerichtshof in case no. 4 Ob 173/02 (Aug. 20, 2002) *reported in* 2004 Gewerblicher Rechtschutz und Urheberrecht 255 (2004).
162. *Id.* An English translation of excerpts from the decision are available at 35 Int'l Rev. of Intell. Prop. & Competition L. 701 (2004).
163. Case C-112/99, Toshiba Europe GmbH v. Katun Germany GmbH, 2001 E.C.R. I-7945.
164. The reason that Toshiba did not pursue the case under a trademark infringement theory is because the ECJ had previously held that use of another person's trademark may be legitimate where it is necessary to inform the public of the nature of the products or the intended purpose of the services offered. Case C-63/97, BMW v. Deenik, 1999 E.C.R. I-905.

in any form which refers, *even by implication*, to a competitor or to the goods or services which he offers.[165] The application of this rule to the facts led to the conclusion that the conduct of Katun amounted to comparative advertising.

In *Aluminiumräder*, however, the German Supreme Court held that an advertisement containing a picture of the competitor's product was not an implicit comparison. The issue in that case was whether an advertisement of an automobile wheel manufacturer using a Porsche car with the wheels of the wheel manufacturer constituted illegal comparative advertising.[166] Porsche objected because it was also active in the market for replacement wheels for its cars. The Supreme Court held that "the mere reference to the products of a competitor, even if intended to make use of the good reputation of the other, does not constitute comparative advertising because it does not compare purchase alternatives."[167]

The third component of the concept of comparative advertising is that the other company whose goods or services are compared must be a competitor. A reference in a McDonald's advertisement to a Ford automobile would not constitute comparative advertising. Moreover, the undertakings must be competitors in the product markets being compared.[168] If, using the prior example, the advertisement was for hamburgers, it still would not be comparative if McDonald's had a subsidiary that manufactured automobiles.

(2) Requirements for Comparative Advertising

The Comparative Advertising Directive sets forth specific requirements for comparative advertising. According to the ECJ, the purpose of these requirements is to achieve a balance between the different interests that may be affected by comparative advertising, that is, the interests of the competitors in stimulating competition between them and the protection of the consumers from unfair advertising practices.[169] If the advertising constitutes comparative advertising, it is permitted if it meets the following conditions:

- it is not *misleading* (i.e., deceives or is likely to deceive the persons to whom it is addressed or whom it reaches and which, by reason of its deceptive nature, is likely to affect their economic behavior or which, for those reasons, injures or is likely to injure a competitor);[170]

- it compares goods or services meeting the same needs or intended for the same purpose;[171]

---

165. *See also* Case C-381/05, De Landtsheer Emmanuel SA v. Comité Interprofesionnel du Vin de Champagne, 2007 E.C.R. I-3152, 3167 ¶19.
166. Decision of the Bundesgerichtshof in case number I ZR 37/01 (July 15, 2004) *reprinted at* 2005 Wettbewerb in Recht und Praxis 219 (2005).
167. *Id.* at 221.
168. Case C-381/05, De Landtsheer Emmanuel SA v. Comité Interprofessionnel du Vin de Champagne, 2007 E.C.R. I-3152, 3172 ¶39.
169. Case C-159/09, Lidl SNC v. Vieryon Distribution SA, 2010 E.C.R. I-11782, 11791 ¶20.
170. *Id.* at 11797 ¶44.
171. The goods or services being compared must display a sufficient degree of functional demand-side interchangeability. Case C-159/09, Lidl SNC v. Vieryon Distribution SA, 2010 E.C.R. I-11782, 11794 ¶28.

- it *objectively compares* one or more material, relevant, verifiable, and representative features of those goods and services, which may include price;[172]
- it does not *discredit or denigrate* the trademarks, trade names, other distinguishing marks, goods, services, activities, or circumstances of a competitor;
- it does not take *unfair advantage* of the reputation of a trademark, trade name or other distinguishing marks of a competitor or of the designation of origin of competing products;
- it does not present goods or services as *imitations or replicas* of goods or services bearing a protected trademark or trade name; and
- it does not create confusion in the marketplace between the advertiser and a competitor or between the advertiser's trademarks, trade names, other distinguishing marks, goods, or services and those of a competitor.

Comparative advertising which does not meet the fairness standards set forth above is generally prohibited. Although it is not codified in the Directive, the inability of an advertiser to substantiate the comparison suggests the illegitimacy of the comparison. For example, if a producer of water claims its water is wetter than that of a competitor, the producer making the claim will have to substantiate it. National courts tend to place the burden for such substantiation on the party making the claim.[173] Although an untrue comparison is improper, it does not necessarily follow that a true comparison is always legitimate. The European courts as well as the national courts have repeatedly reviewed the legality of true comparisons.

With the possible exception of blatantly untrue comparisons, it is difficult to identify specific categories of advertisements which are per se unfair. Even the use of a competitor's logo or trademark for purposes of comparative advertising is legitimate, provided all of the other conditions of permissible comparative advertising are met. In *Pippig Augenoptik v. Hartlauer Handelsgesellschaft mbH*, the ECJ held that price comparisons are not per se misleading even if the compared products are of a different quality (in this case eyeglasses).[174] In that case, the plaintiff unsuccessfully argued that it was misleading to compare prices of other eyeglasses with its eyeglasses because the quality of the compared

---

172. Case C-356/04, Lidl Belgium GmbH & Co. KG v. Etablissementen Franz Colruyt NV, 2006 E.C.R. I-8501, 8501 ¶58. The verifiability criterion requires that the elements of the products being compared "be capable of being individually and specifically identified on the basis of the information contained in the advertisement." Case C-159/09, Lidl SNC v. Vieryon Distribution SA, 2010 E.C.R. I-11782, 11802 ¶60.
173. *See, e.g.*, Decision of Aug. 20, 2002 of the Austrian Oberster Gerichtshof, Case Nr. 4 Ob 173/02, *reported in* 2004 Gewerblicher Rechtsschutz und Urheberrecht 255 (2004), where a milk producer was not able to substantiate its claim that its milk stayed fresh longer than other brands of milk.
174. Case C-44/01, Pippig Augenoptik v. Hartlauer Handelsgesellschaft mbH, 2003 E.C.R. I-3127, 3156 ¶80.

eyeglasses was significantly lower. If, however, the advertisement compares the prices of two products and omits the fact that the more expensive product is a well-known brand name, the advertisement may be misleading.[175]

As comparative advertising often uses the registered trademark of a competing company, the issue arises whether the owner of the trademark right can prevent the use of its trademark in this context. In *O2 Holdings Ltd. v. Hutchinson 3G UK Ltd.*, Hutchinson, a UK mobile phone services provider, used a trademark of O2 to compare its services to those of O2.[176] O2 claimed that this use of its trademark violated applicable trademark law. The ECJ held, however, that if the conditions for permissible comparative advertising are met, the holder of the trademark rights cannot rely on those rights to prevent the comparative advertising.[177]

Absolute claims are generally more difficult to justify than relative claims. This is illustrated in the experience of a poster for eBay that stated "GUESS WHAT? 25% CHEAPER THAN THE HIGH STREET ON BRAND NEW ITEMS." In response to a complaint, the UK Advertising Standards Authority (ASA) concluded that the advertisement was misleading because "readers were likely to infer from the headline claim that they could expect a new item purchased on eBay to be 25 percent cheaper than one purchased in the high street on every occasion." As the ASA pointed out, it was possible that the high street stores sold some products at cheaper prices than eBay. The inclusion of small print at the bottom of the advertisement stating that the statement was obtained by comparing the average sold price of 288 new products on eBay.co.uk with the price in six mainstream retail stores was insufficient to make the advertisement not misleading. In the opinion of the ASA, the "small print was of insufficient size to avoid being overlooked."

5. Product Safety and Defects

The main EU legislative acts applicable to the condition of products and responsibility for defects in products are the Product Safety Directive[178] and the Defective Products Directive.[179] As is discussed in greater detail below, there is a conceptual distinction between an unsafe product and a defective product. The safety of a product refers to its design. A product could be manufactured

---

175. Case C-159/09, Lidl SNC v. Vieryon Distribution SA, 2010 E.C.R. I-11782, 11800 ¶53; Case C-44/01, Pippig Augenoptik v. Hartlauer Handelsgesellschaft mbH, 2003 E.C.R. I-3127, 3148 ¶53.
176. Case C-533/06, O2 Holdings Ltd. v. Hutchinson 3G UK Ltd., 2008 E.C.R. I-4254.
177. *Id.* at 4269 ¶45.
178. Directive 2001/95/EC of the European Parliament and of the Council of 3 December 2001 on general product safety, 2002 O.J. (L 11) 4 [hereinafter Product Safety Directive].
179. Council Directive 85/374/EEC of 25 July 1985 on the approximation of the laws, regulations and administrative provisions of the member states concerning liability for defective products, 1985 O.J. (L 210) 29 [hereinafter Defective Products Directive].

without a defect in the manufacturing process and yet be unsafe. A defective product, on the other hand, is one which has not been manufactured properly.

5.1 Safety

The Product Safety Directive requires the member states to make sure that producers place only safe products on the market. A product is considered a "safe product" if, under normal or reasonably foreseeable conditions of use, it does not present any risk (or only the minimum risks compatible with the product's use) to the safety and health of persons.[180] The mere fact that there may be alternative ways to make the product safer does not necessarily mean that the product does not qualify as safe.[181] The term "product" in this context means any product—including products supplied together with a service—which is intended for consumers (or likely to be used by consumers even if not intended for them), and is supplied or made available in the course of a commercial activity.[182] The Directive covers not only new products, but also used or reconditioned products. The fact that the products may be provided for free does not take them outside the scope of the Product Safety Directive.

The Product Safety Directive gives the member states broad latitude in determining which products are safe or not safe. In determining whether a product constitutes a safe product, the member states are instructed to consider applicable standards; European Commission recommendations setting guidelines on product safety assessment; product safety codes of good practice in force in the sector concerned; the state of the art and technology; and reasonable consumer expectations concerning safety.[183] There are, however, certain circumstances in which products will be considered presumptively safe. Compliance with EU legislation or with national standards gives rise to a presumption that the products qualify as safe.[184] This presumption can be overcome. The member states can prevent or restrict the sale of products which are presumptively safe if there is evidence that, despite their conformity with the requirements of the presumption, they are dangerous.[185]

5.2 Defects

The Defective Products Directive is intended to harmonize the member state laws on strict liability for damages resulting from a defective product. At its core, the Directive requires the member states to impose "liability without fault" on the producer of a product in the event of damage caused by a defect in its product. Once the inured party proves damages, defect, and the causal relationship between the damages and defect, the assumption is that the producer was at fault. The member states are prohibited from implementing a product liability system that is more stringent than that provided for in the Directive.[186]

---

180. Product Safety Directive at art. 2(b).
181. *Id.* at art. 2(b).
182. *Id.* at art. 2(a).
183. *Id.* at art. 3(3).
184. *Id.* at art. 3.
185. *Id.* at art. 3(4).
186. Case C-52/00, Comm'n v. France, 2002 E.C.R. I-3827.

(a) Defective Product

The first requirement for the imposition of strict liability on a producer is that the product is defective. The term "product" means all movables even though incorporated into another movable object or into an immovable object.[187] Although the definition is quite broad - for example, it would apply to things such as a bathroom faucet installed in a home as well as a defibrillator implanted in a human[188] - it is a narrower definition than employed in the consumer protection legislation discussed above.

A product is "defective" when it does not provide the safety which a person is entitled to expect.[189] In making this determination, the courts are to take into account such factors as the presentation of the product, the use to which it could reasonably be expected that the product would be put, and the time when the product was put into circulation.[190] The claim is automatically precluded if it is not brought within 10 years after the product was introduced into commerce.[191] The time consideration reflects a recognition that because "products age in the course of time, higher safety standards are developed and the state of science and technology progresses …it would not be reasonable to make the producer liable for an unlimited period."[192] A product is not considered defective for the sole reason that a better product is subsequently put into circulation. If, for example, the producer of a bathroom faucet improves the safety of the faucet by introducing an anti-scalding valve, this improvement cannot be used as prima facie evidence that the original faucet was defective. The injured party has the burden to prove the existence of the default and the causal relationship between the defect and the damages.

It is not always necessary that the specific product be shown to be defective if a sufficient number of other products in that same series have proven to be defective. This is illustrated in *Boston Scientific Medizintechnik GmbH v. AOK Sachsen-Anhalt*. One of the issues in that casse was whether a person who had received an implant of a heart pacemaker manufactured by Boston Scientific could claim that his pacemaker was defective based on evidence that other similar pacemakers in the same series were defective. Although there was no evidence that this particular person's pacemaker was defective, the ECJ held that "where it is found that such products belonging to the same group or forming part of the same production series have a potential defect, it is possible to classify as defective all the products in that group or series, without there being any need to show that the product in question is defective."[193]

---

187. Defective Products Directive at art. 2.
188. See, e.g., Joined Cases C-503/13 and C-504/13, Boston Scientific Medizintechnik GmbH v. AOK Sachsen-Anhalt, 2015 E.C.R. I-____.
189. *Id.* at ¶37.
190. Defective Products Directive at art. 6.
191. *Id.* at art 11.
192. *Id.* at recital.
193. Joined Cases C-503/13 and C-504/13, Boston Scientific Medizintechnik GmbH v. AOK Sachsen-Anhalt, 2015 E.C.R. I-____ at ¶41.

(b) Damage

The term "damage" only applies to material damages.[194] The reference to "material" is not a quantitative qualification but rather a limitation on the types of damages: there must be an injury to person or property. The producer is not liable for nonmaterial damages such as economic loss. Liability for nonmaterial damages continues to be governed by national law and not the Defective Products Directive.[195]

There is no required limit on the amount of damages that can be claimed in individual cases.[196] However, for damage to property, the Defective Products Directive imposes a de minimis threshold: if the damages to property do not exceed €500, the member states are precluded from applying a strict liability standard to the producer.[197] An additional limitation on property damage claims is that the property damaged must be of a type ordinarily intended for private use or consumption and was in fact used in that context. For example, damage caused to a piece of manufacturing equipment in a factory does not fall under the Defective Products Directive. Regardless of the type of material damages (to person or property), the injured party carries the burden of proof concerning damages and the causal relationship between damages and the defect.[198]

(c) Apportionment of Liability

The strict liability mandated by the Defective Products Directive is imposed on the producer. The term "producer" is interpreted broadly to include not only the manufacturer of the product but also the manufacturer of any raw material or component part or even a company that presents itself as the manufacturer by putting its name, trademark, or other distinguishing mark on the product.[199] For example, a company that outsources the production of products it subsequently sells under its own brand is still considered the producer even though it did not actually manufacture the products. If the producer of the product cannot be identified, each supplier of the product is considered the producer unless such supplier informs the injured party of the identity of its supplier. Two or more producers liable for the same damage will be held jointly and severally liable.

The term producer would not include a service provider using the defective product to provide services. In *Centre hospitalier universitaire de Besançon v. Dutrueux*, for example, a hospital patient was injured by a defective heated mattress not manufactured by the hospital. When the injured patent brought an action against the hospital, the issue was whether the Defective Products Directive even applied. The ECJ held that the liability of a service provider using defective products not manufactured by it is not regulated by the Defective Products Directive.[200]

---

194. Defective Products Directive at art. 9.
195. Case C-203/99, Veedfald v. Århus Amtskommune, 2001 E.C.R. I-3586, 3599 ¶27.
196. Member states may provide a cap of €70 million on serial defects, i.e., damage caused by identical items with the same defect. Defective Products Directive at art. 16(1).
197. *Id.* at art. 9. *See, e.g.*, Case C-154/00, Comm'n v. Greece, 2002 E.C.R. I-3879.
198. Defective Products Directive at art. 4.
199. *Id.* at art. 3(2).
200. Case C-495/10, Centre hospitalier universitaire de Besançon v. Dutrueux, 2011 E.C.R. I-14174, 14185 ¶27. Although the Defective Products Directive does not cover service providers, it is possible for a member state to impose liability on the service provider in its legislation implementing the Defective Products Directive. *Id.* at 14189 ¶39.

The Defective Products Directive expressly allows the member states to have contributory negligence laws.[201] In the event that the injured party is partially at fault for the damage, the applicable national liability laws need to be consulted. The liability of the producer in such cases may be reduced or disallowed entirely.[202]

(d) Defenses

Although the Defective Products Directive requires the member states to impose strict liability on producers of defective products that cause material damage, the producer is given defenses.[203] For example, the producer is not liable as a result of this Directive if it can prove that it did not put the defective product into circulation. Additional defenses exist if the producer can prove:

- that the defect which caused the damage did not exist at the time when the product was put into circulation by that producer or arose after it put the product into circulation; or

- that the product was neither manufactured by it for sale or any form of distribution for economic purpose nor manufactured or distributed by it in the course of its business; or

- that the defect was due to compliance of the product with mandatory regulations issued by the public authorities; or

- that the state of scientific and technical knowledge at the time when it put the product into circulation was not such as to enable the existence of the defect to be discovered; or

- in the case of a manufacturer of a component, that the defect was attributable to the design of the product in which the component has been fitted or to the instructions given by the actual manufacturer of the product.

According to the ECJ, these defenses are to be interpreted narrowly.[204] In *Veefald v. Århus Amtskommune*, a local Danish hospital prepared a kidney flushing fluid which, when used to flush a patient's kidney, proved to be defective. The hospital argued that the Product Defect Directive provided a defense under Article 7(a) of the Directive as the fluid was never "put into circulation" and the injured party was receiving a service and not a product. The ECJ held, however, that "a defective product is put into circulation when it is used during the provision of a specific medical service."[205]

---

201. Defective Products Directive at art. 8(2).
202. *Id.* at art. 8.
203. *Id.* at art. 7. The list of defenses in Article 7 is exhaustive. Case C-203/99, Veefald v. Arhus Amtskommune, 2001 E.C.R. I-3586, 3596 ¶15.
204. *Id.*
205. *Id.* at 3597 ¶18.

Index of Legislation and Common Names[1]

Accounting Directive	Directive 2013/34/EU of the European Parliament and of the Council of 26 June 2013 on the annual financial statements, consolidated financial statements, and related reports of certain types of undertakings, amending Directive 2006/43/EC of the European Parliament and of the Council repealing Council Directives 78/660/EEC and 83/349/EEC, 2013 O.J. (L 182) 18
Ancillary Restraints Notice	Commission Notice on restrictions directly related and necessary to concentrations, 2005 O.J. (C 56) 24
Anti-Dumping Regulation	Council Regulation (EC) No. 1225/2009 of 30 November 2009 on protection against dumped imports from countries not members of the European Community, 2009 O.J. (L 343) 51
Anti-Subsidy Regulation	Council Regulation (EC) No. 597/2009 of 11 June 2009 on protection against subsidized imports from countries not members of the European Community, 2009 O.J. (L 188) 93
Article 102 Guidelines	Commission Guidance on the enforcement priorities in applying Article 82 of the EC Treaty to abusive exclusionary conduct by dominant undertakings, 2009 O.J. (C 45) 7
Artists Resale Rights Directive	Directive 2001/84/EC of 27 September 2001 on the resale right for the benefit of the author of an original work or art, 2001 O.J. (L 272) 32

---

1. All legislation is as amended July 1, 2015.

Berne Convention	Berne Convention for the Protection of Literary and Artistic Works, Sept. 9, 1886, completed at Paris on May 4, 1896, revised at Berlin on Nov. 13, 1908, completed at Paris on May 4, 1896, revised at Berlin on Nov. 13, 1908, completed at Berne on Mar. 20, 1914, revised at Rome on June 2, 1928, at Brussels on June 26, 1948, at Stockholm on July 14, 1967, and at Paris on July 24, 1971, 1161 U.N.T.S. 3
Biotechnology Patent Directive	Directive 98/44/EC of the European Parliament and of the Council of 6 July 1998 on the legal protection of biotechnological inventions, O.J. 1998 (L 213) 13
Brussels I Regulation	Regulation (EU) No. 1215/2012 of the European Parliament and of the Council of 12 December 2012 on jurisdiction and the recognition and enforcement of judgments in civil and commercial matters, 2012 O.J. (L 351) 1
Collective Redundancies Directive	Council Directive 98/59/EC of 20 July 1998 on the approximation of the laws of the member states relating to collective redundancies, 1998 O.J. (L 225) 16
Computer Software Directive	Council Directive 91/250/EC on the legal protection of computer programs, 1991 O.J. (L 122) 42
Consolidated Jurisdictional Notice	Commission Consolidated Jurisdictional Notice under Council Regulation (EC) No. 139/2004 on the control of concentrations between undertakings, 2008 O.J. (C 95) 1
Consumer Credit Directive	Directive 87/102/EEC of 22 December 1986 for the approximation of the laws, regulations and administrative provisions of the member states concerning consumer credit, 1987 O.J. (L 42) 48
Consumer Guarantees Directive	Directive 1999/44/EC of the European Parliament and of the Council of 25 May 1999 on certain aspects of the sale of consumer goods and associated guarantees, 1999 O.J. (L 171) 12

Consumer Interest Injunctions Directive	Directive 98/27/EC of the European Parliament and of the Council of 19 May 1998 on injunctions for the protection of consumers' interests, O.J. 1998 (L 166) 51
Consumer Product Pricing Directive	Directive 98/6/EC of the European Parliament and of the Council of 16 February 1998 on consumer protection in the indication of the prices of products offered to consumers, 1998 O.J. (L 80) 27
Consumer Guarantees Directive	Directive 99/44/EC of the European Parliament and of the Council of 25 May 1999 on certain aspects of the sale of consumer goods and associated guarantees, 1999 O.J. (L 171) 12
Consumer Rights Directive	Directive 2011/83/EU of the European Parliament and of the Council of 25 October 2011 on consumer rights, 2011 O.J. (L 304) 64
Copyright Term Directive	Directive 2006/116/EC of the European Parliament and of the Council of 12 December 2006 on the term of protection of copyright and certain related rights, 2006 O.J. (L 372) 12
Counterfeit Goods Regulation	Regulation (EU) No. 608/2013 of the European Parliament and of the Council of 12 June 2013 concerning customs enforcement of intellectual property rights and repealing Council Regulation (EC) No. 1383/2003, 2013 O.J. (L 181) 15
Cross-Border Merger Directive	Directive 2005/56/EC of the European Parliament and of the Council on cross-border mergers, 2005 O.J. (L 310) 1
Current Insolvency Regulation	Council Regulation (EC) No. 1346/2000 of 29 May 2000 on insolvency proceedings O.J. 2000 (L 160) 1
Customs Code Implementing Regulation	Commission Regulation (EEC) No. 2454/93 of 2 July 1993 laying down provisions for the implementation of Council Regulations (EEC) No. 2913/92 establishing the Community Code, 1993 O.J. (L 253) 1

Data Privacy Directive	Directive 95/46/EC of the European Parliament and of the Council of 24 October 1995 on the protection of individuals with regard to the processing of personal data and on the free movement of such data, 1995 O.J. (L 281) 31
Database Directive	Directive 96/9/EC of the European Parliament and of the Council of 11 March 1996 on the legal protection of databases, 1996 O.J. (L 77) 20
Defective Products Directive	Council Directive 85/374/EEC of 25 July 1985 on the approximation of the laws, regulations and administrative provisions of the member states concerning liability for defective products, 1985 O.J. (L 210) 29
De Minimis Notice	Comm'n Notice on agreements of minor importance which do not appreciably restrict competition under Article 101(1) of the Treaty on the Functioning of the European Union, 2014 O.J. (C 291) 1
Design Regulation	Council Regulation No. 6/2002 on Community Designs, 2002 O.J. (L 3) 1
Distance Selling Directive	Directive 97/7/EC of the European Parliament and of the Council of 20 May 1997 on the protection of consumers in respect of distance contracts, 1997 O.J. (L 144) 19
Distance Marketing of Consumer Financial Services Directive	Directive 2002/65/EC of the European Parliament and of the Council of 23 September 2002 concerning the distance marketing of consumer financial services and amending Council Directive 90/619/EEC and Directives 97/7/EC and 98/27/EC, 2002 O.J. (L 271) 16
Division of Companies Directive	Sixth Council Directive of 17 December 1982 based on Article 54(3)(g) of the Treaty, concerning the division of public limited liability companies, 1982 O.J. (L 378) 47

Domestic Mergers Directive	Directive 2011/35/EU of the European Parliament and of the Council of 5 April 2011 concerning mergers of public limited liability companies, O.J. 2011 (L 110) 1
DSU	Understanding on Rules and Procedures Governing the Settlement of Disputes, Apr. 1, 1994, Marrakesh Agreement Establishing the World Trade Organization, Annex 1C, 33 I.L.M. 112 (1994)
ECJ Rules of Procedure	Rules of Procedure of the Court of Justice, 2012 O.J. (L 265) 1
ECJ Statute	Statute of the Court of Justice of the European Union, 2010 O.J. (C 83) 210
E-Commerce Directive	Directive 2000/31/EC of the European Parliament and of the Council of 8 June 2000 on certain legal aspects of information society services, in particular electronic commerce, in the Internal Market, 2000 O.J. (L 178) 1
ECSC Treaty	Treaty establishing the European Coal and Steel Community, Apr. 18, 1951, 261 U.N.T.S. 140
Electronic Signatures Directive	Directive 1999/93 on a Community framework for electronic signatures, 2000 O.J. (L13) 12
Eleventh Company Law Directive	Eleventh Council Directive 89/666/EEC of 21 December 1989 concerning disclosure requirements in respect of branches opened in a member state by certain types of company governed by the law of another state, 1989 O.J. (L 395) 36
Employer Insolvency Directive	Directive 2008/94/EC of the European Parliament and of the Council of 22 October 2008 on the protection of employees in the event of the insolvency of their employer, 2008 O.J. (L 283) 36

ePrivacy Directive	Directive 2002/58/EC of the European Parliament and of the Council of 12 July 2002 concerning the processing of personal data and the protection of privacy in the electronic communications sector, 2002 O.J. (L 201) 37
Equal Opportunities Directive	Directive 2006/54/EC of the European Parliament and of the Council of 5 July 2006 on the implementation of equal opportunities and equal treatment of men and women in matters of employment and occupation, 2006 O.J. (L 204) 23
Equal Treatment Framework Directive	Council Directive 2000/78/EC of 27 November 2000 establishing a general framework for equal treatment in employment and occupation, O.J. 2000 (L 303) 16
EU Treaty	Treaty on European Union, Feb. 7, 1992, O.J. 1992 (C 191) 1
EU Unitary Patent Regulation	Regulation (EU) No. 1257/2012 of the European Parliament and of the Council of 17 December 2012 implementing enhanced cooperation in the area of the creation of unitary patent protection, 2012 O.J. (L 361) 1
European Council Rules of Procedure	Rules of Procedure of the European Council, 2009 O.J. (L 315) 52
European Patent Convention	Convention on the Grant of European Patents, Oct. 5, 1973, 13 I.L.M. 268 (1974)
Foodstuffs Advertising Directive	Directive 2000/13/EC of the European Parliament and the Council of 20 March 2000 on the approximation of the laws of the member states relating to the labeling, presentation and advertising of foodstuff, O.J. 2000 (L 109) 29

Framework Consultation Directive	Directive 2002/14/EC of the European Parliament and of the Council of 11 March 2002 establishing a general framework for informing and consulting employees in the European Community, O.J. 2002 (L 80) 29
GATT	General Agreement on Tariffs and Trade, Oct. 30, 1947, 61 Stat. A-11, T.I.A.S. 1700, 55 U.N.T.S. 194
General Court Rules of Procedure	Rules of Procedure of the General Court, 2010 O.J. (C 177) 37
Geographical Indications Regulation	Council Regulation (EC) No. 510/2006 of 20 March 2006 on the protection of geographical indications and designations of origin for agricultural products and foodstuffs, 2006 O.J. (L 93) 12
Horizontal Cooperation Guidelines	Guidelines on the applicability of Art. 101(3) of the Treaty on the Functioning of the European Union to horizontal cooperation agreements, 2011 O.J. (C 11) 1
Horizontal Merger Guidelines	Guidelines on the assessment of horizontal mergers under the Council Regulation on the control of concentrations between undertakings, 2001 O.J. (C 31) 5
Information Society Directive	Directive 2001/29/EC of the European Parliament and of the Council on the harmonization of certain aspects of copyright and related rights in the information society, 2001 O.J. (L 167) 10
Interstate Commerce Guidelines	Guidelines on the effect on trade concept contained in Articles 81 and 82 of the Treaty, 2004 O.J. (C 101) 81
Late Payment Directive	Directive 2000/35/EC of the European Parliament and of the Council of 29 June 2000 on combating late payment in commercial transactions, O.J. 2000 (L 200) 35

Limited Liability Company Directive	Directive 2009/101/EC of the European Parliament and of the Council of 16 September 2009 on coordination of safeguards which, for the protection of the interests of members and third parties, are required by member states of companies within the meaning of the second paragraph of Article 48 of the Treaty, with a view to making such safeguards equivalent, 2009 O.J. (L 258) 11
Madrid Agreement	Madrid Agreement Concerning the International Registration of Marks, Apr. 14, 1891, 23 U.S.T. 1353
Madrid Protocol	Madrid Protocol for the International Registration of Marks, June 28, 1989, 2003 O.J. (L 296) 22
Market Abuse Regulation	Regulation (EU) No. 596/2014 of the European Parliament and of the Council of 16 April 2014 on market abuse, 2014 O.J. (L 173) 1
Market Definition Notice	Notice on the definition of relevant market for the purposes of European Community competition law, 1997 O.J. (C 372) 5
Medical Products Advertising Directive	Directive 2001/83/EC of the European Parliament and of the Council of 6 November 2001 on the Community code relating to medicinal products for human use, O.J. 2001 (L 311) 67
Merger Control Regulation	Council Regulation (EC) No. 139/2004 of 20 January 2004 on the control of concentrations between undertakings, 2004 O.J. (L 24) 1
Merger Treaty	Treaty Establishing a Single Council and Single Commission of the European Communities, April 8, 1965, 4 I.L.M. 776 (1965)
Misleading and Comparative Advertising Directive	Directive 2006/114/EC of the European Parliament and of the Council of 12 December 2006 concerning misleading advertising and comparative advertising, 2006 O.J. (L 376) 21

Index of Legislation and Common Names 747

New Insolvency Regulation	Regulation (EU) 2015/848 of the European Parliament and of the Council of 20 May 2015 on insolvency proceedings, 2015 O.J. (L 141) 19
Package Vacation Directive	Council Directive 90/314/EEC of 13 June 1990 on package travel, package holidays and package tours, 1990 O.J. (L 158) 59
Paris Convention	Paris Convention for the Protection of Industrial Property of 1883, March 20, 1883, 25 Stat. 1272, 828 U.N.T.S. 305, as revised at Stockholm on July 14, 1967, 53 Stat. 1748, 21 U.S.T. 1630
Paris Convention of 1883	Paris Convention for the Protection of Industrial Property of 1883, March 20, 1883, 25 Stat. 1272, 828 U.N.T.S. 305, as revised at Stockholm on July 14, 1967, 53 Stat. 1748, 21 U.S.T. 1630
Patent Cooperation Treaty of 1970	Patent Cooperation Treaty, June 19, 1970, 28 U.S.T. 7645, 1160 U.N.T.S. 231, 9 I.L.M. 978 (1970)
Private Actions Directive	Directive 2014/104/EU of the European Parliament and of the Council of 26 November 2014 on certain rules governing actions for damages under national law for infringements of the competition law provisions of the member states And of the European Union, 2014 O.J. (L 349) 1
Product Safety Directive	Directive 2001/95/EC of the European Parliament and of the Council of 3 December 2001 on general product safety, 2002 O.J. (L 11) 4
Proposed Utility Model Directive	Proposal for a European Parliament and Council Directive approximating the legal arrangements for the protection of inventions by utility model, O.J. 1998 (C 36) 13

Prospectus Directive	Directive 2003/71/EC of the European Parliament and of the Council of 4 November 2003 on the prospectus to be published when securities are offered to the public or admitted to trading and amending Directive 2001/34/EC, 2003 O.J. (L 345) 64
Public Company Capitalization Directive	Directive 2012/30/EU of the European Parliament and of the Council of 25 October 2012 on coordination of safeguards which, for the protection of the interests of members and others, are required by member states of companies within the meaning of the second paragraph of Article 54 of the Treaty on the Functioning of the European Union, in respect of the formation of public limited liability companies and the maintenance and alteration of their capital, with a view to making such safeguards equivalent, 2012 O.J. (L 315) 74
Racial and Ethnic Discrimination Directive	Council Directive 2000/43/EC Implementing the Principle of Equal Treatment Between Persons Irrespective of Racial or Ethnic Origin, 2000 O.J. (L 180) 22
R&D Block Exemption	Commission Regulation (EU) No. 1217/2010 of 14 December 2010 on the application of Article 101(3) of the Treaty on the Functioning of the European Union to certain categories of research and development agreements, 2010 O.J. (L 335) 36
Regulation 2003/1	Council Regulation (EC) No. 1/2003 of 16 December 2002 on the implementation of the rules on competition laid down in Articles 81 and 82 of the Treaty, 2003 O.J. (L 1) 1
Rental Rights Directive	Directive 2006/115/EC of the European Parliament and of the Council of 12 December 2006 on rental right and lending right and on certain rights related to copyright in the field of intellectual property, 2006 O.J. (L 376) 28

Resale Right Directive	Directive 2001/84/EC of the European Parliament and of the Council of 27 September 2001 on the resale right for the benefit of the author of an original work of art, 2001 O.J. (L 272) 32
Safeguards Regulation	Council Regulation (EC) No. 260/2009 of 26 February 2009 on the common rules for imports, 2009 O.J. (L 84) 1
Sales Representative Directive	Council Directive 86/653/EEC of 18 December 1986 on the coordination of the laws of the member states relating to self-employed commercial agents, 1986 O.J. (L 382) 17
Satellite and Cable Directive	Council Directive 93/83/EEC of 27 September 1993 on the coordination of certain rules concerning copyright and rights related to copyright applicable to satellite broadcasting and cable retransmission, 1993 O.J. (L 248) 15
SE Regulation	Council Regulation (EC) No. 2157/2001 of 8 October 2001 on the Statute for a European company, 2001 O.J. (L 294) 1
Shareholders Rights Directive	Directive 2007/36/EC of the European Parliament and of the Council of 11 July 2007 on the exercise of certain rights of shareholders in listed companies, 2007 O.J. (L 184) 17
Specialization Block Exemption	
Statute of the ESCB and ECB	Protocol on the Statute of the European System of Central Banks and of the ECB, 1992 O.J. (C 191) 68
Takeover Directive	Directive 2004/05 of the European Parliament and of the Council of 21 April 2004 on takeover bids, 2004 O.J. (L 142) 12

Technology Transfer Block Exemption	Commission Regulation No. 316/2014 of 21 March 2014 on the application of Article 101(3) of the Treaty on the Functioning of the European Union to categories of technology transfer agreements, 2014 O.J. (L 93) 17
Technology Transfer Guidelines	Guidelines on the Application of Article 101 of the Treaty on the Functioning of the European Union to technology transfer agreements, 2014 O.J. (C 89) 3
Term Directive	Directive 2006/116/EC of the European Parliament and of the Council of 12 December 2006 on the term of protection of copyright and certain related rights, 2006 O.J. (L 372) 12
TFEU	Treaty on the Functioning of the European Union (consolidated version), 2012 O.J. (C 326) 1
Timeshare Directive	Directive 2008/122/EC of the European Parliament and of the Council of 14 January 2009 on the protection of consumers in respect of certain aspects of timeshare, long-term holiday product, resale and exchange contracts, O.J. 2009 (L 33) 10
Toy Safety Directive	Directive 2009/48/EC of the European Parliament and of the Council of 18 June 2009 on the safety of toys, O.J. 2009 (L 170) 1
Trade Barriers Regulation	Council Regulation (EC) No. 3286/94 of 22 December 1994 laying down Community procedures in the field of the common commercial policy, 1994 O.J. (L 349) 71
Trade Quotas Regulation	Council Regulation (EC) No. 717/2008 of 17 July 2008 establishing a Community procedure for administering quantitative quotas, 2008 O.J. (L 198) 1

Trademark Directive	Directive 2008/95/EC of the European Parliament and of the Council of 22 October 2008 to approximate the laws of the Member States relating to trade marks, 2008 O.J. (L 299) 25
Trademark Regulation	Council Regulation (EC) No. 207/2009 of 26 February 2009 on the Community trademark, 2009 O.J. (L 78) 1
Transfer Directive	Council Directive 2001/23/EC on the approximation of the laws of the member states relating to the safeguarding of employees' rights in the event of transfers of undertakings, businesses or parts of undertakings or businesses, 2001 O.J. (L 83) 16
Transparency Directive	Directive 2004/109/EC of the European Parliament and of the Council of 15 December 2004 on the harmonization of transparency requirements in relation to information about issuers whose securities are admitted to trading on a regulated market and amending Directive 2001/34/EC, 2004 O.J. (L 390) 38
Transparency Implementing Directive	Commission Directive 2007/14/EC of 8 March 2007 laying down detailed rules for the implementation of certain provisions of Directive 2004/109/EC on the harmonisation of transparency requirements in relation to information about issuers whose securities are admitted to trading on a regulated market, 2007 O.J. (L 69) 27
Treaty of Amsterdam	Treaty of Amsterdam amending the Treaty on European Union, the Treaties establishing the European Communities and certain related acts, 1997 O.J. (C 340) 3
Treaty of Lisbon	Treaty of Lisbon amending the Treaty on European Union and the Treaty establishing the European Community, signed at Lisbon, 13 December 2007, 2007 O.J. (C 306) 1

Treaty of Nice	Treaty of Nice amending the Treaty on European Union, the Treaties establishing the European Communities, and certain related acts, 2001 O.J. (C 80) 1
TRIPS Agreement	Annex 1C to the Agreement on Trade-Related Aspects of Intellectual Property Rights, Apr. 15, 1994, Marrakesh Agreement Establishing the World Trade Organization, 33 I.L.M. 81 (1994)
Unfair Commercial Practices Directive	Directive 2005/29/EC of the European Parliament and of the Council of 11 May 2005 concerning unfair business-to-consumer commercial practices, 2005 O.J. (L 149) 22
Unfair Terms Directive	Council Directive 93/13/EEC of 5 April 1993 on unfair terms in consumer contracts, 1993 O.J. (L 95) 29
Union Customs Code	Regulation (EC) No. 450/2008 of the European Parliament and of the Council of 23 April 2008 laying down the Community Customs Code, 2008 O.J. (L 145) 1
Universal Service Directive	Directive 2002/22/EC of the European Parliament and of the Council of 7 March 2002 on universal service and users' rights relating to electronic communications networks and services, 2002 O.J. (L 108) 51
Vertical Mergers Guidelines	Guidelines on the assessment of non-horizontal mergers under the Council Regulation on the control of concentrations between undertakings, 2008 O.J. (C 265) 6
Vertical Restraints Block Exemption	Commission Regulation (EU) No. 330/2010 of 20 April 2010 on the application of Article 101(3) of the Treaty on the Functioning of the European Union to categories of vertical agreements and concerted practices, 2010 O.J. (L 102) 1

Vertical Restraints Guidelines	Guidelines on Vertical Restraints, 2010 O.J. (C 130) 1
WIPO Copyright Treaty	World Intellectual Property Organization Copyright Treaty, adopted by Diplomatic Conference at Geneva, Dec. 20, 1996, 36 I.L.M. 65 (1997)
Workers Free Movement Regulation	Regulation (EU) No. 492/2011 of the European Parliament and of the Council of 5 April 2011 on the freedom of workers within the Union, 2011 O.J. (L 141) 1
Works Council Directive	Council Directive 2009/38/EC of the European Parliament and of the Council of 6 May 2009 on the establishment of a European Works Council or a procedure in Community-scale undertakings and Community-scale groups of undertakings for the purposes of informing and consulting employees, 2009 O.J. (L 122) 28
WTO Agreement	Agreement on Trade-Related Aspects of Intellectual Property Rights, Apr. 15, 1994, Marrakesh Agreement Establishing the World Trade Organization, 33 I.L.M. 81 (1994)

Index

A

Article 29 Working Group. *See* Data Protection Working Party
Abuse exception, freedom of establishment, 386–388
Abusive conduct, 207–224
    average avoidable costs, 213*n*418
    bundling, 210–211
    conditional rebate schemes, 223
    copyright, 218
    discrimination, 212
    exceptional circumstances, 217–219
    excessive pricing, 207–210
    exclusive dealing, 220
    patents, 218–219
    predatory pricing, 212–214
    rebate and discount schemes, 220–224
    refusal to deal, 215–216
    refusal to license, 216–219
    regulatory action petitions, 214–215
    tying, 210–211
    unfair terms, imposition of, 210
    vexatious litigation, 214–215
    volume discounts, 212
Accounting Directive, 404–406
Acquisitions
    asset acquisitions, 246–247
    bankruptcy, 508
    concentrations, 246–247
    control, 245
    domestic mergers by, 410, 414
    inside information, 458
    insolvency law, 508
    intangible asset acquisitions, 246–247
    mergers by, 410, 414
Active selling, defined, 174
Admission Temporaire/Temporary Admission (ATA), 313
Ad valorem rates, 306–309

Advertising
    bait advertising, 709
    behavioral, 673–676
    comparative, 657–659, 712, 728–733
    defined, 728
    electronic commerce, 657–659, 673–676
    Internet, 673–676
    misleading advertising, 728–733
Agency agreements, 139–143. *See also* Sales agency law
Agents, 254–255, 479–481. *See also* Sales agency law
Aggressive sales practices, 708, 715
Agricultural products trademarks, 557–563
American Bar Association, 699
Ancillary restraints, 287–291
    generally, 157
    bilateral restraints, 157
    doctrine, 288–289
    intellectual property rights, 290
    noncompetition clauses, 289
    specific restraints, 289–291
    supply or purchase obligations, 290–291
Annual corporate governance statements, 409
Annual reports
    limited liability companies, 404–405
    reporting obligations, 443–444
Anti-dumping, 320–353. *See also* Anti-Dumping Regulation
    adjustment factors, 331–332
    after-sales costs, 332
    ancillary costs, 332
    captive production, 339
    circumvention, 351–353
    Combined Nomenclature, 350*n*277
    commissions, 332
    comparison requirement, 330–332

755

constructing normal value, 327–330
cooperating Union producers, 337–338
customs duties and charges, 349–350
discounts, 331
dumping, defined, 320
duties, imposition of, 349–350
excess capacity, 333
existence of dumping, 321–330
export price, 323–324
handling and loading, 332
import charges, 331
indirect taxes, 331
initiation of proceedings, 347–349
injury to Union industry, 332–341
investigation, 349
like product, 323
market share loss, 333
material injury to Union industry, 332–341
normal value, 324–330
ordinary course, 325–327
physical characteristics, 331
price reductions, 333
procedure, 347–350
product concerned, 321–322, 322n133
profits, 333
rebates, 331
safe harbor, 349
sales price as normal value, 324–327
technical assistance and services, 332
transportation, 332
Union interest, 341–347
volume discounts, 331
warranty costs, 332
Antidumping Act of 1916 (U.S.), 363
Anti-Dumping Regulation, 319–321, 331–332, 335, 351, 353, 361–362, 366–367. *See also* Anti-dumping
Anti-Subsidy/Countervailing Measures Regulation, 320, 355–356, 361–362, 366–367. *See also* Countervailing measures
Appreciability requirement, 144–145, 150–152

Appropriation, trademarks, 571
Apps, 673–676
Arbitrary discrimination, 80–81
Artists' resale rights, 624
Artists' Resale Rights Directive, 624
Asset acquisitions, 246–247
Association decisions, 141–142
ATA (Admission Temporaire/Temporary Admission), 313
Average avoidable costs, 213n418

B

Bad faith, Union trademark, 581–582
Bait advertising, 709
Bait and switch, 709
Banking crisis of 2007–2008, 22
Bankruptcy. *See* Insolvency law
Behavioral advertising, 673–676
Behavioral restraints, 245
Benchmark information, 461
Berne Convention for the Protection of Literary and Artistic Works, 363, 606–607
Bilateral restraints, 133–192
agency agreements, 139–141
agreements, 133–134
ancillary restraints, 157
appreciability requirement, 144–145, 150–152
association decisions, 141–142
block exemptions, 156
collective boycotts, 160
collusion, 133–142
commercialization, 167–168
common market effects, 145–152
competition, defined, 145
concept of restraint, 145–147
concerted practices, 134–135
consumer benefit, 154–155
contract manufacturing, 184
cultural and linguistic diversity, 190
defined, 129
De Minimis Notice, 151–152
distribution and division of markets, 171–175
dual distribution, 184–185

economic benefit, 154
EEA Agreement, 7
effect on trade between member states, 142–145
elements of violation, 133–152
environment, 191
exclusive dealing, 175
exclusive supply, 175
exemptions, 153–156
fundamental rights, 191–192
grant-back clauses, 183–184
hard-core restraints, 158–163
horizontal block exemptions, 156
horizontal cooperation, 163–169
horizontal hard-core restraints, 158–163
indispensability, 155
individual exemptions, 153–155
information exchanges, 160–162
intra-brand restraint, 172
intra-undertaking conspiracy, 138–139
joint ventures, 185–188. *See also* Joint ventures
license agreements, 180–184
market division, 159, 171–175
no challenge clauses, 184
noncompete agreements, 176
noneconomic considerations, 189–192
non-price terms of sale, 159
object or effect, 148–150
output limitation, 160
per se rule compared, 150, 158
potential effect, 143–144
price restraints, 158–159
production cooperation, 164–166
purchasing cooperation, 166–167
R&D cooperation, 163–164
rebate and discount schemes, 179–180
resale price maintenance, 169–171
Research & Development Block Exemption, 156, 164
sectorial block exemptions, 156
selective distribution, 176–179
social policies, 189–190
Specialization Block Exemption, 156
standardization, 168–169
strategic data exchanges, 162
substantial competition, 155
tacit acquiescence, 136–138
Technology Transfer Block Exemption, 156, 180–183
tying, 179
vertical agreements with horizontal implications, 184–185
vertical block exemptions, 156
vertical restraints, 169–184. *See also* Vertical restraints
Vertical Restraints Block Exemption, 156, 174–176, 180–181, 184–185
Binding tariff information (BTI), 298–299
Biology Directive, 51
Biotechnology Patent Directive, 600–601
Biotechnology patents, 599–603
  biotechnological inventions, defined, 600
  human cloning, 601
  material, 602–603
  patentability, 600–602
  plant and animal varieties, 601
  public policy, 601–602
  scope, 602–603
Boycotts, collective, 160
Breakthrough rule, 426
Bricks-and-mortar stores, 664
Broadcasting
  copyright, 623–624
  electronic commerce, 655
Brokerage costs, 307
Brussels Convention, 659
Brussels I Regulation, 243
BTI (Binding tariff information), 298–299
B2B. *See* Business-to-business (B2B) exchanges
Bundling, 210–211, 280–282
Business-to-business (B2B) exchanges, 660–661, 716

Buy-Back Implementation Regulation, 421
Buybacks. *See* Share buybacks

C

Caching, 609–610, 672
Capacity usage, 272–273
Capital
    defined, 102
    free movement of, 102–113. *See also* Free movement of capital
    limited liability companies. *See* Capitalization of limited liability companies
    nonfungible capital, 432
    subscribed capital, 397–399
Capitalization of limited liability companies, 397–403
    hostile takeovers, 400–401
    increases in share capital, 401–402
    initial capitalization, 397–399
    in-kind contributions, 399, 402
    loans, 401
    money market instruments, 399
    reduction of share capital, 402–403
    share buybacks, 400–401, 421, 462
    subscribed capital, 397–399
    transferable securities, 399
Captive production, 339
Causation
    confusion, 712–713
    countervailing measures, 356–357
    solicitation of sales, 713, 714
CCC (Customs Cooperation Council), 300
CCT. *See* Common Customs Tariff
ccTLD (Country code top-level domain) authorities, 548, 665–666
CE (Conformité Européene) mark, 125
CEN (European Committee for Standardization), 124, 168–169
CENELEC (European Committee for Electrotechnical Standardization), 124, 168–169
Center of main interest (COMI), 469
Certain and direct requirement, 72–73

Certification service providers (CSPs), 652
Charge equivalent to customs duty, defined, 60
Charter of Fundamental Rights of the European Union, 40, 649
Choice of law rules, insolvency law, 476–477
Circumvention of anti-dumping, 351–353
Clayton Act (U.S.), 246
Codes of conduct, 713
Collective boycotts, 160
Collective dominance, 204–206
Collective marks, 549
Collective Redundancies Directive, 515, 517
Collective redundancy, 514–517
    consultation requirements, 516–517
    establishments, 516
    notification of, 517
    qualification of, 515–516
Collusion, 133–142
    agency agreements, 139–143
    agreements, 133–134
    association decisions, 141–142
    bilateral restraints, 133–142
    concerted practices, 134–135
    intra-undertaking conspiracy, 138–139
    tacit acquiescence, 136–138
Colors, trademarks, 553–555
Combined Nomenclature, 295–297, 300, 350n277
COMI (center of main interest), 469
Commerce Department, U.S., 691–694
Commercial agents, 479–481
Commercialization, 167–168
Common commercial policy, 313–368
    anti-dumping, 320–353. *See also* Anti-dumping
    competitive strategy, 367–368
    countervailing measures, 353–360. *See also* Countervailing measures
    dispute settlement, 315–318

Index

DSB, 315–318
international regimes, 313–319.
  See also International regimes
parallel application of trade and competition law, 367
political considerations, 317–318
procedure, 362
relation to competition law, 367–368
remedies, 366
safeguard measures, 361–362
trade barriers, 362–366. *See also* Trade barriers
trade instruments, 319–320
trade law vs. competition law, 367–368
trade measures, relationship between, 366–367
Uruguay Round, 314–315
WTO, 313–314
WTO Appellate Body, 316, 318
Common Customs Code, 297–298
Common Customs Tariff (CCT), 294–298, 300, 309
Company law, 369–428
  annual corporate governance statement, 409
  corporate forms, 384–385
  corporate governance, 408–409
  divisions of companies, 417–420
  external directors, role of, 409
  freedom of establishment, 385–388. *See also* Freedom of establishment
  legislation, 389
  limited liability companies. *See* Limited liability companies
  mergers, 409–417. *See also* Mergers
  national company law, 384–385
  overview, 369–370
  pan-European corporate forms, 370–385. *See also* Corporate forms
  private limited companies, 393
  private limited partnerships, 392–393
  registration systems, 404
  remuneration of directors, 408
  shareholder meetings, 393–397.
    See also Shareholder meetings
  takeovers, 420–428. *See also* Takeovers
  taxonomy, 389–393
Comparative advertising. *See* Directive on Comparative Advertising; Misleading and comparative advertising
Compensation right, 483–485
Compensatory fees, 62
Competition, regulation of, 127–291.
  See also Market manipulation; Merger Control Regulation; Mergers
  active selling, defined, 174
  ancillary restraints, 157
  bilateral restraints. *See* Bilateral restraints
  block exemptions, 156
  Brussels I Regulation, 243
  character of competition law, 128
  claims for damages, 242
  competition, defined, 145
  competition law vs. trade law, 367–368
  consumer benefit, 154–155
  context, 127–129
  contingency fees, 242
  corporate veil, 237
  damage claims, 242
  dawn raids, 158n147
  economic benefit, 154
  electronic commerce, 660–664
  employees or workers, 131
  EU law, extraterritorial application of, 235–236
  EU law, parallel application of, 234–235
  EU law vs. national law, 232–234
  European Commission, 9, 128
  European courts, 128
  exemptions, 153–156
  free movement rules, relationship to, 128–129

funding actions, 242
horizontal block exemptions, 156
horizontal issues, 660–662
indispensability, 155
individual exemptions, 153–155
intellectual property rights vs., 649–650
intra-brand restraint, 172
jurisdictional issues, 232–236
liability for violations, 236–240
multilateral restraints, 133
natural persons, 131
parent company liability, 236–238
passive selling, defined, 174
piercing corporate veil, 237
private enforcement, 240–243
purpose, 127–128
relation to national law, 232–234
Research & Development Block Exemption, 156, 164
sectorial block exemptions, 156
Specialization Block Exemption, 156
state action, 226–232. *See also* State action
structural restraints, 243–291. *See also* Structural restraints
substantial competition, 155
successor liability, 239–240
taxonomy, 129
Technology Transfer Block Exemption, 156, 180–183
trade law vs., 367–368
undertakings, 130–133
unilateral restraint. *See* Unilateral restraint
vertical block exemptions, 156
Vertical Restraints Block Exemption, 156, 174–176, 180–181, 184–185
vicarious liability, 238
violations of, 236–240
Complex products, 627n592
Compulsion, 230–232
Compulsory license, 643
Computer programs
consumer protection, 707
copyright, 620–622
interoperability, 622
requirements for protection, 621
routers, 609–610
scope of rights, 621–622
servers, 609–610
term, 622
Computer Software Directive, 608, 621, 640, 644–645
Concentrations, 245–255
agents, 254–255
asset acquisitions, 246–247
common ownership, 245–246
contractual control, 247–249
control, acquisition of, 245
control, concept of, 246–247
de facto control, 247–249, 257
distributors, 254–255
franchisees, 254–255
intangible asset acquisitions, 246–247
joint and sole control, 249–251
joint ventures, 186–187, 249–253
legal control, 247–249
minority interests, 247n603
procedural analysis, 245–255
related parties, 254–255
same parties, 253–254
sole and joint control, 249–251
strategic decisions, 246
types, 245–246
Concentrative joint ventures, 186–187
Concerted practices, 134–135
Conciliation Committees, 46
Conditional rebate schemes, 223
Conferral, 48–49
Confidentiality
anti-dumping, 349
conflicts of interest, 396
data privacy, 696
employee consultation, 526
Conflicts of interest, 396. *See also* Confidentiality
Conformité Européene (CE) mark, 125
Confusion

Index 761

likelihood of, 563–568, 573–574, 586–587
OHIM, 564
practices causing, 712–713
Conglomerate effects, 280–283
Consumer benefit, bilateral restraints, 154–155
Consumer contracts, 715–728
   B2B, 716
   concluding, 715–723
   content, 724–728
   distance sales, 715–723. *See also* Distance sales
   information society services, 716*n*83, 720
   model withdrawal forms, 721
   off-premises sales, 717, 720, 723
   on-premises sales, 717, 720–721, 723
   pre-contractual information obligations, 718–721
   price terms, 728
   taxes, 728
   types of consumer sales, 715–717
   unfair terms, 724–728
   VAT, 728
   withdrawal rights, 721–723
Consumer Credit Directive, 653, 702, 706
Consumer Guarantees Directive, 653, 702
Consumer Interest Injunctions Directive, 653, 702
Consumer interests, 359–360. *See also* Consumer protection
Consumer Product Pricing Directive, 653, 702, 728
Consumer protection, 701–737
   B2B commerce, 716
   comparative advertising. *See* Misleading and comparative advertising
   consumer, defined, 654*n*19, 705
   damages, 736
   defective, defined, 735
   defects, 734–737
   defenses, 737
   digital content, 707
   electronic commerce, 652–655
   enforcement, 703–704
   goods and services, 706–707
   legislation, 701–703
   liability, 736–737
   misleading and comparative advertising, 728–733. *See also* Misleading and comparative advertising
   national law, 707
   online transactions, 707
   producer, defined, 736
   product, defined, 734, 735
   product safety and defects, 733–737
   safety, 734
   sales, 704–728. *See also* Sales
   scope, 704–707
   software, 707
   strict liability, 736
   traders, 704–705
   unfair commercial practices, 707–711
Consumer Rights Directive, 702, 707, 715–716, 718*n*97, 719, 721–724
Contingency fees, 242
Contract manufacturing, 184
Controller, defined, 683
Convention on the Grant of European Patents, 592
Conversion, 375–376, 380, 438
Convertible debt, 431–432
Cookies, 673–676
Copenhagen Criteria, 5
Copyright, 605–624
   abusive conduct, 218
   artists' resale rights, 624
   broadcasters, 623–624
   caching, 609–610
   circumvention, 669
   computer programs, 620–622
   database protection, 614–620. *See also* Database protection
   distribution rights, 613, 668
   duration of protection, 613–614, 620
   electronic commerce, 667–671

EU copyright law, 608
exceptions, 609–611
exhaustion of rights doctrine, 644–645
films, 605, 609, 613, 623, 668
international conventions, 606–608
lending rights, 622–623
license refusal, 218
performers, 623–624
phonograms, 605, 607–609, 613–614, 623, 668
public communication rights, 612–613, 668–669
public, defined, 612–613
remedies, 670
rental rights, 622–623
reproduction rights, 608–611, 667–668
resale rights, 624
routers, 609–610
servers, 609–610
source of rights, 606–608
transient reproductions, 609–610
Copyright Act (U.S.), 363
Copyright Directive, 613
Copyright Term Directive, 608
Corporate forms, 370–385
    EEIG, 382–384. *See also* European Economic Interest Grouping
    national company law, 384–385
    SE, 370–382. *See also* Societas Europeae
Corporate governance, 408–409
Corporate veil, 237
Council of Europe, 7–8
Countervailing measures, 353–360.
    See also Anti-Subsidy/Countervailing Measures Regulation
causation, 356–357
consequences, 360
consumer interests, 359–360
elements, 354–358
injury, 355–356
public body, defined, 354–355
subsidy, defined, 354
Union interest, 358–360
WTO Agreement on Subsidies and Countervailing Measures, 353
Country code top-level domain (ccTLD) authorities, 548, 665–666
Country of origin, duty amount determinations, 303–306
Credit institutions and securities law, 432
Creditors' rights, 474–475
Cross-border mergers, 414–417.
    See also Mergers
experts, 416
impact reports, 416
implementation, 415–417
limited liability companies, 415, 417
pre-merger certificates, 416–417
recognition of, 415
share-exchange ratio, 416
Cross-Border Mergers Directive, 392, 415–417, 512–514
Cross-elasticity of demand, 194–196
CSPs (Certification service providers), 652
Customs Cooperation Council (CCC), 300
Customs duties and charges
abolition of, 59–62
amount determinations, 298–310.
    See also Duty amount determinations
anti-dumping, 349–350
CCT, 294–298, 300, 309
charge equivalent to customs duty, defined, 60
Combined Nomenclature, 295–296, 300, 350n277
compensatory fees, 61–62
duties, defined, 293
duty rates, 296–297
external transit, 310–311
internal taxation, 61–62
internal transit, 313
inward processing, 311–312
mixtures, 301–302

Index 763

outward processing, 312
processing under customs control, 312
prohibition of, 59–62
purpose, 294
quotas, 309–310
relief from, 310–313
TARIC system, 297
temporary importation, 312–313
TFEU, 59–60, 62
TIR carnet, 311
warehousing, 311
Customs law, 293–313
   absolute quotas, 294
   CCT, 294–298, 300, 309
   Combined Nomenclature, 295–296, 300
   Common Customs Code, 297–298
   customs unions, 8–9, 11, 57–58, 293–294
   duties and charges. *See* Customs duties and charges; Duty amount determinations
   external transit, 310–311
   Implementing Regulation, 297
   internal transit, 313
   inward processing, 311–312
   outward processing, 312
   processing under customs control, 312
   quotas, 294, 309–310
   tariff quotas, 294
   temporary importation, 312–313
   Union Customs Code, 297–299, 309, 311–312
   Union goods, defined, 293–294
Customs territory, defined, 57*n*1
Customs unions, 8–9, 11, 57–58, 293–294
Customs warehousing, 311
Cybersquatting, 665–666

D

Damages. *See also* Remedies
   competition, regulation of, 242
   consumer protection, 736
   electronic commerce, 670

Dassonville Formula, 68
Database Directive, 608, 614–617, 620
Database protection, 614–620
   copyright protection, 616–617
   database, defined, 615
   duration, 620
   electronic commerce, 665
   exhaustion of rights doctrine, 645
   extraction, 619–620
   reutilization, 619–620
   scope, 620
   sui generis right/database right, 617–620
   types, 615–620
Data integrity, 693
Data privacy, 677–699
   applicable law, 681
   breaches, 697
   compliance alternatives, 687–695
   confidentiality, 696
   consent, 694–695
   controller, defined, 683
   data processing, 679–680
   data subjects, 684
   derogations, 694–695
   discovery vs., 698–699
   enforcement, 682–684
   legal norms, 677
   national law, 680–681
   permitted processing, 685–686
   personal data, 678–679
   preemption, 680–681
   private enforcement, 683–684
   processing principles, 684–685
   prohibited transfers, 686–687
   public enforcement, 682–683
   registration, 682
   relation to U.S. discovery, 698–699
   scope, 678–680
   security obligations, 695–697
   transfers to nonmember states, 686–695. *See also* Data transfers to nonmember states
   U.S. compliance codes, 697–698
   whistleblowers, 697–698

Data Privacy Directive, 42, 676–699
Data processing, 679–680
Data Protection Working Party, 678–679, 682, 689, 697–699
Data subjects, 684
Data transfers to nonmember states, 686–695
   access, 693
   adequacy determinations, 688–690
   Argentina, 687
   Canada, 687
   contractual clauses, 690–691
   data integrity, 693
   enforcement, 693–694
   framework, 689–690
   Guernsey, 687
   Hungary, 687
   notice, 692
   onward transfer, 692
   safe harbor, 691–694
   security, 692–693
   self-assessment, 693
   Switzerland, 687
   TRUSTe, 693
   United States, 687–688
   WebTrust, 693
Dawn raids, 158n147
Debt instruments, 431
Deceptive practices, 711–712
De facto control, 247–249, 257
Default works council, 525
Defective, defined, 735
Defective Products Directive, 653, 702, 733–737
Defenses
   consumer protection, 737
   failing firm defense, 283–285
   takeovers, 425–427
Deficit procedure, 15–20
Demand substitution, 194–196
De Minimis Notice, 151–152
Depositary receipts, 431
Derogations, 14–15
   data privacy, 694–695
   Euro Group, 14–15
   GATT, 58

Descriptive marks, 539–541
Designation of origin, 558–560, 562
Design Directive, 626
Design patents, 587
Design Regulation, 626–627, 632, 634
Design rights, 625–637
   complex products, 627n592
   components, 627
   concept of design, 627
   conflict with other designs, 635
   design, defined, 625
   disadvantage of registration, 636
   duration, 634
   exhaustion of rights doctrine, 644
   failure to meet requirements, 634–635
   freedom in developing, 631–632
   function, not dictated by, 632–633
   individual character, 629–632
   informed user, defined, 629–630
   invalidity, 634–636
   newness, 627–629
   OHIM, 625–636
   public morals, 632
   public policy, 632
   registration, 633, 636
   requirements for protection, 627–633
   scope of protection, 633–634
   source of law, 626
   successors in interest, 633–634
   trademarks, 625
   unauthorized incorporation, 635–636
   unregistered designs, 636–637
   user, defined, 629
Digital content, 707
Direct discrimination, 495
Directive on Comparative Advertising, 12, 659
Directive on Transparency Requirements for Issuers of Public Securities, 42
Directive on Unfair Terms in Consumer Contracts. *See* Unfair Terms Directive

Directives. *See also specific directives*
   freedom to conduct business, 100
   harmonization, 123–124
   regulations vs., 41
   as sources of law, 41–43
Directors
   external directors, role of, 409
   remuneration of, 408
Disclosure requirements
   inside information, 456–457
   limited liability companies, 403–404
   market abuse, 463–464
   securities law, 446
   takeovers, 424–425
Discounts. *See* Rebate and discount schemes
Discovery, 32–33, 241–242, 698–699
Discrimination
   abusive conduct, 212
   arbitrary discrimination, 80–81
   direct discrimination, 495
   equal treatment, 85–86
   ethnic discrimination, 502–504
   gender discrimination, 55, 500–502
   indirect discrimination, 495–496
   intellectual property rights, 638
   nationality discrimination, 53, 490–499
   occupational requirements, 502
   racial discrimination, 502–504
Dispute settlement, 315–318, 363, 365–366, 666
Dispute Settlement Body (DSB), 315–318
Dispute Settlement Mechanism (DSM), 315–318
Distance Marketing of Consumer Financial Services Directive, 653, 702, 706
Distance sales, 715–723
   as consumer contract, 715–717
   language issues, 719
   pre-contractual information obligations, 718–720
   withdrawal rights, 721–723
Distance Selling Directive, 80, 654, 656–657
Distinctiveness, 539–544, 566, 585–587
Distribution and division of markets
   bilateral restraints, 171–175
   markets, 159
   vertical restraints, 171–175
Distribution license, 643–644, 668
Distribution rights
   copyright, 613, 668
   electronic commerce, 668
Distributions to shareholders, 403
Diversity, cultural and linguistic, 190
Division of Companies Directive, 417–420
Divisions of companies, 417–420
   experts, 419
   implementation, 419–420
   prospectus, obligation to publish, 438
   recognition, 418–419
   shareholder meetings, 419–420
Domain names, 547–548
Domestic mergers, 409–414
   by acquisition, 410, 414
   experts, 413
   by formation, 410–411
   implementation, 412–414
   public limited liability companies, 412
   recognition, 410–412
   shareholder meetings, 413–414
   subsidiaries, 411, 412n212
   terms of, 412–413
Domestic Mergers Directive, 376n28, 391, 409–414, 415
Dominance, 192–204
   collective dominance, 204–206
   cross-elasticity of demand, 194–196
   demand substitution, 194–196
   dimensions of relevant market, 193
   evidence to define markets, 197–198
   factors beyond market share, 200–204
   geographic dimension, 198–200
   intellectual property rights, 202–203

market entry, 201–202
market share, importance of, 192–200
product market definition, 193–198
profits and prices, 203–204
relative market share, 200–201
relevant market dimensions, 193
substantive analysis, 266
supply substitution, 196–197
vertical integration, 201
DRAMs (Dynamic Random Access Memories), 317
DSB (Dispute Settlement Body), 315–318
DSM (Dispute Settlement Mechanism), 315–318
Dual distribution, 184–185
Dualist legal systems, 52n252
Dumping. *See* Anti-dumping
Duty amount determinations, 298–310. *See also* Customs duties and charges
ad valorem rates, 306–309
brokerage costs, 307
BTI, 298–299
CCT administration, 298, 309
classification, 298–303
container costs, 307
country of origin, 303–306
declaration, 298–299
fixed rates, 306–309
Generalized System of Preferences, 304
insurance costs, 307
license fees, 308
mineral products, 304
mixtures, 301–302
packaging costs, 307
quotas, 309–310
royalties, 308
sales commissions, 307
transport costs, 307
value, 306–309
Dynamic Random Access Memories (DRAMs), 317

E

ECB. *See* European Central Bank
ECJ. *See* European Court of Justice
E-commerce. *See* Electronic commerce
E-Commerce Directive, 653–657, 659–660, 703, 720, 724
ECSC Treaty (Treaty of Paris), 1–2
EEA (European Economic Area), 6–7
EEC. *See* European Economic Community
EEC Treaty (Treaty Establishing the European Community), 2–3
EEIG. *See* European Economic Interest Grouping
EFTA (European Free Trade Association), 6–7
Electronic commerce, 651–699
advanced electronic signatures, 652
advertising, 657–659, 673–676
applicable law, 659–660
apps, 673–676
behavioral advertising, 673–676
bricks-and-mortar stores, 664
broadcasting, 655
B2B exchanges, 660–661
caching, 672
ccTLDs, 665–666
challenges, 651
circumvention, 669
comparative advertising, 657–659
competition law, 660–664
consumer, defined, 654n19
consumer protection, 652–655
contract content, 657
contract formation, 652, 655–656
cookies, 673–676
copyright, 667–671
CSPs, 652
cybersquatting, 665–666
damages, 670
database protection, 665
data privacy, 677–699. *See also* Data privacy
distribution rights, 668
electronic mail, 655, 676

encryption, 669
file sharing, 651
fingerprinting, 675–676
framing, 672
gTLDs, 665–666
horizontal issues, 660–662
information society services, 655, 660, 720
injunctive relief, 670
Internet promotion, 657–659
Internet, regulation of commercial practices involving, 673–676
Internet solicitation, 657–659
ISPs, 670
keyword searches, 666–667
linking, 671–672
meta tagging, 672–673
promotion, 657–659
public communication, 668–669
qualified certificates, 652
remedies, 670
reproduction rights, 667–668
rights-management information obligations, 670–671
scrambling, 669
secure-signature-creation device, 652
smart phones, 675
solicitation, 657–659
spam, 676
standardization, 660–662
tracking devices, 673–676
trademarks, 665–667
transactions involving consumers, 655–657
URLs, 671
vertical issues, 662–664
withdrawal rights, 656–657
Electronic mail, 655, 676
Electronic means, defined, 655
Electronic signatures, 652
Electronic Signatures Directive, 652
Employee consultation, 521–527
    applicable law, 521
    confidentiality, 526
    default provisions, 525–526
    default works council, 525
    employee information and consultation procedure, 522–525
    good faith negotiation, 523
    group of undertakings, 522n179
    inability to reach agreement, 525–526
    non-EU companies, application to, 526–527
    small and medium-sized companies, 527
    works council establishment, 522–525
Employee share plans, 436, 438, 461
Employees or workers
    confidentiality, 526
    consultation. *See* Employee consultation
    employee, defined, 518
    employee rights, 509–514
    employee share plans. *See* Employee share plans
    employer insolvency, protection in event of, 519–520
    negotiating with employees, 514
    part-time workers, 493
Employer Insolvency Directive, 518–521
Employer insolvency, protection in event of, 517–521
    employee, defined, 518
    exceptions, 520–521
    guarantee institutions, 519–520
    protections for employees, 519–520
    scope of Directive, 518
Employment, access to, 496–497
Encryption, 669
Environment, 11, 191
EPO. *See* European Patent Office
ePrivacy Directive, 676, 696–697
Equal treatment, 85–86
Equal Treatment Framework Directive, 502
Equity securities, 431
ERM II, 20

ESCB (European System of Central Banks), 20–21
ESMA. *See* European Securities and Markets Authority
Establishment. *See* Freedom of establishment
Ethnic discrimination, 502–504
ETSI (European Telecommunications Standards Institute), 124, 168–169
EU Council
   configurations, 28
   European Council distinguished, 27–29
   fiscal discipline, 17–20
   group presidency, 28
   as institution, 23, 27–29
   legislative procedures, 45–47
   organization, 28–29
   product concerned, 322
   recommendations, 43–44
   suspension of membership, 6
   Union Customs Code, 309
   withdrawal agreements, 5
EU dimension
   initial test, 257–258
   lack of, 258–260
   legitimate interests of member states, 264
   procedural analysis, 255–265
   referral to member states, 263
   review procedure, 260
   sales, 256–258
   structural restraints, 255–265
   supplementary test, 257–258
   thresholds, 255–258
   transactions as concentrations under national law, 264
EU patent court, 47
EU Patent Regulation, 598
Euratom Treaty, 1–2
Euro Group. *See also* European monetary union
   Austria, 14
   Belgium, 14
   convergence criteria, 14–15
   Cyprus, 14–15
   defined, 13
   derogations, 14–15
   ESCB, 20
   Estonia, 14–15
   euro, introduction of, 13
   exchange rate criterion, 14
   expulsion, 18
   Finland, 14
   fiscal discipline, 15–20
   France, 14
   Germany, 14
   Greece, 14–15
   inflation rate criterion, 14
   interest rate criterion, 14
   Ireland, 14
   Italy, 14
   Latvia, 14–15
   Lithuania, 14–15, 20
   Luxembourg, 14
   Malta, 14–15
   membership, 13–15
   Netherlands, 14
   Portugal, 14
   price stability, 14
   public deficit criterion, 14
   Slovak Republic, 14–15
   Slovenia, 14–15
   Spain, 14
European Atomic Energy Community, 1–2
European Central Bank (ECB)
   ERM II, 20
   ESCB, 20–21
   exchange rates, 20
   as institution, 23
   Monetary Committee, 17
   monetary policy, 21–22
European Coal and Steel Community, 1–2
European Commission
   CCT, 309
   College of Commissioners, 24
   delegated acts, 25–26
   enforcement, 39
   as executive branch of EU, 26–27

fiscal discipline, 16–17
Guidelines on the Effect on Trade Concept, 45
implementing acts, 25–26
as institution, 23–27
Interstate Trade Guidelines, 45
jurisdiction, 10
legislative functions, 25
legislative procedures, 45–47
makeup of, 9
nonlegislative acts, 25–26
number of commissioners, 24
organization, 24–25
recommendations, 43–44
referrals by, 263
referrals to, 258–260
review procedure, 260
suspension of membership, 6
Union interest, 344
European Committee for Electrotechnical Standardization (CENELEC), 124, 168–169
European Committee for Standardization (CEN), 124, 168–169
European Convention on Human Rights, 7–8
European Council
consumer protection, 703
EU Council distinguished, 27–29
as institution, 27
European Court of Auditors, 23, 31
European Court of Human Rights, 7–8
European Court of Justice (ECJ)
enforcement, 39
European Commission function, 26–27
as institution, 23
interpretation methods, 37–39
legal system, 10–12
legislation, challenges to, 50
preliminary rulings, 33–34
ratio legis, 38
referrals to, 33–34
sanctions imposed by, 35–36
statutory interpretation, 38
structure, 31–32
TFEU, 32
European courts, 31–39. *See also specific courts*
codified legal norms, 36–37
composition, 31–33
enforcement, 39
evidence, 32–33
function, 31–33
interpretation methods, 36–39
jurisdiction, 33–36
language issues, 37, 39, 47, 190
law sources, 40–48. *See also* Sources of law
preliminary rulings, 33–34
structure, 31–33
European Data Privacy Supervisor, 682
European Data Protection Officers, 682
European Data Protection Panel, 694
European Economic Area (EEA), 6–7
European Economic Community (EEC)
establishment, 1
institutional and legal context, 1–3
membership, 4
European Economic Interest Grouping (EEIG), 382–384
amendment of formation agreements, 383
corporate form, 370
duration, 383
establishment, 382–383
joint and several liability, 384
liability, 384
management, 383–384
purpose, 383
taxation, 384
European Free Trade Agreement, 8
European Free Trade Association (EFTA), 6–7
European General Court
jurisdiction, 36
statutory interpretation, 38–39
structure, composition, and function, 31–32
European Investment Bank, 18
European Issuers, 394
European monetary union, 13–23

ECB. *See* European Central Bank
ERM II, 20
ESCB, 20–21
Euro Group. *See* Euro Group
Eurosystem, 22
excessive deficit procedure, 15–20
exchange rates, 20
fiscal discipline, 15–20
institutions of, 20–23
SSM, 22–23
European Parliament
as institution, 23, 29–30
legislative procedures, 45–47
makeup of, 9
political powers, 30
powers, 9, 29–30
suspension of membership, 6
withdrawal agreements, 5
European Patent Convention, 47, 588, 592–600, 603
European Patent Office (EPO), 592–599, 620
European patents, 592–599. *See also* Patents
advantages, 599
disadvantages, 599
industrial application, 597
inventive step, 595
nonpatentable subject matters, 594–595
novelty, 595–597
patentability, 593
process for securing, 597–598
requirements, 593–597
unitary effect, 598
European Securities and Markets Authority (ESMA), 429, 431, 433, 443, 460, 462
European System of Central Banks (ESCB), 20–21
European Telecommunications Standards Institute (ETSI), 124, 168–169
Eurostat, 15
Eurosystem, 22
Excessive deficit procedure, 15–20

Excessive pricing, 207–210
Exclusive dealing, 175, 220
Exclusive supply, 175
Exhaustion of rights doctrine, 639–647
compulsory license, 643
consent of IP owner, 642–644
copyright, 644–645
database, 645
design rights, 644
distribution license, 643–644
intangible products, 641–642
license to distribute, 643–644
patents, 644
plant variety rights, 645
repackaging limitation, 645–647
sale in EEA, 640–642
trademark, 646–647
Export price, 323–324
Expressions, trademarks, 545–547
External directors, role of, 409
External liability, 407
External trade, 293–368
common commercial policy, 313–368. *See also* Common commercial policy
customs law, 293–313. *See also* Customs law
External transit, 310–311

F
Failing firm defense, 283–285
Fairness, presumption of, 428
Fair, reasonable, and nondiscriminatory terms (FRAND terms), 219
False or misleading information, 461
False practices, 711
Federal Trade Commission (U.S.; FTC), 245, 694
Fictitious devices, 460
Fiduciary duties, 379–380
Fifth Company Law Directive, 408
File sharing, 651
Films, 605, 609, 613, 623, 668
Financial institutions, supervision of, 109
Financial services
contracts, 716

insolvency law, 477
Financial statements, 404–405
Fingerprinting, 675–676
Fiscal discipline, 15–20
Fiscal supervision justification, 118–119
Fisheries policy, 11
Fishing rights, 59
Fixed rates, 306–309
Foodstuffs Advertising Directive, 703, 706
Foodstuffs trademarks, 557–563
Forum, 469–472, 476–477
Forum shopping, 476–477
Framework Consultation Directive, 521–522
Framing, 672
Franchisees, 254–255
FRAND terms (fair, reasonable, and nondiscriminatory terms), 219
Freedom of establishment. *See also* Right of establishment
   abuse exception, 386–388
   company law, implications for, 385–388
   free movement of capital and, 105
   limitations, 386–387
   mutual recognition, 385
   services vs., 82–85
Freedom to conduct business, 82–102
   application sphere, 88–90
   cross-border element, 91–93
   deterrence of, 86–87
   directives, 100
   equal treatment, 85–86
   EU nationality, 88–90
   exceptions, 93–100
   freedom of establishment vs. services, 82–85
   free movement of goods compared, 100–102
   judicially created exceptions, 95–98
   legal bases, 82–85
   official authority, 94–95
   overriding requirements, 95–98
   preconditions for exceptions, 98–100
   prohibited restrictions, 87
   public health, 93–94, 100
   public interest, 99–100
   public policy, 93–94
   public security, 93–94
   restriction, defined, 85
   right of establishment, 88–89, 91–93
   services, defined, 83
   services, right to provide, 89–90
   state measures, 90–91
   substantive standard, 85–87
Free movement of capital, 102–113
   basic prohibition, 102–106
   capital, defined, 102
   exceptions, 107–113
   financial institutions, supervision of, 109
   freedom of establishment and, 105
   free movement of services and, 105–106
   geographic scope, 104
   Golden Share cases, 104, 112
   indistinctly applicable restrictions, 104
   overriding requirements, 107–109
   private restrictions, 106
   proportionality, 111
   public policy, 107–109
   public security, 107–109
   relationship to other free movement principles, 105–106
   requirements for application of exceptions, 111–113
   restrictions, 102–104
   right of establishment, restrictions on, 109–110
   state measures, 106–107
   supervision of financial institutions, 109
   third countries, exceptions applicable to, 110
Free movement of goods, 59–82
   certain and direct requirement, 72–73
   customs duties and charges, abolition of, 59–62. *See also* Customs duties and charges

exceptions, enumerated in TFEU, 73–77
freedom to conduct business compared, 100–102
goods benefiting from, 81–82
imperative requirements doctrine, 71–72
intellectual property rights, 76–77, 638–639
limitations by ECJ, 68–73
public morality, 74
public policy, 74
public security, 74
quantitative restrictions and equivalents, 62–68. *See also* Quantitative restrictions and equivalents
requirements, 71–73
selling arrangements, 68–71, 80
Free movement of labor, 490–499. *See also* Employees or workers
access to employment, 496–497
beneficiaries of prohibition, 493–495
deterrence of, 496
direct discrimination, 495
employment, access to, 496–497
entry and residence, 497
family, 498
indirect discrimination, 495–496
internal market, 82
interstate commerce requirement, 492
limitations on, 498–499
part-time workers, 493
public service, 499
relocation, 497
remuneration, 493–494
social benefits, 497–498
state measures, 491–492
substantive protection, 495–498
Free movement of services, 7, 83, 90, 101, 105–106
Free speech, 48
Free trade areas, 8, 57–58. *See also* North American Free Trade Agreement (NAFTA)

FTC. *See* Federal Trade Commission
Fundamental rights, 191–192. *See also* International law

G

GATS (General Agreement on Trade in Services), 315
GATT. *See* General Agreement on Tariffs and Trade
Gender discrimination, 55, 500–502
General Agreement on Tariffs and Trade (GATT)
Article I, 58
Article XXIV, 58n3
background, 314–315
derogations, 58
protective action, 361
quotas, 309
tariff concessions, 297
General Agreement on Trade in Services (GATS), 315
Generalized System of Preferences, 304
Generic top level domains (gTLDs), 665–666
Generic trademarks, 580
Geneva Act, 626
Genuine use, 578–580, 584
Geographical indication, 558–560, 562
Geographic dimension, 198–200
Geographic origin marks, 556–557
Golden Share cases, 104, 112
Gramm-Leach-Bliley Act (U.S.), 680
Grant-back clauses, 183–184
Graphic representability, 537–538
Group of undertakings, 522n179
gTLDs (Generic top level domains), 665–666
Guarantee institutions, 519–520
Guernsey, data transfers to nonmember states, 687
Guidance on Vertical Restraints, 663
Guidelines on the Effect on Trade Concept, 45
Gustatory marks, 556

H

Hague Agreement for the International Registration of Industrial Designs, 626
Hard-core restraints
    horizontal. *See* Horizontal hard-core restraints
    vertical, 183
Harmonization, 123–125. *See also* Office of Harmonization in the Internal Market
Harmonized Commodity Description and Coding System (HCDCS), 295–296
Harmonized System of Explanatory Notes, 295
Hart-Scott-Rodino Antitrust Improvements Act of 1976 (U.S.), 243–245
Havana Charter, 313
HCDCS (Harmonized Commodity Description and Coding System), 295–296
Health, protection of. *See* Public health
Holding companies, SE as, 373–375
Home member states, 434, 439–442, 447–448
Horizontal block exemptions, 156
Horizontal cooperation, 163–169
    commercialization, 167–168
    production cooperation, 164–166
    purchasing cooperation, 166–167
    R&D cooperation, 163–164
    standardization, 168–169
Horizontal hard-core restraints, 158–163
    collective boycotts, 160
    information exchanges, 160–162
    market division, 159
    non-price terms of sale, 159
    output limitation, 160
    price restraints, 158–159
    strategic data exchanges, 162
    Technology Transfer Block Exemption, 182
Horizontal issues, electronic commerce, 660–662
Horizontal mergers, substantive analysis, 269–270
Hostile takeovers, 400–401
Host member states, 439–442, 447
Human cloning, 601

I

ICANN. *See* Internet Corporation for Assigned Names and Numbers
Identical marks, 563, 572–573, 582–583
IFRSs (International Financial Reporting Standards), 449
IMF (International Monetary Fund), 313
Impact reports, 416
Imperative requirements doctrine, 71–72
Implementing Regulation, 297
Indemnification payment, 485
Indirect discrimination, 495–496
Indirect taxes, 331
Information exchanges, 160–162
Information Society Directive, 608, 667–668, 671–672
Information society services, 655, 660, 716n83, 720
Informed user, defined, 629–630
Initial capitalization, 397–399
Injunctive relief, 670. *See also* Consumer Interest Injunctions Directive
In-kind contributions, 399, 402
Inside information, 450–458
    authorized persons, 457
    components, 452–455
    disclosure of, 456–457
    good faith trades, 458
    insider dealing, 450–455
    insider dealing, recommending or inducing, 455–456
    insider, defined, 451
    legitimate conduct, 457–458
    market makers, 457
    public mergers and acquisitions, 458
    reasonable suspicion, 453
    recommending or inducing insider dealing, 455–456
    unlawful disclosure of, 456–457
Insolvency law, 467–477

acquisitions out of bankruptcy, 508
applicable law, 472–473
automatic mutual recognition,
  473–474
choice of law rules, 476–477
COMI, 469
creditors' rights, 474–475
employer insolvency, protection
  in event of, 517–521.
  See also Employer insolvency,
  protection in event of
establishment, defined, 471
forum, 469–472, 476–477
insurance and financial industry, 477
jurisdiction, 469–472
language, 474–475
main solvency proceedings, 470
mutual recognition, 473–474
overview, 467–468
reorganization, 471
reservation of title, 475
scope, 468–469
title reservation, 475
Insolvency Regulation, 467–470,
  472–477
Intellectual property rights, 529–650
ancillary restraints, 290
competition law vs., 649–650
copyright, 605–624.
  See also Copyright
counterfeit goods from outside EU,
  647–649
creation, 529
design rights, 625–637. *See also*
  Design rights
discrimination, 638
dominance, as evidence of, 202–203
electronic commerce, 665–673
exceptional circumstances, 217–219
exhaustion of rights doctrine,
  639–647. *See also* Exhaustion
  of rights doctrine
foreclosure, 276
FRAND terms, 219
free movement of goods, 76–77,
  638–639

as goods, 59
intangible asset acquisitions,
  246–247
intellectual property, defined, 529
limitations, 637–650
patents, 587–605. *See also* Patents
refusal to license, 216–219
Trademark Directive, 34
Trademark Regulation, 12
trademarks, 529–587. *See also*
  Trademarks
treaty principles, 637–638
TRIPS, 315
tying, 211
types, 529
unitary patents, 47
Internal trade
common market, 57
customs territory, defined, 57n1
customs unions, 8–9, 11, 57–58
freedom to conduct business,
  82–102. *See also* Freedom to
  conduct business
free movement of capital, 102–113.
  See also Free movement
  of capital
free movement of goods, 59–82.
  See also Free movement
  of goods
free movement of labor/workers, 82
free trade areas, 8, 57–58
harmonization, 123–125
internal market, 11, 57
preferential tariff treatment, 57
taxation and free movement
  principles, 113–123. *See also*
  Taxation and free movement
  principles
Internal transit, 313
International copyright conventions,
  606–608
International Court of Justice, 235
International Financial Reporting
  Standards (IFRSs), 449
International law, 10, 40, 191–192
International Monetary Fund (IMF), 313

Index 775

International Organization of Securities
    Commissions, 443
International regimes, 313–319
    dispute settlement, 315–318
    DSB, 315–318
    EU law vs. WTO agreements,
        318–319
    GATS, 315
    GATT, 314–315. *See also* General
        Agreement on Tariffs
        and Trade
    political considerations, 317–318
    TRIMs, 315
    TRIPS, 315
    Uruguay Round, 314–315
    WTO, 313–315
    WTO Appellate Body, 316, 318
International Trade Organization
    (ITO), 313
Internet
    advertising, 673–676
    apps, 673–676
    behavioral advertising, 673–676
    ccTLD authorities, 548, 665–666
    ccTLDs, 665–666
    commercial practices involving,
        673–676
    cookies, 673–676
    cybersquatting, 665–666
    distance sales, 715–720
    domain names, 547–548
    electronic commerce, 673–676
    electronic mail, 655, 676
    encryption, 669
    framing, 672
    ISPs, 670
    keyword searches, 666–667
    linking, 671–672
    meta tagging, 672–673
    online transactions, 707
    passwords, 669
    promotion to consumers, 657–659
    regulation of commercial practices
        involving, 673–676
    routers, 609–610
    scrambling, 669
    servers, 609–610
    solicitation to consumers, 657–659
    spam, 676
    tracking devices, 673–676
    trademarks, 547–548
    websites, 547–548
Internet Corporation for Assigned
    Names and Numbers (ICANN),
    547, 666
Internet service providers (ISPs), 670
Interstate commerce, 492
Interstate Trade Guidelines, 45
Intra-brand restraint, 172
Intra-undertaking conspiracy, 138–139
Invalidity and design rights, 634–636
Inventive step, 595
Investors, protection of, 442
Invitations to purchase, 713–714
Inward processing, 311–312
ISPs (Internet service providers), 670
ITO (International Trade
    Organization), 313

J

Joint and several liability, 384
Joint and sole control, 249–251
Jointly owned subsidiaries, 375
Joint ventures, 185–188
    breakups, 254
    concentrations, 249–253
    concentrative and nonconcentrative,
        186–187
    defined, 185–186
    legal analysis, 187–188
    Merger Control Regulation, 185,
        187–188
    parent companies, 253
    same parties, 253–254
    start-up periods, 253
Jurisdiction
    competition, regulation of, 232–236
    European Commission, 10
    European courts, 33–36,
        232–234, 319
    European General Court, 36
    insolvency law, 469–472

preliminary rulings, 33–34
TFEU infringement, 33–36, 232–234, 319
Trademark Regulation, 12
Justice Department, U.S., 245

K
Keyword searches, 666–667

L
Labor law, 489–527
   collective redundancy, 514–517. *See also* Collective redundancy
   employee consultation, 521–527. *See also* Employee consultation
   employer changes, 504–514. *See also* Employer changes
   employer insolvency, protection in event of, 517–521. *See also* Employer insolvency, protection in event of
   ethnic discrimination, 502–504
   free movement of labor, 490–499. *See also* Free movement of labor
   gender discrimination, 500–502
   insolvency, protection in event of, 517–521
   nationality discrimination, 490–499
   occupational requirements, 502
   other discrimination, 499–504
   racial discrimination, 502–504
   sources, 489–490
Language issues
   creditors' rights, 474–475
   cultural and linguistic diversity, 190
   distance sales, 719
   EU legal system, 37
   insolvency law, 474–475
   interpretation by EU courts, 39
   reporting obligations, 446–447
   unitary patent, 47
Late Payment Directive, 703

"Layering" transactions, 460
Legal control, 247–249
Legal systems
   dualist legal systems, 52*n*252
   ECJ, 10–12
   EU, 10–12, 37
   language issues, 37
   pan-European legal systems, 6–8
Legislation
   challenges to, 50
   company law, 389
   consumer protection, 701–703
Legislative functions, 25
Legislative principles, 48–50. *See also* Laws; Legislation
   conferral, 48–49
   proportionality, 50
   subsidiarity for shared authorities, 49
Legislative procedures, 45–47
Lending rights, 401, 622–623
Letters, trademarks, 545–547
Leveraging, 280–282
Liability
   competition, violations of, 236–240
   consumer protection, 736–737
   EEIG, 384
   external, 407
   joint and several liability, 384
   limited liability companies, 390–393. *See also* Limited liability companies
   managers, 407–408
   mergers, 412
   noncontractual liability, 53–54
   parent company liability, 236–238
   post-incorporation, 407–408
   pre-incorporation, 407
   prospectus, obligation to publish, 443–444
   shareholders, 407–408
   strict liability, 736
   successor liability, 239–240
   vicarious liability, 238
Licenses
   abusive conduct, 216–219

agreements, 180–184
bilateral restraints, 180–184
concentrations, 247
fees, 308
Merger Control Regulation, 247
refusal to license, 216–219
vertical restraints, 180–184
Likelihood of confusion, 563–568, 573–574, 586–587
Like product, 323
Limited liability companies, 390–393
    annual reports, 404–405
    branch offices, 405–406
    capitalization, 397–403
    cross-border mergers, 415, 417
    disclosure requirements, 403–404
    distributions to shareholders, 403
    financial statements, 404–405
    governing documents, 404n186
    mergers, 412
    registration systems, 404
    shareholders, 397, 403
Limited Liability Company Directive, 390–392
Linking, 671–672
Lome Convention, 294

M
Maastricht Treaty, 2–3
Madrid Agreement, 532–535
Madrid Protocol, 532–535
Main solvency proceedings, 470
Map of EU, 5
Marine biological resources, 11
Marjolin Memorandum, 13
Market abuse, 449–465
    criteria, 459–460
    enforcement, 463–464
    geographic scope of prohibition, 464–465
    inside information, 450–458. *See also* Inside information
    market manipulation, 458–462. *See also* Market manipulation
    notification and disclosure obligations, 463–464

    own shares, trading in, 461–462
    sanctions, 463
    share buybacks, 462
    stabilization programs, 462
    types, 450–461
Market Abuse Directive, 421
Market Abuse Regulation, 450, 452, 456–462, 464–465
Market makers, 457
Market manipulation, 458–462. *See also* Competition, regulation of
    benchmark information, 461
    false or misleading information, 461
    fictitious devices, 460
    "layering" transactions, 460
    manipulative dissemination of information, 461
    misleading signals, 458–460
    "pump and dump" transactions, 460
    "trash and cash" transactions, 460
    types, 458–461
Market power, 276
Markets. *See also* Common markets; European Securities and Markets Authority (ESMA); Internal trade; Market abuse; Market manipulation; Market shares; Regulated markets
    bilateral restraints, 159, 171–175
    distribution and division of markets, 159, 171–175
    dominance, 197–198
    foreclosure, 275–276
    horizontal hard-core restraints, 159
    market entry barriers, 273–274
    securities law, 429–430, 432–433
    transparency, 205
    vertical restraints, 171–175
Market shares
    aggregate market shares, 267
    anti-dumping, 333
    cross-elasticity of demand, 194–196
    customer size, 274–275
    demand substitution, 194–196
    dimensions of relevant market, 193
    evidence to define markets, 197–198

geographic dimension, 198–200
importance of, 192–200
loss, 333
product market definition, 193–198
relative market share, 200–201
substantive analysis, 267–270
supply substitution, 196–197
Market Standards for General
    Meetings, 394
Medical Products Advertising Directive,
    703, 706
Mercosur, 8
Merger Control Regulation. *See also*
    Competition, regulation of;
    Mergers; Structural restraints
    asset acquisitions, 246–247
    Clayton Act (U.S.), compared, 246
    common ownership, 245–246
    control, 421
    dominance, 266
    EU dimension, 255–265. *See also*
        EU dimension
    extraterritorial application, 264–265
    initial test, 257–258
    intangible asset acquisitions,
        246–247
    joint ventures, 185, 187–188
    legal consequences, 264–265
    legitimate interests of member states,
        264
    mergers outside EU, 10
    minority interests, 247n603, 249
    multiple premerger filings, 259
    noncompetition concerns, 287
    parent company liability, 238
    preemption, 12
    procedural analysis, 244–265. *See*
        also Procedural analysis
    review procedure, 260
    same parties, 253–254
    as secondary law source, 40–41
    substantive analysis, 244
    supplementary test, 257–258
    tacit coordination, 278–279
    taxonomy, 129

TFEU Articles 101 and 102 vs.,
    260–262
transactions as concentrations under
    national law, 264
Mergers. *See also* Competition,
    regulation of; Employer changes;
    Merger Control Regulation
    by acquisition, 410, 414
    company law, 409–417
    cross-border, 414–417. *See also*
        Cross-border mergers
    defined, 409
    domestic, 409–414
    by formation, 410–411
    horizontal mergers, 269–270
    inside information, 458
    outside EU, 10
    pre-merger certificates, 416–417
    prospectus, obligation to publish, 438
    public limited liability
        companies, 412
    public offerings, 436
    share-exchange ratio, 416
    shareholder meetings, 413–414
    subsidiaries, 411, 412n212
    terms of, 412–413
Merger Treaty (Treaty Establishing
    a Single Council and Single
    Commission of the European
    Communities), 3
Meta tagging, 672–673
Mexico and NAFTA, 57
Mineral products, 304
Minority interests, 247n603, 249,
    422–424
Misleading and comparative advertising.
    See also Misleading and
    Comparative Advertising
    Directive
    advertising, defined, 728
    comparative, defined, 729–730
    consumer protection, 728–733
    electronic commerce, 657–659
    misleading, defined, 729
    requirements, 731–733

scope, 730–731
trademarks, 712, 733
Misleading and Comparative Advertising
    Directive, 576, 653, 657–658,
    702, 704, 728–733
Misleading sales practices, 708, 711–714
Misleading signals, 458–460
Misleading trademarks, 581
Mixed vs. pure bundling, 280–282
Mixtures, duty amount determinations,
    301–302
Model withdrawal forms, 721
Monetary Committee of the European
    Central Bank, 17
Monetary policy, 11
Monetary union. *See* European
    monetary union
Money Laundering Directive, 100
Money market instruments, 399, 431
Morocco, EU membership application, 5
Movies. *See* Films
Mutual recognition, 385
Mutual Recognition Agreement, 125

N
NAFTA. *See* North American Free Trade
    Agreement
Nationality discrimination, 53, 490–499
National law
    company law, 384–385
    competition, regulation of, 232–234
    consumer protection, 707
    corporate forms, 384–385
    data privacy, 680–681
    employer changes, 513
    EU dimension, 262–264
    EU law vs., 232–234
    patents, 591–592
    preemption of, 12
    sales, 707
    structural restraints, 262–264
    trademarks, 530, 535–536
    transactions as concentrations
        under, 264
Neologisms, 545–547

Neutrality rule, 426
Newness, design rights, 627–629
Nice Agreement, 543, 575
No challenge clauses, 184
Noncompete agreements, 176, 289
Noncompetition concerns, 287
Nonconcentrative joint ventures,
    186–187
Noncontractual liability of member
    states, 53–54
Noneconomic considerations, bilateral
    restraints, 189–192
Nonequity securities, 431–432
Nonfungible capital, 432
Nonlegislative acts, 25–26
Nonpatentable subject matters, 594–595
Nonprofit associations
    prospectus, obligation to publish, 432
    securities law, 432
    Transfer Directive, 505
Normal value, 324–330
North American Free Trade Agreement
    (NAFTA), 8, 57
North Korea, exports of goods and
    technology to, 110
Notice and notification
    bilateral restraints, 151–152
    collective redundancy, 517
    data transfers to nonmember
        states, 692
    De Minimis Notice, 151–152
    employer changes, 511
    market abuse, 463–464
    means of issuing notice, 394
    notice of general meeting, 393–395
    notice period, 393–394
    shareholder meetings, 393–395
    sources of law, 44–45
Novelty, 595–597

O
Offer to the public, defined, 433
Office of Harmonization in the Internal
    Market (OHIM)
    appeals from, 36

confusion, 564
design rights, 625–636
distinctiveness, 566, 585–587
generic marks, 580
identical marks, 573
invalidity declarations, 581–583
misleading marks, 581
registration date, 577
revocation of trademarks, 577
trademarks, 534–544, 547–551, 554–557, 563, 566
Off-premises sales, 717, 720, 723
Olfactory marks, 555
Omissions, 713–714
Online transactions, 707
On-premises sales, 717, 720–721, 723
Ordinary course, 325–327
Origin, designation of, 303–306, 363, 556–560, 562
Output limitation, 160
Outward processing, 312
Overriding requirements, 96–98, 107–109

P

Package Vacation Directive, 703, 706
Packaging costs, 307
Packaging, trademarks, 549–553
Pan-European corporate forms, 370–385. *See also* Corporate forms
Pan-European legal systems, 6–8
Parallel application of trade and competition law, 367
Parent companies
    joint ventures, 253
    liability, 236–238
Paris Convention, 530–532, 589
Paris Convention for the Protection of Industrial Property, 626
Parliamentary Assembly (Council of Europe), 7
Part-time workers, 493
Passive selling, defined, 174
Patent Cooperation Treaty, 589–591
Patents, 587–605

biotechnology patents, 599–603. *See also* Biotechnology patents
design, 587
European patents, 592–599. *See also* European patents
exhaustion of rights doctrine, 644
industrial application, 597, 604
industrial property rights, 587
international regimes, 588–591
international searching authorities, 590–591
inventive step, 595, 604
national law, 591–592
novelty, 595–597, 603–604
Paris Convention, 589
Patent Cooperation Treaty, 589–591
patent, defined, 587
plants, 587
refusal to license, 218–219
registration, 604–605
source of rights, 588–592
state of the art, 603–604
TRIPS Agreement, 591
unitary effect, 598
unitary patent, 47
utility, 587
utility model patents, 603–605
Performers, copyright, 623–624
Per se unfair practices, 708–711
Personal data, 678–679
Phonograms, 605, 607–609, 613–614, 623, 668
Piercing corporate veil, 237
Plant and animal varieties, 601, 645
Plant patents, 587
Plant Variety Regulation, 645
Pleading thresholds, 241
Political considerations, 317–318
Political criterion, 5
Political dimension, 9
Political powers, 30
Portfolio effect, 282–283
Post-incorporation liability, 407–408
Predatory pricing, 212–214
Pre-incorporation liability, 407
Pre-merger certificates, 416–417

"Preserves its autonomy," defined, 510
Presumption of fairness, 428
Pricing
    average avoidable costs, 213*n*418
    bilateral restraints, 158–159
    consumer contracts, 728
    dominance, 203–204
    excessive pricing, 207–210
    predatory pricing, 212–214
    price stability, 14
    resale price maintenance, 169–171
    vertical restraints, 169–171
Privacy. *See* Confidentiality
Private Actions Directive, 241–242
Private enforcement, 240–243, 683–684
Private limited companies, 393
Private limited partnerships, 392–393
Private restrictions, 106
Privileged undertakings. *See* Public and privileged undertakings
Product differentiation, 270–272
Production cooperation, 164–166
Product market definition, 193–198
    cross-elasticity of demand, 194–196
    demand substitution, 194–196
    evidence to define markets, 197–198
    supply substitution, 196–197
Product safety and defects, 733–737
Product Safety Directive, 653, 702, 733–737
Programs. *See* Computer programs
Proportionality principle, 50
Prospectus Directive, 430–444, 447
Prospectus, obligation to publish, 430–444
    admission for trading on regulated market, 432–433
    approval, 438–439
    convertible debt, 431–432
    credit institutions, 432
    debt instruments, 431
    depositary receipts, 431
    divisions, 436, 438
    employee share plans, 436, 438
    enforcement, 443–444
    equity securities, 431
    exemptions, 434–438
    format, 439
    home member states, 434, 439–442
    host member states, 439–442
    investors, protection of, 442
    liability, 443–444
    mergers, 436, 438
    money market instruments, 431
    no consideration, 437
    nonequity securities, 431–432
    non-EU issuers, 433–434, 440–441
    nonfungible capital, 432
    nonprofit associations, 432
    offerings on regulated market exemptions, 436–438
    offer to the public, defined, 433
    precautionary measures, 442
    prior registrations, 437
    publication, 438–439
    public offering exemptions, 434–436
    public offerings, defined, 433
    qualified investors exemption, 434–435
    secondary registrations, 436–437
    securities, defined, 431–432
    share dividends, 436, 438
    share exchange or conversion, 438
    share substitutions, 435–436, 437–438
    small offerings, 435
    state or government authorities, 432
    takeovers, 436, 438
    third countries, 442–443
    types of securities, 431–432
Protocol on the Convergence Criteria, 14–15
Protocol on the Excessive Deficit Procedure, 15–20
Proxy voting, 396
Public and privileged undertakings, 227–229
    defined, 227
    limits on member states, 227–228
    limits on public and private undertakings, 228–229
Public body, defined, 354–355

Public communication rights, 612–613, 668–669
Public Company Capitalization Directive, 404n186, 422
Public, defined, 612–613
Public health
  exceptions, 74–76
  freedom to conduct business, 93–94, 100
  free movement of goods, 74–76
Public interest, 99–100, 116–117
Public limited liability companies, 393–397, 412
Public mergers. See Mergers
Public morality, 74, 632
Public offerings
  defined, 433
  divisions, 436
  employee share plans, 436
  exemptions, 434–436
  mergers, 436
  qualified investors exemption, 434–435
  share dividends, 436
  share substitutions, 435–436
  small offerings, 435
  takeovers, 436
Public policy
  biotechnology patents, 601–602
  design rights, 632
  exceptions, enumerated in TFEU, 74
  freedom to conduct business, 93–94
  free movement of capital, 107–109
  free movement of goods, 74
  Union trademark, 538, 578
  use requirement, 578
Public security
  exceptions, 74
  freedom to conduct business, 93–94
  free movement of capital, 107–109
  free movement of goods, 74
Public service, 499
"Pump and dump" transactions, 460
Purchasing cooperation, 166–167
Pure vs. mixed bundling, 280–282

Q
Qualified certificates, 652
Quality marks, 709
Quantitative restrictions and equivalents
  defined, 63
  distinctly applicable state measures, 66–67
  elimination of, 62–68
  equivalents, effects of, 65–67
  indistinctly applicable state measures, 66–67
  state measures, 63–65
  trade between member states, effect on, 67–68
Quotas, 294, 309–310

R
Racial discrimination, 502–504
  Racial and Ethnic Discrimination Directive, 502
R&D (Research and development) cooperation, 163–164
Reasonable suspicion, 453
Rebate and discount schemes, 179–180, 212, 220–224, 331
Record date, defined, 394n119
Refusal to deal, 215–216
Refusal to license, 216–219
Regulated markets, 429–430, 432–433, 436–438
Regulatory action petitions, 214–215
Relative market share, 200–201
Relocation, 497
Remedies. See also Damages
  common commercial policy, 366
  copyright, 670
  electronic commerce, 670
  injunctive relief, 670
  sanctions, 463
Remuneration
  company law, 408
  of directors, 408
  free movement of labor, 493–494
  right of, 481
  sales agency law, 481

Rental rights, 622–623. *See also* Rental Rights Directive
Rental Rights Directive, 608, 622–623, 668
Reorganization, 471. *See also* Insolvency law
Reporting obligations
   additional disclosures, 446
   annual reports, 404–405, 443–444
   cross-border mergers, 416
   home member states, 447–448
   host member states, 447
   impact reports, 416
   language, 446–447
   limited liability companies, 404–405
   major shareholdings changes, 445–446
   periodic requirements, 444–445
   securities law, 444–449
   semi-annual reports, 443–444
   third country equivalence, 448–449
Reproduction rights, 608–611, 667–668
Resale price maintenance, 169–171
Resale Right Directive, 608
Resale rights, 624
Research & Development Block Exemption, 156, 164
Research and development (R&D) cooperation, 163–164
Reservation of title, 475
Restraints. *See* Competition, regulation of; *specific types*
Reutilization, 619–620
Revocation of trademarks, 577
Right of establishment, 88–89, 93, 109–110, 405. *See also* Freedom of establishment
Rights-management information obligations, 670–671
Routers, 609–610
Royalties, 308
Rule of national treatment, 531
Rule of priority, 531

S

Safeguards Regulation, 320, 361–362, 366–367
Safe harbor, 349, 691–694
Sales agency law, 479–487
   applicable law, 479
   commercial agents, 479–481
   commission right, 481–483
   compensation right, 483–485
   indemnification payment, 485
   mandatory character, 486–487
   protections offered, 481–487
   remuneration right, 481
   scope, 479–481
   statute of limitations, 486
   termination, 483–485
   termination compensation, 485
   types of compensation, 483
Sales commissions, 307
Sales price as normal value, 324–327
Sales Representative Directive, 479–487
Sanctions
   ECJ, imposed by, 35–36
   market abuse, 463
Satellite and Cable Directive, 608
Scrambling, 669
SE. *See* Societas Europeae
Second Company Law Directive, 389, 391, 422
Sectorial block exemptions, 156
Secure-signature-creation device, 652
Securities law, 429–465
   admission for trading on regulated market, 432–433
   capitalization of limited liability companies, 399
   convertible debt, 431–432
   credit institutions, 432
   debt instruments, 431
   depositary receipts, 431
   disclosure requirements, 446
   equity securities, 431
   home member states, 434, 439–442
   investors, protection of, 442
   market abuse, 449–465. *See also* Market abuse

markets, 429–430, 432–433
money market instruments, 399, 431
nonequity securities, 431–432
nonfungible capital, 432
nonprofit associations, 432
offer to the public, defined, 433
prospectus, obligation to publish, 430–444. *See also* Prospectus, obligation to publish
public offerings, defined, 433
regulated markets, 429–430, 432–433
reporting obligations, 444–449. *See also* Reporting obligations
securities, defined, 431–432
state or government authorities, 432
supervisory authorities, 429
transferable securities, 399
transparency, 444–449
types of securities, 431–432
Security obligations, 692–693, 695–697
SE Directive, 513–514
Selective distribution, 176–179
Selling arrangements, 68–71, 80
Sell-out rights, 424
Semi-annual reports, 443–444
SE Regulation, 370–371, 377–379, 414
Services
    consumer protection, 706–707
    defined, 83
    freedom of establishment vs., 82–85
    free movement of. *See* Free movement of services
    right to provide, 89–90
Services Directive, 87
Settlement. *See* Dispute settlement
Shapes, trademarks, 549–553
Share buybacks, 400–401, 421, 462
Share capital, 401–403
Share dividends, 436, 438
Share exchange or conversion, 438
Share-exchange ratio, 416
Shareholder meetings, 393–397. *See also* Shareholders
    agendas, 395
    conflicts of interest, 396

content of notice, 394–395
correspondence voting, 396
divisions of companies, 419–420
domestic mergers, 413–414
electronic participation, 395–396
means of issuing notice, 394
mergers, 413–414
notice of general meeting, 393–395
notice period, 393–394
participation, 395–396
proxy voting, 396
record date, defined, 394n119
results, 397
voting, 395–396
Shareholders. *See also* Shareholder meetings
    distributions to, 403
    liability, 407–408
    limited liability companies, 397, 403
    major changes, reporting requirements, 445–446
    minimum number, 397
    minority interests, 247n603, 249, 422–424
    SE, 377
Shareholders Rights Directive, 370
Share substitutions, 437–438
Signatures, electronic, 652
Single European Act, 3, 57
Single Supervisory Mechanism (SSM), 22–23
Sixth Company Law Directive, 391
Slogans, 548–549
Small and medium-sized companies, 527
Smart phones, 675
Social cohesion, 11, 287
Social policies
    bilateral restraints, 189–190
    EU, 11
Societas Europeae (SE), 370–382
    administrative organ, 378–379
    capital, 376
    conversion, 375–376, 380
    employee participation, 380–382
    fiduciary duties, 379–380
    formation, 371–376

as holding company, 373–375
jointly owned subsidiaries, 375
managing bodies, 377–379
merger of public companies, 371–373
one-tier system, 378–379
registration, 376
SE Regulation, 370–371
shareholders, 377
structure, 377–379
subsidiary of, 376
termination, 380
two-tier system, 378–379
Software. *See* Computer programs; Computer Software Directive
Sole and joint control, 249–251
Solicitation of sales, 707–715
    aggressive practices, 708, 715
    ambiguity, 714
    bait advertising, 709
    bait and switch, 709
    causation, 713, 714
    codes of conduct, 713
    commercial intent, 714
    company policies, 713
    confusion, practices causing, 712–713
    contract terms, 710
    copycat packaging, 713
    deceptive practices, 711–712
    false practices, 711
    Internet, 657–659
    invitations to purchase, 713–714
    misleading actions, 711–713
    misleading practices, 708, 711–714
    omissions, 713–714
    per se unfair practices, 708–711
    quality marks, 709
    service availability, 709
    trademark, 712
    transaction decision, defined, 711n61
    trust marks, 709
    unfair commercial practices, 707–711
Solvency. *See* Insolvency law
Sound marks, 555–556

Sources of law, 40–48. *See also* Laws
    decisions, 43
    directives, 41–43
    general principles of law, 47
    guidelines, 44–45
    hierarchy of norms, 47–48
    international law, 40
    language issues, 37, 39, 47, 190
    legislative procedures, 45–47
    notices, 44–45
    primary law, 40
    recommendations, 43–44
    regulations, 40–41
    secondary law, 40–47
Spam, 676
Specialization Block Exemption, 156
Squeeze-out rights, 427–428
SSM (Single Supervisory Mechanism), 22–23
Stabilization programs, 462
Standardization, 168–169, 660–662
Standing, trade barriers, 364–365
Start-up periods, 253
State action, 226–232
    compulsion, 230–232
    public and privileged undertakings, 227–229
    sovereign actor, state as, 226–227
State measures
    freedom to conduct business, 90–91
    free movement of capital, 106–107
    free movement of labor, 491–492
    quantitative restrictions and equivalents, 63–65
Statute for a European Co-Operative Society, 390
Statute of limitations, 486
Statute of the ESCB, 21
Strategic data exchanges, 162
Strategic decisions, 246
Strict liability, 736
Structural restraints, 243–291. *See also* Merger Control Regulation
    behavioral restraints compared, 245
    EU dimension, 255–265. *See also* EU dimension

minority interests, 247n603, 249
national law role, 262–264
procedural analysis, 244–265.
  See also Procedural analysis
substantive analysis, 266–291. See
  also Substantive analysis
taxonomy, 129
thresholds, 255–258
Subscribed capital, 397–399
Subsidiaries
  jointly owned, 375
  mergers, 411, 412n212
  of SEs, 376
Subsidiarity for shared authorities, 49
Subsidy, defined, 354
  noncoordinated effects, 266–277
  portfolio effect, 282–283
  potential competition, 273–274
  product differentiation, 270–272
  pure vs. mixed bundling, 280–282
  relevant effects, 266–287
  social cohesion, 287
  structural restraints, 244
  sustainability, 279
  timeliness, 274
  tying, 280–282
  unilateral effects, 266–277
Substantive protection, 495–498
Substantive standard, 85–87
Successor liability, 239–240
Successors in interest, 633–634
Sui generis right/database right, 617–620
Supervision of financial institutions, 109
Supply or purchase obligations, 290–291
Supply substitution, 196–197
Suspicion, reasonable, 453
Sustainability, 279

T

Tacit acquiescence, 136–138
Tacit coordination, 278–279
Tagging, 672–673
Takeover Directive, 370, 391, 393, 420–429
Takeovers, 420–428
  breakthrough rule, 426
  consideration, form of, 423–424
  control, 421
  defenses to, 425–427
  disclosure requirements, 424–425
  fair market conditions, 422
  fairness, presumption of, 428
  financing, 422
  limitations of defenses to, 425–427
  minority shareholder protection, 422–424
  neutrality rule, 426
  post-bid squeeze-out rights, 427–428
  presumption of fairness, 428
  prospectus, obligation to publish, 436, 438
  scope of EU law, 420–422
  sell-out rights, 424
  squeeze-out rights, 427–428
  tender offers, 424–425
TARIC system (Tarif Intégre Communautaire), 297
Tariff quotas, 294
Tarif Intégre Communautaire (TARIC system), 297
Tastes, trademarks, 556
Taxation
  abuse or tax avoidance, counteracting, 118
  anti-dumping, 331
  coherence of tax system, safeguarding, 119–121
  consumer contracts and price terms, 728
  customs duties and charges, 61–62.
    See also Customs duties and charges; Duty amount determinations
  EEIG, 384
  free movement principles, 113–123.
    See also Taxation and free movement principles
  indirect taxes, 331
  internal taxation, 61–62
  internal trade, 113–123
  VAT, 728

Taxation and free movement principles, 113–123
    abuse or tax avoidance, counteracting, 117–118
    coherence, safeguarding, 119–121
    fiscal supervision justification, 118–119
    imperative requirements in public interest, 116–117
    justifications, 116–123
    taxing authority, allocation between EU and member states, 113–114
    tension between, 114–116
    TFEU codification of justifications, 121–123
Technology Transfer Block Exemption, 156, 180–183, 649
Temporary importation, 312–313
Tender offers, 424–425
Territorial cohesion, 11
TFEU. *See* Treaty on the Functioning of the European Union
Third countries
    CSPs, 652
    equivalence, 448–449
    free movement of capital, 110
    prospectus, obligation to publish, 442–443
    reporting obligations, 448–449
    TFEU, 110
Timeshare Directive, 703, 706
TIR carnet, 311
Title reservation, 475
Toy Safety Directive, 703
Tracking devices, 673–676
Trade Act of 1974 (U.S.), 317
Trade associations, 348
Trade barriers
    adverse effect, 364
    common commercial policy, 362–366
    elements, 363–365
    international trade rules, 363–365
    obstacle to trade, 363–364
    standing, 364–365
    Union interest, 365
Trade Barriers Regulation, 320, 362–366
Trade instruments, 319–320
Trademark Directive
    applicability, 34
    EEA sales, 641
    harmonization, 586
    national law and, 535–536
    non-use, 579–580
    preemption, 583
    shapes and packaging, 549
Trademark Regulation
    confusion, 712
    generic marks, 580
    identical marks, 573
    jurisdiction, 12
    local significance, 583–585
    registration, 626
    shapes and packaging, 549
    unfair advantage and detriment, 568
    Union trademark, 536–537
    unregistered marks, 583–585
    use exception, 553
Trademarks, 529–587
    agricultural products, 557–563
    appropriation, 571
    ccTLD authorities, 548, 665–666
    collective marks, 549
    colors, 553–555
    comparative advertising, 712, 733
    cybersquatting, 665–666
    defined, 529–530
    descriptive marks, 539–541
    designation of origin, 558–560, 562
    design rights, 625
    detriment, 568–570
    distinctiveness, 539–544, 566, 585–587
    domain names, 547–548
    electronic commerce, 665–667
    European law and international treaties, 535
    exhaustion of rights doctrine, 646–647
    expressions, 545–547

foodstuffs, 557–563
genuine use, 584
geographical indication,
  558–560, 562
geographic origin, 556–557
gTLDs, 665–666
gustatory marks, 556
identical marks, 563, 572–573,
  582–583
internal trade, 76–77
international regimes, 530–535
international treaties and European
  law, 535
Internet, 547–548
keyword searches, 666–667
letters, 545–547
likelihood of confusion, 563–568,
  573–574, 586–587
local significance, 583–585
Madrid Agreement, 532–535
Madrid Protocol, 532–535
Madrid system, 532–535
misleading marks, 581
national treatment, 531, 535–536
neologisms, 545–547
OHIM, 534–544, 547–551, 554–557,
  563, 566
olfactory marks, 555
packaging, 549–553
Paris Convention, 530–532
prior distinctiveness determinations,
  543–544
priority, 531
refusal grounds, 563–571
revocation, 577
rule of national treatment, 531
rule of priority, 531
shapes, 549–553
slogans, 548–549
sounds, 555–556
sources of rights, 530–536
tastes, 556
traditional specialty guaranteed
  designation, 562–563
TRIPS Agreement, 532

types, 544–563
unfair advantage, 568–570, 574–575
Union trademark, 536–571. *See also*
  Union trademark
unregistered, 583–585
use requirement, 534–535
websites, 547–548
WIPO, 532–533
words, 545–547
Trade measures and common commercial
  policy, 366–367
Trade-Related Aspects of Intellectual
  Property Rights (TRIPS), 315,
  363, 532, 591, 606, 626
Trade-related investment measures
  (TRIMs), 315
Traders, 704–705
Traditional specialty guaranteed
  designation, 562–563
Trans-European networks, 11
Transferable securities, 399
Transfer Directive, 42–43, 504–514
Transfers
  data. *See* Data transfers to
    nonmember states
  undertakings. *See* Employer changes;
    Transfer Directive
Transient reproductions, 609–610
Transparency Directive, 444,
  447–448, 464
Transparency Implementing
  Directive, 448
Transport costs, 307
Transports Internationaux Routiers
  Treaty, 311
"Trash and cash" transactions, 460
Treaty Establishing a Single Council
  and Single Commission of the
  European Communities (Merger
  Treaty), 3
Treaty Establishing the European
  Community (EEC Treaty), 2–3
Treaty of Amsterdam, 3
Treaty of Lisbon, 3
Treaty of Nice, 3

Treaty of Paris (ECSC Treaty; 1951), 1–2
Treaty of Rome (1957), 1–2
Treaty on the Functioning of the
    European Union (TFEU)
  Article 16, 677
  Article 28, 59, 81
  Article 29, 67, 81
  Article 30, 59–60, 62, 73, 95, 101
  Article 31, 66
  Article 34, 59, 61–64, 66–74, 76–78,
      81, 101, 128, 638–639
  Article 35, 59, 61–63, 67, 69, 71–74,
      76–78, 128
  Article 36, 67, 72–73, 75, 77–81,
      638–639
  Article 45, 84–85, 94, 131,
      490–495, 498
  Article 45(2), 53, 495
  Article 45(3), 498
  Article 45(3)(a), 496
  Article 45(3)(b), 497
  Article 45(3)(c), 497
  Article 45(3)(d), 497
  Article 45(4), 94, 493
  Article 46, 489
  Article 48, 88
  Article 49, 83, 85, 88, 90–93, 114,
      369, 385
  Article 49(2), 89
  Article 50, 85, 90, 369, 389
  Article 52, 93, 95–98, 101
  Article 54, 130, 385, 389
  Article 56, 83–85, 90–91, 93, 101,
      115, 497
  Article 56(1), 89
  Article 59, 85
  Article 62, 93
  Article 63, 102–104, 106–107
  Article 64, 46
  Article 65, 102, 106–107, 109
  Article 65(1)(b), 107–109
  Article 65(2), 109
  Article 66, 110
  Article 75, 110
  Article 81(1)(a), 121–122
  Article 101, 27, 45, 53, 63,
      128–129, 132–133,
      138–141, 145, 147,
      150–151, 153, 157,
      189–192, 224–225
  Article 101(1), 131–134, 136–142,
      145–153, 157–158
  Article 101(2), 133
  Article 101(3), 133, 146, 149,
      153–156
  Article 102, 27, 45, 63, 128–129,
      192–225
  Article 103, 128
  Article 104, 128
  Article 105, 27, 128
  Article 105(2), 43
  Article 106, 128
  Article 106(1), 227–228
  Article 106(2), 229
  Article 106(3), 128
  Article 110, 61–62
  Article 110(1), 61
  Article 114, 123
  Article 115, 46, 78
  Article 126(1), 15
  Article 126(9), 19
  Article 157, 500
  Article 157(1), 55
  Article 157(3), 489
  Article 185, 701
  Article 185(1), 701
  Article 206, 319
  Article 207, 319–320
  Article 215, 110
  Article 223(2), 46
  Article 225, 36
  Article 226, 46
  Article 228(2), 32
  Article 228(4), 46
  Article 230, 36
  Article 245(2), 32
  Article 247, 32
  Article 256, 36
  Article 258, 35, 41, 52
  Article 259, 34

Article 260, 35
Article 262, 46
Article 263, 19, 27, 35, 319
Article 263(4), 35
Article 265, 35, 36
Article 268, 35, 36
Article 270, 36
Article 272, 36
Article 273, 35
Article 286(7), 32
Article 288, 40
Article 294, 45
Article 296, 43
Article 318(11), 35
Article 326, 46
Article 327, 46
Article 328, 46
Article 329, 46
Article 330, 46
Article 331, 46
Article 332, 46
Article 333, 46
Article 334, 46
Article 340, 35, 36
Article 340(2), 36
Article 345, 535, 638–639
agency agreements, 139–141
ancillary restraints, 157
appreciability, 145
arbitrary discrimination, 80–81
association decisions, 141–142
authority to act, 49
bilateral restraints, 129, 133, 145–153
B2B exchanges, 661
certain and direct requirement, 72–73
company law, 369–370, 389
compensatory fees, 62
competition laws, 27, 128
consumer protection, 701
convergence criteria, 14
coordinated effects, 277–279
cross-border sales, 101
customer or territorial restraints, 173
customs duties and charges, 59–60, 62

database protection, 614
data privacy, 677
decisions, 43
deficits, 15–20
direct effect, 52
discrimination, 80–81, 638
ECJ, 32
economic policy, 9
EEA Treaty compared, 7
enforcement, 26
equal treatment, 85
ESCB, 21
EU based on, 3
EU nationality, 88–90
European Commission, 27
European General Court, 36
exceptions, enumerated, 73–77
excessive deficit procedure, 15–20
exclusive dealing, 175
exemptions, 153–156
exercise of official authority, 94
financial institution supervision, 109
fishing rights, 59
freedom of establishment, 385
free movement of capital, 102–104, 106–107
free movement of goods, 59, 68, 81
free movement of labor, 82
free movement of services, 83
gender discrimination, 55, 500
Guidelines on the Effect on Trade Concept, 45
harmonization, 123
information exchanges, 161
institutions, creation of, 23
intellectual property rights, 59, 76–77, 535, 638–639
intra-undertaking conspiracy, 138–139
joint ventures, 185–187
judicially created exceptions, 95–98
jurisdiction of EU courts, 33–36, 232–234, 319
language issues, 39
legal interpretation, 37
legal procedure, 45

legal system, 10–11
legislative acts, 46
license agreements, 182–184
Merger Control Regulation vs., 260–262
nationality discrimination, 53, 490–499
noneconomic considerations, 189–192
non-price terms of sale, 159
opera singers, 131
passive selling, 174
preemption, 78–80
price restraints, 158
as primary law, 40
proportionality, 77–78
public and privileged undertakings, 227–228
public health, 74–76
public morality, 74
public policy, 72, 74, 107–109
public security, 74
purchasing cooperation, 166–168
quantitative restrictions, 63, 66
R&D cooperation, 163–164
rebate and discount schemes, 179
refusal to license, 216–219
regulations vs. directives, 41
right of establishment, 88–89, 93, 405
selective distribution, 177
selling arrangements, 68–70
standardization, 169, 662
state compulsion, 230
state measures, 90–91
structural restraints, 243
tacit acquiescence, 136–138
taxation, 61–62, 121–123
third countries, 110
tying, 179, 280–282
undertakings, 130
unilateral restraints, 192–225
U.S. Constitution compared, 48
vertical restraints, 170
TRIMs (Trade-related investment measures), 315

TRIPS. *See* Trade-Related Aspects of Intellectual Property Rights
TRUSTe, 693
Trust marks, 709
Twelfth Company Law Directive, 391–392, 397
Tying, 179, 210–211, 280–282

U

UDRP (Uniform Dispute Resolution Procedure), 666
UK. *See* United Kingdom
Unfair advantage, 568–570, 574–575
Unfair Commercial Practices Directive, 100, 702, 705–711
Unfair Terms Directive, 653, 701–702, 724–728
Uniform Dispute Resolution Procedure (UDRP), 666
Unilateral restraint, 192–225
  abusive conduct, 207–224. *See also* Abusive conduct
  collective dominance, 204–206
  dominance, 192–204. *See also* Dominance
  effect on trade between member states, 224
  national vs. EU law, 233–234
  substantial part of Union, 206–207
  tacit coordination, 205–206
  taxonomy, 129
Union Customs Code, 297–299, 309, 311–312
Union interest
  anti-dumping, 341–347
  countervailing measures, 358–360
  European Commission, 344
  trade barriers, 365
Union trademark, 536–583. *See also* Trademarks
  advantages, 585–587
  agricultural products, 557–563
  appropriation, 571
  bad faith, 581–582
  cancellation, 577–583
  ccTLD authorities, 548, 665–666

collective marks, 549
colors, 553–555
conflict with prior rights, 583
contrary to absolute grounds for refusal, 581
designation of origin, 558–560, 562
detriment, 568–570
disadvantages, 585–587
distinctiveness, 539–544
domain names, 547–548
duration, 577
earlier identical mark, 582–583
expressions, 545–547
foodstuffs, 557–563
generic, 580
genuine use, 578–580, 584
geographical indication, 558–560, 562
geographic origin, 556–557
graphic representability, 537–538
gustatory marks, 556
identical marks, 563, 572–573, 582–583
invalidity, 581–583
letters, 545–547
likelihood of confusion, 563–568, 573–574, 586–587
limitations, 575–576
local significance, 583–585
misleading, 581
neologisms, 545–547
non-use, 577–580
olfactory marks, 555
packaging, 549–553
prior distinctiveness determinations, 543–544
property rights, 576
public policy, 538, 578
refusal grounds, 563–571
registration requirements, 537–544
revocation, 577–581
scope of rights, 571–576
shapes, 549–553
slogans, 548–549
sounds, 555–556
tastes, 556
traditional specialty guaranteed designation, 562–563
types, 544–563
unfair advantage, 568–570, 574–575
unregistered, 583–585
websites, 547–548
words, 545–547
Union Trade Marks Bulletin, 537
Unitary effect, 598
Unitary patents, 47
Universal Service Directive, 702, 706
Unregistered designs, 636–637
URLs (Universal Resource Locators), 671
Uruguay Round, 314–315
Utility Model Directive (proposed), 603–605
Utility model patents, 603–605
Utility patents, 587

V

Value-added tax (VAT), 728
Vertical agreements with horizontal implications, 184–185
Vertical block exemptions, 156
Vertical integration, 201
Vertical restraints, 169–184
    contract manufacturing, 184
    distribution and division of markets, 171–175
    dual distribution, 184–185
    exclusive dealing, 175
    exclusive supply, 175
    grant-back clauses, 183–184
    intra-brand restraint, 172
    license agreements, 180–184
    markets, 171–175
    no challenge clauses, 184
    noncompete agreements, 176
    pricing, 169–171
    rebate and discount schemes, 179–180
    resale price maintenance, 169–171
    selective distribution, 176–179
    TFEU, 170

tying, 179
vertical agreements with horizontal implications, 184–185
Vertical Restraints Block Exemption, 156, 174–176, 180–181, 184–185
Vexatious litigation, 214–215
Vicarious liability, 238
Vienna Convention on the Law of Treaties, 38
Volume discounts, 212

W

Warehousing, 311
WCO (World Customs Organization), 295–296
WebTrust, 693
Werner, Pierre, 13
Werner Report, 13
Whistleblowers, 697–698
WIPO (World Intellectual Property Organization), 532–533
    Copyright Treaty, 607, 613, 667
    Gazette of International Marks, 533
    Performances and Phonograms Treaty, 607–608, 613, 667
Withdrawal rights, 5–6, 721–723
Words, trademarks, 545–547

Worker Adjustment and Retraining Notification Act (U.S.), 514
Workers, free movement of, 82. *See also* Employees or workers; Free movement of labor
Working Time Directive, 489
Works Council Directive, 521–527
Works council establishment, 522–525
World Bank, 313
World Customs Organization (WCO), 295–296
World Intellectual Property Organization (WIPO), 532–533
World Trade Organization (WTO)
    Agreement on Rules of Origin, 363
    Agreement on Subsidies and Countervailing Measures, 353
    Anti-Dumping Code, 319
    Appellate Body, 316, 318
    background, 313–314
    creation of, 315
    dispute settlement, 315–318
    Dispute Settlement Procedure, 363, 365–366
    EU law vs. WTO agreements, 318–319
    rules, conforming to, 10

About the Author

Andre Fiebig has studied, practiced, and taught EU business law for almost three decades both in Europe and the United States. Mr. Fiebig is a graduate of IIT/Chicago-Kent College of Law and also holds a Doctorate of Laws degree from the University of Tübingen in Germany. Prior to coming to the United States, he practiced EU business law in Brussels with one of the leading European law firms, where he focused on EU competition and merger law. Mr. Fiebig is currently a partner in the Chicago office of Quarles & Brady LLP, where he continues to focus on transatlantic business law issues advising both European companies doing business in the United States and U.S. companies doing business in Europe. He is the author of many publications on international business law and serves as Adjunct Professor at Northwestern University School of Law and regularly as visiting professor at Bucerius Law School in Hamburg, Germany, and Hong Kong University School of Law.